A Level Business Studies for AQA

ALAIN ANDERTON

Causeway Press

Cover design by Tim Button.
Images provided by PhotoDisc, DigitalVision.
Graphics by Caroline Waring-Collins and Tim Button.
Cartoons by Brick www.brickbats.co.uk.
Photography by Andrew Allen, Dave Gray and Alain Anderton.
Page design by Caroline Waring-Collins.
Edited by Dave Gray.
Readers - Mike Kidson, Sue Oliver, Heather Doyle, Jan Gray.

Every effort has been made to locate the copyright holders of material reproduced in this book. Any errors or omissions brought to the attention of the publishers are regretted and will be credited in subsequent printings.

British Library Cataloguing in Publication Data
A catalogue record of this book is available from the British Library.

ISBN 1-902796-02-0

Pearson Education,
Edinburgh Gate,
Harlow,
Essex, CM20 2JE
First impression 2005

Design and page origination by Caroline Waring-Collins (Waring Collins Limited).
Printed and bound by Scotprint, Haddington.

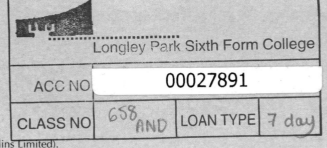
Acknowledgements
The publisher and author would like to thank the following for the use of photographs and other material in this book.

Accountemps p166(l), Action Press/Rex Features p420, Aga-Rayburn p228, Alvey & Towers p91,201(b), Anglian Water Group p291, Apex Photo Agency p188, Austin Reed Group p287, Bath Store p22(b), BBC Worldwide p74(b), Bently Jennison p166(t), Billiton p94(r), Bob Watkins/photofusion p504, Bristan p22 (c), Caroline Waring-Collins p269, Condé Nast p74(t), Co-op/Fair Trade p264, Corel pp103,126,145(t),305,502, Dan Chung/ Reuters/ popperfoto p204, Dick Baldwin/Reuters/popperfoto p154, DigitalVision pp6,20,23,65,93,129,169,187,192,194,200,201(l),207,209,212, 233, 237,245,249,256,261(r),267,315,336,343,348,365,366,392,414(t),423,451,453,522,526, Dixons p73,p78(l), EMI p58, Emap Group plc pp81,277, *Express & Star* pp53,284, Express Dairies p105, *Financial Times* pp99,195, Food Ferry p88, Ford p78(t), Frank Casimiro/Rex Features p347(r), Fyffes p9(b), Geest p29, Glenmorangie plc p297, HSBC p286, Ian Sager p232, IWP International plc 144, Jamil Bittar/Reuters/popperfoto p262, John Downing/Rex Features p477, John Powell/Rex Features p543, Jonathan Player/Rex Features p399, Keith Tollman/ Reuters/ popperfoto p220, Kingfisher pp8,10, Manganese Bronze Holdings plc 79, Menzies Group plc p23, MFI pp43,152, Minivator p446, Monotub p112, NatWest p286, Nils Jorgensen/Rex Features p492(l), OneSaturdayNight plc p282, Pascal Rossignol/Reuters/popperfoto p210, Paula Sollaway/Photofusion p308, Perry Joseph p199, Philippe Hays/Rex Features p425, PhotoDisc pp13,19,35,66,67,84,94(c),95,104,107(t),108,116, 121,122, 123,133,148,156,160,64,172, 205,221,236,256,261(l),272,273,274,276,292,293,304,307,311(b),317(b),318,324,326,339,342,345,355,356,358,370,373,374,380,384,391,413, 414(b),435,445,456,468, 488,489,505, 527,531,545, Rex Features Limited/Ray Tang p80, Rex Features Limited pp87,168,189,242,265,492(r), Richard Burns/Reuters/popperfoto p46, Royal Bank of Scotland p111, Ryanair p246, Safeway p72, Saga p12, Sam Morgan/Rex Features p408, ScottishPower p258, Silentnight Holdings plc p231, Sipa Press/Rex Features pp9(c),442,523, Sony p215, Stagecoach p89, Stan Gamester/Photofusion p459, Stockbyte pp25,39,49(r),107(b),114,117,119,124,127,131,135,137,140(b),142,143,145,147,170,173,175,177,180,201(r),227,234,235,238,243,252,271,278,279, 285(b),294,300,311,331(t), 334,337,397,422,427,507, Stuart Atkins/Rex Features p310, Suma p402, TCM Guitars p49(l), TGI Friday's p159, Tim Jones/ Photofusion p504, Tomkins p288, Topfoto/ImageWorks pp150,347(l),539, Topfoto/PA p149, Topfoto/Photonews pp38, 182, Topfoto/Picturepoint p351, Topfoto pp9(l),59, TRH Pictures/Ewan Partridge p186, The National Magazine Company p74(c), Ulster Bank p167, Vaillant p218, Virgin Group p12, Wales News Service p216, WDS p441.

All other material is acknowledged at source.

Preface

A Level Business Studies for AQA has been designed for use as the core textbook for students studying the A Level Business Studies specification for AQA (including AS and A2 Levels). It has been designed in colour to give candidates a distinctive and unique resource for use both in and out of the classroom. The book has a number of key features.

Comprehensive The book systematically covers the content of the A Level specification (including AS and A2 Levels). However, it has been designed to be used flexibly, allowing teachers, lecturers and students to adapt the book to suit their own scheme of work.

Unit structure The material has been organised into 116 short units. Each unit contains
• text covering the content of the specification;
• case studies;
• short answer questions;
• definitions of key terms.

Case study based Each unit contains a number of case studies. The opening case study is laid out to illustrate the key skills of knowledge and understanding, application, analysis and evaluation. Most units contain one or two case studies with accompanying questions within the text to illustrate specific aspects of the specification. At the end, there is a case study covering the content of the whole unit. These have questions which specifically test the different skills required by the AQA AS and A2 Level examinations.

I would like to thank Dave Gray for editing the book so superbly. Various proof readers checked the work with great skill. The page origination of the book was sensitively accomplished by Caroline Waring-Collins. Not least, I would like to thank my wife for all her help with the project.

The author and Causeway Press would welcome any comments you have to make about the book. We hope it will greatly help you in your learning and teaching of Business Studies.

Contents

1 Marketing

EXIT

Psion

Knowledge In July 2001, Psion announced that it was leaving the market for handheld organisers. These are small portable electronic machines which combine a variety of features, including a diary, an address list, a memo pad and a calculator. Psion had been the first company worldwide to sell such a product in 1982.

Application Psion organisers had faced fierce *competition* in the *market*. First it was Japanese companies, followed by US companies such as Palm and Handspring. The cost of constantly developing new models was heavy and *sales* were not always *profitable*. Its *marketing* was not effective enough

Analysis The Psion organiser was a well respected product. Psion recognised the need to bring out new models regularly. This was to satisfy the needs of customers and to beat off competition from copycat products. But it found it hard to sell in sufficiently high quantities or at a high enough price to yield consistent profits. By 2001 the company felt that it was not going to be able to compete profitably against its rivals in future. So it pulled out of the market.

Evaluation Did Psion make the right decision? Many of its loyal customers were disappointed. They argued that the Psion organiser was the best product on the market at the time. But having a good product and satisfied customers is only part of the marketing story. If the business can't make a profit selling a product, there is no incentive for it to continue offering that product for sale. Customers might have been disappointed. But Psion took the view that withdrawal from the market was in its best long term interests.

Adapted from the *Financial Times*, 12.7.2001.

What is marketing?

Coca-Cola produces soft drinks. The Ford Motor Company produces cars. Microsoft produces computer software. But making or supplying a product, whether it is a good or a service, is only part of the function of a business. Products have to be sold to customers. This function in a business is called MARKETING.

Marketing is a process which involves a number of different elements, as shown in Figure 1.1. The UK Chartered Institute of Marketing defines marketing as the 'management process involved in identifying, anticipating and satisfying consumer requirements profitably'.

Process Marketing is a process. It requires planning and executing over a period of time. It uses up resources, such as management time. Because it is a process, it can also be evaluated. Management can judge whether it has been a success or a failure and can analyse how it can be changed to make it more effective.

Identification Businesses have to understand what customers want to buy. It is easy for a business to offer products for sale which it thinks are excellent, but which fail to sell. For example, in the late 1990s, Marks & Spencer, the retailer, saw its sales and profits fall sharply because too much of its clothing stock proved unattractive to consumers. **Market research** (see units 4-8) can help businesses identify those customer needs.

Anticipation Businesses have to understand what customers want in advance. In some cases this is easy. For example, butchers will stock up with turkeys before Christmas. In other cases it is more difficult. Will teenage girls dress mainly in black this season or will another colour become fashionable? A chain of stores with the wrong colours might find it difficult to sell their stock.

Satisfaction Successful businesses have to build up a customer base which will keep buying their products. To do this, customers have to be satisfied with the product and be prepared to buy again. Kellogg's, for example, has to satisfy the needs of those buying its Corn Flakes. British Airways has to satisfy the needs of the passengers flying on its planes. This can be seen as one side of an exchange contract. The business supplies a product which consumers want to buy.

Making a profit This is the other side of the exchange contract. Nearly all businesses have profits as an objective (see unit 9). Profit is the reward to the business and its owners for bringing products to the market for customers to buy. Making a loss will, in the long term, force a business to close. Without profit, there will be little or no investment in the long term future of the business. So marketing must not just aim to satisfy customer needs. It also has to satisfy the need of the business to make a profit from its transactions with customers.

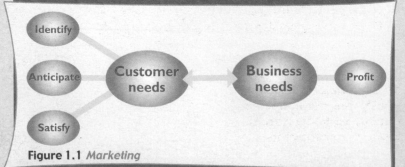

Figure 1.1 *Marketing*

Table 1.1 *Marketing definitions*

There are many other definitions of marketing. Some are given in Table 1.1.

The marketing mix

Some definitions of marketing refer to the 'major tools' of marketing. These are commonly known as the '**4 Ps**' (product, price, promotion and place). They make up the MARKETING MIX. **Product** (see units 12 to 14) is about the good or service itself. It is about research and development, quality and how technical specifications help satisfy the needs of customers. **Price** (see units 15 and 16) is about the price charged for the product. This will not just be affected by business costs, but also by what customers are prepared to pay and the sales volumes that the business wishes to achieve. **Promotion** (see unit 18) is about communicating the value of the product to customers through means such as advertising, direct mail, public relations and personal selling. **Place** is about getting the product to the customer in the right place, at the right time. Channels of distribution are important parts of this (see unit 19).

Product vs market orientation

Every business has a slightly different marketing **strategy**, a marketing plan designed to achieve its goals (see unit 9). One way of grouping these different strategies is to compare product and market orientated businesses.

Product orientation A PRODUCT ORIENTATED BUSINESS is one which puts most of its management effort into developing and making a product which it believes consumers want, and will sell well. For example, a copper mining company is likely to be product orientated. It will focus on extracting copper bearing ore and refining metal from the ore. Many manufacturing companies in the past were product orientated. They concentrated on making products which were technically 'sound'.

Market orientation A MARKET ORIENTATED BUSINESS is one where products are developed in response to customer needs. A market orientated business will try to find out what the market wants through market research. It will then design and sell products which reflect what it has found out about its customers' needs.

Most businesses at the start of the 20th century could be categorised as product orientated. 100 years later, businesses tend to be more market orientated. However, some businesses today are competitive, despite being product orientated.

- In industries producing certain COMMODITIES, such as wheat, beef, copper or aluminium, there is little opportunity for the use of sophisticated marketing techniques. Market forces, for example, determine the price. It could be argued that an advertising campaign would give little benefit to a business because it would not get customers to distinguish its product from those of other businesses.
- Some industries produce manufactured goods or services which are highly standardised. Most manufacturers of nuts and bolts, for example, make products to specifications which are standard in the industry.
- Many small businesses don't have the resources for

Marketing is not a recent invention. In the 19th century, many of today's most famous brands such as Cadbury's chocolates and Boots the Chemists were created. Another success story was the Singer sewing machine, first sold in the USA in the 1850s. This was a revolutionary development. It brought a sewing machine into the home for the first time and allowed ordinary people to sew, mend and make their own clothes.

Isaac Merritt Singer was not the first to invent or sell a domestic sewing machine. His unique contribution was to mass market the machine. He took an existing design, slightly modified the stitching mechanism, and sold it as his own invention. Then he targeted rural US households for sales. They tended to make their own clothes or have their clothes made for them by a neighbour wanting to earn extra cash. But rural households were often poor and couldn't afford the $100 price. Singer got round this by inventing 'hire purchase', where people could pay in instalments. His sewing machine was also sold in a wooden box which could easily be converted into a work table for the machine. This was important in an era when furniture was scarce.

The Singer Company went on to sell sewing machines around the world. But the company began to fall on hard times after the 1960s and 1970s when people stopped making their own clothes or repairing them.

Adapted from *The Guardian*, 15.5.1999.

1 **Marketing can be defined as 'the process of identification, anticipation and satisfaction of the customer's needs, profitably'. Suggest how Isaac Singer (a) identified, (b) anticipated and (c) satisfied customer's needs.**
2 **Suggest why Singer has experienced problems over the past twenty years.**

Over the past 10 years, it has been fashionable for large diversified chemical companies to reinvent themselves as speciality chemical companies. Diversified chemical companies produce large amounts of a relatively small number of bulk commodity chemicals, concentrating their efforts on safety, quality and reduction of costs. Speciality chemical companies, in contrast, concentrate on producing low volumes of a large range of chemicals, targeted at particular customer markets. However, many of the new speciality chemical companies have had disappointing results. Some observers blame this on the operating culture inherited from their parents. Many managers have been in the industry for 20 years or more. As a result, the companies have not changed their way of doing business. They are insufficiently customer orientated and have failed to invest enough in developing strong links with customers.

Adapted from the *Financial Times*, 25.9.2001.

> 1 **Explain whether speciality chemical companies are product orientated or market orientated businesses, according to the article.**
> 2 **Suggest possible problems that a speciality chemical company might have in being product orientated or market orientated.**

sophisticated marketing. They survive by providing the same quality of good or service over and over again to their customers. For example, most hairdressers concentrate on giving the same service to their customers over the years. Hair styles might change and so the way in which hair is cut and dyed might change. But these market orientated changes are, perhaps, only a small part of what is a product orientated service.

- Where a business has little or no competition (i.e. it is a **monopolist**, see unit 49), it may feel little need for marketing. UK water companies, for example, are monopolists. They concentrate their efforts on delivering a product and service to their customers. Every household and business needs a water supply and so there is no need to get customers. Pricing is determined by a government regulator. When competition is introduced into the water market, as it has been in the gas and electricity supply market, then water companies may become more market orientated. However, even in the gas and electricity industries, it could be argued that competing companies concentrate mainly on providing a service to customers rather than adopting aggressive market orientated strategies.

In many industries, though, businesses have had to become market orientated to survive.

- In markets where customer tastes change quickly and constantly, businesses have to understand and produce for their market. Clothing retailers, for example, must have the right mix of clothes in their shops each season to be successful.
- Market orientated strategies have enabled a few businesses to dominate their markets. In the world market for soap powders and washing liquids, two firms, Unilever and Procter & Gamble, use a variety of marketing tools to ensure continued dominance. Market orientated strategies are used then to deter competition from other businesses.
- Finding out what customers want before launching a product is important when getting a product to market is costly. For example, launching a brand new car is extremely expensive for a global car manufacturer. So market research, and then continued marketing support for the product once launched, is essential to recover the investment.

All firms have to pay some attention to the product they sell and all have to market their product. So the distinction between product and market orientation could be seen as a spectrum (see Figure 1.2) with businesses being somewhere along it. A mining company like Ashanti Goldfields is likely to be at the product orientated end. A retailer like Marks & Spencer might be at the market orientated end.

Asset-led marketing

Both market and product orientated approaches have their limitations. Many businesses have failed because they have offered a high quality product, but have not met the needs of their customers. Perhaps the product was too expensive or the business failed to persuade enough retailers to stock it. Equally, market orientated businesses might fail because they put great effort into certain aspects of marketing, but fail to get the right product to the customer.

Another approach is ASSET-LED or ASSET-BASED MARKETING. A business which is asset-led is responsive to the needs of the market. But equally it takes into account its own strengths and weaknesses when producing a good or providing a service. Its strengths, for example, might include its product, production techniques, goodwill and branding, experience and knowledge.

A tobacco company, for example, might come up with the idea of offering life insurance

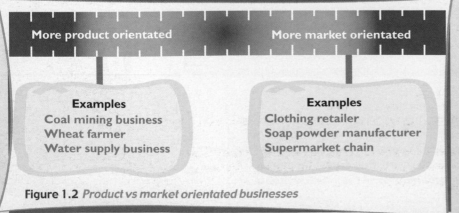

More product orientated	More market orientated
Examples Coal mining business Wheat farmer Water supply business	**Examples** Clothing retailer Soap powder manufacturer Supermarket chain

Figure 1.2 *Product vs market orientated businesses*

to smokers. It could offer lower premiums (prices) to its customers than other insurance companies which group smokers and non-smokers together. It also might have a large customer database of users who could be contacted to advertise the insurance. However, selling insurance is a very different business from manufacturing and selling cigarettes. There are likely to be few **synergies**, or links, between the different businesses. The tobacco company has great expertise in the production of cigarettes, but little in selling insurance. Simply because market research shows there is a potentially profitable business opportunity does not mean to say that a business should take it up.

keyterms

Asset-led or asset-based marketing - where a business combines its knowledge of the market with an understanding of its strengths and weaknesses to decide what products to bring to market.
Commodity - a standard product, typically made in large quantities, such as wheat, copper or timber.
Marketing - the process of identification, anticipation and satisfaction of the customer's needs, profitably.
Marketing mix - the combination of factors which help the business sell a product, usually summarised as the 4Ps, which are product, price, promotion and place.
Market orientated business - a business whose strategy is to find out what customers want to buy and then develop products which will suit their needs.
Product orientated business - a business whose strategy is to make and introduce products to the market which it believes will sell and satisfy the needs of customers.

✓checklist

1 What is the difference between production and marketing?
2 '60 per cent of UK households own a microwave oven.' What needs might a business identify from this statistic?
3 'The cool colour this Autumn will be green.' How might a clothing retailer like Top Shop or Oasis use this information for marketing purposes?
4 A company spends £50 million developing a new type of textile hailed by designers as a 'wonder textile'. But in the first five years of sale it makes a loss of an average £2 million a year. Is this good marketing?
5 What are the four elements of the marketing mix?
6 Distinguish between a product orientated business and a market orientated business.
7 What types of business might be successful and product orientated?
8 Using the concept of asset-led marketing, explain whether an ice cream manufacturer could successfully expand into manufacturing crisps.

In 1990, Perrier was the world's number 1 brand of bottled mineral water. It started in 1904 when St. John Harmsworth was recuperating from a car accident at the spa town of Vergeze, France. He was given some of the natural sparkling water from the local spring which was thought to have health giving properties. He realised the commercial potential of the water and bought the spring from his doctor, Louis Perrier. By 1922, his company was producing 6 million bottles a year, going from strength to strength.

The brand was always supported by strong promotion. Initially, Harmsworth marketed Perrier under the slogan 'the champagne of table waters'. After World War Two, leading poster artists were commissioned to produce promotional campaigns. In 1969, for example, a colour advertisement by the famous Surrealist artist, Salvador Dali, appeared in French newspapers. A variety of other types of promotion have also been used. In 2000, for example, Perrier bought the rights to be the official mineral water supplier to the Wimbledon tennis championships for that year.

However, disaster struck in 1990. Routine testing in the USA found traces of benzene in 12 bottles of Perrier. The company initially withdrew 72 million bottles from the US market, but failed to recall bottles in other world markets. It claimed that the benzene levels found were not dangerous. At first it blamed the problem on a cleaner's dirty rag. Later it admitted that gas filters at the bottling plant had not been changed. Public pressure and threats of legal action forced it to recall all bottles worldwide, a total of 280 million bottles. But this was not before consumers had boycotted the water, fearing poisoning. They turned to other brands and failed to return when Perrier had sorted out its problems. In the USA where it had been the number 1 brand in 1989, it was only 22nd in 2000.

Perrier, the company, was bought out by the international giant, Nestlé, in 1992. It now forms part of its Perrier-Vittel division, which has 55 brands including Perrier, Vittel and Buxton water.

Adapted from *The Guardian*, 17.6.2000.

1 What is meant by the term 'marketing'? (3 marks)
2 Explain TWO ways in which Perrier water has been marketed. (6 marks)
3 Analyse why Perrier suffered so badly in 1990 when traces of benzene were found in its product. (10 marks)
4 'It could be argued that the way in which Perrier handled the crisis in 1990 was a case of how NOT to deal with such problems.' Discuss whether it is always in the interests of a business to recall products that might have problems. (11 marks)

2 Market size, growth & share

The DIY market

Knowledge Three companies account for around half of the DIY (do it yourself) sales in the UK, as Figure 2.1 shows. These are Focus Wickes, which owns the Focus Do It All and Wickes chains, Homebase and B&Q (owned by Kingfisher).

Application These *companies* operate in the DIY *market*. In this market, *suppliers* such as B&Q offer DIY goods for sale to *customers*. These *customers* are *consumers* and small building *businesses*. B&Q has the largest *market share* of the major chains.

Analysis The DIY market is growing, as Figure 2.2 shows. Partly this is because consumers and small builders are buying goods at DIY outlets which before they bought in other types of shop. For example, DIY retailers have taken trade away from garden centres and lighting shops. Partly it is because consumers feel more confident about their DIY skills, encouraged by television programmes. Partly it is due to rising disposable incomes, which allow households to spend more.

Evaluation B&Q may turn out to be the main winner of changes in the DIY market. It has invested heavily in large DIY 'sheds' which offer low prices and large choice. It has been predicted that its market share within the next ten years could reach 40 per cent. This would make it even more dominant in the market.

Adapted from *The Observer*, 12.12.2000 and 23.6.2002, Mintel, Verdict Research.

Figure 2.1 *The DIY market: market share of largest retailers*

Figure 2.2 *The DIY market: total sales*

Sales (£bn): 1995: 6.26, 1996: 6.70, 1997: 7.14, 1998: 7.64, 1999: 8.14 est, 2000: 10.4 forecast

Markets

Every business operates within a MARKET. There are many different types of market, but all share the same characteristics - they are places where buyers and sellers meet to exchange goods and services. Street markets are a good example. In a street market, shoppers buy goods from sellers, the stall holders. **Money** is used in the transaction. In the past, and sometimes even today, goods would be **bartered**. This means that buyers and sellers would swap one good for another rather than using money.

Today, it could be argued that businesses operate in a single **global** or **international** market. Modern communication and trade links allow customers to buy from all over the world. GLOBALISATION, the process of integration between national economies and markets, is increasing the size of many markets.

However, most markets are not global. Some, for instance, are **local markets**. An example is the market for hairdressing services. Customers rarely travel outside their local area to have their hair styled. There is also a local market for petrol. Motorists fill up at local filling stations and won't be prepared to travel long distances just to save 1p a litre.

Other markets are **national markets**. For example, there is a national market in the UK for magazines like *Sugar* and *Loaded*. There is also a national market for cars in the UK. Unlike most of the rest of the world, UK cars are left hand drive. This, together with UK safety specifications, means that car manufacturers make cars specifically for the UK market. Equally, UK drivers rarely buy cars outside the UK.

Which market?

Distinguishing between local, national and international markets is one way of classifying markets. But there are others. For example, markets can be classified:

- by industry, such as motor vehicles, food processing or mining;
- by the three sectors of industry - **primary** (extraction), **secondary** (manufacturing) and **tertiary** (services);
- as INDUSTRIAL or PRODUCER MARKETS, where one business sells to another, or CONSUMER MARKETS, where businesses sell to consumers;
- by customer **needs**, such as the need for transportation, the need for accommodation, leisure needs and medical needs;
- by size and, in particular, whether they are **mass markets** or **niche markets** (see unit 11).

A business can make a product which could be classified in several different markets. For example, a tyre manufacturer, producing tyres for cars, could be classified as being in the rubber products market. Or it could classified as being in the motor vehicle component manufacturing industry. Or it could be classified as being part of the transportation industry.

Being aware of this is important in marketing. For example, an ice-cream manufacturer knows that it is in the ice-cream market and faces competition from other ice-cream manufacturers. But it is also in the market for 'treats'. When consumers go into a newsagents and buy an ice-cream, they could have bought a chocolate bar, a packet of crisps or a magazine instead. It is in the market for 'puddings' as well. A shopper could choose to buy a cake or ice-cream to serve at the end of a meal. When targeting a market a business has to

1 **What is a 'market'?**
2 **Explain in what ways McDonald's operates in (a) local markets and (b) the global market.**
3 **It could be argued that McDonald's operates in the market for restaurant food. Or some might argue that it is in the fast food market. Others might say that it operates in the food take away market. Discuss which of these you think provides the best description of the market within which McDonald's operates.**

be clear as to how this market is defined.

Market size

Markets differ in size. For example, the world car market is larger than the world market for cricket equipment. There are two main ways in which market size can be measured.

By volume This is a physical amount. For example, 1 350 million tonnes of packaging were produced and sold worldwide in 2000 as shown in Table 2.1.

By value This is an amount of money. The total value of spending on packaging worldwide, for example, was €443 billion in 2000.

Volume and value might not change by the same proportion over time because prices change. Say that the average price of packaging per tonne in 2002 was €450 and 1 500 million tonnes were sold. The total value of spending would be €675 billion (€450 x 1 500 million). By 2010, the **volume** of packaging output might grow by 20 per cent, to 1 800 million. But if the average price fell by 5 per cent, to E427.5, the **value** of sales would be €769.5 billion (€427.5 x 1 800 million). So the value of sales would only have grown by 14 per cent (€769.5 billion - €675 billion ÷ €675 billion x 100).

In markets for **commodity products** (see unit 1), prices tend to fall over time because more efficient ways are found of producing the product. The size of these markets by volume tends to increase faster than when measured by value. Businesses in such markets tend to be **product orientated**, concentrating on making a product at a low enough cost to

make a profit. When businesses can differentiate their products by creating **branded** goods or services (see unit 10), prices are less likely to decline over time. Maintaining a price is part of the marketing strategy of businesses which tend to be **market orientated** (see unit 1).

Market share

Nearly all businesses face competition in their market. They sell only a proportion of the total sales in the market. This proportion, usually expressed as a percentage, is the MARKET SHARE or MARKET PENETRATION of a business. As a formula, it can be expressed as:

$$\text{Market share (or penetration) of Business A} = \frac{\text{Sales of Business A in the market}}{\text{Total sales in the market}} \times 100\%$$

For example, a business might sell £3 million worth of goods in a market with total sales of 100 million. Its market share would then be 3 per cent ([£3 million ÷ £100 million] x 100%) by value.

	Value (€bn)	Market share by value (%)	Volume (m tonnes)	Market share by volume (%)
Paper/board	150	38.9	500	37.0
Plastics	130	29.3	300	22.2
Metal	112	25.3	150	11.1
Glass	28	6.3	400	29.6
Others	23	5.2	n/a	n/a
Total	443	100.0	1350	100.0

Adapted from World Packaging Organisation.

Table 2.1 *World packaging sales, 2000*

Market share can be expressed by **volume**. For example, in Table 2.1, 'plastic' packaging businesses have 22.2 per cent of the world market for all types of packaging. More commonly, though, market share tends to be expressed by **value** of sales. 'Plastic' packaging has a higher average price than other types of packaging. So 'plastic' packaging businesses have a higher share of the market by value, ie 29.3 per cent.

Market share or penetration is often used in the context of an individual business. But it can also be used in the context of a type of product or an individual brand. In Table 2.1, for example, 'glass' packaging in 2000 had a global market share by value of 6.3 per cent. Virgin Cola, a branded cola drink, had 2 per cent of the UK cola market in 2000 by value.

The larger the market share of a business, the greater its market power. Commodity producers, for example, tend to have low market shares. They have little or no control over the price at which they sell. Businesses with high market shares have much greater control over prices and profits.

Market growth

Market size is unlikely to remain the same over time. Markets change in size. Some markets grow, whilst others decline. For example, the world market for personal computers is growing. The market for coal in the UK over the past 30 years has declined.

Large businesses, with a relatively high market share, may be able to affect the overall size of the market in the short term. For example, they may be able to expand the size of the market through advertising and other forms of promotion. Alternatively, they may restrict sales volumes to drive up the price at which they can sell. In the long term, though, the size of a market tends to be determined by factors outside the control of an individual business, however large.

- Rising incomes, associated with long term economic development in the industrialised countries of the world and developing countries in Africa, Asia and Latin America, has tended to increase the size of markets.
- Changes in technology have affected the size of markets. For example, the large market for goods associated with horse driven transport was all but wiped out by the arrival of the motor car. The market for mobile phones has grown

'key terms'

Consumer markets - markets in which businesses sell to consumers.
Globalisation - the process of ever-increasing specialisation, trade and interdependence between different parts of the world economy, which creates world markets for products and labour.
Industrial or producer markets - markets in which one business sells to another business.
Market - where buyers and sellers meet to exchange goods and services.
Market share or penetration - the proportion (usually expressed as a percentage) of sales (by value or volume) that a business has compared to the total sales of the market.

✓ checklist

1 What are the (a) similarities and (b) differences between a local market for garage repair services and the global market for oil?
2 A textile company manufactures cloth which it sells to another company manufacturing garments. This company sells its products to retailers. Explain which of the three companies operate in (a) industrial markets and (b) consumer markets.
3 What is the difference between market value and market volume in the market for footwear?
4 'Wilkeman's market penetration in the paint market is 24 per cent, with its best selling branded paint having a 13 per cent market share.' Explain what this means.
5 Explain briefly FOUR factors which might affect the changing size of a market over time.

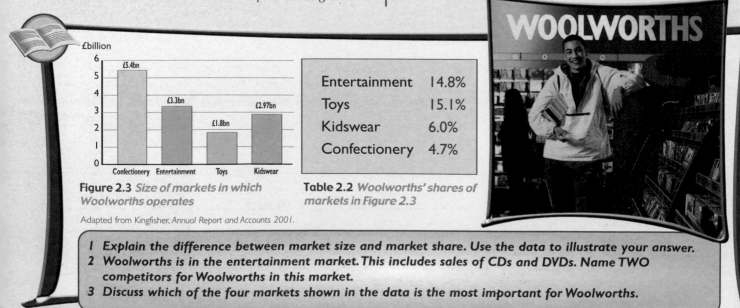

Figure 2.3 *Size of markets in which Woolworths operates*

Entertainment	14.8%
Toys	15.1%
Kidswear	6.0%
Confectionery	4.7%

Table 2.2 *Woolworths' shares of markets in Figure 2.3*

Adapted from Kingfisher, Annual Report and Accounts 2001.

1 **Explain the difference between market size and market share. Use the data to illustrate your answer.**
2 **Woolworths is in the entertainment market. This includes sales of CDs and DVDs. Name TWO competitors for Woolworths in this market.**
3 **Discuss which of the four markets shown in the data is the most important for Woolworths.**

from zero in less than 20 years.
- Social change is important too. For example, the way we dress is dictated by a complex mix of factors. Over the past 50 years, the UK markets for hats and corsets have shrunk to a fraction of what they were 100 years ago. In contrast, the UK market for women's trousers has grown from almost zero in 1900 to its position today.
- Demographic change (i.e. change in population) is fuelling changes in market size worldwide. In many developing countries, population is increasing rapidly, creating the

opportunities for expanding markets for goods and services. In Europe and Japan, the population is forecast to shrink over the next fifty years, which will tend to reduce market size. Different markets are likely to be affected in different ways because of changes in the structure of the population. In the UK there are forecast to be more people aged 65 and over. This could create opportunities for businesses offering sheltered housing and medical care. On the other hand, there will be fewer young people. This might reduce markets for education and children's clothing.

Freeserve is an internet service provider. When anyone goes online, it has to be through an internet service provider like Freeserve, AOL (America On Line), BT Internet or NTL.

When it was launched in 1998, Freeserve was an instant success. Before, internet service providers often charged over £100 a year for their services to household customers, and more to businesses. On top of that, customers also had to pay telephone charges. Freeserve provided internet access free to households, but they still had to pay the telephone charges.

Like any internet service provider, Freeserve had costs. There were staff costs and promotion costs, such as free software disks given away to get households online. Then there was computer hardware to service the needs of customers accessing the internet through Freeserve. The plan was for Freeserve to recoup these costs by charging businesses to advertise on Freeserve sites. Freeserve would also take a cut of any sales made by businesses on its sites.

Today, such financing is no longer fashionable. Advertising and e-commerce revenues have proved disappointing. So free internet service providers are increasingly trying to move customers onto subscription plans.

AOL has always charged customers for its service. Its success in gaining customers has been largely due to heavy advertising and promotional activity. In 2001, it spent an estimated £100 million on promotion.

NTL has chosen a different route. It has sold internet access through its cable television services. By signing up to cable television, it offers cheaper telephone calls than BT and gives free internet access. What's more, the cable internet access is broadband, allowing faster downloading speeds than the usual narrow band connection via a telephone line.

BT has the advantage that it has a near monopoly on telephone services to households. It has used its marketing power with customers to advertise its internet services. Importantly, it has also offered free telephone charges in return for a fixed monthly fee, the BT Click scheme. Its market share has grown from 10 to 15 per cent since January 1999. On top of that, another 3 per cent has signed up for BT Click.

Freeserve has lost market share to its three main rivals. It says that this is because it stopped advertising in January 2001. It too has been trying to move its customers from a free service to a subscription service like BT Click, where customers pay a fee to having unlimited access to the internet free of telephone charges. It claims that at the start of the year it did not have enough hardware to cope with subscription customers, who were spending much longer online. But it would shortly be renewing its advertising campaign. It hoped to regain market share within a growing market.

Adapted from *The Independent* ,16.11.2001.

	Aug 00	Jan 01	Feb 01	May 01	Aug 01
Freeserve	27	21	21	18	19
AOL	10	15	13	17	16
BT Internet	10	10	12	12	15
NTL	5	9	8	8	9

Adapted from Oftel

Table 2.3 *Household UK market share (%)*

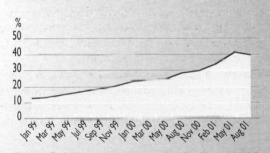

Figure 2.4 *Internet penetration by household*
Adapted from OFTEL.

1 Explain what is meant by the following terms:
   (a) market share; (3 marks)
   (b) market growth. (3 marks).
2 Using Table 2.3 and Figure 2.4, explain how market share of the internet provider market has changed as the size of the market has changed. (6 marks)
3 Analyse why market share has changed over the period shown in Table 2.3. (8 marks)
4 In the first half of 2001, Freeserve made an estimated loss of £28 million, having earned £32.3 million in revenues. In 2002 Freeserve charged £13.99 a month for its Anytime internet access service. Discuss whether Freeserve should, in fact, have continued to offer only a free internet service to customers. (10 marks)

3 Market segmentation

The Internet

Knowledge The Internet took off in the second half of the 1990s. By 2000, there were over 11 million Internet users in the UK and 100 million in the USA.

Application Within the *global market*, there are many *market segments*. For example, *Internet* users can be *segmented* by region. Users in France are likely to be different from those in the UK. They can also be segmented by age. In the UK, for example, around 20 per cent of *Internet* users in December 2000 were aged 50+.

Analysis Internet companies have tended to target the youth market. Their reasoning has been that young people are more likely to use the Internet. However, Internet use amongst older people is growing fast. Those over 50 are also more likely to be heavy users. In a French survey in March 2000, people aged 50+ made up 16 per cent of all users, but 23.7 per cent of heavy users. What is more, the over 50s have higher average incomes than the 'youth' segment of the market. Those aged 50-59 are likely to have money to spend and also be interested in fashion, finance, computers, mobile phones and cars.

Evaluation Many Internet companies have failed to exploit the potential to sell or advertise to the over 50s. Businesses need to be aware that these 'silver-surfers' are an affluent market segment. With the right approach, they could generate large orders. If major companies fail to seize the opportunity, they could lose sales to specialist companies like Saga, which has been successful in targeting the unfashionable grey market.

Adapted from the *Financial Times, Connectis*, October 2001.

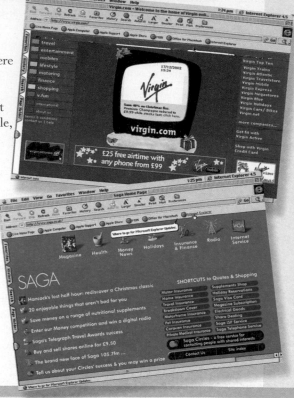

Market segments

Who would buy a magazine on farming? Would they also buy a book *The History of Lancashire Textiles* or a first class airline ticket? In fact, the buyers of these three products are likely to be quite distinct groups of people. They are part of different MARKET SEGMENTS - groups of customers who share similar characteristics.

One way of segmenting buyers might be to distinguish between those in **industrial markets** and **consumer markets** (see unit 2). This unit considers buyers in consumer markets. There are four main ways in which consumers tend to be segmented:

- geographically - by where they live;
- demographically - by their age, income or religion;
- psychographically - by their social class, lifestyle and personality;
- behaviourally - by how they act, for example whether they make repeat purchases, buy on impulse or want high quality products.

Geographic segmentation

Markets can be segmented by area. For example, there is a North American market and a European market. There is also a market in the Newbury area and a market in the Reading area. Different areas tend to have different spending patterns. This can be based on climate. Consumers in Alaska are likely to spend more on heating than consumers in Florida, for example. Spending can also be based on tradition. Toasters are a standard piece of kitchen equipment in the UK. But fewer are bought in France because the type of bread bought is different.

Geographic segmentation can help a business focus its promotion efforts. For example, a hairdressers in Newbury might advertise in the local Newbury newspaper. But it might not advertise in a Reading paper. People in Reading are unlikely to travel the 30 miles to Newbury to have their hair styled.

It may also be possible for a company to price goods differently in different markets. For example, car manufacturers sell the same cars at different prices in different countries in the European Union. The price will depend, in part, on what they think customers are prepared to pay.

Demographic segmentation

DEMOGRAPHY is the study of population. Demographic segmentation splits people up into different groups according to different characteristics.

Age The population can be split up into age groups. For example, the over 65s could be seen as one segment, whilst teenagers aged 14-18 could be seen as another. Rap CDs might be marketed to teenagers, whilst a Frank Sinatra CD is more likely to be attractive to older buyers.

Gender Men and women often have different spending patterns. Cosmetics, for example, are marketed mainly at females. Shaving equipment tends to be marketed mainly at men.

Family and household Households differ in size and composition. For example, there are single households, perhaps with one retired person or a young adult living on their own. There are single parent households with one adult and children. There are also 'traditional' households of two adults with children. Each type of household has different typical spending patterns and, importantly, different typical incomes. For example, single parent and retired households tend to have lower incomes. Therefore they are unlikely to be targeted by businesses selling luxury items.

Income The population can be split up into income groups and targeted accordingly. So a Cartier watch is likely to be marketed at the highest income groups. Baked beans might be marketed to lower income groups.

Occupation Occupation can affect spending habits. For example, it can be a guide to the income of consumers. Different occupations might also have different priorities for spending. A teacher might spend more on books than a bricklayer. A sales representative is likely to spend more on transport than a sales assistant in a shop.

Religion, race and nationality Within a population, there may be religious, racial or national groups with distinct purchasing characteristics. For example, there is a market for Jewish kosher food which conforms to strict Jewish dietary laws. In West Indian communities in the UK, grocery shops may stock vegetables and fruit such as yams and plantain bananas. In Indian communities, there are business opportunities to sell traditional garments such as saris. In the United States, businesses may target Italian, Hispanic or Chinese communities.

Psychographic segmentation

Geographic and demographic segmentation have limitations. For example, there is a wide variety of spending patterns amongst females aged 16-18 living in Manchester. Yet people in this consumer group share the same gender, age and location. An alternative way of grouping customers is through psychographic segmentation. This groups customers according to their beliefs, attitudes, opinions and lifestyles.

Social class It is often argued that social class affects spending decisions. Table 3.1 shows a classification used by the Institute of Practitioners in Advertising (IPA). It splits the population into six classes and gives each a grade from A to E. As, for example, are upper middle class workers, such as doctors, lawyers and company directors. D's, in contrast, are the semi-skilled and

Social grade	Social status	Head of household's occupation
A	Upper middle class	Higher managerial, administrative or professional such as doctors, lawyers and company directors
B	Middle class	Intermediate managerial, administrative or professional such as teachers, nurses and managers
C1	Lower middle class	Supervisory or clerical and junior managerial, administrative or professional such as shop assistants, clerks and police constables
C2	Skilled working class	Skilled manual workers such as carpenters, cooks and train drivers
D	Working class	Semi-skilled and unskilled manual workers such as fitters and store keepers
E	The poorest in society	State pensioners or widows, casual or lower grade workers, or long term unemployed

Table 3.1 *Socio-economic groups – IPA classification*

unskilled working class, such as fitters and storekeepers.

Social class is not just about income and how much a household can afford to spend. It is about a complete lifestyle and way of viewing the world. Social groups A and B, the upper middle and middle classes, for example, tend to place emphasis on planning for the future. Their children's education is a priority, as is planning for retirement. So they tend to spend more on children's books, university fees and pension payments as a proportion of their income than other groups. Businesses aiming to sell to the most affluent often target 'ABC1s'.

Another system is the Registrar General's classification, as shown in Table 3.2. It is used as the basis of government surveys and statistics shown in government publications. It divides social class into eight categories. They are based on whether a person is employed, self-employed or an employee. They also take into account the nature of the employment, ranging from a secure job with promotion prospects to the long term unemployed.

'If you get your youth marketing 1 per cent wrong, you might as well get it 100 per cent wrong, because your brand will look like your drunk uncle trying to dance at a disco.' This is the warning from Tim Millar, senior planner at Agency Republic.

His advertising agency is directly involved in targeting university students. In the last five years, the UK student population has grown by 10 per cent and will hit 2 million this year. 34 per cent of the 18-21 age group now enters higher education, compared to just 16 per cent 10 years ago. They will spend an estimated £6 billion while at college. When they graduate, they will be the new generation of ABC1 consumers. Marketers want to begin building a relationship with this group while they're young and all in one place.

However, it is important not to see all students as the same. Marketers need to identify different segments, from the 'ambitious go getter' to the 'London sociable'.

Adapted from the *Financial Times*, 25.9.2001.

1 **Explain FOUR different ways of segmenting the market described in the data.**
2 **Explain TWO reasons why a company like a bank or a drinks manufacturer might want to target student campuses for marketing.**
3 **Discuss what might be the dangers for a company like a drinks manufacturer of marketing to students.**

Class 1	Higher managerial and professional occupations
	1.1 Employers in large organisations (eg corporate manager)
	1.2 Higher professionals (eg doctor or barrister)
Class 2	Lower managerial and professional occupations (eg journalist, actor, nurse)
Class 3	Intermediate occupations (eg secretary, driving instructor)
Class 4	Small employers and own account workers (eg publican, taxi driver)
Class 5	Lower supervisory, craft and related occupations (eg plumber, butcher, train driver)
Class 6	Semi routine occupations (eg shop assistant, traffic warden)
Class 7	Routine occupations (eg waiter, road sweeper)
Class 8	Never worked/long-term unemployed

Table 3.2 *Socio-economic groups – Registrar General's classification*

Lifestyle Consumers can be segmented into different lifestyle groups. There is no standard classification for this. Different advertising agencies and companies have different classifications. However, they all group consumers by how they live. For example, one classification proposed by Joseph Plummer in 1974 was to segment consumers according to their activities (e.g. holidays, entertainment, sports, work), their interests (e.g. family, home, fashion, food, media), their opinions (e.g. politics, business, education, culture) and demographics (age, etc. as described above).

Personality and self-concept It may also be possible to group people with similar personalities, self-concepts or self-images. For example, some consumers see themselves as 'fun loving'. Adverts aimed at this market segment might associate outgoing activities with a product. Other consumers see themselves as good at getting value for money. They might be attracted by adverts stressing low prices or bargains.

Behavioural segmentation

Behavioural segmentation attempts to segment markets according to how consumers relate to a product.

Usage rate Consumers can be segmented according to how often they buy a product, for instance never, occasionally or frequently. A business can then target whichever group it feels would be most likely to buy its product.

Loyalty Consumers can be categorised according to their product loyalty. Certain consumers always buy a particular brand. Others like to change products, but will regularly come back to the original brand. Some have no loyalty, buying the brand that is cheapest perhaps.

Occasions Consumers often buy products which are associated with specific occasions. Children might buy flowers on Mothers Day. Turkeys are bought at Christmas. Cereals are bought to be eaten at breakfast time. Businesses can use this knowledge to reinforce buying patterns or to get consumers to buy for other occasions. For example, cereal manufacturers have promoted cereals as a food to be eaten as a snack at any time of the day, rather than just at breakfast.

Awareness Customers can be segmented according to their awareness of a product. Some customers might be prepared to buy, but simply don't know about a product. Others might be aware, but not feel the need to buy at this point. Some are seeking out alternatives, one of which they will buy. Others are at the point of buying. Businesses can use this knowledge to develop their marketing strategies and tactics. For example, a multinational company introducing a product for the first time into the UK will need to raise customer awareness about the product and make sure that it is available when customers decide to buy.

Benefits sought Different consumers look for different benefits from a product. For example, some consumers want value for money. Others want particular qualities, such as air conditioning in a car. Some want to create an image, so they buy designer labelled clothes.

Market segmentation and strategy

Certain businesses make little use of market segmentation. Some simply adopt an **undifferentiated strategy** towards marketing. They try to promote their product to the entire market, rather than to a segment as shown in Figure 3.1. For example, a local newsagents will want to sell to the entire market. The nature of the service it offers means that this market will be local. But the newsagents won't try to target young customers at the expense of old age pensioners, or professional customers at the expense of unskilled manual customers.

Equally, many businesses have little need to segment their markets. If a business is producing a **commodity** (see unit 1) sold in bulk, like wheat, copper or oil, there is no need to

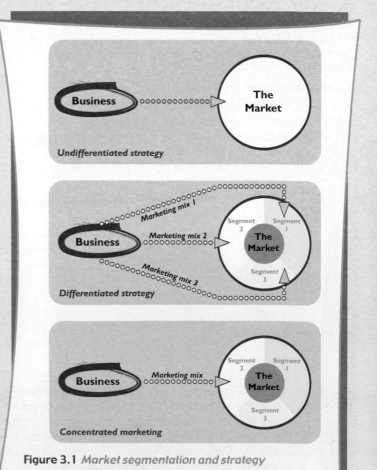

Figure 3.1 *Market segmentation and strategy*

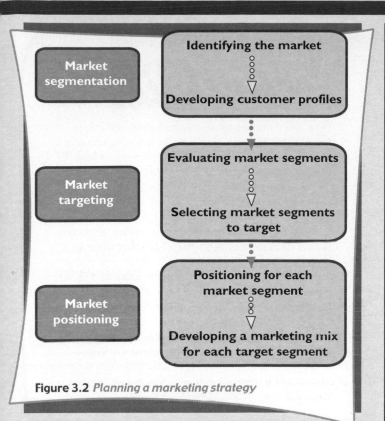

Figure 3.2 *Planning a marketing strategy*

produce specific products for specific segments of the market. Customers want to buy a standard product. It could also be that the cost of producing different products or services to satisfy different market segments far outweighs what customers are prepared to pay for the differentiation. Customers might prefer to buy a cheap undifferentiated product rather than an expensive one tailored precisely to their needs.

Some businesses even deliberately produce brands to appeal to all customers. They want to capture as much of the market

as possible with an undifferentiated product. For example, in the UK tea brands such as PG Tips or Typhoo Tea are aimed at the mass market.

However, many businesses develop marketing strategies for particular segments of a market. A **differentiated strategy** would aim to target different market segments with different marketing strategies. A detergent manufacturer might sell cleaning products to consumers and to cleaning companies. But it could use different packaging for the two markets and offer cleaning companies much larger packs. It could also use different advertising and other promotion in the two market segments.

Another alternative is to focus on just one market segment. This **concentrated marketing** is used, for example, by luxury brands such as Dior or Gucci. Dior does not attempt to sell clothes to consumers in every segment of the clothing market. It concentrates on selling to consumers with high incomes by producing high quality, expensive clothing.

Segmentation, targeting and positioning

The stages through which a business might plan a differentiated or concentrated marketing strategy are shown in Figure 3.2.

Segmenting the market The business will try to identify how it might segment its markets.

Developing customer profiles The business will find out exactly who its customers are in each market segment. This might be done through **market research** (see unit 4). It might then draw up a CUSTOMER PROFILE (or CONSUMER PROFILE if the buyers are consumers). This is an analysis of the characteristics of customers in the market or market segment. It could include age, income, budgets, **channels** through which purchases are made (see unit 19) and reasons why customers buy the product.

Evaluating market segments The business then needs to evaluate which market segments it is worthwhile targeting. A manufacturer of vacuum cleaners may find that 30 per cent of households have not bought a new cleaner in 15 years. But there might be little point in targeting these customers if three quarters of them are in the bottom 40 per cent of the income range. This might indicate that most would not have the income to buy a new vacuum cleaner. On the other hand, it might find out that young people aged 20-30 are three times as likely to buy a vacuum cleaner as old age pensioners. With higher average incomes too, young people might be worth targeting.

Selecting market segments to target Once a business has evaluated its market segments, it must then choose which will be its **target market** (see unit 11). The vacuum cleaner manufacturer might decide to target more affluent young people as the most promising way of increasing sales.

Positioning the product for the target segment Having chosen which market segments to target, the business must now make decisions about **positioning** its products

Table 3.3 shows average household spending in three categories of total expenditure as well as total expenditure per week for five regions of the UK, and the average for the UK itself.

	Food & non-alcoholic drink	Clothing & footwear	Alcohol & tobacco	£ per week All spending
North East	50.1	19.7	20.6	285.4
South East	61.4	21.4	18.9	392.5
South West	55.4	17.3	18.0	332.2
Scotland	57.7	21.0	23.0	317.3
Northern Ireland	67.3	25.3	21.2	316.9
UK average	**58.5**	**21.0**	**20.5**	**348.2**

Adapted from the *Social Trends*, Office for National Statistics.

Table 3.3 *Household expenditure by region*

1 'Table 3.3 shows household expenditure segmented by region.' Explain what this means.
2 (a) What are the differences in spending between the regions shown in the data?
   (b) Discuss how (i) a supermarket chain and (ii) an alcoholic drinks manufacturer might use this data to make marketing decisions.

within that market (see unit 11). In particular, it must consider the competition it faces and how it will differentiate its product from others.

Developing a marketing mix for each target segment Finally the business must develop a **marketing mix** (see unit 1). This would take into account the product, price, promotion and place suited to the market segment. By doing this, the business will have responded to the needs of the market and its customers, i.e it would be **market orientated**.

keyterms

Customer (or consumer) profile - an analysis of the characteristics of customers (or consumers) in a market or market segment, e.g. by their age, income or where they shop.
Demography - the study of population, its composition and how it is changing over time.
Market segment - part of a whole segment which contains a group of buyers with similar characteristics, such as age, income, social class or attitudes.

✓ **checklist**

1 How can a market be segmented geographically?
2 Explain THREE ways in which the spending patterns of females aged 25-35 with children who are in paid employment might differ from those of males aged 55-65 who have taken early retirement and whose children have left home.
3 (a) What is meant by 'social class'?
   (b) Give TWO ways in which the spending of social class A households might differ from that of social class D.
4 How might understanding the personality of different groups of consumer help in the marketing of a product?
5 Briefly explain FIVE ways in which consumers might be segmented on a behavioural basis.
6 What is the difference between a differentiated marketing strategy and a concentrated marketing strategy?
7 How might a business plan a concentrated marketing strategy?

The first pilsner beer, Pilsner Urquell, was created by a Czech brewery in 1842. But it has been Western European and US brands, particularly Heineken, Budweiser and Beck's, owned by other companies, which have become the top international Pilsner brands.

South African Breweries (SAB) bought the Czech brewery in 1999. It wants to put that very first Pilsner beer back onto the international market and begin to rival the best selling brands. It has a head start as it is generally agreed by beer experts that Pilsner Urquell is a good tasting, high quality beer. This distinguishes it from many 'international' beers, which are criticised for being bland and bought only because of heavy promotion.

SAB defined its target market segment for Pilsner Urquell as 25-40 year olds, 'transitional' consumers who are neither 'promiscuous' in their brand allegiances nor yet hardened in their ways. Promotion of the brand would emphasise Pilsner Urquell's status as the 'original golden beer'. It would develop a theme called 'Inspiring Originality' which aimed to tap into a consumer's aspirations to be mould-breaking, charismatic and uncompromising.

Sales have already doubled since SAB bought the Czech brewer two years ago. There are now encouraging signs that Pilsner Urquell could become an internationally recognised beer brand. Sales to the USA have increased considerably, whilst the availability of the beer in European markets such as Germany, Poland, Hungary and Slovakia has improved.

Adapted from the *Financial Times*, 26.9.2001.

1 What is meant by the term 'market segment' (third paragraph)? (3 marks)
2 Explain the main characteristics of the market segment into which South African Breweries hopes to sell Pilsner Urquell. (8 marks)
3 Examine the possible factors which could prevent Pilsner Urquell from becoming a brand to rival Heineken, Budweiser and Beck's. (8 marks)
4 The beer is being sold at a 'premium price'. This means that its price is higher than that of the average mass market beer. Discuss whether this is likely to help increase sales of Pilsner Urquell to (a) the market segment targeted by SAB and (b) other consumers. (11 marks)

4 The role of market research

Puma

Knowledge Puma is number four in the world market for trainers behind Adidas, Nike and Reebok. Most trainers are bought as much as a fashion accessory as footwear. This is particularly true for those consumers who buy more than one pair of trainers a year.

Application Puma carries out *market research* to find out what the next trend in fashion trainers will be. It employs researchers and designers who spend their time on the streets, in shops and in clubs looking at what people are currently wearing. They will talk to *consumers* who buy trainers and try to find out what other *products* are being bought. This is an example of *field* or *primary research* to gather *primary data*.

Analysis Market research gives Puma the insights it needs to compete successfully against other companies that make trainers. It provides knowledge which can be used in the design process to make next year's models. Without market research, designers would have to rely on their own perceptions of what consumers want to buy. These could be very different from consumers' views.

Evaluation Market research is vital for the success of Puma. But equally, the success of the latest product range depends upon the ability of Puma designers to use information gathered in the design process. It is the combination of market research and designs based upon it that leads to high selling products.

Adapted from TV series 'Coolhunters'.

Defining market research

Businesses that want to survive and succeed need to keep in touch with their customers. For example, a business starting up should consider who might buy its products. A business suffering falling sales needs to understand why sales are falling before it can develop a response. A business wanting to launch a new product onto the market should consider whether customers will buy the product in sufficient quantity to make it profitable.

This process is known as MARKET RESEARCH. It has a number of key elements.
- Deciding what information needs to be collected. This might be information on consumer reactions to a prototype or figures on the size of a market.
- Deciding what is the most appropriate way to collect information. For example, would it be best to look at published statistics or to conduct a survey?
- Collecting the information using the chosen method.
- Collating the information. This means putting it together. For example, in a survey, the percentage of respondents who answer 'yes' to a particular question needs to be calculated from the individual survey forms.
- Analysing the information. This means drawing out what the information is saying in response to the questions that are asked and seeing whether any clear conclusions can be drawn.
- Communicating the results of market research to those who need to know about the findings.

The uses of market research

Market research is used by businesses for a variety of reasons.

Keeping in touch with customers The main purpose of market research is to keep a business informed about the wishes of actual and potential customers. This helps in decision making.

Monitoring market performance Some market research is carried out to give feedback on how well a business is doing. For example, an airline will have information on its sales, the number of passengers it is carrying, what routes they are travelling and how much revenue it is receiving. But the airline might also wish to find out whether its passengers are happy with its service. Unhappy passengers today could lead to lower ticket sales tomorrow. Equally, it might want to find out how the competition is performing. If the market share of the airline is falling in a market which is growing, does this indicate poor performance?

Identifying market opportunities Market research can be used to find possible new markets. The airline might be considering what new routes to fly. Market research could identify which of the many new routes would be profitable. Equally, an aircraft manufacturer might carry out market research to identify what sort of planes will sell to the world's airlines in the future.

Generating, refining and evaluating marketing decisions The airline might identify an opportunity for a new route from London to Delhi. But there are many decisions that need to be taken before any plane flies the route. How many flights a day will there be? Will the service be different at weekends than on weekdays? How large will the aircraft be flying the service? Which airport will they use in London and in Delhi? Will there be any stopovers, and if so where? What will be the fare structure? How will the service be promoted? Market research can help when making these marketing decisions. Initial decisions can be changed and refined in the light of market research information. Market research can also help to judge whether the decisions have been successful or not.

Reducing risk By taking action on the basis of good market research, a business is able to reduce the risks it faces. The extra information provided by market research aids decision making. For example, it can be used to take action to minimise the effect of a downturn in the market. It can be used to

Smile as you walk down that aisle, because retailers have you in their sights. New technology being examined by high street stores uses cameras to analyse which products catch shoppers' gaze. They can tell whether a purple display attracts more attention than a red one. They know how long you spend staring at the beer and whether women or men are more likely to be swayed by a special offer. Brand manufacturers are also trialling the system, hoping that it will help them target promotions more successfully.

Retail psychologist Tim Denison of Solution Products Systems, which devised the system, said: 'As consumers, we are often unaware of our in-store movements, actions and thoughts. We filter out many of the sub-conscious processes, so brand guardians and retailers gain only limited benefits from traditional consumer research methods in determining in-store behaviour'.

Crude customer footfall measures help stores work out basic conversion rates (sales per shopper). But they are too broad. For example, an 18-month-old child would be counted walking into Mothercare, but would be unlikely to make a purchase.

Adapted from the *Daily Mail*, 2002.

1 **Explain why the 'new technology' would gather primary rather than secondary data.**
2 **Suggest THREE ways in which a supermarket could use the market research data gathered.**

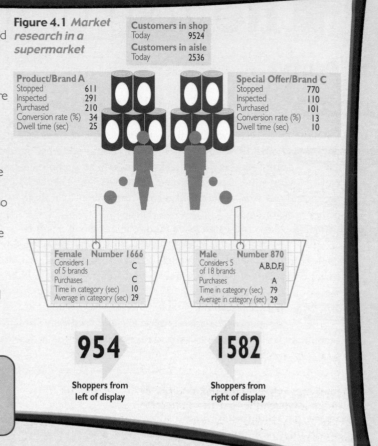

Figure 4.1 *Market research in a supermarket*

Customers in shop	
Today	9524
Customers in aisle	
Today	2536

Product/Brand A
Stopped	611
Inspected	291
Purchased	210
Conversion rate (%)	34
Dwell time (sec)	25

Special Offer/Brand C
Stopped	770
Inspected	110
Purchased	101
Conversion rate (%)	13
Dwell time (sec)	10

Female   Number 1666
Considers 1 of 5 brands	C
Purchases	C
Time in category (sec)	10
Average in category (sec)	29

Male   Number 870
Considers 5 of 18 brands	A,B,D,F,J
Purchases	A
Time in category (sec)	79
Average in category (sec)	29

954

Shoppers from left of display

1582

Shoppers from right of display

counter threats posed by competing firms. It can also help to successfully launch new products, change prices or develop a new marketing campaign.

Desk research and field research

There are two ways of collecting data in market research. DESK RESEARCH (sometimes called SECONDARY RESEARCH) involves collecting data which have already been gathered for another purpose, called SECONDARY DATA. Looking up a list of business addresses in *Yellow Pages*, reading a report on the hotel trade by a market research agency, or studying figures on inflation published by the Bank of England would be examples of desk research (see unit 5).

FIELD RESEARCH (sometimes called PRIMARY RESEARCH) involves collecting new data which are not present before the research began, called PRIMARY DATA. The data are generated by the researcher for a new purpose. Observing the behaviour of consumers in a supermarket, discussing a new product in a focus group or conducting a telephone survey would be examples of field research (see unit 7).

Quantitative and qualitative research

Market research can also be divided into quantitative research and qualitative research. QUANTITATIVE RESEARCH collects data in the form of numbers that can be analysed statistically. This is known as **quantitative data**. It often involves collecting data from a large number of people. The information may come from a postal survey or from business sales data, for example. It may show that 15 per cent of customers aged over

65 bought a product. Or it may show sales of a product rose by 20 per cent from 10 000 to 12 000 over a year.

QUALITATIVE RESEARCH explores people's opinions and judgments. It involves the collection of **qualitative data**. These are data that are not in the form of numbers. They might include descriptions of consumers' motivations, attitudes and behaviour. They can often be found through one-to-one interviews and small focus groups. For example, a small group of young people being interviewed may say that a brand is 'not cool'. Or a consumer may say that it was 'difficult to find the product they were looking for' on a company's website.

Researchers ideally want research to produce data which are **valid** and **reliable**. Data are valid if they present an accurate measurement. They must also measure what they are supposed to measure. For example, production figures are valid if they provide an accurate measurement of the number of products a business makes. Data are reliable when researchers using the same methods produce the same results. An example might be a number of market research agencies interviewing the same people and all agencies having the same opinion about consumers' views of a product.

Data can be reliable but not valid. For example, a number of market research agencies, using the same methods, might find out that a particular product is the UK market leader. The data would then be reliable. But the market research agencies might all have failed to include sales of the second largest business in Scotland. In fact, it is this business's product which is the UK market leader. Although the original data are reliable, they are not valid because they have failed to pick up the Scottish sales.

1 Explain briefly the key elements of market research.
2 List the ways in which a business can use market research.
3 Explain the difference between (a) desk research and field research; (b) quantitative and qualitative research.

Market research and marketing research

A distinction may be made between **market research** and **marketing research**. Market research is research into a particular market, like the cosmetics market or the foreign holiday market. Market research would consider who buys a particular product or their perceptions of the product. Marketing research, in contrast, is the broader function of linking the customer to the business through information. For example, marketing research for a motor company could involve finding out what consumers perceive to be the environmental damage caused by motor cars. Or it could be researching whether it would be profitable to export all of a company's products to the Far East.

Market research is therefore a part of broader marketing research. However, the two terms are often used interchangeably. In this book, the term 'market research' will be used to refer to all research associated with marketing.

"keyterms"

Desk (or secondary) research - the gathering of information, called secondary data, which has already been collected for another purpose.
Field (or primary) research - the gathering of new information, called primary data, which has not been collected before.
Market research - a process of identifying data needed to understand the relationship between the customer and the business, its collection, collation analysis and communication to decision makers.
Primary data - information which has not been collected before.
Qualitative research - research which collects qualitative data, i.e. data that are not expressed as numbers. This might include opinions, judgments and attitudes.
Quantitative research - research which collects quantitative data, i.e. data that are expressed as numbers and can be statistically analysed.
Secondary data - information which has already been collected for another purpose.

Men and women in their 50s are breaking out of the stereotypes of typical middle age. But their experiences increasingly depend on how well they have done at work and whether they stayed married. As life expectancy increases, 'people in their 50s will redefine the meaning of 'age'', says Professor Richard Scase, one of the authors of a report from the Economic and Social Research Council.

The quantitative study, which uses current trends to predict what it will mean to be 'fit and 50' in a decade's time, says: 'More will see themselves as young, and engage in a diversity of active, creative leisure pursuits. Reaching 50 will no longer be a predictor of changes in spending, saving and consumption patterns. This will have huge ramifications for retailers as age and income cease to be relevant categories for advertising, marketing and selling. We are witnessing the evaporation of standard income and age categories into various "lifestyle" tribes shaped by diversities in personal life and employment.'

The study, a piece of desk research, shows that people in their 50s share the attitudes of those in their 30s and 40s rather than those in their 60s and adapt well to new technologies. But growing concern for 'one's own good' suggests more separation and divorce, often with financial consequences for the less well-off and for some women. Equally, differences in income and wealth are greater among those in their 50s. The top 10 per cent typically have £65 000 in liquid assets and the next 10 per cent £10 000. Most others have only a few hundred pounds.

Adapted from the *Financial Times*, 20.11.2000.

1 Explain what is meant by the terms (a) 'quantitative' (3 marks) and (b) 'desk research'. (3 marks)
2 Explain why the report described in the passage is a piece of 'marketing research' rather than 'market research'. (6 marks).
3 A high street women's fashion retailer owns three chains of stores. One is aimed at teenagers aged 14-19; another focusses on young adults, 18-25; a third stocks clothes for women aged 25-45. How might this retailer respond in the long term to the information about changing trends contained in the report? (8 marks)
4 A travel operator specialises in adventure holidays, from white water rafting in Wales to treks by camel across the Sahara. Its marketing has always been focussed on males in their 20s and 30s. However, there has been a small, but growing number of retired males in their 50s booking holidays. Consider whether the company should make the over 50's the main focus of its marketing. (10 marks)

5 Desk or secondary research

Researching the pipe and fittings market

Knowledge A large company selling into many different countries developed a new pipe and fittings system.

Application This *multinational company* felt that the system was superior in design to *competing* systems in the UK *market*. It commissioned a *market research report* from a *market research company*. The *multinational* company wanted to find out about the UK *market*: the *market size*, the *market structure*, processes and attitudes within the *market*, and the *opportunities* and *threats* for a new *product*.

Analysis The market research consisted of both field research and desk research. For the desk research, the agency undertook a literature search, looking for any existing research on the topic. For example, it reviewed publications from trade associations and trade magazines and gathered relevant government statistics. It also gathered sales literature from competing companies to develop an understanding of their product range, pricing and strengths and weaknesses.

Evaluation By using market research, the multinational company was better able to see how to target its product at the market. In particular, it gained a better understanding of potential distribution channels for its product and which key advantages of its new system to emphasise in marketing. It was money well spent given the investment needed to launch the new product and promote it in the future.

Desk research

Desk research (sometimes called **secondary research**, see unit 4) is the process of collecting data which have already been complied for another purpose. These secondary data already exist in one form or another.

There are two main types of secondary data. **Internal data** are data which are available from the records of the business conducting the desk research. **External data** are data which have been obtained from sources outside the business.

Internal data

Businesses keep records for a variety of purposes. These records can be used for market research purposes. A variety of internal records will be available to the researcher.
- **Sales figures**. These give information about past sales patterns and can be used to predict future sales.
- **Customer databases**. Information about customers may be kept. So it may be possible to find out who are the most important clients of a business, for example. This information could be used to target these customers.
- **Customer responses and complaints**. A business may keep an ongoing record of customer complaints. Or customer attitudes might be monitored regularly through feedback. These records might be used to identify where quality needs improving or where there may be scope for new products.
- **Previous reports, minutes and memos**. There may be documents produced as part of previous market research which could be used now. Or day to day written records may include material of use in researching a market.

External data

There are many sources of information available outside the business. Traditionally they have been available in paper form. Increasingly this information is also available on disk, on Internet websites or on CD Rom.

Other businesses Other businesses, including competitors, publish a wide variety of information. For example, a company must produce a set of publicly available accounts (see unit 20) which can be used to assess its financial position. In some industries, like car manufacturing, businesses publish production figures. Product specifications may be available, particularly to businesses bidding for contracts. Some businesses have their own publications, such as *Ford News*.

Governments, international organisations and research institutes There is a wealth of data published within the **public sector** or by government-funded organisations. The UK government, for example, funds its own statistics body, the **Office for National Statistics (ONS)**. This publishes a range of statistics in books, such as *Social Trends*, the *Annual Abstract of Statistics* and *Economic Trends*. The ONS also has an Internet site where data can be obtained. Large amounts of data are also available from international bodies such as the European Union, the World Bank and the United Nations. National research institutes, such as National Institute for Economic and Social Research (NIESR), also publish reports and statistics.

The trade press Many industries in the UK have their own newspapers or magazines which publish industry news and data. Examples include *Farming Weekly* and *The Grocer*.

The local, national press and international press and media
Newspapers, magazines and journals can also provide data. Magazines may publish stories about competitors. Newspapers may produce reports on particular industries or countries. Even television and radio may carry reports which can be used as part of market research.

Trade associations A TRADE ASSOCIATION is a body which represents the interests of a particular industry. Examples are The Association of British Travel Agents, The Salt Manufacturer's Association and the Guild of Hairdressers. Trade associations are financed by subscriptions paid by businesses within the industry. In return, they provide members with a variety of services, which may include market research and reports.

Chambers of Commerce Chambers of Commerce represent all businesses in a local area. They provide a variety of information on the local economy and on local businesses.

Directories and registers A variety of directories and registers are published. Some, like *Yellow Pages*, are aimed both at businesses and households. A small business wanting some electrical work done, for example, might look up *Yellow Pages* to draw up a list of potential contractors. Businesses wanting names and addresses of households in a local area to send out advertising leaflets may use the Electoral Register. There are other directories aimed solely at businesses. For example, CBB Research publishes the *Directory of European Industrial and Trade Associations*, listing trade associations throughout Europe.

Market research organisations There is a number of commercial organisations which conduct their own market research and sell their findings to customers. They include Mintel, Keynote Reports, Verdict and the Economist Intelligence Unit. Some are widely distributed. For example, some Mintel and Keynote Reports are bought by reference libraries throughout the UK. They can be read by the general public and businesses for free. Most reports, though, are sold only to businesses. Where the number of potential buyers is small, a market research organisation may charge thousands of pounds for a copy of a 100 page report. Customer companies are prepared to pay these prices because it would be more costly to undertake their own research.

Internet website pages Many businesses have their own websites on the Internet. A website might include a variety of information about a business, including its product range, company history and aims, prices, sales and past accounts.

The advantages of desk research

Desk research has a number of advantages compared with field research.
- Secondary data is usually relatively cheap to collect, particularly where sources are known by the researcher. For example, a company might buy a subscription to a magazine or a regular report on market trends.
- It can be collected in a fairly short period of time. It is not, for example, like a survey of customers which might take months just to set up.
- It is often possible to collect data on the same marketing area from several sources. This allows the data to be cross checked and verified because secondary data is not necessarily accurate.

- Historical data can be collected to establish a trend or perhaps an absence of trends.
- Valid, accurate data can be obtained without using sophisticated research techniques. This makes it suitable for small and medium sized businesses which cannot afford to employ an agency to conduct research.
- It is often useful to conduct desk research prior to field research. This may help to establish the 'right' questions to be asked before carrying out more expensive and complex field research.

The problems with desk research

Desk research does have a number of problems.
- It can be difficult to find the right data to answer the question which has been set by the market researcher. For example, secondary data is unlikely to be available about customer attitudes to a particular product. Or a set of data may relate to households when the researcher wants data on individuals.
- Secondary data can easily be too old to be relevant. This is particularly true where markets are changing rapidly.
- Researchers must always be aware of how the data has been collected and the problems involved. For example, the results of a survey may be published, but the footnotes may state that the sample size was too small for much confidence to be placed on the findings.
- Researchers must be aware of bias. Company reports and accounts may try to show figures in an optimistic light to satisfy shareholders. Governments may try to manipulate official statistics to encourage businesses to invest.
- Desk research uses data that have already been collected for another purpose. They may not be suitable for the particular research being carried out.

keyterms

Trade association - a body which represents the interests of the businesses which are its members. Typically, trade associations represent businesses in a particular industry.

✓checklist

1. What is the difference between internal data and external data in desk research?
2. A market research agency wishes to conduct research for a client on the market for chilled foods. What external sources of data might it use for this research?
3. Explain the advantages of desk research compared to field research.
4. What might be the problems in using secondary data?

Jeffersons is a company which specialises in market research. For a fee, it will produce a market research report for a client.

A business selling bathroom and kitchen products approached Jeffersons to gain a more detailed and accurate understanding of how its products and their prices compared to those of other suppliers in the UK market. The review Jeffersons undertook covered 40 different companies and 150 products. The features of the products, prices and options, such as different colours, were all reviewed. The research was conducted over 2 months and a report written. The cost to the client was around £12 000.

One way in which information was gained was to obtain sales literature either from distributors or manufacturers of rival products. The sales literature showed what products were available in the market and their prices.

Another way was to visit showrooms or distribution outlets. This enabled researchers to look at the product and its quality. It allowed the researchers to assess the sales approach adopted by the selling company.

A third way of gaining information was to ask for quotations from manufacturers and distributors for a range of products. Prices for the range could then be compared to the prices charged by the client.

Jeffersons also provided background data on competing businesses. Through desk research, it obtained figures for the number of employees, sales turnover and profits of competitors.

1 Explain what is meant by the terms:
  (a) 'market research'; (3 marks)
  (b) 'desk research'. (3 marks)
2 Outline TWO ways in which the Jeffersons research agency gathered data by using desk research. (6 marks)
3 Analyse the advantages of using desk research in this study. (8 marks)
4 Consider how the client company might have used the information gained by the market research. (10 marks)

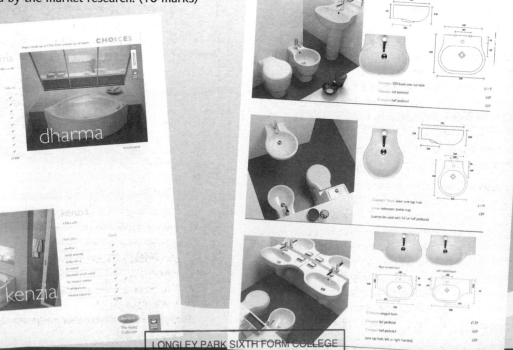

6 Business data

TY Gaylor

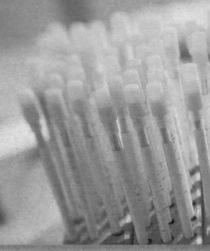

Knowledge — TY Gaylor is a company which specialises in the production of high quality products used in the medical profession. It produces large amounts of data.

Application — These *data* are used in a variety of ways. *Customers* are given *specifications* about products in *sales brochures*. The *accounts department* uses *data* to monitor past *financial transactions* and to predict what might happen in the future. The *managing director* and the rest of the *board of directors* use *data* to help them make decisions about the future of the *company*. *Shareholders* can find details of *company performance* in the *Annual Report and Accounts*.

Analysis — Data are essential to the effective running of the business. The sales team, for example, uses moving averages to smooth out sharp monthly changes in sales volumes. This enables it to have a clearer picture of trends in monthly sales.

Evaluation — Without a sophisticated use of data, TY Gaylor would not be as successful as it is now. In a quality niche market, use of data in every part of the company is essential to sell and manufacture products which satisfy the needs of customers and are profitable.

Presenting data

Businesses gather a variety of data. Some data are used **internally**, within the business. Some are available to people outside the business, such as customers, suppliers or the government. Data can be presented in a variety of ways.

In words Data can be presented in written form. For example, a report might state that 'first quarter sales in 2002 were £1.2 million, falling to £1.1 million in the second quarter and £0.8 million in the third quarter, whilst rising to £1.5 million in the fourth quarter'. A QUARTER here is a period of three months. If too much data is presented in a report it can be difficult to read and understand. It can also be difficult to tell at a glance what is happening. For these reasons, data is often presented in a table or chart.

Tables Table 6.1 shows the data from the report in the form of a table. When presenting a table, it is important to number the table clearly if it is to be referred to elsewhere. It must also be given a title, which explains what the table shows. If the data refer to a period of time, this should be shown clearly in the title or on the table. Units of measurement must also be included, usually as a label for the table. In Table 6.1, the unit of measurement is '£ million'. Tables have the advantage over graphs that exact figures can be read. For example, in the fourth quarter, sales were exactly £1.5 million. This is more difficult to read off the line graph or bar graph in Figures 6.1 and 6.2. When there is a great deal of data, though, it can often be difficult to identify trends or see relationships between different variables in a table.

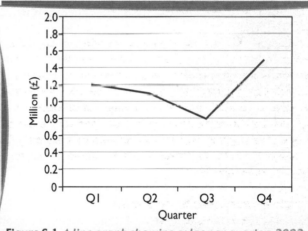

Figure 6.1 *A line graph showing sales per quarter, 2002*

Line graphs Line graphs show the relationship between two variables. Figure 6.1 is a graph showing the data in Table 6.1. The two variables are time and quarterly sales. On a line graph, time is usually shown on the horizontal axis. The number of times something occurs, the FREQUENCY, and the value or

	£ million
Quarter	Sales
Q1	1.2
Q2	1.1
Q3	0.8
Q4	1.5

Table 6.1 *Sales per quarter, 2002*

Menzies Group plc is a company which specialises in logistics - transporting products from one place to another for other businesses. Table 6.2 shows the value of its profit between 1997 and 2001.

	1997	1998	1999	2000	2001
£ million	30.6	28.6	13.4	33.3	15.1

Table 6.2 *Menzies Group plc, profit before taxation 1997-2001*
Adapted from Menzies Group, *Annual Report 2001*.

1 **Describe in words the change in profit of the company.**

2 **Construct a line graph showing profit between 1997 and 2001.**

3 **Construct a bar chart showing the information in Table 6.2.**

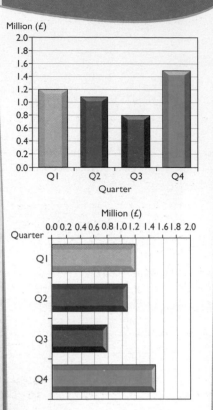

Figure 6.2 *A bar chart showing sales per quarter, 2002*

	£ million	£ million
Quarter	2001	2002
Q1	1.5	1.2
Q2	1.3	1.1
Q3	0.9	0.8
Q4	1.7	1.5

Table 6.3 *Sales per quarter, 2001 and 2002*

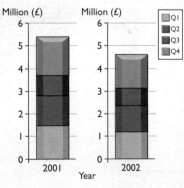

Figure 6.3 *A component bar chart showing sales per quarter, 2001 and 2002*

Cost of sales order, £	Number of orders
0-1 000	30
1 001-3 000	80
3 001-6 000	60
6 001-10 000	20

Table 6.4 *Sales dispatched by cost of order, third quarter 2002*

amount, such as sales, are usually shown on the vertical axis. Line graphs are good for showing trends which can be seen at a glance. On the other hand, values of variables can be difficult to read accurately from the scale on the vertical axes. There can also be difficulties in constructing or reading line graphs where there are several lines showing more than two variables, with widely differing values. For example, it would be difficult to construct a readable line graph with 2002 quarterly sales figures for 10 companies with sales ranging from £30 000 to £250 million. A table would be far more effective at showing this information.

Bar charts A BAR CHART shows information in the form of bars. Table 6.1 has been converted into two types of bar chart in Figure 6.2. The first is a vertical bar chart, the most often used of the two. As with line graphs, time is usually placed on the horizontal axis. The second is a horizontal bar chart. Here time is shown on the vertical axis. A horizontal bar chart is simply a vertical bar chart turned

clockwise through 90 degrees.

A **component bar chart** allows more complex data to be presented clearly on a bar chart. Table 6.3 shows the 2002 value of sales for the business in Table 6.1. But it also adds the 2001 figures. Figure 6.3 shows two bars, one for total sales in 2001 and the other for 2002. But each bar is broken up according to the sales for each quarter. These quarterly sales when added together make up the total yearly sales.

One advantage of using a bar chart is that it is often easier to read off values from a bar chart than a line graph, but less so than from a table. As with a line graph, it is often easier to see trends from a bar graph than from a table. However, the more information and variables displayed on a bar graph, the more difficult it is to read.

Histograms A HISTOGRAM looks similar to a bar chart. However, in a vertical bar chart the value of a variable (its frequency) is shown by the **height** of the bar. In a histogram, it is shown by the **area** of the bar.

Table 6.4 shows the number of orders dispatched in the third quarter of 2002 by the cost of the order. For example, there were 30 orders sent out costing between £0 and £1 000 and 20 orders costing £6 001-£10 000. If the data were drawn as a vertical bar chart, as in Figure 6.4, there would be four bars of equal width with values (i.e. frequencies) of 40, 80, 60 and 20. On the horizontal axis, the bars would be labelled '£0-£1 000, £1 001-£3 000, £3 001-6 000 and £6 001-10 000'.

If the data in Table 6.4 is drawn as a histogram, as in Figure 6.5, the unequal **ranges** of the cost of deliveries are now taken into account. The horizontal axis is divided up into equal ranges. From the data in Table 6.4, an easy division would be to mark every £1 000. Then the bars are drawn.
- There are 30 orders in the first £1 000 range. This is shown by a bar with a height of 30 orders.
- There are 80 orders in the range £1 001 to £3 000. This is made up of two £1 000 ranges, whose average value is 40 orders (80 ÷ 2). So the height of the bar is 40 orders and its horizontal length is two £1 000 ranges (i.e. from £1 001 to £3 000). The **area** of the bar is 2 x 40 orders, i.e the 80 orders shown in Table 6.3.
- There are three £1 000 ranges between £3 001 and £6 000. So, with a total of 60 orders over this range, the height of the bar will be 20 orders (60 orders ÷ 3).

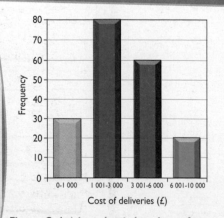

Figure 6.4 *A bar chart showing sales dispatched by cost of order, third quarter 2002*

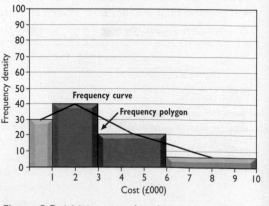

Figure 6.5 *A histogram showing sales dispatched by cost of order, third quarter 2002*

- With four £1 000 ranges between £6 001 and £10 000, the height of the last bar will be 5 orders (20 orders ÷ 4).

Looking at a histogram compared to a bar chart, the visual difference is that the bars are of different horizontal length. Note too that there is never any gap between the bars. The bars form a continuous area. This is because the histogram records **continuous data** - data which covers a complete range of values.

Sometimes, a **frequency curve** is added to a histogram. This is a line which connects the horizontal mid points of the vertical value of each histogram bar. This is shown in Figure 6.5. The area bounded by the frequency curve and the horizontal and vertical axes is called a **frequency polygon**.

Pie charts A pie chart represents data as segments of a circle. The pie chart in Figure 6.6 is drawn from the data in Table 6.5. This shows the value of sales for the four largest companies in a market, and sales of all other businesses in the market. The pie chart has five **segments**, representing the value of sales for each company together with the 'all other businesses' component. The number of degrees of each segment is calculated by finding the proportion of total sales for each company and multiplying it by 360°. As a formula:

$$\frac{\text{Value of the part}}{\text{Total}} \times 360°$$

For example, the segment representing sales for Reading's would be equal to:

$$\frac{£0.9m}{£4.2m} \times 360° = 77°$$

Pie charts are useful for getting an idea of the relative values of the various parts of a total. However, unless clearly labelled with the absolute quantities of the parts, it can be difficult to read an accurate value off the chart. Pie charts are unsuitable for displaying complex data with many components. They are also not particularly suited for showing changes over time.

Mean, medium and mode

Frequently, businesses want to calculate an average. There are three types of average commonly measured.

The mean The arithmetic MEAN is perhaps the most often used average measure. Say that a business had sales over the last five years of £0.9 million, £1.2 million, £1.7 million,

£1.7 million and £1.5 million. The mean is calculated by adding together the value of sales and dividing by the number of values. So the mean is:

$$\frac{£0.9m + £1.2m + £1.7m + £1.7m + £1.5m}{5} = £1.4m$$

The median The MEDIAN is the 'middle value'. It is found by placing values in rank order, from the least to the most. Placing sales values in rank order would be:

£0.9m, £1.2m, £1.5m, £1.7m, £1.7m

The middle value or median is the third number of the sequence of five numbers which is £1.5 million.

If there had been six numbers, the median would have been found by taking the mean of the third and fourth values, the middle two values. Assume that sales in the sixth year were £0.8 million. Then the rank order would be:

£0.8m, £0.9m, £1.2m, £1.5m, £1.7m, £1.7m

The middle two values are £1.2 million and £1.5 million. So the median would be:

$$\frac{£1.2\text{ million} + £1.5\text{ million}}{2} = £1.35\text{ million}$$

The mode The MODE is the most frequently occurring number. In the sales figures only one number occurs more than once. This is 1.7. So 1.7 is the mode.

Table 6.6 shows the number of customers visiting a supermarket chain in four age ranges.

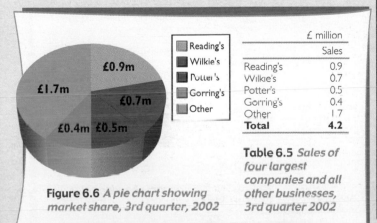

Age range of customers	Number of customers (millions)
10-19	0.6
20-39	1.4
40-69	2.4
70-79	0.3
Total	4.7

Table 6.6 *Number of customers visiting a supermarket chain*

1 Draw a histogram showing the number of customers in each age range. Note that there will be four blocks. Put age on the horizontal axis and frequency of customers on the vertical axis.
2 On your histogram, draw a frequency curve.
3 Explain in words where the frequency polygon is located on your diagram.
4 Draw and label a pie chart to show the data in Table 6.6. Note that each segment of your pie chart will represent the number of customers in a particular age range.

	£ million
	Sales
Reading's	0.9
Wilkie's	0.7
Potter's	0.5
Gorring's	0.4
Other	1.7
Total	**4.2**

Reading's, Wilkie's, Potter's, Gorring's, Other

£0.9m, £1.7m, £0.7m, £0.4m, £0.5m

Figure 6.6 *A pie chart showing market share, 3rd quarter, 2002*

Table 6.5 *Sales of four largest companies and all other businesses, 3rd quarter 2002*

These three methods of calculating an average are useful in different circumstances. The mean uses all the data available. However, one untypical value can lead to a distorted picture. For example, assume that sales in one of the five years was not £1.7 million but £12 million due to a one-off special order. The mean for the five years would then be £3.46 million (£0.9m + £1.2m + £1.7m + £12m + £1.5m ÷ 5) and not £1.4 million. This is over twice as high as the values in the other four years. One advantage of the median and the mode is that a £12 million order would not influence the average because it would be an extreme figure. On the other hand, if there is relatively little data, the mode can produce unhelpful results. For example, can it really be said that two years when sales were £1.7 million were typical simply because the mode is £1.7 million?

Moving averages

Sometimes, data can be subject to fluctuations. For example, most clothes retailers are faced with large changes in sales over the year. In the run-up to Christmas, sales peak and may be four times greater than those in August. It can be difficult to spot a trend from such figures. One way around this is to calculate a MOVING AVERAGE. This smooths out fluctuations, allowing a trend to become clearer.

Table 6.7 shows quarterly sales figures for a business over three years. There are great fluctuations in sales between quarters. So it is not immediately obvious whether the business is performing better at the end of the period than at the beginning. Calculating a moving average should help make the trend clearer.

Moving averages can be calculated using any period of time. In Tables 6.7 and 6.8, they are calculated for three quarters or four quarters. The longer the period chosen, the more fluctuations from period to period will tend to be smoothed out.

A three period moving average Look at Table 6.7. Using a period of three quarters for averaging, the moving average for Q2 in 2000 is £3.3 million. This is calculated by adding together sales in the two quarters either side of Q2, ie Q1 and Q3, to Q2 itself and dividing the total by 3:

$$\frac{£5m + £3m + £2m}{3} = £3.3m$$

Similarly for Q3, the moving average is:

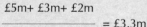

$$\frac{£3m + £2m + £8m}{3} = £4.3m$$

No moving average can be calculated for the Q1 2000 because there are no sales figures for Q4 1999. Similarly, the moving average for Q4 2000 cannot be calculated because there is no figure for Q1 2003.

Odd number moving averages are easier to calculate. This is because there is a **mid-point** in the series. The mid-point of a seven period moving average, for example, would be the fourth period, as there are three periods either side.

A four period moving average Even number moving averages are more complex. No single period provides a mid-point around which an average can be calculated. For example, the mid-point of Q1, Q2, Q3 and Q4 of 2000 in Table 6.8 lies **in-between** Q2 and Q3. Calculating a four period moving average for this in-between point would be:

$$\frac{£5m + £3m + £2m + £8m}{4} = £4.5m$$

Calculating a four period moving average for the mid-point of Q2, Q3, Q4 of 2000 and Q1 of 2001 would be:

$$\frac{£3m + £2m + £8m + £6m}{4} = £4.75m$$

To resolve this problem, a process called CENTRING is used. This allows an average to be plotted against a central figure. Look at Table 6.8. How can a four period moving average for Q3 2000 be calculated? One method is to take an average of the two figures above. This gives a centred average of:

$$\frac{£4.5m + £4.75m}{2} = £4.625$$

Mathematically, it is often quicker to add together the eight numbers which form the four period moving averages and

				£ million
Year	Quarter	Actual sales	3Q moving average
2000	QI	5	
	Q2	3	3.3
	Q3	2	4.3
	Q4	8	5.3
2001	QI	6	5.7
	Q2	3	3.7
	Q3	2	4.0
	Q4	7	4.3
2002	QI	4	4.3
	Q2	2	2.7
	Q3	2	3.7
	Q4	7	

Table 6.7 *A 3 period moving average: quarterly sales figures for a clothing retailer*

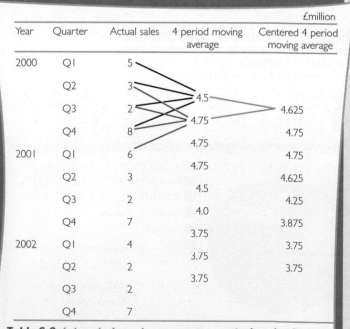

				£million
Year	Quarter	Actual sales	4 period moving average	Centered 4 period moving average
2000	QI	5		
	Q2	3		
			4.5	
	Q3	2		4.625
			4.75	
	Q4	8		4.75
			4.75	
2001	QI	6		4.75
			4.75	
	Q2	3		4.625
			4.5	
	Q3	2		4.25
			4.0	
	Q4	7		3.875
			3.75	
2002	QI	4		3.75
			3.75	
	Q2	2		3.75
			3.75	
	Q3	2		
	Q4	7		

Table 6.8 *A 4 period moving average: quarterly sales figures for a clothing retailer*

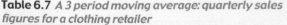

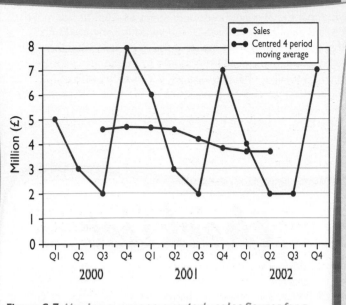

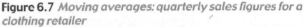

Figure 6.7 *Moving averages: quarterly sales figures for a clothing retailer*

Eco-Gaveda is a business which specialises in selling eco-friendly products by mail order. New customers are sent a catalogue with their first order. Table 6.9 shows the number of catalogues sent.

Year	Quarter	Actual catalogues
2000	Q1	500
	Q2	300
	Q3	100
	Q4	10 400
2001	Q1	540
	Q2	340
	Q3	170
	Q4	11 100
2002	Q1	580
	Q2	350
	Q3	210
	Q4	11 200

Table 6.9 *Numbers of catalogues sent to customers*

1 **Calculate (a) a three period moving average; (b) a four period moving average; (c) a centred four period moving average from the data in Table 6.9.**
2 **Plot (a) the actual number of catalogues; (b) the three period moving average data; (c) the centred four period moving average data onto a graph.**
3 **Discuss what the data indicate about the sales of Eco-Gaveda.**

divide by 8 rather than calculating the two averages and dividing by 2. For example, to calculate the centred average of Q3 in 2000:

$$\frac{(5+3+2+8) + (3+2+8+6)}{8} = 4.625$$

To calculate the centred average for Q4 of 2000 would be:

$$\frac{(3+2+8+6) + (2+8+6+3)}{8} = 4.75$$

It is possible to plot the data from Table 6.8 on a graph, as shown in Figure 6.7. Looking at Figure 6.7, a clearer **trend** picture can be seen from the centred 4 period moving average than from the sales data. Trading conditions deteriorated in 2001, but may have stabilised towards the end of 2002.

Index numbers

Table 6.10 shows sales figures for two companies over a five year period. It is not obvious which company has performed better. One way to make comparisons easier is to present the data in INDEX NUMBER form. This converts one value into the number 100. The rest of the values are then changed so that their proportions remain the same. For example, Heart's sales in 1998 were £742.3 million. They increased to £769.6 million in 1999. If £742.3 million is 'called' 100, then the index value of £769.6 million is 103.7. This is calculated as:

$$\frac{1999 \ value}{1998 \ value} \times 100$$

i.e. 769.6 : 742.3 x 100 = 103.7. The same process is used to calculate the index numbers for sales in 2000-2002, shown in Table 6.11.

One advantage of using index numbers is clear from Table 6.11. It is much easier to see at a glance how Heart's has performed. Instead of the large numbers used before, it can be

seen that over the five period sales rose by 11.3 per cent. It is also possible to compare the performance of Tyler's with Heart's. The 1998 value of sales for Tyler's is also 'called' 100, since 1998 is the BASE PERIOD. This is the year around which all other values are compared. In relative terms, Tyler's has outperformed Heart's. Its sales over the five year period increased 22.9 per cent, compared to 11.3 per cent for Heart's.

The disadvantage of using index numbers is that they do not give absolute values. For example, just using the data in Table 6.11, it is not possible to say how much in £ million were the

	£ million			1998=100	
	Heart's	Tyler's		Heart's	Tyler's
1998	742.3	487.4	1998	100.0	100.0
1999	769.6	521.5	1999	103.7	107.0
2000	801.5	560.5	2000	108.0	115.0
2001	802.6	587.8	2001	108.1	120.6
2002	826.5	599.0	2002	111.3	122.9

Table 6.10 *Heart's and Tyler's, value of sales, £ million, 1998–2002*

Table 6.11 *Heart's and Tyler's, index of the value of sales, 1998–2002, 1998=100*

sales of Heart's in 2002. Nor is it possible to say which of the two companies had the largest sales turnover.

Index numbers can be used to simplify the presentation of a single set of data, as in Tables 6.10 and 6.11. They are also used when the results of complex averages are presented. The index most often mentioned in the news is the **Retail Price Index** (see unit 53). This is an average of the prices of a typical basket of goods and services bought in the UK by the average household. It is calculated monthly from thousands of different prices which are averaged out using a complex formula based on the relative amounts spent on different items. Rather than saying that the average household spent £1 263.98 last month on this typical basket of goods, the value is converted into index number form. This makes it much easier to see the relative **change** in prices from month to month and year to year. This relative change in prices is called the **rate of inflation** (see unit 53). It is easier to see that the rate of inflation was approximately 2 per cent when the index of prices rises from 106 to 108 than if the price of the average basket went up from £1 263.98 to £1 289.26.

Severn Trent and South Staffordshire Group are two UK water companies. They are also active in related industries such as waste disposal. Table 6.12 shows the value of sales of the two companies between 1997 and 2001.

| | £ million | |
	Severn Trent	South Staffordshire Group
1997	1 215	66
1998	1 251	84
1999	1 364	101
2000	1 567	125
2001	1 682	151

Table 6.12 *Sales turnover: Severn Trent and South Staffordshire Group*

Adapted from Severn Trent and South Staffordshire Group Annual Accounts.

1 **(a) Convert the sales figures for Severn Trent into index number form using 1997 as the base year. (b) Do the same for South Staffordshire Group.**
2 **Compare the sales performance of the two companies between 1997 and 2001.**

checklist

1 What is the difference between a line graph and a bar chart?
2 What is a component bar chart?
3 What is the difference between a bar chart and a histogram?
4 Total sales for a company are £300 million. Of this, £200 million comes from the UK and £100 million from the USA. If you were drawing a pie chart to show this, how many degrees would you measure to draw the segment for (a) UK sales and (b) US sales?
5 Using an example, explain the difference between the mean, the median and the mode of a set of sales figures.
6 Using an example, explain the difference between the way that a three period moving average would be calculated and the way a four period moving average would be calculated.
7 Sales for company A increased by 10 per cent between 2002 and 2003. Over the same period company B saw its sales increase by 20 per cent. Using 2002 as the base year, explain how this data could be expressed in index number form.

keyterms

Bar chart - a graphical presentation of data where the value of a variable (its frequency) is shown by the height of a block on a vertical bar chart, or the length of a block on a horizontal bar chart.
Base period - the period, such as a year or a month, with which all other values in a series are compared.
Centring - a method used in the calculation of a moving average where an average can be calculated for a particular period rather than in between periods. It is used where there is an even number of periods, such as two periods or four periods, to be averaged.
Frequency - the total number of times a variable occurs; on a graph or vertical bar chart, it would be shown as a value on the vertical axis.
Histogram - a graphical presentation of data where the value of a variable (its frequency) is shown by an area on the chart rather than, as with a vertical bar chart, the

height of a block.
Index number - an indicator showing the relative value of one number to another from a base of 100.
Mean - often called the average, it is a method of representing a set of numbers by adding up the value of the numbers and dividing by the quantity of numbers.
Median - the middle value of a set of numbers when the data is put in rank order.
Mode - the value which occurs most frequently in a set of data.
Moving average - a method of smoothing out fluctuations in data by calculating an average for several periods around a single period and recording it as the average for that period.
Quarter - a period of a quarter of a year, i.e. three months.

Geest plc

Geest plc is a UK based company which specialises in creating and producing high quality fresh prepared foods. It sells its products to retailers, who in turn sell them on to consumers. Fresh prepared food is a fast growing segment of the UK market. In 2000, it grew by 10 per cent compared to just 2 per cent for all food.

		1971 = 100	
	Food	All household spending	
1971	100	100
1981	104	121
1991	115	166
2001	137	232

Table 6.13 *Real[1] household spending, UK 1971–2000, index numbers*

1 i.e. after inflation has been taken out of the figures.
Adapted from *Social Trends*, Office for National Statistics.

Although the fresh prepared foods sector continues to grow strongly, it still represents only 9 per cent of total food purchases by value. Less than one-third of consumers buy fresh prepared foods in any month, and for most product categories it is less than 10 per cent of consumers. In addition, the average purchase is two items per month or less. These statistics suggest that there is considerable scope for further growth.

Adapted from Geest, *Annual Report* 2001.

1 Explain what is meant by an 'index number' (Table 6.13). (3 marks)

2 Using Table 6.14, calculate (a) the mean growth rate of those UK markets in which Geest is active; (b) the mean growth rate of those UK markets into which Geest does not sell; (c) the name and size of the median sector of the freshly prepared food market; (d) the name and size of the mode of the sectors of the freshly prepared food market. (8 marks)

3 Examine and compare the growth rate of total UK household spending with that of the UK food sector, freshly prepared food, and the sectors within it. (8 marks)

4 Comment on whether Geest is pursuing a strategy which will optimise its growth and profit. (11 marks)

	Total UK market, £m	% UK market growth year on year
Sectors into which Geest sells products		
Ready meals	961	14
Prepared salads	302	1
Prepared leaf	260	20
Pizza (inc. instore delicatessen)	260	6
Prepared vegetables	120	41
Fresh pasta	92	8
Chilled breads	68	6
Fresh sauce	67	10
Fresh soup	63	2
Dips	58	2
Stir Fry	49	11
Prepared fruit	42	17
Other major fresh prepared food sectors but into which Geest does not sell		
Yoghurt/fromage frais	700	0
Sandwiches (multiple retailers & stores)	505	10
Hot eating pastry products	427	3
Dairy desserts	322	15
Chilled cake	227	15
Cold eating pastry products	202	3
Quiche & flan	151	11
Hot eating desserts	88	29
Party food	61	8

Table 6.14 *UK market for fresh prepared food*

Adapted from Geest, *Annual Report* 2001.

7 Field or primary research

Researching television advertising

Knowledge BARB is the standard way of measuring audience figures for adverts on television. It measures the number of a people in a room where a television is playing. In 2002, Mark Ritson of the London Business School conducted some research which showed that many people in a room where the television was playing were not actually watching the television.

Application Both BARB and Mark Ritson's *studies* used *surveys* for their findings. The BARB *survey* is a continuous minute by minute *survey*, using a *sample* of 5000+ households. Mark Ritson's *study* was conducted over 8 weeks with just 8 households in the *sample*. Both *surveys* are *observational studies*, recording the behaviour of *respondents*.

Analysis Mark Ritson argued, on the basis of his study, that advertisers were being misled by the BARB figures. To know that 5 million people were in a room when an advertisement was played does not mean that 5 million people were watching the advertisement. His critics argued that his survey was flawed. How could 8 households observed for just 8 weeks be representative? Equally, advertisers already know that many viewers don't watch advertisements attentively. However, they do pick up characters, colours, tunes and products even though they may be talking to someone else in the room at the time, reading the newspaper or playing a game. TV advertising can be highly effective in terms of consumers buying products even when those consumers don't sit attentively through a 30 second commercial.

Evaluation Billions of pounds are spent each year in the UK on television advertising. Companies using the medium therefore want to know that they are getting value for money. Mark Ritson's field research suggested that one common way of measuring this, the BARB viewing figures, was seriously flawed. Not surprisingly, the advertising industry strongly disagreed and they were probably right. Almost certainly, a lot of television advertising is absorbed by people in a room where the advert is playing even when they are not watching the advert. The power of advertising should never be underestimated.

Adapted from the *Financial Times*, 11.2.2003.

once you pop you can't stop

Millions of prizes to sing about

Field research

Field research (or **primary research**) is about the collection of **primary data** (see unit 4). This is data which is not present before the research began. It is generated for a new purpose.

Primary data might be gathered directly by a business. This may be the case if the business or the number of respondents is small. For example, a small business that buys in an **industrial market** (see unit 2) may survey its few local suppliers to find out whether delivery times are likely to change in future.

Where the business is large or the method of collecting the data is complex, a **market research organisation** may be used. This is a business which specialises in conducting market research. Many **advertising agencies**, which organise advertising campaigns for businesses, have market research departments too.

There is a number of field research methods that can be used. A business must choose which method is most suitable to find the information it is seeking.

Surveys

One method of primary research is a SURVEY. Individuals or businesses are contacted and interviewed. Those interviewed are called RESPONDENTS because they reply to the survey. Surveys make use of a **questionnaire** (see unit 8). This is a list of questions to be asked and from which the survey results will be compiled. Most surveys rely upon **sampling** to make the

collection of data feasible and to cut down on the cost of the survey. This means choosing to survey only a small number of potential respondents. There are various types of survey.

Postal surveys In a postal survey, a questionnaire is sent out to a sample of people and returned via post. Postal surveys are relatively cheap to organise. However, questions cannot be changed once the questionnaire has been sent out. There is also little opportunity to follow up on interesting responses as there would be with a personal interview, for example. Response rates to postal surveys are usually poor. This can affect the validity of the findings (see unit 4). The success of the questionnaire depends on how well it has been constructed. If questions are obscure or key questions are left out, this will affect how much can be learnt from the responses.

Personal interviews In a personal interview, the respondent is interviewed face-to-face. This may be in the street, at home, at work or in some other place. The interview may be **structured**. Here the interviewer asks a series of set questions which often require short, factual answers. Structured interviews are good for gathering **quantitative data** (see unit 4). An unstructured interview does not follow a set pattern. Here, the interviewer follows up responses with questions which may be unscripted. Unstructured interviews are good for collecting **qualitative data**. Personal interviewing can be highly labour intensive and costly. Valid findings depend upon the quality of the questionnaire and the skills of the interviewer.

Telephone interviews Telephone interviews allow both

structured and unstructured interviews to take place. They can be carried out quickly with enough interviewers. But they might be more labour intensive than postal surveys and so tend to be more expensive. It may be difficult to reach respondents or persuade them to give responses over the telephone. Interviewees often feel that the interview is an excuse for trying to persuade them to buy a product. They also have no control over when the interview takes place and so may resent the time wasted on the interview.

Focus groups FOCUS GROUPS involve bringing a group of people together to answer and discuss questions. Questions are likely to be open ended, allowing many different responses. The researcher leading the group can 'focus' in on particular aspects of the research during the group meeting. The main advantage of a focus group is that researchers can see how individuals react with each other. Sometimes, the response of individuals on their own to a question they are asked can be very different from when they are part of a group. Focus groups are good for gathering qualitative data. They can also be relatively cheap to run. However, only a small number of people are likely to be interviewed. Researchers then have to use their judgment to decide whether the focus group was typical of the market.

Consumer panels A CONSUMER PANEL is a group of people who are consulted on a regular basis about a product or group of products. Unlike focus groups, they tend to be semi-permanent groups, whose views will be researched again and again. Members of a consumer panel can be brought together to discuss a product. But more often they record their reactions individually in their homes and send in their comments, known as a **mail panel**. At times they may be interviewed face-to-face or over the telephone. Some consumers are asked by a business to keep **consumer purchase diaries** of the products they buy. A consumer panel is more expensive than conducting a one-off survey and the results are not necessarily valid. However, it can be useful to build up a relationship with a group of individuals who are seen as having an insight into a product.

Internet based surveys The use of the Internet allows a quick, easy and fairly inexpensive way of carrying out surveys. Internet surveys can ask simple questions that collect quantitative data, such as how many times a week do you buy a product? Or they can be more like 'chat rooms' which collect qualitative data. One problem with such surveys is a lack of face-to-face contact with the respondent. Also, respondents may not be representative of the market. People using the Internet tend to have higher incomes and be younger than the average consumer.

Computer assisted surveys Increasingly surveys are making use of communication technology. On-site computer interviews, for example, allow respondents to fill in a questionnaire on a computer monitor. These may be sited in a supermarket or shopping centre. Computer assisted telephone interviews allow an interviewer to record the responses given over the phone on computer. This can be done with a touch sensitive screen or a keyboard. The use of computers speeds up the research process. It also allows data to be collected, stored and analysed more easily.

Observation

Sometimes information can be gained by watching how consumers behave. For example, in a supermarket, researchers could observe how consumers react to a new product on the shelves or to a new store layout. In the home, researchers may observe how consumers react to a new piece of kitchen equipment and what features are most used. Cameras can be used to provide information. Their advantage is that sequences can be played over and over again when something interesting takes place.

Consumer behaviour is not the only thing that can be observed. For example, businesses may employ 'mystery shoppers' to visit their premises and act as customers. The 'shoppers' then make observations in response to a questionnaire given before the visit. These include comments on how staff react to customers and how the shop looks. Or a car service may be booked by researchers and then cancelled, to observe the attitude of the receptionist to the lost business.

Observation has the advantage over surveys that it tells the

Following trials, Boots, the chemist and cosmetics chain, has decided to drop plans to open between 50 and 60 male-grooming stores around the country. The chain had invested £2 million developing the concept and opening two trial stores in Bristol and Edinburgh. The concept was for the stores to offer a range of men's health and beauty products. They would also offer services such as facials and head massages.

A Boots spokesperson admitted: 'Men are not that fussed about having their own stores'. The chain also admitted that the failure was partly because of the low numbers of men visiting their traditional stores. In a recent survey, the company found that 93 per cent of its customers were women. The spokesperson said: 'A lot of men either shop with their partner or their partner shops for them under instruction'.

Despite the setback, Boots insisted that the market for men's toiletries remained buoyant.

Adapted from *The Times*, 11.6.2001.

1 'The two trial shops in Bristol and Edinburgh were examples of test marketing by Boots.' Explain what this means.
2 What did the trial and other market research show about the shopping habits of men?
3 Discuss whether Boots would be better off removing all male toiletry products from its shops and using the shelf space to stock goods or provide services aimed at women.

In April 1996, Derwent Valley Foods successfully launched a Coriander Chutney flavoured poppadom product into the UK market under the Phileas Fogg label. Wanting to capitalise on the success of the launch, Derwent Valley Foods prepared another three flavours for possible addition to the range.

The company employed North East Market Surveys (NEMS), a market research company, to evaluate which of the three flavours should be put into production and sold. As part of the research, NEMS conducted five separate product tasting sessions during September 1996. The sample consisted of 300 consumers, with equal numbers of females and males, aged 18-34 years old and within A, B or C1 socio-economic groups. The products were identified only by a code reference to preserve their anonymity in this blind test. Respondents were invited to taste at least two sample poppadoms of each flavour. They were invited to comment on four criteria - spicy, strength, authentic (Indian), and overall appeal. They were also asked whether they would buy each of the flavours if available in shops, and whether they would buy them as well as, or instead of, the original Coriander Chutney flavoured poppadoms..

Adapted from www.nems.demon.co.uk.

1 **Suggest what were the objectives of the market research carried out by NEMS.**
2 **Discuss whether the research method was to use personal interviews or consumer panels.**
3 **Suggest why the 300 respondents were selected by age, sex and socio-economic group rather than simply chosen at random from the whole population.**

researcher about how those being observed actually behave. In an interview or postal survey, for example, the danger is that the interviewee will exaggerate or not tell the truth. However, observation depends on the ability of the observers to interpret what is taking place. It also tends to be a fairly expensive method of research.

Experiments

Researchers can conduct experiments using consumers. This might involve changing variables, such as price or promotion. It often takes place before a product is launched. For example, a test might be carried out to see how people react to different prices being charged for a new cereal after tasting the product and its main rivals. A problem with this research method is that it is difficult to control humans in the same way as animals in laboratory experiments. So results tend to be less reliable.

One type of experiment used by large companies is TEST MARKETING. This is when a business sells a new product to a limited group of customers to assess their reaction. If the response is favourable, the product can then be sold to the whole market. If not, it may be withdrawn. It can be very costly to sell a new product to the whole market. New products often need heavy promotion. Large numbers of goods may need to be made prior to launch to satisfy potential demand. If the product fails, the business will have wasted its spending on promotion and be left with unsold stock. The cost of failure in a test market is much smaller. Test marketing in the UK tends to take place in a small geographical area, like the North East.

Retail audits

RETAIL AUDITS use information from systems already present in retail outlets. The most comprehensive is the Epos system (Electronic Point of Sale). Most goods are now labelled with a bar code. Retailers use them to process a good as it goes from arrival from the supplier to sale to the consumer. It is possible to conduct research into a product from Epos. For example, in a chain of stores, Epos information should show in which areas of the country sales of a good are particularly high. If the Epos system is linked to till receipts, it could be possible to see whether there is a correlation between sale of an item and the total amount spent in the store. It should also be possible to see whether sales of certain products are linked. Are buyers of tinned spaghetti hoops more likely to buy baked beans than the average customer?

Another source of information is store loyalty cards. Information gathered from these cards should allow a store to identify heavy buyers of, say, wine, cheese or frozen food. Because the store has the name and address of customers, they can be targeted for special promotions on these products.

In practice, retailers and other businesses have failed to exploit retail audits fully. Mainly, this is because information systems have not been set up for the purpose of market research. They have been installed to improve handling of stock or make movement through the tills more efficient. So it is often difficult to use the system to find the information that the researcher wants. It is also costly to undertake research and to act on it. It is likely, for example, that the cost of finding and contacting heavy wine buyers and setting up a wine tasting promotion for them would be greater than any revenue from increased sales.

Advantages and disadvantages of field research

Field research has a number of advantages over desk research.
● Data can be collected which directly applies to the issue being researched. Secondary research uses data which are likely to have been collected for a different purpose.
● Secondary data may be unavailable in a particular area. This is often the case when the researcher wishes to gather qualitative data. Qualitative data tend to focus on particular issues, which may not apply to other areas.
However, there are potential problems when carrying out

✓ *checklist*

1 Who might a large business employ to undertake market research?
2 What is the difference between a postal survey and a face-to-face interview?
3 What is the difference between a focus group and a consumer panel?
4 Explain why a business might employ a 'mystery shopper'.
5 What is meant by 'test marketing'?
6 'Large retailers, such as supermarkets, often hold an enormous amount of information about individual customers but have failed to exploit this.' Explain this statement.
7 What are the advantages and disadvantages of field research?

field research.

- If the research techniques are flawed, so too will be their findings. A poorly worded questionnaire, for example, may not provide the data a business wants.
- Primary data is usually gathered from a small number or **sample** of the population (see unit 8). If the sample is too small, the findings may not be representative of the whole population. When information is deliberately gathered from small groups, researchers have to decide whether the opinions of this group can still help the research.
- Field research tends to be more expensive and take longer than desk research. This is why businesses will often pay for reports about their markets from market research bodies. It is cheaper and easier to buy this secondary data than to gather the primary data contained in the report.

keyterms

Consumer panel - in market research, a group of people who are consulted, perhaps on a regular basis, about a product or group of products.

Focus group - in market research, a group of people brought together to answer usually open ended questions about a product, brand or issue.

Respondent - a person or business who replies to questions asked in market research.

Retail audit - in market research, the gathering together of data by a retailer of information already held within its systems.

Survey - where respondents provide information to researchers about their actions, habits, attitudes and perceptions.

Test marketing - in market research, when a product is sold to a limited group of customers to see their reaction before making a decision about whether to abandon the product, refine it or roll it out to the whole market.

Long established brand icons, such as Toblerone chocolate, Camel cigarettes and Polo mints would be considered unacceptably innovative by marketers if launched today according to Sutkar Gidda, sales and marketing director of SieberHead, a leading design consultancy. They would 'either be strangled at birth or sent back to the drawing board' he said . 'Every new product or pack concept is researched to death nowadays - and many great ideas are thrown out simply because a group of consumers is suspicious of anything that sounds new.

Conservatism among the buying public, twinned with a generation of marketing directors who won't take a chance on something that breaks new ground, is leading to supermarkets and car showrooms full of "me-too" products, line extensions and minor product tweaks.' Mr Gidda believes that the notion of triangular chocolate - launched in 1908 - would today be considered too 'difficult and risky' as a proposition, as would a mint with a hole, introduced 40 years later.

One answer would be a different type of market research. Most product research looks back at what consumers have bought in the past rather than what they might be persuaded to buy in the future. Market research company, FutureSearch, for example, looks at future needs. 'When we researched a new tea-shop/tea bar concept for a client recently, we were well aware that if they came to it cold, consumers would say negative things like 'only grannies like tea-shops' or 'tea isn't fashionable like coffee', says Simon Avlson, New Solutions' managing director. In order to establish the tea bar chain as contemporary in feel, New Solutions created a cuttings file of 'articles' about it, siting it in fashionable areas such as Soho and Brighton. The market research sessions took place after participants had read through the cuttings. 'Because our consumers felt that the tea bar was already up and running, and was wholly contemporary, rather than 1940s, they became very enthusiastic about the whole idea'.

Adapted from the *Financial Times*, 17.6.2002.

(a) Explain what is meant by the terms 'market research'. (3 marks)
(b) Outline TWO methods of field research a company could undertake to find out whether a new tea shop/teabar chain would be successful. (6 marks)
(c) Analyse why potential new products are 'researched to death'. (10 marks)
(d) Discuss the problems of using field research prior to the launch of a new, cutting-edge product. (11 marks)

8 Questionnaires and sampling

Experient

Knowledge Experient, a market research business, was commissioned by a US financial services company to undertake market research. The company had a corporate website aimed at shareholders, career seekers and the media. It also ran a further 48 websites, each providing a different service. For example, some had online services for credit card customers, others for bank account customers. The team running the corporate site believed that it should provide a full range of services to customers to improve the company's competitiveness.

Application Experient drew up a sophisticated *questionnaire*. Over two days, visitors to the corporate website were *randomly sampled*. Every 30th visitor was invited to fill in the online *questionnaire*. 16 per cent of those *sampled* completed the *questionnaire*. In total there were 252 *respondents*.

Analysis The results of the questionnaire backed the views of the business team running the corporate website. 42 per cent of respondents said they were current customers, the largest group of visitors. Of these, 84 per cent came to the website to make an online payment, access their account or find customer service information. Out of the 84 per cent, 53 per cent failed to be able to do this. This was not surprising since the corporate website didn't offer these facilities. But 47 per cent said they had been successful. This showed that nearly half of customers were using links on the corporate website to get onto one of the 48 customer service websites. So, around 20 per cent of the people visiting the corporate website were using it successfully to make customer transactions, a use for which it was not designed. Another 22 per cent were trying to make customer transactions but failing.

Evaluation Experient believed that its research showed clearly that the corporate website should provide a unified one stop shop for all the customers of the US financial services company. By linking in the many different services offered to customers, more services will be sold online. So the US company will save money because its customers will use online services more and call centres less, and the brand will become better known.

Adapted from www.experient.biz/market.html

Questionnaires

Questionnaires are the main method of gathering data in surveys (see unit 7). They are often used when field or primary research is being carried out. A QUESTIONNAIRE is a list of questions. It is given to a respondent, who is asked to answer the questions. Questionnaires have a number of features.

- They can have **closed** and **open** questions. Closed questions have a range of responses set by the researcher. For example, a respondent might be asked: 'Have you visited a local cinema never, once, twice, or more than twice in a week?'. An open question asks respondents to answer in their own words, such as: 'How do you think the services in this cinema could be improved?'
- Questionnaires provide data that are **quantifiable** (see unit 4). For example, the data from a survey might show that the percentage of people visiting a cinema aged 0-16 is 35 per cent, aged 17-50 is 50 per cent and aged over 50 is 15 per cent. The data can then be compared or used to make decisions. For example, the cinema might decide from the results of the survey that it needs to find ways to promote more to younger people.
- Questionnaires can be carried out in a number of ways. They can be self-completion questionnaires. These are left with respondents to fill in and either picked up later or returned by post. Or an interviewer can ask a respondent questions and record the answers. Some businesses use questionnaires which can be answered using an Internet website or receive responses by email.

Sampling

Sometimes a business or market research organisation is able to conduct a survey of all its **target population** - those whose views it wants to find out. For example, a business making components might only supply five companies with parts. So it should be fairly easy to survey all of its customers.

But in most cases it is impractical to survey the whole population. It would take too long and would be too costly to gather and process the information. Instead, researchers take a SAMPLE of the population. This is a number of people from the whole population. Samples should be REPRESENTATIVE. They should have the same characteristics as the whole population. If they don't, results from the sample which are generalised to the whole population may be inaccurate. For example, a survey may be carried out by a food company to find out how many people would buy a new, up-market product. If it only asked pensioners on low incomes, it would almost certainly find that the survey predicted fewer sales than would actually be the case. This is because the sample chosen did not accurately reflect the whole population. In this case SAMPLING BIAS is present.

Size of sample

The SAMPLE SIZE will influence how representative the sample is of the population. Larger samples tend to be more representative. For example, say that the target population is 10 000 customers. If the sample were the same size as the target population, 10 000, it would be totally representative. A sample of 9 000 people is more likely to reflect the characteristics of the target population than 10 people surveyed on the street. So decisions based on the results of the larger sample are more likely to be accurate. But the larger the sample, the longer and more complicated will be the survey. And it is also likely to be more expensive. So businesses, therefore, often use smaller samples.

Type of sample

There are different types of sample and sampling methods that can be used. Each has its own advantages and problems.

Random sampling RANDOM SAMPLING involves choosing respondents at random. So each member of the population has an equal chance of being chosen in the sample. There are many ways of picking a random sample. Market researchers sometimes use random numbers generated by a computer. Every name in the population is given a number. Those selected for the sample have numbers which match those of the random numbers.

As long as the sample is large enough, a sample chosen at random will probably have the same characteristics as the population. So it should be representative. However, this is not always the case. For example, if the target population is people aged 18+, the electoral register could be used. This might appear to give a list of all adults from which a random sample could be taken. But it excludes those who have not registered to vote. A disproportionate number of those who are elderly and on low incomes don't register.

A further problem with this method is that it can be difficult to obtain all the names of the target population. This may be the case if there is restricted information about the population, for example users of a particular medicine whose records are confidential.

Systematic sampling SYSTEMATIC SAMPLING is where the researcher chooses every 5th, 10th or nth name on a list, for example, to include in the sample. It is, therefore, not a random

A pharmaceutical (drugs) company wanted to commission a study on male health worldwide. The results would be used to make major marketing decisions.

A market research agency was commissioned to carry out the study. It set about conducting a two phase research project using survey techniques. In the first phase, 20 000 interviews were completed with target respondents in eight countries. A combination of phone and web interviewing was used. In the second phase, an algorithm was developed to allow the random selection of about 5 per cent of the initial respondents for participation in a second interview. These interviews were conducted on the Internet for those with access or through the use of a paper questionnaire.

The research methods used meant that the same questions were put to all respondents and answers collated in an identical manner. Random sampling meant that sample bias was eliminated.

1 **The market research agency interviewed 20 000 males in eight countries. Suggest why they interviewed: (a) males only; (b) respondents from eight countries rather than just one country; (c) 20 000 people rather than 1 000 or 500 000.**

2 **'Random sampling meant that sample bias was eliminated.' Explain what this means.**

survey and may not be representative of the population. But it is easier to choose those to be surveyed than in a random sample. It is also likely to cheaper and quicker.

Stratified random sampling STRATIFIED RANDOM SAMPLING is a method of sampling that divides the population into 'strata'. Strata can be based on characteristics such as age, gender or income. A random sample which reflects the proportions of these characteristics in the population is then chosen from the strata. For example, a business might know that 30 per cent of people earning less than £10 000, 50 per cent of people earning between £10 000 £40 000 and 20 per cent of people earning over £40 000 buy its products. For a sample of 100 people, it will therefore choose, at random, 30 people earning less than £10 000, 50 people earning £10 000-£40 000 and 20 people earning over £40 000.

The advantage of this method is that it ensures each group in the sample reflects its proportion in the population. It should therefore be more representative than a random sample. However, it relies on researchers being able to stratify accurately the population and derive a random sample from the strata. Surveys based on stratified random sampling techniques are likely to be more expensive to conduct than those using other methods.

Quota sampling QUOTA SAMPLING is similar to stratified sampling. However, the difference is that respondents are not selected at random from each stratum. They are chosen simply to fill the **quota**. For example, a business might know that 50 per cent of its customers are less than 25 years old, 30 per cent are aged 25-45 and 20 per cent are over 45. For a sample of 100 it would need 50 people below the age of 25 to fill its quota from that stratum. So it might choose the first 50 people it meets in a street to fill the quota.

Quota sampling is cheaper, quicker and easier than stratified random sampling. As a result, many high street surveys often use quota sampling techniques. But it is less likely to produce a sample that is representative of the population. This is because researchers can choose who to interview. So people in the same strata do not have an equal chance of being selected. For example, picking 50 people in an out of town shopping centre is likely to exclude many people without their own transport, who may be on lower incomes.

Cluster sampling One way of reducing interview costs is to interview **clusters** of respondents in a geographical area. For example, a bank might want to survey university students across the UK. A random sample would almost certainly require it to interview a few students on every university campus. With CLUSTER SAMPLING, researchers concentrate their interviews on just a few campuses, interviewing as many students as possible. The method is unlikely to produce a representative sample. The students are not selected randomly, nor are they stratified. They could have very different views from the majority of students. On the other hand cluster sampling is a cheap, quick method of getting the views of a target population.

Snowball sampling Sometimes it is difficult to know who to survey. SNOWBALLING attempts to solve this problem by starting off with a few known respondents. These people are then asked to find others who fit the sample. For example, four people who buy a magazine might be asked their views about the latest issue. Each person could then find four other friends who also buy the magazine, and so on. Hopefully, the number of respondents interviewed will get larger and larger as time goes on - hence the term 'snowball'.

The major problem with snowballing is that the sample is not random and may not be representative of the population. So market researchers need to use any results with care.

Statistical significance

The only way to get an accurate picture of a population is to have all relevant data about the population. But this takes time and is expensive. So researchers take a sample and the results obtained from the sample are then applied to the whole population. But how **confident** can a business be about the results of such a survey?

When analysing data from a sample, researchers are interested in certain statistics.
- The mean. This is the average result (see unit 6). For example, the average amount spent on a Monday by a shopper may be £10. On Saturday it may be £20.
- The STANDARD DEVIATION. This tells researchers about the **spread** of results. Standard deviation measures the average difference (deviation) of each item of data from the mean. For example, the standard deviation from the average amount spent may be £2 on Monday and £5 on Saturday. Comparing the means shows that shoppers spent twice as much on Saturday than on Monday. The standard deviations show that the spread of amounts spent was greater on Saturday as Monday. So on Monday, the amounts spent by shoppers varied less and were generally closer to the mean.
- Researchers also make use of a NORMAL DISTRIBUTION curve. This is a 'bell shaped' frequency distribution. It shows the results that can be usually be expected when the whole population is surveyed.

There is a relationship between the normal distribution, the mean and the standard deviation. The mean is in the centre. Most results cluster around the mean, with a few high and low values away from the mean. The data is symmetrically distributed around the mean, so that 50 per cent of results lie either side of the mean, as in Figure 8.1. In a normal distribution:
- about 68 per cent of values lie within 1 standard deviation of the mean on either side;
- about 95 per cent of values lie within 2 standard deviations of the mean on either side;
- about 99.8 per cent of values lie within 3 standard deviations of the mean on either side.

Look at Figure 8.2. What if a business did not know the mean (average) spending, but a sample found that it was £12? How would it know whether this was an accurate reflection of the population? To do this a range of values must be taken either side of £12, which will hopefully include the unknown mean' spending. A 95 per cent CONFIDENCE LEVEL could be set, where values of 2 standards deviations either

DPX is a market research company. In 2003, it completed a report for a manufacturer of building materials and fittings which had seen an unexpected fall in sales over the previous 12 months. The manufacturer wanted to find out how its immediate customers, DIY chains such as B&Q and Wickes, and the larger number of builders' and plumbers' merchants, viewed its products. For example, it wanted to find out whether customers saw its products as giving value for money compared to those of competitors, whether the fittings were reliable and whether the range of products was large enough. It also wanted information about sales and profits of rival businesses to see if they had experienced a similar downturn.

DPX devised a telephone questionnaire for customers. In its sample, it interviewed all the large DIY chains. But it only conducted 30 interviews with smaller builders' and plumbers' merchants. The sample of 30 was judged to be representative of all smaller builders' and plumbers' merchants and a 95 per cent confidence level was given for the responses.

The research showed that a major rival company had completely updated its range over the previous 24 months. The products of the manufacturing company commissioning the research had lost competitiveness as a result. For example, they were said by respondents to be giving less good value for money than before.

> 1 **Explain what is meant by 'a 95 per cent confidence level was given for the responses' from the smaller plumbers' and builders' merchants.**
> 2 **How might the business reduce the chance that its results did not reflect the views of all small builders and plumbers' merchants?**
> 3 **Discuss ONE strategy the manufacturing company might develop to reverse the decline in its sales.**

side of the mean are included. The business would then know that in 95 out of 100 (19÷20) cases the unknown mean would fall within the range either side of the £12 sample mean. If it wanted to reduce the margin of error, it could set a confidence level of 99 per cent. This would involve a larger range of results. So the business could be more certain that the sample reflected the population.

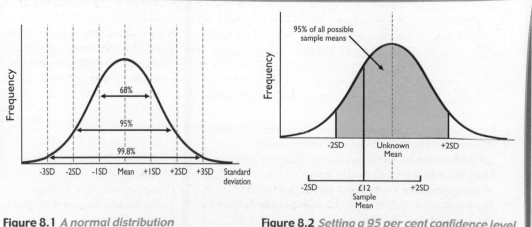

Figure 8.1 *A normal distribution*   **Figure 8.2** *Setting a 95 per cent confidence level*

Researchers often use 95 per cent and 99 per cent confidence levels. For a normal distribution, a 95 per cent confidence level spans 2 standard deviations either side of the population mean. A 99 per cent confidence level spans just under 3 standard deviations either side of the mean.

What about the sample size? In terms of time and cost, the smaller the sample, the better. But to give meaningful results from random or stratified samples, researchers argue that the size of the sample should be over 30. As the sample gets larger the variance of results decreases. So there is less chance that there would be a 'distorted sample', which would give an inaccurate picture of the population.

✓checklist

1 Why do most surveys involve a sample of a population rather than all the population?
2 What is the difference between a random sample and a systematic sample?
3 What is the difference between stratified random sampling and cluster sampling?
4 What does standard deviation show?
5 Explain the meaning of 'confidence levels'.

keyterms

Cluster sampling - where respondents are chosen for interview in a few locations, to reduce the cost of research, rather than being spread evenly across the population.
Confidence level - expresses as percentages an indication of how likely results obtained from a sample can be applied to the population. A 95 per cent confidence level, for example, indicates that the results will be representative 95 times out of 100.
Normal distribution - a naturally occurring frequency distribution where many of the values cluster around the mean, and where there are few high and low values away from the mean.
Population - everyone in the group to be studied in a survey.
Questionnaire - a list of questions, given to a number of respondents to answer, which provide data.
Quota sampling - where respondents are selected for interview in a non-random manner in the same proportion as they exist in the whole population.
Random sampling - where respondents are selected for interview at random.
Representative (sample) - a sample which has the same characteristics as the population.
Sample - a selection of part of the population.
Sampling bias - where the sample chosen is not representative of the population studied.
Sample size - the number of people chosen for the sample from the whole population.
Snowballing - a non-random method of market research where a small number of selected respondents are asked to nominate further potential respondents for interview and so on.
Standard deviation - a measure of the average difference (deviation) of each result from the mean.
Stratified random sampling - a method of quota sampling where respondents are chosen at random.
Systematic sampling - a non-random method of sampling where a researcher chooses respondents by taking every nth name on a list

Local authority Trading Standards Departments are responsible for enforcing over 70 Acts of Parliament, European Directives and other regulations, as well as providing advice to consumers and businesses. For example, Trading Standards Officers inspect business premises regularly where food is prepared or sold.

A County Council hired AMA Research, a market research company, to produce a report. This report was designed to help the County Council understand more fully the needs of consumers and the relative importance these consumers placed on specific services provided.

The basic methodology for this research was to interview consumers within the relevant County boundaries. The first stage involved the design of a questionnaire to meet the research objectives. Following design, proposals were developed to interview a sample size with socio-economic and demographic characteristics, similar to those held by the region as a whole.

The method of interviewing was face to face 'street' interviews as this would allow the interview to raise the issues of spontaneous awareness without stating the Department's identity.

The sample size in this project was governed to some extent by the budget available, with a sample of around 1 000 interviews considered to be sufficient to generate a reasonably high degree of accuracy with the results and yet be within budgetary constraints.

Adapted from www.amaresearch.co.uk.

1 Explain what is meant by the terms:
   (a) 'sample size'; (3 marks)
   (b) 'questionnaire' (3 marks).
2 Explain TWO reasons why the research was commissioned. (6 marks)
3 Analyse the research methods used by AMA Research. (8 marks)
4 Discuss whether AMA Research would have been better off using a random sample with 40 000 respondents. (10 marks)

9 Objectives, strategy and marketing

Aston Martin merchandise

Knowledge Aston Martin is a UK manufacturer of luxury cars. It is owned by Ford, the world's second largest motor manufacturer. In 2001, Aston Martin launched a range of merchandise, including silver handcuff key rings and leather underwear. A catalogue advertising the products was sent to 3 800 Aston Martin customers. Months later, Ford insisted the catalogue was withdrawn. A new catalogue was launched containing more conventional products, such as pens and briefcases.

Application Aston Martin is an *up-market brand*. The *launch* of the *merchandise range* was an attempt to *stretch* the *brand* and move into associated *markets*. The *market leader* in *branded merchandise* is Ferrari, the Italian rival to Aston Martin.

Analysis Stretching a brand across other product areas can be a profitable marketing strategy. Virgin is often quoted as an example of a brand which has achieved success in this. Aston Martin is a recognised brand name, partly because of its association with James Bond films. Their 'racy' image was reflected in the merchandise in the new catalogue. Commentators felt that the decision to withdraw the catalogue reflected Ford's conservative values. But it also reflected a change in Ford's corporate strategy. Between 1998 and 2001, Ford's chief executive tried to diversify into related consumer products, but lost his job when profits fell sharply. He was replaced by a new chief executive who promised to go 'back to basics', concentrating on the manufacture of vehicles.

Evaluation Management at Aston Martin felt that if Ferrari could operate a highly profitable merchandising business, so could they. The 'racy' merchandise probably reflected the tastes of Aston Martin owners. Today's James Bonds might buy a pair of leather boxer shorts. But it is difficult to see them getting excited by Aston Martin pens. So it could be argued that Ford made the wrong marketing decision in getting Aston Martin to withdraw its original catalogue.

Adapted from the *Financial Times*, 26.1.2002.

Marketing objectives, strategy, planning and tactics

Businesses have objectives, strategies, plans and tactics for their marketing.

Marketing objectives These are the goals that a business wants to achieve from its marketing. Marketing objectives are often more effective if they have a target and a time limit. For example, a marketing objective might be to increase market share by 10 per cent in the next three years.

Marketing strategy A strategy is a set of **plans** designed to meet the objectives of a business. A business will devise a suitable strategy to achieve its marketing objectives. For example, a business may decide that the best way to increase market share is to promote a product to a wider range of customers.

Marketing planning Plans are detailed programmes of action about what the business will do in the future. They can be short term, medium term or long term plans. A short term plan for a business might cover the next 12 months. A long term plan might cover the next 3-5 years.

Marketing tactics Tactics are small scale, short term, individual ways in which objectives might be achieved. For example, a marketing objective might be to see continuous rises in sales. A tactic to achieve this over the next 3 months might be to increase spending on advertising by £200 000, or run a 'buy one get one free' offer.

It is also important that a business chooses suitable marketing tactics and strategies to allow it to achieve its marketing objectives. There might be, for example:

- a marketing objective - to increase market share by 10 per cent;
- leading to a marketing strategy - to promote to a wider range of customers;
- leading to a marketing tactic - to increase advertising spending.

Marketing objectives

MARKETING OBJECTIVES are what a business wants to achieve from its marketing. Marketing objectives should support the overall objectives of the business. A business might have marketing objectives in a number of areas.

Sales Probably the most commonly found marketing objective is sales. For example, the objective might be to increase sales by 10 per cent a year. Sales could be sales **volume**, the number of products sold. Or it could be sales **value**, the revenue earned from sales. Achieving growth in sales value could come from changing price as well as volume sold.

Profitability Increasing profits is likely to be an overall objective of a business. It becomes a marketing objective because increased profits are likely to come from increased sales or higher prices. New products could also help raise profits.

Gains in market share Gaining market share (see unit 2) is important when a few businesses control most of the market. In such markets, increased sales are likely to come from taking sales away from a rival business. In markets such as cars or home entertainment equipment, individual businesses will often set themselves marketing objectives of increasing market share.

Improvements in consumer satisfaction Many businesses recognise that consumers must like a product if they are to continue to buy it. Consumer satisfaction can therefore be a marketing objective.

Customer awareness of products Customers won't buy if they are not aware of what is for sale from a business. Raising the awareness of customers, for example through advertising or through direct contact by a sales force, can therefore be an important marketing objective.

Product introduction In many markets, such as computers or mobile phones, businesses have to introduce new products on a regular basis to remain competitive and survive. New products can also become the mature products which earn high profits for the business. Product innovation, a marketing objective, can therefore be part of an overall business objective such as remaining competitive, survival or maintaining profits.

Product innovation Most new products launched into a market are variations on existing products. However, some new products are genuinely innovative. Innovation can then give the business a lead over rivals. At best, such as with the Windows operating system from Microsoft, innovation can lead to market domination. So product innovation can be an important marketing objective for some businesses.

Marketing strategy

A MARKETING STRATEGY is a set of plans about marketing designed to fulfil the objectives of a business. A marketing strategy might, for example, set out plans about product development, pricing and promotion to achieve marketing objectives such as breaking into new markets or increasing sales of existing products.

A marketing strategy is a set of plans about the future. A successful marketing strategy must have plans which are achievable and realistic. Marketing plans in practice may simply be the 'wish lists' of the marketing department, which have little chance of success. For example, at the moment it may be unrealistic for Waitrose to have as its marketing strategy 'the growth of the business so that it becomes the number 1 supermarket chain in the UK within 2-3 years'. It is so far behind the current no 1, Tesco, that within 3 years it highly unlikely that it would achieve this. But a realistic strategy could be to 'increase market share at the expense of small independent grocery retailers'.

Marketing strategy will differ from one business to another. Partly this is because there are many different markets and industries in which they operate. But even businesses in the same market adopt different marketing strategies. For example, the marketing strategy of Aldi and Netto in the grocery market is to offer goods at lower prices than larger rivals such as Sainsbury or Tesco. The marketing strategy of Sainsbury and Tesco places more importance on their product range and the quality of their products.

Another reason why marketing strategy differs is because no two businesses have identical resources. Jaguar cars, for example, has expertise in developing, producing and marketing luxury cars. Vauxhall in the UK may have more expertise in the family car market. So their marketing strategies are likely to be different.

Developing a marketing strategy

There are many ways in which a marketing strategy can be developed.

For a small, established business, a marketing strategy could be simply to continue as before. Only if circumstances change

---

BT Retail provides telecom services to 21 million UK business and residential customers. It is part of the BT company, which has businesses worldwide. Its 2001 Annual Report and Accounts stated: 'BT Retail's strategy is to maintain turnover and (... profit) margins in the medium term at 2001 levels by seeking ongoing productivity improvements from existing businesses and new business opportunities in higher value Internet and broadband services.'

In 2000 a new chief executive, Pierre Danon, was appointed. At the time customer service at BT was perceived as poor. The 'abandonment rate' rate was 50 per cent. So half of all callers to BT were unable to get through and put their phones down. Also, for every 30 incoming calls, 70 were made out. These were usually by BT marketing 'advisers' trying to persuade customers to buy new services.

Danon changed this. For every 70 calls received by BT, only 30 were made out. As a result, customers wanting to report a fault got through more quickly and were less likely to receive a sales call. The abandonment rate fell to 5 per cent as a result. Over the same period, the backlog of outstanding faults on BT customer lines was reduced from 50 000 to 15 000.

Making it easier to contact BT and dealing with faults quickly increased consumer satisfaction. Whilst BT might have been selling fewer new packages, it was retaining customers who might have moved to another operator. Retaining customers and increasing satisfaction were important in helping BT achieve its marketing objectives. It also cut costs and increased profit. The quicker a fault is corrected, the fewer the number of phone calls to BT about the fault. So fewer staff were needed to receive incoming calls.

Adapted from *The Times*, 25.6.2001; BT, *Annual Report and Accounts* 2001.

1 **Using your own words, explain what were the objectives of BT Retail in 2001.**
2 **How might (a) calling customers to sell new BT services and (b) reducing the number of outstanding faults have helped BT achieve these objectives?**
3 **Discuss whether reducing the number of outstanding faults should be a tactic on the part of BT or part of its long term marketing strategy.**

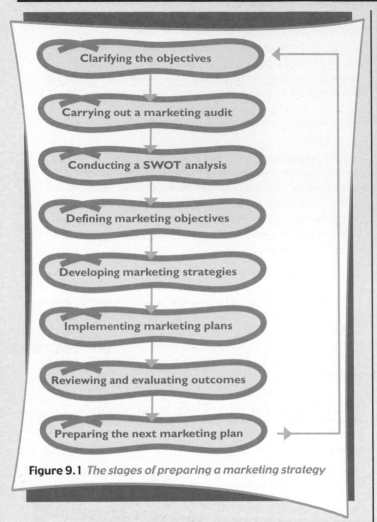

Figure 9.1 *The stages of preparing a marketing strategy*

Stages shown:
- Clarifying the objectives
- Carrying out a marketing audit
- Conducting a SWOT analysis
- Defining marketing objectives
- Developing marketing strategies
- Implementing marketing plans
- Reviewing and evaluating outcomes
- Preparing the next marketing plan

might a business change its marketing strategy. This is an example of a rational marketing strategy if the objective is to continue making the same level of profit. Developing a marketing strategy requires time and resources. It also involves predicting how a market will develop, which could be wrong. Formal planning, therefore, would be costly and could be of little value.

Similarly, in businesses where there are charismatic leaders (see unit 39), planning may be pointless. The leader may be constantly making decisions as events change. These decisions might have little to do with a prepared strategy.

However, many larger businesses use a method of preparing marketing strategies which is logical and rational. The main stages of this method are shown in Figure 9.1.

Clarifying overall objectives

It is difficult to develop a strategy unless the objectives of a business are clear. After all, a strategy is a set of plans to meet given objectives. So those developing a marketing strategy must understand the overall corporate objectives of the business (see unit 63). If the business has no clear overall objectives, it may simply set marketing objectives and plan strategies to meet those objectives. The danger then is that marketing objectives may be in conflict with objectives set by the production department or the finance department. This is likely to weaken the competitiveness of the business.

The marketing audit

A MARKETING AUDIT is a systematic analysis of business procedures, activities, operations, systems and the external environment which may affect how the business markets its products. It should identify the marketing strengths and weaknesses of the business. The audit is carried out to analyse the position of the business now and explain how it arrived at this position. The audit should come in two parts - an internal audit and an external audit.

The internal audit The internal audit considers those aspects of a business over which it has some control. These are likely to be within the business. It might cover areas such as:
- sales - what has been the recent history of sales and who is buying products;
- product - what products are being sold and what new products are in the pipeline;
- prices - what prices are being charged and what pricing strategies are being used;
- promotion - how products are being promoted;
- place - where products are available for sale and what channels of distribution are being used;
- organisation - how the marketing department is organised;
- planning - what plans are already in place and how they are being carried out.

External audit The external audit looks at the environment in which the business operates, over which it has little or no control. The external audit could cover areas such as:
- the market - how big it is and how is it changing;
- the competition - what competitors the business faces;
- the macro-economic environment - how variables such as inflation, unemployment and growth in the whole economy are affecting the business;
- the political environment - how laws, such as labour laws or consumer laws are affecting the business;
- the social and cultural environment - how areas such education or demographic (population) changes are affecting the business;
- technology - how technology is changing the way the business operates;
- the environment - how environmental issues affect marketing.

Sometimes, analysis of the political, economic, social, technological and environment (green) issues is called a **PEST-G** analysis (see unit 64).

SWOT analysis

The information gathered in the external and internal audits needs to be organised so that it is useful to planners and decision makers. There are many ways in which this could be done. One method is to conduct a **SWOT analysis** (see unit 64). This examines the internal strengths (S) and weaknesses (W) of the business. It also takes into account the external opportunities (O) and threats (T) that the business faces.

Marketing objectives

After carrying out a marketing audit and analysing the information using techniques such as SWOT analysis, marketing objectives can be set. They may be in the areas explained earlier in this unit.

The marketing objectives must support the overall, corporate objectives of the business. They should also be realistic. For example, they must take account of the resources available to the business and to the marketing department in particular. These resources may be available internally, such as a research department that develops new products. Or the business may have to buy in outside expertise, such as the skills of an advertising agency.

Developing marketing strategies

Marketing strategies are based upon the marketing objectives of a business. How can these objectives be achieved? There are many different types of marketing strategy.

Competitive marketing strategies Strategies may be devised to achieve the objective of becoming more competitive. One strategy might be to become the lowest cost producer in the market. Another might be differentiation. This involves offering products which are different from those of competitors. Another might be focus, where a business concentrates on selling into a particular market segments (**niche marketing**, see unit 11), rather than selling to the whole market.

Market positioning Another set of strategies relates to the 'position' of a business in its market. In some markets, there is a MARKET LEADER. This is usually the business with the largest market share. The market leader tends to set prices. It sells the products which other businesses attempt to match. Its products have the highest consumer awareness. Market leaders may adopt strategies to expand their share of the market, expand the size of the whole market and their sales within it, or defend their market position against competitors.

MARKET FOLLOWERS are businesses which adopt strategies which react to those of the market leader. If the market leader increases prices, for example, so will they. If the market leader launches a new product, they will launch a similar product. Market followers can adopt strategies such as price cutting to win market share from the market leader. This could be a high risk strategy, however, if the market leader engages in a price war. The market follower could be forced out of business. Market followers, therefore, often try to adopt strategies which will not directly attack the market leader. They might, for example, simply aim to mirror the actions of the market leader. Or they might compete in small (niche) market segments which the market leader sees as unimportant.

Growth strategies Businesses may set themselves the objective of increasing their sales. Not all businesses are in a position to do this. In markets which are shrinking in size, it can be difficult enough for a business to maintain sales. But, where growth is possible, a business can use the ANSOFF MATRIX to analyse its strategies. H I Ansoff, in a 1957 article, suggested that a business had four possible strategies if it wanted its sales to grow. These are shown in Figure 9.2.

● It could leave its products and the markets into which it sells unchanged. But its objective would be to increase its **market penetration** (or market share, see unit 2). Existing customers

In October 2001, the US company Polaroid filed for bankruptcy, faced with a $1 billion debt. Founded in the 1950s, its core product was cameras which made instant prints. Despite spending almost nothing on marketing, and developing just one new product per decade, Polaroid created one of the best-known brands in the world.

The 1990s were more difficult. Photolabs offering almost instant processing of film had sprung up in shopping centres and supermarkets. There was also growing competition from digital cameras linked to computers. Polaroid found it hard to generate the sales revenue needed to cover the high cost of its research expenditure into potential new products.

In 1995, a new chief executive, Gary DiCamillo, was appointed. He vowed to change Polaroid from a technology business to a consumer marketing company. His ideas were influenced by Swatch, the Swiss company that turned precision watches into mass-market fashion items. Instead of concentrating all of Polaroid's resources on a single breakthrough technology, he decided to fund a range of novelty products. For example, the company developed a pink Barbie Polaroid camera aimed at children. The biggest success was the I-Zone camera. This was a cheap camera, often sold at supermarket checkouts, which produced postage stamp-sized photographs of poor quality. It had immense initial success, particularly with Japanese teenagers, but sales quickly fell away.

In May 2001, the company announced two promising technologies. There was a camera giving pictures that could be run out on an ink jet printer at photo quality. And there was a camera which enabled digital prints to be made from wireless devices. But by October the business had run out of money to put the products on the market.

Adapted from the *Financial Times*, 13.10.2001.

> 1 **Polaroid changed its competitive marketing strategy in the mid-1990s. Explain this change.**
> 2 **Use the Ansoff Matrix to evaluate (a) whether this strategy could ever have succeeded and (b) whether its previous strategy would have been more successful in the long term.**

		Product	
		Existing	New
Market	Existing	Market penetration	Product development
	New	Market development	Diversification

Figure 9.2 *The Ansoff Matrix*

might be persuaded to buy in greater quantities or sales could be taken away from competitors. This could be achieved, for example, by cutting prices or increasing spending on promotion.

- It could maintain its existing product range, but enter new markets. This is **market development**. A UK supermarket chain, for example, could expand into Hungary or Poland. Or a builder's merchants which had before sold exclusively to the building trade could reposition (see unit 11) itself by selling to ordinary consumers.
- It could maintain its markets but change its product range - called **product development**. New products could help to increase sales. Existing products could be modified and upgraded to boost demand.
- It could DIVERSIFY by changing both its products and the markets into which it sells. For example, Virgin owned by Richard Branson has a long history of **diversification**. It has established companies in markets such as music, air travel, financial services and soft drinks.

Diversification is the most risky of the four strategies since both product and market are new to the business. It is the strategy which is most likely to fail. On the other hand, successful diversification can reduce risk in the long term for the business because it no longer relies on a particular set of markets or products. The safest strategy is market penetration, since neither market nor product will change. However, it may be more difficult to achieve sales growth than with a market or product development strategy.

Implementing plans

Marketing strategies need to be **implemented** - to be put into effect. This is done through marketing **tactics** - the day to day ways in which objectives will be achieved. Cutting prices, reducing costs, increasing spending on advertising or getting the product into more stores are examples of tactics.

Reviewing and evaluating outcomes

It is important to review and evaluate the outcomes of a marketing strategy. Businesses need to learn what has been successful and what has failed. This information is vital when the next marketing strategy is planned.

In practice, marketing strategies can sometimes fail. There is a number of reasons for this.

- The marketing strategy may have been badly thought out, unrealistic targets may have been set or little thought may have been given to conflicts of objectives in the plan. For example, a marketing department may have set itself the objective of selling better quality products at lower prices, to be achieved by lower costs. It is often not possible to improve quality and cut costs at the same time.
- Those making marketing decisions on a day to day basis may think that planning is a waste of time. They may simply see plans as extra paperwork to be completed. As a result they may work in different ways to that outlined in the marketing plan.
- Strategies followed by the marketing department could come into conflict with the strategies being followed by other departments, such as production or finance. For example, the marketing department may have planned to spend £1 million on an advertising campaign for which the finance department refuses to release the funds. This comes about when those at the top of an organisation have not coordinated the strategies of different departments. Or it occurs when other departments don't follow their strategy when the marketing department is carrying out its strategy.
- The marketing strategy can be knocked off course by events outside the control of managers. For example, the economy may suddenly go into an unexpected **recession** (see unit 50). A competing business may become more aggressive in its marketing tactics. A fire may destroy a factory, cutting the output of the business in the short term.

Preparing the next marketing strategy

The medium to long term marketing strategy needs to be reviewed and reworked on a regular basis, such as once a year. This doesn't mean that the whole strategy needs to be rewritten. There is likely to be some continuity from year to year. But the strategy needs to be reworked in the light of events and recent successes and failures. The strategy needs to be responsive and flexible.

❝key terms❞

Ansoff Matrix - a model which identifies growth strategies for businesses based on an analysis of their products and markets.
Diversification - expansion by a business into new product markets.
Market follower - a business which tends to mimic the actions of the larger business in the market, the market leader.
Market leader - usually with the largest market share, this business tends to set the trends in pricing, product development and other areas which smaller competing

businesses tend to follow.
Marketing audit - a systematic analysis of business procedures, activities, operations, systems and the external environment which may affect how the business markets its products. It should identify the marketing strengths and weaknesses of the business.
Marketing objectives - the goals that the business wants to achieve from its marketing.
Marketing strategy - a set of plans designed to achieve the marketing objectives of a business.

checklist

1 Explain the difference between a marketing objective, strategy and tactic.
2 'A marketing strategy should be achievable and realistic.' Explain what this means.
3 Why might the marketing strategy of a luxury car manufacturer like Land Rover or Porsche differ from that of a mass market car manufacturer like Vauxhall (part of General Motors) or Ford?
4 What are the main stages in developing a marketing strategy?
5 Explain the difference between an internal marketing audit and an external audit.
6 What is SWOT analysis?
7 Why should the marketing objectives of a business support the objectives of the business as a whole?
8 What is meant by 'competitive marketing strategies'?
9 Explain the difference between a market leader and a market follower.
10 What sales growth strategies could a business pursue?
11 Explain how the Ansoff Matrix could be used by a business to analyse its growth strategy.
12 Why might marketing strategies fail?

When John Hancock became chief executive at MFI Furniture in March 1999, all the talk was of falling sales and rising losses, high debts and a low share price, cutting costs and cutting the dividend. Today the company is very different, with rising sales, profits and dividends.

Hancock's first important decision was to build on the group's strength as a vertically integrated business. MFI was not just a chain of shops. It was also a manufacturer of kitchen and bedroom units. But the factories that made the units for the shops were underutilised. Increasing sales would increase the throughput of the factories. Average costs in the manufacturing side would fall and so profits would increase.

One element of Hancock's marketing strategy was to give the core out-of-town MFI stores a facelift. The Conran Design Group was hired to update the design of the stores to entice 'the customer for the 2000s, not the 1980s'. He also experimented with small high-street stores of around 4 000 sq ft. Without the rest of the business, these would not be profitable. But by piggy-backing the existing factories and delivery network, they could earn a decent profit. In 2000, there were nearly 20 such stores, with 50 planned by 2003.

MFI also did a deal with Curry's, the electrical retailer, to sell kitchens alongside the Curry's appliances. That venture is now breaking-even, and the plan is to double it from 50 to 100 stores in the next six months.

In terms of international marketing, MFI is planning to expand its profitable business in France where John Hancock believes 'we can double sales and treble profits in three to four years'. A four-store joint venture in Taiwan promises to open up another market.

But one of the fastest growing businesses within MFI does not even have the MFI name. Howden is a chain of depots selling kitchen solutions to small builders. Outlets are located on industrial estates where rents are low, and are often close to plumbers' merchants. They have a small showroom with a larger warehouse. Builders can take brochures to show their customers, along with computer designs that staff help the builder to draw up. The kitchen cupboards are ready-made, not flat-pack, saving the builder time and improving quality. Howden staff generate business by contacting local builders with mail shots and phone calls, rather than waiting for them to come in. The success of Howden comes from a combination of local staff relating to local customers and the back-up of the MFI infrastructure. When John Howden took charge, there were 100 depots. Today there are 200 and it is hoped there will be 350 in two or three years' time.

For the future, John Hancock is experimenting with selling bathrooms, currently being tested in 12 MFI stores. Diversification could also come with further international expansion.

Adapted from the *Financial Times*, 9.10.2001.

1 Explain what is meant by 'marketing strategy'. (3 marks)
2 Outline TWO advantages for MFI of increasing its sales. (6 marks)
3 Analyse what types of marketing strategy MFI used between March 1999 and October 2001. (10 marks)
4 Discuss the possible problems that MFI might face in the future in its marketing strategy to increase sales. (11 marks)

10 Branding

Heineken

Knowledge Heineken is one of two beers that can truly be said to be a major international brand, the other being Budweiser. It is sold in 170 countries around the world by the Dutch company Heineken which gave the name to the brand.

Application Heineken in most countries is sold as a *premium brand*. This means that it is sold at a *higher price* than the *average beer price* in the *market*. The *higher price* is justified by the *unique selling points* of the *brand*: factors such as the quality of the drink and its consistent taste.

Analysis The formulation of Heineken is the same around the world. Taste and appearance are uniform. This is a deliberate policy to promote the value of the brand to customers over time. Marketing differs from country to country, however. For example, in the USA stronger glue is used on the labels because beer is often cooled by putting bottles into ice buckets. In Jamaica and Taiwan, 20cl bottles are produced because customers fear that the beer will warm up before it is finished. The British market is one of the few where giant bottles are demanded. The British market is also unique in having a strength that is weaker than Heineken sold in other countries. Historically, this was because Heineken judged that British drinkers preferred weak beer when the brand was first introduced into the UK market.

Evaluation By marketing a premium beer worldwide, Heineken has been highly successful in penetrating markets and exploiting the market to earn substantial profits. In the UK, Heineken may well upgrade the strength of the beer in the near future and reprice it to place it clearly within the premium product range. There are great risks in such a move. But if the company could achieve this without losing too many customers, the brand would be more profitable in the UK.

Adapted from the *Financial Times*, 19.9.2001.

Homogeneous products

Some products are HOMOGENEOUS or GENERIC. This means that they are standard products. They are the **same** whether produced by one business or another. For example, carrots from one farm are the same as carrots from another farm. Copper from one mine is the same as copper from another mine. Ball bearings from one manufacturer are the same as ball bearings from another manufacturer.

Frequently, there are industry standards set for homogeneous products. Supermarkets, for example, may set standards about the size, colour and and shape of the carrots they are prepared to buy from their suppliers. There are standard sizes for ball bearings and standard specifications for the materials used in their manufacture.

Businesses which produce homogeneous products cannot distinguish their products from those of their rivals. Customers therefore tend to buy the cheapest on the market. This means that suppliers have to cut their prices to the minimum to gain sales. This minimum price includes a profit margin. If it didn't, businesses would cease to supply the product in the long term. Profit is, after all, the reward to the owners for risking their capital in the business. But the profit margin will tend to be the minimum necessary to keep that business in production of that good or service in the long term.

Branded products

Many products, however, are unique to the business which produces it. So Coca-Cola is different to Pepsi Cola. A Wall's Magnum is different to a Nestlé Fab. A Beatles CD is different to an Eminem CD. These are examples of BRANDS. A brand is a name, design, symbol or any other feature that identifies a business's products from those of others.

A brand may identify an individual product. So Fiesta, Clio, and Nova are all BRAND NAMES of small cars. A brand may also be used to identify a **range** (see unit 13) of products. For example, Persil is a brand of washing product, including washing powder, liquid detergent, biological and non-biological washing powders and washing up liquid.

Some businesses also make their own **business** into a brand. Virgin is a good example. The Virgin brand covers products from airlines to railways to financial products to cola drinks. In doing this, Virgin is attempting to say that all these different products have some similar characteristics which distinguish them from other products on the markets. One is that they represent good value. Another is that Virgin is on the side of customers when it sells its products. So the product is low in price or high in quality. Some of the world's most famous brands include company names such as Sony, Disney and IBM.

Creating and maintaining a brand

Brands distinguish products from those of rivals. Creating a brand is a strategy a business can use for ADDING VALUE. This means that a business increases the worth of a product to the customer. Customer value is the difference between the costs and benefits of buying a product to the customer. The benefits are affected by the image the consumer has of the product. A strong brand image may increase the value of products to customers compared to competing products. So, for example, a business buying a lorry may choose a well known brand because it thinks it will get a more reliable product or a better after sales service. A family may choose a holiday from a well known company because it feels safer about the flights and accommodation.

Successful brands also tend to have a UNIQUE SELLING PROPOSITION or POINT (USP). This is a characteristic of a product which makes it different from any other product on the market. The USP is promoted by businesses to customers as being the 'best'. For example, cars may be advertised as being the smoothest ride or giving the safest journey.

The added value in a brand and its unique selling point come about through manipulation of the **marketing mix** (see unit 1).

Product Branded products tend to have a different formulation to other similar products. For example, a Ford Fiesta has a slightly different shape and performance to a Renault Clio. Coca-Cola is made with a different mix of ingredients to Pepsi Cola or Virgin Cola. A British Airways flight from London to New York provides a different service to a Virgin flight over the the same route.

Branded products which are more expensive than similar rival products tend to be of superior quality. It could be argued that a BA flight from London to Paris is of higher quality than an EasyJet flight to the same destination. BA uses main airports with plenty of ongoing connections. EasyJet uses airports which are further from city centres, with fewer opportunities to connect to other flights. The food and drink may be better on a BA flight and there may be greater choice.

Some brands need regular improvement. For example, the specification on a Ford Fiesta is continually changed and new models are introduced. Ford could not survive if it failed to produce better cars over time. Other brands, however, have remained the same over time. The product formulation of Coca-Cola is the same as it was 50 years ago.

Key to the success of a brand is **uniformity**. Customers must know that the brand is the same every time they buy. Large variations in the quality of a brand could damage the brand image. Customers would not know what they were buying.

Promotion Businesses often have to remind customers of the unique qualities of their brands. They therefore need to be promoted. For example, Virgin might run an advertising campaign for its airline, Virgin Atlantic. Or Kellogg's might run an offer of free tickets to a theme park on its cereals packets. The amount of promotion spending on brands is often linked to the volume of sales. So promotion often affects demand for the brand.

Place The success of a brand depends on the ability of customers to purchase where and when they want to. The success of Coca-Cola, for example, has been strongly linked to its availability through stores or vending machines within a few minutes walk of any customer.

Price Brands are often able to command a PREMIUM PRICE, a price above the market average. In part, this reflects higher costs. The branded product may be of higher quality than rival products, but this increases costs of production. Promotion and distribution costs may also be higher.

Charging a premium price may send a signal to customers that the brand is a premium product. If the price is set too low, customers may decide that the quality of the product is also low. The higher price also allows the business to earn a higher profit than the market average. This is the reward to the business for selling a successful brand.

Some brands are successful because they offer **lower** prices than their competitors, perhaps for the same quality of product. The reward to the business then comes not from higher profit margins but from increased sales. Businesses like Asda (part of the US giant Wal-Mart) and EasyJet have low profit margins. But they aim to earn high profits by selling large volumes.

Own brands

Large retailing chains may offer OWN BRANDS for sale. These are products which are manufactured by suppliers but sold under the name of the retailer. For example, Tesco offers 'Tesco baked beans' for sale in its stores. Tesco does not manufacture the baked beans. This is done by a supplier which puts the Tesco label onto the product.

Own brands are an attempt by the retailer to use the brand name of the company to sell products. They are often lower in price than the leading brand in the market. So Tesco baked beans tend to be cheaper than Heinz baked beans. However, retailers attempt to make the quality of the own brand product as high as the leading branded product. Own brands therefore present a major competitive threat to manufacturers' brands.

Retailers gain from selling own brands in two ways.
● Selling products at a lower price helps increase the competitiveness of the retailer itself against other retailers.

Ferrero Rocher, made by Ferrero and KitKat, made by Nestlé, are two successful brands of chocolate confectionery. KitKat has consistently been the best selling chocolate confectionery bar in the UK for many years. Ferrero Rocher has seasonal demand, with sales rising sharply in the Christmas period.

1 **What are the unique selling points of each brand? In your answer consider (a) product, (b) promotion, (c) place and (d) price.**
2 **Discuss whether either of the two brands could be considered to be a premium product.**

A firm from Walsall Wood in the West Midlands has won an order to provide electrical wiring for the world-beating Sabaru rally cars raced by drivers such as Richard Burns. Teepee Electrical Systems said that the wiring had been subjected to extensive testing by Prodrive, the company running the rally team, to ensure it met the standards of reliability and performance needed for rally cars.

Teepee Electrical Systems, and its parent company Craig & Derricott, is involved with a range of industries, from railway rolling stock, to conveyor belt systems at airports and even the submarine controls in the last James Bond film. Kevin Jones, managing director of the company, put the success of the company down to the skills its workers bring to the business. 'A wiring loom is a wiring loom, but our people add engineering skills from widely diverse fields.'

Adapted from the *Express and Star*, 17.4.2000.

1 **Teepee Electrical Systems sells electrical wiring to other businesses. Suggest why it could find it difficult to establish a strong brand in this market.**
2 **To what extent do you think Teepee Electrical Systems could sell its wiring at premium prices?**

When Tesco sells own label baked beans, this is part of its strategy to win customers away from rival supermarkets like Asda and Sainsbury. It also helps take customers away from local small grocery stores.
- Own brands sometimes have higher profit margins for the retailer than leading brands.

Branding vs homogeneity

Sometimes it is argued that the goal of a business should be to establish strong brands.
- Consumers with BRAND LOYALTY will return to buy their favourite brand and ignore others.
- Brands can often be sold at premium prices.
- PESTER POWER can influence sales of brands. Children often want brands of toys or clothing and put pressure on their parents or other relations to buy the products for them.

For certain businesses, however, this may not the most suitable strategy.
- Some businesses operate in markets where the products sold are homogeneous. Branding may not be possible in these markets.
- Some businesses are in markets where there is a clear BRAND LEADER. It may be difficult to establish a strong brand, outsell the brand leader or charge premium prices in these markets. It may then be more profitable to sell a product in the same market which is not strongly branded. The savings on marketing costs may be far greater than the loss in price the business has to accept to create demand.
- Creating a new brand is often difficult. Large companies such as Unilever or Nestlé spend large amounts of money each year on launching new products only to see them fail. Small businesses may simply not have the resources to create a new brand.

"key terms"

Adding value - creating greater worth for products. Adding value can be achieved through branding or creating a USP.
Brand - a name, design, symbol or any other feature that identifies a business's products from those of others. Brands can be about a product, a range of products or a business.
Brand leader - usually the brand with the highest sales in a market, although it can also be simply a brand with high sales.
Brand loyalty - the extent to which customers of a brand repeat their purchases of the brand rather than buying another brand.
Brand name - a unique name of a product, range of products or business that distinguishes it from others.
Homogeneous or generic product - a product made by a number of different businesses which is broadly identical and where customers see little or no difference between the product made by one business and another.
Own brand - a product sold under the brand name of a retailer like Tesco or B&Q, which is manufactured by a supplier of the retailer.
Pester power - the ability of children to persuade their parents, or other adults making purchases, to buy the product they wish to consume.
Premium price - a price which is above the average price for the market for that type of product.
Unique selling proposition or point (USP) - a characteristic of a product, such as its design, function, image or service, which makes it different from other similar products on the market and which therefore helps sell it to customers.

checklist

1 Explain the difference between a homogeneous and a branded product.
2 'A business may try to make its name into a brand.' Explain why it might do this.
3 How can a brand add value for customers?
4 What might be the USP of (a) a car, (b) a holiday, (c) an airline flight?
5 Why is uniformity important to the success of a brand?
6 Explain briefly why promotion and place are important to the success of a brand.
7 How might (a) higher and (b) lower prices of brands increase the rewards to a business?
8 How might a retailer gain from selling own brand products?
9 How can a business selling a brand benefit from pester power?
10 'Brands can always be sold at premium prices.' To what extent is this true?

200 years ago, travellers had to put up at the local inn where standards could be excellent or very poor. Today, the hotel trade is made up of thousands of independent hotels individually owned, together with chains of hotels. The chains all want to establish a strong brand loyalty amongst customers. The fastest growing segment of the market is the budget, no frills sector. In 1992, there were only 6 000 rooms in this category, most either Travel Inns or Travel Lodges. Today there are over 40 000, with many more planned. The Travel Inn and Travel Lodge chains are still expanding with nearly 500 hotels between them. But foreign companies have also now moved into the market. The French chain Formule 1 has built 10 hotels to date. US companies Days Inn and Express by Holiday Inn have over 50 hotels in the UK between them, and Sleep Inn has just entered the UK market too.

The attraction of these hotels to travellers is simple. They offer consistent quality wherever you are staying. At the top end of the budget market, the premier brands offer facilities on a par with three and even four star hotels, such as large beds, direct-dial telephone, modem, satellite TV, tea and coffee maker, trouser press and hairdryer. Pricing is also transparent. The price is per room and there are no hidden extras. Prices are lower than in a conventional hotel because budget hotels don't offer facilities such as gyms, pools, multiple bars and room service.

Business customers are increasingly aware of the excellent value offered by budget chains. Leisure travellers are perhaps less aware, many still thinking that a local B&B might be best for them. However, leisure travellers are becoming more sophisticated. They are less and less willing to put up with highly variable standards offered by B&Bs and small hotels. These businesses are likely to be the main casualties of the expansion of budget chains.

Adapted from *The Guardian*, 6.1.2001.

1 Explain what is meant by the following terms:
(a) brand loyalty; (3 marks)
(b) premier brand. (3 marks)
2 Outline TWO segments within the hotel market. (6 marks)
3 Examine TWO factors which encourage travellers to stay at a branded chain of budget hotels such as Travel Inn or Travel Lodge rather than at an independent hotel or B&B. (8 marks)
4 To what extent do independent hotels and B&Bs have a long term business future in the UK? (10 marks)

Levi Jeans

Knowledge In 2001, the European Court of Justice ruled that Tesco could not sell Levi jeans that it had bought from a supplier other than Levi's outside the European Union (EU). Levi Strauss, the US company which manufacturers Levi jeans, welcomed the decision.

Application The Levi name is a powerful *brand* in the jeans *market*. Levi Strauss wished to retain its power to *position the brand* within its *target market* and not where retailers such as Tesco might push it. In this case, Levi Strauss wanted to retain Levi jeans as an *up-market brand*.

Analysis Levi Strauss fought hard to retain control of its distribution channels in the EU. It feared that supermarket chains would sell Levi jeans at a low price, which would equate the brand with baked beans and soap powders. Although it might sell more in the short term, Levi Strauss feared that the product would lose its exclusive, up-market brand image. Low prices would also lead to lower profits for Levi Strauss. Instead, Levi Strauss wanted to retain its ability to sell its jeans through more up-market outlets at premium prices.

Evaluation Levi Strauss was probably the winner from the court ruling. It retained its ability to control its distribution channels. Tesco was a loser because it lost sales and profits that it could have made from selling discounted Levi jeans. As for the consumer, Tesco might argue that its customers were losers because they would now have to pay more for Levi jeans. Levi Strauss might argue that the customer benefited because buying Levi jeans from Tesco ultimately devalued the power of the brand. Why buy Levi jeans if they don't show to other consumers that you can buy a superior brand?

Adapted from *The Independent*, 21.11.2001.

Positioning a product

Businesses must choose which markets to sell into. These are their TARGET MARKETS. A target market will consist of consumers with similar needs. For example, Kelloggs sells cereals into the market for breakfast food and snack foods. The need of one consumer to have food for breakfast is similar to that of another consumer. Businesses with **branded** products (see unit 10) can also manipulate their characteristics to make them appear the same as or different from other competing brands.

Both of these decisions will influence the brand's MARKET POSITION. This is the relationship of one brand to others in the market. For example, Harrods is a brand known worldwide. It is one brand amongst many in retailing. Competitors include Marks & Spencer, Harvey Nichols and Selfridges. Harrods is a London department store, selling everything from clothes to hi-fi equipment to food. It aims to provide an up-market service. It is successful because it attracts customers who will pay high prices for high quality goods sold in a quality environment.

In contrast, Iceland is a specialist retailer of mainly frozen foods. It attracts customers who are looking for value for money. Its prices therefore must be competitive with those of supermarket chains, such as Tesco and Asda. The range of its products must be attractive to a wide market.

Perceptual maps

The positioning of a brand is influenced by **customer perceptions** rather than those of businesses. For example, a business may feel its brand is a high quality, up-market product. But if customers see it as low quality and down-market, it is their views that will influence sales.

So, if a business wants to find out where its brand is positioned in the market, it might carry out **market research** (see unit 4). This will help it to understand how customers see the brand in relation to others in the market.

A business may also wish to launch a new brand. Having decided the target market, market research might show what characteristics the brand must have to succeed in that market. It could reveal the price that customers are prepared to pay. It could also suggest what sort of promotional support will be needed. For example, will a national television advertising campaign be used? Will promotion to retailers be a better strategy?

The results of market research can be displayed on PERCEPTUAL MAPS (sometimes also called MARKET MAPS or POSITIONING MAPS). Typically, the maps are drawn in two dimensions, as in Figure 11.1. This allows two of the attributes of the brand to be shown visually. More maps need to be drawn if more than two attributes are shown.

Figure 11.1 shows a perceptual map for cars. Two characteristics are displayed - the price of a new car and its 'sportiness'. So Bentley cars might be highly priced, but considered traditional. Morgans might be less costly, but considered more sporty. Cateram produces cheaper sporty 'kit cars' which must be self-assembled.

Drawing maps can help a business make marketing decisions about new or existing brands. **Market mapping** reveals the extent to which brands are similar or different from those of rivals. A business can then choose to emphasise those similarities or differences through promotion. Or it can change the characteristics if current sales are poor. It could, for example, change its price or its promotion. Perhaps the brand itself needs redesigning. Changing the characteristics will help REPOSITION the brand in the market.

Mass marketing

Some businesses choose not to target particular consumers. Instead they use MASS MARKETING. They try to offer almost the same product and promote it in the same way to all consumers in a large market. Examples today might include Kellogg's Corn Flakes, Fairy Liquid and the Sony Playstation.

Mass market products generate high sales. This enables businesses producing them to enjoy **economies of scale** (see unit 42). Large volumes of production reduce the cost of producing each item. For example, large car manufacturers can negotiate lower prices for the components they buy than smaller manufacturers. Economies of scale allow businesses to charge lower prices than their competitors, or earn higher profits.

However, higher profits are not guaranteed. If a mass market producer faces fierce competition, it may have to charge low prices to customers and earn low profits to survive. Equally, a mass market product may be in the decline phase of its **product**

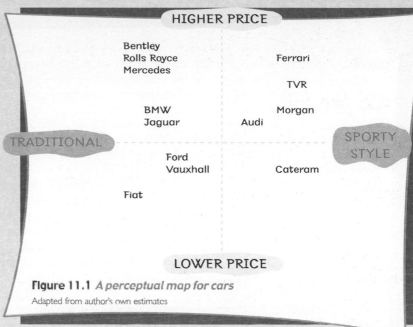

Figure 11.1 *A perceptual map for cars*

Adapted from author's own estimates

life cycle (see unit 12). With demand falling, total profits will fall too, even if the profit per item sold remains the same.

Mass market products are often sold across many national markets. GLOBAL MARKETING gives a business the opportunity to sell in very high volumes. Companies which pursue global marketing strategies include household names

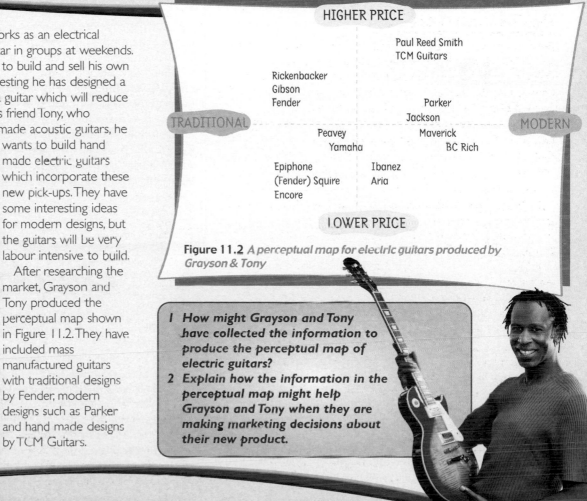

Grayson Lampkin works as an electrical engineer and plays guitar in groups at weekends. His ambition has been to build and sell his own guitars. After years of testing he has designed a new style pick-up for a guitar which will reduce noise. Together with his friend Tony, who currently makes hand made acoustic guitars, he wants to build hand made electric guitars which incorporate these new pick-ups. They have some interesting ideas for modern designs, but the guitars will be very labour intensive to build.

After researching the market, Grayson and Tony produced the perceptual map shown in Figure 11.2. They have included mass manufactured guitars with traditional designs by Fender, modern designs such as Parker and hand made designs by TCM Guitars.

TCM Glory Custom™

Shetley Blue Optional Stain Finish

Figure 11.2 *A perceptual map for electric guitars produced by Grayson & Tony*

1 **How might Grayson and Tony have collected the information to produce the perceptual map of electric guitars?**
2 **Explain how the information in the perceptual map might help Grayson and Tony when they are making marketing decisions about their new product.**

Ben and Jerry's is a luxury ice cream brand. Luxury ice cream accounts for around 10 per cent of the ice cream market worldwide. In 2000, the company was bought by one of the world's largest food manufacturers, Unilever. The company also happens to be the world's largest ice cream manufacturer with mass market brands such as Walls, Magnum and Cornetto.

The rationale for buying Ben and Jerry's was simple. It is very difficult for any business to create a successful brand. Large multinational companies like Unilever are no more successful at this than smaller companies despite large research and development departments and the fire power of intense promotion. Ben and Jerry's is a good example. It was founded by two hippy dropouts in a disused petrol station in Vermont, USA in the 1970s. A good product combined with anti-establishment marketing saw the company grow into a leading luxury ice cream brand. Buying brands is a safer and cheaper way for a large company like Unilever to grow than attempting to establish new brands in the market.

What Unilever can bring to Ben and Jerry's is quality management and the financial resources to expand. For example, Unilever has renegotiated deals with suppliers to reduce costs. It is planning to double sales within five years. Ben and Jerry shops will increase from 250 to over 1 000 through franchising.

Unilever knows that expansion will only be possible if the Ben and Jerry brand image remains broadly unchanged. It has to be fun but socially committed. These attributes may be very different from those for many other Unilever products. But successful market positioning doesn't imply uniformity across a company with thousands of different brands.

Adapted from from *The Times*, 10.12.2001.

1 **Explain why Ben and Jerry's operates in a niche market.**
2 **What are the potential benefits to Unilever of acquiring Ben and Jerry's?**
3 **Discuss why the marketing of Ben and Jerry's should be different to Unilever brands such as Magnum, Cornetto, Persil or Flora.**

such as Coca-Cola, Ford, McDonald's and Sony. For UK based businesses, membership of the European Union has led to PAN-EUROPEAN MARKETING over the past 20 years. Companies such as Unilever and Ford increasingly organise production, sales and marketing on a European level.

Niche marketing

Not every business can produce mass market products. An alternative strategy is NICHE MARKETING. This is where a business **targets** a small group within a segment of a larger market. For example, luxury car brands, such as Porsche or Morgan, don't aim for the mass market. Instead, they sell a few thousand cars a year to enthusiasts within the car sports market.

Successful niche marketing is based on:
- finding a part of a market which is poorly served by existing suppliers;
- understanding the precise needs of the small group of customers;
- identifying a small part of a market segment where there are few or no competitors. If there are already suppliers in the niche market, it is likely to be difficult to generate enough sales at a high enough price for profits to be made.

Niche marketing tends to be undertaken by small businesses. Large businesses are big partly because they sell into mass markets. For them, it is not worth spending resources on producing a targeted product for, say, just 1 or 2 per cent of a market. But for a small business, that 1 or 2 per cent may be more than enough to justify producing for that niche market.

Costs of production are often higher for niche products than for mass market products. Small producers are unable to exploit the economies of scale available to large producers. So prices for niche products tend to be higher than for mass market products.

Whether a business can make a profit in a niche market typically depends upon just how much customers are prepared to pay extra for the niche product. Niche market car companies like Porsche, for example, have traditionally found it difficult to make profits over the long term. This is despite charging very high prices for their cars. This suggests that demand over a long period of time has not been high enough to sustain so many luxury car manufacturers in this market niche. On the other hand, there are many speciality butchers in the UK which are prospering despite intense competition from supermarkets. By providing high quality products, they can attract customers prepared to pay high prices for better quality.

checklist

1 'Marks & Spencer has positioned itself at the premium end of the food market'. Explain what this means.
2 How might market research help a business draw a perceptual map for one of its products?
3 What is the difference between mass marketing and niche marketing?
4 Explain the difference between global marketing and pan-European marketing.
5 Why might a niche marketing company be more profitable than a mass market company?

keyterms

Global marketing - where a business markets its products not just in its own country, but across the world.

Market position - the position of one brand in the market in relation to its rivals, in the opinion of consumers in the market.

Mass marketing - occurs where a business offers almost the same product and promotes it in the same way to all consumers in a large market.

Niche marketing - occurs where a business positions a product to appeal to customers in a small segment of a larger market.

Perceptual maps, positioning maps or market maps - typically a two dimensional diagram which shows two of the attributes or characteristics of a brand and those of rival brands in the market.

Pan-European marketing - where a business based in one European country markets its products across Europe.

Repositioning - changing the positioning of a brand in its market.

Target market - the market into which a business aims to sell.

In the 1990s, Ford, traditionally a mass market car manufacturer with a single US luxury car brand, Lincoln, bought a number of European luxury car makers. These were Volvo, Jaguar, Aston Martin and Land Rover. In the late 1990s, Ford decided to put these luxury car brands together into one group - the Premier Automotive Group (PAG).

The rationale was simple. First, costs could be cut across these luxury marques through common sourcing of products and common design. So parts which might be found in a Volvo might also now be found in Jaguar or a Lincoln car. A component designed for a new Land Rover model might also be used in a new Aston Martin model. Second, marketing could be co-ordinated across the brands. Volvo would not attempt to compete with Jaguar. Land Rover might be sold through the same distributors as Lincoln in the USA. The marketing philosophy is to expand the customer base for each marque with newer products and better marketing, whilst retaining and enhancing the premium niche that each occupies.

One way in which rival luxury car manufacturers, such as Mercedes or BMW, have expanded their markets is to move into the small car market. This attracts new customers who either want a luxury small car or who are unable to afford a large luxury car. If the customer is young, it may well lead to further sales of larger cars when the customer grows older. This is likely to be a strategy now pursued by Ford. Another way of expanding the market is to produce different types of car. For example, Volvo could produce a sports car.

Different brands within PAG currently have different problems and challenges. But in ten years' time, Ford hopes that the group will have sorted out its problems and be a major contributor to profits.

Adapted from the *Financial Times*, 23.10.2001.

1 Explain what is meant by the term 'mass market ... manufacturer'. (3 marks)
2 Outline TWO possible ways in which a brand within PAG could reposition itself in the market. (6 marks)
3 Examine TWO benefits to Ford of putting its luxury car brands into one group. (8 marks)
4 Discuss whether it would be beneficial for Ford if it could turn Volvo into a mass market brand. (11 marks)

12 Product life cycle

Red Bull

Knowledge Red Bull is an energy drink favoured by young clubbers, students, sports players and drivers. The product was first marketed in 1987 in Austria. Since then, it has been sold in most EU countries and has recently been launched in the USA.

Application Total *sales* of Red Bull worldwide show that the *product* is still in its *growth phrase*. However, in *markets* such as Austria and the UK, where the *product* was *launched* in 1987 and 1993, it has entered the *maturity stage*. The *company* has considered *extension strategies*, such as a ready-mixed alcoholic cocktail, to take on rival drinks such as Smirnoff Ice and Bacardi Breezer. But, as yet, it has decided to focus on *launching* Red Bull in new geographical areas.

Analysis Red Bull has successfully filled a niche in the carbonated drinks market. It sells at a premium price, generating large profits in its more mature markets. To date, these profits have been used to finance expansion. As a result, the business is relatively debt free. Its single biggest failure occurred when the product was launched in Germany in 1994. Sales soared and the company ran out of its distinctive 250 ml cans. It took 3-4 months to get the product back on this shelves due to lack of capacity. In the meantime, a competitor had rushed out a similar product and taken the market.

Evaluation Red Bull is fortunate in being able to make sufficient profit to finance expansion. By focussing on the introduction of one product, the management of the company can devote all its energies to this one task. However, sooner or later, sales worldwide are likely to peak. The company will then have to pursue extension strategies or launch a completely new product if it wishes to grow further.

Adapted from the *Financial Times*, 3.4.2001.

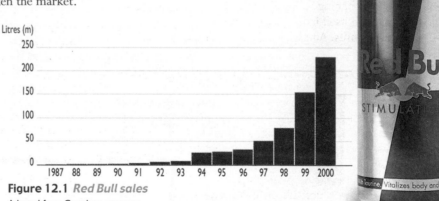

Figure 12.1 *Red Bull sales*

Adapted from Canadean, company.

Stages of the cycle

Product is one of the 4Ps in the marketing mix (see unit 1). It is therefore a key element in a business's marketing. A useful way in which a business can consider changes that occur over the life of a product is to look at the PRODUCT LIFE CYCLE. This shows how a product passes through a number of stages over time, as in Figure 12.2. Each stage has certain features.

Development stage This is when product ideas are developed and tested.

- **Research**. A business might research a problem. For example, producers might investigate how to develop faster micro-chips. Market research might also be carried out (see units 4, 7 and 8) to give feedback about what products customers are prepared to buy and the price they will pay.
- **Sales and costs**. Sales will be zero. But the business will have to pay the high costs of researching the idea.
- **Failure**. Most ideas for new products fail to get through this stage. It may be technically impossible to make a product. Or market research may show that there will be too little demand. Alternatively,

an idea may be rejected because it is not possible to make the product at a price that customers are prepared to pay.

Introduction stage This is when a product first appears on the market.

- **Launch**. A product might be launched in one market or in many markets at the same time. But it might be launched in stages. The Sony PlayStation was sold first in Japan and only later in the USA and Europe. A business might adopt this strategy to get feedback, giving it time to change the product before launching into other markets. Sometimes the launch

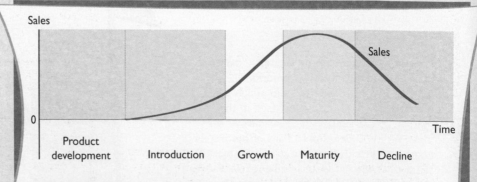

Figure 12.2 *The product life cycle. A typical product passes through various stages during its life, from development to launch, growth, maturity and decline before being withdrawn from the market.*

of a product may have to be accompanied by the launch of a complementary product. In the games market, for example, software must be launched at the same time as a games machine.

- **Promotion**. Different promotion strategies might be used (see unit 18). Businesses often spend heavily on promotion at first to build up sales and market share. Advertising may also be more effective at this stage. But promotion might be kept to a minimum at launch. Perhaps a business does not have the money. Or it might have low stocks and not want to disappoint customers.
- **Pricing**. Businesses might set high prices to pay for promotion costs. A business may also set a high price if the product is novel and customers are prepared to pay to be the first to own it. Flat screen televisions, for example, were launched at very high prices. This is an example of **market skimming** (see unit 15). But the price may be set low to encourage customers to try the product. The price could then be raised later to allow the product to be profitable. This is an example of **penetration pricing**. Sony, for example, when launching its PlayStation, set its price below full cost to establish itself in the market quickly.
- **Sales, costs and profits**. After launch, sales will start to rise

slowly. But the business will still be recovering its research costs and will also be spending on promotion. So profits will be negative, or at best very low. As a result, products with poor sales may be withdrawn at this stage.

- **Distribution and competition**. Few outlets may stock the product until they feel confident it will sell. This was the case with DVD players until after the year 2000. However, there is likely to be little competition. For example, when Phillips released its first DVD player in 1996 it was the only player on the market.

Growth stage This is when a product becomes established.

- **Sales, costs and profits**. Sales grow most rapidly in this stage. Customers make repeat purchases and new customers buy the product. As production rises, costs may fall as businesses gain economies of scale (see unit 42). Profits will increase as a result of falling unit costs and rising sales.
- **Pricing and promotion**. Businesses need to consider their pricing and promotion strategies. For example, if a business has adopted a market skimming policy, at what point will it lower its price? Businesses may spend on advertising to encourage brand loyalty (see unit 10).
- **Distribution and competition**. Competitors will be attracted to the market by profits. There are likely to be improvements and changes to products. Greater sales will encourage more outlets to sell a product. This is what happened to DVDs after 2000.

Maturity stage There are two parts to the maturity stage.

- **At first**. Sales will reach their peak in this stage. The business will continue to make profits as the fixed costs of development will have been paid for.
- **Saturation**. At some point the market will become saturated. Sales will then start to fall. Businesses may reduce prices or use promotion to maintain sales. But this may result in lower profits. Some products will be forced out of the market. During this saturation phase, consumers might not buy new products because they own an existing product. In the late 1990s, for example, sales of video players were falling because of market saturation. Fortunately for electronics manufacturers, sales of DVD players began to take off after 2000.

Decline stage This is where the product is losing its appeal. In the decline stage, sales will fall quickly. Profits are also likely to be falling. Eventually the product will be withdrawn from the market or sold to another business. The decline phase might still be profitable if a business is spending little on new product development or promotion, but is still able to charge a high price.

Different product life cycles

The product life cycle of a typical product is shown in Figure 12.2. Not all products conform exactly to this pattern, however. Some are disastrous from launch and are quickly withdrawn. Styles of clothing or designs may have a number of peaks in sales over time as they become popular again and again. **Fads** often have very short life cycles, with rapid rises and falls in sales.

It is also suggested that products tend to have longer life cycles than brands. For example, toothpaste has had a fairly long life cycle, since its introduction in Victorian times. But toothpaste with fluoride was only introduced in the 1960s.

Classic Glass and Dishwashing is a Staffordshire based company which specialises in the manufacture of dishwashers aimed at the industrial market. It estimates that it currently has 25 per cent of the market and is the market leader.

Earlier this month, it launched a new range of dishwashers. The XL range was the culmination of a three-year programme carried out by the firm's research and development team. The machines are made to high specifications incorporating energy saving features. They are being aimed at large breweries and major groups.

Initial sales suggest that the new range is being well received by customers. The company has already taken on 10 extra workers to cope with the extra production work generated from the XL range. The firm is confident that more jobs will be created as sales increase.

Adapted from the *Express & Star*, 26.3.2001.

1 **Explain where the XL range of dishwashers was in its product life cycle on 26 March 2001.**
2 **Using a diagram, (a) explain the life cycle of the XL range before 26th March 2001; (b) discuss how the life cycle of the XL range might develop over time.**

Extension strategies

No business with a successful product wants sales to fall. So they may use EXTENSION STRATEGIES to prevent falling sales. These attempt to prolong the life of the product. There is a variety of ways in which extension strategies can be implemented.

Product development To keep pace with competition, the product may be redesigned or reformulated. Sony, for instance, spent $500 million launching a new 128 bit version of the PlayStation in 1999. It could be argued that this was a completely new product. On the other hand, it could be seen as an extension strategy for the PlayStation brand. Many products are reformulated. Formulations of long running brands of soap powder like Persil or Ariel are regularly changed to maintain sales in the face of competition.

Face-lifts A business may make small cosmetic changes to a product to give it a face-lift. For instance, the packaging on a brand of cereals might be changed. Car manufacturers tend to change their models regularly in small ways, sometimes slightly altering the style or adding new features. The scent in a soap powder may be changed.

New markets Products can be launched into new markets. Often this needs the business to be creative. Changing the size of a product can be a useful extension strategy. For instance, chocolate bar manufacturers in the 1980s began packaging their successful bars into smaller bite sized bars, suitable for children's parties or lunch boxes. Alternatively, a move might be made into an established adjoining market. For instance, coffee manufacturers like Nestlé have attempted to sell iced coffee in cans to compete with soft drinks. Cereal manufacturers have promoted existing products into the health food market by pointing out their high fibre or low fat content.

The effects of extension strategies can be seen in Figure 12.3. Extension strategy 1 prolongs the life of the product by lifting sales from what they would otherwise have been. Equally, extension strategy 2 gives the product a second boost in sales. Extension strategies are often used in the maturity stage. But they can also be used to boost sales in the growth stage or to support sales in the decline stage.

Cash flow and the product life cycle

Cash flow is the difference between the cash going into a business and the cash flowing out (see unit 27). Cash might flow in from sales or from interest on investments. Cash flows out as a business pays for its raw materials, rent, electricity, workers' wages and tax. The concept of cash flow can also be applied to a product. There is negative cash flow if the receipts from sales of the product are less than the costs associated with the product.

Figure 12.4 shows the relationship between cash flow and the product life cycle for a typical product.

Development stage In the development and introduction stages, there is likely to be negative cash flow. During the development stage, a business must pay the costs of research and development. But there is no revenue because the product is not yet being sold.

Introduction stage During the introduction stage, production costs must be paid. These may be high if small quantities are being produced, so economies of scale cannot be exploited. There will also be other costs, such as promotion. Revenue will tend to be low because sales take time to build. If the business has adopted a penetration pricing policy, prices will also be set below cost, further limiting sales revenue.

Growth stage At some point during the growth stage, cash flow should become positive. Partly this is because sales will be rising and price is less likely to be low. Average costs might also be falling. Promotion costs, possibly heavy at launch, might be falling. Average costs of production should be falling as economies of scale begin to be achieved.

Maturity stage Average costs may still be high in the growth stage if the investment needed to make more products is particularly expensive. For some products, like perfume, there may still be expensive promotion costs during the growth phase. In cases like this, cash flow may only become positive in the maturity stage. Thereafter, cash flow should be positive.

Decline stage In the decline stage, cash flow will start to fall. As sales fall rapidly, so will cash flow. Eventually, it will become negative, so more money will be spent on a product

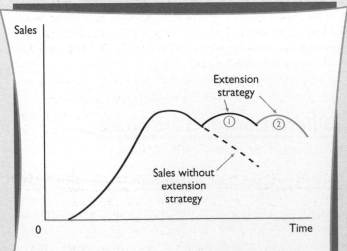

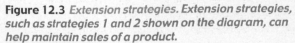

Figure 12.3 *Extension strategies. Extension strategies, such as strategies 1 and 2 shown on the diagram, can help maintain sales of a product.*

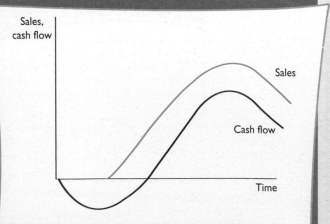

Figure 12.4 *Cash flow and the product life cycle. Cash flow is likely to be negative for a new product until sales and revenues have grown sufficiently, and costs such as promotional costs have fallen. This is likely to take place in the growth phase, but could be delayed until the maturity phase.*

Rachel's is a manufacturer of organic dairy products. The business is very much a farm based enterprise. In 1952, Brynllys, a farm in Wales, began the process which made it into the first organic farm in the UK. Initially, its dairy production was confined to selling organic milk. But in 1982 it branched out into making and selling cream and butter, initially sold locally. 1984 saw the first commercial production of yoghurt. By 1987, Marigold, a leading London health food supplier, was an enthusiastic buyer, and in 1989 Rachel's yoghurts were on sale in Harrods.

In 1990, the owners of the business, the husband and wife team of Gareth and Rachel Rowlands, decided to expand. They borrowed the money, using their farm as collateral, to build a state-of-the-art dairy. It was capable of processing not just the 330 000 litres of organic milk a year from their farm, but 3 million litres - the entire organic output of Wales. Their decision to take this risk was helped by their first large contract to supply a supermarket chain, Sainsbury.

In 1999, they sold the business to Horizon Organic, the biggest wholly organic dairy supplier in the US. Horizon has introduced three new yoghurt flavours: low fat vanilla, whole-milk with maple syrup and Greek style with honey. This month sees the debut of Rachel's organic fat-free yoghurt and a Welsh butter with bilingual packaging. However, Horizon promised not to alter Rachel's yoghurts in content or concept.

Adapted from the *Financial Times*, 24.11.2001.

1 **Discuss whether the introduction of (a) organic yoghurt in 1984 and (b) organic fat-free yoghurt in 2001 were examples of a new product being brought to the market or an extension strategy for an existing product.**
2 **Discuss the cash flow requirements of Rachel's yoghurts during and after the decision in 1990 to build a new state-of-the-art dairy.**

cash until they were needed. There would be less risk that the new capacity would be greater than sales. But, if sales were higher than expected, the business might find it difficult to invest quickly enough to prevent shortages.

Alternatively, new capacity could be created **before** sales take place. But this carries the risk that the investment would be wasted if sales did not grow in line with expectations. The cash to pay for the investment would flow out of the business earlier. Average costs would be higher too because the cost of creating and running spare capacity at launch would have to be paid for. However, it would easier to deal with unexpectedly high sales than if investment took place when sales happened.

Utilising existing capacity There is less risk if a business uses existing capacity. If a business is operating at less than full capacity, it could use the spare capacity to launch a new product. This would help reduce cash outflow associated with new products. Or a business may be working at full capacity, but have products which are at the end of their life cycle. These could be taken out of production and replaced by the new lines.

A problem with this approach is that the average costs of production, excluding the cost of any investment, may be higher than if new capacity had been built. For example, it may cost 60p to produce an item on old machinery but only 40p if the latest equipment is used. The decision about whether to buy new equipment will depend upon the relationship between the cost of the new equipment and the saving on running costs. If a business only saves £10 000 a year on running costs by buying £100 000 of new equipment, then it probably won't buy. If it saves £90 000 on running costs for an investment of £100 000, it will probably purchase the new equipment.

As explained above, average costs of production may be higher at launch and during the growth phase if existing capacity to cope with high levels of sales is set aside for use at launch. But again, if sales exceed expectations, the business is more likely to cope if there is spare capacity.

than comes into the business. The business would then stop producing the product.

Capacity utilisation and the product life cycle

The product life cycle and cash flow can be affected by the CAPACITY of a business. A business's capacity is the maximum or potential amount it can produce over a period of time. For example, the capacity of a car plant might be 200 000 cars per year. The capacity is fixed by the size of the premises, the amount of plant and machinery and the way in which the plant is laid out.

CAPACITY UTILISATION is the proportion of actual output to capacity. For example, if the car plant produces 150 000 cars a year when its capacity is 200 000, its capacity utilisation is 75 per cent (100 x [150 000÷200 000]). Here the car plant is operating **below capacity**. It is sometimes possible to operate **above capacity** by getting workers to work overtime or hiring extra equipment, for example.

Capacity utilisation is an issue for businesses over the product life cycle. In the development, launch and growth phases a business has a number of alternative strategies.

Creating new capacity A business may decide to build new capacity to deal with sales of a new product. New capacity could be created as sales **grow**. This would delay outflows of

Uses and problems of the product life cycle

The product life cycle has a number of uses for businesses.
- It helps to evaluate when a product needs to be withdrawn from the market and new products introduced.
- It encourages understanding and planning for times when sales of a product will no longer grow.
- It helps to plan different strategies to cope with different stages in the life of a product.

- It warns against overcharging or complacency when a product is selling well. The product life cycle predicts that competition will enter the market encouraged by high sales and profits.

There may be problems, however, when using the product life cycle model in business. The product life cycle is a useful tool showing changes that have occurred over the life of products. But it is not a **prediction** of how sales will change in future. In practice, every product has a different shaped life cycle. A few products, like Cadbury's Dairy Milk chocolate, are arguably still in the maturity or saturation stage 100 years after they were first produced. Other products fail completely on launch.

Also, it is important that businesses and managers do not allow the product life cycle to **determine** their actions. If sales are in decline, for example, managers may assume that there is nothing that can be done to stop this. But it could be that sales are falling because of insufficient promotion for the product. Or the product may lack adequate distribution. Getting the product sold in new and different places could lift sales. A decline in sales may be more about poor management than where a product is in its life cycle.

checklist

1 Explain briefly the differences between the development and launch stages of the product life cycle.
2 Compare the growth stage with the maturity stage of the product life cycle.
3 Why might different products have different product life cycles?
4 What different extension strategies might a business pursue for a product?
5 Contrast the different cash flows of a product in its development stage and introduction stage with its growth stage and maturity stages.
6 Explain briefly the link between capacity utilisation and the product life cycle.
7 (a) How might a business use its knowledge of the product life cycle to determine strategy? (b) What are the main problems which could arise from this?

keyterms

Capacity - **the maximum or potential amount a business, factory or outlet can efficiently produce over a period of time.**
Capacity utilisation - **actual output as a percentage of capacity.**
Extension strategies - **strategies used to extend the life of a product and prevent it falling into decline.**
Product life cycle - **the stages through which a product passes from its development, through growth and maturity to decline and finally being withdrawn from sale.**

Martyn Dawes set up Coffee Nation in the mid-1990s. He was looking for a new business idea when he went to New York and noticed that every corner shop sold coffee. When he came back, he installed some instant coffee machines in a few downmarket corner shops. But he quickly realised that this was not going to make his fortune. Neither the coffee sold or the locations were particularly attractive to potential customers. He decided to go up-market, both in product and location. Four machines offering a variety of coffees were installed in mainstream retail sites and were an immediate success, both for Coffee Nation and the owner of the location. Revenues were split between the site owner and Coffee Nation. The site owners incurred no extra costs because machines were installed and maintained by Coffee Nation. But research shows that customers buying a cup of coffee also spend on average another £3 at the site on other merchandise, such as food or magazines.

At this stage, in order to expand further, Martyn needed extra finance. The machines were profitable but not profitable enough to see the business concept taken nationwide within a reasonable timescale. So he sought out a business angel, a person who would put money into the business venture for a share of the company. Martyn found someone willing to put in £100 000. Since then, he has raised another £4.2 million to fund expansion.

Today, the company has machines in 120 locations, from garage forecourts to airports, theme parks and motorway service areas. What's more, Coffee Nation is now expanding fast, installing 30 new machines a month. This year the business is expected to double in size. The UK potential is around 2 000 machines and Martin Dawes is already thinking of expanding abroad.
Adapted from *The Times*, 29.6.2002.

1 Explain what is meant the terms 'downmarket' and 'up-market'. (3 marks).
2 Using a diagram, outline the stages of the product life cycle through which Coffee Nation had passed by June 2002. (8 marks)
3 Examine the cash requirements of the business through its product life cycle. (8 marks)
4 Consider what extension strategies Coffee Nation could use in future once its current business concept has reached maturity. (11 marks)

13 Product portfolio analysis

Coca-Cola

Knowledge Coca-Cola is the largest soft drinks supplier in the world. Since the company was founded, Coca-Cola, the carbonated drink, and other brands owned by the company, such as Sprite, have broadly enjoyed rising sales, both in its home country (the USA) and abroad.

Application In many *markets*, *sales* of Coca-Cola, the carbonated drink, began to *stagnate* in the late 1990s. The *product* turned from being a *star* to a *cash cow* for the *company* in these *markets*. In 2002, there was speculation that Coca-Cola would launch a new *brand* of vanilla-flavoured Coke.

Analysis Launching Vanilla Coke could create a new star product for Coca-Cola. However, it would essentially be an extension strategy for the existing basic product. Sales could easily peak within 12-18 months and then tail off without the product establishing any maturity of sales. It would pass straight from being a star to a dog. On the other hand, sales may stabilise as they have with Cherry Coke, creating a successful cash cow for the company.

Evaluation Coca-Cola could be taking a risk in launching Vanilla Coke. If it turned into a dog, it could harm the image of the main Coca-Cola brand. On the other hand, it could help growth in sales of carbonated drinks at Coca-Cola. With the main brand stalled in some of its key markets, new ideas are needed if growth is to be resumed.

Adapted from the *Financial Times*, 2.4.2002.

Product mix and product line

Most businesses sell a range of products. For example, a manufacturer of electrical products may sell products as varied as televisions, electronic games machines, MP3 players and DVD players. This range of products represents the PRODUCT MIX or PRODUCT PORTFOLIO of the business. The product portfolio will be made up PRODUCT LINES. A product line is a group of products which are very similar. For example, the business might sell flat screen, widescreen and portable televisions. Televisions are an example of a product line of the business.

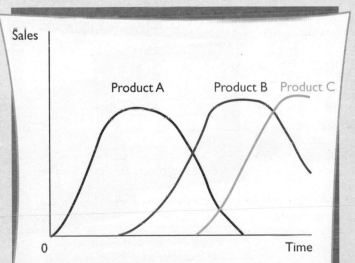

Figure 13.1 *Managing the product portfolio. This business is launching new products at regular intervals to replace declining sales from older products. This keeps overall sales constant or growing.*

Some businesses have a wide product portfolio, producing many different product lines. Examples include Virgin, Sony and General Motors. A small business may have only one product line.

Product portfolio analysis

Businesses need to manage their product portfolios. For example, drugs are patented, typically for 25 years. This gives pharmaceutical companies a monopoly on their production and sale during this time. Once out of patent, however, successful drugs are copied by other companies and **generic** products (i.e. identical products) appear on the market. Prices tend to fall and the company with the original patent also loses sales to the new competitors. The result is a drop in sales revenue and an even sharper drop in profits for the pharmaceutical company. So the company needs to keep finding new drugs to replace those which are nearing the end of their patented life. Figure 13.1 shows a company which has been successful in maintaining its revenue. As one product comes to the end of its patented life, another is growing to replace it.

The Boston Matrix

One way for a business to analyse its product portfolio is for it to use the BOSTON MATRIX. This is a technique developed by a US management consultancy company, the Boston Consulting Group (BCG).

Products are categorised according to two criteria.
* **Market growth.** How fast is the market for the product growing? The market may be declining, as for example with jams and preserves. Or it may be expanding strongly, as with frozen convenience meals. Sales of a product in a fast expanding market have a much better chance of growing

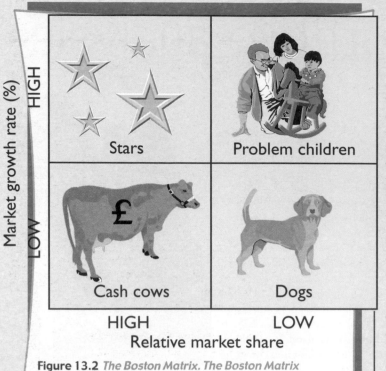

Figure 13.2 *The Boston Matrix. The Boston Matrix classifies products according to the rate of growth of their market and their relative market share. Products then fall into one of four categories – stars, cash cows, problem children or dogs.*

than a product in a stagnant or declining market.

- **Relative market share.** How strong is the product within its market? Is it the **market leader** (see unit 19)? Is it a product which is twelfth in terms of sales? To measure this, the market share of the product is compared to the strongest rival product. For example, if Product X has a market share of 10 per cent, whilst the market leader has a market share of 40 per cent, then the **relative** market share of product X is 0.25 (10 per cent ÷ 40 per cent). If Product Y is the market leader with a market share of 50 per cent, whilst the next most important product has a market share of 25 per cent, then the relative market share of Product Y is 2.0 (50 per cent ÷ 25 per cent).

Using these two criteria, the products of a business can be placed in one of four categories, shown in Figure 13.2. Each of these categories is given a name - stars, cash cows, problem children and dogs - to show their value to the business.

Stars A STAR is a product which has high market growth and a relatively high market share. Stars are likely to be very valuable to a business in the future. The product is in a strong position within its market because it has a relatively high market share. It therefore is well positioned to take advantage of a fast growing market. A star is already likely to be **profitable** because it has relatively high market share. But the business will need to **invest** strongly in the product to cope with a growing market and growing sales. For example, spending may be needed on new production facilities or promotion to fend off competitors anxious to exploit the growing market. Overall **cash flow** is likely to be nearly zero. Profits will be high, bringing cash into the business. But high investment will lead to an outflow of cash. So the two balance each other.

Cash cows A CASH COW is a product with a relatively strong market share. It is therefore well positioned in its market and is likely to be highly profitable. But the market itself has relatively weak growth. So the prospects for increases in sales and profits are poor. There is likely to be little need for investment. For example, with only slow growth in sales, or perhaps even declining sales, there should be little call for investment in new production facilities. Cash cows, as the name implies, have strong positive cash flow. The profits coming into the business are not matched by investment flowing out of the business.

Problem children A PROBLEM CHILD (or QUESTION MARK or WILDCAT) is a product with relatively low market share in a fast growing market. It is a problem for the business because it is unclear what should be done about the product. On the one hand, it is performing weakly compared to rival products. It is therefore unlikely to be very profitable. On the other hand, it is in a fast growing market. The potential is there to make this

To music purists, it's a typical case of corporate pop mediocrity. But to 70 million customers over 18 years, it's a must have product. The *Now That's What I call Music!* brand this week reached a venerable half century. First launched in 1983, EMI, the record company behind the series, has just launched *Now 50*. One million copies have been printed in time for the Christmas rush. Previous editions have sold between 500 000 and 2 million copies each, far beyond what would be considered a runaway hit for an individual artist.

The formula has remained the same over the 50 albums. Reproduce the best acts that have recently been in the charts, are in the charts now or will be within the next few weeks. As one record executive put it: 'Now and other compilations are basically a cash cow. And labels love milking them. It allows the labels and artists to recycle their recent chart hits and get the royalties for the song a second time round in a form that offers something for everyone - it's musical Quality Street. There's no doubt that it's a money spinner. The customer gets a sort of four-month summary of the latest hits for the price of a CD and we can rely on a windfall from the recent back catalogue.'

Adapted from *The Independent*, 21.11.2001.

1 Using the Boston Matrix,
(a) explain why 'Now' is a cash cow for EMI;
(b) discuss whether 'Now' could be turned from a cash cow to a star.

McDonald's is not yet in crisis, but it does have a problem. Sales in the US are at best stagnant and at worst falling. Elsewhere in the world it is expanding - 1 500 stores were opened in 2000. But new foreign outlets do not necessarily add to profits. In the last quarter of 2000 net income was down 7 per cent, mainly due to weakness of the euro.

McDonald's has tried to stimulate sales in the US market by launching new products, such as McPizza. They have all failed. In the past 15 years only Happy Meals and Chicken Nuggets have been successful innovations. So the company began a new strategy - buying into small, growing companies in other food sectors. It now has a stake in Boston Chicken and Donatos Pizza, and the UK business Pret a Manger.

Pret a Manger is a fast growing sandwich chain. It has recently successfully opened a branch in New York. Pret a Manger and McDonald's might seem different. Pret a Manger has prided itself on selling high quality, fresh food, mainly to office workers. McDonald's sells value food mainly to children, young people and families. But McDonald's doesn't want to turn Pret a Manger into a sandwich McDonald's. It wants to keep the successful up-market brand. What it will add is its skills in franchising, operations, marketing and managing property. Pret a Manger will find it easier to expand in the US market with McDonald's backing. McDonald's hopes that at least one of its acquisitions will grow into a major profit earner to supplement profits from its main chain.

Adapted from *The Sunday Times*, 4.2.2001.

1 **Suggest, using the Boston Matrix, how the senior management of McDonald's views its main chain of stores.**
2 **How might the Boston Matrix have helped management at McDonald's to make the decision to buy new food chains such as Pret a Manger?**

---

product into a star. Cash flow is likely to be either zero or negative. Weak relative market share means that the product will not be particularly profitable. But investment will be needed to cope with expanding sales in a fast growing market.

Dogs A DOG is a product with relatively low market share in a low growth market. These are products which have poor prospects for future growth in sales or profits. They may generate some positive cash flow because there is likely to be little investment, whilst some profits may be earned on sales. Equally though, the product might be struggling to **break-even** (see unit 22) or it might be loss making. In this case, cash flow will be zero or negative.

Strategy and the Boston Matrix

Having analysed their product portfolio, managers of a business can then decide on a suitable product strategy.

Stars Stars are the products which have the greatest future potential. Already successful, they are in the growth phase of the **product life cycle** (see unit 12). When the market matures, they will be the cash cows of the business. So although they are likely to contribute little to current cash flow due to heavy investment, they need to be encouraged. The appropriate strategy is therefore to BUILD the brand or product. Sales must be increased. If possible, so too should market share. Competition needs to be fought off. If possible, the product should have the largest share of the market since this will be the most profitable position in the long term.

Cash cows Cash cows are highly valuable to a business. They are likely to be in the maturity or saturation phase of the

product life cycle. With little need for investment, the product can be MILKED for cash. This provides the finance for investment in other products of the business, in particular stars. Some problem children need investment too. In certain industries, cash cows provide the funds for large research and development budgets for the products of the future. Cash cows still need defending from competition, however. So promotion is an important part of the defensive strategy for a cash cow. Some investment may also be needed to finance **extension strategies** (see unit 12) for the product. Overall, though, the most appropriate strategy for cash cows is HOLDING - spending just enough on promotion and product development to maintain sales and market share.

Problem children Managers have to make difficult decisions about problem children, as their name implies. They have three main choices.

- The first is to **build** the product or brand. In putting extra resources into the product, managers are gambling that the product will increase its market share and its growth rate of sales. For this strategy to be successful, the product must be turned into a star. Failure of the strategy will almost certainly mean that the business will make a loss on the product and divert management time from potentially more successful products.
- The second strategy is HARVESTING. This means maximising profit and cash flow, probably by raising prices and cutting marketing spending. Sales are likely to fall, but the profit per unit sold (the profit margin) will increase by a larger percentage, giving the rise in profit. Harvesting is a strategy that is likely to reduce the

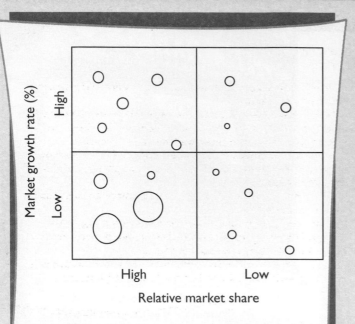

Figure 13.3 *A desirable product mix. Each product is represented by a circle. Revenue from its sale is shown by the size of the circle. This business has an excellent product mix. It has significant cash cows with a number of stars ready to become the cash cows of the future. It has some problem children , but these are few in number. It also has some dogs, but they are relatively insignificant.*

remaining lifetime of the product. Whilst sales last, however, as much benefit is squeezed from the product as possible.

- A third strategy is DIVESTMENT. This means either dropping the product or selling it. Withdrawing the product from sale is likely to indicate that the product is generating negative cash flow and is unprofitable. The finances of the business will therefore improve if the product is dropped. Selling the product will yield some profit and is therefore preferable to simply dropping the product. But a buyer needs to be found and this could be difficult.

Dogs Dogs provide little or no cash flow or profit to the business. Some may be both unprofitable and yield negative cash flow. In many cases, the most appropriate strategy to adopt is **divestment**. However, some dogs are worth **harvesting** if they are still profitable.

In an ideal situation, most of a business' revenue will come from stars and cash cows. Figure 13.3 shows such a situation. Each circle represents a product. The size of the circle indicates the value of its revenue. The exact location of the circle shows where it is in relation to market growth and relative market share.

But a business may find that it has far too few cash cows and stars. This means that it is finding it difficult to finance the development of new products. Too few stars means that future cash flow and profitability are at risk. Too many problem children could be an opportunity for the business if it can turn these into stars. But they are a liability if many of them prove to be dogs. As for dogs, they are likely to be low profit, negative growth products.

Using the Boston Matrix

The Boston Matrix is a tool for analysing the product portfolio of a business. However, it needs to used with caution. A simple 2 x 2 matrix is a crude way of categorising products or basing strategy upon it. Problems with the matrix include the following.

- Cash flow and profit can be different for individual products than predicted by the model. For example, a dog might have strong cash flow and be highly profitable despite falling sales. A star might have negative cash flow if the market is growing extremely fast or there is fierce competition.
- Products may be linked. A dog might be an important part of a product range for customers, who might not buy a star or cash cow if they can't also buy less popular products. Divesting the dog might affect sales of stars and cash cows. Take ice-cream as an example. The best selling product in a freezer cabinet by the seaside might be a Wall's Magnum. Cheap ice lollies might be 'dogs' for the ice-cream vendor. But families may choose to buy elsewhere if they can't find something cheap to buy for their children.
- There are examples of businesses which have made a success out of owning mainly problem children and dogs. For example, **venture capitalists** (see unit 25) specialise in investing in businesses that develop or make problem children products. They accept that most of these products will remain problem children or even could become dogs. But a few will turn out to be stars. The profit from the development of one star is greater than the zero or negative return on the products which fail to make the grade.

The Boston Matrix, like the product life cycle model (see unit 12), can provide valuable insights for businesses. But in some cases it may lead them into making the wrong decision. Managers ideally need a fully rounded view of a business to judge what is an appropriate strategy at a particular point in time.

1 Explain the difference between a product range and a product line.
2 Explain briefly why a business needs to manage its product portfolio.
3 In the Boston Matrix, what two criteria are used to judge products?
4 What is the difference in the Boston Matrix between (a) a star and a dog and (b) a cash cow and a problem child?
5 How can a business build its star products?
6 How might a business manage its cash cows?
7 What might be the difference in the way a dog and a problem child are managed by a business?
8 Why does the Boston Matrix need to be used with caution by a business?

keyterms

Boston Matrix - a 2 x 2 matrix model which analyses a product portfolio according to the growth rate of the market and the relative market share of products within that market. Products are placed in one of four categories - stars, cash cows, problem children or dogs.

Building - a strategy for increasing the sales and market share of a product.

Cash cow - according to the Boston Matrix, a product which is in a low growth market but has a relatively high market share.

Divestment - for a product, a strategy of either ceasing its production or selling it to another business.

Dog - according to the Boston Matrix, a product which is in a low growth market and has a relatively low market share.

Harvesting - a strategy for maximising cash flow and/or profit from a product even if this means a decline in its sales and a shortening of its product life cycle.

Holding - a strategy for maintaining the sales and market share of a product.

Milking - a strategy of using the cash and profit generated by one product to finance other strategic objectives such as the development and growth of another product.

Product line - a group of products produced by a business which are very similar, such as a brand of paint offered in 20 different colours.

Product mix, portfolio or range - the combination of products that a business sells.

Problem child, question mark or wildcat - according to the Boston Matrix, a product which is in a high growth market but has a relatively low market share.

Star - according to the Boston Matrix, a product which is in a high growth market and has a relatively high market share.

Sunny Delight was launched in the UK by Proctor & Gamble (P&G) in 1998. It was an instant success. Children liked it and parents were happy to buy it as a healthy orange juice alternative to carbonated drinks. The label on the bottle said it all: a 'vitamin enriched citrus drink'. By 2000, two years after launch, it was the second biggest selling UK soft drink with sales of £150 million, second only to market leader Coca-Cola.

But then Sunny Delight was hit by a PR disaster. Some parents complained to the press that only 5 per cent of the drink was orange juice. The rest was mainly water and sugar. Every 200 ml bottle contained 14 grams of sugar, just as much as Coca-Cola or Pepsi. The low point came when a story broke that the skin of a three year old girl had turned orange after drinking 1.5 litres of Sunny Delight every day. The fact that it later turned out that the cause was over-consumption of beta carotene, found in the 5 per cent of the drink that was orange juice, didn't prevent damage to the brand. Between October 2000 and October 2001, sales slumped 38 per cent.

The brand was too valuable to P&G to be abandoned. Indeed, P&G defended its marketing. Sally Woodidge, P&G's head of external affairs, said 'When a brand becomes as successful as Sunny Delight, it becomes an icon and attracts coverage and comment that could have been directed towards many (soft drink) brands.' She said that any deception around the brand was more in the mind of the media than parents buying it for their children. 'Our research shows the actual numbers of consumers who were confused about Sunny Delight was very low. People who bought it knew what it was.'

Despite this defence, next month will see the launch of new varieties of Sunny Delight. They will have a higher fruit juice content of 15 per cent and will contain only natural sugars totalling 1.3 grams in a 100 ml bottle. The new flavours will be Orange Outburst, Tropical Tornado, Blackcurrant Blast and Apple and Kiwi Kick. Original Sunny Delight will, however, remain on sale.

Sunny Delight's brand managers insist that the new format and a significant marketing budget can revitalise Sunny Delight. However, Andrew Seth, a former marketing chief of Lever Brothers, which in the mid-1990s had its own disaster with Persil Power, said: 'I don't think P&G have really owned up over Sunny Delight. The brand name is now damaged and simply has not been around long enough to have the kind of heritage that allows you to recover consumers' trust.'

Adapted from *The Times*, 27.02.2002.

1 Explain what is meant by the terms:
   (a) 'market leader'; (3 marks)
   (b) 'brand name'. (3 marks)
2 Explain TWO reasons why Sunny Delight sales fell in 2001. (6 marks)
3 Using the Boston Matrix, how might you categorise Sunny Delight in the UK (a) between 1998 and October 2000;
   (b) between October 2000 and February 2002? (8 marks)
4 Consider whether the new marketing campaign, including the launch of new varieties in March 2002, could rebuild the Sunny Delight brand. (10 marks)

14 Product design and development

Voss

Knowledge Voss is a brand of bottled water from Norway. It claims to be the cleanest water in Northern Europe. It is sold through 'up-market' outlets.

Application Voss is a *consumer good*, sold through *consumer markets*. The *product* has certain *characteristics* or *attributes*. It is a pure spring water. It is sold in a cylindrical glass bottle, making it look like expensive perfume. Consumers drink the water to quench their thirst, a *tangible benefit*. The product is sold in top restaurants and hotels, at high price of £4 for a 750ml bottle. So consumers might gain the *intangible benefits* of feeling a sense of exclusivity and trend setting when buying the water.

Analysis To succeed, Voss must persuade consumers to pay high prices for a product which they could get free from a tap. Pure water is also available from other bottled water products. So the aesthetically pleasing design of the bottle might be what distinguishes Voss from its competitors.

Evaluation Launching a new product is a gamble. By carefully positioning its product in the market, Voss stands some chance of success in establishing itself as a premium brand.

Adapted from the *Financial Times*, 3.4.2001.

Product

A PRODUCT is anything that can be exchanged and is able to satisfy customers' needs. It might be a tangible physical GOOD, such as a car or a packet of peas. Or it might be an intangible, non-physical SERVICE, such as a foreign holiday, a medical examination or defence.

When a product is bought, the customer receives a mix of 'inputs'. For example, when buying a foreign holiday, the customer is getting:
- the services of workers who provide everything from baggage handling at an airport to a meal in a hotel;
- the ability to use a place, the holiday destination, for sleeping, eating, lying on the beach or going on a trip;
- the use of goods, such as food, petrol, airliners or deckchairs;
- ideas from the individuals who put the foreign holiday together to the technology which powers aeroplanes.

A distinction can be made between PRODUCER (or INDUSTRIAL) PRODUCTS and CONSUMER PRODUCTS. Producer products are used to make other goods and services or in the operation of the business. For example, a coffee machine and a building are two producer products used by Starbucks to make a cup of coffee served to consumers. Producer products are sold by one business to another in **industrial markets** (see unit 2). The cup of coffee is a consumer product because it is bought by individuals or households for personal use. A car bought from a dealer by an individual would be a consumer product bought in a **consumer market** (see unit 2). In contrast, a car bought by a business for use as a company car would be a producer product.

A distinction can also be made between CUSTOMERS and CONSUMERS. A customer is any person, business or organisation which purchases a product. So Starbucks is a customer of property companies that rent premises for its coffee shops. Equally, an individual buying a coffee from Starbucks is also a customer. Consumers, on the other hand, are individuals or households who buy and then use up a product.

Product attributes

PRODUCT ATTRIBUTES are the **characteristics** of a product. For example, a car (a good) might be red, seat five people, be an estate, and be able to go up to 120 miles per hour. A holiday (a service) might be in Ibiza for two weeks, in a hotel 200 metres from the sea, in peak season in August. A Wolverhampton Wanderers' home football match (a service) might be between 3-5 o'clock on a Saturday afternoon at the Molyneux stadium, where spectators can watch 22 players trying to kick a ball into a net.

Consumers buy products because of the benefits given by these attributes. TANGIBLE BENEFITS are benefits which can be measured. For example, the benefit of a train journey might be that it gets you from London to Glasgow in four hours. The benefit of a washing machine might be that it will wash for five years without breaking down.

INTANGIBLE BENEFITS are benefits which, though present, cannot be measured. Some products are bought because of the image they convey. For example, wearing a t-shirt in the colours of a national football team might have been considered 'cool' during the World Cup of 2002. Other intangible benefits might be pleasure or peace of mind. Cadbury's adverts stress the pleasure gained from eating a Cadbury's Flake. Insurance to cover funeral expenses is often sold to give peace of mind to the person who is going to die.

'Good' products

What are the characteristics of a 'good' product?
- It should be functional and fulfil the needs of customers. For example, food should taste good. A train service should be fast, frequent and reliable. A television set should give good quality pictures. A lawn mower should cut grass well.
- It should be aesthetically pleasing. Good design is not just about working properly. It is also about how a product looks to the customer. In some industries, such as clothing, cars and kitchen equipment, aesthetics and design have a great

effect on how consumers spend their money.

- It should be affordable. Many people would like to take a journey into space, but at present it is too expensive for all but a few. On the other hand, a furniture company like IKEA has become extremely successful because it sells goods which are affordable to most. So the product should be capable of being produced within the purchasing budgets of the target market.
- The product must conform to legal requirements. Toys, for example, should not contain lead paint. Food sold to people should be fit to eat.
- Ideally, products should be environmentally and socially friendly. Increasingly, products are being bought by consumers on the strength of their 'ethical' credentials. For example, people want paper made from recycled paper. They might also refuse to buy trainers made in factories with poor work conditions in low income countries.

Developing new products

Many businesses operate in changing markets where competitors constantly bring out new products. Developing new products is therefore important to stay competitive. Product development may go through a number of stages, as shown in Figure 14.1.

Ideas The first stage is the generation of ideas for new products. These can come from a variety of sources.

- **Market research** (see unit 4) may indicate that existing products could be improved. Or it might show a gap in the market for a new product.
- RESEARCH AND DEVELOPMENT (R&D) may lead to new products being created. R&D can be **pure research** into new ideas or theories. Or it can be **applied research**, where existing research is used to create new products or improve existing products.
- Individuals or groups may come up with ideas which they think will be commercially viable. An example of this is the US company, 3M, where employees are allowed to use 15 per cent of their work time to devise new products. Sometimes, **brainstorming techniques** are used. This is where a group of people is asked to generate a large number

In 1933, Bialetti, an Italian company, launched a new coffee maker which has come to be the world's best selling stove-top coffee machine. The pot had a unique eight sided aluminium design. Since the 1950s, nearly 300 million pots have been sold. Current sales volumes are 10 million a year. The pot was designed to sit on the ring of a cooker. Water in the pot is heated up and passed over coffee beans to produce coffee.

Today, the product is being 'extended'. Bialetti is collaborating with Strix, a company based in the Isle of Man. Strix is the world's biggest maker of kettle controls. The idea is to produce an electric coffee pot which, it is hoped, will be particularly popular in Northern Europe, North America and Asia.

A team of eight engineers, drawn from Strix and Bialetti, spent six months perfecting the design of the pot. This has ensured that the rate at which heat is applied using the electrical system to the water inside the pot is comparable to what happens with the stove-top model. Strix says the system gives a more consistent cup of coffee than the stove-top model. Also, because the electrical system switches itself off, it is safer. Sometimes people leave the traditional Bialetti coffee maker on the stove too long. This causes the aluminium parts to melt.

The new pot will retail for about £30, twice the price of a stove-top model. Strix hopes that sales by 2005 will be 2-3 million a year. This would represent an increase of 10 per cent in total sales for Strix.

Adapted from the *Financial Times*, 29.1.2002.

1 What might make the electric coffee pot a 'good' product?
2 Outline the key stages in the development and launch of the electric Bialetti coffee pot.
3 Discuss what are the advantages for Bialetti and Strix of working together to create the new electric coffee pot.

of ideas in a short time. The ideas can be realistic or unrealistic. From this, one or two ideas might be used for further development.

- Competing products may provide ideas. For example, a business might develop a product which mimics the successful product of a competitor.

Once ideas have been generated, they must be analysed. Decisions must be made about which ideas will go forward. The technical feasibility of making the product will need to be investigated. Market research may be used at this point to indicate whether there is a likely demand. Potential products will need to be costed to see if they can be sold at a price which customers are prepared to pay.

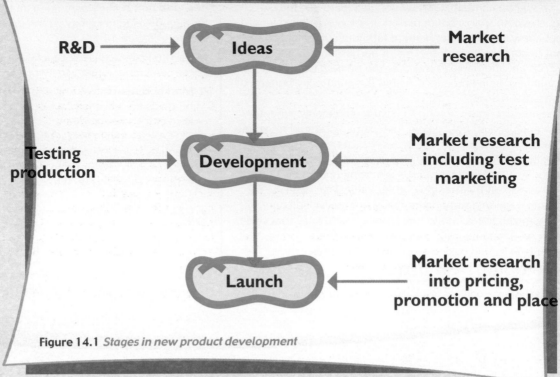

Figure 14.1 *Stages in new product development*

Development The next stage is to develop the product. Some ideas may prove impossible to produce. Hopefully, however, **prototype** products will result from the development process. These are sample products created before a product is put into final production. Prototypes may then be tested in two ways.

- In some cases, it is important to test whether a product can be made in bulk. Making a product in a laboratory can be very different from making it in large quantities. Sometimes, businesses find it impossible to 'gross-up' production to a commercial scale and a product has to be abandoned.
- Sometimes, businesses choose to **test market** (see unit 7) a new product. This is to see whether customers in a small area will buy the product in sufficient quantities to justify the costs of a full scale launch.

Launch If a potential new product has survived this far, it will now be ready for launch. Its long term success will depend mainly on how well it satisfies the needs of customers. But in the short term, success for some products can be affected by other elements of the marketing mix - price, promotion and place. Some businesses may use market research at this stage to make decisions about how to launch a product.

Constraints on new product development

The ability of businesses to launch new products is affected by many factors.

- Businesses have limited funds. A business selling £500 000 worth of products a year is unlikely to spend £1 million a year on developing new products. Most businesses spend only a few per cent of their turnover on new product development.

- Technology and the final price can prove an obstacle. This is particularly true for businesses in the high technology sector. Pharmaceutical companies, for example, spend huge sums on developing new drugs which in the end do not work. Equally, manufacturers have spent decades trying to create a flat screen television with a screen size over 40 inches. So far, they have developed a variety of technologies to achieve this. But they have not been able to reduce the final price to a level which most consumers will pay.
- There can be legal constraints. Businesses have to be careful not to infringe the patents and copyrights of other businesses (see unit 59). New products also have to conform to laws which set standards. Toys, for example, can't contain lead paint in the UK.

checklist

1 What is a product?
2 What is the difference between a consumer product and a producer product?
3 What is the difference between the tangible benefits derived from the consumption of a product and the intangible benefits?
4 Explain briefly the attributes of a 'good' product.
5 How can ideas for a new product be generated?
6 What is meant by (a) a prototype product and (b) test marketing?
7 What are the constraints on business in the launch of new products?

keyterms

Consumers - individuals or households that purchase products and use or consume them.

Consumer products - goods and services which are sold to individuals or households for personal consumption.

Customers - individuals, households, businesses or organisations which purchase products from suppliers.

Good - a physical product such as a car, a cabbage or a container. Goods are tangible because they can be touched, seen, smelt and heard.

Intangible benefits (of a product) - product benefits which cannot be measured, such as image, satisfaction and reputation.

Producer (or industrial) products - goods or services which are sold by one business to another business.

Product - anything that can be exchanged and is able to satisfy customers' needs. Products are either goods or services which have particular product attributes.

Product attributes - the characteristics of a product, such as size, weight, colour, image, after-sales service or place which satisfy consumer demand.

Research and Development (R&D) - the process of scientific and technological research (both pure and applied research) and the development of that research into creating new products.

Services - non-physical products, such as a haircut, a train journey, a foreign holiday or education. Services are intangible in that they are not physical products.

Tangible benefits (of a product) - product benefits which can be measured, touched and seen, such as colour, speed and durability.

Pyroban is a Sussex based company with annual sales of £9 million which specialises in fire protection systems. 90 per cent of its sales come from the company's core activity: retro fitting specialised shielding equipment to lift trucks. This is to prevent fires being ignited by sparks from their engines. Some companies need to use fork lift trucks in areas where there are highly flammable materials. A spark from an engine, or simply too much heat, could lead to a fire. Pyroban solves this problem by fitting a shield to a standard lift truck engine.

Pyroban is the European market leader in this niche producer product market. It has a market share of around one third. It currently converts about 400 trucks a year of many different makes and sizes. These customised specialist jobs cost on average around £16 000, typically up to twice the price of a new truck. Fire protection is therefore an expensive option for companies buying from Pyroban.

Despite a solid base of sales, Pyroban is aiming to expand out of its niche market into related products. It has a 10 person development team working on a variety of new ideas. One promising market is for hazard warning systems. These would be fitted to trucks and other industrial vehicles which might stray into areas where there are flammable gases. Possible customers include airlines which maintain aircraft engines, where jet fuel spillage is a potential hazard.

Another new development would be to provide engine management techniques to satisfy tougher laws aimed at controlling pollution. These could be fitted at the same time as shielding equipment to lift trucks and similar vehicles.

Adapted from the *Financial Times*, 7.10.1999.

---

1 Explain what is meant by a 'producer product market'. (3 marks)

2 Outline (a) TWO product attributes and (b) ONE tangible benefit to customers of Pyroban's shield system for lift engines. (6 marks)

3 Examine the possible characteristics that the hazard warning system being developed by Pyroban should possess. (10 marks)

4 Discuss the case for and against Pyroban moving into new product areas. (11 marks)

15 Pricing methods

The restaurant trade

Knowledge In the restaurant trade there is a rule of thumb about the pricing of meals. If the food ingredients cost £1, the restaurant charges around £3 to the customer.

Application The 1:3 ratio is an example of *cost-plus pricing*. The price of a meal is determined by one of the main *production costs*, its ingredients.

Analysis In practice, there are factors other than cost which determine the price of a meal. For example, if ingredients cost £3.06, the restaurant might not charge £9.18 for a meal. This is because £9.18 is not what customers would expect to pay. They might expect a price of £10.00. The business might even decide to charge £9.99 because it seems psychologically lower than £10.00. The restaurant might also judge that items would be too cheap or expensive in relation to the rest of the menu if cost-plus pricing were used. For example, ingredients for a 'starter' might cost 40p, so the price could be £1.20 (40p x 3). But the restaurant might want to set a minimum £2.00 price on any first course. The restaurant may also be aware of local competition. If rivals charge £5.95 for a set menu at lunchtime, a restaurant may set its lunchtime price at £5.95 too.

Evaluation Exactly what mix of pricing strategies a restaurant uses will depend on many factors. These include the costs of the business, the willingness of customers to pay particular prices for meals and competition in the area. To survive in the long term, however, the restaurant must be able to sell meals at prices which allow it to cover its costs and make a profit.

Price and the marketing mix

Price is one of the elements of the marketing mix (see unit 1). Businesses have to decide at what price to sell their products. This unit considers the three main pricing methods used by businesses - cost based pricing, market orientated pricing and competition-based pricing. Unit 16 considers how these methods can be used within a pricing and marketing strategy. Unit 17 then considers in detail how the demand for a firm's products is affected by their prices and the income of consumers.

Cost-based pricing

COST-BASED PRICING is where a business uses production costs to determine prices. Costs are important in pricing because unless price is greater than total cost, the sale will result in a **loss**. The greater the difference between price and total cost, the greater will be the **profit** (see unit 21). There is a number of cost-based pricing methods.

Cost-plus pricing Businesses aim to make a profit on their sales. So an easy way of pricing is to add a MARK-UP to the fixed and variable (or full) cost of a product as in Figure 15.1. This is known as COST-PLUS PRICING or FULL COST PRICING. For example, a business may routinely add a 20 per cent mark-up to its products. So if the full cost of production (i.e. variable cost plus fixed cost) was £1.00 per unit, it would add 20p (£1.00 x 20%) to this and sell it for £1.20.

In some industries, prices are based on just some of the costs faced by a business. Clothing and shoe shops, for example, typically add 100 per cent to the cost of stock (their main **variable cost**, see unit 21) that they buy from manufacturers to arrive at a price. So a pair of shoes might cost £20 from a shoe factory. The shoe shop then sells

them at £40. The £20 margin here is not just profit. It also has to cover all the other costs of the business, such as wages of staff, rent and insurance.

The size of the mark-up is likely to be based on past experience. A business might know what level of mark up will generate a reasonable level of profit, but won't be so high as to drive customers away. In the short term, the mark-up may also be driven by market conditions. If the demand for the product is strong, the mark-up may be high. If demand is weak, the mark-up may be low. Businesses are then likely to offer **discounts** or have a **sale**, i.e. accept a reduced mark-up for their products. In the long term, full cost represents a minimum price that the business will accept. If market conditions force it to accept less than this, the business might stop producing the item.

There are two advantages to cost-plus pricing. First, it is an

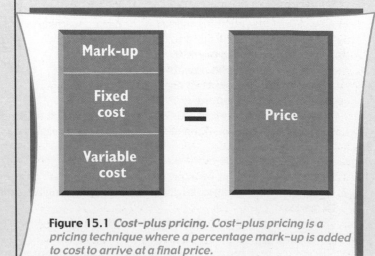

Figure 15.1 *Cost-plus pricing. Cost-plus pricing is a pricing technique where a percentage mark-up is added to cost to arrive at a final price.*

Gordon Hancocks is a landscape gardener. He has one employee and, between them, they do all the work. Contracts come mainly from residential customers. They might have bought a new house and need a garden laying out. Or perhaps some trees need taking down and the area re-landscaping.

Gordon does all his own pricing. He calculates the material costs of a job. Then he adds wages for himself and his employee. There are also costs such as his van, the telephone and paying to have his accounts done. For these, he averages them out and charges per day worked. Finally, he adds 20 per cent as a profit margin.

Work is usually easy to come by between Easter and November. But the winter can be difficult. There may be weeks when he has no work on at all. But he still has costs such as the wages of his employee or the repayments on his van.

What he finds most difficult is when a customer rings round contractors trying to knock their price down. Last week, Gordon quoted a customer £2 000 for a job. This week, the customer rang back saying that another business would do the job for £1 500 and did Gordon want to revise his price? Gordon knew that he had no work booked in for the following two weeks of January. Should he revise his quote down to £1 450?

1 **'The materials needed for a job are a variable cost for Gordon.' Explain what this means.**
2 **'The repayments on his van are a fixed cost for Gordon.' Explain what this means.**
3 **Gordon uses cost-plus pricing for his jobs. Calculate the price Gordon would quote for a job if his fixed plus variable costs are: (a) £2 000; (b) £5 000; (c) £8 000 per job.**
4 **'Using contribution pricing methods, Gordon should accept a price of £1 450 for the job in January since he has no alternative work booked in.' Discuss whether he should accept the contract at this price.**

easy pricing method to use. Businesses add the mark-up which they have traditionally added to their products. Second, it is easy to see whether a sale will be profitable or not. This encourages the business to market its product in a profitable way and not to chase market share or sales volumes.

A problem with cost-plus pricing is that it can be inflexible to market conditions. A business may lose customers to cheaper products, when in fact a slightly lower price would still have given a reasonable level of profit. It can also be difficult to work out the **fixed cost** (see unit 21) of an individual product. Fixed costs of a business are those which don't change with output. For example, a business may run a factory making 30 different products. The rent on the factory is a fixed cost because it still has to be paid whether it is working flat out or production has stopped. But how should the rent on the factory be allocated to each individual product made? There are standard methods of doing this, but all have their advantages and drawbacks. So finding out the true total cost of a product on which to add a mark-up is not necessarily easy or accurate.

Contribution (or marginal) pricing As explained above, the costs of a business can be divided into two types. **Variable costs** are costs which change as output changes. For example, leather is a variable cost for a shoe manufacturer. The more shoes that are made, the more leather is used. **Fixed costs** are costs which stay the same whatever the level of output. For example, the shoe manufacturer may rent a factory. The rent is a fixed cost because it has to be paid whether a million pairs of shoes are made or zero.

Say that the variable costs for an order of 5 000 pairs of shoes were £40 000. If the order were priced over £40 000, it would cover its variable costs of production and make a **contribution** (see unit 23) towards the fixed costs and profit of the business. Contribution is defined as:

Contribution = revenue - variable costs

So, if the order were priced at £50 000, it would make a £10 000 contribution. If it were priced at £65 000, it would make a £25 000 contribution.

CONTRIBUTION PRICING can be used to decide whether to accept a lower price. This is shown in Figure 15.2. The usual price of shoes might be £20. If fixed costs were £8 per pair, costs would be £18 (variable costs of £10 + fixed costs of £8). Profit may be £2 per pair. Should the business accept a lower price for an order?

This pricing method would suggest that it could accept any price as long as it was at least £10, the variable cost of production. At a price of £12, for example, each pair makes a loss of £6 (£12 price - £10 costs). But it still makes a contribution of £2 per pair (£12 price - £10 variable cost). If it doesn't take the order, the business will be worse off. There will be no £2 contribution per pair of shoes.

In the long run, businesses have to cover all their costs and make a profit to survive. So the total contribution on sales has to be greater than fixed costs. But in the short run, the contribution method of pricing suggests that businesses might accept orders where the price fails to cover total costs, so long as the contribution is positive.

There are certain advantages of using contribution pricing.
● It encourages flexibility when pricing. Variable costs represent the minimum acceptable price. After that, the business can try to maximise the amount of contribution it can earn from any single sale.
● Products in high demand can be sold at high prices. Where there is intense competition, or the product is not popular with customers, the price can be lower.
● It may lead to one-off orders being accepted at a lower price.
● It may be used to break into new markets. Products can be sold at lower prices to attract initial customers (known as

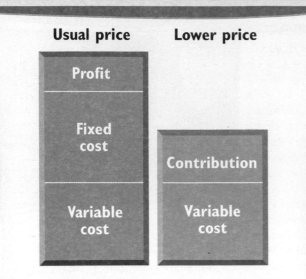

Figure 15.2 *Contribution pricing. A business might accept a lower price for an order as long as it covers variable costs and makes a contribution to fixed costs.*

entry pricing, see below).

- It may encourage the use of **excess capacity** (see unit 43) at times of the year when there is low demand. This is often the case in the printing or airline industries.

The main disadvantage is that those in charge of sales can focus too much on sales and not on selling at a profit. If all businesses in an industry adopt contribution pricing, this may lead to widespread selling below full cost. Businesses compete with each other for sales and the business with the lowest price can often increase market share. This puts a downward pressure on prices.

Market-orientated pricing

MARKET-ORIENTATED PRICING is a method of pricing based upon an assessment of market conditions. There is a number of market-orientated pricing methods used by businesses.

Penetration pricing A business may want to launch a new product or sell an existing product in a new market. It may adopt a strategy of PENETRATION PRICING with such products. This involves selling a product at a low price in the short term.

A disadvantage of this method is that it could be costly in the short term. The product will often initially be sold at below the full cost of production. The low price will hopefully attract large numbers of buyers. But each purchase will increase the loss being made.

On the other hand, market share can be gained quickly. Once prices are raised, sales and market share are likely to fall. However, if the product is as good as other products in the market, sales should stabilise. So, in the long term, it could be a relatively cheap way of acquiring market share quickly and establishing the product in the market.

New magazines are often launched using penetration pricing. The first issue is priced below the cover price. In some cases, the first two issues are sold together at the price of just one issue. There may also be expensive 'give-away' products

with the magazine.

Loss leaders A LOSS LEADER is a product which is sold at a very low price, often below full cost, to attract customers to buy other products. For example, a supermarket chain may advertise cut price bread for sale. This attracts customers, who then buy products apart from bread.

This can be a successful pricing method if overall sales and market share increase because of the loss leaders. Success can also be judged if the profit earned from the extra sales exceeds the losses made on the loss leaders.

The danger is that competitors will match any price cuts on selected items. Then the business won't see any increase in overall sales and will lose profit if it is selling loss leaders at below full cost.

Price discrimination Different groups of customers are prepared to pay different prices for the same product. For example, a business sending an executive to a meeting might be prepared to pay £150 for a return rail ticket. A student might only be prepared to pay £20 to travel on the same train. PRICE DISCRIMINATION is a pricing method where a business charges different prices to different customers, maximising the revenue from each group of customers.

Price discrimination is not possible in many markets. For example, in the UK market for DVDs, companies can't sell DVDs at a higher price to some customers than others. This is because they couldn't stop customers being charged a high price from buying DVDs at a lower price. However, companies can price discriminate internationally because they can control distribution through copyright laws. So they tend to sell DVDs in the USA at a lower price than in the UK. This is because UK buyers are less price sensitive than US buyers. So profits are kept higher in the UK by charging a higher price rather than a lower price.

Many successful examples of price discrimination are **time based**. For example, rail companies charge higher ticket prices to those travelling at peak time. Telephone companies charge more for calls during weekdays than in the evening and at weekends. Customers can often be kept in separate groups because most of those charged the higher price have to use the product at that time. Commuters, for example, have to travel at peak times to get to work.

Market skimming MARKET SKIMMING is the opposite of penetration pricing as shown in Figure 15.3. It involves charging a higher price when a product is launched and lowering it later.

Market skimming tends to be used when those buying the product first are relatively insensitive to the price they pay. For example, some cinema goers are prepared to pay twice the price for a ticket if they can see a newly released film a few days earlier than anyone else. Some enthusiasts are prepared to pay a high price to get hold of the latest technology, such as large flat screen televisions.

Market skimming allows a business to maximise its revenues and profits over the life cycle of the product (see unit 12). At launch, revenue and profit is maximised by charging a high price. Later on, profit is maximised by lowering price and increasing sales.

Psychological pricing In many markets, consumers have expectations about what price they should pay for a product.

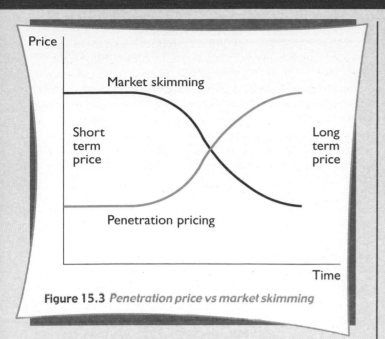

Figure 15.3 *Penetration price vs market skimming*

Businesses may use PSYCHOLOGICAL PRICING in these markets. For example, there is often a range of PRICING POINTS which guide buying decisions. A budget price CD might sell for £4.99. A full price CD might sell for £14.99. A budget CD priced at £6.50 could be seen as 'poor value for money' by consumers. Equally, customers might question what was wrong with a CD which they expect to sell for £14.99 if it were sold for £4.99.

Pricing points are also important in making decisions about the exact price to charge. Many products are priced at just below a certain figure. For example, cars may be priced at £14 999 rather than £15 000. A magazine may be priced at £2.99 rather than £3.00. Businesses might not charge £1 or 1p more because psychologically the product might look more expensive, which could affect sales.

Sometimes, however, figures are rounded up or down. For example, set menus for meals may be £5, £10 or £20. This is a simple figure which customers understand. The same choices 'a la carte' might add up to £6.18, £12.54, or £24.67. Where prices are rounded down, it suggests that the customer is being given value for money. It encourages them to buy more food than they might otherwise have done.

Prestige pricing PRESTIGE PRICING (or PREMIUM PRICING) is a method used to price high quality, luxury, up-market goods. Such products are set at a high price as part of their marketing mix. Their price implies that these are high quality, desirable products. The price is set not just to increase revenue and profit for the business. The high price is there to reassure customers that they are buying 'the best'.

Discounts In many industries, businesses set a fixed price for their products. For example, consumer goods often have a **recommended retail price**. This is a price set by the manufacturer and acts as a guide to retailers as to what to charge. Sometimes the fixed price is called the **list price**. The 'list' is a list of prices issued by the business to its customers.

A business may then offer DISCOUNTS on the fixed price. Discounts are usually intended to encourage customers to buy the product, or buy it more frequently or in greater quantities. For example, a car dealer may offer a discount if a car is bought this month. Or a car parts manufacturer may offer discounts to business customers who buy in greater bulk.

Sales Sales are typically used to sell stocks of goods which have proved difficult to sell. For example, shops have sales in January for stock which has not sold in the peak selling season of September to Christmas. In some cases, businesses will run a sale on all their stock, whether it has been selling slowly or not. This attracts customers who are seeking a bargain.

Dairy farmers who went organic on the advice of retailers and the government are now facing falling prices because consumer demand was widely overestimated.

About half the organic milk now produced is having to be sold as non-organic. Instead of receiving the expected 30p a litre for organic milk, farmers have to accept the wholesale price of about 20p, said the Organic Milk Suppliers' Co-operative.

The glut of organic milk arose because many dairy farmers in early 1999 decided to convert to organic production. They were attracted by the high prices and strong consumer demand for organic products. It takes two years to turn a farm organic. Hence, there has been a surge in organic milk production from 32.5 million litres in 2000 to 70 million litres in 2001.

Brian Walters, a Welsh farmer who went organic, said: 'We were told that the price of organic milk would remain stable for five years - the leading lights in the dairy sector and politicians were telling us that. Now there is over-supply because too many of us have converted in a short period of time.'

The Soil Association, the organic campaign group, admitted that there had been a glut, but said the long-term trends still justified farmers making the transition to organic production. The overall organic market grew 33 per cent last year, with three-quarters of all organic produce being imported.

Adapted from the *Financial Times*, 18.12.2001.

1 **'Organic milk farmers have no choice but to accept the going rate for their product.' Explain what this means, illustrating your answer from the data.**
2 **Discuss the possible long term trends for the price of Brian Walters's organic milk.**

✓checklist

1 What is the different between 'cost' and a 'mark-up'?
2 A business calculates that the cost of producing a product is £60. It then adds a 20 per cent mark-up to arrive at a final price before VAT. What is this final price?
3 A business calculates that the variable cost of a particular job is £2 500 whilst the fixed cost is £1 500. (a) If it receives £3 000 in revenue for the job, what is the contribution made? (b) Explain why it might have accepted the job even though it makes an overall loss on it.
4 Explain the difference between market skimming and penetration pricing.
5 Why might a product be priced at '£3.99' rather than '£4.00'?
6 Explain why the makers of luxury goods tend to use prestige pricing methods and would not use them as loss leaders.
7 What is the difference between a discounted price and a sale price?
8 Explain the difference between a price leader and a price follower.
9 Explain the difference between going rate pricing and destroyer pricing.

Competition-based pricing

COMPETITION-BASED PRICING is a method where prices are based upon those of rival businesses.

Going rate pricing GOING RATE PRICING is a pricing method where a business sets its price according to the prices of similar products in the market. Often there is a **market leader** (see unit 9), a business which is dominant enough to take on the role of PRICE MAKER or PRICE LEADER. Businesses aiming to sell goods of similar quality will sell at the same price (the going rate) as the price leader. They then become PRICE FOLLOWERS. Businesses that sell what is perceived to be an inferior product will sell at a lower price than the going rate. For example, supermarket own brands sell for less than best selling branded products because consumers would tend to buy branded products if the prices were the same.

Businesses tend to adopt going rate pricing in markets where setting a different price would harm sales. If a business set its price above the going rate, it could lose sales to other businesses. If it set its price below the going rate, other businesses would drop their prices too. A price war could break out where businesses would see no increase in sales but revenues would fall because of lower prices. This would lead to a fall in profits. In this situation, there is no incentive to adopt a different price to the going rate price.

In some industries, businesses have no option but to accept the going rate. This is because there are many businesses in the market producing identical products (there is **perfect competition**, see unit 49). Businesses in this type of market

"key terms"

Competition-based pricing - a group of pricing methods where a business bases its prices on those of its competitors.
Contribution (or marginal) pricing - where price is set above the variable cost of production and a contribution is made towards fixed costs and profit.
Cost-based pricing - a group of pricing methods based on the cost of making a product.
Cost-plus pricing (or full cost pricing) - where price is set by calculating the full cost (variable plus fixed cost) of a product and adding a profit margin.
Destroyer (or predatory) pricing - where the price of a product is set at a very low level in order to force a competing business out of the market.
Discount pricing - where a product is sold below its list price.
Going rate pricing - where price is set to be equal to the price of similar products produced by competing firms in the market.
Loss leader - a product which is sold at a low price in order to encourage customers to buy other full price products from the business along with the loss leader product.
Mark-up - in full cost pricing, this is what is added to full cost of a product and is therefore equal to the profit made on it.
Market-orientated pricing - a group of pricing policies where price is set according to conditions in the market.

Market skimming - where price is set very high for a new product before the price is lowered to attract a wider customer base.
Penetration pricing - where price is set very low for a new product with the aim of rapidly gaining market share before price is raised to a profitable level.
Prestige (or premium) pricing - where the price of a product is maintained at a high level to reinforce its high quality, luxury image.
Price discrimination - where different groups of customers pay different prices for the same product based on their ability to pay.
Price follower - a business which sets its own prices by considering the prices set by another business in the market, the price maker business.
Price maker (or leader) - a business which sets prices in a market around which other firms (price followers) set their own prices.
Price taker - a business which is unable to choose at what price to set its products but has to accept the prevailing market price.
Pricing point - a price which is judged to be a psychological barrier for customers above or below which the product is seen as too expensive or too cheap.
Psychological pricing - where prices are set based upon the psychological expectations of customers about the price of a product.

cannot fix the price at which they sell. They have to accept the market price. They are then called PRICE TAKERS. Examples of price takers are farms producing agricultural commodities, mining companies producing commodities, such as copper or coal, and commodity steel producers.

Destroyer (or predatory) pricing DESTROYER PRICING (or PREDATORY PRICING) occurs when one business deliberately lowers its price to force another out of the industry. For example, a bus company might have a local monopoly in a town. A new company could set up in competition on some of the routes in the town. The monopolist might then cut its prices on those routes. Its will aim to make the rival business make losses so that it is forced to close down its operations. Either the rival company will find it hard to attract passengers onto its buses at the previous higher fare. Or it will be forced to cut its own fares, lowering revenues. Once the rival has withdrawn from the market, the dominant business will raise its prices to restore long term profitability.

Tenders In some industries, businesses have to tender for contracts. This means stating in advance how much they will charge for a job if they get the contract. The buyer then chooses the tender which offers best value for money. All other things being equal, the business quoting the lowest price will win the tender.

Virgin Trains operates a complex fair structure on its route from Wolverhampton to London depending upon the class of the ticket, when the ticket is booked and the time passengers travel. Table 15.1 shows just five out of the eleven types of ticket offered by Virgin on this route for adults without a Railcard. In addition, there are child fares and tickets for those with Railcards (bought annually and entitling the holder to reduced fares).

Virgin Trains has based its pricing system on that operated by airlines. This type of fare structure is designed to price discriminate between customers to maximise revenues for the train company. Virgin knows, for example, that many of those travelling First Class have tickets paid for them by their employer. So price may not be an important determinant of whether they travel or not. In contrast, old age pensioners or students that travel are highly price conscious. The pricing structure is also designed to spread passenger numbers across the day. It aims to discourage passengers from travelling at peak times, when trains tend to be full of workers travelling to meetings in London or commuting to work, and encourage price conscious customers to travel off peak.

Adapted from *The Times*, 27.02.2002.

Type of ticket	Class	Return fare	Booking deadline	Availability of tickets on any train	Time of travel
First open return	First	£160	None	Unlimited	Any time
Standard open	Standard	£98	None	Unlimited	Any time
Saver	Standard	£35.10	None	Unlimited	After 10.10 am
Virgin value 7 day advance	Standard	£15	7 days in advance	Limited	Off peak only
Virgin Value 3 day advance	Standard	£22	3 days in advance	Limited	Off peak only

Table 15.1 *Virgin fares, Wolverhampton to London, Autumn 2002*

1   Explain what is meant by the term 'price discrimination'. (3 marks)

2   Outline why Virgin Trains charges £160 return for a first class return ticket on the Wolverhampton to London route. (8 marks)

3   Examine the problems that Virgin Trains might face if it charged a single price for all standard class tickets. (10 marks)

4   Discuss what pricing strategies Virgin Trains could adopt if another train company were given the right to run a rival train service along the same route into London Euston. (11 marks)

16 Pricing strategies and tactics

Safeway

Knowledge Safeway (now part of Morrisons) was, in 2002, Britain's number 4 grocery retailer in size after Tesco, Sainsbury and Asda. In the 1990s, it struggled to make profits because of fierce competition from the market leaders. In 1999, it appointed a new chief executive, an Argentinean, Carlos Criado-Perez.

Application In the 1990s, Safeway struggled to find a successful *marketing strategy*. It found itself up against Tesco and Asda, which used *competition-based pricing strategies*. Its *short term pricing tactics* failed. Also, its *purchasing costs* were higher than those of the big three.

Analysis Criado-Perez began to turn round the business. He realised that there was no point in competing with the big three on price. Their size meant that they could drive prices from suppliers down further than was possible for the smaller Safeway. Instead, he adopted a high-low price strategy for the main supermarkets and hypermarkets. On most products Safeway prices are higher than Asda or Tesco. But a few key branded products are sold at greatly discounted prices for a limited period. These special offers are backed up by leaflets delivered to many households near to each store. The larger stores are being revamped to stock a much larger proportion of up-market products. Fresh foods and service foods, such as fresh pizza, take up a larger proportion of floor space than in, say, the typical Asda. In today's Britain, there is a big market for quality food, where customers are not too concerned about getting the lowest price.

Evaluation By the end of the 1990s, Safeway had to change. By shifting pricing policy away from competition based pricing to a more market orientated approach through stocking a distinct range of products, Criado-Perez tried to find a formula which would allow Safeway to carve out a distinctive niche in the UK grocery market. However, the strategy was not good enough. In 2004, Safeway was bought by the UK's number 5 grocery retailer, Morrisons, and lost its separate identity.

Adapted from the *Financial Times*, 5.2.2002.

With over 5,000 price cuts and unmissable weekly deals Safeway has to be fantastic value.

● Over 5,000 low prices on a wide range of products around the store ☑

plus

● All the fantastic weekly deals we know you love ☑

Pricing strategy as part of corporate strategy

A **strategy** is a set of plans designed to meet objectives. PRICING STRATEGY is part of the marketing strategy of the business (see unit 9). Other strategies such as product and distribution strategy also make up a marketing strategy. Marketing strategy is then part of the corporate strategy of the business (see unit 64). Other strategies include production and financial strategy.

Pricing strategy is therefore a set of plans about pricing which help a business to achieve its marketing and corporate objectives. For example, a corporate objective might be to double in size over the next five years. A marketing objective to achieve this might be to take the products of the business 'up-market'. The pricing strategy developed from this could be to increase the average price of the products made by the business.

Pricing strategies and the market

To be successful, strategies must be realistic. Both plans and objectives must be achievable. For example, in a growing market with a dominant competitor, a business might be able to increase sales by 20 per cent over five years. But it might not be realistic to expect market share to increase by 20 per cent.

Pricing strategies too must be realistic and achievable. The pricing strategy a business adopts is likely to be influenced by a number of factors.

Costs Over time, a business must earn enough profits to survive. So in the long term, the average market price of its products must be greater than the average cost of making them. If the business produces a range of products, some products may contribute more to profit than others. Some, for example **loss leaders** (see unit 15), may even be permanently unprofitable. But cost must be one factor in the pricing decision.

The market The nature of the market will determine which pricing policies are effective. For example, if the market is dominated by one firm, a **monopolist** (see unit 49), it is likely to be able to **price discriminate** (see unit 15). A business in a commodity market with a large number of producers, like a farm, has to accept the going price to make a sale. A business selling a strongly branded product can, to some extent, choose what price to set.

Demand The higher the price set, the lower will be the quantity sold. Exactly what effect a higher price will have on sales depends on the **elasticity of demand** for the product (see unit 17). So any pricing policy must take into account the trade-off between higher prices and lower sales.

The marketing mix Price is just one element in the **marketing mix** (see unit 1). A business must consider other aspects of the marketing mix when deciding on a pricing strategy. For example, if a business sells a luxury, up-market good, then a high price strategy is likely to be the only option available.

WIDESCREEN TV

£748.70

SONY
28" flatscreen and Virtual Dolby for great sound
- 100Hz flat screen ● 66cm visible screen size

CONVENTIONAL TV

EXCLUSIVE
£189.99

PHILIPS
Want something a bit bigger for the bedroom? Then this 21" TV is just right
- Nicam stereo ● Parental controls ● 51cm visible screen size

> 1 'Toshiba is using market skimming methods to price its widescreen TVs, whereas it is using cost-based pricing for its conventional TVs.' To what extent do you think that this is true?

Laws and regulations The law may affect the price that a business can charge. For example, a retailer may be forced to sell a product at a price set by the manufacturer if the law gives manufacturers the power to set prices. The government may impose maximum prices for a product, such as electricity. The government may also place such high taxes on products like petrol that large changes in manufacturers' prices have little effect on the final 'after-tax' price.

Strategies for new products

When launching a new product, a business might decide to set a price which it does not expect to change greatly over time. However, there are two other pricing strategies which it could adopt.

Market skimming Market skimming (see unit 15) is where the business sets a higher price for the product initially, but drops the price later. Market skimming is common in the market for home entertainment equipment, such as televisions, DVDs and hi-fis. The latest equipment or newest format is typically sold at a high price. Later, manufacturers drop their prices. This should increase sales substantially, moving the product from a **niche product** (see unit 11) to a mass market product. Market skimming tends to occur in markets where the new product contains the latest technology and development costs have been high.

Market skimming allows manufacturers to capture the high prices that a few are willing to pay to get the latest equipment. It helps finance the investment that has already been undertaken. It also generates revenues for the new investment spending that will be needed if the product is to produced in large quantities. However, it is not a strategy which will lead to high sales quickly.

Penetration pricing Penetration pricing (see unit 15) is where a business sets a very low price for the product initially. But it

raises the price once sufficient market share has been gained. It tends to be used where the new product is very similar to others already on the market. For example, penetration pricing techniques might be used to launch a new magazine or a new brand of washing up liquid. Low prices, together with promotion costs such as advertising, often mean that the product makes a substantial loss during its launch phase. Once the launch has been successful, the price must be put up to a level where the product will be profitable in the long term.

Strategies for existing products

The pricing strategy for an existing product will depend on a variety of factors. These include the type of product, market conditions, competition and legal constraints (see unit 49). For example, a monopolist might be able to price discriminate. This strategy would not be possible for a business in a market with a large number of competing firms. This is because customers being charged a high price by one business could buy instead from another business charging a low price.

In general, though, businesses tend to use a mixture of the three main types of pricing strategy.
- **Cost-based pricing** techniques tend to set a minimum price at which a product can be sold in the long term. This is because a business must at least cover its costs to survive over time. Cost-based pricing is often used in industries where businesses have to bid for contracts. For example, building firms often bid for work by estimating the cost and then adding a profit margin. Professionals, such as accountants or lawyers, also tend to calculate fees by multiplying an hourly rate by the number of hours worked.
- **Market-orientated** pricing techniques tend to be used by businesses that have considerable market freedom about the price they set. Such businesses often produce a branded product. So price is just one of the elements of the

marketing mix which is used to generate sales and profits.

- **Competition-based pricing** can often be found in markets where there are one or two firms with high market share. **Price leader** or **price follower** patterns may then emerge. But competition-based pricing can also be a characteristic of markets where businesses have to tender for contracts. Instead of putting in a bid based on cost-plus techniques, firms may instead choose to second guess the price of contracts by competitors. **Predatory pricing** may be used when a competitor enters the market in an attempt to drive the rival business out and maintain market share.

Pricing tactics

Tactics (see unit 9) are short term, specific ways in which the short term objectives of the business can be achieved. Tactics are used to achieve objectives this week or this month, for example. In contrast, strategy is about a much longer period.

Examples of tactics could include:

- discounts on purchases made this month;
- special-offer pricing, such as a 'two for one' offer, on a product for a month to boost sales and product awareness;
- loss leaders, such as a supermarket slashing the price of baked beans this month to attract customers into the shop;
- using psychological pricing for a period, such as in a sale, by reducing a price from £10.00 to £5.99 instead of £6.00.

✓ checklist

1 What is the difference between a pricing strategy and a marketing strategy?
2 Explain briefly what factors might affect the pricing strategies that a business chooses to adopt.
3 Explain the advantages and disadvantages of using market skimming rather than penetration pricing as a strategy for a new product.
4 Explain briefly the three main types of pricing strategy a business could use for an existing product.
5 What is the difference between a pricing strategy and a pricing tactic?

key terms

Pricing strategy - **a set of plans about pricing which will contribute to the achievement of the marketing and corporate objectives of the business.**

Glamour, a new women's magazine, was launched in April 2001. It quickly achieved sales of 450 000 per month. *Glamour* was different from rival magazines such as *Company* and *Eve* in two ways. First, although it had the same number of pages, it was physically half the size of a typical women's magazine. This was small enough to fit into a large handbag. Second, it was cheaper. At £1.50 it was half the price of similar competing products selling for around £2.50-£3.00.

Glamour's publishers, Condé Nast, deny that the magazine is making a loss. Although the publisher's costs are the same, significant savings have been made on printing. It uses nearly half the paper of a conventional magazine, for instance. Also, the amount paid to those in the distribution chain, including retailers which sell to consumers, is the same percentage of price. But it is half in money terms (at around 75p) that of a typical £3.00 magazine. On the revenue side, *Glamour* is said to be charging its advertisers the same rates as it would it if were double the size. Advertisers are attracted to the magazine because of its high circulation figures and are less concerned about the size factor.

Competitors have reacted in different ways. One of the main rivals, *Company* magazine, published by The National Magazine Company, saw its sales fall 14 per cent over the first six months. It responded by cutting its price in half from £2.60 to £1.50 permanently. Two other magazines responded by discounting prices for just one issue. *Eve*, published by BBC Worldwide, cut its price from £2.80 to £1.00, whilst *Real*, published by H Bauer, cut its price from £1.50 to 75p.

It is likely that competition will intensify as publishers launch their own women's magazines in the new smaller format, at the lower price. But the new magazines may not have it all their own way. There are signs that magazine distributors will refuse to deal with the new low priced magazines. Already, some small newsagents have refused to stock the discounted £1.50 *Company* because they now get half the amount per sale than they did before. Supermarkets would like to increase sales of selected magazines by discounting them further. The fear then would be that publishers would lose control over the price at which magazines were sold. The supermarket chains would become major retailers of a few selected, deeply discounted, magazines. Independent newsagents would be squeezed hard and many would cease stocking magazines altogether. The publishers would then face having to negotiate directly with supermarkets. Given the buying power of supermarkets, the publishers would then lose out.

Adapted from the *Financial Times*, 18.9.2001 and 15.1.2002.

1 Explain what is meant by the term 'discounting'. (3 marks)
2 Outline TWO pricing strategies which a magazine company could use to launch a new magazine. (8 marks)
3 Examine the possible reasons why *Company* was cut in price from £2.60 to £1.50. (8 marks)
4 To what extent do magazine publishers, such as Condé Nast and H Bauer, base their pricing strategy mainly on cost factors? (11 marks)

17 Elasticity of demand

Nutraceuticals

Knowledge Recently in the UK there has been a large increase in demand for 'functional foods' or nutraceuticals. These are designed to combat diseases of old age, such as heart disease or diabetes. Examples include Benecol, a spread that helps cut cholesterol levels, and Yakult, a fermented milk drink that helps to maintain a favourable balance of bacteria in the digestive system. Baby-boomers, people born in the decade after the Second World War, are the most important market for these foods. They are now entering the highest risk age group for the ailments that nutraceuticals try to prevent.

Application Baby-boomers have relatively high levels of *disposable income*. This allows them to afford the *premium prices* charged for nutraceutical *brands*. Younger *consumers* are another *target market*. But they have lower *incomes* and are less likely to be able to afford to buy these *products*. Nutraceuticals therefore have a *positive income elasticity of demand* - the higher the *income*, the higher the average *spending* on these foods.

Analysis One way for nutraceutical manufacturers to increase the quantity demanded of their products would be to reduce the prices they charge. However, this would only increase total revenue from the sale of the products if price elasticity of demand was elastic - that is, the percentage increase in products bought was greater than the percentage fall in price. Even then, there might not be an increase in profit because greater sales could mean greater production costs.

Evaluation With incomes rising over time and a positive income elasticity of demand, manufacturers of nutraceuticals can look forward to increasing sales in the future. But this is likely to attract more products onto the market. With an increasing range of products to choose from, manufacturers will have to spend heavily on promotion and distribution to ensure their products get noticed by consumers.

Adapted from the *Financial Times*, 5.2.2002.

Demand

DEMAND for a product is the quantity bought over a given time period. For example, demand for cars in 2002 was 2.7 million vehicles. The quantity bought of a product is affected by a number of factors. These include:

- price - the lower the price, the higher tends to be the quantity demanded; the higher the price, the less tends to be bought;
- the income of customers - for most goods, the higher the income of customers, the more will be bought and vice versa. However, there are some goods, called **inferior goods**, where customers buy less of the good as their incomes rise;
- the price of other goods - for example, if one chocolate bar goes up in price by 10 per cent, demand for other chocolate bars is likely to increase if their price remains constant;
- advertising - successful advertising can increase demand for a product;
- seasonal factors - many goods, from ice creams and beer to toys and foreign holidays are affected by the time of year and the weather. For example, hot summer weather increases demand for ice creams and beer. The run up to Christmas is the peak selling time for toys and clothing.

Price elasticity of demand

Demand theory suggests that quantity demanded varies with price. The higher the price, the lower the quantity demand and vice versa. But it doesn't say by **how much** the quantity demanded will fall or rise if there is a change in price. This varies from product to product. The relationship between the effect of a change in price on quantity demanded is known as PRICE ELASTICITY OF DEMAND.

If there is a **large** percentage change in quantity demanded when price changes by a small percentage, there is said to be ELASTIC DEMAND. The word 'elastic' is used to give an idea that there would be a large response. Think of an elastic band. When you pull it, can you easily double its length? Then it is 'elastic'. But if it is thick, it may be difficult to change its length. It is 'inelastic'. This is also the case with price elasticity. If a large percentage change in price brings about only a **small** percentage change in quantity demanded, there is said to be INELASTIC DEMAND.

Take the example of a Mars Bar made by Mars Corporation. If it puts up the price by 10 per cent, and there is a fall in quantity demanded of 30 per cent, then the demand for Mars Bars is elastic. The percentage change in quantity demanded of Mars Bars is much bigger than the percentage change in price which caused it. But if quantity demanded fell only 5 per cent when prices went up by 10 per cent, then there would be inelastic demand. The percentage change in quantity demanded is smaller than the percentage change in price.

It is important to realise that price elasticity compares **percentage** changes in quantity and price. Percentages allow the relative changes to be measured and compared.

The formula for price elasticity of demand

The exact value of price elasticity of demand can be calculated by using the formula:

$$\text{Price elasticity of demand} = \frac{\% \text{ change in quantity demanded}}{\% \text{ change in price}}$$

For example, say that the price of Mars Bars increases by 10 per cent.

- If the quantity demanded falls by 20 per cent as a result of the 10 per cent price rise, then price elasticity of demand is:

$$\frac{-20 \text{ per cent}}{+10 \text{ per cent}} = -2$$

- If the quantity demanded rises by 5 per cent as a result of the 10 per cent price fall, then price elasticity of demand is:

$$\frac{+5 \text{ per cent}}{-10 \text{ per cent}} = -0.5$$

Price elasticity of demand is always negative. This is because a rise (+) in price is always followed by a fall (-) in quantity demanded and vice versa. A plus divided into a minus is a minus. Because it is always minus, the sign is normally left out when talking about price elasticity of demand.

Elastic and inelastic demand

It is possible to give a more precise definition of elastic and inelastic demand using the formula for price elasticity.

Price elastic demand Demand is **price elastic** when it is **greater than 1**. This means that the percentage change in quantity demanded (on the top of the formula) is greater than the percentage change in price (on the bottom of the formula). A 12 per cent rise in quantity demanded resulting from a 10 per cent fall in price would give a price elasticity of +12 per cent ÷ -10 per cent or -1.2. This would be an example of elastic demand.

Price inelastic demand Demand is **price inelastic** when it is **less than 1**. This means that the percentage change in quantity demanded (on the top of the formula) is less than the percentage change in price (on the bottom of the formula). An 8 per cent fall in quantity demanded resulting from a 10 per cent rise in price would give a price elasticity of -8 per cent ÷ +10 per cent or -0.8. This would be an example of inelastic demand.

Estimating price elasticity

There is no easy way to find out the exact price elasticity of demand for a particular product. The business environment is constantly changing. So when the price of a product changes, it is likely that other factors will change too. For example, competing businesses may all change their prices at roughly the same time.

One way of estimating the price elasticity of demand is to assume that all these other factors remain the same. Then a business could consider the impact of its price changes on demand in recent years. If it has changed price four times in four years, it could estimate the impact this has had on quantity demanded each time and calculate a price elasticity figure for each price change. These four figures might be averaged to provide an approximate price elasticity.

Alternatively, a business could use market research (see units 4, 5 and 7). It could ask customers how much they would buy of a product at different prices. Price elasticity of demand for the sample could then be calculated. A problem is that what respondents actually do can be different from what they say they will do in a survey.

A business could consider the behaviour of its customers. For example, the price elasticity of demand for the gas that British Gas sells to households might be inelastic. A 10 per cent rise in price is likely to have little effect on quantity demanded. This is because households tend not to turn off

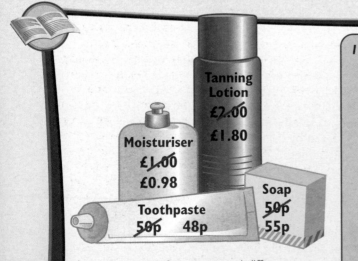

A company manufactures several different types of toiletries. It has recently changed the prices of its main brands, but its competitors have kept their prices the same.

1 **Calculate the price elasticity of demand for each of the following.**
(a) The price of its shampoo was raised by 6 per cent. As a result, quantity demanded fell by 12 per cent.
(b) The price of its moisturiser was cut by 2 per cent. As a result, quantity demanded rose by 1 per cent.
(c) The price of its hair conditioner was raised by 3 per cent. As a result, quantity demanded fell by 9 per cent.
(d) The price of its toothpaste was cut by 4 per cent. As a result, quantity demanded rose by 1 per cent.
(e) The price of a bar of its soap was raised from 50p to 55p. As a result, quantity demanded fell from 100 000 bars to 95 000 bars.
(f) The price of its tanning lotion was cut from £2.00 to £1.80. As a result, quantity demanded rose from 20 000 bottles to 25 000 bottles.
2 **Which products had (a) elastic demand and (b) inelastic demand?**

their central heating when the price of gas rises. Most customers, also, won't switch to another gas company.

In contrast, a small clothing manufacturer might face elastic demand. All its work could come from larger companies that only want limited quantities of dresses or trousers. There are many UK businesses doing this sort of work and others in countries like India or China. So if it quotes a slightly higher price for a contract it is unlikely to get the order. In this industry, businesses find it difficult to raise their prices without losing many customers.

Price elasticity and sales revenue

Price elasticity of demand is important when developing a **pricing strategy** (see unit 16). This is because the price of a product affects **sales revenue** (see unit 21). Sales revenue is the amount a business receives from the sale of its products. It is calculated by multiplying the price of the product by the quantity sold. For example, a business selling 1 million products at £10 each would have sales revenue of £10 million (£1 million x £10).

Sales revenue is affected by the price at which a product is sold and price elasticity of demand. Assume that the product sold at £10 has a price elasticity of 2.

● This means that a 10 per cent increase in price would lead to a fall in quantity demanded (and therefore sales) of 20 per cent. Sales revenue would then fall from £10 million (1 million x £10) to £8.8 million (800 000 x £11).

● If, on the other hand, price was lowered by 10 per cent, quantity demanded (and therefore sales) would rise by 20 per cent. Sales revenue would then rise from £10 million (1 million x £10) to £10.8 million (1.2 million x £9).

This is an example of a more general rule. If demand is price elastic, then putting up price will lead to a fall in sales revenue. The increase in price will be more than offset by a decrease in sales. Conversely, lowering price when demand is price elastic will lead to a rise in sales revenue. The fall in price will be more than offset by an increase in sales.

Equally, the opposite relationship applies if price is inelastic. A rise in price will lead to a rise in sales revenue whilst a fall in price will lead to a fall in sales revenue. For example, if price elasticity of demand is 0.7, then a 10 per cent rise in price leads to a 7 per cent fall in sales. This leads to an approximate 3 per cent rise in sales revenue. This relationship between price elasticity and sales revenue is shown in Table 17.1.

Changing the price can therefore affect sales revenue. But the exact effect, and whether it leads to an increase or decrease, depends on the price elasticity of demand.

Price elasticity and profit

Price elasticity also has an effect on **profit**. Profit is calculated

1 Explain how revenue would change in each of the following cases.
(a) A business puts up its prices by 10 per cent when the price elasticity of demand for its product is - 2.0.
(b) A business reduces its prices by 10 per cent when its price elasticity of demand for its product is - 0.5.
(c) A business puts up its prices by 5 per cent when the price elasticity of demand for its product is - 0.4.
(d) A business reduces its prices by 6 per cent when the price elasticity of demand for its product is - 1.5.

as sales revenue minus costs (see unit 21). Costs are likely to change with sales. The more that is produced, the higher the costs.

If demand is price inelastic, a rise in price will lead to lower sales but increased sales revenue as explained earlier. But the lower sales will mean lower costs. So profits will increase, not just from higher sales revenue but also from lower costs.

If demand is price elastic, an increase in sales revenue can be achieved by lowering price and raising sales. But higher sales also mean higher costs. In this situation, higher profits will only occur if the increase in sales revenue is greater than the increase in costs.

Factors affecting price elasticity of demand

The value of price elasticity of demand for a product is mainly determined by the ease with which customers can switch to other similar SUBSTITUTE products. A number of factors is likely to determine this.

Time Price elasticity of demand tends to fall the longer the time period. This is mainly because consumers and businesses are more likely to turn to substitutes in the long term. For example, fuel oil is highly price inelastic in the short term. If the price of petrol goes up 20 per cent in a week, the fall in quantity demanded is likely to be only a few per cent. This is because car owners have to use their cars to get to work or to go shopping. But over a ten year period, car owners will tend to buy more fuel efficient cars. Businesses with boilers using fuel oil may replace these with gas boilers. Homeowners with oil fired central heating systems might install more insulation in their houses to cut running costs or change to gas boilers. As a result, demand for oil in the long run is likely to be price elastic.

Competition for the same product Some businesses face highly price elastic demand for their products. This is because they are in very competitive markets, where their product is either identical (i.e. are perfect substitutes) or little different from those produced by other businesses. Farmers, for example, when selling wheat or potatoes are in this position.

	Elastic demand	Inelastic demand
Price increase	Revenue down	Revenue up
Price decrease	Revenue up	Revenue down

Table 17.1 *Effect on sales revenue of a change in price*

If they push their prices above the market price, they won't be able to sell their crop. Customers will simply buy elsewhere at the lower market price.

Branding Some products are **branded** (see unit 10). The stronger the branding, the less substitutes are acceptable to customers. For example, many buyers of Kelloggs' corn flakes do not see own label brands, such as Tesco or Asda cornflakes, as good substitutes for Kelloggs. They will often pay 50 per cent more to buy Kelloggs rather than another brand. Successful branding therefore reduces the price elasticity of demand for the product.

Product types vs the product of an individual business Most products are made and sold by a number of different businesses. Petrol, for example, is processed and sold by companies such as Shell, Esso and Total. The major supermarkets also sell petrol which they have bought from independent refiners. The demand for petrol is price inelastic in the short term. But the demand for Shell petrol or Esso petrol is price elastic. This is because petrol has no real substitutes in the short term. But Esso petrol is a very good substitute for Shell petrol. In general, a product category like petrol, carpets or haircuts has a much lower price elasticity of demand than products within that category made by individual businesses.

However strong the branding and however little the competition that an individual product faces, it is still likely that a business will sell at a price where demand is price elastic. To understand why, consider a product which has inelastic demand. As explained above, raising the price of the product would increase sales revenue. It would also reduce sales and costs of production would fall. So profits would rise. A profit maximising firm should therefore continue raising price until demand is price elastic.

If demand is price elastic, raising price leads to a fall in sales revenue, but also a fall in costs because less is sold. At the profit maximising point, any further increase in price would see the fall in sales revenue being greater than the fall in costs.

This would suggest that even strongly branded goods, such as Coca-Cola or McDonald's meals, have a price elasticity of demand greater than one at the price at which they are sold. It also suggests that luxury brands, such as Chanel or Gucci, also have elastic demand at their current price.

Income elasticity of demand

Price is not the only factor which affects demand. Income is another. For most goods, an increase in the income of customers will lead to an increase in demand for a product.

INCOME ELASTICITY OF DEMAND measures the responsiveness of changes in quantity demanded to changes in income. The formula for income elasticity is:

$$\text{Income elasticity of demand} = \frac{\%\ \text{change in quantity demanded}}{\%\ \text{change in income}}$$

For example, if quantity demanded increases by 10 per cent when income increases by 20 per cent, then income elasticity of demand is:

$$\frac{+20\ \text{per cent}}{+10\ \text{per cent}} = +2$$

Normal and inferior goods

Most products have a positive income elasticity. When income rises, so too does demand for the product. These products are called NORMAL GOODS.

However, for some products, a rise in income leads to a fall in their demand. Their income elasticity of demand is negative (because in the formula there is a plus sign on the top and a minus sign on the bottom or vice versa). These products are called INFERIOR GOODS. Examples of inferior goods might include:

- bread - as incomes rise, consumers eat less bread and more expensive foods;
- bus transport - as incomes rise, travellers tend to use trains or cars;
- sugar - increased income tends to be associated with a better diet and a greater awareness of the problems of having too much sugar.

Most products are normal goods. However, some products have a higher income elasticity than others. For example, over the past 20 years, with rising incomes, the demand for services has increased faster than the demand for goods. Services, such as holidays and meals out, have expanded particularly fast.

> l **Discuss which of these products you think might be a normal good and which might be an inferior good.**

keyterms

Income elasticity - the responsiveness of quantity demanded to changes in incomes. It is measured as the percentage change in quantity demanded ÷ percentage change in income.

Inferior good - a product which has a negative income elasticity. This means that when incomes rise, the quantity demanded falls and vice versa.

Normal good - a product which has a positive income elasticity. This means that when incomes rise, the quantity demanded rises, and vice versa.

Price elasticity of demand - the responsiveness of quantity demanded to changes in price. It is measured as percentage change in quantity demanded ÷ percentage change in price.

Price elastic demand - when price elasticity is greater than 1, which means that the percentage change in quantity demanded is greater than the percentage change in price which caused it.

Price inelastic demand - when price elasticity is less than 1, which means that the percentage change in quantity demanded is less than the percentage change in price which caused it.

Substitute product - a product which has similar characteristics to another good. For example, gas is a substitute for oil as a fuel in heating systems. Shell petrol is a good substitute for BP Amoco petrol for use as a fuel in cars.

✓checklist

1 Explain, without using the formula, what is meant by 'price elasticity of demand'.
2 'The demand for journeys taken on the London Underground is price inelastic.' Explain what this means.
3 (a) What is the formula for price elasticity of demand?
   (b) How does it differ from the formula for income elasticity of demand?
4 How can a business estimate the price elasticity of demand for one of its products?
5 Explain why a rise in price would lead to higher revenues if demand for the product were price inelastic.
6 Explain the link between price elasticity of demand and profit.
7 Explain why strongly branded goods such as Coca-Cola or Chanel perfumes are likely to be price elastic at the price at which they are currently sold.
8 Using the concept of income elasticity of demand, explain the difference between a normal good and an inferior good.

Bill Finch is a London taxicab driver.

Towards the end of 1999, all the talk amongst taxicab drivers was about the new Millennium - whether they were going to drive or be out partying on New Year's Eve. In November 1999, the government, which sets London taxicab fares, announced that London taxis would be able to charge double rate for journeys taken between 8 pm on December 31 and 6 am on January 1st. Those taking journeys long enough to cost more than an ordinary fare of £25 would have to pay a flat rate £25 supplement. This compared to the usual New Year supplement of £3 per journey.

Bill decided he would drive on the Millennium eve, expecting that demand would be highly price inelastic. But he was disappointed with his takings. Many party goers had decided to stay at home because restaurants, pubs and clubs as well as taxis were charging double or more on the night. There was a general feeling amongst the public that they were going to be ripped off if they went out. Where journeys were necessary, many took a private car and agreed in advance which of the party goers would be the non-drinking driver. Bill Finch found that he carried 30 per cent fewer passengers than he typically did on a normal Saturday night in the winter months. None of his journeys on the Millennium eve exceeded the £25 limit.

1 Explain what is meant in the passage by 'demand would be highly price inelastic'. (3 marks)
2 Explain (a) why it was expected that demand for taxi cab rides would rise on Millennium eve; (4 marks)
   (b) how this might have affected the ability of travellers to get a taxi cab ride on that night if fairs had NOT risen from their normal levels. (6 marks)
3 Using the concepts of price elasticity of demand, revenue and profit, discuss whether Bill made the right decision to drive on Millennium eve. (11 marks)

18 Promotion

Coca-Cola and Harry Potter

Knowledge In 2000, Coca-Cola negotiated an exclusive marketing deal with Warner Brothers to sponsor the film Harry Potter and the Philosopher's Stone. By the release of the film in 2001, it had budgeted to spend $150 million on a global marketing programme. Part of the budget was spent on a global reading programme inspired by Harry Potter. In the USA Coca-Cola donated $18 million to 'Reading is Fundamental', a non-profit group helping to install thousands of classroom libraries. In the UK, Coca-Cola targeted its reading efforts at disadvantaged youngsters.

Application Coca-Cola, like any *company*, has a limited *marketing budget*. It chose to spend around 10 per cent of its worldwide *marketing budget* on the Harry Potter *promotion*. The *promotional campaign* took many forms. There was traditional *advertising*, as well as changes to *packaging* and *in-store displays*. The spending on the global reading programme was an attempt to gain positive *public relations (PR)*.

Analysis Linking Coca-Cola with Harry Potter was an attempt by the company to target children without alienating adults. Children are important consumers of Coca-Cola drinks in their own right. They are also the consumers of the future. If Coca-Cola fails to attract children now, they might not be loyal customers in future. Hence, Coca-Cola was prepared to spend such a large amount of its marketing budget on just one tie-in with a film.

Evaluation The promotional campaign was one element in Coca-Cola's long term marketing campaign to keep its customers loyal and to introduce new customers to its drinks. The link with reading was a skilful attempt to use PR to promote the brand. The reading campaign could be seen as Coca-Cola acting as a responsible company in a world where social issues are important to its customers.

Adapted from the *Financial Times*, 15.11.2001.

Promotion and the marketing mix

Promotion is one of the 4Ps of the marketing mix (see unit 10). Promotion is often said to be ABOVE-THE-LINE or BELOW-THE-LINE. Promotion above the line is usually only classed as media advertising. But there are many other types of promotion. These are commonly referred to as 'below the line' methods of promotion. They are becoming increasingly important for businesses today.

The objectives of promotion

Businesses have a variety of objectives when they promote themselves and their products which include making customers:

- more aware of an existing product;
- aware of the launch of a new product;
- compare the qualities of a rival product with the product of that business;
- aware of extra features added to an existing product or of new prices;
- want to purchase a product immediately or more frequently;
- appreciate the qualities of a brand;
- aware of the business itself, so that the business brand will then itself act as a promotion for products.

Marketing departments sometimes use **models** to help them devise promotional campaigns. The AIDA model says that effective advertising will:

- grab consumers' Attention (A);
- encourage Interest in the product (I);
- and develop Desire (D);
- so that consumers will Act to buy the product (A).

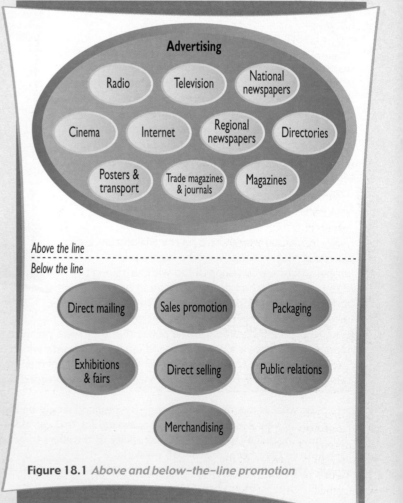

Figure 18.1 *Above and below–the–line promotion*

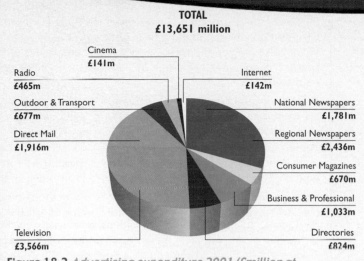

TOTAL £13,651 million

Cinema £141m
Radio £465m
Outdoor & Transport £677m
Direct Mail £1,916m
Television £3,566m
Internet £142m
National Newspapers £1,781m
Regional Newspapers £2,436m
Consumer Magazines £670m
Business & Professional £1,033m
Directories £824m

Figure 18.2 *Advertising expenditure 2001 (£million at constant 1995 prices)*

Adapted from *Advertising Statistics Year Book*, 2002.

	TV		Womens weeklies		Womens monthlies	
	Total spending (£m)	% change on previous 12 months	Total spending (£m)	% change on previous 12 months	Total spending (£m)	% change on previous 12 months
Total	1,725.08	-6.6	38.61	25.7	48.97	18.8
Procter & Gamble	87.82	-21.2	5.40	15.8	8.47	19.9
British Telecom	40.42	-36.1	0.92	1,526.0	0.27	1.9
Ford Motor Company	48.52	29.8	0.73	44.6	1.51	68.4
Renault UK	36.51	-15.7	0.19	3,491.3	1.71	47.7
Loreal Golden	34.62	-30.2	1.25	117.0	7.35	8.7
Unilever Bestfoods UK	36.52	-24.4	0.99	-12.9	2.14	51.8
Vauxhall Motors	26.29	-36.0	0.09	211.2	0.62	28.4
Mars Confectionery	36.72	-10.8	0.27	-30.3	0.52	55.1
Kelloggs (GB)	36.12	-18.8	1.15	-12.8	1.39	20.3
Sainsburys Supermarkets	28.77	15.2	2.09	161.1	0.48	66.4

Table 18.1 *Changes in advertising: TV compared to women's magazines*
Adapted from AC Nielsen MHS.

'Recession? What recession?' is the reaction of the consumer magazine sector to the downturn in the economy which has hit advertising. The top 100 company spenders on advertising spent 3.3 per cent less in the 2000-2001 year to July than in 1999-2000. But the fall in spending masks very different stories for different advertising media.

Spending on television advertising fell 6.6 per cent. In contrast, the top 100 companies spent 25.7 per cent more on women's weekly magazines, 18.8 per cent more on women's monthlies and 19.9 per cent more on outdoor media, including billboards.

In 1999-2000, television advertising saw a boom. Many non-traditional TV advertisers, such as dot-com businesses, had used television as an advertising medium. The television companies raised their prices for adverts as a result of this increased demand. Traditional TV advertisers responded by spending less on advertising. When TV advertising rates fell in 2000-2001, as the businesses cut back on advertising, the large traditional advertisers failed to return to their former levels of spending.

But there is also a growing perception that television advertising is not sufficiently targeted. For example, four women's celebrity magazines, *Hello!, OK!, Now* and *Heat* have a combined circulation of more than 2.2 million with a readership several times more. These celebrity magazines can provide a targeted audience which is more attractive than, say, a daytime soap on TV.

Equally, it is still true that women's magazines provide a much cheaper advertising medium for companies. Many advertisers simply can't afford a TV campaign, whereas they can afford to advertise widely in women's magazines. Even for large advertisers, such as Procter & Gamble or Ford, the same mass coverage can be bought in women's magazines for half the price of television advertising.

Adapted from the *Financial Times*, 4.9.2001.

1 **How has advertising changed over the period (i) 1985 to 2001 and (ii) 1999-2000 to 2000-2001?**

2 **Explain why expenditure on television advertising fell between 1999-2000 and 2000-2001.**

3 **Discuss which of the companies in Table 18.1 is most likely in future to increase the proportion of its advertising budget spent on women's magazines.**

Another model is DAGMAR (Defining Advertising Goals for Measured Advertising Results). It says that effective promotion should move a consumer through various levels:
• from being unaware of the product;
• to being aware of the product;
• recognising the product and what it does to (comprehension);

• to preferring the product to others (conviction);
• to purchasing the product (action).
A similar model by Lavidge and Steiner suggests six stages - awareness, knowledge, liking, preference, conviction and purchase.

Above-the-line promotion

Above-the-line promotion is ADVERTISING through the media. There is a variety of media which businesses can choose:

- commercial television, whether terrestrial such as ITV1 or Channel 4, or satellite such as BSkyB;
- commercial radio, which in the UK is local radio;
- national newspapers, such as *The Sun* or *The Times*;
- regional newspapers, such as the *London Evening Standard* or the *Birmingham Evening Post*;
- magazines, such as *Cosmopolitan* or *Loaded*;
- trade newspapers and journals, such as *The Grocer* or *Accountancy Age* which are read by workers or businesses in a particular industry, trade or profession;
- directories, including the telephone directories *Yellow Pages* and *Thomson Directory*;
- posters and transport, such as billboards by the side of the road or advertisements on the side of buses;
- the Internet.

Choice of medium

The medium that is chosen will depend on a variety of factors including:

- cost - most businesses could not afford television adverts, for example. Cost also has to be measured against effectiveness - how much extra new business will be generated by each £1 of advertising expenditure;
- media reach - what media will best get to the audience the advertiser wishes to reach;
- delivery of the chosen message - what media would best persuade consumers to change their brand of washing powder, for example, or give customers a telephone number to call if their washing machine broke down;
- the marketing mix - an advertising campaign may be part of a wider campaign using other elements of the marketing mix, such as below-the-line promotion or pricing. These other elements may help determine which media to use for advertising;
- the law - there are legal restrictions on the use of different media for advertising certain products, such as cigarettes.

The choice of media will also to some extent depend upon whether the advertisement is to be informative or persuasive. INFORMATIVE ADVERTISING is where the aim of the advert is to convey **information** to the potential customer. Small ads in a newspaper are often informative because they contain facts about what is on offer for sale, together with contact addresses or telephone numbers.

PERSUASIVE ADVERTISING is where the aim of the advert is to change or reinforce the perception of a product in the mind of a customer. Persuasive advertising may have little or no informative content. Instead, it tries to associate ideas such as sex, strength, softness, caring or coolness with a product.

Below-the-line promotion

There are many other forms of promotion apart from advertising. These form part of below-the-line promotion.

Direct mailing DIRECT MAILING is where potential customers are contacted directly through the post. Direct mailing is often unsolicited. This is where customers are sent information even though they have not asked for it. Lists of names and addresses of potential customers can be obtained from various sources. A business might have its own list of past or existing customers. Or lists may be bought from other organisations. Direct mailing through the post is often called JUNK MAIL. When the message is sent via email, it is called **spam**. The equivalent of direct mail using the phone is called **cold calling**.

Exhibitions and fairs In some markets, exhibitions and fairs are important ways of buying and selling. There are exhibitions and fairs for goods ranging from defence equipment to caravans to wedding materials. Having a stand at an exhibition or fair may be the most important way in which a business sells to customers.

Sales promotions SALES PROMOTIONS are methods often used to boost sales in the short term. Examples of sales promotions include:

- money off purchases, such as 'two for the price of one', 'buy one get one free' (known as BOGOF) or '30p off this week';
- coupons given out, for example in magazines, which can be redeemed on purchase;
- free gifts, such as free CDs or make-up with the purchase of a product;
- special credit terms, such as 'interest free loans' if a good is purchased on loan;
- competitions, such as 'win a holiday for two to Florida';
- better value offers, such as '20 per cent extra free';
- product placing, where products are given free to celebrities in the hope that other potential customers will see them and want to buy them;
- reward systems, such as Boots Advantage card or Air Miles, where customers gain points for spending which can be exchanged for cash or products.

Direct selling DIRECT SELLING or personal selling is where customers are sold a product directly by the manufacturer without using an intermediary (see unit 19). Some direct selling takes place door-to-door, such as Avon cosmetics, Betterware household products or double glazing. A few companies, such as Tupperware or Anne Summers, sell through parties organised in people's homes. In industrial markets, businesses often employ sales representatives to visit potential customers. Direct selling can also take place over the phone. Telesales have become increasingly important in some industries. Some direct selling is now done over the Internet. Internet direct selling has helped transform the air travel industry. No frills airlines such as EasyJet and Ryanair have cut out the intermediary, the travel agent, and can offer lower prices as a result.

Merchandising MERCHANDISING is where manufacturers provide POINT-OF-SALE MATERIAL at the place where a sale could take place, for example in a shop. This material might be posters, bins and displays which are used to draw the customer's attention to a particular product. Retailers and wholesalers themselves can also affect what is sold by the layout of stores. Products stocked on shelves at eye-level, for example, might sell more than if they are stocked at the bottom of a display rack. Products displayed at checkouts might sell more than if they are stacked in the aisles.

Packaging The way in which a product is packaged might affect sales. Packaging is an important part of '**product**'

(see unit 14) within the marketing mix. Packaging should be designed so that the product reaches the customer safely and in perfect condition. But much of the design of the packaging aims to promote the product. The colours that are used on the packaging, for example, are important statements about the nature of the product. Overpackaging (when there is far more packaging needed than is necessary to protect the product) is often used to convey the message that the product is an expensive, up-market product.

Public relations PUBLIC RELATIONS (PR) is the promotion of a positive image about a product or a business through the giving of information to the general public, the media, other businesses or government. For example, Virgin Trains organised a media event at Euston Station in London to launch the first of its tilting trains for the West Coast route in 2002. With Richard Branson present, Virgin received a large amount of free publicity as the event was widely reported on television, radio and in newspapers. PR is often conducted through press releases, press conferences, well-advertised

donations to charity or sponsorship. Good PR can provide considerable promotion for a product or a business at little cost.

The promotional mix

Businesses usually use a range of different types of promotional methods at any one time. This range is the PROMOTIONAL MIX employed by the business. For example, a business launching a new product might advertise it, but also offer a discount (an example of sales promotion). Packaging will have been designed to promote the product. The business might also send a press release to the newspapers and magazines that it thinks might cover the story.

The promotional mix, chosen from the range of possible types of promotion shown in Figure 19.1, will be determined by a number of factors.

The type of product A manufacturer of industrial cookers might rely heavily on sales reps and advertising literature to promote its products to businesses. An ice cream manufacturer, however, might concentrate on media advertising to the public.

The type of market This includes its size, geography, **socio-economic characteristics** (see unit 3) and whether it is a consumer market or an industrial market (see unit 2). For example, a small local newsagent might spend all its promotional budget on placing its telephone number in *Yellow Pages*. But this would be a very small part of the budget for a major retailer such as Marks & Spencer. It is likely to use a variety of above and below the line promotion.

The budget available for promotion A local cleaning service with few funds for promotion might distribute leaflets in the area. A national cleaners might advertise in newspapers and magazines and sell to businesses via reps or trade fairs.

The promotional mix of competitors If competitors are spending a great deal on advertising, a business may feel the need to respond with its own advertising campaign.

The stage of the product in its product life cycle The promotional needs of a product at its launch may be very different from that in its decline phase of the product life cycle (see unit 12).

♥ **key**terms

Above-the-line promotion - promotion in the form of advertising through the media.
Advertising - a form of communication between a business and its customers where the business pays to have visual or pictorial images presented in the media to encourage customers to purchase a product.
Below-the-line promotion - promotion that is not media advertising.
BOGOF - 'buy one get one free'.
Direct mail - advertising promotions sent to the address of the potential customer.
Direct selling - a form of promotion which involves face-to-face contact between the seller and the buyer.
Informative advertising - advertising where the aim is to convey information to the potential customer.
Junk mail - direct mail which is unsolicited by the potential

customer.
Merchandising - promotions and displays at the point-of-sale.
Persuasive advertising - advertising where the aim is to change or reinforce the perception of a product in the mind of a customer.
Point-of-sale material - promotion of a product in the place where it is bought by the customer. Examples include special displays or distribution of leaflets in shops.
Promotional mix - the mixture of promotional techniques such as advertising, merchandising and public relations used by a business to promote itself or its products.
Public relations (PR) - the promotion of a positive image about a product or a business through the giving of information to the general public, the media, other businesses or government.
Sales promotion - methods of promoting a product in the short term, such as money off offers, competitions or free gifts.

In 1998, tobacco manufacturers in the US reached an agreement with 46 states. Part of the deal was a severe cut back in cigarette promotion. Sponsorship of sporting events and advertising were curbed. The use of cartoon characters, product placement in movies and 'ads' in magazines aimed at young readers were also banned.

Tobacco companies, however, remain some of the largest spenders on promotion in the USA. Following the signing of the agreement, tobacco companies had to be more inventive about how to spend their promotion budgets.

Philip Morris, maker of Marlboro, the world's best selling cigarette brand, spends more than $2 billion a year on advertising. The company is continuing to sponsor the Marlboro Penske car racing team. It is also heavily advertising its 'Marlboro Ranch party'. This is a sweepstake which sends winners to a five-day ranch holiday in 'Marlboro country', mountainous states such as Montana and Arizona. These promotions are often held in bars in big cities. Prizes also include cameras, sunglasses, jackets and bags, all in Marlboro colours. 'This kind of promotion is very niche-orientated' according to David Adelman, a tobacco analyst for Morgan Stanley Dean Witter. 'People tend to smoke the cigarettes their friends smoke and brands have momentum. It is very hard to get people to try a new brand because it is about loyalty, image and taste.'

The agreement also put an end to another popular promotion. Cigarette manufacturers could no longer exchange lighters, clothing and other products bearing their logos for coupons included in cigarette packs. But the tobacco companies retained the list of past customers who redeemed those coupons. Their names formed part of a database used for marketing.

Another company, R.J. Reynolds, sends a glossy 16-page magazine to more than a million customers who smoke its Dural brand. This direct marketing includes restaurant reviews, recipes and coupons for Dural brand products. In addition, the company sponsors regular 'smoker appreciation' parties in cities around the US. They involve games and country music, with cigarettes given as prizes.

Another manufacturer, Brown and Williamson Tobacco, has targeted office workers who are forced to go outside to smoke. The company has teams who visit office buildings in cities such as New York in the winter months. They hand out hot mugs of coffee to smokers banished from their warm offices.

Adapted from the *Financial Times*, 13.6.2000.

1 Explain what is meant by 'direct marketing'. (3 marks)
2 Outline TWO reasons why tobacco companies might have wanted to promote their products to low income 'young readers' of magazines. (6 marks)
3 Examine the various forms of promotion that US cigarette companies are currently using and their possible effectiveness in maintaining consumer loyalty. (10 marks)
4 Discuss whether the tobacco companies would have been even more profitable than they are today if the agreement had banned all forms of cigarette promotion. (11 marks)

19 Place

Beer distribution

Knowledge Beer is distributed by brewers through pubs, wholesalers, off-licences and supermarket chains, such as Sainsbury and Tesco. In November 1999, the major supermarket chains warned brewers that from now on they would only stock the best selling brands of beer.

Application The 'route' that beer takes from the brewer to the consumer is known as the *distribution channel*. The *channel of distribution* through pubs has been declining in importance, whilst *sales* through large supermarkets have been increasing.

Analysis Brewers face increasingly difficult market conditions. The trend towards home drinking makes brewers rely more on sales through major supermarkets. But supermarkets are such large buyers that they are able to negotiate lower prices. This forces down brewers' profits. Supermarkets also are able to dictate which beers they will stock. Without a supermarket channel of distribution, 'second tier' brands such as Skol, Harp or Kestrel could find it difficult to survive.

Evaluation To what extent do supermarket chains alone influence the distribution of beer through supermarkets? Supermarkets aiming to maximise sales and profits only want to stock the most popular brands. But it could be argued that brewers' actions also lead to fewer brands of beer being available in supermarkets. This is because a beer's popularity often reflects how much promotion it is given by brewers. Brewers might kill the incentive for supermarkets to stock a beer by not promoting it heavily. 'Place' in this example is linked to promotion, another element of the marketing mix.

Adapted from *The Guardian*, 15.11.1999.

Place and the marketing mix

Place is one of the 4Ps of the marketing mix (see unit 1). It is no less important than the other Ps of product, price and promotion. However good the product, if it isn't available to customers to buy at the right place and at the right time, it won't sell.

The right place Products need to be available to customers in the place where they want to buy. For example, 75 per cent of all groceries in the UK are now bought from large supermarket chains. So if a grocery product is not available in a supermarket, its sales will be severely restricted. Equally, a car manufacturer might insist that parts are delivered to its plant by the component manufacturer. Unless the business agrees to deliver, it won't get the order.

The right time Products need to be available to customers at the time they want to buy. For example, often at Christmas there is a toy which becomes popular. Supplies may run out in shops. The manufacturer of the toy knows that unless it can increase supply to meet demand before 25th December, the sales it could have made will be lost. Equally, if there is a strike at the printers of a daily newspaper and a day's production is lost, those sales will never be recovered. Nobody will want to buy yesterday's newspaper today.

Coca-Cola has become the world's largest soft drinks distributor by making sure that its drinks are available to consumers not just in the right place, but also at a time when consumers want to buy. Coca-Cola vending machines, for example, are part of this strategy.

Distribution channels in consumer markets

The DISTRIBUTION CHANNEL for a product in a **consumer market** (see unit 2) is the route it takes from manufacturer to the consumer. Figure 19.1 shows some common channels of distribution. They can be distinguished by the number and type of intermediary involved. A MARKETING INTERMEDIARY is a business or individual which acts as a link between the producer and customer.

Manufacturers to consumers DIRECT MARKETING involves a business selling its product straight to consumers. A manufacturer might advertise its products directly for sale to the public through advertisements in magazines. It might also operate a mail order catalogue or offer on-line ordering through a website on the Internet. It might even sell via its own sales representatives. Some manufacturers have factory shops where consumers can buy products. **Services** are also usually distributed straight to the customer, for example solicitors or accountants.

Direct marketing is a **zero level channel** because there are no intermediaries between manufacturers and consumers.

Manufacturers to consumers via retailers A RETAILER is a service business which sells goods to consumers. Retailers are typically called **shops**. But there are many other names for retailers, such as department stores, supermarkets and hypermarkets, superstores and convenience stores. Jewellers, butchers, grocers and hardware stores are also examples of shops.

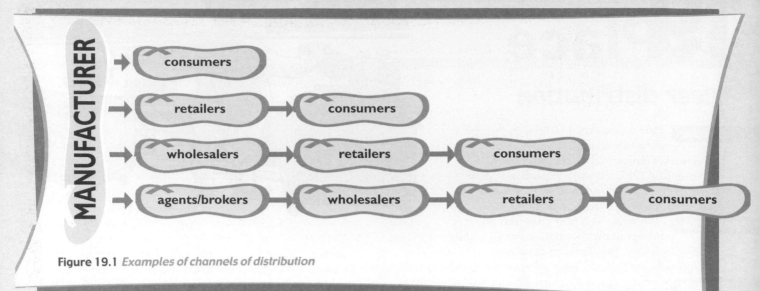

Figure 19.1 *Examples of channels of distribution*

Retailers provide certain services. First, they BREAK-BULK. They buy large quantities from suppliers and sell in smaller quantities to consumers. For example, a supermarket chain might buy 1 million packets of butter from a food manufacturer, but sell butter to consumers in single packets. Breaking-bulk is a service both to manufacturers and consumers. Most manufacturers don't want to sell in small quantities to consumers. Equally, consumers don't want to buy large quantities from manufacturers.

Retailers also sell goods in locations which are convenient to consumers. A yoghurt manufacturer may have a plant in Wales, for example. But consumers in London don't want to travel to Wales every time they want to buy a yoghurt.

Retailers also provide other services which add value to the good being sold. These may include home delivery, repair services, extra guarantees and gift wrapping.

Manufacturers selling to customers via retailers is a **one level channel** because there is a single intermediary between manufacturers and consumers.

Manufacturers to consumers via wholesalers and retailers A WHOLESALER is a business which buys goods from manufacturers and sells them to retailers. Some wholesalers call themselves a **cash-and-carry** because their customers, usually small shops, visit the premises and take away what they have purchased. In most cases, though, wholesalers deliver to retailing customers.

Like retailers, wholesalers provide two main services. They break-bulk and they are located or deliver to a location which is convenient to the retailer. They may also offer services such as trade credit (see unit 25).

The use of wholesalers is an example of a **two level channel** because there are two intermediaries between manufacturers and consumers.

Manufacturer to consumers via agents and/or wholesalers and retailers A manufacturer may use an intermediary called an AGENT or BROKER. They bring buyers and sellers together. Agents are often used when selling into a foreign country. They often have better knowledge of the laws, needs of consumers and trading conditions in that country.

The choice of distribution channel

Which distribution channel is used depends upon a variety of factors.

Cost The longer the supply chain, the greater may be the cost to the final consumer. This is because each intermediary has its own costs to cover and wants to make a profit. Large supermarket chains often reduce these costs by cutting out the wholesaler and buying directly from the manufacturer.

However, in some cases short supply chains can be more costly than long supply chains. For example, a small upmarket food manufacturer may find that supermarkets will not stock its goods. To survive, it might have to supply directly to the customer, by mail order or the Internet. But the cost of a catalogue, an Internet site and delivery may be far more than the cost of supplying through a retailer. Some businesses employ sales representatives to sell directly. These can also be very costly.

Distribution Manufacturers may find it difficult to reach large numbers of consumers without an intermediary. This might be because the manufacturer lacks resources. It may not be able to afford to run a sales team, for instance. Equally, a manufacturer such as Heinz or Kellogg may want to sell to every household in the country. The only way it can achieve this might be to use the large network of retailers, including supermarket chains.

Another factor may be knowledge of the market. A UK company that wants to sell a small quantity of goods to Australia may know nothing about this market. By using an agent to sell the goods, it will gain the agent's expertise.

Control Some manufacturers want to control the distribution channels they use carefully. For example, manufacturers of luxury goods or up-market brands, such as Chanel or Levis, don't want their goods being sold in supermarkets. This is because the place of sale can give important messages to consumers about the product. Expensive perfumes or jeans sold in Tesco or Asda detract from the exclusive image of the brand, according to their manufacturers. It is then going to be more difficult to sell these luxury goods at a high price and high profit margin.

Safety may be another issue. Some products require careful installation or maintenance. The manufacturer may find it

In 2000, Pringle, an up-market and exclusive knitwear brand, was bought by a Hong Kong textiles company. The previous owners had seen the company fall into loss, with declining sales. The new owners brought in a new chief executive, Kim Winser, who within two years transformed the fortunes of the company. By producing new designs aimed at younger customers, and by reinforcing the new image with updated promotion, sales nearly doubled.

An important element of the new marketing mix was changes in the channel of distribution. Pringle sold through a mixture of exclusive independent retailers worldwide. By July 2001, it had withdrawn supply from 508 outlets, mainly because they were failing to buy and sell enough of the product. When Kim Winser took over, half of all sales were to retailers which sold less than 100 items per year. But it had also signed up 90 new retailers who were now major customers. By July 2001, under 1 per cent of Pringle retailers were selling less than 100 items per year.

Pringle now plans to open a few shops of its own, starting with a flagship fashion store in London. A sportswear shop could follow, and Pringle could develop a chain in selective UK and international cities.

Adapted from the *Financial Times*, 10.7.2001.

1 **Describe the channel of distribution used by Pringle (i) before July 2001 and (ii) after July 2001 if its plans are implemented.**
2 **Analyse the possible advantages to Pringle of selling through its own stores rather than just through independent retailers.**
3 **Discuss how Pringle should react if it were approached by a large UK supermarket chain for an order for Pringle clothing.**

easier to control safety aspects if it sells directly to the customer.

Legal factors The law may affect how a product is distributed. For example, drugs which need a doctor's prescription can only be sold through licensed chemists.

Distribution channels in producer markets

The distribution channel for a good in an **industrial** or **producer market** (see unit 2) is the route it takes from the manufacturer to another business. As in consumer markets, there can be none, one or more intermediaries. For example, some businesses sell directly to others using their own 'sales reps'. Small tradespeople and businesses in the building industry, such as plumbers or carpenters, often buy from builders' merchants or building wholesalers. These intermediaries distribute products for the building industry. Agents might also be used by a producer dealing with a manufacturer in a foreign country.

Services are often distributed straight from one business to another, for example cleaning services, or through an agent, such as secretarial help.

The number of intermediaries depends upon a variety of factors, including cost and ease of distribution.

Distribution targets and objectives

A business that wants to be successful is likely to have clear **marketing objectives** (see unit 9). These are the goals that the business wants to achieve through its marketing, such as increasing sales.

When choosing which distribution channels it will use, a business will set DISTRIBUTION TARGETS. These are plans which might include, for example, the quantity to be sold over a future time period and to whom products will be sold. They will take into account marketing objectives. For example, a toy manufacturer that has the objective of increasing sales may set a target of selling 5 000 extra toys a month. It might decide that the best way to do this is to sell in bulk to wholesalers. Or a new computer magazine may want to target computer users. It may decide to sell directly over the Internet for a charge, allowing buyers to download and print out the magazine.

checklist

1 Explain why it is important for businesses to have goods available for sale (a) at the right price and (b) at the right time.
2 What is the difference between a zero level channel of distribution and a two level channel of distribution?
3 Explain why a mail order catalogue is an example of direct marketing.
4 What is the difference between a retailer and a wholesaler?
5 What services do retailers provide to consumers?
6 What services do wholesalers provide to retailers?
7 What factors determine which channel of distribution is used by a manufacturer?
8 What channels of distribution might there be in producer markets?
9 Why are distribution targets important for achieving marketing objectives?

keyterms

Agent or broker - an intermediary which arranges contracts for the sale of products between a supplier and a customer.

Break-bulk - dividing a larger quantity of goods ordered from a supplier and selling them in smaller quantities to customers. A key function of retailers and wholesalers is to break-bulk.

Direct marketing - selling by manufacturers direct to consumers without passing through retailers or wholesalers.

Distribution channel - the path taken by a product as it goes from manufacturer to the ultimate customer.

Distribution targets - goals set by a business for future sales of goods, for instance, through particular channels of distribution.

Marketing intermediary - a business or individual which acts as a link between the producer and customer.

Retailer - a type of business which buys goods from manufacturers and wholesalers and sells them, typically in smaller quantities and in a place convenient to the buyer, to customers.

Wholesaler - a type of business which buys goods from manufacturers and sells them in smaller quantities to retailers.

In the late 1990s, it was easy to get carried away with the idea that the Internet would be the dominant channel of distribution for goods in future. Today, it is easier to see that the Internet, at best, will only cater for a fraction of total spending.

Foodferry, based in London's New Covent Garden, is a case in point. The company, started in 1990, allows Londoners unable or unwilling to visit their local supermarket to order weekly groceries by telephone and fax. The groceries are then delivered to the door. Today, Foodferry has a sales turnover of £2.2 million and is still growing.

In 1997, it launched a website which allowed on-line ordering. It assumed on-line ordering would become the most popular way for customers to order. Today, only 17 per cent of orders come from the website, with the phone taking 50 per cent and fax 33 per cent. What's more, the average on-line order is only £100, compared to £130 for phone and fax.

The company has a number of explanations for the poor performance of on-line ordering. One is that most customers find it more complicated and time consuming to order over the Internet than to use a telephone or fax. Despite its running an award winning website, most customers did not find the site easy to use. Another problem is that customers like to see and feel the groceries they are buying. A mail order operation like Foodferry can't provide this, unlike a supermarket. But many Foodferry customers find placing an order with a real person on the other end of a phone a reasonable substitute for 'physical shopping'. The Internet doesn't provide that personal touch.

What is more, Foodferry found that running the website was costly. It required a team of expensive, competent and dedicated staff. To provide the same level of service as phone or fax ordering, the company reckoned that the staff cost of on-line ordering was roughly double that of off-line ordering.

In the long term, the company will maintain a website to advertise its services and explain how to order over the phone and by fax. The cost of maintaining such a website is relatively low and it attracts new customers. But there is doubt about whether to maintain on-line ordering. Possibly the last chance for on-line ordering is the adoption of a customer list which has proved highly popular with fax customers. Customers are supplied with a form listing items which they have previously ordered. They then indicate what they want to buy this time and write in any new item not previously ordered. Average fax orders have increased from £100 to £130 since the introduction of this list. Foodferry is currently adapting this idea for its website to on-line customers.

Adapted from the *Financial Times*, 3.1.2002.

1 Explain what is meant by a 'channel of distribution'. (3 marks)
2 Outline (a) one advantage and (b) one disadvantage that Foodferry has compared to a traditional supermarket in the distribution of food. (6 marks)
3 Examine why Foodferry's Internet strategy has had to change in the light of experience. (10 marks)
4 Discuss whether manufacturers of food products, such as Cadbury or Unilever, and UK farmers which currently supply meat and vegetables to supermarkets, should market directly to consumers via the Internet. (11 marks)

20 Accounts

Stagecoach

Knowledge Stagecoach Holdings is a company which operates bus and rail services worldwide.

Application Its *Annual Report and Accounts* for 2001 showed that its *turnover* (i.e. the money it received from *sales*) was over £2 billion for the year to 30 April 2001. Its *financial accounts* included much more financial information about what had happened in the past year. The *Annual Report and Accounts* did not, however, contain *management accounts*, which would have included *plans* and *projections* about future *finances*.

Analysis Its 2001 Annual Report and Accounts showed that the company made a loss for the year on ordinary activities before taxation of £316.5 million. This compared with a £182.3 million profit for 2000.

Evaluation The financial story told by the 2001 Accounts was mixed. On the one hand, parts of the company, such as the Hong Kong operations, performed well. On the other hand, other parts, particularly the US operations, performed poorly. Overall there was a deterioration in the performance of the company over the period 2000-2001. Management accounting would be one tool for the company to improve its performance in the 2002 financial year.

Adapted from *Stagecoach, Annual Report and Accounts*, 2002.

Accounting

Many people compile accounts to keep track of their money. You might note down what you think you will spend over the next week to see if you can afford it. Taxpayers might compile a list of their income to put on a tax return to the Inland Revenue.

Just as individuals keep accounts, so do businesses. But for businesses, accounting is a necessity, not an option. Businesses must keep financial records of their past transactions for legal reasons. For example, tax authorities can demand to see their accounts. Also, businesses need to plan for the future, so they need to be able to draw up financial forecasts.

ACCOUNTING is defined by the the American Accounting Association as 'the process of identifying, measuring and communicating information to permit informed judgements and decisions by users of the information'. This definition distinguishes between the **collecting** of financial information and the **use** which is made of that information. Accounts are simply numbers on a piece of paper. But their **purpose** is to tell a story and allow the reader to make judgments and decisions.

Accounts are used by the **stakeholders** (see unit 56) of the business. They might be people who are outside the organisation but have an interest in it (external users). Or they might be people who are within the business (internal users).

External users of accounts

Tax authorities The Inland Revenue (responsible for collecting income tax and corporation tax), Customs and Excise (responsible for collecting VAT and excise duties) and the Department for Social Security (responsible for collecting National Insurance contributions) use the accounts of a business to assess how much it owes in tax.

Suppliers Suppliers to a business usually give **trade credit** (see unit 25). Typically this means that they will give the business 30 days to pay for any goods or services provided. However, there is always a risk that a business may cease to trade with bills unpaid. Accounts are one way in which suppliers can find out if a company is at risk.

Bankers If a bank were to lend a business money, it would want to be satisfied that it would be paid back. The accounts of the business give evidence of its financial soundness. Typically, banks want to see both accounts of how the business has performed in the past and forecasts of how it will perform in the future.

Investors and advisors Anyone thinking of investing or who has already invested in a business would want to have as much financial information about it as possible. For example, a person wanting to buy shares could find out some information about a company through its published Report and Accounts. Shareholders, as owners of the company, are likely to be very interested in its performance. The accounts may indicate whether their shares could rise or fall in value and whether they might receive a dividend.

Financial advisers would use accounts to base decisions on whether to advise clients to buy or sell. Public limited companies often give briefings to investment analysts from the City of London to give information to potential investors.

The media Financial journalists are interested in accounts because they write articles about companies. These may give investment advice or they may use accounts to back up other stories on, say, job creation or environmental issues.

Competitors Competitors use the accounts of other businesses as part of their decision making process. For instance, a company might **take over** another company if it sees that it has valuable assets but is failing to use those to make reasonable levels of profit. Competitors might want to **benchmark** (i.e. compare, see unit 48) their performance against their rivals. Businesses might also look at the financial strength of potential competitors if they were to **diversify** (see unit 48) into new markets.

The community The local community is interested in the businesses located in its area. For instance, local businesses create jobs in the local area. They provide opportunities for local suppliers to increase trade, so further increasing prosperity in the local community. The financial performance of local businesses is therefore vital to the economic well being of the local community.

The government Apart from collecting taxes from businesses, government is also interested in the well being of the economy. Government and its agencies, like the Bank of England, use the accounts of businesses to see how well the economy is doing and if it needs to change its policies. Falling company profitability, for example, might be a sign that the economy is going into recession. So the Bank of England might cut interest rates to boost spending (see unit 51). Governments will also want to see the accounts of companies when they apply for grants from government.

Internal users of accounts

Management The management of a business uses financial records to report back on how well the business has been doing. But, perhaps more importantly, management uses accounts to plan for the future. For example, accounting information might be used when deciding whether to launch a new product or invest in a new piece of machinery.

Employees and their representatives Employees are affected by the success or failure of a business. If the business is doing badly, for example, there are likely to be job losses. If the business is expanding it may relocate its premises, forcing workers to move. Employees also expect to receive regular pay rises. The accounts of a business are one way in which employees can gain information about possible changes and whether pay rises are affordable. Some employees may be represented by trade unions. They use accounts to back up their arguments in negotiations with employers.

Managers and other employees might also be shareholders in a company. The accounts might indicate whether their shareholding is a worthwhile investment.

Financial accounting

One type of accounting is FINANCIAL ACCOUNTING. This is the keeping of financial records to satisfy the needs of external stakeholders in the business. Financial accounting tends to be concerned with what has happened in the past. It provides a historical record of the finances of a business. There are three main financial statements.

The profit and loss account This shows sales revenues and costs. From this, it is possible to calculate profit (see unit 21). The profit and loss account also shows how that profit has been distributed - whether it was retained in the business or given to

In 2001, it became apparent that Enron, the 7th largest company in the USA at the time, had falsified its accounts. Subsequently, it filed for bankruptcy. The accounting irregularities were designed to inflate sales and profits and minimise costs and losses. The company had achieved this mainly through creating new companies which it owned and putting into them sales, costs and debts which it didn't want outsiders to see. The accounts of the main company then looked much better than was actually the case if all the 'special vehicles' were taken into account.

The stakeholders of Enron all lost out. For example, taxpayers lost out because Enron failed to pay the right amount of tax. Suppliers to Enron lost out because they were left being owed money when it went into bankruptcy. Banks lost out because Enron had borrowed large sums from them which were unlikely to be repaid.

If Enron had kept accurate accounts, it would never have grown to the size that it became immediately prior to going bankrupt. Stakeholders would have had a much better picture of what was going on at the company and they would have been more wary in their dealings with it.

Adapted from various articles, 2001.

---

1 **List FOUR items, mentioned in the case study, which would have appeared on a full set of accounts for Enron.**

2 **Explain how bankers and suppliers were affected because Enron had falsified its accounts.**

3 **Explain how TWO sets of stakeholders not mentioned in the case study might have been affected by Enron's falsification of its accounts.**

---

shareholders. Profit and loss accounts are usually drawn up for a 12 month period. **Interim accounts** typically show the six monthly position.

The cash flow statement This shows the past flow of cash (defined as all types of money, including cheques and credit card receipts) through the business (see unit 27). It shows the sources of the cash that the business has received. It also shows how money was spent.

The balance sheet This shows the value of what the business owns (its **assets**) and what it owes (its **liabilities**). For a company, it will also show the value of the shareholders' capital which has been used to purchase any net assets.

Financial accounting reports tend to contain fairly general information about the whole of the business. They provide an overview of the recent financial history.

Some accounts need to be produced to satisfy the requirements of the law. For example, companies have to produce an Annual Report and Accounts, which includes a statement from the directors about the past year and possible future prospects. It also includes a profit and loss account, balance sheet and cash flow statement with supporting tables, giving a fuller picture of these summary accounts. In addition, there is normally a chairperson's statement concerning the past year and future prospects. The accounts must also conform to standards set by the Accounting Standards Board

The accounts need to be AUDITED. This involves getting an outside firm of accountants to check over the books and accounts to confirm that they represent a 'true and fair' record of

Eurotunnel is the company which owns the Channel Tunnel between Folkestone and Calais. Opened for business in 1996, it has yet to make a profit.

For it to make a profit in any one year, its revenues must be greater than its costs during that year. In 2001, its revenues were greater than its operating costs by £322 million. These costs were the costs of running the tunnel on a day to day basis. But its main costs are interest and repayments on its huge £8 billion debt. Interest charges in 2001 were £330 million. There were also other non-operating costs of £139 million. As a result, the net loss for the year was £132 million.

In 2002, there was still little likelihood that Eurotunnel would improve its financial position just to break-even (i.e. for revenues to equal costs). To break-even, there would have to be a significant increase in traffic through the tunnel, which is unlikely in the circumstances.

Adapted from *The Independent*, 12.2.2002.

1 **The newspaper article reports a number of figures which would be seen on the financial accounts for Eurotunnel for 2001. Give THREE examples of these.**
2 **The newspaper article also reports on aspects of management accounting. Give ONE example of a management account given in the article.**
3 **Discuss TWO ways in which Eurotunnel could increase its revenues.**

what has taken place. Audits are one way in which the interests of shareholders are protected from the possibility that directors or managers in the company are defrauding it for their own benefit.

Management accounting

Financial accounting reports at best provide only background information for managers when they are making decisions about the future. When making decisions, managers usually need more detailed financial information. This information typically needs to be targeted on a small area of the finances of the business, such as the finances of a department or a decision about whether or not to buy a new piece of equipment. It also needs to relate not to the past, as with financial accounting, but to the future. And it must be available regularly, so management accounts are often prepared monthly, weekly or even daily.

MANAGEMENT ACCOUNTING seeks to provide this sort of financial information. It is not aimed, like financial accounting, at outside users of information, such as the tax authorities or outside shareholders, but at decision makers within the organisation.

Two important management accounting statements are:
● **budgets** - plans of income and spending for the whole business or parts of a business, such as a department or a division (see unit 29);
● **cash flow forecasts** - projections of future inflows and outflows of money (see unit 27).

When making decisions about whether or not to invest in new capital equipment, accountants can carry out an **investment appraisal**, giving a prediction of its profitability. **Break-even analysis** (see unit 22) and **contribution statements** (see unit 23) are also used when making decisions about production and investment.

Compiling accounts

Like other financial records, there has been a revolution in recent times in the way in which accounts are compiled. Before, accounts were kept by hand and recorded on paper. Today, many businesses use computers to keep their accounts. This doesn't mean that paper is not used. Bills and invoices are still typically sent out in paper form. Equally, some management accounts are still prepared using pencil, paper and a calculator. But as accountants and employees become more computer literate, as computers become the norm in business and as software programmes are written for specific tasks, computers are becoming increasingly important.

Computers are particularly useful when information needs to be recalled or exchanged. For example, retailing chains are able to use **EDI (electronic data exchange)** to send information about sales today in one store back to head office. The company then has almost instant information about sales across the whole chain.

Intranets are also used by larger businesses. These allow one computer to communicate with another like the larger Internet. But with an intranet, the communication is confined to computers within the business. This prevents outsiders being able to access confidential information. So a manager, for example, when preparing a budget for a department can access information about costs and revenues from the intranet of the business.

Numbers in accounts are often seen as being 'true'. However, it is important to remember that accounts often contain errors. Numbers can be entered incorrectly. Data which should be inputted is omitted through human error. Equally, accounts can be manipulated and falsified. There are various ways in which companies, for example, can manipulate their profit figures to make them look better worse. Businesses also have an incentive to manipulate or falsify records in order to pay less tax. Managers who want to increase their departmental budget may put in over-optimistic projections about increases in sales to justify their bid. So accounts should always be read with caution.

Social auditing

Financial and management accounts are valuable in giving information about a business. But they only represent one of many ways of viewing a business. For example, a business may make a profit of £10 million on a factory it owns in a low income country. But what the £10 million might not say is that the factory pays very low wages to employees and working conditions are below the minimum standard that would be expected in the UK.

To present a fuller picture, some businesses now present SOCIAL AUDITS. These attempt to quantify aspects of the social impact of the business. For example, figures might be presented on the impact of the business on the environment, or employment statistics might be given.

Critics argue that social audits might just be a public relations exercise by businesses that have been criticised for their social and environmental impact. They are a way of making the company look as though it is socially concerned. They also suggest that social auditing masks the real goal of a company, which is to maximise profits.

Companies that make social audits, however, would argue that the process makes them more aware of the social cost of the profit that is generated. Where this social cost is too high, it might not be in the company's interest to carry on with the activity. This is particularly the case if it risks a consumer backlash.

✓checklist

1 What is meant by 'accounting'?
2 Explain the difference between an external user of accounts and an internal user of accounts in the case of a company.
3 Explain the difference between financial accounting and management accounting.
4 How has information technology changed how accounts are compiled?
5 Explain why a company may compile a social audit.

keyterms

Accounting - **the process of identifying, measuring and communicating information to allow informed judgments and decisions by users of the information to be made.**
Auditing - **verifying the accuracy of accounts prepared by a business or other organisation. Auditors tend to be accountants from outside the business.**
Financial accounting - **the keeping of financial records to satisfy the needs of external users such as shareholders, investors and the tax authorities. Financial accounting tends to represent a historical record of the finances of a business.**
Management accounting - **aimed at those making decisions within the business, this type of accounting tends to be about planning and projections.**
Social auditing - **collecting information and reporting back on the impact of the business on society and the environment.**

Some of Britain's largest companies are failing to provide meaningful information on issues such as customer service, innovation and staff performance in their Annual Report and Accounts. As a result, they leave a lot to be desired if they are to be used by investors to make an informed judgment, said the Foundation for Performance Measurement in its second annual review.

'It is surprising that companies choose to place so little emphasis on subjects such as customer service, innovation, R&D, staff performance and learning, brand development, management and the supply chain relationship.' Sixty one of the largest companies on the London Stock Exchange failed to include any measure of customer service, seventy four failed to measure innovation and seventy five did not measure R&D.

Few companies published targets, including financial ones, the study showed. Only thirteen of the largest one hundred companies released a target for financial returns, and only five of these were targets for shareholder value.

Companies by law must publish an Annual Report and Accounts each year. The Accounts must show a minimum given set of financial information. For example, they must show the profit and loss made for the previous two years. However, they don't have to give all the financial information available to the company at the time. To do so would make the Annual Report and Accounts an enormous volume and be very costly to prepare and print. It would also give competitors and anyone thinking of buying the company a large amount of information which they could use against it. The result of this is that companies tend to give the minimum amount of information they can get away with in their Annual Report. So the findings of the Foundation for Performance Measurement are perhaps hardly surprising.

Adapted from the *Financial Times*, 7.12.1999.

1 Explain what is meant by the terms:
  (a) 'investors'; (3 marks)
  (b) 'customer service'. (3 marks)
2 The Annual Report and Accounts of a company is an example of financial accounting. Explain what this means. (6 marks)
3 Give TWO groups of stakeholders in a company which might be interested in reading its Annual Report and Accounts and explain why they would be interested. (8 marks)
4 Discuss why companies may be reluctant to give more than the minimum necessary information in the company Annual Report and Accounts. (10 marks)

21 Costs, revenue and profits

Jennings Ltd

Knowledge Jennings Ltd is a printer of full colour brochures and leaflets. It manufactures advertising material with print runs varying from as little as 500 to a maximum of 100 000.

Application In the financial year to 31 March 2001, the business earned *sales revenue* of £900 000 from producing brochures and leaflets. It had *direct costs* of £765 000. Its indirect costs were £100 000, so its total *costs of production* amounted to £865 000. The difference between its *total revenue* and *total costs* was £35 000. £6 650 was paid in *corporation tax*, the tax on profits, leaving a *profit after tax* of £28 350. From this, £24 000 was distributed in *dividends* to *shareholders* and the rest, £4 350, was *retained profit* for the *company*.

Analysis Sales revenue fell in the 2002 accounting year compared to 2001, from £900 000 to £750 000. This was partly due to the business ending a long term contract to provide a company with brochures, where the cost of the materials used in printing the brochures was very high. In part it was also due to the retirement of an older sales representative who was not replaced. However, the retirement of the older sales representative reduced the indirect costs of the business. Also, the business found that some of the work it got in to replace the lost brochures could be manufactured with far cheaper materials. Both these factors led to a profit after tax of £28 350 in 2001 being turned into a larger profit after tax of £64 800 in 2002.

Evaluation The loss of business and the retirement of the sales representative affected the revenue of Jennings Ltd. But the company felt that it was necessary to improve its long term profitability.

Adapted from material provided by John Collins, Waring Collins Ltd and Chris Sawyer, Sawyer & Quine.

Production costs

The COSTS of a business are the expenses that it incurs when producing and supplying products and services to customers. Businesses face many different costs. For example, most will either rent or buy a factory, shop or office premise to carry out their business. Business rates must be paid on these premises to the local authority. Manufacturers will need to buy raw materials, components and machinery, and hire workers to make products. A travel service will need to employ travel agents and buy computers to show transport and accommodation details. Businesses will need to pay for heating and lighting. Products will also usually need some form of promotion.

Information about costs is vital for business decision making. It may be used, for example, when:
- setting the price of a new product;
- deciding how profitable a product will be;
- forecasting the cash flow of the business;
- calculating the value of stocks held in the warehouse.

Fixed, variable and semi-variable costs

One way of dividing the costs of a business is to classify them as fixed, variable and semi-variable costs.

FIXED COSTS are those costs which do not change as the level of **output** changes. For instance, the cost of buying or renting a factory for a manufacturer stays the same whether production falls by 20 per cent or increases by 20 per cent. Business rates on the factory, the charge which the company has to pay on its property to the local authority, are constant whatever the level of production. Other examples of fixed costs for a business might be building or employee insurance, interest charges and depreciation.

VARIABLE COSTS are costs which change directly with the level of output. The more produced, for instance, the more materials are used. If production falls, so too will the number of materials that need to be bought. Examples of variable costs might be raw materials and components or packaging.

Some costs, though, might contain both a fixed and variable cost element. These are called SEMI-VARIABLE COSTS. Examples of semi-variable costs might include:
- heating and lighting. A business will usually pay a certain regular amount for energy costs a week. But at peak times it may stay open longer and use more power;
- telephone charges. There is usually a 'fixed charge' on telephone calls and then payments based on the number and length of calls. In peak periods more calls may be made to cope with greater demand;
- maintenance. There is likely to be regular planned maintenance of machinery by businesses. However, at peak times more repairs may be needed to correct faults;
- travel. Some travel costs are fixed, such as vehicle licences. The travel costs of sales representatives are also likely to be fixed. But if demand rises sharply, more deliveries may be made and there may be more visits, for example to new customers.

Earnings may be fixed, variable or semi-variable. Some managers are paid a fixed salary no matter how long they work. Some workers are paid only on commission or are paid piece rates (see unit 34). Their earnings are related to their sales or to output. But sometimes workers are paid a basic wage (a fixed cost) and then overtime (a variable cost) when the business is producing beyond its normal capacity.

1 **Explain which of the costs shown in the photographs might be (a) fixed costs; (b) variable costs; and (c) semi-variable costs.**

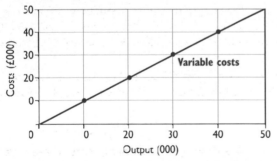

Figure 21.1 *A fixed cost curve.* **The fixed cost curve is horizontal at £20 000 because whatever the level of output fixed costs do not change.**

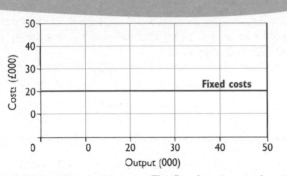

Figure 21.2 *A variable cost curve.* **The variable cost curve is drawn on the assumption that the cost per unit is £1.**

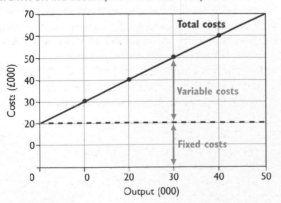

Figure 21.3 *A total cost curve.* **The total cost curve is upward sloping, starting at £20 000 because this is the fixed cost.**

Fixed, variable and total cost curves

Fixed and variable costs can be illustrated on a diagram. The business in Figure 21.1 has fixed costs (FC) of £20 000. This is shown as a horizontal line at £20 000. These costs do not change as output changes. Hence, fixed costs remain the same on the graph whatever the level of output.

Figure 21.2 shows variable costs. The variable cost (VC) line is upward sloping. As output increases, so do variable costs. For instance, if the variable cost of producing one unit is £1, then at an output level of 1 unit, variable costs will be £1. At an output level of 10 000 units, they will be £10 000 (£1 x 10 000). At an output of 50 000 units, they will be £50 000 (£1 x 50 000).

TOTAL COSTS can be shown too. If we assume that all costs are either fixed costs or variable costs:

Total costs = fixed costs + variable costs

On Figure 21.3, the fixed cost is shown as a horizontal dotted line at £20 000. Then the variable cost is added to this. So the total cost of producing zero units is £20 000 (£20 000 + £0). The total cost of producing 30 000 units is £50 000 (£20 000 + [£1 x 30 000]) and the total cost of 50 000 units is £70 000 (£20 000 + [£1 x 50 000]). If there were any semi-variable costs, they must be split into the amounts that are fixed and the amounts that are variable.

The short run and the long run

Over a period of time, a business can change all its costs. In the LONG RUN, all costs are variable. For example, a business can move from larger premises to smaller premises, reducing costs such as rents and insurance. A business can also shed permanent staff. It is, therefore, only in the SHORT RUN that a business has fixed costs.

The period of time needed to change all costs varies from business to business and industry to industry. In **capital intensive industries** (see unit 44), the long run tends to be decades. It is unlikely, for example, that a business would build a £500 million chemical plant one year and then scrap it the next. In **labour intensive industries**, however, the short run is likely to be a few years. But it can be as little as months or even weeks.

Elaine Potter runs a bakery. Her monthly costs are as follows.

Rent and rates	£200
Average cost of ingredients per batch	£0.50
Wages of permanent staff with no overtime	£300
Other non-variable costs	£100

1 **Which costs are (a) variable costs and (b) fixed costs?**
2 **(a) Draw a fixed cost line on a graph between output levels of 0 and 600 per month.
    (b) Draw the variable cost line on the same graph.
    (c) Draw the total cost line on the graph.**

Direct and indirect costs

Another way to distinguish between costs is to divide them into direct and indirect costs. DIRECT COSTS (sometimes called PRIME COSTS) are costs which are linked with production. For instance, the materials used in the manufacture of a children's toy would be a direct cost. So too would be the cost of workers employed in making the toy. Direct expenses, such as the cost of hiring a specialist piece of machinery or commissioning a specific design, might also be direct costs.

INDIRECT COSTS or OVERHEAD COSTS are costs which cannot be linked directly to production. The pay of the office workers or a sales team would be examples. So too would be insurance, business rates and maintenance costs on office buildings.

Total costs can also be calculated using direct and indirect costs where:

Total cost = direct cost + indirect cost

Look back at the photographs shown in the case study on page 94.

1 **Explain what (a) direct costs and (b) indirect costs are shown in the photographs.**

Direct costs are often variable costs. For example, the materials used by the toy manufacturer are a direct cost. They are also variable, because the cost of materials rises the more that is produced. However, some direct costs are fixed costs. For instance, the cost of hiring a specialist design for a toy is likely to be fixed by the designer.

Indirect or overhead costs are often fixed costs. For example, the rent paid by a toy manufacturer for premises is unlikely to vary with output. But they can be variable. For instance, the sales staff of the toy manufacturer may be paid commission only, i.e. they are paid according to how many sales they make. The orders they obtain determine the level of production. Hence, commission-only sales staff are arguably a variable cost.

Average cost

Total costs can be used to calculate the AVERAGE COST of production. This is the cost **per unit** of production. For instance, assume that the total costs of producing 10 000 magnets of a particular specification were £30 000. Then the average cost of each magnet is £3. This is calculated by dividing the total costs, £30 000, by the output or quantity produced, 10 000, where:

$$\text{Average cost} = \frac{\text{total costs}}{\text{output}}$$

Marginal cost

Total costs can also be used to calculate the MARGINAL COST of production. The marginal cost is the extra cost of producing more output. If the cost of producing 10 000 magnets is £30 000, and the cost of producing 10 001 is £30 002, then the marginal cost of production of 1 extra unit is £2. If the cost of producing 11 000 magnets is £32 000, the marginal cost of producing 1 000 extra magnets is £2 000 (or £2 per unit).

The marginal cost is the difference between the total costs of the higher level of output and the existing level of output.

Accounting and opportunity costs

So far this unit has dealt with **accounting costs**. These costs deal with the value of resources used up in production. For example, when a business buys materials they might cost £10 000. Cost and management accountants calculate the production costs and sales revenue of a business (see unit 20). This information is used by management to make decisions. Financial accountants show the financial position of a business, taking into account costs and revenues, in accounts such as the profit and loss account (see unit 20). They must follow strict guidelines when presenting these figures.

However, it can sometimes be helpful for a business to think of the OPPORTUNITY COST of a decision. This is the benefit foregone from the next best alternative to that chosen. If a business buys a new machine costing £300 000, the opportunity cost might the benefits lost because it couldn't spend £300 000 training staff and making them more productive.

Revenue

SALES REVENUE is the revenue or income a business receives from selling its products. It is also sometimes referred to as SALES TURNOVER or TOTAL REVENUE. It can be calculated using the formula:

Total revenue = quantity sold x average selling price

If the quantity sold increases at the same price, then total revenue will increase. For example, if a business increases sales from 10 000 to 20 000 units at an average price of £2, total revenue will increase from £20 000 to £40 000 (10 000 x £2 to 20 000 x £2).

The average selling price is the same as the AVERAGE REVENUE (or AVERAGE TURNOVER). Both are equal to:

$$\frac{\text{total revenue}}{\text{quantity sold.}}$$

Equally, a rise in price will increase total revenue if sales remain constant. For example, if a business sells 10 000 units and prices increase from £2 per unit to £2.50, total revenue will increase from £20 000 to £25 000 (10 000 x £2 to 10 000 x £2.50).

If businesses raise their price, they may find that the number of sales declines. How much sales are affected depends upon the **elasticity of demand** for the product. In turn, whether the percentage change in sales is large or small then affects the impact of the price change on sales revenue (see unit 17).

A total revenue curve can be drawn on a graph, as in Figure 21.4. Total revenue is put on the vertical axis and output on the horizontal axis. The average price of £2 per unit remains the same however much is sold. So if 10 000 are sold, total revenue is £20 000. If 50 000 are sold, total revenue is £100 000. If price changes as sales change, then the curve will be a different shape depending upon how one variable changes with the other.

Most businesses sell at least two products or product variations. So the 'average price' received on **all** sales is the average price over the product range. But businesses often calculate total revenue for sales from just one product. They might, for example, want to know how total revenue would be affected if they put up prices. So total revenue can be applied to the total sales of a business, or just one product line.

Some businesses attempt to maximise their sales revenue because the costs of producing extra units of output are very small. Maximising sales revenue is a way of maximising profit. These businesses are then said to be **revenue orientated**.

Profit

PROFIT is the difference between revenue and costs:

Profit = total revenue - total cost

If a business makes a LOSS, it means that total revenue is less than total costs. A loss is a negative profit. Sometimes, a business making a loss is said to be **in the red** and a business making a profit is **in the black**. These expressions come from bookkeeping entries in past times, when plus figures were written in black ink and minus figures were written in red ink in business accounts.

There are many different types of profit shown in the accounts of businesses. The definitions vary because different measures of revenue and cost are used. Some of the key types of profit are as follows.

Gross profit GROSS PROFIT is sales revenue minus cost of sales. COST OF SALES are the direct costs of production. So gross profit is the profit made from sales of goods before overheads (indirect costs) have been taken into account. For a construction business it could be the revenue from the sale of houses minus the direct costs of production, such as materials and wages of construction workers. It would not include overhead costs, such as the wages of office staff or promotion. For a clothing shop, it could be revenue from sales of shoes minus the cost of buying in shoes and wages of shop staff. It would not include indirect costs, such as administration costs at head office.

Gross profit = sales revenue - cost of sales

Operating profit OPERATING PROFIT is total sales revenue minus both the direct costs and indirect costs of production. It is therefore gross profit minus indirect costs (or overheads):

Operating profit = sales revenue - (cost of sales + overheads)

Pre-tax profit This is also called **profit on ordinary activities before taxation**. It is all revenues minus all costs. So it is operating profit **plus** non-sales revenues, such as interest received or income from the sale of part of a business **minus** other costs such as interest paid or exceptional items. Exceptional items are costs which the business deems to be one-off costs, such as making large numbers of workers redundant.

Sometimes the term **net interest** is used. This is the difference between interest earned and interest paid. If net interest is positive (interest earned is greater than interest paid) then it is added to operating profit to show profit before tax is taken into account. If net interest is negative (interest paid is greater than interest earned) it is taken away from operating profit.

Profit after tax This is pre-tax profits minus corporation tax, a tax on company profits.

Most profit made by businesses is recurring profit. It is made from continued sales of goods and services over time.

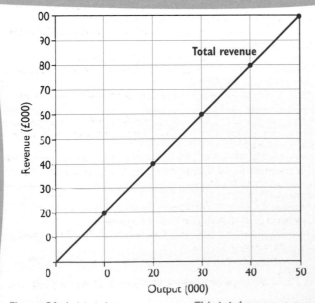

Figure 21.4 *A total revenue curve.* **This total revenue curve is drawn on the assumption that the price of each unit is £2 per unit.**

But some profit is 'one-off' profit. For example, a business may sell part of its operations to another business. This can only happen once. Some financial journalists talk about 'profit quality'. If profits are of high quality, it means that they are likely to recur in the future. Low quality profits are one-off profits.

The uses of profits

A business **utilises** its profits after tax in two main ways.

Distribution to owners The owners of the business may receive a share of the profit made. In a company, this is known as the DIVIDEND.

Retained or undistributed profit The business may choose not to distribute profits after taxes to its owners. It may keep back the profit. In a company, this RETAINED or UNDISTRIBUTED PROFIT is added to its RESERVES. In future years, the reserves can be used for a variety of purposes. They can be used to buy other businesses or to pay for investment, for example building new factories or buying new machinery. Or they can be used to continue paying the owners of the business a dividend even when it has not made enough profit to pay for (or **cover**) that dividend. The dividend in a bad year for the business is therefore being paid from the profits made in previous years.

The significance of profit

The world today is dominated by capitalist economies such as the USA, the UK, Germany and Japan. In a capitalist economy, profit plays a vital role in allocating resources.

Businesses and industries which are successful in selling products that customers want tend to make high profits. This acts as a signal to the businesses themselves and to competitors. Attracted by the high profit, businesses invest in order to generate further profit. Output expands, giving customers more of what they want to buy.

On the other hand, if businesses are making losses, they will tend to shrink in size. Loss making businesses will find it more difficult to generate cash to pay for new investment. Ultimately, a loss making business will be forced to close down. Businesses make losses because they cannot sell the products at a profit. Customers are not prepared to buy enough or to pay a high enough price. Losses are a signal that the business is not providing what customers want to buy.

For individual businesses, high profits provide cash for expansion. Most investment by UK businesses is paid for from retained profit. But high profits allow a business to get loans if necessary. They also make the business attractive to new investors if it is prepared to sell new shares.

There are different ways of judging whether a business is making particularly high profits.

- The size of the business must be taken into account. BT, for example, should make much higher profits than a local builder because BT is much larger if measured by its sales and the value of its assets.
- Profitability tends to differ from industry to industry. A business may be highly profitable compared to other businesses in its industry. But it could be making below average profits for the whole economy. A good measure to use when comparing profits within an industry is the PROFIT MARGIN. This is profit as a proportion of revenue. If one business is making £6 profit on £100 of sales (a profit margin of 6 per cent), it is perhaps doing better than another business in the same industry making only £3 of profit on £100 of sales (a profit margin of 3 per cent).
- Profitability often depends on the state of the economy. If the economy is in **recession** (see unit 50), businesses may struggle to make a profit. If the economy is in boom, it may be easier to make profits.

66key terms 99

Average revenue or turnover - **the average selling price, equal to total revenue ÷ quantity sold.**

Average cost - **the cost per unit of production, calculated by total costs ÷ output.**

Cost of sales - **an accounting term for direct costs.**

Costs - **the expenses a business incurs when producing goods or supplying services.**

Direct or prime costs - **costs which are linked directly to production of a good or service.**

Dividend - **the part of profit given to the shareholders of a company.**

Fixed costs - **costs which remain the same whatever the level of output of the business.**

Gross profit - **total sales revenue or turnover minus cost of sales (the direct costs of production).**

Indirect costs or overhead costs - **costs which cannot be identified directly with production of a specific good or service.**

Long run - **period of time over which all costs are variable costs and there are no fixed costs.**

Loss - **the opposite of profit, when total revenues are less than costs.**

Marginal cost - **the cost of producing an additional unit of output.**

Operating profit - **total sales revenue minus both the direct costs and indirect costs of production.**

Opportunity cost - **the cost of a decision as measured by the benefits foregone of the next best alternative.**

Pre-tax profits - **in accounting terms this is profit on ordinary activities before taxation.**

Profit - **the difference between revenue and cost.**

Profit after tax - **all revenues minus all costs after the tax on profits has been deducted.**

Profit margin - **profit as a proportion of revenue, expressed as a percentage.**

Profit utilisation - **how a business uses its profits once made.**

Reserves - **past profits which have been kept back for future use by the business.**

Retained or undistributed profit - **profit which is not distributed to the owners of a business but is kept back to put into its reserves for future use.**

Sales revenue (or sales turnover or total revenue) - **the flow of cash into a business from sales of goods and services. It can be calculated as quantity sold x average price.**

Semi-variable costs - **costs which have both a fixed cost and variable cost element.**

Short run - **period of time over which there is at least one fixed cost.**

Total cost - **the sum of all costs of a business over a period of time.**

Variable costs - **costs which vary directly with the output of the business.**

checklist

1 What is the difference between fixed and variable costs?
2 What is the difference between the short run and the long run for a business?
3 'Wages can be both a direct cost and an indirect cost.' Explain why.
4 A business produces 100 units of output per week at a total cost of £2 000. (a) What is its average cost of production? (b) If it could produce 101 units for £2 010, what would be its marginal cost?
5 A business produces 39 units of output per month at a total cost of £1 180. If its marginal cost of production is £20, what would be (a) the total cost and (b) the average cost of producing 40 units?

6 What is the difference between accounting cost and opportunity cost?
7 How can the sales revenue of a business be calculated?
8 Draw a total revenue curve on a graph for sales between 0 and 1 000 assuming that each unit is sold for £5.
9 Distinguish between gross profit and profit after tax.
10 Explain how businesses use their profit after tax.
11 A coal mining company has been making losses for the past three years and there is little sign that it will return to profitability. What are the implications of this for (a) the company and (b) the allocation of resources in the economy?

Talbot Ltd is a company which makes time pieces commissioned to order. It has been making clocks and sun dials for the past twenty years, ranging from small clocks costing £500 to a £100 000 sundial for a company headquarters in Hong Kong. The costs of the business last year are shown in Table 21.1 when it worked on 60 commissions and its sales revenue was £320 000.

During last year, the company failed in a bid for a commission priced at £100 000. The manufacturing cost of the commission would have been £50 000, with no changes in other costs.

The company has four directors, all of whom work full time for the business in various capacities. Kim Talbot is the creative director and Fiona Buckton is production director. Matthew Filby is responsible for marketing and spends much of his time visiting potential customers. Bill Shannon runs the office and the office staff. Although each of the four has a main role, they all share the work whenever necessary. If Matthew can't visit a client, for instance, any of the other three may go instead. Most importantly, all have an input into the design work, contributing ideas and technical knowledge.

Banking charges and interest	10 000
Insurance	3 000
Accountancy fees	2 000
Directors' salaries	130 000
Total manufacturing costs	120 000
Rent and rates	12 000
Other overhead costs	23 000

Table 21.1 *Costs (£)*

1 What is meant by the term 'sales revenue'? (2 marks)
2 (a) Explain which costs would be classified as (i) fixed costs and (ii) variable costs for the company if all costs are either fixed or variable. (6 marks)
   (b) Explain how TWO of the 'Other overhead costs' might be semi-variable costs . (4 marks)
3 Table 21.1 shows the costs of the business.
   (a) Draw a graph showing the fixed cost line for the company. Plot between 0 and 60 commissions on the horizontal axis.
   (b) The variable cost of 60 commissions was £120 000. Assuming that variable cost of each commission is the same, draw a variable cost line on a graph with between 0 and 60 commissions on the horizontal axis.
   (c) Using your answers to (a) and (b) plot the total cost line onto a graph with between 0 and 60 commissions on the horizontal axis. (8 marks)
4 Analyse the possible effects on profit last year if the company had won the £100 000 commission. (10 marks)
5 Discuss the possible advantages and disadvantages to the company of the directors being able to share roles within the company. (10 marks)

22 Break-even analysis

Virtual music stores

Knowledge The world of recorded music is in a state of flux. Take, for example, a machine made by Virtual Music Stores (VMS). It looks like a listening post. But this machine contains a range of music several times larger than what is on offer physically on the racks. The music is supplied via a satellite, so the range of music potentially on offer is limitless. Customers can choose tracks or whole CDs. Then a CD is burned for them by another machine in a back room. The result is a custom made CD. The machines are currently on trial in the Reading area.

Application The *break-even point* of the machines - the level of *sales* where it just covers its *costs* - is just 52 CD sales per week to stores. VMS is charging rent of £500 a month to hire its machines. The retailer receives 20 per cent of the price of each CD it sells at an average price of £11.20.

Analysis In theory, the VMS machines could be installed anywhere, from supermarkets to corner stores. In practice, 52 CD sales per week just to break-even means that there must be a reasonable existing demand for CDs. However, VMS is less worried about store take-up than the attitude of the music companies supplying the music. To date, it has only persuaded EMI/Virgin, BMG and a number of small independent labels to licence around 5 000 tracks. For the VMS machine to become a mass market provider, VMS needs to sign up the big world labels, such as Sony and Warner.

Evaluation Sony and Warner have so far resisted attempts to move away from distributing their music on pre-recorded CDs. Some argue that they are burying their heads in the sand. Pirated music, particularly via the Internet, is a growing problem. VMS could provide them with a way of offering huge amounts of their music to potential customers browsing in a store. Without their co-operation, however, VMS won't take off.

Adapted from the *Financial Times*, 6.11.2001.

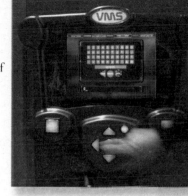

Break-even

To survive in the long term, businesses must make a profit (see unit 21). So it is important for a business to know how much it needs to sell before it starts to make a profit. This is where its total revenue exactly equals its total costs, known as the BREAK-EVEN POINT. At this level of output or sales, the business is neither making a **profit** (where total revenue is greater than total costs) nor making a **loss** (where total revenue is less than total costs). Any extra sales will push the business into profit. Any fewer sales and the business will start to make a loss.

Take as an example a sandwich business selling 500 sandwiches per week.
- It charges its customers an average £1 per sandwich. So if it sold 500 sandwiches per week, **total revenue** (see unit 21) would be £500 (500 x £1).
- It has **fixed costs** (see unit 21) of £800 per week.
- Its **variable costs** (see unit 21) are 60p per sandwich. If it sold 500 sandwiches, its total variable costs would be £300 (500 x £0.60). Or if total variable costs are £300, the variable cost per sandwich would be £0.60 (£300 ÷ 500).
- The **total costs** of producing 500 sandwiches per week are therefore £1 100. This is fixed costs of £800 added to the variable costs of £300.
- It is currently making a **loss** of £600 per week. This is the difference between total revenue of £500 and total costs of £1 100.

So how much more does it need to sell to break-even? The break-even point is 2 000 sandwiches per week. Selling 2 000 sandwiches would bring in total revenue of £2 000 (2 000 x £1). Total costs would be £2 000 too. This is made up of fixed costs of £800 and variable costs of £1 200

(2 000 sandwiches x £0.60).

There are three main ways in which the break-even point can be calculated.

- Through trial and error. Choose a level of output and work out whether a profit is being made or a loss. If it is a profit, reduce the level of output and make the calculations again. If it is a loss, increase the level of output. Carry on doing this until the break-even point is found.
- Calculate the **contribution** made (see unit 23). This is a quicker way of calculating break-even than through trial and error.
- Use a BREAK-EVEN CHART. The advantage of doing this is that the chart also gives information about the range of profit to be made as output varies.

Break-even charts

One way of finding out the break-even point is to draw a graph from cost and revenue figures. Table 22.1 shows the costs and revenue of the sandwich business at different levels of output.

Costs Fixed costs, including rent, wages and repayments on a loan, are £800 per week. The variable costs, which are mostly the costs of the ingredients to make the sandwich, are 60p per sandwich. Fixed costs stay at £800 per week whatever the level of output. However, variable costs are zero when no sandwiches are made. They increase from £300 when 500 sandwiches are made to £1 800 when 3 000 sandwiches are made. The total costs are the fixed costs plus the total variable costs. So when 3 000 sandwiches are made, total costs are £800 + £1 800 = £2 600.

Revenue Assume that sandwiches are sold at £1.00 each. So

Output (Number of sandwiches per week)	Fixed cost £	Variable cost £	Total cost £	Total revenue £	Profit (+)/loss (-) £
500	800	300	1100	500	- 600
1000	800	600	1400	1000	- 400
1500	800	900	1700	1500	- 200
2000	800	1200	2000	2000	0
2500	800	1500	2300	2500	+ 200
3000	800	1800	2600	3000	+ 400

Table 22.1 *Costs, revenue and profits for a sandwich business*

when no sandwiches are sold there is no revenue. If 1 000 sandwiches per week are sold, total revenue is £1 000. If 3 000 sandwiches are sold per week, total revenue is £3 000.

Break-even It is possible to read off the break-even point from Table 22.1. It is at 2 000 sandwiches per week, where both total costs and total revenue equal £2 000.

The break-even chart in Figure 22.1 is drawn from the data in Table 22.1.

Total revenue and total cost lines The total revenue and total cost lines are upward sloping. They show that revenues and costs increase as output increases. The fixed cost line is drawn as a dotted line on the diagram. It is horizontal because fixed costs remain the same whatever the level of output. Total variable costs are the vertical distance between the total cost line and the fixed cost line.

Break-even The break-even point is where the total revenue and the total cost line cross. This is at an output of 2 000 sandwiches, the break-even level of output or sales.

Profit and loss If output is to the right of the break-even point,

the business will make a profit. If output is to the left of the break-even point, the business will make a loss. The amount of profit or loss is shown by the vertical distance between total revenue and total costs and can be read off the vertical axis. Figure 22.1 shows that:

- profit is £400 per week if 3 000 sandwiches are sold per week (revenue of £3 000 - total costs of £2 600);
- there is a loss of £400 per week if sales are 1 000 sandwiches (revenue of £1 000 - total costs of £1 400).

The margin of safety

If a business is making a profit, sales must be at a higher level than the break-even level. The difference between actual profitable sales and the break-even level is the MARGIN OF SAFETY. For example, in Figure 22.2, if current output is 3 000 sandwiches per week, then the margin of safety is 1 000 sandwiches (3 000 minus the break-even level of 2 000).

The greater the margin of safety, the less **risk** there is likely

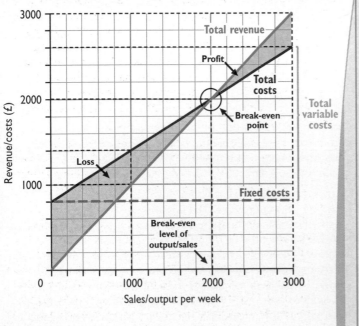

Figure 22.1 *A break-even chart*

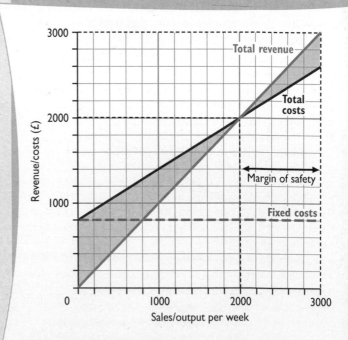

Figure 22.2 *The margin of safety*

Paul Roberts makes Spanish guitars from a rented room in a rural business park. Figure 22.3 shows a break-even chart for his business.

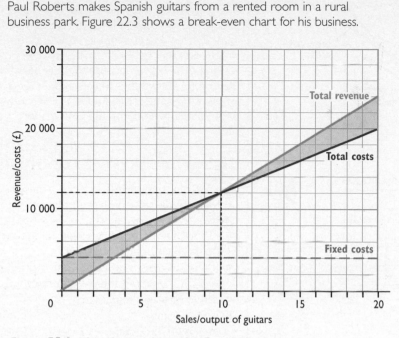

Figure 22.3 *A break-even chart for Paul Roberts' business*

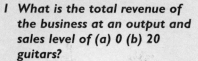

1 **What is the total revenue of the business at an output and sales level of (a) 0 (b) 20 guitars?**
2 **What are the fixed costs of the business?**
3 **(a) What is the break-even level of output? (b) What are the revenue and costs at this level?**
4 **What is the margin of safety if the business sells (a) 12 guitars; (b) 20 guitars?**
5 **If the business produces and sells 15 guitars, what would be the:**
   (a) total revenue; (b) total costs; (c) profit or loss
   (d) total variable costs;
   (e) variable cost of each guitar?

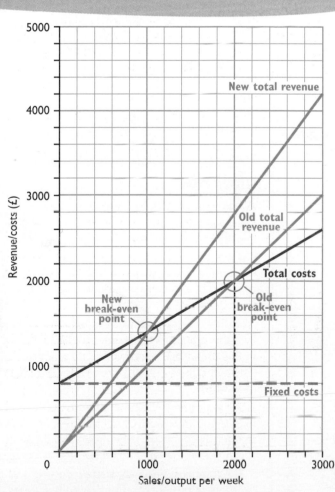

Figure 22.4 *A rise in price leads to a fall in the break-even level of output*

to be that the business will fall into loss.

Changing revenue and costs

Break-even analysis can be used to see what would happen if prices or costs changed.

Changes in price If prices **increase**, total revenue at any given level of output will rise. For instance, the sandwich business may increase its price from £1.00 to £1.40. So total revenue would increase from £3 000 to £4 200 when 3 000 sandwiches were sold. As Figure 22.4 shows, the total revenue line becomes steeper with a price increase. The break-even point falls from 2 000 to 1 000. So the business has to sell fewer sandwiches at the higher price to break-even. At an output of 3 000 the margin of safety also rises, from 1 000 to 2 000.

If the business **cut** prices, the total revenue line would become shallower, the break-even output would rise and the margin of safety would be smaller. Lower prices means it has to sell more sandwiches to break-even.

Changes in fixed costs If fixed costs rise, the total cost curve will shift up by the amount of the rise in fixed costs. For instance, if fixed costs rose by £200 per week, from £800 to £1 000, then total costs would also rise by £200 per week. The break-even output would rise to 2 500 sandwiches. The business would need to sell more sandwiches to break-even because costs have risen. This is shown in Figure 22.5 (over the page). If 3 000 sandwiches were actually sold, the margin of safety would fall from 1 000 to 500

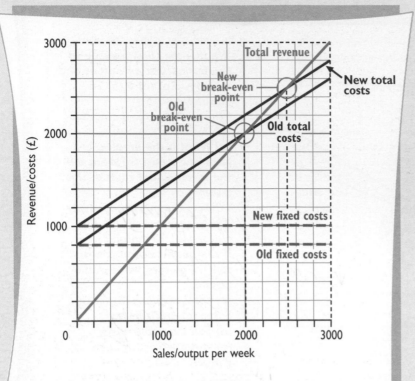

Figure 22.5 *A rise in fixed costs leads to a rise in the break-even level of output*

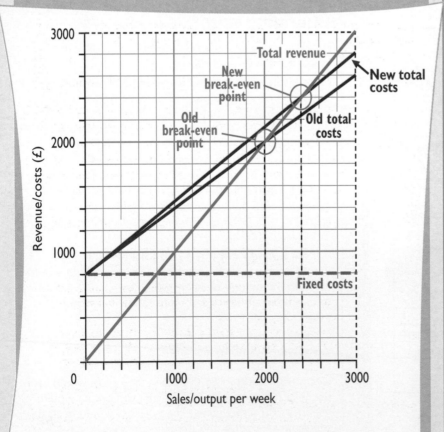

Figure 22.6 *A rise in variable costs leads to a rise in the break-even level of output*

sandwiches.

Changes in variable costs A rise in variable costs will lead to the total cost line becoming steeper. At any given level of output, fixed costs stay the same. But variable costs and therefore total costs will be greater. The break-even level of output will rise because the business has to sell more sandwiches to cover its costs. This is shown in Figure 22.6. And if 3 000 sandwiches were actually sold, the margin of safety would fall.

Using break-even analysis

Break-even analysis is used in business as a tool to make decisions about the future. It helps answer 'what if' questions. For instance:
- if price went up, what would happen to the break-even point?
- if the business introduced a new product line, how many would the new product have to sell to at least break-even?
- if the business is just starting up, what has to be the level of output to prevent a loss being incurred?
- what will happen to the break-even point if costs are forecast to rise?
- would the break-even point be lower if components were bought in from outside suppliers rather than being made in-house?

Break-even analysis is also found in **business plans**. Banks often ask for business plans when deciding whether or not to give a loan. So break-even analysis can be vital in gaining finance.

Problems with break-even analysis

Break-even analysis is a simple tool for assessing financial viability. It can be used to consider the break-even point of the whole business. It can also be used to assess the break-even point of a new product, a product range, or a part of a business operation. But it does have drawbacks.

Non-linear relationships Most businesses do not face the straight cost and revenue lines shown in this unit. Costs and revenue may not rise at a constant rate as output increases for a number of reasons.

Some businesses face a fall in total revenue at high output. For example, a business may have to offer discounts on large orders. So the total revenue line may be curved.

The total cost line may also be curved. For example, a business can buy in bulk at lower costs. So costs may fall as output rises. Or a business may face higher costs if workers have to be paid overtime to increase output.

Ryestairs is a Benedictine monastery which earns part of its living by running The Haven, a guest house and retreat centre. It charges £80 per day for full board and overnight stay per person. The variable costs of items such as food and laundry cleaning come to £30 per day per visitor. The fixed costs of running the business venture are £50 000 per year.

1 Draw a break-even diagram for The Haven. The horizontal axis will be the 'number of overnight stays per year'. Label the axis up to 1 500 overnight stays per year. Mark on it the break-even level of output.

2 The management of The Haven decide to raise the price to £110 per day. (a) Draw a new total revenue curve on your diagram for question 1. (b) Show on the diagram what has happened to the break-even level of output.

3 If prices remained at £80 per day and variable costs are still £30, but The Haven cut its fixed costs to £40 000 per year, what would happen to the break-even level of output? Illustrate your answer by drawing a new diagram.

4 Prices remain at £80 per day and fixed costs remain at £50 000, but The Haven manages to reduce its variable costs. Explain, using a diagram, the effects of this on: (a) the break-even point, (b) the margin of safety assuming the number of overnight stays is 1 200 a year.

Uncertain data Break-even analysis is only as good as the figures that are used. For instance, if a business overestimates the price at which it can sell its product, it will underestimate the break-even level of output. If it underestimates its variable costs, it will underestimate the break-even level of output. Recessions, changes in interest rates or world economic crises can all affect prices and costs. In these cases, a business may be unable to accurately predict revenue and costs.

Unsold output Break-even analysis assumes that all production is sold. But every product that is made is not always sold. Some goods are made, but remain unsold as they go out of fashion. Also production may be put into **stock** (see unit 45) rather than being sold. If goods remain unsold, production costs will not relate to the number of goods sold, only the number produced. So predictions from break-even analysis are likely to be inaccurate.

Multi-product businesses Many businesses sell a variety of products, each with its own price and costs. But the fixed costs of a business usually relate to more than one product. A business may find it difficult to decide what proportion of fixed costs to allocate to a particular product. Unless this is accurate, break-even analysis may be incorrect.

Stepped fixed costs Break-even charts show that fixed costs do not change as output rises. In practice, fixed costs are often 'stepped'. They stay the same as output rises. But a business may reach a point where it has to buy new machinery to produce any more products. Fixed costs will rise sharply at this point.

❝keyterms❞

Break-even chart - **a graph giving total costs and total revenue lines over a range of output, and where the break-even point is shown.**
Break-even point - **where the total costs of a business are exactly equal to the total revenue. It is the level of output or sales where a business makes no profit or loss.**
Margin of safety - **the difference between the level of output at which a business breaks-even and the actual or projected level of output greater than the break-even point.**

checklist

1 What is the difference between total revenue and total costs?
2 A business has fixed costs of £1 million and variable costs of £2 million when it produces 100 000 units. What is its break-even point?
3 What lines might be drawn on a break-even chart?
4 Why is the total cost line likely to start at greater than zero on the vertical axis?
5 A business is currently producing 100 units per month and earning £60 000 in profit. It calculates that its break-even level of output is 80 units per month. What is its margin of safety?
6 Explain what would happen to the break-even point for a business if (a) it were forced to accept permanently lower prices for its products; (b) its insurance premiums were cut by 20 per cent; (c) the Bank of England cut interest rates substantially.
7 Why might a business conduct a break-even analysis?
8 What problems are there in using break-even analysis?
9 State whether the business is making a profit, a loss or breaking-even if:
(a) total revenue is £2 million and total costs are £1.5 million;
(b) total revenue is £250 000, fixed costs are £100 000 and total variable costs are £150 000;
(c) the average selling price is £5, the variable cost per unit is £2, fixed costs are £10 000 and 3 000 units are produced and sold.

The market for very lightweight bicycle frames is small. But some riders are prepared to pay high prices for a frame to compete in races. Li Chen runs a business making these frames to order. Each frame is unique, in that it is made up to the size of the rider. His current price is £2 000 per frame.

Li makes the frames in a business unit on a business park in South London. Rent and wages are his main fixed costs, which come to £40 000 per year. The variable cost per frame is £1 200. He is currently producing 60 frames per year.

The order book for the business is more than full, with customers having to wait three months for delivery. Li is thinking that perhaps he is selling his frames too cheaply and that he could push the price up to, say, £2 500.

Alternatively, he could expand, but this would mean moving to larger premises and taking on more staff. Fixed costs would rise to £80 000 but the variable cost per frame could be cut to £1 000 with Li being able to negotiate better prices for his inputs.

Li is undecided about what might be the best course of action: to stay as he is, put up his prices or increase productive capacity.

1 Draw a break-even chart for his business at the moment. On it mark (a) the break-even level of output and (b) the margin of safety. (6 marks)
2 What is his current profit or loss? (2 marks)
3 If he were to increase his price to £2 500, explain what would happen to the break-even point and his level of profit if his current level of output (a) remains the same or (b) were to fall to 50 frames per year. (6 marks)
4 Explain what will happen to the break-even level of output if he expands his productive capacity. (4 marks)
5 Discuss whether Li should expand, raise prices or stay as he is. Justify your answer, looking at both financial and non-financial factors. (12 marks)

Express Dairies

Knowledge Express Dairies is a company which processes and delivers milk and related products to millions of doorsteps in the UK. In 2000, it announced a trial to deliver Littlewoods catalogues in the North West of England.

Application How much could delivering *mail order* catalogues *contribute* towards paying the *fixed costs* of the delivery system and how much could it *contribute* in *profit* to the *company*?

Analysis The variable cost of delivering catalogues to Express Dairies is likely to be low. The catalogues have to be handled and sorted at milk delivery depots in the North West. Then they have to be delivered by workers on their rounds. However, the extra time spent delivering catalogues is likely to be small because workers will pass the front of any house to which a catalogue has to be delivered. Even less cost would be incurred if the catalogue were delivered to an existing Express Dairies customer. So most of the amount paid by Littlewoods to Express Dairies for deliveries is likely to contribute either to paying the fixed costs of the dairy company or to earning profit.

Evaluation Express Dairies has, over the years, experimented with delivering a variety of products apart from milk to its customers. The potential for such deliveries to contribute towards fixed cost and profit is considerable. Its main problem seems to be finding products apart from milk which customers want to buy or which suppliers wish to deliver to homes. Perhaps mail order catalogues could be added to orange juice and bread on the milk floats? Only time will tell whether it is profitable to both Littlewoods and Express Dairies.

Adapted from *The Guardian*, 11.11.2000.

Contribution

CONTRIBUTION is the difference between sales revenue and variable cost. For example, say that the owner of a sportswear shop buys trainers at £50 a pair and sells them for £110. The shop is small and the only variable cost of the business is the cost of buying in stock. All other costs are fixed. So the £60 earned from selling a pair of trainers is a contribution. It is a contribution:
- first to paying off the **fixed costs** of the business;
- and then towards making a **profit**.

As a formula:

Contribution = sales revenue - variable cost
(£60 = £110 - £50)

Contribution per unit and total contribution

It is possible for a business to distinguish between the unit contribution of a product and its total contribution.

Unit contribution A manufacturer may produce a lathe for a variable cost of £100 000. If it sells the lathe for £150 000, the contribution of this product is £50 000. This is the unit contribution. It is the contribution from selling a **single** item or unit. As a formula:

Contribution per unit = selling price per unit - variable cost per unit
(£50 000 = £150 000 - £100 000)

Total contribution The manufacturer may sell 20 machines this year at a price of £150 000. The total revenue would then be £3 million (£150 000 x 20). If the total variable cost of production this year was £2 million, total contribution

would be £1 million. Total contribution is the value of total sales over a time period minus total variable cost. As a formula:

Total contribution = total revenue - total variable cost
(£1 million = £3 million - £2 million)

Total contribution can also be calculated by adding the contribution of each item sold (i.e. adding all the contributions per unit) using the formula:

Total contribution = contribution per unit x number of units sold
(£1 million = £50 000 x 20)

If a business sells a number of different products, total contribution can be calculated for each product. Table 23.1 shows a manufacturer making lathes and milling machines. It sells in total £5 million worth of lathes, whose total variable cost is £4 million. So lathes make a total contribution of £1 million. Milling machines, in comparison, have total sales of £10 million and total variable costs of £6 million. So milling machines make a total contribution of £4 million. Sales of both machines make a total contribution of £5 million (£1 million + £4 million). This £5 million contribution is used to pay the £3 million fixed costs of the business and generate a profit of £2 million for the year.

Contribution costing

Contribution can be used as a decision making tool by a business. CONTRIBUTION COSTING (or MARGINAL COSTING) considers the variable cost of a product or product range, and the contribution it makes towards fixed cost and profit. In Table 23.1, for example, milling machines are

	Lathes	Milling machines	Both machines
Quantity sold	40	200	
Price	£125,000	£50,000	
Variable cost per machine	£100,000	£30,000	
Total sales revenue	£5 million	£10 million	£15 million
Total variable cost	£4 million	£6 million	£10 million
Total contribution	£1 million	£4 million	£5 million
Total fixed cost			£3 million
Profit			£2 million

Table 23.1 *Contribution made by lathes and milling machines over a twelve month period*

making much more of a contribution than lathes. The machine tool business could, on the basis of this, decide to specialise in milling machines and stop the production of lathes. On the other hand, it could judge that it would be difficult to expand sales of milling machines at a profit. Lathes might make less contribution, but it is still a £1 million contribution. The business could judge that this would be more than the extra contribution to be made from closing down lathe production and expanding milling machine production.

Contribution pricing

Contribution pricing (or **marginal pricing**, see unit 15) is a method of pricing based upon contribution. What if the manufacturer in Table 23.1 is approached by a customer and asked to supply a lathe at a price of £110 000? Usually the price of lathes sold is £125 000 and the variable cost is £100 000. So each lathe sold makes a contribution of £25 000. On this order it would only be £10 000 (£110 000 - £100 000). Should it accept the order at the price of £110 000?

Contribution pricing would suggest that it probably should accept the order. This is because £10 000 of contribution is £10 000 towards paying the fixed costs of the business and helping it to make a profit. The alternative (the **opportunity cost**, see unit 21) is to reject the order. Without the order, there will be no contribution. £10 000 of contribution will be lost.

So with contribution pricing, the manufacturer should accept any order so long as it makes a positive contribution. This is true even if it is clear that the order will not make a profit, i.e. cover **both** its variable costs and fixed costs. Assume that the business expected the fixed costs of a lathe to be £12 500. The £10 000 contribution is less than the fixed cost. But £10 000 towards paying the fixed cost is still better than nothing, which would be the case if the order was turned away.

In the long term, a business has to make a total contribution which is greater than fixed costs. This is because businesses have to make a profit in the long term to survive. Accepting new orders which fail to cover fixed costs might make poor business sense in the short run in certain situations.

- If production is running at full capacity, then accepting new unprofitable orders will push back delivery dates for existing, hopefully profitable, orders. This could damage the reputation of the business for reliability.
- If existing customers, paying a higher price, force the business to extend lower prices to their orders, then the

business could suffer a sharp drop in profitability. If the business is to set different prices for different customers (**price discrimination**, see unit 15), it must be able to stop customers currently buying at a high price from buying at lower prices.

Contribution and break-even

Contribution can be used to find the **break-even** level of output (see unit 22). At the break-even level of output, the business is neither making a profit or a loss. Sales revenue is just covering total costs, made up of the fixed and variable costs of production. Contribution is sales revenue after variable costs have been taken into account, which is used to pay off the fixed costs of a business and then to earn profit. So at the break-even level, where variable costs are paid but no profit is made, contribution must be equal to fixed costs.

Assume that a manufacturer sells lathes for £125 000 each. The variable cost of production is £100 000. So contribution per lathe is £25 000. If the fixed costs of the company are £250 000, how many lathes does it need to sell just to pay off its fixed costs, i.e. to break-even? The answer is 10 lathes because 10 x £25 000 is equal to £250 000.

This can be expressed as a formula.

$$\text{Break-even level of output} = \frac{\text{total fixed costs}}{\text{selling price per unit - variable cost per unit}}$$

$$= \frac{\text{total fixed costs}}{\text{contribution per unit sold}}$$

So, if total fixed costs are £250 000, the selling price is £125 000 and variable costs are £100 000.

$$\text{Break-even level of output} = \frac{£250\ 000}{£125\ 000 - £100\ 000} = \frac{£250\ 000}{£25\ 000} = 10$$

With fixed costs of £250 000, any sales **above** 10 lathes makes a profit. If sales are less than 10 lathes, the business will make a loss.

If fixed costs were £1 million, the business would need to sell 40 lathes to break-even because 40 x £25 000 is £1 million. If fixed costs were £2 million, the business would need to sell 80 lathes to break-even.

Contribution and profit

Contribution can be a useful way to calculate profit and loss. Assume that a manufacturer sells 30 machines and fixed costs are £250 000. If the contribution per lathe is £25 000, then total contribution will be 750 000 (£25 000 x 30).

Profit can be calculated using the formula:

Profit = total contribution - fixed costs

So profit is £500 000 (£750 000 - £250 000).

This method of calculating profit is often used in management accounting when a business is planning for the future. Questions such as 'How many do we need to sell to break-even?' or 'How many do we need to sell to make a profit of £200 000?' can be answered quickly and simply if the business knows the contribution per unit.

Deneuve is a small exclusive manufacturer of high quality necklaces. Selling at an average price of £500, they certainly aren't cheap. Cherie Deneuve is working out some financial projections for next year. The variable cost per necklace she estimates to be £300. Her fixed costs are likely to be £200 000.

1 Calculate her break-even level of output using the contribution method. Show your calculations carefully.
2 What would be the break-even level of output per year if: (a) variable costs per necklace were £400, selling price was £600 and fixed costs for the year were £400 000; (b) variable costs per necklace were £300, selling price was £600 and fixed costs for the year were £600 000; (c) selling price was £500, variable costs per necklace were £100 and fixed costs for the year were £200 000?
3 Using the initial data, calculate using the contribution method, the profit or loss if she sold: (a) 1 500 necklaces per year; (b) 800 necklaces per year; (c) 1 200 necklaces per year.

✓ checklist

1 'Contribution is used to pay the fixed costs of a business and then to provide profit.' Explain what this means.
2 What is the difference between the contribution made by an individual product and the contribution made by the business as a whole?
3 What is meant by contribution costing?
4 Explain why a business might be prepared to accept an order which is priced below the total cost (i.e. variable cost plus fixed cost) of production.
5 Explain how the break-even point can be calculated using the contribution method.

keyterms

Contribution - **what is left over from sales revenue once variable costs have been paid (i.e. sales revenue - variable cost). It contributes towards paying the fixed costs and profit of a business.**
Contribution (or marginal) costing - **a system of costing where variable costs of production are calculated for individual products, product ranges or production facilities, but fixed costs are only taken into account at the level of the whole business. Fixed costs are therefore not assigned to individual products.**

Helen Lockett is the manager of a 250 room hotel in London. Trade for the past year has been poor. US tourists, in particular, were reluctant to fly after September 11th 2001, fearing terrorist attacks. London tourism was a casualty of this. Occupancy levels at hotels went down and the prices that hotels could charge fell. In early October Helen received a phone call asking whether she had room for 130 conference delegates for Monday 15th October for four nights. The conference organisers would only place the order if all places could be guaranteed. She knew what was coming next if she said yes - a haggle over price.

On the one hand, the conference organisers clearly had a problem. Another hotel may have cancelled. Perhaps the organisers had underestimated demand. Or perhaps the conference was organised at the last minute. Urgent late bookings meant Helen might be in a strong position to negotiate the price. On the other hand, the conference organisers knew that there were plenty of spare hotel rooms in London because of the downturn in the tourist industry. Her hotel might not be the only one where the organisers may find rooms available.

The list price for a night's stay with an evening meal and breakfast usually ranged from £110 to £160. Helen would have to offer a single price per person. She would start the negotiations by asking for £100 per person. If she had to reduce the price, there was a minimum price she could accept. The variable cost for each person staying at the hotel was £40 per night.

Helen estimated that if she took the booking, she would probably have to turn away 50 customers per night who would, on average, have paid £135. The fixed costs of running the hotel were £10 000 per day.

1 Explain the meaning of the term 'fixed cost'. (3 marks)
2 (a) Calculate the contribution per conference guest if Helen Lockett negotiated a price of £80 per person. (1 mark)
  (b) What would be the total contribution made per night for 130 conference delegates at a price of £80 per person? (1 mark)
  (c) What would be the total contribution made by 50 customers staying for one night each paying a price of £135? (1 mark)
3 Assume that the 130 rooms for the week of 15 October would have been vacant. Explain why 'the minimum price she could accept' for hosting the conference delegates would be a little over £40. (5 marks)
4 Analyse whether, at a conference price of £80 per delegate per night, she should accept the booking, or turn it away and receive the 50 customers at an average £130 per customer per night. (8 marks)
5 Discuss the implications for break-even and profitability on London hotels of a rise in confidence on the part of US and other tourists and their greater willingness to travel abroad. (11 marks)

Fearon & Hemphill

Knowledge Fearon & Hemphill is a business based in Northampton that specialises in manufacturing bespoke kitchens, studies and wooden conservatories. In 2002, it took over the Sussex based company Stennet Ltd, which had gone out of business after making a £500 000 loss on a single order. Fearon & Hemphill paid £400 000 for the Sussex firm and expected to invest an equal amount to make it profitable again.

Application Fearon & Hemphill needed to find £800 000 to integrate Stennet Ltd into its business. The need for extra *finance* arose because the *takeover* represented an opportunity for Fearon & Hemphill to expand into a new, potentially *profitable*, geographical *market*. The £800 000 could be raised either *internally*, from within the business, or *externally*, from sources outside.

Analysis The owners of Fearon & Hemphill chose to finance the deal internally. In recent years, profits had been high and £500 000 had been put aside in retained profit. The business also had spare land at its Northampton site, which it aimed to sell for £200 000. The remaining £100 000 would be raised from improved credit control, possible sale of property in Sussex or reductions in stock levels.

Evaluation As a financially cautious business, Fearon & Hemphill hoped to finance the entire deal internally. If it had taken out a loan instead, it would have had to pay interest and repay the loan over time. However, there is still the risk that the £800 000 to be invested in Stennet Ltd could be wasted if Fearon & Hemphill failed to turn the business around. At worst, problems at Stennet Ltd could force the new integrated company out of business. At best, the takeover could considerably increase Fearon & Hemphill's profitability and underlying value.

Why finance?

When a business is first set up, it will almost certainly need money. This finance is usually used for two main purposes.

- The business will need CAPITAL EQUIPMENT, such as machines, vehicles or plant. It may also buy property and premises. Capital equipment and property that a business purchases make up the FIXED ASSETS of the business. The need for capital expenditure varies from business to business and industry to industry. A mobile hairdresser, for example, needs a car and some hairdressing equipment. A car manufacturer will need a large amount of capital equipment, from presses to assembly line robots to paint shops.
- The business also needs **working capital** (see unit 28). These are assets that can be used to pay for the day to day running of the business. They include cash and stocks of materials, and finished goods for sale which can be changed into cash relatively quickly.

Existing businesses may also need finance. The business may want to expand. This will mean that more fixed assets and working capital will be needed. Finance will also be needed simply to keep the business going over time. Capital equipment will wear out and will need replacing. Markets may change, which could increase the need for working capital. If the business makes losses, it will also need finance to cover the loss.

A new business will need EXTERNAL FINANCE to start up. This is money from outside the business and will be discussed in unit 25. An existing business may also use INTERNAL FINANCE. This is money generated from within the business.

Retained profit

Retained profit is the most important source of finance for a business. Businesses need to make a profit if they are to survive in the long term. The profit can be given to the owners of the business (in the case of a company, the shareholders). But it can also be kept back (or **retained**) within the business and used when required. So it is a form of internal finance. An estimated two-thirds of all finance for businesses comes from retained profit in a typical year in the UK.

One advantage of retained profit is that the business does not have to pay interest or dividends on the money, unlike a loan from a bank or a new share issue (see unit 25). It is also a relatively safe way of obtaining finance. There is little risk of not being able to repay the money as with a loan. The business is clearly able to afford this finance because it is coming from within its own profit.

However, there can be a conflict of interests. The owners of the business might want to be paid a higher share of the profits, whilst managers might want to retain profit to reinvest in the business. Further, businesses able to retain large amounts of profit do not always use that profit wisely. They may, for example, expand but fail to make a profit on the expansion.

Sale of assets

Another form of internal finance is the sale of assets. A business may own assets, such as offices or land, which it can sell. The money raised can then be used to finance investment by the business. If the asset being sold is no longer being effectively used by the business, it makes sense to sell it and use the money more profitably. However, sometimes businesses are forced to sell assets when they get into financial trouble. The assets that are sold may be important to the continued profitability of the business.

Sometimes, a business may choose to release cash in property through a **sale and leaseback** arrangement (see unit 27). This is where a property company buys the property from the business and simultaneously agrees to lease (or rent) the property back to the business. The advantage is that the business gets the value of the property in cash immediately. The property company may also become responsible for the upkeep of the building. The disadvantage is that in the long term the business now has to pay rent on the property.

Tighter credit control

Some businesses give customers **trade credit** (see unit 25). They allow the customer to take delivery of goods and pay at a later date, typically after 30 days. However, not all customers pay on time. Businesses often have lists of aged debtors, showing the length of time of outstanding bills, i.e. 30, 60, 90 or over 120 days. Improving credit control should reduce the amount owed and the time taken to pay by trade debtors. This will leave the business with more finance. A problem, however, is that the relationships with customers may be affected if the business puts too much pressure on them to make earlier payments.

Reducing stock levels

Money is tied up in stocks. The business will usually have to pay for stocks of materials well before they are changed into products and sold to raise revenue. Holding too many stocks is also unproductive for the business. The money could be used to finance the purchase of equipment, for example.

But there are dangers in reducing stocks too much. A sudden increase in demand may mean the business is unable to produce the orders that customers want. This could lead to a loss of orders and harm the reputation of the business.

keyterms

Capital equipment - **machines, vehicles and plant used in the production process.**
External finance - **funds obtained from sources outside the business, such as loans from banks or from the sale of shares in a company.**
Fixed assets - **assets (what the business owns) used up over a long period of time, such as machines, vehicles and plant.**
Internal finance - **funds obtained from sources within the business, such as retained profit.**

checklist

1 Why might (a) a new business and (b) an existing business need finance?
2 What is the difference between internal and external finance?
3 Explain how retained profit can be used to finance a business.
4 A business has underutilised assets. How can they be used to finance a new investment project?
5 How can reducing stock levels (a) benefit and (b) harm a business?

Shellam's is a local Nottinghamshire based business specialising in soft drinks. It sells still and carbonated drinks under its own brand name, 'Shellam's', mainly to local stores and caterers. 30 per cent of production by value is on own label products for one of the large supermarket chains.

Turnover has been steadily growing over the past ten years and there is no spare capacity on existing production lines for future growth. The existing carbonated drinks line is now 20 years old and badly outdated. A state-of-the-art production line would double that capacity with the same workers and the same factory space. It should also considerably reduce the amount of downtime for repairs. The existing line is out of action because of faults for up to 30 per cent of any working shift.

However, a new carbonated drinks line will cost £1 million. Installation will cause considerable disruption to supply for up to two weeks and possibly more.

Shellam's in the past has been very conservative about financing. If a new production line is installed, management would want it to be financed internally. The company has £700 000 in the bank in an average week. Although at peak production times of the year this part of its working capital can drop to £400 000. It owns its own site. At the southern end of the site is a parade of shops which is rented out to tenants, bringing in £80 000 a year.

If necessary, though, Shellam's may be forced to consider financing at least part of the investment project externally.

1 Explain what is meant by (a) 'financed internally'; (3 marks)
  (b) 'working capital'. (3 marks)
2 Outline two possible advantages to Shellam's of financing the new production line from retained profit. (6 marks)
3 Examine two alternative ways that Shellam's could finance its new investment internally. (8 marks)
4 Evaluate the risk that Shellam's is taking by spending £1 million on new capital equipment. (10 marks)

25 External finance

CargoLifter

Knowledge CargoLifter is a German company set up in 1996 to build airships. The goal of the company is to produce a huge manned airship which will have the capacity to lift and transport loads of up to 160 tonnes over distances of several thousand kilometres.

Application In 2002, at its *Annual General Meeting*, the *company* acknowledged that it did not have enough *funding* to continue with the *development* project. It would need an additional €420 million (about £250 million). It hopes to get the money from three sources: the sale of new *shares* in the *company*, a *long term bond issue* and a substantial *grant* from *government*.

Analysis Whether it gets the additional funding depends upon potential investors. They need to be convinced that the company will succeed in building the airship and that the company can then make a profit from it. Lending money to the company, through buying its bonds, or buying additional shares are both high risk options. Equally, the government will want to be convinced that jobs will be created in the long term if it is to give financial grants to the company.

Evaluation Costs are likely to rise further and the date at which a prototype would be ready is likely to be put back. Already, the launch date for the prototype has shifted from 2003 to 2005. However, the project has caught the imagination of many investors and there is a need for the service that the airship could offer. The future of the company is therefore on a knife edge and it is difficult to predict whether it will survive or not.

Adapted from the *Financial Times*, 19.3.2002.

Sources of external finance

Businesses in the UK fund part of their financial needs internally, mainly from retained profit (see unit 24). However, **external finance** remains an important way in which businesses can increase the funds available to them, for example for new investment. It involves obtaining funds from sources outside the business itself. The main types of external finance are shown in Figure 25.1. They are sometimes divided into short term and long term sources. These terms tend not to have exact definitions. It could be argued, however, that long term sources are where repayment is only due after a number of years.

The major sources of external finance are borrowing and new equity.

Borrowed money This accounts for over 90 per cent of external funds in the UK. There is a number of different ways in which money can be borrowed, from a bank overdraft, to trade credit, to a debenture. Interest usually has to be paid on borrowed money. So there is a cost to borrowing. The amount borrowed will have to be repaid at some point in the future. So there may be a risk that payments on the borrowing will not be met. Failure to pay debts could lead to the collapse of the business.

New equity EQUITY is the monetary value of a business. The equity of a business belongs to its owners. For example, in a company, equity is owned by the shareholders. In a partnership, it is owned by the partners. With a new business, the owners will put in some money to finance the start up. Existing businesses may choose to ask existing owners or potential new owners to put more money into the business. For a company, this would mean selling new shares.

One advantage to the business of raising new equity is that the money received never has to be repaid, unlike with a loan. Moreover, payments of dividends to the owners (the equivalent of interest on a loan) don't have to made if the business is doing badly or profit needs to be retained for future investment. In this sense, new equity is less risky to the long term viability of the business than taking on a loan. However, where there are several owners of an existing business, the issue of new equity will dilute the value of existing equity.

Bank overdrafts

Most businesses open a current account with a bank or a building society. This is an account into which they can pay

SHORT TERM	LONG TERM
Bank overdraft	Owners' funds/shareholders' funds
Hire purchase/leasing	Hire purchase/leasing
Factoring/invoice discounting	Loans
Trade credit	Government grants

Figure 25.1 *External business finance*

Today, around 30 000 companies use factoring in some form. One such company is Shukla Packaging, a Watford based company which makes wrapping paper and accessories. Its decision to use a factor goes back to 1991 when the UK economy was in recession. At the time, the company experienced a growing problem of getting customers to pay outstanding invoices. This is typical in a recession when so many businesses experience difficulties. Shukla Packaging had seen its customers adding 15-20 days to their payments. It was heading towards a cash flow crisis. Moreover, to cope with this, the managing director of the company, Jitu Shukla, was spending increasing amounts of his time chasing debtors.

So he decided to employ Lombard, now part of Royal Bank of Scotland Commercial Services, to provide factoring services. He went for a comprehensive package of services - advancing cash on security of invoices presented, collecting all monies owed on invoices and providing insurance against any bad debts.

The cost of the credit management and bill collection service has varied from 1-2 per cent of total invoices. This, Mr Shukla says, 'is a fraction of the cost of hiring a sales ledger clerk and a credit controller to chase debts throughout the UK, not to mention the possible legal costs'. The insurance against bad debt paid off in 1992 when Athena, a retailer which owed 40 per cent of Shukla Packaging's total trade credit, collapsed. Without the insurance, Shukla Packaging would have collapsed too.

Adapted from the *Financial Times*, 24.1.2002.

Collecting money

A reference guide

The Business Bank

The Royal Bank of Scotland

1 **Explain the services that Shukla Packaging buys from Royal Bank of Scotland Commercial Services.**
2 **What are (a) the advantages and (b) the disadvantages to Shukla Packaging of employing a factor?**

cash and cheques. Customers might also make payments into the account using debit cards, credit cards, standing orders, direct debits, or direct transfers from the bank of one business to another. Businesses can then withdraw cash from the account or make payments direct from the account, usually by cheques or debit cards.

Current accounts are often kept in credit, where there is a positive amount of money in the account. But they can be in debit, where the business takes more out of the account than it pays in. Usually, a bank would want the business to remove this quickly. But a business can negotiate with the bank to allow it to spend more than is in its account. This amount is the size of its OVERDRAFT. The maximum amount that the bank will allow a business to be overdrawn is the OVERDRAFT LIMIT or CREDIT LIMIT.

The main advantage of an overdraft is its flexibility. The business can reduce the amount borrowed at any time. However, banks charge interest on any amount overdrawn and sometimes increase charges for running an account if it is overdrawn. The amount of interest may also vary according to how reliable the bank thinks the customer will be. A bank often asks to see details of projected cash flow and profit before granting an overdraft. It can ask for immediate repayment of the overdraft at any time. Banks may also want SECURITY against an overdraft. Businesses usually put up assets such as property as security against an overdraft or loan. If they fail to repay money, the bank can sell the property to collect the money it is owed.

Hire purchase

HIRE PURCHASE is where a business takes delivery of equipment, for example, and makes regular payments over a period of time. Ownership only passes to the business after a fixed number of payments. For example, a business may buy a photocopier from a manufacturer and take out a hire purchase agreement with a FINANCE HOUSE. The manufacturer would be paid for the photocopier by the finance house. The business might make an initial payment of £280, followed by 12 monthly payments of £60 to the finance house. With the final payment, the photocopier becomes the property of the business.

The advantage is that payments can be spread over time and don't have to be made in one large lump sum. But the hire purchase price is higher than the purchase price, reflecting the charge that the finance house makes. Also, a business that does not keep up payments may find the asset is repossessed by the finance company.

Leasing

Instead of buying equipment or property outright, a business might lease it. LEASING is a form of renting. So a business may lease a machine or a company car. The company which leases equipment or property usually maintains the asset. So this cost would be included in the lease payment. Leasing is attractive to a business because it doesn't have to pay the full cost of the equipment at the start. It will also get new equipment. A business could lease a £12 000 new piece of equipment for £200 a month over two years, for example. Leasing is also suitable for equipment that is only needed for a particular period, such as a digger on a construction job. Over a long period, though, leasing will almost certainly be more expensive than buying.

If a business takes out a **finance lease**, often over more than three years, it may be given the option to buy the asset at the end of the period. An **operating lease**, however, is usually for

Monotub is a washing machine manufacturer. It has developed a revolutionary new washing machine, the Titan, which has a very large capacity drum and a removable basket. However, the company has experienced problems. The launch of the Titan, Monotub's only product, was delayed twice by technical problems. In January 2001, the company saw its share price halved after it reported a problem with the drive shaft. In September 2001 it finally launched the machine in 7 selected Currys stores.

In October 2001 Monotub announced that it would raise a further £3 million through a new share issue. It intended to sell 2.4 million new shares at 130p each. Monotub will use the money raised to develop more sophisticated tooling processes to cut the cost of making the Titan. The rest will be used to expand production and launch the machine in the continental European market and fund research into a US launch.

Adapted from the *Financial Times*, 27.10.2002.

1 **Explain how Monotub intends to raise finance.**
2 **For what will the finance be used?**
3 **What will be the impact on existing shareholders of the new share issue?**

a shorter period.

Trade credit

Trade credit is usually given by a business to its business customers. The supplier allows the business a period of time (usually 30 days) to pay the invoice for goods or services delivered. So a business buying goods or services from another business can 'borrow' money from its suppliers between the time the goods are delivered to the time they are paid for.

A supplier might offer, say, 30 days trade credit. Trade credit terms can be shorter or longer. A new business with no track record of trading may receive no trade credit. It is too risky for another business to deliver goods and wait for payment from a business which may cease trading before it pays. On the other hand, large businesses making large purchases may be able to negotiate much longer periods of trade credit. A car manufacturer buying £50 million worth of exhausts a year may be able to negotiate a 91 day (i.e. 3 months) credit period with its supplier.

Businesses often pay late. This extends the period of their borrowing. To encourage prompt payment, a discount might be given on the amount owed on the invoice. So the business borrowing the money will pay back less.

Trade credit allows a business to borrow money. But the business is likely to have to extend trade credit to its own business customers in turn (see unit 28). The net amount the business borrows - the difference between the trade credit it receives from its suppliers (its creditors) and the amount it gives to its customers (its debtors) - can then be small.

Factoring

Factoring is a service offered by a financial business, such as a bank, known as a **factor**. The factor takes over the collection of money owed to a business. It pays the business 80 or 90 per cent of the value of outstanding INVOICES (i.e. bills) straight away. The business receives the remaining 10-20 per cent when all the invoices are paid. In effect, the business is 'borrowing' against the money that will be paid in future by its debtors. The charge made by the factor is usually a percentage of the turnover of the business.

This can be a useful service for a business that wants to concentrate on other aspects of its operation than collecting debts from customers. So it is sometimes used by small businesses with few staff. It can also improve cash flow. But it can be expensive and may indicate to others that the business is having financial problems.

Sometimes a business can simply borrow from a factor based on the money it is owed by debtors (known as **invoice discounting**). The responsibility to collect the debt remains with the business. The money must be repaid to the factor within a short period, such as 60 or 90 days.

Loans

A loan is where money is provided by a lender. It then has to be paid back with interest over a period of time by the borrower. A small business, for example, might take out a five year loan with a bank. It would then have to make monthly repayments over the five years.

Banks assess the risk of **default** (i.e. not being paid back) carefully before giving a loan. One way of reducing risk is to demand security. A loan where property is the security, for example, is often called a MORTGAGE.

Large companies are able to borrow on stock markets by issuing CORPORATE BONDS (also known as STOCKS or DEBENTURES). Typically, the company sells the stock at the start, with a promise to repay the amount borrowed at a future point in time. In the meantime, interest will be paid on the stock. The stock will be sold to a number of buyers, who are the lenders. During its lifetime, parts of the stock can be bought and sold in financial markets. So if lenders want to cash in the stock before it is due for repayment, they can do this by finding someone who will buy the stock from them.

Owners' or shareholders' funds

The finance of a business will vary according to its legal organisation (see units 60-61). **Sole traders** often put some of their own money into a business when it first starts. For example, a sole trader setting up a cleaning service might put £1 000 into the business to buy equipment. In a **partnership**, some of the partners often use their own money to start the business. The business might also take on a new partner after a period because it needs an injection of finance.

The owners of a **company** are its SHAREHOLDERS. A new company might be launched by the sale of shares to shareholders. An existing company could raise finance through selling new shares. **Public limited companies**, companies which are listed on a stock exchange can issue new shares relatively easily. This is because the shares can then be traded second hand on the stock exchange. There is no open market for shares in **private limited companies**. So shareholders often tend to be the people who start the business and their family and friends.

New shareholders can be difficult to find. One source of finance for a fast growing private limited company is a VENTURE CAPITALIST. Most venture capitalists are

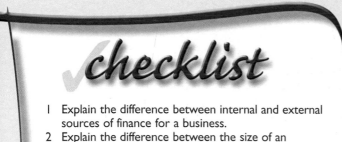

checklist

1 Explain the difference between internal and external sources of finance for a business.
2 Explain the difference between the size of an overdraft and the overdraft limit.
3 Explain one advantage and one disadvantage of hire purchase for a business.
4 How might factoring help a business financially?
5 A business offers 30 days trade credit to its customers. It sent an invoice to a customer 60 days ago. Why does it have a problem?
6 A company wishes to raise finance from its shareholders. How could it do this?
7 Suggest why security might influence whether a business can obtain an overdraft or a loan.
8 What is the difference between a bank loan, a mortgage and a debenture?
9 Why might a business decide to lease equipment on a two year lease but not a ten year lease?

"keyterms

Corporate bonds or debentures or stocks - long term loans by companies, typically from 10-25 years. The loan is often split into small slices so that each part can be traded second hand on stock markets.
Equity or equity capital - the monetary value of a business. This value belongs to the business owners. In a company, equity is the value of the shares.
Factor - a financial business such as a bank which advances money owed to another business on trade credit. Factors also offer the further service of collecting all money owed on trade credit to a business.
Finance house - a financial institution, typically a bank, which specialises in providing hire purchase finance and finance for leasing.
Invoice - a bill which a business issues to a customer for payment of goods or services received. The invoice is likely to state when the bill must be paid, such as in 30 days time.
Hire purchase - a form of purchase scheme for equipment where, in law, regular rental payments are made by an individual or business. With the last rental payment, the equipment becomes the property of the individual or business.
Leasing - renting equipment or premises.
Mortgage - a loan where property is used as security.
Overdraft - a way of borrowing from a bank by drawing out more money than is actually in a current account. Interest is charged on the amount overdrawn.
Overdraft or credit limit - the maximum amount that the bank will allow a customer to become overdrawn on its current account.
Security - specific assets of a borrower, such as property or shares, identified when taking out a loan or an overdraft which can be sold by the lender if the borrower fails to repay the loan with interest.
Shareholders - owners of a company, who own part of the company through owning its shares.
Trade credit - given when a supplier allows a customer to receive goods or services but pay for them at a later point in time. Typically, trade credit is given for 30 days.
Venture capitalist - usually a business which specialises in providing finance for small to medium sized businesses which it believes has potential for fast growth.

businesses that specialise in buying a stake in smaller companies. They attract money from financial institutions and **business angels** - individuals who want to invest in businesses with potential. The money provided by venture capitalists is used to finance expansion. If successful, the venture capitalist will then sell its shares at a profit. But it can be risky. On average, venture capitalists only make a profit on 20 per cent of the companies in which they invest.

Government grants

A business may be able to get a government grant, to finance start up or expansion. The important advantage of a grant is that it is free. However, businesses may put a great deal of effort into applying for a grant only for it to be turned down. Also, grants can only be obtained for specific purposes, such as creating jobs.

A year ago, Syreeta Bailey was attempting to gain external finance for a proposed new business venture. She wanted to set up a business service centre aimed at foreign companies looking to set up in central London. The idea was simple. Clients would be charged a membership fee of £100 a month. They would then pay by the day to rent office space and computers. Other services, from telephone calls to taxis and flowers, would be charged at cost plus 10 per cent.

Initial finance was needed to set up the business. Syreeta was prepared to put £100 000 of her own money in. She wanted to borrow another £150 000 - £200 000. Banks, however, were unwilling to lend that much. In the end, she found a bank which offered her a £40 000 loan with a £30 000 overdraft facility. A further £50 000 came from friends and relatives prepared to buy shares in the new company.

1 Explain what is meant by the term 'external finance'. (3 marks)
2 (a) Calculate the cost of finance in the first year if none of the loan was repaid and the rate of interest on the loan was 7 per cent, an average £20 000 was borrowed on overdraft at a rate of interest of 6 per cent, and a dividend was paid to shareholders of 4p for every £1 share issued. (4 marks)
   (b) How would this cost have differed if Syreeta had secured the finance she originally hoped for? (4 marks)
3 Analyse TWO possible disadvantages to Syreeta of taking out the loan from the bank. (8 marks)
4 Discuss the potential benefits and risks that Syreeta's friends and relatives face by investing in the business. (11 marks)

26 Choice of finance

KMI

Knowledge — KMI (Knowledge & Merchandising Inc.) is a UK company which sells up-market men's shaving creams. The trade name it uses is King of Shaves. The company is a virtual company, employing just 12 people. It outsources everything from manufacture to logistics to sales.

Application — Founded in 1993, it now has 8 per cent of the fiercely *competitive* British shaving cream *market* by *value*. In 2000, it had *sales* of £5.5m and the company was still growing fast. *Profit* was £100 000. The *company* needs *finance* to expand *further*.

Analysis — So far, it has solved its working capital needs through factoring. However, it cannot use this form of financing for large investment in product development or advertising. The company is still too small to become a public limited company and gain finance through a share offering. Banks are reluctant to lend large amounts because the company has no tangible assets to offer as security.

Evaluation — Like many businesses, KMI finds itself restricted in its choice of finance. Options that are open, such as gaining finance from a venture capitalist company, are unattractive because that would give too much control away to the new shareholder. However, KMI should perhaps look to retained profit as a source of finance. Currently, it is making very low profits on its sales. If it could expand profitability, it could then use that profit to fund its expansion plans.

Adapted from *The Sunday Times*, 2.9.2001.

Short, medium and long term finance

Different types of finance are required for different situations. Finance needed to fund working capital (see unit 28), for example, tends to come from short term sources. This includes overdrafts, which in theory are repayable on demand to the bank. It might also include trade credit, some hire purchase and leasing and money received through factoring (see unit 28). Reducing stock levels may also be a short term tactic used by businesses that require finance.

Longer term finance comes in a number of forms. It is often used for investment and the development of the business over time. Bank loans may be repayable in the medium term, within say 1-5 years. Some loans, however, are negotiated for a longer period. Leasing and some hire purchase contracts can also last for more than 12 months. A business may issue shares or debentures to raise finance. It would not expect to repay the money it borrows for a long time, and in some cases never. Retained profit might also be regarded as a longer term source of funds (see unit 24).

Size and type of business organisation

The size and **organisation** (see units 60-61) of a business can determine what methods of finance are available and suitable. Table 26.1 summarises this.

Small businesses are usually sole traders, partnerships or private limited companies. They will rely mainly on retained profit, overdrafts, trade credit and loans for their finance. They may lease equipment or buy it on hire purchase. Sale of assets may also provide extra finance. Owners' or shareholders' funds are likely to be a source of finance when the business is started up, but can be difficult to obtain if the business grows.

Medium sized businesses will be private or public limited companies. They will rely on the same mix of finance as small businesses. Public limited companies have the advantage that they can issue new shares more easily than private limited companies.

Large UK businesses are almost all public limited companies. They have access to money markets and stock markets. They still use all the different types of finance used by small businesses. But they have access to stock markets to issue new shares and corporate bonds.

	Sole trader	Partnership	Private limited company	Smaller public limited company	Larger public limited company
Bank overdraft	✓	✓	✓	✓	✓
Trade credit	✓	✓	✓	✓	✓
Leasing	✓	✓	✓	✓	✓
Hire purchase	✓	✓	✓	✓	✓
Factoring	✓	✓	✓	✓	✓
Bank loans	✓	✓	✓	✓	✓
Mortgages	✓	✓	✓	✓	✓
Venture capital	✗	✗	✓	✓	✗
Share issues	✗	✗	✓	✓	✓
Retained profit	✓	✓	✓	✓	✓
Debentures or stocks	✗	✗	✗	✗	✓
Sales and leaseback	✗	✗	✗	✗	✓

Table 26.1 *Sources of finance for different types of business organisation.* **Note: ability to conclude sale and leaseback deals or issue debentures has more to do with the size of the business than its legal organisation.**

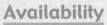

Lucia Cardoza owned four bars. Every day to her was a holiday because she enjoyed her job so much. She loved serving customers, dealing with suppliers and seeing her pubs prosper. But she was way behind in paying her invoices. At the bank, she was overdrawn by £65 000 and she had just negotiated to increase her overdraft facility to £90 000. There were mortgages on all her bars and her house, and a further £20 000 bank loan.

When the salesperson from the cash machine company came to see her, Lucia was delighted. For around £5 000 per ATM (Automatic Teller Machine or cash machine), she could own a cash machine in a bar. Customers withdrawing money paid a handling charge, part of which came back to her. What's more, evidence showed that sales increased by 4.5 per cent in pubs where cash machines were installed. Having calculated that the machines would pay for themselves in two years, she ordered four machines and financed them by increasing her overdraft.

Within 12 months her bank, alarmed at her financial situation, had called in her overdraft and forced her into bankruptcy.

1 **What evidence is there that Lucia Cardoza's business was overtrading?**
2 **Explain why Lucia Cardoza's choice of finance for the cash machines was inappropriate.**

Availability

Many businesses, particularly small firms, have little choice about which type of finance to use. For example, their owners may be unwilling or unable to put extra money into the business. Some can't use the stock market to raise finance because they are too small. Suppliers may put limits on how much trade credit they will be given. Their bank may refuse to give an overdraft or raise the overdraft limit. They may be making a loss and so there is no retained profit to use. A mortgage may not be an option because the business or its owners do not own property to use as security on the loan. In general, the larger the business, the more sources of finance are likely to be available.

Cost

Businesses will consider the cost of different types of finance when making a decision. The great advantage of using retained profit, for example, is that it seems costless. In practice, however, there is a cost because the money could be used, say, to earn interest in a bank account. Loans carry interest charges and possibly an arrangement fee. Leasing charges are higher than buying equipment outright. Issuing new shares is likely to mean that dividends will have to be paid to shareholders each year with no time limit.

Risk

Choosing an suitable form of finance reduces risk. For example, buying a machine using a loan rather than an increased overdraft reduces the risk that the business will fail because of an unexpected downturn in orders. Retained profit and issuing shares are also less risky than borrowing or leasing. With nearly all forms of borrowing, the business has to pay interest on a regular basis whether it is making a profit or a loss. If it is a loan, repayments will also be required. But no repayments can be required for retained profit or the issue of new shares. Managers can also decide not to pay owners a share of the profit if finance is needed for the future of the business, or if the business is making a loss.

Control

Issuing shares to raise finance can have major implications for control of a business compared to other forms of finance. If the business takes out a loan, it should have no impact on who owns and controls the business. However, if it issues shares or asks owners for funds, ownership and control may change.

For example, if a sole trader expands by taking on a partner and turning the business into a partnership, then he or she will lose some control of the business. If the partnership is set up so that each partner has equal control and takes half the profits, this is far different from being a sole trader with total control who receives all the profits.

If the business is a limited company, sale of shares will again dilute control and the share of profit. For example, a company might have 1 million shares. It then issues 500 000 more. The holder of an existing share will now receive only one third less of the total profit distributed to shareholders than before. The holder will also have one third less of the total voting rights.

In a small family company, changes in shareholding can be very important. Take a company with 100 shares, where family members own 60 shares. They then decide to expand. They finance this by issuing 50 shares to a venture capitalist. The venture capitalist will then own one third of the total shares (50 ÷ 150 x 100%). The family will now own only 40 per cent of the shares (60 ÷ 150 x 100%). This might cause it to lose control of the business, since in theory it needs at least half the total shares to outvote other shareholders.

Financing problems

Businesses sometimes fail to have adequate finance. This inevitably causes problems. There are two main types of problem.

Lack of finance Sometimes a business expands too quickly, placing a strain on its financial resources. This can cause the business to have too little working capital (see unit 28), a situation known as OVERTRADING. A business which is overtrading has liquidity problems.

For example, the production of a business may be growing fast. The business may have to order more stock from

suppliers to cope. The suppliers may want payment 30 days after stock has been delivered. But the business may not have sufficient working capital to meet its needs. It might take 15 days to turn the stock into finished goods and dispatch it to customers. Their payment may come in 30 days afterwards because they have been given trade credit terms. So cash may not come quickly enough from the sale of the final goods to pay for the stock. Businesses sometimes try to get around this by not paying their suppliers on time or by persuading their bank to increase their overdraft limit. But the danger is that suppliers will refuse to supply and the bank will refuse any increase in the overdraft limit. The business can fail because of a lack of adequate working capital, despite having full order books.

Imbalanced finance Sometimes businesses obtain unsuitable finance. For example, a business might buy an expensive machine. It is expected to be used for at least five years and will not show a profit before 24 months. Financing it on overdraft is risky. If the business got into financial difficulties, its bank might **call in** the overdraft (i.e. asking for it to be repaid). With no easy way of getting cash, the business could fail. A long term loan for the machine would be more suitable. The bank could not force the business to repay the loan until the date in the contract.

Equally, trying to raise working capital by long term finance can cause problems. For example, a business may have a £200 000 'one-off' order. A business may choose to finance this through an increase in the overdraft because the overdraft can be repaid once the buyer has paid for the order. A long term loan is likely to be unsuitable. The business

would have to continue paying interest on the loan well after it had the money to repay it.

checklist

1 Explain the difference between short-term finance and long term finance.
2 Why might it be important for the financial security of a business not to finance long-term investment projects through increased overdraft borrowing?
3 Briefly explain what sources of finance are available to a large company that are not open to a sole trader.
4 'Retained profit and issuing shares are less risky than borrowing or leasing.' Explain why this is likely to be the case.
5 Why should a business have sufficient finance to maintain adequate levels of working capital?

keyterms

Overtrading - **a situation when a business has too little working capital to support its level of production and sales.**

Louise Davies-Harper has always loved getting shoes as gifts. Her father, Michael Davies-Harper, was in a good position to provide them. He owned a chain of exclusive designer shops with branches in London, Paris, Milan and New York.

Having left school, Louise worked for a time in her father's company. She tried everything from being a sales assistant to personal secretary to working in accounts. Now she wanted to set up her own company in collaboration with an old school friend, Lucy Parker. Lucy had taken a degree in Textile Design, specialising in shoes. After study, she worked for two years for a top shoe design company which makes shoes for some of the world's most exclusive fashion houses.

Finance was going to be a problem. Neither of them had any money to start the business. Louise's father was prepared to put in all or part of the start-up capital. But in return he expected to own most, if not all, of the company. Having worked for him, Louise knew that her father would get involved in the day to day running of the company. This was something she was anxious to avoid.

Louise and Lucy drew up a business plan which they showed to a bank. They calculated that they needed £50 000 to start the business. Then, as the business grew, it would need further financial capital. The bank liked the plan and indicated that it might give the company an overdraft and a loan, but only if most of the start-up capital was in place beforehand. It also gave them details of factoring services which could be provided once the company had been operating for a year.

Louise and Lucy began to despair. But then Louise's grandmother stepped in. She offered them a £20 000 loan at 7 per cent interest per annum, repayable in two years' time.

1 Explain the meaning of the terms:
   (a) 'overdraft'; (3 marks) (b) 'factoring services'. (3 marks)
2 Explain why the proposed company would need to obtain finance to start up and survive in business. (6 marks)
3 Analyse two possible disadvantages of starting up the company with the £20 000 loan from Louise's grandmother. (8 marks)
4 Discuss whether Louise and Lucy should accept Michael Davies-Harper's offer to provide the start up capital for their business. (10 marks)

27 Cash flow

Webvan

Knowledge   Webvan was a US online grocery retailer. Customers would order their groceries over the internet and Webvan would deliver to the door. Stock was kept in large automated warehouses, 18 times the size of a typical supermarket. Founded in 1996, it raised over $1 billion of cash from investors in its brief five year history.

Application   Webvan attempted to '*re-engineer*' the *supply chain* from grocery *manufacturer* to *customer*, i.e. it tried to reinvent how groceries were delivered to the home. Building very large *warehouses* was supposed to give Webvan *economies of scale*, i.e. lower *average costs*, than the typical supermarket. This would offset the high *cost* of home delivery. Webvan failed because it had negative *cash flow* and eventually ran out of *cash*.

Analysis   In the five years before Webvan filed for bankruptcy, it managed to spend $1 billion on building up its business. Each of the 26 warehouses it opened across the USA cost $35 million. But not only was cash flowing out of the company to pay for its new warehouses. For most of its existence, it was also making losses on each order it delivered. The cash flowing into the company from customers paying for groceries was less than the cash flowing out to pay for costs. The warehouses themselves were underutilised because the volume of business was less than predicted.

Evaluation   With hindsight, it is possible to see why Webvan failed. In the late 1990s, everyone thought that Internet buying was the way forward. Who would want to go to the supermarket when they could sit in the comfort of their homes to order their groceries? What some businesses failed to appreciate was that Internet shopping is little different from catalogue shopping. It is a small niche market, attractive to only a few per cent of shoppers. Building such huge warehouses in so many locations quickly drained the company of cash. Not surprisingly, investors were not prepared to give it yet more cash in 2001 to bail it out. So the business went into bankruptcy.

Adapted from the *Financial Times*, 10.7.2001.

Defining cash flow

CASH FLOW is the term used to describe the movement of cash into and out of the business.

CASH is not just notes and coins. It is any form of financial asset which can immediately be used for paying debts or turned into notes and coins. For most businesses, their cash is almost all held in a current account at a bank. But a small market trader might hold mainly notes and coins. A large company may have money invested which earns interest apart from an account used to process cheques and cash. So long as the money is available within 24 hours without incurring a penalty for early withdrawal, it is classified as cash.

Cash flows **into** a business from different sources. The main inflow is likely to be from the sale of goods and services. But a business could receive interest on investments or cash from the sale of a building.

Cash flows **out of** a business to pay for items such as wages of staff, materials, taxes and equipment.

NET CASH FLOW is the difference between total cash inflows during a period and total cash outflows.

- There is POSITIVE CASH FLOW if cash inflows are greater than outflows. For example, a small business may receive £5 000 from sales of goods this month but only pay out £4 000 in wages and other bills. Net cash flow would be positive at £1 000 (£5 000 - £4 000).
- There is NEGATIVE CASH FLOW if inflows of cash are less than the outflows. For example, the same small business last month might have received £4 000 from the sale of goods but had to pay out £6 000 in wages and other bills. Cash flow would then be a negative at £2 000 (£4 000 - £6 000).

The importance of cash flow

Cash flow is vital for a business. If cash flow is positive, then there will be more cash coming into a business than leaving it. The business will be in a better position to survive and be profitable.

If cash flow is negative, the business could be in financial trouble. Take a small business which needs to pay out £5 000 in cash per month but only receives £4 000 in a month. It has negative cash flow of £1 000. The cash to finance that negative cash flow has to come from somewhere. Hopefully, the business will have reserves of cash. If not, it could borrow the money from its bank. But what if it can't find any cash to pay the shortfall of £1 000? The danger is that the business may have to cease trading.

Cash flow problems are the main reason why businesses

fail. Businesses are highly vulnerable to cash flow crises when they are first set up. The owners of the business often fail to put in enough money at the start for it to survive. Costs are often greater than planned, whilst the start of production is often delayed. Sales can also take time to build up to at least their break-even level. The result is a cash crisis. Costs are too high and there is too little revenue. It is estimated that 70 per cent of new companies that fail in their first year do so because of cash flow problems.

Cash flow and profit

Positive cash flows are likely to be an indication that a business is making a profit. Positive cash flow over a period of time also enables a business to finance expansion. It could take over another business, for instance, with the cash it is accumulating. Alternatively, it could use the cash to finance internal expansion, buying new fixed assets like buildings, machinery or equipment.

However, cash flow and profit are not the same. A business can be highly profitable and yet have cash flow problems. Equally, a business can have a positive cash flow and be making a loss.

For instance, a manufacturer may be offered a contract to make £200 000 of goods. The profit on the contract will be £50 000. But it is a small company. Having accepted the contract, it orders £100 000 of materials. The materials arrive, but they have to be paid for one month later. The company finds that it does not have the cash to pay these bills. It is forced to close. But the contract which caused the failure would still have generated £50 000 of profit if it had been completed. The problem was that it had to pay £100 000 for the materials before it received the £200 000 for the contract.

Equally, a business can have positive cash flow and be making a loss. Eurotunnel is a good example. Whilst the tunnel was being built in the late 1980s and early 1990s, Eurotunnel borrowed over £10 billion. When Eurotunnel received the cash from a loan, this was an inflow of cash for the company. Cash was then flowing out to pay the contractors building the tunnel. For most of the period, inflows of cash from loans were greater than outflows. The company had positive cash flow. However, since the tunnel was not finished, the company was not earning any revenue from customers. It was therefore making a loss. Many new businesses have positive cash flow at the start due to inflows of cash from loans and grants. But they make a loss on trading because the business is not established.

Cash flow is a key financial indicator in the short term. If there is positive cash flow, the business is in a better position to survive. If there is negative cash flow, the business could be forced to stop trading. In the long term, though, profit is the more important financial indicator. A business which has a small positive cash flow in the long term but is barely making a profit is likely to cease to exist. Its owners are likely to want to sell it or close it down so that they can earn a higher return on their investment elsewhere.

Cash flow forecasts

A CASH FLOW FORECAST is a prediction of how cash will flow through a business over a period of time in the future.

Rachael Shapcott has just started up in business as an interior designer. Her first few jobs were small ones, for rooms in houses of friends. One of these owned a restaurant. She was so impressed with Rachael's work that she offered her a contract to redesign the interior of the dining room. Rachael had £1 000 in the bank and had just negotiated a £500 overdraft. The restaurant owner said she would pay Rachael for the work on 'normal trade terms'. By this she meant 'one month after completion'. Rachael knew that refurbishing the restaurant would cost at least £10,000, but she could probably earn around £3,000 profit on the contract. It would also act as a showcase, helping her to win future contracts with other customers.

I Should Rachael begin negotiations with the restaurant owner on a contract?

Table 27.1 shows a monthly cash flow forecast for a business over the next 6 months. The forecast is made up of a number of elements.

Receipts Receipts (or **cash in** or **cash inflows**) are the cash coming into the business in each time period. The main cash inflow in Table 27.1 is from sales of products. But other receipts are also shown in August and November. The cash flow forecast shows that the business has seasonal trade. As Christmas approaches, sales increase.

Payments Payments (or **cash out** or **cash outflows**) are the cash leaving the business in each time period. Examples are wages and materials.

Net cash flow This is the difference between receipts and payments. In months where receipts are greater than payments, as in December and January, net cash flow is positive. In months where receipts are less than payments, as in September to November, net cash flow is negative.

Opening balance This shows the amount of cash owned by the business at the start of the month. In August, for example, the business had £22 000 in cash.

Closing balance This shows the amount of cash owned by the business at the end of the month. The opening balance and the closing balance are linked by the net cash flow. Take November and December. The opening balance in November

	August	September	October	November	December	January
Receipts						
Sales	60 000	70 000	80 000	90 000	100 000	100 000
Other receipts	10 000	0	0	5 000	0	0
Total receipts	70 000	70 000	80 000	95 000	100 000	100 000
Payments						
Wages	20 000	21 000	22 000	26 000	24 000	24 000
Materials	40 000	45 000	52 000	59 000	55 000	40 000
Other costs	10 000	11 000	12 000	15 000	11 000	11 000
Total payments	70 000	77 000	86 000	100 000	90 000	75 000
Net cash flow	0	-7 000	-6 000	-5 000	10 000	25 000
Opening balance	22 000	22 000	15 000	9 000	4 000	14 000
Closing balance	22 000	15 000	9 000	4 000	14 000	39 000

Table 27.1 *Example of a cash flow forecast (£)*

was £9 000. Net cash flow for the month was a negative £5 000. So the closing balance was £4 000, the opening balance plus the negative net cash flow, i.e £9 000 + (- £5 000). The closing balance at the end of November becomes the opening balance at the start of the next month, December. So the opening balance in December is £4 000.

Net cash flow in December is a positive £10 000. Hence the closing balance is £14 000, made up of the opening balance of £4 000 **plus** the positive net cash flow of £10 000.

Interpreting cash flow forecasts

Every cash flow forecast tells a story about the finances of the business.

In Table 27.1, it shows that as Christmas approaches, both payments and receipts are predicted to increase. But payments are going up faster than receipts between September and November. The result is that net cash flow is negative. The net outflow of cash has to be financed from somewhere. In this case, there was enough cash in the business at the start of August to finance the net cash outflow. If negative cash flow continued each month then the cash within the business would be used up to finance this.

In December and January, net cash flow becomes positive. Receipts are greater than payments. Partly this is because more goods are sold at Christmas and in the January sales. Partly it is because costs fall as less is produced. The business is ordering fewer materials and other goods because it has already stocked up for Christmas. The business is also likely to have been given extended **trade credit** (see unit 25). This is where payments for goods ordered and received from other businesses only have to be made some time after delivery.

But what if the business had only started in August with £5 000? In this case the cash flow for the business would have been as in Table 27.2. The business would have run out of cash in September. It does not have enough cash from the previous months to cover this. It has negative closing balances until January. If it couldn't get any cash to cover these months, it could have been forced to cease trading. Usually, though, it is possible to get around this by borrowing money from a bank. Many businesses negotiate an

overdraft limit (see unit 25) with their bank which allows them to borrow up to a certain amount when they need the cash. Negative cash balances then tend to indicate how much has been borrowed on overdraft.

Note that over the six month period, the business was profitable. Receipts were greater than payments. This shows that a business can be profitable but still have negative cash flow in certain months.

The purpose of cash flow forecasts

There are two main purposes of cash flow forecasts.

Business use Businesses should always be planning for the future. Preparing a cash flow forecast is part of that planning. The cash flow forecast will tell a business whether it will have enough cash to survive, and to meet its other plans. For example, if the business expects to increase sales by 20 per cent over the next year, it will almost certainly require more cash. The cash flow forecast should indicate just how much more cash will be needed and when it will be needed.

Loans and investments Cash flow forecasts are also usually required if a business wants to increase its outside financing. For example, if it wants to take out a loan from the bank, the bank will want information about the finances of the business. This will include a cash flow forecast. This should show that the business will be able to make payments on the loan to the bank. It also shows that the business has taken planning for the future seriously.

Accuracy of cash flow forecasts

Cash flow forecasts are unlikely to predict exactly the cash flow through a business. There is a number of reasons why this might be the case.

Lack of data A new business setting up will find it difficult to estimate cash flow accurately because it has no previous sales or costs figures to work from. New businesses also tend to be too optimistic about their performance in the first year. There are often unexpected delays in starting up the business. Sales are often lower than expected, whilst costs are often higher.

	August	September	October	November	December	January
Receipts						
Sales	60 000	70 000	80 000	90 000	100 000	100 000
Other receipts	10 000	0	0	5 000	0	0
Total receipts	70 000	70 000	80 000	95 000	100 000	100 000
Payments						
Wages	20 000	21 000	22 000	26 000	24 000	24 000
Materials	40 000	45 000	52 000	59 000	55 000	40 000
Other costs	10 000	11 000	12 000	15 000	11 000	11 000
Total payments	70 000	77 000	86 000	100 000	90 000	75 000
Net cash flow	0	-7 000	-6 000	-5 000	10 000	25 000
Opening balance	5 000	5 000	-2 000	-8 000	-13 000	-3 000
Closing balance	5 000	-2 000	-8 000	-13 000	-3 000	22 000

Table 27.2 *Example of a cash flow forecast (£), opening balance of £5 000*

This means that the cash needs of a new business tend to be far greater than that predicted. Even existing businesses may find it hard to forecast if they are moving into new markets, or if there will be change in their existing market.

Manipulating the forecast Cash flow forecasts for existing businesses should be far more accurate because they have actual cash flow figures from previous years from which to work. But, even then, estimates may be inaccurate. For example, a business wanting to increase its borrowing from its bank may put in highly optimistic figures for future cash flow. Better cash flow figures might improve its chances of getting the loan. Or senior managers may be under pressure to improve the performance of the business. Putting in optimistic sales figures or lower costs is one way in which these managers can reduce the pressure at the moment, even if there was little chance of achieving the figures. Alternatively, managers might put in data which deliberately underestimate future performance. When performance turns out to be much better than forecast, they can take the credit and even get larger bonuses than they would otherwise have done.

Changes in the business environment Cash flow forecasts are likely to be inaccurate the more there is change in the business environment. For example, the economy going into an unexpected **recession** (see unit 50) is likely to lower sales revenue for most businesses. Higher **inflation** (see unit 53) than forecast is likely to push up costs. For some businesses, changes in the weather can have an important impact on sales. Beer sales and ice cream sales in the summer are dependent on good weather. A poor summer depresses clothes sales because consumers don't buy so many summer clothes.

Because cash flow forecasts can be inaccurate, businesses should consider what would happen if their forecast proved to be wrong. Cash flow forecasts today tend to be done on spreadsheets. So it is easy to produce forecasts which show what would happen if, for example, sales were 10 per cent lower than the main forecast, or costs were 10 per cent higher.

keyterms

Cash - notes and coins but also typically money on deposit with banks and building societies which can be withdrawn instantly, for example by paying out a cheque.

Cash flow - the movement of cash into and out of a business over a period of time.

Cash flow forecast - a prediction of how cash will flow through a business over a future period of time. It includes a summary of receipts and payments during each period of time.

Negative cash flow - where cash outflows are greater than cash inflows over a period of time.

Net cash flow - cash inflows minus cash outflows over a period of time like one month, a quarter or a year.

Positive cash flow - where cash inflows are greater than cash outflows over a time period.

Bill and Jenny Henry run a small hotel in Devon. It has a restaurant and two bars, which are used by people in the local area as well as the guests staying at the hotel. Their cash flow forecast for the six months May to October is shown in Table 27.3.

1 In Devon, the tourist trade is seasonal. How is this shown in the cash flow forecast?

2 What does it mean when in May their net cash flow is - £3 000?

3 Why is their forecast closing balance at the end of October larger than their forecast opening balance in May?

4 Last year, their net cash flow in the winter months from November to April averaged a negative £4 000 per month. If this were repeated this year, would this be a problem for the business? Explain your answer.

	May	June	July	August	September	October
Receipts						
Sales	25 000	34 000	38 000	40 000	31 000	22 000
Other receipts	0	0	0	0	0	2 000
Total receipts	25 000	34 000	38 000	40 000	31 000	24 000
Payments						
Wages	10 000	11 000	12 000	12 000	11 000	9 000
Food and drink	4 000	5 000	6 000	6 000	5 000	4 000
Other costs	14 000	14 000	15 000	15 000	14 000	13 000
Total payments	28 000	30 000	33 000	33 000	30 000	26 000
Net cash flow	-3 000	4 000	5 000	7 000	1 000	-2 000
Opening balance	5 000	2 000	6 000	11 000	18 000	19 000
Closing balance	2 000	6 000	11 000	18 000	19 000	17 000

Table 27.3 *Cash flow forecast for the hotel (£)*

Large companies may carry out risk appraisals to calculate the likelihood of particular changes. For example, what would be the implications for the company if there was a 5 per cent chance that revenues over the next six months were 25 per cent lower than predicted? But even small businesses should be aware of the impact of possible changes in cash flow. Their survival may be at stake if their forecasts prove to be too optimistic.

checklist

1 What is the difference between a cash inflow and a cash outflow for a business?
2 'Last month, there was a positive cash inflow of £2 000.' Explain what this means.
3 Bethson is a business which specialises in manufacturing metal components. Identify which of the following would be outflows of cash for the business and which would be inflows.
(a) Wages of workers.
(b) Receipts from sales of coil springs.
(c) Payments for electricity used.
(d) Business rates (a tax) on its factory.
(e) Payment for buying another business.
(f) Expenses of the sales team.
(g) Interest on short term deposits.
4 Why is negative cash flow a potential problem for a business?
5 Explain the difference between cash flow and profit.
6 Explain the two main purposes of cash flow forecasts.
7 Why might a cash flow forecast be inaccurate?

Benzing's is a supplier of catering clothing with an annual turnover of £3.4 million. Exports account for around one-third of sales. A recent downturn in the world economy has had a serious effect on Benzing's. Overseas orders have still been coming through. But twice in the past six months, a large overseas customer has failed to pay for an order.

In one sense, Benzing's has not lost out. This is because it tends to supply overseas customers through 'bills of collection'. Goods are shipped out to the foreign country, but held by the freight company on arrival until payment is received by the customer. So Benzing's at least kept the goods when the overseas customers failed to pay. On the other hand, Benzing's had to pay for the goods to be dispatched back to the UK and put into stock. Not only did it fail to receive cash from the order, but it had to pay out cash to the freight company.

The finance director at Benzing's has prepared a cash flow forecast for the next six months based upon sales for the same period six months ago. This is shown in Table 27.4. The managing director, however, is concerned that she has not taken sufficient account of the downturn in the world economy. This could be important because the company currently only has a £120 000 overdraft facility with its bank.

1 Explain the meaning of the term 'cash flow forecast'. (3 marks)
2 Calculate the following:
(a) home sales for May;
(b) total payments for July;
(c) the closing balance for October.
(3 marks)
3 The finance director has calculated what would happen to the opening cash balance for November if, instead of the figures shown in Table 27.4, export revenues for October were 20 per cent down and freight costs were 20 per cent up. Showing your workings, complete this calculation. (5 marks)
4 The finance director has suggested that the company should increase its marketing to export markets. Analyse TWO possible disadvantages of this for the business. (8 marks)
5 The managing director is extremely concerned about the business export markets. Write a short report from the finance director to the managing director discussing the implications for cash flow for the period May to October if export receipts were halved. (11 marks)

	May	June	July	August	September	October
Receipts						£000
Home sales	?	200	190	180	160	190
Export sales	100	100	100	90	80	90
Other receipts	10	10	10	10	10	10
Total receipts	330	310	300	280	250	290
Payments						
Wages and materials	205	205	195	175	195	205
Freight costs	15	15	15	15	15	15
Other costs	60	60	80	90	60	60
Total payments	280	280	?	280	270	280
Net cash flow	50	30	10	0	-20	10
Opening balance	-160	-110	-80	-70	-70	-90
Closing balance	-110	-80	-70	-70	-90	?

Table 27.4 *Cash flow forecast for Benzing's*

28 Improving cash flow

Stevens Locksmiths

Knowledge Holly Stevens owns a small locksmiths business in Willenhall in the West Midlands. The firm has a long family history, stretching back 150 years. But it is currently in financial trouble. A year ago, Holly was forced to sack half her staff due to competition in the lock business from Far East manufacturers. At the time, she also sacked her financial controller and decided to do all the financial paperwork herself with the help of a secretary.

Application By *specialising* in small quantity, *high value orders*, *sales* have been strong recently. Holly has carefully *priced* orders so that they should be *profitable*. Yet she is constantly battling against *cash flow problems*. It is always a struggle, for example, to find the *cash* to *pay her workers* on *pay day*.

Analysis There is a difference between profitability and positive cash flow. Holly's basic problem was that she didn't have enough cash in the business to deal with day to day trading. In the short term, she had major problems with collecting money owed to her from customers. She didn't have the time to chase up debts. The result was that the average debt repayment period had risen from 65 days a year ago to 96 days today. Her bank overdraft was constantly stretched to its credit limit and so she couldn't borrow extra money when she needed. Stocks of raw materials were also too high, 70 per cent of the total compared to two years ago. But she was now only producing half the number of locks. In the long term, she faced major problems with her existing level of financing. Downsizing the firm a year ago had drained much of the finance from the business. Even if she sorted out her short term financing problems, she would still have a cash shortage. Ideally, Holly needed to invest some new financial capital into the business.

Evaluation Like many small business owners, Holly has not paid enough attention to her cash flow. She needs to tighten up her financial control procedures and to have an injection of long term finance if the business is to survive.

The short term

There is a number of ways a business can improve its cash flow position in the short term. It does this by manipulating its WORKING CAPITAL. This is the net value of the short term assets of a business. It is defined as:

Working capital = (cash + stocks + debtors) - (short term borrowing + creditors + taxation)

Working capital is therefore the difference between the short term or **current assets** (what it owns, i.e. cash, stocks and debtors) and its short term or **current liabilities** (what it owes, i.e. short term borrowing, its creditors and taxation).

In the short term, there are various ways that a firm can change its assets and liabilities to increase the amount of cash in the business.

Reducing stock levels STOCKS are materials and goods which are owned by a business ready to be processed or delivered. A business is likely to hold stocks of materials ready to be processed. For example, a car manufacturer will hold stocks of steel, whilst a coffee shop will hold stocks of coffee beans or powder. Businesses in the primary and secondary industries will hold stocks of semi-finished goods. For example, a car manufacturer will hold stocks of semi-finished cars on its production line each day. Businesses in primary and secondary industries will also hold stocks of finished goods waiting delivery to customers. For example, the car manufacturer will hold stocks of finished cars waiting to be dispatched to car dealers.

Stocks cost money to hold. Reducing stock levels will therefore increase the cash in a business. For example, a business may decide to cancel all deliveries of stock for the next 7 days. Cash flow will improve by the amount that would have been spent on that stock. Or a business may cut stocks of finished goods by reducing production levels. The business will then have to order fewer materials and may be able to cut down on its wage bill. The money saved will improve the cash flow position. A shop could convert its stock into cash quickly by holding a sale.

Reducing debtors DEBTORS are those who owe a business money for goods or services delivered. The debtors of a business are likely to be other businesses. This is because it is usual to give TRADE CREDIT to other businesses. Trade credit is typically 30 days, although it can be longer. So a business has to wait 30 days for payment of goods or services that it has delivered to another business. A business can make a once and for all increase in cash if it can reduce the amount outstanding which it is owed. There is a variety of ways of doing this.

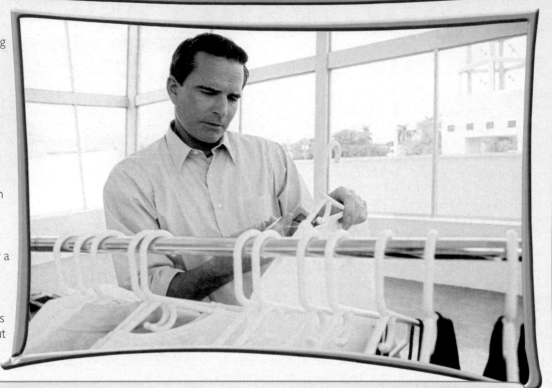

Adrian Talbot owns and runs a small garment manufacturing business. He employs 12 workers, using rented premises in London. Cash flow is always a problem for him. The businesses that buy from him often pay late whilst the profit margins he earns are wafer thin in an industry notorious for cut throat competition. At least finished stock is never a problem. He makes a sample and wins orders based on that. As soon as an order is complete, it is sent out to the purchaser.

I Suggest and explain THREE ways in which Adrian Talbot could possibly improve his cash flow situation.

- It could reduce the trade credit period it offers to its customers. For example, it could cut the trade credit period from 30 days to 20 days. Although this should improve its cash flow, it risks losing customers to competitors which are still offering 30 days trade credit. It could also stop giving extended trade credit, longer than 30 days.
- It could be more efficient at collecting its debts. Although the typical trade credit period offered is 30 days, the average time it takes for a business to receive payments is 75 days in the UK. Partly this is because some businesses offer more than 30 days trade credit. But much of it is due to customers not paying their bills on time. A business that is owed money should have an efficient system for chasing up late payers. It might offer a discount on the bill to those who pay early or even just on time, although this reduces revenue and cash received. It might threaten to add interest to a bill which is paid late, although this is hard to enforce legally. It could also refuse to sell to customers which pay persistently late, although this risks losing valuable future sales and cash flow.
- It could employ a FACTOR. A factor is often a bank which offers various services to businesses in debt collection. The factor is likely to offer to lend a business 80 per cent of what it is owed by debtors at any time. It charges interest on the loan. For a further fee, it will take over the collection of debts completely from the business. The bank collects what is owed to a business and passes the money through to it on time. Factoring improves cash flow because at least 80 per cent of the money owed to a business by its debtors is paid on time. If the business opts to have its debts

collected by the factor, the factor should provide an efficient service, again speeding up the time it takes to collect debts. Cash flow should therefore see a once and for all improvement. The disadvantage to the business is that it has to pay the factor for the services it provides.

Increasing creditors CREDITORS are those to whom a business owes money. For example, a business may have taken delivery today of £10 000 worth of steel. The supplier offers 30 days trade credit. So the business doesn't have to pay for the steel till 30 days later. One way of increasing the cash in a business is to find suppliers which will give better trade credit terms. Buying steel from a supplier offering 60 days trade credit rather than 30 days will give a once and for all increase in cash flow.

Equally, a business could simply increase the time it takes to pay its bills. Not paying any bills this month, even though the money is due, will increase cash flow this month. This tactic won't work forever. A business which keeps increasing the amount of time taken to pay its bills may find that suppliers will refuse to sell it goods and services. Paying late could mean that valuable discounts for paying on time are missed. It could find itself threatened with legal action. At worst, a supplier could get a court order to seize whatever they can to pay off the bill. Many businesses, however, choose not to pay bills in months when they are facing cash flow problems. Or they prioritise their payments. They pay those businesses which apply a lot of pressure on their debtors to pay up. They don't pay those businesses which are inefficient in collecting debts.

Increasing the overdraft Most businesses have an **overdraft facility** (see unit 25) with their banks. An overdraft is a type of flexible loan. The borrower can choose to borrow up to a certain sum of money agreed with the bank, called the **overdraft limit**. But they are free to pay back part of the money borrowed at any time and don't have to be borrowing money to have an overdraft facility. A business can increase its cash by borrowing more money on its overdraft. For example, it might have an overdraft limit of £5 000. It is currently borrowing £3 000. So it could borrow up to £2 000 extra.

There is more of a problem if it is already borrowing up to its overdraft limit. Then it has to negotiate with its bank to increase its overdraft limit. There is no guarantee that the bank will do this. A business experiencing cash flow problems could well be a business in difficulties. The bank won't want to increase lending to a business which could cease trading in the immediate future. The bank is likely to want to see a **cash flow forecast** (see unit 27) to judge whether or not the business will be able to pay the interest on the overdraft and the overdraft itself in the future.

The main disadvantage of borrowing more is that interest has to be paid on the overdraft. Interest is an outgoing for the business and therefore leads to a deterioration in cash flow.

The long term

A business may be able to improve its cash flow by becoming more efficient in its use of short term assets like stocks or debtors. Often, though, manipulating its working capital is a sign that the business is in financial trouble. What it needs is a long term solution to its cash flow problems. There is a variety of ways cash can be increased in the long term.

Increased financial capital Cash can be increased if the owners of the business are prepared to invest more in it. If it is a company, this would mean selling new shares (see unit 25). If it is a partnership, it means the partners putting more of their own money into the business. A sole trader would have to use his or her own funds.

Increased long term borrowing A business could take out long term borrowing. It might, for example, borrow £20 000 from its bank to be repaid over three years. The £20 000 is an immediate increase in cash flow. The downside is that each month, a repayment will have to made on the loan, reducing that month's cash flow.

Sale and leaseback Many businesses own premises and other property. If it is a large business, it may be able to negotiate a SALE AND LEASEBACK deal with a property company. The property company agrees to buy the property, but then leases it (a form of renting) back to the business. The business gets a large one off increase in its cash flow from the purchase. But after that, it has to pay rent, which is an outgoing on its cash flow.

Leasing rather than buying Many businesses buy the equipment they use. But there are many types of equipment where they could lease (i.e. rent) instead. For example, photocopiers and company cars are often leased rather than owned. One advantage to the business is that it doesn't have to pay out one large sum for the equipment, which would be negative cash flow. Instead, it can spread the cost of the equipment, and therefore the negative cash flow, over a longer period of time. Equally, a business may choose to rent new premises rather than buy them, which would have the same effect.

keyterms

Creditors - **those to whom a business owes money for goods or services delivered but not yet paid for.**
Debtors - **those who owe a business money for goods or services delivered but for which they have not yet paid.**
Factor - **a financial business, such as a bank, which advances money owed to another business on trade credit. Factors also offer the further service of collecting all money owed on trade credit to a business.**
Sale and leaseback - **a method of raising finance where a business sells typically property it owns, at the same time agreeing with the purchaser to lease (i.e. rent) the property.**
Stocks - **materials and goods owned by a business either awaiting to be used to produce goods or services, or finished products awaiting to be delivered to customers.**
Trade credit - **given when a supplier allows a customer to receive goods or services but pay for them at a later point in time. Typically, trade credit is given for 30 days.**
Working capital - **the net value of the short term assets of a business. It is defined as short term assets (usually cash plus stocks plus debtors) minus short term liabilities (usually short term borrowing, creditors and taxation).**

✓checklist

1. List three possible short term assets and three short term liabilities of a business.
2. Why does it cost money for a business to hold stocks?
3. Explain the difference between a debtor and a creditor of a business.
4. Why could (a) reducing stock levels and (b) reducing the level of debtors increase the amount of cash in a business?
5. What services does a factor offer to businesses?
6. Why might increasing the repayment time on invoices help increase the amount of cash in a business?
7. Explain why borrowing more money on overdraft (a) could increase cash in a business but (b) will have no effect on working capital.
8. Briefly outline FOUR different ways a business could inject more cash into its operations in the long term.

Jill and Chris Fawcett retired in 2000. They decided to move to the Lake District and open a bed and breakfast (B&B) business. The move was to be financed by the sale of their existing house and the cashing in of all their existing savings. Having bought a large house, they set about converting it into a luxury B&B. Each bedroom needed an ensuite bathroom installed. The central heating system had to be replaced. A new kitchen was installed. The whole place was redecorated, including new carpets and curtains. New furniture had to be bought. There were also payments to be made for advertising in holiday brochures. The conversion went over budget and the Fawcetts had to borrow £5 000 from their bank. The loan was for two years, repayable in fixed monthly instalments. But the cash flow forecast for the new business drawn up by the Fawcetts showed that the repayments were easily affordable.

In February 2001, they were ready to open. Almost immediately, foot and mouth disease struck the UK. This affected cloved hoof animals such as cattle and sheep. Cumbria, which includes the Lake District, was particularly badly affected. Footpaths were closed, images of burning slaughtered cattle were broadcast internationally, and the number of visitors to the Lake District plummeted. Small businesses in farming and the tourist trade were badly affected. Many, as Figure 28.1 suggests, were forced to borrow money to cover their negative cash flow.

Then, just as the foot and mouth crisis seemed to be finishing, terrorists demolished the World Trade Centre in New York. The September 11 attack frightened many US tourists off flying abroad. The Fawcetts had forecast that American tourists would be a small but significant market for their B&B given that they were charging above average prices for their luxury accommodation. The hoped for upturn in trade in the autumn of 2001 was disappointing. Some UK trade returned, but there were hardly any bookings from European or American visitors.

The Fawcetts made a profit of £2 000 in the year to January 31, 2002, when their forecast was for a profit of £25 000. This profit did not include any payment to themselves for all the work they had put into the business. They had also saved cash by not employing the staff they had planned for in their cash flow forecast. Luckily, they had their own private pensions to live off. If they hadn't, they would have been forced to borrow more money or to sell the B&B.

Their plight was nothing compared to some of the local farmers who made losses over the period. These local farmers had to pay out cash for items such as wages of employees, feed for their animals and taxes when they were unable to sell any of their animals.

1 Explain what is meant by the term 'cash flow'. (3 marks)
2 Suggest what happened to the cash flow of the Fawcetts from the time they sold their existing house to the time when they opened their B&B for business. (6 marks)
3 Analyse why the Fawcetts had few opportunities to improve their cash flow in the short term in 2001. (10 marks)
4 The Fawcetts had planned to spend £5 000 on advertising in 2002. From (a) a cash flow viewpoint and (b) a profit viewpoint, discuss whether or not they should have cut their spending on advertising from this planned level. (11 marks)

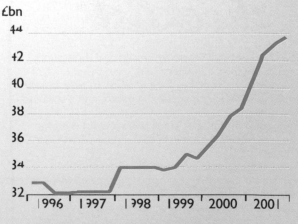

Figure 28.1 *Small business borrowing*
Adapted from BBA and CEBR.

29 Budgeting

ACW

Knowledge ACW is a privately owned car dealer network with six showrooms in the UK.

Application Each year, *management* agrees on *sales goals* for the *company*. These are split between new car sales and servicing and repairs. Individual *departments* within the *company* then prepare their own *budgets* based upon these *objectives*. This year, there was a significant *adverse variance* on new car *sales*.

Analysis Drawing up a budget for next year was a difficult task for the sales side of the business. Sales this year fell 15 per cent short of the current year's budget, due possibly to increased competition from Internet rivals. Management wanted to set a goal next year of matching this year's sales. But a 15 per cent cut in costs would be required. Those responsible for setting sales budgets argued that cost cuts were simply not possible, even if this year's disappointing sales were to be maintained. A 15 per cent budget cut would mean redundancies of staff with many years of experience. Staff morale would plummet. They also argued the fall in sales could easily be reversed, but only if the budget was maintained. Indeed, increasing staff and promotion could lead to an even greater than 15 per cent rise in sales.

Evaluation Cutting budgets is usually a difficult process. However, one of the purposes of setting budgets is to plan for the future, so that a company remains profitable. Staff typically resist budget cuts. Management could resist the temptation to give in to the sales department and impose its decision through the budgetary process. The new budget could give sales staff more realistic targets. In the long term this could be more motivating than chasing unrealistic targets.

Defining cash flow

A BUDGET is a plan of future operations. Typically, budgets are short term plans drawn up for 12 months, which may be split up into monthly periods. The process of BUDGETING allows a business to plan its future costs and revenues. Budgets have three important features.

Quantifiable Budgets are quantifiable - they can be given a value. This is often, though not always, in monetary terms. The sales budget of a business, for instance, is based on planned future sales revenues. A sales budget for a chair manufacturer for six months of the year is shown in Table 29.1. Table 29.2 shows a simple production costs budget. Businesses may have budgets in a number of areas including sales, stocks, production levels and costs, purchases of materials, production and sales overheads, debtors or creditors, or cash.

Achieving objectives Budgets and business objectives (see unit 63) are closely linked. All budgets must be prepared to enable the business to achieve its objectives. For example, if a business objective is to increase sales by 10 per cent per year, then this 10 per cent increase should be shown in the sales budget. This will then have implications for all the other budgets within the business, such as the production budget.

A budget is a plan Plans are different from forecasts. A forecast predicts what may happen in the future. A delivery business, for instance, might forecast on current trends that it will earn £500 000 in January next year. A plan, however, shows what it wants to achieve. The business may set an objective of earning sales revenue of

£550 000 in January. Budgets and strategies then have to be drawn up to allow this objective to be achieved.

The purpose of budgets

Budgeting is a management tool for controlling the business and effecting change. It has a number of purposes.

Control and monitoring Budgeting allows management to control the business. It does this by setting objectives and targets (see unit 63). These are then translated into budgets for, say, the coming year. Success by the workforce in achieving those targets can be found by comparing the actual results with the budget. The reasons for failing to achieve the budget can then be analysed and appropriate action taken.

Planning Budgeting forces management to think ahead. Without budgeting, too many managers would work on a day

	January	February	March	April	May	June
						£
Traditional chair	80 000	72 000	72 000	84 000	92 000	96 000
Modern chair	120 000	108 000	108 000	123 000	126 000	150 000
Stacking chair	60 000	58 000	56 000	61 000	65 000	70 000
Total	260 000	238 000	236 000	268 000	283 000	316 000

Table 29.1 *Sales budget, January – June*

	January	February	March	April	May	June
						£
Materials costs	120 000	110 000	110 000	125 000	140 000	160 000
Labour costs	20 000	20 000	20 000	20 000	30 000	30 000
Other costs	90 000	92 000	95 000	100 000	102 000	110 000
Production costs	230 000	222 000	225 000	245 000	272 000	300 000

Table 29.2 *Production costs budget, January – June*

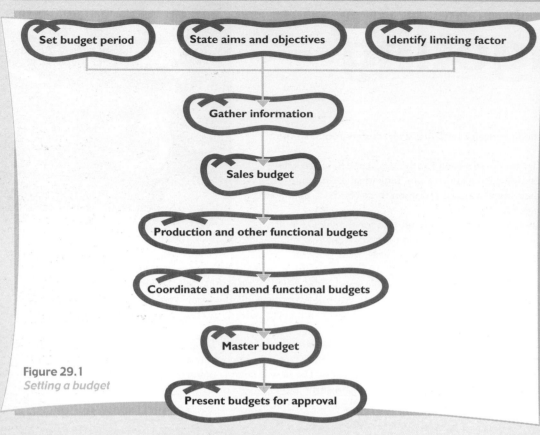

Figure 29.1
Setting a budget

by day basis, only dealing with opportunities and problems as they arise. Budgeting, however, plans for the future. It anticipates problems and their solutions.

Co-ordination Larger businesses often have complex organisations. There may be many departments and different production and administrative sites. A multinational company will have workers spread across the world. Budgeting is one way in which managers can co-ordinate the activities of the many areas of the business.

Communication Planning allows the objectives of the business to be communicated to the workforce. By keeping to a budget, managers and workers have a clear framework within which to operate. So budgeting removes an element of uncertainty within decision making throughout the business.

Efficiency In a business with many workers, it becomes important for management to **empower** staff by **delegating** (see unit 31) decision making. In a medium to large business, senior management cannot efficiently make every decision on behalf of every employee, department or site. Budgeting gives financial control to workers who are best able to make decisions at their level within the organisation.

Motivation Budgeting should act as a motivator to the workforce. It provides workers with targets and standards. Improving on the budget position is an indication of success for a department or group of workers. Fear of failing to reach budgeted targets may make workers work harder.

Setting budgets

Setting a budget can be a complicated process, as Figure 29.1 shows. At the start, the business must set overall **objectives** and the budgetary period. For instance, it might want to increase sales by 10 per cent, reduce costs by 2 per cent or improve skills levels of workers over the next year. These objectives need to be reflected in budgets that are drawn up throughout the business.

Typically, the first budget to be set is the sales budget. This is because sales are likely to be the KEY BUDGET FACTOR or LIMITING BUDGET FACTOR. This is the factor which limits the activities of a business. For example, a business may plan revenue in January to be £6 000. If the price of its product is £100 then it would plan production to be 60 goods. It would also need to take into account other factors. For example, if it had stocks of 10 and wanted to be left with stocks of 20, it would plan production to be 70 (60 + 20 - 10).

Once the sales budget has been set, draft budgets can be prepared. These will include budgets in functional areas such as the production and purchasing department. The draft budgets need to be coordinated, to make sure that they do not conflict with each other. This is often done by a budget officer or budget committee.The budgets can then be brought together into a MASTER BUDGET. This is a summary of all the other budgets. It shows the cash flow budget, budgeted profit and loss and balance sheet of the business (see unit 20).

Budgets are sometimes difficult to prepare for a number of reasons.

- It may be difficult to plan future revenues or costs. This may be the case where the external environment is changing rapidly. For example, the mobile phone market might have expanded by 20 per cent last year. In this market it may be difficult to predict whether it will expand by 10 per cent or 30 per cent next year. But for budgeting purposes, there is a large difference between these two figures.
- The larger the business, the more difficult and time consuming will be the process of drawing up budgets.
- Negotiations about budgets with departments can be difficult. Every budget-making group will want to defend and even expand its work. The marketing department, for example, could argue that sales could be increased if more money were allocated to marketing. The accounts department could argue that its budget cannot be cut because its workload will remain the same even if sales fall. The research department could argue that it needs a much larger budget if new and innovative products are to be made.

Zero budgeting

Most businesses prepare their budgets using the previous period's budget as a guide. The wage costs of an accounts department last year may have been £230 000. So it is

Povey's is a manufacturer of light trucks. It has just launched a new generation of trucks to replace its existing product range. Management is keen to cut costs since the company will make a projected £750 000 loss this year. The head of the R&D department has been told that the launch has been a great success. There has been positive feedback from customers who have tried out the new range. However, the range will not need replacing for at least another five years. In the meantime, the R&D department will only be required to research any problems with the new range, and produce additional variations depending on customer demand.

Traditionally, budgets have been drawn up on the basis of past costs. The projected costs of the R&D department for the current year are shown in Table 29.3. The head of R&D has been asked to draw up a zero-based budget for the forthcoming year. He has been warned that substantial cuts will be expected from his department.

1 **Why might future costs of the R&D department be lower than past costs?**
2 **What might be the advantages of using zero budgeting techniques in this case?**

	£
	Projections 2002
Wages	400 000
Premises	34 000
Equipment	230 000
Materials	53 000
Other costs	67 000
Total	784 000

Table 29.3 *Projected costs, R&D department, 2002*

relatively easy to say that next year they will be £230 000 plus an allowance for an annual pay increase. This assumes that the size of the accounts department will remain the same.

An alternative method of budgeting is ZERO BUDGETING. Here, departments and managers do not base their future budgets on past budgets. Just because spending took place on an item in the last budget does not mean it will take place in the next budget. Instead, budgets are drawn up from 'zero', and every item which appears on the budget must be justified. So a particular item of spending must generate enough benefit to the business for money to be allocated to it in the budget.

The advantages of zero budgeting are that:
- it forces managers to look at every item of revenue and expenditure on their budget and justify it;
- it helps senior managers identify spending in the business which is no longer needed to achieve its objectives;
- it tends to put a downward pressure on costs because every cost is reviewed on a regular basis.

Zero budgeting can have disadvantages for a business.
- It can be time consuming and expensive to construct budgets from nothing every budgeting period. This time may be better used on other tasks.
- It does nothing to resolve the problem of managers being able to exert undue control over the budgetary process to benefit themselves and their departments at the expense of the rest of the business.

The benefits and drawbacks of budgetary control

Budgeting has a number of benefits for a business.

Planning and coordination It allows management to plan for the future in the light of the objectives that have been set. When budgeting works, different parts of a business can help to achieve these objectives by keeping to their budgets. The different parts are then working together, rather than pulling in different directions financially.

Control Budgeting provides a means of controlling expenditure. This helps the business to control its cash flow and avoid possible financial difficulties in future. It also allows management to monitor the performance of individuals, groups or departments. This can be done by comparing actual figures with budgeted figures. This then lets managers use MANAGEMENT BY EXCEPTION. It is a technique where managers concentrate on individuals or groups who have not made their budgets and do not spend too much time on those that have. This saves time and costs. So, for example, management may investigate why the marketing department had budgeted to spend £2 million this year but actually spent £2.5 million. But it may not be too concerned with why other departments had spent a little less than they budgeted.

Motivation Budgets motivate staff by giving them clear goals to achieve. They also provides a way in which the performance of departments and individual staff can be evaluated.

However, there are disadvantages to budgeting.

Cost The time spent drawing up and evaluating budgets could have been spent on other tasks. For example, sales managers could be gaining new customers and increasing revenue for the business instead of drawing up this year's budget. Time spent on paperwork and attending meetings in the production department means less time spent on production itself and increases costs.

Over-ambitious objectives Sometimes businesses set over-ambitious objectives. When this happens, the budgeting process is pointless because budgets are being drawn up for targets which are unachievable. The budget then ceases to become a benchmark with which to compare the outcome.

External influences In some industries, it is difficult to plan ahead because of large and unpredictable changes in the external environment. In farming, for instance, there can be variations in price from year to year and the weather can have large effects on output. This doesn't mean that businesses in such industries should not draw up budgets. However, it can be difficult to analyse outcomes against the budget. It may be unclear if external influences or the way in which a business is run have affected whether a budget is achieved or not.

Motivation In some businesses, workers are left out of the planning process. If workers are not consulted about the budget, it will be more difficult to use that budget to motivate them. Budgets which are unrealistic can also fail to motivate staff.

Manipulation Budgets can be manipulated by managers. For example, a departmental manager might have great influence over those coordinating and setting budgets. The manager may be able to arrange a budget which is easy to achieve and makes the department look successful. But the budget may not help the business achieve its objectives.

Rigidity Budgets can sometimes constrain business activities. For instance, departments within a business may have different views about when it is best to replace vehicles. The more often vehicles are replaced, the higher the cost. However, the newer the vehicle, the lower the maintenance cost and the less likely it will be off the road for repairs. The budget may be set so that older vehicles have to be kept rather than replaced. But this may lead to customer dissatisfaction and lost orders because deliveries are unreliable.

Variances

A business may budget to sell £1.8 million worth of engineering products next year. If it actually sells £2 million, there is a **difference** between the budgeted figure and the actual figure of £0.2 million. This difference is called a VARIANCE.

Variances can be favourable or unfavourable.

Favourable A FAVOURABLE VARIANCE (which may be shown as F in a table) is where the actual performance is better than the budgeted performance. It increases profit above that which was budgeted. Look at Table 29.4. Favourable variances can occur in two ways.
- If actual revenue is **more** than budgeted revenue. In 2002,

	Budgeted	Actual	Variance
			£ million
2002			
Revenue	2.0	2.1	0.1 F
Costs	1.8	1.5	0.3 F
Profit	0.2	0.6	0.4 F
2003			
Revenue	2.6	2.4	0.2 A
Costs	2.2	2.4	0.2 A
Profit	0.4	0.0	0.4 A

Table 29.4 *Variances*

actual revenue is £2.1 million and budgeted revenue is £2 million. So actual revenue is £0.1 million more than budgeted revenue.
- If actual costs are **less** than budgeted costs. In 2002, actual costs are £1.5 million and budgeted costs are £1.8 million. So actual costs are £0.3 million less than budgeted costs.

Actual profit is now £0.4 million more than was budgeted.

Adverse An ADVERSE VARIANCE (which may be shown as A in a table) is where the actual performance is worse than the budgeted performance. It makes profit lower than that which was budgeted. For example, in Table 29.4, an adverse variance was when:
- actual revenue in 2003 was £0.2 million **less** than budgeted;
- actual costs in 2003 were £0.2 million **more** than budgeted.

Actual profit is now £0.4 million worse than was budgeted.

Interpreting variances

Variances are calculated to alert managers to differences in planned outcomes from budgets. They can then take action. For example, if sales are lower, it could be that marketing needs to be increased. If costs are higher, managers need to see if there is any way that costs can be cut back.

However, variance analysis needs to be treated with caution. Table 29.5 shows budgeted and actual revenues and costs for a business over four quarters.

	Budgeted	Actual	Variance
			£ million
Revenue			
Q1	1.2	1.5	0.3 F
Q2	1.3	1.3	0
Q3	1.1	1.0	0.1 A
Q4	1.6	1.4	0.2 A
Costs			
Q1	1.0	1.1	0.1 A
Q2	1.1	1.2	0.1 A
Q3	0.9	1.1	0.2 A
Q4	1.4	1.6	0.2 A

Table 29.5 *Variances*

- In the first quarter, there is a favourable revenue variance, but an unfavourable cost variance. Management might not be too concerned, however, at the increase in costs if the rise in costs has occurred because of increased production to cope with increased sales.
- In the second quarter, there is no variance for sales but an adverse variance for costs. Management should be concerned that actual costs have risen when sales have remained the same.

- In the third and fourth quarters, the business is performing poorly. Not only are there adverse variances in revenues, but there also adverse variances in costs. Revenues have gone down but costs have risen.

Considering why variances have occurred is called VARIANCE ANALYSIS. It may be due to changes in levels of expenditure, efficiency and usage, for example.

keyterms

Adverse variance - **when the variance is likely to lead to a reduction in profit, typically due to lower actual revenues or actual higher costs than budgeted.**
Budget - **a plan of operations for a future accounting period.**
Budgeting or Budgetary control - **the process of setting a budget, comparing the outturn and taking action based upon the information gained.**
Favourable variance - **when the variance is likely to lead to an increase in profit, for example, if there are higher actual revenues or lower actual costs than budgeted.**
Key budget factor or limiting budget factor - **the factor which limits the activities of a business. This has to be taken into account when drawing up budgets.**
Management by exception - **a technique where managers**
spend most of their time on individuals, groups or departments that have not achieved budgeted figures rather than those that have.
Master budget - **the budget which summarises all the budgets of different parts of the business.**
Variance - **in budgeting, the difference between the budgeted or planned figures for costs or income and the actual figures.**
Variance analysis - **explaining why differences between budgeted figures and actual figures have occurred.**
Zero budgeting (or Zero-based budgeting) - **a system of budgeting where every item of income or expenditure is assumed have a value of zero unless a positive figure can be justified by those preparing the budget.**

1 **Complete the last column in the table by filling in the size of the variance and stating whether it is favourable (F) or adverse (A).**
2 **Discuss whether the company has performed well or poorly over the four month period January to April.**

Table 29.6 shows the budgeted and actual sales revenue and costs for a wholesaling chain of tools and electrical goods.

	Budgeted	Actual	Variance
Revenue			
January	12	13	
February	14	15	
March	13	12	
April	15	16	
Costs			
January	10	12	
February	12	14	
March	14	14	
April	15	13	

Table 29.6 *Budgeted and actual sales revenue and costs, £m*

checklist

1. What is the link between a budget and the objectives of a business?
2. Explain the difference between a budget and a forecast.
3. Briefly explain the different purposes of a budget.
4. Explain how a budget is set.
5. Why might a business set a zero budget for its departments?
6. Explain briefly the disadvantages of budgeting to a business.
7. What is the difference between a favourable variance and an adverse variance?

Tadminster Football Club plays in a local football league. It uses budgets as part of its financial control system. The budgets for the 2001-02 and 2002-03 seasons are shown in Table 29.7. The table also shows the actual revenues and costs (the outturn) for 2001-02.

It was a disappointing season both on and off the pitch for the club. On the pitch, the club struggled to avoid relegation. Off the pitch, a budgeted profit turned into a loss, mainly due to higher than budgeted costs. As the club enters its 2002-03 season, it hopes that the new players it has bought will improve performance on the pitch. However, the new players come at a price and the club has budgeted for a deficit for 2002-03.

1. Explain what is meant by the term 'budget'. (3 marks)
2. (a) Was the variance on profit for 2001-02 positive or adverse? (1 mark)
   (b) Calculate the variance on revenue for 2001-02. (2 marks)
   (c) Outline TWO factors which caused the club to fail to meet its budget for profit in 2001-02 (6 marks).
3. The club increased its ticket prices for the 2002-03 season by 10 per cent. Analyse reasons why the club has not budgeted for a 10 per cent increase in total sales of match tickets. (8 marks)
4. Discuss the club's financial strengths and weaknesses as it goes into the 2002-03 season. (10 marks)

	2001-02 Budgeted	2001-02 Actual	2002-03 Budgeted
Revenue			
Match receipts	60 000	50 000	62 000
Retailing and merchandising	5 000	6 000	6 000
Conference, banqueting and catering	4 000	5 000	6 000
Sponsorship, advertising and other income	10 000	8 000	8 000
Total revenue	79 000	69 000	82 000
Costs			
Staff and players wages and associated costs	55 000	56 000	68 000
Stadium and match costs	10 000	9 000	11 000
Retailing and merchandising	2 000	3 000	4 000
Conference, banqueting and catering	4 000	5 000	7 000
Costs associated with sponsorship, executive suites, advertising and other income	2 000	2 000	2 000
Total costs	73 000	75 000	92 000
Profit for the year	6 000	- 6 000	-10 000

Table 29.7 *Tadminster Football Club, budget and outturn 2001–03 (£)*

30 Cost and profit centres

Page Recruitment

Knowledge John and Marilyn Page run a recruitment agency in the London area. It has six branches and specialises in secretarial placements.

Application Each branch is a separate *profit centre*. It is set *targets* for each quarter. How it achieves those targets is left to the *manager* in charge of the *branch*. Each branch has a different sized *sales turnover* because of different *performance* over the 12 years the *company* has been in existence. Last quarter, *branches* were set *two targets*. One was to increase *sales turnover* by 5 per cent. The other was to make a 20 per cent *profit* on *sales turnover*.

Analysis Three branches achieved both targets. Two saw sales increase by only 3 per cent, but achieved the 20 per cent profit target. The other fell short on both targets. It achieved only 1 per cent higher sales and made only a 14 per cent profit. This branch has underperformed consistently for the last two years. The manager has already been warned that performance must improve. John and Marilyn have now decided that the time has come to take action.

Evaluation By splitting the business into profit centres, John and Marilyn can see how different branches are performing. This might give them a competitive edge in a market where there are many similar companies providing the same service. However, it is important that they use their financial data alongside other information. There may be good reasons why one branch is not doing particularly well. Perhaps it is situated in an area where businesses are not doing as well as in the rest of the London area. If the business takes the wrong action, this could be demotivating for staff at the branch.

Cost and profit centres

Businesses often find that they can operate more efficiently if they break down their organisation into smaller units. One way of doing this is to establish cost and profit centres.

Cost centres A COST CENTRE is a section of a business for which costs are seperately identified and collected.

It might be:
- a department, like the production department or the accounts department;
- a geographical area of the business, like the North West of England or France;
- a product which is made by the business;
- an outlet or set of premises, such as a shop, a factory or offices;
- a person, such as a sales representative or a maintenance worker;
- a machine, like a photocopier or a telephone line.

Profit centres A PROFIT CENTRE is similar to a cost centre. But revenues as well as costs are identified and collected. This enables a profit for the centre to be calculated.

Cost and profit centres prepare **management accounts** (see unit 20) for their operations. These accounts allow managers to monitor, control and plan the operations of cost and profit centres. For example, a cash flow forecast may be prepared for a production department or a budget may be prepared for an operation in France.

Reasons for operating cost and profit centres

There are reasons why businesses establish cost and profit centres.

Decision making To make decisions, managers need information. In a large business, it is important to know how the whole business is doing financially. But it is also important to have financial information about different parts of the business.

Organisational control Financial information about different parts of the business allow those parts to be monitored and controlled. For example, if the sales department has seen its costs rise by 20 per cent when total costs of the business have only risen 4 per cent, this could indicate that sales have been inefficient and wasteful in their use of resources. A business which owns a chain of shops can compare the performance of each shop by considering sales, costs and profit. Decisions can then be taken to improve the performance of those parts of the business which are underperforming.

Motivation Cost and profit centres will be controlled by managers and workers. By setting targets for each centre, management can motivate its staff to achieve those targets. Success in hitting targets can be rewarded in a variety of ways. It may just give staff job satisfaction to know that they have achieved their targets. Hitting targets may be one aspect of the process of recruitment to more senior positions. Targets can also be linked to bonus payments. For example, the furniture department in a department store might be given a target of increasing its profit by 5 per cent over the next 12 months. If the target is achieved, each member of staff in that department might be given a bonus worth 5 per cent of their salary. Problems with bonuses can arise, however, if workers outside the cost or profit centre feel that they have made a significant contribution to achieving the target but they are not rewarded. Equally, targets can be set which would be so difficult to achieve that staff don't even try to achieve them.

Advantages and disadvantages of cost and profit centres

Cost and profit centres allow businesses to monitor the financial

"**key**terms"

Cost centre - a section of a business for which costs are separately identified and collected.
Profit centre - a section of a business for which profits are calculated.

✓ checklist

1 What is the difference between a cost centre and profit centre?
2 What sections of a business might be suitable for the creation of cost or profit centres?
3 Why might a business operate a profit centre?
4 Explain briefly the possible disadvantages of creating cost centres to a business.

performance of parts of their organisation. This enables them to assess their performance and identify strong and weak performing areas. Delegating authority for achieving costs and profit targets can also motivate for staff. However, cost and profit centres can have disadvantages.

Cost allocation Businesses have fixed costs. For example, there is the cost of the managing director's salary. Or perhaps there is a headquarters for the business. No single cost or profit centre can be said to incur these costs on its own. These costs have to be spread out somehow across cost or profit centres. There is a variety of ways of doing this, such as allocating fixed costs according to the costs or revenue of a cost or profit centre. However, no single method is perfect. Choosing the wrong method can give a distorted picture of the performance of a cost or profit centre compared to others in the business. Individual cost or profit centres may also feel that they are being made to pay too much of the overheads of the business and hence their performance is being dragged down through no fault of their own. This can be demotivating for staff.

The costs of resources Financial information must be gathered, collated and analysed if it is to be of use. This takes up staff resources which could be used elsewhere. Sometimes it is simply not cost effective to create a cost or profit centre. The benefits outweigh the costs of gathering the information.

Insufficient skills Staff given control over costs and revenues must be capable of handling the responsibility. Sometimes, authority to make decisions is pushed too far down the organisation to staff who do not have enough skills to cope successfully. This can demotivate staff.

Conflict Cost and profit centres may create a sense of identity for staff within the centre. But it can also create a 'them and us' attitude within a whole organisation. Centres may work in their best interests at the expense of other cost and profit centres. This can damage the efficiency of the whole business.

External factors The performance of a cost or profit centre may have more to do with external factors than with the work and effort of staff within the centre. For example, falls in profits may be due to rising energy costs in world markets, rather than a lack of costs control. This could be demotivating for staff, especially if performance is judged on fixed targets set by management.

Westacott is a furniture manufacturer. Its factory is in Sunderland and up till four years ago it sold only in the UK. At the time, it wanted to expand and thought that it would be easier to do this in Europe than in the UK. So it set up two sales offices, one in Paris, the other in Berlin. Both were operated as profit centres and set profit targets. In the first year, it was recognised that both would make a loss as contacts were built up amongst potential customers. The second year, the profit centres were expected to break-even. For the past two years, targets have been set and missed by both profit centres, as can be seen from Table 30.1.

The sales managers in Paris and Berlin have different ways of working. Henri Ducas in Paris tends to be cautious in his operations. He keeps a tight control on costs and always aims to meet targets. Paul Stengelhofen is more revenue-orientated. Gaining a sale is what gives him most satisfaction. The difference showed up two months ago. Stengelhofen succeeded in selling some furniture to the Lille office of a German company. Lille is in Northern France. When Henri Ducas heard about it, he faxed a memo of complaint to Sunderland and Berlin. Ducas argued that any sales in France should have gone through the Paris office which had the expertise to deal with French customers. Stengelhofen simply replied that 'a sale was a sale' and why bother to make a fuss about who dealt with it.

	2000	2001	2002	2003
Paris office				
Sales turnover	30, 000	90,000	300,000	500,000
Costs of sales	15,000	45,000	150,000	250,000
Overheads	120,000	150,000	150,000	150,000
Total costs	135,000	195,000	300,000	400,000
Profit	-105,000	-105,000	0	100,000
Target profit	-100,000	0	100,000	200,000
Berlin office				
Sales turnover	40, 000	130,000	380,000	660,000
Costs of sales	20,000	65,000	190,000	330,000
Overheads	130,000	150,000	180,000	200,000
Total costs	150,000	215,000	370,000	530,000
Profit	-110,000	-85,000	10,000	130,000
Target profit	-100,000	0	100,000	200,000

Table 30.1 *Westacott: management accounts for Paris and Berlin offices: 2000–2003. **Note: Cost of sales is the value of goods delivered from Sunderland, including transport charges. Goods are charged to each profit centre at the cost of manufacture before any profit has been included.***

1 Explain the meaning of the terms:
   (i) profit centre; (3 marks); (ii) management accounts. (3 marks)
2 Using Table 30.1, outline TWO possible reasons why both the Paris and Berlin offices failed to reach their target profits between 2000 and 2003. (6 marks)
3 Analyse possible reasons why Westacott decided to operate its Paris and Berlin offices as profit centres. (8 marks)
4 Senior management at Westacott is considering closing one of the two continental offices and organising all non-UK sales from one office based in Berlin. Discuss the possible advantages and disadvantages of this change in strategy. (10 marks)

School structure

Knowledge Secondary schools in the UK tend to take pupils from 11-18. They can range in size from 500 to 2 000 pupils.

Application Secondary schools need to have an *organisational structure* to work effectively. At the top of the *hierarchy* is the Headteacher. Then there will be at least one *Deputy Headteacher*. The *organisation* then tends to split into two. On the one hand, there is an academic structure responsible for the teaching of subjects. For example, there will be a Head of Science, *responsible* for a number of science teachers. On the other hand, there is a pastoral structure, responsible for the welfare of pupils. A Head of Year or Head of House will be responsible for a number of tutors, each responsible in turn for a small group of pupils. In this *chain of command*, the *span of control* can vary enormously. The Head of Mathematics, for example, might have *line authority* over her 8 full time maths teachers and 4 part time teachers. The Head of Physical Education might have *line authority* over just three teachers. Different Headteachers have different *management styles*. In some schools, decision making is highly *centralised* with the Headteacher making all the key decisions. In other schools, decision making is highly *decentralised* with decision making powers being pushed down the *chain of command*.

Analysis No two schools have exactly the same organisational structure. Also, as new demands are placed on schools, organisational structures can change considerably. For example, in the 1950s in state schools, pastoral care tended to be given informally. Today, pastoral care is very important, from the legal requirement to monitor attendance to reviewing a child's overall progress to giving references for university or work.

Evaluation There is no 'best' organisational structure for a school. However, schools need to change their organisational structures to cope with changing demands. The extent to which school organisations should be centralised depends upon the talents and skills of individual staff, particularly the Headteacher. The Headteacher will almost certainly be the single most important influence on the effectiveness of the organisation. A Headteacher who skilfully manages a highly centralised organisation can be as effective as Headteacher who is skilled at managing a decentralised organisation.

Organisational structures

Every business with more than one person working in the organisation must have an ORGANISATIONAL STRUCTURE or BUSINESS STRUCTURE. This structure is the way in which positions **within** the business are arranged.

The organisational structure of a business defines:
- the roles of employees and their job titles;
- the route through which decisions are made;
- who is responsible and accountable to whom, and for what activities;
- the relationships between positions in a business;
- how employees communicate with each other and how information is passed on.

Structure is important for all businesses. It helps them to divide work and coordinate their activities so they achieve their objectives. But it is likely to become more important the larger the business. A plumbing business with two workers, for example, is likely to have fewer problems deciding exactly 'who does what' than a company with businesses in many countries.

Organisation charts

The formal organisation of a business can be shown on an ORGANISATION CHART or ORGANISATION TREE. It illustrates the formal relationships (set by written rules and procedures) between different people in a business. Figure 31.1 shows an organisation chart for a manufacturing business. This business is split into six **functional** DEPARTMENTS - sales, marketing, finance and administration, production, human resources, and research and development. But it could have been organised into geographical regions or by different products, for example.

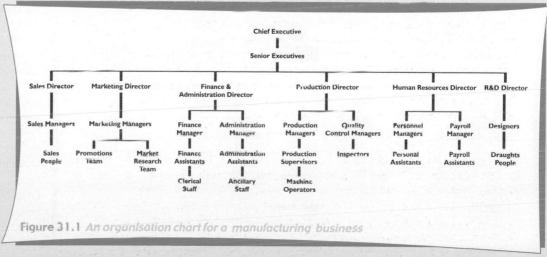

Figure 31.1 *An organisation chart for a manufacturing business*

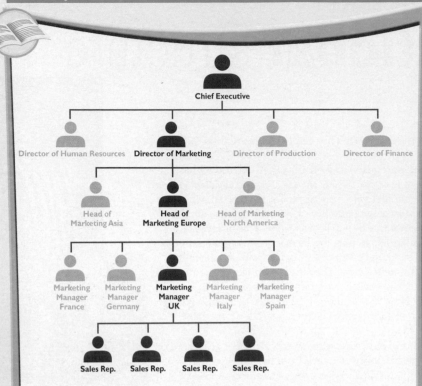

Figure 31.2 *Part of an organisation chart for a multinational engineering company*

> *Figure 31.2 shows part of an organisation chart for a multinational engineering company.*
>
> 1 **The company sells into both European and North American markets. How can this be seen from the chart?**
> 2 **Describe the chain of command from Chief Executive to UK sales representative.**
> 3 **How large is the span of control of the European Head of Marketing?**
> 4 **Who is immediately subordinate to the Director of Marketing?**
> 5 **The Chief Executive is considering streamlining the management organisation through a process of delayering. (a) Suggest ONE way in which this could be done and (b) describe its effects on the chain of command and the span of control within the organisation.**

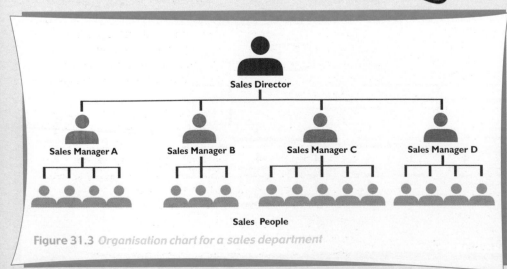

Figure 31.3 *Organisation chart for a sales department*

There is a clear HIERARCHY within the business - the way in which it is organised from 'top to bottom'. For example, departmental directors are responsible to the senior executives. Underneath each department director are the other employees of the business. For example, in the production department there are machine operators and production supervisors. Figure 31.1 also shows clearly the LINE MANAGERS within the organisation. These are employees responsible for the group of workers below them in the vertical line of the organisation.

Features of organisations

Figure 31.1 can be used to illustrate a number of important features about organisations.

Chain of command The CHAIN OF COMMAND is the path down which orders are passed. For example, in Figure 31.1, orders would be passed down from the senior executives to the departmental directors. In turn, they would pass orders down to the workers below them. For example, the production director would pass orders to the quality control manager.

The number of workers in the chain of command is important to the efficiency of the business. On the one hand, the more workers in the chain, the more **specialised** each becomes. The division of labour helps increase output because each worker can become highly skilled (see unit 42). On the other hand, too long a chain of command can make it very difficult to communicate from top to bottom and vice versa. The chief executive of a large multinational will have no direct regular contact with workers at the bottom of the chain. The more layers a message has to go through, the less likely it is to be sent or received accurately. A long chain of command can also mean that too many staff are employed to make the chain operate effectively, rather than being employed in making the end product.

In the 1990s, many large businesses went through a process of DELAYERING. This is where positions within the hierarchy are abolished. This reduces the length of the chain of command. For example, in Figure 31.1, the position of sales manager might be abolished so that salespeople are directly responsible to the sales director. Delayering cuts costs and means that lines of communication from top to bottom are shorter. However, the danger is that there are too few middle managers and that essential work is not done.

Span of control The SPAN OF CONTROL is the number of people who report directly to a person in a superior position. In Figure 31.3, an organisation chart for the sales

Ansuya Chopra was an accountant with a large UK accountancy firm. However, she didn't find much job satisfaction and decided to join the family carpet manufacturing business in Kidderminster. Asuya learnt to do everything, from running the books of the company to working machines and using design programmes. Eventually, she took over, becoming its owner manager.

Ansuya had wanted to make changes to the business for some time. She felt that workers were given too much authority to make decisions. The company would be more efficient if the decisions were made by her. She was determined to shake things up. So she set about restricting the decisions that could be made by individual workers. Decisions that before had been made by ordinary shop floor workers now had to be referred to senior team leaders. In turn, team leaders now had to get Ansuya's approval on many more issues than before.

1 'Ansuya removed some responsibility from her workers and centralised decision making within the company.' (a) Explain what this means. (b) What might be the advantages and disadvantages to the company of this centralisation.

department is drawn. There are 4 sales managers under the sales director. The span of control for the sales director is therefore 4 workers. The span of control of the sales managers varies from 3 to 5 salespeople. The salespeople are SUBORDINATES of the sales managers because they work under them and receive orders from them.

The span of control is important for the efficiency of the business. Henri Fayol, a French industrialist, in his book *Administration Industrielle et Generale* (1916), suggested that the span of control should be between 3 and 6 subordinates. The exact number would depend on the complexity of the work done by subordinates. The more complex the work, the less should be the span of control. This would ensure tight managerial control of the business. It would also give the managers time to do this part of their work. The wider the span of control, the more time a superior is likely to have to spend controlling subordinates. If there are too many subordinates, control will become ineffective. Superiors will have to rely on their subordinates to make the right judgments. On the other hand, a wide span of control will lead to increased DELEGATION. Giving authority to subordinates to make decisions can increase their motivation and their job satisfaction. Delayering (i.e. removing layers of management from the hierarchy) will increase the span of control of managers who are left.

Authority AUTHORITY is the power given by the organisation to undertake a certain task. For example, the sales director may have the authority to place advertisements in the media, while sales managers do not. The finance and administration director may be the only person with the authority to sign cheques for a very high amount. The lower down the hierarchy, the less authority a member of staff is likely to have. However, even workers at the bottom of the hierarchy may have authority which those higher up do not have. For example, a shop floor employee may be the first aid worker

for a section of the factory. If a worker collapses in front of a senior executive and this employee, the first aid worker would have the authority to help the collapsed worker, not the executive.

There are three types of authority in a hierarchy. **Line authority** is the authority that a worker has over a subordinate. So commands can be passed **down the line** in an organisation. **Staff authority** and **functional authority** occur when workers have a role outside their main area. These workers operate across the hierarchy, not up and down the hierarchy. For example, a member of the accounts department may be authorised to work with the production department to draw up a budget. Workers with **staff authority** can only give advice. They have no power to enforce their decisions. In contrast, workers with **functional authority** have the power to make decisions. So, for example, a finance manager may be given functional authority over another department to control costs.

Responsibility RESPONSIBILITY means being accountable for work. Workers given responsibility for a task are obliged to complete the task. So the sales director may be responsible to the senior executives for the level of sales in the last quarter. The sales director would have to give reasons if sales were below those forecast. Ultimately, the sales director could be dismissed if he or she consistently fails to meet sales targets set by senior executives.

Centralisation and decentralisation CENTRALISATION means that all important decisions are made at the centre or core of an organisation. These decisions are then passed down the hierarchy to be carried out lower down the organisation. DECENTRALISATION means that decision making is pushed down the chain of command. Decision making is then DEVOLVED to lower parts of the organisation.

Centralisation has a number of advantages.
● Senior management can keep a tight control on the business. The smaller the business, the more senior

'key terms'

Authority - the right given by the organisation to a worker to make a decision in a particular situation.

Bureaucracy - a workplace organisation where there are clear, formal structures designed to achieve specific goals.

Centralisation - a type of business organisation where major decisions are made at the centre or core of the organisation and then passed down the chain of command.

Chain of command - the path down which orders are passed. In a company, this goes from the board of directors down to shop floor workers.

Decentralisation - a type of business organisation where decision making is pushed down the chain of command and away from the centre of the organisation.

Delayering - removing layers of management from the hierarchy of an organisation.

Delegation - passing down of authority for work to another worker further down the hierarchy of the organisation.

Department - a grouping of employees doing similar jobs within an organisation, such as the finance department or the marketing department.

Devolved decision making - where authority to make decisions is passed down the chain of command to subordinates.

Hierarchy - vertical structure of different levels of authority in a business organisation from the lowest to the highest.

Line manager - a manager who has direct authority over other employers down the chain of command.

Organisation chart or tree - a diagram which shows the internal formal structure of an organisation.

Organisational or business structure - the way in which the business is arranged internally to perform its economic activities.

Responsibility - the obligation to complete a particular task and to be accountable for the task.

Span of control - the number of workers who report directly to a worker in a superior position within the hierarchy.

Subordinate - workers in the hierarchy who work under the control of a more senior worker.

---

management can direct even the smallest details of how a business is run.

- There is less dependence on the decision making skills of subordinates, which may vary. Assuming that experienced senior management are making the right decisions, the business will benefit from good decision making.
- Workers may try to make decisions which benefit themselves rather than the organisation as a whole. Centralisation reduces the risk of this because decisions are made at the top.
- There is likely to be consistency of procedures throughout the organisation. For example, centralisation in a fast food chain is likely to lead to common hygiene standards in each outlet.
- Economies of scale (see unit 42) may arise because there is more likelihood of common purchasing policies.

However, decentralisation also has its advantages. Delegating authority for decision making can:

- motivate subordinates because they have more control over their work, leading to greater job satisfaction;
- allow staff who are closer to the actual work being done to design more effective, non-standard solutions to problems;
- speed up decision making at lower levels of the hierarchy. Decisions can be made on the spot rather than having to be passed up and then back down the hierarchy;
- free senior management from making minor decisions, allowing them to concentrate on more important strategic decisions;
- help junior and middle management staff to gain decision making skills, which will be useful to them if they are promoted within the business.

Bureaucracy Some organisations are fluid. There are few formal structures and workers are expected to perform a variety of tasks when the need arises. Other organisations are bureaucratic. In a BUREAUCRACY, there are clear formal structures. Workers have strict job descriptions. Employment and promotion is based on qualifications and merit. Work is completed according to pre-set rules. Work is also monitored carefully. Where meetings take place, records of the meeting and any decisions made are kept. There is a high degree of specialisation.

Max Weber, a German sociologist, in his book *The Theory of Social and Economic Organisations* (tr.1947), argued that bureaucracies were highly effective forms of organisation. They could be devised in a scientific way to make an organisation as rational as possible. Today, 'bureaucracy' is often seen in a negative way. It is associated with rigidity, over-complexity and wasteful pen-pushing. In a bureaucracy, workers' individuality is suppressed and they become institutionalised. However, this is one extreme view. Weber argued that organisations work better if there are clear structures and rules about how workers should relate to the work environment. An unstructured work environment, where workers are unclear about their roles, will lead to inefficiency.

checklist

1. Why is the organisational structure of a business important?
2. How does the organisational chart of a business show the hierarchy within the business?
3. What is the link between specialisation of workers and the chain of command within a business?
4. Explain the relationship between authority, subordinates and delegation.
5. What is the difference between line authority and functional authority?
6. Explain the difference between centralisation and decentralisation with a business structure.
7. What is the link between bureaucracy and formal structures?

Avalanche control operations at the Lake Louise Ski Area have a history spanning nearly thirty years. Lake Louise is in the Banff National Park in Canada. The area currently receives half a million guests per year for skiing, snowboarding and related activities. Safety is a key aspect and part of that relates to the danger of avalanches of snow burying skiers in their wake. The ski resort covers over 17 square kilometres and there are over 100 places where avalanches can occur. In addition, some skiers deliberately go outside the resort area for the thrill of skiing in uncrowded, uncontrolled areas. But this increases the number of potential avalanche areas.

In the 1980s, there were effectively three separate departments working on the mountain. The main responsibility of the Ski Patrol was pre-hospital care for skiers who had accidents. For the Warden/Ski Patrol Avalanche Crew, it was monitoring and controlling avalanches. For the Trail Crew, it was managing the slopes including putting up fencing. However, there was overlap between the three departments. Members of the Trail Crew, for example, if they were first on the scene at an accident, would organise help.

These three departments were then reorganised into one Snow Safety Department. This was partly prompted by budget costs. The previous three departments had over 40 staff. The new single department was now just 25 staff. The efficiency gain from downsizing was possible because staff were used more intensively. In particular, on the mountain, patrollers were expected to perform any of the functions which before had been the main responsibility of just one of the departments.

Under the new structure, shown in Figure 31.4, a Snow Safety Manager was put in charge of the whole department, answerable to the Area Manager for the ski resort. Beneath the Snow Safety Manager in the hierarchy were three Snow Safety Supervisors. Two of these were Avalanche Forecasters and one was a Patrol Leader. Working under the the Snow Safety Supervisors were 4 Senior Avalanche Patrollers. Their main duties were as Team Leaders in snow research and avalanche control. In addition, they have become involved in other facets of the department, such as training and acting as roving 'troubleshooters'. They are not scheduled into the daily routine of run checks and accident coverage or to patrol specific areas. In addition, there are 5 Senior Patrollers and 13 Patrollers who have as their primary responsibilities pre-hospital care and risk management (in the form of run checks and trail work). These 18 people also act as Avalanche Team Members on a rotating basis wherever needed. Generally, 2-5 teams are used daily for research and control, depending on conditions.

Adapted from a paper by Mark Klassen, Skiing Louise Ltd, Alberta, Canada.

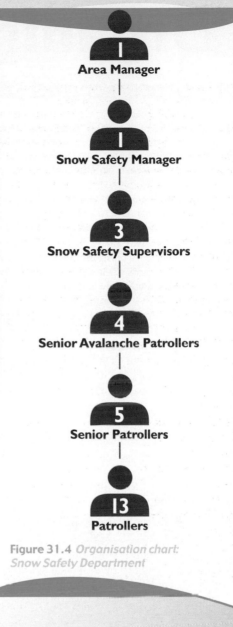

Figure 31.4 *Organisation chart: Snow Safety Department*

1 Explain what is meant by the terms:
  (a) 'hierarchy'; (3 marks)
  (b) 'department' (3 marks).
2 (a) Explain what is the span of control of the Snow Safety Manager shown in Figure 31.4. (3 marks).
  (b) Explain to whom the Patrol Leader, who is one of the three Snow Safety Supervisors, might delegate a task. (3 marks)
3 Analyse the change in structure between the 1980s and the 1990s described in the data. (8 marks)
4 Discuss the possible costs and benefits of downsizing the organisation further by removing the 4 Senior Avalanche Patroller posts. (10 marks)

32 Organisational design

Fabry Groceries and Sainsbury's

Knowledge George Fabry runs two grocery stores close to each other in North London. In contrast, Sainsbury's plc has nearly 500 stores in the UK.

Application George Fabry's *business* has an *entrepreneurial structure*. He makes all the decisions, orders the *stock* and pays the *staff*. In contrast, Sainsbury's has a *bureaucratic structure* within its stores *division*.

Analysis The grocery store business of George Fabry is small enough to work with an entrepreneurial structure. He considers himself to be responsible for every member of his staff. The only workers in the hierarchy between himself and the shop assistants are two store managers and they have relatively little power to make decisions. George wants to keep a firm control on his business. So his business could be said to possess a power culture. Sainsbury's, in contrast, is too large a business for a power culture to be effective. Instead, it has a role culture where the hierarchy of the business is clearly laid out and where every worker has a job description which explains their function within the organisation.

Evaluation Using an entrepreneurial organisational structure, George Fabry is able to achieve his objectives. Using a more complex structure would be simply inappropriate given the size of the organisation. Similarly, Sainsbury's is too large to be organised except through a bureaucratic structure. However, Sainsbury's lost its position as number one grocery retailer in the UK to Tesco in the late 1990s. It can be argued that its organisational structure failed to allow the innovation that was needed to enable it to compete against a more entrepreneurial Tesco.

Different organisational structures

Different types of organisational structure can be chosen by a business.

The bureaucratic or pyramid structure The structure shown in Figure 32.1 is a BUREAUCRATIC or PYRAMID STRUCTURE. It may also be referred to as a FORMAL or TRADITIONAL HIERARCHY, or a LINE AND STAFF ORGANISATION. It is outlined in unit 31. It has certain features.

- It is **bureaucratic**. There are clear formal structures where each member of staff has a defined role and place in the structure.
- It is a **pyramid** structure. The further up the hierarchy, the fewer the workers.
- It is a **formal** structure. It shows how the business expects its workers to relate to each other.
- It is **hierarchical**. Work is delegated down the organisation from the worker at the top.
- It is a **traditional** hierarchy. Through much of the 20th century this was considered to be the most effective way to organise a business.
- It is a **line** and **staff** organisation. Authority is exercised both down the hierarchy and across it.

This type of organisation provides workers with clear roles. Typically, workers are organised into departments which allow the development of expertise and specialisation. Channels of communication are formalised, so workers in the hierarchy have a clear understanding of who should be communicating with whom.

However, such a structure can find it difficult to cope with change. Because every worker and every department has a place, staff and departments can adopt rigid positions. Loyalty of staff can be mainly to fellow workers or to their department rather than to the organisation as a whole. If the chain of command is long, as it is likely to be in a large business, communication can break down because it passes through so many layers. The actual aim of the organisation can become one of self-preservation rather than serving customers or earning profit for the owners. This is because so many workers are involved in maintaining the hierarchy rather than dealing directly with customers or the owners of the business.

Product or geographical structures A traditional pyramid structure can become so large that it becomes too inefficient. One way of getting around this problem is to break a single pyramid into several smaller pyramids. This can be done by breaking a business up into sections or divisions, typically based either on product or on geographical areas. For example, an engineering company might split itself into four divisions, grouping similar products in a single division. Or a food manufacturer might split itself into three geographica; divisions, North America, Europe and the rest of the world. Each division is headed by a executive under whom there is a traditional hierarchy of workers. The divisional executive is then answerable to the chief executive based at the

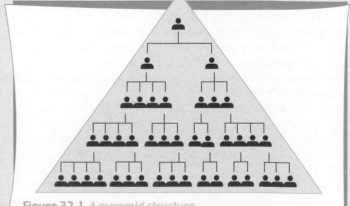

Figure 32.1 *A pyramid structure*

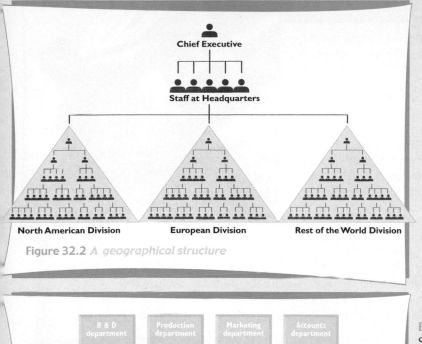

Figure 32.2 *A geographical structure*

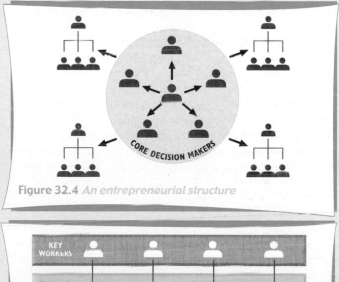

Figure 32.3 *A matrix structure*

- They value workers for the expertise they can bring to a team. This can be highly motivating for staff because it empowers workers (the structure fits McGregor's Theory Y, see unit 39).
- It also provides flexibility when businesses face fast changing markets, where speed, creativity and market awareness are needed for survival.

But there are also disadvantages.
- Empowering workers further down the hierarchy may result in senior management losing some strategic control of the business. Different teams may be pulling in different directions.
- Matrix structures can also be expensive in terms of support staff.
- There may be a conflict of interest. Departments may want their members to concentrate on tasks important to the department. But teams may want experts from the departments to spend time on the team's project. Workers themselves may feel they have divided loyalties.

Entrepreneurial structures ENTREPRENEURIAL (or WEB) STRUCTURES, shown in Figure 32.4, tend to be found in small businesses. A strong central person will run the business (the ENTREPRENEUR). This individual will often have founded the business, may own it and will make many of the important decisions. The rest will be taken by a few trusted subordinates. Decision making is therefore concentrated in a few hands and there may be little consultation.

headquarters of the whole company. This structure is shown in Figure 32.2.

The matrix structure A MATRIX STRUCTURE, shown in Figure 32.3, is where groups of workers are organised flexibly by task. An organisation may have traditional departments. But workers are pulled out of those departments to be part of a team of workers undertaking a particular project. MATRIX MANAGEMENT describes the management task of organising such a team.

For example, a medical insurance company may have teams to process claims. Instead of an insurance claim being passed from department to department, a group of workers from these different departments with different expertise may work together.

Or a chocolate manufacturer may be developing a new chocolate bar. Instead of development being passed from the R&D department to the production department to finance to marketing, a team with different departmental expertise could be put together. In a traditional development process, the R&D department would create a new product. The production department would then comment on whether it was technically possible to produce it. Accounts would comment on what price and sales volumes would be needed for it to be profitable. Marketing would comment on whether the new bar could be marketed effectively in the current market. Doing this in order could take time as it passes from department to department. By putting a team together, there can be almost instant feedback between those involved. Development time could be reduced greatly.

Matrix structures have certain advantages.

This type of structure works extremely well if the entrepreneur is good at decision making and the business has a small number of employees. Entrepreneurs have great influence on their businesses and so their skills are crucial to its success or failure. In a business with few employees, it is fairly easy for the entrepreneur to direct and monitor work of subordinates.

Figure 32.4 *An entrepreneurial structure*

Figure 32.5 *An informal structure*

Perera is a multinational food group. It is split into three divisions, Europe, North America and South America. Within each division, there is a number of subsidiary companies, which specialise in market segments such as frozen foods, ready meals, dairy products and snacks. For example, in the European division there are 26 subsidiary companies with bases across Europe. Not all the divisions have the same range of foods represented. Perera has grown by acquiring small local producers with promising brands and building these up.

The headquarters of the group is in the UK, sharing the same offices with the divisional staff of the European division. The chief executive of the group keeps in daily contact with the three divisional chief executives. They in turn supervise the work of the managing directors of the individual subsidiaries in their geographical area.

A new chief executive for the group was appointed in 2003. He is keen to shake up the group and change its structure. He wants to reorganise the group so that divisions are based on products rather than geographical areas. His belief is that there is currently far too little exchange of information and ideas between companies in the group making the same range of products. By bringing them together into the same division, there could be a much greater sharing of best practice in manufacturing, and a development of brands from the local to the international. The three divisional chief executives are known to be opposed to this, arguing that manufacturing techniques and brands cannot easily cross continents.

1 **Draw a diagram showing the organisational structure of Perera.**
2 **Explain why the organisation of Perera is an example of a hierarchical structure.**
3 **What might be the advantages and disadvantages of having a geographical structure to the group rather than a product structure?**

However, if the number of workers employed grows, it may become difficult for the entrepreneur to keep direct control over the whole business. Decision making may become paralysed if every decision, however small, has to go through one person. Even if the entrepreneur delegates some decision making to a few trusted workers, they can become overwhelmed if there are too many workers within their span of control.

Informal structures INFORMAL (or INDEPENDENCE or CLUSTER) STRUCTURES, shown in Figure 32.5, exist in smaller businesses which need little structure. Typically the structure exists to support the work of one or a few key highly skilled workers. Examples include doctors' practices, barristers' chambers, management consultants, small accountancy firms and architects' practices. The key worker will interact with a few support staff and possibly a few other key workers who might share the support staff. The advantage of an informal structure is that it gives maximum professional freedom to the key workers. However, the structure does not allow for enough control and co-ordination to allow a business to grow to any size.

Factors influencing organisational structures

There is a number of factors which influence which organisational structure is chosen by a business.

Size The larger the business, the more control and co-ordination is required. So entrepreneurial structures and informal structures are less suitable than structures such as pyramid organisations or matrix organisations. Size is also likely to increase the length of the chain of command in a hierarchy. There will be more layers of management to cope with the increased size.

Control Owners who wish to retain day to day control of their businesses tend to adopt informal or entrepreneurial business organisations where spans of control are small. When owners do not run the business, as in most large companies, other types of business structure tend to be more common. Delegation tends to be associated with wider spans of control.

Culture of the organisation Charles Handy, in *Understanding Organisations*, argued that the culture of an organisation affects its choice of organisation.
- Where roles of workers have become very important, the organisation is likely to be a pyramid organisation. This is a **role culture**.
- Where the emphasis is on completing jobs or projects, a matrix organisation is more likely to emerge. In a **task culture**, there is less emphasis on rules, procedures and job titles.
- In a **power culture**, the organisation tends to be dominated by a single powerful individual. So an entrepreneurial structure tends to emerge.
- In a **person culture**, the work of a few key professionals is all important. An informal structure therefore may be appropriate.

Workforce skills Businesses which have many highly skilled workers are less likely to have pyramid type structures. This is because pyramid structures tend to stifle creativity and initiative. Instead, matrix structures will be more common. In small organisations, entrepreneurial or informal organisations are more likely to exist.

Design versus development Small businesses will almost certainly have an entrepreneurial structure. As businesses grow larger, they may change their structures. Some do it organically, making small changes as the need arises. Others make a sudden and deliberate change which has been designed before hand. Even with the largest of businesses, some changes to the organisational structure are small and piecemeal, others are large and involve thousands of managers. An example of a deliberate change in the organisational design would be a change from a geographical structure to a product structure.

External factors Changes in the external environment can affect organisations. Improvements in technology can cut layers within a pyramid organisation. For example, the ability of managers to use personal computers has greatly reduced the need for administrative support. In a recession, pressures to cut costs to survive can lead to delayering of an organisation. In a fast changing market, entrepreneurial or matrix structures may be more responsive than a pyramid structure.

Formal and informal organisation

The FORMAL ORGANISATION of a business is created by senior management. It decides how staff are supposed to relate to each other. By creating formal structures, such as hierarchies and departments and giving workers job descriptions, senior management imposes a way of working on the business.

However, a business may also have an INFORMAL ORGANISATION. This is the network of relationships which staff create themselves. For example, information to members of the accounts department might have to pass up and down the hierarchy through the head of the accounts department. But a member of the accounts department may play squash with a member of the sales department. They may exchange information informally, bypassing the formal channels. Or a senior member of the production department may be inefficient and difficult to work with. Other members of the production department may cut this worker out of the decision making process, contrary to what the formal structure states should happen.

Informal structures can increase efficiency. They can speed up the flow of information around a business. Workers can gain more control over their work, leading to greater motivation and job satisfaction. However, they can also damage the organisation. Sensitive information can be leaked. Gossip can lead to individual workers being victimised. Incorrect information can also be passed on, leading to poor decision making and loss of morale amongst staff.

In any organisation, informal structures will exist. Senior management can influence them by supporting those that are positive and discouraging the less positive. For example, informal networks can be encouraged by putting on social activities for staff or taking people away on staff training. Rumours can be corrected if staff are kept well informed about business matters.

✓ checklist

1 Explain the difference between a bureaucratic organisational structure and a matrix organisational structure.
2 Why do some businesses adopt product or geographic structures?
3 What are the main advantages of matrix organisational structures?
4 Explain the reasons why some businesses adopt entrepreneurial structures.
5 Briefly outline the factors which affect what type of organisational structure might be chosen for a business.
6 Distinguish between formal and informal structures within an organisation.

Rumours that there were going to be staff redundancies had been circulating for at least a month before the official announcement. No one at the Wrens Road factory knew exactly who would go or how many would go. Some said that Catlin's, the owner of the factory, was going to close the whole plant. Others said that the company wanted simply to slim down the operation.

Jeff Clarkstone was in charge of invoices in the accounts department at Wrens Road. He asked his boss, Jane Belk, whether there was any truth in the rumours. Jane said she didn't know anything official and certainly hadn't been told anything by her boss, the manager of the factory Mike Ruffle. Jane had a number of contacts with other employees in a similar position to hers at other factories. She also had a contact at head office. But telephone conversations with them didn't get any hard facts. Some of her contacts had heard the rumours, but sounded rather relieved that they were about the Wrens Road factory and not their factories.

On March 6 2003, the manager at Wrens Road called a meeting for 9.30 of all the staff. He read out a letter from senior management of the company thanking them for all their hard work, but explaining that the factory was losing money and there would have to be a rationalisation of production. Wrens Road would close within three months and production would move to the underutilised Downton site 25 miles away. Some of the staff would be offered new jobs at the Downton site. But the rest of the workforce at Wrens Road would unfortunately be made redundant.

1 **Identify THREE relationships between workers at the Wrens Road factory which would be part of the formal organisation of the company.**
2 **Identify TWO examples of the informal organisation of the business given in the data.**
3 **Discuss the impact on motivation of the workers at Wrens Road of the rumours flowing through the informal organisation at the factory.**

keyterms

Bureaucratic structure - **a form of organisation where there is a hierarchy, workers have defined roles, rules and procedures govern operations, workers are appointed to posts on merit and there is a system of promotion. It is sometimes called a pyramid structure, a formal or traditional hierarchy, or a line and staff organisation.**

Entrepreneur - **a person who, usually, sets up and runs a business and takes the risks associated with this.**

Entrepreneurial (or web) structure - **where an individual is at the centre of an organisation and takes all the important decisions, perhaps delegating some decision making to a few key trusted individuals.**

Formal organisation - **the relationships between individual workers determined by the organisation, which can be shown on an organisation chart.**

Informal organisation - **the network of relationships in a** workplace which staff in an organisation form themselves, based upon friendship and common interest.

Informal (or independence or cluster) structure - **a type of business organisation where the organisation supports the work of one or a few key highly skilled workers, such as doctors, accountants or architects.**

Matrix management - **the management of a group of workers with different skills and from different departments, placed together, typically on a short term basis, to complete projects.**

Matrix structure - **a business structure where groups of workers with different skills and from different departments are placed together, typically on a short term basis, to complete projects and are reassigned to another project when the first is completed.**

IWP International plc is a 'leading international manufacturer, distributor and marketer of high quality, fast moving consumer goods and related products'. It is organised into three divisions, the Household Products Division, the Personal Care Division, and the Distribution and Labels Division. The Personal Care Division manufactures cosmetics, perfumes and after-shaves, toiletries such as soap, and shampoos.

In its financial year 2000-2001, IWP reorganised its divisional structure. In its *Annual Report*, it stated: 'The disappointing performance in the Personal Care Division reflects the level of change that has been undertaken during the year. It became increasingly clear to us that in order to maximise our opportunities in our marketplace, we should combine our cosmetics, toiletries and fragrance divisions under one common management structure. By focussing our sales effort and developing a more targeted approach to both domestic and export markets we have the ability to rationalise our product portfolio. This allows us to target more resources behind the development of creative products in this division. The restructuring of the division and the change in approach has inevitably resulted in the need for a change in the organisational structure. This has led to a number of redundancies in both our Dutch and UK operations, particularly at management level.'

Adapted from IWP International plc, *Annual Report and Accounts*, 2000-01.

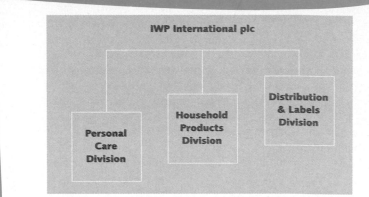

Figure 31.6 *Group structure of IWP International plc*

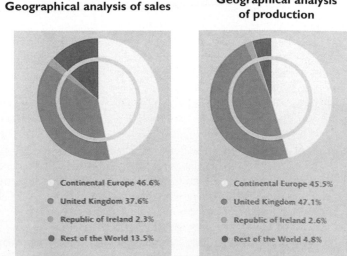

Geographical analysis of sales

- Continental Europe 46.6%
- United Kingdom 37.6%
- Republic of Ireland 2.3%
- Rest of the World 13.5%

Geographical analysis of production

- Continental Europe 45.5%
- United Kingdom 47.1%
- Republic of Ireland 2.6%
- Rest of the World 4.8%

Figure 31.7 *IWP International production and sales: geographical analysis, 2000-2001*

1 Explain what is meant by the terms:
  (a) 'divisional structure'; (3 marks)
  (b) 'product portfolio'. (3 marks)
2 Compare the sales of IWP in 2000-2001 with where its products were made. (6 marks)
3 Analyse why IWP reorganised its Personal Care Division. (8 marks)
4 Discuss whether IWP would need to adopt a different organisational structure if it doubled in size over the next five years. (10 marks)

33 Management by objectives (MBO)

The Highbridge Hotel

Knowledge Hanna Kemboi bought her hotel in rural England in 2001. She had got a good price because the previous owners had carried out no major repairs on the building for at least ten years. But she quickly found that that was not the only problem with the hotel.

Application It became apparent from day one of the *takeover* that the *staff* were not working as a *team*. Everyone seemed to have their own *goals*. No one was interested in working together to serve the guests. Assistant *managers* failed to *organise* their *staff* properly. *Command and control* structures were weak. Co-ordination was appalling. The hotel *staff* were simply out of *control*.

Analysis Within six months, Hanna had turned the situation around. She compiled a plan detailing objectives for the hotel and, working downwards, for every group of hotel staff and every individual. Each member of staff was given a clear job description. The assistant managers were given firm instructions to co-ordinate and control the work of their subordinates. Personal rivalries between members of staff couldn't be eliminated in such a short space of time. But how well members of staff were getting on with other members formed part of the performance appraisal conducted by Hanna with assistant managers.

Evaluation By adopting the approach of management by objectives, Hanna was able to communicate her objectives to the staff. Turning round the staffing situation was only part of what was needed to make the hotel a success. But it was, arguably, the most difficult part. Spending money on upgrading the facilities at the hotel and marketing the hotel was relatively straightforward.

Management functions

Managers play a key role in medium to large businesses. But what do they do? What are the **functions** of managers?

Henri Fayol was the general manager (the top manager) of a French mining company for many years. In 1916, he published a book called *General and Industrial Administration*. The book analysed the role of management in a business. He argued that there was a number of key elements of management.

Forecasting and planning Managers have to **predict** what will happen in the future. Unless they do this, they cannot prepare their business for future events. Once the future has been assessed, managers have to decide what needs to be achieved and **plan** how to meet these objectives (see units 63 and 64). For example, managers may predict that spending will fall next year. They may decide to prevent the fall in sales revenue that may result. So they could have the objective of raising sales revenue by, say, 5 per cent over a 12 month period. Managers need to plan what tactics and strategies they will use to achieve this growth in sales revenue.

Organising Managers must organise resources to achieve their objectives. For example, workers need to be allocated to different types of production. Managers must organise the purchase of supplies.

Commanding Managers must exercise command of other workers lower down the hierarchy of management (see unit 31). They must direct their activities by giving orders. They must also motivate subordinates.

Co-ordinating On a day to day basis, managers must manage a variety of activities which contribute towards achieving business objectives. Co-ordinating activities and the work of subordinates is therefore vital.

Controlling Managers must monitor the activities for which they are responsible. They must measure how far they are being successful in achieving the objectives set out in their plans. For example, a marketing manager must compare actual sales of a product with forecast sales. A production manager must monitor whether quality levels are being achieved.

Fayol's ideas formed the basis of what came to be called **classical management theory** or **scientific management**. This school of thought argued that there were certain principles of management which could be applied to every business to make it run efficiently. For example, businesses where managers failed to plan would soon run into trouble. A failure of co-ordination on the part of management will lead to disorganisation and wastage.

Managerial roles

Fayol argued that managers had five important functions. Henry Mintzberg in the 1980s suggested that managers also performed three important roles.

Interpersonal roles An interpersonal role is a role arising out of the interaction of managers with other staff but where the manager has formal authority. For example, managers have **figurehead** roles where they represent the business organisation in ceremonies such as giving a speech at a retirement party or cutting the tape at the opening of a new facility. They have a **leadership** role in areas such as recruitment of staff or motivating employees. They also have a liaison role, talking or networking with other managers, staff and contacts outside the business. Managers build up a large store information from this, which can be used to make decisions.

Information roles Because of their contacts, managers act as channels of information between departments, other managers and members of staff, and those outside the business.

Decision making roles Managers are decision makers. They are ideally placed to make decisions because of their knowledge gained through networking with other colleagues and departments.

Management by objectives (MBO)

In 1955, Peter Drucker, a US business adviser and writer, published a book called *The Practice of Management*. In the book, he suggested that managers had five functions:

- setting objectives;
- organising work;
- motivating employees and communicating information to them;
- job measurement - checking that tasks have been performed and objectives met;
- developing people, including organising training.

Drucker argued that businesses could run into problems if managers and employees worked towards different objectives. For example, the marketing department might want to launch a new product. This could raise revenues, but would also increase costs. In contrast, the finance department might frustrate those plans by not agreeing to any increase in spending for the next six months.

So Drucker put forward the idea that a business could be run and controlled through:

- the setting out of objectives;
- making plans to realise those objectives;
- carrying out those plans;
- monitoring whether objectives have been reached.

This is MANAGEMENT BY OBJECTIVES (MBO). It is a scientific approach to management, where the same principles can be applied to different businesses and different situations. MBO requires managers to use the skills identified by Drucker as essential to their role as managers.

In a large organisation, the system to implement management by objectives is likely to be complex. This is because there is a large number of employees who must be involved at different levels in the hierarchy of the business.

In a large organisation, objectives or goals for the whole business (**corporate objectives**, see unit 63) are set by senior managers and the directors of the company. Those objectives are derived from their **aims** (sometimes written out in the **mission statement** of the business, see unit 63). Senior management then has to plan how to achieve those objectives.

The next stage is to involve the next layer of management in the hierarchy. A corporate objective might be to increase sales by 30 per cent over the next three years. Senior management of a subsidiary company of the business would then be asked how they could contribute to realising that goal. Following discussions and analysis, they could agree on their objective. They might, for example, agree to an objective of increasing sales by 10 per cent. Planning is then required to map out how the 10 per cent increase will be

Alison Broomes had a typical morning as personnel manager for a company employing 750 people.

8.00	In her office dealing with her emails.
8.10	Interrupted by the production manager asking whether she had any luck in getting applications for the toolsetter's job.
8.30	Secretary arrives and they go through her diary appointments for the day.
8.40	Meeting with accounts manager to discuss the wording of an advert and job description for an accounts executive. Interrupted by mobile phone call from managing director's personal secretary confirming 3.45 meeting.
9.20	Back into the office to deal with the mail. Delegate tasks arising from the mail to her 2 assistants and 1 secretary in their open plan office.
9.40	Meeting with trade union representative to discuss disciplining of a worker for persistent lateness.
9.50	Review file for interviews taking place the following day. Interrupted by phone call from managing director's personal secretary to ask if the meeting could be moved to 4.00 p.m.
10.10	Checks progress on two job vacancies with one of her assistants.
10.30	Monthly meeting with head of marketing to discuss current personnel issues in her department.
11.30	Attendance at small ceremony where 15 employees are given their CIEH Basic Health and Safety awards.
11.50	Back in the office reading over letters and documents that are to be sent out by her secretary which require her signature.
12.10	Discussion with one of her assistants about a pay issue that has cropped up.
12.25	Accesses emails and replies to them.
12.40	Calls assistant head of production about application for training course from two of his workers.
12.55	Working lunch with her 2 assistants in the office.

> **1 Explain what functions of management Alison Broomes has fulfilled during her morning according to (a) Fayol's theory of management and (b) Mintzberg's theory.**

achieved.

This might then be taken down to managers of individual departments within the subsidiary company. What objectives would those departments have to help achieve the 10 per cent increase in sales?

Ultimately, it can be taken down to the level of individual workers. Through systems of **performance appraisal** (see unit 37), individual workers can be set goals, say for the next year. Achieving these goals will form a small part of the way in which the objectives of the whole business will be achieved.

Over the past five years, sales at Holthan International, an international engineering group, had grown at an average 5 per cent per annum. This average masked very considerable differences in performance by the divisions within the group. The Hardware Division, the largest division, had consistently outperformed the other divisions with average growth of 8 per cent per annum. The Lifting Products Division and Power Systems Division had grown by approximately 4 per cent. The Logistics Division had seen growth of only 1 per cent.

The chief executive of Holthan, Phil Dagnall, concerned at the performance of the Logistics Division, had persuaded his board of directors three months ago to fire its chief executive. A new chief executive, Iseo Inamoto, was appointed and given the objective to increase sales by 3 per cent in his first year and 5 per cent in his second year. Profits had to increase in line with sales.

Iseo Inamoto, on his first day in office, called a meeting with his senior marketing managers and outlined the targets set. He asked them to produce a plan detailing how sales could be grown profitably within the time scale set. He wanted the plan with supporting documentation ready for a presentation in three days time. During that time, Mr Inamoto familiarised himself as much as possible with the previous work of the marketing department. He called in all the senior managers one by one for an interview. The presentation took place over one day with Mr Inamoto questioning every aspect of what was being proposed.

Over the next seven days, the marketing team was restructured. Three senior members of the team, including the head of marketing, whose performance Mr Inamoto thought was inadequate, were told that they would lose their jobs. The former assistant head of marketing was promoted to head of marketing and there was a reorganisation of roles within the department. A new marketing plan was thrashed out with clearly identifiable targets for the department as a whole, broken down by country and product. Individual marketing managers, who had contributed to the construction of the plan, were made responsible for achieving those targets.

The implications for increasing sales were then worked out for each of the other departments within the division. The emphasis was upon drawing up plans which would see modest increases in costs to ensure that the sales increases generated growth in profits. The personnel department helped devise an incentive scheme for individual members of the marketing department to reward them for achieving their objectives.

> **1 What are the key features of 'management by objectives'? Illustrate your answer with examples from the data.**

Participation

The MBO process should encourage participation and negotiation. Orders should not simply be passed down the **chain of command** (see unit 31). Instead, objectives and how to achieve them should be the subject of discussion and negotiation. There are two main reasons for this.
- Those lower down the chain of command often have a better understanding of what is possible than those further up the chain. Their knowledge and experience should be used rather than ignored. So they should be fully involved in objective setting, planning and execution.
- Participation is likely to increase **motivation** (see unit 35). Managers and workers are likely to be committed to achieving goals which they have helped to set.

Compensation

Compensation of individual workers or groups of workers can be linked into the achievement of objectives. **Bonuses** (see unit 37) can be paid to managers and workers who meet targets. Bonus systems should be designed to reward those who achieve. They should therefore motivate managers and workers.

Reward-based compensation systems also force businesses to be clear about whether they have achieved their objectives. Information about what has been achieved must be collected to decide whether or not to award bonuses are to be paid.

They force everyone to concentrate their attention on what is to be achieved and what has been achieved.

Advantages of MBO

MBO has a number of advantages.
- Managers and workers in the organisation will know their objectives. So the business can work to a single purpose.
- Objectives and plans can be co-ordinated throughout the organisation. So one part of an organisation should not be working in a way which will frustrate the objectives of another part of the organisation.
- Clarity of purpose, negotiation and payment systems should lead to workers and managers being better motivated.
- MBO allows senior managers to control the organisation. The MBO system allows them to steer the business in the direction in which they have agreed to go.

Problems of MBO

Some large organisations have attempted to adopt MBO, although perhaps not as a complete management system. Others have not, for a number of reasons.

Time and resources Properly implemented, the system requires a considerable amount of time and resources to be allocated to it. Involving managers at all levels of an organisation is costly. It can be argued that these costs outweigh the benefits to be gained from implementation.

Obstruction MBO assumes that managers and workers can be moulded into employees who will understand objectives and carry out plans which will fulfil those objectives. But each manager and worker is different. Some are highly motivated and are good at seeing objectives and implementing them. Others might have less positive attitudes towards work. They might have little interest in seeing the business achieve its objectives. Equally, many workers and managers find it difficult to understand large scale objectives and plans. In their view, getting on with familiar routine tasks is all that is important. Meetings to them are mostly a waste of time, whose outcomes are usually best ignored. There are also employees who find it difficult to work in ways which are fixed by others. They are not necessarily good team members because they do things in the way which suits them. But they can be highly valuable to an organisation, particularly where individuality and creativity are needed. So, many managers and workers won't conform to the type of working required by the MBO system. This reduces its effectiveness.

Creativity Some argue that MBO fails to recognise the importance of creativity and spontaneity in a successful business. MBO is a system of control to ensure that managers carry out the objectives and plans of senior management. But success in many businesses comes about because workers react as individuals to individual situations. MBO stifles that initiative and makes it more difficult for managers to react to an unpredictable environment.

A changing environment MBO assumes that the environment in which a business find itself is likely to be fairly predictable. But in practice, the business environment can be volatile. Objectives set one month can be unrealistic the next. War, recession, collapsing markets or new competitors can completely change what is possible. So, too much planning can be a waste of resources. Even worse, it can paralyse a business when circumstances change. Managers can carry on working to old objectives and plans when these have become redundant.

In practice, all medium to large businesses have formal or informal **strategies** (plans to meet objectives, see unit 64) and systems to implement those strategies. These systems include elements of MBO. But most accept that management by objectives is not the only way to run a successful business.

✓checklist

1. (a) According to Fayol, what are the functions of management? (b) How do these differ those suggested by Mintzberg?
2. What are the functions of management according to Drucker?
3. Explain what is meant by 'management by objectives'.
4. Explain the role, in management by objectives, of (a) participation and (b) compensation.
5. Compare the advantages and disadvantages of management by objectives.

❝**key**terms❞

Management by objectives (MBO) - **a management system where a business is run and controlled through the setting of objectives and the implementation of plans to achieve those objectives at every level of the business.**

Management by objectives was the driving management philosophy of a bank. For example, each month bank branches would be given a new target. One month it would be the number of new savings accounts opened. Another month it would the number of loans sold. Another month it would the number of student accounts opened. Quite what was the plan of head office was unclear, but bonuses for the staff at the branches depended on hitting those targets month after month.

The branch manager at one of the Bournemouth branches, Patricia McGuire, regularly went on 'away' days. At these conferences, the objectives that head office were setting its managers were explained. Patricia was expected to communicate those objectives to her staff - get them to see the big picture of how they fitted into the big plan. But many branch managers found it difficult to be motivated by these training sessions. Often, the targets were completely unattainable. Take the target in September for signing up students. Her branch was in Bournemouth, capital city of England for senior citizens. She would be lucky to sign up one student, let alone the target of 50.

At Patricia McGuire's annual performance appraisal, her line manager didn't seem unduly worried that her branch had missed its target for 9 out of the previous 12 months. She concentrated on other aspects of Patricia's work and recommended that she be given her individual bonus for the year. During the interview Patricia expressed her frustration that she had no control over what targets were set for her branch staff. The line manager said that the system was not designed to incorporate feedback from staff further down the line. Head office decided what it wanted and that was what went out to the branches.

1. Explain the meaning of the terms:
   (a) 'objectives'; (3 marks)
   (b) 'performance appraisal'. (3 marks)
2. Outline TWO possible reasons why the bank was setting monthly targets for its branches. (6 marks)
3. Examine how management by objectives was being carried out in the bank. (8 marks)
4. Discuss whether the management by objectives approach of the bank was effective. (10 marks)

The Post Office

Knowledge In 2001-02, the Post Office faced a financial crisis, making losses of hundreds of millions of pounds. One of the main ways in which they hoped to resolve this crisis was by introducing new ways of working for their staff. At one point, up to 30 000 jobs were predicted to be lost. The trade union representing most postal workers, the Communication Workers Union, launched strikes and threatened more action.

Application The Post Office had developed a poor reputation for *industrial relations* between *workers* and *management*. *Productivity* was low and workers were highly resistant to change. Worker *motivation* was poor.

Analysis The situation at the Post Office might seem to confirm the views of Frederick Taylor, an American who wrote at the beginning of the 20th century. It could be argued that Post Office management had failed to manage their workforce effectively. Management had allowed outdated working practices to continue, resulting in low productivity and high costs.

Evaluation The solution to the Post Office's problems was, arguably, for management to decide how best work should be organised. Post Office workers would receive higher pay for agreeing to sweeping changes in work practices, but thousands of jobs would have to go. Paying workers more would be sufficient to motivate them. But this approach could be criticised. Perhaps there is more to motivating postal workers than just pay. Postal workers are also more than simple cogs in a machine.

Adapted from the *Financial Times*, 16.10.2001, 16.12.2001, 14.6.2002, *The Times*, 23.11.2001.

The importance of motivation

MOTIVATION in the workplace is the desire to complete a task. It can be argued to have three components.

- Direction - the extent to which a worker completes an assigned task, such as finishing the writing of a report, rather than completing other tasks, such as talking about holiday photographs with a colleague.
- Effort - how hard a worker is trying to complete the task.
- Persistence - how long a worker keeps trying to complete the task despite possible setbacks.

Motivation is important in any business for a number of reasons.

Productivity The more motivated a workforce, the higher is likely to be its PRODUCTIVITY. Worker productivity is the output per person. A demotivated workforce is likely to spend as little time as possible on work assigned to them. Demotivated workers might make little effort to complete work quickly and might be easily discouraged when problems occur. This means that far more workers might be needed to produce a certain output than in a business with a highly motivated workforce.

Quality Motivated workers are more likely to produce goods and services of the required quality. Demotivated workers might not care about the quality of their work.

Absenteeism Poor motivation is often linked to absenteeism. Poorly motivated workers are more likely to take time off work. Partly this is because having a day or week at home becomes more attractive than going to work. Partly it is because poorly motivated staff tend to suffer more from stress at work, which can lead to illness.

Retention Staff turnover is likely to be higher, the poorer the motivation. If staff are bored, feel unappreciated or dislike work, they might look for other jobs. Recruiting staff is an expensive process for a business. If workers also have to be trained once they are taken on, there is a further cost if the turnover of staff is high.

Industrial relations There is likely to be more industrial unrest if workers are demotivated.

Public relations Businesses where worker motivation is high may get a boost to their public relations (see unit 18). In the past, companies such as Cadbury Schweppes and Marks & Spencer have attracted positive publicity because they have been seen to treat their workers well. Their workers have responded by being more motivated.

Scientific management

One view of motivation forms part of a larger theory of SCIENTIFIC MANAGEMENT. The most influential writer in this area was an American, Frederick W Taylor (1856-1915). He worked for many years at Midvale Steel Company in Philadelphia, eventually becoming chief engineer. At 45, he retired and spent the rest of his life lecturing, writing and acting as a consultant. In 1911, he published *The Principles of Scientific Management*, in which he outlined his ideas.

In his experience of working in American industry, management had little control over how workers performed their tasks. 'Foremen' (as they were often called at the time) played a crucial role. They often decided who was to be employed and laid off, how work was organised and when rest breaks were taken. Workers were typically expected to provide their own tools. Training consisted of learning from more experienced workers on the job. No two workers performed tasks in exactly the same way. They were left to decide for themselves how best to approach a job. Workers were inclined to do as little as possible, labelled by Taylor as 'natural soldiering'. But 'systematic soldiering' also took place.

McDonald's was a small company in California serving fast food until Ray Kroc came along in the 1950s. He saw that a moderately successful business could be turned into something much greater. But even he probably did not foresee just how successful McDonald's would become.

Ray Kroc's philosophy was to achieve a winning formula and replicate that exactly through every outlet. Before he took charge 'there was inefficiency, waste and temperamental cooks, sloppy service and food whose quality was never consistent.' What was needed was 'a simple product that moved from start to completion in a streamlined path'.

This meant standardising everything from the raw ingredients, to how they were cooked and served, to the outlets and advertising. For example, workers cook hamburgers in exactly the same way, for the same time, in Paris, Chicago or Sydney. Workers have to clean equipment using the same instructions wherever they are in the world. Problems with 'temperamental cooks' have been eliminated because McDonald's serves a very limited menu and uses standardised equipment. It means that any worker can, with the minimum of training, be an expert in how to cook a McDonald's meal.

Adapted from www.spunk.org/library/food/mcdonalds/sp001158.txt

1 **Suggest why there might be 'inefficiency, waste and temperamental cooks, sloppy service and food whose quality was never consistent' in a fast food restaurant which is not part of a large chain.**
2 **Suggest how the principles of 'scientific management' have been applied by McDonald's.**

This was where groups of workers did a minimum amount of work to keep management satisfied, even though it was well below what the group could achieve. Workers who worked harder than the rest in their group were pressured by their fellow workers to slow down to the norm within the group. After all, greater output by one worker could indicate to management that the rest of the workers were slacking.

Taylor believed that work could be organised scientifically. He argued that the objectives of scientific management were to:

- increase efficiency (i.e. increase output per worker) through better working practices and reduced soldiering;
- improve the predictability of job performance through the division of labour (see unit 42);
- establish firm control by imposing discipline on workers through a chain of command (see unit 31) where the policies of management could be implemented.

Taylor suggested that tasks could be scientifically analysed. By understanding the best or optimal way of working, this could be made the norm for workers. Productivity and predictability would then be maximised. He gave an example of how this could be done for a particular task.

- A number of good steady workers should be chosen for study.
- Time how long it takes them to complete the task.
- Make adjustments to the equipment used to see whether this could increase output.
- Study and record the actual movements of arms, body and legs.
- Having decided the optimal way to perform the task, train all workers to do it in this way.
- Management is then responsible for making sure workers continue to perform the task in exactly the same way. Taylor

wrote that: 'It is only through enforced standardisation of methods, enforced adoption of the best implements and working conditions, and enforced cooperation that this faster work can be assured. And the duty of enforcing the adoption of standards and of enforcing this cooperation rests with the management alone.'

Taylor's work showed the gains that could be made by scientific management. In 1898, he was hired by the Bethlehem Iron Company to improve work methods. One task he studied was that done by pig iron handlers. These moved finished pig iron from the blast furnaces to outside yards. He found that the 75 pig iron handlers moved, on average, twelve and a half tons per worker per day. Reorganising how they worked raised their productivity nearly four fold to 48 tonnes per day per worker.

'Taylorism' had an enormous impact on management thinking and industrial relations. Researching the way in which workers performed their tasks came to be called a TIME AND MOTION STUDY. It was usually resisted by workers because they saw it as something which would lead to change in traditional work practices. It would make them work much harder. Increased division of labour, with the introduction of labour saving equipment, would deskill workers. Work would become more monotonous because workers would perform a much narrower range of tasks. It could also lead to large scale redundancies. Increased productivity meant that fewer workers were needed to do the same job. Management, on the other hand, saw Taylorism as a way of reducing costs and either increasing profit or reducing profit to survive in a competitive market. Today, aspects of Taylorism can be seen in a wide variety of work place settings from fast food restaurants, to car assembly plants to nurses answering calls on NHS Direct.

Linton Brick is a specialist brick manufacturer based in Manchester. Simon Linton, managing director, acknowledges that motivation of staff is linked to a variety of factors. For example, communication is important. 'By communicating we get people interested in the fortunes of the company rather than feeling they are just a cog in the machine.' Investment in training is also essential. By investing in training, staff can be motivated to remain with the company rather than seek jobs elsewhere.

However, money is also a key motivator. 'People must be rewarded financially. There is nothing more sincere - money never lies.' Linton staff can earn extra if they raise productivity, and there is a team-based profit-share system that awards annual bonuses according to how successful the company has been in beating its targets. In addition, Mr Linton has introduced a company pension scheme, matching employee contributions with an equal amount paid by the business. 'It's not massive, but it is much better than you would usually get in a company of this size.'

Adapted from the *Financial Times*, 20.2.2003.

1 **Explain how workers at Linton Brick are motivated to work harder by financial inducements.**
2 **Discuss whether motivation of staff would be higher if Linton Brick reduced the wages of its workers by 10 per cent and spent the money saved on improved training for staff.**

Scientific management and motivation

Taylor had a very simple view about worker motivation. He assumed that workers were motivated solely by the pay they received. The higher the level of pay, the more motivated they would be. He recognised that if ways of working were reformed, workers would have to be paid more to compensate them for the changes. He wrote that: '... management must also recognise the broad fact that workmen will not submit to this more rigid standardisation and will not work extra hard, unless they receive extra pay for doing it.' In his view, gains from productivity arising from work reorganisation had to be split between employer and employee if workers were to accept the changes.

Taylor saw PIECE RATES as an ideal payment system for

employers because pay was linked to production. For pig iron handlers, for example, pay could be based on how much pig iron they move during a day, rather than the number of hours worked during the day. If pig iron handlers then engaged in 'soldiering', they would suffer because they would get less pay, rather than the employer. Pay was therefore an INCENTIVE to work hard.

He put forward a piece rate system which would motivate workers in two ways. He suggested that piece rates should be low up to a level of production which a worker could achieve comfortably in a day. Thereafter, piece rate per item produced should be much higher. 'Soldiering' would result in workers getting a very low overall pay packet. But by working hard, workers would be generously rewarded.

This tiered piece rate system was tried out, but was immensely unpopular with workers. They saw it as unfair and recognised that it put them under pressure to achieve much higher levels of output than before. They resented working harder with most of the benefits going to the factory owners.

Criticisms

Taylor and the scientific management school have been criticised in a number of ways.

- Taylor has been attacked for holding simplistic views on motivation. Later thinkers on motivation recognised that pay was just one factor amongst many in motivating workers (see unit 35).
- He has been criticised for seeing workers as cogs in the machine of an industrial process, to be pushed around and manipulated as if they were just another type of capital equipment. In particular, his view that productivity can be improved by narrowing down the range of tasks performed by a worker is contrary to much modern management thinking (see unit 36).
- Taylorism can be be seen as giving intellectual backing to modern mass production methods. In particular, Taylorism is often linked to the introduction by Henry Ford of the first production line. On the production line, workers are forced to work to the pace of the production line and not to the pace that workers may choose themselves.
- Taylorism is often criticised for giving more power to trade unions and creating industrial unrest. If workers were to be aggressively managed by the owners of factories, there was an even greater incentive for them to join trade unions to protect their interests. Any change in work practices could then be seen as serving the interests of the owners of businesses. So they should be fiercely resisted unless workers received higher pay.

However, some argue that whilst pay is not the only motivator, it is the most important for many workers. It can also be argued that workers could be more productive if a way was found of eliminating 'soldiering'. Many modern management techniques, such as **quality circles** or **lean production** (see units 47 and 48), are successful in raising productivity because they reduce the power of traditional informal groups amongst workers.

So even though alternative theories have suggested workers may be motivated by other factors (see unit 35), Taylor's ideas still influence the ways many businesses pay and organise their workforces.

'keyterms'

Incentive - **a reward received by someone to encourage them to complete a task, for example, a worker might receive a bonus of £100 for achieving a target.**
Motivation - **in the workplace, the desire to complete a given task which will contribute towards the business reaching its goals.**
Piece rates - **a system of payment for workers where they are paid according to how much they produce.**
Productivity - **output per worker.**
Scientific management - **a theory of management, associated with Frederick Taylor, which suggests that, by observation and rational thinking, an optimal way of working can be devised which will maximise output and produce efficiency in production.**
Time and motion study - **the observation of workers completing a task, analysing their movements and timing them, with a view to improving the method of work and increasing productivity.**

✓ *checklist*

1 State three components of motivation.
2 Why is motivation important for a business?
3 What was 'soldiering'?
4 What did Taylor put forward as the objectives of scientific management?
5 How did Taylor suggest that management could find out what was the optimal way of performing a task?
6 What is the role of management in ensuring high productivity amongst workers according to Taylor?
7 Explain what, according to Taylor, motivates workers.
8 Explain briefly FOUR criticisms that could be made of Taylor's arguments.

In 2000, MFI, the furniture retailer, decided to trial a programme to improve the productivity of its warehouse staff. The programme, called PACE (Performance Achieves Customer Expectations) had been developed in the USA. According to Tim Nealon, MFI's logistics director, 'It measures the performance of workers but in addition it pays the individuals for their performance. It is an opportunity for the better to be paid more than the ones who weren't so good.'

To see how productivity could be improved, a PACE team was set up which spent time on the ground at the company's home delivery centre in Sidcup, Kent. Working with local management, they found out how warehouse employees worked. They then identified potential for improvement. For example, staff had been using a heavy 'shopping basket' to pick out goods. The goods were badly positioned in the warehouse, causing staff to zigzag between different areas, while heavy or bulky items were disrupting their flow. A purpose built trolley was designed and produced, with the help of staff. The floor was rearranged in a more logical way. Heavy products were put at the bottom of pallets whilst lighter ones were put on top.

Bonuses and incentives were then redesigned. Bonuses kicked in when employees achieved 80 per cent of the target performance. If they achieved 100 per cent, they earned a bonus of 23 per cent of their basic pay. Targets were carefully set so that a trained individual, using the right procedures and working at a sustainable pace, should be able to achieve the 100 per cent target. Additional incentives were also given. Management at a centre were given £15 000 to reward staff at their discretion. Awards including buying staff lunch, weekend trips and buying consumer items such as TVs and DVD players.

The result was a more than 50 per cent productivity increase at the three home delivery centres where the programme had been implemented. As a result of this increase in output per worker, MFI was able to consolidate its home delivery centre network and close two out of 14 sites. Individual workers earned more, but total labour costs actually fell by 15 per cent as fewer workers were needed. The PACE programme will be rolled out to cover all home delivery centres and three primary warehouse sites by the end of 2002.

Adapted from *The Times*, 19.2.2002.

1 Explain the meaning of the terms:
(a) 'productivity'; (3 marks) (b) 'incentives'. (3 marks)

2 Explain TWO ways in which the PACE programme increased the motivation of staff. (6 marks)

3 Examine the costs and benefits (a) to warehouse employees and (b) to the company of implementing PACE. (8 marks)

4 Assess what problems MFI might experience in rolling out the PACE programme to all its home delivery centres and warehouses. (10 marks)

35 Motivation and the human relations school

C&A

Knowledge

C&A used to be a familiar sight on British high streets. It was a clothing retailer which competed with chains like Marks & Spencer and British Home Stores.

Application

The Dutch owners found it more and more difficult to make a *profit* in the 1990s. By the late 1990s, UK stores were making annual *losses* running into tens of millions of pounds. In June 2000, the owners announced that C&A in the UK would be closed down and all its stores sold off. Staff at C&A would all be made *redundant*. However, C&A management instituted a number of measures to *motivate* staff and keep morale high. *Redundancy payments* would be twice the legal minimum for staff who stayed to the end. Monthly *bonuses* were given based upon the performance of the store in which the members of staff worked. C&A devoted large resources to providing *careers advice* and *job-search training*.

Analysis

Mass redundancies should have completely demotivated C&A staff. According to Maslow's theory of needs, staff were threatened at the most basic level by the loss of their livelihoods. Equally, according to Herzberg's two factor theory, certain redundancy meant that hygiene factors were not being met. However, the generous redundancy scheme and the monthly bonus payments counteracted this. So too did the careers advice and training. Nearly every member of staff succeeded in getting a new job. Some simply stayed in the store and were taken on by its next occupants, chains such as Gap or Next. Others got better jobs with more pay. This secured their basic needs. C&A staff also felt that the company was looking after them, satisfying their need for love and belonging according to Maslow's theory.

Evaluation

The C&A closure could have been a disaster both for the company and the staff. Demotivated staff could have caused considerable damage in the months leading to the final closure. As it was, C&A management succeeded in keeping staff motivated. This contributed to the fact that for the first time in years, C&A UK made a profit in its closing down period.

Adapted from *People Management*, 7.3.2002.

Elton Mayo

Elton Mayo (1880-1949) was an Australian. Initially a philosopher with psychoanalytical training, he migrated to the USA in 1922 and became Professor of Industrial Research at the Harvard Business School in 1924.

In 1927, he was asked to carry out research at the Hawthorne plant of the Western Electric Company in Cicero, Illinois. This was because of problems with earlier research. In the early 1920s, the US company General Electric (GE) wanted to promote the sales of light bulbs to businesses. It had paid for a number of experiments to show that better lighting using bulbs increased workers' productivity. But the tests were criticised by academics as being less than objective when GE started using the results in promotional materials. So a more independent set of experiments was set up in 1924 to be carried out at the Hawthorne plant. By 1927, however, they had shown no clear link between lighting and productivity.

The Hawthorne effect The original experiments of 1924-27 studied a large production area within the factory. Mayo and his team decided to focus on just six female workers from the relay assembly department. They were withdrawn from their production area and put in a separate room. The research team chose two female workers who were friends, who then chose four other workers.

The group was studied between 1927-33. Over a period of time, working conditions were changed as Figure 35.1 shows. At the start, they worked the then standard 48 hours a week, including Saturdays with no tea breaks. Tea breaks and rests were introduced, as well as changes to hours of work. Working conditions at the end were restored to their initial position.

Figure 35.1 shows that productivity climbed throughout the changes, even when working conditions came full circle at the

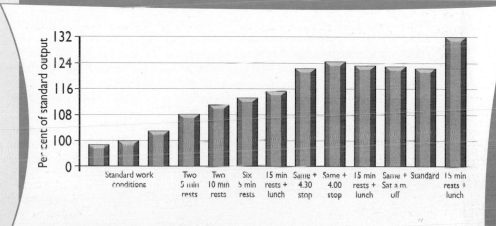

Figure 35.1 *Relay assembly test room experiments: how productivity changed*
Adapted from *Behaviour in Organisations*, J. Greenberg and R.A. Baron, Prentice Hall.

end. Mayo and his team published the results of their research in 1939. They suggested that a major reason for the improvement in productivity was the interest taken in the six workers by the researchers. This became known as the HAWTHORNE EFFECT. The researchers also suggested that team working helped increase productivity, as did giving the group of six workers more control over their work environment through consultation and less intensive supervision.

Informal groups In 1928, Mayo's research team began to interview workers at the Hawthorne factory. Between 1928-30, over 20 000 interviews were carried out. A key finding of the interview programme was that there was a network of strong **informal groups** (see unit 32) within the factory. These existed in parallel with the formal organisation of the factory.

To test this further, researchers set up another experiment with 14 male bank wiring workers. In the bank wiring observation room experiments, conducted in 1931-32, the workers were organised into three sub groups. Each group was made up of three wirers and a supervisor. There were also two inspectors who checked the work of all three groups. Researchers found that within the three formal groups, there were two informal groups, one with four workers and the other with five workers, including one inspector. Two workers were semi attached to the two groups and three seemed to be independent.

The informal groups controlled how much work was done. If a worker was producing too much, he was labelled a 'rate-buster'. If he produced too little, he was a 'chiseller'. Workers who told supervisors anything which would get another worker into trouble were 'squealers'. Workers who offended these norms were punished by the informal group. Verbal abuse such as 'the slave' or 'speed king' might be directed at the worker. At worst, the offender would suffer total rejection by the group.

The researchers suggested that workers were being less productive than they could be. This was despite the fact that they lost pay as a result, since each worker's pay depended on the output of the group. However, this was argued to be a rational response to their situation. They feared that if they worked harder, management would cut the rate of pay per item produced. They would then have to work harder for the same amount of pay as before. Also, fewer workers would be needed, so some would lose their jobs.

Human relations

Frederick Taylor and the scientific school of management emphasised the importance of the physical environment to productivity. For example, giving the right tools to workers was

Microsoft is the best company to work for in Britain, according to a *Sunday Times* survey. Microsoft employs 1 595 workers in the UK, 90 per cent of them based at a 'campus' in Reading, Berkshire. The site is spectacular, with a lake where charity rowing teams train, a forest and picnic tables. 93 per cent of staff surveyed feel proud to work for Microsoft and say it 'makes a positive difference to the world we live in'. 92 per cent are excited about where it is going and would miss it if they left. About nine in ten praise Microsoft's positive and faith-inspiring leadership, together with its high regard for customers, and 89 per cent say they love working there.

'We work long hours but it doesn't feel like work most of the time: it is cool stuff and very upbeat', says Maxine Edwards who joined as a graduate trainee nearly two years ago. 'One of our directors sent an email saying he doesn't want to see us after 6pm. I've never heard of anything like that before.'

Steve Harvey, another employee, is grateful for the well-being clinic, offering everything from a mechanical massage chair to well-man clinics. There is a 'bump' club to help pregnant mothers before their 18 weeks' fully paid leave, on-site nurses and doctor, and even a facility to donate bone marrow. The firm has opened a creche with 50 places for £35 a day, has four cafes, a subsidised restaurant and Xbox games terminals for entertainment. Sports are given a boost with a £260 000 social budget and the business subsidises outings to shows or trips abroad.

Mike Dixon, an account systems engineer, says: 'It is like a family. I met my wife, Moira, at work and when we got married the canteen even offered to bake our cake!'

Although staff say the business is not the top payer in the industry, two-thirds earn more than £40 000 a year. There is free private healthcare (including 'life partners' and family) and a four-month sabbatical (unpaid) after four years. Flexible options to be introduced this year include dental cover, childcare vouchers for staff in London and Edinburgh and for those working from home, and the chance to buy days off.

Adapted from *The Sunday Times*, 2.3.2003.

---

1 Using Maslow's hierarchy of needs, discuss whether workers at the Reading site of Microsoft are likely to be highly motivated.

essential if output was to be maximised. Important too for manual workers was their precise physical actions in doing a job. Finally, the key motivator for workers was pay.

Mayo's work suggested that there were other dimensions to motivation and productivity. Social and psychological factors were important too. The experiment with the six women in the relay assembly department suggested that factors such as recognition, security and a sense of belonging were important. Group identity contributed positively to increased productivity. But the bank wiring observation room experiments also showed that groups could work against the aims of an organisation.

Frederick Taylor had recognised that informal group norms could work against management aims. The conclusion of the scientific management school of thought tended to be that informal groups should therefore be broken up where possible. Mayo and his followers came to the opposite conclusion. They suggested that the power of the informal group needed to be aligned with management aims.

Following on from Mayo's work, businesses began to create personnel departments focused on serving the needs of workers. Teamwork and good communications between workers and management became fashionable.

However, just as 'Taylorism' had only a limited impact on industry, so too did what became called the HUMAN RELATIONS SCHOOL of thought. There are many businesses today in the UK where informal groups of workers have an important and negative influence on productivity and where management fail to provide social and psychological support for workers. On the other hand, there are equally many businesses where teamwork is key to their success and where workers are supported in their work.

Abraham Maslow and the hierarchy of needs

Motivational theories, such as Taylor's, which argue that how people behave is dependent upon rewards and punishments is called INSTRUMENTALITY THEORY. In *Motivation and Personality* (1954), Abraham Maslow, an American psychologist, put forward another theory. CONTENT THEORY or NEEDS THEORY suggests that we are motivated because we wish to satisfy our needs.

Maslow suggested that there is a HIERARCHY OF NEEDS for human beings, as shown in Figure 35.2.

Physiological needs These are basic human needs for survival. They include the need for food, drink, shelter or air to breathe. If these needs aren't satisfied, human beings mightl die.

Safety needs These are the needs for security and protection against danger. People want to be protected against danger in their environment, such as fire in their homes and accidents on roads and in the workplace. There are also psychological safety needs, such as freedom from anxiety or stress.

Social needs (or love and belonging) People are social animals. They want to belong to families, tribes and nations. They value friendship and seek contact with other human beings. In the workplace, they want to be part of a group or team. As Mayo discovered, being part of the informal group of workers can be more important than being part of the formal organisation of the workplace.

Esteem needs People need to have self-respect. They want to be confident individuals who have status within their families, at work and within society. They seek recognition and enjoy titles from 'mother' to 'site supervisor' to 'MP' which show their role.

Self-actualisation (or self-fulfilment) needs People want to fulfil their potential. They want, as Maslow wrote, 'to become everything that one is capable of becoming'. A talented musician might dream of becoming a professional soloist and be unfulfilled if she ends up teaching music. A production worker may want to become a manager and feel unfulfilled by his current job.

Maslow argued that a **hierarchy** exists in these needs. An individual might not be motivated by a need further up the hierarchy unless the needs lower down the hierarchy have been met. This hierarchy then has implications for management in motivating the workforce.

- A worker might not be motivated by an initiative which appeals to a higher need if a lower need is not being fulfilled. For example, a worker threatened with the sack might not be motivated by training designed to increase his sense of belonging in the workplace.
- Needs which are already satisfied are not motivators. For example, if a worker is paid £20 000 and considers this a reasonable wage on which to live, she might not be motivated to work harder by a wage increase. On the other hand, if physiological and safety needs are already being met, a worker might work harder if she were praised more and felt as if she belonged in the workplace.
- Individuals aim to reach the next rung on the hierarchy once they have achieved the one below. Workers who have achieved all their needs apart from self-actualisation will seek opportunities to fill this highest order need.
- Many jobs do not allow workers to go very high up their hierarchy of needs. Take, for example, a temporary cleaning job on the minimum wage for a single parent aged 35. Physiological needs might just be met, but with no job security safety needs might not be met. Social or self esteem needs are most unlikely to be met and there will be no scope in the job for self-actualisation to take place. Workers who are most likely to fulfil all their needs are those at the top of any organisation. The chief executive of a large multinational, for example, could have considerable scope to satisfy all needs in Maslow's hierarchy.

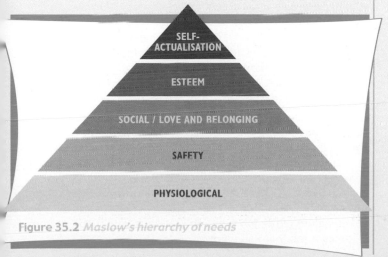

Figure 35.2 *Maslow's hierarchy of needs*

A consensus has developed among organisations and academics that work is getting worse. Dissatisfaction grew during the 1990s, researchers found. But this picture has been questioned by personnel managers. The Chartered Institute of Personnel and Development's continuing research into the 'psychological contract' between employer and employee has found commitment to be fairly high. Most workers are happy with both their jobs and their pay.

This year's survey of 1 000 workers agrees job satisfaction has declined - most starkly among public sector workers and more marginally in the private sector. But it reports that only 10 per cent of employees are 'seriously dissatisfied', whilst a surprising 84 per cent are either very or quite proud to tell people who they work for.

Most workers believe organisations keep the promises they make and tend to trust their immediate boss, while remaining suspicious of the motives of senior managers. Levels of commitment have not changed over the past few years and are good by international standards. Work is seldom 'just a job', but is centrally important to only about a third. Those with the longest service, and therefore who have less chance of promotion, tend to be less happy. Job security is neither declining nor is it especially important to people, it finds. Many people hope to jump ship shortly of their own accord. Employee involvement in the workplace has gone down. Commitment appears to be lower for people working under a regime of tight control and surveillance.

Against expectations, the study found that anxiety over the balance of work and life appears to have faded, possibly due to greater adoption of family-friendly policies. Yet stress remains a serious problem, with a quarter of workers finding their employment 'very stressful'. The survey also worried over workplace monitoring regimes. A total of 52 per cent of employees say their performance is being measured all the time, whilst 27 per cent are under constant observation.

Adapted from the *Financial Times*, 3.12.2002.

---

1 (a) List the motivators that Herzberg found in his study. (b) How do these compare with the factors affecting employees in the survey described in the data?

2 (a) List Herzberg's hygiene factors. (b) How do these compare with the factors affecting employees in the survey described in the data?

It should also noted that although the hierarchy applies to most people, it does not necessarily have to be in the order shown in Figure 35.2. For example, some people might value self esteem more than love. Or creative people might aim to satisfy higher needs even though they have not yet satisfied safety needs.

Maslow's hierarchy has been criticised in a number of ways, particularly when applied to work situations.
- Some rewards can fit into more than one level. For example, a pay rise may satisfy the physiological needs of some workers helping them to buy more food or clothing.

For others, it may satisfy their self-esteem needs.
- For people within the same level, motivating factors might not be the same.
- It is difficult, if not impossible, to measure when a need has been satisfied in practice.
- People do not necessarily satisfy their needs just through the work situation.

Herzberg's two-factor theory

Another example of a content theory of motivation was given by an American psychologist, Frederick Herzberg. In 1966, he published an article about research he had conducted on 203 professional engineers and accountants in the Pittsburgh area, USA. They were asked about the events they had experienced at work which had made them feel good or bad about their job and to give reasons why. This led to a two-factor theory.

Motivators Herzberg gave the name MOTIVATORS to those factors which, if present, motivate workers. As Figure 35.3 shows, the main motivators which came from his survey were:
- achievement - such as accomplishing a particularly difficult task or passing professional examinations;
- recognition - superiors showing that they know the worker has done a good job;
- the nature of the job itself - the satisfaction that comes from doing a job that you enjoy;

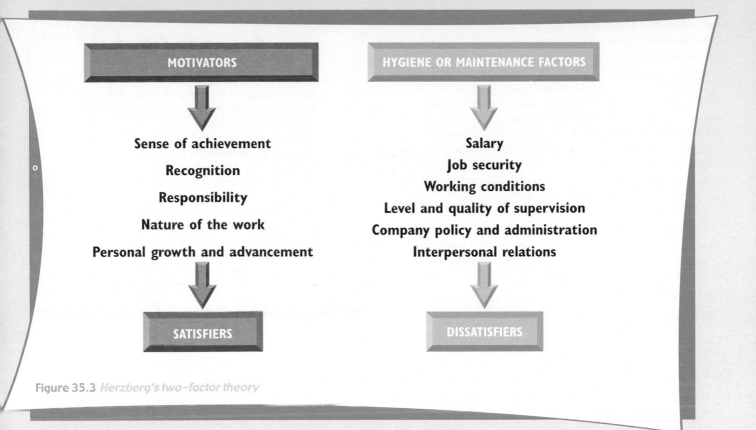

Figure 35.3 *Herzberg's two–factor theory*

- responsibility - such as being in charge of a project or a group of workers;
- personal growth and advancement - such as being promoted to a new job.

Hygiene factors The factors which result in dissatisfaction, if absent, Herzberg called HYGIENE (or MAINTENANCE) FACTORS. Herzberg used the word 'hygiene' to indicate that these were mainly preventative and environmental factors. They prevented dissatisfaction. The main hygiene factors were:

- company policy and administration - such as adequate safety rules;
- level and quality of supervision - such as proper help and guidance when using difficult equipment;
- salary - such as being paid the salary that workers think they deserve;
- job security - such as knowledge that they will not be made redundant in future;
- interpersonal relations - such as getting on with co-workers ;
- working conditions - including adequate heating, car parking and drink facilities.

Herzberg argued that the first group of factors motivated workers. For example, promoting a worker and giving her an award as recognition of her achievements would be motivating to that worker. This would lead to job satisfaction.

The second group of factors did not motivate workers. So, giving all workers an annual pay rise in a company would not motivate them. They would see the annual pay rise as part of normal running of the company. However, not giving them an annual pay rise because the company was performing poorly would lead to dissatisfaction. But giving them the pay rise would prevent this dissatisfaction.

Herzberg's work was used to promote **job enrichment**

(see unit 36), where jobs were redesigned to make them more fulfilling for the individual worker. Workers have been given a wider range of tasks to enable them to do a whole task. The theory suggested that being able to complete a whole task would give a sense of achievement and be more intrinsically

keyterms

Content or needs theory - **the theory that we are motivated because we wish to satisfy our needs.**
Hawthorne effect - **that those taking part in an experiment and are under observation will behave differently than they otherwise would.**
Hierarchy of needs - **placing needs in order of importance; in Maslow's theory, this starts from basic human needs and finishes with the need for self-actualisation.**
Human relations school of thought - **an approach that considers the social factors at work and the behaviour of employees in an organisation. It concentrates on the variety of factors that satisfy workers' needs.**
Hygiene or maintenance factors - **in Herzberg's theory, factors which can result in a reduction in job satisfaction.**
Instrumentality theory - **theories of motivation which argue that how people behave depends upon rewards and punishments.**
Motivators - **factors which motivate individuals; in Herzberg's model, these include achievement, recognition, responsibility the nature of work and personal advancement.**

interesting that doing a small part of a job. Issues such as quality should be the responsibility of the individual worker and not a supervisor or quality inspector. Feedback on work should also be given regularly.

Herzberg's work has been criticised for a number of reasons.

- It has been argued that the work is methodologically flawed. The original sample (see unit 8) of 207 workers was too small and covered too narrow a range of workers. Using only US workers also suggested that the findings would not necessarily be applicable to other countries and cultures.
- No attempt was made to measure the relationship between satisfaction and actual performance. The survey concentrated on satisfaction and experiences which the respondents themselves recalled.

Despite these criticisms, Herzberg's work has been highly influential in the field of business. It is an easy and self-intuitive theory which has led to changes in the way some jobs have been designed.

checklist

1 What did Mayo's experiments in the relay assembly department show about improving productivity?
2 What did Mayo's experiment in the bank wiring observation room show about the power of informal groups over the productivity of individual workers?
3 What did Mayo's work suggest are the main motivators of workers?
4 What is the difference between instrumentality theory and content theory?
5 Explain Maslow's hierarchy of needs.
6 What are the criticisms of Maslow's theory?
7 What is the difference in Herzberg's theory between motivators and hygiene factors?

Plans by the London Borough of Wandsworth to punish staff who persistently take days off sick could create more problems than they solve, according to workplace experts. In 1999 the council was in dispute over proposals that would force staff who persistently have days off without a doctor's note to take a cut in pay or work longer to make up for lost time. It was proposed that staff who have taken more than five single days off work or exceeded 10 days off in three or more periods would reimburse the employer as part of a 'workback/payback' scheme.

A spokesperson for Wandsworth said the details of the scheme, covering 3 700 manual and office-based workers, had yet to be worked out. But a pilot was successful in one department where absenteeism due to sickness has been cut dramatically. Absence rates had been reduced from an average 11.2 days per employee in 1990 to 8.3 days in 1998. Despite its success, the council believed it could cut its £5 million absence bill further and hit a target of 6.2 days per employee.

Jessica Learmond-Criqui, co-author of the *A-Z of Absence & Sickness*, argued that short-term absences could affect employers dramatically. One method of calculating the cost to an employer multiplies the length of time by the number of occurrences and squares the total. The cost of someone off work for a three-week period in a year gives 9. But the cost of someone who is absent for a period of three days, five times per year, gives a figure of 225. The high figure for short-term absences is due to the havoc they cause, she said.

Unions claimed that the plans failed to recognise the strains of working in the public sector. They also feared that managers could use the scheme to single out employees thought to be 'troublemakers'. Occupational therapists pointed out that stress could greatly undermine such a scheme. They suggested that an organisation cracking down on staff who are frequently sick might make problems worse. Stress is now one of the top three causes of sickness absence, along with neck and back problems and hearing and breathing difficulties. Disciplinary regimes that try to restrict absences due to sickness can add to stress and cause a serious breakdown in relations between and employers.

Gary Cooper, professor of organisational psychology at University of Manchester Institute of Science and Technology, said the idea that you take a big stick to staff to solve the problem is flawed. 'In principle, I believe that policies which reward people are more effective than those that punish.' He argued that public sector organisations have an even greater problem than their commercial or industrial counterparts. 'It's no good punishing people you are already paying badly. And public sector staff are mostly paid badly compared to the private sector. They will only become more resentful and the underlying problems remain', he said

Adapted from *The Guardian*, 27.12.1999.

1 Explain what is meant by the terms:
  (a) 'absenteeism; (3 marks)
  (b) 'working conditions'. (3 marks).
2 Outline how Wandsworth is proposing to reduce average absenteeism rates through sickness. (6 marks)
3 Examine the reasons why Wandsworth wants to reduce the average number of working days per employee lost through sickness. (8 marks)
4 Discuss the impact that Wandsworth's scheme is likely to have on the motivation of its staff. (10 marks)

TGI Friday's

Knowledge TGI Friday's is a restaurant and bar chain with 42 outlets in the UK.

Application *Job design* has been carefully thought through. On the one hand, there are strict procedures to ensure that the *corporate identity* is enforced. For example, cooks have to present meals in a particular way. On the other hand, *staff* are free to 'be themselves'. *Managers* of *outlets* are *empowered* to set up their own *reward schemes* for *staff*, which might include free beer or a weekend's use of a company car. *Employees* are encouraged to have fun to complement a high level of service to the *customer*. *Job enlargement* is available to *employees* who undergo *training*. The *business* gives *staff* an average 80 hours of *training* a year.

Analysis Management at TGI Friday's want their staff to give customers a fun experience with excellent levels of service. Empowering their workers and helping them to form teams in each outlet leads to high levels of motivation. This is then communicated to customers, ensuring that they make repeat visits.

Evaluation TGI Friday's is arguably one of the best companies in Britain for which to work. In 2003, *The Sunday Times* gave it a ranking of number 52 out of the top 100 best companies. By motivating staff, TGI Friday's should continue to grow in the years to come.

Adapted from *The Sunday Times*, 2003.

Motivation and the size of the business

Approximately two million workers in the UK are self-employed. Effectively, they run and work in their own businesses, often called sole proprietorships (see unit 60). They have to be **self-motivating**. If they take time off work to go shopping, this is time when they can't be working. Money is a key factor in motivating the self-employed. But there are many other factors which motivate them, including wanting to see a job well done, preferring one type of work to another and loyalty to customers.

In a larger business, most workers will be employees and will have no ownership stake in the business. Neither will they have freedom to choose how they work and what work they do. Motivation then becomes an issue for management and owners. How can staff be motivated to work in a way which meets the **objectives** of the business?

In a new business, management and owners can establish their own culture of work from the start. In an established business, changing an unsatisfactory culture can be difficult. Both Frederick Taylor (see unit 34) and Elton Mayo (see unit 35) argued that workers tend to adopt the culture and work attitudes of their peers, their immediate fellow workers. If this small group culture approves of doing the minimum amount of work or pretending to be sick to take holidays, for example, new members will tend to adopt these working practices. Workers who didn't would be shunned by fellow workers.

This suggests that changing the culture of an organisation requires management and owners to change the culture of these informal groups. This could involve:
- changing the way in which staff work;
- changing the work which is done by individual members of staff;
- giving training to staff to equip them with the skills for new methods of working.

Job design

The work of researchers from the **human relations school** (see unit 35) led to a greater interest in the concept of JOB DESIGN. It has been suggested that the design of a job can affect workers' motivation and the performance of a business.

Job design is about the relationship between workers, the nature and content of their jobs, and the tasks involved in their jobs. It attempts to meet worker's needs by reorganisation of their work. Job design is important because:
- workers want to be employed in jobs which interest them and give them job satisfaction and challenges which they could meet;
- businesses want workers to be productive and efficient, producing high quality work which satisfied the needs of 'customers'. They are more likely to do this if they are motivated.

A number of different ways of approaching job design have been suggested. These include job enrichment, job enlargement, empowerment and team working.

Job enrichment

JOB ENRICHMENT was first advocated by Frederick Herzberg in the 1960s and taken up by other researchers in the human relations school (unit 35). It is a process where workers are given more challenging and complex tasks. This is a process sometimes called VERTICAL LOADING because they are doing more complex tasks within their current role. Job enrichment requires a mixture of the following.

Combining tasks Workers should not be given narrow, repetitive tasks to perform. Rather, they should perform a

Call centres now employ more than 400 000 people, more than coal, steel and car manufacturing put together. Call centres are dedicated facilities for receiving phone calls from customers or for selling over the telephone. Some large businesses run their own call centres. Many businesses, though, outsource this work to specialist call centre companies.

Call centres have come to have a bad reputation. Wages are typically low, staff are tied down to their desks during working hours, there is little job satisfaction and staff turnover is very high. On the other hand, call centre employment naturally attracts people who are looking for short-term contract work. Stephen Thomas, managing director of Convergys, which operates 45 call centres in Europe, the Middle East, Africa and Asia says: 'A call centre can offer people a structured environment for six, nine or 12 months. We have a lot of students working for us, for example, and mothers returning to work. It is a good role for people who otherwise would not feel confident applying for an office job.'

Training appears to be crucial to employees' feeling of well-being and presumably to their motivation for staying in their jobs. A report published in 2000 by David Holman of the University of Sheffield and Sue Fernie of the London School of Economics found that call centre workers rated training even higher than pay as an important influence on their job satisfaction, and this in a sector that usually pays well below average earnings.

At Convergys, an average 12 per cent of staff time is given over to training. This allows staff to take on more complex jobs, which gives them greater job satisfaction and reduces staff turnover. Variety of work, such as processing emails and faxes rather than just taking calls, is a major incentive to stay on in the job.

Adapted from the *Financial Times*, 15.1.2002.

1 **Suggest why motivation is often not high in call centres.**
2 **Why might training contribute to job enlargement for call centre workers?**
3 **Discuss whether motivation of workers is important to call centre companies if most of their workers have left within 12 months.**

range of tasks. This range should give variety to workers and enable them to use a wider range of skills and talents. This could be called **job enlargement** (see below).

Making an identifiable contribution Workers should make an identifiable contribution to producing a good or service. For example, a personal secretary who writes letters, answers the phone, keeps the appointments diary and does a variety of other tasks is likely to be more satisfied than an administrative assistant who only word processes letters. The personal secretary is more likely to see that he or she is making a contribution to the effectiveness of the organisation. The administrative assistant who is constantly typing is unlikely to get much job satisfaction from the task.

Interaction with known individuals Most workers prefer to deal with people they know. For example, a worker who orders supplies usually prefers to deal with a person they have dealt with before at the suppliers. Establishing relationships within an organisation and outside it therefore helps motivation. It also allows the individual to receive feedback from others in day to day dealings.

Vertical loading An important part of job enrichment is vertical loading. Workers are given more responsibility to manage their work. Studies have shown that workers who have little or no responsibility and no power to change their work environment are more likely to suffer stress and have the least job satisfaction. Vertical loading is likely to increase job satisfaction and make work less stressful. Workers are likely to need training to undertake their new responsibilities.

Feedback Assuming extra responsibilities is likely to increase the amount of informal feedback workers receive about their performance. Workers should also receive formal feedback, such as regular performance appraisals. Feedback should identify whether workers are coping with the extra responsibilities given and identify training needs where they are not.

The term 'job enrichment' today is not particularly fashionable. However, the ideas behind job enrichment are mostly contained in the concepts of 'empowerment' and 'team working' (see below), both of which are important in business today.

Some have argued that workers don't want job enrichment. This is because they don't necessarily want extra responsibilities, particularly if they are not paid more for taking them on. This is most likely to be true of manual workers who are least likely to see work as something which fulfils their needs for self-esteem and creativity (see unit 35). However, for white collar workers, job enrichment is a way in which their higher order needs can be satisfied.

Job enlargement

JOB ENLARGEMENT occurs when workers are given a greater variety of tasks to complete. For example, an administrative assistant who mainly types may also be given the task of answering the phone. Or a worker on an assembly line, instead of doing the same task all day, may spend the morning doing one task and the afternoon doing another. Job enlargement results in HORIZONTAL LOADING. The extra

In 2001, Travel Inn, a chain of budget hotels owned by Whitbread, launched a new customer satisfaction scheme. Any customer who complained that they had not had the promise made by the chain of 'providing anything you want for a good night's sleep' would get their money back.

Staff were sceptical, believing that it would encourage customers to complain. In practice, less than 0.5 per cent of sales turnover is refunded. But this is worth the cost because customers with complaints are far more likely to carry on using the chain. What's more, customer satisfaction is increased because the scheme empowers staff to fix the problems that caused the complaint in the first place.

When a refund is made, the complaint is meticulously recorded and then analysed by the relevant team the following day. That team is then empowered to fix the problem. For example, at the County Hall Hotel in central London, a customer complained about the heat in the room on a summer's night. The housekeepers' team responded by buying electric fans from a local shop. Another customer complained that they had run out of the small cartons of milk in their room to make coffee. Now throughout the chain there are baskets of milk cartons and biscuits on the reception desk so customers can help themselves if they run out.

Empowering workers to fix problems has not just improved customer satisfaction. Staff turnover (the percentage of staff resigning from their job over a period of time) is down 29 per cent, which Travel Inn believes is partly down to increased empowerment and job satisfaction.

Adapted from *People Management*, 7.11.2002.

> **1 How has empowerment of staff at Travel Inn benefited (a) the staff themselves; (b) customers; (c) the company?**

tasks undertaken are at the same level of competence as the original task. So job enlargement doesn't involve workers taking on extra responsibilities as with job enrichment.

Job enlargement tends to come about in three ways.
- **Job enrichment**. Job enlargement can be one part of job enrichment.
- **Job rotation**. JOB ROTATION occurs when a worker switches from one job to another on a regular basis. This typically provides more variety.
- **Job loading**. Job loading occurs when workers are given extra tasks to perform because fellow workers are off sick or because they have left and not been replaced. Job loading has come to be seen as particularly important in production line work. Here, absent workers can be highly disruptive to overall productivity.

Job enlargement can raise productivity by increasing variety for workers. It also makes workers more flexible and can allow the business to cope more easily with staff absences or sudden surges in demand for a product. However, it can involve higher costs. Training may need to be given. Workers may need extra time to move from one task to another. Also, workers may be less skilled and productive doing, say, three different tasks at different times than if they were just concentrating on one. They may also find that it simply increases the number of lower levels tasks they do, without really satisfying and challenging them.

Empowerment

EMPOWERMENT of workers means giving workers greater freedom, authority and self control over their work. It also involves giving them the right to make decisions.

In one sense, empowerment is simply a more fashionable word today for **delegation** (see unit 31). However, delegation tends to be associated with the passing down of power to perform a particular task. It is narrow and specific. Empowerment is broader and wider ranging. It is about giving employees responsibility for achieving activities in the best way possible. Empowerment implies a trust in workers, liberating them to make decisions.

Empowerment is motivating for a variety of reasons.
- Workers are more likely to be able to use their skills and talents in their jobs.
- Workers will have greater control over their working lives through increased decision making.
- Empowerment creates a sense that the organisation trusts workers and recognises their talents.
- Successful empowerment is likely to be linked to training. Workers initially may not have all the skills need to make correct decisions.
- Workers will feel less frustrated by more senior staff making decisions which they feel are incorrect.
- Empowerment gives workers greater control over the working lives. This increases job satisfaction and reduces stress.

From the business viewpoint, output is likely to be raised if workers are more motivated. It is also possible to **delayer** (see unit 31) management, taking out management posts. This is because decisions are now being made lower down the management **hierarchy** (see unit 31). This reduces the wage bill.

However, the same criticisms that apply to job enrichment

also apply to empowerment because empowerment is a key feature of job enrichment. Training has to be given to staff to enable them to become empowered which increases costs to the business. Moreover, not all workers want to be empowered. Many workers, particularly at the bottom of any hierarchy, prefer to be told what to do rather than have to think about how to respond to a situation. Empowerment can be highly demotivating if a worker makes wrong decisions.

Teamworking

TEAMWORKING became fashionable in management theory in the 1980s and 1990s. Managers have often operated as teams in the past. But in the 1980s, European and US manufacturers became aware of teamworking in Japanese plants, particularly car plants. **Production cells** (see unit 47), where a group of workers were responsible for producing a particular item, were seen as important to high Japanese productivity. **Quality circles** (see unit 47) also became fashionable in management theory, although relatively few businesses actually operated them in practice. These were teams of workers drawn from a variety of backgrounds within a business. The quality circle looked at a particular aspect of the running of the business to see how it could be improved.

Teams within a business are likely to have some or all of the following characteristics.
- Workers with a number of different skills are part of the team. But there is also an element of MULTI-SKILLING where different workers are able to do more than one task within the team.
- The team is set a goal by management, but the team is empowered to decide how best to achieve that goal.
- Teams are encouraged constantly to think about better ways of performing a task. In Japanese management theory, this is part of **Kaizen** (continuous improvement, see unit 47).

Teamworking has a number of advantages.
- It creates possibilities for workers to interact. This can be motivating and can lead to high productivity.
- Multi-skilling is useful when staff are absent or there is a sudden surge in demand for a particular product.
- Teamworking is likely to lead to job enrichment, job enlargement and empowerment with all their benefits.

However, there can be problems.
- Not everyone works best in a team. Some individuals work more productively on their own and some tasks are better accomplished by individuals. Some workers may resent others slowing them down or getting rewards when they have contributed little to team efforts.
- People in a team may not get on with each other. There may be discrimination against some team members. A strong character may bully others into their way of thinking.
- Businesses may say 'in this office, we are all part of the same team'. Yet in practice some people may work in different conditions to others.
- Some businesses do not have the organisation for teams to work. They may not have support staff, effective communication between team members or clearly differentiated job roles.

Motivational theory

Concepts such as job enrichment, job enlargement, empowerment and teamworking have come out of the work of the **human relations school** (see unit 35). This suggests that management can increase motivation within their organisations through ways other than paying workers more.

However, it can be argued that different workers respond differently to different types of scheme. Some workers don't want responsibility and don't want to be empowered. Others don't want to work in teams. Others don't want to learn new skills. But they might work longer hours if they were paid more. Some work situations are also more suitable for, say, teamworking, than others. So in practice it is important for managers wanting to motivate their workforce to think clearly about what might and might not be effective in their particular circumstances. No one method is necessarily the best method for every business organisation.

keyterms

Empowerment - **occurs when workers are given more responsibility and freedom to make decisions.**
Horizontal loading - **occurs when workers are given a greater range of tasks to do but at the same level of difficulty as their previous tasks.**
Job design - **creating a pattern of work for an employee which would answer the needs of the business organisation for productivity, efficiency and quality and of the worker for job satisfaction.**
Job enlargement - **occurs when workers are given a greater variety of tasks to complete.**
Job enrichment - **occurs when workers are empowered and given a greater range of more complex tasks to perform.**
Multi-skilling - **where workers, through training, have several skills allowing them to perform a variety of jobs.**
Teamworking - **when workers are grouped together and set a task to perform.**
Vertical loading - **occurs when workers are given more complex tasks to perform.**

checklist

1 Why must the self-employed be self-motivating if they are to be successful?
2 How can the culture of a business affect motivation of staff?
3 Why is job design important?
4 What is the difference between job enrichment and job enlargement?
5 Explain the difference between vertical loading and horizontal loading.
6 What is the difference between empowerment and delegation?
7 Why might some workers not wish to be empowered?
8 What are the advantages and disadvantages of teamworking?

Salary rises, bonus schemes and share options are the traditional tools managers use to motivate employees based on the simple idea that cash is the most effective carrot in the work-place. But experts say that money is not a long-term motivator. 'It doesn't matter how much their salaries are, unhappy employees will not be as dedicated to their work' according to Peter Done of Peninsula, the employment law adviser. To inspire staff, businesses should be looking at alternative ways that are often far more effective and longer lasting than pay rises. Ensuring that workers feel involved and that their opinions matter to the company is an important incentive.

St Luke's Communications, a London advertising agency, has removed symbols of hierarchy in the office because its managers feel they act as barriers to productivity. There are no private offices, not even for the chairperson. Staff are encouraged to contribute to projects other than those to which they have been specifically assigned. Everyone has the right to stumble in meetings. They can mention incomplete ideas without reproach since these thoughts often inspire others.

Innocent is a health-drink maker based in west London, whose main product is 'smoothie' fruit juices. When 25 year old Ailana Kamelmacher arrived for work on her first day, she found a mug with her name on it in the staff kitchen and a two week timetable showing her the different members of staff who would be taking her out to lunch. 'These lunches gave me a thorough introduction to the company', she says. 'But they also enabled me to chat and make friends with almost half the staff.' The warm welcome is not just special treatment for new employees. It is part of co-founder Richard Reed's management ethos. 'We're a company of only 24 people' he says. 'Our success is intrinsically linked with these employees. It's vital that they're interested in the product and the growth of the business. The best way of maintaining this is by making sure they're happy.' Sales targets at Innocent are painted for all to see on the side of a large smoothie bottle called the Drinkometer. When each target is met, the managers organise fun days as a reward. The last one was a sports day in the park for the whole team, complete with egg-and-spoon races. The next one is a group yoga session. As Reed says: 'The days help to show our employees that we value their efforts. They are simple to organise and have fostered a real family atmosphere in the company.'

Adapted from *The Sunday Times*, 14.6.2002.

1 Explain the meaning of the terms:
  (a) 'motivator'; (3 marks)
  (b) 'team'. (3 marks)
2 Outline TWO examples of job design from the data. (6 marks)
3 Using examples from the data, analyse how a company might empower its work and so raise motivation. (8 marks)
4 Discuss whether being part of a successful team is a more important motivator to workers than the salary they earn. (10 marks)

37 Motivation: financial methods

Consultants

Knowledge In 2002, hospital consultants in England and Wales rejected a contract which would have given them more pay. The proposed new contract between the NHS and the hospital consultants would have meant consultants working 40 hours a week for the NHS. It would also have meant that the health service would have had first call on their time before they undertook private work.

Application The new contract was intended to *motivate* consultants to work longer hours for the NHS. However, the consultants had been annoyed at the introduction of *performance targets* into hospitals. Instead of consultants deciding what work should be done, increasingly these decisions were being made by *managers* responding to *targets* such as cutting waiting list times set by *government*.

Analysis The rejection of the new contract by consultants was partly financial. Consultants didn't want to give up any of the lucrative private health care work that they were currently doing. But it also reflected a rejection of the increasing trend towards professional management in the NHS. NHS consultants were not sufficiently motivated by the extra money being offered to them by the government to sign the new contract.

Evaluation Arguably, the rejection of the contract was not a rejection of higher pay. It was the consultants expressing their frustration at their current working conditions. With the government determined to push ahead with reforms of the NHS, it seems likely that the consultants will have to back down at some stage and accept an element of performance related pay.

Adapted from People Management, 21.11.2002.

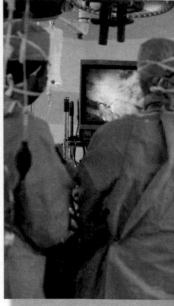

Salaries and wages

For nearly all workers, the main reason for going to work is to earn money to buy goods and services. Most workers in the UK are either paid a wage or a salary.

Wages WAGES tend to be associated with lower paid workers and BLUE COLLAR WORKERS (i.e. MANUAL WORKERS). Wages are typically expressed as hourly TIME RATES of pay, such as £5.50 an hour or £12.75 an hour. This then forms weekly rates of pay, such as £250 a week, for a fixed number of hours work, such as 38 hours. The 38 hours would then be the **basic working week**.

Waged employees often have the opportunity to work OVERTIME. These are hours worked over and above the basic working week. To motivate workers to accept overtime, employers often pay higher rates of pay. If the basic wage is £10 an hour, overtime might be paid at time and a quarter (£12.50 an hour) or time and a half (£15 an hour). Saturday or Sunday overtime working might be paid at higher rates than weekday overtime, to encourage people to work at weekends.

Salaries SALARIES tend to be associated with better paid workers, particularly WHITE COLLAR WORKERS (i.e. NON-MANUAL WORKERS). Salaried staff are typically paid each month. Some salaried staff might earn overtime because they are only expected to work a fixed number of hours per week. However, most salaried staff are paid to do a particular job. There might be a recommended number of hours work per week, like 38 hours. But they are often expected to work as many hours as it takes to complete the job. A yearly salary is usually higher than that which could be earned by workers if they were in a less senior job and paid a wage.

The main long term factors which determine the level of wages and salaries are the forces of demand and supply. Businesses have to pay the 'market rate' for the job if they want to retain existing staff and recruit new staff. Paying below the market rate can also demotivate staff. They might feel that they are not valued by their employer. Paying above the market rate can be motivating. Workers might feel that their contribution is being rewarded by higher pay.

Piece rates and commission

Not all workers are paid wages or salaries. Some are paid piece rates or commission.

Piece rates Piece rates (see unit 34) are payments for each unit produced. For example, a worker might be paid £0.50 per parcel delivered or £1.00 per kilo of strawberries picked. Piece rates were recommended by Frederick Taylor, founder of the **scientific management school** (see unit 34). He thought they were an ideal way to motivate workers. Workers who produced more were more highly paid.

However, piece rates are only suitable for jobs where it is easy to identify the contribution of an individual worker. It would be difficult to devise a piece rate system for, say, secretaries or managers. Piece rates have been criticised on health and safety grounds. They might encourage workers to take dangerous short cuts in a bid to reduce the amount of time taken for each item. Rushing production might also affect the quality of the product.

Commission COMMISSION is a payment system mainly used with white collar workers. Commission, like piece rates, is a payment for achieving a target. For example, car salespeople may get a commission of £100 for each car they sell. Some white collar workers are paid entirely on commission. A salesperson, for example, may be paid entirely on the basis of their sales record. Alternatively, a worker may be paid a basic salary and then receive commission on top. Commission based pay systems are intended to 'incentivise' workers by tying in pay with output.

Fringe benefits

FRINGE BENEFITS are benefits received over and above that received from wages or salaries. Fringe benefits are payments 'in kind' rather than in cash. Typical examples of fringe benefits include contributions to pensions, a company car, private health insurance, subsidised meals including luncheon vouchers, and subsidised loans or mortgages.

One reason why fringe benefits are given is because they are a tax-efficient way of rewarding employees. It may cost a business less to give the fringe benefit than the equivalent sum of money needed to buy it by the employee. Some fringe benefits help the running of the business. For example, private health care might reduce the number of days off sick by employees and give the business greater control about when an employee has an operation.

Businesses also give fringe benefits as a way of motivating staff. They can act as a motivator in two ways.
- Many satisfy the basic physiological and safety needs of workers, as outlined by Maslow (see unit 35). They also meet the hygiene factors as outlined in Herzberg's two-factor theory (see unit 35).
- The awarding of fringe benefits can be linked to achievement and promotion. Free private medical health care insurance, for example, is sometimes only available to more senior members of staff within an organisation

In 1999, the UK company Zeneca and the Swedish company Astra merged to form AstraZeneca. Both were pharmaceutical companies making medicines and drugs. The two companies offered different benefit packages to their employees and these were merged into one called AZAdvantage. Under this, staff are given a salary and a budget for buying fringe benefits. However, they have the freedom to spend that budget as they wish. Fringe benefits include lifestyle options such as extra holiday and retail vouchers; health options such as dental cover; financial options such as enhanced retirement benefits; and protection options which include insurance services. Each benefit is priced. Employees have the further option of simply receiving part or all of the budget as extra cash added to their salary.

Both AstraZeneca and its staff gain from offering the fringe benefits. These gains come either from paying less tax and National Insurance or from obtaining discounts from benefit providers such as insurance companies. The company reckons that an individual employee can add between 5 and 15 per cent extra value to the total pay package through AZAdvantage.

The company believes that AZAdvantage was one factor in keeping staff turnover low through the difficult time of the merger. It also helped attract new staff to join the company.

Adapted from *People Management*, 7.11.2002.

1 **Explain what is meant by a fringe benefit, giving examples from the data.**
2 **Why can fringe benefits be financially beneficial both to the employer and the employee?**
3 **Using the example of AstraZeneca, explain how fringe benefits can motivate staff.**

Performance related pay

PERFORMANCE RELATED PAY (PRP) is a pay system designed specifically to motivate staff. Introduced in the 1980s and 1990s, it is now used widely in the UK amongst white collar workers, especially in the financial services industry, such as banking, and in the public sector.

PRP gives workers extra pay for achieving targets. The extra pay may be a lump sum such as £1 000 or it could be a percentage of salary. Some PRP systems make distinctions between levels of achievement. For example, one worker may be rated 'excellent' and receive a 10 per cent bonus, another 'good' and receive a 5 per cent bonus, another 'satisfactory' and receive no bonus.

The targets are likely to be set through a system of APPRAISAL. This is where the performance of individual staff is reviewed against a set of criteria. These criteria could include factors such as arriving for work on time, ability to get on with other workers, improving skills through training or achieving a particular task within the job. Staff are likely to have a performance appraisal interview where someone more senior, such as their **line manager** (see unit 31), conducts the appraisal.

PRP is widely used because it directly links performance with pay. According to the **scientific management school** (see unit 34), it should motivate workers to achieve the goals set for them by the organisation.

However, PRP and performance appraisal have been widely criticised for a number of reasons.
- The bonus may be too low to give workers an incentive to achieve their targets.
- Achieving the targets may have far more to do with the smooth running of machinery or technological systems, or how a group of workers perform than the performance of an individual. For example, a worker may set a goal of increasing forms processed by 5 per cent. But the number of forms she receives may depend on how many are processed by other members of her team or whether the printing machines are working smoothly. Where teamworking (see unit 36) is an important management tool, it is likely to be better to give bonuses based on the output of a team rather than an individual.
- Targets may be difficult or even impossible to achieve in the eyes of workers. If this is the case, then they are unlikely to make any effort to achieve them.
- Few staff see appraisal as an independent objective procedure. Staff are quite likely to put their failure to achieve a grade in an appraisal interview down to the unfairness of the interviewer. This is particularly true when there are already problems in the relationship between, say, a worker and his or her boss. Staff who do achieve highly in appraisal interviews may be seen by others as 'favourites' of the interviewer.

Failure to receive a high enough grade in the appraisal process may act as a demotivator of staff. Instead of staff wanting to improve their performance, they may simply give up attempting to change their behaviour and attitudes. Failure to receive a PRP bonus could challenge the physiological needs of staff in Maslow's hierarchy of needs because it deprives them of money (see unit 35). It could also make them feel less 'loved' by the organisation, challenging their need for love and belonging. It will almost certainly knock their self-esteem.

accountemps®
Specialised Financial Staffing

Purchase Ledger Clerk - Wolverhampton
Temporary to permanent position working in a large organisation at their Head Office. Good team player and previous purchase ledger experience essential. £7.00 per hour.

Accounts Assistant - Telford
Temporary to permanent role, working part time 30 hours week. The successful candidate will be working for a s organisation assisting the company accountant. £7.50 hour.

Finance Assistant - Wolverhampton
Maternity cover to start May 2003. General accounting d to include - cash reconciliation, budget preparation spreadsheet work. £8.50 per hour.

Credit Controller - Telford
Solid credit controller required for a short-term assignm reduce debtor days, to start as soon as possible. £7.75 per hour.

Accounts Clerk - Shropshire
Temporary ongoing assignment, working in a large team resolving invoicing queries, previous accounting experience essential. £6.50 per hour.

Finance Manager - Shropshire
Temporary to permanent assignment to start as soon as possible, the successful candidate will be required to supervise a small team and complete all round general accounting duties. £10.00 per hour.

Payroll Clerk - Wolverhampton
Temporary to permanent assignment, the successful applicant will be responsible for a 150 monthly payroll covering all aspects. Previous payroll knowledge essential. £5.50 per hour. For more information on these and other positions please contact Melissa Brown, Claire Marshall or Penny Witcherley on 01902 317200.

FINANCE DIRECTOR
Burton on Trent £60k + Benefits
My client is a rapidly expanding business, involved in the commercial Vehicle Leasing market. Due to the group's success they are looking to appoint a Finance Director to run the growing finance department.
Reporting to the board your remit will be to provide accurate and effective financial information, from the production of management accounts, to special ad hoc projects. You will have a strong commercial acumen, and demonstrate strong managerial skills. You will be a proactive hands on accountant, with the ability to communicate at all levels.
Supervising a team of three, you will be results driven, possess the skills to develop the finance function for future requirements.
Experience within a similar sector, or the finance sector would be advantageous, but is not essential.
For further information please forward your CV to:
Alan Webb
BENTLEY JENNISON
15-20 St Paul's Square, Birmingham B3 1QT
No agencies

Wanted
Salespeople with or without experience

We are looking for well motivated and ambitious people aged 25-45. The successful candidates will earn over £30,000 a year and will be allowed the use of a company car. You will be given a travel allowance each week and all the training required to become a success. There is no cold calling. We provide at least 10 appointments per week. Payment is based on commission, but you can also take advantage of the great holiday incentives for you and a partner.

Call now for more details on
01112 98766 and ask for Mel Peterson

> 1 **Compare the different payment systems shown in the advertisements.**
> 2 **What fringe benefits were being offered?**
> 3 **Discuss what might happen if any of the employers advertising were offering a remuneration package which was below the market rate for the job.**

Profit sharing

Some businesses have PROFIT SHARING schemes. In a **company**, profits would normally be distributed to shareholders. Profit sharing occurs when some of the profits made are distributed to workers as well as shareholders.

Profit sharing can motivate workers to achieve the **objectives** (see unit 63) of the business. Shareholders want higher profits. So too do workers if they are to receive a share of them. Profit sharing therefore unites the goals of both shareholders and workers for extra money. Profit sharing can also be a way of showing staff that they are appreciated. In Maslow's hierarchy of needs, it may help satisfy the need for love and belonging (see unit 35).

However, most individual workers will have little or no control over how much profit their company makes. If they make extra effort to raise sales or reduce costs, the benefit of that extra effort will be shared between all the other workers. There is no link between individual effort and individual reward in profit sharing. Profit sharing is also unlikely to motivate financially if the amount received is fairly small.

A UK business which shows the effects of profit sharing is the John Lewis Partnership which owns the John Lewis department stores and the supermarket chain Waitrose. The John Lewis Partnership is owned in trust for its workers. So all the profits after tax and retentions are distributed to its workers. The amount given varies according to the salary of the worker. In a good year, Waitrose workers will receive a profit share handout of more than 20 per cent of their salary. This is a substantial sum. Whether it motivates John Lewis Partnership workers to work harder is debatable.

Share ownership

Some have argued that workers would be motivated by owning a share of their business. They would then have an incentive to work hard because their efforts would contribute to profit. They would benefit from high profits because they would get part of those profits. The value of their shares in the business would also rise if the business were successful.

There are many ways in which employees might acquire shares. One is through **save-as-you-earn schemes**. Here, employees are able to save a regular amount of money from their pay over five years. At the end of five years, they are able to buy shares in the company at the price that they were five years previously. If the share price has gone up over the five years, the saver will make a capital gain.

The granting of **share options** has become a common way of rewarding senior managers and chief executives of large companies. A member of staff is given the option to buy shares

✓checklist

1 Explain the difference between payment systems frequently found for blue collar workers and white collar workers.
2 Explain the difference between piece rates and commission.
3 Why might fringe benefits motivate workers?
4 Explain the role of targets in performance related pay systems.
5 How might profit sharing schemes motivate workers?
6 Explain the difference between a save-as you-earn scheme for buying shares and share option schemes.

in the company at a fixed point in the future, say three years, at a price agreed today. This price may be below, above or at the same level as today's share price. Share options are supposed to be an incentive to senior management to act in a way which will raise the share price significantly. This means that senior management have the same objective as shareholders.

Share options have been controversial. Some chief executives have been able to earn millions of pounds from **exercising** their share options (i.e. buying the shares at the end of the period and then, usually, selling them immediately, make a large capital gain). But when the stock market is rising, the performance of a company can be average and still its share price will rise. So chief executives can earn large amounts even though their company has not done particularly well.

keyterms

Appraisal - **where the performance of an individual worker is reviewed against a set of criteria.**
Blue collar (or manual) workers - **workers who do mainly physical work, like assembly line workers.**
Commission - **payment made, typically for achieving a target such as a sales target.**
Fringe benefits - **payment in kind over and above the wage or salary paid, such as a company car or luncheon vouchers.**
Overtime - **time worked over and above the basic working week.**
Performance related pay (PRP) - **a payment system, typically** where workers are paid a higher amount if they achieve certain targets set for them by their employer.
Profit sharing - **where workers are given a share of the profits made by the company which employs them.**
Salary - **pay, usually of non-manual workers, expressed as a yearly figure but paid monthly.**
Time rates - **rates of pay based on an amount of time, usually per hour.**
Wages - **payments made to employees for work done, usually given weekly to manual workers.**
While collar (or non-manual) workers - **workers who do non-physical work like office workers or teachers.**

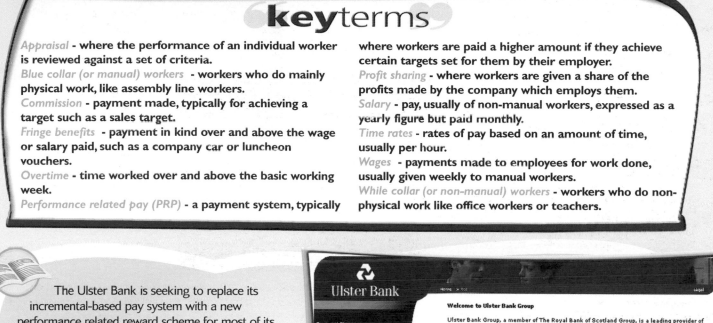

The Ulster Bank is seeking to replace its incremental-based pay system with a new performance related reward scheme for most of its 1 000 staff in the Republic of Ireland. The bank's proposals have been resisted by members of the banking union, the Irish Bank Officials Association (IBOA). They have, however, been accepted by its staff in Northern Ireland.

Informed banking sources suggest that the resistance to the measures by its staff in the Republic may be due to a fear among the younger staff about how their performance will be appraised. There is also a level of frustration among older staff that their contribution is no longer valued.

Ulster Bank's new performance-related scheme is aimed at junior staff ('bank official' grade). Most have joined the bank during the past seven years, but they now find promotional prospects are restricted as the junior grade attracts no additional incremental increases after eight years of service. The existing incremental-based pay scales would be replaced by four new grades, allowing for performance related progress.

Ulster Bank says that at least 80 per cent of staff who agree to come within the new structure would receive an annual performance rating which would entitle them to a 6 per cent salary increase. This would be in addition to cost-of-living increases due under Ireland's centralised pay agreement, Partnership 2000. The main thrust of the proposals is to give incentives to younger employees and to reward performance more accurately, the bank maintains. It insists that the measures are not aimed at cost reduction.

Adapted from eironline, European Foundation for the Improvement of Living and Working Conditions.

1 Explain what is meant by the terms:
   (a) 'performance related reward scheme'; (3 marks)
   (b) 'incentives'. (3 marks)
2 Outline TWO differences between performance related pay and an incremental pay system. (6 marks)
3 Analysis how the introduction of performance related pay might help the Ulster Bank perform better as a company. (8 marks)
4 Discuss whether performance related pay will help increase motivation of workers at the Ulster Bank. (10 marks)

38 Workforce planning

Consignia/Royal Mail

Knowledge Consignia, due to be re-named The Royal Mail Group in 2003, has been undergoing radical change over the past five years. The next three years will see even more radical change.

Application To remain *profitable* and *competitive*, it has plans to shed 30 000 *staff* over the next three years. This includes *senior managers* at the top of the *organisation*.

Analysis Currently there are around 320 senior managers, of whom around 120 form the 'Top Y', the most senior group, and 200 are part of second tier management. The 120 most senior managers have had to apply for the 90 jobs that will now form the top of the Consignia hierarchy. The 30 who do not find a job can still apply for the 100-150 jobs that will become the second tier of management. But with only 190-240 senior management posts to go around, some of the existing 320 senior managers will not be reappointed. To help decide who will get a job, Consignia brought in Kiddy & Partners, a firm of business psychologists that uses 'business simulation' methods. Its role has been to scrutinise attitudes, experience and achievements among every one of Consignia's highest-paid staff and to assess them against comparable post-holders outside the group.

Evaluation Having senior managers who are commercially aware will help drive Consignia forward against the wave of competition that it will soon face. Without effective workforce planning, both in terms of numbers of staff and the quality of staff, Consignia could find that it loses large amounts of market share, leading to further redundancies.

Adapted from the *Financial Times*, 26.2.2002.

Human resource management

HUMAN RESOURCE MANAGEMENT is the process of administering and controlling the workforce of a business to achieve its objectives. Human resource managers are responsible for a variety of tasks including:

- human resource planning (see below);
- recruitment and selection (see unit 40)
- promotion and redeployment (see below);
- redundancies and dismissals (see below);
- staff development and training (see unit 41);
- staff appraisal (see unit 37);
- motivation of staff (see units 34-37)
- pay and conditions of service (see unit 37);
- working conditions and staff welfare (see unit 36);
- as well as discipline and ensuring staff operate within the law (see unit 55).

Human resource management came out of the pioneering work of researchers such as Elton Mayo (see unit 35) in the 1930s. Initially, large firms began to set up personnel departments to deal with staffing issues. This led to the idea of PERSONNEL MANAGEMENT, managing workers in the business. In the 1980s, greater emphasis was placed on using personal management to achieve business objectives. This led to the term human resource management.

Human resource planning

HUMAN RESOURCE PLANNING or WORKFORCE PLANNING is the process of determining the labour needs of the business now and in the future, including the number of workers and their skills, and ways of achieving labour targets. It has several aspects.

How many The business must plan how many workers its needs. A food business that is planning to expand, for example, might require an extra 34 workers next year. When deciding how many staff are needed, the business must take into account whether workers are full or part time and how many hours they will be expected to work.

Skills The types of workers and their skills must be decided upon. Of the 34 workers, there could be a need for 1 office worker, 15 production workers with no previous qualifications or skills, 2 supervisors with previous experience in the catering trade, and so on.

When needed The business must decide when new workers will be needed. Is a worker needed immediately or will a vacancy arise in 12 months time?

Where needed In larger businesses, there may be many sites where employees are based. So the workforce plan must specify where the employee will be needed.

Achieving targets The human resource plan should identify what changes to staffing will be needed and indicate how this might be achieved. Staffing might need to increase. This can be done in a number of ways.

- Existing staff might have to be **trained** (see unit 41) to increase their skills to cope with new demands in their existing job.
- Staff might have to be REDEPLOYED (i.e. change their jobs) within the organisation. This is also likely to mean staff will need to be trained, perhaps to learn different skills.
- New staff may have to be **recruited** from outside the business (see unit 40).

Alternatively, the number of staff required may need to fall. A business may need to **rationalise**.

- This might be achieved through NATURAL WASTAGE. This is where staff who leave because of retirement, to look after children or to get a better job in another business are not replaced.
- A VOLUNTARY REDUNDANCY scheme may be offered to workers. This is where staff are invited to resign from their jobs. Business often offer inducements, such as generous redundancy payments, to persuade workers to take voluntary redundancy.
- Those nearing retirement age might be offered an early retirement package. They will be able to draw their pension now rather than at the age of retirement.
- As a last resort, the business may be forced to make COMPULSORY REDUNDANCIES. This is where selected employees are told they will lose their jobs. A business is legally able to make workers REDUNDANT if their job 'no longer exists' and they do not intend to appoint another worker to do that job.

Anticipating demand

Businesses use a wide variety of information to calculate their existing and future demand for labour. The starting point is likely to be existing employment patterns. A business knows what it can produce with a given amount of labour. For example, McDonald's knows from previous experience how many staff are needed to run an outlet. A construction company might know how many workers it needs to build a new housing estate. A taxi firm will know how many drivers it needs on a Saturday night.

Then, human resource managers can build in a variety of factors which may affect current or future demand for workers by the business.

Staff turnover STAFF or LABOUR TURNOVER is the proportion of staff leaving a business over a period of time. Staff leave for a variety of reasons. Some may retire and some leave their jobs to look after their children. Others leave because they want a different job. Labour turnover is measured by the formula:

Stemper International is an oil extraction company. It specialises in buying and then operating oil fields which large oil companies judge to be nearing the end of their lives. But even for Stemper, there comes a time when oil fields have to close.

The company faced one such example in 2003. It had 50 employees based in Aberdeen in Scotland working a field which it had bought in the mid-1990s. The 50 employees would no longer have a job and there was no other field owned by Stemper which was serviced from Aberdeen.

The personnel department therefore had to work out how to manage this situation. A quick sort through the files showed up some clear groups of people:

- workers aged 50-65;
- workers who were likely to be immobile because their partners had jobs in the Aberdeen area, or who had spent their whole lives in Aberdeen;
- workers who had skills which could be used elsewhere in the company if those workers were prepared to move internationally;
- workers who with training could be developed and offered new jobs in the company, again assuming they were prepared to move internationally.

The workers aged 50-65 could be offered an early retirement package which some might find attractive. The company was prepared to put some cash into this. But it was not prepared to pay very much more than what it would cost to make these workers compulsorily redundant.

The company had few options for the immobile workers. Having interviewed the workers and found out what their career hopes were following the closure, the personnel department put some resources into trying to find these workers a job with other major employers in the area. Personnel also gave out information about training and job search courses.

The workers with skills in short supply were offered posts elsewhere in the group. Some took these up. Others used the opportunity either to gain a job with another oil company working out of Aberdeen or to gain promotion with another company.

One third of those offered retraining took up the offer, whilst the rest proved reluctant to move out of the UK.

The personnel department was on the whole pleased with the way it had handled the closure. Staff in Aberdeen, although sad, remained motivated up to the end. A survey showed that 83 per cent felt that they had been treated fairly by the company. Nearly three quarters of the staff had either secured another job or taken retirement by the time of the closure.

1 **Explain why there was a need for the personnel department at Stemper to be involved with the Aberdeen operations.**
2 **How did it succeed in rationalising staff?**
3 **Suggest why '83 per cent felt that they had been treated fairly'.**

Penny Dunseith is director of personnel at Pickerell's, a nationwide chain of retailers selling a wide range of goods, including perfumes. Every year she has to present a report to the board of directors outlining the work of the personnel department over the previous twelve months and the personnel issues likely to face it over the next 12 months. In an appendix to the report is a detailed statistical breakdown of staffing requirements. Part of a table from this report is shown in Figure 38.1.

In 2003, she reported that turnover of management the previous year had been 22 per cent, which was roughly what it had been over the previous five years. Turnover of full time staff below manager level in stores was 38 per cent, whilst for part time staff excluding weekend staff it was only 52 per cent. Turnover of part time weekend only staff was 125 per cent.

Part time weekend only staff were mainly 16-25 year old students looking for a little extra money to supplement their pocket money or student grants. In London, there were also a significant minority of young people, mainly from the EU, who had come to the capital to acquire language skills and see the sights. They would often take a weekend job immediately on arrival to start earning some cash and then quickly leave to work more hours.

Ordinary part time staff who worked during the week as well as weekends were typically again either students, young people from overseas or young females with at least one small child. Full time staff below manager level were on average five years older than part time staff. For many, the job was simply one of a succession of jobs, where the worker was constantly looking for a job at the same level offering better pay or working conditions, or nearer to their home. For some, though, it was a stepping stone into management. Penny wanted to devote more resources to training this category of worker, both to reduce staff turnover and to make it easier to recruit at store management level.

	Number of posts
Full time store staff below managerial level	6258
Weekday part time store staff	4 780
Weekend only part time store staff	3 524

Table 38.1 *Average number of employees, 2002*

---

1 **Assuming that labour turnover rates and overall staffing levels remained the same in 2003 as in 2002, calculate to the nearest whole number the number of staff that need to be recruited in 2003 in the following categories:**
   (a) full time staff below manager level;
   (b) weekday part time store staff;
   (c) weekend only part time store staff.
2 **How would your answer to 1 (a) differ if, through the provision of extra training in 2003, the labour turnover of full time staff below manager level fell 20 per cent?**
3 **Suggest why posts filled by students aged 16-25 are likely to have a higher labour turnover than posts filled by young women aged 21-30.**

$$\frac{\text{Number of staff leaving over a period of time}}{\text{Average number of staff in post during the period}} \times 100\%$$

Labour turnover varies enormously between different types of job, between industries and between businesses. McDonald's, for example, has a staff turnover of around 100 per cent per quarter in the UK. This means that on average staff only stay three months in their job. Staff turnover for most jobs is much lower than this. Human resource managers have to take staff turnover into account when planning for the future. Businesses with high staff turnover must recruit more frequently than those with low staff turnover. If staff turnover is concentrated amongst just a few jobs in the business, then recruitment will focus on those jobs.

Sales A change in the level of sales for a business is likely to lead to different staffing needs. A business that forecasts a drop in sales of 20 per cent over the next 12 months is likely to

need fewer employees. An expanding business is likely to need more. In larger businesses, the type of sales that are expanding and contracting will affect staffing levels. If US sales are falling but UK sales are rising for a fast food chain, then the number of US employees is likely to fall but in the UK numbers will rise. Within a management consultancy firm, expanding contracts for IT consultancy will require more IT experts, whilst falling contracts for financial consultancy will require fewer accountants.

Competition Competition between businesses will affect staffing. In manufacturing today, there is fierce competition between firms in the supply of household goods. Some manufacturers have ceased production in the UK as a result. Others have been forced to become more efficient, producing more output with fewer resources and so bringing down prices. Fewer staff have often been needed. Remaining staff often have to have higher levels of skill and to be flexible.

Technology Changes in technology will probably change the skills needs of a business. In general, improved technology requires more skilled workers to use it. Office technology today requires many white collar workers to be computer literate and able to use software programs. Improved technology is also likely to be labour saving. Fewer workers are needed to produce the same amount of output.

Changing production techniques There can be considerable differences in productivity (output per worker) between businesses. Changing how employees work with existing resources such as machinery can considerably improve productivity. Teamworking (see unit 36), for example, can improve productivity. Improved productivity will mean that fewer workers are needed to produce the same amount of output. Equally, they often need greater skills, changing the composition of the workforce.

Analysing supply

Understanding how the demand for labour will change over time is only one side of workforce planning. The supply of labour must also be taken into account.

Human resource managers must first understand the skills and talents of existing staff. This might be done by conducting a SKILLS AUDIT, a survey of the skills of the workforce. They must also decide whether existing employees are likely to remain in their posts or not. They must carry out projections on staff training needs and whether staff can be recruited from within the business or from outside.

A number of factors may then affect the current and future supply of labour.

Staff development and training Over time, the job requirements of a business may change. Instead of making some workers redundant and employing new workers with appropriate skills, it may be possible to redeploy staff, training them to deal with new types of work and giving them new jobs. This can prevent demotivation of staff as they see fellow workers lose their jobs. It can be motivating as staff acquire new skills. It also saves the business from paying the cost of redundancies and recruitment. Staff development and training can also help a business promote employees into more responsible positions. Internal promotion can often be a more cost effective and motivating solution than recruiting a new employee from outside.

Changing work practices There is an increasing trend towards more flexibility in work. Employees may want to go from part-time to full time or vice versa. They may want to work flexible hours, where they have more control of exactly when they work during the day or during the week. A few workers job share, sharing one full time post between them. Some workers find it tax advantageous to be self-employed and work for a business rather than being an employee. Although traditional full time or part time jobs are still the norm, human resource managers, particularly in large organisations, are likely to find examples of employees wishing to adopt a more flexible work pattern which suits their needs.

External recruitment Often there is no alternative to recruiting new workers from outside the business. The human resource manager must decide when this is more appropriate than moving someone internally into the vacant post. However, recruiting externally can have its problems.

- There might be a shortage of the particular type of worker in the labour market.
- Potential workers may have to be offered a range of fringe benefits (see unit 37) if they are to take the job.
- It might be better to recruit at certain times of the year than others.
- Human resource managers need to know which is the best way to advertise a job.
- Workers may not be available where they are needed, due to high house prices or transport problems, for example.

✓ checklist

1 What is the possible difference between personnel management and human resource management?
2 Explain the functions of workforce planning.
3 Explain the difference between (a) voluntary redundancy and compulsory redundancy; (b) redeployment and natural wastage.
4 What factors might affect the demand for labour by a business?
5 Explain the factors that might affect the supply of labour to a business.

keyterms

Compulsory redundancy - **when employees are dismissed from their job without their consent**
Human resource management - **the process of administering the workforce of a business to achieve its objectives.**
Human resource planning or workforce planning - **the process of determining the labour needs of the business now and in the future and how to achieve labour targets.**
Natural wastage - the day to day loss of staff by an employer due, for example, to retirement, staff leaving to look after children, sick or elderly relatives, or gaining a better job with another employer.
Personnel management - **the process of administering the workforce of a business.**
Redeployment - **moving an employee from one job to another job.**
Redundancy - **the termination of an individual's employment when the employer no longer needs the worker.**
Skills audit - **a survey of the skills of the workforce.**
Staff or labour turnover - **the proportion of staff leaving a business over a period of time. It is usually measured as a percentage by dividing the average number of staff employed into the number of staff leaving over a period of time.**
Voluntary redundancy - **when employees choose or volunteer to lose their jobs, sometimes in return for early retirement benefits or an enhanced redundancy package.**

Garness & Rollay is a firm of estate agents. Currently it has 19 branches in the North West of England and is planning to open a 20th branch in eight weeks' time. With the current housing boom, the firm is fully stretched in terms of its workforce. So the extra staff needed will have to be recruited externally.

Workforce planning shows a need for two full time office staff, two sales agents and one chartered surveyor. The plan is to take staff from nearby offices of the business to start up the new branch. Their places will be taken by the new recruits. This will ensure that the new branch is staffed by experienced workers who are familiar with the standards and procedures set by the firm.

One of the sales agent's posts is likely to be given to an existing office worker. Since coming to the business two years ago, she has shown exceptional talent and six months ago, with the firm's support, started professional training to become a sales agent.

At the same time as recruiting to replace the staff going to the new branch, the business has to replace those leaving for whatever reason. Labour turnover on a staff of 120 was 20 per cent last year. This was 5 per cent higher than the industry average. The partners in the business, aware of the considerable cost of recruiting new staff and making them effective, have striven to understand why they have a relatively high labour turnover. They put it down to other estate agent businesses poaching their staff by offering higher pay. However, some in the business believe it is due to an autocratic management style, where the senior partners fail to consult with branch managers, and where branch managers are encouraged to adopt aggressive tactics with staff to ensure sales.

1 Explain what is meant by:
    (a) 'workforce planning'; (3 marks)
    (b) 'labour turnover'. (3 marks)
2 Showing your workings, calculate:
    (a) the number of staff who left Garness & Rollay in 2002; (2 marks)
    (b) the number of staff who would have left had Garness & Rollay had a labour turnover equal to the national average for the industry. (2 marks)
3 Explain how and why Garness & Rollay is planning to increase its workforce. (10 marks)
4 Discuss how best Garness & Rollay might reduce its labour turnover. (10 marks)

39 Leadership and management styles

McFadzen

Knowledge McFadzen is a family owned construction company in North London. The company is run by Michael McFadzen who founded the company over 30 years ago. He is now nearing retirement and has not been in very good health recently.

Application The *company* is owned by Michael McFadzen and his wife, who between them have 90 per cent of the *shares*. The other 10 per cent were given to his son, Patrick, who is now in his late 40s and who works in the *business*. Michael had hoped that Patrick would be able to take over the running of the *company*. However, Patrick proved to be a poor *manager* and it became obvious that he lacked any *leadership* qualities. Last year, Michael appointed a *managing director*, Janine, who was told that she would be responsible for day to day control of operations. However, Michael 's *autocratic style of leadership* has meant that the new *manager* is thinking of resigning.

Analysis The problem is one too often found in family owned businesses. An outsider is brought in to run a company, but the family members find it difficult to give control over the business to the new manager. Michael has become so used to having total control of his company that he has found it almost impossible to keep out of the running of his business. His autocratic style has made matters worse because he interferes in difficult decisions that have to be made by the new manager which can affect the future of the business.

Evaluation Michael McFadzen has to make some hard choices. Either he stops interfering on a day to day basis or he lets the new manager go and returns to running the company himself. Facing worsening health, he is probably better off taking the former course of action. He can assess whether the new manager has the right leadership qualities. Then he should tie the manager into the company by allowing her to acquire part of the shareholding of the company. This will safeguard the financial future of his family.

Leadership and management

Unit 33 explained that management had a number of functions. For example, managers, according to the management theorist Henri Fayol, should predict what will happen in the future, plan to achieve their objectives, organise resources, exercise command over staff lower down the hierarchy, co-ordinate day to day tasks and monitor how well objectives are being achieved. Peter Drucker, writing 40 years later, added motivating and communicating with staff and giving them training opportunities to this list.

Some writers make no distinction between management and leadership in an organisation. Managers are leaders because of the roles they play. Others, however, suggest that leaders are not necessarily the same as managers. Leaders may perform the same functions as managers. But in addition, they may do some or all of the following.

- Leaders can be **visionaries**, understanding where an organisation is at today and seeing the direction in which an organisation has to change to survive and flourish.
- Leaders tend to be good at carrying through the **process of change**. Because they understand the starting point and the end point, they can chart a route from one to the other. Where others may see only chaos and think the organisation is taking the wrong road, the leader has the ability to see through the details and small setbacks which are a part of any change.
- Leaders are often excellent at **motivating** those around them, allowing them to perform at their best. They are particularly good at motivating others to change both themselves and the organisation.

It could be argued, that in large businesses, leaders devise **strategies** (see unit 64) whilst managers are responsible for implementing them. However, sometimes leaders do get involved in implementation because they appreciate that it is just as important to implement change as to devise strategies. In small businesses, leaders often have the skills to both devise and carry out a strategy.

The characteristics of leaders

Some argue that leaders only become leaders because of the position they find themselves in. For example, faced with major problems a leader might emerge to take control of a business and guide it through the crisis. Others argue that leaders are born and will rise to the top in whatever circumstances they find themselves.

It is likely that both theories are to some extent correct. Leaders need to have the right context in which to exercise leadership skills. But they must also possess certain characteristics or TRAITS which mark them out from others, as in Figure 39.1. These traits include:

- being an expert in at least one part of their job, but also possessing a wide all round knowledge in the rest;
- possessing vision and ability to solve problems in innovative ways;
- an ability to focus on completing a job;
- a willingness to act decisively and change direction if the need arises;
- a strong sense of responsibility and personal integrity;
- self motivation;
- self confidence;

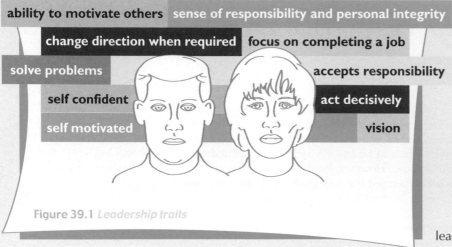

ability to motivate others   sense of responsibility and personal integrity

change direction when required   focus on completing a job

solve problems   accepts responsibility

self confident   act decisively

self motivated   vision

Figure 39.1 *Leadership traits*

- an ability to motivate others and get them to change;
- a willingness to accept responsibility even when things go badly.

Not all leaders possess all of these traits. Also, some possess some of these traits more than others. Hence, leaders can operate in very different ways and still be just as effective. This might suggest that there is no such thing as a 'typical' leader.

Leadership styles

Although there might be no typical leader, different styles of leader can be identified.

Authoritarian or autocratic leadership AUTHORITARIAN or AUTOCRATIC leadership is where leaders set objectives and goals and give orders so that they can be achieved. **Subordinates** (see unit 31) are expected to obey and carry out the orders given. There is no discussion between subordinates and superiors about what should be done. Authoritarian leadership styles were common in the past when subordinates had little education or few skills. By giving instructions and being obeyed, leaders could achieve an outcome far greater than if the subordinates were left to make decisions. This is an argument which would have been used by Frederick Taylor (see unit 34) and the scientific management school of thought. Authoritarian leadership is also essential in any situation where subordinates could each come to very different decisions and create chaos. For example, in the army, discipline is often essential. Finally, authoritarian leadership can work well in any situation where a leader has outstanding vision and understanding of how to achieve goals. The success of the whole organisation can be driven by the orders of one individual.

However, authoritarian leadership has its limitations. If the leader lacks leadership qualities, then the whole business could perform poorly. Also, some workers find it difficult to be motivated in an environment where they are only expected to carry out orders from further up the hierarchy. Further, workers often create informal power structures amongst their peer group which frustrate the orders given from above (see units 34 and 35). Finally, problems might arise if subordinates have to make their own decisions but no orders are given by the authoritarian leader. For example, there might be a breakdown in deliveries from abroad. If no decision is made about what to do by the leader, different subordinates might try to solve this

in different ways, leading to chaos.

Paternalistic leadership PATERNALISTIC LEADERSHIP is similar to autocratic leadership. The leader makes the decisions and expects them to be obeyed by subordinates. However, a paternalistic leader is one who places great importance on the welfare of subordinates. The business might make less profit, or profit may be retained to invest back into the business, rather than being paid out to shareholders. In the past there has been a number of famous paternalistic leaders including George Cadbury and Joseph Rowntree. By putting the welfare of staff high on the list of objectives for the business, paternalistic leaders can command high loyalty from staff. This type of leadership might motivate employees more than authoritarian styles. However, as with autocratic leaders, paternalistic leadership still does not give subordinates control over decision making.

Democratic leadership DEMOCRATIC LEADERSHIP (or PARTICIPATIVE LEADERSHIP when there is a great deal of 'democracy') is where leaders allow subordinates to be involved in decision making. This can take place in a variety of ways.

- Leaders may seek the advice of subordinates when making a decision.
- Subordinates may be set objectives and allowed to devise their own strategies to achieve those objectives (i.e. management by objectives, see unit 33).
- Decision making may be collective, where groups of

Sir Clive Thompson is Chief Executive of Rentokil. The company operates in 40 countries and is the world's largest business services company.

Thompson has an autocratic management approach. 'I'm a relatively aggressive person so I know what the company needs and I drive for it. But I don't think my style in running the company is necessarily aggressive,' he says. 'I encourage success and I think it's important to identify and remove failure. If failure has come about by internal performance, we will note it and if it happens again, eradicate it. I don't think that there is any point in carrying a big carrot unless you carry at least a small stick.'

While he is comfortable with delegation, Thompson clearly spells out what role is expected of each director. But he firmly believes that you cannot carve up the ultimate responsibility for the company into small pieces and share it out - the buck stops with him. He says: 'People know exactly what their job is, they know what tools they have to do their job. They know the frame in which they operate - I do not do their jobs. There's a fine line between delegation and abdication.'

Adapted from *The Sunday Times*, 3.6.2001.

1 **What style of leadership does the article suggest is used by Sir Clive Thompson?**
2 **Suggest why he delegates tasks to his directors.**

Leadership is the big idea in today's management development business. Companies are desperately searching for leaders. They are needed to run the show and to take responsibility at all levels.

One aspect of leadership is values. To be effective as a leader capable of inspiring and turning the ordinary into something extraordinary, our leader must be different from the rest of us. If our boss is neither better nor worse, then the company is unlikely to get the leadership most employees say they want. Leaders are set apart by their strong sense of values. They know what matters and repeatedly convey this.

A survey by J Hunt of 24 000 people working for companies and governments showed a strong convergence on certain values. The respondents were workers who either worked directly for the chief executive of a business or the permanent secretary of a government department. They were asked to write down what they thought their boss believed to be the four values most important to their organisation. The most frequently cited value could be summarised as 'people matter the most' which was quoted by 23 per cent of respondents. Second was 'be the best', with 22 per cent. Third was 'be active/task oriented' with 19 per cent. Next was 'networks matter' with 12 per cent. Next came 'results matter most' with 11 per cent. Sixth was 'provide good customer service' with 7 per cent. And last came 'innovate to survive' with 6 per cent.

Adapted from the *Financial Times*, 27.9.2000.

1 **Why do companies need leaders?**
2 **How might the values of the leaders given in the survey help a company to be successful?**

individuals rather than a single individual are responsible for making decisions.

- The organisation may have a culture of openness where subordinates are encouraged to comment on decisions or prospective decisions made by their superiors and where leaders have to justify their decisions to their subordinates.

Democratic leadership has become much more common in business. Research shows that democratic leadership leads to greater commitment and motivation of staff. When unsupervised, staff under democratic leadership tend to be as productive as when supervised. In contrast, staff under autocratic leadership tend to work less hard and less effectively when not being supervised. By being more involved in decision making, subordinates are more likely to satisfy their higher order needs as defined by Maslow. Workers today are also much better educated and trained than fifty years ago. They are therefore often more capable of being involved in decision making. Finally, democratic leadership may work more effectively than authoritarian leadership styles today because organisations are often more complex than fifty years ago. The amount of knowledge involved in doing a task is often much greater and so leaders cannot possibly absorb all the information needed to make decisions on their own. They need the advice and the expertise of others to come to decisions.

However, democratic leadership requires more complex communication networks than authoritarian leadership. With authoritarian leadership styles, it is important that orders flow down the hierarchy and that information which the leader must have to make decisions flows up. With democratic leadership styles, communication needs not just to flow up and down the hierarchy but also across the organisation at the same level. The communication skills of the leader must also be greater because there is likely to be much greater interaction between the leader and subordinates.

Laissez-faire leadership LAISSEZ-FAIRE LEADERSHIP occurs when leaders allow subordinates to make decisions rather than the leader making the decisions. Decisions are often made at random by those in the organisation who decide they are best at making that decision. The leader will be available to give advice, but will not interfere in decisions.

Laissez-faire leadership is unlikely to be effective because the ability to make good decisions is one of the key aspects of leadership. Businesses which have laissez-faire leaders typically lack direction and purpose. Motivation of staff is often poor because staff work best when they feel secure in the knowledge that their business is achieving its objectives.

McGregor's Theory X and Theory Y

A key function of leadership is to motivate workers. How this is done depends upon how a leader views subordinates. In 1960 a US researcher, Douglas McGregor, published *The Human Side of Enterprise*. In the book, he contrasted two management views.

One, which McGregor called THEORY X, was that workers disliked work, were motivated by earning money, that they were inherently unambitious, lazy, irresponsible and untrustworthy, and that they needed to be closely controlled and monitored by management. The other view, called THEORY Y, was that workers enjoy work and money is only one among many factors why they work. Theory Y workers are motivated, want to take responsibilities and organise themselves, but don't want to be too closely supervised. In their jobs, they want to satisfy their higher order needs, such as self-actualisation.

Theory X corresponds to the scientific management view of workers (see unit 34). If leaders believe Theory X, then they are likely to adopt an autocratic or paternalistic management style where they can closely control the work of subordinates. Organisations are likely to be strongly hierarchical with centralised decision making. Strong emphasis will be placed on financial rewards to motivate staff, whilst workers who fail to perform will be disciplined.

Theory X managers believe

- Workers are motivated by money.
- Workers are lazy and dislike work.
- Workers are selfish, ignore the needs of organisations, avoid responsibility and lack ambition.
- Workers need to be controlled and directed by management.

Theory Y managers believe

- Workers have many different needs which motivate them.
- Workers can enjoy work.
- If motivated, workers can organise themselves and take responsibility.
- Management should create a situation where workers can show creativity and apply their job knowledge.

Table 39.1 *McGregor's Theory X and Theory Y*

Theory Y corresponds to the human relations view of workers (see unit 35). If leaders believe Theory Y, they will tend to adopt a democratic leadership style. Staff will given greater input to decision making and may be **empowered** (see unit 36) to make decisions themselves. A variety of ways of motivating staff apart from financial rewards will be used by the organisation and staff will be encouraged to find ways of satisfying all their needs.

Team-based leadership

Teamworking (see unit 36) has become more common in UK businesses since the 1980s. Teamworking has implications for styles of leadership.

Under a traditional hierarchy, information formally tends to flow up and down the hierarchy. Superiors are supposed to know more about the job than their subordinates. Leaders are often employees who start at the bottom of the organisation in their teens with no qualifications and work their way up to the top of the business. Such leaders have a natural authority over subordinates because of their expertise.

However, in today's world, work is often highly complex. No single worker can expect to have an understanding of all aspects of the workplace. In this environment, the warehouse truck driver can know more about the operation of the warehouse than the chief executive. Grouping workers into teams recognises that a task might be best done with a number of workers with different skills. Each worker is an expert in their own right.

This then has implications for leadership. The leader of a team is not someone who gives orders and has a clear understanding of how a task is to be accomplished. Rather, the leader is someone who has the skills to enable the rest of the team to accomplish the task. Leaders then become workers who:

- understand the objectives set by the organisation;
- know the resources that are available to achieve a task which achieves those objectives;
- can enable and motivate subordinates in the team to accomplish a task;
- monitor and evaluate whether a task has been achieved successfully.

Because the leader is part of the team, traditional hierarchical methods of organisation are unhelpful. There has

therefore been a move towards SINGLE STATUS organisations. In a single status organisation, every worker is treated the same. In the past in large organisations, different groups of workers had different working conditions. There might be separate canteens for shop floor and administrative staff. Dress codes for different types of staff would be different. Those higher up the organisation might have reserved spaces in the car park nearest to the building in which they worked. In some businesses, moving up the management hierarchy could mean a bigger office, a bigger desk, a better chair, a more expensive office carpet and a larger company car. The result was a 'them and us' mentality amongst workers and management.

In a single status organisation, it is recognised that every worker, from top to bottom of any hierarchy, makes a contribution. So there is only one staff canteen, no reserved spaces in the car park and the same quality carpet and chairs throughout. Workers are paid differently, but this reflects differences in the pay rates of different workers in the economy. 'Them and us' attitudes are broken down so that every worker feels part of the business.

Consultation and delegation

Consultation and delegation are important features of any leadership style.

Consultation CONSULTATION occurs when leaders seek the advice of others before making a decision. For example, a chief executive may consult other directors of the company. Or a supervisor might consult with a subordinate worker about how best to do a job. The purpose of consultation is for leaders to gain information and opinions which will inform their decision making. The best leaders are not necessarily the ones who know the most or even who on their own would come to a good decision. Rather, the best leaders are often the ones who know who to consult and can spot which person or group is making the best proposal for action.

Delegation Delegation (see unit 31) occurs when a superior gives authority for a subordinate to perform a task. For example, a chief executive delegates the day to day running of the financial affairs of the business to the finance director. The purpose of delegation is to create the time and energy for the leader to concentrate on making leadership decisions and allow others to do other tasks. Delegation can also motivate subordinates because they are making more decisions. It also prepares subordinates for promotion, allowing them to perform tasks which might otherwise not be part of their job specification.

Consultation and delegation are features of any style of leadership. Autocratic leaders, however, are least likely to consult because they often prefer to make decisions on their own. Paternalistic leaders are likely to consult more because they want to listen to the views of employers. Democratic leaders are consulting all the time because they are allowing subordinates to share in decision making. With laissez faire leaders, there may be consultation. However, there is a tendency for different parts of the business to make their own decisions about consulting other parts.

All leaders delegate. However, autocratic and paternalistic leaders tend to delegate the least because they want to keep as much decision making in their own hands as possible. With laissez-faire leadership, decision making has a tendency not so much to be delegated by the leader as taken over by subordinates.

Since the 1980s in the UK, greater emphasis has been placed on pushing power to make decisions down the hierarchy. This has been inevitable, for example, when companies have delayered (see unit 31), cutting out layers of middle management. Equally, team working has tended to result in more delegation. Responsibility for making decisions has been given to a team rather than a more senior member of management. Also many businesses are now operating quality circles and Kaizen groups (see unit 47). These groups are often given some delegated authority to make their own decisions. It is argued that giving them delegated powers makes them more effective, which helps the efficiency of the business.

keyterms

Authoritarian or autocratic leadership - **a leadership style where the leader makes all the key decisions and expects obedience from subordinates.**
Consultation - **where those in authority seek the views of subordinates or other interested parties before making a decision.**
Democratic or participative leadership - **a leadership style where leaders take the advice of subordinates and allow that advice to influence their decision making.**
Laissez-faire leadership - **a leadership style where subordinates are given the freedom by the leader to make their own decisions and where there is little attempt to co-ordinate those decisions at the highest level.**
Paternalistic leadership - **an authoritarian leadership style where the leader takes account of the welfare of employees when making decisions.**
Single status - **for workers, where every worker, whether manual or non-manual, enjoys the same conditions of work such as access to a common staff canteen, company pension scheme or car parking facilities.**
Theory X - **put forward by McGregor, the theory that workers disliked work, were inherently unambitious, lazy, irresponsible and untrustworthy and were motivated to work mainly by earning money.**
Theory Y - **put forward by McGregor, the theory that workers enjoy work, want to take responsibilities and organise themselves and are motivated to work by a much wider number of factors simply than earning money.**
Traits (of leadership) - **features or characteristics that make people effective leaders.**

checklist

1 Explain the possible differences between a manager and a leader.
2 What are the characteristics or traits of leaders?
3 Explain the difference between autocratic and paternalistic leadership styles.
4 Explain the difference between democratic and laissez-faire leadership styles.
5 What is the difference between the Theory X view of workers and the Theory Y view of workers as put forward by McGregor?
6 What are the implications for leadership of (a) teamworking; (b) single status structures?
7 Explain the link between leadership styles and (a) consultation; (b) delegation.

Martin Guntac owns a small chain of four car dealerships in the Yorkshire area. Part of the business is selling cars, both new and second hand. The other half provides servicing and repairs for customers. When he first started the business 30 years ago, he had two employees doing repair work from a run down garage in the back streets of Leeds. Today, he has over 100 employees spread across four premium sites. Each site has a manager, with a head of sales and a head of servicing and repairs underneath them.

Martin relies heavily on the four site managers. They have day to day operational control of the business. He monitors their work and keeps a careful check on the performance of each site. Performance is checked both against previous periods and site to site. Martin is capable of making hard decisions. For example, five years ago he sacked one site manager who had been in the post for just 18 months when his site consistently underperformed the other sites in the group.

This was a difficult decision, though, for Martin. He sees himself as a 'people person', and believes strongly in teamworking. Employees are encouraged to develop their own capabilities with a heavy emphasis on staff training and empowerment. Workers are encouraged to make decisions for themselves. Occasionally mistakes are made, but Martin believes firmly that this is an inevitable part of taking responsibility.

Each week, he has a three hour meeting with the four site managers, his 'board of directors' as he likes to call them. Everything to do with the running of the business is discussed at these meetings. Martin expects his site managers to be frank and there can be major differences of opinion about how to develop the business. Ultimately, he has to make the key decisions but he always consults with others to hear what they have to say.

1 Explain what is meant by the terms:
  (a) 'teamworking'; (3 marks)
  (b) 'consults'. (3 marks)
2 Explain TWO factors which would suggest that Martin is a democratic leader. (6 marks)
3 Analyse whether Martin Guntac would hold McGregor's Theory X view of management or a Theory Y view. (8 marks)
4 Discuss the strengths and weaknesses of Martin Guntac's leadership style of empowering his subordinates. (10 marks)

B&Q

Knowledge   B&Q is the UK's largest DIY retailer. It is a major employer and, for example, receives 200 000 applications a year for 15 000 customer adviser jobs in its stores.

Application   B&Q has to select from this large pool of *applicants*. It does this initially by using a *psychometric test*. By asking standard questions of *applicants*, it claims to be able to find out who is suitable for a customer adviser post. Those passing the *psychometric test* go onto a *database*. When there is a local *vacancy*, store *managers* draw up a *shortlist* to *interview* in the traditional way from the *applicants* on the *database*.

Analysis   B&Q claims that the use of psychometric tests helps eliminate some of the bias in selection. When selecting those for interview, for example, B&Q store managers are not told the names of applicants, their gender, age or ethnic origin. It also allows the company to test for attitude. B&Q wants its workers to fit into the culture of the company. As evidence to support the validity of the tests, B&Q states that its employee turnover has fallen since the system was adopted in 1999 from 35 per cent a year to 29 per cent a year today.

Evaluation   The use of psychometric tests in recruitment is controversial. Some claim that they have little validity. Others, like B&Q, claim that they can help sift through applicants to find those with the right attitudes, qualities and experience. Their growing popularity, however, suggests that employers have some confidence in them.

Adapted from the *Financial Times*, 5.12.2002.

Recruiting staff

Medium to large businesses tend to recruit new staff on a regular basis. Natural wastage (see unit 38), if nothing else, means that there is a regular turnover of staff. Some employees retire and some leave to get better jobs elsewhere.

Recruiting new workers imposes costs on a business. It takes management time to go through the recruitment process. Outside agencies may be hired and advertising space might have to be bought. Getting the right person for the job is, however, worth the expense if they perform well. Appointing the wrong person can be highly damaging to the business.

Job descriptions and person specifications

In a small business, it may seem obvious to the employer what will be required of a new recruit. The employer may put in an advert for, say, an 'administrative assistant' and explain at the interview what the job entails.

However, where the business is larger, and if there is a personnel department, more formal procedures are likely to be adopted.

First, a JOB DESCRIPTION will be drawn up. This gives the title of the job. It is a statement of the tasks to be undertaken and responsibilities of the employee holding that job. The job description may describe the employee's place in the hierarchy of the business. Working conditions may also be specified, such as rates of pay or holiday entitlements. An example of a job description is shown in Table 40.1.

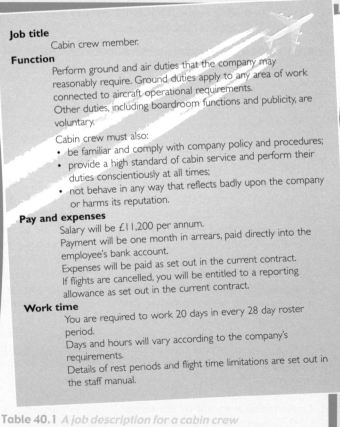

Job title
   Cabin crew member.

Function
   Perform ground and air duties that the company may reasonably require. Ground duties apply to any area of work connected to aircraft operational requirements.
   Other duties, including boardroom functions and publicity, are voluntary.

   Cabin crew must also:
- be familiar and comply with company policy and procedures;
- provide a high standard of cabin service and perform their duties conscientiously at all times;
- not behave in any way that reflects badly upon the company or harms its reputation.

Pay and expenses
   Salary will be £11,200 per annum.
   Payment will be one month in arrears, paid directly into the employee's bank account.
   Expenses will be paid as set out in the current contract.
   If flights are cancelled, you will be entitled to a reporting allowance as set out in the current contract.

Work time
   You are required to work 20 days in every 28 day roster period.
   Days and hours will vary according to the company's requirements.
   Details of rest periods and flight time limitations are set out in the staff manual.

Table 40.1 *A job description for a cabin crew assistant with an airline*

In many cases, the job description for the new recruit will simply be the job description of the person leaving the job. Large businesses, where many employees do the same job, such as a sales assistant or production line worker, might have a common job description for a particular job.

Job descriptions tell the new employee what is expected of them. It can be used when appraising the performance of a worker (see unit 37). If the worker fails to perform satisfactorily and is threatened with dismissal, it can also be used by the employer as evidence to support the dismissal.

A job description can be used to draw up a PERSON SPECIFICATION. This is a description (or profile) of the personal qualities that match the requirements of the job specification. The person specification might include the educational and professional qualifications needed for the post. Previous experience required might be outlined. General skills and character traits could also be described.

The person specification can be used to 'screen' applicants. If there are many applicants, selectors will be able to discard those which don't match the person specification. If there are only a few applicants, and none match the specification exactly, the employer may have to compromise and decide which aspects of the person specification are most important. Alternatively, the employer might decide to readvertise the post.

Internal recruitment

INTERNAL RECRUITMENT is recruitment from **within** the business. An employee may be chosen to be offered a post. Or the business may advertise internally, asking employees to apply for the vacancy. The advertisement may be sent round via email or posted on a noticeboard. Larger organisations

Figure 40.1 *How employees obtained their current job (within the last three months)*
Adapted from *Labour Market Statistics*, August 2002, Office for National Statistics

may have regular newsletters devoted to internal vacancies or notices may be put in the company magazine or on the company website.

Internal recruitment has a number of advantages compared to external recruitment.
- It is often cheaper because no adverts have to be placed and paid for at commercial rates.
- Internal recruits might already be familiar with the procedures and working environment of the business. They may, therefore, need less induction training (see unit 41) and be more productive in their first year of employment.
- The qualities, abilities and potential of the candidates should be better known to the employer. It is often difficult to foresee exactly how an external recruit will perform in a particular work environment.
- Regular internal recruiting can motivate staff. They might see a career progression with their employer. Even for those who aren't seeking promotion, internal recruitment suggests that the employer is looking after existing staff. This satisfies the need for security and sense of belonging identified by Maslow (see unit 35).

External recruitment

EXTERNAL RECRUITMENT is when someone is appointed from outside the business. External recruitment has two main advantages over internal recruitment.
- The employer may want someone with new and different ideas to those already working in the business. Bringing in experience of working in different organisations can often be helpful in keeping a business competitive.
- External recruitment might attract a larger number of

Job Designation: Broadcast Journalist
Grade: Towers Perrin Level 5/7

Ref: 59858

JOB PURPOSE
To initiate and produce, as part of a team, a wide variety of news and current affairs material for Radio and/or Television.

KEY BEHAVIOURS
1. To carry out in-depth research to a broad brief, with minimal supervision across the whole range of Regional Broadcasting news and current affairs output.
2. To write material for programme scripts, bulletins and links, exercising editorial judgment, maintaining professional journalistic standards and adhering to BBC policy and legal and contractual guidelines.
3. To undertake interviewing and reporting duties, under broad direction in both recorded and live situations, in studio or on location, for both Radio and Television.
4. To prepare and present bulletins, including assessing incoming copy, sub-editing news copy and deploying the necessary resources.

Adapted from BBC.co.uk.

1 **Explain what is meant by a 'job description', illustrating your answer with examples from the data.**
2 **The job being advertised was for the presenter of the Good Afternoon Show on BBC Radio Leeds. Discuss whether the BBC was likely to recruit internally or externally for the post.**

applicants than internal recruitment. The employer then has more choice of whom to appoint.

External recruitment requires the employer to communicate with potential employees. Ideally, every person who is suitable and who might consider the job should apply. That way, the employer will have the maximum number of candidates from which to choose. There is a number of ways in which an employer can do this.

Word of mouth According to the official statistics shown in Figure 40.1, the commonest way for a person to hear about a job is through word of mouth. This means a person hearing about a job from someone else, often someone who works in the place of employment. For example, a person might hear

about a vacancy for a hospital porter from their next door neighbour who works as a nurse in a local hospital.

Direct application Many jobseekers send their details to employers for whom they would like to work on the off-chance that they would have a vacancy. An employer might then use these to recruit if a vacancy arises.

Advertising The employer may place advertisements in local or national newspapers and specialist magazines and journals. The Internet is another medium for job advertisements. Advertisements may appear on a company website. Not surprisingly, the largest sector covered by Internet advertising is jobs in IT. Advertisements on a board or window on the employer's premises can also be successful. Advertisements are sometimes costly. But they can reach a wide number of potential applicants. People wanting to change their job are likely to seek out advertisements.

Private employment agencies The business may employ a private employment agency to find candidates. Private employment agencies are probably best known for finding temporary workers (temps). However, many also specialise in finding permanent staff. At the top end of the range, private employment agencies tend to call themselves executive agencies. They specialise in recruiting company executives and finding jobs for executives seeking a change or who have been made redundant.

For some posts, such as chief executive of a company, it may be possible to **headhunt** a candidate. This is where the agency draws up a list of people they think would be suitable for a job. Having cleared the list with the organisation making the appointment, the agency will approach those on the list and discuss the possibility of them taking the job. Some will say no. Others will indicate that, if the terms were right, they might take the job. A final selection is then made and one person is offered the job. Nobody has formally applied or been interviewed. Headhunting works best where there is only a limited number of people who potentially could take on the post and where the agency knows about most of those people.

Using an employment agency should take much of the work out of the recruitment process for the employer. But it can be costly because the employment agency charges a fee. Private employment agencies sometimes have a website where specialist workers can look for jobs or advertise their services.

Jobcentres Businesses can advertise vacancies through Jobcentres run by the government. Jobcentres are often used by the unemployed and vacancies tend to pay less than the average wage. So a cleaner's post is more likely to be advertised in a Jobcentre than a chief executive's post. For a business, this is a relatively cheap way of advertising, but it is not suitable for many vacancies.

Government funded training schemes Some businesses take on trainees from government funded training schemes. The current main scheme is called the New Deal. The schemes are designed to give the unemployed a chance to work for 6 or 12 months with some element of training. Businesses may choose then to offer these workers a permanent job if there is a vacancy and they have proved satisfactory.

Selection

Having advertised the post or gone through an employment agency, a business needs to select the right candidate. Those

Pete Roghey owns and runs a small building company with 20 employees. Turnover of staff is relatively high. Skilled workers are constantly in demand and he can find that they have been poached by another company, often on short term contracts, to work at higher rates of pay.

This week, Pete needs to hire three workers. There is a part time office cleaner's job, working in the evening from 5-7 five nights a week. He is looking for a skilled full time bricklayer. Then there is a general labourer's job, which could suit a young person just starting.

There never seems to be a right way to get hold of new staff. Sometimes, Pete advertises in the local newspaper and gets no replies. Other times, he can be spoilt for choice. More often than not, he gets approached by someone who has heard about the job vacancy from one of his workers. But there is never any guarantee that anyone will turn up this way.

1 **Discuss the advantages and disadvantages for Pete Roghey of using word of mouth to fill job vacancies compared to placing adverts in local newspapers.**

2 **What might be the advantages of placing an advert in a local newsagent for the cleaner's job?**

expressing an interest may be sent details about the post and how to apply. Sometimes, a business has an **application form** that it wants filling in. Sometimes, it simply asks candidates to send a CURRICULUM VITAE (CV), possibly with a letter explaining why they want the post. A CV is a short document which gives the main details about a candidate. It should show information such as their name, address, age, gender, qualifications and job experience. For unskilled jobs, candidates may simply be asked to come to an INTERVIEW without having to send in any details.

If a business receives many applications, it is likely to **short list** or **long list** candidates. This involves selecting a small or large number of candidates who appear most suitable from their applications. Some or all of these candidates might then be interviewed. Short and long listings might reduce the cost of selection for a business as it would be time consuming and costly to interview, say, two hundred applicants.

At an interview, applicants will be asked questions about themselves and about issues related to the job. Applicants may have the chance to ask their own questions about the job. Almost every selection process involves some sort of interview. Applicants may even be put through several interviews with different interviewers or panels of selectors. Interviews may be conducted by the personnel department or by department heads.

Some research has shown that interviews are poor at selecting the best candidate for the job. Some candidates are very good at interviews, but poor at their job. Others are bad at interviews, but are excellent employees. Interviewers tend to look for someone with qualities similar to their own rather than qualities required by the job and person specification. Judgments are often formed within the first few minutes of most interviews.

Because interviews are so unreliable, some businesses choose to use additional selection techniques.
- Candidates may be asked to **role play** or take part in a **simulation** relating to the job. This involves interviewees acting out a situation. It gives assessors a better insight into how a candidate might perform in a post.
- **Tests** may also be used. These could be simple numerical or literary tests to see whether candidates can perform calculations and write effectively. There could be complicated tests, such as IQ tests. PSYCHOMETRIC TESTS aim to uncover the personality of the candidates. This helps selectors gain insights, for example, into whether a candidate would be good with customers, a useful part of a team, or could cope with stress.
- A number of large organisations today use **assessment centres** for some of their appointments. These are specialist organisations that deal only with making appointments. They use a variety of selection techniques to gain as wide a picture of candidates as possible. Even so, they can recommend unsuitable appointments, showing that selection procedures are not 100 per cent accurate.

Appointment

The successful candidate for a job will be **appointed** by the business. Candidates might be offered a job **conditionally**. For example, if, after the interview, they fail medical tests or police checks the offer of the job may be withdrawn. Employers also usually take up **references** from previous employers. A current or previous employer may give unflattering references because they don't want to lose the employee or simply out of spite. This is one reason why most employers don't ask for references before the interviews. However, a reference may turn up something like a police conviction which would again mean the offer of the job being withdrawn.

Legal constraints

Businesses recruiting and selecting new staff are bound by various employment laws.
- The Sex Discrimination Act 1975 and the Race Relations Act 1976 state that there must be no discrimination against applicants, whether male or female, or whatever ethnic origin. Discrimination can occur at any stage of the recruitment process. For example, an advertisement saying 'Males only need apply' might be a case of discrimination. Cases are also brought against employers through **employment tribunals** (courts which deal with employment law) mainly by women or those from ethnic minorities arguing that jobs were given not to the best applicant, but on gender or race grounds.
- The Disability Discrimination Act 1995 states that it is unlawful for businesses to discriminate against an applicant with a disability, unless there is **justification**. Justification might be shown if the employer had to take unreasonable measures to allow the person with the disability to work successfully. For example, an employer might not be able to reject a candidate in a wheelchair if there were a few steps at the entrance to the place of work because a ramp could easily and cheaply be installed. However, it might be unreasonable to expect an employer to move premises just to employ the disabled worker.
- There is no law against discriminating on the grounds of age, although this is possible in the UK in future. So employers might place an advert which states 'Candidate aged 20-50 sought'. However, some businesses are now recognising the benefits of employing older workers, who might have useful experience.
- After appointment, employees must be given a contract of employment detailing their duties and their rate of pay, for example (see unit 55).

✓ checklist

1. What is the difference between a job description and a person specification?
2. Compare the advantages of recruiting internally with recruiting externally.
3. Briefly explain the different ways in which a business might recruit externally.
4. Explain the difference between a short list and a long list.
5. What techniques may a business use to select candidates for a post?
6. Briefly explain the legal constraints on employment.

"key terms"

Curriculum vitae - **a brief description of an individual's personal details, experience and qualifications.**

External recruitment - **when an employee looks for applicants for a job from outside the organisation.**

Internal recruitment - **when an employee seeks to find applicants for a job from inside the organisation.**

Interview - **a meeting where an applicant answers questions from and asks questions of selectors for a job.**

Job description - **a statement of the tasks to be undertaken and responsibilities of the employee holding the job.**

Person specification - **a description (or profile) of the personal qualities that match the requirements of the job specification.**

Psychometric tests - **tests which aim to uncover the personality of individuals.**

Pret a Manger is a chain of 118 shops which make and serve coffee and sandwiches. It has 2 400 staff of whom 1 900 work in the shops themselves. Staff turnover was 98 per cent last year with 1 500 vacancies advertised. In most industries, such high staff turnover would be disastrous. But in the fast food industry, it is excellent since the average for the industry is 150 per cent staff turnover. What's more, there were 55 000 applicants for those 1 500 jobs.

The selection procedure at Pret a Manger has always involved on-the-job experience. But before that happens, applicants are initially given a competency based interview. Most don't get through that first interview because they lack the right personality. 'We want people who are outgoing, have a positive attitude to life, want to work for the company and know a bit about us', says Esther O'Halloran, head of recruitment at Pret a Manger. 'We aren't necessarily looking for people with experience making coffee and sandwiches.'

If they make if through the initial interview, applicants are asked to turn up at 6.30 a.m. at the Pret a Manger shop where they might work. This is the start of the working day for the staff. One in three applicants fails to make it. 'It's a good test', O'Halloran says. 'Can they get there on time and stay awake?' A team member will be assigned to act as the candidate's guide and mentor for the day. But the aim is to get them working with as many other team members and doing as many different jobs as possible. It is an organised process with staff asked to take the person through the different tasks. So they might help to make sandwiches, clear the workbench, or deal with customer queries. 'They are simple but relevant things that we ask them to do', O'Halloran says.

Throughout the process, their future colleagues assess them against core competencies, such as enthusiasm and their ability to follow instructions. This is because the workers in the shop will vote on whether the interviewee will get the job. The workers have to be able to justify their vote for, or against, and Pret a Manger has to ensure the process is fair and legal.

Meanwhile, the shop manager takes time out to interview the applicant over a cup of coffee. The manager doesn't get a vote but can lobby for or against someone. Towards the end of the shift, the manager gathers team members' votes and lets the candidate know the result. Half of those who take part in on-the-job experience fail to make the grade. But they go away with £30, a free lunch and some comprehensive feedback on their performance. New recruits also receive feedback, which might be fed into a training plan, and they are put straight on the payroll.

So successful is on-the-job experience as a recruitment tool that Pret a Manger insists all managerial and head office recruits also go through a shorter version. But while Pret a Manger seems to have made huge inroads into getting its recruitment right, O'Halloran is well aware that recruitment will always be a major business activity for the firm. 'London has a transient population. We attract people who only come here for six months, and that will continue', she says.

Adapted from *People Management*, 16.5.2002.

1 Explain the meaning of the terms:
   (a) 'recruitment'; (3 marks)
   (b) 'interview'. (3 marks)
2 Outline TWO different skills which Pret a Manger might put on a person specification for a job in one of its shops. (6 marks)
3 Explain why using on-the-job experience might help reduce the turnover of staff at Pret a Manger. (8 marks)
4 Evaluate whether Pret a Manger should solely recruit internally for management posts. (10 marks)

41 Training

Red Mill Snack Foods

Knowledge Red Mill Snack Foods is a manufacturer of snacks with two sites, one in Wednesbury in the Midlands and the other in Bolton, Lancashire.

Application Red Mill Snack Foods encourages *employees* to engage in *continuous learning*, telling them that if they are *trained* up, it will not *recruit* from outside. Every *department* within the business has benefited from *training*, with even the *managing director* having undertaken *training* in such areas as *employment law*. *Training* also takes place at every level within the *organisation*. The *company* currently employs several engineering *apprentices*, 400 *employees* are soon to complete a CIEH Basic *Health and Safety* course, 28 are studying ISM Insignia *training* for *team leaders*, and six are studying NVQ Level 3 in *supervision and management*. The *personnel manager* is studying for a Masters Degree in *Human Resource Management* at Wolverhampton University. The *company* was recently re-accredited for *Investors in People*.

Analysis Gary Nield, the managing director, is clear about the benefits of training. 'Our only real competitors are the big boys in the snack food industry - so we have to be very flexible in case we win a huge order at a moment's notice, having to produce more efficiently than the competition. It takes the confidence that ongoing training brings to feel sure that we can fulfil the promises we make. This is one of the reasons we have grown our turnover by 15 per cent in the last three years.'

Evaluation Red Mill has clearly thought out the benefits that systematic training can bring to a company. By being so committed to training, it is likely that it will continue to grow in the future, and be able to compete better with other businesses in the industry.

Adapted from the *Express & Star*, 17.6.2002.

Why train?

TRAINING is the process of increasing the knowledge and skills of workers so that they are better able to perform their jobs. The objectives of training differ from business to business but they include:

- making workers more productive by teaching them more effective ways of working;
- familiarising workers with new equipment or technology being introduced;
- educating workers in new methods of working, such as shifting from production line methods to cell methods;
- making workers more flexible so that they are able to do more than one job;
- preparing workers to move into a different job within the business, which could be a new job at a similar level or a promotion;
- improving standards of work in order to improve quality;
- implementing health and safety at work policies;
- increasing job satisfaction and motivation, because training should help workers feel more confident in what they are doing and they should gain self esteem;
- assisting in recruiting and retaining high quality staff, attracted by the quality of training offered.

Sometimes, individual employees request training or undertake training without the financial or time support of their employers. For example, a manager may take an MBA university course in her own time. More frequently, training is provided by the employer. The need for training is sometimes identified in the **appraisal process** (see unit 37).

Induction training

Many businesses put on training for people starting a job. This is known as INDUCTION TRAINING. It is designed to help new employees settle quickly into the business and their jobs. Exactly what is offered differs from business to business and job to job. For example, a small business might simply allocate another worker to look after the new employee for a day to 'show them the ropes'. A young person just out of university might have a year long induction programme to a large company. They might spend time in a number of departments, as well as being given more general training about the business. But most induction training attempts to introduce workers to the nature of the business and work practices, including health and safety issues (see unit 55).

On-the-job training

ON-THE-JOB TRAINING is training given in the workplace by the employer. There are many ways in which this could happen.

Learning from other workers An employee might simply work next to another worker, watch that worker do a task and with their help repeat it.

Mentoring This is where a more experienced employee is asked to provide advice and help to a less experienced worker. The less experienced worker can turn for help and advice to another more experienced worker at any time.

Job rotation This is where a worker spends a period of time doing one job, then another period of time doing another job

It's official - furniture repairing is a dying art and one of the areas most affected is Wolverhampton. A national furniture repair firm is desperate to recruit craftsmen and women with traditional skills from Wolverhampton, but is finding it impossible to fill its growing vacancies.

Regency@Home has the largest independent network of repairers in the UK, working for retailers such as Courts and J Harveys and manufacturers like Divania and Nicoletti. When a retailer or manufacturer has a customer with a damaged item of furniture, Regency@Home goes out to the client's home to repair the goods. The company, which often acts as a service centre for larger retailers, currently handles more than 100 000 claims per annum and looks set to double in size in the next six months.

General Manager Andy Doran said: 'We are one of the UK's leading furniture repair companies. We have many contracts with major manufacturers and retailers, with more coming on stream every week. Since launching earlier in the year our business expansion has been phenomenal. But despite the huge demand for furniture repairs we cannot find the crafts people to do the work. We could create 20 plus repairers' positions nationally every month if we could find suitable candidates. One of the biggest areas where we need staff is Wolverhampton.'

In today's throwaway society, furniture repairing seems to be a dying art, he said. The pool of qualified employable repairers is diminishing. 'To help meet the need for skilled furniture repairers we are starting a national training and apprenticeship scheme, believed to be the first in the country, and we are keen to train up people who are interested in learning the skills. We are looking for 10-15 apprentices in any area.'

Adapted from the *Express & Star*, 4.3.2002.

1 **Explain why Regency@Home needs to train furniture repairers.**
2 **Discuss whether setting up a 'national training and apprenticeship scheme' is the most effective way for Regency@Home to recruit the workers it needs.**

and so on. Eventually they have received the broad experience needed to do a more specialist job.

Apprenticeships In the past, workers in traditional skilled trades, such as carpentry or engineering, would undertake training over, say, 3-5 years in an **apprenticeship**. This would involve a mix of training methods. When the business decided they had 'qualified' they would be employed as a full time worker. Many of these schemes died out due to the cost for the business, the decline in traditional trades, mechanisation and the need for more flexible work practices.

Graduate training Medium to large sized businesses may offer graduate training programmes. They are typically designed to offer those with university degrees either professional training, such as in accountancy or the law, or managerial training.

Off-the-job training

OFF-THE-JOB TRAINING is training which takes place outside the business by an external training provider like a local college or university. For example, 16-25 year olds might go to college one day a week to do a catering course or an engineering course. A trainee accountant might have an intensive course at an accountancy college or attend night classes before taking professional exams. A graduate manager might do an MBA (Masters in Business Administration) course at a Business School in the evening and at weekends.

Off-the-job training can provide courses which a business internally would be unable to provide. But it can be expensive, particularly if the business is paying not just for the course but also a salary for the time the employee is attending the course.

Training initiatives

The government promotes training through a variety of initiatives and schemes.

Learning and Skills Councils These are bodies which have been set up by government to cover the the whole of the UK. Each area of the UK has its own regional Learning and Skills Council. They are responsible for promoting training and manage funding for a wide range of schemes such as modern apprenticeships (see below). They are funded by the government from taxes. But businesses taking part in training may also be required to contribute towards the cost of training which directly benefits them.

Modern apprenticeships In the past, apprenticeships were the most common way for a school leaver to become a skilled manual worker with a qualification. In the 1970s, with a sharp decline in employment in manufacturing industry, most businesses scrapped their apprenticeship schemes. Today, the government sponsors Modern Apprenticeships. This scheme aims to give young people an apprenticeship training which will equip them for a specific job in an industry. Businesses run Modern Apprenticeships and then receive a subsidy from the government for each apprentice on the scheme. Typically the Modern Apprenticeship training runs for three years.

The New Deal Since the late 1970s, governments have run a variety of schemes aimed at getting unemployed workers, particularly young workers, into a job. The latest such scheme is the New Deal. It promises to give any young unemployed person under the age of 25 either full time training or work experience. The New Deal also offers older long term unemployed workers a similar package.

Investors in People (IiP) IiP is a national standard developed by industry bodies such as the CBI and TUC with the support of the Employment Department, which businesses have to meet if they wish to gain IiP accreditation. To get accreditation, they have to show that the need for training is considered at every level and in every major decision made by the business. Businesses which go through the process of gaining IiP accreditation typically find that there are inefficiencies in the way the business operates because staff have not been trained properly. These training needs then have to be addressed. Gaining IiP is a useful marketing tool for a business. This is because customers perceive that, by gaining IiP accreditation, the business is a modern, forward thinking business where staff are properly trained to deal with their work.

Labour market failure

It can be argued that, if left to free market forces, too little training would take place. This is an example of MARKET FAILURE. In the labour market, it occurs for two reasons.

- Businesses spend too little money on training because it is often cheaper for them to recruit new workers who have already been trained by another business or on a government training scheme.
- Individual workers don't spend enough on training themselves because they don't want to get into short term debt. They also fail to realise how much more they could earn if they had better training.

In the past, traditional apprentices might have signed an agreement to stay with their employer a number of years after they became qualified. This meant they could not be 'poached' by a rival business. Today, linking training with staying on in the business is rare. There is nothing to stop a newly trained worker from leaving one business to take up a post at a higher salary elsewhere.

Generally, when there is market failure, it is argued that the government should step in to correct that market failure. Governments have two broad ways of doing this.

- They can provide training themselves and pay for it from tax revenues. Currently, the UK government provides training for the unemployed through its New Deal programme for example. Training is also provided through free college or further education courses.
- The government can pay grants to industry bodies or individual businesses to undertake training. This can be funded from general taxation or by a levy on all businesses in the industry. For example, in the UK construction industry, businesses have to pay a levy (effectively a tax) to pay for the work of the Construction Industry Training Board. This provides training for construction workers.

Spending on training per worker tends to be higher in countries such as France, Germany and Sweden because their governments and businesses spend much more on training. It is often argued that the UK spends too little on training and this is one of the reasons why productivity (output per worker) is significantly lower than in other countries.

Staff training helped Internet marketing company Panlogic to survive the end of the Internet boom, says managing director William Makower. Panlogic's employee numbers rose in the past four years from 12 to 27 and fell back down to the current 14. Mr Makower says the company's staff training helped it to survive because it kept everyone up to date with industry developments in a fast-moving market and because the staff 'value learning'. Everyone is encouraged to share information with colleagues. Customers, who include household names such as Honda and Garnier, like continuity and 'training is key to motivating and retaining staff'. 'Our process is well honed but it is still ad hoc', says Mr Makower, who believes policy makers 'should recognise that the end-game is dissemination' of skills. The challenge for small businesses is to share the benefits of informal and formal training internally.

'When I was a Courtaulds trainee returning from a course, the manager would say: "Brilliant, let's talk about it next week" - and of course next week never came.' When Panlogic started paying for staff to do external training, 'I was determined to bring the learning back in to the business'. Panlogic's experience of external courses has been mixed. Last week, the creative director returned from a 'useless' innovation conference to report that it had been 'uninspiring, too much theory and way below our level'. The value of the course was the networking opportunities it offered. Another employee, however, found a government-backed course on applying for government contracts useful. 'But attending was only a fifth of the value - the other four-fifths came from her sharing the information back at the company.' One measure of the success of that course and the report-back, he adds, will be how Panlogic succeeds in its application to go on the Central Office of Information roster.

Adapted from the *Financial Times*, 27.3.2003.

1 **Using examples from the data, explain the difference between on-the-job training and off-the-job training.**
2 **What are the advantages to Panlogic of on-the-job training?**
3 **Discuss the costs and benefits to Panlogic of using off-the-job training for its employees.**

keyterms

Induction training - **training which occurs when a worker starts a job with a business.**
Market failure - **when the operation of free market forces fails to provide an optimal level of output.**
Off-the-job training - **training which takes place outside the business through an external training provider like a local college or university.**
On-the-job training - **training given in the workplace by the employer.**
Training - **the process of increasing the knowledge and skills of workers so that they are better able to perform their jobs.**

✓checklist

1 List the reasons why a business might train its employees.
2 Why might a business offer induction training?
3 Explain the difference between mentoring and job rotation.
4 What is graduate training?
5 Who benefits from training through the New Deal programme?
6 What is Investors in People?
7 What is the role of Learning and Skills Councils in training?
8 Explain why businesses might spend less on training than is desirable.

Monarch is a small airline company in the UK, comprising Monarch Aircraft Engineering and Monarch Airlines. Monarch Aircraft Engineering is an aircraft maintenance company. Since 1971, it has run an apprenticeship scheme.

Today, this is a four year advanced modern apprenticeship in aeronautical engineering. In the first year, apprentices spend two day a week at college. The rest of the week is spent doing practical work in the company's training workshops. In the second year, apprentices spend a period of time in each different area of the organisation. They start studying for their NVQ level 3. In the third and fourth year, apprentices begin to specialise, and work largely in the hanger area where aeroplanes are brought in for maintenance. College courses are completed by the end of year three.

Since 1971, Monarch has trained over 600 apprentices. It currently spends £60 000 training each advanced modern apprentice over four years. It receives a subsidy from government of just £12 000 to offset part of this cost. However, Monarch thinks this cost is well worth while.

The trainees, once they have completed their apprenticeship, are under no legal obligation to stay with Monarch. They are free to go and get a job with another airline. However, trainees are encouraged to stay and most if not all are offered a job at the end of training. This helps the company by cutting down on recruitment costs. It also helps ensure that there is a regular supply of young people coming into the company to replace those retiring or moving to another company. Given that there is a shortage of qualified staff who have good quality, recognised training in the industry, this is especially important.

Ultimately, though, it is about safety. In the airline industry, any fault in maintenance of an aeroplane can lead to a disaster. As Bronwen Philpott, Monarch's director of personnel, says: 'If we train the right people, we are looking at having people of high calibre for a lifetime. Given the nature of our business, we can't have the wrong people. The investment is worthwhile.'

Adapted from *People Management*, 7.3.2002.

1 Explain the meaning of the terms:
   (a) 'training'; (3 marks)
   (b) 'apprenticeship'. (3 marks)
2 Outline ONE example of on-the-job training in the modern apprenticeship at Monarch and ONE example of off-the-job training. (6 marks)
3 Examine the advantages to an 18 year old of accepting a modern apprenticeship with Monarch rather than doing a university degree. (8 marks)
4 Discuss whether Monarch could increase its profitability by shutting down its modern apprenticeship scheme. (10 marks)

The brewing industry

Knowledge The brewing industry has traditionally been fairly fragmented worldwide. Even in national markets, such as the UK or the USA, a few national brewers face competition from regional and small local breweries.

Application There are *economies of scale* in brewing: that is, average *costs* of *production* fall as *output* rises. For example, there are *technical economies of scale*, *marketing economies* and *purchasing economies*. Successful brewers are also more likely to be *productively efficient*, producing at lowest cost.

Analysis A large brewer is more likely to use a brewery to its full capacity compared to a smaller brewer which might only need that capacity at certain times of the year This indivisibility contributes to technical economies of scale. Marketing economies arise when a brand is able to gain strong regional, national or international recognition. There are purchasing economies because a large brewer placing a large order is able to get better prices from suppliers than a small brewer. Large brewers are able to transfer best practice from one brewery to another, thus achieving productive efficiency. Small breweries often lack the knowledge to achieve lowest cost production. The presence of economies of scale has been one of the reasons why there has been consolidation amongst breweries. A few international brewing companies have emerged over the past 20 years, such as Interbrew and Heineken.

Evaluation Whether the large international brewers will further tighten their grip on local markets is debatable. Although they have cost advantages over smaller brewers, local customers typically have strong loyalty to local brands. Often, only by buying up these brands can larger brewers dominate the local market.

Operations management

OPERATIONS MANAGEMENT (or PRODUCTION MANAGEMENT) is the administration or management of the process by which inputs, such as labour, materials and machinery, are transformed into final products. Production managers are therefore responsible for making decisions about:

- what production methods are to be used (see unit 44);
- what levels of input of labour, machinery and materials are needed to produce a given quantity of output;
- what stock levels are required to support production (see unit 45);
- how to ensure that work is completed on time;
- how best to ensure quality (see unit 46).

Decisions about the entire business that affect production also need to be made .

- What is the optimal size for a business? Should there be five employees or 500 000 for example?
- Where should production take place? On one or two sites? In the UK or the Far East?

Productive efficiency

One objective of production managers is to achieve PRODUCTIVE EFFICIENCY. This occurs when the average cost per unit of output is at its lowest. So if a business produced bolts at 6p per 1 000 when it could produce them at 4p per 1 000, then it would be **productively inefficient**. It would only be productively efficient if average costs were 4p per 1 000.

There are many reasons why businesses can be productively inefficient. For example, from a production viewpoint, they might:

- not be paying the cheapest price for the materials its buys in;
- be employing more workers than is necessary;
- be using outdated technology;
- hold too much stock;
- have badly organised or inappropriate production methods.

Inefficiency can also be caused by failing to manage human resources effectively. For example, workers might:

- be demotivated and not be working as hard as they might (see units 34-37);
- have not received sufficient training (see unit 41);
- apply for a job, but fail to get it despite being the best candidate because of poor recruitment procedures (see unit 40);
- suffer from weak leadership and be less productive;
- be in a poorly organised business where the organisational structure is a barrier rather than a help to efficient working;
- be underemployed and have too little to do because of over recruitment due to poor workforce planning (see unit 38);
- be unable to do their job fully because poor workforce planning has led to underrecruitment of staff (see unit 38).

How can small businesses gain the benefits of economies of scale? One way is to grow into a larger business. But another way is to combine with other small businesses to form an alliance.

The Heather Marketing Company is one such example. It was set up by five small heather growers. Heathers are produced in nurseries and sold mainly to garden centres. The five growers are in different areas of the country: Kent, Northern Ireland, Somerset, Dorset and Essex. Each markets its products on behalf of all five nurseries. So if a large order comes in to one nursery which it is unable to cope with, it can share the order with another nursery. This way, the five growers are able to take on much larger orders than before. This also gives them access to orders in areas of the country where before they were unrepresented. For example, the nursery in Essex can now receive part orders from Dorset customers which would not have been likely before.

The Heather Marketing Company has already hired a marketing consultancy to increase its marketing effectiveness. It is about to distribute common brochures.

Adapted from the *Financial Times*, 6.6.2002.

1 **Explain why the five growers are able to exploit marketing economies of scale by being part of the Heather Marketing Company.**
2 **Discuss whether the five independent businesses could exploit other economies of scale in the future.**

Productive efficiency and economies of scale

The size of a business has a major impact on average costs of production. Typically, there is a range of output over which average costs fall as output rises. Over this range, larger businesses have a competitive advantage over smaller businesses. This is shown in Figure 42.1 over the range O to A. There may then be a range of output over which average costs remain the same as output rises. This is the range A to B

in Figure 42.1. At output levels higher than OB, the business gets too large and average costs rise.

When average costs are falling as output rises, there are said to be ECONOMIES OF SCALE. When average costs are at their lowest, between A and B in Figure 42.1, there are said to be CONSTANT RETURNS TO SCALE. At output levels higher than OB, there are DISECONOMIES OF SCALE, with average costs rising.

A business is **productively efficient** when it has achieved the lowest average cost of production possible. So a business is productively efficient at any level of output between A and B in Figure 42.1. The business is productively inefficient when it has failed to exploit fully the economies of scale possible. So a business operating at output levels below A could achieve lower costs by expanding output. Equally, the business is productively inefficient when it is too large and is producing beyond the lowest average cost level of output. So it is productively inefficient if it produces beyond B.

Sources of economies of scale

Economies of scale occur for a number of reasons.

Technical economies The size of machines, equipment, plant or factories can have a major effect on average costs. In many processes, larger size of capital equipment leads to lower costs. This link between average cost and the size of machinery, capital or plant is known as the **principle of increased dimensions**. For instance, all other things being equal, a McDonald's fast food outlet that seats 100 people is

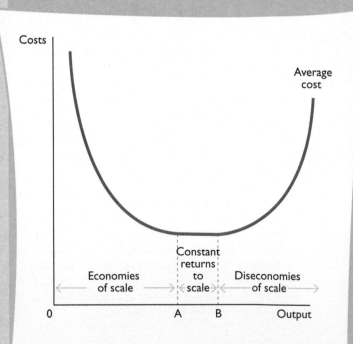

Figure 42.1 *Economies and diseconomies of scale*
Economies of scale exist between output levels 0 and A. There are constant returns to scale between output levels A and B. At output levels higher than B, there are diseconomies of scale. A business is productively efficient only if it operates at its lowest average cost level, between A and B.

In the 1970s, it was argued that large companies could be very profitable if structures were crystal clear and rational. Through these means, human error or deviance could be minimised. But in the 1990s, a variety of studies were conducted which showed that around 1 000 employees in one location is about the maximum size for any company if it is to retain the advantages of economies of scale and minimise the human diseconomies arising from adding more people.

Take the case of IBM, the world's first large computer company. In the 1970s and 1980s, IBM came to symbolise the success of big business. It had pioneered the manufacture of large mainframe computers. But by 1993, it was in trouble, losing £5.6 billion in that year alone. It had failed to move with the times. Part of the business was saying that the future lay with cheap small personal computers. Part of the business was making a profit from computer software. Those at the top failed to listen and persisted in thinking that the future lay with expensive mainframes.

A new chief executive, Lou Gerstner, was appointed. He reduced IBM's workforce by 50 per cent. The company was refocussed on providing e-business services and solutions, research and design and semiconductor architecture. Very importantly, the company was segmented into small operational units. IBM employees were remotivated to develop services, discover solutions and be innovative.

Adapted from the *Financial Times*, 4.1.2002.

> **1 Explain what is meant by 'diseconomies of scale' and , using the example of IBM, explain why they occur.**

more costly to build per person than one which seats 500 people. If a shipping company doubles the length, breadth and height of a cargo carrier, the ship can carry eight times the amount of cargo.

Technical economies also arise because of **indivisibilities**. These occur because a business might need to buy a piece of equipment, like a lorry or a machine, but won't necessarily use it 24 hours a day, 7 days a week. The purchase of a lorry is indivisible because you can't buy part of a lorry because you only want to use it for 20 hours a week. The larger the producer, the more likely the equipment will be used all the time, i.e. the more likely it is to achieve maximum capacity utilisation (see unit 43). The more the piece of equipment is used, the lower its cost per unit of output that it produces. Another example would be a fast food outlet. For a given size of outlet, the more customers it has, the greater the length of time all its facilities, including the kitchen equipment, will be used. Hence, the lower the cost per customer of food served.

A third source of technical economies is SPECIALISATION. The larger the business, the more likely it is to employ specialised methods of production. Small manufacturers may have to use equipment which is not specifically designed to do a particular job. One machine might have to perform six different tasks. It might take time to change the tooling of the machine for every new task that is undertaken. A larger business is more likely to be able to employ machinery dedicated to performing one task.

Specialisation of workers In a large business, workers can specialise. In a large company, for instance, there are accountants, sales personnel, production engineers and personnel officers. In a very small business, one individual might have to do all these jobs. That person might not have

any great expertise in any of them. This might be expensive in terms of the time taken and the costs of the job. Being able to employ specialist workers can therefore reduce average costs.

Purchasing economies For any business, buying in bulk is likely to reduce costs. Asda or Tesco are more likely to be able to buy products directly from manufacturers at lower average costs than the local corner store. Purchasing economies arise for two reasons.

- There are cost savings in selling in bulk. Transport costs are typically lower. Businesses selling goods don't have to employ such large sales forces. Promotion costs can be lower. There is also less paperwork.
- Buyers can force sellers to take lower profit margins. Taking a bulk order from Asda will help a supplier make a profit. But the profit per unit sold is likely to be lower than on a smaller order from another buyer.

Marketing economies In marketing, there are economies of scale. It costs the same **total** amount to buy advertising space on television whether a product has sales of £1 million a week or £10 million. But the **average** cost of that advert is ten times lower for the product selling £10 million than for that selling £1 million.

Equally, the total cost of an advertising display in a supermarket is the same whatever the sales of the product. But the higher the sales, the lower the average cost.

Average costs of marketing can also be reduced through bulk buying. A large company buying £50 million of advertising space on television can usually get a lower rate per minute than a smaller company buying £1 million of space.

Financial economies Small businesses often have difficulty raising finance (see unit 26). Banks might be reluctant to lend them money because of the risk that the business will fail and the money not be repaid. When banks do lend money, they will often charge higher rates of interest and impose higher charges per pound borrowed to small businesses than larger businesses. A large multinational company has access to world financial markets. It can choose from a wide variety of sources of finance. Most of these would be denied to a small business. It will be able to shop around for the lowest rate of interest. Large companies are also usually seen as less likely to default on repaying their loans than small companies. So they can negotiate lower rates of interest from lenders.

Research and development (R&D) economies The larger the size of the business, the more likely there are to be R&D (see unit 14) economies. Large companies are likely to sell larger volumes of products than small companies. So the total cost of developing a new product is spread over a much larger volume of sales. For example, if it costs £200 million to develop a new car, the R&D cost per car is £100 if 2 million cars are sold (£200m ÷ 2m). But the R&D cost per car rises to £1 000 if only 200 000 are sold.

Diseconomies of scale

DISECONOMIES OF SCALE occur when average costs rise as output rises. In Figure 42.1, diseconomies of scale occur at output levels higher than OB. Unlike economies of scale which are widespread across all businesses and industries, diseconomies of scale are not inevitable. Diseconomies of scale tend to arise due to poor management of a business. A well run company, whatever its size, should not have diseconomies. There is a variety of sources of diseconomies of scale.

Co-ordination One of the problems with a large business is co-ordination. Senior managers have to supervise the running of a business, which could be spread across a number of sites. There may be a number of **subsidiary companies**. Sites and companies may also be spread across the world. Parts of the business might be poorly monitored as a result. Costs may be allowed to rise and sales to fall. No business is too large to be effectively controlled. However, co-ordination can be far more of a problem with a company the size of, say, Ford or General Motors than with a sole trader.

Communication Poor communication can lead to higher costs. Different parts of a company might not pass on information about the prices of supplies, for example. As a result, some parts of the company might pay more than they need to for components. At worst, poor communication can be severely disruptive. If, for example, the R&D department fails to communicate with the production department, it might be more costly to bring in new models because the production department has not been involved in the planning process.

Motivation In a large organisation, it can be difficult to motivate workers. They can easily lose sight of the interests of the business and choose to pursue their own interests instead. This might involve gaining the highest earnings possible for doing the least work. In a well run business, management is able to motivate its workers in a variety of ways. In a poorly run business, motivation and morale of workers can be low which leads to a loss of **labour productivity** (output per worker).

Factors influencing the scale of operation

The scale of operation differs widely from industry to industry. In industries like leather making and furniture manufacture, economies of scale tend to be relatively small. In car assembly or the chemicals industry, they tend to be large. The reasons why they differ are related to the sources of economies of scale.

Technical economies In some industries, there are considerable technical economies. In car manufacturing, for instance, plants need to be a certain size to reach the lowest average cost scale of production. In leather manufacturing, however, even quite small businesses can be highly efficient because the machinery required is relatively little and relatively cheap.

Specialisation In car manufacturing, the organisation of production is complex and there are considerable opportunities to exploit specialisation of labour and capital. In leather manufacturing, the organisation of production is relatively simple with far fewer opportunities to gain the benefits of specialisation.

Purchasing economies Car manufacturers buy billions of pounds of components each year. So there is scope for a large business like Ford to negotiate large discounts compared to a small manufacturer like Morgan cars. In leather manufacturing, the market is much smaller. So no business would ever approach the size of orders that are common in

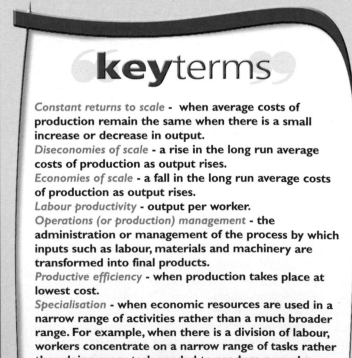

keyterms

Constant returns to scale - **when average costs of production remain the same when there is a small increase or decrease in output.**
Diseconomies of scale - **a rise in the long run average costs of production as output rises.**
Economies of scale - **a fall in the long run average costs of production as output rises.**
Labour productivity - **output per worker.**
Operations (or production) management - **the administration or management of the process by which inputs such as labour, materials and machinery are transformed into final products.**
Productive efficiency - **when production takes place at lowest cost.**
Specialisation - **when economic resources are used in a narrow range of activities rather than a much broader range. For example, when there is a division of labour, workers concentrate on a narrow range of tasks rather than doing every task needed to produce a good or a range of products. Specialisation occurs when machines are built which can only be used to perform one task. Businesses specialise in making a limited range of products rather than every product that customers might purchase.**

car manufacturing. Hence the difference in purchasing power between small and large firms in the industry is greatly reduced.

Marketing economies In marketing, Ford markets models which sell in their millions around the world. The cost of marketing per car is therefore likely to be far less than, say, for Morgan cars that sells only a few hundred per year. In leather manufacture, it is difficult to mass market any product because leather goods tend to be produced in small quantities to individual designs which are constantly changing. So larger manufacturers are unlikely to have much lower marketing costs per unit sold than small manufacturers.

Because of these factors, leather manufacturers tend not be large. On the other hand car manufacturers are amongst the larger companies in the world.

checklist

1 What is meant by 'operations management'?
2 Explain why a business may be productively inefficient.
3 What is the difference between economies of scale and diseconomies of scale?
4 Explain the principle of increased dimensions.
5 What is the difference between purchasing economies and marketing economies?
6 Why might diseconomies of scale arise?
7 Suggest why the oil extraction industry tends to be dominated by large businesses (e.g. BP Amoco or Shell) whilst hairdressing is dominated by small businesses.

In 1999, Volvo, a Swedish company, sold its car division to Ford, the US multinational. Since the takeover, Volvo cars has prospered in a way that would have been inconceivable when it was still under Swedish ownership. Ford has funded a strong programme of new model development, both to replace existing cars and to enter new sub-markets such as off road vehicles. As a result, sales have increased and there has been a strong positive consumer reaction to the changes.

However, the cost of production development and production itself is lower than it would have been if Volvo cars had remained with its Swedish parent company. Volvo has achieved greater productive efficiency. This is because it is now able to exploit the economies of scale available to the whole Ford group. Development costs have been lower because Volvo has been able to include many already available parts in new vehicles. This has included everything from car chassis to headlamps to petrol caps. Using common components across a number of car models also means that Ford now buys larger quantities of many components. Volvo is able to benefit from the cheaper prices that global purchasing brings. Ford has also approved an aggressive expansion of the Volvo brand in its home US market. Again, the cost of this expansion has been less than if Volvo were not part of Ford because it is able to make use of Ford's formidable marketing power in the USA.

Volvo cars now looks far more secure than when it was under independent Swedish ownership. Sales look set to double in the medium term. Costs are lower because of economies of scale. Models will be replaced far more regularly than before. Volvo is also less at risk if one model fails. Before, a single model failure could have led to the collapse of the whole company because development costs were so high in relation to company profits. Today, development costs for a model are far lower, but represent only a fraction of Ford's annual profit. Both Volvo cars and Ford have benefited from the 1999 acquisition.

Adapted from the *Financial Times*, 4.3.2002 and *The Times*, 5.3.2002.

1 Explain the meaning of the terms:
   (a) 'economies of scale'; (3 marks)
   (b) 'productive efficiency'. (3 marks)
2 Explain TWO reasons why Volvo has been able to increase sales of its cars. (6 marks)
3 Analyse the different reasons why Volvo has been able to reduce its average costs. (8 marks)
4 To what extent can Ford's policy of increasingly sharing components between different models of cars benefit both the company and its customers? (10 marks)

Car manufacturing

Knowledge Car manufacturing has a more than one hundred year history. Over the years, car manufacturers such as Ford, General Motors and Fiat have built plants all over the world.

Application Car plants have a *capacity*, fixed by the amount of equipment and physical space in each plant. The nearer a car plant achieves 100 per cent capacity output, the greater its *efficiency* and the lower the *average costs* of *production*. Currently worldwide there is *excess capacity* in the motor industry. In Europe, for example, *excess capacity* stood at approximately 20 per cent in 2003.

Analysis Individual car manufacturers are often reluctant to cut capacity. They hope that demand will pick up for their models and don't want to face the pain of rationalising their production facilities by closing them down. The result can be that parts of individual plants are mothballed in the short term. However, in the long term, car manufacturers have been forced to cut capacity to reduce costs and increase profitability. In the UK, for example, Ford closed its Dagenham plant and General Motors (Vauxhall) closed its Luton plant between 2000 and 2002.

Evaluation Car manufacturers will be forced to close more plants in the future, however much bad publicity and resistance from trade unions and governments they receive. Ultimately, car producers are in business to make a profit. Under-utilised car plants are too much of a drain on profitability in the long term. What is likely to happen is that car production from closed down plants will be transferred to other plants to raise their capacity utilisation, reducing costs and so increasing profits.

Utilising capacity

Capacity utilisation (see units 12 and 49) compares actual output with capacity output. Capacity output is the potential output of the capital employed in a business.

The formula to calculate capacity utilisation is:

$$\frac{\text{current output}}{\text{maximum potential output}} \times 100\%$$

For example, a business might operate its factory for 50 hours in one week. Potentially, the factory could be run 24 hours a day, 7 days a week. So it has a capacity of 168 hours of production time. The capacity utilisation of the factory would then be [50 ÷ 168] x 100% or 30 per cent.

Capacity can also be measured directly in terms of output. So a car factory might have the capacity to produce 200 cars a day. If today it only produced 150 cars, then it was running at 75 per cent capacity ([150 ÷ 200] x 100%).

Capacity utilisation and productive efficiency

Increasing capacity utilisation is likely to increase **productive efficiency** (see unit 42). This is because increasing capacity utilisation tends to reduce the **average** cost of production.

The reason for this is that capital equipment and buildings are mainly **fixed costs** (see unit 21). Their cost does not change whether they are used 8 hours a day, 16 hours a day or 24 hours a day. Increasing capacity utilisation allows the business to spread these fixed costs out over a greater output.

For instance, a business might have fixed costs of £1 million and other costs of £2 million. Its total costs would then be £3 million. The business might double its output. If it does this, fixed costs remain the same at £1 million because fixed costs don't change with output. But other costs double to £4 million. Total costs have now risen to £5 million, an increase of only 66.6 per cent or two thirds. With output doubled but costs only up two thirds, average costs fall. Hence, productive efficiency has increased.

Ways of increasing capacity utilisation

There is a number of ways in which capacity utilisation can be increased.

Increasing sales Low levels of capacity utilisation occur because not enough is being produced. Increasing sales will mean higher levels of production are needed. So capacity utilisation will increase. Productive efficiency should also increase. Many businesses with low capacity utilisation levels are not able to increase sales profitably. So this might not be an option.

Rationalisation RATIONALISATION in business is the process of reducing the number of resources needed to produce a given quantity of output. Businesses can all too easily find they have surplus factory space, carry too much stock, have too many workers or have too much equipment for current production levels. Businesses in declining industries are most likely to find themselves with EXCESS or SURPLUS CAPACITY - too much capacity for the actual level of output.

Rationalisation can be achieved in a number of ways.
● Workers can be made redundant or given early retirement.
● Stock can be sold off.
● Factories, outlets or offices can be sold off or have their leases terminated.
● Parts of the business may move to smaller premises.
● Plant may be MOTHBALLED. This is where machines, equipment or building space are left unused, but maintained, so they could be brought back into use if necessary.

Sub-contracting Capacity utilisation can vary considerably within a business. Where capital equipment has low utilisation rates, it might be more efficient for the business to SUB-CONTRACT or OUTSOURCE the work. This means hiring or contracting another business to do work which was previously done in-house.

For instance, a business might run a small fleet of delivery vans which on average are on the road for 4 hours per day. It is likely that it would be cheaper for the business to sell the vans and employ a company to make the deliveries. The delivery company will be more efficient because it will be running its vans for much longer during the day. There may also be cost savings in terms of staff. If the business employed full time drivers for the vans, they would have been under-utilised on 4 hours per day.

Sub-contracting can also lead to other cost advantages. The delivery business will be a specialist business. It should operate its delivery service more efficiently than a business with a few vans and little knowledge of the industry. If nothing else, it should have greater buying power. It might be able, for instance, to negotiate lower prices for its vans because it is buying more vans. If it is a very small business, its hourly wages may be less than, say, a union negotiated rate at the larger business.

An alternative outsourcing strategy is to take on outsourcing contracts for other businesses. For example, a major manufacturer of soap could accept contracts from rival soap manufacturers to improve its capacity utilisation. Outsourcing then becomes a strategy for increasing demand for the business.

Problems of working at full capacity

Working at full capacity might seem to be a goal to which every business should aim. Working at full capacity:
● allows a business to achieve lowest average fixed costs of production helping to increase profits;

keyterms

Excess or surplus capacity - when a business has too many resources, such as labour and capital, to produce its desired level of output.
Mothballing - when machines, equipment or building space are left unused but maintained so they could be brought back into use if necessary.
Rationalisation - reducing the number of resources, particularly labour and capital, put into the production process, usually undertaken because a business has excess capacity.
Subcontracting or outsourcing - hiring or contracting another business to do work which could be done in-house by a business.

checklist

1   What is the difference between actual output and capacity output?
2   Why would increasing capacity utilisation reduce costs?
3   Explain why increasing sales is likely to increase capacity utilisation for a business.
4   What is the difference between working at full capacity and having excess capacity?
5   'A business mothballs plant.' What does this mean?
6   How might outsourcing allow a business to increase its capacity utilisation?

● is an indicator both to its workers and to customers that the business is doing well.

However, very few businesses work at full capacity all the time.
● Inevitably there are unforeseen equipment breakdowns or workers don't turn up to work, which prevents 100 per cent capacity utilisation on a particular day.
● Working to full capacity imposes strains on both management and workers who have to be totally focussed on working to the limits of production imposed by equipment.
● It is not necessarily the most profitable way of organising production if orders have to be turned away when they exceed the production limit of the business, or if work has to be sub-contracted.

Zaman & Nazran is a business which specialises in the manufacture of diecast zinc and aluminium products. It produces components for a variety of industries. Since being founded in the mid-1990s, it has grown to today's workforce of 14 employees. Sales were up 7 per cent last year and 50 per cent up from five years ago. It is confident that in the next five years, it can increase its sales by another 50 per cent.

Table 43.1 shows the number of hours that machinery and equipment were used during each week between July and August 2003. Management works on the assumption that 60 hours per week represents full capacity for the business. This reflects the maximum number of hours that the existing labour force would be prepared to work, including overtime.

Currently, equipment in a typical week is used to 75 per cent capacity. Working to 100 per cent capacity in any week, such as in the second week of July 2003, is unusual and difficult to maintain because machines break down or employees are off work sick. In fact, in the second week of July, the business was forced to sub-contract some of the work to rival companies because it couldn't cope with delivery deadlines set by customers. Seasonal factors affect demand. Orders often fall in late July and early August because customers tend to produce less due to their workers taking summer holidays.

Management has considered rationalisation to reduce costs. Equally the business is committed to an investment programme to buy the latest equipment, which will increase productive efficiency and allow for expansion of sales in the future.

	July				August			
Week	1	2	3	4	1	2	3	4
Hours worked	44	60	47	31	41	45	45	47
Capacity utilisation (%)	73	100	?	?	?	?	?	?

Table 43.1

1 Explain what is meant by:
   (a) 'capacity utilisation'; (3 marks)
   (b) 'rationalisation'. (3 marks)
2 Calculate capacity utilisation for weeks 3-4 in July and weeks 1-4 in August. (6 marks)
3 Analyse TWO ways in which the business could increase capacity utilisation. (8 marks)
4 Discuss whether the business would perform better in the long term if it sold off half its plant and equipment, moved to smaller premises, sacked half the workforce and used sub-contractors to complete work which it could not manufacture to meet delivery deadlines from customers. (10 marks)

44 Types of production

Ercol

Knowledge Ercol is a medium-sized furniture maker based in High Wycombe near London. The company buys in wood, textile covering and foam material and from these raw materials manufactures a variety of furniture from chairs to cabinets to tables.

Application Around 2 500 *components* are *manufactured* at its *factory*, which are *assembled* into approximately 4 000 variants of different types of furniture. *Components*, such as chair legs or furniture catches, are *manufactured* in *batches* and put into store for when needed. Finished pieces of furniture tend also to be made in *batches*. However, in the case of settees, customers are able to choose individual finishes. This work is an example of *job production*. There are no examples of *flow production* at Ercol.

Analysis The furniture manufacturing industry is made up of many relatively small businesses. With customers wanting a large variety of choice, businesses are, for the most part, unable to mass manufacture furniture. Production runs are too small to justify the investment that would be required for flow production. Ercol, as an up market manufacturer, is more interested in providing quality products than low prices. So job and batch production techniques are used.

Evaluation By being an up market producer, Ercol has been able to establish a profitable niche for itself in a highly competitive market. The emphasis on quality of production and design should allow Ercol to survive in the future.

Adapted from the *Financial Times*, 10.7.2001.

How to produce

Operations management is concerned with how to transform inputs such as materials, workers and machines into completed products efficiently. The method of doing this will be very different for a company making electricity from a nuclear power plant, a potter making pots for the tourist trade, or a retailer selling furniture.

Production can be placed on a spectrum, depending upon the relative inputs of labour and capital, as in Figure 44.1.
- At one end is CAPITAL INTENSIVE PRODUCTION. This is where there is a large amount of capital, such as machines, equipment and buildings, used in the production process relative to labour. For example, a nuclear electricity plant may cost billions of pounds to build. But it can be run with just a few workers.
- At the other end is LABOUR INTENSIVE PRODUCTION. This is where relatively little capital is used, but there is a high labour input. A window cleaning business might have a number of workers, but little capital except ladders, buckets and cloths. Services, such as education, retailing and entertainment, are often labour intensive.

Production methods can broadly be put into four categories. These are job production, batch production, flow production and process production.

Job production

JOB PRODUCTION occurs when a single good or service is produced from start to finish. Each product is often unique. For instance, the building of an office block or a bridge would be an example of job production. So too would be the design of a leaflet to advertise space for rent in an office block. In the service sector, the job done by a cleaner working in an office block would be another example. Job production is often labour intensive.

Batch production

BATCH PRODUCTION occurs when a number or amount of the same products is made at the same time. For instance, a business might make 100 000 rivets of one size. Then it would change the settings on its machines to produce rivets of another size. So production of rivets occurs in batches. When a company orders brochures from the printers, they will be printed in a batch before the printer moves onto the next order. The traditional textbook example of batch production is the making of bread. A batch of dough is made, the individual loaves are shaped and the batch is then baked in an oven.

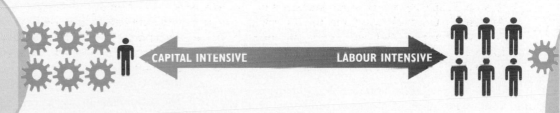

Figure 44.1 *Capital vs labour intensive production*

CAPITAL INTENSIVE → LABOUR INTENSIVE

Titanium is a strong light metal used in a variety of products from aircraft to golf clubs and artificial hips. Although the minerals in titanium occur naturally in abundance, titanium up till now has been too expensive to be used in mass market products such as car parts because it is produced in small batches. It is also tricky to incorporate into alloys.

British Titanium (BTi), a small UK company, has been working for three years on a continuous production process, discovered by scientists at the University of Cambridge, which could cut production costs substantially. The first test was successful and the company is hoping to secure funds for a full-scale pilot soon. If that works, it intends to commercialise the process by licensing the technology to manufacturers and becoming a niche producer itself.

An article in the *New Scientist* last month suggested that BTi technology could slash the cost of the metal by up to three-quarters, and bring it or its alloys into everyday use in anything from lightweight personal mini-helicopters to saucepans, washing machines and cookers.

Adapted from the *Financial Times*, 19.6.2002.

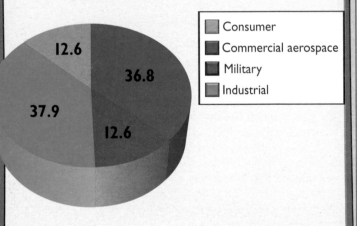

Key:
■ Consumer
■ Commercial aerospace
■ Military
■ Industrial

12.6
36.8
37.9
12.6

Figure 44.2 *Division of world titanium shipments by markets, 1999 (%)*

Adapted from *Roskgill Information*.

1 **Explain what is meant when it says that titanium 'is produced in small batches' but that in future it might be made in a 'continuous production process'.**
2 **Explain TWO reasons why sales of titanium would increase if it were made using a continuous production process.**

Flow production

FLOW PRODUCTION occurs when a product is made continuously. Cars on an **assembly line** are made using flow production techniques. The car moves from one point to another with the same process being completed at each point on the assembly line for every car. Some car components are also made using flow production techniques. Flow production is used in other industries. A processed food product, like a chocolate bar or a packet of corn flakes, might be produced continuously, passing from the initial mixing of ingredients to the final packaging.

Repetitive flow production refers to flow production where identical products are made and the same processes are used time and time again. For instance, a press might be part of the production line where a single pressing machine is making a part 24 hours a day. Flow production is often capital intensive.

Process production

PROCESS PRODUCTION is a technique where a product is made continuously by being passed through a production plant rather than on an assembly line. Petrol, for instance, is manufactured using process production techniques. Oil is put through an oil refinery and is chemically changed into petrol as it passes through pipes, vats and tanks. Process production takes place at a **plant**, like a chemical plant, and not in a factory. It tends to be highly capital intensive.

Factors affecting which production method is used

Different production methods are used in different situations. A number of factors determine which production method is likely to be most suitable.

The nature of the product In some cases, there is little choice about which production method to use. For instance, the building of a bridge across a river could only be done by job production because the bridge will be unique.

A mass market product, where millions of identical products are made, is unlikely to be suited to job production. Batch or flow production is more likely to be used. The more standardised the product, the more likely it is to be suited to flow production techniques because flow production is the least flexible of the methods of production.

In some cases, quality dictates production methods. If company executives take clients to dinner, they often expect individual service. This might only be produced through job production. Cars, on the other hand, could not be made to modern quality standards without the use of sophisticated machinery suited to batch or flow production methods.

The level of demand For flow production to be used, a business must be able to make a product continuously. The market must then be big enough to sell what is made from continuous production. So, a chocolate manufacturer might use flow production for a chocolate bar which has very large mass market sales.

Batch production is often used where demand for the product does not justify continuous production. So a chocolate manufacturer might use batch production methods for less popular bars. Ten days might be spent producing one chocolate bar and then the machinery might be changed to produce another chocolate bar.

Job production methods tend to be used where the market is very small. For instance, the building of a completely new car assembly plant is unlikely to occur more than once a decade in the UK.

The technology in use Technological processes sometimes dictate the method of production. For instance, baking bread or firing pots cannot be done using flow production methods.

In a factory near Derby, 50 high-tech machines whir 24 hours a day, producing lace that ends up in 3 000 colours, and is incorporated into women's underwear by manufacturers around the world. The factory is owned by Sherwood Group.

Since 1995, Sherwood Group has been forced to slim down drastically. In 1995, it had sales of £170 million and employed 3 500 people worldwide. Today, after sell-offs following heavy losses in 1999 and 2000, it is expected to have sales of about £40 million and some 400 employees. Its problems stem from international competition. It can't compete at the bottom end of the market with producers in low labour cost countries such as China and Thailand.

Its survival strategy involves investments in automation and a focus on design and linking up with global customers. In the past five years, Sherwood has spent £12 million on the latest German equipment for making high-quality lace in a large number of variants and with minimal involvement by employees on the shop floor. It has spent smaller sums on increasing its ability to come up with new patterns through an eight-person design studio, which turns out about 200 lace designs each year. It has also bought in dyeing equipment that ensures the lace can be made in many shades.

It has relationships with several hundred design and textile companies around the world, which design garments and make them. It also has relationships with 20 large retailers that sell the finished product. The retailers include Marks and Spencer, Tesco and the French supermarket chain Auchan. It can produce a new lace design in a matter of hours so that - after being made somewhere in the world into the finished garment - the product can end up on the retailer's sales floor just week after it has been designed, fitting in with the lingerie world's thirst for new fashions.

Adapted from the *Financial Times*, 13.11.2002.

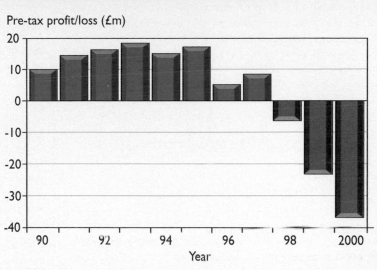

Figure 44.3 *Sherwood Group: pre-tax profit/loss (£m)*
Adapted from Thomson Financial Datastream.

---

1 **Explain what difficulties Sherwood Group faced in the late 1990s.**
2 **Discuss how Sherwood Group has attempted to regain competitiveness.**

They have to be done in batches or one at a time. In car manufacturing, many of the processes now cannot be undertaken to the right level of quality by workers. Machinery has to be used and this may force a business to use batch or flow production rather than job production.

Labour and capital inputs Sometimes the nature of the labour and capital used in the production process dictates the production method used. For instance, in job production there is often a large amount of skilled labour used which cannot be replaced by machinery. If company executives take clients out to dinner, the labour content in the preparation of the meal will be high. Each client is likely to order something different from the menu and so each meal needs individual preparation. If the clients were taken to a fast food outlet instead, the food might be prepared in batches by relatively unskilled workers trained in basic cooking techniques.

Batch and flow production may require higher levels of capital input and less skilled labour. In car production, some of the capital that is used is so expensive that a business could not justify buying it unless it was used continuously. In batch production, workers and machines often need to be flexible. A print machine, for instance, might need to handle different sizes of paper because the size of a brochure might

be different from, say, the size of poster or a business compliment slip. Workers need to be trained to cope with differing batch requirements. Some businesses are unable to use job production techniques because they cannot recruit enough skilled workers to undertake the work at the wage rates offered. Fast food chains, for instance, tend to operate batch production systems because their workers don't have the skills that the staff of a high quality restaurant would have.

Cost of capital The cost of capital is sometimes an influence on production techniques. Small businesses may not be able to afford expensive machinery. So they might use labour intensive methods of production. These are likely to be job or batch production rather than flow production. Flow production tends to be associated with large inputs of capital. Therefore it is more likely to be found in large businesses that can afford to install machinery.

Cost of production Job production tends to be more expensive per unit than batch or flow production. Some small car manufacturers might use job production for much of the building of a car. But this is more expensive than the mass production methods used by larger manufacturers because it limits the amount of capital that can be used and requires more skilled labour input. In job production, there is often less **specialisation** (see unit 42) of labour and capital which increases costs.

Batch production tends to be more expensive per unit than flow production because it takes time to move from production of one batch to another. For instance, machines are likely to need to be reset. They may have to be cleaned. Different raw materials might need to be brought in from the warehouse. Flow production techniques are most likely to exploit fully potential **economies of scale** (see unit 42) and therefore lead to lowest cost.

Implications of different production methods

Different methods of production have different implications for a business.

Motivation of workers Job production is likely to motivate workers. This is because workers can see the whole process through and be responsible for creating an end product. The work is also likely to be more skilled and more satisfying.

Flow production can be associated with the deskilling of workers. Modern car manufacturing methods emphasise the need for skills on the production line. Traditionally, though, car assembly plants were associated with boring, routine work which could be completed by unskilled labour. The jobs tended to be demotivating to workers. This causes problems for businesses, such as absenteeism, poor quality of work and poor industrial relations. It should be remembered, however, that the method of production is only one factor amongst many which determines motivation (see units 34-37).

Flexibility Flow production is relatively inflexible. A car plant, for instance, cannot easily be turned into a factory making saucepans. Equally, it is costly to convert a production line from making one model of car to another. Batch and job production tends to be more flexible. Less specialised machinery is often involved, which can be used to make different products.

Stocks Different methods of production produce different **stock** needs (see unit 45). For instance, in batch production, a batch might need storing when it is completed. With job production, stocks of raw materials might have to be stored for long periods of time because it would be uneconomical to buy in small quantities when they are needed. Flow production has seen the greatest use of **just-in-time** production techniques (see unit 47). This is where stocks are kept to an absolute minimum.

Disruption to work There are many causes of disruptions to work. For instance, workers may go on strike. There may be a fire at a suppliers that prevents new stocks arriving. A business may be unable to recruit a worker quickly enough.

If job production techniques are used, these disruptions might only have a limited impact because workers can get on with other tasks, for instance. They are likely to be most important in flow production. Here disruptions to a small part of the chain of production can lead to the shutting down of the whole production process. For instance, if the supply of seats to a car manufacturing plant did not arrive, production at the whole plant might stop.

Implications for international competitiveness

For the past fifty years, the volume of world trade has been growing at a faster rate than the output of the world economy. A larger and larger proportion of what is bought in a country is imported from other countries. Exports to other countries have also become a larger and larger proportion of what is produced in a country like the UK.

This growth in world trade, part of what is called **globalisation** (see unit 2), has been caused partly by the reduced cost of transporting goods and improved communications. Cheaper transport means that production of goods will tend to be sited in the countries that have the lowest production cost. Improved communication means that it is almost as easy for a British retailer to buy goods manufactured in Thailand or China as it is from London or Glasgow.

Many countries, such as India, China or Indonesia, have a plentiful supply of cheap unskilled labour. The UK too has a certain supply of unskilled labour. But in the UK, such labour has to be paid a minimum wage, in excess of £4 an hour. In some far eastern countries unskilled workers might be paid as little as 20p an hour. Not surprisingly, labour intensive production, where the labour needed is unskilled, has tended to shift from countries like the UK to countries with low wages.

Countries like the UK have a relatively high supply of capital. So capital intensive production has tended to remain in such countries. Some businesses have been able to fight off competition from countries with low labour costs by making

✓checklist

1 Explain the difference between labour intensive production and capital intensive production.
2 (a) In a top restaurant, all main courses are prepared and cooked once a customer has placed an order. Explain why this would be an example of job production.
   (b) In the same restaurant, one of the puddings is prepared during the afternoon and chilled. Why is this likely to be an example of batch production?
3 Explain the difference between flow production and process production.
4 What influence does (a) the level of demand for a product and (b) the cost of production have on the production method used to make a product?
5 Explain why many jobs on production lines have tended to demotivate workers.
6 A toy manufacturer, which has 75 per cent of its sales between August and December, makes toys in batches. What impact is this likely to have on stocks of finished goods?
7 Why has much labour intensive manufacturing industry relocated from countries like the UK and Germany to Thailand or Malaysia?
8 Explain why UK manufacturing companies might retain competitive advantage if their production processes are capital intensive.

their production even more capital intensive. For example, a UK textile manufacturer might employ 500 workers, but can not compete with an Indian producer. One way around this might be to buy more automated machinery and cut the workforce to 50.

Some countries like China and India also have a large supply of skilled and educated workers who will work for lower wages than in, say, the UK or the USA. Businesses in these countries have become more competitive against UK and US firms. For example, India now has a large pool of IT workers. The result is that Indian software companies have been able to win subcontracted work from software companies in the USA and Europe. In future, low skill labour intensive production is likely to continue to be attracted to the lowest wage areas of the world. So India or Thailand may lose much of its industry to, say, Uganda or Nigeria. Those industries will be replaced by higher skilled labour intensive industries or more capital intensive industries. UK businesses, open to foreign competition, must concentrate on either more capital intensive production or labour intensive production with a high labour skill element in it to survive.

'key terms'

Batch production - method of production where a product is made in stages, with a particular operation being carried out on all products in a group or batch.
Capital intensive production - when large amounts of capital are used with relatively small amounts of labour in the production process.
Flow production - a method of production where a product is made continuously, often through the use of an assembly line. Mass produced goods are most suitable for this type of production.
Job production - a method of production where a product is made individually from start to finish like a bridge or an aeroplane. Each product is likely to be unique.
Labour intensive production - when large amounts of labour are used with relatively small amounts of capital in the production process.
Process production - a method of production where a product is made continuously by being passed through a production plant rather than on an assembly line.

Smiths, the UK engineering group, is the world's second largest manufacturer of tracheotomy tubes, accounting for around one quarter of the global market. Tracheotomy tubes are inserted into the windpipe in surgical procedures to allow a patient to carry on breathing. The tubes are manufactured in Hythe in Kent, as well as in smaller satellite facilities in Folkestone and in northern France. Around 1 000 people are employed making tracheotomy tubes and other devices which aid breathing. Sales from these factories totalled around £75 million last year with production having increased by an average of 10 per cent a year in recent years.

Success has come about for three reasons. First, Smiths' tracheotomy tubes have been vigorously marketed across the world. Currently, it sells into 90 countries including Japan where it has a market share of 80 per cent and the USA where its market share is 15 per cent.

Second, Smiths has adopted an innovative approach to product design. One sixth of sales last year came from products less than three years old. This proportion is regarded as fairly high in an industry where new products are not necessarily taken up quickly because of rigorous safety and regulatory conditions. Recent new designs will improve the supply of air to the patient, make sterilisation easier to combat infection risks, or make the devices easier to fit.

A third area to which Smiths has had to pay increasing attention is manufacturing efficiency. The Hythe factory has several automated processes in which machines extrude or mould small pieces of plastic, together with many extremely fiddly operations in which the plastic parts are assembled. Because the tracheotomy tubes - made at the rate of about 1 million a year and in about 40 broad variants - have to be produced in relatively small batches, the focus is on labour intensive production techniques, using people for these assembly jobs rather than machines. Even so, because of the continual requirement to cut manufacturing costs, some assembly jobs may be cut back in the next few years as machinery takes over more of them or work is transferred to other of Smiths' manufacturing operations in lower cost parts of the world such as Mexico.

Adapted from the *Financial Times*, 11.3.2002.

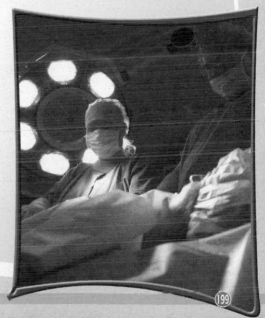

1 Explain what is meant by:
   (a) 'produced in relatively small batches'; (3 marks)
   (b) 'labour intensive production' (3 marks).
2 Outline TWO reasons why tracheotomy tubes are not made using flow production techniques at the Hythe factory. (6 marks)
3 Analyse the reasons why Smiths does not use more process production methods at Hythe. (8 marks)
4 Discuss whether Smiths should move all of its production of tracheotomy tubes to countries in the Third World such as Mexico. (10 marks)

45 Stock control

Yeuell & Gilling

Knowledge Yeuell & Gilling is a manufacturer of springs. For nearly all its existence, its major customers were lock making businesses in the Black Country region of the West Midlands. However, since most lock making work has gone to the Far East, it has had to diversify, selling to the aerospace, gunmaking and defence industries.

Application The *company* keeps *stocks* of materials including many grades of wire coil which will ultimately be shaped into springs. The *company* aims to keep a *minimum level of stock* at all times. When *stock* falls to a particular level, it is *reordered*. The *lead time* between the ordering of *stock* and its arrival at the factory is around 5 working days on most items. It doesn't keep *stocks of finished goods* because all items are made to order.

Analysis Yeuell & Gilling needs to keep stocks of raw materials so that production is not disrupted on a day to day basis. It could have stock delivered within 24 hours, but it has to use a different supplier than normal and it has to pay higher prices for this service. Cost is very important since there is so much foreign competition. Unless it keeps costs down, it could lose many of its remaining customers to cheap labour factories in the Far East.

Evaluation In the long term, Yeuell & Gilling would like to deal with suppliers which were prepared to offer lowest prices and same day or next day delivery. The company could then cut its stock levels and not have to worry about delivery of stock if there were a sudden large rush order.

Purchasing

Nearly all businesses buy in materials to produce goods and services. These materials need to be purchased and then stored. When deciding where to buy their materials, businesses consider which supplier offers the best **value for money**. There is a number of factors which affect value for money. One is cost - all other things being equal, the lower the cost the better the value for money. Another is quality - are materials consistently of the right quality for the task? Flexibility in terms of being able to change the quantity or range of supplies ordered is important too. The time taken before supplies are delivered could be crucial: if ordered from the Far East, it could take 6 weeks for bulky supplies to arrive by ship in the UK. Suppliers should also be reliable and creditworthy.

Stocks

STOCKS are goods held by a business for one of three purposes.

To make other goods Some stocks will be goods that the business has bought in and are waiting to be used to make other goods. These might be raw materials, such as coal or oil. They could be components, such as fastenings, nuts or screws. In the case of retailers and wholesalers, they would be finished goods to be sold on to customers.

Partly finished goods Some stocks are the WORK IN PROGRESS of a business. They are UNFINISHED GOODS that a business has started to make, but has not completed. For example, cars left half finished on a production line overnight would be work in progress.

Finished goods FINISHED GOODS are goods on which work has been completed and they are waiting to be delivered to a customer. The goods might already have been ordered. Or a business might have made them so it has goods ready for sale when a customer wants to buy. Some businesses, such as toy manufacturers or farmers, are affected by seasonal demand or supply. They then often carry larger levels of finished goods than average. The toy manufacturer has to STOCKPILE (or PRODUCE FOR STOCK) through much of the year before retailers and wholesalers are prepared to buy in August to December. Farmers may stockpile crops they have harvested and sell them off over a period of time after the harvest.

The levels of stocks in business today are often monitored through the use of computer software programs. In a sophisticated system, movement of stocks in, through and out of the business can be recorded via invoices, bar coding systems and production systems. However, businesses might also carry out manual STOCK TAKES, for example once a year, to check on stock levels. This is where someone visually counts the physical number of goods that are in stock. There is a number of reasons for this.

- Stock may be recorded on the system, but might be damaged and unusable.
- Stock may have been stolen.
- There might have been a human error in inputting data to a computer system. This could lead to over or under recording of stock levels.

Stock control

Businesses need to manage their stocks to ensure efficient production and sales. A business wants to keep as little stock as possible because stocks are a cost to the business. Equally, it doesn't want to run out of raw materials and so stop production. Nor does it want to lose orders because it has no finished stock to sell when a customer wants to purchase goods. One way of managing stocks efficiently is to keep stock levels within a minimum and a maximum range.

Minimum stock levels The minimum stock level is called the BUFFER STOCK. If stock levels fall below this, there is a danger that stocks will run out before new raw materials arrive from suppliers or when customers want to buy. The

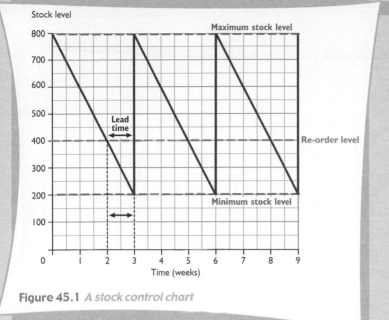

Stock level

Figure 45.1 *A stock control chart*

minimum stock level can be shown on a **stock control chart**, as in Figure 45.1. This shows stock levels of raw materials, but a similar chart could be drawn for stocks of finished goods. The minimum stock of raw materials is 200 units.

The minimum stock level is determined by a number of factors.
- The frequency with which stocks can be delivered or produced. If new supplies can be delivered within 24 hours of being ordered (i.e. the LEAD TIME is 24 hours),

for example, fewer buffer stocks need be kept than if the lead time is 14 days. This is because production is often uneven. If there is a sudden unexpected large order which must be completed within 5 days, there could be major production problems if the lead time for delivery of stocks is 14 days.
- The reliability of supplies and production. If suppliers promise 24 hour delivery but this often becomes 48 hours or longer, then more stocks will be needed to cope with emergencies. Similarly, if the business can always produce an item within 24 hours of an order being received, less stock is needed than if the lead time is two months.
- The level of production. A small business is likely to have smaller minimum stock levels than a large business.
- The type of product. For example, a steel producer can store stocks of coal and iron ore without risk of deterioration. But a cheese maker cannot hold high minimum stock levels of milk because milk deteriorates within days of delivery from the farm.

Maximum stock level The maximum stock level is the largest amount of stock the business could efficiently hold. In Figure 45.1, the maximum stock level is 800 units. The maximum stock level may be determined by a number of factors.
- The physical amount of stock holding space in the business. This could be warehouse space, for example.
- As a multiple of stocks needed for production or sales. For example, a business might decide that the maximum stock of raw materials should be the amount used in a typical

> Look at the photographs. Explain which photographs show
> (a) raw materials;
> (b) work in progress;
> (c) finished stock.

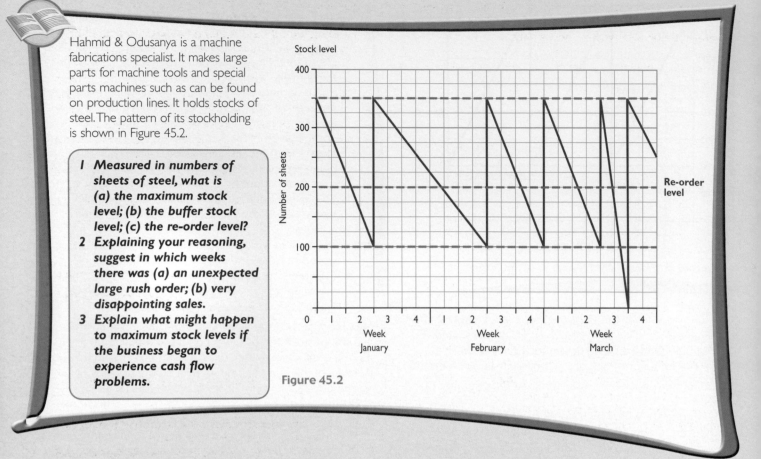

Hahmid & Odusanya is a machine fabrications specialist. It makes large parts for machine tools and special parts machines such as can be found on production lines. It holds stocks of steel. The pattern of its stockholding is shown in Figure 45.2.

1 **Measured in numbers of sheets of steel, what is (a) the maximum stock level; (b) the buffer stock level; (c) the re-order level?**
2 **Explaining your reasoning, suggest in which weeks there was (a) an unexpected large rush order; (b) very disappointing sales.**
3 **Explain what might happen to maximum stock levels if the business began to experience cash flow problems.**

Figure 45.2

month of production. Or the maximum stock of finished goods should be two weeks' worth of sales.
● The ability of a business to finance the holding of stock. A business with cash flow problems (see units 27-28), for example, may have lower maximum stock levels than is efficient in order to reduce cash outflows.

The RE-ORDER LEVEL is the level of stock at which the business will order new stock. In Figure 45.1, this is at 400 units. In Figure 45.1 the **lead time** is one week. It takes one week from ordering for stock to arrive. The business has a **reorder quantity** of 600 units each time it places an order for stock.

The re-order level is determined mainly by the lead time on replacing stock. So if it takes one week to receive supplies from ordering, then the reorder level will be the minimum stock level (200) plus the amount of stock used up in one week (200 in Figure 45.1).

Figure 45.1 shows a pattern of production and stock use which is uniform from week to week. In practice, this is most unlikely to be the case. Even in businesses where production is relatively stable, there will be some weeks when machinery breaks down, and bank holidays or illness of staff disrupt production. So stock control charts as in Figure 45.1 are too simplistic for everyday use. However, much more complicated stock control charts, typically generated by past records on computer, can be used to monitor stocks. They can also be used to analyse stock control. For example, if supplies are always arriving late, then it could be the fault of the suppliers, or office staff at the business itself failing to put in orders on time.

Stock management

Stocks need to be managed efficiently by a business. One aspect of this is STOCK ROTATION. Most stock is perishable or can be damaged in storage. So it makes sense to use the oldest stock first. This principle is FIRST-IN-FIRST-OUT (FIFO). In shops, for example, new stock added to shelves is put behind existing stock. So customers picking up goods from the front of the shelf automatically take the oldest stock. In an automated warehouse, the computer management system will identify which stock should be taken out first.

Minimising STOCK WASTAGE is also important. Stock might be used inefficiently or 'wasted' in a number of ways.
● Too much stock can be used in the production process. For example, poor design might lead to 30 per cent more steel than is necessary in the production of a cooker. Or workers might use too many ingredients making products.
● Poor production and errors might result in large numbers of goods being rejected. The goods might have to be reworked to bring them up to the right standard. Or they may have to be scrapped or sold off as seconds.
● Stock can be damaged in transit or in storage. For example, peaches can be bruised during delivery or they might become ripe too quickly in storage before being sold. Either way, the value of the peaches will be reduced on sale.
● Stock may be stolen (called **wastage** in retailing) by staff or customers. So security is vital in a business to prevent this.

The costs and benefits of holding stock

Holding stock is a major cost for a business.

- Stock needs to be handled and stored. So there is a labour cost to handling the stock. There is also the cost of the warehouse or area where stock is kept.
- Stock often deteriorates or gets damaged over time. At worst, stock becomes unsellable because it has passed its 'sell by date' or because a new model has been introduced.
- Finance tied up in stocks has a cost. If a business has £1 million of stocks, that £1 million might have been borrowed. In this case, interest will have to be paid on the £1 million. Alternatively, the £1 million might belong to the business itself. But that £1 million then has an opportunity cost - benefits that could be gained by using the money in its next best alternative use. For example, the £1 million could perhaps be used to buy new equipment, which would reduce operating costs and boost profits. It could be used to finance research and development which would lead to new products, higher sales and higher profits. Or it could be used to spend on promotion, again boosting sales and profits.
- At worst, holding too much stock could lead to a business having a cash flow crisis and being forced to cease trading.

However, holding too little stock can also be a problem.

- Holding too little stock of materials or semi-finished goods could cause production to come to a halt. On a car production line, for example, the whole line can be brought to a stop if items such as car seats, engines or light fittings are not available.
- Holding too little stock of finished goods might lead to customers being turned away. For example, a fashion retailer might order 50 000 of a particular design which sells out within one week of being put into stores. Customers might come in looking for the design, but not find it. Sales will then be lost.
- Both of the above can lead to long term damage to customer relations. For example, a supermarket which persistently has large numbers of **stock outs** (i.e. where a store has run out of stock of a particular item and so it isn't available on the shelves for customers to buy) could lose customers to other supermarkets.
- Holding too little stock and then making frequent orders for small quantities of supplies can be expensive if suppliers give discounts on larger orders. A business can then lose the advantages of **purchasing economies of scale** (see unit 42). Buying small orders can also add to costs because processing each order can be expensive. For example, a corner shop owner may go to the cash and carry wholesaler daily to buy stock because of cash flow problems. Not only does the owner have to give up time to make the trip. It also costs money for petrol. Note, though, that frequent delivery of stock is the basis of just-in-time techniques (see unit 47) which have revolutionised stock control.

Stock control and IT

Information technology (IT) has allowed many businesses to

checklist

1 What is the difference between unfinished goods and finished goods?
2 Why do businesses have stock takes?
3 Explain the difference between the minimum stock level and the maximum stock level.
4 What is the link between the re-order level and lead times for re-order stock?
5 What advantages are there to a business in minimising its stock levels?
6 Explain the problems a business might face if it holds too little stock.
7 How has information technology affected stock control?

keyterms

Buffer stock - in stock control, the minimum stock level a business intends to keep to cope with unforeseen circumstances such as late delivery of stock from suppliers or an unexpected increase in production.

Finished goods - goods which have been processed by a business and are awaiting sale or delivery to customers.

First-in-first-out (FIFO) - a system of stock rotation where the oldest stock is used first.

Lead time - the amount of time between ordering supplies and their delivery.

Maximum stock level - the highest quantity of stock which a business wants to keep; this influences how much new stock is bought.

Produce for stock - making products and putting them into stock rather than immediately dispatching them to customers.

Re-order level - the level of stock at which the business will order new stock.

Stock rotation - the movement of stock in and out of storage, ideally in a way which maximises efficiency and minimises wastage. FIFO is an example of a stock rotation system.

Stock wastage - stock which is damaged in transit or in storage and is therefore either unusable or which has lost part of its value.

Stockpile - ordering or making products and putting them into stock in order to build up stocks.

Stock take - counting the amount of stock held at a point in time in order to calculate the total stock level held.

Stocks - goods held by a business either waiting to be used in the production process, semi-finished goods, or finished goods waiting to be delivered to customers.

Work in progress or unfinished goods - products which are in the process of being made.

keep a much better track of stock. At its simplest, a computer system will hold details of existing stock. Employees will then manually enter quantities of stock that arrive at and leave the business. Work in progress can also be monitored in this way if the business thinks this is important. The computer system can also be programmed to reorder stock automatically when the re-order level of stock is reached.

The system becomes easier to handle and more accurate if stock is bar coded. Stock can be scanned and monitored as it moves through the production system. Bar codes have long been used by retailers, particularly supermarket chains, because they allow stock to be scanned at checkouts. This speeds up the check out time for customers. It also provides more accurate bills and means that the supermarkets don't have to price every single item on their shelves. More sophisticated uses of bar coding and stock control, such as automatic reordering when stocks fall to a certain level, have

only recently been used widely in the UK.

In the future, many goods are likely to have electronic tags. These are small microchips attached to or built into the product. They can be read by a sensor. For example, a supermarket trolley full of goods could be pushed past the sensor and instantly recorded without having to take them out of the trolley. Electronic tagging will automate the recording of stock. It will enable businesses to keep an even closer control over the stock and its geographical location.

Just-in-time (JIT)

Just-in-time manufacturing has had a considerable impact on both stock control and production. This is where stocks are kept to a minimum and ordered just before they are needed for production. This process is discussed further in unit 47.

MG Rover, the largest UK-owned car maker, has halted production for a week in an effort to resolve a crisis in spare parts supply that threatens to damage customer relations. The business has stood down most of 3 300 production workers at its Longbridge site in Birmingham, allowing components produced by suppliers to be diverted for use as spares.

Kevin Howe, chief executive, said: 'Our dealers and customers are experiencing frustrating delays ... We are taking incredible steps to address the problem.' The shut down, implemented under flexible working arrangements, began on Monday and is expected to end on June 17. Lost production of 3 500 vehicles will be made up later.

Suppliers claimed the long-running shortage of stocks was undermining the service provided by dealers, delaying repairs and maintenance for many Rover customers. One supplier said: 'It's causing complete chaos. There has been a foul-up in the distribution and logistics systems.'

The main cause of the problem is that component manufacturers, damaged by two years of falling car sales and exports, were struggling to cope with a rebound in demand.

The distribution of spare parts is worth £250 million a year to MG Rover. Operating profit on components is close to 10 per cent of cost compared to just 2 per cent for a finished car.

Adapted from the *Financial Times*, 13.6.2002.

1 Explain what is meant by the terms:
  (a) 'suppliers';
  (3 marks)
  (b) 'stocks' (3 marks).

2 Outline TWO possible reasons why MG Rover decided to divert spare parts from its factory to car dealers. (6 marks)

3 Explain why MG Rover, car dealers and manufacturers of parts for MG Rover all found themselves in difficulties in June 2002. (8 marks)

4 Discuss whether MG Rover should in future hold far more stock of parts at its Longbridge plant. (10 marks)

46 Quality

Greenside Baking

Knowledge Greenside Baking, was hit hard by the BSE crisis in the late 1990s. BSE is a fatal disease which affects cows and which can be passed on to humans through eating contaminated beef. The crisis caused a sharp drop in demand for beef products, including the beef pasties and pies which were made by Greenside Baking. To secure the survival of the business and its 50 employees, the bakery switched to making Danish Pastries.

Application After the main BSE crisis had passed, Billy Kenrick, who owned the bakery, was approached by his local Business Link to see if he would be interested in rebuilding his beef *market* using *quality* beef. He met with farmers who produced beef fed solely on grass. Grass fed beef didn't suffer BSE because they hadn't been in contact with the contaminated feed at the heart of the BSE crisis. They negotiated a deal whereby, using this premium beef, Greenside Baking would rebuild its trade in beef pies and pasties. The customer could then trace the *quality* of the final *product* through the *supply chain*.

Analysis Greenside Baking is a small producer that is committed to ensuring high quality products for its customers. Billy Kenrick believes that products have got to have added value and quality if they are to compete with the big producers. He argues that quality is something you have to work at and that it starts with good ingredients. 'To that, you must add committed and well-trained staff' he said.

Evaluation By putting quality as its top priority, Greenside Baking has created an effective marketing tool. In an age where quality food can command premium prices, this is likely to be prove a highly successful strategy against larger competitors which are not using premium beef supplies.

Defining quality

QUALITY in business has a number of meanings which aren't necessarily compatible.

A superior product The traditional meaning relates to a superior product. This is one which is clearly better than others on the market. For example, luxury brands such as BMW, Harrods and Gucci claim that their products are superior in quality to mass market brands.

A consistent product In production terms, quality tends to be associated with consistency. For Heinz, for example, this means that the contents of every tin of its baked beans must be the same. For this to be achieved, there must be a standard to which the product conforms. This standard may be set by the business. It may be an industry standard, drawn up by an external body such as the British Standards Institution (see below). Or it may be a standard imposed on the business by its customer.

Standards imply that there will be few or no defects. Over the past 20 years, manufacturing has moved closer towards achieving ZERO DEFECTS. This is where the number of faults per million parts produced is almost zero. Zero defects are essential for modern production methods such as just-in-time deliveries (see unit 47). Consistency does not imply anything about quality in the sense of a superior product. A McDonald's hamburger, for instance, is unlikely to be classified as a superior luxury food product. But it does achieve consistency in that a McDonald's hamburger is the same in London as in Paris or Moscow.

Value for money A third meaning of quality associates it with value for money. Asda, the supermarket chain, promotes itself by saying that customers can buy quality products from its stores, but at a cheaper price than its rivals. It therefore provides a better quality service than its competitors.

Another way of looking at quality is to consider what properties a good or service must have for it to satisfy the needs of customers. These quality properties are likely to include the following.

- Fitness for purpose. Does the product do what it says it will? For a motor manufacturer, is the car seat which is arriving from a supplier always of sufficient quality that it can be fitted into a car?
- Reliability and durability. Does a product always work? Will a product still be working perfectly in ten years time? For a railway company, do their services always run on time? For a car manufacturer, how long will a clutch last before it needs replacing?
- After-sales service. Once a product is sold, what back-up service will be available to the customer? For a car manufacturer, are parts easily available for repairs? For a retailer, does it provide a repair service?

Traditional quality control

Achieving quality has traditionally been done through QUALITY CONTROL procedures. A good or service was produced and then checked afterwards, often against a quality standard or specification. This laid down the minimum qualities or properties that were acceptable for the product. In this system, most workers were not directly responsible for ensuring quality. This was the job of **quality controllers** or **quality inspectors**.

When work was of unsatisfactory quality, it might be scrapped if it was, say, processed food or nuts and bolts. Or it might be reworked, as with a car which arrives at the end of the production line with faults. It might even be sold to the customer. If a hotel room is not cleaned, for instance, during the stay of a customer, the customer can still enjoy many of the other aspects of the hotel service being given. The problem, though, is that the customer might choose not to use the hotel again as a result.

Quality systems which rely on work being checked after it has been done tend to perform poorly. This is partly because it is difficult and sometimes impossible to check for quality once a product has been created. Partly, it is because the cost of operating the quality control system, scrapping or rectifying products, or losing customers because of poor quality is considerable. In the 1970s, for instance, one third of the cost of producing quality cars such as BMWs was estimated to be the cost of rectifying faults once cars had come off the production line.

Quality assurance

In the 1980s, a different approach to quality emerged in the UK and the USA. Instead of quality being seen as something which was checked at the end of the production process, quality became part of that process. Everyone became responsible for ensuring quality. Instead of quality being a factor to be controlled, it became something which was assured because it was built into the production chain. The objective was to prevent problems, rather than identifying them after they had occurred.

One approach to QUALITY ASSURANCE was TOTAL QUALITY MANAGEMENT (TQM). The central idea behind TQM is that all workers contribute and are responsible for quality.

Design Quality starts at the design or planning stage for a product. Quality has to be built into the design. For example, the fewer the number of parts in a product, the less likely on average that faults will occur during its assembly or in use by the customer. The ease with which a part can be manufactured also affects quality. A part which is difficult to make is more likely to be defective than one which is simple to make. Designers also need to understand how customers view quality. Designers therefore need to liaise with production managers and with those responsible for marketing before the launch of a product or service.

Suppliers and materials Quality can only be built into a product if suppliers are sending high quality materials to the business. Suppliers are part of the QUALITY CHAIN. However, suppliers are not just external to the business. All workers and all departments within a business are suppliers too, supplying goods and services to customers in the organisation. Take the example of a production line. If parts are faulty when they are put onto the line, this could affect workers further down the line in the work they are doing. Even workers who have nothing to do with production itself are part of the quality chain. If office staff fail to calculate pay accurately, or fail to ensure that it is paid on time, then production workers may become dissatisfied. This could affect their motivation and the quality of their work. Production workers can then be seen as the 'customers' of the office staff dealing with pay.

Process Quality needs to be built into the production process. Everything from the layout of machinery, the production processes used, the materials and the use of labour needs to be considered from the viewpoint of quality. Instead of checking quality at the end, quality becomes an inevitable part of production itself.

Measurement Wherever possible, quality should be measured. This can be done, for example, through STATISTICAL PROCESS CONTROL (SPC). This is a method for collecting and then analysing data on the performance of a process. It makes use of control charts and computer software. For example, bags of sweets are sold by weight. Measurements can be taken of samples of bags to ensure that

In 2001, Ford, the world's number two motor manufacturer, was in trouble. The most visible sign of that was the sacking of its chief executive, Jack Nasser, just two years after he had been appointed. Jack Nasser had worked his way up through Ford from heading its Australian operations, before moving to head Ford in Europe and then Ford operations in North America. He had made his reputation as a cost cutter and hence his nickname of 'Jack the knife'. As chief executive, though, he oversaw a series of blunders, for which in the end he took the blame.

Much of the problem lay in the area of quality. JD Power, a marketing information firm, reported in May 2001 that vehicles built by Ford had an average of 162 faults per 100 vehicles, the highest of the big three of General Motors, Ford and Chrysler. In October 2001, Ford announced it was recalling 1 million vehicles to fix a defective window-wiper switch that could cause fires. Just one week before, it agreed to pay for $2.7 billion worth of repairs on millions of cars and trucks with a flawed ignition system that has been blamed for a number of deaths. Analysts attributed some of these problems to the relentless cost-cutting. Suppliers, who have been subjected to six consecutive years of price cuts, often cut corners.

The worst quality problem, though, related to Ford's highly profitable Explorer vehicle. In August 2000, the vehicle had been involved in a series of accidents, allegedly caused by defects in its tyres made by Firestone. Both companies initially denied there was a problem. Eventually, in May 2001, Ford decided to stop buying any tyres made by Firestone. But not before the tyre problem had turned into a huge public relations disaster for Ford.

Adapted from *The Sunday Times*, 4.11.2001.

1 **Explain why a failure to secure quality in its supply chain damaged Ford.**
2 **Discuss how Ford could have improved quality in its supply chain.**

A generic standard for management might seem like a nightmare for companies to implement. But ISO 9000, the international set of standards for quality management, has been enthusiastically adopted by more than 250 000 organisations in 143 countries. Although ISO 9000 is not intended as a quality label or guarantee, it has become an important differentiator for businesses. It covers 'quality management' - what an organisation does to ensure that its products conforms to customer requirements. Any organisation accredited with ISO 9000 has had its management systems independently audited and approved.

At HSBC Asset Management, ISO 9000 was adopted recently to improve back-office management in seven international branches. 'We wanted to enhance quality procedures in our back offices, but we are now looking to tailor it for other areas. Even if we did not retain accreditation, the system would still be maintained', says Steve Gibbon, group operations development manager at HSBC Asset Management, London.

The ISO 9000 logo has a special cachet in the Far East and the Pacific rim region, where some countries are said to regard it as a badge of honour. Even those who regard the standard essentially as a preventative tool concede its value in ensuring that things are 'done by the book'.

In the UK, British Gas has won company-wide registration after a two-year process involving the auditing of its entire business. 'We needed to show our management systems meet and exceed customer expectations. The British Standards Institution (BSI) assessed our onsite activities, examined our procedures and surveyed operations throughout the UK', says Roger Wood, managing director of British Gas Services.

At Vodafone, Steve Hudson, senior quality manager, says: 'You can be as innovative as you wish with ISO 9000 or just meet requirements - it gives you a clear mechanism for identifying problem areas.'

Adapted from the *Financial Times*, 30.11.1999.

---

1 **Explain what it means when it says that ISO 9000 is an 'international set of standards for quality management'.**

2 **Why do businesses spend management time and resources to gain ISO 9000 accreditation? Use examples from the data to illustrate your answer.**

---

the production process is manufacturing them within tolerance. This information highlights problem areas which need to be tackled to improve quality.

Workers As part of this process, workers must become responsible for checking the quality of the work they do. In car manufacturing, workers may be organised into teams where each team is responsible for quality in the section where it works. Team working encourages each worker to deliver quality because if they don't, the rest of the members of the team will have to pick up the responsibility for it.

Total participation TQM will only work if every member of the business is committed to implementing it. This means a chief executive and managing director must be as committed to quality as a shop floor worker. If this fails to happen, there will be gaps in the quality chain within the organisation itself.

Many businesses in the 1980s and 1990s implemented TQM with mixed results. Some of the problems were due to a failure to implement the initiative fully. There was a variety of reasons for this. Businesses failed to put sufficient resources into training staff. There wasn't the willpower to implement the procedures required by TQM, such as regular audits of performance. TQM was also often only implemented effectively in part of the business, whereas a key aspect of TQM is that it is a whole organisation approach to quality.

Other management techniques, such as benchmarking, Kaizen and quality circles have been used to improve quality. These are discussed in detail in units 47 and 48.

Training and employee development

TQM and other similar quality programmes can only be successful if staff are properly trained. For example, staff could develop their skills, through courses and gaining qualifications. The importance of training can be indicated through the **appraisal system** (see unit 37), where pay increases could be directly linked to the achievement of additional qualifications.

Partly, though, training is about taking responsibility for quality. If staff believe that quality is someone else's responsibility, then it is unlikely that the organisation will be able to deliver a quality product. A business which gives its staff responsibility for quality is also likely to be giving it responsibility over many other aspects of their work. Training for quality is part of a general **empowerment** (see unit 36) of workers, where traditional command and control structures are broken down.

In the UK, this quality is encouraged through a variety of initiatives. For example, Investors in People (IiP) was developed in the 1990s by industry bodies such as the CBI with the support of the Employment Department. It is a national standard for training quality. A business can achieve Investors in People status by showing assessors approved by IiP that its policies and procedures conform to the standard. To do this, a business must show that it is able to identify its **aims and objectives** (see unit 63) and how it can achieve these. Inevitably, in doing so, the business will realise that there is a gap between the skills of its current workforce and the skills that will be needed. Therefore, a training programme will need to be established to bridge this gap. Investors in People is therefore not just concerned with quality, but quality is likely to be a key training issue identified by the programme.

Quality standards for individual products

Many businesses set their own quality standards. However, there are independent bodies which set standards for both products and processes. In the UK, the most important body is the British Standards Institution (BSI). It issues standards for individual products, ranging from types of steel to door locks to child car seats.

A business can apply to the BSI to have its product registered as conforming to a BSI standard. For many products, this means that the product can then carry a BSI **kitemark**, a logo which shows customers that the product has met the standard.

There are other bodies which also issue standards and codes of practice, such as:
- the British Electrotechnical Approvals Board, which inspects domestic electrical equipment;
- the Association of British Travel Agents (ABTA), which has a code of practice for travel agents;
- the Wool Marketing Board for manufacturers of woollen garments;
- the British Toy and Hobby Association (BTHA) for toys.

Local authorities, through Trading Standards departments, are responsible for enforcing law relating to quality issues. The main body of law covers:
- weights and measures, ensuring that the customer receives the quantity stated in a sale;
- food protection, ensuring that food is fit for human consumption;
- individual safety regulations for specific products, such as no lead in toys, or night dresses being inflammable.

ISO 9000

Businesses can qualify for quality standards issued by the British Standards Institution and other independent bodies. ISO 9000 is an internationally agreed quality standard. It is based on the former UK quality standard BS5750. ISO 9000 shows that a business has quality assurance procedures in place throughout its business. To gain ISO 9000, a business has to:
- document its business procedures, from how an invoice is dealt with to how a product is made;
- prepare a quality manual, including how quality is to be built into the making of a product;
- assess its quality management systems, addressing such

issues as training for staff and how to deal with customer complaints.

Once a business has gained ISO 9000 accreditation, it is regularly inspected to ensure that standards are being maintained.

The importance of quality

Quality is essential for a business in a competitive market place. Poor quality is likely to lead to a loss of customers to rival businesses. Even if a business is a monopoly (see unit 49) with no competition, quality is important. The railways in the UK, for example, have seen customers leave their services to take to their cars or use buses and planes because of such poor quality service in recent years.

Quality is also important for costs. Poor quality typically means that products have to be remade or there is considerable wastage in production. Poor quality means higher costs and lower profits.

Gaining quality assurance certification, like ISO 9000, can have considerable benefits for a business. By using the certification on marketing material, it can persuade customers to buy from the business rather than a rival. The process of gaining and keeping certification is likely to reduce costs through more efficient production. Staff motivation is likely to be higher because workers will gain satisfaction from producing to a quality standard. ISO 9000 is also likely to be associated with training and empowerment of workers, both of which are likely to be motivating. Just-in-time manufacturing has had a considerable impact on both stock control and production. This is where stocks are kept to a minimum and ordered just before they are needed for production. This process is discussed further in unit 47.

keyterms

Quality - achieving a standard for a product or service, or a production process, which meets customers' needs.
Quality assurance - a commitment by a business to maintain quality standards throughout its organisation.
Quality chain - a series of links between workers within an organisation or workers and customers from other organisations where the interaction is considered in terms of quality of product or service.
Quality control - ensuring the quality of a product meets specified performance criteria.
Statistical process control (SPC) - inspecting and analysing data from business processes to make judgments about their level of quality and to identify solutions to problems.
Total Quality Management (TQM) - a production philosophy which states that all workers in an organisation contribute to and are responsible for quality.
Zero defects - when there are no faults in products because products are made to a quality standard every time.

checklist

1 Explain three different ways of defining quality.
2 What is the function of a quality controller?
3 Why is it expensive to achieve quality in a traditional quality control system?
4 Explain the main features of Total Quality Management.
5 What is the role of training in achieving quality?

6 Explain the role of the British Standards Institution (BSI).
7 Why might a business want to gain ISO 9000 accreditation?
8 Why is quality important for a business?

It is difficult to argue against the idea that companies should strive to improve quality. But legitimate questions can be raised about their chances of success. Quality improvement programmes come in many different flavours. There are more similarities than differences between them. The common belief is that companies should aim for 'zero defects' in all aspects of their operations, achieved by relentless improvements in business processes. Common techniques include a team-based approach to problem-solving and a highly quantitative approach to measuring results.

Yet the financial record of US companies that have pioneered the pursuit of quality is hardly inspiring. In the early 1980s, for example, Xerox was one of the first US companies to adopt the ideas of quality gurus W Edwards Deming and Joseph Juran. These management consultants had been hugely influential in Japan and helped companies such as Canon and Ricoh to mount a dramatic assault on the US market. Xerox needed to fight back or face extinction. At first the company registered some important victories. It regained market share from its Japanese rivals after 10 years of retreat. But success did not last. A combination of strategic errors in the late 1980s and management mistakes in the late 1990s undermined its position. Xerox is now trying to recover from an accounting scandal and a near-miss with bankruptcy.

Joseph Juran points out that it took Japanese companies more than 30 years to transform their collective reputation for poor product quality. 'I know of no company that took less than six years to achieve a position of quality leadership within their industry. Usually it took closer to 10', he says.

Perhaps the responsibility for quality initiatives really to take hold in the long term comes from a failure at the top. In practice, most top executives are reluctant to introduce quality processes that may hamper their freedom of action. It is fine for those lower down the hierarchy to follow quality procedures. But those at the top shy away from adopting them to govern their own actions. Mike Beer, professor of business administration of Harvard Business School, comments: 'Few management teams are willing to address their own quality and shortcomings. Experience tells me that they won't get any lasting benefit from these programmes unless they do.'

Adapted from the *Financial Times*, 15.7.2002.

1 Explain the meaning of the following terms:
   (a) 'zero defects'; (3 marks)
   (b) 'quantitative approach to measuring results' (3 marks).
2 Outline TWO advantages for a business of implementing a quality improvement programme. (6 marks)
3 Analyse how ONE quality improvement programme with which you are familiar leads to improved quality within a business. (8 marks)
4 Discuss whether quality management techniques such as TQM should be applied to senior management as much as to shop floor workers. (10 marks)

47 Lean production (1)

Toyota

Knowledge Toyota is the world's third largest car manufacturer and Takaoka is its largest car production facility in Japan, making almost 700 000 vehicles a year.

Application At Takaoka, *management* has pioneered *lean production techniques* over the past 30 years. These include *Kaizen*, and *just-in-time production*. But with *competitors* catching up, Toyota is committed to a new *efficiency* drive designed to reduce *costs* by £5.6 billion by 2005. This new *restructuring* emerged from a *benchmarking* exercise where Toyota compared itself to other car manufacturers. Toyota found that the *company* still had a lead in *quality* but it was slipping in the area of *cost* reduction and parts *procurement*.

Analysis Other manufacturers have made considerable savings on the procurement (i.e. purchasing) of parts over the past 5 years. Toyota has set itself the goal of cutting 30 per cent off its supply costs of parts and modular systems. It is committed to working with its suppliers to help them cut their own costs sufficiently to remain profitable after their prices have fallen by 30 per cent. This reflects Toyota's close long term association with a key number of suppliers.

Evaluation Toyota has, arguably, been the world's most efficient car producer over the past three decades. Other car producers, however, have been forced to implement changes and learn from Toyota's lean production techniques to survive. To stay ahead, Toyota has to continue changing and innovating.

Adapted from the *Financial Times*, 13.12.2001.

Purchasing

In the early 20th century, Henry Ford revolutionised production techniques through the introduction of the assembly line at his car plants. By mass producing goods in large quantities, he could reduce costs of production. This in turn led to lower prices and competitive advantage over rivals. Mass production enabled producers to gain economies of scale (see unit 42).

However, it was the Japanese who realised that mass production systems tended to be both wasteful and inflexible. Eiji Toyoda, a member of the family which founded Toyota, visited Ford's plant in Detroit in the 1950s for three months. He found that production was inefficient and wasteful (called 'muda' in Japanese). On his return, he looked for ways to reduce inefficiency and wastefulness within Toyota. By the 1980s, Japanese car production plants were typically far more efficient than those of US or European rivals. The result was that Japanese cars were taking a larger and larger share of US and European markets.

It was at this time that the term LEAN PRODUCTION was first used. It occurs when inputs to the production process are **minimised**. Lean production is not about just one technique. It occurs because of a variety of methods used to minimise labour inputs, the amount of materials used, stock levels and capital inputs, and to optimise design and product quality. These are shown in Figure 47.1 and described in this unit and in unit 48.

Central to all lean production techniques is PEOPLE-CENTRED MANAGEMENT. It is employees, whether management or workers, who are going to see what needs to be changed, implement the change and then operate the new systems. With traditional mass production techniques,

there was typically a huge gulf between management, representing the owners, and workers who were represented by trade unions. Workers often resisted change because it could lead to employees having to work harder, in worse conditions or being made redundant because of increased efficiency. Lean production assumes that there is no gulf between workers and management. Part of being a worker is a willingness not just to accept change but to create change when this will improve working practices. The gulf between workers and management ceases to exist because everyone is committed to the same goals.

Continuous improvement/Kaizen

KAIZEN means continuous improvement in Japanese. Its philosophy includes a number of aspects which affect business operations.

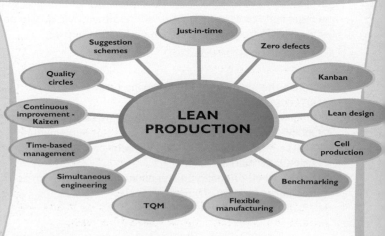

Figure 47.1 *Lean production techniques*

Continuous improvements The production philosophy behind Kaizen is that improvements are difficult to make in large, sudden jumps. For example, management may know that they could achieve 20 per cent cost savings if they moved to a purpose-built factory and replaced all existing machinery. But this is far too large a change for most businesses to undertake, especially in the short term.

The alternative Kaizen strategy is to make many small changes continuously rather than suddenly. In themselves none of these changes might be very significant. But when taken together they can be very important. For example, assume a business carried out 50 changes during the year, each of which reduced overall costs by 0.1 per cent. The total cost savings over the year would be 5 per cent (0.1 per cent x 50).

Empowerment and teamwork Kaizen would not be effective if it were implemented simply by managers. The Kaizen philosophy assumes that every employee will be involved in change. One way is to **empower** (see unit 36) workers to make changes themselves. For example, a group of workers may be organised into a cell (see below) or into a **team** (see unit 36). The team may have the authority to decide how to work and accomplish the goals or targets which have been set for them. Members of the team will also be responsible for making changes, such as improving quality or reducing costs. Best practice in one team can then be spread across all teams.

Another way of empowering workers is to establish Kaizen groups. A Kaizen group is a team of workers specifically set up to consider ways of changing work practices to bring about improvements in efficiency and quality. The Kaizen group may meet regularly and makes suggestions which will be passed onto management. The group may choose which areas of work it wishes to consider or it may be directed by management to consider a particular area. Kaizen groups are empowering for workers because, having set them up, management is likely to accept their suggestions for change. In some businesses where Kaizen has been adopted, Kaizen groups operate as 'quality circles' (see below).

Training Pushing responsibility down the management hierarchy (see unit 31) means that workers must be capable of taking on responsibilities such as checking their own work or making simple repairs to machines. This is likely to raise **training** (see unit 41) issues. Management cannot implement Kaizen unless it is prepared to put resources into raising the skills levels of its workers.

Shared goals Kaizen assumes that workers share the goals of management to make improvements in the production process. It is a philosophy that will only really be effective if all employees of the business are committed to the approach. The business must see its employees as a valuable resource. Employees must work towards the same aims and objectives as managers.

Kaizen offers many benefits to businesses that adopt its philosophy. It can improve productivity and quality as shown in Figure 47.2. By empowering staff and giving them more control over their work environment, it can increase the motivation of workers.

However, many UK businesses have never heard of Kaizen, particularly outside of the manufacturing sector, as shown in Figure 47.3. Where it has been adopted, it has not always worked. The major problem in implementation occurs when senior management treat Kaizen as a bolt on technique rather than seeing it as a technique which must permeate the whole work system. As with Total Quality Management (TQM, see unit 46), every employee must be committed to making constant improvements in the way they and their team work. Sometimes, it is claimed that management tried to implement Kaizen but dropped it after encountering worker resistance. This indicates that management is not performing its job properly, rather than being a criticism of Kaizen. Management which can't implement change in the workplace is likely to see its business become uncompetitive in the long term. Kaizen might also not be implemented on cost grounds. It requires training of staff and may involve some capital investment if it is clear that problems occur mainly because of lack of the right sort of equipment. However, Kaizen has been shown in many studies to reduce costs quickly and improve sales because of improved quality or reduced lead times on

A West Midlands engineering firm has used Japanese business techniques to double its production in less than a week. Midland Pneumatic has been taking its departments through a process called 'Kaizen Blitz'. In a series of intensive sessions everyone, from the shopfloor workers to the managing director, is allowed to express their views on how their job could be done better.

Geoff Pye, managing director at Midland Pneumatic, which makes hydraulic and pneumatic cylinders, totally reorganised its layout and ways of working in three days. 'We stripped everything out, cleaned it all up, and put it back in the new layout. In one of our cylinder cells, production increased by more than 90 per cent immediately, from 60 cylinders a week to 60 in two and a half days. We've been through that process five times now in different departments.'

The process also involves changing production methods and making the company more open to ideas from the shop floor. 'There was some resistance from people initially, but virtually everyone has recognised the benefits now. The job isn't finished yet, but we have come a long way', said Mr Pye.

The firm has also brought in Peter Kitson as production controller to oversee work in the new production cells. He said: 'All the ideas for reorganising things came from the shop floor. They are the experts, it was simply a case of getting them to show us what they could do.'

Paul Higgs, the union shop steward at the company, is another convert to the new system. 'It has definitely changed the atmosphere in the place - people feel a lot more involved, that their views are being listened to.'

Source: adapted from the *Express & Star*, 24.9.2001.

1 What is a 'Kaizen Blitz'?
2 Giving examples from the data, explain the role of empowerment and teamwork in Kaizen.
3 Discuss whether workers and managers at a company using Kaizen are likely to have shared goals if (a) a large order is received which will increase output over the next 12 months by 20 per cent; (b) orders fall such that 20 per cent less production is forecast for the next 12 months.

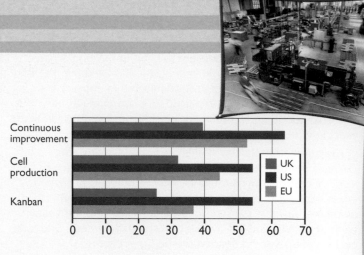

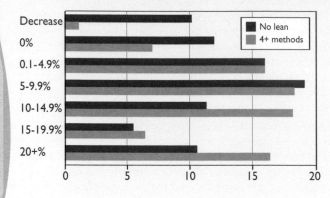

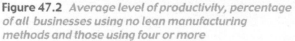

Figure 47.2 *Average level of productivity, percentage of all businesses using no lean manufacturing methods and those using four or more*

Figure 47.3 *Percentage of businesses undertaking lean manuacturing methods*

Adapted from Engineerng Employer's Federation.

orders. The time period over which initial costs is repaid is typically a few months and not years. Kaizen is not the solution to every management problem. But evidence suggests that, where properly implemented, it has a considerable impact on the long term competitiveness of a business.

Suggestion schemes

Another way of involving employees is for management to seek suggestions for improvement from workers. In small businesses, this can be done informally because management is likely to be working alongside employees. In medium to large businesses, management may implement a SUGGESTION SCHEME. Employees are invited to put suggestions for improvements in writing to the management or to a team of managers and workers with responsibility for improvement. Most suggestions are unlikely to work for a variety of reasons. But the ones which do are then implemented.

Quality circles

Businesses might also motivate employees to improve quality and productivity by setting up QUALITY CIRCLES. These are small groups of employees who often work together in a similar area of the business. They are set up to improve continually and maintain the quality of products, services and jobs. They are usually 'first line' workers, such as shop floor workers who meet on a regular basis. Their suggestions are presented to management, who will decide whether to implement changes. These changes are then implemented and monitored by the employees themselves. Some larger businesses have a company wide quality control programme with many quality circles. Originally in the 1950s, when quality circles first appeared in Japan, the focus was on meeting to control quality. However, today their purpose has changed to include any improvement to methods of work.

Just–in–time production (JIT)

JUST-IN-TIME (JIT) production techniques are linked to the holding and use of **stocks** (see unit 45). They were pioneered by the Japanese shipbuilding industry in the 1950s. At the time, they had traditionally held large stocks of steel. They realised that they could hold far less stock if suppliers would deliver more frequently and nearer the time when the stocks would be used in production.

With just-in-time production, stocks levels are held at a minimum. Ideally, a business will hold no stock at all. For example, in a car factory, parts will be delivered several times a day from suppliers straight to points on the production line. Small quantities of stock will therefore be held for a few hours before being replenished. As the cars come off the production line, they will be immediately put on transporters and delivered to car dealers. The car dealers themselves may well have sold the cars prior to arriving. All they do is hold the cars whilst they are prepared for the customer.

Benefits Just-in-time production has a large number of advantages.

- Holding stock is costly to a business. If it has £1 million tied up in stock, that £1 million could have been used elsewhere in the business, for example to reduce debt or invest in new machinery. Stock also needs space to be held, such as in warehouses. Workers will need to be employed to deal with stock. The less stock held, the less space is needed to store stock and the fewer workers need to be employed. Reducing stock levels is likely to improve both cash flow (see unit 28) and profit (see unit 21).
- Stock can deteriorate or disappear (for example through theft) whilst held in storage. Reducing or eliminating stock reduces this problem.
- With reduced or no stock levels, supplies must be of the right quality and delivered on time. For example, if car seats are being delivered three times a day to a car production plant, the whole production could be brought to a halt if one batch of seats is defective or if the delivery is an hour late. Just-in-time production therefore requires **zero defects** (see unit 46) in supplies. Just-in-time techniques are tools for ensuring quality throughout the production process. They require perfect timing for delivery on the part of suppliers.
- Co-operation with suppliers is likely to be improved. Buyers and suppliers have to work much more closely. Some Japanese companies in the UK, for example, have

Just-in-time delivery techniques aren't just confined to car plants or shipbuilders. They are here on the high street being used by Zara, a Spanish fashion retailer which now has over 1 000 outlets throughout Europe, Japan and North America.

In a traditional UK high street fashion store, designers draw up a collection which is manufactured either in the UK or in the Far East. Or buyers from the store chain purchase a range of clothes already designed by the manufacturer. Either way, stock eventually arrives in the store after anything from one to three months after the order is placed. Then the stock might stay on the rails for a few more months if it proves unpopular and end up in a sale where the retailer has to cut its profit margins to off load it to bargain conscious shoppers. UK suppliers tend to give quicker delivery, but are higher cost. Far Eastern suppliers have longer delivery times, but tend to be lower cost.

Zara operates in a different way. It designs and manufactures all the clothes it sells in its own stores. The manufacturing headquarters and factories are on the outskirts of La Coruna in Spain. There are 250 designers and 14 000 production workers. In addition, there is a team travelling the globe, visiting university campuses, discos and other venues to observe what the young and the hip are wearing. That information also gets fed back to Zara's headquarters - often using hand-held computers that transmit images as well as data. From that information, designs are produced and small quantities manufactured which are sent out to stores. Managers of those stores are then in daily contact with head office saying what has been selling and what has not. They reorder quantities of stock which have sold rapidly. If something hasn't sold well, there is not a particular problem because only a small amount of the stock will have been delivered initially and it won't get reordered. Manufacturing back in Spain is geared up to incredibly fast turnaround times from placing of the order by the store manager to delivery.

The result is that Zara has far less stock in its system than a normal fashion retailer. Almost all the stock is sold at full price because most items are produced in response to fast sales of initial stock in stores. Customers are happy because there is a continuous turnaround of new stock in the stores from which they can choose. Zara, despite having higher manufacturing costs than the norm for the industry, has such an efficient supply chain that profit margins are the same as for industry leaders such as Gap. But, by supplying the very latest fashion, its stores tend to sell more per square metre of floor space. It has proved a winning formula.

Adapted from the *Financial Times*, 26.9.2000.

1 **Explain how Zara could be called a 'just-in-time' manufacturer and retailer.**
2 **Assess the financial benefits to Zara of operating a just-in-time system.**

sent in teams to suppliers to identify ways in which the supplier could improve production methods.
- Workers are likely to be more motivated. There are likely to be fewer breakdowns in the production process because of zero defect stocks.

Problems Just-in-time production techniques also have disadvantages.
- The supply chain is highly vulnerable to any disruption. A strike or a disaster such as a fire at a supplier can bring production to a halt very quickly further down the supply chain.
- Large businesses can force suppliers to deliver just-in-time and secure low prices because of the volumes being bought. But small to medium size businesses may be unable to take advantage of both purchasing economies of scale (see unit 42) and just-in-time deliveries. A supplier might charge a higher price per unit for small deliveries compared to large deliveries. The buyer then has to choose between higher priced more frequent deliveries and low priced less frequent deliveries.
- Suppliers may have to accept lower profits if their customers insist on just-in-time deliveries because their delivery costs increase. Even buyers may find that costs associated with accepting deliveries, ordering and paying invoices rise.
- A buyer which is let down in any way by a just-in-time supplier may find its reputation damaged.

Despite these possible disadvantages, just-in-time techniques have become commonplace in industry worldwide. Stock levels have fallen considerably. Large manufacturing businesses in particular have revolutionised their production techniques through just-in-time. This is because there are substantial cost and quality advantages to adopting just-in-time methods.

JIT, along with other lean production practices, has also led to the adoption of people-centred management practices. JIT can only be carried out if workers are empowered to make decisions about stock management. To do this, they might have the authority to order new stock or stop the production line if stock is faulty. They will almost certainly be responsible for their own quality control. Training and working in teams are likely to be central features of any business with JIT.

JIT is also an essential feature of **flexible manufacturing** (discussed more fully in unit 48).

Kanban

KANBAN is a Japanese term which can be translated as 'sign board' or 'visible record'. It is a simple, yet powerful way of controlling the flow of stocks and work in **progress** (see unit 45) through the production system.

In a traditional flow system, work is **pushed** through from start to finish. So on a car production line, 20 car doors might be delivered to a work station each day because that is the number that has been decided beforehand. The result is that stock can build up in areas where production has not been as fast as anticipated. Equally, stock can run out if production has been faster, or the delivery of stock has for some reason been reduced.

With a Kanban system, work is **pulled** through from start to finish. This is because workers at a workstation or production cell are responsible for ordering more stock when it is needed. At its simplest, a workstation has two boxes of stock in use. When one is finished, it is taken back to those making the components with a card showing what component is needed and to where it is to be delivered back. In more complex systems, workers can key in their stock requirements into a computer. This then can tell:

* workers at a previous workstation to manufacture more stock;
* warehouse workers to take stock out of the warehouse and deliver to a point in the factory;
* a supplier to deliver supplies to the factory.

Kanban is a powerful way in which businesses can

minimise the level of stock within the system.
* Stock is only ordered when it is needed.
* Stock cannot build up at points within the system.

It is also a way of empowering workers. They become responsible for ensuring that they have enough stock to work with at any point in time.

Cell production

CELLULAR MANUFACTURING involves production being broken down into small cells, as in Figure 47.4. Cells are usually U-shaped or horse shoe shaped because this minimises the distance that materials have to be transported. Each cell completes a number of tasks which either makes a product or completes a process. Workers within the cell act as a **team** (see unit 36) and often individual workers are multiskilled and so can do the work of other workers in the cell. This allows much greater flexibility if a worker is absent, perhaps because of illness or being on holiday. Multi-skilling also allows workers more variety if they choose to perform a variety of tasks during their work (**job enlargement**, see unit 36).

Production cells are often created by breaking up a traditional production line. Compared to production lines, production cells have a number of advantages.

* The amount of factory space needed for a number of production cells is usually far less than that needed for a production line completing the same work. So factory space can be released for alternative uses.
* Production times are reduced because materials don't have to be transported such great distances. Ideally, cells should be organised so that workers minimise the amount of walking, stretching, handling or carrying that they do.
* Teamworking helps motivate workers. By sharing work and being responsible for quality and output, the team of workers can develop an identity which increases motivation.
* Quality should improve because workers in cells can be more clearly identified as being responsible for particular work. They are also responsible for checking their own work.
* 'Downtime' due to machine breakdowns should be reduced because the team of workers in the cell will

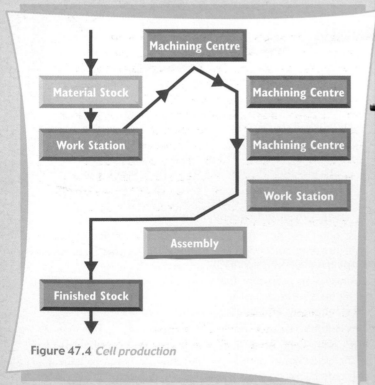

Figure 47.4 *Cell production*

1 Explain why (a) mass production and (b) lean production can both lower costs of production.
2 How can continuous improvement lead over time to large changes?
3 Why is Kaizen associated with (a) empowerment of workers and (b) teamwork?
4 Explain the difference between a Kaizen group and a quality circle.
5 What are (a) the advantages and (b) the disadvantages of holding as small a level of stock as possible?
6 Explain why a Kanban system 'pulls' work through a factory.
7 What is the difference between a production line system and cellular manufacturing system?

co-operate to repair the machine.
- It is easier for management to set targets for workers in a cell than if they were on a production line. On a production line, workers simply have to keep pace with the line.

Cellular manufacturing has become common in UK manufacturing industry since the 1990s. Changing over to production cells has often resulted in considerable increases in **productivity** (output per worker).

'key terms'

Cellular manufacturing - **where production is organised into small cells, each with its own team of workers and equipment.**
Kaizen - **in Japanese, 'continuous improvement' - a production philosophy where a business is committed to making continuous small scale improvements to its way of working, leading to greater efficiency.**
Kanban - **in Japanese a 'sign board' or 'visible record' - a system where new stock is ordered to be made by the production group which requires the stock by the placing of a Kanban card in a stock bin.**
Just-in-time (JIT) production - **where stocks or raw materials, work in progress and finished products are kept to a minimum through supply chain systems which ensure that stocks are delivered only when they are needed.**

Lean production - **a system which attempts to reduce all inputs to a minimum in the production process, from workers to raw materials to factory space to stocks.**
People-centred management - **a management approach which recognises the value and skills of workers and seeks to give them the training and skills needed to undertake their work effectively.**
Suggestion schemes - **where workers are invited to make suggestions about how to improve methods of working, some of which will be implemented by management if they improve efficiency.**
Quality circles - **small groups of workers who meet together regularly to discuss quality issues which affect them and either make suggestions for improvements to management or are empowered to make changes themselves.**

Last summer, Sony did something unusual. It brought production of camcorders back from China to Japan. The move highlights the success of a wide ranging revamp of Sony's global manufacturing and distribution system that has helped to boost the profit margins and competitiveness of its electronics goods.

Sony has been under intense pressure to improve its ability to respond flexibly and speedily to market demand. 'Digitalisation has made the product life cycle even shorter than before', says Tadakatsu Hasebe, president of Sony Logistics. 'In the past, because the market was growing, it was fine to make as much product as you had the capacity (for). But now it is necessary to adjust product to market demand as closely as possible.' Failure to do so results in poor sales and high stock levels of finished goods, which puts pressure on cash flow. 'The key challenge was to cut the time it takes to get product to the end user', says Mr Hasebe.

An important step towards that goal has been the introduction of cell-based manufacturing, where products are made in small lots by small groups, or cells. This system makes it easier to control the volume of production - unlike traditional, mass production factory lines, which are difficult to stop once they are started. Cell based manufacturing, which Sony claims was first developed by Tatsuyoshi Kon, one of its managers, makes it possible to shift quickly from making one camcorder model to another, depending on which is selling better. This is important as Sony makes 200-300 models of camcorder. Cell-based manufacturing is critical to Sony's supply chain management system, which has enabled the group to determine which products are selling well, adjust production accordingly and deliver within a very short time without the need to accumulate vast stocks. Electronics stocks of finished products fell from 923.4 billion Yen in the third quarter of 2000 to 627.5 billion Yen in the third quarter of 2001 and again to 506.5 billion Yen (£2.6 billion) in the third quarter of 2002. 'Inventory (stock) is a business risk in a fast-changing market', Mr Hasebe says. As a result of cutting stocks, cash flow also improves. With the new system, Sony can manufacture a product one day after an order is taken and deliver the product the next day in Japan. If the order is in the US, the product is air-freighted. A customer in the US can place an order for a camcorder accessory online and receive the product, which is made in Japan, 48 hours later.

Adapted from the *Financial Times*, 12.2.2003.

1 Explain what is meant by:
   (a) 'stock'; (3 marks)
   (b) 'cell-based manufacturing'. (3 marks)
2 Outline TWO advantages for Sony of reducing stocks of finished camcorders. (6 marks)
3 Explain why cell-based manufacturing at Sony for camcorders has led to lower stock levels. (8 marks)
4 To what extent, in a world market where customers demand high levels of service and differentiated products, can a company like Sony mass produce any product? (10 marks)

48 Lean production (2)

Industry Forum

Knowledge South Wales Forgemasters is a company which makes components for the automotive industry. In 1998, it called in the Society of Motor Manufacturers and Traders' Industry Forum, at a cost of £9 000, to look at its ring roll cell-making transmission parts. Industry Forum is led by eight master engineers from Honda, Nissan, Toyota, General Motors and Volkswagen.

Application Industry Forum runs master classes for *companies* in how to cut *costs*, improve *production times* and increase *quality*. The master engineers have a long experience of implementing *lean production techniques* and are aware of the *industry benchmarks* for *industrial processes*.

Analysis Nissan's Yoshio Suzuki led the master class. He saw the priority was to reduce job change times, which would improve all productivity measures. Job change time is the time it takes to change the equipment from making one component to another. Every task and piece of equipment was analysed. The gantry was repositioned, tools were given standard places to cut search time and non-vital items were removed. After the first trial, job change times fell from 269 minutes to 160 minutes and then to 90 minutes. The target is 70 minutes, which could improve sales by up to 75 per cent.

Evaluation £9 000 is a small price to pay for such significant increases in productivity. This example shows that there is much work still to be done to bring British manufacturing to world class standards. Unless British manufacturers implement lean production techniques, they are likely to continue to lose competitiveness in world markets.

Adapted from the *Financial Times*, 7.12.1999.

Benchmarking

BENCHMARKING (or BEST PRACTICE BENCHMARKING, BPB) is a technique for comparing business performance. For example, one business may compare how long it takes for its invoices to be paid with another business. Ideally the businesses used for comparison should be those businesses which are 'best in class', i.e. the most efficient in its industry or process. This could mean locally, nationally or internationally. The technique is used in order to implement change. If, on average, your customers are taking 93 days to pay their invoices when for the best business in your industry it is just 43 days, then there must be a reason for this. Benchmarking involves finding out the reasons for the difference in performance and then making changes in your business.

Benchmarking focusses on individual business processes, such as how invoices are dealt with or what rust treatment is given to a piece of equipment. It doesn't focus on a wide range of issues all at once because this would be far too large a task.

Figure 48.1 shows the steps which are followed in a typical benchmarking exercise.

Selection A business selects what process it wishes to improve. Usually, it already has evidence that rival businesses are much more efficient in this area.

Planning The business must then plan how it will carry out the benchmarking exercise. A team of people, preferably those with responsibility for implementing any changes at the end of the process, must be identified. Resources need to be allocated to the team, including time to carry out the exercise and a budget for expenses. Then the team must understand, measure and document the existing process within the business.

Identification Other businesses must then be identified to benchmark against. Usually, the business will be in the same industry, making, say, the same range of products, or having the same potential customers. Sometimes, however, it is useful to compare businesses in other industries. For example, an airline company looking at how to turn round a plane at an airport in the shortest possible time might look at how a Formula 1 racing team makes pit stop changes. Or a train company looking at how best to manage the sale of tickets might look at how airlines manage this.

Agreement An agreement must be reached between the two businesses to allow the benchmarking procedure to take place. The business being benchmarked will want an assurance that all data gathered will be treated confidentially. It will also almost certainly ask for all information gathered to be shared, including the data gathered at the business doing the benchmarking. The advantage to the business being benchmarked of co-operating is that it is likely to see ways from the study of how it could improve its own process. Not all businesses are prepared to be studied by another. Sometimes it is possible within a large business for one part of the business to study the process in another part of the business.

Gathering data Data must now be gathered. Usually this involves at least one visit to the business being benchmarked. Questionnaires, direct observation and print outs of past

Figure 48.1 *The benchmarking process*

[Flowchart boxes:]
- Select a business process
- Plan the benchmarking exercise
- Identify the business or businesses against which benchmarking will take place
- Reach an agreement with the other business or businesses to permit benchmarking
- Gather the data and evidence
- Analyse the data
- Produce an action plan for change and implement it

Textron is a US industrial conglomerate which manufactures a range of products, from helicopters and fastenings to lawn mowers and fuel tanks. Sales last year were £8.4 billion from 15 main business divisions in 40 countries. Traditionally, each business and each division have operated autonomously. But Lewis Campbell, chief executive of Textron, has become convinced that the way to drive the group forward is to share best practices across all 15 business divisions. A team of 500 'black belts' have been trained to cajole employees in different businesses to give up details of their best initiatives to others elsewhere in the group. There has also begun a drive to standardisation. For example, currently there are 154 medical schemes operating in different companies providing private medical insurance for employees. Campbell would like to see that shrink to just one, the one that gives best value for money.

At Eaton, a rival US conglomerate whose products include control equipment, circuit breakers, engine parts and clutches, the chief executive Alexander Cutler has used the Internet to spread best practice. The company has a website accessible to all 48 000 employees that records operating details plus ideas related to ways to improve productivity and quality for the company's 200 worldwide plants. To ensure rigour, the Internet data are reviewed by an internal team of 300 Eaton assessors who visit the plants regularly. "I want to encourage a new culture in the company that people should steal shamelessly (from other divisions) to improve. I reject the the notion that doing this is too complicated', says Mr Cutler.

Adapted from the *Financial Times*, 2.7.2002.

1 **Explain how both Textron and Eaton have attempted to benchmark their business practices.**
2 **Suggest what might be the (a) advantages and (b) disadvantages of benchmarking within a group of companies like Textron rather than benchmarking against companies outside the group.**

performance data are some examples of the ways in which relevant data can be collected.

Analysis The data are then analysed to show the differences in performance between the two businesses and, importantly, why there is this difference in performance.

Action planning An action plan is drawn up showing how change is to be implemented. The action plan must then be put into action.

Benchmarking has a number of advantages.
- It is a technique where a team within a business doesn't have to 'reinvent the wheel'. It can copy or, more likely, adapt best practice to suit its own circumstances.
- An understanding of best practice in the industry can prevent a business from becoming uncompetitive. In the car industry today, for example, benchmarking is a frequently used tool. It has helped US and European car producers to close the gap that had developed between themselves and Japanese car producers in the 1970s and 1980s. It continues to motivate car producers to keep up with their rivals.
- The frequent use of benchmarking helps a business to maintain a 'change culture'. It empowers teams and individual workers to make changes to improve efficiency.

The disadvantages of benchmarking are that:

- it uses up resources within the business which have an opportunity cost (see unit 45);
- the process may not be properly implemented, for example management may not implement the changes recommended in the action plan of the benchmarking team because of the costs.

Re-engineering

RE-ENGINEERING or BUSINESS PROCESS RE-ENGINEERING is in some ways the opposite of Kaizen (see unit 47). It was first put forward by Michael Hammer and James Champy and introduced into UK businesses in the early to mid-1990s. The Kaizen philosophy is that a large change can be achieved over time by making a large numbers of small changes. Re-engineering is a fundamental and large scale change in a business process achieved relatively quickly. It is designed to make immediate and large improvements in performance such as cost, quality or service.

Re-engineering starts with management identifying business

processes which have to be re-engineered. The process and the work practices involved are then changed. When implemented, there are likely to be major gains in efficiency resulting from better use of capital equipment, resource inputs and labour. Typically, there is:

* empowerment of staff lower down the hierarchy;
* decisions being made more quickly by people dealing with the problem;
* several jobs being combined;
* flatter organisational structures with fewer middle managers and fewer levels in the hierarchy;
* work organised around processes rather then staff organised in different departments.

For example, there may be problems with payments being made on time by a business for stock which is purchased. This might be because of poor communication between the production department that handles stocks and the finance department. A traditional solution might be to try to improve communication, perhaps with computers. A re-engineered solution could be to re-engineer the process, so that employees work together in a 'stock payments team' and payments are made by employees who also receive the stock.

Change is often difficult for staff, especially if it is sudden and large scale. Greater efficiencies resulting from re-engineering are likely to lead to workers losing their jobs or changing their job titles. So for re-engineering to be successful, it must have the backing of senior management prepared to cope with these human resource management issues (see unit 38).

Time-based management

TIME-BASED MANAGEMENT is a group of lean production techniques to minimise the use of time in business processes. Time is a scarce resource and has an opportunity cost. This

For the past century Vaillant has been the pioneering name in the heating industry, developing even better systems and products for greater efficiency and reliability. Click on one of the images above for your product information.

1st October 2002. ecoMax pro - the new condensing boiler range for traditional openvent systems availab

Vaillant is Europe's biggest maker of central heating boilers with current sales of €1.7 billion (£1.1 billion). However, traditionally the market has been highly fragmented because there is a huge variation in customer tastes and building standards across the continent. As a result, individual countries' boiler markets have largely been dominated by local suppliers, with cross-border selling much less highly developed than in most other industries.

Since the appointment of joint managing directors in 2000, the company has been determined to use best practice in manufacturing to overcome these obstacles. Boilers will still be developed to meet the set specifications of individual countries, but they will have as many common features (such as burners and controls) as make sense. In this way, the costs of the 'customisation' that is essential in this industry can be minimised, without narrowing the choice for the consumer.

Other major changes have been made in the area of design. For example, the company has 300 research and development staff and 80 component purchasing staff working across sites in Europe. 16 of these have been appointed to keep abreast of trends in eight specific areas of components that are common to virtually all types of boiler, such as gas valves, pumps and heat exchanges.

Another change is that representatives of all parts of the company - marketing, production, R&D and purchasing - are pulled together in teams of up to 30 people to work on new products. At any time, several dozen teams will be working on such initiatives, with the groups meeting periodically - sometimes chartering a light aircraft for a gathering in one of Vaillant's factories - and the rest of the time exchanging information, predominantly in English by phone or email. This fluidity is vital if the company is to maintain its rate of introducing products. In the past three years, the company has replaced four-fifths of its 500 wall-hung models and the aim is to keep up a similar rate of change of 10-15 per cent of products being replaced.

Adapted from the *Financial Times*, 10.12.2002.

1 **Explain why boiler production in Europe has been traditionally high cost.**
2 **How is Vaillant using lean design techniques to speed up and lower the cost of product replacement?**
3 **Discuss the possible benefits of flexible manufacturing to Vaillant.**

can be seen in a number of different areas.

Product development Often, in the past, new product development was a long and slow process. In a large business, the design process typically involved:

- the marketing department which looked at whether there was a market for a potential product;
- the research and development department which developed prototypes;
- the production department which was responsible for seeing whether it could be produced in large enough quantities at the right price and the right quality level.

The process of design tended to be sequential. The idea was considered by the marketing department, then passed to the production department, then passed to the technical department and so on. In contrast, in lean design, the different departments are involved simultaneously with a design project. All departments are working on a project at the same time. This allows the development cycle to be much shorter. Designing products in this way is known as SIMULTANEOUS ENGINEERING.

Flexible manufacturing One of the reasons why **flow production techniques** (see unit 44) tend to lead to lower average costs than **batch production** or **job production** is because time is not lost changing tools or other equipment to make a new product. For example, a chocolate manufacturer could easily lose a day or two days' production when changing from production of one chocolate bar to another using batch production techniques. Machines have to be completely cleaned to prevent contamination and tooling within the machines has to be changed.

FLEXIBLE MANUFACTURING aims to reduce or even eliminate changeover time from one product to another so that it becomes as cheap to produce 10 units of one item, 8 of another, and 12 of a third as 30 units of the same item. On a car production line, the ideal is for every car produced to be unique. It might be the same model with different specifications. Or it might be two or more models being made at the same time. Flexible manufacturing is achieved by using equipment which can be changed from one use to another use very quickly and ideally instantaneously. It also means that workers must be flexible too, having the skills to deal with different products. Flexible manufacturing requires the back-up of other lean production techniques. For example, on a vehicle production line, if there are 14 different sets of doors fitted during a shift, each a different colour, then there must be just-in-time production techniques used to deliver those doors to that work station at the right time. Otherwise flexible manufacturing would require huge levels of stocks. Similarly, every worker must be responsible for the quality of work done.

Just-in-time production Just-in-time (JIT) manufacturing can be seen as another example of time-based management. JIT cuts the amount of time that stocks are held by a business. In a car manufacturing company, for example, car seats may have been held on average 10 days at the factory in the 1970s before being assembled into a car. Today, the average stock time held may be 3 hours because seats are being delivered three times a day to the car plant.

Critical path analysis Time-based management can also be incorporated into more traditional techniques such as CRITICAL PATH ANALYSIS (CPA). This is a technique used to show the shortest time to make a product and the effects of any delays.

For example, an engineering business might take 10 days to design a machine, 20 days to make it, 5 days to deliver it and 2 days to install it. Task must be done in this order. It might take 3 days to install the wiring at the factory where the machine will work. But this task must be carried out at the same time as the machine is being delivered. So the least time (the critical path) it will take to carry out the job is 37 days (10 + 20 + 5 + 2). A delay in any task except the wiring will delay the whole job. But the wiring can be delayed by 2 days (5 - 3) before the whole job is delayed.

Time based management should ensure that the business is able to keep to its timetable. If it finds that there are likely to be delays, then it can use lean techniques to prevent them.

keyterms

Benchmarking (or Best Practice Benchmarking, BPB) - **a technique which compares business practices in one business with those in other businesses, ideally those businesses which are 'best in class' worldwide in order to implement change.**

Critical path analysis - **a method of planning, scheduling and implementing projects to identify minimum times and the effects of delays.**

Flexible manufacturing - **a system designed to allow a number of products and product variants to be produced using the same resources over a short space of time.**

Simultaneous engineering - **where tasks in the whole design process, from initial idea to product launch, are carried out together to save time.**

Re-engineering or business process re-engineering - **a fundamental and large scale change in business processes designed to make immediate improvements in performance, such as cost, quality or service.**

Time-based management - **a group of lean production techniques to minimise the use of time in business processes.**

 checklist

1. Explain how a business might use benchmarking to improve its performance.
2. Compare the advantages and disadvantages of benchmarking.
3. Explain the difference between Kaizen and simultaneous engineering.
4. How might the use of common platforms help contribute to lean design?
5. Explain how a manufacturer of domestic cookers might benefit from the use of flexible manufacturing techniques.

Ford, the world's second largest car maker, has rebuilt its Rouge plant in Chicago. It is a landmark in Ford's history because the Rouge plant was the first Ford plant to be built and it is now the first Ford plant built to use flexible manufacturing techniques. The shift to flexible production will allow workers at the new plant to produce nine different models, giving Ford the ability to respond rapidly to changes in demand. 'It is really a preview of the new Ford Motor Company', said Bill Ford, chairman, while showing journalists the vast plant.

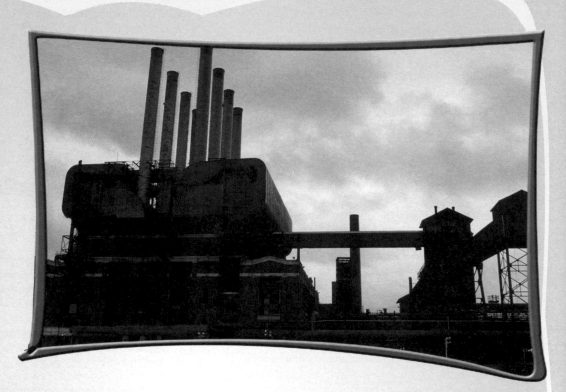

Turning a traditional car plant into a flexible one able to produce multiple models is expensive and time-consuming. The crucial requirement is that cars and trucks be designed along similar lines, sharing the maximum possible number of common parts and having attachment points in the same places. The plants themselves also require heavy investment to make them flexible, with conversion of body shops - where the metal is made - the single biggest cost at $150-200 million. Jigs, which hold the vehicles and parts as they travel along the production line, also need to be flexible so they do not have to be replaced every time the model produced is changed. And robots must be able to run multiple programmes.

Given all the benefits of flexibility, the surprise is that it has taken US manufacturers so long to start emulating their Japanese rivals. Roman Krygier, head of manufacturing and quality at Ford, says Nissan, Honda and Toyota were forced into producing flexible plants to gain economies of scale as they entered the US market. Because they had low volumes from each vehicle, the only way to produce cars cost-effectively was to use one plant for multiple models.

The potential advantages to Ford can be seen from the example of their rival General Motors (GM). It is running three traditional mass production truck plants in Pontiac, Fort Wayne and Arlington overtime to meet the demand for its large pick-ups and sports utility vehicles (SUVs). But in Baltimore and New Jersey, it is running factories at 50 per cent of full capacity making less popular people carriers and older SUVs. If the Baltimore and New Jersey factories were fully flexible they could be converted cheaply and quickly to produce a more popular model, keeping them running full time. Equally, production of the popular large pick-ups and SUVs could be shifted out of the busy factories to cut overtime costs.

Adapted from the *Financial Times*, 13.2.2003.

1 Explain the meaning of the terms:
   (a) 'flexible manufacturing' (3 marks);
   (b) 'mass production'. (3 marks)
2 Outline TWO advantages to Ford of creating flexible production plants. (6 marks)
3 Explain why Ford's use of flexible manufacturing could be seen as the outcome of benchmarking its Japanese rivals. (8 marks)
4 Discuss whether the use of benchmarking could ever give Ford a competitive lead over other car manufacturers. (10 marks)

The farming industry

Knowledge The farming industry worldwide is made up of hundreds of millions of relatively small individual businesses producing crops. In contrast, some of the industries which supply products to the industry, such as seed manufacturers, equipment manufacturers including tractor companies, and fertiliser and pesticide businesses, are relatively large.

Application The farming industry is an example of *perfect competition*. Many small *businesses compete* on *price*, producing *homogeneous products*. It is relatively easy to set up in farming because barriers to entry are low. In contrast, agricultural supply industries, such as tractor companies, are often *oligopolies* with just a few firms dominating national and even international markets. *Barriers to entry* are often high because of the high *cost of capital* to start up *production*.

Analysis The farming industry in the UK has suffered badly since the mid-1990s. The BSE crisis hit sales and prices of British beef. Overproduction of wheat and other cereals led to falling prices. Government production subsidies have also fallen. Farmers have responded by reducing capacity, producing less and by diversifying to obtain alternative sources of income. Agricultural supply industries have also suffered as orders have fallen from cash strapped farmers. They too have reduced capacity.

Evaluation Farmers want to see much higher prices for their production. This would also be likely to benefit their suppliers who could increase sales and push up their prices. The farming industry, however, is likely to see sustained downward pressure on prices as worldwide production expands. In the European Union, farmers will see increased competition from the new member states in Eastern Europe, such as Poland and Hungary. This in turn will make it difficult for agricultural supply industries to force through price increases.

External influences on the business

Businesses don't operate in a vacuum. They are faced on a daily basis with a wide variety of pressures being exerted from outside the business. The main EXTERNAL INFLUENCES, summarised in Figure 49.1, are:

- the degree and nature of competition from other businesses in the market (discussed in this unit);
- the level of interest rates in the economy (see unit 51);
- the exchange rate level (see unit 52);
- the level of inflation in the economy (see unit 53);
- unemployment and the level of economic growth (see unit 54);
- the law, both national and EU law (see unit 55);
- the social and ethical environment (see unit 56-57);
- technological change (see unit 58).

Markets

In Unit 2, it was explained that:
- a market exists in any place where buyers and sellers meet to exchange goods and services;
- the place may be a physical one, such as a street market, or a supermarket. Equally, many transactions today take place by post, fax, over the phone or on the Internet;
- markets can be local, national or international;
- some markets, such as that for cricket bats, are small. In some, such as the car market, sales are so large that they dwarf the output of many countries in the world today.

Competition

Almost every business has to compete in the market place. COMPETITION can take a variety of forms depending upon the particular market in which a business operates. One simple way of characterising competition is the 4Ps of marketing (see unit 1). All other things being equal:
- the lower the price charged, the more sales there will be;
- businesses which sell superior products to their rivals will sell more;

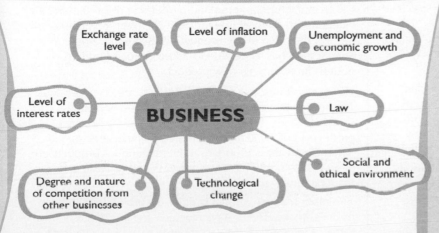

Figure 49.1 *External influences on a business*

It isn't difficult to set up in the grocery industry. A few tens of thousands of pounds will give you a grocery store on a little parade of shops giving personal service to the local inhabitants. But don't expect to survive or make a large profit because the grocery industry today is dominated by just a few supermarket chains.

Supermarket chains are valued in the billions of pounds. They do change hands from time to time. Asda, for example, was bought by the US giant Walmart in the late 1990s. Safeway was the subject of a fierce takeover battle in 2003 and was eventually bought by Morrisons. Somerfield made a huge mistake when it took over the KwikSave chain in the mid-1990s. However, it would be almost impossible now for a new chain to set up from scratch because it is so difficult to acquire sites for large new supermarket stores.

There is no rocket science involved in running a supermarket. Success is about making a few key decisions. What mix of goods are you going to sell? How are your stores going to present the goods for sale? How much are you going to charge and how much will you make in profit on each item? How are you going to organise your supply chain? What price will you offer your suppliers? Different supermarkets offer different mixes. Asda, for example, combines groceries with other goods such as clothes. Its market share has increased in recent years due both to this and to its low price policy.

1 **What is the relative size of businesses in the grocery industry?**
2 **What barriers to entry exist?**
3 **How do supermarkets differ in what they offer?**
4 **To what extent is knowledge about how to run a supermarket chain available to all grocery store and supermarket owners?**
5 **If Tesco increases its sales, what could be the impact on Asda?**

- promotion can help increase sales;
- getting products to customers at the right place and at the right time will stimulate sales.

Market characteristics

Not all markets are the same. They have different MARKET STRUCTURES. These are the main characteristics or features of markets.

Number and relative size of businesses in the market In some markets, such as farming, a large number of businesses compete with each other. None of these businesses is particularly large compared to other businesses in the market. So the market share (see unit 2) of any single business is small.

In other markets, a few businesses dominate the market, even though there might be a large number of other small firms. For example, in the UK washing powder and liquid detergent market, two businesses (Unilever and Procter & Gamble) have over 80 per cent of the market between them.

In some markets, there is only one business, a monopolist. For example, on most railway routes in the UK, there is only one train company operating a service.

Barriers to entry In some markets, it is easy for a new business to set up. Many people each year set up small shops selling everything from groceries to clothes to toys. This is because the BARRIERS TO ENTRY are low. It doesn't cost much to open a shop. The amount of knowledge of the industry required is fairly little. In most cases, there are no special licences or other legal obstacles in the way. In certain markets, barriers to entry are high. In the rail transport industry or mobile telephone industry, the government gives licences to a limited number of businesses to operate. In the drug industry, newer drugs are protected by patent. This prevents other businesses from copying them.

In other markets, the cost of starting up a business are large. Car manufacturing, aeroplane production or oil refining are examples. In the perfume industry, the main companies spend most of the price of the product on marketing. Any new entrant then has to be able to afford to spend millions of pounds launching its new product.

The product In some markets, products are homogeneous. This means that they are the same whichever business produces them. Typically, there are standards to which products conform. So nine carat gold is the same quality whatever business produces it. Homogeneous products are often found in raw materials markets and in basic manufacturing, such as steel.

In other markets, products differ according to which business makes them. A McDonald's meal is different from a Burger King meal. Ford cars differ from Volkswagen cars. Heineken lager is different from Budweiser lager. Individual products or product ranges can then be **branded** (see unit 10). The stronger the perceived difference, the stronger the brand.

Knowledge In some markets, buyers and sellers have access to all the information they need to make rational decisions. Buyers, for instance, would be able to find out the best price in the market. Sellers would have open access to the most efficient methods of production. This is known as having perfect knowledge.

In other markets, knowledge is not available to all. One business might not be able to find out how much a rival business is charging for its products. A consumer might not know which of 20 washing machines washes clothes best. If there is imperfect information in the market, this can give a competitive advantage to some businesses over others.

Interrelationships within markets In some markets, the actions of one business have no effect on another business. Businesses are independent of one another. In farming, the decision by one farmer to plant a field with carrots has no impact on a nearby farm in terms of the price it will receive or how much it produces.

In other markets, such as or car production, increased sales by one business will mean reduced sales by another business if the size of the market remains the same. Businesses are then interdependent.

Classifying markets

Markets can be classified into a number of different types according to their mix of characteristics.

Perfect competition In PERFECT COMPETITION, there are many small businesses, none of which has any significant market share. They are independent of one another. The actions of one business have no effect on other businesses. In a perfectly competitive market, businesses produce homogeneous (i.e. identical) products. So there is no product branding by individual businesses. Barriers to entry are low, allowing freedom of entry to new businesses.

The main example of a perfectly competitive market is agriculture. It is called 'perfect' competition because it is at one extreme of the spectrum of competition.

Perfectly competitive businesses, such as farms, have little or no control over the price at which they sell. They are price-takers. A farmer taking cattle to market has to accept whatever price is set at the auction. A farmer selling potatoes from a farm shop has to price them at roughly the same price as in local shops.

Monopolistic competition In MONOPOLISTIC COMPETITION, there are many small businesses competing in the market. However, there is very weak branding of products. As with perfect competition, barriers to entry are low and so new businesses can set up easily. Branding means that businesses can choose the price they set. They are price-setters. However, their influence over price is weak because the power to brand is weak.

An example of monopolistic competition is the sportswear retail market. There are a few large sportswear chains of shops. But there are also thousands of independent sportswear retailers. Each shop has a brand image and can

Around 90 per cent of all personal computers have one thing in common: they use a version of the Windows operating system produced by Microsoft. There are competitors. Apple has been around for over 20 years and was the first to produce the desktop screen with a mouse as a navigational tool that is standard today. However, Microsoft is less worried by Apple than by a relative newcomer to the market, an operating system called Linux. This is not owned by any single company, having been deliberately written by programmers as a 'free' alternative to Windows. However, companies, such as IBM, produce and sell versions of Linux which are consumer friendly.

Windows has the great advantage that its users are fairly certain they will be able to communicate with another user, for example through email or the Internet. Windows also has by far the largest amount of other software written for it, including the very commonly bought Office software which includes Word, the world's standard word processing package.

Microsoft would like to extend its monopoly into other areas where computer systems are used. First, it has spent large amounts of money producing the X Box, a game machine to rival the PlayStation produced by Sony and the Game Cube produced by Nintendo. Second, it has attempted to get its operating system adopted as the standard for the new third generation mobile phones. The X Box has been successful since launch but is still third by sales behind the PlayStation and Game Cube. As for mobile phones, mobile phone producers have developed their own operating system. They didn't want to get trapped, as PC producers have been, in being forced to buy an operating system from Microsoft where the operating system makes much more profit than the product itself.

Adapted from The Guardian, 29.1.2002.

1 'Microsoft has a virtual monopoly on personal computer operating systems.' Explain what is meant by a 'monopoly', using Windows as an example.

2 'The games machine market is an oligopoly.' Explain what is meant by an 'oligopoly', using the X Box as an example.

3 Suggest why mobile phone manufacturers, such as Nokia, didn't want Microsoft to become a monopoly provider of the software system used in third generation mobile phones.

choose where it wants to position itself in the market in terms of price, products sold, promotion and location. These will all affect how much each sells. For instance, the higher the price charged, all other things being equal, the lower will be the volume of sales.

Oligopoly In OLIGOPOLY, a few businesses dominate the market. For example, there might be 2 000 businesses in the market. But if three of them have 80 per cent of the market between them, then the market would be oligopolistic. Because a few firms dominate the market, they are interdependent. This means the actions of one business affect other businesses. For example, if the market share of one business grows from 25 per cent to 30 per cent, other businesses must have lost market share.

Often oligopolies exist because there are high barriers to entry. In car manufacturing, one barrier is cost. When car assembly plants can cost billions of pounds and a new model £500 million to develop, it is not surprising that there are relatively few businesses in the market. Another major barrier to entry may be the existence of strong brands, often supported by high levels of marketing spending.

Branding is a main characteristic of oligopolistic markets. Brands don't just deter competition. They also allow businesses to charge premium prices and sometimes to earn high profits. So oligopolistic businesses are price setters. Branding, though, most favours the top brand in the market. Being number 2 or number 3 in terms of market share can make it difficult to charge premium prices and earn high profits.

Monopoly With MONOPOLY, there is just one business in the market. An example is a railway company which has the exclusive right to provide a service along a rail route. Water companies might also be monopolies, as they might have the exclusive right to provide water to houses in a particular area.

Monopolies exist because there are barriers to entry to the market. National monopolies in the UK today tend to be ones where the government has legally restricted competition to the market. However, there can be local monopolies for other reasons. For example, in rural areas, there may only be one large supermarket which effectively has a monopoly on supermarket grocery sales. Or a bus operator may provide the only service along a route even though other bus operators may be legally entitled to run a rival service. In both these cases, the market is not large enough to allow two businesses to offer a service a make a profit.

Monopolies may be able to exploit their market by charging high prices and earning high profits. For this reason, governments either make monopolies illegal or monitor their activities to prevent them from exploiting the market. In the UK, a number of industries, such as water, rail and telecommunications, are regulated and maximum prices are set.

Capacity

Capacity is the amount that a business can produce with the resources it owns (see unit 12). For example, a biscuit factory may be able to produce 20 000 packets of biscuits a day.

Capacity utilisation is the proportion of the capacity that is currently being used. If the biscuit factory makes 12 000 packets of biscuits per day, then capacity utilisation is 60 per cent ([12 000 ÷ 20 000] x 100%). Spare or excess capacity is the amount of capacity which is lying idle and is not used. So the biscuit factory making 12 000 packets of biscuits a day would have spare capacity of 8 000 packets or 40 per cent ([8 000 ÷ 20 000] x 100%).

What if the market would actually allow the business to produce and sell 14 000 packets a day? In this case the business has a CAPACITY SHORTAGE of 2 000 packets. It does not have enough capacity to cope with potential orders.

Excess capacity and capacity shortages will affect the strategy of a business.

key terms

Barriers to entry - factors which make it difficult or impossible for businesses to enter a market and compete with existing producers.

Capacity shortage - when a business does not have sufficient resources to meet the demand for its products.

Cartel - a group of businesses (or countries) which join together to agree on pricing and output in a market in an attempt to gain higher profits at the expense of customers.

Collusion - in business, where several businesses (or countries) make agreements among themselves which benefit them at the expense of either rival businesses or customers.

Competition - rivalry between businesses offering products in the same market; competition may take forms such as price competition, distinctive product offerings, advertising and distribution.

Dumping - the sale of products at a price which is below the full cost of production.

External influences - factors outside a business which affect its operation.

Market structures - the characteristics of a market, such as the size of the barriers to entry to the market, the number of businesses in the market or whether they produce identical products, which determine the behaviour of businesses within the market.

Monopolistic competition - a market structure where there is a large number of small businesses producing differentiated, branded products, where barriers to entry are low and businesses are price setters.

Monopoly - a market structure where there is a single business in the market and there are barriers to entry.

Oligopoly - a market structure where a few large businesses dominate the market producing differentiated, branded, products, where barriers to entry are typically high and where businesses are price setters.

Perfect competition - a market structure where there is a large number of small businesses producing identical products, where barriers to entry are low and where businesses are price-takers.

Excess capacity Many businesses suffer falls in sales when the economy experiences a general downturn or recession (see unit 50). During a boom, a business may have installed capacity to cope with a high level of sales. In a downswing, sales are lower and so the business operates at less than full capacity. Alternatively, a business may have been too optimistic about future sales and installed too much capacity. It is then left with spare capacity.

There is a number of strategies a business could use to cope with excess capacity.

- It could use the capacity to produce goods and put the excess into stock. This would only be sensible if the business expected an upturn in demand in the near future to sell off the stock. Stocks cost money to keep (see unit 45). There is also the risk that stocks will remain unsold.
- It could seek out new markets. Tough trading conditions can force businesses to be more creative about their markets. For example, a business might try to export goods abroad.
- It could diversify and use its excess capacity to produce different types of products. For example, a coffee shop chain might introduce new types of food or offer new types of coffee. The risk is that customers will not want to buy the new products. There is also a limit to diversification. A coffee shop chain with excess capacity couldn't diversify into manufacturing coffee pots, for example.
- It could simply increase its marketing efforts in its existing markets. Most likely is that it will lower its prices. Competitors are likely to be suffering similar difficulties and they too couldl be cutting their prices. Lower prices will stimulate demand, but also cut profit margins. However, profits will rise or losses will fall so long as the profit on the extra units sold is greater than the lost profit from lower prices on existing sales.

In a recession, downward pressure on prices is common in markets suffering excess capacity. However, businesses may plan for excess capacity as part of their normal operations. Many UK hotels, for example, have excess capacity during the winter season. Businesses that manufacture for the Christmas market are likely to have excess capacity at the start of the year. So excess capacity is not necessarily a sign that a business is doing badly.

Capacity shortages Just as businesses can suffer from excess capacity, sometimes they can suffer from lack of capacity. In a boom, for example, many businesses may be unable to cope with the number of orders. Businesses can adopt a number of strategies.

- They may be able to delay sending out orders, for example by establishing waiting lists or prolonging delivery dates.
- They may increase prices to dampen demand.
- They could reduce marketing spending, such as advertising.
- In the short term, plant may be run beyond its long term capacity. Workers may be asked to work extra overtime. Shift work may be introduced. Temporary workers may be employed. Regular maintenance work which puts capacity out of use may be postponed.
- If it was judged that demand was going to continue to outstrip capacity in the long term, businesses are likely to invest in extra capacity.

Too little capacity amongst existing businesses combined with rising prices should attract new businesses into the industry. Equally, excess demand may be met from abroad through imports. So having too little capacity can be damaging in the long term to existing businesses because it may introduce new competition into the market.

Fair and unfair competition

Competition between businesses is generally seen as being in the best interests of customers. They can shop around between businesses offering the same or similar products for the best deal. This means that businesses have to offer what the customer wants or face closing down through lack of customers.

In contrast, monopoly is usually argued to be bad for customers. They are forced to buy from one supplier whatever the quality of the product and whatever the prices. The monopolist has enormous power over customers and acts to maximise the benefits to itself.

Monopolies, therefore, tend to be controlled by governments. In the USA, they are illegal. In the UK and the rest of the European Union, monopolies can exist legally so long as they do not exploit customers.

A monopolist exists where there is only one firm in a market. However, firms in a market can act as if they were a monopoly by COLLUDING. This means they get together, usually to fix prices and output in a market. They then have formed a CARTEL. For example, a group of firms making vitamins may fix a high price between themselves at which they will sell vitamins to customers. Then they have to restrict output between themselves to sustain those high prices.

There are many ways in which firms can compete unfairly. For example, a dominant business may want to get rid of an existing competitor or stop a new competitor setting up. To do this it might engage in predatory pricing (see unit 15). This is where it cuts its prices and often makes losses for a time. The weaker firm is forced either to lose sales or cut its prices too. Either way, it makes such high losses that it is forced to leave the industry. The dominant firm then puts back up its prices and returns to making high profits.

Sometimes, businesses complain about 'unfair competition'

✓ checklist

1. How do businesses compete with each other?
2. Explain THREE possible barriers to entry to a market.
3. What is the difference between a branded product and a homogeneous product?
4. What is the difference between (a) a perfectly competitive market and a monopoly; (b) an oligopolistic market and one with monopolistic competition?
5. How might the marketing strategy of a business be affected if it has excess capacity?
6. Explain TWO ways in which businesses can engage in unfair competition.

from foreign companies. For example, steel producers in Russia might offer lower prices to UK customers than UK steel manufacturers. One reason why foreign businesses might be able to offer lower prices is because they pay their workers much lower wages. This might give them a competitive advantage rather than being an example of 'unfair competition'. However, some foreign governments give subsidies to their domestic producers which result in lower prices. This would be regarded as giving those producers an unfair advantage.

Equally, sometimes foreign producers sell their products for export at below the full cost. This is called DUMPING. Persistent dumping is also usually seen as unfair competition.

Colluding to fix prices is illegal in the UK unless it has been agreed with government authorities, in this case the Office of Fair Trading (OFT). So it was not surprising that Argos and Littlewoods, two of Britain's top toy sellers, were fined £22 million by the OFT in February 2003. They had colluded to fix prices with Britain's largest toy manufacturer Hasbro, maker of toys such as Monopoly and Action Man.

Hasbro operates a dual distribution system for its products. It sells directly to its largest buyers, including Argos, Littlewoods Index, Toys 'R' Us and Woolworth's. Then it also sells to wholesalers, who in turn sell on to independent shops and smaller chains.

Hasbro, Argos and Littlewoods wanted to maintain their profit margins. They were afraid that wholesalers might sell Hasbro products on to small retailers at a low price. This could have meant small retailers being able to sell at lower prices than large retailers such as Argos and Littlewoods. Worse still, large aggressive competitors such as Asda, the supermarket chain, had already been buying Hasbro products from the 'grey' or unofficial market via retailers or wholesalers at lower prices than those offered by Hasbro directly. This would have hit sales at Argos and Littlewoods and therefore their profits. It would also have hit Hasbro because it would have come under pressure from Argos and Littlewoods wanting to negotiate lower prices to keep them competitive against the likes of Asda.

So management at Hasbro between early 2001 and July 2001 signed agreements with 10 wholesalers preventing the wholesalers from selling Hasbro toys and games to retailers for less than Hasbro's list price without Hasbro's permission. Retailers buying from wholesalers would have to buy at the price that Hasbro's dictated. This meant that Argos and Littlewoods could charge high prices and still be more price competitive than other retail outlets. Competition in the market was arguably controlled to the benefit of Argos, Littlewoods, Hasbro and their profits.

Adapted from the *Financial Times*, 30.11.2002 and the *Daily Mail*, 20.2.2003.

1 Explain what is meant by the terms:
   (a) 'competition in the market'; (3 marks)
   (b) 'collusion'. (3 marks)
2 To what extent was competition in the UK toy market limited the price fixing arrangements in 2001? (12 marks)
3 Discuss the possible impact on Hasbro UK of the abandonment of the price fixing agreements. (12 marks)

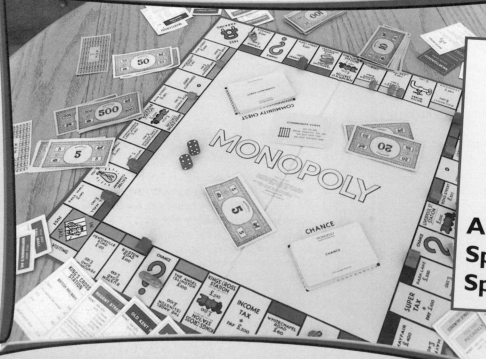

ARGOS CATALOGUE PRICE FOR MONOPOLY

Autumn 1999 £14.99
Spring 2001 £17.99
Spring 2003 £13.99

UK recession and boom

Knowledge In 1991, the UK economy was in trouble. Unemployment had risen to 3 million and output in the whole economy was shrinking. In 1999, in contrast, the economy was doing well. Unemployment had fallen below 1.5 million and output in the whole economy was growing at a historically fast level.

Application In 1991, the *economy* was in a deep *recession*, sometimes called a *depression*. *Recovery* began in 1992, but it wasn't until the late 1990s that the *economy* began to enjoy a *boom*.

Analysis For many businesses, the recession of 1990-92 was a disaster. Some were forced to close because they became unprofitable. Other loss making businesses only survived by borrowing more or running down their reserves. For most businesses, profits fell as less was sold. In contrast, the boom years of the late 1990s saw high profits and growing sales. Confidence in the economy led many businesses to increase their investment spending. In particular, there was a boom in spending on ICT (information and communications technology).

Evaluation Businesses would prefer not to have to cope with a cycle of boom and bust in the economy. By creating uncertainty, it makes it difficult to plan for the future. The majority of businesses would prefer the economy to be in boom. Then they can see fast growth in sales and growing profits.

Economic growth and the business cycle

For the past 50 years, the UK economy has grown at an average rate of 2.5 per cent. ECONOMIC GROWTH is measured by changes in the size of NATIONAL INCOME. This is the value of total income in the economy. It is also equal to the value of total spending and total production or output. There is a number of different ways of calculating national income. The method most often used by economists and the media is GROSS DOMESTIC PRODUCT or GDP.

Economic growth means that more is produced. In turn, this means that households and individuals can, on average, consume more goods and services. The standard of living enjoyed by the typical family today is far higher than 25 or 50 years ago as Figure 50.1 shows.

The business cycle

GDP does not rise at a steady rate each year. There are fluctuations and in some years the level of GDP may even fall. These fluctuations tend to occur on a regular basis and follow the same broad pattern. This is known as the BUSINESS CYCLE or TRADE CYCLE or ECONOMIC CYCLE. There are four phases to the business cycle, shown in Figure 50.2.

Boom In a BOOM, the economy is doing well.
- Output is high and the economy is growing strongly.
- Consumer spending is high. Also consumers are willing to borrow to finance their purchases.
- House prices are likely to be growing, helped by high mortgage lending by banks and building societies.
- Unemployment is low and businesses may find it hard to recruit new workers.
- Wages are likely to be rising at a fast rate, as businesses compete to employ a limited pool of workers.
- Strong growth in demand for goods and services, combined with above average increases in

Figure 50.1 *Income per person at constant 2001 prices, £, UK 1956–2004. Income is GDP at constant 2001 market prices*
Adapted from *Economic Trends*, ONS.

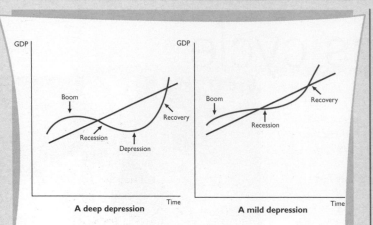

Figure 50.2 *The stages of the business cycle. In a cycle where GDP falls over several quarters, the economy will experience a depression. In a milder cycle, recession is characterised by a less harmful fall in growth of GDP.*

wages, might increase inflation rates. Inflation (see unit 53) is the rise in the general level of prices in the economy.

● With many domestic businesses working at full capacity, they could find it difficult to provide all the products that customers want to buy. So demand for imports might grow at a faster than average rate.

● There might be bottlenecks in certain sectors of the economy. This is where customers want to buy products, but they aren't available in sufficient quantities from domestic producers or importers. Delivery times might be longer. In some industries, waiting lists may develop.

● Businesses, encouraged by strong demand, will tend to increase their investment spending to increase their capacity.

● Record numbers of new businesses will be created, attracted by the possibility of earning high profits.

Recession In a RECESSION or DOWNSWING or DOWNTURN or ECONOMIC SLOWDOWN, the rate of growth of the economy begins to fall.

● Lower growth in demand will cause unemployment to rise, which in turn will lead to even lower demand growth.

● Wage increases will start to slow and businesses will find it more difficult to push through price increases. So the rate of inflation will start to fall. Some sectors of the economy might be more affected than others.

● Many businesses will see a fall off in growth of sales and some will see an absolute fall.

● Profit growth will falter and could become negative.

● The rate of growth of imports will fall as the the rate of growth in overall spending by UK customers slows.

Depression The bottom of the business cycle has a number of different names. If economic growth becomes negative, i.e. GDP falls, then it tends to be called a DEPRESSION or SLUMP. The last major prolonged depression in the UK economy occurred during the 1930s. However, there were short depressions in 1974-75, 1980-82 and 1990-92.

When GDP is still growing, but at a relatively low rate at the bottom of the cycle, this phase is usually given the same name as the downswing, i.e. a **recession**. So a recession here refers both to the slowdown in economic growth and its bottoming out.

At the bottom of the business cycle:
● unemployment is relatively high and inflation relatively low;
● low increases in demand or, at worse, falls in demand will lead to workers being laid off;
● it will be difficult for businesses to increase their prices without losing sales;
● investment by businesses will be low and there will spare capacity in the economy.

Recovery In a RECOVERY or UPSWING, the economy begins to pick up again, and:
● the rate of growth of GDP starts to increase or moves from being negative to positive;
● unemployment begins to fall as businesses take on more workers to cope with the rise in economic activity;
● inflation might start to increase as the rate of growth of demand increases;

Aga Foodservice makes cookers and commercial kitchen equipment. Its most well known products are Rayburn and Aga cookers. In January 2003, it announced that the company had performed well over the past 12 months despite growing evidence of recession in both the UK and US markets. In particular, sales of Aga branded cookers exceeded 9 000 a year for the first time, putting it well on track to reach its 10 000 a year target.

However, the company is vulnerable if recession really takes hold. On the commercial side, it could see sales of equipment to catering companies, hotels and restaurants fall as they cut back on their investment. On the consumer side, homeowners would quickly cut back on luxury expenditure like a £6 000 Aga cooker if wage increases and bonuses fell, whilst the threat of unemployment became more of a reality.

Adapted from The Independent, 17.1.2003.

1 *Explain why, in a recession, Aga could 'see sales of equipment to catering companies, hotels and restaurants fall'.*

2 *Explain why homeowners might buy fewer products from Aga Foodservice in a recession.*

3 *Aga and Rayburn are both strong consumer brands. To what extent might this help Aga Foodservice survive a recession better than its competitors?*

Wax Lyrical, the candle shops chain, became the first significant high street casualty of the economic slowdown yesterday when its US parent called in the receivers.

Blyth, one of the world's biggest makes of candles, said it could no longer sustain Wax Lyrical's losses as department stores ate into its market share and customers stayed away because of the slowdown. The company said it had taken the decision to abandon Wax Lyrical after disappointing sales in the run-up to Christmas. Administrative receivers have been appointed, making it likely that some or all of the 35 outlets will be closed and up to 175 jobs could be lost.

Wax Lyrical was set up in 1990 by the management consultants Marjorie Bannister and Mark Chessel after seeing the variety of decorative candles used in Icelandic homes. With the help of the prolonged upswing in the economy from 1992, the concept grew from a single store in Richmond, south-west London, to be the biggest chain of its kind, with stores from Glasgow to Brighton. It has annual sales of £11 million.

Adapted from *The Independent*, 28.12.2002.

1 **(a) Explain why the 'economic slowdown' led to lower sales for Wax Lyrical.**
  (b) Explain THREE other ways in which the economic slowdown has had an impact on the company.
2 **Discuss whether the economic slowdown was the main factor in causing Wax Lyrical to fail.**

- businesses will begin to increase their investment spending as business confidence increases.

Causes of changes in the level of economic activity

The causes of the business cycle are complex. Major slumps in the UK are arguably caused by international trade. In the 1930s, the Great Depression was triggered by a slump in the US economy, which led to a fall in UK exports. This was made worse by many countries, including the USA, putting up trade barriers such as taxes on imports (called **tariffs**) or limits on the amount that could be imported (called **quotas**). In the 1970s and 1980s, the two depressions of 1975-6 and 1980-82 were arguably caused by steep rises in the price of oil on world markets. On the other hand, the depression of 1990-92 was caused by the British government putting up interest rates to 15 per cent to reduce rising inflation. The depression was made worse by an exchange rate of the pound which was too high, hitting exports.

This does not explain why economies recover but then go back into recession on a regular basis, about every five years for the UK economy. There is a number of factors which can cause these regular fluctuations.

Consumer durables During the recession phase of the business cycle, households will delay buying consumer durables. These are consumer products, such as furniture, cookers, carpets, television sets and cars which are used up (or consumed) over a number of years. This causes a fall in growth of demand for these products or even a negative growth in demand, i.e. there is a fall in sales.

As the recession progresses, there comes a point when some households are forced to replace consumer durables. A car, for example, might cost so much to repair this time that it is better to buy a new car. This is often helped by government policy. At the bottom of the cycle, government often cuts interest rates to stop the economy falling further into recession. Consumer durables are often bought on credit. Low interest rates reduce repayments and so encourage consumers to buy.

At the top of a boom, in contrast, the government often raises interest rates to slow down the economy and reduce inflation. This rise in interest rates chokes off demand for credit and so buying of consumer durables falls.

Stock levels At the top of a boom, businesses will expand production. However, small falls in the rate of economic growth will leave them with excess stocks. These might be finished goods which they can't sell. Or businesses might have bought in stocks of raw materials which, because of lower demand for their products, they haven't used up.

Businesses will then start to DESTOCK, i.e. reduce their stock levels. This can have a significant effect on demand. Assume that a business suffers a small fall in sales and ends up with two weeks' worth of extra raw material stocks. At some point it will reduce its stock orders or it might simply cancel stock deliveries for two weeks. This has a knock-on effect on suppliers. A customer that cancels two weeks' worth of orders can lead to a significant downturn in production. This effect is then magnified because reducing stock is an easy way of stemming a cash flow crisis (see units 27 and 28). Businesses in financial trouble in a recession can get much needed cash to survive by running down their stocks. Destocking then fuels a downward spiral in demand in the economy.

At the bottom of the cycle, there is a point when businesses can no longer destock without going out of business. Many will be operating with too little stock for greatest efficiency. So stock buying will start to increase. Once this happens, there is an upward spiral of spending which contributes to recovery and eventually boom.

Investment At the top of a boom, businesses will be investing to expand their capacity. However, growth in production can become unsustainable with bottlenecks emerging. For example, very low unemployment means that some businesses will be unable to recruit all the labour they need. Suppliers may not be able to keep up with all the orders they receive and will delay deliveries. New production capacity, the result of that extra investment, will come onstream which is not fully utilised. At this point, some businesses will cut back on their investment to better match their production and capacity. Also at the top of a boom, the government may have put up interest rates if it feels the need to reduce inflationary pressures in the economy. Higher interest rates increase the cost of borrowing to finance new investment. So some businesses will abandon investment plans.

If investment spending begins to fall, this reduces demand in the economy. Businesses which make investment goods, such as construction companies building offices and factories or machine tool manufacturers, will suffer first. They could lay off workers, which further reduces demand in the economy. This leads to a downward spiral known as a recession.

At the bottom of the business cycle, businesses will have been putting off investment because of financial difficulties. However, there will come a point when they have to invest to replace worn out capital equipment. This decision may be helped by low interest rates set by government more worried about recession than inflation. A small increase in investment starts an upward spiral of demand in the economy. More spending by one business leads to more jobs and more spending.

The impact of the business cycle on business

Changes in the level of economic activity affect all businesses. But some are affected more than others.

Output The major impact of the business cycle is on output and sales. In a boom, output and sales will be growing.

In a recession, growth will be sluggish at best. At worst, output and sales will fall. Some businesses will be more affected than others. Businesses that make or sell consumer necessities (i.e. products with a low income elasticity of demand, see unit 17), such as food, gas or petrol will not be too affected. People will continue to buy these products. Businesses which make luxury products or products whose purchase can be delayed, such as restaurant meals or cars, will suffer more.

Profit In a boom, it is easier for even inefficient businesses to make a profit. Markets are buoyant and there is often little pressure to lower prices.

In a recession, inefficient businesses or those making products that are not necessities can often make losses.

Business start ups, expansion and closures In a boom, with sales and profits relatively easy to make, there is likely to be a high number of business starts up. Existing businesses might expand.

In a recession, businesses are forced to close down or abandon investment and expansion plans. Many businesses will contract in size, closing unprofitable areas. In a prolonged recession, there will be far more businesses closing down than starting up.

Employment In a boom, businesses will tend to take on workers to cope with expanding demand. However, recruitment may be difficult because unemployment is low and there are fewer workers looking for jobs. There will also be pressure on businesses to raise wages to stop staff leaving for better paid jobs.

In a recession, businesses will tend to reduce their workforces. Staff leaving may not be replaced, a process known as **natural wastage** (see unit 38). There may also be a need for compulsory redundancies.

Stocks and investment In a boom, stock levels and investment will be high, as explained above.

In a recession, both will fall, typically at a faster rate than the fall in demand.

Government and the business cycle

The government often intervenes to reduce the impact of the business cycle through:

- FISCAL POLICIES - policies on government spending, taxes and government borrowing;
- MONETARY POLICIES - policies on interest rates, the price of money.

In boom periods In a boom, the government is likely to be worried about rising inflation. So it will tend to reduce the impact of the government sector on demand. It can do this by reducing its spending or by raising taxes. The effect will be to reduce the amount it has to borrow (if spending is greater than its revenues including taxes) or increase the amount it saves (if revenues are greater than spending).

Control of monetary policy today lies with the Bank of England. In a boom, if inflation is rising above the target rate of 2.5 per cent, it will tend to increase interest rates. This dampens demand for borrowing and hence spending on investment and on consumer durables.

In recessions In a recession, the government is likely to be worried about rising unemployment. So it will tend to increase its spending or lower taxes, or some combination of both.

Inflation is likely to be low and so the Bank of England will be able to push down interest rates. This will increase demand, particularly for investment goods and consumer durables.

checklist

1 Explain the link between the standard of living and economic growth.
2 What are the differences between (a) a boom and a depression, (b) a recession and a recovery?
3 Explain possible causes of major slumps in an economy.
4 How can each of the following affect the level of economic activity: (a) consumer durables; (b) stocks; (c) investment?
5 Explain how businesses might be affected by a recession.
6 How might government react to a recession?

keyterms

Boom - the peak of the business cycle, when the economy is growing fast and unemployment is low but there could be problems with rising inflation.

Business cycle or trade cycle or economic cycle - regular fluctuations in the level of output of the economy, going from boom through recession and depression to recovery.

Depression or slump - the bottom of the business cycle when economic growth is negative and there is high unemployment; if economic growth remains positive at the bottom, then it is usual to refer to a recession rather than a depression

Destocking - when a business reduces its levels of stock held.

Economic growth - the change in the productive potential of the economy; it is usually measured by changes in national income and in particular GDP.

Fiscal policy - policies by government on government spending, taxes and government borrowing.

Gross Domestic Product (GDP) - the commonest way in which national income is measured.

Monetary policy - policies implemented by the Bank of England on interest rates, the price of money.

National income - the value of total income in the economy; it is also equal to the value of total spending and total production or output.

Recession or downswing or downturn or economic slowdown - when the rate of economic growth begins to fall and unemployment begins to rise.

Recovery or upswing - when the rate of economic growth begins to increase following a recession or depression and unemployment begins to fall.

The UK economy in 2000 was still in boom after a long period of economic growth since 1992. Businesses were generally doing well and consumer confidence was strong. The housing market was booming with a record number of houses being bought and sold.

This benefited Silentnight Holdings Plc. The company was the market leader in two sectors of the UK domestic furniture market: assembled cabinet furniture and beds. Sales on ongoing operations increased in value by 4.7 per cent. Of this, sales by value of beds increased by more than 9 per cent. In contrast, sales of cabinet furniture were disappointing, with turnover falling by 3.3 per cent.

However, overall profits fell. For ongoing operations, profit fell by £1.4 million, an 8.5 per cent fall. There was a variety of reasons for falling profits. One was that the company spent £700 000 on a national television advertising campaign for Silentnight Beds, the first television advertising campaign for a number of years. It was designed to reinforce brand awareness and lead to higher sales in future. Another was high investment of £9.7 million in manufacturing plant and factory development in order to maintain the company's competitive position and to improve efficiencies.

The average number of workers employed increased from 3 760 to 4 071 over the year. Part of this increase was due to the expansion of the company. During the year, it took over Ducal, a manufacturer of up market mainly pine furniture, and Cornwell Parker, manufacturer of the Parker Knoll range of furniture. Although both were loss making businesses, Silentnight intends to turn round both operations and make them profitable.

Adapted from Silentnight Holdings plc, *Annual Report and Accounts*, 2001.

1 Explain the meaning of the terms
  (a) 'boom'; (3 marks)
  (b) 'economic growth'. (3 marks)
2 Discuss possible ways in which the economic boom affected the company. (12 marks)
3 To what extent might the company have been affected if the UK economy had gone into recession after 2000? (12 marks)

The Bank of England and interest rates

Knowledge In February 2003, the Bank of England announced a cut in its interest rate from 4 per cent to 3.75 per cent. This was the first change in interest rates in 15 months.

Application The *Bank of England interest rate*, called the *base rate*, is important because it strongly influences the *rates* of *interest* which *banks* and *building societies* charge on *saving* and *borrowing*. Those *rates of interest* have an important impact on *spending* on *consumer durables*, *investment* by *businesses*, *stock levels* and the *exchange rate*.

Analysis The small fall in interest rates in January 2003 was important psychologically for consumer and business spending. It signalled that low interest rates were likely to stay in the short term. This encouraged consumers to continue borrowing at high levels, preventing a fall in sales by businesses. It also encouraged businesses to continue investing. Sales would remain buoyant and the cost of borrowing to finance investment would remain low.

Evaluation Low interest rates are generally welcomed by businesses. At 3.75 per cent, UK interest rates were unlikely to fall much further. However, many businesses would probably have been better off with even lower interest rates to reduce the cost of their borrowing further and to encourage sales.

Interest and interest rates

If a business or an individual borrows money, they usually have to pay **interest** on the loan. Equally, if they put their savings into a bank or building society, they expect to receive interest.

The INTEREST RATE is the price of borrowing or saving money. For example, if a small business borrows £10 000 from a bank for one year, and the interest rate is 7 per cent, it has to pay £700 in interest. Equally, if a business has £1 million in the bank for a year which it uses as working capital, and the rate of interest the bank offers is 3 per cent, it will earn £30 000 in interest.

Different interest rates

A business might be able to borrow money on overdraft at 6 per cent. If it took out a five year loan, the interest rate might be 7 per cent. A consumer buying a house might be offered a mortgage rate of 8 per cent. The interest rate on a credit card might be 15 per cent.

These are just four of the thousands of interest rates in an economy. Each interest rate is set within a market for money. In each market, there is a **demand** for money. This comes from those who want to borrow money. There is also a **supply** of money from those who want to lend money. The forces of demand and supply will fix the price of money in that market, which is the interest rate.

Many money markets are influenced by the rate of interest set by the central bank of a country. In the UK, the central bank is the Bank of England. It has the power to fix the rate of interest charged and offered by the major banks in the UK on short term loans and savings. Banks such as Barclays or HSBC will change their BASE RATE when the Bank of England declares a change in interest rates. The base rate of a bank is the rate around which all its other interest rates are structured. For short term savings with the bank, it will offer interest rates below the base rate. For borrowing, it charges above the base rate. The profit it makes out of borrowing and lending has to come from the difference between the lower rate of interest it gives to savers and the higher rate of interest it charges to borrowers.

Base rates are linked to other rates of interest in the economy. When base rates fall, so do long term rates of interest. The rate of interest on other types of borrowing, such as borrowing through a credit card, also tends to fall. But there is no direct link between these other interest rates and the base rates set by the Bank of England. So short term interest rates can change and long term interest rates can remain unaffected. Sometimes, long term interest rates can be rising when short term interest rates are falling. It depends on market conditions.

Effect on business overheads

Changes in interest rates are likely to affect the overheads of a business. Interest charges are part of overhead costs (see unit 21). If interest rates rise, businesses are likely to have to pay higher interest payments on their borrowing. For example, a business might borrow £10 000 on overdraft. The annual payments on this would rise from £600 to £700 if the rate of interest rose from 6 to 7 per cent a year.

Not all borrowing is at variable rates of interest. Variable rates mean that banks or other lenders are free to change the rate of interest on any money borrowed. Many loans to businesses are at fixed rates of interest. This is where the bank cannot change the rate of interest over the agreed term (the time over which the loan will be paid off) of the loan. A rise

Dalton's is an industrial manufacturer of canning products. It currently has an overdraft of £1.2 million and loans of £4.3 million. Of these loans:

- £1.3 million are variable rate loans, with interest at 2 per cent above base rate;
- £1 million is at a fixed rate of 8 per cent;
- the remaining £2 million is at a fixed rate of 9 per cent.

1 **Explain why interest on borrowings is an overhead cost for Dalton's.**

2 **Base rates in the economy fall from 6 per cent to 5 per cent. As a result the overdraft rates for Dalton's falls from 7 per cent to 6 per cent. Calculating the change in interest payments, explain how this will affect the company's overhead costs.**

in interest rates in the economy won't affect the overheads of a business with only fixed term loans. But, if a business wanted to take out new loans, it would have to pay the higher rates of interest the bank or other lender was now charging. So overhead costs would rise.

Effect on investment decisions

Changes in the rate of interest affect the amount that businesses invest, for example in new buildings, plant and machinery. There are four main reasons for this.

The cost of loans Investment projects are often financed through loans. A rise in interest rates increases the cost of borrowing money. So projects financed this way will find that the total costs have risen, reducing profitability. This might be enough to persuade some businesses to shelve their investment plans. Total investment in the economy will then fall.

Attractiveness of saving Businesses have the alternative of putting their funds into savings schemes rather than investing in machinery or buildings, for example. A rise in interest rates makes putting money into financial assets relatively more attractive. For example, if interest rates rise from 5 to 8 per cent, a business might decide to shelve an investment project

and save the funds instead.

Paying off existing loans A rise in interest rates will increase the cost of existing variable rate borrowing. A business could choose to pay off existing loans rather than increase its investment. This will reduce its costs. It also reduces the risk associated with borrowing.

A fall in demand A rise in interest rates is likely to reduce total spending in the economy, as explained below. This might affect the profitability of many investment projects. For example, a business might forecast that an investment project would be profitable with 20 000 sales a year. But if sales were projected to be only 15 000 a year because of a downturn in demand, then the investment project could be unprofitable and might not go ahead.

Effect on demand

The level of interest rates affects aggregate demand (i.e. total demand) for goods and services in the economy. A rise in interest rates will tend to push down aggregate demand. A fall in interest rates will tend to increase demand.

Businesses are directly affected by changes in demand. When demand falls, their sales go down because less is being bought. If demand rises, businesses receive more orders and more sales.

There are many different ways in which changes in interest rates lead to changes in the sales of businesses.

Domestic consumption Consumers will be hit by a rise in interest rates. The cost of loans will rise. This will deter consumers from buying goods bought on credit, such as cars, furniture and electrical equipment. These goods are known as CONSUMER DURABLES because they are 'used up' over a long period.

In the UK, people who have a mortgage (a loan to buy a house) are also likely to see their monthly repayments rise because most mortgages are variable rate loans. Existing mortgage holders will then have less to spend on other goods and services. Some potential new home buyers will be put off because they can't afford the repayments, directly hitting the new housing market. If unemployment begins to rise because of less spending, consumer confidence will fall. This will make consumers even less willing to take out loans and spend.

Domestic investment As explained above, businesses are likely to cut back plans for new investment if interest rates rise. Investment goods, like new buildings or machines, are made by businesses. So these businesses will see a fall in their demand.

Stocks Businesses keep stocks of raw materials and finished goods (see unit 45). Stocks cost money to keep, because a fall in stock levels could be used to finance a fall in borrowing and interest payments. So a rise in interest rates will increase the cost of keeping stock. This will encourage businesses to destock, i.e. reduce their stock levels. This will be especially true if the rise in interest rates has hit demand in the economy. With fewer sales, less needs to be produced. So less stock needs to be kept. But cutting stock reduces orders for businesses further up the chain of production. For example, a retailer cutting stocks affects demand from its suppliers. Destocking due to higher interest rates will therefore cause a

Bill Lockington was devastated when his business went up in flames. He made a range of tyres, manufactured from existing worn out tyres. His 'retreads' had proved popular with customers because of their high quality and low prices compared to brand new tyres. Due to the high cost of insurance, he was uninsured at the time of the accident and it looked as though ten years' hard work had come to an abrupt end.

However, having got over the psychological shock of seeing £250 000 worth of equipment and stock destroyed overnight, he decided that it was possible to rebuild the business. Two important things had not disappeared. First, he still had a list of customers who wanted to buy his tyres. Second, he had the knowledge and a skilled workforce to produce quality retreads. Low interest rates were vital to success too. He could not have afforded to borrow the money to restart the business if he could not have borrowed at 7 per cent from his bank. The retread business was also highly dependent on buoyant consumer confidence. Low interest rates encouraged customers to buy vehicles and motorcycles and so create the demand for retreads in the longer term.

Even so, he had to make economies. Before the fire, he had built up stocks worth £100 000 of used tyres. Such large levels of stock were unnecessary for the efficient running of the business. His new business started with just £20 000 worth of stock.

1 **Explain carefully how low interest rates affected Bill Lockington's business.**
2 **Suggest why he only bought £20 000 worth of stock to restart the business when previously he had held £100 000 worth of stock.**
3 **Discuss whether Bill Lockington could have recovered from the fire if interest rates had been high at the time.**

fall in demand throughout much of industry.

Exports and imports As explained in unit 52, a rise in interest rates tends to lead to a rise in the value of one currency against others. A rise in the pound, for example, will make it harder for UK businesses to export profitably. At the same time, foreign firms will find it easier to gain sales in the UK domestic market because they will be able to reduce their prices. The result is likely to be a fall in exports and a loss of sales to importers in the domestic market. Both will reduce

demand and hit UK businesses.

Variable impact on businesses

Changes in interest rates affect different businesses in different ways. Businesses that are most likely to be affected are those which:
- have high levels of borrowing at variable rates of interest;
- sell consumer goods, typically bought on credit;

✓checklist

1 A business has borrowed £100 000 on overdraft. Bank base rates rise. How is this likely to affect the amount of interest the business pays?
2 What is the difference between variable and fixed rates of interest for a business that has borrowed money?
3 Explain briefly why the investment plans of a business may change if there is a fall in the rate of interest.
4 (a) How might consumers react to a fall in the rate of interest and (b) why might this benefit businesses?
5 Why might businesses destock if interest rates rise?
6 Why might a fall in interest rates lead to a change in export orders?

keyterms

Base rate - the rate of interest around which a bank structures its other interest rates. A rise in the base rate will result in a rise in most saving and borrowing rates and vice versa.
Consumer durables - consumer goods such as televisions, furniture and cars which are used over a long period of time. They are often bought on credit.
Interest rate - the price of borrowing or saving money. There are many different interest rates charged in an economy because there are many different markets for borrowed funds.

- are directly linked to the housing market, such as house builders;
- produce investment goods for other businesses;
- depend on exports or are in markets where competition from imports is particularly strong.

A rise in interest rates might have little impact on some of these. For example, a rise in interest rates might not deter consumers from taking out loans because their confidence is high. Or the rise might have little impact on the value of the pound and so not affect exports and imports. The impact depends very much on what else is happening in the economy.

There are also many businesses that are unlikely to see much change in their demand even if other businesses are suffering. For example, consumers tend not to cut back on their spending on food even when times are hard. So supermarkets are often unaffected by changes in interest rates. A hairdressers or a village post office are unlikely to be much affected either.

In 1991 bank base rates had been at the crippling level of 14-15 per cent for nearly two years. The economy was in the midst of a deep, prolonged recession which had begun in 1989. Al Farrall had run his fastening business for 23 years, but he had never known conditions like this.

He manufactured fastenings mainly for the car and furniture industries. Bolts, castor pegs, nuts and pins were the staple products. Like many businesses, he had expanded in the mid-1980s. Furniture sales were booming in the climate of relatively low interest rates. The housing market was also booming, which encouraged home owners to buy new furniture as they moved house.

At the same time, car production picked up, first for the domestic market and then later for export. But, in 1989, the bottom dropped out of this market. Bank base rates had gone from a low of 7.5 per cent in mid-1987 to 14 per cent by mid-1989. Car production fell back and furniture sales slumped. He not only lost sales volumes, but found himself having to offer ridiculously low priced contracts to win orders.

By early 1991, Al's business was facing closure. He had already been forced to cut the workforce from 20 in 1989 to 12 in 1991, helping to swell the ranks of the UK unemployed which had risen from 1.5 million to 3 million over the period. Whilst his workforce shrank, his borrowing just kept growing. With the benefit of hindsight, he knew that he had made a huge mistake to borrow £150 000 to buy new equipment in 1988. A third of his equipment now lay idle because of lack of orders. His borrowings stood at an unsustainable £200 000 given that the business had made a loss of £25 000 in 1990 and was on track to make a loss of £30 000 in 1991. The business desperately needed a cut in interest rates and a return to growth in the economy.

1 Explain what is meant by:
  (a) bank base rates; (3 marks)
  (b) recession. (3 marks).
2 To what extent were Al Farrall's business problems caused by overborrowing in the late 1980s? (12 marks)
3 Bank base rates fell from 14 per cent in February 1991 to 6 per cent in February 1993. Discuss whether this change could have helped Al's business to survive.
  (12 marks)

AorTech

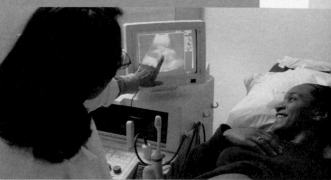

Knowledge   AorTech International plc is a medical device company. It is
researching a number of new products, but in 2000-2001 it
was mainly selling monitoring systems for medical services.

Application   *Exports* accounted for about 80 per cent of *sales* by value for
the company in 2000-2001. During the 12 months, the
exchange rate of the pound was relatively high.

Analysis   The high value of the pound meant that AorTech could afford
to lower its prices in foreign currency terms whilst
maintaining its prices in pounds sterling. Lowering the foreign currency
price made the company's products more competitive and therefore helped to boost sales.

Evaluation   AorTech chose to use the advantage gained by the high value of the pound to lower foreign currency prices and so
increase exports. It could instead have chosen to maintain foreign currency prices and so increase profit margins.
However, as a relatively new company rolling out a range of new high technology products, it was probably better for the company
to increase sales in order to promote brand awareness amongst customers. It will benefit from brand awareness when it launches
new products in the future.

The exchange rate of a currency

An EXCHANGE RATE is the price of one currency against
another. For instance, the exchange rate of the pound might
be €1 = £0.58 or £1 = US$1.60. At these exchange rates, a
business wanting to buy €1 million through its bank would
have to pay £580 000 (€1 million x 0.58) plus a
commission.

Currencies can change in value. If the exchange rate
changed to €= £0.60, the business would now have to pay
£600 000 (€million x 0.60) plus commission.
- A **rise** in the value of the pound against other currencies
  means that the pound will buy more foreign currency. For
  example, if the value of the pound changed from
  £1 = €1.60 to £1 =€1.75, this would be a rise in the
  value of the pound. Each pound is now worth€0.15 more
  than before. A rise in the pound is sometimes called an
  APPRECIATION of the currency.
- A DEPRECIATION or **fall** in the value of the pound would
  mean that the pound would buy less foreign currency than
  before. A change from £1 = $1.50 to £1 = $1.30
  would be an example. The pound buys $0.20 less
  than before.

Sometimes, the value of a currency is said to be high.
This means that it can buy more foreign currency
compared to the recent historical average. For example,
the recent historical average value of the pound against
the euro might be £1 =€1.40. If the actual value of the
pound today were £1 =€1.60, the value of the pound
would be high. On the other hand, it would be low if it
were well below the £1 =€1.40 level. So, for example,
it would be low if the exchange rate were £1 =€1.20.

Changes in exchange rates

Exchange rates are affected by the demand for and
supply of currencies. Buyers of one currency demand
another currency. Sellers of one currency supply

another currency.

Demand for a currency Demand for a currency like the
pound, for example, comes from three main sources.
- **Exports**. A US business buying goods priced in pounds
  from a UK business would need to buy pounds to pay the
  invoice. The US business would be buying an export from
  the UK. So buyers of UK EXPORTS, goods or services sold
  abroad, would demand pounds.
- **Capital transactions**. Foreign individuals, businesses or
  other organisations might want to buy UK owned assets.
  For instance, a French company might decide to buy a UK
  company. It would need to buy pounds to buy out the UK
  company's shareholders. Or a German citizen might want
  to buy shares on the London stock exchange in Barclays
  Bank. She would need to exchange euros for pounds to do
  this.
- **Speculation**. The largest source of demand for pounds on a
  day-to-day basis is foreign currency speculation. Dealers in
  foreign currency buy and sell pounds. They hope to sell at
  a higher price than they buy, to make a profit.

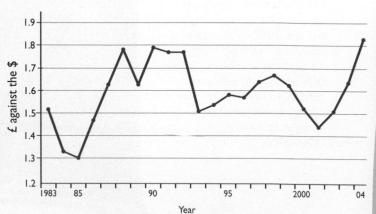

Figure 52.1 *The value of the pound against the US dollar*
Adapted from *Economic Trends*, ONS.

Supply of a currency The supply of a currency also comes from three main sources.

- **Imports**. If a UK company bought components from a United States manufacturer, it would need to buy US dollars and sell pounds to pay the invoice. So UK IMPORTS create a supply of pounds.
- **Capital transactions**. If UK citizens, businesses or organisations want to buy foreign assets, such as shares, factories or companies, they will need to sell pounds for foreign currency.
- **Speculation**. Foreign currency speculators dominate day-to-day transactions. They buy and sell, hoping to make a profit.

The rate of exchange changes minute by minute depending upon how much is demanded and how much is supplied. Foreign exchange rates, therefore, tend to be volatile. Figure 52.1 shows how the pound has changed against the US$ over 20 years.

Exports and exchange rate changes

Businesses can be directly or indirectly affected by changes in the exchange rate. Those most affected are likely to be EXPORTING (selling goods and services to foreign governments, businesses and individuals) or IMPORTING (buying goods and services from abroad).

Take a UK company that exports marmalade abroad. The price of a pot of marmalade is 50p. If the value of the pound is £1 =€1.60, a company abroad buying a pot of marmalade will pay €0.80 for it (1.60 x 0.50p). What if the value of the pound now appreciates (i.e. rises) to £1 = €1.80? How might the UK business react?

Keep the price in pounds the same The UK company could keep the price in pounds the same. So at 50p per pot, it would now cost the foreign company €0.90 (1.80 x 0.50p). This rise in price from €0.80 to €0.90 will affect demand (i.e. the quantity bought). It is likely that the quantity demanded would fall. The UK company would see a fall in sales abroad. By how much depends on how price sensitive is demand. If it is highly price sensitive (i.e. price elasticity of demand is high, see unit 17), the percentage fall in sales will be high. If demand is fairly insensitive (i.e. price elasticity of demand is low), then there will be little effect on sales.

Keep the foreign currency price the same The UK company could keep the foreign currency price the same, i.e. keep the price of the pot of marmalade at €0.80. If it does, the price it will receive in pounds will fall to around 44p (€0.80 ÷ the exchange rate = €0.80 ÷ €1.80). By adopting this pricing strategy, demand for marmalade should remain unchanged. But profits from marmalade sales will fall. It might even be the case that at 44p the business will make a loss on the sale.

So for an exporting business, a **rise** in the value of the pound is likely to result in either a fall in export sales, a fall in profits on those sales, or both. Which of these occurs depends on the pricing policy the exporting company adopts following the appreciation of the currency.

The reverse is true if the value of the pound **falls**. Exporting companies can choose to let the foreign currency prices of their goods fall. This should lead to a rise in export sales. Or they can improve their profit margins by raising the price in

Betteny is a UK paint manufacturer. It produces paint for domestic and industrial use worldwide. The fall in the value of the pound in the early part of 2003 both against the US dollar and the euro was welcome news to the company. With the pound so high in 2001-2002, the company had struggled along with many UK exporters to remain profitable.

The directors of the company had met to discuss their pricing strategy in the light of the fall. On the whole, they decided that they wanted to restore profit margins on export contracts by trying to maintain their prices in pounds sterling. However, the fall in the value of the pound meant that they could afford to offer slightly better prices to overseas customers if it meant that they would win a contract. In the UK market, Betteny would be better able to compete against importers which had eaten into their market share in 2001-2002.

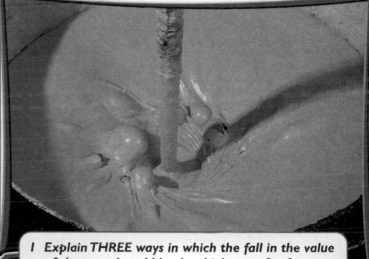

1 **Explain THREE ways in which the fall in the value of the pound could lead to higher profits for Betteny.**

pounds to a level where the foreign currency price is unchanged. Or they can do a combination of the two, seeing some increase in sales and some increase in profits.

Imports and exchange rate changes

Businesses that import goods are affected by exchange rate changes too. For example, the marmalade manufacturer might import oranges from Spain. What happens if the value of the pound changes?

A rise in the value of the pound If the price of the pound goes up against the euro, it means that the company can now buy more euros for £1. So the price of imports should fall. For example, assume that it can buy 10 kilos of oranges for €1.60. At an exchange rate of £1 =€1.60, 10 kilos cost £1. But if the exchange rate of the pound now appreciates to £1 = €1.80, the cost of 10 kilos of oranges, still priced at €1.60, falls to around 89p (€1.60 ÷€1.80).

A fall in the value of the pound The opposite occurs if the value of the pound falls. For example, the pound might depreciate from £1 =€1.60 to £1 =€1.40. Before, 10 kilos of oranges cost E1.60 or £1. After, 10 kilos of oranges still cost

Rugol & Flynn's is a company which manufactures household goods. The managing director, George Rugol, is an outspoken critic of Britain's failure to join the European Monetary Union. Over the years, he has seen large fluctuations in the value of the pound against European currencies and against the US dollar. Within a matter of weeks, the pound can go up or down against key trading currencies by 5 per cent or more. This is highly disruptive to his business since his company exports mainly to Europe but also to the USA.

George Rugol is very careful to ensure that all export contracts are hedged - that is, the company buys or sells foreign currency in advance so that it knows how much it will receive in pounds on any given order. But this takes both time and money to arrange with its bankers. The company wouldn't have to do this for sales in Europe if the UK used the same currency, the euro, as its main trading partners.

Equally, Rugol's imports raw materials. The exact price to be paid is uncertain because of day to day exchange rate fluctuations. Again, the company hedges all contracts but this adds to the costs of the contract.

George Rugol wants it to be as risk free to sell his products to German or France as it is to London or Scotland. This means that Britain must adopt the euro.

1 **Rugol's signs a contract to export goods to France in one month's time for 50 000 euros. A week later, the value of the pound rises by 5 per cent against the euro. Explain whether the company would gain or lose out as a result?**

2 **Explain whether the UK joining the euro would help Rugol's with its exports to the USA.**

€1.60. But the price in pounds is around £1.14 (€1.60 ÷ €1.40). A fall in the value of the pound leads to higher import prices.

As with exports, foreign companies could adjust their own prices to compensate for the change in the exchange rate.

So, if the value of the pound **rises**, import prices in pounds will fall and foreign firms will become more competitive in the UK market. Instead of selling more exports to the UK, however, foreign firms could choose instead to raise prices in their currency. If they raised them so that the price in pounds remained the same, they wouldn't sell any more products to the UK. But they would increase their profit on each sale.

If the value of the pound **falls**, import prices in pounds will go up and foreign businesses will find it more difficult to sell into the UK market. By cutting prices in their own currency, foreign firms can bring the price in pounds back to what it was before. They, however, suffer lower profits as a result.

Direct and indirect effects of exchange rate changes on a business

Businesses can be affected directly and indirectly by changes in the exchange rate.

Directly Businesses might be affected by changes in the exchange rate directly because they sell abroad or buy imports. Many of these businesses are both exporters and importers. For them, exchange rate changes can have complicated effects.

• A UK business that buys roughly the same amount of imports as it exports can be unaffected by an exchange rate change. If the pound falls in value, the extra cost of imports can be offset by rises in the UK price of its exports.

• A UK business that has high levels of exports, but imports little, is likely to benefit from a **depreciation** of the pound. It can either allow foreign currency prices to fall and so become more competitive overseas, or it can increase its prices in pounds and so increase profit margins.

• A UK business that has high levels of exports, but imports little is likely to suffer from an appreciation of the pound. Either it will have to put up foreign currency prices and become less competitive or it will have to absorb the exchange rate rise by lowering its prices in pounds, resulting in lower profit margins.

Indirectly UK businesses can also suffer indirectly from exchange rate changes. This is because of the effect of a change in the value of the pound on inflation (a general rise in prices in the economy, see unit 53).

A **depreciation** in the value of the pound will mean that the price of imported goods and services is likely to rise. UK businesses that import these products could pass on some of the rise in price to customers, many of which will be other businesses. So a business that doesn't import anything may still pay higher prices for supplies because of a fall in the exchange rate.

Similarly, an **appreciation** of the pound can lead to importing businesses passing on the saving made on imports to their customers in the form of lower prices.

Exchange rates and the rate of interest

Changes in interest rates can lead to changes in exchange rates. A fall in interest rates, for example, is likely to lead to a fall in the exchange rate. Lower interest rates discourage saving and investment in a country. So if UK interest rates fall, fewer pounds will be bought to invest in the UK. A rise in interest rates is likely to raise the exchange rate.

How might lower interest rates and exchange rates affect a business? Lower interest rates can **benefit** UK businesses:
- borrowing money in the UK, as they pay back less;
- selling to the UK market, because lower interest rates will encourage UK consumers to borrow and spend more;
- selling exports. They can either sell more since prices will be cheaper to foreigners or increase their prices and profit margins.

A fall in interest rates is likely to **harm** UK businesses:
- because inflation in the UK may increase as a result of higher import prices;
- UK businesses that import materials from abroad because a fall in the exchange rate cause import prices to rise.

The opposite is true if interest rates rise.

Strategy and exchange rates

Many businesses find that exchange rate changes can have a major effect on their finances. They have to develop strategies to cope with exchange rate changes.

Balancing exports and imports A business could try to balance the value of exports and products that are imported. Some car manufacturers operating in the UK have adopted this strategy. If the value of the pound rises, the manufacturer lowers its export prices in pounds to leave the foreign currency price the same. But the lower revenues it earns in pounds are matched by the lower prices it has to pay for imported products. The net result is that profit is unaffected.

Similarly, if the value of the pound falls, import prices will rise for the business. But it can offset this by raising the price of its exports in pounds, which leaves the foreign currency price to its customers the same.

Becoming more competitive Changes in the value of the pound can affect two main groups of businesses. If the value of the pound rises:
- exporters will find that the foreign currency price of their goods will rise if they maintain existing prices in pounds. This will damage export sales;
- imports are likely to fall in price. This will harm sales of UK businesses that make products competing against imports.

A fall in the value of the pound will help both UK exporters and those UK businesses in competition with imports.

Both exporters and UK businesses that compete against imported products can attempt to become more COMPETITIVE. They can do this in two ways.

First they can try to reduce their costs so they can reduce their prices to customers. If the value of the pound rises by 10 per cent, for example, UK exporters need to cut their prices in pounds by 10 per cent to maintain the same price in foreign currency. Greater price competitiveness can be achieved by more efficient methods of production. The business might be able to get better prices on the products it buys in from suppliers. The workforce may need to be reduced in numbers, with the remaining workers working more efficiently than before. In a few cases, businesses have been forced to cut the wages of workers to achieve cost savings.

Second, they can become more competitive by adding value to the products they sell. Their products might be more reliable or better designed than those available from overseas competitors. Or the UK business might promise faster delivery times.

Marketing changes One response to a rise in the value of the pound for an exporter would be to pull out of the export market. If the business judged that it simply couldn't compete at the new higher exchange rate, then it should concentrate on the domestic market. The opposite strategic response might come from a UK business which suffers competition from abroad. A rise in the value of the pound will make imports cheaper and so give foreign companies a competitive advantage. To compensate for lower UK sales, the UK business may decide that it must expand into foreign markets and so it will start to export products.

Similarly, if the value of the pound fell, this would make UK products more competitive abroad. This could be a marketing opportunity for existing exporters to expand their markets. It could also be an opportunity for a UK firm which hadn't exported before to seek out new markets abroad.

Joining the euro

By the time you read this book, the UK might or might not have joined the European Monetary Union (EMU). If it had joined, the pound would no longer exist. Instead, the UK would use the euro when buying or selling abroad. This would have considerable implications for UK businesses.

Over 50 per cent of all UK exports and imports go to and come from other European Union countries. Joining the euro would mean that the price of those exports and imports would

checklist

1 What is the difference between an appreciating pound and a depreciating pound?
2 Why do currencies change in value against other currencies?
3 (a) An exporter charges £20 for a product sold to the USA. What would be the price in US$ if the exchange rate were (i) £1 = $1.60; (ii) £1 = $1.85; (iii) £1 = $1.35? (b) At what exchange rate would the exporter be most competitive?
4 The value of the pound changes from £1 = $1.70 to £1 = $1.40. How might a UK exporter to the USA change its prices as a result and what would be the effect on sales?
5 Why might a rise in the value of the pound force UK exporters to become more competitive?
6 How might exchange rate changes affect marketing?

be fixed for UK businesses. There would be no more appreciation or depreciation of the UK currency against other European currencies. Selling to France or Italy would be the same as selling to Northumberland, London or Northern Ireland. As a result, businesses trading with other euro countries wouldn't have to pay commission to banks to change pounds into foreign currencies. It would also remove the uncertainty caused by changing exchange rates. What will be the exchange rate when payment is made on the import or export contract?

However, UK businesses would still face these risks when selling or buying outside the eurozone. Just as the pound can fluctuate against the US dollar or the Japanese Yen, so does the euro.

keyterms

Appreciation of a currency - a rise in the value of the currency.
Competitiveness - the extent to which a business or a geographical area such as a country, can compete successfully against rivals.
Depreciation of a currency - a fall in the value of a currency.
Exchange rate - the price of one currency in terms of another currency.
Exports - goods or services produced domestically and sold to foreigners.
Exporting - selling goods and services produced domestically to foreigners.
Imports - goods or services produced outside the country and purchased from foreigners.
Importing - buying goods and services produced outside a country from foreigners.

Joseph Wolff is a major importer of hot dogs to the UK. He founded his business 20 years ago and imports mainly from Germany and Denmark. Over the years, he has had to cope with large changes in the value of the pound against both the old German deutschmark, the German currency, and the Danish krona. Today, he is no better off. The German deutschmark has been replaced by the euro. But the Danish krona still exists because Denmark, like the UK, refused to adopt the euro as its currency in 2002 when the euro was launched.

The hot dog business is fiercely competitive. When the pound depreciates in value, Wolff is unable immediately to put up prices to his UK customers. He simply has to see his profit margins reduced. On the other hand, his short term profit margins improve when the pound appreciates in value against the euro and the krona. Over a longer period of time, he make small price adjustments, but he has to be careful not to put up his prices too much or else he would lose orders from customers.

Over the years, Wolff has tried to reduce exchange rate risks by seeing if he could buy hot dogs from UK sausage manufacturers. The quality of the UK product has been disappointing though. UK manufacturers seem to have little idea of how to make a truly great hot dog.

1 Explain the meaning of the terms:
  (a) 'importer'; (3 marks)
  (b) 'the pound depreciates in value'.
  (3 marks)
2 Discuss the possible impact of changes in the value of the pound on Wolff's hot dog business. (12 marks)
3 Consider whether Wolff would be better off setting up his own hot dog manufacturing business in the UK. (12 marks)

53 Inflation

Asda

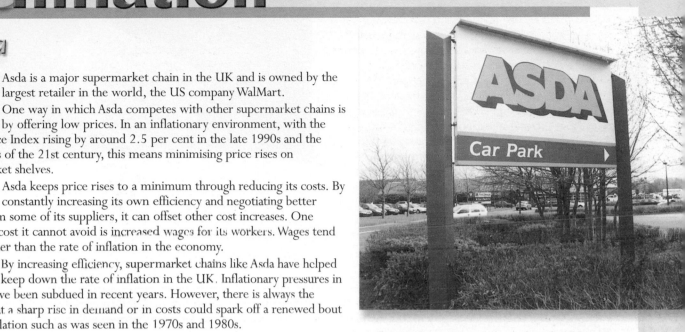

Knowledge Asda is a major supermarket chain in the UK and is owned by the largest retailer in the world, the US company WalMart.

Application One way in which Asda competes with other supermarket chains is by offering low prices. In an inflationary environment, with the Retail Price Index rising by around 2.5 per cent in the late 1990s and the early years of the 21st century, this means minimising price rises on supermarket shelves.

Analysis Asda keeps price rises to a minimum through reducing its costs. By constantly increasing its own efficiency and negotiating better prices from some of its suppliers, it can offset other cost increases. One increased cost it cannot avoid is increased wages for its workers. Wages tend to rise faster than the rate of inflation in the economy.

Evaluation By increasing efficiency, supermarket chains like Asda have helped keep down the rate of inflation in the UK. Inflationary pressures in general have been subdued in recent years. However, there is always the danger that a sharp rise in demand or in costs could spark off a renewed bout of high inflation such as was seen in the 1970s and 1980s.

The meaning of inflation

INFLATION is a general **rise** in prices in the economy. A 5 per cent inflation rate over the past 12 months, for example, means that the average increase in prices across the economy during the past year was 5 per cent.

DEFLATION is a **fall** in average prices. Deflation means that, on average, the products are cheaper to buy than before. Note, however, that the term 'deflation' is also used to describe a recession in the economy, when the inflation rate is falling but inflation is still positive.

Figure 53.1 shows inflation since 1959 for the UK economy. There have been considerable fluctuations in the yearly rise in prices, from a low of 0 per cent in 1959 to a high of 24.1 per cent in 1975. At its worst in 1975, a basket of products which cost £1 at the start of the year had risen in price to £1.24 at the end of the year. Today, the Bank of England is given the responsibility of keeping inflation at around 2.5 per cent per year.

Figure 53.2 shows price changes for Japan since 1990. It experienced deflation in a number of years during the 1990s. Average prices were falling in Japan.

The measurement of inflation

In the UK, inflation is usually measured by calculating the change in the RETAIL PRICE INDEX (RPI). This is sometimes called the 'headline rate of inflation'. The RPI is a measure of

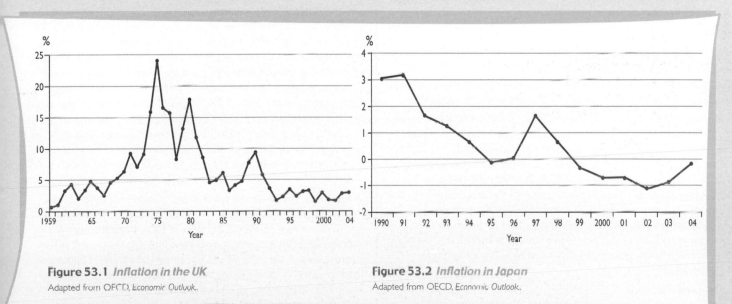

Figure 53.1 *Inflation in the UK*
Adapted from OECD, Economic Outlook.

Figure 53.2 *Inflation in Japan*
Adapted from OECD, Economic Outlook.

In 2002, Britain's firefighters put in a claim for an inflation-busting pay increase of 40 per cent. They argued that they had fallen behind workers with similar responsibilities and facing similar dangers. In Autumn 2002, they staged a series of strikes to bring pressure on their employers, local councils.

With inflation running at just 2.5 per cent, the government was in no mood to see the firefighters get anywhere near the 40 per cent. Any pay increase much over the rate of inflation would have had to be financed from grants from central government to local authority employers. That could have meant higher taxes to pay for the wage increases.

The government was also concerned about the effect a 40 per cent wage increase would have had on other workers. If the firefighters go much more than a 2.5 per cent pay increase, there would be calls from other public sector workers such as ambulance operators, nurses or soldiers for pay increases to match those of the firefighters. Then there would also be calls from private sector workers for high pay increases. Overnight, the government's whole anti-inflation strategy could be demolished.

Adapted from various newspaper sources 2002-2003.

1 **Explain why giving the firefighters a 40 per cent pay increase could have (a) led to businesses being pressured to give large pay increases to their workers and (b) then led to increased inflation throughout the economy.**

average prices. Each month, around 12 000 prices of more than 600 goods and services are taken around the UK from all different businesses that sell these products. An average price for that month is then worked out and changed into an index number (see unit 6). The month's figure can then be compared to last month's average price, or that of 12 months ago, to calculate the percentage rise in prices over the period (i.e. the inflation rate).

Over time, the products that are included each month change. The exact 'basket' of products is derived from an annual survey of households (the Family Expenditure Survey). Each household taking part has to record everything it spends over a period. From the data, a profile of the 'typical household' in the UK emerges and how it spends its money. Researchers then go out and price up this average basket of products bought by the average family each month.

The causes of inflation

Inflation can be caused by two main sets of factors - demand and costs.

Demand-pull inflation DEMAND-PULL INFLATION is caused by too much demand in the economy as a whole. Typically, the economy is **booming** (see unit 50) and output (AGGREGATE SUPPLY) is not keeping up with the spending of consumers and businesses (AGGRFGATE DEMAND). Shortages may develop in some parts of the economy because businesses are working at maximum capacity. In these circumstances, businesses are under little pressure to give discounts to buyers. So prices rise towards their list price. Many might also put up their list prices without losing customers.

Cost-push inflation COST-PUSH INFLATION occurs when costs of production rise without there being a rise in aggregate

demand in the economy. Costs may rise for a number of reasons.

- Over the past 50 years, cost-push inflation in the UK has occurred mainly due to sharp rises in the cost of imported goods, such as oil. In 1973-74, for example, the price of oil quadrupled, from around $5 a barrel to $20 a barrel. These 'supply-side shocks' led to large price increases throughout the economy. Inflation in 1975 reached 24.1 per cent, for instance.
- Rises in wages might cause cost-push inflation. In the 1960s and 1970s, there was an increase in trade union militancy. Some argue that this caused wages to rise more than they would otherwise have done. On the other hand, in the 1980s, tough new laws were introduced by government that limited the powers of trade unions and strike action. It can be argued that reducing the power of trade unions reduced cost-push inflationary pressures.
- Other causes of cost-push inflation can be rises in taxes or profits. If the government increases taxes on goods and services, inflation will rise. In 1979, for example, the government increased VAT from 8 per cent to 15 per cent. This added around 5 per cent overnight to the inflation rate for that year. Equally, if the economic climate changes, as it did in the 1980s, and businesses decide that they need to earn more profit, this is likely to come about through price increases.

Wage-price spirals and expectations Cost-push inflation and demand-pull inflation tend to feed off one another. This is known as a WAGE-PRICE SPIRAL. It often starts through a supply-side shock, such as a sudden increase in import prices. Businesses put up their prices to remain profitable. Higher prices lead to workers demanding large pay rises. If they don't get wage rises which are at least as large as the increase in inflation, their standard of living will fall. This is because their wages

Zeenat is a small garment manufacturer in Bradford with 15 employees. It makes up clothes for a variety of buyers, including a couple of high street chains. The past four years have been very difficult for the company. Prices paid have been falling consistently as retailers have increasingly sourced clothes from the Far East. In January 2003, for example, official statistics were published showing that the price of clothes on the high street had fallen 1.8 per cent in one month alone, December 2002.

It had all been different when the company was started up ten years previously. Then, prices could be increased each year to cover increased costs such as wage increases or raw material price rises. Today, costs were still going up but prices were falling. Take, for example, the minimum wage which the company had to pay its remaining workers. In March 2003, it was announced that at the end of 2003 the minimum wage would be increased from £4.20 an hour to £4.50 an hour.

1 **Why are falling prices a problem for a company such as Zeenat?**
2 **Discuss whether high inflation would pose worse problems for Zeenat than mild deflation.**

won't be able to buy as much as before at the new high prices. Large wage increases lead to an increase in aggregate demand as workers spend their pay increases. However, businesses are forced to put up their prices again because their wage costs have increased. This leads to more wage demands and so on.

Wage-price spirals might be restricted by government policy to control inflation. However, at the end of the spiral, inflation tends to stabilise at a certain level anyway, for example 2 per cent in the late 1990s or 5 per cent in the mid-1980s. Stable inflation is maintained through the role of **expectations**. If all economic agents in the economy expect inflation to be the same as before, then they will act in a way which ensures that it is achieved. For example, if everyone expects inflation to be 2 per cent, then workers will negotiate pay rises of 2 per cent plus a little more to give them higher spending power than before. If workers expect inflation to be 20 per cent, they will negotiate for wage rises in excess of 20 per cent.

Similarly, businesses will base their price rises on expected inflation. If expected inflation is 2 per cent, businesses will tend to raise their prices by a few per cent. If expected inflation is 20 per cent, they will put up their prices by around 20 per cent. The whole system can be stable if every economic agent acts on common expectations. But it can be unstable if different economic agents have different economic expectations. For example, a wage price spiral may begin if workers suddenly demand and obtain pay increases of 10 per cent when expected inflation has been 5 per cent.

Inflation, deflation and businesses

Inflation is not necessarily a problem. If prices are rising by a few per cent each year, and the inflation rate is fairly constant, inflation is likely to have little impact on businesses.

The situation is different if inflation is high. At 5 per cent and over, businesses have to be managed to cope with

inflation. When inflation gets over, say, 20 per cent per annum, there are serious consequences for businesses. This is particularly true if inflation is fluctuating. For example, if yearly inflation goes from 5 per cent to 25 per cent to 150 per cent back down to 10 per cent in a four year period, then a business could easily be forced to close.

Equally, even quite low levels of deflation can have a significant impact on business. So there is considerable difference between 2 per cent inflation per year, which has little or no effect on business, and 2 per cent deflation.

Effects of inflation on businesses

High and particularly fluctuating inflation is likely to be damaging to business for a number of reasons.

Increased costs High or fluctuating inflation imposes a variety of costs on businesses.

- With suppliers' prices rising all the time, but at different rates, time must be spent researching the market for the best deals. Equally, more time has to be spent tracking the prices of competitors to decide when and by how much to increase your own prices. These costs are called **shoe leather costs** because before the age of the telephone and the Internet, businesses would have to send their employees round on foot to gather this information.
- Raising prices costs money. Customers have to be informed of the new prices. Brochures might have to be reprinted and sent out. Web sites might have to be updated. The sales force has to be made familiar with new prices. These costs are called **menu costs** because, for a restaurant, increasing prices means that it has to reprint its menus.
- Management is likely to have to spend more time dealing with workers' pay claims. Instead of being able to sign a two or three year deal, annual pay negotiations are likely to be the norm. If there is **hyperinflation**, where inflation is running into 100 per cent per annum or over, pay

negotiations may have to take place each month. There is also a much larger risk of strikes because workers and managers will probably have different views of future inflation rates. Workers will be worried that any deal they make will leave them worse off after inflation. So they might be more willing to take industrial action to get high pay settlements.

Uncertainty With high and fluctuating inflation, businesses don't know what prices will be in three or six months time, let alone in one or five years. But decisions have to be made now which will affect the business in the long term. For example, businesses need to invest to survive. But how much should they invest? The price of a new machine, a shop or a new computer system will probably be higher in six months than today. But are they worth buying if interest rates are at very high levels? What if the new machine is bought, financed by very high cost borrowing and there is a **recession** (see unit 50), where demand for goods and services falls?

Another problem with uncertainty is linked to entering long term contracts. A customer might approach a business wanting to buy products on a regular monthly basis for the next two years. How can the supplier put a price on this contract if it doesn't know what the inflation rate will be over the next 24 months?

Borrowing and lending Borrowing and lending becomes an opportunity and a problem for businesses. On the one hand, the real value of debts incurred in the past can become quickly eroded by inflation. If inflation is 100 per cent per annum, the real value of money borrowed a year ago is halved in one year. Inflation initially benefits borrowers and harms lenders.

But in an inflationary environment, interest rates rise to match inflation. If inflation is 100 per cent, interest rates might be 110 per cent. If there is prolonged inflation, interest rates are likely to become INDEX LINKED - linked to the index of prices. So interest might be charged at the rate of inflation plus 5 per cent or plus 10 per cent.

Consumer reactions Consumers react to inflation as well as businesses. Prolonged inflation tends to lead to more saving. Inflation unsettles consumers. They become less willing to borrow money, not knowing what will happen in the future. The value of savings tends to fall as inflation erodes its real value. So people react by saving more to make up savings to their previous real value. Increased saving means less spending and so businesses will sell less.

If inflation is very high, consumers will adopt different spending patterns which may affect businesses. For example, if there is hyperinflation, prices will be changing by the day. Consumers will then tend to spend wages or interest as soon as they receive them. On 'pay day' there can be huge activity in shops. Supermarkets have to be geared up to selling most of the weekly or monthly turnover in just a few hours. Suppliers of fresh produce to supermarkets have to be geared to delivering most of their goods on one day a week.

International competitiveness High inflation poses problems for businesses that buy or sell abroad.

If the inflation rate in the UK is 10 per cent, but is only 2 per cent in France, then UK **exporters** will become uncompetitive against French businesses. For example, if a UK product is priced at 58 pence, it would be sold at €1 in France (assuming the exchange rate is €1= £0.58). Now assume there is inflation

in the UK and the manufacturer has to put its prices by 10 per cent to 63.8p or €1.10. In contrast, competitors in France only experience 2% inflation and put their prices up to €1.02. The UK exporter has therefore lost price competitiveness and will find it harder to sell into the French market.

UK businesses facing competition from French firms will also suffer because French **imports** to the UK will be relatively cheaper. UK companies might have to put up their prices by 10 per cent because of cost-push pressures in the UK economy when French competitors are only putting up their prices by 2 per cent. UK companies will therefore lose market share in their home market.

Effects of deflation on businesses

Deflation, a fall in prices, can also lead to problems for businesses.

A stagnant economy Deflation tends to be associated with an economy which is not growing in size. It might even be shrinking. This is because falls in price are often associated with falling levels of demand. Consumers are reluctant to spend money. Businesses don't want to increase their investment because their output is stagnant. Demand for exports may also be stagnant, perhaps because of a recession in the world economy. In a stagnant economy, problems could be made worse by rising unemployment. This also tends to reduce the willingness of consumers to spend and borrow. Faced with deflation, businesses will find it difficult to expand their own production. Many could face falling demand for their products if they are selling into markets which are in decline because of changes in spending patterns.

Reducing costs Deflation means that businesses are being forced to cut their prices. When deflation initially occurs, businesses may choose to pay for the price cuts by simply cutting their profits or accepting a loss for the year. But if deflation is prolonged, businesses have to cut their costs to survive. Cost cutting year on year is very difficult. It may be possible to achieve lower costs through more efficient production methods. An alternative is to cut the wages of workers. This is likely to lead to demotivation and threats of industrial action. It is perhaps more difficult to manage a business that continually has to cut its prices than one where prices can be slowly pushed upwards.

checklist

1. What is the difference between inflation and deflation?
2. How is inflation generally measured in the UK?
3. What is the difference between demand-pull inflation and cost-push inflation?
4. Why are expectations important in determining inflation?
5. Explain the problems that a business might face if:
   (a) there is very high inflation of 25 per cent per year;
   (b) there is high inflation and it does not know whether inflation will rise or fall next year;
   (c) it has financial reserves of £2 million deposited with its bank and there is high inflation;
   (d) it is a major exporter and inflation is much lower in other countries;
   (e) prices in the economy are, on average, falling.

'key terms

Aggregate demand - total demand within the economy, which is equal to total output and total spending.

Aggregate supply - total supply within the economy, equal to total output of the economy.

Cost-push inflation - inflation which is caused by changes in aggregate supply, typically increases in the price of imports or increases in wages.

Deflation - strictly defined, it is a fall in the general price level within an economy. It is often used, however, to describe a situation when the rate of economic growth is falling or is negative and when inflation is falling.

Demand-pull inflation - inflation which is caused by changes in aggregate demand, such as a large increase in consumer spending, or a sizeable increase in spending by businesses on capital equipment (i.e. investment), or a significant increase in exports.

Index linked - in the context of inflation, adjusting the value of economic variables such as wages or the rate of interest in line with a measure of inflation such as the Retail Price Index.

Inflation - a general rise in prices.

Retail Price Index (RPI) - the average price of the average basket of products bought by the average household in the UK converted into index number form. Percentage changes in the RPI is the most commonly used measure of inflation in the UK, sometimes called the headline rate of inflation.

Wage-price spiral - the process whereby increases in costs, such as wages, lead to increases in prices and this in turn leads to increases in costs to businesses.

McGinnel's is a small independent oil supply company in the south west of England. It buys oil on the open market from refineries and sells to businesses and home owners with oil fired central heating systems. Its green and white liveried tankers are a familiar sight in its local market.

The single largest cost for the company tends to be the oil it buys. The price of crude oil over the years has fluctuated enormously. The result has been that the cost base of the business has also fluctuated significantly.

Another major cost facing the company has been the wage costs of employees, together with related costs such as National Insurance contributions, pension contributions and training. These costs have tended to rise at roughly the same rate as average inflation in the UK. Although tanker drivers' pay has risen faster than the rate of inflation, this has been, to some extent, offset by rises in productivity. Through improved working practices and the introduction of new technology, fewer staff have been needed to deliver the same amount of oil.

Other costs include running a small fleet of tanker trucks for delivery of oil to customers and the overhead costs of the central office and plant for storing oil. Over time, these costs have risen at a little over the average rate of inflation for the economy.

The price that the company charges its customers is very much affected by the price charged by its competitors, the oil majors such as BP Amoco or Texaco. McGinnel's has survived the competition over the years by giving very slightly better prices to customers than the oil majors. Sometimes this pricing policy has caused financial problems because McGinnel's has had to pay higher prices for its oil supplies, but has been unable to pass on the higher cost because the oil majors have left their prices constant. Equally, McGinnel's has sometimes had a profit windfall when oil prices have dropped but the oil majors have been slow to respond with falls in the price of oil to customers. Over time, though, the oil majors have adjusted their prices in line with changes in the price of crude oil.

More importantly, perhaps, for sales, McGinnel's has offered customers excellent service. It has been prepared, for example, to offer same day delivery to customers who suddenly find they have run out of oil. By being a highly efficient, value for money 'local' company, McGinnel's has built up a very loyal customer base.

1 Explain the meaning of the terms:
   (a) 'inflation', (3 marks)
   (b) 'productivity'. (3 marks)
2 To what extent is McGinnel's affected by inflation in the wider economy? (12 marks)
3 Discuss whether McGinnel's should change its pricing policy to one where its prices changed immediately the price of its oil supplies changed. (12 marks)

54 Unemployment

Ryanair

Knowledge Ryanair is an Irish airline company.

Application In November 2002, it announced another set of excellent results, with a substantial rise in *profits* fed by a 37 per cent rise in passenger numbers. Ryanair is a low-cost carrier, *competing* by charging low prices. It planned to double its *sales volumes* between 2002 and 2007. However, what would happen if there was a significant *downturn* in the world economy with rising *cyclical unemployment* in key *markets* such as Ireland, the UK and the USA?

Analysis A sharp rise in unemployment is likely to lead to a fall in demand for airline flights. There would be fewer people going on holiday abroad and less business trips being made. Ryanair, though, could benefit as other airlines suffer. Ryanair offers a no frills budget service. Travellers may trade down to Ryanair from higher cost airlines, allowing Ryanair to continue growing. Ryanair's low prices could also mean that the majority of its potential customers would keep on flying. They would respond to high unemployment cutting down on purchases of high cost goods, such as new furniture or a new car, rather than flights.

Ryanair is one of the companies which has considerably broadened the market for air travel. A rise in world unemployment is likely

Evaluation to make trading more difficult. But it could well find itself suffering far less than its full fare competitors. At best, it might even benefit as customers switch to its low price services. So the future for Ryanair looks bright. Its main concern has to be competition from other low cost airlines such as EasyJet or British Midland.

Adapted from *The Independent*, 5.11.2002.

Unemployment and underemployment

There are always unemployed workers in a market economy. However, the level of UNEMPLOYMENT can vary as Figure 54.1 shows. Official statistics on unemployment tend to measure those who do not have a job, but are actively looking for work.

There are many more, however, who would take on a job if it were available, but are not actively seeking work. The largest group of these **underemployed** people is women who remain at home to look after children. Another large group is the over-50s. Many have taken early retirement because they were made redundant from an existing job. However, they would re-enter the workforce if there were a suitable job available.

Types of unemployment

There is a number of different types of unemployment. Each type is related to a different **cause** of unemployment.

Frictional unemployment Often workers voluntarily leave their jobs or are made redundant before they have another job. Or they may leave one job but their next job only starts in, say, two weeks' time. In between jobs, they are classified as unemployed. This type of unemployment is called FRICTIONAL UNEMPLOYMENT.

Seasonal unemployment In some industries, it is common for workers to be employed only at certain times of the year. In tourism, for example, workers are taken on just for the tourist season. In the construction industry, outdoor construction workers can often be laid off in the winter when building conditions become difficult. In agriculture, extra workers are taken on at harvest time. In general, unemployment tends to go up in the winter and down in the summer because of this SEASONAL UNEMPLOYMENT.

Cyclical unemployment Unit 50 described how economies can go from boom to recession. The unemployment caused by the move to recession is called CYCLICAL UNEMPLOYMENT.

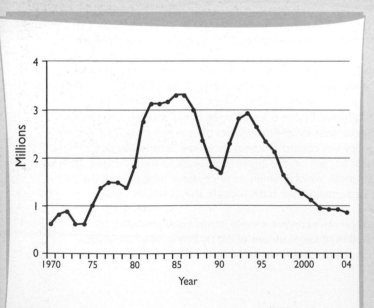

Figure 54.1 *Unemployment, claimant count, millions, not seasonally adjusted.*
Adapted from *Economic Trends*, ONS.

Usually it occurs because aggregate (or total) demand in the economy stops growing at a rate that is fast enough to maintain current levels of employment. At worst, the economy can go into a depression and aggregate demand can fall. With less demand for goods and services, unemployment will rise.

Structural unemployment Today, the pace of change in an economy can be very fast. These changes can lead to STRUCTURAL UNEMPLOYMENT. This is unemployment caused by changes in the structure of an economy.

There is a number of different types of structural unemployment.

- **Technological unemployment** is caused by changes in technology which allow different methods of production to be used or permit new goods to be made. For example, computer technology has transformed much of manufacturing. It has reduced the number of workers needed to produce a given output. Equally, it has created jobs in industries such as computer manufacturing. However, the workers who lost their jobs in manufacturing are unlikely to live in the place where the new jobs are created. Even if they were, they might not have the right skills. They might not even want the new jobs if the new jobs are at a much lower rate of pay.
- Where a whole region is affected by a run down of major

industries, **regional unemployment** is said to exist. The reason for the run down may be changes in technology. Or it could be that major industries in a region have become uncompetitive. In the UK, for example, much of manufacturing has closed down and the jobs have been transferred to the Far East where wages are much lower. It could be that demand for the product of a region has fallen. Lace making in Nottingham or coal from Wales are examples.

- **Sectoral unemployment** is said to exist when major industries collapse leaving large numbers of unemployed workers.

These different types of structural unemployment are usually linked. Structural unemployment would not exist if there were perfect **mobility of labour** within an economy. If the labour market were perfect, workers would be able to move from job to job instantly. They would have the skills to move from being a coal miner to being a computer technician. They could move from Wales to London. They would also be able to understand that they might have to take a cut in pay to get a job.

In the real world, however, there are barriers to mobility. Workers don't have transferable skills. Housing costs are a major barrier to mobility. Workers might not want to leave the town where they were brought up. There might be

2002 was a watershed year for McDonald's, the US fast food chain. For the first time, it made a loss. Outside of the USA, the company is still expanding profitably. But in its core US market, it has experienced significant difficulties. Competition has been intense and US consumers have begun to desert McDonald's for fast food chains offering healthier alternatives.

Problems for McDonald's have been made worse by a downturn in the US economy which has seen rising unemployment. The result has been that fast food chains have suffered from a lack of lunchtime foot traffic. The company claims that it is fairly recession proof because 'when people are cutting back we tend to be one of the last things to be eliminated because our product is not very expensive'. However, to offset rising unemployment and increased competition, the company recently introduced a $1 menu.

A sign that not everything was well with McDonald's was the announcement in October 2002 that it would be closing 175 outlets, many in the US where there were simply too few customers due to fierce local competition. Some analysts believe that a more savage cut in capacity in the USA, particularly where McDonald's outlets were very close to each other, would boost profits.

Adapted from *The Times*, 7.12.2002.

1 **What type of unemployment is caused by a 'downturn in the economy'?**
2 **Explain why rising unemployment could lead to problems for McDonald's.**
3 **Discuss whether closing outlets in the USA in a recession would be a sensible strategy for McDonald's to adopt.**

discrimination against unemployed workers in their 50s trying to get jobs.

Effects of unemployment on businesses

Changes in the unemployment levels in a local area, region or country can have major effects on businesses.

Output Rises in unemployment are likely to affect output and sales of businesses. For example, a small town may have a factory that employs 10 per cent of its workers. If that factory closes, shops in the town will almost certainly see a downturn in trade because unemployed workers will spend less. Suppliers to the factory, perhaps in the local area, will also see a fall in sales.

Low unemployment, on the other hand, is associated with rising output as employed workers spend their wages and other firms invest.

Redundancies and recruitment A fall in output because of rising unemployment could lead to businesses making some of their workers redundant. Redundancies have many effects on businesses. It can be costly if redundancy pay is given. It takes management time to organise. It leads to demotivation amongst staff (see unit 35). On the other hand, if a business is able to recruit in a high unemployment period, it could have a large number of applicants from which to choose. High unemployment can also help put downward pressure on pay and reduce the willingness of workers to take industrial action to support a pay claim.

Low unemployment, on the other hand, is associated with recruitment of workers in tight labour markets. So businesses may have relatively few workers applying for a job. There is also upward pressure on wages because the demand for labour is high and the supply relatively low.

Capacity If unemployment is rising and a business is suffering falling orders as a result, it is likely to suffer from excess capacity (see unit 43). Machines will be idle and office and factory space will be underutilised. This can raise average costs because fixed costs won't change, but less will be produced. Eventually, businesses will be forced to cut their excess capacity by closing sites, not replacing equipment and moving to smaller premises.

On the other hand, falling unemployment leading to higher output is likely to increase capacity utilisation and reduce average costs. Eventually, businesses will increase their capacity, which will fuel demand in the economy further.

Government spending and taxes In a downturn, with rising unemployment, government spending will increase. This is because there will be a rise in social welfare payments to the unemployed. The government is unlikely to raise taxes at this point for fear of reducing spending in the economy even further.

However, if unemployment starts to fall, the government may begin to raise taxes to reduce their borrowing. Higher taxes may be targeted at households, which will slow down the pace of recovery. Taxes could also be targeted at businesses. For example, corporation tax, a tax on company profits, might be raised. This would hit profits.

Sectoral and regional effects Some businesses would be more affected than others by rising unemployment. If the rising unemployment was structural, then businesses in certain industries or certain regions would be affected. For example, the decline of heavy industry in the UK between 1950 and 1990 hit regions such as Scotland, Wales, Northern Ireland and Northern England very hard. Many service industries in these regions were then affected by the knock-on decline in demand from workers who became unemployed.

If the rising unemployment was cyclical, then industries which provided essential goods and services would suffer far less than industries providing luxury goods. For example, in the UK recession of 1990-92, supermarket chains were relatively unaffected as households maintained spending on food. However, the car industry was badly affected because many households and businesses delayed buying new cars and made do with their existing vehicles.

Social issues Long term unemployment tends to create areas of poverty where the unemployed tend to live. Vandalism, crime and other types of antisocial behaviour can result in those areas. This will affect any business located there. For

keyterms

Cyclical unemployment - **when there is insufficient demand in the economy for all workers to be able to get a job. Cyclical unemployment occurs in recessions.**
Frictional unemployment - **when workers are unemployed for short lengths of time between jobs.**
Seasonal unemployment - **when workers are unemployed at certain times of the year, such as building workers or agricultural workers in winter.**
Structural unemployment - **when the pattern of demand and production changes, leaving workers unemployed in labour markets where demand has shrunk. Examples of structural unemployment are regional unemployment, sectoral unemployment and technological unemployment.**
Unemployment - **when those actively seeking work are unable to obtain a job.**

checklist

1　Explain the difference between (a) frictional unemployment and seasonal unemployment; (b) cyclical unemployment and structural unemployment.
2　Explain why 300 workers being made redundant in a small town could affect services industries in the local area.
3　Why might rising unemployment lead to overcapacity in industry?
4　Why might a business be deterred from setting up in an area of high unemployment?

example, business premises may be broken into, equipment stolen, or vandals may set fire to the premises. New businesses thinking of setting up in such areas might be deterred, whilst existing businesses may relocate or shut down, making the problems of unemployment worse.

The UK textile industry employs around 300 000 workers, more than farming, car manufacturing or the chemicals industry. When a car production plant like Dagenham in Essex or Longbridge in Birmingham faces closure, it is national news. But the 41 000 job losses in the textiles industry last year passed almost unnoticed by the media. One difference between textiles and these other industries is that the textile job losses being experienced are almost all amongst low paid women. In car production, farming and the chemicals industry, the workforce is often better paid male workers.

Maggie Rowley provides an example of the story. She worked as a machinist for Coates Viyella, a major supplier to Marks & Spencer, for 20 years. She was one of 450 women made redundant 18 months ago when M&S moved its manufacturing base for the trousers on which she worked to Morocco. Her factory was one of two in Rossington, an old mining village outside Doncaster. On the one road into the village is the pit where her brothers, all miners, were once employed; one still is, the rest work on chicken farms.

Maggie Rowley was lucky enough to get another textiles job after the factory closed, but it was two bus rides away and only paid at the national minimum wage rate. She was quickly made redundant from that job too and now she works in a lighting components factory. Commenting on her job loss at Coates Viyella, she said that it was caused because 'there was no investment, no training, no planning. Now we're losing a whole industry and it's devastating.'

There are significant centres of textile production around the country with a quarter of the industry based in the East Midlands. In Maggie Rowley's home area, 1 000 textile jobs have gone, plus more jobs lost in Doncaster itself. Closures can hit an area hard. Often, textile plants close in areas where there is already high unemployment, particularly male unemployment. Women working in textiles may well be the only wage earner in their household. They often don't have cars and find it difficult to travel far to get a job.

Adapted from *The Guardian*,16.5.2000.

1 Explain what is meant by the terms:
   (a) 'textiles industry'; (3 marks)
   (b) 'unemployment'. (3 marks)
2 Discuss the possible effects of textile closures on manufacturing and service businesses in the Doncaster area. (12 marks)
3 'There was no investment, no training, no planning.' To what extent can a UK business avoid closing down plants and making workers redundant by investment, training and planning? (12 marks)

55 UK and EU Law

Volkswagen

Knowledge Volkswagen is one of the world's largest car manufacturers, with plants and markets around the world.

Application In the UK, Volkswagen has significant *market share*,
although all its cars are *imported* from plants on the
Continent. Its UK *employees* are responsible for *marketing* in the UK
and liaison with the network of Volkswagen dealers. Like any UK
employer, it has to conform to UK and EU *laws* on *health and safety*
and *employment*. Volkswagen dealers are subject to *consumer protection
laws*. Volkswagen is also subject to UK and EU *competition legislation*.

Analysis One example of the way in which Volkswagen is subject
to EU law occurred in 2001 when the company was
fined £19 million. This was not the first time the company had been
fined for restrictive practices by the EU. In 1998, it had been fined
for attempting to stop mainly German car drivers buying VW cars
in Italy where they were cheaper. In 2001, the fine was for intimidating VW dealers in Germany to prevent them from offering
discounts on the new Passat model.

Evaluation UK and EU law in areas such as health and safety, employment law, competition and consumer protection is designed to
protect workers and consumers from abuses by businesses. It can be argued that businesses are far less able today to treat
their workers or their customers unfairly than 50 or 100 years ago. On the other hand, legislation can be argued to have placed such a
heavy burden on industry that European businesses are uncompetitive against Third World firms.

Adapted from Bulletin EU 1/2 - 1998, *The Times*, 31.5.2001.

The law

Businesses must operate within the law. So the law acts as a
constraint on their activities. Businesses face two main types
of law.

- **Criminal law** is enforced by government. Under criminal
  law, individuals or businesses can be **prosecuted**. If found
  guilty of having broken the law, they can be fined or
  imprisoned.
- **Civil law** allows an individual or business to **sue** another
  individual, business or the government to gain
  compensation.

For example, a business may sell food which is unfit for
human consumption. It can then be prosecuted by
government and fined. But it could also be sued by a
consumer who has fallen ill as a result of eating the food.

The body of the law in the UK has emerged from a number
of sources.

- Acts of Parliament are laws which have been passed by the
  UK Parliament at Westminster. The regional assemblies in
  Wales and Scotland also have the power to pass their own
  laws. For example, the Scottish Parliament made hunting
  with dogs illegal in 2002 when it was still legal to hunt in
  England and Wales.
- Common law originates in custom and practice before
  Parliament existed. Judges have made rulings about what is
  legal or illegal. These judgments are then used as
  precedents in future cases of a similar nature. Common
  law continues to evolve because not every legal
  circumstance is covered by Acts of Parliament.
- European Union directives (i.e. EU law) are becoming

increasingly important. To become a true **common
market**, businesses in the EU must operate within the
same legal framework. If laws are different, it could give
businesses in one country an unfair competitive
advantage against businesses in another. EU law
overrides the laws of individual nation states. So when
the EU issues a directive, the UK introduces legislation in
Parliament to change UK law to conform to the
directive. However, the UK does have an input into the
intense negotiations which take place between member
states on any new EU legislation.

In addition to the law, some industries have **voluntary codes
of practice**. These are regulations which businesses or groups
of businesses have drawn up. For example, the advertising
industry has a voluntary code of practice policed by the
Advertising Standards Authority (ASA). The ASA is funded by
contributions from businesses that operate in advertising. Its
code of practice lays down guidelines about what is
acceptable or not in advertising. Individuals or businesses can
complain about individual adverts or campaigns. If the ASA
rules that the advert or campaign does transgress its code, it
will ask for the advert to be withdrawn or the campaign
stopped. Businesses don't have to comply, but generally do so.
If the rules of the ASA were widely flouted, businesses know
that the government might step in and pass legislation which
could easily be harsher than the current voluntary code.

Health and safety legislation

There has been health and safety legislation in the UK since
the nineteenth century. However, the main Act of Parliament

Sixteen years ago, Vince Regan set up Sports Tours International. The Manchester company, employing 16 people, organises sports teams' trips abroad, for training or for matches. He has the same problems as most managers in keeping up with the government's enthusiasm for employment legislation.

To cope with the flood of new and existing regulations, Regan pays an employment law firm to act as a helpline and to keep him abreast of the changes. It may seem an extravagance, but he knows it is worth it. Last year, a female member of staff felt that she was being sexually discriminated against because it was always the men who were given work abroad. The first Regan heard about her grievance was in a letter from a lawyer. 'We have a small but happy team, so the letter came as a real shock', he says. 'The fact is that we needed to send experienced athletes on these trips. They happened to be men.' But Regan did not make the mistake of underestimating the threat. He immediately sought expert advice on how he should respond. 'I followed instructions on replying to the letter, explaining my position and organising meetings with the employee', says Regan. 'I'm glad I did. Left alone, I would have done things differently and could have faced a large fine.'

Plenty of managers might not have been as careful, but experts say they need to be. The number of employment tribunal cases brought against bosses has more than trebled since 1990, with 128 000 cases being filed last year. The maximum award limit has risen from £12 000 to £50 000 over that time. At the same time, government red tape has multiplied, placing a heavy burden on small businesses.

Adapted from *The Sunday Times*, 24.11.2002.

---

1 **(a) What Act of Parliament deals with sexual discrimination in the workplace? (b) What was the grievance brought against Sports Tours International by the female employee?**

2 **(a) What were the costs to Sports Tours International of dealing with grievance? (b) Suggest what might have been the potential cost to Sports Tours International if the company had not followed proper legal procedures.**

3 **Explain the cost to businesses of having to comply with 'government red tape' in the field of employment.**

---

which governs health and safety today is the Health and Safety at Work Act, 1974. Under the Act, government departments can issue further **regulations** when needed to cover new situations.

The Act states that employers have a duty to 'ensure, so far as it reasonably practicable, the health, safety and welfare at work' of all staff. It also states that employers must protect the safety of the public from the activities of employees. So, for example, employees in a supermarket should not carry such heavy loads that they are likely to suffer back injuries. Equally, if a bottle of milk is spilt in the shopping area, staff must clean it up as quickly as possible to prevent customers from slipping and injuring themselves.

'Reasonably practical' measures are those for which employers can weigh up the cost against the benefit. For example, if it costs £100 000 to install a lift, when there was a 1 in 400 000 chance per year that employees might hurt themselves carrying loads up or down stairs, then this might not be 'reasonably practical'.

Some of the key provisions of the Act are that:

- employers must prepare a general policy on health and safety in written form;
- this written policy should be on public display;
- employees have a legal obligation to comply with health and safety procedures;
- the business must give training, information, instruction and supervision to employees on health and safety issues;
- trade unions which appoint safety representatives can inspect premises and investigate the cause of accidents;
- businesses must provide safety equipment and clothing to employees free of charge.

The Act is enforced by the **Health and Safety Executive**. This is a government body which has the power to issue new codes of practice to govern safety issues as they arise. It also has a team of inspectors responsible for inspecting premises. Inspectors can order changes to be made or, if the situation is serious enough, an immediate closure of the premises until faults are rectified. Sometimes, businesses are taken to court for infringements of Health and Safety legislation, typically when a worker has been injured or killed. Courts have the power to fine businesses for infringements.

Businesses are affected in different ways by health and safety legislation. Businesses where there is little risk of industrial injury find it easy to comply at little cost. However, where there is a strong likelihood of injury, such as in mining or construction, complying with health and safety legislation can be extremely costly and time consuming. Large businesses tend to take health and safety issues seriously. Partly this is because they have the resources to do so and partly because they do not wish to suffer adverse publicity if there is a bad accident. Small businesses in construction and farming tend to have poor safety records. They are often unclear about the law and find it too costly to comply with anyway. In construction, there are major problems because many workers are self-employed and move from site to site picking up work. Pay might be more important to them than health and safety.

Some businesses claim that they are internationally uncompetitive because of having to comply with health and safety laws in the UK. Businesses in, say, the Far East have lower costs because they do not provide as safe a work environment as is required in the UK. However, working in a safe environment should motivate staff. For example, according to Maslow's theory (see unit 35), safety is a fundamental need of human beings.

Employment law

Laws relating to employment can be divided into two categories. **Collective labour law** deals with trade unions and industrial relations. **Individual labour law**, however, deals with the rights and obligations of individual employees. Individual labour law tends to be dealt with through **industrial tribunals** rather than courts of law. Industrial tribunals were originally set up so that workers could represent themselves and, at little cost, pursue a claim against an employer. In practice, industrial tribunal cases tend to be dealt with by lawyers. Workers taking cases to the industrial tribunal are often represented by lawyers working for their trade union.

Different **employment rights**, **relations and protection acts** deal with the rights of workers in a number of areas. For example, employees have the right to receive a **contract of employment** when they start work. This will state the conditions of work, such as how long an employee has to work for per week or month or year, and the rate of pay. Workers are protected from unfair **dismissal**. If an employer wants to dismiss or make a worker redundant, the law lays down procedures for this. Workers are entitled to maternity and paternity leave. Employers cannot ask workers to work more than 48 hours a week except in 'exempt professions'. The **Data Protection Act, 1998** protects information about employees and allows them access to the information.

A number of pieces of legislation also promote equality at work.

The Equal Pay Act, 1970 This stated that workers were entitled to the same pay rates and conditions as other workers in a place of employment doing the same or 'broadly similar'

work. It was intended to stop discrimination against women workers who were often paid less than their male counterparts for doing the same job. The Act was strengthened in 1983. Women could now claim equal pay for work which made the same demands on them in terms of skills, effort and duties as male workers.

The Sex Discrimination Act, 1975 This Act made it unlawful to discriminate on grounds of gender or marital status. It had a number of implications for employers. They couldn't stipulate the gender of applicants in job advertisements. In appointing to a post, they couldn't choose on the basis of gender of the applicant. Employers couldn't make a worker redundant on the basis of gender. Nor could they offer different conditions of work to males and females or married and unmarried workers. Sexual harassment was also made illegal. The **Equal Opportunities Commission** was set up to promote equal opportunities.

Race Relations Act, 1976 This had broadly the same implications as the Equal Opportunities Act in the area of race. It became illegal for employers to discriminate on grounds of colour, race, nationality or ethnic origin. The **Commission for Racial Equality** was set up to promote good race relations.

The Disability Discrimination Act, 1995 This made it illegal

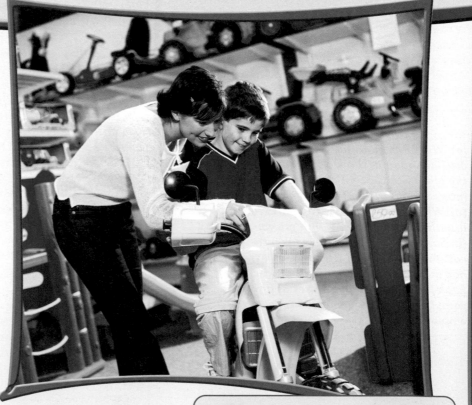

Vanessa Charles had a bad day on April 23rd. It was her son's birthday. She had bought him a motorised cycle from a large high street chain of stores. When he tried it out, though, the motor wouldn't work. She rang the store worried that she might not have carried out all the instructions properly to get it working. It suggested checking the connections in the motor. When she undid the screws and pulled off the plate, the motor was covered in dirt and had obviously been used already.

At least there was the party to look forward to. In the afternoon, she cooked all the foods that children like, including some mini sausages from the local butcher. Some of the children fell ill after the party, all of them having eaten the sausages. All the children who didn't eat the sausages had no problems.

When she took the cycle back to the store, they were extremely apologetic, and offered her a replacement cycle and 10 per cent of the price back as a 'goodwill gesture'.

1 **What rights in law did Vanessa Charles have concerning (a) the faulty cycle and (b) the sausages?**
2 **Discuss the costs and benefits to large chains of retailers of offering 'goodwill gestures' to complaining customers.**

European Commission investigators yesterday carried out dawn raids at Coca-Cola's largest European bottler in a widening probe into its practices in European markets. Coca-Cola typically doesn't bottle its products itself. It sells concentrate to independent companies in local countries or regions round the world. They make up the concentrate, bottle the drink and then distribute it to wholesalers and retailers. Coca-Cola often owns a part share in its bottlers. The raids on the offices of Coca-Cola Enterprises in London - partly owned by the Coca-Cola company - and its Belgian subsidiary came 10 months after

Commission officials targeted Coca-Cola bottlers in Germany, Austria and Denmark.

The move marks a broadening of the investigation into whether Coke has abused its dominant position in European markets by offering retailers incentives to increase sales volumes, carry the full range of Coke products, or stop selling competitors' drinks. The EU investigation is thought to have been triggered by complaints from rivals including PepsiCo and Virgin. If found guilty of abuses of dominant position, the companies could theoretically be fined up to 10 per cent of turnover.

Adapted from the *Financial Times*, 19.5.2000.

1 **Explain how Coca-Cola distributes its products.**
2 **Analyse how Coca-Cola might have 'abused its dominant position' and harmed sales of Pepsi and Virgin drinks.**
3 **Why is the EU involved in this case?**

for an employer with over a given number of employees to discriminate against a worker with a disability. This means that those workers with a disability should not be treated less favourably than other workers unless there is a justified reason. This justified reason might be that it would cost an unreasonable amount to adapt a workplace to accommodate the worker with disabilities. However, where adaptations could be made at relatively little cost, employers are under a legal obligation to do so.

The Minimum Wage Act, 1998 This established a national minimum wage for workers. 18-21 year old workers could be paid a reduced minimum wage. But all adult workers, whether part time or full time, were entitled to a minimum wage rate. In 1998, this was set at £3.60 an hour.

Employment law is an area where small and medium sized businesses feel vulnerable. There is a large amount of legislation and, without expert legal help, small businesses might infringe the law, particularly in areas such as dismissals

and contracts of employment. Small to medium sized businesses also complain about the cost of implementing legislation. '**Red tape**', the jargon word for a large amount of complicated rules and regulations imposed by government, has severely dented competitiveness and profitability according to some businesses, and forced others to close. Businesses trading abroad often claim that red tape has made them uncompetitive against cheap labour Third World country producers.

Consumer protection

Consumers have long been protected by the law from businesses attempting to exploit them. Weights and measures legislation which prevented traders from giving underweight amounts existed in the Middle Ages. As consumers became increasing affluent in the twentieth century and became able to buy a great variety of products, so the need for consumer protection became more important. This was linked to the growth of CONSUMERISM. By grouping together in associations such as the Consumers' Association in the UK, consumers were able to put greater pressure on businesses to provide good quality, safe products with excellent after sales service. Pressure was also put on government to pass laws which would give greater legal safeguards for the consumer.

The major consumer legislation acts in **criminal law** are as follows.

Weights and Measures Acts, 1951, 1963 and 1985 These acts made it an offence to sell goods which were underweight or undervolume. Using false or unfair weighing equipment was also an offence. The 1985 Act introduced metrification.

Trade Descriptions Act, 1968 This made it an offence to sell goods with a false or misleading description. This included advertising and other promotional material and packaging.

Consumer Credit Act, 1974 This Act protects consumers when borrowing money to purchase goods. For example, credit can only be given by financial institutions with a licence. Consumers must be given a copy of the credit agreement they have signed.

Consumer Safety Act, 1978 This issued regulations about the safety of individual products, including children's toys and electrical goods.

Food Safety Act, 1990 Legislation which makes it illegal for businesses to supply food unfit for human consumption has been in existence for a long time. This 1990 Act enlarged the scope of existing legislation, bringing food sources such as farmers under food regulations. Under this Act, the **Food Safety (General Food Hygiene) Regulations** were issued in **1995**, which regulated the preparation and storage of food and equipment. The **Food Labelling Regulations 1996** stated the information which had to be included on food packaging.

The acts described above allow government to prosecute offenders and fine or imprison them. The acts are policed by local authority **trading standards departments**. Trading standards officials inspect premises on a regular basis, particularly food premises. They will also investigate dangerous products.

However, for consumers to win compensation against injury or faulty products, they must use **civil law**. The two main consumer protection acts in civil law are as follows.

Sale of Goods Act, 1979 This states that consumers can sue a business if the goods it sells are not of merchantable quality, fit for the purpose for which they were sold or as described by the business. So a shirt sold with a hole in it is not of merchantable quality. Envelopes which do not stick down are unlikely to be fit for the purpose for which they were sold. A case of six bottles of wine which contains only five is not as described by the business.

Supply of Goods and Services Act, 1982 This extended consumers' rights into the area of services. So services sold have to be of merchantable quality and sold at a reasonable price. Plumbers, for example, who do a bad job and charge very high prices can be sued under this act.

Sale and Supply of Goods Act, 1994 This amended the previous two Acts. So, for example, a customer could reject part of a good or service that was not fit for the purpose.

Consumer protection legislation has increased costs to businesses. However, this varies from product to product.

Businesses involved in food sales have probably seen the highest increase in costs because they have had to change work practices and often buy expensive equipment to conform to the law. Consumer legislation, though, is unlikely to affect the competitiveness of individual businesses since all businesses have to conform to these laws. This is true of imported goods as well. Toys manufactured in China or Thailand for sale to the UK market have to conform to the same safety standards as toys made in London. The cost of improved standards can also be passed on to the consumer.

Larger businesses now often have customer services departments to deal with customer complaints. Their aim is to ensure that customers can get a refund or a repair quickly if something has gone wrong. Businesses want to avoid being taken to court and then having bad publicity. Television programmes such as Watchdog can also give businesses bad publicity.

Some businesses have made it a unique selling point (USP, see unit 10) to give consumers more rights than they have in law. Many clothing chains, for example, allow consumers to bring back goods they decide they do not like and give full refunds. Electronics goods manufacturers might give a one year warranty on a good. In the future, quality of goods and services is likely to be increasingly important. The move to zero defect manufacturing (see unit 46) has considerably improved quality of consumer products.

Competition law

Competition in the market is generally considered to be beneficial to customers. Competing firms have to offer good value products if they are to survive. Good value might be in terms of the quality of the product or in terms of lowest price for a given quality of product. However, competition may be limited for two reasons.

- **Monopolies** (see unit 49) may exist. In economic theory, a monopoly is the sole business in a market. In practice, there are very few monopolies. Railtrack, which owns all the rail infrastructure in the UK, would be one example. But there are many businesses which have very high **market shares** (see unit 2). In UK law, a monopoly is said to exist if a single business has more than 25 per cent of the market. Monopolies can be created by the **merger** of two or more businesses. Therefore mergers must be of concern to any government which wants to promote competition.

- Businesses in a market may **collude** (see unit 49). This means that they get together to fix prices, sales or any other factor which will benefit their profits. The measures that they take are called RESTRICTIVE PRACTICES because they restrict trade. An example of a restrictive practice would be a supplier forcing retailers to sell only at a price which has been set by the supplier. The supplier can then charge high prices to retailers knowing that the customers will be forced to pay the high price. This in turn allows the supplier to charge a high price to the retailers and so enjoy high profits. Another example would be a group of bus companies getting together to fix tenders for contracts. They share out the contracts between them, deciding in advance which firm will win which contract. The lowest bidder on each contract has in fact put in a high price to make high profits. The other bus companies simply put in an even higher price to allow the one bus company to win the contract. The result is that customers have to pay high prices.

In general, UK and EU law forbids businesses to collude unless government permits them to do so in the public interest. Monopolies are not illegal unless the monopolist acts in a way which harms customers. Equally, mergers which create monopolies are not illegal unless customer interests are likely to be harmed.

There is a number of important institutions which play a role in competition policy.

- **The Office of Fair Trading** was established in 1973 under the **Fair Trading Act, 1973**. The Office of Fair Trading is responsible for UK competition policy and consumer protection. It can refer a situation where it believes that a monopolist is abusing its power or there are restrictive trade practices in existence to the Competition Commission.
- The **Competition Commission**, established under the **Competition Act, 1998**, is the body which investigates alleged cases of abuse of monopoly power and restrictive trade practices. It has the power to stop activities and impose fines on businesses which it finds are engaged in uncompetitive behaviour.
- **Regulatory watchdogs such as Oftel, Ofwat and Ofgem** Between the end of the 1940s and the beginning of the 1980s, many key industries in the UK were state owned monopolies. In the 1980s and 1990s, most were PRIVATISED but many remained monopolies, such as the water industry. Or competition was restricted as with telecommunications or electricity supply. For these reasons, many privatised industries were given an individual regulatory watchdog which had the power to limit price increases and encourage competition.
- **The European Commission** is empowered to investigate cases of anti-competitive behaviour when it affects more than one country. For example, pharmaceutical companies might fix the price of competing drugs between them across the whole of the European Union. They would then be in breach of EU law.

There is a number of laws which relate to competition policy.

Competition Act, 1998 This prevents businesses from taking part in activities which might prevent competition, although there are exclusions. It also prevents businesses from abusing a dominant market position. The Act gave the Office of Fair Trading (OFT) power to investigate businesses that might be engaged in such practices. If it finds that they are, it can refer them to the **Competition Commission** to carry out enquiries and make judgments. Business can appeal to the Competition Commission if they disagree with a judgment .

Articles 85 and 86 of the Treaty of Rome The Treaty of Rome, signed in 1956, set up the European Union. Article 85 of the Treaty prohibits restrictive practices across the EU. Article 86 prohibits any business from abusing a dominant position in their market. The EU can also prohibit large mergers which are likely to be against the public interest.

In the first half of the twentieth century, monopolies and restrictive practices were both legal and common in the UK.

In one sense, this benefited many existing businesses because they were able to make higher profits than if there was competition in the market. However, businesses which were outside cartels, or small businesses in a market with a dominant supplier suffered as a result. Competition law is designed to give all businesses a 'level playing field' in their market. It allows new businesses to be created and challenge existing businesses in the market. Ultimately, the purpose of competition law is to prevent customers from being harmed. However, all businesses are customers of other businesses, so they benefit as well as consumers. Competition law is not there to prevent businesses making a profit. The UK government and the EU recognises that profits are the essential incentive for businesses to produce goods and services. The business community can therefore be argued to be a major beneficiary of competition law.

keyterms

Consumerism - **the growth in power of consumers acting together, through associations such as the Consumers Association in the UK, to pressure businesses to make better products and government to pass legislation giving consumers greater rights over businesses.**
Privatisation - **the sale of government owned assets, such as state owned companies, to the private sector.**
Restrictive practices - **measures taken by businesses in a market to limit competition with the goal of raising their profits.**

checklist

1 Explain the difference between civil and criminal law.
2 What are the main provisions of the Health and Safety at Work Act, 1974?
3 To what extent does health and safety legislation benefit businesses?
4 Summarise the main provisions of the law relating to (a) employment and (b) consumer protection in the UK.
5 To what extent does (a) employment law and (b) consumer protection legislation benefit businesses?
6 Outline both UK and EU law relating to competition.
7 To what extent does competition law benefit businesses?

Peter Tildersley runs a software company in London which specialises in contract work for City financial firms. In 2002, with the stock market having crashed to its lowest levels since the early 1990s, City institutions were shedding staff and cutting back on investment. Tildersley's company felt the backwash of this downturn and sales fell by a third over just six months.

He felt that the downturn could be prolonged and knew that the company was making a substantial loss at current sales levels. The only option was to slim down his staff, his major cost. He calculated that he would need to make 15 staff redundant. It was at this point that things began to go wrong. Not understanding the law, he called in the staff he had chosen to go, one by one, and told them they were going to lose their jobs. Nine of them had worked for the company for more than two years and therefore would be entitled to redundancy pay. Three of those chosen he found 'difficult' as employees. Two of them were in jobs which no one else on the staff could do and Peter knew he would have to spend money on training other staff to take on the jobs. One of the members of staff, told in the morning that he would be made redundant, was part of a small team seeing a new client in the afternoon, hoping to win a major contract. He was so demoralised that the presentation to the client was a disaster and the company failed to win the contract. Two of the staff subsequently took the business to an industrial tribunal for unfair dismissal. The staff that remained were angry about what had happened and Peter lost three of his key workers within two months as they could get other jobs.

Peter Tildersley consulted a lawyer about the cases brought against the business. The lawyer explained that he would lose the two cases because he hadn't followed the law. He was legally obliged to consult with his employees before making anyone redundant. It could be that some staff would have gone voluntarily or some would have been prepared to work reduced hours. Only after consultation could he issue redundancy notices. He also was not entitled to dismiss workers because he found them 'difficult'. If the redundancies were about a fall in demand, then legally he had to be able to show that those workers made redundant no longer had work to do. The lawyer pointed out that he should have foreseen the other problems he encountered and taken steps to avoid them.

1 Explain the meaning of the terms:
  (a) 'downturn'; (3 marks)
  (b) 'redundant'. (3 marks)
2 Discuss whether Peter Tildersley should have made 15 staff redundant. (12 marks)
3 To what extent did the problems he encounter over the dismissals arise from having to comply with government 'red tape'? (12 marks)

Starbucks

Knowledge Starbucks, founded in 1985, is a US coffee shop company which has outlets throughout North America and Europe.

Application Starbucks claims to be a *socially responsible* company. In 1991 it began to support Care, an international relief organisation, and became the first privately owned US *company* to offer a *stock option (share) scheme* that included *part time employees*. It also now pays its coffee growers in the *Third World* a *premium price* for coffee *supplies* - today around $1.20 a pound against a world price of less than 50 cents. It has long term direct-*contracts* with its farmers in the *Third World*. It invests in clinics, schools and credit schemes in growers' communities.

Analysis Despite being socially responsible, Starbucks has come under attack from pressure groups for not being responsible enough. For example, the US Organics Consumers Association wants Starbucks to use only milk which is certified free of the growth hormone rBST which is given to cows. Other groups argue that it is not good enough for Starbucks to say that it is helping coffee growers by paying them high prices. The growers themselves must grow coffee in a sound ecological way and not destroy forest to plant new bushes or use pesticides. Coffee growers must pay decent wages to their employees and provide them good conditions of work. Anyway, they argue that there is no independent verification of the fact that Starbucks is paying its coffee growers the price it says it is.

Evaluation One reason why Starbucks might have been targeted by pressure groups is that it is highly visible, with 5 200 outlets across the globe. Also, the fact that it claims to be socially responsible has made it more of a target than companies such as Nestlé, Procter & Gamble and Kraft Foods, all of which sell coffee products. The Organic Consumers Association dismisses the attempts of Starbucks to audit its social responsibility policies as 'greenwash' - environmental public relations that allows a company to escape wider criticism. However, it could be argued that the criticism is unfair. At least Starbucks is some way down the road towards its outlined social responsibility goals, which is surely better than nothing.

Adapted from the *Financial Times*, 11.3.2002.

Social responsibilities

Businesses are often said to be run for the benefit of their owners. In the case of companies, this means being run for the benefit of **shareholders** (see unit 61). However, workers, customers, government and other groups are also an important part of business decision making. This is because it is argued that businesses have SOCIAL RESPONSIBILITIES towards all those affected by their activities, their STAKEHOLDERS.

The main stakeholders in a business, shown in Figure 56.1, are likely to be owners, employees, customers, suppliers, and local communities politically represented by local government. Large businesses may impact on national communities represented by central government and international communities represented by a variety of organisations such as the United Nations. Environmental issues also suggest that animals and plants are possibly stakeholders, as well as future generations of human beings.

It could be argued that, in the UK and the USA, workers, customers and governments act as a constraint on the business achieving its objectives. In countries such as France or Japan, there is a much greater sense that workers, customers, government and other groups should be as important as shareholders in business decision making.

The owners of a business

The owners of a business are stakeholders because they have put up the capital which runs the business. Their reward is the gain they make from owning the business. If owners were unable to get any reward for investing in the business, no one would bother to invest.

In a company, rewards are a mix of the share of the profits

Figure 56.1 *Stakeholders in a business*

made and the capital gain from any increase in the value of shares (the **shareholder value** see unit 63). With a sole trader and partnership, it is a mix of the drawings from the business (part wage, part profit) together with any increase in value of business assets, such as shop or factory premises.

Employees

Employees have a stake in the business for which they work. For example, the business pays them a wage on which they have to live. It might also give them a variety of fringe benefits (see unit 37). Job security is important because workers have bills to pay in the future such as a mortgage. Jobs can give workers satisfaction and a sense of self worth. Training is important both in accomplishing the current job and in giving skills in new jobs. Health and safety and the environment in which the employee works are affected by business policies. A 'good employer' is one which compares well with other similar businesses on employment issues.

Customers

Business have responsibilities to their customers. They have a duty to sell them a well made product which is reasonably priced. Individual products and different customers have different needs. For a business customer, delivering orders on time might be very important, particularly if it is operating just-in-time manufacturing (see unit 47). For a household buying a car or a DVD player, reliability might be very important.

It should be remembered that, in a capitalist market economy, the ultimate function of businesses is to provide customers with goods and services. Giving profits to shareholders is the incentive that the market mechanism offers to the owners of businesses to get them to do this. Equally, wages are the incentive for employees to go to work. But they are only the means to the end of getting businesses to make products. So it could be argued that customers are the most important stakeholders in a business.

Suppliers

Suppliers rely upon customers that are businesses to buy their products. Businesses have a social responsibility to act fairly to their suppliers, paying reasonable prices for products, for example. They should also respect contracts which they have signed with suppliers.

ScottishPower is a power company mainly supplying electricity and gas in the UK and the USA. In 2002-03, it had sales of £5 200 million and earned profits before tax of £697 million. ScottishPower Learning was set up in 1996 as a way of turning some of the parent company's strong training traditions into a wider community benefit. The organisation, a joint venture with ScottishPower's unions, aims to create learning opportunities for the unemployed, provide curriculum and other support for schools in deprived communities, and more generally encourage lifelong learning. ScottishPower Learning accounts for 27 per cent of the company's total community expenditure in the UK - it costs £1.84 million a year to run.

The benefits of ScottishPower Learning's activities are not confined to the young people who gain qualifications or enter employment. ScottishPower emphasises that there are business benefits as well. These include connecting the company with the community in which it operates, and giving it a 'platform across various policy debates on social exclusion, employability and skills development, and an opportunity to directly influence curriculum development which in turn benefits ScottishPower as a major employer.'

Adapted from Business in the Community, *Financial Times*, December 2002 and http://www.ScottishPower.com

1 **Explain how ScottishPower is acting in a socially responsible way.**
2 **How much is ScottishPower spending on community projects relative to its sales and profits?**
3 **Discuss the costs and benefits to ScottishPower of adopting a stakeholder approach.**

Tough environmental laws impose a burden on many mid-market companies which are forced to spend heavily to meet new regulations. One such company is Zeus Aluminium, a foundry making engine castings. In recent years, it has invested heavily in modern technology to enhance quality and productivity and to ensure the environmental acceptability of what it does.

In many instances Zeus has gone beyond what is required by law. But the time and resources spent reaching these goals have imposed heavy burdens. Gary Roper, Zeus's engineering manager, now spends up to half his time dealing with environmental issues. The company has to contend with the anti-pollution requirements of local councils, which takes up a lot of management time. Because of the company's expansion, Zeus could fall within the remit of the Environment Agency rather than the local council. This would increase its costs further. What's more, continued changes in legal regulations mean that the company is having to 'run fast just to stand still'. For example, since April it has had to contend with the energy tax, part of the climate-change levy. The new tax has wiped out earlier savings made by using fuel more efficiently and led to additional costs of £50 000 in the first year alone. Tax paid will increase if the company continues to grow.

Zeus is aware that it must be environmentally friendly to go on winning work. Car makers are putting pressure on their suppliers such as Zeus to adopt more environmentally friendly policies. The car makers know that their reputation with their customers is at risk if the automobile industry doesn't attempt to reduce environmental damage. Zeus will go on meeting its environmental targets, but there are no positive spin-offs from doing so. 'Money spent meeting environmental goals means less to spend on new efficient machinery,' says Peter Harpin, managing director of Zeus.

Adapted from *The Sunday Times*, 17.6.2001.

> 1 **Outline (a) the benefits and (b) the costs to Zeus of being a socially responsible company.**
> 2 **Discuss whether Zeus would have adopted such environmentally friendly policies if it had not been forced to do so by laws and government regulations.**

If a business is in danger of failing, this can have an important effect on suppliers. Not only might suppliers lose future sales, but they may also have trade credit outstanding to a customer. In some cases, suppliers are forced to cease trading themselves when a customer fails because they are owed so much money.

Local, national and international communities

Businesses have social responsibilities to the communities in which they operate. Such social responsibilities can come in many forms.

- The economic prosperity of a community depends upon particular businesses. For example, businesses provide jobs in the local community, which in turn support other businesses such as shops where wages are spent. In some communities, a single business may provide a large proportion of the jobs. The prosperity of the local community can then become totally dependent upon one employer. This can be true of nations too. In Africa, for example, some small countries are highly dependent on single mining companies or oil companies.
- A few businesses play important roles in their communities by supporting local charities or getting involved with schools and colleges. In the past in the UK, and in some countries today, businesses have also built and owned the housing in which their workers live. Rowntree in York or Cadbury in Birmingham were examples.
- Some businesses, such as McDonald's or The Body Shop, have a very high media profile. Arguably, they have an important influence upon the way we live. In France, for example, it is suggested that McDonald's, by encouraging

people to eat fast food, has led to a change in eating habits away from traditional French cuisine. The Body Shop, by its ethical stance, has perhaps encouraged other businesses to be more ethical.

The environment and future generations

In recent years, businesses have been lobbied by environmental groups, such as Greenpeace, animal welfare groups, such as the World Wildlife Fund, and ecological groups, such as Friends of the Earth. These PRESSURE GROUPS have raised the awareness of both government, communities and businesses of the impact that business activity has on the environment. Recycling has become more common among businesses even when it fails to increase profits. In industries such as mining or oil extraction, where damaging the environment is almost inevitable, most companies have reduced some of the damage they cause. Many also present a case to the public that they are environmentally responsible.

However, businesses face a dilemma. Nearly all business activity is to some extent damaging to the environment. Employees travelling to work by car for their business have a negative impact on the environment. So businesses have to weigh up the demands of environmentalists with what they see as legitimate business activities.

Businesses face another problem if their activities impact on future generations of human beings. Building a nuclear power plant today means almost certainly that future generations will be left clearing up the nuclear waste created. Taking a barrel of oil from the ground today means that it will not be

checklist

1 List the major stakeholders in a typical business.
2 Outline THREE benefits which a socially responsible employer might provide for its employees.
3 In some hospitals, companies have their name on products. To what extent are these companies 'socially responsible'?
4 Can any mining company which takes away scarce resources that can never be replaced be 'socially responsible'?
5 Explain TWO ways in which a company could be socially responsible and as a result increase its profits.
6 Has the ban on cigarette advertising in the UK made tobacco manufacturers more socially responsible?

available to people 200 years from now. Sending a lorry to deliver goods 100 miles away probably contributes to global warming. Business is typically geared up to what is happening today, or over the next three months or a year. Five years is quite a long time horizon for most businesses. What will happen in twenty years time is perhaps seriously considered by only a few companies worldwide.

Some large businesses now carry out SOCIAL and ENVIRONMENTAL AUDITS. These set out criteria upon which the performance of a business will be judged. For example, an environmental audit may consider how much pollution is delivered into the atmosphere by the business. Policies can then be worked out either to maintain or improve the environmental record of the business.

Costs and benefits to businesses of adopting a stakeholder approach

Adopting a socially responsible approach means taking the needs of stakeholders into account when making business decisions. In practice, it often means giving less importance to the interests of owners and more importance to other stakeholders than the typical business. The costs and benefits to businesses of adopting such an approach tend to be measured in terms of their impact on profits, sales, revenues and accounting costs. The advantages include the following.

● Having good employment policies. This should attract better applicants for posts and help motivate and retain existing staff. Improved motivation and retention should lead to increased profits.
● Effective customer care policies should lead to higher sales and hence higher profits.
● Working well with suppliers should enable the purchaser to get value for money. It should be much easier to sort out problems such as late deliveries or defective work with suppliers with whom there is a good relationship.
● Putting something into the community, such as giving to local charities, taking on workers or backing training projects should give the business good public relations (PR, see unit 18). This might help sell products or attract good applicants for jobs.

● Being environmentally friendly could lead to lower overall costs. For example, recycling heat in a boiler might cost money for new equipment, but quickly save money because of lower fuel inputs needed. Being seen as environmentally friendly may help sales of products and thus increase profit.
● For some high profile companies, becoming more socially responsible deflects the criticisms of pressure groups. Companies such as Monsanto (over GM crops) or Nike (over poor conditions of work in factories making trainers in the Third World), for example, have found bad publicity affects sales. In the mid-1990s, Shell faced a consumer boycott of its petrol filling stations over its plans to dispose of a North Sea oil platform by sinking it in the middle of the Atlantic Ocean. The nuclear power industry has found it almost impossible to win new contracts to build nuclear power stations because of the concerns of environmentalists and local community groups. Spending money on becoming more socially responsible is a way of reducing the risks to sales and profits that would come from bad PR.

The main disadvantage of the stakeholder approach is that, in practice, it tends to add to costs and can lower profits for most businesses. If this were not the case, every employer would give large sums of money to local charities or to pursue environmentally friendly policies.

Of course, being seen as socially responsible might lead to an increase in sales. So in practice businesses have to weigh up the benefits of being socially responsible against the extra costs that this might incur.

Social responsibility and the law

Becoming more socially responsible can increase the costs and reduce the profits of business. So they sometimes ignore stakeholder concerns to prevent this. It is for this reason that governments over the past 200 years have introduced legislation to force businesses to become more socially responsible and to take more care of their stakeholders. Everything from banning the use of child labour, to minimum wages, to paternity leave, to consumer protection laws, to bans on advertising of certain products and limits on pollution have changed the way in which businesses operate.

Because the law is such a powerful way to change how businesses operate, pressure groups, from trade unions to the Consumers' Association to Friends of the Earth, spend large sums of money lobbying governments to get laws changed.

keyterms

Pressure groups - groups which attempt to influence business, government and individuals, such as trade unions or environmental charities.
Social and environmental audits - measures of the performance of businesses against social and environmental criteria.
Social responsibilities - duties that a business owes to those affected by its activities.
Stakeholder - an individual or group which is affected by a business and so has an interest in its success of failure.

Social reporting is accelerating. A growing number of leading companies, especially in Britain and other countries in northern Europe, are providing information about how well they are performing on issues affecting employees, local communities and society at large. But this enthusiasm for joining the social reporting bandwagon is rarely matched by rigour in documents and websites, which are dominated by what Tom Woollard, a director of the international environmental consultancy ERM, describes as 'corporate gloss'.

ERM has carried out a review of the material published this year by the UK's top 100 listed companies. Mr Woolland says few of these companies are prepared to publish hard data or tackle tough issues. 'A lot of companies say they are committed to being transparent and sustainable but they report data on an incredibly narrow and conservative range of parameters', he says.

ERM's study found that 70 of the top 100 companies published some information on social performance - twice as many as a year ago. But three-quarters of those companies provided no quantitative data to back up their claim. It is as if the board of a company has asked its shareholders to believe sales were forging ahead, without revealing the numbers to prove it.

And Mr Woollard has no truck with complaints that corporate social reporting is a difficult area where numbers are hard to come by, at least as far employees are concerned. 'All companies should be able to say whether the women who work for them are paid the same as the men, what their ethnic mix is, or the gap between the lowest and highest paid. These are basic human resources statistics', he says.

It is not just a question of data. The other gap concerns the issues companies are prepared to deal with. Typically they are not the controversies that most people would be interested in. Mr Woollard explains: 'If you take telecommunications, there are only two issues people want to know about: masts and handsets. But you get reports full of data about training and the accident rate. In the pharmaceuticals world, the hot topic is drugs and the developing world but the reports are fairly silent about that. Banks say in reports that they are committed to sustainable development but they don't tell people what they will and won't invest in.'

Adapted from the *Financial Times*, 11.12.2001.

1 Explain what is meant by the terms:
 (a) 'social reporting'; (3 marks)
 (b) 'quantitative data'. (3 marks)
2 To what extent are businesses providing accurate social reports to their stakeholders in the UK? (12 marks)
3 Discuss whether it is in the best interests of companies to publish comprehensive social reports which are supported by statistical evidence. (12 marks)

Number of safety incidents
Days lost through illness
Charitable spending
Employee fundraising
Number of community complaints
Wages
Training days
Training budget
Number of staff appraisals
Employee ethnicity/gender/disability analysis
Employee satisfaction statistics

Table 56.1 *Social indicators used by companies*

57 Business ethics

GM Crops

Knowledge Monsanto was one of a number of US companies developed GM crops in the 1980s and 1990s. Genetically modified seeds are seeds which have been modified in the laboratory by changing one or more of their genes. This allows familiar plants such as wheat or tomatoes to have new properties. For example, one Monsanto GM wheat strain was made resistant to a popular Monsanto pesticide, Roundup.

Application In the second half of the 1990s, Monsanto *launched* its *products* in the USA without any major problems. But when it attempted to *sell* into Europe, there was a storm of protest from environmental *pressure groups* such as Greenpeace. They argued that it was *unethical* to sell these new crops because no one knew exactly what might happen to the *environment* following planting or to *consumers* eating food.

Analysis Monsanto developed GM crops because it thought they were the crops of the future. They would be environmentally welcomed because they were designed to use less pesticides than normal crops. Farmers would use them because their costs would fall. The reaction in Europe caught it totally unawares. Monsanto failed to foresee that some would argue that it was morally wrong to plant the new crops.

Evaluation In failing to foresee the ethical dimension of its new products, Monsanto has arguably missed an enormous opportunity to expand sales and profits. Greenpeace might be overreacting when it writes on its website that: 'Genetic scientists are altering life itself - artificially modifying genes to produce plants and animals which could never have evolved naturally.' However, whether Greenpeace is right or not, European consumers have reacted negatively to GM foods. Only by regaining the moral highground can Monsanto win round sceptical Europeans.

Adapted from the *Financial Times*, 8.3.2002.

Social responsibilities

ETHICS is about morality and doing 'what is right' and not 'what is wrong'. All businesses have to make many ethical decisions. Some are affected by the law. For example, it is illegal for businesses to dump waste by the roadside or send their drivers out on the road in unroadworthy vehicles. However, many ethical decisions have to be made without the help of the law. For example, should an employer allow a worker to take a day off work to look after a sick child and still be paid? Should a company stop buying goods from a factory in the Far East where it knows that work conditions are poor and wages are very low?

Making ethical decisions can be complicated because of differences of opinion. Some argue that it is wrong for businesses to manufacture toy guns to sell to children. Others suggest that they do no real harm. Muslim restaurant owners might face a dilemma about whether to sell alcoholic drink because the Koran forbids the drinking of alcohol. Other restaurant owners might not face such an ethical dilemma. Despite these differences, in many situations most people often take the same ethical stance. For example, most would agree that a company should not use employees' money in a pension fund to bail it out if it is making a loss.

Ethical issues

All businesses have to make ethical decisions. Should a self-employed plumber charge an old age pensioner extra when a job takes longer than estimated? Should a finance manager delay payments if the business has cash flow difficulties?

Over the past twenty years, a number of issues have arisen for large firms which require decisions based on ethics.

The environment In countries like the UK or the USA, the law prevents businesses from polluting or destroying the environment. However, businesses must decide whether to adopt even more stringent measures to protect the environment. For example, should a business recycle materials, especially if this will lower profits? Multinational businesses often face lower environmental standards in Third World countries. Should they lower their own environmental standards in the Third World to take advantage of this?

Animal rights Some companies, such as pharmaceutical companies or cosmetics manufacturers, might use animals to test products. Animal rights groups argue this is unethical. Other companies, particularly food manufacturers or oil groups, can destroy habitats and endanger animals. Wildlife conservation groups argue against farming which destroys forests or oil installations, which can pollute the environment leading to the destruction of animal life.

Workers in the Third World A number of companies have been criticised for exploiting workers in Third World countries. Companies manufacture in the Third World because it reduces their costs. However, there is an ethical question about the extent to which low costs should be at the expense of low paid workers.

Corruption In some industries, such as defence, bribes might be used to persuade customers to sign contracts. It has been suggested that this takes place in the Third World, where civil servants or government ministers want money from any deal to buy arms. The ethical question is whether it is right to use bribes even if a business knows that its competitors do.

New technologies Some industries are at the cutting edge of science and technology. Most new products developed, such as DVD players or a new chocolate bar, do not cause problems. But since the 1950s, nuclear power generation has been an issue. In the 1990s, GM crops hit the headlines. In the future, many biological processes, such as cloning, could arouse strong ethical reactions.

Product availability If a poor family cannot afford an expensive car, most would not see this as an ethical issue. But if an Aids sufferer in South Africa cannot afford drugs for treatment because pharmaceutical businesses charge such a high price, many would argue that it is an ethical issue. The direction of research is also important. Companies might research new drugs for complaints suffered by only a few in

the industrialised world. Or they might research illnesses such as malaria which kill millions each year in the Third World. The choice that businesses make is an ethical issue.

Trading issues Some countries have been condemned internationally for the policies pursued by their governments. They may even have had sanctions or trade embargoes placed upon them. Companies must decide whether to trade with or invest in these countries.

Codes of practice

In recent years, some large businesses have adopted ETHICAL CODES OF PRACTICE. These lay down how employees in the business should respond in situations where ethical issues arise. Ethical codes will differ from one business and one industry to another. However, they may contain statements about:
- environmental responsibility;
- dealing with customers and suppliers in a fair and honest manner;
- competing fairly and not engaging in practices such as collusion (see unit 49) or destroyer pricing (see unit 17).
- the workforce and responding fairly to their needs.

Ethics and profitability

As with social responsibility (see unit 56), there might be a conflict between business ethics and profitability. Acting ethically when not required to do so by the law can have a negative impact on profit in two ways.
- It can raise costs. For example, paying higher wages than is necessary to Third World workers increases costs. Having to find other ways than animal experiments to test a new drug might add to costs. Adopting an ethical code of practice can raise costs. Staff have to be made aware of it and trained to implement it. It takes management time to prepare a code of practice.
- It can reduce revenues. A business might lose a contract if it refuses to give a bribe. Selling medicines to the Third World at low prices might increase sales, but total revenue is likely to be lower. Refusing to develop GM crops might mean a competitor getting into the market first and becoming the market leader. Acting ethically might even mean the destruction of the company. For example, a cigarette manufacturer which took full account of the costs it causes to customers would probably decide to cease trading.

However, adopting an ethical stance can produce benefits.
- Some companies have used their ethical stance for marketing purposes. In the UK, for example, the Co-operative Bank and The Body Shop have both increased sales by having a strong ethical stance and drawing in customers which are attracted by this. But adopting an ethical stance is no guarantee of success. Since the mid-1990s, The Body Shop has had disappointing sales growth. An ethical stance which may catch the mood of today's customers may not interest them ten years later.
- For most companies which have taken ethics seriously, it is the equivalent of an insurance policy. They don't want to be caught out behaving unethically and face serious penalties for breaking the law or see sales fall as customers

Huntingdon Life Sciences is a company which carries out scientific experiments on animals for commercial clients. It has been involved in a long running dispute with animal rights activists which want to close the company down. The long term term aim of the animal rights activists is for all animal experimentation to be banned.

What has been unusual about the dispute is its length and ferocity. The company's main laboratory is picketed every day. Workers and managers have been subject to threatening telephone calls. The managing director has been attacked by animal rights activitists.

Failing to close down the company, the protesters turned to shareholders and financial companies dealing with Huntingdon Life Sciences. Shareholders were picketed outside their homes. Stockbrokers and bankers were subjected to a campaign of abuse. The result was that most shareholders sold their shares in the company, and the banks and stockbrokers in the UK refused to deal with the company anymore. The campaign has now spread to the USA, where customers and financial institutions dealing with the company have been targeted.

Adapted from *The Sunday Times*, 21.1.2001, the *Financial Times*, 15.10.2001, 5.6.2002.

1 **Discuss whether Huntingdon Life Sciences can ever be an 'ethical' company.**
2 **Evaluate whether customers, such as pharmaceutical companies developing new drugs, should continue to use Huntingdon Life Sciences.**

protest against this behaviour. In 2002, two major companies paid the price for unethical behaviour. Enron, a large US energy trading company, collapsed. It was found to have manipulated its accounts to inflate its profits. Senior management had acted unethically by hiding this from shareholders and government. This also led to the collapse of one of the world's top five accounting firms, Arthur Anderson. It had audited Enron's accounts and was accused of hiding the irregularities. As a result, it began to lose its major customers and decided to close down.

Ethics has become a serious issue for large companies. Customers and society have become less tolerant of businesses which behave in a way they see as unethical. However, most companies tend to follow trends and adopt ethical policies which will prevent them from coming to harm in the market place or by law. A few have adopted an aggressive ethical stance which sometimes has led to them gaining more customers. Often, small to medium sized businesses do not have management time or resources to draw up an ethical code of practice. Their ethical stance and behaviour is influenced by the society in which they operate.

✓checklist

1 Give TWO examples of ethical decisions an oil production company might have to make.
2 Explain which types of companies might be particularly affected by ethical issues relating to:
(a) the environment; (b) animal rights issues; (c) Third World labour; (d) bribery; (e) new technologies; (f) access to products; (g) trading with politically unacceptable countries.
3 What might be contained in an ethical code of practice?
4 To what extent can businesses increase profits by becoming more ethical?

"keyterms

Business ethics - ideas about what is morally correct or not in a business situation.
Ethical code of practice - a statement about how employees in a business should behave in particular circumstances where ethical issues arise.

The Co-operative Group is to convert all its own-brand chocolate bars to the ethically-sound Fairtrade label. Terry Hudghton, head of brands at the Co-op, which was the first to bring Fairtrade bananas to Britain, said: 'We want to make Fairtrade mainstream.' If successful, the move would double the amount of Fairtrade chocolate eaten in Britain. The Co-op sells almost £3 million worth of own-brand chocolate a year and hopes to convert all these sales to the new bars.

However, success would affect only a small part of the market. Britons spend £185 million a year on chocolate bars. None of the big chocolate companies includes an ethical chocolate bar in its product line up.

Fairtrade is an independent consumer mark and is intended to give producers a more stable income and a higher price for their goods by cutting out intermediaries and offering longer term contracts. However, research by the Institute of Grocery Distribution, the food industry research body, indicated that consumers were more influenced by price and taste of an item than by the conditions in which it was produced or traded. The Co-op hopes that rather than beat the competition, the likes of Nestlé, Cadbury and Mars will follow suit. 'If the major manufacturers were to carry just one Fairtrade product in their range, the benefits for the poverty-stricken cocoa grower would be phenomenal', said Mr Hudghton. 'We have made chocolate our primary focus because of the obscene contrast between the pleasure derived from eating it and the suffering that can go into supplying its key ingredient.'

Adapted from the *Financial Times*, 26.11.2002.

88 Fair Trade

Milk Chocolate
Rich and smooth milk chocolate
150 g ℮

FOR BEST BEFORE DATE: SEE REVERSE OF PACK
STORE IN A COOL, DRY PLACE

FAIRTRADE — Guarantees a better deal for Third World Producers
Approx. per ⅓ bar — Cals 280 Fat 18g Salt Nil
Suitable for Vegetarians

1 *What might be the advantages to the Co-op of adopting an ethical buying policy for its own-label chocolate?*
2 *Discuss the possible costs and benefits to a major chocolate manufacturer of adopting Fairtrade principles in its chocolate buying.*

Nike is the world's number one trainer brand. It doesn't manufacture anything though. It designs shoes and markets them. Production is subcontracted to hundreds of factories around the world. Today, around 500 000 workers make Nike footwear and apparel.

So how did such a successful company come to face a negative ethical campaign? It started in 1992 when Jeff Ballinger, a US-based activist working in Indonesia, published a report about conditions in the country's factories, detailing labour abuses, unsanitary conditions and forced overtime. Nike, as a high profile US company, became a symbol for the activists wanting to change the system. Student groups in the US lobbied for independent monitoring of factories of companies selling goods on US campuses, threatening Nike's share of a $2.4 billion business in college wear. Activist groups, such as Global Exchange, bombarded the media with anti-Nike stories.

In response, the company implemented a code of conduct that dealt explicitly with labour rights in 1992. There then followed a series of further initiatives. Ernst & Young, the international firm of auditors, began monitoring labour conditions in 1994. Nike joined President Bill Clinton's Fair Labour Campaign in 1996. The company asked Andrew Young, a prominent black American who had been Ambassador to the United Nations, to review factories in Vietnam, China and Indonesia. The company also set out to improve the lives of workers. It launched lending programmes for workers, adult education and better factory monitoring. In 1999, it joined the World Bank and Mattel the toy maker to launch the Global Alliance, an adult training programme.

Despite these initiatives, Nike still received criticism. In 2000, for example, a BBC documentary accused Nike of using child labour in Cambodia. The company as a result reviewed all 3 800 workers' records and interviewed those it suspected were under age. But it couldn't verify that all the workers were adult. As a result, it pulled out of production in Cambodia. Oxfam Community Aid Abroad, the Australian-based organisation that closely monitors Nike, alleges that the company has 'consistently moved production of its sneakers to wherever wages are lowest and workers' human rights are most brutally oppressed'. It says most of Nike's Indonesian workers who are parents are forced by their financial circumstances to live apart from their children. Nike's factory monitoring programme 'looks good on paper but ... in practice achieves very little'.

Nike itself admits that it is not perfect. In its first 'corporate responsibility report', published in October 2001, it said that making Nike trainers was 'tedious, hard and doesn't offer a wonderful future'. Workers in factories that make Nike products were harassed by their superiors who showed scant regard for the rules on overtime. Nike said it knew far too little about what happened in the factories it uses. Finally, it admitted that its monitoring system did not work well enough.

Nike knows that it will continue to be targeted by activists unless it uses factories with Western style conditions of work, if not pay. To do that could turn a highly profitable company into one making losses, which could find it difficult to compete against other companies using cheap Third World labour. It also knows that almost all large clothing manufacturers, or giant retailers such as Wal-Mart (which owns Asda), routinely buy from Third World factories where conditions of work are just as poor, if not poorer, than in Nike factories. So Nike is now resigned to continuing to receive criticism despite its efforts to improve working conditions in supplier factories.

Adapted from the *Financial Times*, 21.12.2000, 7.3.2002 and 18.6.2002.

1 Explain the meaning of:
   (a) 'number one trainer brand'; (3 marks)
   (b) 'ethical campaign'. (3 marks)
2 Discuss whether the criticisms levelled at Nike by activists are justified. (12 marks)
3 To what extent would Nike benefit if it implemented the sort of ethical policy its critics would like to see adopted?

Hamed & Sehmi

Knowledge Hamed & Sehmi is a small manufacturing company making specialist turned parts, fasteners and machine parts for a wide range of industrial sectors.

Application In 2003, it purchased its first *CNC (Computer Numerically Controlled) machine* costing £135 000 with the help of a £20 000 government *grant*. The *investment* was a large one for the *company*, but it felt that to remain *competitive* it had to replace some of its *machinery*, much of which was at least 30 years old.

Analysis Hamed & Sehmi, like many small businesses, faced a dilemma. On the one hand, it was struggling to match the prices being offered by competitors who were better equipped. On the other hand, investing in excess of £100 000 on new machinery, financed through borrowing, was a gamble. Fortunately, the six workers the business employed were keen to work with the new machine. If nothing else, they knew that their jobs were at risk if the company failed to invest. Two of the workers underwent extensive training to operate the machine.

Evaluation Introducing new technology can be risky, especially for a small business like Hamed & Sehmi. A sharp cut back in orders for a few months could throw their business plan into complete disarray. However, the business was probably right to invest. The investment will help it to match at least some of the productivity of rival companies.

Technological change

The use of TECHNOLOGY is one of a number of characteristics which separate human beings from most other animals. Over time, humans have developed a range of technologies, such as the wheel, water power, steam power, electricity and telephony. The latest technology to transform society has been the microchip. This has given rise to computers and information and communication technology. The next major wave of technologies is likely to centre around biotechnology.

It has been argued that technological change is **exponential**. This means that the rate of change accelerates over time. 2000 years ago, the rate of technological change hardly altered at all over a person's lifetime. 100 years ago, there was significant change for many people in industrialised countries over their lifetime. Today, major changes take place almost every decade.

Business opportunities

Technological change provides businesses with two main opportunities.

New products In some industries, developing new products is vital to the competitiveness of a business. For example, vehicle, domestic appliance and electronic goods manufacturers all survive by constantly bringing out new and improved products. The **product life cycle** (see unit 12) varies from industry to industry. In the car industry, models may be changed every five years, although there will be minor modifications made each year. With a new product like a DVD player, the product life cycle may be less than one year.

In these industries, failure to bring out new products based on the latest technology is likely to lead to falling sales and the survival of the business may be threatened.

However, in other industries, new technology has little if any impact on the product. Heinz Baked Beans, for example, are sold with the marketing message that they haven't changed over time. Today's baked beans are the same as the 'original'. New technologies can also be fiercely resisted by customers. Foods containing GM (genetically modified) crops have had to be withdrawn from supermarket shelves in the UK because some consumers didn't want to buy the products.

So the introduction of technologically improved products is vital in some industries. At the other other end of the scale, some businesses are successful because the product is the same as before, unaffected by technological change.

Product processes Even though Heinz Baked Beans have not changed over time, the technology used in their production is likely to have changed. Much of manufacturing industry has been transformed over the past thirty years, partly due to the introduction of microchip technology. This has resulted in further AUTOMATION of processes where workers have been replaced by machines.

For example, COMPUTER NUMERICAL CONTROLLED (CNC) lathes and milling machines are now standard in UK manufacturing. In design, COMPUTER AIDED DESIGN (CAD) packages are commonplace. These are programs which allow a design to be completed on a computer rather than on paper. The package is also able to do the numerical calculations necessary for the job. COMPUTER AIDED MANUFACTURING (CAM) (or CAD/CAM ENGINEERING) links CAD packages with CNC machines. The CNC machines can be programmed from the CAD package. Computers are also used in other departments of manufacturing companies. Accounts are likely to be produced using an accounting program and financial information stored on computer or disks. Deliveries can be tracked online with some delivery companies.

Service industries too have been transformed. Even a traditional restaurant, for example, is likely to use a till which is controlled by a microchip. People might pay for a meal using a swipe card. In the kitchen, cookers, refrigerators and utensils will have changed from thirty years ago. In many service industries, there has been a revolution in the way in which the service is delivered. Computerisation has swept away the keeping of manual records. Email communication is becoming more common than written letters. The Internet allows advertising and sales to be made directly to customers via computer link.

Using technology to change the way in which work is done has several benefits. One is that production becomes more efficient, reducing costs. Another is that the quality of production can be improved. Email allows a faster response time to a query. The use of robots lets car manufacturers achieve zero defects in production. Improved technology can be used to improve the health and safety of workers. By automating dangerous processes, workers can be protected from harm.

Impact of changes in technology

New technology can present businesses with considerable opportunities. But it can also be pose a major threat. There is a variety of ways in which this occurs.

Implementing technological change Buying a new computer system, installing a new CNC machine or developing a new product with the latest technology will not necessarily be successful in improving productivity or sales. The introduction of new technology is often a high risk process. Many new products fail. It may prove impossible to integrate the new machine into the existing production process. Computerisation may not save a worker time compared to a pen and paper system.

The introduction of new technology might also affect business organisation. Improvements in communication might mean changes in work practices, such as a reduction in face to face meetings. It might also allow a business, for example, to set up in another country and keep in regular contact to better meet the needs of a foreign market.

Managing technological change requires skill and often a certain amount of luck on the part of a business.

Competition and survival It is often expensive to install new technology in production processes. Designing new products containing new technology is also costly. Many businesses don't make enough profit or generate the cash flow to be able to afford this investment. However, they risk being left behind in the market if they don't invest. In the UK, manufacturing companies which have consistently failed to invest have become less and less cost competitive. Many businesses have been forced to close due to competition from cheap labour producers in the Far East. In a competitive market place, the businesses that survive are those which invest enough and manage the new technology successfully.

The workforce New technology will have an impact on the workers in a business. Introducing new technology in production is likely to require **training** (see unit

Ever since General Motors installed the first industrial robot in its Trenton, New Jersey, plant in 1962, the car industry has been in the vanguard of robotics. Robots do not demand pay rises, do not join trade unions and are happy to do dirty, smelly, dangerous jobs. They are also pinpoint accurate time after time, an essential ability if your job is to weld together hundreds of thousands of cars a year. Yet car factory automation seems to have reached its peak for two different reasons.

First, car makers have come to realise that robots are expensive compared to workers. Not only is their initial purchase cost high, but they are costly to maintain. Breakdowns are costly too. 'We had to realise in the car industry that a high degree of automation in the factory will give you reliability problems and then you will have downtimes - and downtimes cost you money', said Noirbert Reithofer, director of production at BMW.

Second, robots have proved too inflexible in final assembly where the variety of options on any individual car explodes. Robots are well suited to making standard movements using standard components. But the complexity of options in final assembly is too great. Even in one of the few areas of final assembly that have been colonised by robots - attaching windscreens - some new factories are reverting to human beings. At the new Honda plant in Swindon, the experience gained with the glazing robot in the old factory gave the company the expertise to fit windscreens manually.

Third, with flexible manufacturing systems, car manufacturers want to be able to switch production from one model to the next relatively quickly. Robots can be too inflexible for this. 'There has been a rebalancing', according to Steve Young, automotive vice-president at consultants AT Kearney. 'There is a better understanding of the real cost of automation from real experience.' In particular, he says, it costs a lot more to reprogram the machine for a new vehicle than was expected - as much as buying the robot in the first place.

Adapted from the *Financial Times*, 1.5.2003.

1 **Explain the link between automation and robots.**
2 **What are the main advantages to car manufacturers of using robots?**
3 **Why have some car manufacturers begun to use less technology in their plants and relied more on human workers?**

41) of workers. This may be on-the-job training or off-the-job training. Not all workers will necessarily be able to cope with the changes. Some workers, for example, may not have the basic skills needed. Others may be reluctant to change to new ways of working. Management may then have to consider redeployment of some staff. Redundancy may also be a possibility. If the new technology is labour saving, and sales are not increasing, then redundancies may be inevitable.

Change can affect **motivation** (see unit 35). Some workers may be highly motivated by working with new products or new processes. Other workers may find it threatening and demotivating. They may be afraid that they will lose their job or their position in the hierarchy. They may worry about having to work with a new group of people or under a different manager. If the workplace is unionised, these fears may lead to trade unions objecting to the changes and attempted to stop, delay or alter them. Management, therefore, need to handle change with great care.

keyterms

Automation - the process of the replacement of workers by machines in production.
Computer Aided Design (CAD) - the use of computers to design products.
Computer Aided Manufacturing (CAM) or CAD/CAM engineering - the use of computers to control production processes, for example from design using **CAD** technology through to manufacture on **CNC** machines.
Computer Numerical Control (CNC) machines - machines in factories which receive instructions about what to do from a computer rather than directly from the actions of a worker.
Technology - a creative process which uses human, scientific and material resources to solve problems and improve efficiency.

checklist

1 Give THREE examples of technological change that has occurred over the past three hundred years.
2 What does it mean to say that the rate of technological change is 'exponential'?
3 How can technological change lead to (a) changes in products and (b) changes in production processes?
4 Why might introducing new technology into a workplace be disruptive to production?
5 What are the human resource implications of introducing new technology?

Kesslers International is one of Europe's biggest makers of display stands for retailers. This is a fast-changing category of product, where success depends on translating design into manufacturing as smoothly as possible. At the company's factory in east London, a piece of metal can be cut into a complex shape on the shop floor using digital instructions generated 20 minutes earlier by a designer sitting at a computer terminal on the other side of a partition. 'We spend half our time working on creative design and the other half turning a concept into a working product without losing the aesthetic appeal', says George Kessler, one of two brothers who run the family-owned company.

Each year the company makes up to 1 000 types of display, selling from just a few pounds to £1 500 each, in production runs that are rarely above a few thousand. The displays use about 70 000 types of component. These are made on a variety of machines, including robot welders, vacuum forming machines, laser cutters, injection moulding systems, silk screen printers and powder coating equipment. About 80 per cent of what it makes will not be repeated the next year because of fashion changes.

The main contacts of customers among Kesslers' 300 employees are with its 30 or so designers and product developers. These people use computer-aided draughting systems to turn ideas into product specifications, normally in a matter of weeks after receiving an order. The close link between the design and manufacturing teams means the company can make late changes to orders on behalf of customers, even a few days before the order is delivered. The customers like the flexibility, for which Kesslers charges extra.

Maintaining such a close link between manufacturing and design requires heavy investment. The company spends up to £500 000 a year on capital equipment and puts another £80 000 a year into training. It is putting its employees through special training courses organised by Cardiff University's lean enterprise implementation group to tutor them in the latest thinking in fields such as just-in-time manufacturing and ways to minimise waste. 'There is absolutely no point in investing in machinery if you don't put substantial sums into improving the capabilities of your employees', says George Kessler.

Adapted from the *Financial Times*, 20.12.2001.

1 Explain the meaning of the terms:
  (a) 'computer aided draughting systems'; (3 marks)
  (b) 'lean enterprise'. (3 marks)
2 Discuss whether technological change in new products or in business processes is more important for Kesslers. (12 marks)
3 Evaluate the problems that Kesslers might face in using new technologies in production. (12 marks)

HorseCare

Knowledge In 2003, Caroline Moore set up a business in south Lancashire looking after horses. Caroline realised that you could put cats into catteries and dogs into kennels. But if you went on holiday there was no-one in the area set up to look after horses.

Application The *business idea* came from looking through a *trade directory, Yellow Pages*. Horse riding was a hobby for Caroline. Her main *job* was as an editor on the local newspaper. She realised there was a *gap in the market* and that she could turn a hobby into a *new business*. Her initial *marketing* was small scale given her limited *budget*. It was just a couple of *advertisements* in the local newspaper. She was now an *entrepreneur*.

Analysis The response was enormous and she is currently looking after 10 horses, with advanced bookings already taken. She has started small, so her capital requirements are minimal. Cash flow has been positive almost from the start. She only has to charge customers more than the cost of hiring a place in a local stables and she can make a profit. Initial market research costs were zero, whilst her marketing costs were very small. If she has satisfied customers, word will quickly spread of her services and she could easily build up a strong customer base. Helen has set up her own business alongside her full time job. The business is currently very small scale. Both these factors reduce the risks to her of potential failure of the business.

Evaluation If the business continues to be successful, Caroline will have to decide whether or not to expand it. Potentially, she could work full time for the business and employ other workers. She could also buy premises to keep the horses. This depends to some extent on the size of the market in the south Lancashire area. It also depends on whether other businesses have started up in competition. She has made an excellent start, but there is a considerable difference between a small business where she works part time and a larger business where she is a full time entrepreneur.

Finding an initial idea

Each year, hundreds of thousands of people set themselves up in business. Instead of working for someone else, they become the owner. Or they move from owning one business to owning another business. If they are successful, they may start to set up a number of businesses. This is what Richard Branson of Virgin has done during his career.

For most 'would-be' entrepreneurs (those who risk their own capital in setting up and running a business), the starting point is the product to be sold. Finding this is not so difficult as it might at first seem. The majority of those who set up in business already have skills and experience. Few, for example, leave education and immediately set up on their own. The Richard Bransons of the business world are also quite rare - he started his first business when he was still at school. More typical is the plumber who has been trained by an employer and then gained experience on the job. He then sets up his own plumbing business. Another example would be a marketing consultant working for an advertising agency setting up her own marketing agency.

There are other ways in which entrepreneurs decide on a line of business. A few turn a hobby into a job. An amateur cyclist might buy a cycle shop. A keen gardener might set up a nursery. Some types of business attract people who want a change of career and to do something different. Setting up a Bed & Breakfast, or running a pub or a local post office are examples. Some people see an opening to set up a business which is related to but not the same as their expertise. A plumber might judge that in his area electricians can charge more for their work. So he might train as an electrician and set himself up as a self employed electrician. A teacher might become a textbook writer.

Small budget research

Many new businesses fail for a variety of reasons. One estimate by GSB Consulting Ltd in 2001, for example, suggests that one in three businesses cease trading within their first three years of life, and two in three within their first ten years. Some businesses will fail, with the business making losses from the start. Many more simply aren't profitable enough to make it worthwhile for the entrepreneur to continue. After all, why have your own plumbing business making £200 a week if you can get a job as a plumber making £300 a week?

The risk of failure could be reduced if the entrepreneur seeks advice and makes plans before setting up. Part of drawing up a **business plan** (see unit 62) is to undertake **market research** (see unit 4). Market research is about finding out about the market into which the product will sell. For example, someone wanting to set up in business making bicycle parts needs to find out who might buy the parts and in what quantities. They need to find out what would be the specifications demanded for the parts. Competition could be analysed using a **market map** (see unit 11), showing where the product of the business will be positioned compared to rival products.

On a limited budget, there is a number of ways in which market research can be conducted.
- **Secondary research** (see unit 5) is finding information which has already been gathered by someone else. For example, looking in *Yellow Pages* to see how many businesses offer the same product might be helpful.

6+ MONTHS

anywayup cup

The Original Mandy Haberman
the original and only
leak-proof anywayup®trainer cup

Designed by real mum, Mandy Haberman.
Mandy knows that award-winning products
are what you need to help your baby.
Whenever, wherever, whatever.

Award-winning ✓
Unique valve ✓
Leak-proof ✓
Germ-free ✓
Easy drink ✓
Easy clean ✓

Mandy Haberman had not intended to become an inventor. But her daughter Emily was born with a condition that made if difficult for her to suck. Mandy was so frustrated at trying to feed her baby, she decided to invent a solution. It took five years of research and improvising to come up with a workable model. But Mandy was determined not to fail. She raised the £20 000 to develop a prototype by writing to hundreds of organisations for help. Then she patented the product. When she was unable to find a company interested in licensing her product, which she called the Haberman Feeder, she set up her own firm and marketed it by mail order to hospitals and parents.

Mandy came up with the idea for a second invention while visiting a friend's house and watching a toddler spill juice on the cream carpet. The result was the Anywayup Cup. It is a toddler-training cup that automatically seals between sips. She made 20 presentations to companies to get them to licence the product, but she failed. So she made her own prototype and then discovered a small Welsh company that was willing to market it. Within months 60 000 cups were being sold every week.

But one month after a new factory had been built to make the Anywayup Cup, Mandy discovered that a rival manufacturer had launched a similar cup using her technology. She decided to take it to court for infringement of her patents and intellectual-property rights. After a lengthy legal battle , the company settled out of court, paying all costs and substantial damages. Her Anywayup Cup now has annual sales of £10 million.

Adapted from *The Sunday Times*, 18.5.2003.

> 1 **What research did Mandy Haberman do on her products?**
> 2 **Explain why it was important for Mandy Haberman to have patented her inventions.**
> 3 **What might be the advantages and disadvantages to Mandy of licensing her products to a US manufacturer for sale in the USA?**

Gathering specialist literature, like trade brochures or articles on the industry from newspapers and trade magazines, is another possibility.

- There could also be a role for **primary research** (see unit 7). This is the gathering of information which is not available in collected form elsewhere. When setting up a shop, going to see its location is vital. Spending a day looking at how many customers enter and leave a shop which is up for sale can be a more accurate measure of its potential profitability than its existing accounts Most new small businesses are unlikely to be able to afford to conduct a large **survey** (see unit 8) with a questionnaire. However, a larger company might be able to afford to hire a **market research company** to do this.

Researching the market can help cut down the possibility of failure. However, ultimately the entrepreneur has got to take the risk of setting up in business. Very few new businesses find that the market is exactly the same as predicted from the market research. For some, sales are better than predicted. For most, sales are disappointing at the start for a variety of reasons. Entrepreneurs have to be able to cope with such setbacks and change their plans to make the business viable.

Small budget marketing

New small businesses are likely to have very limited budgets for **marketing**. Typically, new small businesses might:

- advertise in *Yellow Pages*, a trade directory;
- place advertisements in local newspapers or trade magazines;
- send out leaflets and brochures to potential customers;
- attempt to get some free publicity, for example in a local newspaper or a trade magazine when a reporter writes up a story about the start up. This is known as using **public relations** (see unit 18);
- offer discounts on products for the first few weeks of operation to lure customers to buy;

- use the telephone to contact potential customers;
- physically go to potential customers, meeting them and trying to persuade them to buy.
- setting up a website on the Internet.

Using patents and copyright to protect the product

A few new business start-ups arise out of the creation of genuinely new products. For example, someone might invent a new type of corkscrew or a new type of coffee machine. New inventions should be PATENTED to stop other businesses from copying the invention. Patents in the UK are registered with the Patents Office. However, it is important to patent new inventions internationally. If a product is patented in the UK but not in the USA, it can be copied free of charge in the USA.

Holders of patents may choose to market the invention themselves by setting up their own business and making the product. However, they could also LICENCE the patent to other businesses. This allows other businesses to use the idea, although they have to pay a fee to the holder of the patent. Under the Copyright, Designs and Patents Act, 1988, patents in the UK last for 20 years. After 20 years, the patent lapses and any business can use the idea. Registering a patent internationally will cost thousands of pounds and is an important start up cost for any new small business. Most patents are taken out by existing medium sized and large firms who register inventions developed by their employees as part of their research programme.

COPYRIGHT exists for books and music. It prevents the copying (often called 'pirating') of original works. Businesses wanting to use the copyright have to pay the copyright holder a ROYALTY or COPYRIGHT FEE. For example, a marketing company that wanted to make a television advertisement using a song by Eminem would have to get the permission of the copyright holders of the song and the recording. Copyright can sometimes be a combination of the songwriter, the artist and the record or publishing company.

✓ checklist

1 How might a would-be entrepreneur decide what to produce when setting up a business?
2 How might entrepreneurs cut down the risk of failing with their new businesses?
3 Explain what market research can be conducted on a limited budget by someone thinking of setting up a small business.
4 What methods of marketing are open to a new business with a limited budget?
5 Explain the difference between a patent and copyright.
6 Why do businesses take out patents?

keyterms

Copyright - **legal ownership of material such as books, music and films which prevents these being copied by others.**
Copyright fee or royalty - **payment to the copyright holder for permission to copy or use material which is subject to copyright.**
Licence - **in the context of patents, permission given by one individual or business or another to use an invention or process which has been patented; typically there will be a licence fee agreed for this use.**
Patent - **right of ownership of an invention or process granted by government for a fixed period of time to the individual or business which registers the original invention or process.**

Dave Sidlow had been passionate about board games since he was a child. He always dreamed about inventing his own board game and it becoming the Monopoly or Trivial Pursuit of his generation. In 2001, he met by chance an accountant, Gina Barrett, who shared a similar passion. Gina worked for a company which made the packaging for some board games sold in the UK and abroad. She therefore had contacts in the games industry as well as having financial expertise in how to run a business.

That meeting spurred Dave to come up with an idea for a game. He test marketed it with Gina and some friends. Over a period of months, they refined and altered the game in the light of comments that were made until they thought they had a hit. At this stage, Gina got to work researching suppliers who would make the various components for the board game. Her own company would make the packaging. Dave and Gina would assemble the games and shrink wrap the boxes ready for sale. Dave and Gina also took time off work from their full time jobs to visit buyers from key retailers who might stock the product. Getting to see the buyers was often difficult and those they did see turned the game down.

At this stage, things looked bleak for the pair. It was going to cost £10 000 to manufacture the first 1 000 copies of the game. But with no outlets to sell them into, they would end up with 1 000 items of unsold stock. They decided to take a gamble. £10 000 was spent from their own savings to buy in the stock of 1 000 games, which were ready in June 2002.

To market the games, a strategy was developed. First, a website was set up to advertise the game. The website was simple and set up by a friend in a few hours. It gave Dave's email address and PO Box number for ordering. Gina arranged for them to be able to accept credit card payments over the phone. The website was written with the right key words so that it came up fairly early on Internet search engines such as Google. Second, Dave and Gina became salespeople for their products. Every relative and friend was approached to buy a copy as the ideal present for Christmas. Independent toy shops in their local area were targeted. In some cases, one copy of the game was left with the shop on a sale or return basis. Any type of fair in the local area, from Christmas fairs to upmarket school fairs, had them taking a stall and energetically selling.

It was hard work and time consuming. But by Christmas 2000 they had managed to sell 700 games at an average price of £18. They worked out that they had spent £2 000 on marketing including petrol, but not including anything for their time. So their profit was £600, plus a stock of 300 unsold games. Perhaps it wasn't much for thousands of hours of effort put in. But Dave and Gina were already planning their next game. And this time they were determined to get at least one big retailer to put it on its shelves.

1 Explain what is meant by the terms:
   (a) 'researching suppliers'; (3 marks)
   (b) 'marketing'. (3 marks)
2 Discuss whether the research for and marketing of the game was effective. (12 marks)
3 To what extent have Dave and Gina set up a profitable long term business? (12 marks)

Liu oriental cuisine

Knowledge Shu Fang Liu opened her first shop selling oriental foods and ingredients in 2001. Its instant success encouraged her to set up another shop in a nearby city with a large ethnic student population.

Application Shu Fang had spotted a *gap* in the *market* in the university town where she lived. There were many students from South East Asia. She had worked for a number of years for her aunt and uncle in a *wholesaling business* and so knew something about *retailing*. Going it alone, she became a *sole trader*. However, she was worried about *unlimited liability* and hoped soon to be large enough to justify founding a *company*.

Analysis Setting up as a sole trader was the quickest and easiest way for Shu Fang to set up in business. It meant she was in total control and could expand the business in the way she wanted. Initially, it was also to her advantage from a tax viewpoint.

Evaluation Shu Fang hoped, however, that her business would soon be too large for it to be appropriate for her to be a sole trader. She would need to reduce risk by forming a company and gaining limited liability. In the meantime, being a sole trader gave her the personal and financial flexibility that she wanted.

Sole traders

In the UK, there are over three million workers who are SELF-EMPLOYED. The majority of these are SOLE TRADERS (sometimes also called SOLE PROPRIETORS). The rest are partners in partnerships. A sole trader is the single owner of a business called a SOLE PROPRIETORSHIP. Most sole traders work on their own. However, larger sole traders can employ other workers. Often these are family members such as wives or husbands. Many small businesses are therefore family businesses.

Setting up a sole proprietorship is relatively simple. The business must fill in tax return forms for the Inland Revenue because sole traders are liable for income tax on the profits of the business. If the **turnover** of the business (how much it sells, see unit 21) is more than approximately £50 000 a year, then the business must notify Customs and Excise because the business will then have to charge Value Added Tax (VAT) on its sales. The business will also have to conform to any relevant laws, such as the **Health and Safety at Work Act** (see unit 55). It might have to gain planning permission from the local authority to extend premises. Equally, in certain trades, such as taxis or setting up as a chemist, sole traders need to get a licence. However, unlike starting up a company (see unit 62), generally there are no registration forms to complete and the sole trader can start business immediately.

Unlimited liability

In law, there is no distinction between the activities of sole traders and their non-business affairs. For instance, if a sole trader running a wine merchant sells 100 bottles of wine to a customer for £500, the money belongs to the sole trader personally. Equally, if sole traders run up business debts, they are personally responsible for paying them off. This is known as having UNLIMITED LIABILITY.

Sometimes, sole traders run up such large business debts that they are forced to declare themselves BANKRUPT before a court of law. Because of unlimited liability, all their assets, apart from a few personal possessions like clothes, are sold and their **creditors** (see unit 28), those who are owed money, get a proportion of the proceeds. So a sole trader owing £400 000 in business debts could be forced to sell his or her house or car to pay the debts.

Advantages of being a sole trader

Most of the three million self-employed workers in the UK are sole traders. So there must be some major advantages to being a sole trader.

Easy to set up and close down A worker can set up in business immediately without any of the formal paperwork involved in setting up a company. Again, if the worker wants to close down the business, there is no formal paperwork to complete.

Easy to run Sole proprietorships are easier to run than other types of business. There aren't any other owners to deal with. There are no legal obligations to file accounts. The accounts which are presented to the Inland Revenue and Customs and Excise can be kept in a simple way and don't needed to be **audited** (see unit 20) by an accountant. Typically, though, sole traders employ accountants to prepare accounts for tax purposes.

Tax advantages Sole traders are treated in a more generous way from a tax viewpoint than employees and companies. Partly this is because they can set more of their work expenses against tax. This reduces the amount of income tax they have to pay on their income. Partly it is because they pay lower rates of National Insurance contributions (NICs). For all except the lowest paid workers, employers have to pay employers' NICs and in addition workers have to pay employees' NICs. Self-employed sole traders, in contrast, pay a flat sum contribution plus a proportion of income which is usually lower in total than employees' NICs alone.

Profits All the profits of the business are kept by the sole trader. They don't have to be split up amongst several or perhaps even millions of others owners or shareholders. This means that there is a link between effort, success and money earned. The harder a sole trader works, and the more successful the business, the more can be earned.

Privacy Sole traders only have to declare earnings to the tax authorities. Unlike with companies, there is no public disclosure of business details.

Control Since a sole trader is owned by one individual, the sole trader is in total control of the business. Sole traders can decide how, when and where to work.

Capital Sole proprietorships can be set up with little or no money in the business. They don't cost anything to set up. So the capital cost of creating a sole proprietorship can be minimal.

Flexibility Sole traders can have greater freedom about when and how they work than employees. Often, they can take time off to suit their needs. However, sole traders tend to work longer hours than employees. Despite this, many sole traders value the freedom and flexibility that being their own boss brings.

Disadvantages of being a sole trader

Whilst there are many advantages to being a sole trader, there are also disadvantages.

Unlimited liability Sole traders stand to lose everything they own if their business does badly. In contrast, shareholders in a limited liability company at most only lose their investment in the shares of the business if it closes. Equally, employees working for a business which fails can only lose their job and their wage.

Risk Sole proprietorships can be risky for their owners. If the business is unsuccessful, sole traders can end up working for nothing or even subsidising the business out of their own private resources. Also, because the business is the sole trader, long term illness can have a devastating effect on it. Becoming an employee is less risky and is one reason why most workers would probably not want to work for themselves.

Long hours Sole traders tend to work long hours. For sole traders engaged in businesses like owning a pub or a restaurant, their jobs tend to become their whole life.

Lack of continuity Sole proprietorships face problems about continuity. Will the business survive if the sole trader dies, takes retirement or simply decides to do something different? Some sole traders run family businesses where parents tend to pass on their business to their children. Farming is one example. However, most sole traders have businesses which won't be passed on to another family member and are likely to disappear. A plumber working on her own, for instance, is unlikely to be able to sell her 'business' to another plumber. So when she gives up working, her business will disappear.

Difficulty of raising capital Sole traders often find it difficult to raise capital. They have fewer ways of doing this than companies (see unit 62). This difficulty can limit the growth of

Jane Mitchell worked as an assistant in a local village school. But she did not particularly enjoy working for someone else. So she decided to set up her own kindergarten in the same village. Premises were found and equipment bought. The local area was leafleted, advertising the new kindergarten which offered a wider range of services than the local school nursery. In particular, younger children and babies could be looked after and the kindergarten would be open from 8 in the morning to 6 at night including school holidays. Jane took on three other staff to cope with anticipated demand. Within 12 months of opening, however, Jane was forced to close. Fees didn't cover her day to day running expenses and she had a £3 000 bank debt from the opening costs. She was forced to sell her car to pay off the bank loan. Running a business was not as easy as she had thought.

1 Jane Mitchell was a sole trader. What are the main features of sole proprietorship as a form of business organisation?
2 Explain why Jane had to sell her car to meet debts incurred by her business.

Brian Walters and Chris Hodges were made redundant from an Internet design company. They used their redundancy pay to set up in partnership running Internet sites for clients. Now they were competing with their former employer for some of the same business.

That was three years ago. Today, their business is thriving. So much so that Brian is thinking they should take on an extra worker. Chris isn't sure, worried about the financial implications of employing someone who will cost at least £15 000 a year. To give the company a better image, Brian also wants to buy their own offices, costing £40 000. This would be financed through mortgage borrowing. Chris definitely doesn't want to do this, worried about what will happen if trade falls off and they can't afford to keep up the mortgage repayments. Chris is even thinking that he would prefer to break up the partnership rather than go along with Brian's expansion plans.

1 **Chris and Brian formed an ordinary partnership when they set up in business. What is an ordinary partnership?**
2 **If Brian took on an extra worker, what would be the implications for Chris?**
3 **Discuss whether Chris should break up the partnership.**

sole proprietorships. There are unlikely to be any large businesses in the UK which are sole proprietorships partly because of this.

Limited specialisation Large businesses can employ specialist workers. A sole trader often has to be purchaser, driver, accountant, lawyer and labourer to run the business. Allowing workers to **specialise** (see unit 42) can lead to lower costs of production per unit. So sole traders can be at a disadvantage competitively which they are forced to make up by paying themselves lower wages.

Limited economies of scale Sole proprietorships are usually small businesses. So they are unable to gain reductions in unit costs of production as the volume of output rises, known as **economies of scale** (see unit 42). Sole traders tend to be concentrated in industries such as farming, where economies of scale are limited.

Partnerships

Another form of business organisation in the UK is a PARTNERSHIP. The typical partnership is, in law, a business with unlimited liability. It can have between 2 and 20 partners or owners. Partners are jointly responsible for making decisions, running the business, sharing the profits and also paying any debts. If the partnership fails, leaving debts, the partners would be responsible for paying those debts. As with sole traders, partners could lose not just their investment in the business but all their personal assets, such as houses and cars, if the partnership has large debts.

Lawyers and accountants always advise those thinking of becoming partners to draw up a DEED OF PARTNERSHIP. It is a legal agreement between the partners. This contract sets out details such as:
- who are the partners;
- how much capital each partner must put into the business;
- how profits should be shared out;
- how many votes each partner has in any partnership meeting;
- what happens if any of the partners want to withdraw from the business or if new partners are brought in.

Without a deed of partnership there are often disputes between partners about how profits should be shared during the running of the partnership and who owns what when a partnership is dissolved. Such disputes can end up in court and be expensive to resolve.

There are two other less common types of partnership. In LIMITED PARTNERSHIPS, one or more partnerships can be SLEEPING PARTNERS. These are partners who play no active role in the running of the business but have money invested in it. In law, sleeping partners can have limited liability. In LIMITED LIABILITY PARTNERSHIPS, all partners, including those working in the business, have limited liability. Limited liability partnerships tend to be found amongst large firms of accountants today.

Advantages and disadvantages of partnerships

Partnerships have both advantages and disadvantages as a form of business organisation.

Legal formalities A partnership, like a sole proprietorship, can be set up with no legal formalities, unlike a company.

However, a company can be set up for a little over £100 by buying one 'off the shelf' from a company which specialises in completing the paper work to set up companies. In contrast, a deed of partnership would need to be drawn up with the help of a solicitor, which is likely to cost more than £100. The accounts of a partnership, like a sole proprietorship, do not need to be independently audited. In contrast, there are strict guidelines about the auditing of accounts and reporting of information to Companies House, which could cost a company at least £500 a year in accountancy fees. However, a successful partnership is likely to use an accountant to deal with the finances of the business.

Disclosure of information Like a sole proprietorship, an ordinary partnership does not need to publish any accounts which may be seen by the public. Only the tax authorities must have access to the accounts of a partnership. In contrast, the accounts of a company are available to anyone who asks to see them via Companies House. The accounts of a limited liability partnership are, however, open to inspection by the public but in a less detailed format than those of a company.

Skills Creating a partnership can bring skills into a business which a sole trader might not have. For example, a sole trader manufacturing pots might go into partnership with someone with marketing expertise.

Finance Some unlimited partnerships are formed because of the need for finance. Sole traders on their own might not have the money to launch and run a successful business. By creating an unlimited partnership, they can bring extra money into the business. However, companies have an advantage over partnerships in attracting finance in that shareholders in a company have limited liability whereas partners in a partnership only have unlimited liability. It is most unlikely that anyone who isn't actively involved in running a business would want to become a partner because of the risk of unlimited liability. In contrast, individuals who have nothing to do with a company are prepared to invest in its shares because the most they stand to lose if the company fails is their shareholding in the company.

Profits Profits have to be shared between the partners. Partners hope that their share of the profits will be higher than if they were working on their own or were employed by another business. However, there is no guarantee that this will be the case. Disputes over profit shares can break out if a partner is ill and is unable to work in the business over a period of time or if a partner works less hard than other partners.

Control Partners share control of the business between themselves. Some partnerships work extremely well because the partners are able to work together. Other partnerships work poorly because partners don't work together and disagree about how the business should be run. Some partners create constant friction by telling other partners how to do the work but doing little of it themselves. A successful partnership is about successful team work. Some individuals aren't good team players. Where this occurs, the partnership often breaks up.

Liability Partners, like sole traders, have unlimited liability, which is less attractive than the limited liability shareholders enjoy in a company. However, they face an additional risk.

Any decisions taken by one of the partners with customers or suppliers are binding on the other partners. For example, if one partner ordered £10,000 of promotional leaflets, the

keyterms

Bankruptcy - a situation where an individual is forced to sell all their possessions to repay debts. A court of law declares the individual bankrupt and all previous debts are then cancelled.

Deed of partnership - the legal contract which governs how a partnership will be owned and organised.

Partnership - an unlimited partnership is a business with between 2 and 20 partners where partners have unlimited liability. A limited partnership is one where at least one partner not involved in the day to day running of the business has limited liability, but the active partners continue to have unlimited liability. A limited liability partnership is one where all partners have limited liability.

Self-employed - workers who work for themselves and not for an employer.

Sleeping partner - a partner who plays no active role in running the business and who usually has limited liability.

Sole proprietorship - an unincorporated business with unlimited liability, owned and run by a single owner, a sole trader or sole proprietor.

Sole trader or sole proprietor - an individual who owns and runs his or her own business called a sole proprietorship. Sole traders are self-employed.

Unlimited liability - a legal obligation on the owners of a business to settle all debts of the business. In law, there is no distinction between the assets and debts of the business and the personal assets and debts of the owner.

checklist

1 'There are over 3 million people who are self-employed in the UK.' Explain what this means.
2 How easy is it for a sole trader to start a business?
3 A sole trader extends her business premises at a cost of £40 000. What is the significance of unlimited liability for this?
4 What are the tax advantages of being a sole trader?
5 Why is there a direct link between effort and profit in a sole proprietorship?
6 What risks do sole traders face?
7 How can taking on a partner allow increased specialisation and economies of scale?
8 Why is drawing up a deed of partnership very important for a new partnership?
9 What happens to a partnership if a partner leaves?

other partners would be liable for the payment whether or not they had agreed to the purchase. At worst, the action of one partner can lead to the bankruptcy of all the partners.

Ending the partnership A partnership ends when one of the partners leaves the partnership. If a partner decided at the end of two years of a partnership to pull out, the partnership would terminate. There is a danger that the partners will disagree about the value of the assets of the partnership to be divided up between them. At worst, if there is no deed of partnership, there can be disagreement about what proportion of the assets should go to each partner. Some partners may also want to continue in business but find it difficult to secure the financing to start out again on their own.

John Powderley owns and runs a butchers shop. It was started by his great grandfather and passed down the generations to him. Now, as he gets older, he wants to give up the business and retire. For the past few years, John has found the work an increasing burden. Often working over 60 hours a week, his health has suffered. He is single, without children, and he has been the only family member working in the business since the death of his father twenty years ago.

Twelve months ago, local authority plans were ratified to pull down his shop. It stood in the way of a new junction for an important dual carriageway scheme. Compensation, of course, would be paid. But John was now facing the prospect of finding new premises and making a move. His existing premises were now a little too small. But to take on larger premises and furnish them could involve an investment of an extra £60 000. It would also probably take time for the business to settle down in its new premises and for refurbishment and building work to be completed. That would take John closer to retirement age.

The prospect of having a lot of time off work due to illness is another worry for John. He has employees whom he relies on heavily. But, John also knows that he has unlimited liability. What would happen, for example, if in the middle of the move, he was suddenly taken ill? Who would control costs sufficiently? Would he be faced with huge bills and declining sales because of mismanagement?

His accountant has for a long time advised him to form a company and gain limited liability. The accountant has also suggested simply selling up now. However, he has pointed out that the business could be sold at a much higher price if the move into new premises had been accomplished satisfactorily.

Adapted from *The Guardian*, 16.5.2000.

1 Explain what is meant by the term 'unlimited liability'. (3 marks)

2 Outline TWO problems which currently face the business. (8 marks)

3 Examine TWO alternative ways in which John could deal with having his current premises demolished. (8 marks)

4 Discuss the advantages and disadvantages to John of being a sole trader. (11 marks)

Companies

Emap

Knowledge Emap is a UK communications and media company. One core activity of the company is publishing magazines such as *Heat*, *FHM* and *Smash Hits* in the UK and abroad. The other core activity is running radio stations and making music related television programmes.

Application Emap is a *company* which is listed on the *London Stock Exchange*. Its *shares* can therefore be bought and sold on the free *market*. It has issued over 250 million *shares*. As a company, its *shareholders* have *limited liability*.

Analysis In the 1990s, Emap enjoyed strong growth and increasing profits. However, it recorded large losses in 2000 and 2001. In 2001, the loss before tax was £527 million. This substantial loss was not large enough to threaten the existence of the company. But the share price fell sharply. The company directors and managers were forced to rethink their strategy to bring the company back to profit.

Evaluation With sales of over £1 billion per year, Emap is a significant player in the publishing and media industry. However, its losses in 2000 and 2001 show that large companies can make strategic mistakes. In the first decade of the 21st century, it needs to ensure that future growth is profitable and sustainable.

Adapted from Emap, Annual Report and Accounts, 2001.

Companies

A COMPANY has a separate existence in law. Like an individual, it can be prosecuted and sued. It is liable for tax. It can own property. It can enter into contracts with other parties. This is different from a sole trader, where the sole proprietorship has no separate legal identity from the individual who is the sole trader.

Shareholders and limited liability

Companies are owned by shareholders. There must be a minimum of two shareholders in a company by law. The shareholders have LIMITED LIABILITY. All companies are limited companies. This means that the assets and liabilities of the shareholder are separate in law from the assets and liabilities of the company. If the company makes a loss, those to whom it owes money cannot force the shareholders of the company to sell their private assets or possessions to pay for the loss. This is different from an unlimited business. If sole traders make a loss on business activities, then they are personally responsible for paying the debts.

The most that shareholders can lose is the value of their shareholding in the company. This would occur if the company became INSOLVENT and went into LIQUIDATION. This means that the company does not have enough assets to cover its debts. The value of shares in the company would then be zero. The company would cease to trade in its existing form. Insolvency for a company is the equivalent of bankruptcy (see unit 60) for an individual. In a case of insolvency, the value of all debts and all assets would be totalled. Those who were owed money by the company might get a proportion of their debts repaid. But the shareholders would not have to pay out anything.

Companies are sometimes known as JOINT STOCK COMPANIES. This is because the stock (an old fashioned name for shares in the UK and still the name for shares in the USA) is held by a number of shareholders jointly.

The running of a company

Most companies are small. The largest companies produce more than the total output of many of the poorest countries in the world. There are three key groups involved in the running of the company.

Managers MANAGERS are employees of the company who are responsible for organising the day to day running of the business. In a large company, there would be managers responsible for different tasks such as production, accounts and sales.

Directors DIRECTORS are responsible for devising longer term strategies for the company. These strategies are implemented by the managers. The main duty of directors is to look after the interests of the shareholders. Indeed, they are elected by shareholders into office at the Annual General Meeting (AGM) of the company. One director will be elected to be the **Chairperson of the Board**, sometimes referred to as the **Company Chairperson**. Some directors, known as EXECUTIVE DIRECTORS, will also be managers of the company. One will be the most senior manager, usually called the **Managing Director** or **Chief Executive**. Other directors are known as NON-EXECUTIVE DIRECTORS. These are directors who are not managers in the company but are appointed directors for their outside expertise.

All companies have executive directors but small to medium sized companies tend not to have non-executive directors. The larger the company, the more likely it is that it will have non-executive directors.

Shareholders Shareholders are the owners of the company. Usually, their sole concern is that the company performs well so that the returns to shareholders are maximised.

Shareholders make a return on their shares in two main ways. First, they receive a dividend, a share of the profits,

A Southampton-based firm is hoping to pick up business manufacturing and supplying period-style fireplaces to the USA.

In ten years, Pastime Fireplaces has turned the idea of making period fireplaces into an international success. The firm employs 20 people and makes fireplaces for customers all over the world. Company founders, directors and shareholders, Clinton and Terri said: 'We have been astounded by the success. We still think we are only scratching the surface of the potential market out there.'

1 *Suggest who owns and runs Pastime Fireplaces.*
2 *What risks do shareholders in the company face if it were to become insolvent?*

each year. Second, the value of their shares can rise, although they can also fall. Rising share prices give shareholders capital gains.

In a small company, all three groups (shareholders, directors and managers) are likely to be the same people. If, for instance, there are just two shareholders, they are likely to be the directors of the company and run it on a day to day basis.

In larger companies, there will still be some overlap between the groups. The founders of the company may still be working for the business, so at least some of the shares will be held by directors who are also possibly senior managers. This is most likely to happen in medium sized companies. In long established large companies, however, the directors and managers are unlikely to have any substantial shareholding in the company. This may cause a problem because of the divorce of ownership from control (see below).

Financing a company

Companies need finance both for their creation and ongoing

activities. Their day to day running costs are paid for by the revenues they receive from the sale of goods and services. However, they need **capital** (see unit 25) for equipment, buildings, stocks and other items. They also need capital if they are to buy other businesses.

Companies are started off with **share capital** or **equity capital**. Shareholders put up money which is then used to buy equipment etc. (see unit 25). A company can issue new shares at any time subject to the approval of the shareholders. Once issued, shares can be traded second hand. For public limited companies (see below), shares must be openly traded on a stock exchange, such as the London Stock Exchange, the Birmingham Stock Exchange or AIM (the Alternative Investment Market). When an investor buys a second hand share, the money paid goes to the investor owning the share and not to the company which originally issued the share.

Shareholders may receive a dividend from their company. This is a share of the profits made. If the company makes a loss in a year, or a disappointing profit, it may choose not to pay a dividend. Alternatively, it may pay a dividend but this money would come out of **reserves** owned by the company rather than the profit made in the year.

In the UK, the most common type of share issued is ORDINARY SHARES. With ordinary shares, it is up to the directors of the company to decide whether to pay a dividend and how much to pay in any year. Companies can also issue PREFERENCE SHARES. These pay a fixed amount of dividend, such as 45p per share, which doesn't change over time. Companies must pay out a dividend on preference shares if they make enough profit to pay for it. If there is not enough profit to cover both preference shareholders and ordinary shareholders, then preference shareholders have priority.

The issue of new shares in a typical year in the UK raises only a few per cent of total funding for companies. Most comes from retained profit, followed by various types of borrowing, particularly from banks. Companies may also issue debentures, a form of long term borrowing. Finance for companies is discussed in more detail in units 24-26.

Creating a limited company

Limited companies are created by applying for incorporation to the Registrar of Companies. The application must include two documents. The first is the MEMORANDUM OF ASSOCIATION. This lays down the constitution of the company and must include:
- the name of the company;
- the address of the office where it is registered and can be contacted;
- its objectives and the nature of its activities;
- the liability of its members;
- the amount of capital raised and the number of shares to be issued.

The second document is the ARTICLES OF ASSOCIATION. This deals with the internal running of the business such as:
- how directors are to be appointed;
- what powers the directors will have;
- the length of service of directors before they need to be re-

elected;

- how often board meetings will take place;
- the rights of shareholders;
- arrangements for auditing the company accounts.

The Registrar of Companies will check that the directors of the company have not been banned from holding directorships because of previous involvement with failed companies or with fraud. The name of the company must also be unique and not be capable of being confused with another company. For instance, no company could now set up as the 'Royal Bank of Scotland' because a company of this name already exists.

If all of this is satisfactory, the company will be awarded a CERTIFICATE OF INCORPORATION. This allows it to begin trading. All the documents relating to incorporation can be seen by anyone for a fee by applying to Companies House in Bristol. Each year, the company must submit a set of audited accounts to Companies House too, which will be made available to anyone inspecting the company's documents. These documents tend to be looked at by businesses which are considering trading with it as part of their assessment of risk.

Private and public limited companies

There are two types of limited companies. The main legal difference between the two concerns the sale of shares.

PRIVATE LIMITED COMPANIES can only sell shares in the company on a private basis. They cannot be advertised for general sale. When existing or new shares in a private limited company are sold, all the existing shareholders must agree. In contrast, shares in PUBLIC LIMITED COMPANIES must be openly available for trade via a stock exchange.

Private limited companies add 'Limited' or 'Ltd' to the end of their name. Public limited companies add 'PLC' or 'plc'.

Private limited companies tend to be much smaller than public limited companies. One of the most important reasons why companies 'go public', 'float on the stock exchange' and become PLCs is because they want to issue new shares and use the money to finance expansion. However, potential purchasers of the shares will not buy unless they know there will be a market in the shares when they come to sell. If the company is very small, there will be too few shares to create a market for daily buying and selling. So the company needs

Colin Jevons started his own building company in 1998, having had experience working for another company in the same industry. Jevons Ltd started out with two shareholders, Colin and his brother, who were also the two directors of the company. There were three employees, Colin, his brother and a salesperson. The company grew quickly and in the last financial year, to January 31 2003, had sales of £1.3 million. Today there are 10 employees.

Colin doesn't regret leaving a secure well paid job. 'Running your own business has its own pressures. But you are in charge and you are responsible for your own destiny', he said. Convincing customers that his new company would be safe to deal with was a worry at first. Being VAT registered from the start provided one indication to customers that they were dealing with a large enough business to do the work. Colin also used the many contacts that he had made during his time working for his former employer to gain orders.

Colin's brother does the day to day financial paperwork. But he also works closely in co-operation with the company's accountants who do the work needed by the tax authorities and Companies House.

The company is still expanding strongly. This year, it intends to buy new equipment at a cost of around £300 000 and will probably need to take on more staff. Colin has been extremely pleased with the way in which the business has developed. The company he worked for previously had sales of around £30 million a year. This gives him a target to work for in the future.

1. **What does 'Ltd' mean in the name of the company?**
2. **Jevons Ltd might be described as a 'family firm'. Explain what this means.**
3. **What might be the advantages and disadvantages to Colin Jevons of having set up a limited company rather than becoming a sole trader or a partnership?**
4. **Discuss whether Jevons Ltd is ever likely to become a public limited company.**

to be of a certain size to generate such a market. Even then, most public limited companies are so small that daily trading in their shares is very low and this can create problems for potential investors. It is one of the reasons why many investors tend to buy only companies in the Financial Times 100 Share Index of the UK's 100 largest quoted companies.

Many private limited companies are **family firms** where the owners are related to each and run the business. Even in public limited companies, family members of the original founders of the company may still play an important part both in ownership and running of the business. For example, there is still a strong family presence in Sainsbury's, Tesco and the Ford Motor Corporation. However, the larger and the older the company, the less likely it is that families will play an important part. Shares are likely to be owned mainly by **institutional shareholders** rather than private individuals. Institutional shareholders are financial businesses such as assurance companies, pension funds, and unit trust and investment trust companies, which buy shares as vehicles for saving on behalf of their customers.

Advantages and disadvantages of limited companies

Limited companies have a number of advantages over sole traders and partnerships, which are unlimited businesses.

- Because the business is limited, its owners, the shareholders, are less at risk than the owners of an unlimited business. If an unlimited business makes losses, owners are totally liable for its debts. In a limited business, the owners can only lose the value of their shareholding in the company.
- This risk makes investing in an unlimited business less attractive than in a limited company. Hence, businesses which want to grow almost inevitably become limited companies. This protects existing owners from risk of failure of the business and makes it attractive for others to buy shares in the business.
- A limited company has a separate legal existence from its owners. If a shareholder dies or sells their shares, the company remains in existence. In an unlimited business, if a sole trader or partner dies or sells up, the business ceases to exist. It may carry on trading having been bought by another person. But this is a new business. So there is more chance of the business carrying on if it is limited rather than unlimited.
- For a wealthy owner of a limited company, it might be more tax advantageous to keep the profits earned by the business in the company rather than distribute them to shareholders. This would be particularly true if the owner was currently having to pay higher rate income tax now but might, for instance on retirement, earn less and pay a lower rate of income tax.
- Some businesses will not deal with unlimited businesses or with businesses that are not registered to pay VAT. This is because they think that limited companies registered for VAT are more likely to be well run, since they have to keep proper accounts and tend to use the professional advice of accountants and solicitors.

Limited businesses have disadvantages though.
- Details of the company and accounts are available for inspection by the general public at Companies House. Hence there is a lack of privacy for owners.
- There is much more paperwork associated with running a limited company. Both the Inland Revenue and Companies House require regular returns relating to the business. The accounts must also be audited by a qualified accountant. The minimum cost of this is likely to be around £500 per year. So a business which earned £5,000 a year for its owners would see a tenth of that used for auditing fees if it were a limited company rather than an unlimited business.
- If the company is small and the owners rely on the company to pay them as employees, they are likely to pay more in tax and National Insurance contributions than if they were sole traders or partners in an unlimited business.

Private vs public limited companies

Private limited companies have both advantages and disadvantages compared to public limited companies. There are several advantages of private limited companies.
- They are less costly to administer than public limited companies. A public limited company has to disclose and publish more information than a private limited company. These costs for a PLC are a minimum of £100,000 per year.
- It is more difficult for a private limited company to be bought by another company against the wishes of some shareholders than a public limited company. Most private limited companies have only a few shareholders. So it is usually difficult to buy more than 50 per cent of the shares without the full support of all the shareholders.
- The owners of private limited companies can to some extent ignore the need to maximise profits in the short term. They can, for example, invest today in new equipment or new ventures, resulting in low profits now but higher profits in the future. Public limited companies, on the other hand, are under the constant inspection of the financial media and financial analysts, not to mention their shareholders. They want to see high profits now. PLCs, it is argued, can then be forced to ignore strategies which would bring high profits in the long run when this involves low profits today.
- Another disadvantage of public limited companies is that there can be a DIVORCE OF OWNERSHIP FROM CONTROL. In a private limited company, the managers, directors and shareholders of the company are likely to be roughly the same people. The owners therefore usually run the company on a day to day basis. So, in the typical limited company, there is no conflict of objectives between shareholders and managers. But in a large PLC, managers and directors of the company often hold hardly any shares. So the people who control the company, the directors and the managers, can be a different group to the owners, the people who are the shareholders. Shareholders want to see the return on their investment in shares maximised. This means earning high profits and seeing long term growth of the company. Directors are supposed to represent the interests of shareholders. But it can be argued that they are more interested in maximising their fees and salaries. Similarly, managers might say they are committed to maximising profit for shareholders whilst at the same time negotiating to get better wages, bigger company cars and

higher pensions. Paying directors and managers more means higher costs and lower profits. So there is conflict of objectives between shareholders and directors and managers. Over the past 20 years, there has been an increasing trend to reward top managers and directors with various types of performance related bonus scheme. These link the size of the bonus with factors such as an increase in sales or profits or increases in the share price. The idea is that this will stop there being any conflict between the objectives of shareholders and the people they pay to run the company on their behalf. These schemes remain highly controversial, however. The pay of top executives in the UK has vastly increased since the 1980s without there being any improvement in the performance of the average PLC. Some have argued that top executives are using their power with companies to take more and more of the profit which should belong to shareholders and put it into their own pockets.

Public limited companies, though, have several advantages over private limited companies.

- Shareholders of public limited companies can sell their shares in the open market at any time. With a private limited company, consent has to be obtained from the majority of shareholders and a buyer has to be found which can take a long time.
- As a result, public limited companies tend to find it much easier to raise equity capital from sale of new shares than a private limited company. Investors are prepared to buy shares knowing that they can easily sell them.
- The ability to raise equity capital means that PLCs are more likely to grow in size than private limited companies.
- Pressures from the financial media and financial analysts as well as the danger that the PLC might be **taken over** (i.e. bought) by another company encourages managers to perform well and make profits. These pressures don't exist in a private limited company where shares are difficult to buy and sell.

Companies and types of industry

Limited companies tend to be larger than unlimited businesses because they have greater access to capital finance. Owners are also less willing to own large businesses unless they have unlimited liability because of the potential risks of the business doing badly. So, limited companies are more common in industries where size gives the business a competitive advantage. There is an above average concentration of limited companies in production, such as car manufacturing, business services, finance and property, wholesaling and dealing, and in transport, such as the railways.

✔ checklist

1 What legal status does a company hold?
2 What are the advantages to shareholders of having limited liability?
3 Explain the role in a company of (a) shareholders; (b) managers; (c) executive directors; (d) non-executive directors.
4 Distinguish between an ordinary share and a preference share.
5 What is the difference between the Articles of Association of a company, its Memorandum of Association and its Certificate of Incorporation?
6 Explain (a) the similarities and (b) the differences between a private limited company and a public limited company.
7 Why might someone decide to set up a company rather than remain as a sole trader?
8 Why might a private limited company 'go public'?
9 Explain why shareholders might suffer if there is a divorce of ownership from control in a large public limited company.

"key terms"

Articles of association - the document which gives details about the relationship between the company, its shareholders and its directors.
Certificate of Incorporation - a formal document which declares that a company has been created.
Company - a business owned by shareholders who have limited liability, and which is incorporated under the Companies Act.
Directors - elected by shareholders at the Annual General Meeting, they are responsible for setting long term strategies which will benefit shareholders.
Divorce of ownership from control - where the owners of a business are not the managers who run the business.
Executive directors - directors who are also managers of the company.
Insolvent - an inability to pay debts. An insolvent company would have its assets seized by a liquidator and sold to pay its debts.
Joint stock company - another name for a limited company.
Liquidation - the distribution of assets to a company's creditors and members which brings the life of a company to an end.
Limited liability - when shareholders of a company are liable for its debts only up to the value of their shareholding.
Managers - employees of the company who are responsible for organising the day to day running of the business.
Memorandum of association - the document which gives details of a company's purpose, its name and address, and its share structure.
Non-executive directors - directors who are not managers of the company.
Private limited company - a joint stock company whose shares are not openly traded on a stock exchange.
Public limited company - a joint stock company whose shares are openly traded on a stock exchange.

OneSaturday Group plc was listed on the UK AIM (Alternative Investment Market) stock exchange in 2000. It was created from the merger of Singles Scene Limited (previously owned by Columbus Group plc) and Club Sirius Limited. OneSaturday provides a range of dating and introduction services for young people. It has three brands, Dateline, Club Sirius and Elite, providing different services for different markets. It attracts most of its customers by advertising in newspapers and magazines, although it is also using the Internet for marketing purposes. Revenue mainly comes from charging subscriptions and receiving income from premium rate telephone calls made when customers call up to hear messages from individuals hoping to find a partner.

During 2000-2001, the company had five executive directors (three of whom resigned during the year) and three non-executive directors. 71.4 million ordinary shares had been issued by April 2001. Of these, 15.6 million shares were held by the non-executive Chairman of the company. Another non-executive director held directly and indirectly 4.1 million shares. Other directors held a further 0.7 million shares. The Group made a loss over the financial year to 30 April 2001. To provide further working capital, the three largest shareholders gave a two year loan to the company to supplement the overdraft negotiated with Barclay's Bank.

In the 2001 *Annual Report and Accounts*, it was stated that 'in accordance with the company's Articles of Association, all directors retire' but they all put themselves up for re-election at the AGM of the company.

Adapted from OneSaturday plc, *Annual Report and Accounts*, 2001.

1 (a) Explain what is meant by the business terms:
   (a) 'limited'; (3 marks)
   (b) 'Articles of Association'. (3 marks)
2 Discuss the advantages and disadvantages to OneSaturday Group of floating on a stock exchange. (12 marks)
3 To what extent is there likely to be a 'divorce of ownership and control' at OneSaturday Group? (12 marks)

OneSaturday
single minded about...

There has never been a more exciting time to join an introductions club. The 'noughties' really has to be dedicated to the 'Decade of Dating'. Single is the new Black. The unattached everywhere are enjoying the fact that dating and introduction agencies are very much in vogue and refreshingly the one time stigmatised perception is now almost defunct. The media infatuation with singledom seems to be developing into its own full-blown love affair. Online dating, speed dating, blind dating, even global dating - everybody is doing it. When choosing a OneSaturday introductions or dating club you are choosing quality and heritage, blended with an informed awareness of the current trends. This is what puts us head and shoulders above our competitors. OneSaturday is the only company in the UK who offer a portfolio of different brands and services to suit every genre, age group and peer group.

Our Club Sirius brand has clearly positioned its place within the OneSaturday Group - and indeed within the industry - as the faction for the intelligent, articulate and well-educated to converge. Club Sirius combines the personal service that comes with an offline introductions company with the added benefit of a fantastically convenient and user friendly online dating service, as well as our members benefit scheme and our extensive calendar of events.

Dateline is your hotline to dating. The service does what its name suggests and introduces members whose criteria matches. Soon we will be adding a new option within Dateline. We aim to give new choice to Dateline members and offer the option of either selecting other online members or having our experts match profiles for you. Most online brands do not offer the same quality of customer service, nor do they offer the customer screening.

When you join Elite Introductions you are appointed your own personal "Relationship Manager" who will guide you through the pitfalls of the dating game. Your relationship manager will be like your new best friend! They will get to know you and together you will build a picture of the type of person you would like to meet, and what sort of relationship you are looking for. Once you have decided who you want to meet your relationship manager will then make all the arrangements!

Those aesthetically blessed and picky amongst you will be guided towards a more exclusive boutique - independently owned Gorgeous Get-togethers, who have a close affiliation with OneSaturday, is more a lifestyle club offering a monthly curriculum of events. It was the first to bring speed dating to the UK. Attracting career minded 24-40 year olds, it has a strict joining criteria. Applicants are only invited to join if they are gorgeous. Clients are vetted for looks, presence and drive.

Gorgeous Get Togethers

Vickridge Video and DVD

Knowledge John Vickridge worked for a major video distribution company. But he decided that he could make more money if he set up on his own.

Application A video distribution company buys the *rights* to *distribute* a video or DVD within a territory such as the UK from the *production company* that owns the *copyright*. The *start-up* was thoroughly *researched*. John drew up a *business plan* which laid out in detail how the *company* would operate. *Finance* would come partly from savings and partly from a *bank loan* secured on his house. His *premises* were within walking distance of where he lived and were the cheapest he could find. His *customer base* would be the *companies* he knew intimately from selling to them for five years. *Cash flow* was a worry because money had to be paid *upfront* for the *distribution rights* before he sold any videos or DVDs.

Analysis Once the company was up and running, the benefits of his planning bore fruit. The cash injected into the company at the start was enough to see it through the first twelve months, by which time cash flow was positive. He worked his contacts in the trade hard and, despite some initial misgivings, they bought his products in the quantities he expected. His premises were certainly not luxurious, but then he never allowed his customers or suppliers to visit. The key was that they were cheap and so helped him increase his profits.

Evaluation John Vickridge's success was probably down to two factors. First, he had an inside knowledge of the industry in which he set up his business. Second, he planned meticulously. Being an entrepreneur, however, always carries some risk. His potential customers could have refused to deal with him, for example. Being successful in business requires a little luck as well as planning.

Finance

Starting up a business will almost certainly require finance. New small businesses get finance from a range of sources.

Savings Some **entrepreneurs** (see unit 59) are lucky enough to have savings. This might include money in the bank or building society or shares invested on the stock market. The money may have come from a redundancy payment or from the sale of private assets. A vintage car might be sold or a capital gain might be made by moving from a larger to a smaller house. It could come from an inheritance or a lump sum given on retirement as part of the pension package. Most new small businesses, though, need other sources of finance as well to start up.

Borrowing from family and friends Another common source of finance is to borrow money from family or friends. Often the money is borrowed free of interest and so this is a cheap source of finance. It can be difficult, though, if the business fails and it becomes impossible to repay the money.

Borrowing from the bank The majority of business start-ups arrange to borrow money from their bank. The borrowing may be in the form of a **loan** where a sum is borrowed up front and has to be paid back in fixed monthly instalments. This is a good way of financing the purchase of machinery or equipment. Alternatively, the business may arrange an **overdraft facility**. This is where the business is allowed by the bank to go into the red on its bank account (i.e. take out money even though there is no money in the account). The bank sets a limit on how much can be borrowed in this way, called the **overdraft limit**. Borrowing through an overdraft is flexible as money can be repaid when it comes into the business. Overdraft borrowing should be used to finance

periods when trading is poor. A Christmas decorations company, for example, should have a positive bank balance over the Christmas period. But it may go into the red in the middle of the year when it is still producing but not selling very much.

Borrowing from a bank has two drawbacks. One is that **interest** has to be paid on borrowing. This adds to costs. Second, the bank may well ask for **security** (sometimes called collateral). Collateral is the assets of the business owner which the bank can sell if the borrowing is not repaid. Often the most valuable asset owned by an entrepreneur is their own house.

Many entrepreneurs are turned down for finance by banks. This is because the bank judges that the client will **default** on the loan (i.e. will not repay it in full). The client is then too risky. The government, however, has a scheme called the Loan Guarantee Scheme where it guarantees the bank that it will repay up to 80 per cent of the loan in case of default. This encourages banks to lend to riskier business start-ups. However, the business has to pay a slightly higher rate of interest on the loan under the scheme.

Trade credit Once the business is up and running, it may be able to get trade credit from its suppliers. Trade credit is when goods or services are provided to the business but it doesn't have to pay for them till later. Typically, trade credit is given for 30 days, although it can be longer. However, the business may find that it has to give trade credit itself to customers which will increase its financing needs.

Other sources Small businesses sometimes can tap into other sources of finance. They may be able to hire equipment long term rather than buying it outright. A few may find a **business angel**. These are individuals who are prepared to invest in a new business if they think it will be successful. They will want a **share** of the business, i.e. to become a co-owner of the business. Often they will also offer helpful business advice in setting up and running the business. A few businesses attract **venture capital**. Venture capitalists are businesses which specialise in providing finance, mainly to existing medium sized businesses for further growth. However, for a new start-up, they would only be interested if the investment was substantial, say a minimum of £250 000.

Location

For many businesses, the exact location of their premises is not important. For a manufacturer or a mail order company, for example, the most important factors about location are likely to be suitability of the premises and the cost. Obviously, for a small business start-up, location is likely to be guided by where the owner is currently living. A plumber in London is unlikely to set up in Northern Ireland simply because premises are cheaper there.

For some businesses, though, the exact location is crucial to success. This is true, for example, in retailing. Having a shop in the middle of a busy street can mean plenty of customers coming into the shop. Being tucked away in a side street may mean hardly any customers. Similarly, the location of a petrol station can determine how many cars stop and fill up with petrol. Location in these circumstances will be linked with costs. The better the location, the higher the rent or the cost of buying outright.

Building a customer base

New businesses need to build a **customer base** to survive. A customer base is a group of customers who make repeat purchases over time. They are loyal customers who have found the product being offering attractive. There is a number of ways in which businesses can build up and maintain a customer base.

- Quality of product is important. Whether it is a good or a service, customers will come back if they are satisfied with what they have bought.
- Price is a key factor in some areas of business. This isn't necessarily the cheapest price. It is the price relative to the quality of the product bought. Value for money is essential.
- The level of service provided is often crucial. For example, a small manufacturer needs to deliver on time. A music shop must be able to get music ordered by customers quickly from publishers. In a restaurant, customers should be able to order their meals when they are ready and service should be efficient. Customers can easily be lost if staff are unhelpful or offhand.
- Good after-sales service is important. This includes dealing with complaints and mistakes made. A customer will often come back if a complaint has been dealt with to their satisfaction. Failure to deal with complaints will lose customers.
- Maintaining contact with customers where possible can be vital. How this is done varies from industry to industry. It may be the norm to send out Christmas cards to customers, for example. Customers may expect to receive regular visits.

The latest addition to Britain's breweries is Blythe Brewery. Situated on a farm in Staffordshire, it is a one-man microbrewery. The brewery is the dream-come-true of former chemicals worker Robert Greenway who is currently producing around 180 gallons a week of his ales.

He set the brewery up with his redundancy pay. When looking for premises, he found that most were too big, around 1 000 square feet, and just too expensive. Eventually he came across some business units on a farm which were the right size and the right price. The farmer paid for the alterations to suit the brewery with a sloping floor and drainage at the front of the unit.

He has made some sales locally at free houses (pubs which are not owned by a large brewery and forced to sell only the brewery's products). He also has a brother who is chairman of the local branch of the real ale campaign CAMRA in Northamptonshire who placed the first batch of beer brewed in free houses in that county.

Adapted from the *Express & Star*, 19.5.2003.

---

1 **Explain how Robert Greenway financed his new business.**
2 **Suggest why (a) he chose to locate his business on a farm and (b) why he doesn't need to be located near his customers.**
3 **Discuss what difficulties he would face if he chose to expand his production substantially.**

Cash flow

Cash flow refers to the way in which cash comes into the business, for example from sales, and leaves the business, for example to pay bills (see units 27 and 28). Managing cash flow is crucial for the survival of a business.

The main problem with start-ups is that cash tends to flow out of the business in much larger quantities than originally planned. For example, businesses often start to trade at a later point in time than expected. A business might plan to have heavy initial expenditure in March so that it is up and running in April. But equipment may arrive late. Building work may run over schedule. There may be complications with getting workers. So instead, the business doesn't start till June. That is two months lost sales with no cash coming into the business.

The best way to prevent cash flow problems is to have

Everything Printing was set up in London in 1986. Since then it has gone from strength to strength. Its customer base is extensive, attracting work from all over the country. It offers something for everyone - from people wanting enlargements of their holiday snaps, to leaflets, brochures, business cards, bound reports and posters to companies requiring high quality four colour print jobs.

Its manager Siobhan Benson, argues that there are several reasons why people trust their work to the business and are assured they will get the most professional of services.

'We always aim to provide a competitive price', she says. 'And the quality of our work seems to ensure that people come back to us again and again. We work for a number of internationally renowned magazines that offer services to the footwear and sports industries. Businesses buying these magazines and using their website see our name and often use our services as well.'

'We also provide a wide range of services to clients and we are flexible. We can print in black and white, two colour or full colour. We can print one offs or long print runs.' The business passes very little of its work out to other suppliers. At times it might use a local business it has worked with for many years to finish a magazine cover, but that's about it. This means it can guarantee both the quality of the work and delivery times.

1 **Explain what is meant by a 'customer base'.**
2 **List FOUR factors which have helped Everything Printing develop a customer base.**
3 **Discuss whether Everything Printing could raise its prices and so increase its profits and still maintain its customer base.**

sufficient finance at the start. But many small business start-ups fail to have a cushion of finance to cope with unforeseen problems. Even if they survive the first year, a lack of cash can cause constant running problems. For example, one way of dealing with poor cash flow is to pay bills to suppliers late rather than on time. Paying a bill two months late means that that cash hasn't flowed out of the business during those two months. But it can be a risky strategy. Suppliers may refuse to supply if bills are unpaid. They may charge penalties for late payment. They might constantly contact the business asking for payment which takes up management time and adds to stress levels.

The business plan

Research shows that start-up businesses which have prepared a BUSINESS PLAN are more likely to survive than ones which have not. The business plan is a plan of how the business will develop over a period of time, like one or two years. Writing a business plan is important for a potential business start-up for three main reasons.

- Writing the plan forces the would-be entrepreneur to look at every key aspect of the future business. It is easy to concentrate on some aspects of running a business, like the product to be sold or its location. But other aspects are often not thought out well, such as finance. The business plan forces the entrepreneur to consider every aspect equally.
- If the business is to borrow money from a bank, the bank will expect to see a business plan. The bank uses the business plan to judge whether the business is likely to be

credit worthy.
- The plan is useful once the business has started to trade. The actual operation of the business can be compared to the forecasts contained in the plans. This will highlight problems that are occurring. The business owner can then take steps to overcome the problem.

The outline of a business plan can be obtained from any of the major banks in leaflets they produce on starting up a business. They give a detailed list of points which must be addressed in the plan. These include the following.

1 Explain briefly the ways in which a start-up small business might obtain finance.
2 Explain whether the exact location of the business is important for the success of (a) a hairdresser; (b) a business manufacturing metal fasteners such as nuts and bolts.
3 Why is building a customer base important for a new business?
4 (a) What is meant by 'cash flow'? (b) Explain why a business which has continuous negative cash flow will be forced to cease trading.
5 Why is it important for a would-be entrepreneur to draw up a business plan?

285

- The business and its objectives. The name of the business, its address, its legal structure (see unit 60-61) and its aims and objectives (see unit 63-64).
- The product or service. A description of the product or range of products to be made, the quantity to be sold and the estimated price.
- The market. The size of the potential market and a description of the potential customers, the nature of the competition, and marketing priorities, backed up with evidence from market research.
- Personnel. Who will run the business, how many employees there will be, and the skills, qualifications and experience of those in the business.
- Buying and production. Where the business will buy its supplies, the production methods to be used, and the costs of production.
- Premises and equipment. The premises to be used and any equipment which needs to be obtained and financed.
- Cash flow and profit. A cash flow forecast together with a profit forecast, including a break-even analysis (see unit 22).
- Finance. Where the finance to start-up and run the business will come from, including savings of owners and borrowing.

keyterms

Business plan - a plan for the development of a business, giving details such as the products to be made and sold and forecasts such as costs and cash flow.

Niall MacArthur is the young pretender to the London sandwich bar throne. He has already opened seven Eat ('excellence and taste') cafes and is on track to raise this to 30, the number in his original business plan.

MacArthur began Eat in 1996 after leaving his job as an investment banker. He saw that the market for sandwiches and coffee was polarised. Pret a Manger dominated the sandwich bar market because of its excellent food. Starbucks was big in the coffee bar market but wasn't renowned for its food. MacArthur aspired to bring the two together in one cafe - great food, including soup and home-baked bread for the sandwiches, with fine coffees.

In his market research, he saw that it was going to be difficult to beat the quality of the Pret a Manger food. But his solution was to go one better than Pret a Manger by building a bakery to produce his own bread rather than buying from outside suppliers. This gave him greater control over quality and with his wife, Faith, he set about creating a range of breads, sandwich fillings and soups that would rival and outdo the best from other chains.

Location of shops is vital. MacArthur has made sure that Eat cafes are in prime sites near high concentrations of London office space, to grab a big portion of the lunchtime trade.

Eat was initially financed by MacArthur himself from his own savings. But it became clear rapidly that he would need outside funding. He got that from venture capitalist 3i, which took a 40 per cent stake in Eat at a cost of £3 million. This £3 million was ploughed into the business. 3i's involvement allowed MacArthur then to get a £4.25 million loan from NatWest. This will be enough to finance the opening of the 30 shops in his original business plan by the end of the year.

Adapted from *The Sunday Times*, 25.7.1999.

1 Explain what is meant by the terms:
   (a) 'market' (3 marks);
   (b) 'funding'. (3 marks)
2 Discuss the advantages and disadvantages to Niall MacArthur of having drawn up a business plan. (12 marks)
3 Evaluate whether Niall MacArthur should have attempted to raise more finance than the £3 million from 3i and £4.25 million from NatWest. (12 marks)

63 Aims and objectives

Austin Reed Group

Knowledge The Austin Reed Group is a public limited company which retails clothes for both men and women under the names of Austin Reed, Country Casuals and Stephens Brothers. The company, according to its 2000-01 Annual Report and Accounts, 'aims to create increasing shareholder value'. It does this by 'investing in the development of premium lifestyle brands in the UK and internationally; delivering high quality, exclusively designed collections of clothing and accessories that meet the needs of each brand's target customer; managing an effective and efficient operating organisation; and enabling management and staff to work in an environment that allows them to excel'.

Application Austin Reed, Country Casuals and Stephens Brothers are *up market brands* for the *business*. To create *shareholder value*, the *company* must earn growing *profits* to pay its *shareholders dividends* and to see *investors* wanting to buy shares in the *company* which will raise the *share price*.

Analysis The aim of the company is to increase shareholder value. To achieve this, it has four main objectives. Two of its objectives relate to its customers. By satisfying the needs of its customers, it will be able to sell clothes in sufficient volume and at a high enough price to generate profit. The other two objectives relate to organisation and staff. By creating an efficient organisation where staff can maximise their potential, costs can be kept down, whilst staff can create clothes collections which will attract customers.

Evaluation One way of judging whether the company is achieving its aim is to look at its profit for the year. In 2000-01, it made a profit (on ordinary activities before taxation) of £72 000 compared to £1 962 000 in the previous financial year and £7 126 000 the year before. This would suggest that the company was in difficulties over this period. In fact, the fall in profits was mainly due to the cost of closing down parts of the business to focus on more profitable activities. Short term costs have been incurred in the hope that profits in the long term will be higher. Certainly, the stock market judged that there was some hope of success for this strategy. The share price of the company rose from 91.5p to 100p over the financial year 2000 to 2001. However, the long term success of the business remains to be seen.

Adapted from Austin Reed, *Annual Report and Accounts*, 2000-01.

Business aims

All businesses have AIMS. An aim is what the business intends to do in the long term - its purpose. Ultimately it is what the business is striving to achieve. Different businesses have different aims. A business might also have more than one aim. What might be the aims of a business?

Profit It could be argued that the main aim of businesses is to make a profit. Some businesses try to PROFIT MAXIMISE. This comes about when the difference between the **revenues** and **costs** (see unit 21) is greatest over a period of time. Profit maximisation is most likely to benefit the owners of the business. For a sole trader, the profit is usually equivalent to the wage drawn from the business. The bigger the profit, the more money can be taken. In a company, the level of dividend paid is likely to depend on the profit made. In a public limited company, quoted share prices too are affected by profits. Companies which the stock market thinks will be highly profitable in the future have high share values. Companies which have poor profit forecasts tend to have low share values. Existing shareholders want the price of their shares to be as high as possible.

Shareholder value In the 1980s and 1990s, it became fashionable for large companies to argue that their aim was to maximise SHAREHOLDER VALUE. Shareholder value can be interpreted in different ways. Shareholders make a return from their shares partly through the dividend they receive, and partly through increases in value of shares on a stock exchange. Increasing dividends and increasing share price may go together for a growing company. However, companies can pay out too much in dividends in the short term to please their shareholders at the expense of the long term success of the business. Profits, instead of being paid out as dividends, can be retained by the company and used for investment (see unit 24). If there is too little investment by the company, it can see sales and profits stagnate and even fall. High dividend payouts can therefore **destroy shareholder value** in the longer term. Maximising

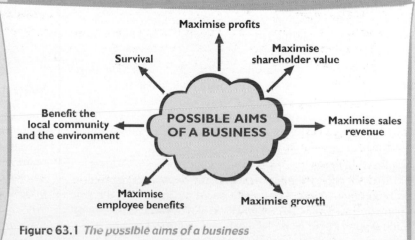

Figure 63.1 *The possible aims of a business*

shareholder value is in the interests of the shareholders. It may even be in the interests of managers too if it secures their jobs.

Survival For some businesses, survival is the main aim. This is particularly true for small businesses just starting up and for larger businesses which have got into financial difficulties. Unless a business survives, it cannot generate benefits for its **stakeholders** (see unit 56) such as profits for its owners or jobs for employees.

Sales revenue An alternative objective for a business might be SALES REVENUE MAXIMISATION. Earning the highest level possible of revenue over a period of time might lead to high levels of profit, so benefiting the owners of the business. But the owners of a business are not its only stakeholders. In medium to large sized businesses, managers are stakeholders too. They control the day to day running of the business. They may have more influence on how the business is run than its owners. Maximising revenue might be more in the interests of managers than maximising profit. The larger the business, the higher the salaries of top managers and their fringe benefits are likely to be. A growing business can be an exciting environment in which to work. There is plenty of opportunity for managers to gain promotion and exercise power over how money is spent, recruitment of staff and new products. The opposite is true in a business which is reducing in size. Job cuts, for instance, are demoralising for all workers. The tendency for managers to pursue revenue maximisation rather than profit maximisation is one of the main reasons why many companies link the **remuneration** (the total pay package) of top managers with profits. It is common today, for instance, for top managers today to be given share options. In small businesses, where the owners are the managers, this conflict of interest between them does not arise.

Growth Another aim of a business might be to grow. Revenue is just one measure of the **size** of a business. A business might aim to be the 'number one company in the market', i.e. have the largest market share. There are other measures of growth, such as capital value, and the number of employees it has. If the owners control a business, they might be prepared to sacrifice short term profits for long term growth which leads to higher profits in the long term. Maximising growth could be in their best interests. If managers are in control, growth may become the main business objective because it suits their objectives more than profit maximisation. As already explained, the pay of top managers and their power tends to be linked with business size.

Customer welfare Many businesses state that one of their aims is to benefit their customers. This might be in the form of providing 'best value', or innovative products, or high quality service. Without customers, businesses could not survive. So some argue that customer satisfaction must be an aim of any business.

Employee benefits Employees are stakeholders in a business too. The success of the business is vitally dependent upon the skills and motivation of staff. So it could be argued that the aim of any business must be to benefit employees. The existence of **trade unions** in the workplace can also put pressure on a business to make employee benefits one of its aims.

Tomkins is a world class global engineering and manufacturing group with market and technical leadership across three businesses; Air Systems and Components, Engineering & Construction Products and Industrial & Automotive.

Tomkins is committed to enhancing shareholder value through increasing the economic value of its businesses by concentrating in product and geographic markets in its chosen sectors where the businesses have sustainable competitive advantage, and which offer prospects for profitable growth.

	1996-97	1997-98	1998-99	1999-00	2000-01
Dividend paid per ordinary share	11.45	13.17	15.15	17.45	12.00
Share price[1]	268.5	351.8	264.3	197.3	156.5
FTSE All Share[2]	268.5	350.7	381.8	377.4	360.8
FTSE Engineering and Machinery[3]	268.5	333.1	299.4	252.2	209.3

1 Share price on 30 April.
2 Average share price of all shares quoted on the London Stock Exchange on 30 April. Prices have been rebased so that 30 April 1997 = 268.5.
3 Average share price of all shares quoted on the London Stock Exchange in the Engineering and Machinery sector on 30 April. Tomkins itself is classified as a company in the Engineering and Machinery sector by the London Stock Exchange. Prices have been rebased so that 30 April 1997 = 268.5.

Adapted from Tomkins, *Annual Report and Accounts*, 2001.

Table 63.1 *Tomkins: share performance compared with other shares*

1 **Suggest the aim of Tomkins as a company.**
2 **Using Table 63.1, compare the financial performance of Tomkins with other companies between 1996-97 and 2000-01.**
3 **To what extent has Tomkins achieved its aim between 1996-97 and 2000-01?**

Benefiting the local community and the environment A few businesses, like The Body Shop, have been set up explicitly with the aim of benefiting the local communities in which they operate and respecting the environment. Equally, some large companies, such as Tesco or BP, have stated aims with regard to community and environmental issues.

What is the main aim of the business?

The main aim of small businesses, such as sole traders or partnerships, is usually to maximise profits. Owners want to maximise the return on their work in a business. There are many exceptions though. For example, doctors working in partnership may make the needs of their patients an important priority.

For companies, though, the situation is more complex. In the UK and the USA, it has been traditional for the needs of shareholders to be most important. So it can be argued that UK and US companies are usually profit maximisers or maximisers

The Body Shop should adapt its hallmark social crusades to move with the times, according to Adrian Bellamy. He has run the US operations of The Body Shop for two years and has now been hired on a two-year consultancy to advise on improving the company's global operations.

'One of Anita Roddick's (the co-founder of the company) favourite expressions is passion before profit', he said in an interview. 'I have a little challenge with that.' In contrast with other companies on whose boards he sits, such as Gap, 'performance is not at the top of the agenda (at The Body Shop) and the social agenda of the company comes first and foremost'.

Asked whether the company needed a change in emphasis, he said: 'I think you have to in a certain way. If you run a business in this day and age you have got to be good or you won't be here tomorrow'. Some of The Body Shop's corporate values, such as crusading against animal testing, had grown 'long in the tooth', he added. The US business was putting more emphasis on campaigns to help families in distress, he said.

Adapted from the *Financial Times*, 19.7.2001.

1 **What, according to Adrian Bellamy, is the aim of The Body Shop as a business?**
2 **Explain why this aim might put the long run survival of the business at risk.**
3 **Discuss whether The Body Shop should change its main aim.**

of shareholder value. This is true even though there is a **divorce of ownership and control** (see unit 61), where the owners are a different group of people from those who run the company.

In continental Europe and Japan, however, workers, customers and the local community are seen as being much more important stakeholders than in the UK or the USA. So a European or Japanese business may have several aims.

It can also be argued that this is true even in the UK and the USA. According to BEHAVIOURAL THEORIES OF THE FIRM, shareholders, managers, workers, customers, local communities and pressure groups, such as environmental activists, share power within a business. The business aims to reconcile the often **conflicting aims** of each group of stakeholders. For example, it PROFIT SATISFICES, making enough profit to keep shareholders happy, but this is not the maximum level of profit it could make. Instead, it spends more than it otherwise would on environmental projects, or servicing the local community. Perhaps it pays better wages to staff than it needs to recruit and motivate them. Senior managers and directors, who have some control over their own pay, are able to negotiate larger remuneration packages than might otherwise be the case.

Over time, the balance of power between stakeholders can change and therefore so can the aims of a business. For example, it could be argued that over the past forty years in the UK the power of employees has gone down as trade union power has decreased. This could be one of the main reasons why the share of profits in the income of the whole UK economy has risen sharply whilst that of earnings has fallen. On the other hand, the power of environmentalists has increased. Forty years ago, few companies acknowledged that the environment was of any importance in their decision making.

Some economists have suggested that in a company, there are in fact only two sets of stakeholders with sufficient power to influence the running of the business. According to the MANAGERIAL THEORY OF THE FIRM, shareholders and managers share power. Managers have to make enough profit to keep shareholders happy otherwise they risk losing their bonuses and jobs. But managers have enough day to day control to be able to reward themselves more than is strictly necessary.

Objectives

The OBJECTIVES of a business are its goals - outcomes or targets which allow it to achieve its aims. Objectives should be practical outcomes from the operation of a business. One way of summarising this is to use SMART criteria. This says that objectives should be:

- **specific (S)** - they must set out clearly what a business is attempting to achieve;
- **measurable (M)** - they must be capable of being measured so that it can judged whether or not they have been achieved;
- **agreed (A)** - everyone responsible for achieving an objective must have agreed with the objective and understood what it meant;
- **realistic (R)** - the objective must be achievable given the resources available and the market conditions;
- **time specific (T)** - the objective must specify over what period of time it is to be achieved.

So a business must choose suitable objectives to help it achieve its aims. There could be many ways in which this could be done.

- The aim of a business might be to make a profit. An objective to achieve this could be to increase sales or cut costs by 20 per cent over the next two years.
- The aim might be to become more environmentally friendly. An objective to achieve this could be to double spending on community projects next year.
- The aim of the business might be to be the number one producer in three years. An objective to achieve this could be to be innovative and change the whole product range within the next three years.

It is important to understand that the same measure could be either an aim or an objective (but not both at the same time). Take, for example, profit maximisation. This is traditionally seen as an aim of a business. But it could be an objective if the aim of the business is to maximise shareholder value. Note that maximising profit is not a SMART objective because it is not measurable. Another example would be market share. Becoming the number one company in a market could be the aim of a business. Equally, it could be an objective if the aim of the business were to maximise profits. This is because becoming the market leader could enable the business to charge higher prices to customers than if it were second or third in the market. Becoming 'the number one' in a market is a SMART objective because it is measurable.

Mission statements, aims and objectives

Larger businesses often have a MISSION STATEMENT. This is a statement, written by the business, of its purpose and its values. It is meant both to state the aims of the business and to provide a vision for its stakeholders.

For example, MSB International PLC is a UK based company which provides other businesses with services in the field of human resources. Amongst other services, it helps businesses recruit temporary and permanent staff. Its mission is: 'To provide human capital solutions that enable our clients to achieve their business goals. Expand our organisation globally both organically and through acquisition, whilst enhancing and broadening the services. We are committed to rewarding shareholders and employees through sustained growth in profitability.'

Mission statements often illustrate the problem of distinguishing between aims and objectives. For example, in the MSB International mission statement, the stated aim is to expand the organisation. It then goes on to say how this will be achieved - through organic growth and acquisition. It is likely that organic growth and acquisition are in fact objectives. They are the means through which the aim of expansion of the organisation will be achieved. But it could also be argued that expansion of the organisation is not an end in itself but is there to increase the rewards to shareholders, another stated aim. Also, is the business equally committed to 'rewarding shareholders' and 'rewarding employees'? Some might argue that rewarding employees is an objective, not an aim, but it is a way of motivating workers to generate high profits for shareholders.

Often, writers use the terms 'aims', 'objectives' and 'goals' as if they were the same to overcome this problem of distinguishing between what is an aim and what is an objective.

checklist

1 What is the difference between maximising profit, maximising sales revenue and maximising shareholder value?
2 Under what circumstances is survival likely to be the main aim of a business?
3 Why might a business aim to (a) maximise employee benefits and (b) maximise customer welfare?
4 Why might the aim of a small business be different from the aim of a large company?
5 What is the difference between managerial theories of the firm and behavioural theories?
6 What is the difference between an aim and an objective for a business?
7 Why should objectives be SMART?
8 What is the purpose of a mission statement?

keyterms

Aim - the intention or purpose of a business; what a business is ultimately striving to achieve.
Behavioural theories of the firm - theories which suggest that businesses have multiple aims set by their main stakeholders.
Managerial theories of the firm - theories which suggest that businesses are controlled by managers who run them for their own benefit subject to the need to make enough profit to satisfy shareholders (profit satisficing).
Mission statement - a statement, written by the business, of its purpose and its values; it is meant both to state the aims of the business and to provide a vision for its stakeholders.
Objective - a goal or target of a business; an outcome which allows a business to achieve its aims.
Profit maximisation - earning the highest profit possible over a period of time.
Profit satisficing - making enough profit to satisfy the needs of shareholders whilst pursuing at least one other aim such as rewarding managers and directors.
Sales revenue maximisation - earning the highest possible revenue over a period of time.
Shareholder value - the value of a company to its owners over a period of time as measured by a combination of the size of its dividend payments and the rise in its share price.
SMART - acronym for the attributes of a good objective - specific, measurable, agreed, realistic and time specific.

It could also be argued that those in business blur the distinction between aims and objectives. Managers and directors might themselves find it difficult to distinguish between the two. They might also be unwilling to reveal their actual aims. For example, large multinational corporations tend to state, that their aim is to benefit shareholders, customers, workers and the environment. But if their actual aim was simply to benefit shareholders, they would be unlikely to admit to this publicly in a mission statement. This is because they could attract a great deal of adverse publicity as 'uncaring', 'greedy', 'capitalist' organisations. In practice, they do have to reward their employees sufficiently to motivate them. They have to be at least environmentally friendly enough to avoid risking prosecution under the law. So, employment and environmental issues must form part of their objectives. But they are not necessarily part of the aims of the company. Mission statements, and what companies say about their aims, should therefore be examined critically and not taken at face value.

Anglian Water Group is a UK based public limited company. Its core activity is the operation of Anglian Water, a water company which provides water and wastewater services in the East Anglian region. Prices charged to customers are regulated by Ofwat and therefore the main way in which the company can increase profits is through reducing costs. However, cost reduction programmes have not come at the expense of quality. In 2000-01, the company came top of the Ofwat league table for overall service to customers.

In order to increase profit substantially, the company has expanded into non-regulated areas of business. It has entered the international market for water supply, for instance by buying Czech and Chilean water companies. Within the UK, it has bought Morrison, a construction company, which builds everything from shopping centres to houses to schools. It specialises in financial management (FM), where it builds and then maintains infrastructure such as shopping centres and schools over a period of time. Included in this is an expansion into the provision of services such as refuse collection, street cleaning, buildings and highways maintenance and other essential services.

Adapted from AWG plc, *Annual Report and Accounts*, 2001.

AWG's aim is to sustain and enhance communities and the lives of our customers through profitable management of infrastructures.

AWG plc, *Annual Report and Accounts*, 2001.

Last year, at a series of vision and values events with staff, I said that we were embarking on three journeys: our objectives were to be the UK water industry's number one by 2002; a global player by 2007; and to grow a thriving facilities management (FM) business. All the while building a business steeped in sustainable principles.

Chief Executive Chris Mellor.

AWG plc, *Annual Report and Accounts*, 2001.

1 What is meant by the term 'global player'? (3 marks)
2 (a) State THREE objectives of AWG. (3 marks)
   (b) Explain how the company is building up its business to achieve those objectives. (6 marks)
3 Analyse how AWG's objectives might help the company achieve its aims. (8 marks)
4 Comment on the problems that AWG might experience in achieving its aims and objectives. (10 marks)

Hurford's

Knowledge Hurford's is a company which owns and runs a group of 23 hotels in the UK, serving mainly the tourist trade. In 2001, it was hard hit by the foot and mouth crisis and by the events of September 11. Foot and mouth was a disease which affected livestock. One government response was to close many footpaths in rural England, damaging tourism. September 11 saw the World Trade Centre buildings in New York destroyed by terrorists. US tourists, already put off from visiting the UK by the foot and mouth crisis, became frightened to travel by plane. UK tourist numbers fell even further.

Application The *aim* of the *company* is to *increase shareholder value*. Its *strategic objectives* are: to expand the group as and when suitably *priced* hotels come onto the *market*; to maintain high levels of occupancy at its hotels whilst maintaining *prices*; to develop its *employees* to enable them to play a full part in the development of the *company*.

Analysis Hurford's plans to meet its objectives in 2001 were ruined by the foot and mouth crisis and by the events of September 11. Occupancy levels fell sharply and it was forced to reduce the prices of many of its hotel rooms. Cash flow was negative and the company felt unable to buy any new hotels. Some workers lost their jobs and training was cut back to reduce costs.

Evaluation Hurford's has had to re-evaluate its plans for 2002. Its main short term objective is to return to occupancy and pricing levels seen in 2000. Even this could be difficult, though, if US tourists continue to stay away from the UK. Problems could be compounded if economic growth in Europe and the US is sluggish or if unemployment in the UK rises. Overall, Hurford's will be lucky to achieve its aims and objectives in 2002.

Strategy

Businesses have **aims** which they hope to achieve through their **objectives** or **goals** (see unit 63). But objectives are not achieved by chance. Many businesses plan how they will achieve their objectives. PLANNING to achieve objectives is known as STRATEGY.

In a large business, strategies should be set at all levels of the organisation.

Corporate strategy CORPORATE STRATEGY is the planning of how to achieve the main objectives of the whole company. For example, companies must decide what markets they wish to sell into and which they should withdraw from. They have to decide on what they are best at doing, their CORE CAPABILITIES (or CORE COMPETENCIES). Activities which don't match their core capabilities should be sold off or closed down. Companies which have significant sales overseas should have a GLOBAL STRATEGY about how they plan to exploit markets worldwide.

Business unit (or divisional) strategy BUSINESS UNIT (or DIVISIONAL) STRATEGY is the planning by each business unit or division within the company of how it will achieve its objectives. These objectives will contribute to the realisation of corporate objectives, the objectives of the whole company. Most large companies comprise a parent company, which sets corporate strategy, and a number of **subsidiary companies**. Each of these subsidiary companies should have a business unit strategy. The whole company may also be split up into several **divisions** (see unit 31), usually based upon common markets and products or geographical market areas. Each division should have its own strategy.

Functional (or operational or department) strategies Large businesses are likely to be organised into **departments** by **function** (see unit 31). For example, there could be a marketing department, a production department, a personnel department and a finance department. Each of these departments should have a strategy which details plans of how it will meet its objectives. An example of a FUNCTIONAL (or OPERATION or DEPARTMENT) STRATEGY would be a plan to cut wastage in the production department by 5 per cent this year in order to achieve the departmental objective of cutting overall production costs by 2 per cent.

Business strategies may also be linked to individual employees. They may be set goals which reflect the objectives of the company, the division or the department in which they work. Individual employee targets or goals may then be used to appraise the worker on a regular basis. Bonuses or the chance of promotion may be linked in with this too.

Developing a strategy

There are many ways of developing strategies, but one standard model is to develop a strategy systematically as follows.

1 Clarify objectives.

Sixcor is a UK private limited company which manufactures food equipment for sale to businesses in the food processing and food retailing sectors. Last year was a difficult year for the company. Sales were down 5 per cent whilst profits fell from £3.5 million the previous year to £0.1 million. Part of the problem was the strength of the pound. Overseas orders were lost to competitors on price. Those orders which Sixcor did gain were at such low prices that they were barely profitable. In the UK market, Sixcor suffered because of the movement of the economy into a mild recession.

However, problems within the company didn't help the situation. During the year, the company moved to a larger site so that production could be expanded. But there was considerable disruption during the move. An estimated four weeks' production was lost as a result. There were continued difficulties recruiting sufficient skilled production workers and as a consequence some orders were sent out late. The marketing department reported that the failure to deliver some goods on time made it more difficult to get repeat orders, whilst the finance department warned that the situation adversely affected cash flow.

The company continued to roll out new products in response to changing customer needs and to advances in technology. Competitors too, though, were bringing out innovative products, making the trading environment difficult. There was considerable debate at board level about whether the expenditure on research and development for new products was too great or too little. Any increase in spending would hit profits in the short term, but could enhance profits in the long term if it gave the company a competitive advantage.

1 (a) From the information given list (i) SIX issues which would be included in an internal audit of the business and (ii) SIX issues which would be included in an external audit. (b) WOULD any issues be included in a PEST-G analysis?
2 Which problems facing the company last year were short term problems and therefore unlikely to affect performance in the long term?
3 Evaluate the most important problems facing the business in the long term.

2 Gain information about the business and its external environment by carrying out an audit.
3 Summarise and analyse the results of the audit by carrying out a SWOT analysis.
4 Make plans to achieve the objectives set.
5 Implement the plans.
6 Review and evaluate outcomes.
7 Prepare the next plan.

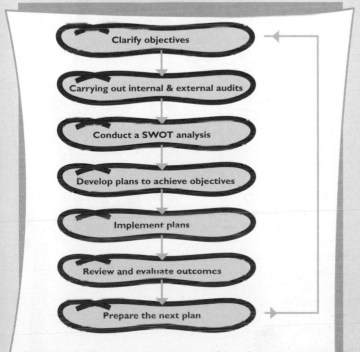

Table 64.1 *Hierarchy of strategy within a large company*

Each of these stages, shown in Figure 64.1, will now be considered in detail.

Clarifying the objectives of the business

The first stage of developing a strategy is to identify objectives. Unless objectives are clear, it will be impossible to devise plans to achieve them. There are different types of objective which can be identified for planning purposes.

Strategic objectives STRATEGIC OBJECTIVES are the main objectives of a business. They are the objectives which will help the business achieve its **aims** (see unit 63). They will almost certainly be LONG TERM OBJECTIVES. This is because it is most unlikely that the aims of a business can be achieved in, say, the next 6 or 12 months. Long term objectives tend to be objectives for the next 3-5 years.

Tactical objectives TACTICAL OBJECTIVES are SHORT TERM OBJECTIVES. They are objectives which will help achieve the strategic objectives set by the business. For example, a strategic objective might be to increase sales by 10 per cent per year over the next five years. A tactical objective to help achieve this could be to increase spending on promotion by 5 per year over the next year. Increased spending on promotion would be a TACTIC employed by the business.

Operational objectives OPERATIONAL OBJECTIVES are very short term objectives which are typically small scale and cover the day to day running of the business. They are set to achieve tactical and strategic objectives. For example, the marketing department might set itself the operational objective of finalising an advertising campaign within the next 7 days. The production department may set itself the objective of getting an important order out on time in 21 days' time.

Strategic planning is therefore concerned with setting out how the strategic objectives of the business can be achieved over the long term. An annual plan for the business will be more concerned with short term objectives. It will set out the tactics to be used to achieve this year's part of the strategic plan.

Auditing the business and its external environment

The next stage in developing a strategy is to audit the business and its external environment.

The internal audit An INTERNAL AUDIT is an analysis of the business itself and how it operates. It attempts to identify strengths and weaknesses of its operations. It would cover areas such as:

- products and their cost, quality and development;
- finance including profit, assets and cash flow;
- production, including capacity, quality, efficiency and stock management;
- internal organisation including divisional and departmental structures;
- human resources including skills, training and recruitment.

In a large business, the internal audit might be conducted by outside **management consultants**, brought into the business to conduct an independent analysis.

The external audit An EXTERNAL AUDIT is an analysis of the environment in which the business operates and over which it has little or no control. It can be split into three parts: the market, competition and the political, economic, social and technological environment.

The audit should analyse the **market** or markets in which

the business operates. For example, it should analyse:

- the size and growth of the market;
- the characteristics of the customers in the market;
- the products on offer;
- the pricing structure;
- how products are distributed;
- how products are promoted;
- industry practices, such as whether there is a **trade association** or government regulation.

The audit should also analyse the **competition** in the market. The nature of the COMPETITIVE ENVIRONMENT will be important in setting strategy. For example, it should analyse:

- the structure of the industry including the number and size of competitors, their production capacity and marketing methods, the likelihood of new entrants to the market or businesses leaving the industry;
- finance including profits of competitors, their investment programmes, costs, revenues, cash flow and assets.

Third, the external audit should use PEST-G ANALYSIS. This is analysis of the political (P), economic (E), social (S), technological (T) and environmental (G for green) issues relevant to the business.

- Politics, government, taxes and the law affect the business. For example, the tax environment will affect the price of goods (through VAT), investment (through corporation tax) and the number of workers employed (through National Insurance contributions and pension legislation). Customers and suppliers will have certain rights in law which need to be taken account of when trading. Trade union legislation will affect employment. Controls on advertising will affect promotion.
- The economic environment is very important to the business. Whether the economy is likely to be in boom or

Phipps is a company which specialises in producing colour pigments. These are used to colour everything from cans, wrappers, cartons, plastic products, textiles to magazines. It is a global company with customers and plants across the world. Its fastest growing market is in the Far East where it has plants in China and Thailand. But it faces intense competition at the bottom end of its market from Far Eastern producers who have even lower costs of production than Phipps.

Economists are predicting a major slowdown in the world economy over the next 12 months led by a recession in the United States. The Japanese market remains weak following a decade of weak or no economic growth. The combination of weakness in demand in the United States and Japan threatens to make any recession in the Far East severe and deep.

Three weeks ago, Graham Downy, the managing director (MD) of the company for the past ten years, left to take up an appointment with a larger rival company. This has left a major gap in the senior management team. Graham was considered to be an excellent MD and had overseen substantial growth in the company. It could take months to find a suitable replacement.

An audit of two plants in the United States found that management there had allowed a substantial stock of pigment to build up. The management has since been replaced, but decisions about what to do with the excess stock have yet to be taken.

A new pigment suitable for metal coatings is about to be launched. It has superior colour retention qualities, but is more expensive to produce than traditional pigments for metal coatings. A debate about pricing policy is taking place within the company.

> 1 **What is meant by SWOT analysis?**
> 2 **Use SWOT analysis to discuss the future of Phipps.**

recession could have an important impact on sales. Levels of unemployment will affect both customer demand and ability to recruit workers. Inflation will impact on pricing policy. Barriers to international trade will affect exports.

- The social and cultural environment covers areas such as education, demographics (i.e. population), migration, religion, roles of men and women and changing consumer tastes. For example, more and more women going out to work has increased the market size for ready made meals and takeaway food. Increased educational attainment over the past 40 years has increased the skills of the workforce.
- Changes in technology can have a radical impact on businesses. Manufacturing has been transformed by automated machinery. Computers have eliminated large numbers of jobs in banking and insurance. Quality has been considerably improved through applications of information technology.
- The impact of environmental changes has been felt by some businesses more than others. Extraction companies, such as oil companies or copper mining companies, have been forced to change the way in which they work because of pressure from environmental groups and governments. Businesses need to be seen to be 'green' if only to create a positive public relations image with both their workers and with consumers.

SWOT analysis

The internal and external audits should yield a large amount of information about the business and its external environment. However, this information needs to be summarised. There are many ways of doing this, but one useful way is to complete a SWOT ANALYSIS.

SWOT analysis involves looking at the internal strengths and weaknesses of a business and its external opportunities and threats.

Strengths These are positive aspects of the business arising from the **internal audit**. For example, it might have a loyal customer base, its products may be seen as amongst the best in the market or it might make large profits.

Weaknesses These are the negative aspects of the business arising from the **internal audit**. For example, fault rates in production may be high, recent promotional campaigns may have failed or staff training may be poor.

Opportunities The **external audit** should show up what opportunities are available to the business. For example, there may be an opportunity to expand into a new market with existing products. Or the weakness of a competitor may enable the business to gain market share. Or technological developments may permit the development of new products.

Threats The **external audit** should also show up what threats face the business. For example, falling numbers of customers in the 16-25 age group may threaten the sales of the business. The government may be about to increase the minimum wage, which would push up the wage bill and overall costs for the business. The business may be liable to come under attack from environmental pressure groups because of its poor record on environmental issues.

SWOT analysis is often carried out in brainstorming sessions before being written up. It can be a powerful way of summarising and building upon the results of internal and external audits.

Developing strategies

The next stage is to develop strategies. The business has identified its objectives. It has carried out an audit and analysed its internal strengths and weaknesses, as well as the opportunities and threats posed by the external environment. So it can now plan how to use its strengths and overcome its weaknesses and seize the opportunities presented, whilst countering threats, to achieve its objectives.

Planning can take place at a variety of levels. There could be a 3-5 year plan for a business, prepared by senior management and designed to meet its corporate objectives. This will have far less detail in it than a departmental plan for the next 12 months by the production department designed to meet short term tactical objectives.

Implementing plans

Plans need to be implemented on a day to day basis. The plan should inform workers about the actions they take and the decisions they make. For example, if the plan is to take a product up market, then managers should work on improving quality and making sure that the supply channels for the product reflect this. If the plan is to increase profit margins by cutting costs, then a cost reduction plan should be implemented.

Reviewing and evaluating outcomes

Having implemented a strategy, it is important for it to be reviewed. Did it achieve the objectives set? If not, what was achieved? What lessons can be learnt from the failures encountered?

There are many reasons why a strategy may fail.

Unrealistic objectives The objectives may have been unrealistic. There is often a tendency for managers to set objectives which are too ambitious. When set, they impress shareholders or more senior managers. But they prove to be unattainable.

Conflicting objectives The objectives may have been poorly thought out and may conflict. This can often be a problem when different layers of an organisation set objectives. The objectives of the marketing department, for example, may conflict with those of the production department. The overall aim of the business might be to increase profit. The marketing department sets itself the objective of moving its product range upmarket, selling fewer goods but at a high price and profit margin. The production department, on the other hand, sets itself the objective of increasing production to exploit economies of scale, reducing cost per unit and so increasing the potential for profit.

Poor planning Plans to achieve objectives may be badly thought out. For example, the production department may plan to increase production by 20 per cent but fail to build sufficient spending on new equipment into its plan to achieve this.

Poor execution of the plan Even if objectives and plans have been carefully and realistically thought through, workers may not implement them. It could be that the workers lack the skills and training to do so. It could also be that workers are not motivated to implement the plan. Many workers see planning and objective setting as a distraction from the 'real work' of making a sale or getting an order out to a customer. So they do what they think is best, rather than following the plan. The plan may also conflict with the interests of individual workers. For example, a plan may call for a 10 per cent reduction in staff in the production department. But the production manager in charge may resist the job losses to defend his or her staff. Or the production manager may think that making workers redundant will be far more time consuming and less pleasant than getting senior management to change their decision.

Corporate culture Many businesses find it difficult to make planned changes because of the BUSINESS (or CORPORATE) CULTURE they face. This is a set of ways of doing things and unwritten rules which dominate how the business is run in practice. If the new plan conflicts with the culture of the business, frequently the plan fails. This is one reason why many large businesses stress the importance of a **change culture** in their organisation. Unless staff are prepared to change, there is often little chance of planning being effective because plans often call for change.

Uncontrollable variables Even if a strategy is well executed within a business, events outside the control of the business can knock the strategy off course. For example, the economy may go into **recession** (see unit 50). This can have a severe effect on sales and profitability. New technology may make existing products obsolete far quicker than expected. Or severe weather conditions may affect production or demand in unexpected ways.

Reviewing the strategy

Strategies need to be reviewed on a regular basis at all levels within a business. For example, the long term corporate strategy might be reviewed every 3-5 years. In the meantime, if it becomes obvious that the strategy is failing, or is not ambitious enough, a new strategy must be worked out. Departments within a business are likely to have yearly plans. They must be reworked every twelve months.

The new strategies will be based on existing or new

✓ checklist

1 What is meant by 'strategy'?
2 Explain the difference between corporate strategy, business unit strategy and functional strategy.
3 How can strategy be linked to individual employee targets?
4 Explain the difference between strategic objectives, tactical objectives and operational objectives.
5 What is strategic planning?
6 Explain the difference between an external audit and an internal audit.
7 What is PEST-G analysis?
8 Explain the role of external and internal audits in SWOT analysis.
9 Briefly outline the reasons why a strategy may fail.

key terms

Business or corporate culture - **the values, beliefs and norms that are shared by people and groups in an organisation.**
Business unit (or divisional) strategy - **strategy of a division or a subsidiary company owned by a parent company.**
Competitive environment - **the nature of the competition which a business faces in its market.**
Core capabilities (or competencies) - **the most important strengths of a business, which should be central to decision making when corporate strategy is devised.**
Corporate strategy - **the strategy of the business as a whole.**
External audit - **an audit of the external environment in which a business finds itself, such as the market within which it operates or government restrictions on its operations.**
Functional (or operation or departmental) strategy - **strategy of a department within a business.**
Global strategy - **strategy of a business relating to sales or production internationally.**
Internal audit - **an analysis of the business itself and how it operates.**

Long term objective - **an objective of a business over the next 3-5 years.**
Operational objectives - **very short term objectives.**
Pest-G analysis - **analysis of the political (P), economic (E), social (S), technological (T) and environmental (G for green) issues relevant to the business.**
Planning - **the process of deciding how a business will run and operate in the future in areas such as production, marketing and finance, deciding what resources will be needed and how they will be used.**
Short term (or tactical) objectives - **objectives of a business which are likely to be achieved within the next 12 months.**
Strategic objectives - **the main objectives of a business designed to achieve its aims.**
Strategy - **a set of plans drawn up to achieve the objectives of the business.**
SWOT analysis - **analysis of the internal strengths and weaknesses of a business and the opportunities and threats presented by its external environment.**
Tactical strategy - **short term strategy using tactics designed to achieve long term strategic objectives.**
Tactics - **short term, specific ways in which the short term objectives of the business can be achieved.**

objectives. They should reflect the past experience of the business at achieving its objectives. They should also take account of the changing external environment.

Small and large businesses

Most businesses do not have written down aims, objectives or strategies. People who run small businesses might not be able to tell you verbally what were their objectives or give a definition of strategic planning. It is mainly in larger businesses that at least some of these issues have been thought through. Even then, there is a large number of examples of large businesses failing to define their objectives, or implement strategies to achieve them.

Equally, simply because a small business may have little understanding of textbook definitions of objectives or strategy, it doesn't not mean that objectives and strategy don't exist. For example, the owner of a small business may be content to run the business making its current level of profit. So in fact one objective of the business might be to maintain current profitability. The strategy (the plan to achieve the objective) might be to continue running the business in the same way. For many businesses in markets where change only occurs slowly, this can be a highly successful, low cost and low risk strategy.

Glenmorangie plc is a leading provider of branded malt whiskies. Based in Scotland, it sells its brands throughout the world. Brands include Glenmorangie, Glen Moray, Ardberg, Martin's Deluxe and Bailie Nicol Jarvie. It owns two Scottish distilleries (sites where whisky is manufactured), Glenmorangie and Glen Moray. Bottling, warehousing and distribution takes place at the company's Broxburn facility.

Adapted from Glenmorangie plc, *Annual Report and Accounts*, 2000-01.

Glenmorangie plc aims to achieve consistent growth in profit and shareholder value over the long term through:
- developing and growing our premium malt brands;
- achieving best use and value from our assets, in particular from our stocks, distilleries and Broxburn facility, to support the growth of our brands;
- being a customer focused organisation supported by the best people, systems and processes;
- having a culture which enables skilled, enthusiastic and creative people to reach their full potential.

Adapted from Glenmorangie plc, *Annual Report and Accounts*, 2000-01.

We have continued to invest strongly in marketing behind our brands. It represented 23 per cent of total cased turnover.

We have just completed the first year of our sales and marketing partnership with the Brown-Forman Corporation. The Corporation has a global network of over 100 sales and marketing professionals who work with our local distributors. Both ourselves and the Brown-Forman Corporation have a passion for developing premium spirit brands. The new partnership has started very well. Our ability to sell into the world's markets has been significantly increased.

This year, we also announced a joint venture supply chain partnership with The Drambuie Liqueur Company Limited (DLC). Drambuie is an internationally known whisky based liqueur. Drambuie will now be bottled and warehoused at our Broxburn facility. This will enable both us and DLC to gain economies of scale in both warehousing and in bottling. The Broxburn facility will be used more intensively whilst costs of packaging including bottles should fall due to larger purchasing.

Adapted from Glenmorangie plc, *Annual Report and Accounts*, 2000-01.

1 Explain what is meant by the terms:
   (a) 'shareholder value'; (3 marks)
   (b) 'premium spirit brands'. (3 marks)
2 According to the data, Glenmorangie has four (strategic) objectives. Choose TWO of these and explain how they might help the company to achieve its aims. (6 marks)
3 Analyse how Glenmorangie plans to increase sales and reduce average costs in the future. (8 marks)
4 To what extent is increasing sales the most important part of Glenmorangie's strategy? (10 marks)

65 Marketing and change

Kinnevik

Knowledge In 1995, Kinnevik, a Swedish conglomerate, launched a free newspaper in Sweden called *Metro*. Since 1995, it has exported the *Metro* model to 25 cities around the world, publishing in 14 different languages and with 13 million readers daily.

Application Prior to the Swedish launch, Kinnevik *analysed the market* thoroughly. It decided that *sales* and *market share* of a new paid-for Swedish newspaper would be too low for it to be *profitable*. By giving away the newspaper to *customers*, however, it could significantly increase circulation and so be far more attractive to *advertisers*. Its business model has remained unchanged as it has expanded into other *national markets*. It can be argued that Kinnevik used an *asset-led marketing* approach to its development of its *Metro* newspapers.

Analysis Kinnevik's media division already had substantial experience in the media industry. So it had substantial strengths in this broad market. It then successfully spotted a gap in the Swedish newspaper market, a gap which in fact existed in many other national and local markets around the world. Using its existing strengths and responding to the needs of the market allowed its asset-led marketing strategy to be very successful.

Evaluation The extent to which Kinnevik can continue to roll out its *Metro* formula across the world depends very much on local business environments. In London, for example, another newspaper group, Associated Newspapers, pre-empted the Swedish company by successfully launching its own copy-cat free newspaper. In Buenos Aires in Argentina, *Metro* had to be closed down when the Argentinean economy went into meltdown and advertising revenue suddenly dried up. However, Kinnevik has had far more successes than failures over the past ten years and there are still many countries and cities where *Metro* could prove to be a success.

Adapted from *International Journal of Media Management*, 2002.

Metro PUBLICATIONS EXAMPLES

Country	Cities	Circulation 2001/2002
Sweden	Stockholm, Malmo, Gothenberg	384,000
Finland	Helsinki	105,000
Denmark	Copenhagen	140,000
Netherlands	National	308,000
Czech Republic	Prague	174,000
Hungary	Budapest/national	302,000
Italy	Rome, Milan	414,000
France	Paris, Marseilles, Lyon	500,000
USA	Boston	183,000

Analysing the market

Marketing is the process of identification, anticipation and satisfaction of the customer's needs profitably (see unit 1). To identify and anticipate customers' needs, businesses must analyse the markets in which they operate. In units 2 and 3, it was explained how this MARKET ANALYSIS might be done.

- The nature of the market itself must to be defined. For example, is it a primary, secondary or tertiary market? Is it a consumer or producer market? Is it a mass market or a niche market?
- The market size needs to be identified. Market size is important because a small business has to ask itself whether it can gain any sales in a large market. For a large business, is it worth marketing products into a very small market?
- What is the market share of existing businesses in the market?
- Is the market growing, is it static or is it in decline?
- How is a market segmented and what are the different segments in the market?

Market analysis should not only identify the various features of a market, but it should show how a market is changing. Some markets see little change over time whilst others see rapid change. For example, the colour television market in the UK was relatively static in the 1980s and 1990s. But in the first decade of the 21st century there is profound change as customers move to flat screen televisions in wide screen format, and from analogue to digital signals. What has happened is that the BUSINESS ENVIRONMENT in which television manufacturers operate has changed. Technology has developed to the point where large flat screen digital televisions are cheap enough to manufacture at prices where large numbers of customers are prepared to buy. Television manufacturers need to respond to changes, bringing out new products at the right price at the right time. Companies which overinvest, or charge too high prices and are left with unsold stock, could face substantial losses. Companies which fail to innovate sufficiently fast could see a substantial loss of market share and falling profitability.

Product vs market orientation

A business may be **product orientated** or **market orientated** (see unit 1). A product orientated business is one which focuses on developing and making products which it then sells to customers. A market orientated business, in contrast, is one which focuses on customer needs and then makes products which it thinks will satisfy those needs.

Which approach is more appropriate depends on the industry in which a business finds itself. If it is a farmer growing wheat or a supplier in the motor manufacturing industry, a product orientated approach may help to maximise profits. A product orientated strategy is most likely to work best in industries where products are standardised, as in commodity markets, or where a business has monopoly control of its market. If it is a business in a fast moving market dominated by the latest fashion, a market orientated approach could be the most profitable.

'Product orientated' and 'market orientated' are standard terms in Business Studies. Some have suggested that there might be a third approach, **asset-led marketing**. Asset-led marketing is a combination of a market orientated approach with an understanding of the strengths and weaknesses (the 'assets') of the business. So a steel company might see that there is a gap in the market for large sized talking teddy bears. But it has no experience of producing and marketing teddy bears. So it would be inappropriate for it to enter this market. On the other hand, it might see that there is a gap in the market for a speciality steel which can withstand very high temperatures. Here, the market-led approach is combined with the strengths of the business (its 'assets') in manufacturing and selling steel.

A fuller discussion of these issues is contained in unit 1.

checklist

1 Briefly outline what is meant by 'market analysis'.
2 Explain why the business environment would be important to a chain of pubs which specialises in offering meals to young families and children.
3 Why might a gold mining company be product orientated whilst a garment manufacturer be market orientated?
4 What are the advantages of an asset-led approach to marketing?

keyterms

Business environment - the background factors in which a business operates such as the state of the economy, the given technology, the size of the population, the legal system, the moral, religious and cultural values of society, and the competition in the market.
Market analysis - the study of a market or markets broken down by key features such as size, growth, segmentation and market share of firms within the market.

Duo is a successful US furniture and homeware retailer. It has carved out a niche for itself in the US market by specialising in affordable but good quality ultra-modern furniture and homewares sold from its own retail outlets situated in low cost locations. Duo has built a reputation for being customer friendly and for delivering bulky furniture items on time.

It wants to expand into Europe and is considering first establishing itself in the UK. Market analysis has shown that the UK market is highly fragmented and barriers to entry are relatively low. However, the same market analysis has revealed that a number of existing UK retailers have plans to expand their share of the market. Ikea, for example, the Swedish flatpack furniture retailer, is hoping to double the number of its UK stores. Argos, the high street discount retailer, is expanding its range of furniture. MFI, the market leader, is trying out new store formats to sell more contemporary designs to compete head on with Ikea.

UK grocery retailers, such as Sainsbury's and Tesco, also have plans to expand into the homeware segment of the market. They are attracted by the higher profit margins that can be earned on sales of non-food items. For the customer, the attraction is that they don't have to make a special trip to a homewares specialist retailer to pick up a vase or some new mugs. They can buy them when they do their weekly shop for the groceries. Tesco in particular has gained a formidable reputation for being able to move into a particular retailing category and quickly gain both significant sales and profits.

Duo's strategy faces further problems. Other foreign retailers are also considering moving into the UK market. Ilva, a Danish homeware retailer, is planning to open stores in the UK and Ka, a Spanish furniture and fabric specialist, is hoping to expand its existing foothold in the British market.

On the other hand, the UK market is expanding. Spending on household goods has risen in line with average earnings in recent years. About 9 per cent of all UK household spending is on household goods. With real incomes rising at between 2-3 per cent each year, real expenditure on household goods is rising between 2-3 per cent per annum too.

Source: adapted from The Sunday Times, 26.10.2003.

Company	1997 %	1998 %	1999 %	2000 %	2001 %	2002 %
MFI	8.8	7.7	6.5	7.0	7.5	7.9
Argos Retail Group	-	4.6	4.5	4.7	5.1	5.6
- GUS	1.9	1.9	1.6	1.4	1.3	1.2
- Argos	2.4	2.7	2.9	3.3	3.8	4.4
DFS	3.4	3.5	3.8	4.2	4.5	4.8
Ikea	2.6	3.3	3.8	4.3	4.5	4.6
Homestyle	0.2	0.3	0.4	2.8	3.2	3.3
Harveys	2.1	2.3	2.4	-	-	-
John Lewis	2.2	2.1	2.2	2.3	2.3	2.3
Courts	2.1	2.2	2.4	2.4	2.3	2.1
B&Q	0.9	1.0	1.2	1.4	1.7	1.9
Magnet	1.4	1.5	1.5	1.4	1.3	1.4
Focus Wickes	-	-	-	-	1.2	1.4
Littlewoods	1.7	1.8	1.8	1.6	1.4	1.3
HomeForm	1.2	1.2	1.2	1.2	1.3	1.3
Furniture Village	0.6	0.8	0.9	1.0	1.1	1.2
Homebase	0.6	0.7	0.8	0.9	1.0	1.2
M&S	1.0	1.0	1.0	1.1	1.1	1.1
Allders	1.0	1.1	1.0	1.0	1.0	1.0
ScS	0.3	0.4	0.4	0.6	0.8	1.0
Sub total	**34.4**	**35.5**	**35.8**	**37.9**	**41.3**	**43.4**
others	65.6	64.5	64.2	62.1	58.7	56.6
Total	**100**	**100**	**100**	**100**	**100**	**100**

Table 65.1 *Furniture retailers' market share, 1997-2002*

Source: adapted from Verdict Analysis.

1 Discuss whether Duo has been production led, marketing led or asset-led in its plans to expand into the UK market. (10 marks)
2 To what extent do you think Duo will be able to establish itself successfully in the UK market? (10 marks)

66 Extrapolation and correlation

Sleek

Knowledge

Sleek is a UK chain of clothes shops. During the 1980s and 1990s it grew rapidly, selling to the 'baby boomer' generation of 20-40 'somethings'. Then in the late 1990s, it began to lose its way. Sales fell for the first time in 20 years. A new chief executive, Rod Hickman, was appointed to turn the company around.

Application

Rod Hickman had a background in grocery manufacture and retailing. He believed strongly in *systems* and *market analysis*. When he came to Sleek, he found a company which had poor control of *inventory* and *costs*. With falling *sales* and frequent *price mark-downs* on goods, *profit margins* were in free fall. He looked at the *trends* and *extrapolated* that sales could halve in five years if the experience of the previous three years was repeated. He also asked mathematical experts to carry out *correlation analysis* on the level of sales and factors,

Analysis

such as advertising, average incomes in the area around each shop, age and price of goods.

Having analysed the data, Rod concluded that Sleek needed to change in two ways. First, costs needed to be brought under control. He introduced sophisticated new software systems which extrapolated what stock was needed in what store at what time. As a result, stock turnover increased substantially and he halved the amount of stock that had to be sold at discount prices. Second, Sleek needed to return to its core market of relatively affluent 20-40 year olds. Market analysis had shown that too much of the merchandise in the late 1990s was either considered to be 'old fashioned' by this age group or 'too hip and trendy'. 40-60 year olds had been attracted into the store by this 'old fashioned' merchandise but they spent considerably below average. As for the 'hip and trendy' merchandise, under 20s rarely visited stores, seeing the chain as selling to 'older' consumers. Correlation analysis also

Evaluation

showed a positive correlation between sales and average incomes in its area. As a consequence, Rod closed down 34 unprofitable stores in less affluent areas.

Rod Hickman needed to make changes to reverse the decline in sales at Sleek. Too many successful businesses suffer sudden declines because they fail to pay attention to the basics of running a business. Markets change over time and businesses must keep up with these trends. What was a successful marketing formula before can become a recipe for losses and poor performance overnight. By bringing costs under control and concentrating on Sleek's core market, Rod was able to turn the company around. With lower costs and increasing sales, profits in the early 2000s began to rise again. Growth did not return to the heady levels of the 1980s and early 1990s, but Sleek was now a more mature business. Rod Hickman succeeded in stabilising the company and setting it in on a steadier growth path.

Extrapolation from trends

Total spending in the UK has been rising over the past 50 years. This is a TREND. The trend rate of growth of real spending (spending after inflation has been taken into account) is approximately 2¼ per cent. But the rate of spending on individual items is not changing at the same rate over time. Spending on foreign holidays, for example, has been rising at a much faster rate than the average growth in spending. Spending on jam in real terms has been falling.

Businesses need to have an understanding of trends to make decisions. A food manufacturer, for example, may know that sales of frozen ready meals have been growing at an average of 8 per cent per year over the past five years. On the other hand, sales of jam may have been declining at 1 per cent per year. These trends are likely to affect decisions about investment in new facilities or machines, how to allocate the marketing budget, or in what areas to recruit new workers.

What will happen in the future can be forecast by looking at past trends. This technique is known as EXTRAPOLATION. For example, if sales have been growing on average at 5 per cent per annum over the past 10 years, then a business might forecast that sales next year are likely to grow by 5 per cent as well.

Forecasting

How might a business predict future values of a variable such as sales? Consider Table 66.1. This shows sales volumes for a company manufacturing sofas over time. Unit 6 explained that a business can calculate a trend using a technique known as a four quarter centred moving average. The trend smooths out fluctuations in actual figures, making it easier to

Year	Quarter	Sales	4 period moving average	Centred 4 period moving average	Seasonal variation
2002	1	600			
	2	100			
			450		
	3	300		400	-100
			350		
	4	800		400	+400
			450		
2003	1	200		500	-300
			550		
	2	500		600	-100
			650		
	3	700		650	+50
			650		
	4	1200		650	+550
			650		
2004	1	200		700	-500
			750		
	2	500		800	-300
			850		
	3	1100			
	4	1600			

Table 66.1 *Sales, 2002-04, sales quantities*

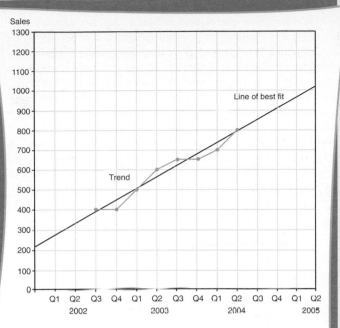

Figure 66.1 *Trend line and line of best fit showing sales forecasts for 2005*

observe the pattern which is taking place. In Table 66.1 the trend in sales has been calculated over three years. It shows that there has been a trend for a rise in sales over the period. The trend is also shown on Figure 66.1 which is a graph drawn from the information.

A business can use the trend line to predict future sales. It is possible to draw a LINE OF BEST FIT through the trend line, as in Figure 66.1. This is a straight line that fits the figures in the trend 'best'. It is possible to draw a line of best fit in two ways.
* The line can be drawn by eye. This means drawing a straight line through the points which appears to represent the general trend that is taking place.
* The line can be drawn using a mathematical technique known as the sum of least squares.

Once the line of best fit has been drawn, it can be extended to forecast sales in a future period. So, for example, in Figure 66.1 the line has been extended so that the extrapolated figure for sales in the first quarter of 2005 is 958 and for the second quarter it is predicted to be 1015. These predictions take into account the trend for rising sales in the past. Whether these predictions are totally accurate will depend on a number of factors, discussed in the next section.

Problems with using trend forecasts

Using trend forecasts can be problematical for a number of reasons.

The future is not necessarily the same as the past Simply because there has been a clear trend in the past does not mean to say that the trend will continue in the future. For example, international airline companies have suffered large drops in demand over the past twenty years whenever there has been a terrorist incident involving airlines. US travellers are particularly sensitive to perceived terrorist activity. New technology can suddenly make an old technology redundant.

So manufacturers of the old technology can face a sudden fall in demand. When CDs took off in the 1980s, there was a sharp fall in demand for cassette tapes. So sudden random shocks can play havoc with a business forecast.

Cyclical variations Capitalist economies tend to experience **business cycles** (see unit 50). These are fairly regular ups and downs in the level of business activity in the whole economy. In a boom, sales tend to be high. In a recession, with increased unemployment, sales can become stagnant or fall. Businesses must take account of where the economy is in the business cycle when forecasting. If the economy this year is at the bottom of the business cycle, sales next year might be higher as the economy recovers. Even if a business takes into account the current position of the economy in the business cycle, its forecasting can still be inaccurate. No two business cycles are the same. The economy might come out of a recession faster or slower than the average in the past. Cyclical variations are subject to randomness, which makes forecasting more difficult.

Seasonal variations Businesses must also take account of seasonal variations when forecasting. For example, ice cream manufacturers sell more in the summer than in the winter. Clothes retailers tend to sell more in the run up to Christmas than at other times of the year. As with the trade cycle, businesses need to know about past seasonal fluctuations to extrapolate future trends. Even then, seasonal variations can be subject to randomness. A spell of very hot weather in August will send ice cream sales soaring. On the other hand, there will be a sharp reduction in the number of customers visiting clothes shops as shopping becomes a less desirable activity than sunbathing or going to the pub.

The prediction from Figure 66.1 can be used to show the effect of seasonal variations. It was predicted from the trend that sales in the second quarter of 2005 would be 1015. However, the trend is a smoothed out version of actual figures, which have seasonal variations depending on which quarter is considered. Table 66.1 shows the seasonal variations in actual sales figures from the trend. The average seasonal variation in the two second quarters shown in 2003 and 2004 is:

$$\frac{(-100) \text{ and } (-300)}{2} = -200$$

So a more accurate prediction for the second quarter might be 815. This is the predicted figure of 1015 but taking into account the average second quarter variation of -200.

Extrapolation of future trends from past trends can therefore be a complex process by the time that cyclical and seasonal trends are taken into account. Even then, random occurrences or sudden changes in the market can make actual outcomes different from forecasts.

Correlation

A CORRELATION exists between two or more variables when a change in one variable results in a change in the other variables. For example, sales of sofas are likely to be related to marketing expenditure by the sofa manufacturer, consumer confidence and levels of unemployment. The greater the level of marketing expenditure and the level of consumer confidence, and the lower the level of unemployment, the greater might be sales of sofas.

Wildmans is a manufacturer of dyes for the textile industry. Table 66.2 shows how its sales have changed between 2002 and 2004.

	£ million		
	2002	2003	2004
Q1	5.3	5.5	5.6
Q2	5.3	5.5	5.7
Q3	5.2	5.3	5.3
Q4	5.9	6.1	6.3

Table 66.2 *Wildmans' sales, 2002–2004*

1 **Draw up a table with the time quarters and the sales figures from Table 66.2. Calculate a three quarter moving average for sales from the figures.**
2 **Draw up another table with the time quarters and the sales figures from Table 66.2. Calculate (a) a four quarter moving average and (b) a centred four quarter moving average.**
3 **Draw the axes for a graph. On the horizontal axis, put quarters 1–4 for the five years 2002–2005. On the vertical axis, start the axis at £5.0 million and extend it to £6.5 million. On the graph, plot (a) the sales figures as shown in Table 66.2 and (b) the centred four quarter moving average of sales figures you have calculated in 2(b).**
4 **(a) From the four quarter moving average, estimate a line of best fit, drawing this on your graph. (b) Extend the line of best fit to the fourth quarter of 2005. What is your estimate of the value of sales in that quarter from the line of best fit?**
5 **Analyse what factors might cause the actual level of fourth quarter 2005 sales to be above or below your estimate.**

Figures 66.2-4 show a SCATTER GRAPH or DIAGRAM where each item of data is shown by a point or a cross. The whole series of data, when plotted, tends to be scattered across the graph. Each point on Figure 66.2 shows the quarterly spending on marketing by the company and its sales in that quarter for the past three years. Sixteen points (4 years x 4 quarters in each year) are therefore shown.

Positive correlation In Figure 66.2 there is a **positive correlation** between sales of sofas and marketing expenditure. As more is spent on marketing, more sofas are bought. However, the correlation in Figure 66.2 is not particularly **strong** because the points are not close to the line of best fit. Mathematically, the degree of correlation can be measured between -1 and +1. There is a positive correlation when it is between 0 and 1. The nearer the correlation is to the value of 1, the stronger the correlation between the two variables.

Negative correlation Figure 66.3 shows a situation where there is a **negative correlation** between the two variables. In this case, it is the level of unemployment in the economy and sales of sofas. When unemployment rises, those made unemployed have less income to spend and hence fewer sofas are bought. Rising unemployment also makes some of those in work fearful of losing their jobs too. They then tend to reduce their borrowing and sofas are often bought through loans. Here there is a strong negative correlation between unemployment and sales. The points on the scatter graph are close to the line of best fit. The stronger the negative correlation, the closer to the value of -1 is the correlation.

No correlation If there is no correlation between two variables, the points on the scatter diagram will be randomly distributed. Figure 66.4 shows the relationship between sales of sofas and sales of baked beans. There is very little or no correlation between the two.

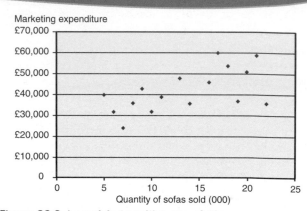

Figure 66.2 *A weak but positive correlation*

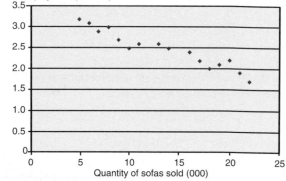

Figure 66.3 *A strong negative correlation*

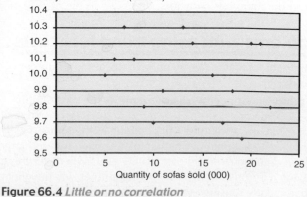

Figure 66.4 *Little or no correlation*

The significance of correlation

Correlation is important for a business. It needs to know what impact, if any, a change in one variable will have on another variable. For example, a rise in interest rates in the economy is likely to lead to a fall in the sale of sofas because borrowing will become more expensive. On the other hand, a rise in interest rates is likely to have no impact on the sale of baked beans. In general, interest rate changes are important for furniture manufacturers but not for food manufacturers.

When targeting particular markets, businesses need to estimate the correlation between marketing expenditure and sales. In the market for soap powders, it has been suggested that the two largest manufacturers in the world, Unilever and Procter & Gamble, can spend up to one quarter of the price of a packet of soap powder on marketing. They believe there is a strong correlation between expenditure on marketing and sales. On the other hand, a local painter and decorator may spend nothing on marketing. Experience may have shown that advertising in, say, the local newspaper doesn't bring in extra work.

Simply because two variables are correlated does not mean that a change in one variable **causes** the other to change. If a manufacturer significantly increases its advertising spending this quarter and sales rise at the same time, then common sense would suggest that the rise in sales is likely to be due to the rise in advertising. But what if, at the same time, interest rates had significantly fallen? It then becomes difficult to know whether the rise in sales was due to the rise in advertising spending or the fall in interest rates or some combination of the two. It could be that the advertising campaign was actually a failure and had no effect on sales. The rise in sales may have been due entirely to the reduced cost of borrowing. So although there was a positive correlation between advertising and sales, in fact increased advertising did not cause the rise in sales.

There are also examples of **nonsense correlations**. Studies have shown that there may be a high correlation coefficient between two variables, but in practice little chance of any real relationship. For example, it has been shown that a strong negative correlation of -0.98 exists between the birth rate in the UK and the production of pig iron in the USA between 1875 and 1920.

It is therefore important for businesses to understand what other variables may have changed at the same time. In a fast moving economy, there may be many changes which have an impact on a variable such as sales.

		Sales £million	Marketing expenditure £million	Average price per unit sold (pence)
2002	Q1	5.3	0.10	80.2
	Q2	5.3	0.10	80.0
	Q3	5.2	0.10	79.3
	Q4	5.9	0.30	77.5
2003	Q1	5.5	0.13	79.1
	Q2	5.5	0.14	78.3
	Q3	5.3	0.15	78.6
	Q4	6.1	0.40	77.1
2004	Q1	5.6	0.17	77.6
	Q2	5.7	0.18	77.2
	Q3	5.3	0.19	78.1
	Q4	6.3	0.50	77.0

Table 66.3 *Wildmans, sales, marketing expenditure and average price per unit sold, 2002-2004*

Table 66.3 shows the sales, marketing expenditure and average price per unit sold for Wildmans.

1 Draw a graph with marketing expenditure on the vertical axis (from 0 to £0.6 million) and sales on the horizontal axis (starting at £5.0 million and going to £6.5 million). Plot each quarter's sales against marketing expenditure to produce a scatter diagram.
2 Draw a second graph with price on the vertical axis (starting at 76p and going to 82p) and sales on the horizontal axis (starting at £5.0 million and going to £6.5 million). Plot each quarter's sales against price to produce a scatter diagram.
3 What sort of correlation is there between (a) sales and marketing expenditure and (b) sales and price?
4 Discuss whether the correlation shown in the data is of significance for Wildmans' marketing strategy.

✓*checklist*

1 Why might a business want to know the trends in sales for a product it makes?
2 'A business can extrapolate future trends by looking at past trends.' Explain what this means.
3 How might a line of best fit be drawn on a scatter diagram?
4 Explain briefly why trend forecasts may prove to be wrong.
5 What is the difference between a positive correlation and a negative correlation?
6 Why might two variables be correlated and yet one variable not be the cause of the other variable?

Propoil is a small oil production and exploration company. It operates globally, but 60 per cent of its production comes from oil fields in Latin America.

Production varies from quarter to quarter, as can be seen from Table 66.4. With existing oil fields, technical problems can force a well to cease production for a time. Equally, some of Propoil's wells are relatively old and the amount of oil that can be pumped out of these wells declines over time. New wells, however, are also coming onstream.

Oil exploration is much riskier than oil production. There is no guarantee that any exploratory well drilled will yield oil. Over the past couple of years, oil businesses had increasing difficulty in finding new sources of oil. Some argue that all the large oil fields around the world have now been discovered. New fields will be smaller and more expensive to develop per barrel of oil recovered. The directors at Propoil have recently discussed whether to stop exploration altogether. If exploration were stopped, the company would in the short term be more profitable. An alternative approach would be effectively to outsource exploration by buying up oil fields that other companies had discovered. Figure 66.5 shows the amount of money spent by Propoil on exploring for new fields and the number of commercially viable fields that it has found as a result. Most of the exploratory wells sunk by Propoil prove to be uncommercial.

1 (a) Calculate a four quarter moving average for Propoil's oil production shown in Table 66.4. (6 marks)
  (b) Plot this four quarter moving average on a graph. (2 marks)
  (c) Using your graph, estimate production in the first quarter of 2006 and the first quarter of 2007. (2 marks)
  (d) Discuss whether your estimates are likely to prove accurate for production in the first quarters of 2006 and 2007. (10 marks)
2 (a) To what extent is there a correlation shown in Figure 66.5 between the amount of money spent by Propoil on exploration and the number of commercially viable wells found? (6 marks)
  (b) Discuss whether the company should continue exploring for oil. (14 marks)

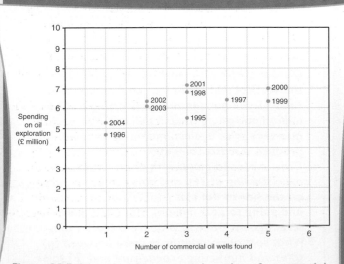

Figure 66.5 *Oil exploration costs and number of commercial oil wells found*

		Oil production, millions of barrels	Brent crude oil, $ per barrel, start of each quarter
2001	Q1	18.3	23.18
	Q2	18.5	23.85
	Q3	18.6	25.96
	Q4	18.8	21.08
2001	Q1	19.4	19.90
	Q2	19.1	26.87
	Q3	19.3	25.53
	Q4	19.7	29.35
2003	Q1	19.4	30.64
	Q2	19.8	27.21
	Q3	19.9	27.93
	Q4	19.5	28.23
2004	Q1	20.3	30.15
	Q2	20.4	32.19
	Q3	20.1	33.64
	Q4	20.8	47.29

Table 66.4 *Propoil: oil production and crude oil prices*

67 Marketing decision making

Mold Hotels

Knowledge Ros Mold owns a chain of small hotels. She got into the industry by chance. On holiday one year in Devon, she stayed in a hotel which was up for sale. She fell in love with the local area and could see the potential in the hotel.

Application The decision to buy the hotel was more of a *hunch* than a *scientific decision*. She worked out a few numbers and checked the *accounts* of the hotel. But she had little idea of how she would develop the hotel. There was no *business plan* or *marketing plan* for example.

Analysis Once she had bought the hotel, the enormity of her decision hit her. It was at this stage that she sat down seriously and drew up a business plan. Included in the business plan was a marketing plan. She used the marketing model to help her identify her objectives, carry out a marketing audit, define marketing objectives and develop a marketing strategy. Fortunately, her initial hunch proved correct. The hotel thrived. Hotel occupancy rates increased, partly through a series of carefully targeted advertising campaigns. The percentage of repeat custom rose from 30 per cent to 45 per cent, helped by regular mailings to previous customers. Since the late 1990s, Ros has also made extensive use of the Internet to reach potential customers.

Evaluation It could be argued that Ros Mold was lucky. Her business instinct proved correct. All too frequently, however, hunches and guesswork in business can end in disaster. That is why larger businesses tend to use more scientific approaches to decision making, such as the use of the marketing model. Ros Mold was right to use the marketing model to put her marketing on the right path once she had bought the business. If she had not developed a clear marketing strategy, occupancy rates and revenues could have been severely affected. Marketing was, of course, not the only issue which Ros faced. She had to get the product right, sort out the staffing and make a profit. But using scientific decision making models was a considerable help in making the right decisions.

Scientific decision making

There are many ways in which marketing decisions are made. In a large company, significant marketing decisions may be made through a formal process. The company may have guidelines and policies about how such decisions should be made. This could be described as a 'scientific' approach to decision making. One such scientific approach was described in unit 9. This approach is sometimes referred to as the MARKETING MODEL. As can be seen from Figure 67.1, it takes a decision maker through different stages, from clarifying business objectives to carrying out a marketing audit to defining marketing objectives, developing marketing strategies and implementing marketing plans.

It could be argued that taking marketing decisions in this way has certain advantages for a business.

- There is a series of steps which must be taken to arrive at a decision. There is therefore both a structure and a process to decision making.
- The marketing model makes use of data. Using data which has been scientifically collected should help bring impartiality to the decision making process.
- It can be used by many people in many circumstances. It therefore provides a common point of reference in decision making.
- It gives consistency to decisions. So, for example, two different decisions can be compared and evaluated.

In practice, scientific decision making may not be carried out in the way described. For a start, progress through the different stages is unlikely to be linear. When defining marketing objectives, for example, managers may want more information than they have from the marketing audit which has taken place. So more research might be conducted in a particular marketing area. Or a particular aspect of the marketing plan may prove impossible to implement. So decision makers may have to go back to their marketing strategy and change part of it.

A 'scientific' model also implies that decision makers are impartial. In practice, their prejudices may play an important role in a particular decision. For example, when conducting a marketing audit, decision makers may put far more resources into researching one area than another simply because they feel that the first is more important.

Scientific models can only give a reliable answer if the data fed into the model is accurate. However, in the marketing model, some of the data may be unsound in one way or another. For example, the market research may include predictions about what will happen in the future in the market. Or actual data may not have been available and so estimated data were included.

A scientific model is unlikely to be the sole determinant of any decision. A marketing department, for example, may have explored whether it was best to enter the Chinese or South Korean market. But the finance department may then say that the company does not have the funds to make this investment. Or the marketing department may argue that there is an opportunity for entering the Indian market. But the board of directors may veto any expansion into India because they do not wish to diversify so far.

Hunches and guesswork

Scientific models are likely to be used only for major marketing decisions, and then only in medium or large sized companies. Smaller decisions and smaller businesses tend to make decisions through hunches and guesswork. This doesn't mean that decisions are made without any reference to data or evidence. Nor does it mean that the decision making is poor and frequently wrong. Hunches and guesswork tend to be based upon previous experience. A decision to reduce prices for the next week on a range of products with flagging sales might be based on a marketing tactic used with success before. A decision to accept a book for publication may be based on an editors liking for the book, and in the past the editor has found that what she likes tends to be what will sell well.

Competitive forces also tend to play a part. Small businesses run by entrepreneurs whose guesses and hunches tend to be wrong will tend to cease trading. Small businesses run by entrepreneurs who can successfully gauge the market will tend to survive and thrive. Equally, decision makers in marketing departments who fail to get it right most of the time will tend to resign, lose their jobs or be transferred elsewhere in the organisation. Decision makers who do make correct decisions will tend to be rewarded and promoted.

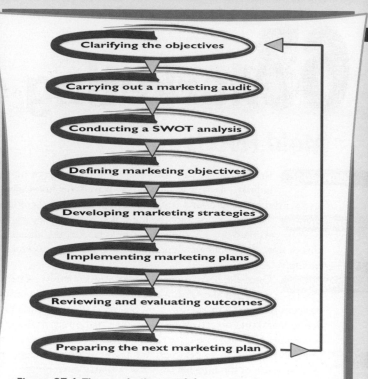

Figure 67.1 *The marketing model*

✓*checklist*

1 List the main stages in decision making in the marketing model.
2 Why should a business use the marketing model in decision making?
3 What are the drawbacks of using the marketing model?
4 Why might a business use hunches and guesswork rather than a more formal scientific decision making model to make decisions about marketing?

"**key**terms"

Marketing model – a scientific approach to the preparation of a marketing strategy, from clarifying business objectives to carrying out a marketing audit to defining marketing objectives, developing marketing strategies and implementing marketing plans.

Garland Banks trained as an estate agent in Birmingham in the boom times of the mid-1980s. By 1988, with house prices soaring and sales at record levels, he decided that he would set up his own estate agent business. He completed an external marketing audit, looking at factors such as local competition, different socio-economic areas within Birmingham and the macro-economic environment. Finance would be a problem. He had only £2 000 in savings. Admittedly he owned a house worth £50 000 which only had a £30 000 mortgage on it. But he calculated he needed £20 000 to start the business from rented premises. This would cover the first year's operations.

From the marketing audit and his cash flow calculations, he was able to develop his marketing objectives. He set himself the target of selling £3 million worth of property in his first year of operations. By the end of his first year, he also wanted to gain a 20 per cent market share of the Birmingham area in which he established his estate agents office. Finally he wanted to break-even over the first twelve months operating period, even though he recognised that during the first six months he would have to dig deep into his working capital.

Garland's marketing strategy was to set up in an area of Birmingham that was relatively poorly served by estate agents. His office would be on a busy local high street where there were no other estate agents. He would offer commission rates which were at the bottom end of those being charged by competing estate agents. He would offer better service by opening his office seven days a week and following up all leads with prospective purchasers.

At the end of the first twelve months, the business had done extremely well, surpassing the marketing objectives set. But then the housing market collapsed almost overnight. High interest rates had killed the market. From being profitable, Banks Estate Agents began to lose money heavily.

One day he received a call from someone wanting to rent out her property. Initially, he told her that he was not in the rental market. But within an hour of getting the phone call, he realised that there might be a gap in the market here. Anyway, any commission was better than none. So he rang her back and agreed to put her property up for rent. From that point on, he began to receive a steady flow of clients. He moved into managing rented properties as well as simply finding tenants for landlords. The introduction by the government of the short assured-tenancy agreement, which meant that landlords could rent out properties without tenants acquiring legal long term rights to rent the property, really opened the market. Today, 75 per cent of his earnings come from arranging lets and managing rented property.

1 Explain the marketing model that Garland Banks used to set up his business. (8 marks)
2 Discuss whether Garland Banks should have used the marketing model to make his decision to move into the property rental market. (12 marks)

68 Marketing plans

Zomgon

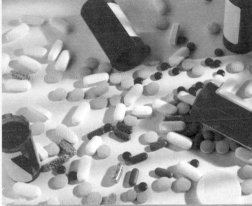

Knowledge In 2004, Lantex, a manufacturer of specialist medicines and drugs, launched a new anti-HIV drug called Zomgon. The company chose to pitch the price of the drug at the 'top end' of the scale. A year's treatment would cost £12 000 for Zomgon alone. Then there would be the cost of other drugs which would have to be used with it, which would push the cost of the whole course of treatment to between £20 000 and £30 000 per year. Some patient groups complained about the high price.

Application The decision to charge a high initial *price* for the drug was part of the *marketing strategy* of the company. Its *marketing plan* laid out a strategy of *price skimming*, charging a high price initially and then lowering the price as *competition* from other new drugs developed. Its *research and development (R&D) costs* for Zomgon had been £400 million. The drug is also highly expensive to *manufacture*, involving 120 separate steps. *Demand* for the drug was forecast to be highly *price inelastic*.

Analysis Lantex could have adopted a number of different pricing strategies. However, it may have chosen a price skimming strategy because it recognised that it was unlikely to secure large sales even if it adopted a relatively low price. A high price low sales strategy was therefore likely to maximise revenues and profits initially. In the marketing plan, estimates were given of how quickly the drug would pay back its initial £400 million investment. The marketing plan also indicated that if a new rival drug came onto the market, the pricing strategy might have to be altered to take account of the greater competition. The expected low sales predicted in the marketing plan was tied in with other plans such as the production plan for other areas of the business.

Evaluation It is unlikely that Lantex was going to achieve massive sales of Zomgon given its market. Adopting a price skimming strategy was probably the best way for Lantex to recoup its large investment in developing the drug. The initial high price did lead to some negative public relations for the company. However, it could be argued that for Lantex to survive in business in the long term, it needs to cover its investment costs and make a profit. Therefore a marketing plan which put it on course to do this was the only sound commercial way to proceed.

Developing and reviewing a marketing plan

In unit 9, it was explained that a marketing strategy is a set of marketing plans designed to fulfil the objectives of a business. The process of developing a marketing strategy was also outlined in unit 9 and summarised in unit 67.

A MARKETING PLAN is a set of proposed marketing actions to be undertaken over a period of time which, if carried out, should enable the business to achieve its marketing objectives. The marketing plan is likely to contain the following.

- There will be a set of dates, stating when the plan starts, when it finishes and points in between when actions might be taken. For example, a three year marketing plan might start on 1st January 2005 and end on 31st December 2007. Within that time period, the advertising budget might be increased by £300 000 for the calendar year starting 1st January 2006.
- A set of actions will be detailed, such as 'extend local advertising to the North West region' or 'ensure product is competitively priced'.
- Responsibilities will be allocated between departments, sections and individuals.
- A marketing budget (see unit 69) will be set which details how the the marketing department will spend its funds.
- Target outcomes will be set for periods within the marketing plan and for the end of the plan.

Much of the marketing plan will centre around the '4Ps' or marketing mix (see units 1 and 12-19). Price, product, promotion and place will be at the core of the actions detailed in the marketing plan.

In a large business, the marketing plan is likely to be developed in outline as part of the overall strategic or corporate plan (see units 64 and 115). A small group of senior marketing managers are likely to be responsible for drawing up the plan. Once this has been agreed, detailed plans will be made within the marketing department. Managers at all levels may be involved in drawing up these more detailed plans.

In a small business, the owner/manager may have drawn up a written marketing plan. This is usually necessary if the business approach a bank for extra loans or a larger overdraft facility (see unit 25). The marketing plan would be a part of the overall business plan (see unit 62). Often, though, the marketing plan is not written down. The entrepreneur has the plan in his or her head. Equally, the owner may have no marketing plan but simply react to events as they arise. Using 'hunches' for decision making (see unit 67) can be effective if the entrepreneur has a good intuitive understanding of the business environment.

Evaluating a marketing plan

A marketing plan should be evaluated at different stages.

At the start Whilst it is being written, managers need to consider whether:

- it meets the objectives set in the marketing strategy and fits in with the corporate strategy of the business;

- the actions described in the marketing plan and their outcomes are realistic;
- the marketing department will be given a sufficiently large budget to carry out its plan.

In operation Whilst the plan is operational, it should be monitored. A number of factors might lead to the plan failing.

- The external environment might become much harsher. For example, it may be difficult to increase sales in a recession.
- Other parts of the overall corporate plan might fail. For example, if the production department planned to increase output by 6 per cent a year, but only manages 2 per cent, then a planned 6 per cent increase in sales is unlikely to come about.
- There might be unforeseen cuts in the marketing budget.
- The original plan may have been too optimistic about the relation between changes to the marketing budget and changes in sales. For example, an expensive advertising campaign may not lead to the increase in sales hoped for. Equally, the marketing plan may have been too pessimistic. For example, the external environment may prove far more favourable than anticipated or an advertising campaign may work far more successfully than predicted.

When a marketing plan clearly is not on target whilst it is operational, managers should adjust the plan to take account of the new realities facing them. If they don't, they risk the plan becoming useless for operational purposes as the predictions of the plan become more and more out of line with what is actually happening.

At the end The marketing plan should also be evaluated at the end of the plan. This evaluation should help those drawing up the next plan to see what has been successful and what has gone wrong with the existing plan. They can then build in these insights into the new plan.

Targets within the marketing plan

Targets should be set within the marketing plan. These should be measurable and understood by those operating the plan. These targets can then form part of the evaluation of the marketing plan. A business could use a number of different criteria.

Sales Sales targets can be set in many forms. For example, sales targets might be set by **value** (i.e. total sales x average selling price, see unit 21) or by **volume** (i.e. the number of sales made). Sales targets could be given for different areas of a country or different countries or continents. A multinational company might have sales targets for North America, Europe, Asia and the rest of the world for example. Sales targets are also likely to be set by product. For example, one product might have a sales growth target of 10 per cent per annum, whilst another might have one of 2 per cent.

Market share Market share (see unit 2) can be an important target indicator of competitiveness. A business which aims to increase market share in its marketing plan is attempting to become more competitive relative to other businesses over time. A business which aims to limit loss of market share is likely to take into account that other businesses are going to become more competitive. As with sales targets, market share targets can be split down into market share by product and by region.

Marketing spending analysis One criticism of marketing spending is that it is impossible to work out whether it has had an effect on sales, sales revenues and profits. For example, a business might spend £1 million on an advertising campaign and sales values might rise by 2 per cent. It could be that the £1 million spending caused the 2 per cent sales rise. But if at the same time the overall economy had grown by 3 per cent, it could be that the rise in sales was simply due

According to the 2001 census, ethnic minorities make up 9 per cent of England's population. Consumers with an ethnic minority background are typically younger and more likely to own a business than other people. They also tend to live in large urban centres, such as London or the West Midlands conurbation, creating opportunities for cost-effective local marketing. Yet British businesses are only beginning to think seriously about the needs of ethnic minority consumers.

One business area which is taking its ethnic minority customers seriously is financial institutions such as banks and building societies. Banks and building societies with branches in the West Midlands conurbation serve large numbers of customers from ethnic minority backgrounds. Some have developed policies of providing help to such customers. For example, some produce leaflets about saving and mortgage products in a number of different languages including Punjabi. Some also employ people from ethnic minorities who are able to talk to customers in their own language. This means, for example, that a Punjabi speaker can arrange a mortgage by talking to a customer adviser who will conduct the interview in Punjabi.

The financial institutions involved have benefited from this approach. Many ethnic groups have a close-knit character that makes word of mouth a powerful force to be reckoned with. Alexandria Hough, a customer services adviser at the Smethwick branch of the West Bromwich Building Society, says 'recommendation is hugely important. A lot of mortgages we sell to Sikh customers come about through parents telling their children about us.'

Source: adapted from the *Financial Times*, 28.3.2003.

1 **The decision to market to ethnic minorities will have been contained in a marketing plan of a building society. Explain three possible features that might be contained in this marketing plan.**
2 **Suggest how a building society in the West Midlands could evaluate the part of its marketing plan relating to ethnic minorities.**

to greater customer spending power. Or the 2 per cent rise in sales values could have been caused by new products entering the product range.

It is possible to produce clear data in some areas. For example, a bank which sends out half a million direct mail (see unit 18) letters offering loans can measure the proportion of customers which respond. In turn, the proportion finally given a loan can be calculated. So the cost per loan given or the cost per £1 loaned of the direct mailing can be calculated.

Equally, a business which is advertising on the Internet can measure the number of 'clicks' on an advert which take a potential customer from the advert to a website. Or the number of 'hits' on a website can be measured and the proportion which lead to a sale on the Internet can be calculated.

But the number of areas where there is such a clear link between marketing spending and sales is limited. Some businesses attempt to get around this problem by using sophisticated mathematical techniques which use correlation techniques (see unit 66) to strip out the effect of changes in other variables. Targets for the effect on sales and profits of marketing spending can then be set. However, most businesses would not set such targets in their marketing plan because of the difficulty of getting accurate and reliable data.

Co-ordinating the marketing plan with the other business functions

Marketing plans should not be written in isolation from the plans of other departments. In a large business, co-ordination is essential if plans are not to conflict with each other. For example, the marketing department might plan to set up an Internet site and require extra staff to run and develop the operation over the next three years. But the human resources department could be planning to reduce overall staff numbers in the business to achieve greater efficiency. These two plans may conflict. Therefore it is important that both departments agree on a plan which has the same effects.

Co-ordination in a large business is often difficult to achieve. Different departments have different and often conflicting agendas. It may need strong and charismatic leadership from the top of the organisation to get a whole business moving in the same direction. Planning can help achieve this unity of direction, but it is unlikely to be a business solution for problems of poor co-ordination.

The advantages and disadvantages of marketing planning

There are both advantages and disadvantages to marketing planning. The main advantages are the following.
- The process of drawing up a marketing plan forces a business to think about how it will act in the future. It can therefore be proactive in its marketing and not just reactive. The larger the business, the more likely it is that successful marketing will only come about through careful planning.
- Because a wide range of employees should be involved in drawing up the marketing plan in a large company, there is

more chance that workers will be committed to ensuring the goals of the company are achieved. It is a way of motivating and informing staff.
- A thorough planning process will mean that the marketing plan is coordinated with other plans in the business. Therefore all departments will be pulling in the same direction.
- Marketing plans are drawn up in the light of the objectives of a business. There is therefore more chance that these objectives will be achieved than if there were no plans.

However, marketing plans have disadvantages.
- Scarce resources, for examples in terms of management and employee time, are used up in creating a marketing plan. Those resources could have been used elsewhere. There is therefore an **opportunity cost** (see unit 21) in drawing up a marketing plan.
- Too many marketing plans are poorly drawn up. They may fail to take account of the objectives of the business. They may be created by a few individuals who see it as a 'paper-pushing' exercise. The marketing plan may be filed away and never used. Those creating the plan may include actions which the business could never do, or it may be far too cautious in its approach. The marketing plan may not be coordinated with other plans in the business.

✓ *checklist*

1 Briefly explain the difference between a marketing strategy, marketing objectives and a marketing plan.
2 In a large company, who might be involved in writing a marketing plan?
3 In a small business, explain why a marketing plan may exist but not be written down on paper.
4 How might a marketing plan be evaluated?
5 What targets might be set within a marketing plan?
6 Why is it important for a marketing plan to be coordinated with other plans in a business?

keyterms

Marketing plan - a set of proposed marketing actions to be undertaken over a period of time which, if carried out, should enable the business to achieve its marketing objectives.

In March 2004, Coca-Cola suffered a marketing setback. It was supposed to launch Dasani, a brand of bottled water, into the UK market. Dasani is the second biggest selling brand of bottled water in the USA. Coca-Cola had ambitious targets for its bottled water sales. Over the previous three years, the company's worldwide water sales had met its targets by growing by over 50 per cent. But in Europe, with Malvern Water in the UK and Bon Aqua in Germany, its existing market share was just 2 per cent. Its future targets could only be met by a launch of a new product into the UK market and using this as a springboard for a launch in Continental Europe.

The launch was to have been accompanied by a £10 million advertising campaign. At the heart of the campaign was supposed to have been a £1 million television advertisement showing Dasani running through a city's streets. A factory in Sidcup, Kent, had been fitted out to produce the water for the UK market.

But its marketing plan hit trouble almost immediately. First, Coca-Cola was forced to admit that it was selling water which came from the mains supply in Sidcup. In Europe, bottled water has always been associated with a natural source. Volvic, for example, comes from the volcanic highlands of the Auvergne in France. San Pellegrino comes from the mountains north of Milan. In Europe, bottled water was called 'mineral water' because each natural source had a different mix of minerals in it. In the USA, in contrast, the leading bottled waters are 'purified waters'. The source of the water is not important. It is the industrial process of creating a purified water which is the unique selling point of the water. Coca-Cola, in its aborted advertising campaign, made much of the 'reverse osmosis' technology used to purify the water at its Sidcup factory. The problem was that the British press ridiculed Coca-Cola for thinking that it could sell water to the English at £1 a bottle when the water it contained could be got free from a tap. The negative PR was so great that it probably would have outweighed the effect of the whole £10 million advertising campaign.

But a second problem came just two weeks later. Tests found that the new 'purified' Dasani water had excessive levels of bromate, a chemical that can increase the risk of cancer. Coca-Cola immediately withdrew all supplies from the market. The two PR disasters coming one after another meant that Coca-Cola decided to abort the launch of Dasani in the UK.

Source: adapted from the *Sunday Times*, 28.3.2004.

1 (a) Examine the reasons why Coca-Cola wanted to launch Dasani in the UK. (8 marks)
 (b) Discuss the likely features of Coca-Cola's marketing plan for Dasani. (12 marks)
2 Consider whether Coca-Cola, as part of its strategy to sell more bottled water in European markets, should relaunch Dasani in the UK in the future. (20 marks)

69 Marketing budgets

Lamaro's

Knowledge   Lamaro's is a small chain of takeaway pizza outlets in the North East of England. First set up eight years ago, it enjoyed considerable success in its first five years, but then over the next two years, sales and profits were flat. Over the last year, however, sales have increased 30 per cent whilst profits are up 50 per cent.

Application   Andy Fearn, who owns Lamaro's, had been worried a year ago that increased *competition* in the local takeaway market would lead to declining *sales* and *profits*. His *marketing budget* had remained the same for three years because he used a *historical budgeting* approach. However, he began to think that a way of increasing *sales* would be to spend more on *marketing* and adopt an *objective and task budgeting method* of setting *marketing budgets*.

Analysis   Andy Fearn had tended to see his marketing budget simply as a cost, something like petrol or the rent, which had to be paid but ideally could be cut back. However, his thinking changed after talking to a business adviser. The adviser suggested that focussing and possibly increasing the marketing budget could be the solution to the previous two years' disappointing sales growth. For example, a combination of special offer leaflets distributed with the local free newspaper, more frequent in-store promotions and rewards such as free garlic bread for repeat customers, could lead to higher sales. The adviser suggested that he needed to experiment with different types of marketing to see what worked and what didn't.

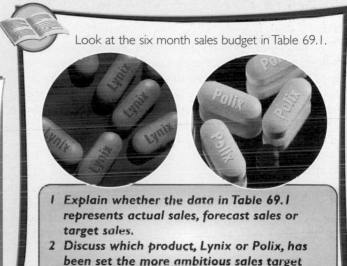

Evaluation   Changing his marketing budgeting method worked for Andy Fearn. Sales increased 30 per cent and profit rose by 50 per cent within six months. A historical budgeting approach seemed to make sense at the time. But in retrospect, Andy Fearn realised that marketing was crucial to continued growth. He knew that if his product wasn't right, no amount of marketing would work. A good pizza delivered promptly and in good condition had to be core to the success of the business. But pizzas need to be marketed effectively in a highly competitive environment. Sometimes an extra £5 000 a month spent on marketing can make all the difference to sales.

Marketing budgeting

In unit 29, it was explained that a budget was a plan of operations for a future accounting period. A MARKETING BUDGET is therefore a plan of operations for a future accounting period which relates to the marketing department. As with all budgets, the marketing budget is:
- **quantifiable**, i.e. expressed in numerical terms;
- linked to the **objectives** of the business;
- a **plan** showing what the business wants to achieve and is different from a forecast.

For example, a **sales budget** sets sales targets over a period of time. Table 69.1 shows part of a sales budget for two different medicine products, Lynix and Polix, within a company's product range. Sales targets are set for each month over a six month period. They are expressed in terms of the physical number of products sold, the average sale price, the value of total sales and the market share for each product. Sales budgets can also break down targets in a variety of other ways. For example, it might be broken down by area or region, by distribution channel, or type of customer.

Other parts of the marketing budget are concerned with expenditure. These set out how the marketing department plans to spend resources allocated to them over a time period. For example, the marketing department has to plan how much to

Look at the six month sales budget in Table 69.1.

	January	February	March	April	May	June
Lynix						
Number of sales (000s)	75	73	72	75	77	79
Average price	1.21	1.24	1.24	1.25	1.26	1.26
Sales value (£000)	90.75	90.52	89.28	93.75	97.02	99.54
Market share (%)	9.6	9.6	9.7	9.7	9.8	9.8
Polix						
Number of sales (000s)	167	162	160	167	170	174
Average price	0.46	0.48	0.48	0.49	0.5	0.5
Sales value (£000)	76.82	77.76	76.80	81.83	85	87
Market share (%)	15.8	15.8	15.9	16.1	16.2	16.2

Table 69.1 *A six month sales budget for two products of a pharmaceuticals company*

1 **Explain whether the data in Table 69.1 represents actual sales, forecast sales or target sales.**

2 **Discuss which product, Lynix or Polix, has been set the more ambitious sales target over the six month period.**

spend on above-the-line and below-the-line (see unit 80) promotion. This is not just spending on advertising but also, for example, on market research, direct sales promotion or the sales force.

Methods of setting budgets

There is a variety of methods which a business might use to set its marketing budgets.

Historical budgeting HISTORICAL BUDGETING (sometimes called **incremental budgeting**) is where the budget in the next time period is based on the outcome of the previous time period. For example, if sales were £220 000 this year, the budget might allow for a 5 per cent increase in sales to £231 000. Historical budgeting tends to rely upon looking at past trends and projecting them forward. This can have its problems because past trends are not always accurate predictors of future events (see unit 70). For example, changing inflation rates, changes in competition or a boom in the economy can alter the value of sales.

Affordable budgeting Businesses have many costs, including raw material costs and labour costs. The AFFORDABLE BUDGETING method bases planned marketing expenditure on what is left over after all these other more essential costs have been paid. The impact of affordable budgeting can be seen when an economy moves from boom to recession. Marketing expenditure is then often badly hit. This is because businesses typically cut their marketing spending before they cut costs such as staffing.

The advantage of affordable budgeting is that businesses only spend on marketing what they can afford. The disadvantage is that there is no attempt to match marketing spending with its effects on sales and profits. In a downturn in the economy, for example, it might make more sense to increase marketing to stabilise sales or minimise their fall. Increased marketing in a recession might also allow a business to gain market share at the expense of businesses which have cut their marketing budgets. Instead, the affordable budgeting method would see a typical business cutting its marketing spending.

Sales-based budgeting SALES-BASED or SALES-RELATED BUDGETING is a method used for marketing expenditure budgets. Marketing expenditure on individual products, product ranges or sales areas in the budget is based on sales achieved. For example, a product which sold £1 million would have ten times the amount of marketing expenditure allocated to it than a product which only sold £100 000.

The **percentage of past sales method** uses past sales to determine the marketing expenditure budget. In contrast, the **percentage of future sales method** uses the figures for future sales. Sometimes, businesses use the **advertising : sales ratio** as a method for planning advertising expenditure. The advertising: sales ratio is the proportion of sales which is spent on advertising. If the advertising: sales ratio were 10 per cent, for example, then for every £10 of sales, there would be £1 spent on advertising.

Sales related budgeting methods are simple to understand and implement. They also allocate scarce marketing resources towards more successful products. However, it is a crude way of planning marketing spending. For example, more sales might be generated by spending an extra pound of advertising on a product with 50 000 sales per week than one with 500 000

sales per week. Advertising a highly successful product may have little impact on sales. Advertising a product with far fewer or declining sales may generate a large number of extra sales. Also, marketing expenditure is not just about gaining extra sales. It is about gaining extra profitable sales. Spending money on promoting high profit margin niche products may be far more profitable than expenditure on the promotion of low profit margin mass market products.

Competitor budgeting COMPETITOR BUDGETING (also known as **competitor-based** or **parity budgeting**) allocates marketing expenditure according to what rival businesses are spending on competing products. For example, a soap powder manufacturer may spend £10 million a year on advertising because a rival soap powder manufacturer is spending this amount.

Competitor budgeting has the advantage that it takes into account market forces. Marketing expenditure clearly has an impact on sales and profits of the average product. It is also simple to understand as a method. However, like sales-related budgeting, it is not necessarily true that matching rivals'

TPG is a magazine publisher with a wide range of titles in the UK, France and the USA. One of its most successful magazines is *Got Ya!*, part of the 'lads mags' segment of the market. Sales of *Got Ya!* in established markets has been declining for the past five years, part of the overall trend for all lads mags magazines. TPG has been unwilling to increase the marketing budget for *Got Ya!* in recent years because it feels that an increased marketing spend would have little impact on sales. The problems with the magazine relate to the decline in the market, the strong product offering of competing magazines and the inability to find a new angle on the product format. Its research also shows that there has been little if any increase in marketing spend by competing magazines.

However, the Chinese market has recently been liberalised, with Western publishers able to sell titles to a potential 1.3 billion customers. TPG has decided to launch a Chinese version of *Got Ya!*. It aims to have initial sales of 250 000 magazines per month rising to 500 000 within three years. It expects the magazine to break even within 6 months and thereafter to have a net profit margin of 20 per cent. It has allocated an extra £800 000 to the marketing budget for *Got Ya!* for the six month period after the launch. It will then review the budget and decide whether further spending is required for the magazine to achieve its sales and profit goals.

Source: adapted from the *Financial Times*, 13.5.2004.

1 **Using a diagram, explain where Got Ya! is in its product life cycle (a) in the UK and (b) in China.**
2 **Discuss what methods of setting marketing budgets are being used by TPG.**

spending is the optimal way to allocate scarce marketing resources. If a rival spends 20 per cent more on advertising a particular product, it may be better for the business not to match this even if sales decline. Instead, there may be more profitable ways of allocating spending where the decline in sales is more than matched by increases in sales and profits on other products. Also, businesses may find it difficult to identify exactly how much rivals spend. Finally, the planned spending may not help the business to achieve its objectives set out in the marketing plan.

Objective and task budgeting OBJECTIVE AND TASK BUDGETING allocates marketing expenditure according to the objectives of the business and the tasks that must be carried out to meet those objectives. For example, if an objective is to increase sales of a product by 20 per cent over three years, then extra marketing resources will probably have to be allocated to that product in the budget. A mature product may need little marketing support if sales growth is not an objective. In contrast, a new product may need heavy marketing to get it past its launch stage successfully. At its most sophisticated, a marketing department may have to justify its spending by calculating its rate of return (see unit 84). Then it can be compared to other possible spending such as investment in training of workers, or investment in new machinery. When marketing departments refer to 'investment in marketing', they are implying that such comparisons can be made.

Objective and task budgeting most clearly ties marketing spending in with objectives and the tasks needed to ensure those objectives are met. As such, it is often seen as the most effective way to plan a budget. However, it requires a sophisticated approach to marketing where no simple rules apply. There is also no guarantee of success. Products launched at considerable marketing expense may fail. Mature products with little marketing expenditure back-up may suddenly go into the decline phase of the product life cycle because a rival business launches a better competing product.

Setting the budget

In practice, the marketing budget in a medium to large sized business is likely to be set by the marketing manager or director together with the managing director. It is the managing director, perhaps with the board of directors, who will determine the overall size of the budget and possibly set the targets for sales and profits. The marketing director will determine how spending is allocated between different products and different types of marketing. In a large marketing department, parts of setting the budget may be delegated further down the chain of command to budget holders. A **budget holder** is an employee responsible for a particular budget area.

How much involvement middle managers will have in preparing the budget will vary from business to business. In a centralised organisation (see unit 31), it is more likely that budgets will be drawn up by those higher up the organisation. In a more decentralised organisation, aspects of preparing the budget may be pushed down the hierarchy. In a centralised organisation, senior management may wish to keep a tight control on decision making, using their expertise to draw up budgets which will further the objectives of the business. In a more decentralised organisation, employees may be more

motivated if they have been part of the decision making process. On the other hand, they may deliberately choose undemanding targets, or inflate their expenditure budgets. If planned sales, for example, are targeted to grow by 1 per cent in the budget when sales have been growing at 5 per cent per annum over the last five years, then the marketing department is likely to achieve its 1 per cent target easily. They can then get the credit for achieving their target even though it was far too low in the first place. Equally, departments have a tendency to inflate their planned costs. It then becomes much easier to stay within budget. It also allows departments to spend on their favourite projects even if it is unlikely that this will benefit sales or profits.

The usefulness of budgeting

There is a number of advantages and disadvantages to a business of budgetary control. These were explained in detail in unit 29. Exactly the same arguments for budgets in general apply to marketing. Equally, in unit 29, it was explained how to calculate variances for budgets. Exactly the same variance techniques can be applied to marketing budgets.

As with any other type of budgeting, marketing budgetary control tends to become more common the larger the size of the business. Without proper marketing budgetary control, it would impossible to run a large business because there would be no effective control of expenditure. Equally, planning for growth would not be present. So budgetary control is an important tool of management for medium to large businesses.

keyterms

Affordable budgeting - a budgeting method where planned marketing expenditure is based on what is left over after all other more essential costs have been paid.
Competitor budgeting (or competitor based budgeting or parity budgeting) - a budgeting method where marketing expenditure is allocated according to what rival businesses are spending on competing products.
Historical budgeting (or incremental budgeting) - where the budget in the next time period is based on the outcome of the previous time period.
Marketing budget - a plan of operations for a future accounting period which relates to the marketing department.
Objective and task budgeting - where the budget is set according to the objectives of the business and the tasks that must be carried out to meet those objectives.
Sales-based budgeting (or sales-related budgeting) - where the size of the marketing budget is determined by the level of sales achieved and where the allocation of the marketing budget between different products, product ranges or sales areas is based on their relative sales.

checklist

1 What might be contained within a marketing budget?
2 What is the difference between a budget set using the historical budgeting method and one set using the affordable budgeting method?
3 What is the difference between a budget set using the sales-based budgeting method and one set using the competitor budgeting method?
4 How might a business set a marketing budget using the objective and task method?

5 Who might be involved in setting a marketing budget in a large company?
6 What are the advantages and disadvantages of involving middle managers in the marketing budget setting process?
7 By revising the material in unit 29, explain the advantages and disadvantages to a business of marketing budgetary control.

Haffner plc is an international cosmetics company. It has four main ranges described in more detail in Figure 69.1. To fix the marketing budgets for its products, it uses the percentage of past sales method. Since 1995, it has allocated 20 per cent of last year's sales to the marketing budget for the current year. Sales and marketing budgets are shown in Table 69.2.

	Emme		Gee		Vee		Cee	£ million
	Sales	Marketing budget	Sales	Marketing budget	Sales	Marketing budget	Sales	Marketing budget
2001	10.6	1.98	23.4	4.74	50.2	10.18	36.8	7.24
2002	10.8	2.12	23.2	4.68	49.2	10.04	37.8	7.36
2003	12.6	2.16	21.8	4.64	47.8	9.84	40.2	7.56
2004	16.6	2.52	20.4	4.36	46.2	9.56	44.6	8.04

Table 69.2 *Annual sales and marketing budgets for Haffner's four main product ranges, £ million*

1 (a) Showing all your workings, and assuming that the method of setting budgets remains the same, calculate (i) the total marketing budget for Haffner in 2004; (ii) total sales for Haffner in 2004; (iii) sales of Cee in 1999; (iv) the marketing budget for Vee in 2005. (8 marks)
(b) Discuss how marketing budgets might have been different if Haffner had used a percentage of forecast sales method to determine marketing budgets over the period 2000-2004. (12 marks)
2 To what extent could Haffner increase its overall profitability if it used a different method of setting budgets than the percentage of past sales method? (20 marks)

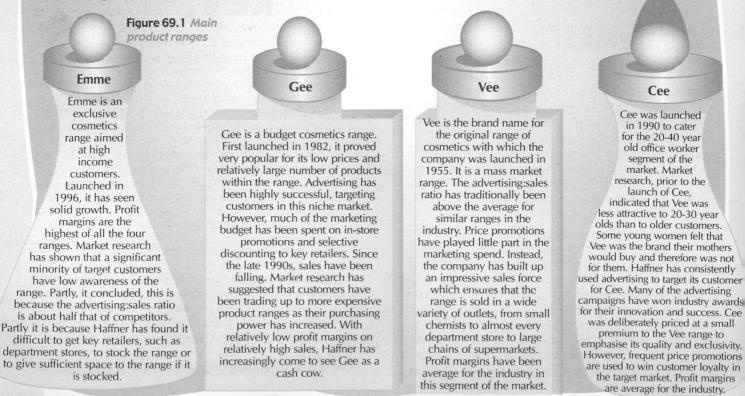

Figure 69.1 *Main product ranges*

Emme

Emme is an exclusive cosmetics range aimed at high income customers. Launched in 1996, it has seen solid growth. Profit margins are the highest of all the four ranges. Market research has shown that a significant minority of target customers have low awareness of the range. Partly, it concluded, this is because the advertising:sales ratio is about half that of competitors. Partly it is because Haffner has found it difficult to get key retailers, such as department stores, to stock the range or to give sufficient space to the range if it is stocked.

Gee

Gee is a budget cosmetics range. First launched in 1982, it proved very popular for its low prices and relatively large number of products within the range. Advertising has been highly successful, targeting customers in this niche market. However, much of the marketing budget has been spent on in-store promotions and selective discounting to key retailers. Since the late 1990s, sales have been falling. Market research has suggested that customers have been trading up to more expensive product ranges as their purchasing power has increased. With relatively low profit margins on relatively high sales, Haffner has increasingly come to see Gee as a cash cow.

Vee

Vee is the brand name for the original range of cosmetics with which the company was launched in 1955. It is a mass market range. The advertising:sales ratio has traditionally been above the average for similar ranges in the industry. Price promotions have played little part in the marketing spend. Instead, the company has built up an impressive sales force which ensures that the range is sold in a wide variety of outlets, from small chemists to almost every department store to large chains of supermarkets. Profit margins have been average for the industry in this segment of the market.

Cee

Cee was launched in 1990 to cater for the 20-40 year old office worker segment of the market. Market research, prior to the launch of Cee, indicated that Vee was less attractive to 20-30 year olds than to older customers. Some young women felt that Vee was the brand their mothers would buy and therefore was not for them. Haffner has consistently used advertising to target its customer for Cee. Many of the advertising campaigns have won industry awards for their innovation and success. Cee was deliberately priced at a small premium to the Vee range to emphasise its quality and exclusivity. However, frequent price promotions are used to win customer loyalty in the target market. Profit margins are average for the industry.

70 Sales forecasting

Emmray's

Knowledge Emmray's is a company which designs and assembles seats for cars, buses and coaches, although it also has some contracts for taxis and ambulances. Founded just two years ago, it has grown rapidly.

Application Rapid growth in *sales* has delighted the two *senior managers*, Emma Chancery and Rique Segura, who founded the *company*. However, problems are now appearing due to the current size of the business. On their current *sales forecast* for the next six months, they won't be able to fulfil all the *orders* received on time.

Analysis An immediate problem is that their premises are too small. They have been looking around for new premises for the past three months and have decided to move locally to a building with 7,000 sq ft, twice their current floor space, and available for immediate occupation. Currently they have 16 staff and need to increase this by another 5 as soon as possible. The new staff will need training which will be done by existing staff. A limited amount of new equipment will need to be bought. From a finance viewpoint, the company will have to increase its working capital. It hopes to finance this through retained profit, which will limit the amount Emma and Rique can take out of the company in dividends. Marketing has so far been highly successful and, with a good track record for repeat orders, expenditure on marketing should remain constant.

Evaluation Emmray's success poses problems for the company, but they are problems which most companies would like to have. There is some risk that its sales forecast is too optimistic. Based on past growth rates and orders already placed, external factors such interest rates or the boom in the economy could change. Equally, its competitors could become far more aggressive in the market to stall the growth of this new company. On the other hand, its sales forecast could be too pessimistic. A few extra orders, or perhaps a large single unexpected order, could push its sales well over the forecast limit. Actual sales of more than plus or minus 20 per cent from the forecast could pose the company serious problems. Emma and Rique need to have strategies in place to cope with these eventualities.

The importance of sales forecasting

SALES FORECASTING is important to any business. The number of sales and the value will have a direct impact on a number of areas.

Profitability and survival Future sales will determine the future profitability of a business. If sales are too low in relation to costs, the business may make a loss. For some businesses, this could mean that they will be forced to cease trading. Low profits or losses could also lead to quoted companies becoming the subject of takeover bids (see unit 111). Equally, if forecast sales are disappointing, this may spur a business to adopt a new strategy, either to boost sales or cut costs.

Production Predicted sales will have an impact on predicted production. For a manufacturer, if sales volumes are forecast to rise by 20 per cent, then the production department must be able to raise its output by this amount to satisfy demand. If production falls short of this, there could be dissatisfied customers who want to buy the product but it is unavailable. If production is above the sales forecast, this could lead to an unwanted increase in stocks. Changes in sales of different products will require changes to what is produced.

Human resources Future sales will have an impact on human resources. Declining forecast sales may alert a business to the fact that it might have to make staff redundant in the near future. Growing sales might mean recruiting extra staff or reorganisation. Changes in sales of different products may mean both recruitment and redundancies having to take place at the same time. Equally, changing sales may have implications for training.

Marketing The marketing department too will be affected by sales forecasts. If sales are forecast to grow too slowly or to decline, then the marketing department may be able to change these trends. Increased expenditure on promotion, for example, might be able to increase sales. Equally, disappointing forecast sales might force the marketing department to consider how it is spending its budget. It might then decide to change the balance of spending on different types of promotion.

Constructing a sales forecast

Sales forecasts can be arrived at in a number of different ways.

Extrapolation from past trends As explained in unit 66, forecasters may attempt to extrapolate future sales figures from backdata. By analysing past data, they may be able to find a trend and then project that trend forwards. The advantages and disadvantages of this method were discussed in unit 66.

Barometric and econometric methods Barometric methods are methods which link the current value of selected variables to future sales. For example, there is some evidence to suggest that a sharp prolonged downturn in stock market prices tends to be followed by a recession in the economy. So a business may reduce its sales forecasts if there is a stock market crash. Or a tour operator selling foreign holidays may find that there is a link between the current strength of rising house prices and future sales of foreign holidays. If the housing market stagnated, it would then cut back on the number of foreign holidays that it expected to sell.

Econometric methods are methods which attempt to provide causal explanations for changes in sales. For example, the demand for new kitchens is linked to the volume of house sales. This is because individuals buying a (second hand) house are more likely to buy a new kitchen than if they hadn't moved. Equally, moving house tends to lead to the purchase of new furniture. So the sales of furniture manufacturers and retailers are directly linked to the volume of house purchases.

The difference between barometric and econometric methods is that barometric methods attempt to link variables which are clearly not causes with changes in sales. With econometric methods, the forecaster is using variables which are causes of changing sales to forecast sales. Both barometric and econometric methods rely upon sophisticated mathematical techniques. They are therefore only likely to be used by large companies which have the personnel able to use such methods, or by market research companies which specialise in producing market research reports for companies.

Market research Market research (see units 4 and 5), including **test marketing** (see unit 7) may help in constructing a sales forecast. For example, there may be no past data from which to extrapolate trends for a new product. Test marketing of a new product, focus groups or shopping surveys should all give some indication of future sales.

Market research may also be able to spot new trends in the market which cannot be picked up by looking at past data. A product, for example, may be about to become 'fashionable' and desirable. Others may be about to go out of fashion. In the 1980s and 1990s, Doc Martin shoes enjoyed cult status amongst some young buyers, but sales fell sharply in the 2000s because they became less fashionable. Denim jeans became unfashionable in the 1990s as young people did not want to look like their parents. New designs using denim after the year 2000 made denim clothing popular again.

Using market research has the advantage that extra information not available from within the business can be used to forecast sales. However, market research is not always reliable, particularly if the methodology (see unit 8) used is inadequate. If test marketing is used, this will give competitors a chance to see the new product and react to it. For example, **viral** or **buzz marketing** techniques, where a well known 'face' in an area is seen with a product such as a car, is used to develop excitement amongst consumers. Competitors may rush forward 'me too' products which are almost identical to the product being test marketed. They may also increase promotion of similar products in the test market area to reduce the sales of the product being test marketed.

Hunches and guesses Small businesses often don't have access to sophisticated past data or market research. Equally, when the market is changing very fast, past data and market research may be an unreliable way of forecasting future sales. So sales forecasts can often be based upon hunches and guesses. Hunches and guesses could be argued to be an unscientific way of producing a forecast. Even when some such forecasts are accurate, this could be simply due to chance and the laws of probability. However, it can also be argued that some individuals have a very good instinctive feel for the market in which they operate. Using their past knowledge, some individuals may be far better at spotting trends than others.

The reliability of forecasts

Forecasts are likely to be more reliable when:

- the forecast is for a short period of time in the future, such as 6 months, rather than a long time, such as five years;
- they are revised frequently to take account of new data and other information;
- the market is slow changing;
- there is plenty of backdata from which to produce a forecast;
- market research data, including test marketing data, is available;
- those preparing the forecast have a good understanding of how to use data to produce a forecast;
- those preparing the forecast have a good 'feel' for the market and can adjust the forecast to take account of their hunches and guesses about the future.

No forecaster is accurate all the time. Even in slow moving markets, sales can change by a few per cent for no apparent reason. One way to take this into account is to produce a forecast range. Forecasts might, for example, prepare three sets of figures – an optimistic forecast, a pessimistic forecast and a central forecast. The two outlying forecasts would have low probabilities of occurring but would indicate a best and worst case scenario. The central forecast would be the forecast which had the highest probability of occurring. By giving these forecasts to other departments, such as production, it would give them an indication of the possible variation they might have to face. They could then prepare their own plans for these eventualities. In a very sophisticated forecast there would be a whole range of possible outcomes, each with a probability attached to its occurring.

Even though forecasts are rarely 100 per cent accurate, they do provide an indication of likely future trends. As such, they are an important tool for any planning or budgeting.

keyterms

Sales forecasting - predicting future demand for products, typically to help other business functions such as production or accounts to construct plans and budgets.

✓checklist

1 Why might a sales forecast be important for a business in (a) human resource planning and (b) financial planning?
2 What is the difference between an econometric and a barometric method of sales forecasting?
3 How might market research help in constructing a sales forecast?
4 What is viral marketing?
5 To what extent can guesses be a successful way of constructing a sales forecast?
6 Why might a sales forecast prove to be inaccurate?

Cardinal is a Scottish sign writing company. Founded 40 years ago, it has enjoyed consistent growth and currently has sales of £5 million per annum. An opportunity has arisen to buy a local competitor with current sales of £2 million per annum. There are many factors which will influence the final decision about whether to buy or not. However, one is future sales.

Cardinal has specialised in shop signs and wall images. Most of the orders received are relatively small, but occasionally a very large order can come through from £200 000 to £2 million. The large chain retailers which places these orders want the work done quickly. So the work tends to be unevenly spread through the year. There can be marked differences in turnover from six month period to six month period and even from year to year. In 2001, for example, a couple of very large orders pushed annual sales over £6 million, when in other years in the five year period 1999-2003 annual sales fluctuated in the £3.5 million to £4.5 million range.

Dowman, the company Cardinal is considering buying, specialises in making signs for house builders. Over the past ten years, the market for new houses and renovations has been extremely healthy and has provided Cardinal with a steady flow of orders. Current sales are running at around £2 million per annum. However, interest rates had increased in 2004 to stem the high growth in house prices that had occurred over the past 5-10 years. If house prices began to fall, as many commentators predicted, the market for new houses might collapse. In the same situation in the late 1980s and early 1990s, the new housing market remained depressed for five years.

If Cardinal were to take over Dowman, it would hope to squeeze costs by bringing both companies under one roof, combining the sales and accounts teams and removing some of the senior management at Dowman. It would also hope to improve efficiency by fusing the best from both companies. Cardinal has a reputation for creative design which could be fed into Dowman's housing market to gain extra sales. On the other hand, Dowman has a reputation for aggressive marketing, which could benefit Cardinal's core market.

Blair McFarlaine, Cardinal's managing director, is concerned, though, that rising interest rates will not just cause a downturn in the new housing market, but also lead to disappointing growth of consumer spending. If retailers experience difficult times, they will cut back on shop refurbishments and investment, posing a threat to Cardinal's core market. All too often in the past, Blair's hunches have proved correct. So he is not convinced that Cardinal can handle the problems of integrating the two companies as well as coping with a downturn in demand.

1 (a) Discuss what forecasting methods Cardinal could use to produce a sales forecast for the merged company if it took over Dowman. (8 marks)
  (b) If Cardinal took over Dowman, evaluate whether sales in the first year of trading as a merged company would be greater than the current £6.5 million sales achieved by the two companies trading separately. (12 marks)
2 Discuss what role a sales forecast could have in planning for the future of a merged company. (20 marks)

71 The profit and loss account

Lincat Group

Knowledge Lincat Group plc is a manufacturer of commercial catering and bar equipment, washing and sanitising equipment and kitchen appliances.

Application In its 2004 *Annual Report and Accounts*, the group published a *profit and loss* account showing *revenues, costs and profit* for the *financial years* 2003 and 2004 ending 30 June. It also published a five year summary, covering the period 2000-2004, of its main financial data.

Analysis Over the 5 year period 2000-04, sales at Lincat increased 23.6 per cent from £25.8 million to £31.9 million. However, costs increased even more. The result was that operating profit fell 25.6 per cent from £5.4 million to £4.3 million. There was a corresponding fall in profit before taxation from £5.5 million to £4.2 million.

Evaluation Profit and loss figures would suggest that Lincat had mixed performance over the period 2000-04. On the one hand, sales are up by a reasonable 23.6 per cent but the company has failed to prevent its costs from rising even more. The result has been a fall in profits. However, the accounts show that profit at least was positive in every year over the period. What the accounts do not show is why Lincat's costs were rising at a faster rate than sales. They also don't show how Lincat's competitors performed. It could be, for example, that Lincat was the best performing company in its industry and that every company experienced rising costs relative to sales. Without such information, it is difficult to give an overall evaluation of the performance of the company.

Adapted from Lincat Group plc, *Annual Report and Accounts*, 2004.

The purpose of the profit and loss account

Businesses need to keep **accounts** (see unit 20) for a variety of reasons. Accounts are records of past events or predictions of future events. Accounts tend to be associated with financial transactions. **Financial accounting** is mainly the recording of what has happened in the past. **Management accounting** tends to be related to the future and what might happen (see unit 20).

One key type of account in financial accounting is the PROFIT AND LOSS ACCOUNT. **Profit** or **loss** is the difference between **revenues** and **costs** (see unit 21):

Profit/loss = revenue - cost

If revenue is greater than costs, the business makes a profit. If costs are greater than revenue, then it makes a loss. The profit and loss account at its simplest shows revenues, costs and the resulting profit or loss made. It also indicates how that profit is used or how the loss is financed.

The profit and loss account is a record of revenues, costs and profit made in the past. The account covers a specific time period, typically one year. For example, a company might compile a profit and loss account for the twelve months to 31 March 2004.

Unit 20 explained that accounts, like the profit and loss account, are compiled because they are needed by the stakeholders of the business.

- Owners (called shareholders if the business is a limited company) want to know how well the business has done in the past. They are also interested in what has happened to any profit that has been made because as owners they are entitled to a share if not all of that profit.
- Managers will use the profit and loss account as an indication of past performance. If it is a company, they will have access to much more detailed information than would be published in the company Annual Report and Accounts.
- Workers in the business, if they have access to the profit and loss account, may use it to argue for improvements in their conditions of service, including pay.
- Potential investors in the business use the profit and loss account as one indication of whether the business is likely to do well in the future.
- The media may publish stories about businesses partly based on their accounts.
- Tax authorities use the profit and loss account to calculate some taxes on businesses. All businesses, including sole traders who are self employed, have to keep records of past revenues and costs and therefore profit or loss made for tax purposes.
- Suppliers may check the profit and loss account of a business to decide whether or not to give **trade credit** (see unit 25).
- Banks will typically ask to see the profit and loss account if a business wishes to borrow money.
- For companies, it is a legal requirement for them to present an audited profit and loss account to Companies House each year (see unit 61).

Profit is revenues minus costs. However, in accounting, there are many different types of profit, like 'gross profit' or 'net profit', depending upon which revenues and which costs are included. There are different measures of profit. Each measure of profit has its own uses and gives different information to those looking at the figures.

The presentation of the profit and loss account

The profit and loss account of a company is made up of three parts.
- The trading account shows profits made before costs not directly related to the goods or services produced by a business are included.
- The profit and loss account shows profits after all costs have been taken into consideration.
- The appropriation account shows how the profit or loss made is distributed.

Note that the second part of the profit and loss account is also called the profit and loss account.

The tables in this unit show four conventions in the presentation of accounts.
- When there are two or more time periods, like two years, being shown, the latest time period is put in the left most column whilst the earliest year is put in the right most column. This may seem as though the numbers in the accounts are being read from back to front. However, the numbers are put in this order because the most important numbers, the most recent ones, are read first going from left to right.
- Any numbers in brackets indicate they are minus numbers. The minus sign '-' is not used in a set of accounts.
- Large numbers are written using commas rather than spaces to indicate thousands. So £6 345 000 in accounts is written as '£6,345,000'.
- Accounts are usually presented in a vertical format. Not all accounts are presented in this form. For example, Table 71.7 shows accounts for one year presented in two columns, which allows subtotals to be shown.

The trading account

The TRADING ACCOUNT shows the level of gross profit made by a business. Gross profit is defined as turnover minus cost of sales.

Turnover - cost of sales = gross profit

TURNOVER is another name for **sales revenue** (see unit 21). In accounting terms, it is defined as the revenue generated from sales over a time period.

Cost of sales is all costs associated with production. For a shoe manufacturer, raw materials costs such as leather and the wages of production workers are likely to be included in cost of sales. So too would heating and lighting the factory and the cost of machinery maintenance. Cost of sales does not include all the other costs of a business such as administration or interest paid on loans. For a retailer, such as a shoe shop chain the costs of buying in stock could be the only cost of sales to the business. The wages of staff in branches who serve customers, rents of branches and their heating and lighting are likely to be placed elsewhere in the profit and loss account.

Gross profit is turnover minus cost of sales. It is the profit made from the sale of goods or services after the costs directly associated with production have been deducted.

An example of a trading account is given in Table 71.1, which shows the trading account of Sipotec Ltd, a private limited company. Sipotec Ltd is a small biopharmaceutical manufacturer which has its own research programme into new drugs but also manufactures drugs and vaccines for larger pharmaceutical companies.

	2005 £000	2004 £000
Turnover	5,893	5,432
Cost of sales	(2,538)	(2,281)
Gross profit	3,355	3,151

Note: a bracket round a number in a set of accounts indicates that it is a minus number. Here, costs of sales is a minus number because it has to be taken away from turnover to give gross profit.

Table 71.1 *Trading account for Sipotec Ltd for the year ended 31 January*

Companies Acts set out the rules of presentation and content of published company accounts. They state what can be included in the trading account of a company. They include the following.

Products delivered but not paid for Any good or service delivered to a customer is counted as a sale even if the customer has not yet paid for the order (this is known as the **realisation concept**)

Stocks Cost of sales is the cost of production of what has been sold in the period covered by the account. However, in that period, say the financial year to 31st January, the business might have produced more than it sold. The extra production will then have had to be put into **stock** (see unit 28). Any production costs associated with the production of stock must be excluded from the cost of sales.

Similarly, a business might have produced less than it sold during a time period. The extra sales will have been of stocks made in a previous time period. The cost of producing those stocks will then have to be added on to the costs of production for that period in which they are sold.

The change in stock is measured by the opening stock at the start of the period minus the closing stock at the end of the period. So the formula for calculating cost of sales becomes:

Cost of sales = cost of purchases + (opening stock - closing stock)

where the cost of purchases is defined as the costs associated with production of goods sold in the same period. The formula for gross profit is then:

Gross profit = turnover - cost of purchases - (opening stock - closing stock)

An example of cost of sales adjusted for stock as might appear in the accounts of a business is shown in Table 71.2.

VAT Any VAT or other sales taxes collected is not included in turnover on the trading account. This is because the tax will have to be passed on to Customs and Excise and will not be retained by the business. Similarly, cost of sales does not normally include any VAT paid by the business on supplies bought because it is deducted from any VAT on sales before being paid to Customs and Excise.

Fixed and variable costs, direct and indirect costs, overheads In unit 21, various types of costs were explained. One was fixed and variable costs. Cost of sales is not the same as

	2005 £000	2004 £000
Opening stock	1,026	756
Cost of purchases	2,749	2,551
Closing stock	(1,237)	(1,026)
Cost of sales	2,538	2,281

Table 71.2 *Cost of sales adjusted for stock, Sipotec Ltd for the year ended 31 January*

variable costs because some fixed costs may be included. However, they are included in cost of sales because they are costs of production. Another distinction made in unit 21 was between direct and indirect costs. Cost of sales include direct costs associated with production. So, for example, they could include the raw materials of a manufacturer. But cost of sales could also include those indirect costs which are attributable to production.

The profit and loss account

The profit and loss account is the name given to the second part of the overall profit and loss account. It shows the level of NET PROFIT made by a business. The profit and loss account for Sipotec Ltd is shown in Table 71.4. The starting point for the account is the level of gross profit made.

From this gross profit, distribution costs and administrative costs (or expenses) have to be deducted. These are overheads not directly linked to production. DISTRIBUTION COSTS or SELLING AND DISTRIBUTION COSTS are costs incurred in the distribution of the product. These could include warehouse costs, advertising and motor expenses for trucks operated by the business. ADMINISTRATION EXPENSES are wages and salaries of administration staff, rent and rates on buildings not directly used for production, telephone bills and insurance.

Included in administration expenses might be two other items.
- **Provision for bad debts**. Businesses often have to extend trade credit. There is always the danger that customers receiving products will not repay the trade credit extended to them. When a business decides that it will never be repaid on a debt, it becomes a **bad debt**. It is then **written off**. In the period when it is written off it appears under 'provision for bad debts' under administration expenses.
- **Depreciation**. Depreciation is the value of wear and tear on fixed assets like machinery, buildings or motor vehicles. It is a cost to the business and therefore must be included as an expense on the profit and loss account. Exactly how depreciation can be calculated is discussed in unit 75.

Sometimes businesses make no distinction between distribution and administration costs in their accounts. In this case, all these costs would be called expenses.

	2005 £000	2004 £000
Turnover	5,893	5,432
Cost of sales	(2,538)	(2,281)
Gross profit	3,355	3,151
Selling, marketing and distribution costs	(326)	(305)
Administrative expenses	(1,829)	(1,604)
Research and development	(176)	(1,482)
Operating profit	1,024	(204)
Interest receivable and other income	24	28
Interest payable and similar charges	(132)	(145)
Profit/(loss) on ordinary activities before taxation	916	(321)
Taxation	(25)	(35)
Profit on ordinary activities after taxation	891	(356)

Table 71.4 *Profit and loss account for Sipotec Ltd for the year ended 31 January*

In Table 71.4, a third type of expense is separated out. This is 'Research and development'. Because Sipotec has a major research and development programme, it lists R&D expenditure separately in its accounts. However, most businesses do not engage in R&D and only a minority who do would list this expenditure separately on their profit and loss account.

Gross profit minus distribution costs and administration expenses is called operating profit. It is the profit that is made from operating or running the business. However, operating profit does not include any interest that is received or paid by the business. The business may receive interest because it might have money placed on deposit with a bank, for

Pink and Black Ltd is a publishing company. Three years ago it published *The Diary of a Bat from Bali* which proved a surprising runaway success.

Table 71.3 shows the trading account for the company for the past three years. It also shows the stock levels at the end of the financial year.

	2005 £000	2004 £000	2003 £000
Turnover	8,471	6,690	?
Cost of sales	(3,856)	?	(3,057)
Gross profit	?	3,219	2,340
Stock levels	634	710	627

Table 71.3 *Pink and Black Ltd, trading account and stock levels for the year ended 31 March*

1 Copy out Table 71.3, calculating the numbers shown by a '?'.
2 (a) Why does Pink and Black need to keep stocks? (b) Explain how stock levels affect cost of sales, illustrating your answer from the data in Table 71.3.
3 To what extent has Pink and Black improved its performance between 2003 and 2005?

example. It may pay interest on loans it has taken out. The difference between interest received and interest paid is NET INTEREST.

Net interest = interest received - interest paid out

Operating profit after net interest has been added or deducted is called PROFIT ON ORDINARY ACTIVITIES BEFORE TAXATION (also known as PROFIT BEFORE TAXATION or NET PROFIT BEFORE TAXATION). UK companies have to pay taxes on their profits. So this tax must be deducted to calculate PROFIT ON ORDINARY ACTIVITIES AFTER TAXATION (also known as PROFIT AFTER TAXATION or NET PROFIT AFTER TAX). This is gross profit adjusted for interest and taxation.

There is a number of other items which can appear on a profit and loss account depending on the particular circumstances of a business and its activities over the accounting period.

Other operating income This is income received which is not part of the trading activities of a business. For example, a fish and chip shop using the ground floor of a building may own and rent out the upstairs part. This rent would be 'other operating income'. It is shown in the profit and loss account after expenses and so any income is included in the figure for operating profit.

Exceptional and extraordinary items EXCEPTIONAL ITEMS are items of expenditure which are part of the day to day expenses of the business. But the item is so unusually large that it is included in the accounts as a separate item. For example, a company might have to make a large payment into the company pension fund because of a fall in the investment value of the fund. In contrast, EXTRAORDINARY ITEMS are items of expenditure which are not day to day expenses of the business. Extraordinary items might include the costs of shutting down part of the business, or making a large number of staff redundant.

The appropriation account

The APPROPRIATION ACCOUNT is the last part of the full profit and loss account of a company. It shows what happens to the profit once it has been earned. Table 71.6 shows the appropriation account for Sipotec Ltd. Profit, once tax has been paid, is either paid out to the owners of the business or is retained by the business for its use.

In a company, the owners are the **shareholders** and they may be paid a **dividend** (see units 21 and 61). The amount paid out in dividends is determined by the Board of Directors. It will depend on the size of the profit made and the needs of the company to retain profit. Dividends may still be paid if the company has made a loss if the directors judge that the company will make a profit in the future

James Beattie is a chain of department stores with 12 outlets across the Midlands. Its profit and loss account for 2003 and 2004 is shown in Table 71.5.

	2004 £000	2003 £000
Turnover	96,124	96,171
Cost of sales	(48,067)	?
Gross profit	48,057	47,916
Selling and distribution costs	(33,442)	(32,581)
Administrative expenses	?	(8,320)
Operating profit	5,553	7,015
Net interest payable	(331)	(384)
Other finance (costs)/income	(40)	380
Profit/(loss) on ordinary activities before taxation	?	7,011
Tax on profit on ordinary activities	(1,599)	?
Profit on ordinary activities after taxation	3,580	4,882

Source: adapted from James Beattie plc, Annual Report and Accounts, 2004.

Figure 71.5 *Profit and loss account for James Beattie plc for the year ended 31 January*

1 Copy out Table 71.5 and fill in the missing numbers shown by '?'.
2 Analyse what happened between 2003 and 2004 to (a) sales, (b) costs, (c) and profit.
3 To what extent did James Beattie perform better in 2003 than it did in 2004?

and there is enough in the reserves to fund the payment.

The business may choose to retain part of the profit to fund future expenditure. This could be investment in new machinery or buildings. Or it could be to fund the takeover of other businesses. It could be simply to hold as savings in case the business makes a loss in a future year which has to be financed.

Plcs usually show earnings per share at the end of the appropriation account. Earnings per share are explained in unit 81.

Profit and loss accounts of sole traders and partnerships

So far this unit has looked at the profit and loss accounts of limited companies. The profit and loss accounts of sole traders and partnerships are similar. However:

	2005 £000	2004 £000
Profit on ordinary activities after taxation	891	(356)
Dividends	(368)	0
Retained profit	523	(356)
Earnings per ordinary share	6.9p	0

Table 71.6 *Profit and loss appropriation account for Sipotec Ltd for the year ended 31 January*

Soyka Krupa
Profit and loss account
for year ended 31.6.04

	£	£
Turnover		125,600
Cost of sales		
Opening stock	35,000	
Purchases	80,000	
	115,000	
Closing stock	42,800	
		72,200
Gross profit		53,400
Expenses		
Casual labour	7,000	
Rent and rates	6,000	
Motor expenses	3,500	
Heat and light	1,650	
Promotion	1,250	
Insurance	2,000	
Telephone	2,500	
Other expenses	6,280	
		30,180
Net profit		23,220

Table 71.7 *Profit and loss account of Soyka Krupa, a sole trader who owns a health food shop*

- administration expenses tend to be broken down in the profit and loss account;
- sole trader and partnership profit and loss accounts have no appropriation account because the profits all belong to the sole trader or partners.

The profit and loss account of a sole trader who runs a health food shop is shown in Table 71.7.

Using the profit and loss account to evaluate performance

The profit and loss account can be used to evaluate the financial performance of a business. But using it for this purpose has limitations for a number of reasons.

Other financial data The profit and loss account only gives data about revenue, costs, profit and how the profit is used. Much more financial data is needed to assess accurately the performance of a business. For example, the cash flow position of the business is a vital indicator of performance. So too is the size of the borrowings of the business.

Other business data The profit and loss account gives data about the finances of a business. But it doesn't say anything about the environmental or social impact of the business and only indirectly gives information about new product development or efficiency of production. Financial data is only one source of data for evaluating the overall performance of a business.

Past, present and future The profit and loss account is a record of the past performance of a business. So it can be used as one piece of evidence to evaluate the performance of the business in the past. But it is not necessarily a good indication of present or future performance. Much can happen within six months or a year to a business. The economy might go into recession. There might be a sudden fall in demand for the products of a business. A new competitor might enter the market and be highly successful. A business whose profit and loss accounts show a period of ten years of successful growth in revenues and profits might suddenly see a fall in turnover and a slump into loss in the eleventh year.

Trends The profit and loss account for a single year is of limited value when judging performance. It gives an indication of the profitability of the business. But one year's figures would not indicate whether the business is growing or declining, or whether the profit is unusually high or low. The more periods of data here available, the more reliable any evaluation can be. For example, some commentators talk about PROFIT QUALITY. There is profit quality if a business is able, period after period, to earn profits. However, there is low profit quality if much of the profit is due to exceptional circumstances, such as the sale of a business or abnormally good weather conditions. Profit quality can only be judged by considering profit over a number of time periods.

The level of detail in the account The more detail in the profit and loss account, the more information available to be analysed. Companies tend to give the minimum information required by law. So anyone looking at published accounts will not necessarily pick up important trends or features within the accounts. Far more background information will, however, be available to managers within the company if they are using profit and loss figures to assess performance. Sole traders and partnerships should have full access to all the detail behind the final profit and loss account drawn up.

'Window dressing' the accounts For sole traders and partnerships, profit and loss accounts are typically prepared for the tax authorities. There is a temptation to minimise profit, for example by not putting some revenue 'through the books' or exaggerating costs. This will then reduce the amount of tax that has to be paid. Companies too may manipulate their accounts to present a better picture than is actually the case (see unit 76 for ways of doing this).

Special characteristics of individual accounts Profit and loss accounts can have special features which need to be noted in evaluating performance. Occasionally a business will change

checklist

1 Why do different stakeholders in a business need to see its financial accounts?
2 What are the three parts of a profit and loss account?
3 How are stocks accounted for in the trading account?
4 What are the similarities and differences between variable costs, direct costs and costs of sale?
5 Explain the difference between exceptional items and extraordinary items on a profit and loss account.
6 What is shown on the appropriation account?
7 Why does the profit and loss account of a sole trader not have an appropriation account?
8 Briefly outline why profit and loss accounts may have limited use in assessing the performance of a business.

its tax year. Accounts might for a single period be presented for 9 months or 15 months, say, instead of the usual 12 months. An increase in profit would be expected if the accounts covered 15 months rather than 12 months. Exceptional and extraordinary items should also be carefully studied. Some businesses are constantly taking over and closing down businesses. Every year they may record extraordinary items in their account as a result. This makes it very difficult to judge performance over time from the profit and loss account. Equally, the costs and revenue sources of these businesses are constantly changing. It becomes very difficult to judge from the profit and loss account whether the operations of the business are being well managed because so much of the profit is coming from new parts of the business.

keyterms

Administration expenses - on the profit and loss account, indirect costs or overheads incurred in the administration of the business, such as wages and salaries of administration staff, telephone bills and insurance.

Appropriation account - part of the profit and loss account which shows how net profit after tax is distributed or apportioned between dividends and retained profit.

Distribution costs or selling and distribution costs - on the profit and loss account, indirect costs or overheads occurred in the distribution of production, such as warehouse costs or advertising.

Exceptional items - on the profit and loss account, items of expenditure which are part of the day to day expenses of the business but which are exceptionally large in that accounting period compared to other periods.

Extraordinary items - on the profit and loss account, items of expenditure which are not part of the day to day expenses of the business and which are exceptionally large.

Net interest - on the profit and loss account, interest received by the business minus interest paid out.

Net profit - broadly defined as gross profit minus operating costs; in the accounts of a limited company, it may be defined as profit on ordinary activities before interest and taxation.

Profit and loss account - a historical record of the revenues and costs of the business, the resulting profit or loss and how that profit or loss has been distributed over a period of time, such as a year.

Profit on ordinary activities after taxation or profit after taxation or net profit after taxation - gross profit minus overheads including net interest payable minus tax on profits.

Profit on ordinary activities before taxation or profit before taxation or net profit before taxation - gross profit minus overheads including net interest payable.

Profit quality - occurs when profits are sustained over a period of time; there is low profit quality if profit in one time period is mainly due to some one-off factor which is not sustainable.

Trading account - the part of the profit and loss account which shows how gross profit is calculated from turnover and cost of sales.

Turnover - in the profit and loss account, the value of sales for a business over a period of time.

(Ricardo is) a fundamentally strong company with an internationally recognised brand and an enviable technical reputation. However, the world's vehicle manufacturers have, with few exceptions, been going through a period of depressed demand and depressed prices and it is inevitable that suppliers to the industry have experienced very difficult trading conditions... .

This has been a very difficult year for the company. In the first half, three sudden programme cancellations by customers impacted the order book. The management team responded quickly to restructure the business to the lower demand levels and this, together with an improved order intake, allowed the company to exit the year with the majority of its activities trading profitably. However, the depressed trading during the first nine months, coupled with the exceptional costs of restructuring, have resulted in an overall loss for the year.

Source: adapted from Chairman's statement, Ricardo plc, Annual Report and Accounts, 2004.

Ricardo plc is a British company with technical centres in the UK, North America, Germany and the Czech Republic. It provides technology, engineering services and strategic consulting to the world's automotive industries. For example, Ricardo now has a leading world position in the development of hybrid vehicle systems which might use a combination of battery power and an ordinary petrol engine. It also is a leading developer of clean diesel and gasoline engine technologies which offer improved fuel economy, reducing CO_2 and low regulated exhaust emissions.

It gains its revenues by selling its technology to companies such as Ford. It also receives contracts from the world's leading motor car companies to develop new technologies and to provide consulting services.

	2004 £000	2003 £000
Turnover	146,242	136,608
Cost of sales	(106,722)	(90,127)
Gross profit	39,520	46,481
Administrative expenses	(41,478)	(31,208)
Operating profit	(1,958)	15,273
Net interest	(800)	565
Profit/(loss) on ordinary activities before taxation	(2,758)	15,038
Tax on (loss)/profit	1,629	(3,160)
Profit on ordinary activities after taxation	(1,129)	12,378
Dividends	(4,632)	(4,677)
Retained (loss)/profit	(5,761)	7,701
Earnings per ordinary share	(2.6p)	24.6p

Source: adapted from Ricardo plc, Annual Report and Accounts, 2004.

Table 71.8 Profit and loss account for Ricardo plc for the year ended 30 June

1 (a) Explain why Ricardo had a difficult year in 2004. (4 marks)
   (b) Use the profit and loss account to analyse the impact of these difficulties on turnover, costs and profits. (16 marks)
2 To what extent does the profit and loss account for 2003 and 2004 show the long term strengths and weaknesses of Ricardo plc? (20 marks)

72 Balance sheets

Cardo plc

Knowledge Cardo plc is a global supplier of specialist fibre products.

Application By law, Cardo has to publish an *Annual Report and Accounts*. In this Annual Report, it has to provide a *balance sheet*. This is a record of its *assets*, such as *fixed assets*, *stocks*, *debtors* and *cash*, and *liabilities*, such as *loans* and *overdrafts* and *trade creditors*, as well as its *capital* and *reserves*.

Analysis The financial year to 31 March 2004 was a difficult one for Cardo. Sales were down and difficult market conditions forced it to engage in rationalisation of some of its operations resulting in redundancies and closures. The effects of this can be seen on the balance sheet. Tangible fixed assets, such as factory buildings and machines, fell by 14 per cent. Stocks, debtors and cash at the bank all fell. So did did short term loans and overdrafts and trade creditors. Some of the cash raised in disposal of assets was used to repay long term loans which fell by 14 per cent. Overall, total net assets, and therefore shareholders funds, fell by 10 per cent.

Evaluation 2003-2004 saw Cardo move from profit to loss. Arguably, its chosen course of action, rationalising and downsizing, was the most effective available to it. Faced with downward pressure on prices from low cost competitors operating out of cheap labour countries like China, it had to cut costs. This was bound to have a negative effect on the balance sheet, reducing the company's net assets. However, it hoped that despite having fewer net assets, it could return to profitability in the future.

The balance sheet

The BALANCE SHEET is a record or account of the assets of a business (what it owns) and its liabilities, capital and reserves (what it owes). It shows the resources owned by a business (assets) and the sources of finance (liabilities, capital and reserves). Unlike the profit and loss account (see unit 71), which is a record of turnover, costs and profit over a period of time, the balance sheet shows assets, liabilities, capital and reserves at a point in time, like 30 April or 31 December.

The balance sheet must always balance. What the business owns must always equal what it owes. This will be explained in more detail below.

Assets

ASSETS are what is owned. They are resources such as buildings, machinery, cash or stocks. These resources are used by the business to produce goods or services. On the balance sheet, assets are divided into fixed and current assets.

- Fixed assests are assets which are held and used by a business over a long period of time. In accounting terms, this is defined as over one year. So buildings and machinery or long term share investments in other companies would be classified as fixed assets. Fixed assets can be tangible assets, financial investments or intangible assets.
- CURRENT ASSETS are those assets held and used by a business for a short period of time. In accounting terms, this is defined as less than one year. The main current assets of a business are likely to be debtors, stocks and cash.

Fixed assets

Fixed assets can be tangible assets, financial investments or intangible assets.

Northgate plc is a company which rents vehicles and sells a range of fleet car products to other businesses. Its core market is in the UK, but it has also expanded into the Spanish rental market. The company's tangible fixed assets are shown in Table 72.1.

	2004 £000	2003 £000
Vehicles for hire	379,346	366,976
Land & buildings	19,601	16,954
Plant, equipment and fittings	2,736	3,519
Motor vehicles	1,005	1,101

Source: adapted from Northgate plc, *Annual Report & Accounts, 2004.*

Table 72.1 *Northgate plc: tangible fixed assets as at 30 April*

1 **Explain, using examples, what are the main tangible fixed assets of Northgate plc.**
2 **Northgate plc was a growing business in 2003-4 with turnover up 5 per cent over the year. How and why have the tangible fixed assets of the group changed between 30 April 2003 and 2004?**

Tangible assets TANGIBLE ASSETS are physical assets ('tangible' means 'touchable'). In accounting, tangible assets are usually referred to as tangible fixed assets, i.e. tangible assets which have a life of more than a year. Tangible fixed assets could include property, machinery, equipment and motor vehicles owned by a business.

Investments INVESTMENTS on the balance sheet are longer term financial assets which will be held for more than one year. An investment could be a long term loan to another organisation. For example, a company might own financial stocks (see unit 25). The British government issues stocks to finance its spending. It pays interest on outstanding stocks which provides an income to any company holding the stocks. Some companies also own shares in other companies. They may have bought the shares hoping to buy the company at a later date or just as an investment. For a shareholding to be classified as an investment on a set of accounts, it has to be less than 20 per cent of the total shares in the other company. If the holding is between 20 -50 per cent, the other company is said to be an **associated company**. If it is over **50 per cent**, the other company is a **subsidiary** and the main company is a **holding** or **parent** company. The shares held in associated companies and subsidiaries would be included in the assets of the main company on the balance sheet.

Intangible assets INTANGIBLE ASSETS are assets which exist but cannot be touched unlike tangible assets. Most intangible assets are not recorded on UK balance sheets. This is because, according to UK Financial Reporting Standards, the value of intangible assets should not be included on the balance sheet unless they have been bought from another business or individual and can be identified separately. This is because of the difficulty in putting an objective valuation on them. However, when intangible assets are bought, they can be classified into a number of different types.

One common type of intangible asset is GOODWILL. The value of a business may be far more than the value of its tangible and financial assets. This is because it may have loyal customers or it may be sited at a favourable location for instance. If you wish to set up in business as a dentist or a general practitioner doctor, it could be easier to buy an existing business practice than to set up from scratch. This is because existing practices have an established list of patients who will carry on using the services offered. Goodwill is the name given to this value of the business over and above its net tangible and financial asset value.

Another intangible asset is the value of **brands** (see unit 10) and **trademarks**. Brands and trademarks like KitKat, Coca-Cola or Gap have an enormous value. They represent established successful products or product ranges within the market. The cost to other businesses of launching new competing products is likely to be high and, even then, the product might not to gain the market share of these established brands. So the value of successful brands and trademarks reflects a mix of these start-up costs and the profit that is predicted to be earned in the future from them.

Patents and copyright (see unit 59) can also be intangible assets because they give a business a competitive edge and the potential for future revenue and profits. Another intangible asset is **research and development**. This contributes to the creation of new products and new streams of income.

Current assets

A current asset is an asset belonging to a business which can easily be turned into cash or is cash. In accounting terms, current assets can be turned into cash within 12 months. The three main current assets are usually stocks, debtors and cash itself (see unit 28).

- **Stocks** are stocks of raw materials, work in progress and finished goods.
- **Debtors** are customers which owe the business money for products which have already been delivered. Debtors arise because many businesses have to extend **trade credit** to their customers.
- **Cash** is either 'cash in hand', in notes and coins, or deposits with a bank which can be withdrawn immediately, such as by writing a cheque.

Current assets are LIQUID ASSETS. The liquidity of an asset is the extent to which an asset can be turned into cash without losing its value. Cash is the most liquid of all assets because it is cash itself. Stocks and debtors are fairly liquid because they can be turned into cash within a few months. A fixed asset like a machine is illiquid. Although it might be possible to sell it on the second-hand market within a few months, the price paid is not likely to reflect its value to the business, as it will have to be sold at a discount.

Liabilities

A LIABILITY on a balance sheet is money which is owed to creditors by a business. There are two main types of liability.

- CURRENT LIABILITIES are monies which are owed and which need to be paid within 12 months. On balance sheets they are sometimes called CREDITORS: AMOUNTS FALLING DUE WITHIN ONE YEAR.
- LONG TERM LIABILITIES are monies which are owed but don't need repaying for at least 12 months. They are sometimes called CREDITORS: AMOUNTS FALLING DUE AFTER ONE YEAR.

Current liabilities There is a variety of current liabilities that a business might have.

- **Trade creditors** (see unit 28) are suppliers which have delivered products but which have yet to be paid. So the business owes these suppliers money.
- Businesses also owe a variety of **tax payments** to government. Businesses keep back part of their employees' wage packets as income tax and employees' National Insurance contributions under the PAYE (Pay As You Earn) scheme. Businesses also have to pay their own tax on wages called employers' National Insurance contributions. They have to pay Business Rates to local authorities on their premises. They are charged taxes on their profits, the main tax being corporation tax. Finally, most businesses charge VAT and other indirect taxes on products to customers. All these taxes have to be paid to the government but they are not handed over immediately on receipt. Instead they are paid every month or three months or a year. So businesses often have tax monies owing.
- **Bank overdrafts** (see unit 25) are monies borrowed from a bank through an overdraft facility on the current account of the business.
- **Short term loans** are typically loans from banks (see unit 25) which must be repaid within the next 12 months.

- **Dividends** are payments to shareholders out of profit which have been announced by a company but which have yet to be paid.
- Some businesses have **lease** agreements which have less than one year to run. These would therefore be classified as a current liability rather than a long term liability.

Long term liabilities The main long term liabilities for a business are likely to be hire purchase and lease payments on equipment or property, and loans including mortgages. Businesses may take out **hire purchase** and **lease payments** (see unit 25) where the contracts last for more than one year. For example, a business may have a lease contract on the premises it uses which has another 10 years to run. Or it has just bought machinery on hire purchase where payments were spread over two years. So these would both be long term liabilities because the contracts today have more than one year to run. The other main type of long term liability is **loans** from banks (see unit 25) where the loan will not be fully repaid within the next 12 months. Where the loan is secured on property, it is called a **mortgage**. Large companies with access to stock markets may also issue **corporate bonds** (also called **stocks** or **debentures**, see unit 25).

Capital and reserves

A business has assets and liabilities. The difference between the two (assets - liabilities) is the **net assets** of the company. This is equal to the CAPITAL AND RESERVES on the balance sheet of a company. The shareholders of a company own the capital and reserves of the business.

Share capital SHARE CAPITAL is the amount of money paid for shares by investors in the company. It does not represent the current value of those shares on a stock market, which may be greater or lesser than the amount originally paid by investors. Share capital usually is not repaid to the shareholders during the lifetime of a business. But it might be repaid, for example, if the business is sold or if there is a share buyback (see unit 81).

Reserves The reserves of the business can take a number of forms.

- **Retained profit or profit and loss account** RETAINED PROFIT or the PROFIT AND LOSS ACCOUNT is the accumulation of monies kept by the company over the years from the annual profit it has made. It is the sum of the retained profit shown on the profit and loss account from previous years. Normally, when the company makes a profit, it will set some of it aside as retained profit and therefore reserves will rise. Part of these reserves might also be used to distribute to shareholders as dividends in future. But reserves can fall if the company has a negative retained profit figure for that year. For example, the company may make a net loss of £2 million after tax. If it decides to pay no dividend to shareholders, the reserves on the balance sheet would go down by £2 million. Reserves are unlikely to be cash held by the company. The reserves have been used to buy a variety of assets, from machines and buildings to brands to stock.
- **Revaluation reserve** Sometimes, the value of a fixed asset like a building increases. So the assets of the business will increase. This increase then has to be balanced in the capital and reserves section of the balance sheet by an increase in the REVALUATION RESERVE.
- **Share premium account** The SHARE PREMIUM ACCOUNT shows the difference between the value of new shares issued by the company and their nominal value. For example, the nominal value of a share might have been £2. The company might decide to issue 2 million new shares. Say the company sold them for £6 each. So each share is worth £4 more than the nominal price, a total of £8 million (2 million x £4). This £8 million would be entered on the share premium account as it is a rise in the reserves of the business.

Company balance sheets

Table 72.3 shows the balance sheet for Telford Homes plc at 31 March 2003 and 2004. Telford Homes is a small new

Total Systems plc is a computer software company. It specialises in providing open software systems for the financial services industry, mainly in the insurance, warranty and pension fund management sectors.

	2004 £	2003 £
Called up share capital	525,744	525,173
Share premium account	82,302	80,189
Profit and loss account	3,345,311	3,730,149
Equity shareholders' funds	3,953,357	3,730,149

Source: adapted from Total Systems plc, *Annual Report and Accounts*, 2004.

Table 72.2 *Total Systems plc: capital and reserves as at 31 March*

1 **Explain how the capital and reserves for Total Systems changed between 2003 and 2004.**
2 **The company runs a share option scheme for its directors which allows directors to buy new shares in the company. On 25 April 2003, one of the directors bought 11,419 new shares in the company. These were the only new shares issued by the company during the year. Explain how this sale affected the capital and reserves.**
3 **Explain whether the company made a profit or loss for the year to 31 March 2004.**

house builder.

Table 72.3 shows the balance sheet in the format published in the company's Annual Report and Accounts. The way in which the balance sheet is laid out must conform with Companies Acts and Financial Reporting Standards issued by the Accounting Standards Board. The Annual Report also contains 22 tables of notes to the accounts. Ten of these give further details about the balance sheet. Notes to the main accounts are found in all published accounts for plcs.

	2004 £000	2003 £000
Fixed assets		
Tangible assets	583	681
Intangible assets	-	-
Investments	255	-
	830	681
Current assets		
Stocks and work in progress	24,444	19,810
Debtors	25,533	18,152
Cash at bank and in hand	848	239
	50,825	38,201
Creditors: Amounts falling due within one year	(29,921)	(25,427)
Net current assets/(liabilities)	20,904	12,774
Total assets less current liabilities	21,742	13,455
Creditors: Amounts falling due after more than one year	(75)	(109)
Provisions for liabilities and charges	-	(4)
Net assets	21,667	13,342
Capital and reserves		
Called up share capital	2,912	2,518
Share premium account	12,310	7,850
Profit and loss account	6,445	2,974
Equity shareholders' funds	21,667	13,342

Source: adapted from Telford Homes plc, *Annual Report and Accounts*, 2004.

Table 72.3 *Telford Homes plc: balance sheet as at 31 March 2004*

Fixed assets Telford Homes owned fixed assets worth £838,000 at 31 March 2004. These were made up of a mix of tangible assets and investments. Its two main tangible assets were properties and motor cars. It had no intangible assets.

Current assets Current assets are stocks, debtors and cash at bank and in hand. One main current asset for Telford Homes is property under construction which it expects to complete and sell within the next 12 months. The other main current asset is debtors. These are customers who have received goods but have not yet paid for them.

Creditors: amounts falling due within one year These are organisations to whom the company owes money that has to be repaid within 12 months. They include banks which have extended overdrafts and short term loans, suppliers who have extended trade credit to Telford Homes, tax authorities owed a variety of taxes, and shareholders owed dividends.

Net current assets/(liabilities) Balance sheets typically show net current assets. This is an important piece of information

because net current assets (current assets minus current liabilities) are the **working capital** (see unit 28) of the company. They show the extent to which the company can pay its immediate expenses.

Total assets less current liabilities This shows the value of all assets less what the company must pay its creditors within the next 12 months. It shows how much the company has in assets to pay its long term creditors, those that need paying after more than one year from 31 March.

Creditors: amounts falling due after more than one year This shows how much the company owes to its long term creditors, those to whom it owes money payable in the period after the next 12 months.

Provisions for liabilities and charges The accounts for Telford Homes show that it has included another liability, 'Provisions for liabilities and charges'. The main provision in 2004 was for **deferred taxation**, tax which the company knows will have to paid at some point in the future.

Net assets NET ASSETS are total assets minus total liabilities. Total assets are the fixed assets plus the current assets of the company. Similarly, total liabilities are liabilities to be repaid in over 12 months' time ('amounts falling due after more than one year') plus current liabilities. The net assets value is equal to the value of capital and reserves.

Capital and reserves Called-up share capital is the amount of ISSUED or AUTHORISED CAPITAL that the business has asked shareholders to pay. When it is paid it is called paid up share capital. The business also has reserves in the form of a share premium account and a profit and loss account.

Telford Homes is a small property construction company specialising in building new homes. It works mainly in the East End of London. The company is relatively new having only been founded in 2000. In the financial year to 31 March 2004, its turnover increased by 62 per cent, after strong growth in previous years. In the last month of the financial year to 31 March 2004, the company issued £4.8 million of new shares, giving it extra finance to fund its growth.

Look at Table 72.3 showing the balance sheet for Telford Homes.

1 **Suggest why the strong growth in turnover for Telford Homes might have led to an increase during the year to March 2004 in:**
   (a) **stocks and work in progress;**
   (b) **debtors;**
   (c) **cash at bank and in hand;**
   (d) **short term creditors.**
2 **Telford Homes saw a significant increase in its profit in the year to March 2004. Explain how this is shown in the balance sheet.**
3 **Explain how the £4.8 million share issue is shown on the capital and reserves section of the balance sheet.**
4 **Using the balance sheet, suggest how the company used the cash it raised in the share issue.**

Note that published company must show figures for a two year period, the previous two financial years.

The balance sheet must always balance

Balance sheets must always balance. The assets of a business show the value of what it owns. The liabilities show what it owes to organisations such as banks, suppliers and the tax authorities. Assets minus liabilities equal the net assets of the business. The owners of the business have a claim on this. For a company, it is equal to the capital and reserves. So:

Assets - liabilities = Net assets = Capital + reserves

The values on balance sheets are constantly changing as assets and liabilities change. To see how these changes might occur and how any change still leads to the balance sheet balancing, consider the following two examples.

Sales have increased An increase in sales will be shown on the profit and loss account (see unit 71). But this increase will almost certainly have an impact on the balance sheet drawn up at the end of the year. An increase in sales is likely to lead to an increase in debtors who have received products but not yet paid for them. Stocks too may rise to cope with increased production. Cash in hand and at the bank may have risen as increased sales could lead to an increase in the flow of cash through the business. These are all current assets. But they will to some extent be offset by an increase in current liabilities. More sales leading to more production is likely to mean an increase in orders to suppliers. They could extend trade credit and so creditors are likely to rise. Increased sales could also mean higher VAT receipts from customers which will be held by the business before being passed on to Customs and Excise. So a rise in current assets is likely to also be associated with a rise in current liabilities, but not by as much. Net current assets (i.e. working capital) could rise and therefore net assets will rise. If this happens, it has to be matched by an increase in capital and reserves. If sales have risen, hopefully those sales will have been profitable. So profits will have risen. Part of that increase in profits may have been kept back by the company as retained profit, shown on the profit and loss account and then transferred onto the balance sheet. If net assets have risen by £300 000, then this will be matched by an increase in the profit and loss account on the balance sheet of £300 000.

A company buys a new factory A new factory will raise the value of fixed assets, say by £2 million. The money to pay the £2 million must have come from somewhere. The company may have taken out a loan, say for £1.5 million which is a liability. So net assets have increased by £0.5 million. The remaining £0.5 million may have come from an issue of new shares, which will increase capital and reserves by £0.5 million. So again the balance sheet has balanced.

The balance sheets of sole proprietors and partnerships

So far this unit has given examples of balance sheets from the published accounts of limited companies. The balance sheets of sole proprietors and partnerships are similar to those for limited companies. They list the assets of the business under fixed assets and currents assets, and the liabilities under current liabilities and long term liabilities. But they differ from those of companies under the capital section of the account. This can be seen from Table 72.4 which shows the balance sheet for a sole trader.

Opening capital This is the amount of money that the sole trader has put into the business to start it up and to finance its growth.

Capital introduced This is the amount of money that the sole trader has put into the business over the past 12 months (or over whatever period the accounts of the business have been drawn up).

Net profit This is the net profit the business has made this year.

	2004 £
Fixed assets	
Van	4 500
Equipment	6 700
	11 200
Current assets	
Stocks	3 500
Debtors	1 400
Cash at bank and in hand	2 300
	7 200
Current liabilities	
Creditors	(1 600)
Working capital	5 600
Net assets	16 800
Financed by	
Opening capital	15 200
Capital introduced	300
Net profit	17 400
	32 900
Drawings	(16 100)
	16 800

Table 72.4 *Balance sheet for Fiona King as at 31 January 2004*

Drawings DRAWINGS are what the sole trader takes out of the business. It is the equivalent of a wage and a dividend which would be paid to a worker and a shareholder in a limited company.

The balance The total capital is equal to the net assets of the business. As with companies, the net assets are equal to the value of what belongs to the owners of the business.

Using the balance sheet to evaluate performance

There is a large number of ways in which a balance sheet can be used to evaluate the performance of a business. To do this, however, almost always involves:
- either comparing balance sheets for the same business over a period of time;
- or comparing businesses in the same industry at the same point in time.

Some key indicators include the following.

Fixed assets A steady growth in fixed assets for a business over time would suggest growing sales and possibly growing profit. If sales and profits are not rising, a growth in fixed assets would suggest inefficiency. More equipment, for example, is not associated with a rise in production. Comparing two similar businesses of the same size by sales in the same industry, a business with significantly higher fixed assets than its competitor would again suggest inefficiency. A sudden fall in fixed assets could indicate a downsizing of the business. This might be a bad sign if the business is in difficulties and being forced to close plant or sell off part of itself. It could be a good sign that it is tackling inefficiency or concentrating its resources on higher profit margin sales.

Long term liabilities Long term liabilities are mainly loans or leases on property or equipment. Sharp sudden rises in long term liabilities might indicate a business in trouble because it is having to increase its borrowings to survive. Equally it could be a sign of strong growth in the business. In order to finance the purchase of fixed assets, or increase its working capital, it has borrowed more money.

Current assets and current liabilities Current assets are mainly trade debtors, stocks and cash. A rise in trade debtors and stocks and a fall in cash could indicate problems. The business could be failing to collect its bills on time. Rising stocks might indicate falling sales whilst production continues at the same level as before. Falling cash levels could indicate cash flow problems. Equally, a rise in trade debtors and stocks could indicate a growth in sales because extra sales are likely to generate higher levels of trade debt and require higher stock levels. Current liabilities include trade creditors and short term borrowing, including overdraft borrowing. A rise in current liabilities could indicate over-purchase of stocks from suppliers and an increase in borrowing to finance payments at a time of falling sales. Equally, it could indicate growth in the business as higher sales lead to higher orders to suppliers and a need for greater borrowing to finance the growth.

Working capital The amount and balance of working capital needed by a business is discussed in detail in units 73 and 77. However, in summary, the balance sheet gives an indication of whether a business has too much or too little working capital. If it has too much, it is being inefficient in its use of resources. If it has too little, it risks overtrading (see unit 26) and potentially being forced out of business by its creditors. The balance sheet also gives an indication of whether current assets and current liabilities are at approximately the right levels. Some businesses, for example, might have the right amount of total working capital but have too much stock and too little cash. Imbalances in the amounts of different types of current asset and current liability will lead to the inefficient performance of a business.

Reserves If there has been a reduction in reserves over a period of time, this could be due to a number of reasons. The first is that the company has gone into loss and is financing the loss from the reserves it has built up over the years. Alternatively, it could be that the company is paying out more in dividends to keep shareholders happy than has been earned in profit after tax. Adopting this strategy one year might be acceptable. However, doing it over a period of years is likely to weaken the company's ability to invest for the future.

Another explanation could be that the company has purchased another company for a price which is greater than its tangible assets. This means that the price has included intangible assets such as goodwill. This is likely to be written

keyterms

Assets - resources which a business owns, such as buildings, machinery, cash or stocks.

Balance sheet - that part of the accounts of a business which shows its assets, liabilities and capital; the balance sheet must balance because assets = liabilities + capital.

Capital or Capital and Reserves - that part of the company balance sheet which shows the value of the business owned by the shareholders; it is equal to assets minus liabilities.

Current assets - assets held and used by a business for a short period of time; in accounting this is defined as less than one year.

Current liabilities - money which is owed by a business and which must be repaid within the next 12 months.

Creditors: amounts falling due within one year - liabilities which a business will have to pay within the next 12 months.

Creditors: amounts falling due after one year - liabilities which a business will have to pay from 12 months onwards.

Drawings - money taken out of a business by a sole trader or partners in a partnership.

Goodwill - the value of the business over and above the rest of its net asset value; it represents intangible assets such as brand loyalty.

Investments - a financial asset which typically is a shareholding in another company but could also be long term loans to other organisations.

Intangible asset - assets which exist but do not have a physical existence, such as trademarks, patents and goodwill.

Issued or authorised share capital - the maximum amount of capital that can be raised by the company by issuing shares.

Liabilities - money which is owed by a business or other organisation or individual to its creditors.

Liquid asset - an asset which can easily be turned into cash without losing its value.

Long term liabilities - money which is owed by a business and which will be repaid in over 12 months time.

Net assets - total assets minus total liabilities.

Retained profit or profit and loss account - on the balance sheet, the cumulative amount of profit that has been retained by a company and not distributed to shareholders during the lifetime of the company. These reserves are owned by the shareholders and are used, for instance, to finance investment, cover losses when the profit and loss account goes into the red, or to pay dividends when the company has not earned enough profit in the year to cover the dividend which is being paid out.

Revaluation reserve - the increase in value of assets such as property which is recorded on the balance sheet and which belong to the shareholders as a reserve.

Share capital - the original value of the shares of a company.

Share premium account - the account on the balance sheet which shows the difference between the amount new shares in the company were sold for and their nominal value.

Tangible assets - assets which are physical; the term usually refers to tangible fixed assets which have a life of more than one year.

off in the accounts by reducing the reserves. Hopefully, the new larger company will be successful. But all takeovers carry risks and it could be that the shareholders' funds will be permanently reduced if the larger company performs poorly.

One number on the balance sheet is unlikely to give much information on its own. To evaluate performance it is necessary to compare a number of figures, perhaps over time or between businesses. One number also cannot be taken in isolation. As the above shows, it is only by looking at several numbers on the balance sheet or the balance sheet and the profit and loss account, that an accurate evaluation can be made.

Limitations of balance sheets as a measure of financial performance

The balance sheet, like the profit and loss account (see unit 71), can be used to evaluate the financial performance of a business. But using it for this purpose has considerable limitations, many of which are similar to those of the profit and loss account.

Trends The balance sheet shows assets and liabilities at a point in time. In most cases, however, it is necessary to compare balance sheets for the same business over a period of time to evaluate performance. A single balance sheet is unlikely to be very informative.

Other businesses It is often useful to compare balance sheets for the same business over a period of time. But equally it is useful to compare balance sheets between businesses in the same industry. Without such financial benchmarking (see unit 48), a single balance sheet for a single business may be of limited use.

Other financial data The balance sheet only gives data about assets, liabilities and capital and reserves. Much more financial data is needed to assess accurately the performance of a business.

Other business data The balance sheet only gives data about the finances of a business. Financial data is only one source of data for evaluating the overall performance of a business.

Past, present and future The balance sheet is a record of the past performance of a business. So it can be used as one piece of evidence to evaluate the performance of the business in the past. But it is not necessarily a good indication of present or future performance.

The level of detail in the account The more detail in the balance sheet, the more information available to be analysed. But published balance sheets, even with notes, found in the accounts of plcs give very limited detail. The less detail, the more difficult it is to evaluate performance.

'Window dressing' the accounts For sole traders and partnerships, balance sheets are typically prepared for the tax authorities. There is a temptation to 'massage' the figures to limit the amount of tax paid. Companies too may manipulate their accounts to present a better picture than is actually the case (see unit 76 for ways of doing this).

Special characteristics of individual accounts Balance sheets can have special features which need to be noted in evaluating performance. Occasionally a business will change its tax year and so the day for which the balance sheet is prepared is not the same date in the year as previously. For some businesses, this can be important. The balance sheet for a clothing retailer like Next, which could be very dependent upon sales in the Christmas period, might show different proportions of current assets and liabilities for 31 December than, say, 30 April. Equally businesses may choose to change ways in which items are recorded. For example, a company might decide to revalue its property holdings upwards, increasing the value of fixed assets but also increasing the revaluation reserve on capital. Often an increase in fixed capital is a sign that the company is expanding and needs more production facilities. But in this case, the increase in fixed assets isn't an indication of increased sales but simply higher property values.

✓checklist

1. What is shown on a balance sheet?
2. What is the difference between a fixed asset and a current asset?
3. What is the difference between a tangible asset and an intangible asset?
4. Why are stocks and debtors classified as assets for a business?
5. What is the difference between a current liability and a long term liability?
6. Why are trade creditors and bank overdrafts a current liability for a business?
7. Explain the difference between share capital and the share premium account on a balance sheet.
8. How would the profit and loss account on a balance sheet be affected if a company made a loss for the year?
9. Explain what a significant rise in long term liabilities for a company might indicate about its economic performance.
10. A company reports that its net assets have increased by 5 per cent over the year. Explain what factors need to be taken into account when considering whether this shows an improvement in the performance of the company.

F.G. Duggins Printing Ltd had two difficult
years in the financial years to February 2004 and 2005.
The company prints security badges and cards, and labels
for manufacturers to place on packaging, as well as
operating a more traditional book printing and paper
supply business. 2004-05 saw profits fall from 2003-04
as trading conditions worsened due to a fall in consumer
confidence and a fall in export orders due to the high
value of the pound. In March 2004, Duggins bought
Defax, a business specialising in the sale of printing
services to small businesses and the general public, for
£11.8 million. It paid for this with a mixture of a share
issue and extra long term borrowings. Unfortunately,
Defax turned out to be in less good shape than thought at
the time of acquisition and its £2 million loss for the year
more than outweighed the reduced profit made in the rest
of Duggins.

During 2005-06, Duggins intends to restructure Defax.
Managers of outlets with less than an annual turnover of
£200 000 will be given 6 months to increase their
turnover or their outlet will close and they will lose their
job. Head office has been given a target of cutting
overhead costs by £1 million. Much greater use will be
made of leasing equipment rather than purchasing it
outright.

F.G. Duggins Printing Ltd
Balance sheet as at 28 February

	2005 £000	2004 £000
Fixed assets		
Intangible assets	6,274	5,395
Tangible assets	28,486	19,476
	34,760	24,871
Current assets		
Stocks	8,437	7,759
Debtors	29,570	20,314
Cash at bank and in hand	12,482	9,523
	50,489	37,596
Creditors: Amounts falling due within one year		
Bank loans, overdrafts and leasing	10,747	7,635
Trade and other creditors	35,639	24,693
Corporation tax	2,647	3,693
Dividends proposed	0	598
	49,033	36,619
Net current assets	1,456	977
Total assets less current liabilities	36,216	25,848
Creditors: Amounts falling due after more than one year		
Bank loans	19,629	15,395
Other creditors	4,694	3,862
	24,323	19,257
Net assets	11,893	6,591
Capitals and reserves		
Called up share capital	4,368	3,760
Share premium account	9,572	0
Revaluation reserve	45	23
Profit and loss account	1,484	2,808
Other reserves[1]	(3,576)	0
Equity shareholders' funds	11,893	6,591

1 Duggins paid more for the Defax than the value of its tangible assets. It decided to account for part of the goodwill thus purchased by putting it into 'other reserves' as a negative value.

Table 72.5 *F.G. Duggins Printing Ltd, balance sheet as at 28 February*

1 (a) Using the balance sheet, examine how the takeover of Defax might have affected tangible assets, debtors and creditors falling due after more than one year. (12 marks)
(b) Discuss whether the capital and reserves on the balance sheet show that 2004-05 was a difficult year for Duggins. (8 marks)
2 To what extent has Duggins performed poorly over the financial period 2004-05? (20 marks)

73 Working capital

Walker Greenbank

Knowledge   Walker Greenbank plc is an international group of companies which design, manufacture, market and distribute wall coverings, furnishing fabrics and associated products for the consumer market. The financial year to 31 January 2004 was a difficult year for Walker Greenbank. It made a loss on ordinary activities before taxation of £4 million although this was down from the £8 million loss the previous year. During the year it had bought Sanderson, an upmarket manufacturer of wall coverings and furnishing fabrics.

Application   Walker Greenback needs to have *working capital*. Its two most important *current assets* are *stocks* and *debtors*. In 2004, these accounted for 85 per cent of total current assets. Its main *current liabilities* were *bank overdrafts*, *loans* and *trade creditors*. These accounted for 82 per cent of current liabilities. *Net current assets*, or *working capital*, was valued at £3.1 million with a *current ratio* of 1.1:1, compared to £7.2 million and 1:1.4 the previous year.

Analysis   The acquisition of Sanderson brought cost savings due to economies of scale. However, when purchased, stocks of the best selling Sanderson ranges had been allowed to run down. This caused delays in getting orders to customers and some sales will have been lost. The Sanderson acquisition also coincided with a 56 per cent fall in the amount of working capital over a period when sales turnover fell only 17 per cent. This was due to a rise in short term loans from £307 000 to £4.3 million to finance the acquisition of Sanderson.

Evaluation   By January 2004, it could be argued that Walker Greenbank had too little working capital. However, the £4 million of short term loans were paid off in May 2004 when the company sold off assets in Milton Keynes and completed a sale and leaseback deal of its Warner Archive. This prompt repayment of the loans helped restore working capital to a healthy level. The company needs, however, to maintain a tight control on its levels of working capital if it is to be profitable.

Adapted from Walker Greenbank plc, Annual Report and Accounts, 2004.

Working capital defined

Working capital (defined in unit 28) is the net value of the short term or current assets (see unit 72) used in a business.

Working capital = current assets - current liabilities

Current assets are typically stocks, debtors and cash. Current liabilities are trade creditors, short term borrowings like overdrafts and other money owed which needs to be paid within the next 12 months, such as tax or dividends (see units 28 and 72). Working capital is usually explained as the capital a business has which can be used in its day-to-day trading, for example to pay electricity and gas bills.

The working capital cycle

Working capital is sometimes called CIRCULATING CAPITAL because current assets and liabilities are continually being created and disposed of in a WORKING CAPITAL CYCLE.

Figure 73.1 shows the working capital cycle for a manufacturer of steel tubes. It has a number of parts.
- To manufacture steel tubes, the business has to purchase materials and components which then become stocks.
- The purchases do not need to be paid for immediately because suppliers usually give trade credit. So trade creditors, a liability, are created.
- Steel tubes are then made and they become finished stock before being sent out to customers.

- Customers are given one month to pay and so become trade debtors.
- When payments are eventually made, this becomes cash.
- The cash is used to pay trade creditors, workers, taxes, interest and loans and dividends to shareholders.
- The cycle restarts as more steel tubes are made.

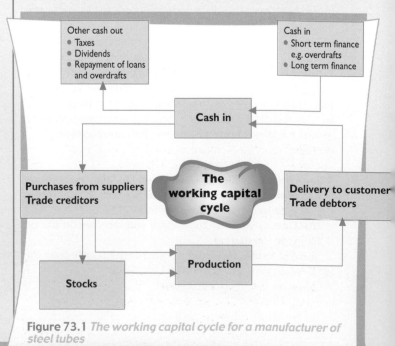

Figure 73.1 *The working capital cycle for a manufacturer of steel tubes*

Different working capital needs

Different businesses have different working capital needs.

Size of business Sales typically generate a need for stocks, trade credit and cash. Hence the larger the business, the larger the amount of working capital there is likely to be. Equally, expanding businesses are likely to need growing amounts of working capital.

Stock levels Businesses in different industries have different needs for stocks. A window cleaning business is unlikely to carry much stock. A retailer is likely to carry considerable amounts of stock. Businesses which are able to adopt just-in-time techniques (see unit 47) will carry lower stocks than other businesses. The more stocks a business needs, the higher will be its working capital, all other things being equal.

Sherwood Group plc is a garment and lace manufacturing business which in 2003 made a loss on ordinary activities before tax of £3.5 million on a turnover of £35.4 million. The Restaurant Group plc is a company which has a portfolio of restaurants, cafes and bars in the UK including Frankie & Benny's and Cafe Uno. In 2003 it made a profit on ordinary activities before tax of £16.6 million on a turnover of £227.4 million.

	Sherwood Group £000	The Restaurant Group £000
Current assets		
Stock	6,420	2,508
Debtors	5,136	15,999
Cash at bank and in hand	6,495	526
	18,051	19,033
Current liabilities		
Trade creditors	3,132	17,795
Other taxes and social security	246	7,153
Proposed dividend	-	6,198
Other creditors	2,771	31,504
	6,149	62,650
Working capital	11,902	(43,617)

Source: adapted from Sherwood Group plc, The Restaurant Group plc, *Annual Report and Accounts*, 2003.

Table 73.1 *Working capital: Sherwood Group plc and The Restaurant Group plc, to 31 December 2003*

1 *Compare the working capital of Sherwood Group with The Restaurant Group.*
2 *Suggest why Sherwood Group had different amounts to The Restaurant Group of:*
   (a) stock;
   (b) debtors;
   (c) trade creditors;
   (d) proposed dividends.
3 *Explain why, at 31 December 2003, Sherwood Group had positive working capital whilst The Restaurant Group had negative working capital.*

Debtors and creditors The time between buying stock financed by trade credit and selling finished products can influence levels of working capital. For example, a builder may need high levels of working capital because the time between starting a project and receiving payment from the client may be long.

At the other extreme, large supermarket chains can often operate with negative working capital (i.e. the current assets are less than their current liabilities). This happens because they buy in stock from suppliers and don't pay them for at least 30 days. The stock though is sold quickly on supermarket shelves, often within days of delivery from suppliers. Customers pay cash. So large supermarket chains can operate safely owing suppliers large amounts, but having very few debtors. The result is negative working capital.

Few businesses are fortunate enough to be able to operate with negative working capital. The textbook rule is that the typical business needs around twice the amount of current assets as current liabilities to operate safely. This means that its current ratio is between 1.5:1 and 2:1 (see unit 77).

Keeping adequate levels of working capital

Businesses need to keep adequate levels of working capital. If they keep too little (ie current assets are too low and current liabilities are too high) they will start to encounter trading problems.

- If a business doesn't carry enough stocks of raw materials, it could find that production is halted when items run out of stock. If it doesn't carry enough finished stock, it might be unable to fulfil orders on time.
- If there is not enough cash in the business, it might not be able to pay its bills on time.
- If it has borrowed too much through trade credit, so it owes too much to creditors, it might be unable to pay invoices when they are due.

On the other hand, a business does not want too much working capital (ie current assets are too high and current liabilities are too low).

- Stocks are costly to keep. The more stock, the higher the cost of physically storing and handling it. The stock will need to be insured whilst it may be liable to shrinkage (a business term for theft usually by employees). Stock is also financially expensive because money tied up in stock could be used to reduce borrowing and so save interest for the business.
- Too much cash is also a problem because the cash is unlikely to be earning very high rates of interest. It could be used, perhaps, to pay back debts or to invest in higher interest long term investments.
- If debtors are high, the company could be allowing its customers too long to pay their invoices. If customers are taking 45 days on average to pay their bills when they only have 30 days credit given, the business would be losing the interest that could be earned on 15 days of credit. They also might have to spend scarce time chasing up late payments. In the UK, according to a 2004 survey by Intrum Justitia, invoices in the UK were on average paid 18 days late. 47 per cent of all invoices are paid late, with 89 per cent of businesses saying that they suffered from late payments. Small businesses are more likely to suffer

from late payment of invoices than large companies. The cost to British businesses of late payment was an estimated £20 billion, although many businesses benefit from themselves paying late.

Reasons why businesses have working capital problems

Many businesses find themselves in difficulties over working capital for a variety of reasons.

Poor control of debtors Too many businesses fail to control their debtors effectively. Partly this is because they fail to collect debts on time. Partly, it is because they give credit to businesses which fail, leaving the debt unpaid. For a small business, a bad debt, one which will not be paid, can be devastating. If large enough, it can lead to the business itself failing.

CREDIT CONTROL systems can help avoid these problems. When a new customer approaches a business wanting trade credit, it should run a credit check on the customer. This could involve getting a bank reference from the customer, checking at Companies House to get the latest accounts of the customer or getting a credit rating agency report. A credit rating agency is a business which specialises in investigating and reporting on the creditworthiness of businesses. The business then has to decide whether to trade with the potential customer and if so set a maximum amount of trade credit that will be extended to it at any one time. Once a customer has received trade credit, the business should chase any overdue payments. This may involve a mixture of telephone calls or emails requesting payment, warning letters and in the last resort taking the customer to court. Customers which are too overdue with payments should be refused any new credit.

Overstocking and understocking Many businesses carry too much stock. Overstocking may arise because the business is being run inefficiently. Managers or owners have failed to realise the business could run with less stock, or they have failed to put in place systems which would minimise stock levels. A less common problem is **understocking**, where businesses carry too little stock. This leads to production problems. For instance, if a shop runs out of a line which is selling well, then it will lose sales.

Overtrading A common problem faced by small growing businesses is **overtrading** (see unit 26). This is when a business has insufficient working capital for its level of turnover. For example, a business might accept orders but then run up against trade credit limits set by its suppliers. It therefore can't order enough stock to complete the orders. It could turn to its bankers to get a higher overdraft limit, but its bankers may refuse because of the risk of failure of the business. The great danger in this situation is that one of the creditors of the business could take legal action to recover debts outstanding. Then the business may be forced to close even though its order book is profitable.

Overborrowing Businesses can borrow too much in the short term. For example, they can take too much trade credit. This might push them up against trade credit limits, risking a refusal to supply on extra orders. If the business fails to pay on time because it does not have the cash to pay, this can lose the business discounts for paying on time. Borrowing on overdraft (see unit 25) from the bank also carries risks. If the

business experiences trading difficulties, its bank may demand repayment of the overdraft afraid that the overdraft will not repaid in the future. Being constantly at overdraft limits also doesn't allow for the unexpected. A small extra bill then could force the business to close because it does not have the cash to pay it.

F&H Welding Products is a Black Country business which specialises in high-value high-specification welding contracts. The company has recently been through difficult times but has emerged stronger and financially more prudent.

The company had always tended to live from hand to mouth financially. There never seemed to be enough cash to pay the bills. Each month, the company would have to put off paying some bills that were due, or would be putting pressure on its bank to increase its overdraft facility. Two years ago, the company took on four large contracts, all of which were completed at roughly the same time. The company offered its customers 45 days credit but was buying from suppliers which were only offering 30 days credit. None of the customers for the four large contractors paid their invoices on time. After 60 days the company was on the verge of going into liquidation because it had exhausted all its sources of cash.

Frank Smith, the managing director, then went to see the four customers personally. He explained his dire situation. Two of the customers paid within 48 hours, enough to stave off the crisis. The other two said they would pay immediately, but in fact took another 30 days to pay.

The crisis had been made worse because the company had ordered extra stock in the belief that there would be an increase in new orders. In fact, orders fell 20 per cent over six months due to fierce competition from overseas suppliers.

Having sought advice, Frank Smith changed the way the company operated. He changed all customer contracts to give only 30 days free credit. He also offered a 5 per cent discount on the invoice for paying on time, which was paid for mainly by raising prices. He refused to accept orders from customers who were persistent late payers. He also reduced his stock levels and moved to ordering from suppliers who were prepared to deliver at short notice. Although the number of orders fell by one third, turnover only fell 15 per cent and profits were hardly down at all.

1 'F&H Welding Products suffered from poor credit control and overstocking.' Explain this statement.
2 Examine how the company overcame these problems.
3 'F&H Welding Products simply didn't have enough working capital.' Discuss whether or not this was the case.

Downturns in demand When the economy goes into recession, the number of business failures increases. Often this is because of problems with working capital. In a recession, orders and sales fall. Businesses often fail to react quickly enough. They allow stocks of finished goods to increase, causing overstocking. They then experience cash flow problems as they have to pay invoices from suppliers but don't have enough cash from sales of their own goods or services. In a recession, debtors also become more of a problem. If all businesses are experiencing difficulties, they will often try to solve short term cash problems by delaying paying their bills. Recessions may also be associated with higher interest rates, as was the case in 1990-92. This increases the cost of running overdrafts and causes further cash flow problems.

Seasonal demand Businesses which face seasonal demand have to be careful that they have enough working capital at times of both peak demand and off peak demand. A toy shop, for instance, may not have enough stock in the run up to Christmas, losing potential sales. On the other hand, it may have too little cash to pay for invoices in August when sales are likely to be very low.

Solving working capital problems

Businesses experience problems with working capital either because they have the wrong amount of working capital or because there is an imbalance between the different constituents of working capital. So how might a business try to deal with such working capital problems?

Too little or too much working capital in total What if the business does not have enough working capital to operate efficiently? There is a number of solutions to this.

- Raise more long term finance (see unit 26). This could be long term loans, a share issue or putting new retained profit into working capital assets for example.
- A business unable to do this may choose to reduce its size to cope. By turning away orders and reducing sales, for example, it will need less stock and will reduce its debtors. In many cases, not enough working capital causes cash flow problems. Typically, a business with this sort of problem is continually short not just of cash but also of stocks and credit with suppliers.
- In some cases, management may manipulate working capital so that there is enough cash in the business (see unit 28). However, cash may be generated by running down stocks to crisis levels, or by increasing overdraft borrowings.

Sometimes businesses have too much working capital. They then need to identify which elements of working capital it would be best to reduce. The cash raised could then be used, for example, to pay off long term debts, increase investment in the business or to pay a higher dividend to the owners.

An imbalance in the constituents of working capital Sometimes businesses have enough working capital in total, but it is badly allocated. For example, a business may not have enough cash to pay its weekly bills (i.e. it has a liquidity problem, see unit 28). But it may be holding more stock than it needs to operate efficiently. Reducing stock levels could increase the amount of cash in the business and so resolve the problem.

Similarly, a liquidity problem might occur at the same time as a business has an excessive amount of debtors. Chasing up debtors and getting more to pay on time through better credit control will inject cash into the business.

Improving cash flow (see unit 28) may not be the problem though. It could be that a business has too much cash but too little stock. Management might be too cautious and hold excessive amounts of cash leading to production problems as stock levels are too low. Equally, management may turn away orders to avoid having to give trade credit to customers when it has more than enough cash to finance an expansion of sales.

Working capital and cash flow

It might be assumed that working capital problems are the same as cash flow problems (see unit 28). Although cash flow and working capital are interlinked, and many working capital problems are cash flow problems as well, they are not the same.

For example, one way of dealing with a cash flow problem is to increase borrowing through an overdraft facility or a short term bank loan repayable within one year. Borrowing more in the short term will lead to an increase in cash, a current asset. So it could solve a cash flow problem. But it won't increase working capital. This is because such borrowing also increases current liabilities. The money borrowed is, in theory, repayable within 12 months.

Another way in which a business can solve a cash flow problem is to run down its stocks. Not reordering stock means that less cash is leaving the business. But improving cash flow in this way leaves the amount of working capital exactly the same. On the balance sheet, all that happens immediately is that the value of stocks falls whilst the value of cash rises.

Equally, a common short term way of dealing with a cash flow problem is for a business to delay paying its bills. This increases the amount of cash in the business. But it also increases the amount of debtors. There is no change in overall working capital.

However, a business with persistent cash flow problems is likely to have a shortage of working capital. The most likely solution to both problems is to increase the equity in the business or to borrow more in the long term.

Working capital and profit

Loss making businesses are likely to have working capital problems. But so do some profitable businesses. Working

key terms

Credit control - systems for monitoring the amount of credit extended to customers, for example through trade credit, and for the prompt collection of debts.
Working or circulating capital - the net current assets (i.e. current assets minus current liabilities) of the business which are used to finance its day to day running.
Working capital cycle - the movement into and out of the business of short term assets and liabilities.

capital and profit are not the same. For example, a business might be offered a contract which would be highly profitable. However, it may be unable to take it because it doesn't have enough working capital. Payment for the contract might only arrive in four months' time, one month after completion. In the meantime, stocks need to be paid for, wages of extra workers will be owed and other costs will be incurred. If the firm's suppliers won't extend any more credit and if the firm's bank won't extend its overdraft, the finance for these expenses will not be available.

In general, businesses which are unprofitable run into working capital problems. Losses drain cash away from the business. This ultimately leads to both cash flow problems and therefore inadequate levels of working capital. However, a business may get around this by raising long term finance. An unprofitable business can survive if long term finance is being used to top up its working capital.

✓ checklist

1 What is the difference between current assets and current liabilities?
2 Why is working capital often called 'circulating capital'?
3 Explain why an expanding business will need to increase its working capital.
4 What problems might a business experience if it has too little working capital?
5 What are the costs to a business of having too much working capital?
6 Explain the difference between overtrading and overborrowing in the context of working capital.
7 How might a business solve a problem of having too little working capital?
8 Explain the difference between a cash flow problem and a working capital problem.

Barbara Frowen owns a small company which manufactures fresh and frozen pizzas. It sells these to the local catering trade as well as to local retailers. In the financial year to January 2005, the company made a small loss for the first time.

Barbara was extremely concerned about this. She contacted a local business adviser who put her in touch with Gillon Foods Ltd, a much larger food company in the same industry. After some discussions, they agreed to benchmark each other for the next 12 months. Included in this was exchanging their Annual Accounts. These were not confidential since they would be available to anyone via Companies House.

Looking at the accounts, Barbara compared her company's levels of working capital with that of Gillon Foods. The comparison is shown in Table 73.2. One thing that jumped out at her was the very low level of working capital at Gillon Foods. In discussion with managers at Gillon Foods, she found they were much more focussed on minimising stock levels and making sure that debtors paid on time. The credit control systems, for example, at Gillon Foods were very sophisticated. In contrast, Barbara realised that the credit control systems at Frowen Pizza were almost non-existent. She began to ask herself whether better management of working capital could be the key to restoring Frowen Pizza to profitability.

1 (a) Compare the current assets and current liabilities of Frowen Pizza with Gillon Foods. (8 marks)
  (b) Discuss whether Frowen Pizza has enough working capital to operate efficiently. (12 marks)
2 2004-05 was not a good year for Frowen Pizza with sales static and the company slipping into a small loss for the year. Evaluate how better management of working capital might help the company return to profitability. (20 marks)

| | at 31 January 2005 | |
	Frowen Pizza £000	Gillon Foods £000
Turnover	2,393	23,473
Profit on ordinary activities before taxation	(145)	2,423
Current assets		
Stocks	360	2,746
Debtors	845	5,134
Cash at bank and in hand	14	98
	1,219	7,978
Current liabilities		
Bank loans and overdrafts	260	2,476
Trade creditors	462	3,297
Dividend proposed	0	542
Taxation and social security	79	964
Other creditors	53	523
	854	7,802
Net current assets	365	176

Table 73.2 *Frowen Pizza Limited compared to Gillon Foods for year ended 31 January 2005*

74 Expenditure and assets

Gatekeepers

Knowledge Laura Cooper owns a small company in Manchester which specialises in making wrought iron gates and fencing. She currently employs three workers and most of her work is for domestic customers. This year, she has bought a £22 000 machine to give her metal a weathered, antique finish.

Application The £22 000 machine was an example of capital expenditure for the company. Laura reckoned that it would also increase revenue expenditure through an increase in turnover.

Analysis Laura calculated that the new machine would save £14 000 in labour costs in its first year. It would reduce the waiting list on delivery of orders from 10 weeks to 4 weeks and allow the company to take on more work. Turnover would therefore increase, in turn increasing revenue expenditure on items such as raw materials. Increased turnover should lead to an increase in profit. So, on the company's profit and loss account, turnover, costs and profit would all be up. On the balance sheet, the machine would be recorded as a fixed asset whilst the loan taken out to fund the purchase would be shown under liabilities with less than one year (the repayments due within the next 12 months) and more than one year (the rest of the loan).

Evaluation The purchase of the machine will almost certainly make production more efficient. With a growing local market, it will enable the company to expand its order book. There is a danger that the local housing market might go into a slump, as in the early 1990s. This would severely damage sales. However, all capital expenditure is risky and Laura Cooper is arguably taking an acceptable risk in increasing her short term costs.

Revenue expenditure

REVENUE EXPENDITURE or REVENUE SPENDING is spending by a business on day-to-day running expenses. In accounting, usually it is spending on items which have a life of no more than one year. Examples of revenue spending include:
- wages of staff employed;
- overheads, such as business rates, road tax on vehicles, advertising, fuel, insurance or rent on a head office;
- materials, such as iron ore for a steel producer or coffee for a coffee shop.

Revenue expenditure is recorded on the profit and loss account (see unit 71) of a business. It is included in either cost of sales or in administration and distribution expenses. An increase in revenue expenditure will be shown as an increase in costs or expenses and will reduce the gross or net profit of the business.

Capital expenditure

CAPITAL EXPENDITURE or CAPITAL SPENDING is expenditure on assets which will last more than one year. Examples of capital spending include:
- purchase of machinery and equipment;
- buying a factory or office;
- expenditure on intangible assets such as goodwill or brands.

Capital expenditure is not recorded directly on the profit and loss account or the balance sheet. However, the effect of capital expenditure might be seen in three ways.

- Spending on a fixed asset, such as machinery and equipment, will raise the value of fixed assets on the balance sheet. For example, assume that a small business had £10 000 worth of fixed assets on the balance sheet one year. Following the purchase of a new machine for £2 000 next year, the total value of fixed assets is £12 000. So capital expenditure can be seen on the balance sheet by the increase in the value of fixed assets. In practice the value of the increase is not necessarily £2 000 because of DEPRECIATION.
- Depreciation is a measure of the reduction in the useful economic life of an asset over time. It measures the wearing out, using up or consumption of an asset. For example, suppose a business buys a machine for £10 000 and estimates that depreciation is £3 000. This £3 000 is the cost of the fixed asset that has been consumed or 'worn out' over the year. So depreciation is recorded as a cost on the profit and loss account. Depreciation also reduces the value of a fixed asset. Depreciation must be deducted from the value of a fixed asset before the value is placed on the balance sheet.
- The cost of buying a new fixed asset must be recorded on the balance sheet somewhere. In practice, though, a balance sheet usually doesn't contain enough information to identify clearly from where the finance for the purchase of new fixed assets has come. For example, perhaps the purchase of a £60 000 machine was financed by increasing long term liabilities. Perhaps the £60 000 has come from greater efficiency in the use of stocks which has reduced stock levels by £60 000.

Profit and expenditure

Both revenue spending and capital spending can affect profit. Revenue spending on workers, materials and overheads like marketing are necessary to produce and sell goods and services. A coffee shop, for example, won't make a profit if it has no coffee beans or shop premises. Equally, capital expenditure is vital for long term profitability. Businesses need to invest in fixed assets, if only to replace equipment which has reached the end of its useful life. But replacement investment will only allow a business to stand still. If it wishes to expand, it will need to invest in more fixed assets. Equally, technological change forces many businesses to invest to remain competitive. Machines and buildings may need to be scrapped long before the end of their productive life because new machinery and new buildings are so much more productive.

But revenue expenditure and capital expenditure are also costs. Wasteful and inefficient expenditure therefore will lower potential profitability. All businesses sometimes buy stocks which have to be scrapped, employ workers who are underutilised or machines which prove surplus to requirements. No business is ever 100 per cent efficient in its use of resources. However, the more efficient it is, the less it will need to spend to earn profit.

In terms of the profit and loss account and the balance sheet, revenue expenditure has an immediate impact on profit. If £1 000 is spent employing a worker, that is a £1 000 cost entered on the profit and loss account. Capital expenditure has a less immediate impact on profit declared on the profit and loss account. This is because only the depreciation on the capital expenditure is calculated as a cost. So if a £1 000 machine is bought which depreciates by £100 over the accounting period, then only £100 is entered

as a cost on the profit and loss account. Over the lifetime of the machine, all its costs will appear on successive profit and loss accounts for the business. But the cost and therefore its impact on profit is spread out over a number of years.

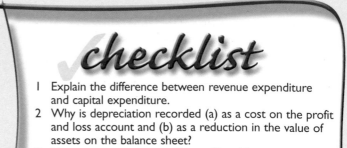

keyterms

Capital expenditure or capital spending - **expenditure on assets which will last more than one year, such as the purchase of machinery and equipment, or expenditure on intangible assets, such as goodwill or brands.**
Depreciation - **a measure of the reduction in the useful economic life of an asset over time; it measures the wearing out, using up or consumption of an asset.**
Revenue expenditure or revenue spending - **spending by a business on day-to-day running expenses such as wages or raw materials; in accounting, usually, it is spending on items which have a life of no more than one year.**

✓checklist

1 Explain the difference between revenue expenditure and capital expenditure.
2 Why is depreciation recorded (a) as a cost on the profit and loss account and (b) as a reduction in the value of assets on the balance sheet?
3 How can revenue expenditure affect (a) turnover; (b) costs; (c) profit?
4 How can capital expenditure affect (a) turnover; (b) costs; (c) profit?

A car parts firm in Darlaston is to create 30 new jobs over the next three years as part of an £8.5 million investment programme. ZF Lemforder UK is a leader supplier of automotive suspension parts for major customers such as Aston Martin, Jaguar, Land Rover, BMW, Ford and Toyota.

The company plans to invest in state-of-the-art plant and machinery at its Heath Road site, upgrade its buildings, expand its technology centre and create a new training facility. There are currently 399 people working at the site and the multi-million pound investment will safeguard 138 jobs and create 30 new ones.

The Darlaston firm is part of the German-based ZF Group, which is a leading worldwide automotive supplier for driveline and chassis technology, employing more than 55,000 people at 119 locations in 24 different countries.

Terry Somerfield, managing director of ZF Lemforder UK said: 'Our buildings are in urgent need of an upgrade, while investment in new plant and machinery will keep us at the cutting edge of automotive technology and enable us to compete for orders against other ZF Group sister companies in Europe, Japan and Turkey. The expansion of the technology centre is essential so that engineers, some of whom are resident at the design centres of our main customers, have the latest computer-based engineering technology at their finger-tips.'

Source: adapted from the *Express & Star*, 28.6.2004.

1 (a) Over the next three years, ZF Lemforder UK plans to expand its operations at its Darlaston site. Outline which aspects of the expansion will increase capital expenditure and which will increase revenue expenditure. (8 marks)
(b) Discuss how this increased revenue and capital expenditure might affect the profit and loss account and the balance sheet of the UK company. (12 marks)
2 To what extent will the proposed increased spending at ZF Lemforder UK increase the profitability of the UK subsidiary company and its parent company, ZF Group? (20 marks)

75 Asset valuation and depreciation

Felles Ltd

Knowledge Felles Ltd manufactures chairs for commercial customers such as hotels, conference centres, hospitals and health centres.

Application Felles has a variety of *assets* including *fixed tangible assets*, such as a freehold property and machinery, *intangible assets* from the takeover of a local rival company three years ago, *stocks* and *debtors*. It uses the *straight-line method* to depreciate its *fixed tangible* and *intangible* assets. It has relatively few *bad debts* which have to be *written off*, although six months ago, Felles was forced to write off £12 000 as a bad debt. This arose from a hotel chain which had taken delivery of an order of chairs but had been put into the hands of the *receivers* before the invoice had been paid.

Analysis Felles depreciates the factory which it owns freehold over a 50 year period. In contrast, equipment and machinery are depreciated over a five year period. Company policy is to invest in the latest equipment when this can be shown to have a good rate of return rather than hang on to outdated equipment. Depreciating equipment over a relatively short period means that profits are lower than they would otherwise have been on the profit and loss account. However, the company feels that this presents a true and fair record of the value of its assets.

Evaluation Choosing a method of depreciation and then a time period over which to depreciate assets is to some extent a subjective decision. The choices made by Felles are as fair a way of depreciating its assets as other ways it could have chosen. As to bad debts, Felles must always be conscious that a customer can become a bad debtor. It needs to monitor the creditworthiness of all its customers. Some bad debts are inevitable in a business with many customers. Equally some bad debts can be avoided if Felles adopts appropriate credit control procedures.

Asset valuation

The balance sheet shows the assets of a business at a point in time. But what value should be put on the assets of a business? How much is a building or a piece of equipment worth on a particular date? This unit will consider some of the issues in asset valuation.

Depreciation and fixed tangible assets

Fixed tangible assets are assets such as machinery, equipment, vehicles and buildings. The value of fixed assets is affected by **depreciation** (see unit 74). Capital goods, such as machines, wear out over time and they also become outdated so that their useful economic life is reduced. Depreciation is a measure of this consumption over a particular period.

When a business depreciates an asset, the value of the asset after depreciation is called its NET BOOK VALUE. It is the value recorded in the accounting books of the business of the asset after it has been **written down** in value. If the business judges that the asset is now worthless, the asset will be WRITTEN OFF in its accounts. Hence, if there is a fire in a factory which destroys a machine, the machine will be a **write off**, i.e. the machine will move from having a positive value on the accounts to having a zero value.

There is a number of different methods a business can use to calculate depreciation.

Straight-line method Perhaps the simplest method is the STRAIGHT-LINE METHOD. Assume a machine costs £10 000 new, lasts for five years and has no value at the end. According to the straight-line method, depreciation is calculated by dividing the original cost of the asset (the

HISTORIC COST) by the number of years over which it will be depreciated. Here it is £10 000 ÷ 5, which equals £2 000 per year. This is shown in Table 75.1

But often fixed assets have a RESIDUAL VALUE. This is the value when a business disposes of the asset second hand. A new machine bought for £20 000, kept for three years, with a residual value of £8 000 when sold, has depreciated by £12 000 over three years. So, using the straight-line method, the annual depreciation would be £12 000 ÷ 3 or £4 000. This is shown in Table 75.2, which shows the depreciation charges and the net book values in each year. The formula for calculating the annual depreciation using the straight-line method is then:

$$\text{Annual depreciation charge} = \frac{\text{Initial cost of asset - residual value}}{\text{Expected life (in years)}}$$

$$\text{Annual depreciation charge} = \frac{\pounds20\ 000 - \pounds8\ 000}{3} = \pounds4\ 000$$

There is a number of advantages with the straight-line method.
- It is easy to calculate depreciation values.
- It spreads depreciation evenly over the expected life of the asset. This can be seen as a 'fair' way of calculating depreciation because the asset is in use over the whole period.
- It is the most commonly used method of depreciation by businesses in the UK. It is an accepted method by accountants and by the Inland Revenue.

However, there are disadvantages to using the straight-line method.

- It is not always possible to predict accurately the residual value of an asset when it is bought because disposal values of assets may change. So the annual depreciation may be too large or too small depending on how residual values have changed.
- Equipment may not last the expected life. Equally, equipment may be in use long after it has been fully depreciated on the accounts of the business. So the accountants' calculation of depreciation may not reflect what has actually happened to the asset.
- Straight-line depreciation values are likely to differ from market values. A car, for example, can lose up to half its market value in its first year. Some specialised machinery has no resale value once bought, i.e. according to market values it depreciates by 100 per cent on purchase. But it might be depreciated by one fifth a year over five years using the straight-line method.

Year	Depreciation cost each year	Net book value
First purchased		£10 000
First year	£2 000	£8 000
Second year	£2 000	£6 000
Third year	£2 000	£4 000
Fourth year	£2 000	£2 000
Fifth year	£2 000	£0

Table 75.1 *Depreciation using the straight–line method, no net residual value*

Year	Depreciation cost each year	Net book value
First purchased	-	£20 000
First year	£4 000	£16 000
Second year	£4 000	£12 000
Third year	£4 000	£8 000

Table 75.2 *Depreciation using the straight–line method, net residual value*

Reducing balance method An alternative method used is the REDUCING BALANCE METHOD (sometimes called the declining balance method). Here, an asset is depreciated by a fixed percentage each year. For example, a machine might be depreciated at 25 per cent per year. So if purchased for £10 000, depreciation in the first year would be £2 500 (£10 000 x 25 per cent). At the start of the second year, it would have a net book value of £7 500 (£10 000 minus the depreciation of £2 500). So depreciation in the second year would be £1 875 (£7 500 x 25 per cent) and the asset would be valued at £5 625 (£7 500 - £1 875). In the third year, depreciation would be £1 406.25 (£5 625 x 25 per cent) and so on. This is shown in Table 75.3.

There is a number of advantages to using the reducing-balance method.

- The second hand value of assets is often better reflected in the reducing balance method. For example, a company car might lose 40 per cent of its market value in the first year, 20 per cent the second year, 15 per cent the third year and so on. A one year old machine might only be worth 70 per cent of its price new. But there might be hardly any difference in the price of a 4 year old machine and a 5 year old machine. So using the reducing balance method brings the value of the asset on the balance sheet more in line with its second hand or market value than, say, the straight-line method.
- The older the equipment, the heavier is likely to be the maintenance and repair costs. A five year old machine, for example, is likely to be more costly to maintain than a one year old machine. By using the reducing balance method, the combined cost of depreciation plus maintenance is better reflected over the lifetime of the asset.

However, there are disadvantages.

- It is a little more complicated to calculate than the straight-line method.
- Depreciating assets most heavily in the early years of the life of an asset will result in heavier costs on the profit and loss account in these years. This might discourage businesses from investing.

Accounting standards do not state exactly which method of calculating depreciation should be used. But they do state that the method chosen should be appropriate and applied in a systematic and consistent way. If the method is changed, this should be explained in the 'Notes to the accounts'.

A Liverpool wheel manufacturer is currently building a £2 million robotic paint plant. The investment is needed to satisfy growing demand for alloy wheels worldwide. It is also further developing its site and is spending £500 000 on buying the freehold of a factory adjoining its site. It continues to invest in its fleet of delivery vehicles. This year it will spend £60 000 on new vehicles.

The manufacturer has a policy of depreciating its assets on a straight-line basis over their estimated useful economic lives as follows.

- Freehold property - 50 years.
- Plant and machinery - 10 years.
- Vehicles - 3 years.

Assume that the expenditure on each of the three items mentioned in the data is recorded at its full historic cost value in the accounts of the company at 31 December 2004.

1 **Calculate the depreciation in the first year on (a) the freehold property; (b) the robotic paint plant; (c) the vehicles; (d) the total of all three items.**
2 **What is the net book value of each item at 31 December 2005?**
3 **What is the net book value of each item after 4 years at 31 December 2008? Show all your workings.**

Year	Depreciation cost each year	Net book value
First purchased		£10 000.00
First year	£2 500.00	£7 500.00
Second year	£1 875.00	£5 625.00
Third year	£1 406.25	£4 218.75

Table 75.3 *Depreciation using the reducing balance method*

Depreciation and intangible assets

Intangible assets (see unit 72) include goodwill (see unit 72), patents, copyright and trademarks (see unit 59), research and development (see unit 14) and brand names (see unit 10). Intangible assets are placed on the balance sheet in two main ways:

- when a business buys another business or part of a business and pays more for it than the value of its tangible nets assets (see unit 72);
- when a business spends money on research and development which results in the creation of brands, patents, copyrighted products and trademark products.

Just as tangible fixed assets are depreciated over time, so too are intangible assets. Depreciation for intangible assets is called **amortisation**. The depreciation period for tangible fixed assets apart from land and buildings is typically between 1 and 10 years. Amortisation for intangible assets is typically spread out over a longer period of time. This reflects the likely period of time of benefit to a business from its ownership of these assets.

Land and buildings

Land and buildings are subject to depreciation in the normal way on the balance sheet. However, unlike possibly a machine, land and buildings may appreciate in value over time. To get around this problem, businesses are allowed periodically to revalue their assets if they have appreciated. A business, for example, may revalue the offices it owns from £3 million to £4 million. This would be shown by an increase in value of fixed tangible assets on the balance sheet. However, the balance sheet must always balance. So there must be an equal and opposite entry. It occurs on the capital part of the account under **revaluation reserve** (see unit 72). Owners' funds are shown to have increased by £1 million.

Valuing stocks

Businesses buy stocks of materials to assist in production (see unit 28). They may also hold stocks of semi-finished goods and completed products awaiting delivery to the customer.

The value of stocks is determined by the price of the stock times the physical amount of stock. The physical amount of stock is calculated by a stock take (see unit 45). Traditionally, this is a physical count of stock by workers. If there is just one stock take per year, this will tend to be just before the financial year end for the business. This then allows a reasonably accurate figure for stock to be used to calculate the value of stock for the business accounts.

In the UK, accounting standards state that the value of stocks must be the **lower** of two figures so that businesses value their assets prudently. One is the historic cost, the original cost to make or buy the asset. For example, a finished machine in stock awaiting sale might have cost £7 000 to build. So the historic cost is £7 000. The other is the NET REALISABLE VALUE (NRV). This is the estimated resale value of stock, less any selling or distribution cost. For example, the machine which cost £7 000 to build might be sold for £8 000. So the NRV is £8 000. In this case, the historic cost is below the NRV. So the item of stock would be valued at £7 000.

It is not always the case that the historic cost is below the

Laser Prompt is a London based sub contract laser cutting firm. From its state of the art plant, it will laser cut materials for a wide variety of uses in manufacturing. To retain its competitive edge, it is constantly investing in the latest technology. Two years ago, it bought a £500 000 cutting machine. This month it is about to take delivery of a £600 000 machine. It moved into its new £800 000 freehold premises just one year ago.

It has a policy of depreciating its assets on a reducing balance basis over their estimated useful economic lives as follows.

- Freehold property - 5 per cent per annum.
- Plant and machinery - 20 per cent per annum.

All plant and machinery is written off after five years.

> **I Complete the following table based on the information in the data.**

Year	Cutting machine		Freehold premises		Cutting machine	
	Depreciation	Net book value	Depreciation	Net book value	Depreciation	Net book value
2003	0	500 000	0	0	0	0
2004	100 000	400 000	0	800 000	0	0
2005	?	?	?	?	0	600 000
2006	?	?	?	?	?	?
2007	?	?	?	?	?	?
2008	?	?	?	?	?	?

Table 75.4 *Laser Prompt depreciation, £*

NRV. Stock might have deteriorated in storage and its NRV might be much lower that its cost. Or, due to changes in fashion or in technology, the NRV of finished goods in stock might be very low. Computer manufacturers, for example, have sometimes been caught with large stocks of computers which have suddenly become out of date compared to the products of rivals. They then have to mark down the sale price to clear the stock, often selling them at a loss compared to the cost of manufacturing them. This stock would therefore be valued at NRV rather than cost.

A furniture manufacturing company has just completed a stock take before its year end when its accounts will be produced. It has materials in stock which were bought for £100 000. It has finished furniture awaiting delivery for which customers will be paying £40 000. It then has some tables in stock which it bought from another manufacturer for £15 000. However, the customer for whom they were bought went into liquidation and the items were never delivered. The company has been struggling to find a buyer for the items and it fears that it may have to sell them at a substantial discount to get rid of them.

1 **Explain how the furniture manufacturing company would value its stocks at its year end.**

Debtors

Debtors are those who owe a business money for goods and services which they have received. Debtors are mainly customers who have obtained trade credit from a business (see units 28 and 72). A problem for businesses is that customers either do not pay on time or even worse, don't pay at all. So long as a business expects a customer to pay,

however late, the debt remains an asset under 'debtors' on the balance sheet. There comes a point, though, when a business has to accept that the debt will not be paid. The debt then becomes a BAD DEBT and is **written off**. The value of this bad debt has to be taken away from the total for debtors on the balance sheet. It also appears as an expense on the profit and loss account.

Recovering debts is part of the process of credit control (see unit 73). One way of deciding whether a bad debt exists is to construct an AGED DEBTORS SCHEDULE. This places debts in age order. A business might then decide that all debts not paid within one year are bad debts. An aged debtors schedule also helps a business to decide which debtors to target for repayment. For example, a business may send out letters to debtors with debts overdue for more than three months, threatening them with court action.

keyterms

Aged debtors schedule - **a list of debtors ranking them according to how long their bills remain unpaid.**
Bad debts - **monies owed to a business which it accepts will not be repaid and therefore must be 'written off'.**
Historic cost - **the original cost of making or buying an asset.**
Net book value - **the value at which an asset appears on the 'books' or accounts of a business, such as on the balance sheet.**
Net realisable value (NRV) - **the estimated resale value of stock, less any selling or distribution cost.**
Reducing balance method - **a method where depreciation is calculated by depreciating an asset by a fixed percentage each time period.**
Residual value - **the value of an asset when it is sold second hand.**
Straight-line method (of depreciation) - **a method where depreciation is calculated by dividing the original cost of the asset minus its residual value by the number of periods over which the asset is to be depreciated.**
Written off - **reducing the value of an asset to zero; for example, in the case of bad debts, accepting that the debt will not be repaid.**

checklist

1 Why has a machine which is five years old depreciated over time?
2 What is the difference between the straight-line method of depreciation and the reducing balance method?
3 Explain the difference between the residual value of a machine and its net book value.
4 When would a business amortise its intangible assets?
5 Explain the difference between the historic costs and the net realisable value of stock.
6 Why do bad debts need to be written off on the balance sheet?

Colin Neams set up Play-It-Again a year ago. The company, based in Newcastle, is a seller of DVDs and computer games. Its main sales come over the Internet, serviced from warehouse premises at the back of its single shop outlet. Popular items are stocked in the shop and warehouse. Less popular items are bought in from a supplier as and when they are ordered by a customer.

The company is relatively asset rich. Colin's family own a string of successful companies and were prepared to invest in the new venture. It was decided to buy the premises because they were located in an up and coming part of Newcastle and would probably appreciate in value relatively quickly in the current Newcastle property boom. There was relatively little structural work needed to the building, but equipment had to be bought, as did stock. The value of the fixed assets at 30 April 2005 is shown in Table 75.6. All assets are depreciated using the straight-line method over the periods shown in Table 75.5.

The company did relatively well in its first year, just about breaking even, although Colin paid himself a salary of only £2 000 and lived rent free with his parents. He hoped to double sales in his second year as word about his website got around. In particular, he was hoping for repeat custom from customers who had been satisfied with the fast and efficient service he had provided on their first order. The shop on its own would clearly have made a large loss. But spreading its overheads with the Internet business meant that it would probably be financially viable in the long term.

At the end of the first year, when Colin did a stock take, he found a number of items which he thought were unlikely to sell at full price. He intended to offer 500 DVDs, which had cost £5 each to buy, at the sale price of £6. Another 200 DVDs, which equally had cost £5 each to buy, he estimated would only sell for £3 each in the sale. The rest of the stock, another 3 000 DVDs which cost 5 each, he estimated could sell for 10 each.

The company had very few debtors because customers paid cash or by credit card for their purchases. However, he had had a bad business experience early on. A man had walked into the shop and said that he owned a small chain of newsagents. He wanted to buy some DVDs in bulk on 30 days' credit to sell through the newsagents and asked for a quote for an initial order of 100 DVDs with a promise that if sales went well, he might put in a regular monthly order. Colin checked the newsagents existed and visited the man in an office at the back of one of the newsagents. The first order worth £600 was placed and paid for, although the invoice was paid one month late. The second order, for £800, was delivered but the chain of newsagents went into liquidation before the invoice was paid. After the event, Colin was told by business friends that he should have been much more cautious about checking the creditworthiness of the customer.

1 (a) Copy out and complete Table 75.6, calculating the depreciation and net book value of both assets (i) by the straight-line method and (ii) by the reducing balance method. (8 marks)
   (b) Assess the advantages and disadvantages to Colin Neams of depreciating assets using the reducing balance method rather than the straight-line method. (12 marks)
2 (a) Calculate the value of the stock of the company at the end of its first year of trading. Show all your workings. (8 marks)
   (b) Evaluate whether the company performed well over its first year. (12 marks)

	Years
Freehold buildings	50
Plant and equipment	5
Motor vehicles	3

Table 75.5 *Depreciation period*

Year	Freehold buildings		Equipment		Car	
	Depreciation	Net book value	Depreciation	Net book value	Depreciation	Net book value
2005	0	200 000	0	50 000	0	0 000
2006						
2007						
2008						
2009						
2010						

Table 75.6 *Fixed assets, value at 30 April; £000*

76 Window dressing

Marconi

Knowledge Marconi is a telecommunications equipment group. In the late 1990s, it sold off its non-telecommunications subsidiaries and invested heavily in acquiring telecommunications equipment companies. With the Internet and the world-wide web taking off, and an explosion in the use of telecommunications networks, Marconi judged that its future lay in telecommunications equipment. In 1999, it bought a US company, Fore Systems for $4.5bn (£3.12bn).

Application The *acquisition* of Fore Systems was paid for in *cash* from the previous *sale* of Marconi owned *companies*. Most of the price paid for the company was recorded as *goodwill* on Marconi's *balance sheet* because the *tangible assets* of Fore were only a fraction of the $4.5bn paid. Subsequently, Marconi began *amortising* the goodwill according to its accounting conventions. In 2001, however, Marconi announced that it would completely *write off* the goodwill from the Fore acquisition.

Analysis In 2000, the market for telecommunications equipment collapsed because companies had been overinvesting in telecommunications networks. Marconi's sales went into freefall. The Fore acquisition was particularly disastrous with much of its sales disappearing. In 2001, Marconi announced that it had made operating losses in just six months of £500 million. However, at the same time, it also announced that it would write off the £4.5bn in goodwill from Fore and other acquisitions. The total pre-tax loss for the six months was £5bn.

Evaluation Many commentators in 2001 argued that Marconi was window dressing its accounts. It had made a loss of £500 million, which effectively reduced its share price to almost zero. There was little difference between a £500 million loss and a £5bn loss so far as shareholders were concerned. However, writing off such large amounts of goodwill would flatter future profits and the rate of return on capital. It would make Marconi's future performance seem better than it would have been if it had not written off the goodwill. Even Marconi admitted that it had 'taken a particularly hard approach to Fore'. But for Marconi's directors, it was better to announce really bad news today than drip feed the goodwill through the profit and loss account over future years.

Adapted from the *Financial Times*, 16.11.2001.

A true and fair record

Accounts must represent a 'true and fair record' of the financial affairs of a business. Legislation and financial reporting standards place limits on the different ways in which a business can present accounts. These limits are designed to prevent fraud and misrepresentation in the compilation and presentation of accounts. However, businesses can manipulate their accounts legally to present different financial pictures. This is know as WINDOW DRESSING. Businesses may want to window dress their accounts for a variety of reasons.

- Managers of companies might want to put as good a financial picture forward as possible for shareholders and potential shareholders. Good financial results will attract praise and perhaps rewards. They might also prevent criticism from shareholders and the financial press.
- If a business wants to raise new capital from investors (see unit 25), then it will want its financial accounts to look as good as possible.
- Where a business has experienced severe difficulties during the accounting period, it may decide to take action which will make the financial position look even worse now but which will improve figures in the future.
- Making the financial picture look worse is often a way of lowering the amount of tax that is paid.
- If the owners of a business want to sell it, the better the financial position shown on the accounts, the higher the price they are likely to get. Equally, a company which wants to avoid being taken over can discourage predators by showing flattering accounts because these accounts

would make the cost of buying the company higher.

There is a number of ways of window dressing accounts explained in this unit.

Manipulating sales

Increasing the level of sales turnover recorded on the profit and loss account will increase profit in that accounting period. This can be done in a number of ways.

Some businesses are able to choose when they record a sale onto the profit and loss account. For example, a software company can choose under UK accountancy practice either to record a software licence deal when a contract has been signed or when the revenue has been received. Choosing to record a deal today will boost profits at the expense of profits in future accounting periods.

Another practice relates to stocks. At the financial year end, a business may make a special effort to dispatch all outstanding orders. This can boost sales in that accounting period and so flatter the profit and loss account figures. It also reduces stocks of finished goods. This can flatter the balance sheet figures, for example, by increasing the stock turnover ratio (see unit 78).

Costs and depreciation

Profits on the profit and loss account can be increased if costs are reduced. One of way of reducing costs is to reduce the cost of depreciation. **Depreciation** (see unit 74 and 75) of assets like buildings, vehicles or machinery takes place over a number of years. Take a building initially valued at £1 million. If the business depreciates the building over 10 years using the straight-line method, then each year the cost of depreciation will be £100 000 (£1 million ÷ 10). This is a cost on the profit and loss account. What if the business were to depreciate the building over 25 years instead? Then the annual depreciation charge would be £40 000 (£1 million ÷ 25 years). For the first ten years, profits on the profit and loss account would then be £60 000 (£100 000 - £40 000) a year **higher** with depreciation over 25 years compared to a depreciation over a ten year period. However, for years 11-25, profits would be £40 000 **lower**. This is because if it has been depreciated over ten years, there is no cost for years 11-25. But if it has been depreciated over 25 years, £40 000 a year is still being accounted for as a cost on the profit and loss account.

Depreciation also has an effect on the balance sheet. In the above example, depreciating the building over 25 years rather than 10 years means that profit on the profit and loss account would be higher in the first ten years because the annual depreciation charge, an expense, would be lower. In later years profit will be lower. On the balance sheet, the reverse is true. Fixed assets will tend to be higher if the asset is depreciated over 25 years rather than 10 years. For example, if the £1 million building is depreciated over 25 years, then it has a fixed asset value of £600 000 at end of year 10 (£1 million x 15 ÷ 25). But if it is depreciated over 10 years, it has £0 value at the end of year 10.

A business can also depreciate its R&D (research and development) costs. Accounting standards allow R&D costs to be written off immediately. Or they can be capitalised', treated it as an intangible asset and then amortised (i.e. depreciated) over a number of years (see unit 75). What if development costs are depreciated immediately instead of over a number of years? This will reduce profits this year on the profit and loss account but increase them in future years. For example, assume that a company has spent £10 million on R&D this year. It could write these off immediately, increasing costs on the profit and loss account by £10 million and so reducing profit by £10 million. Or it could capitalise the R&D and depreciate it over, say, 10 years. Then each year, including the first year, there would be a cost on the profit and loss account of £1 million (£10 million ÷ 10 years) reducing profit each year by £1 million.

A business must be consistent in the method of depreciation it uses. Businesses don't frequently change their method of depreciation. Indeed, accounting standards only allow a business to change methods if there are 'justifiable reasons'. However, businesses occasionally do change their method of depreciation, for instance by lengthening the period of depreciation or changing the way in which R&D is amortised. This can provide a boost to profits over a number of years and is helpful to a company which is perhaps experiencing low profits and is being criticised by shareholders.

Extraordinary items

Businesses are allowed to classify some costs as **extraordinary items** (see unit 71). These are 'one off' costs such as the costs associated with shutting down a factory or

Pennell's plc is a medium sized car dealership in East Anglia. This year has been very disappointing for sales. Despite record sales nationally, Pennell's sales have actually declined. Senior management were worried about the impact this would have on the share price and on shareholder reaction. They therefore agreed on a strategy to boost sales in the all important last financial month of the year to 30 April.

All car sales staff were offered twice the bonus they normally received for selling cars during April so long as the customer took delivery of the car and paid for it in full by the last day of the financial year. As the end of the month approached, sales staff were having to be very persuasive to get some customers who had chosen a car and placed a deposit on it to take delivery of the car on the 30 April rather than in early May.

At the same time, employees were told to cut all unnecessary expenses. There had been a ban in place since mid-February on replacing existing staff who left. Stocks of parts were also run down as far as possible. All this led to some operating difficulties. Waiting times for a service lengthened from around 3 days to 4 days, whilst some customers found that their repairs took a day longer because parts, normally kept on site, had to be ordered specially from suppliers.

> 1 **Explain how the managers at Pennell's manipulated (a) sales and (b) costs to window dress the profits of the company at its year end.**
> 2 **Discuss what impact this window dressing might have had on revenues, costs and profits for the next financial year.**

writing off the goodwill from the acquisition of a company. Writing off assets in this way might seem to put a business in a bad light with investors or shareholders. But some companies choose deliberately to write off assets in an accounting period when the business has done badly anyway. Getting all the 'bad news' out at once is better than having continued poor performance over a number of years.

For example, take a business which made some disastrous acquisitions in the past. The companies it bought have performed very poorly. It also paid more for the companies taken over than the value of their tangible assets. Hence, there is now, say, a £100 million entry on the balance sheet as goodwill, an intangible asset. This year, the company is due to announce a £50 million loss. So its directors decide to get all the bad news out at once by writing off the £100 million in goodwill. The loss this year then becomes £150 million. But in future years, reported profits will be higher because there will be no depreciation on the goodwill.

Writing off assets like this also improves future rates of return on capital (see unit 80). In the example, the company now has higher future profits from writing off the £100 million. But in future it will also have £100 million less in assets. Since the rate of return on capital is profit divided by assets, the rate of return will inevitably increase.

Bad debts

A business may chose to write off its some of its bad debts. This has exactly the same effect as writing off fixed assets. In the short term, profit is reduced by the value of the bad debts. But future profit figures are likely to be improved. This is because most of those bad debts would have had to be written off anyway. A few of the debts may, however, suddenly be paid. This would then be counted as part of revenue boosting profit.

Changing asset values

A business can increase the value of tangible fixed assets such as land and buildings, where this is justified by property valuations. Unlike equipment, land and property can increase in value over time, rather than depreciate. A business choosing to revalue its property on the balance sheet would boost the value of its assets, possibly making the balance sheet look stronger. Note that a company which chooses to do this must make an equal and opposite adjustment under capital on the balance sheet under the revaluation reserve (see unit 72).

Boosting liquidity

A business may be able to boost **liquidity** on its balance sheet. Some businesses have too little liquidity, giving rise to cash flow problems (see unit 28) as well as working capital problems (see unit 73).

One way to boost liquidity is to use sale and leaseback (see unit 24) with property. By selling property to a property company and arranging for that property to be leased back to it, a business can release cash tied up in a fixed asset. In the first year, the cash benefit to the business is the value of the property sale minus the lease payment. Sale and leaseback therefore is a way of increasing liquid assets through the sale of fixed assets. If the cash generated from a sale and leaseback scheme is used to pay off long term loans, the business will also be able to reduce its gearing (see unit 79). Gearing is loans ÷ equity expressed as a percentage. If equity was £20 million and loans £30 million, then gearing would be high at 150 per cent (100% x £30 million ÷ £20 million). If a sale and leaseback deal generated £8 million, loans could be reduced to £22 million (£30 million - £8 million) and gearing would fall to 110 per cent (100% x £22 million ÷ £20 million).

Current assets and liabilities

Some businesses have problems with aspects of their current assets and liabilities. The year end can be a time when the business makes a special effort to improve its performance. For example, a business can improve its debtors' data by making a special effort to collect in money owed by late paying debtors. This is likely to increase the amount of cash in the business or reduce short term borrowings on overdraft. It also improves debtors' ratios (see unit 78). It can attempt to improve its creditors' position by repaying as much as possible, for example by repaying early. It could also get discounts for doing this, which might help show its accounts in a better light.

As explained above, a business could try to hide a problem of excessive stock levels by not ordering new stock towards the year end and by making a special effort to dispatch finished stock to customers.

keyterms

Window dressing - **the legal manipulation of accounts by a business to present a financial picture which is to its benefit.**

checklist

1 Explain why a company may want to window dress its accounts.
2 How can a company manipulate (a) its sales and (b) its costs to flatter its recorded profits on the profit and loss account?
3 How might (a) extraordinary items and (b) exceptional items be used to window dress accounts?
4 How might bad debts be manipulated to window dress accounts?
5 How might liquidity be boosted on the accounts?
6 How might a company manipulate its current assets and liabilities to window dress its accounts?

1400 Smith Street

Enron was a US energy company which saw astonishing growth in sales and profits in the 1990s and early 2000s. But in late 2001 Enron was found to have manipulated its accounts in such a way that what looked like a highly profitable company was in fact bankrupt. There was a $5 billion hole in its balance sheet. Shareholders saw the value of their shares fall to nothing. Particularly hard hit were Enron workers, many of whom had invested large amounts of their pension funds in Enron shares. Most of the same Enron workers also lost their jobs in the bankruptcy.

There were many ways in which Enron used tax laws and accountancy standards to its benefit. For example, in February 2001, it signed a contract with Quaker Oats, the food company, to supply gas and electricity to 15 plants in the USA, and to maintain energy equipment. Enron forecast a $36.8 million profit over the 10 year deal, but immediately put $23.4 million of that onto its accounts as profit for that quarter before it had turned on any of Quaker's lights. Booking profits as having been made now when it fact they would not materialise for years was all too common at Enron. What is more, to get the contract Enron put in very low prices based on very optimistic forecasts of future energy prices. Ten years later, if energy prices had been higher than forecast, which was quite likely, the contract would have been making a loss and not a profit.

Enron used an aggressive tax avoidance strategy. According to Citizens for Tax Justice, a Washington advocacy group, Enron's pre-tax profits between 1996 and 2000 totalled $1.79 bn and yet it received net US federal tax rebates of $381 million. The US taxpayer was giving money to Enron even though it was highly profitable. In only one year did Enron pay Federal Tax at all and that was $17 million in 1997.

Another major manipulation of Enron was to create special purpose financial vehicles. These were companies set up in partnership with other investors but which Enron effectively controlled. It would transfer debt to these companies, making it look as though the balance sheet of Enron itself was relatively debt free. It would also make complicated transactions between these companies and itself around the critical times of the year when accounts had to be compiled for shareholders. Selling assets at high prices to a company just before, say, the financial year end, and then buying them back at lower prices at the start of the new financial year, allowed Enron to boost its reported profits when in fact no extra profit had been made. What happened, of course, was that for every extra $1 of profit reported by Enron, there was a $1 loss for the special purpose financial vehicle company. But shareholders, tax authorities and government regulators weren't aware of the complex web of loss-making vehicles in existence.

Source: adapted from the *Financial Times*, 7.2.2002.

1 Evaluate, using Enron as an example, whether window dressing benefits the stakeholders of a business. (20 marks)

77 Liquidity ratios

Seelford Ltd

Knowledge
Application
Seelford Ltd is a UK manufacturer of perfume and hygiene products. Over half its *sales* are *generic products* sold as supermarket *own labels*. It also has some *branded products* but these tend to be *stocked* only by one major shopping chain wishing to sell a higher *profit margin* line. *Sales* over the past year have been disappointing whilst *costs* have been rising. The result has been a reduction in *working capital*. The *current assets* of the business have fallen whilst the *current liabilities* have risen, leading to a fall in both the *current ratio* and the *acid test ratio*.

Analysis
Current assets have fallen. The fall in sales has hit cash flow with the result that cash in hand and at the bank has fallen sharply. Debtors have fallen too because of lower sales. Stocks have risen because it has been difficult to contract production fast enough to match the fall in sales. Current liabilities have risen, partly because there has been an increase in borrowing through the company's overdraft. Worryingly, the company is nearing its overdraft limit. The firm's tax liability has also increased because it still owes tax from the previous year which had seen an expansion of sales. The management is worried about the fall in the current ratio because it is a clear sign of the difficulties that the company is now facing.

Evaluation
The company faces a number of problems, one of which is the fall in its current ratio and acid test ratio. Management must recognise the importance of the fall in cash and an increase in short term borrowings of the company. Approaching its overdraft limit means that either it must stem the net outflow of cash from the business or it must find extra longer term sources of finance to increase its working capital levels. This may prove difficult if sales are still falling and the prospects for the company are poor.

Ratios

In 2003-04, Somerfield, one of the top supermarket groups in the UK, had a sales turnover of £5 billion. Pownells is a business with convenience stores around Newcastle. It had sales of £2 million over the same period. Which was the most successful business?

It is likely to be difficult to answer this question at this stage for two reasons.
- The term 'successful' has not been defined. Will success be judged on sales, profit, quality of product or environmental record for example?
- Judging success involves making a comparison. For example, in 2003-04, sales at Somerfield were almost identical to those in 2002-03. Pownells' sales were up 10 per cent over the same period. So although Pownells had much smaller total sales, it might be argued that the growth in sales suggests the business was doing better than Somerfield.

One important way to make comparisons is to use RATIO ANALYSIS. This is the numerical comparison of two variables, expressed as a ratio. Ratios fall in various categories.
- Liquidity or solvency ratios (see below) assess the ability of a business to pay its bills on a day to day basis.
- Activity or efficiency ratios (see unit 78) assess the efficiency with which resources have been used within a business by looking at issues such as credit control and stock control.
- Gearing ratios (see unit 79) assess how much of a burden

long term borrowing is to the business. This is a measure of the financial risk a business is taking in the way that it raises finance.
- Profitability or performance ratios (see unit 80) assess how profitable a business is in relation, for example, to its sales turnover or capital employed.
- Shareholders' ratios (see unit 81) assess the relative importance of the returns and dividends paid to shareholders.

Limitations of using ratios to analyse performance

Ratios are widely used in business to monitor and evaluate performance, analyse problems, spot opportunities and make decisions. The significance of individual ratios are discussed later on in this unit and in units 78-81. However, ratio analysis needs to be used with caution.
- Ratios are only accurate if the underlying data used in the ratio is accurate. If the wrong information is fed into the ratio equation, the resulting number will be misleading.
- Some ratios, like the gearing ratio (see unit 79), can be defined in different ways. It is therefore important when making comparisons that the same formula is used. If slightly different measures are used, comparisons can be misleading.
- Accounting standards allow companies, within limits, to classify and treat different items in different ways. For example, companies can choose whether to depreciate

assets using the straight line method or the reducing balance method (see unit 75). When comparing ratios, it is therefore important that exactly the same accounting conventions have been used. If they haven't, then the comparison is likely to be misleading.

- Care must be taken when comparing ratios from the same company over time. Many companies remain broadly in the same industrial sector over time. But others can diversify and change very rapidly. Equally, some companies remain the same size over time. Others grow rapidly or shrink quickly. Such factors can affect the way in which ratios can be used as a measure of performance. The measures of performance of a small company which starts off in the defence sector and grows rapidly to become a leading telecommunications equipment manufacturer will change over time. The value of a particular ratio that is appropriate for the company will therefore change. This must be taken into account when comparing ratios.

- Caution must also be used when comparing ratios between companies at a point in time. Comparing the ratios of two companies which make broadly the same products is likely to say something about their relative performance. But comparing the ratios of a supermarket chain with a cement manufacturer is unlikely be helpful in most cases. The two companies, for example, will have different working capital needs, different profit margins and different asset turnover ratios.

- Ratio comparison is useful in decision making. For example, a company may see from comparing ratios that a rival company has much higher net profit margins, even though their gross profit margins are the same. This would tend to show that the company's overhead costs are too high. But it doesn't necessarily follow that cutting overheads is the right course of action. A ratio is only one piece of evidence that stakeholders could be using when making decisions. They need to look at a much wider range of evidence before coming to any conclusions.

The current ratio

Liquidity (see unit 72) is important for a business. It must have enough funds to pay its day to day bills, such as wages and invoices due for payment of materials. It also must have enough liquid assets, such as stocks, to ensure that production goes smoothly and that orders can be delivered to customers on time.

One measure of liquidity in a business is the value of its **working capital** (see units 28 and 73). This is defined as current assets minus current liabilities. A small business will need much less working capital than a large business because its day to day bills and need for stock will be smaller. However, the CURRENT RATIO or WORKING CAPITAL RATIO is one way of measuring relative liquidity for any business whatever its size.

The current ratio is the ratio of current assets to current liabilities:

$$\text{Current ratio} = \frac{\text{current assets}}{\text{current liabilities}} :1$$

The current ratio is shown as a ratio rather than a percentage or a fraction. For instance, if a business had current assets of

£6 million and current liabilities of £3 million, then the current ratio would be:

$$\frac{\text{£6 million}}{\text{£3 million}} :1 \quad = \quad 2:1$$

The current assets of most businesses tend to be larger than the current liabilities. This is because current assets provide the liquidity to pay for current liabilities, such as debtors or short term loans, and leave money over to pay day to day expenses. Companies that are in a financial position to do this are more likely to stay in business.

It is sometimes argued that the current ratio should be between 1.5:1 and 2:1. If it is, say, 1:1, the business faces the risk of running out of liquid assets at a point in time to pay its bills. If it is more than 2:1, the business probably has too many current assets. It could put those assets to more profitable use, for example by running down stocks, reducing its debtors or buying more equipment (see unit 73).

Not all businesses have current ratios within this range. Large supermarket chains may be able to operate safely with very low current ratios. This is because customers pay immediately in cash for their purchases, but supermarkets pay their suppliers of those goods at least one month after. Some manufacturers, in contrast, need to keep high levels of stock and this may put their current ratio above the 2:1 range. The current ratios of three UK businesses are shown in Table 77.1.

Acid test ratio

The ACID TEST RATIO (or QUICK RATIO or LIQUID RATIO or LIQUIDITY RATIO) is a shorter term measure of liquidity than the current ratio. It is the ratio of current assets minus stock to current liabilities.

$$\text{Acid test ratio} = \frac{\text{current assets - stocks}}{\text{current liabilities}} :1$$

Like the current ratio, it is expressed as a ratio such as 1:1 or 0.5:1. For example, if a business had currents assets minus stocks of £4 million and current liabilities of £3 million, then the acid test ratio would be:

$$\frac{\text{£4 million}}{\text{£3 million}} :1 = 1.33:1$$

Stocks are the least liquid of current assets, i.e. stocks are likely to be the most difficult liquid asset to convert into cash at short notice, such as within a month. Debtors and cash itself are more liquid assets than stocks. By excluding stocks, the acid test ratio gives a better measure of short term liquidity than the current ratio.

It is sometimes suggested that the acid test ratio for the typical business should be approximately 1:1. This gives a business sufficient liquidity for it to run smoothly, paying its bills on time. However, as with the current ratio, different businesses will have different needs for liquidity. Large supermarkets might have acid test ratios which will be considerably less than 1:1, whilst some manufacturers need an acid test ratio greater than 1:1. Acid test ratios for three UK businesses are shown in Table 77.1.

Taking action

If the current ratio or acid test ratio for an individual business is too high, then it has too much liquidity. If it has too much cash, for example, it could invest some of its excess cash in cost-saving equipment to earn higher profit. If it has large amounts of debtors, it might be because it is inefficient in collecting debts. It should then make more effort to collect debts on time.

If the current ratio or acid test ratio is too low, the business runs the risk of having either a working capital crisis or a cash flow crisis or both. The main solutions are either to increase the amount of working capital by injecting long term funds into the business, or to reduce the volume of sales which would reduce the need for both working capital and cash.

Ways of changing the amount of working capital and cash in a business are discussed in greater detail in units 28 and 73.

					(£ millions)
	Current assets	Current assets minus stocks	Current liabilities	Current ratio	Acid test ratio
Somerfield (supermarket chain) at 24 April 2004	536.5	244.9	673.4	0.8	0.4
Pilkington (glass manufacturer) 31 March 2003	864	510	605	1.4	0.6
Renishaw (manufacturer of measuring tools) 30 June 2004	87.9	65.6	26.0	3.4	2.5

Table 77.1 *Current ratio and acid test ratio for three UK companies*

Source: adapted from company accounts.

checklist

1 Why might ratios be more useful in considering the performance of a business than absolute numbers?
2 What are the limitations of using ratios?
3 What is the difference between the current ratio and the acid test ratio?
4 Explain why, for many businesses, (a) the current ratio should be between 1.5:1 and 2:1; the acid test ratio should be approximately 1:1.
5 What actions should a business take if its current ratio is (a) too high and (b) too low?

keyterms

Acid test (or quick or liquid or liquidity) ratio - **the ratio of current assets excluding stock to current liabilities; it is a measure of short term liquidity.**
Current ratio or working capital ratio - **the ratio of current assets to current liabilities; it is a measure of the liquidity of a business.**
Ratio analysis - **the numerical comparison of two variables, expressed as a ratio, to help understand the significance of data.**

Radstone Technology plc is a technology company which has two core businesses. The Embedded Computing Business provides computing subsystems for equipment used in the defence industry. Foundation Technology is a manufacturer of small to medium size batches of complex electronic products for military equipment.

Redrow plc is a UK home building company. Because of long lead times in gaining planning applications and the difficulty of finding suitable sites for potential development, housebuilders in the UK tend to own substantial 'landbanks'. This is land which has potential for building, but which is not currently being developed. A builder may, for example, buy a plot of land for development but only begin building on the site ten years later. Around 60 per cent of Redrow's stocks is accounted for by the value of its landbank.

	Radstone Technology plc		Redrow plc	
	2004	2003	2004	2003
	£000	£000	£m	£m
Current assets				
Stocks and work in progress	9,266	9,450	713.4	579.0
Debtors	13,870	13,248	11.6	11.0
Cash at bank and in hand	9,150	4,406	1.2	6.2
Current liabilities				
Bank and other borrowings	2,733	939	27.2	4.8
Trade creditors	4,208	5,735	102.1	94.1
Other creditors	6,904	4,685	106.3	75.6

Table 77.2 *Current assets and current liabilities, Radstone Technology plc and Redrow plc*

Source: adapted from Radstone Technology plc, *Annual Report and Accounts*, 2004; Redrow plc, *Annual Report and Accounts*, 2004

1 *Calculate (a) the current ratio and (b) the acid test ratio for both Radstone Technology and Redrow for the two years 2003 and 2004.*
2 *Suggest and explain ONE reason why Redrow might have a higher current ratio than Radstone Technology but a lower acid test ratio.*

In November 2004, Courts plc announced that it had called in the administrators. Courts was a furniture retailer with 88 stores in the UK and a strong international division of more than 250 stores stretching from Thailand to Trinidad. The UK business had been experiencing difficult trading conditions for the past few years and in the financial year to 31 March 2004 the company had made a pre-tax loss of £34.4 million compared to a £11.5 million profit the previous financial year. Whilst the international operation was profitable, in the year to 31 March 2004 the company had made a trading loss of £34 million on its UK operations. This, together with £22 million of overheads for the whole group, had more than outweighed the trading profit overseas.

When those figures were announced in June 2004, the board of directors replaced key personnel and appointed Alan Fort, a turnaround specialist, as head of the UK business. He faced a very difficult task. The UK stores had failed to keep pace with the times. In the past, it had attracted customers by offering credit deals on furniture. The credit offered influenced customers to buy what was an increasingly unattractive range of products. However, in recent years, other furniture retailers like DFS had offered both more attractive products and better finance deals. 'They'd completely lost the plot in the UK. I was shocked at the in-store standards', said one analyst at Retail Knowledge Bank. Alan Fort decided to adopt a strategy of increasing customer spending by selling more upmarket products. For the strategy to work, Courts needed to clear its existing, more dowdy stock by slashing prices over the autumn of 2004. Unfortunately, the plan backfired with shoppers snapping up the bargains and ignoring the more expensive products. The result was a drain of working capital from the business.

In November, the company attempted to persuade its bankers to lend it the £20 million it needed in working capital to keep trading in the short term and it was also negotiating a £125 million loan to ensure its longer term survival. They refused and this pushed the company into administration. At the time, the company already owed its bankers £280 million.

Source: adapted from Courts plc, *Annual Report and Accounts*, 2004, *The Daily Telegraph*, 5.12.2004, *The Times*, 30.11.2004.

1 (a) Calculate the current ratio and acid test ratio for Courts for 31 March 2003 and 2004. (8 marks)
   (b) Discuss whether these ratios and the figures for working capital from the 2004 accounts show an improvement or a deterioration in Courts' financial position between 2003 and 2004 (20 marks)
2 Discuss whether the strategy of 'increasing customer spending by selling more upmarket products' had any chance of success. (20 marks).

	2004	2003
	£m	£m
Current assets		
Stocks	82.0	90.9
Debtors	208.8	220.9
Cash and short-term bank deposits	48.3	52.3
Total current assets	339.1	364.1
Current liabilities		
Bank loans and overdraft	109.2	93.2
Trade creditors	54.9	47.3
Other	70.3	65.7
Total current liabilities	234.4	206.2

Table 77.3 *Courts plc, working capital at 31 March 2003 and 2004*

Blacks

Knowledge Blacks Leisure Group plc is a wholesaler and retailer of outdoor and boardwear products. It owns a number of chains of shops including Millets, Blacks and Just Add Water. Its financial efficiency can be measured in a number **Application** of ways including reviewing its *stock turnover*, *debtors' collection days* and *asset turnover ratio*, all of which can be calculated from its *balance sheet* in its *Annual Report and Accounts*. Its 2004 accounts showed that stock turnover on continuing operations had remained broadly the **Analysis** same between the financial years 2003 and 2004 at 2.9. Debtors collection days had slightly deteriorated from 19.2 days in 2003 to 20.9 days in 2004. Asset turnover, measured using net assets as the denominator, increased slightly from 2.66 times to 2.87 times over the period. **Evaluation** These three efficiency ratios would suggest that there was little change in financial efficiency between 2003 and 2004 for Blacks Leisure Group. The extent to which Blacks is financially efficient overall could also be judged by benchmarking the company against similar retailers. This would require additional data.

Adapted from Blacks Leisure Group plc, *Annual Report and Accounts*, 2004.

Efficiency ratios

EFFICIENCY RATIOS (sometimes called ACTIVITY or ASSET UTILISATION RATIOS) measure how efficiently a business uses its resources. These resources are its working capital (see unit 73) and its fixed capital (see unit 72). Three efficiency ratios are considered here: stock turnover, debtor collection period and asset turnover.

Stock turnover

STOCK TURNOVER is the number of times stock is used up over a time period, such as a year. It can be measured by dividing the cost of sales over a time period by the value of stock, which can be found in the final accounts.

$$\text{Stock turnover} = \frac{\text{cost of sales}}{\text{value of stock}}$$

For example, a business may have £1 million worth of stock at 31 December and the cost of sales over the previous 12 months may have been £5 million. The stock turnover would then be:

$$\frac{£5 \text{ million}}{£1 \text{ million}} = 5 \text{ times per year}$$

An alternative way of expressing stock turnover is to calculate the average time period for which stock is held. For stock which is held for sale, this is the average time period on average it takes to sell stock. If the time period is 12 months, then this is given by the formula:

$$\text{Stock turnover} = \frac{\text{value of stock}}{\text{cost of sales}} \times 365 \text{ days}$$

For the business with £1 million worth of stock at the end of the period and £5 million cost of sales over the period, it would be:

$$\frac{£1 \text{ million}}{£5 \text{ million}} \times 365 \text{ days} = 73 \text{ days}.$$

Stock turnover is important for a business. In general, the quicker stock is used up and the faster the stock turnover, the more efficiently the business is using its resources. Keeping stock is costly for a business. Money is tied up in stock which could be used elsewhere in the business, such as reducing the size of an overdraft. Stock also requires handling and storing, both of which use up the resources of a business. A business which can reduce its stock whilst still maintaining its production levels will become more efficient.

However, stock turnover differs sharply between industries. A vegetable market trader, for example, may buy stock twice a week and sell all the stock over the week. Stock turnover would then be approximately 182 times a year or 3.5 days. In contrast, an upmarket ladies fashion

	£ million	
	2003	**2004**
Turnover	114.8	153.7
Cost of sales	67.1	88.8
Value of stock at 31 January	20.5	28.5
Debtors at 31 January	4.0	4.7
Net assets at 31 January	26.0	37.4

Source: adapted from Ottakar's, *Annual Report and Accounts*, 2004.

Table 78.1 *Selected financial statistics, Ottakar's plc*

Ottakar's is a UK chain of specialist book stores. At 31 January 2004, it had 122 outlets across the UK. In April 2003, it bought another company, Hammicks Bookshops Limited, which had 24 outlets. These 24 outlets accounted for £24.4 million worth of sales for the twelve months to 31 January 2004.

1 **Calculate for 2003 and 2004 the (a) stock turnover ratios; (b) debt collection periods; (c) asset turnover ratios.**
2 **To what extent do these ratios indicate that Ottakar's has improved its financial efficiency?**
3 **Assess one way in which Ottakar's could improve its (a) stock turnover ratio; (b) debt collection period; (c) asset turnover ratio.**

boutique may buy in stock four times a year for each new season's fashions. Stock turnover would then be 4 times a year or approximately 91 days. A manufacturer of cars will have different stock levels to a tyre manufacturer. So businesses which want to benchmark (see unit 48) their stock turnover need to do so against their competitors in the same sector of a market.

Stock turnover can be improved by reducing the amount of stock held whilst maintaining sales. This, for example, is what should happen if a manufacturing business introduces just-in-time techniques (see unit 47). Equally, if a business can increase sales whilst maintaining the same level of stock, stock turnover will improve.

Debtors' collection period

DEBTORS' COLLECTION PERIOD or DEBTOR DAYS (also known as the average settlement period) measures the average number of days taken for the debtors of a business to pay what is owed or the average number of days it takes for a business to collect its debts. It is measured by the formula:

$$\text{Debtors' collection period} = \frac{\text{debtors}}{\text{turnover}} \times 365 \text{ days}$$

For example, a large business might have £24 million of debtors outstanding at 31 December. The turnover for the previous 12 months was £146 million. The debtors' collection period was therefore:

$$\frac{24}{146} \times 365 \text{ days} = 60 \text{ days}$$

Offering trade credit to customers is a way of encouraging them to buy from a business. The longer the period of free credit offered, the greater the incentive to buy from the business. In industrial markets (see unit 2), business customers expect to be offered trade credit. Businesses not offering trade credit facilities would therefore be at a competitive disadvantage to their rivals which did offer trade credit.

However, trade credit is costly to the business which offers it. A business, for example, may have to borrow money and therefore pay interest on the loan, to raise the money needed to finance its trade credit. Also, there is always the risk that a debtor will default (i.e. never pay what it owes) and so the business will lose money. It is therefore in the interest of a business to minimise the debtors' collection period.

There is a variety of ways in which the debtors' collection period can be minimised. Some businesses employ a factor (see unit 28). Most businesses, however, collect debts directly themselves. They should then concentrate their resources on pursuing those debtors:
● with the largest amounts outstanding;
● most overdue in paying their debts.
An efficient business will conduct an AGED DEBTORS' ANALYSIS. This is a list showing debtors according to when their payments are due (i.e. 30, 60, 90, 120 days) and the amounts outstanding at the end of this period. They should then have systems in place to pursue outstanding debts, such as sending out reminders to customers slightly overdue in payment, to taking customers to court if payments are a long time overdue. Pursuing debtors rigourously will reduce both debtor days and the risk of default by customers.

A more long term method of reducing the debtors' collection period is to reduce the average credit period offered to customers. For example, reducing the trade credit period from 60 days to 45 days should reduce debtor days by one quarter. However, reducing trade credit periods risks alienating customers and losing sales.

Asset turnover ratio

The ASSET TURNOVER RATIO measures the ability of the assets of a business to generate sales. This is expressed by the formula:

$$\text{Asset turnover} = \frac{\text{sales turnover}}{\text{assets employed}}$$

Sales turnover is the value of sales over a period of time, such as a year. Assets employed can be measured in a number of different ways, each of which will give a different value for asset turnover. For example, assets could be fixed assets or current assets. The two asset figures often used are:

- total assets, which is fixed assets plus current assets and doesn't include any liabilities; so the asset turnover ratio would be sales turnover ÷ total assets;
- net assets where net assets are defined as total (i.e. fixed plus current) assets less current liabilities; so the the asset turnover ratio would be sales turnover ÷ net assets.

If the period of time over which sales have been measured is a year, then the asset turnover is expressed as 'times per year'. For example, if annual sales turnover were £6 million and assets were £2 million, the asset turnover would be 3.0 times per year (£6 million ÷ £2 million).

Increasing asset turnover is likely to be an indication of increased efficiency in a business. For example, if a car manufacturer increases its sales of cars this year by 500 000 with exactly the same assets as last year, it is likely that output per unit of capital employed has increased. Improved efficiency is likely to lead to higher profits.

However, increased sales may have been achieved by lowering average prices. Profit margins (see unit 80) may have fallen and, at worse, total profits may have gone down. So increased asset turnover is not always a positive sign for a business.

Asset turnover varies enormously between markets and industries. Primary industries, such as mining or oil extraction, tend to need large amounts of capital to output produced. In contrast, service industries, such as retailing, tend to require much lower levels of net assets to sales. So comparisons of different asset turnovers are most valid either within the same business over a period of time or between businesses in similar markets.

Increasing asset turnover is likely to arise in two ways.

Increasing sales from the same net assets For example, an oil company producing and then selling more oil without increasing its net assets would increase asset turnover. This is sometimes known as 'making assets sweat', i.e. making assets work harder.

Selling off underutilised assets Reducing assets which are relatively unproductive will tend to raise asset turnover. For example, a business might have eleven factories, ten of which result in sales of £10 million with assets of £5 million and one of which has sales of £2 million with assets of £4 million. The overall asset turnover is 1.33 (sales of £10 million + £2 million divided by net assets of £5 million plus £4 million). Closing down the the eleventh factory will almost certainly raise the asset turnover of the business. Assume a fairly bad

outcome, that it will cost £4 million to close down this factory in redundancy payments etc. In this case, the eleventh factory is worthless. The business would then be left with ten factories and an asset turnover of 2.0 (sales of £10 million ÷ net assets of £5 million).

keyterms

Aged debtors' analysis - **a summary of debtors ranked according to how long the debts have been outstanding.**
Asset turnover ratio - **measures the ability of the assets of a business to generate sales; two commonly used measures of asset turnover are sales turnover ÷ total assets and sales turnover ÷ net assets.**
Debtors' collection period or debtor days - **the average number of days taken for the debtors of a business to pay what is owed. It can be measured by: 365 days x debtors ÷ turnover.**
Efficiency ratios or activity or asset utilisation ratios - **ratios which measure how efficiently a business uses its resources such as working capital and fixed capital; they include stock turnover, debtor collection period and asset turnover.**
Stock turnover - **the average number of times stock is used up over a time period, such as a year. The formula for stock turnover is cost of goods sold ÷ value of stock.**

checklist

1 What is an efficiency ratio?
2 Explain why the following might be an indication of improved efficiency for a business:
   (a) an increase in its stock ratio;
   (b) a reduction in its debtors' collection period;
   (c) an increase in its asset turnover ratio.
3 Why do stock ratios differ between industries?
4 What is the purpose of a business conducting an aged debtors' analysis?
5 Explain how a business might improve the following:
   (a) its stock ratio;
   (b) its debtors' collection period;
   (c) its asset turnover ratio.

Harry Tewson bought his first pub six years ago. Since then, he hasn't looked back and now owns a small chain of pubs in the South East of England. Although the chain is profitable, Harry is aware that it could become more financially efficient.

To benchmark his performance, Harry has compared his 2003 and 2004 performance with those of two large national competitors, JD Wetherspoon and Yates plc. These comparisons are shown in Table 78.2. The figures confirmed that his chain has some way to go to match the two national chains.

In particular, he is aware of three problems. There is too much stock at any one time in his company. His head of purchasing, in his opinion, doesn't do her job very well and tends to overorder. She claims that this prevents pubs running out of stock but he isn't aware that national chains like Wetherspoon and Yates have problems with lack of stock.

Debtors take too long to pay. Most customers, of course, pay for their drinks and food when they buy it. But the chain does have some corporate customers who organise parties or events at the pubs. They insist on being given trade credit but typically fail to pay on time.

Sales per pub don't seem to be as great as the national chains. On a Friday night, Harry Tewson can go into a Yates pub and it is crowded with customers. A street away, he can go visit one of his pubs and it is only moderately full.

1 (a) Refer to Table 78.2. Complete the table by calculating the missing numbers for the ratios marked with '?'. (8 marks)
(b) Consider whether the data in Table 78.2 would support Harry Tewson's analysis of three problems his pub chain faces. (12 marks)
2 Evaluate possible solutions to the problems of financial inefficiency that face Tewson's. (20 marks)

	Tewson		JD Wetherspoon		Yates plc	
	2003	2004	2003	2004	2003	2004
Turnover £m	6.8	7.1	730.9	787.1	153.2	151.3
Cost of sales £m	6.1	6.4	621.9	672.3	124.5	127.7
Value of stock £m	0.2	0.2	10.6	12.0	3.2	2.0
Debtors £m	0.4	0.5	27.8	20.9	7.0	7.8
Net assets £m	11.5	11.9	680.7	677.7	188.7	180.7
Stock turnover ratio	30.5	32	58.7	?	38.9	63.85
Debtors' collection period, days	21.5	25.7	13.9	9.69	?	18.8
Asset turnover ratio	0.6	0.6	1.1	1.2	0.8	?

Source: adapted from J D Wetherspoon and Yates plc, *Annual Report and Accounts*, 2004.

Notes
1 Tewson's accounts to 30 April, J D Wetherspoon to 25 July, Yates plc to 28 March.
2 Value of stock, debtors and net assets at year end for each company.
3 Net assets defined as total assets minus current liabilities.
4 Cost of sales defined as all costs excluding administrative costs.

Table 78.2 *Selected financial statistics, Tewson, JD Wetherspoon and Yates plc*

The gearing ratio

Sondex plc

Knowledge Sondex plc is a supplier of technology to the worldwide oil and gas industry. It manufactures technical equipment for use in the oil and gas industries.

Application At 29 February 2003, the company had *long term borrowings* of £28 million whilst its equity, measured by *shareholders funds*, was slightly negative at £595 000. This meant that it was *high geared*. One year later, it had long term borrowing of £10.25 million, whilst its shareholder funds had increased to £24.2 million. This meant that its gearing had considerably fallen.

Analysis The fall in the gearing ratio between 2003 and 2004 was achieved through a flotation of the company on the London Stock Exchange. Approximately £25 million was raised through the issue of new shares in June 2003. Of this, approximately £18 million was used to reduce long term debt, whilst much of the rest was used to increase the working capital in the business. The fall in long term debt and the rise in equity transformed the company from one which was very high geared to one which was moderately geared.

Evaluation The very high gearing of the company in 2003 made it more vulnerable to sudden changes in the external environment. A sharp downturn in oil and gas exploration or a large rise in interest rates could have led to problems. Reducing the gearing ratio made the financial position of the company more stable and less vulnerable to unexpected changes in the external environment. Using much of the proceeds from the flotation to reduce long term debt put Sondex on a much sounder financial footing.

Adapted from Sondex plc, *Annual Report and Accounts*, 2004.

Gearing

Businesses have two main methods of obtaining long term finance. Either they acquire financial capital through borrowing money or they acquire new equity capital from their owners or potential owners. Gearing measures the relationship between these two forms of long term financing. Gearing is expressed as a percentage. Because there are many ways of defining long term borrowing and equity capital, there are many different ways in which gearing can be measured.

One definition of gearing is the ratio of long term borrowing to equity in the business. As a formula:

$$\text{Gearing} = \frac{\text{Long term borrowing}}{\text{Equity}} \times 100\%$$

Long term borrowing is sometimes called loan capital or long term loans. It includes long term loans and debentures. Equity includes the nominal values of shares plus reserves. On the balance sheet, equity is called shareholders' funds (see unit 72). For example, if a company had £3 million of long term loans and £2 million of debentures due for repayment on 31 December 2015, its total borrowing would be £5 million. If its share capital plus reserves were £10 million, then its gearing would be:

$$\frac{£5 \text{ million}}{£10 \text{ million}} \times 100\% = 50\%$$

Another definition of gearing relates fixed cost capital to long term capital. As a formula:

$$\text{Gearing} = \frac{\text{fixed cost capital}}{\text{long term capital}} \times 100\%$$

Fixed cost capital is any capital where payments on the capital have to be made. For example, long term loans are part of fixed cost capital because interest has to be paid on the loans. Interest will also have to be paid on debentures. Long term capital is variable cost capital plus fixed cost capital. Variable cost capital is almost always share capital and reserves (i.e. shareholders funds) where the company has the discretion whether or not to pay out a dividend. For example, if a company had £3 million of long term loans and £2 million of debentures, its total fixed cost capital would be £5 million. If its share capital plus reserves were £10 million, its long term capital would be £15 million. This is £10 million plus the £5 million in fixed cost capital. Its gearing would be:

$$\frac{£5 \text{ million}}{£15 \text{ million}} \times 100\% = 33.33\%$$

Mathematically, gearing measured by fixed cost capital to long term capital will, in almost all cases, give a lower value for the gearing ratio than gearing measured by loans to equity. This is because fixed cost capital is added to the bottom of the formula in the former definition which makes the bottom of the equation a larger number.

Pyron plc is a food manufacturer, making a variety of processed foods mainly for the large UK supermarket chains.

1 **Copy out Table 79.1 and calculate the company's gearing using the two measures of gearing given.**
2 **Explain why the figures for gearing you have calculated are always higher for the gearing defined as borrowing/equity.**

Table 79.1 *Pyron plc, financial data*

	2004	2003	2002	2001	2000
Long term bank loans	354	321	389	298	240
Debentures	50	50	50	50	50
Equity Shareholders funds	402	389	350	320	304
Gearing % (Borrowing equity)					
Gearing % (Fixed cost capital/ long term capital)					

Pyron Foods

Gearing risks and rewards

The greater the proportion of borrowing to monies raised from equity, the greater the risk that the company will fail and be forced into receivership. This is because a company incurs regular outgoings on its borrowing. Interest has to be paid and, often, repayments of the borrowing have to be made in instalments. If a company fails to pay interest or meet its repayments, it can be forced into receivership by banks and others who are owed money.

In contrast, shareholder capital does not always have to be repaid. Also, the company is able to decide whether or not to pay any dividends to shareholders. If the company is in financial trouble, it will almost certainly choose not to pay a dividend. So a company which has twice the amount of borrowing to equity (i.e. a gearing ratio of 200 per cent) is far more at risk than a company which has half the amount of borrowing to equity (i.e. a gearing ratio of 50 per cent).

It is suggested that on the first definition of gearing, borrowing to equity, a gearing ratio of more than 100 per cent is an indication that the company could be at risk of failing. This company would be described as being **high geared**. A **low geared business** would have a gearing ratio of less than 100 per cent.

On the second definition which includes long term debt added to shareholders' funds on the bottom of the equation, a business would be concerned if the ratio was around 50 per cent. More than 50 per cent and the business would be high geared. Less than 50 per cent and it would be low geared.

Being very low geared, however, is not always beneficial to a business.

* It might have turned away profitable business because it didn't want to borrow funds to finance the orders.
* It might be in the interests of existing owners for a business to borrow rather than issue new equity capital. By borrowing, existing shareholders keep their control and their share of the dividend. If a company finances itself by issuing new shares, existing shareholders will find that

their share of control and their share of the dividend will fall.

However, being high geared has other disadvantages than simply increasing the risk that the business will fail.

* Excessive borrowing will act as a drag on profits and therefore dividends because so much is flowing out of the business in interest payments.
* Businesses which are high geared will find it difficult to attract new long term funds. Banks will be more reluctant to lend because they will fear the business will fail and so not repay its debts. Potential shareholders will be discouraged from investing in new shares in a company which is risky.

Businesses which judge they are too low geared will tend to finance expansion through new borrowing rather than new equity. Businesses which judge they are too high geared have a number of options for reducing gearing.

* Parts of the business can be sold off and the receipts used to pay down debt.
* New equity capital can be raised, which in itself will reduce gearing. If the proceeds are used to repay borrowing, then gearing will fall even further.
* Retained profit can be used to pay back debt rather than being used to finance investment in the business or pay dividends to shareholders.

checklist

1 Explain two different ways in which gearing can be calculated.
2 Explain the link between risk and gearing.
3 What might be an acceptable level of gearing for a company?
4 What are the disadvantages to a company of (a) being high geared and (b) having a very low gearing ratio?

FJY Boatbuilders is a medium sized boatbuilding company with a shipyard in Southampton. Founded just five years ago by the husband and wife team of Fiona and Jim Yeomans, the company has grown to an annual turnover this year of £1.2 million with profits of £60 000.

Fiona and Jim are pleased with their success so far, but are frustrated that they are having to turn away potential orders. Their 25 000 square foot shipyard is too small to build some of the boats for which they have been invited to tender. Ideally, they need to find a 50 000 square foot site, but such a site would cost around £350 000 a year to rent. This would dramatically increase their costs given that they are paying less than half this on their current site.

An alternative to renting would be to purchase a site. This would cost them millions of pounds, however. When the company was first started five years ago, a friend put up £70 000 in equity for 33.3 per cent of the shares. The rest of the shares were split equally between Fiona and Jim. The balance sheet as at 31 March this year shows the initial £210 000 in share capital plus £190 000 in reserves. Long term bank loans stood at £200 000. The company is currently worth an estimated £1 million if it were sold. To use new equity capital to buy a new site would see Fiona and Jim lose control of their company. They are not prepared to go down this route. On the other hand, using a mortgage to finance the outright purchase of a new shipyard would see a large jump in their gearing. A mortgage provider, such as their bank, might be very reluctant to lend such large amounts of money anyway to a business with relatively few fixed assets and only five years old.

Fiona and Jim are optimistic about the future. They forecast that sales will grow by 25 per cent a year for the next five years on their existing site. However, they calculate they could double their turnover in two years if they moved to the larger site. These forecasts assume that the world economy will continue to grow. They are dependent for sales from high income earners not just in the UK but in Europe and the USA. A deep world recession could see their orders dry up overnight. On the positive side, they are not particularly worried about competition. Jim Yeomans spends much of his time marketing the company's products and services. He feels that FJY Boatbuilders has a competitive edge both in design and cost over most rivals.

1 (a) Calculate the company's gearing 'as at 31 March this year' and show how it would change if it took on a £1.8 million mortgage on a new boatyard. (8 marks)
(b) Analyse how a substantial increase in gearing for FJY Boatbuilders arising from the purchase of a new boatyard would increase risk for the company. (12 marks)
2 Evaluate whether or not the company should stay in its current premises. (20 marks)

Supermarkets

Knowledge The large supermarket chains dominate food retailing in the UK. Tesco alone accounts today for £1 in every £8 spent by consumers on all goods and services in the UK.

Application Food *manufacturers* are *suppliers* to the supermarkets. They can adopt two routes to getting their goods through the *supply chain* to *consumers*. Either they can supply *branded goods*, or they can become suppliers of *own label products*. Branded goods tend to carry higher *profit margins* and enjoy a higher *rate of return on capital employed*, but require support in terms of *product development* and *marketing* direct to the consumer. Own label products carry lower profit margins for suppliers but, once awarded a *contract* to supply by a supermarket, the marketing is done by the supermarket itself.

Analysis Ideally, food manufacturers would like to sell higher profit margin branded goods. But new brands are notoriously difficult to establish. Instead, food manufacturers tend to rely on extending their existing brands, creating brand names which cover a variety of products. At the same time, most food manufacturers which produce branded goods compete to manufacture own label products for the supermarkets. Though profit margins and rates of return on capital employed are lower, own label products still allow these food manufacturers to earn an acceptable profit margin. Many smaller food manufacturers also produce no branded products. They rely solely for survival on own label products.

Evaluation Supermarkets are constantly putting pressure on their suppliers to lower their prices. Food manufacturers need to resist such pressure as much as possible if they are to preserve their profit margins. Arguably, it is not in the interests of consumers to have too low prices because this would simply drive food manufacturers out of business, leading to a failure in the supply chain. Equally, it can be argued that consumers overpay for products when food manufacturers of branded products are able to charge high prices and earn very high profit margins.

Adapted from the *Financial Times*, 19.9.2001.

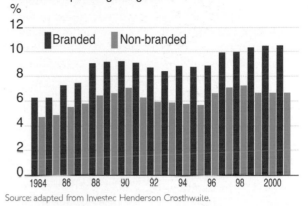

Branded and non-branded UK food manufacturers
Estimated operating margins

Source: adapted from Investec Henderson Crosthwaite.

Main retailers' private sales and overall market share

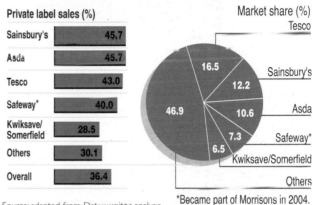

Private label sales (%)

Sainsbury's	45.7
Asda	45.7
Tesco	43.0
Safeway*	40.0
Kwiksave/Somerfield	28.5
Others	30.1
Overall	36.4

Market share (%)

Tesco	16.5
Sainsbury's	12.2
Asda	10.6
Safeway*	7.3
Kwiksave/Somerfield	6.5
Others	46.9

Source: adapted from Datamonitor analysis.

*Became part of Morrisons in 2004.

Profitability ratios

PROFITABILITY RATIOS or PERFORMANCE RATIOS measure the relative profitability of a business. Knowing that a business has achieved a £20 000 profit might not be very useful without also knowing, for example, the value of sales or the size of the business. In this unit, three profitability ratios are considered: the gross profit margin, the net profit margin and the rate of return on capital employed.

Gross profit margin

The GROSS PROFIT MARGIN measures the ratio of gross profit to sales turnover. Gross profit is calculated as turnover minus cost of sales (see unit 21). The gross profit margin is measured as a percentage. The formula is:

$$\text{Gross profit margin} = \frac{\text{gross profit}}{\text{sales turnover}} \times 100\%$$

For example, a business might make a gross profit of £20 000. If its sales turnover were £40 000 then the gross profit margin would be:

$$\frac{£20\ 000}{£40\ 000} \times 100\% = 50\%$$

Gross profit margins differ between industries. One reason is that stock turnover (see unit 78) differs. A supermarket chain like Tesco, for example, turns its stock over at a very high rate. It can continue to operate on relatively small gross profit margins because it is earning a small amount of profit per item sold but selling a large number of items over a year. In contrast, an antique shop may only turn over its stock twice a year. It has to make much higher profit margins to stay in business. So to compare gross profit margins, it is best either to compare a single business from year to year or to compare businesses in similar markets.

Higher gross profit margins can be achieved in several ways.

Raising prices whilst keeping cost of sales constant Assume that a business increases the price of an item from 20p to 25p and that cost of sales is 15p. Gross profit has therefore gone up from 5p to 10p. If it sells 1 item, sales revenue has increased from 20p to 25p. Therefore the gross profit margin has gone up from 25% ([5p ÷ 20p] x 100%) to 40% ([10p ÷ 25p] x 100%).

Cutting the cost of sales whilst keeping sales revenue constant Cutting the cost of sales will raise gross profits if prices are kept constant. With sales revenue unaffected because of constant prices, gross profit margins will rise. For example, if 1 item is sold for 20p and the cost of making it, its cost of sale, falls from 10p to 5p, then gross profit will rise from 10p to 15p. Gross profit margins will therefore increase from 50% ([10p ÷ 20p] x 100%) to 75% ([15p ÷ 20p] x 100%).

Net profit margin

The NET PROFIT MARGIN measures the ratio of net profit to sales turnover. The figure for net profit used here is profit before interest and taxation. It is the profit on the trading activities of the business. It is measured as a percentage. The formula is:

$$\text{Net profit margin} = \frac{\text{net profit}}{\text{sales turnover}} \times 100\%$$

For example, a business might make a net profit of £3 million. If its sales turnover were £30 million, then the net profit margin would be:

$$\frac{\text{£3 million}}{\text{£30 million}} \times 100\% = 10\%$$

In general, a rise in net profit margins for a business should lead to higher net profit. This might not be the case, however, if higher net profit margins have been achieved through raising prices. Then sales might fall, resulting in lower net profit.

There should be much less difference between the net profit margins of individual businesses than gross profit margins. This is because net profit margins include all costs and not just cost of sales.

Comparing gross and net profit margins should indicate changes in indirect costs. For example, if over the past year a business has seen its gross profit margin increase but its net profit margin fall, this must be because indirect costs have risen compared to cost of sales. This could suggest inefficiency and a failure to control indirect costs.

As with gross profit margins, there are several ways in which a business can increase net profit margins.

Raising the price of a product This will increase the net profit margin made on each item sold. However, net profit on all items sold will fall if the increase in price has led to a sufficiently large fall in the volume of sales.

Reducing costs of sales As with gross profit margins, reducing the direct costs of making an item will reduce cost of sales and therefore increase net profit and the net profit margin.

Reducing indirect costs Reducing indirect costs will also increase net profit margins. If a business can reduce its overheads, such as administration expenses, it will increase its net profit and its net profit margin.

Rate of return on capital employed (ROCE)

The RATE OF RETURN ON CAPITAL EMPLOYED (ROCE) or PRIMARY RATIO or PRIMARY EFFICIENCY RATIO measures the relationship between profit and capital employed. It is measured as a percentage. As a formula:

$$\text{Return on capital employed} = \frac{\text{operating profit}}{\text{capital employed}} \times 100\%$$

For example, if operating profit were £2 million and capital employed were £50 million, then the return on capital employed would be:

$$\frac{\text{£2 million}}{\text{£50 million}} \times 100\% = 4\%$$

Operating profit is profit before interest and tax have been paid (see unit 71), sometimes called earnings before interest and tax (EBIT) or trading profit. Operating profit is also often the profit figure used as net profit when calculating the net profit margin.

Capital employed can be measured in a variety of ways, giving different measures of the rate of return on capital employed. It is therefore important when making comparisons between time periods for the same business and between different businesses for the same definition of capital employed to be used. One measure of capital employed is total assets less current liabilities to be found on the balance sheet (see unit 72). This is equal to shareholders' funds plus long term loans (usually called on the balance sheet 'creditors: amounts falling due after more than one year').

The significance of the ROCE can be appreciated if it is compared to interest on a bank account. The operating profit is the equivalent of the interest received. Capital employed is the equivalent of the amount in the bank account. The ROCE is the equivalent of the interest rate paid. The higher the ROCE, the more the business is earning as a percentage on its capital invested. It is therefore a key measure of performance for any business.

The ROCE of a business should be higher than current bank interest rates. Owners might be able to get 5 per cent interest by putting their financial capital into a bank or building society account. They therefore will want to see higher returns if it invested in a business. This is because, whilst investing in a bank is largely risk free, investing in a business is a high risk option. Owners could at worst lose all their capital if the business fails. In the UK, large businesses may expect to make a ROCE on new investment of a minimum of 15-20 per cent. The difference between this and bank interest rates represents the risk premium of investing in business.

The rate of return on capital employed can be increased in two main ways.

Increasing operating profit Increasing operating profit on the top of the formula will raise the ROCE. Operating profit can be increased in a wide variety of ways, from increasing prices, increasing sales levels or reducing costs.

Reducing the amount of capital Reducing the amount of capital on the bottom of the formula will raise the ROCE. Reducing the amount of capital whilst maintaining operating profit is another example of 'making the assets sweat' of the business. For example, underperforming assets could be sold and the proceeds used to pay off long term loans. Or some of the retained profit of the company could be given to shareholders as a special dividend, reducing shareholders' funds and so reducing capital.

✓ checklist

1 Explain the difference between gross profit margins and net profit margins.
2 How could a business raise its gross profit margins?
3 Explain how the rate of return on capital employed is calculated.
4 How can a company increase its rate of return on capital employed?

key terms

Gross profit margin - **the proportion of gross profit earned on sales. It is measured by gross profit ÷ sales turnover.**
Net profit margin - **the proportion of net profit earned on sales. It is measured by net profit ÷ sales turnover.**
Rate of return on capital employed (ROCE) or primary ratio or primary efficiency ratio - **the relationship between profit and capital employed. It is measured by operating profit ÷ capital employed.**
Profitability or performance ratios - **measure the relative profitability of a business. Ratios include the gross profit margin, net profit margin and return on capital employed.**

Marks & Spencer

Marks & Spencer was once called 'Britain's favourite retailer'. From humble beginnings in 1894 when Michael Marks and Tom Spencer formed a partnership, the company gradually expanded and by the 1920s and 1930s, the brand format of good quality clothing and food was established. By the mid-1990s, Marks & Spencer seemed unstoppable, expanding sales and market share. But then everything began to go wrong. Sales faltered and profits fell. Marks & Spencer was accused of having 'lost its touch' of appealing to middle aged, middle class women shoppers. Its core womenswear collections no longer had a competitive edge in either quality or

fashion appeal. Its food lines suffered every increasing competition from supermarket chains which were launching products appealing to the high quality end of the market.

Marks & Spencer was also accused of being 'arrogant'. For example, Marks & Spencer was the only major retailer to refuse to accept credit cards for payment. Instead, it had its own credit card which it offered as part of a profitable package of financial services aimed at customers.

By the late 1990s, it was apparent that something needed to be done. A whole range of initiatives were taken, from shutting loss making stores abroad, to bringing in George Davies to design a new range of women's clothes called 'Per Una', to dropping the iconic 'St Michael' brand logo in favour of other brand names. The initiatives had some success, but by 2005 it was still generally felt that the company had not sorted out all its problems.

Source: adapted from various sources.

	2004	2003	2002	2001	2000
Marks & Spencer[1]					
Turnover £m[2]	8,301.5	8,019.1	8,135.4	8,075.4	8,195.5
Operating profit £m	842.6	729.2	318.3	131.6	403.3
Capital employed £m	5,492.4	5,000.2	5,441.0	5,711.8	5,852.7
Net profit margin	10.1%	9.1%	3.9%	?	4.9%
Return on capital employed	15.3%	14.6%	?	2.3%	6.9%
Next[1]					
Turnover £m[2]	2,516.0	2,206.6	1,817.7	1,588.5	1,425.4
Operating profit £m	370.6	301.5	258.6	213.8	186.8
Capital employed £m	592.4	331.4	585.7	275.5	315.9
Net profit margin	14.7%	13.7%	14.2%	13.5%	?
Return on capital employed	62.6%	?	44.2%	77.6%	59.1%

Source: adapted from Marks & Spencer plc, Next plc, *Annual Report and Accounts*, 2001-2004.

Notes
1 Accounts for Marks & Spencer plc to year end 3 April, Next plc to year end 31 January.
2 Net profit margin calculated using operating profit as net profit.

Table 80.1 *Marks & Spencer plc and Next plc, selected financial statistics[1]*

Next
Next's retailing success story started in the early 1980s when the chain was established under George Davies, later to go on to found the George range of clothing at Asda and then the Per Una range at Marks & Spencer. Next appealed to women in their 20s and 30s who were fashion conscious but also wanted a quality product. Sales grew rapidly and the company diversified into a number of markets from mail order to a newspaper shop chain to soft furnishings. In the late 1980s, it suffered a financial crisis as the economy went into recession, pulling down sales, at a time when it had overborrowed to pay for expansion. When George Davies left and the company pulled back to its core activities of selling women's clothing. However, by the early 1990s, the company had resolved its financial difficulties. Its product offering remained popular with customers and sales expanded. By 2000, it was clear that Next had a winning formula compared to many of its competitors, including Marks & Spencer. Indeed, it was pulling traditional Marks & Spencer customers into its shops to sell them precisely the good quality mid-priced clothes at which Marks & Spencer had traditionally excelled.

Source: adapted from various sources.

1 (a) Refer to Table 80.1. Complete the table by calculating the missing numbers for the ratios marked with '?'. (8 marks)
   (b) Analyse how the data in Table 80.1 might support the view that the period 2000-2004 were difficult times for Marks & Spencer but that Next was a highly successful company over the period. (12 marks)
2 'Marks & Spencer could solve all its problems if only it could increase its profit margins.' Evaluate this view. (20 marks)

81 Shareholders' ratios

GWR Group

Knowledge In 2004, GWR was a company which provided local radio services within the UK. Its stations included Classic FM, Plymouth Sound FM and Essex FM.

Application Table 81.1 gives selected financial statistics for GWR for its financial years 2000-04. *Turnover* and *profit/loss* figures are given. *Dividend yield* and *dividend per share* are calculated from the *market share price*, the total *dividend* and the number of *ordinary shares* issued.

Analysis 2002-04 were difficult times for GWR. In 2000, it was expanding by buying up radio stations internationally, launching Internet services and rolling out digital radio services in the UK. However, its international stations failed to make a profit and in 2002, the company reversed its strategy. By 2004, it had sold all its overseas radio stations but not before it had had to take large losses on the disposals. Investment in digital radio proved disappointing because so few listeners owned digital radio sets. By 2004, half a million sets had been sold, but listeners with digital sets still represented only a small percentage of GWR's audience. From 2001 onwards, advertising revenues fell as the UK economy went into a very mild recession. Advertising is the main source of revenue for GWR. However, by 2003-04, revenues were beginning to increase again. The share price reflected these trends, falling sharply between 2000 and 2003 before rising again.

Evaluation Stagnant revenues and losses in 2002 and 2003 may be put down to a problem with investment strategy and a general fall in UK advertising. Despite these setbacks, the company decided to increase its total dividend and dividend per share throughout the period. This was possibly done to maintain confidence in the company and to prevent the share price falling even further. With a falling share price and a rising dividend, the dividend yield increased between 2000 and 2003, increasing the attractiveness of the shares to potential investors. Despite the fact that dividends per share were 26 per cent higher in 2004 than in 2000, the 2004 share price was only a fraction of its 2000 value. Investors were probably still wary of the future prospects for the company.

Source: adapted from GWR Group plc, *Annual Report and Accounts*, 2001 to 2004.

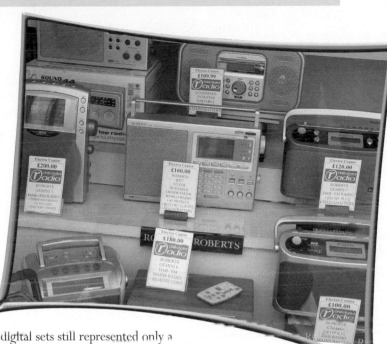

	2004	2003	2002	2001	2000
Turnover £m[2]	128.7	127.1	128.4	127.2	102.3
Profit/loss before taxation £m[2]	14.8	-14.9	-15.1	5.2	17.6
Market share price pence[1]	275	142	255	426	943
Total dividend £m[2]	8.3	7.5	7.2	7.2	5.6
Number of ordinary shares million[1]	130.9	130.5	124.7	124.4	111.7
Dividend per share pence	6.3	5.7	5.8	5.8	5.0
Dividend yield	2.3%	4.0%	2.3%	1.4%	0.5%

1 At financial year end 31 March.
2 For the financial year 1 April to 31 March.

Table 81.1 *Selected statistics, GWR Group*

Shareholders' ratios

SHAREHOLDERS' RATIOS (or SHAREHOLDER RATIOS) provide information which is useful for shareholders. They measure the returns to the shareholders of a company. Shareholders own shares because they want to make a return on them. They do this mainly in two ways.

- They may receive a dividend from the company, a share of its profits.
- The share price may rise, giving shareholders a capital gain if shares are sold.

The two are linked through profit. Rising profit indicates that the company might be able to pay more in dividends in the future. It also increases the value of the company to other companies that might want to buy it. This takeover value is reflected in the price of the shares. So profit and dividends are important indicators for shareholders of how well a business is performing.

Dividend per share

DIVIDEND PER SHARE measures the amount of dividend

paid per each ordinary share issued by a company. It is measured in monetary amounts, typically pence in the UK. The formula is:

$$\text{Dividend per share} = \frac{\text{total dividend}}{\text{number of ordinary shares}}$$

For example, if a company pays out a total dividend of £200 000 and there are 400 000 ordinary shares issued, the dividend per share would be:

$$\frac{£200\ 000}{400\ 000} = £0.50$$

Over time, the total dividend paid to shareholders should rise if profits rise. This should lead to rising dividends per share paid to shareholders. So increasing dividends per share are likely to be beneficial to shareholders. Sometimes, though, companies choose to keep their dividend per share constant or even lower it to finance future investment. This could raise long term profitability and so benefit shareholders in the future.

It is difficult to compare the performance of different companies by using dividend per share. This is because different companies issue different numbers of shares which are unrelated to the value of the company.

A company can increase earnings per share in a number of ways.

- It can increase its profitability and so afford to pay higher dividends.
- It could choose to increase dividends and pay these out of its reserves (i.e. from past profit made but retained by the company). This can be done in the short term but is likely to be unsustainable in the long run.
- It can buy back shares from shareholders, so reducing the number of shares on which it pays dividends. In recent times, SHARE BUY BACKS have been a popular way in which companies have attempted to increase shareholder value. The main reason why companies choose to use share buy backs rather than simply increase the dividend is that it tends to be more tax efficient for shareholders. If individual shareholders receive a dividend, they have to pay income tax on the dividend. If there is a share buy back, the share price should rise. Individual investors can then choose whether to sell some of their shares and possibly pay capital gains tax on them, or to keep them and, at the moment, pay no tax.

Dividend yield

DIVIDEND YIELD measures the dividend paid on each ordinary share in relation to the market price of an ordinary share. It is measured as a percentage. The formula is:

$$\text{Dividend yield} = \frac{\text{dividend per share}}{\text{market price per share}} \times 100\%$$

For example, if dividend per share were 5p and market price per share were 100p, then the dividend yield would be

$$\frac{5p}{100p} \times 100\% = 5\%$$

Different companies have different policies about dividend yield. Some have high dividend yields. Others have low dividend yields or none at all. Companies which have a policy of paying no dividends tend to be those which need to retain cash for investment. They may be growth companies. Those with high dividend yields may be mature companies with mature products and little need for investment. However, it is difficult to use dividend yields to compare the performance of companies without knowing much more about the companies being compared.

An increase in dividend yield is not necessarily good for individual shareholders. If dividend yields have increased because the amount paid in dividend has increased, then this benefits the shareholder. However, a rise in dividend yields can also result from a fall in the share price with the dividend remaining unaltered. Falling share prices are not beneficial to the shareholder. In general, companies find it difficult to manipulate dividend yield.

keyterms

Dividend per share - the amount of dividend paid per each ordinary share issued by a company. It is calculated by total dividend ÷ number of ordinary shares

Dividend yield - the dividend paid on each ordinary share in relation to the market price of an ordinary share. It is calculated by 100% x dividend per share ÷ market price of an ordinary share.

Share buy backs - when a company buys back its own shares from shareholders with the purpose of raising the price of remaining shares and so creating capital gains for shareholders and reducing the number of shares, so increasing the dividend per share paid.

Shareholders' or shareholder ratios - measure the returns to the shareholders of a company; shareholders' ratios include dividend per share and dividend yield.

checklist

1 Why might a shareholder be interested in the shareholders' ratios of a company?
2 How can a company increase its dividend per share?
3 Explain the difference between the dividend per share and the dividend yield.

BN plc is an international engineering group. The period 2000-04 proved difficult for the company. Sales and profits increased in 2000-01 as the world economy expanded and the company made a number of acquisitions. However, the world trading environment proved more difficult between 2001 and 2004 as the world economy went into a period of slower growth.

BN was also affected by much fiercer competition from the Far East and particularly China. The group, in most cases, had to shut down production of low value-added products in the UK and the USA because labour costs in those countries were too high. Instead, the company refocussed its strategy on making high value-added engineering products. Closing facilities, however, led to a significant fall in turnover. Profits fell too as profit margins on remaining low value-added products were slashed, there were heavy costs and write offs arising from closure of factories and subsidiaries and increased investment was required to develop new high value-added lines.

The share price of the company collapsed from 734p at 30 November 2001 to 96p at year end 2004. Admittedly, the share prices of other UK engineering companies performed poorly over the period. Even so, BN performed particularly poorly. The board of directors had to make hard decisions over the period 2001-04. In the financial year 2003, the board of directors approved a cut in the dividend to reflect falling profits. This released a little cash to pay for more factory closures and increased investment. A motion to further cut the dividend in 2004 was voted out. However, the company cannot continue to pay out dividends if it is making losses.

	2004	2003	2002	2001	2000
Turnover £m[2]	120.6	126.7	149.6	156.2	127.5
Profit/loss before taxation £m[2]	-8.7	1.7	11.5	20.4	17.5
Market share price pence[1]	96	134	347	734	469
Total dividend £m[2]	2.0	2.0	4.9	4.9	4.0
Number of ordinary shares million[1]	47.1	46.8	46.5	46.3	46.2
Dividend per share pence	4.2	4.2	10.5	10.5	?
Dividend yield	?	3.1%	3.0%	1.4%	1.8%

1 At financial year end 30 November.
2 For the financial year 1 December to 30 November.

Table 81.2 *BN plc: selected financial statistics*

In 2005, estimates suggested that sales would be down a further 10 per cent and that the loss for the year could be as high as £15 million. In the light of this, some directors in 2005 were recommending that the dividend be cut altogether.

1 (a) Refer to Table 81.2. Complete the table by calculating the missing numbers for the ratios marked with '?'.
(8 marks)
(b) Analyse how the data in Table 81.2 supports the view that the period 2000-04 were difficult times for BN.
(12 marks)
2 Evaluate whether or not shareholders would benefit in the short term and in the long term from cutting the dividend to zero in 2005. (20 marks)

82 Break-even analysis and contribution

Shipping freight

Knowledge The shipping freight industry is a vital link in the world trading system.

Application The shipping market is highly *cyclical*. For much of the 1980s and 1990s, shipping lines were forced to charge *prices* which were below the *break-even* level of prices. Single journey contracts were effectively each a *special order* and shipping lines were glad to make at least some *contribution* to their *overhead costs*. However, in the early 2000s, prices surged ahead and suddenly ship owners were making record *profits*, well above their break-even level.

Analysis The surge in shipping freight prices was due to increasing globalisation and the surge in trade from the Far East and particularly China. The sudden profitability of freight shipping, where revenues exceeded costs by a considerable margin, led to a surge in demand for the building of new ships. Shipyards in the 1980s and 1990s had found it difficult to break-even and many, particularly in Europe and Japan, had closed for lack of orders. In the 2000s, the remaining shipyards were working at full capacity. They were able to considerably increase their prices with each ship being seen as a 'special order'. This was in stark contrast to the repression years of shipbuilding when buyers of new ships were able to negotiate prices which barely covered the shipbuilders' variable costs.

Evaluation The shipping lines should enjoy their high profits whilst they last. History suggests that they will respond by ordering so many new ships that there will be an over-supply and prices will come tumbling down. Being in the shipping industry can be seen as high risk. Fortunately for the world's trading economy, there doesn't seem to be a shortage of such entrepreneurial risk takers.

Break-even analysis

In Unit 22, it was explained that the **break-even point** for a business was where total revenue = total cost. This is where the business is making no profit, but equally it isn't making a loss.

The break-even point can be calculated using figures for total revenue and total cost. This is shown in Table 82.1. Figure 82.1 is drawn from this data.

- It is assumed in the table and diagram that the business makes just one product and charges the same price however much is sold. So the more sales, the higher the level of **total revenue**. The total revenue line in Figure 82.1 is therefore upward sloping.
- The business has a certain level of **fixed costs**. These are costs such as interest charges on borrowing or rent on premises which don't change as output changes. Fixed costs on Figure 82.1 are shown by a broken horizontal line.
- **Variable costs** are the costs such as raw materials which do change as output changes.
- Fixed costs must be added to variable costs to find **total costs**. The total cost line in Figure 82.1 is upward sloping, but starts at the level of fixed costs on the vertical axis.

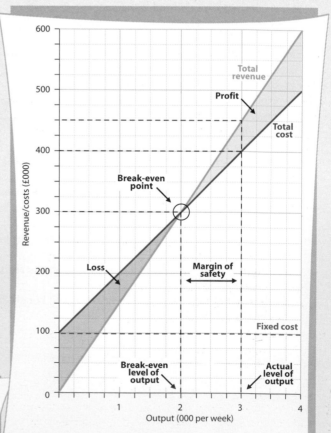

Figure 82.1 *A break-even chart showing the margin of safety*

Output per week	Fixed cost	Variable cost	Total cost	Total revenue	Profit (+)/loss (-)
1,000	£100,000	£100,000	£200,000	£150,000	-£50,000
2,000	£100,000	£200,000	£300,000	£300,000	£0
3,000	£100,000	£300,000	£400,000	£450,000	+£50,000

Table 82.1 *Costs, revenue and profits*

- The **break-even level of output** is where total costs equal total revenue, at 2 000 units per week.
- **Profit** or **loss** is shown by the area between the total revenue and total cost lines. If the actual output of the business is 3 000 in Figure 82.1, the profit is £50 000 (revenue of £450 000 - costs of £400 000).
- If a business is making a profit, the **margin of safety** is the difference between the actual level of output and the break-even output. In Figure 82.1, the business is producing 3 000 units per week and the break-even output is 2 000. So the margin of safety is 1 000 units per week (3 000 units - 2 000 units).

Product ranges and individual products

It might be assumed that the break-even point is calculated for a business as a whole. In reality, small businesses might use break-even calculations like this. Larger businesses, though, are more likely to use break-even analysis to estimate the break-even point of an individual product or a product range.

For example, a business might be thinking about introducing a new product. It intends to sell the product at £10 each. The variable cost per unit is £8. It is not always immediately obvious how much are the fixed costs for the product. For example, if the business pays £20 000 a year on interest on its borrowings, how much of this should be **apportioned** to the new product? There are various methods of apportioning or allocating total fixed costs to individual products, product ranges or parts of a business. Assume that fixed costs are £50 000. Then, as Figure 82.2 shows, the break-even level of output is 25 000 units. Total revenue is £250 000 (25 000 x £10). Total costs are also £250 000 (fixed costs of £50 000 plus total variable costs of £200 000 [25 000 x £8]).

Another way of finding the break-even level is to use the concept of **contribution** (see unit 23). Contribution is the amount that sales contribute towards the payment of fixed costs. If the business has reached the break-even point, contribution can then start earning the business a profit. As a formula, contribution is revenue minus variable cost. In the example above, contribution is £2 (£10 - £8) per unit, i.e. every unit sold contributes £2 towards paying off fixed costs. If total fixed costs are £50 000, the business needs to sell 25 000 units to break-even (£2 x 25 000 units = £50 000). Every £2 contribution after sales of 25 000 is profit for the business.

To calculate the break-even point for a product range, a business would need to calculate the average price of products sold in the range and, their average variable cost and then apportion fixed costs to the range. For example, if the average selling price of a range of washing machines were £300 per washing machine and the average variable cost were £200, then contribution per washing machine would be £100. If total fixed costs were £5 million, the break-even point would be 50 000 machines (£5 million ÷ £100).

Decision making using break-even

Break-even analysis can be an important tool for businesses in their decision making. This is because managers can see the effects that changing their prices or their costs will have on the break-even level of output. There is a large number of variables that could be changed which would affect break-even. Some examples are given here.

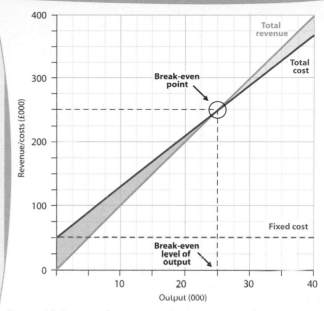

Figure 82.2 *A break-even chart showing the break-even level of output of 25 000 units*

Changing price Break-even analysis can be used to consider the effect of a change in price. Assume a UK business decides that it must cut its prices to compete with new cheap overseas imports. On a break-even chart, a fall in prices will be shown by a downwards rotation of the total revenue line, pivoting around the 0 point on the graph. This is shown in Figure 82.3. At every level of output, total revenue will fall because of the fall in sales price.

This results in a rise in the break-even level of output. The business has to sell greater quantities of the product to break-even. The fall in price should result in higher sales. Whether the fall in price results in higher revenue depends upon the price elasticity of demand of the product (see unit 17). Whether it results in high profits depends not just on the price

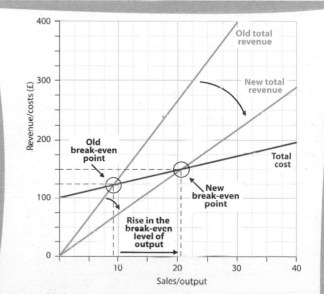

Figure 82.3 *A fall in price. The break-even level of output will rise if the price of a product falls, leading to lower total revenue at every level of output.*

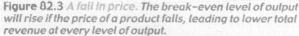

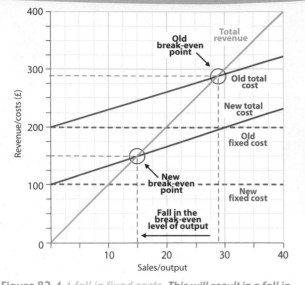

Figure 82.4 *A fall in fixed costs.* **This will result in a fall in the break-even level of output.**

elasticity of demand but also what happens to costs. Selling larger quantities is likely to lead to higher costs. Only if the increase in total revenue is greater than the increase in costs will profits rise.

If the business decides to increase prices, the break-even level of output will fall, as can be seen in Figure 22.4 in unit 22.

Changing fixed costs Businesses can take decisions which will change their fixed costs. Examples where fixed costs would fall include:
● moving to smaller rented premises where the monthly rent was lower than before;
● reducing spending on advertising;
● repaying some loans which would decrease monthly debt and interest repayments;
● leasing less equipment such as photocopiers or cars;
● cutting the number of administrative staff;

● reducing expenditure on research and development.
Decisions by businesses to cut their fixed costs will result in a shift down in the fixed cost curve in Figure 82.4. This will reduce the break-even level of output and will lead to a rise in profitability if both revenues and variables costs remain the same. Cutting fixed costs without affecting sales and variable costs is therefore good for the performance of the business, making it more efficient.

The effects of a rise in fixed costs are shown in Figure 22.5 in unit 22. The Break-even level of output will rise and, all other things being equal, profit will fall.

Changing variable costs Businesses can affect their variable costs. For example, car manufacturers or supermarket chains are constantly seeking to reduce the prices that their suppliers charge them for products. Businesses might have to raise the wages of their production workers to retain and recruit staff. Management deliberately decide to improve the quality of a product to move it more up-market but this will increase the variable costs of production.

Figure 82.5 shows the effect of a fall in variable costs which would come about if a business negotiated better prices on some of its raw materials. The variable cost curve will pivot downwards round the point where it meets the vertical axis. At every level of output, variable costs and therefore total costs are now lower. So too will the break-even level of output. If sales prices and fixed costs remain the same, profit will rise.

The effect of a rise in variable costs is shown in Figure 22.6 in unit 22. A rise in variable costs will increase the break-even level of output.

Changing two or more variables A business may decide to change more than one variable from its costs and revenues. For example, a business may choose to take a product 'down market'. This is because it is facing competition from foreign imports which are poorer in quality than its products but are

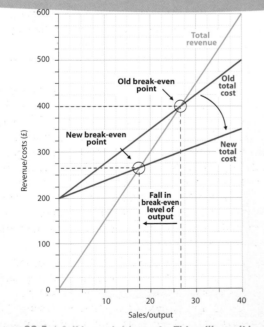

Figure 82.5 *A fall in variable costs.* **This will result in a fall in the break-even level of output.**

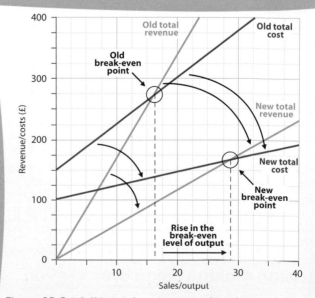

Figure 82.6 *A fall in total revenues and total costs resulting from a fall in both fixed and variable costs here results in a rise in the break-even level of output. However, the break-even level of output could equally fall if the change in total revenues were greater than the change in total costs at every level of output.*

Stepien Ltd is a company which makes foundry products in Willenhall in the West Midlands. Total revenue and total costs for one of its product lines are shown in Figure 82.7. The price of each unit sold is £80 whilst the variable cost is £30 per unit. Fixed costs are £5 000. **Either** by drawing a break-even chart **or** using the concept of 'contribution', calculate and explain what would happen to the break-even level of output in the following circumstances.

1 An increase in demand for foundry products allows Stepien to increase its prices without affecting demand to £100 per unit.
2 The rent on the foundry is increased and £1 000 per week of this is allocated to this product line.
3 The cost of raw materials falls, equivalent to a £5 per unit fall in variable cost.
4 All three events, described in 1 to 3, occur at the same time.

Figure 82.7

also much lower priced. So it needs to reduce its prices and hence total revenue at any given level of output. The only way of doing this and remain profitable is to reduce costs. A large cut in price will almost certainly necessitate a cut in both fixed and variable costs.

Figure 82.6 shows the effect of a cut in all three variables - total revenue, fixed costs and variable costs. In Figure 82.6, the break-even level of output rises. This is because the cut in total costs is greater than the cut in total revenue. However, the break-even level of output could fall if the cut in total costs were less than the cut in total revenue. In Figure 82.6, whether the break-even level of output rises or falls depends upon how much the total revenue line shifts to the right compared to the change in the total cost curve.

Special order decisions

Contribution is what is left over from sales revenue after variable costs have been paid. It is a 'contribution' first to the payment of fixed costs and then to profit.

Many businesses sell their products at fixed prices, their 'normal terms' of trade. For example, Staples, the office supplies chain, sells both to businesses and consumers at the prices displayed in their shops and catalogues. However, sometimes a business may be approached by a customer which wants to negotiate a SPECIAL ORDER. A special order is a one-off order and is not part of the normal trade of the business. Special orders are likely to be negotiated at a special price. Usually this is a price below normal trading terms, but sometimes it is a price above normal trading terms.

Prices lower than the normal price Assume that a business usually sells a product for £10 per unit. A customer approaches the business and offers to buy 5 000 units at £8 per unit. Should the business accept the special order? There is a number of important factors in the decision.

● One factor is the contribution that the order could make. If the variable cost is above £8 per unit, the order should be refused. Assume the variable cost is £9. The business will make an immediate loss on every unit made of £1 and no contribution will be made to paying fixed costs. However, what if the variable cost were below £8? If it were £6, then each unit would make a contribution of £2 to fixed costs and profit (selling price of £8 - variable costs of £6). The total contribution from the order would be £10 000 (£2 x 5 000 units). Whether the order should be accepted will depend on other factors. But at least the order is making a contribution of £10 000. If the order were turned down, that £10 000 would be lost to the business. Either losses would be £10 000 greater or profit would be £10 000 less.
● Another factor is whether the business has spare capacity. If the business is working at full capacity (see unit 43) and selling its output at its normal trade price, there is no advantage to accepting the special order. The opportunity cost (see unit 21) of accepting it would be not to produce an order at the normal price. It would lose money by doing this. However, if the business has spare capacity, then taking the special order might be attractive because of the contribution it would make.
● Accepting the order may push up costs. For example, workers may have to work overtime or materials may have to be ordered at above their normal price for quick delivery. This extra cost must be calculated before any decision about contribution can take place.
● The business has to consider the long term implications of accepting the special order. Other customers paying the normal price might hear of the cheaper price of the special order. They might then want to negotiate lower prices. A short term decision could adversely affect the long term pricing strategy of the business. On the other hand, the special order might add a long term customer for the business. So it might bring added sales in the long term.
● The business must be sure that the special order won't simply be sold on to its regular customers. It would then be undercutting itself in its own market.

Prices above normal price Assume that a business usually sells a product for £10 per unit. A customer approaches the business and offers to buy 5 000 units at £12 per unit. Should the business accept the special order? It might seem obvious that the business should accept the order. After all, the contribution on the special order would seem to be £2 per unit more than on a normal order. However, there are two factors which the business needs to take into account when making a decision.

- The special order may require such fast delivery that workers have to work overtime to complete it, driving up cost. Or it may require special packaging, or better quality materials. These extra costs will reduce contribution and could be so great that the order should be turned down.
- In the longer term, taking on the order may drive away existing customers. For example, if taking on the order means that other orders are delivered late because the business is already working at full capacity, then the business could lose customers.

Sandhu's is a small company which manufactures welded products. It has been approached by one of its customers to make a special order. Sandhu's calculates that the cost of materials plus all other variable costs for the order would be £15 000. The order would take five working days to complete using all the company's production facilities. Annual total fixed costs for the company are £500 000. Working 250 days a year, it apportions fixed costs to orders by the time taken to complete them. So in this case it would apportion £2 000 per day to this order.

I Discuss whether it should accept the special order if the price offered by the customer were (a) £10 000; (b) £20 000; (c) £30 000.

keyterms

Special order - **a one-off order which is not part of the normal trade of the business.**

checklist

1 How might break-even analysis help a business decide whether to launch a new product?
2 Fixed costs for a product line are £100 000. The contribution made on each unit sold of the product is £2. Explain how you would calculate the break-even level of output from this data.
3 Explain how the following would affect the break-even level of output: (a) a fall in total fixed costs; (b) a fall in average variable costs; (c) a rise in the price or average revenue of a product.
4 Why might a business price a special order differently from regular orders?
5 Explain why a business might be prepared to sell a product at less than its full cost.

The past couple of years have been excellent for Sease Ltd. Its order book has been so full that it has had to turn away business. A full order book has also meant that it has not had to discount its prices to win enough orders to keep its production facilities operating at full capacity.

However, turning away orders and not pursuing new business has been frustrating for the company. Marvin Sease, the managing director, reckons that the company could have sold an extra 20-30 per cent by value if it had had the capacity. He is therefore now seriously looking at moving to larger premises, buying more machinery and taking on extra workers. In the long term, there are excellent prospects for the company and so Marvin would like to build in room for expansion over a 3-5 year period. Having to move and then to move again when the new premises proved too small would be time consuming for all staff and costly.

Marvin Sease is looking at possible premises about half a mile from the existing site. Fixed costs at the existing site are £600 000 per annum and variable costs are £10 per unit of output. At the new site, fixed costs would be £1 million but greater efficiencies would reduce variable costs to an estimated £8 per unit of output if it were operating at full capacity. Moving to the new site would raise full capacity output 50 per cent, from 100 000 units of production per year to 150 000 units.

There are many considerations which Marvin has to taken into account before making a decision as to whether to move. However, first he needs to work out whether this new site would make economic sense or whether he needs to look further.

1 (a) Either by drawing a break-even chart or by using contribution, calculate the break-even point at the existing premises and at the new premises. Assume that revenues per unit do not change as output increases. (8 marks).
  (b) Evaluate whether or not moving to the proposed new site makes 'economic sense'. (12 marks)
2 Assume that the company has moved to the new site and its current monthly production averages 124 000 units per year. A customer approaches the company, asking Sease to quote for a special order of 1 000 units. Assess the factors which should be taken into account by Sease when setting the price for this possible order.

NTL

Knowledge NTL is a US company whose operations are mainly in the UK and other European countries. In the 1990s and early 2000s it went from being a small company to a major player in the cable, telephone and Internet markets.

Application NTL grew through *acquisition*, buying up *companies* from cable operators to telephone companies to football clubs. In the process it had amassed a £12 billion *debt* by 2001. However, the banks which had lent this money underestimated NTL's future *cash flow*.

By the end of 2001, it was becoming clear that the cash flow needed to meet repayments on the debt was insufficient. NTL responded to this cash flow crisis by

Analysis adopting a strategy to boost revenues, cut costs and raise cash through sales of non-core operations. 4 000 out of 17 000 staff were due to be made redundant by the end of 2002. Capital investment was slashed. NTL hoped that its revenues would rise as existing customers add services to their existing packages. The company forecast that in 2002, average subscriber revenue would rise from £39.50 a month to £50.00 a month. Some of its businesses were put up for sale, including its mobile phone mast business. The measures taken by NTL's top management proved ineffective. In May 2002, the company filed for bankruptcy

Evaluation because its cash flow was insufficient to pay its debts.

NTL had been overambitious in its acquisition spree. It paid too much for the companies it bought. Also, its capital investment, mainly in laying new cables for cable television, failed to bring the promised returns. It was too optimistic about the take-up of cable television and telephone and Internet services. Buying into tomorrow's technology is a great risk for any company. NTL was just one of the companies which paid the price of that risk taking in the dot.com bubble of late 1990s.

Adapted from the *Financial Times*, 15.12.2001, BBC News 2.1.2003.

FREE Installation

Broadband, Digital TV and Phone package
only £30 a month

ntl:

Cash flow

The importance of **cash flow** to a business was explained in unit 27. Cash flow is the movement of cash through a business. Typically, the main day to day source of cash flowing into a business is from payments for products by customers. Cash can also come in when a business borrows money from a bank. Or a company can raise money by issuing new shares. Cash flows out of a business when it pays for materials, pays the wages of its workers, or makes repayments on a loan for example.

Cash flow is likely to be uneven through the year. Figure 83.1 shows the amount of cash in a business over a 12 month period.
● When the cash line is going upwards, cash flow is positive. More cash is coming into the business than is going out.
● When the cash line is going downwards, cash flow is negative. More cash is flowing out than coming in.
This business, like many others, has to use an **overdraft facility** (see unit 25) with its bank to cope with the periods of the year when its **cash balance** is negative (i.e. less than £0).

Cash flow forecasts

As part of their normal financial planning, businesses

forecast cash flow. This allows them to plan for changes in the pattern of cash flowing into and out of the business over a period of time. If a business, for example, plans to make a large one-off investment in new machinery, it must work out where the cash to pay for the investment will come from and when the cash will be needed.

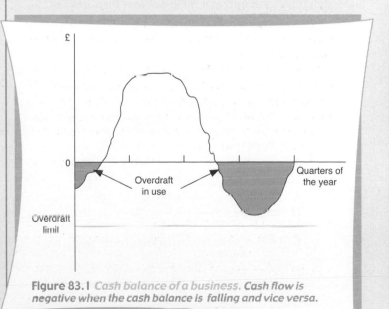

Figure 83.1 *Cash balance of a business. Cash flow is negative when the cash balance is falling and vice versa.*

There is a number of variables which could change the cash flow which is forecast.

Sales Some businesses have sales which are fairly predictable. A local corner grocery or a large supermarket chain, for example, are unlikely to see large sudden changes in their sales over a six to 12 month period.

However, other businesses can experience large, sudden and unexpected changes. For example, airlines over the past 15 years have seen several sudden large falls in demand due to terrorism or war. Demand has often taken years to recover.

Some businesses, such as marketing companies or investment bankers, are strongly affected by the business cycle (see unit 50). When the economy goes into recession and total output goes down, by perhaps 1 per cent, these businesses can see demand for their services cut by 25 per cent or 50 per cent. Businesses suffering a fall in sales could easily slash their marketing budget or put back plans to use investment bankers to take over another business.

In the toy market or in clothes retailing demand might rise or fall due to fashions. Getting the product which everyone wants to buy into the shops at the right time can see sales rise unexpectedly by 20 or 40 per cent. Getting the wrong product in front of customers can mean that sales fall by 20 or 40 per cent.

Costs Costs are unlikely to change as much as sales in the short term. But there can still be large swings in the price of raw materials, such as oil. For a road haulage company, a 10-20 per cent rise in the price of petrol within a period of months can have a very damaging effect on overall costs and profitability.

Prices Most businesses have a large amount of control over their prices. But some businesses are price takers (see unit 15). Farmers, for example, have to accept the market price for their product and so have little or no control over prices. They therefore find it difficult to forecast cash flow because the price they put into their prediction is unlikely to be the exact price they finally receive.

Start-up cash flow Many businesses which are starting up fail to predict their cash flow accurately. Partly this is because they don't have the information to put into their forecast. They only have a vague idea of what their sales might be. Without knowing their production and sales, they can't

accurately forecast costs. But partly it is because most entrepreneurs who start up businesses are too optimistic about cash flow. Typically, costs are larger than forecast and it takes longer to begin production than anticipated. So sales revenues start coming in later than forecast. This combination can have a devastating effect on cash flow during the first few months of a business.

Risks and uncertainties

When drawing up cash flow forecasts, businesses must understand the risks they face if the forecast turns out differently.

- If cash flow is greater than expected they might be left with an excess of funds.
- If cash flow is less than expected they might run out of money to pay bills. If they can't borrow or raise the money elsewhere they may be forced to close down.

They also need to assess the likelihood of the forecast being achieved.

- Some businesses operate in highly stable markets where the quality of the data used in the forecast is excellent. Other businesses operate in unstable markets where past data are a poor predictor of what will happen in future.
- New businesses often don't have accurate or valid data on which to base forecasts.
- The further away the period being forecast, the more variables are likely to change.

All these factors need to be taken into account in decision making.

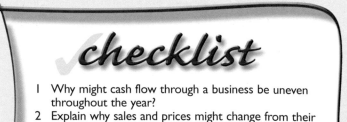

checklist

1. Why might cash flow through a business be uneven throughout the year?
2. Explain why sales and prices might change from their predicted values over a year.
3. Why do new businesses have more difficulty than established businesses in forecasting cash flow?
4. Why is risk important for a business?

For Jill and Ken Matchett, the past twelve months have been very difficult. This time last year they were hoping for a turnaround in their farming business after three years of losses. The cash flow forecast they prepared at the time for 2004 is shown in Table 83.1. However, a combination of factors conspired to bring about yet another poor financial year. Large amounts of rain around harvest time reduced their wheat yields and revenues by 50 per cent whilst the price of flowers also fell by 25 per cent. At the same time, they had to contend with rising oil prices and higher fertiliser costs which added 20 per cent to their materials costs.

	January–March	April–June	July–September	October–December
				£000
Receipts				
Wheat	0	0	0	10
Flowers	8	8	8	8
Other receipts	7	9	11	11
Total receipts	15	17	19	29
Payments				
Wages	1	1	1	1
Materials such as oil, feed and fertiliser	5	5	5	5
Other costs	6	6	6	6
Drawings	5	5	5	5
Total payments	17	17	17	17
Net cash flow	-2	0	2	12
Opening balance	-7	-9	-9	-7
Closing balance	-9	-9	-7	5

Table 83.1 *Cash flow forecast for four quarters, 2004*

The Matchett's overdraft increased by around £5 000 because they withdrew more from the business than the cash it generated. The overdraft now stands at approximately £12 000, and at one point they touched their overdraft limit of £16 000. For 2005, they cannot afford to add to their overdraft and ideally would like to reduce it.

They are aware of the risks they face as farmers. In preparing the cash flow forecast for this year, they have left their revenue predictions the same as last year as shown in Table 83.1. However, they have factored in the increase in materials costs and consequently their net cash flow forecast is lower than the forecast for 2004. If they have another bad year, they may be forced to give up the farm they have rented for the past 35 years, although they have no idea how they would pay off the overdraft if it came to this.

1 Recalculate the cash flow forecast shown in Table 83.1 to produce the cash flow outturn for 2004. To do this, copy out the table putting in new values where appropriate. (20 marks)
2 Discuss the risks that the Matchetts face in 2005 and evaluate TWO ways in which they might reduce those risks. (20 marks)

84 Investment decision making

Juniper Pattern and Tool Company

Knowledge Juniper Pattern and Tool Company is a small company specialising in the manufacture of mould tooling, fixtures and patterns.

Application It is considering making an *investment* in a new state-of-the-art CNC lathe. The new lathe would allow it to *compete* for high precision work, enabling it to *differentiate* its *product* from *low cost producers* in the Far East. The *cost* of the lathe is £60 000. The managing director, Bill Juniper, is aware that there is a variety of *investment appraisal* methods to help him decide whether the investment should go ahead. These include the *payback method*, the *average rate of return method* and the *net present value method*. He wants to see a *rate of return* on his investment of at least 15 per cent. The machine will be *financed* through a *bank loan*.

Analysis Having done the calculations, Bill Juniper sees that the payback period is three years. The average rate of return is 18 per cent and the net present value, assuming a life of 10 years for the machine with a discount rate of 15 per cent, is £150 000.

Evaluation The markets into which Bill Juniper sells are highly competitive. He is concerned that a three year payback period exposes the company to the risk of default on the loan if there is a sudden downturn in orders. Equally, he knows that without continued investment in the latest technology, his company is at risk from losing orders to lower cost overseas competitors. The net present value investment appraisal method shows that, on current best estimates, in the long term the investment could be highly profitable. On balance, he therefore decides to take the risk and buy the machine.

Capital investment

Buildings and **capital equipment** (see unit 24) such as machinery, vehicles and plant, are all examples of **physical capital**. Businesses need physical capital to make the products they sell. CAPITAL INVESTMENT takes place when a business buys new capital equipment and buildings. Capital investment is investment in physical assets which will be used over a period of time. During that time, they will **depreciate** (see unit 75) and eventually, without further capital investment, will become worthless.

How does a business decide whether to undertake capital investment? One way is to make use of numbers, data and mathematics. This is QUANTITATIVE DECISION MAKING. Quantitative decision making takes into account factors that can be **measured**. They might be, for example, the amount of profit in pounds, the amount of cash flowing into or out of the business in pounds, the length of time in years or the return as a percentage.

There is a number of quantitative techniques of INVESTMENT APPRAISAL, three of which will be considered in this unit. Investment appraisal is a process of:
● working out whether an investment project should go ahead or be rejected;
● appraising a variety of investment projects to determine which will be chosen because it is likely to give the highest financial return.

Net cash flow and cumulative cash flow

This unit considers three methods of investment appraisal - the payback method, the average or accounting rate of return method, and the net present value method which makes use of discounted cash flow. These methods take into account the cash flow from an investment. They analyse:
● Net cash flow resulting from an investment. This is the difference between the cash flowing into the business and the cash flowing out of the business. The inflow of cash is the income that is being earned by the business as a result of the investment. The outflow of cash is the costs that result from the investment. These include the initial costs and any extra costs of running the machine each year.
● CUMULATIVE CASH FLOW. This is the running total or addition of all the net cash flows to date. When cumulative cash flow is positive, the investment has become profitable.

Look at Table 84.1 which shows a business which has bought a machine for £100 000. The initial investment causes a **cash outflow** of £100 000. The **cash inflow** for the year is zero because the machine is not yet earning for the business. So the **net cash flow** for the period is -£100 000.

In the first year of operation, the machine earns the business £60 000. This is the cash inflow. The machine costs £20 000 to run. This is cash outflow. The net cash flow in year 1 is £60 000 - £20 000 = £40 000. The **cumulative cash**

flow is the total of the net cash flows so far, ie -£100 000 + £40 000 = -£60 000. Only in year three does the cumulative cash flow become positive at £10 000 and the investment become profitable.

	Initial cost	Year 1	Year 2	Year 3
Cash inflow	£0	£60 000	£70 000	£40 000
Cash outflow	£100 000	£20 000	£20 000	£20 000
Net cash flow	(£100 000)	£40 000	£50 000	£20 000
Cumulative cash flow	(£100 000)	(£60 000)	(£10 000)	£10 000

Table 84.1 *Net cash flow from investment*

The payback method

The PAYBACK METHOD is the simplest method of investment appraisal. Table 84.2 shows the expected net cash flows of an investment project to buy a new machine over five years. The business predicts that it will take time for sales to build up. The machine will therefore operate at less than full capacity in its first few years. It also predicts that it will take a year to train staff to use the machine, which will result in higher than normal costs.

If the cost of the machine is £50 000, the PAYBACK PERIOD is three years. The payback period is the amount of time taken to recoup the initial £50 000 after taking into account the running costs of the investment. It is the point where the cumulative cash flow becomes £0. This can be seen from Table 84.2 because the net cash flow in the first three years is £50 000 (-£10 000 + £20 000 + £40 000), equal to the initial £50 000 investment. From this point on, the investment will start earning a profit for the business.

If the initial investment were £90 000, and other costs were the same, then the payback period would be 4 years (£90 000 = - £10 000 + £20 000 + £40 000 + £40 000).

The payback period is often not an exact number of years. Say the initial cost of the investment is £75 000. Then £50 000 will have been repaid after three years. The remaining £25 000 is then repaid during the fourth year when net cash flow is £40 000. So it will take:

$$\frac{\text{Cash required}}{\text{Net cash flow for year}} = \frac{£25\ 000}{£40\ 000} = 0.625$$

of the year to repay the investment. Multiplying this by 12 to get the number of months, it is 7.5 months. Rounding this up, the total payback period is 3 years and 8 months.

In reality, the net cash flow is likely to be uneven in any year. Many businesses, for example, have better cash flows at the start of the year and the end of the year because of the effect of Christmas on sales. A more sophisticated payback analysis would take this into account.

There are two ways in which payback might be used.
- A business may have a policy that no investment project will go ahead unless the payback period is less than a certain length of time, such as two years.
- A business may compare payback periods on different investments and invest in the project with the shortest payback period. Table 84.3 shows the net cash flows (or net income) from three possible investment projects, A to C. They have different net cash flows and cease to have any net cash flow after 7 years. The total net cash flow from each investment is also different. Assume that the initial cost of each investment is £35 000. The project with the shortest payback period is Project C, which is 2 years. If the business can only afford one investment project, according to the payback method, it would choose Project C.

									£000	
Year	0	1	2	3	4	5	6	7	Total net cash flow	Payback period
Project A										
Net cash flow	(35)	5	10	15	20	25	20	15	75	3yrs3mts
Cumulative cash flow	(35)	(30)	(20)	(5)	15	40	60	75		
Project B										
Net cash flow	(35)	10	10	15	15	15	15	15	60	3yrs
Cumulative cash flow	(35)	(25)	(15)	0	15	30	45	60		
Project C										
Net cash flow	(35)	20	15	10	5	0	0	0	15	2yrs
Cumulative cash flow	(35)	(15)	0	10	15	15	15	15		

Table 84.3 *Expected net cash flow from three investment projects*

Advantages The payback method has a number of advantages.
- It is simple to use. This is probably the most important reason why it is the most widely used method of investment appraisal by businesses.
- The payback method minimises the **risk** of investment. Income and cost streams three, five or ten years out from the initial investment are difficult to predict. The quicker the investment is repaid, the less risk that the investment will be unprofitable. This is especially important for businesses in high risk, fast changing industries.
- Businesses experiencing **cash flow problems** need to boost their cash flow as quickly as possible. Minimising the payback period ensures that this happens.

Disadvantages There are also some disadvantages with the payback method.
- It ignores the value of expected net cash flow and therefore profit earned after the payback period. Table 84.3 shows this clearly. Project C has the quickest payback period but by far the expected lowest total return.
- It is difficult to use if competing investment projects have different initial costs. For example, in Table 84.3, what

	Initial cost	Year 1	Year 2	Year 3	Year 4	Year 5
Cash inflow	£0	£10 000	£30 000	£60 000	£60 000	£60 000
Cash outflow	£50 000	£20 000	£10 000	£20 000	£20 000	£20 000
Net cash flow	(£50 000)	(£10 000)	£20 000	£40 000	£40 000	£40 000
Cumulative cash flow	(£50 000)	(£60 000)	(£40 000)	£0	£40 000	£80 000

Table 84.2 *Expected cash flow from an investment project*

if Project C had an initial cost of £20 000 whilst Project A had an initial cost of £15 000? Project C then has the lower payback period of one year compared to Project A with two years (£10 000 + £5 000). However, spending £20 000 is riskier than spending £15 000. So payback here does not necessarily reflect the amount of risk in investment.

							£ million
Year	0 Initial cost	1	2	3	4	5	6
Project W							
Cash inflow	0	2.5	2.8	3.5	3.5	3.0	2.0
Cash outflow	4.2	1.2	1.3	1.5	1.5	1.2	0.4
Net cash flow							
Project X							
Cash inflow	0	3.5	3.8	4.5	4.5	4.0	3.0
Cash outflow	6.6	2.5	2.8	3.0	3.0	2.6	1.8
Net cash flow							
Project Y							
Cash inflow	0	5.5	5.5	5.0	4.0	3.0	1.0
Cash outflow	8.0	5.0	4.0	3.0	2.0	1.0	0.4
Net cash flow							
Project Z							
Cash inflow	0	4.0	4.0	4.5	5.5	6.5	2.3
Cash outflow	8.0	1.8	1.8	1.9	1.5	1.1	0.5
Net cash flow							

Table 84.4 *Expected net cash flow from four investment projects*

Durkan's is a component manufacturer for the aviation industry. It is currently considering four investment projects, codenamed W, X, Y and Z. Cash outflows and inflows of the projects are shown in Table 84.4. The investments cease to produce any net cash at the end of year 6.

> 1 **Calculate (a) the net cash flow for each investment project in each year; (b) the payback period for each investment project.**
>
> 2 **Explain why, if it could only go ahead with one investment project, it might choose Project W if it used the payback method of decision making.**

The average rate of return

The AVERAGE RATE OF RETURN (ARR) or ACCOUNTING RATE OF RETURN method of investment appraisal calculates the average percentage return on an investment. This is measured by the formula:

$$\text{Average rate of return} = \frac{\text{Average net return (or net profit) per annum}}{\text{Initial outlay (or initial cost) of investment}} \times 100\%$$

The method can be compared to saving money in a building society account. Assume that you put £100 into a savings account and earned £5 interest in the first year, £7 in the second year, and £6, £5, and £7 in the three remaining years. In total the interest earned was £30 (£5 + £7 + £6 + £5 + £7). On average, the interest per year was the total interest £30 divided by the number of years invested, 5 years. This makes £6 per year. So the average interest rate was £6 divided by the amount in the account, £100, making 6 per cent.

For a business making an investment, interest is the equivalent of profit. However, in a building society, the saver doesn't lose the £100 saved. But, for a business, the cost of the investment is a cash outflow and therefore must be deducted from the profit earned each year from the investment to arrive at the total net profit.

Look at Tables 84.3 and 84.5. How can the ARR be calculated?

- Projects A, B and C have net cash flows for seven years. The initial outlay is £35 000. The total net cash flow is shown in the next to last column in Table 84.3 and the second column in Table 84.5.
- This is then divided by the number of years over which profit is generated, in this case seven years, to arrive at average annual profit.
- The average annual profit is divided by the cost of the investment and converted into a percentage to find the average rate of return.

The ARRs range from 6 to 31 per cent. A figure of around 20 per cent might make a sound investment return for British industry today given the risk involved in the investment. Figures much over 20 per cent would be highly attractive investments. A business would be unlikely to invest if the projected return were just 6 per cent.

	Net total cash flow	Average return per year over 7 years	Initial outlay	Average annual rate of return
	£	£	£	%
Project A	75 000	10 714	35 000	31
Project B	60 000	8 571	35 000	24
Project C	15 000	2 142	35 000	6

Table 84.5 *Average annual rate of return on three investment projects*

Advantages The main advantage of the ARR method over the payback method is that it takes into account all the income streams from the investment, not just those in the payback period. It is also relatively easy to perform the calculations necessary.

Disadvantages The main disadvantage of the method is that it fails to take into account that the value of £1 of profit declines the later it is earned. It is therefore an inferior method in this respect to the discounted cash flow method explained later in this unit.

Look at Table 84.4 in the case study on page 376.

1 **Calculate for each of the projects W to Z (a) the net total cash flow; (b) the average return per year in pounds; and (c) the average rate of return as a percentage on each of the projects W to Z.**

2 **Explain why, if it could only go ahead with one investment project, it might choose Project Z if it used the average rate of return method of decision making.**

Discounted cash flow

When making an investment decision a business might take into account what cash flow or profit earned in future is worth now. Look at Table 84.6. This shows that £100 invested today at a compound interest rate of 10 per cent would be worth £161 in five years' time.

- In one year's time, the investment would be worth £110. Of this, £10 would be the interest and £100 would be the initial investment.
- In two years' time, it would be worth £121. With compound interest, the interest is based not on the initial investment but on the investment at the end of the first year. So interest is 10 per cent of £110, making £11. Then this has to be added to the £110 value at the end of the first year to make a total of £121 for the second year.

This carries on until the value after five years is £161.

Year	1	2	3	4	5
Value of £100	£110	£121	£133	£146	£161

Table 84.6 *Value of £100 invested over five years at 10 per cent per annum compound interest*

If £100 today is worth £161 in five years' time, it must be true that £161 in five years' time is worth just £100 today. This is an example of an important insight of DISCOUNTED CASH FLOW techniques. Money in the future is worth less than the same amount now (the PRESENT VALUE). This is because money available today could be invested and it could earn interest.

Note that this is a completely different idea to the fact that money in the future can also become devalued due to the effects of inflation. Inflation does indeed affect future values of money. So there are two effects on the value of future money. Discounted cash flow techniques just deal with one of these, the effect of interest rates.

DISCOUNT TABLES can be used to show by how much a future value must be multiplied to calculate its present value. Table 84.7 shows a discount table with five different rates of interest. If an investment project were predicted to give a net cash flow of £10 000 in three years' time, and the discount rate were 10 per cent, then reading off the table, the £10 000 would need to be multiplied by 0.75. To arrive at its present value the calculation would be:

$$£10\ 000 \times 0.75 = £7\ 500.$$

So £10 000 received in five years' time at a DISCOUNT RATE/interest rate of 5 per cent is worth £7 500 today. Cash flow or profit of £15 000 from an investment project received in 5 years' time, a discount/interest rate of 20 per cent, would be £15 000 x 0.40 or £6 000.

The discount table shown in Table 84.7 also shows two features of discounting.

- The higher the rate of discount, the less the present value of cash flow in future. This is the reverse of saying that the higher the rate of interest, the greater will be the value of an investment in the future.
- The further into the future the cash flow or earnings from an investment project, the less is their present value. So £1 000 earned in five years' time is worth less than £1 000 earned in one year's time. Again this is simply the opposite way of saying that £1 000 invested today at a fixed rate of interest will be worth more in five years' time than in one year's time.

Year	5%	10%	15%	20%	25%
					Rate of discount
0	1.00	1.00	1.00	1.00	1.00
1	0.95	0.91	0.87	0.83	0.80
2	0.91	0.83	0.76	0.69	0.64
3	0.86	0.75	0.66	0.58	0.51
4	0.82	0.68	0.57	0.48	0.41
5	0.78	0.62	0.50	0.40	0.33
6	0.75	0.56	0.43	0.33	0.26
7	0.71	0.51	0.38	0.28	0.21
8	0.68	0.47	0.33	0.23	0.17
9	0.64	0.42	0.28	0.19	0.13
10	0.61	0.39	0.25	0.16	0.10

Table 84.7 *Discount table*

Net present value method

The NET PRESENT VALUE METHOD makes use of discounted cash flow. It calculates the rate of return on an investment project taking into account the effects of interest rates and time. Using discount tables, it is possible to calculate the net present value of an investment project.

Table 84.8 shows three investment projects. The initial cost of each investment project is £50 000, shown in the Year 0 row. In years 1 to 10, each produces a stream of net cash flow. When added up, these come to far more than the initial £50 000. So it might appear that each investment project is profitable. However, if the net cash flow is discounted using a discount rate of 20 per cent, the picture is very different.

- **Project A**. The sum of the present values in years 1-10 for Project A is just £41 700. The net cash flow each year is constant at £10 000. But the present value of each of those £10 000 falls the further away it is received. By year 10, the present value of £10 000 discounted at 20 per cent is just £1 600. The NET PRESENT VALUE can be calculated simply by totalling the present value figures in years 0-10, including subtracting the initial cost. Or it can be calculated using the formula:

Net present value = present values - initial cost = £41 700 - £50 000 = - £8 300.

So project A is unprofitable according to discounted cash flow techniques.

Year	Project A Net cash flow £	Project A Present value £	Project B Net cash flow £	Project B Present Value £	Project C Net cash flow £	Project C Present Value £	Discount table Rate of discount at 20%
0	(50 000)	(50 000)	(50 000)	(50 000)	(50 000)	(50 000)	1.00
1	10 000	8 300	5 000	4 150	20 000	16 600	0.83
2	10 000	6 900	8 000	5 520	16 000	11 040	0.69
3	10 000	5 800	10 000	5 800	14 000	8 120	0.58
4	10 000	4 800	12 000	5 760	12 000	5 760	0.48
5	10 000	4 000	12 000	4 800	12 000	4 800	0.40
6	10 000	3 300	12 000	4 000	12 000	4 000	0.33
7	10 000	2 800	12 000	3 360	12 000	3 360	0.28
8	10 000	2 300	14 000	3 220	10 000	2 300	0.23
9	10 000	1 900	16 000	3 040	8 000	1 520	0.19
10	10 000	1 600	20 000	3 200	5 000	800	0.16
Total net cash flow before discounting	50 000		71 000		71 000		
Present values years 1-10		41 700		42 850		58 300	
Net present value (NPV)		(8 300)		(7 150)		+8 300	

Table 84.8 *Net present value of three investment projects discounted at 20 per cent*

- **Project B**. The total net cash flow before discounting is higher than for Project A, £71 000 compared to £50 000. But once discounted, there is little difference in the sum of the present values. This is because net cash flow in Project B is weighted towards later years. The net present value of this project is £42 850 - £50 000 = - £7 150. Again, Project B is unprofitable according to discounted cash flow techniques.

- **Project C**. The total net cash flow before discounting is the same as with Project B. Indeed, the pattern of net cash flow is an exact reverse of those of Project B. Here, the higher net cash flow figures are concentrated at the start and fall off towards the end. This means that the total present value is much higher than with Project B. The net present value of Project C is £58 300 - £50 000 = £8 300. This is the discounted profit that the business will make on this project.

The net present value method would suggest that a business should go ahead with any investment projects that have a positive net present value. If a business has to make a choice between investment projects for whatever reason, it should go for those with the highest net present value. So in this case it would choose Project C.

Advantages
- The net present value method, unlike the payback method and the average rate of return, correctly accounts for the value of future earnings by calculating present values.
- The discount rate used can be changed as risk and conditions in financial markets change. For example, in the 1990s, the cost of bank borrowing for many businesses fell from over 15 per cent to 7-8 per cent. Investment projects therefore did not need to make such a high rate of return to be profitable and so the rate of discount could be lowered.

Disadvantages
- Calculating discounted cash flow is the most complex of the three methods. It certainly can't be done 'on the back of an envelope' as can the other two methods. As such, it is rarely used by small businesses.

- The rate of discount used is critical in determining what is and is not profitable. The higher the discount rate, the fewer investment projects are likely to be profitable.

An alternative method to the net present value method is the INTERNAL RATE OF RETURN METHOD. With the net present value method, a discount rate is chosen which reflects the rate of return a business would like to earn on its capital investment. If the net present value is positive, then the discount rate has been more than achieved, i.e. the rate of return is greater than the discount rate. In comparison, the internal rate of return method calculates what the discount rate would be if the net present value were exactly zero. This discount rate is then the exact rate of return the business would earn on its capital investment.

The mathematics to calculate the internal rate of return (IRR) is complicated but handheld financial calculators have a program which will calculate it if the net cash flows for each time period are put into an equation. So it is relatively easy for a business to calculate the IRR.

Gethings is a garment manufacturer in London. It is considering making an investment in one of two machines, A and B. The projected net cash flows for each machine are shown in Table 84.9.

							£000
Year	0 Initial cost	1	2	3	4	5	6
Machine A							
Net cash flow	(600)	100	150	200	300	200	100
Discounted cash flow							
Machine B							
Net cash flow	(600)	200	300	200	150	100	100
Discounted cash flow							

Table 84.9 *Expected net cash flow from two investment projects*

1 **Calculate the discounted cash flow for each machine and each year using a discount rate of 15 per cent from the discount table, Table 84.9.**
2 **Calculate the net present value for each machine.**
3 **Explain why Gethings might buy Machine B if it uses the net present value method of decision making.**

To decide whether to go ahead with an investment, a business should compare the IRR of a project with the minimum rate of return it expects to earn from investment. If the IRR on a project is 25 per cent and the minimum rate of return required is 15 per cent, then the project should go ahead. If the IRR is only 12 per cent, however, it is not high enough to proceed.

The limitations of quantitative techniques

The answers given by quantitative techniques are likely to form only part of the decision making process for investment. There is a number of reasons for this.

- One problem with relying on quantitative investment appraisal techniques is that there is no single technique which provides a 'right' answer. For example, the simple payback method provides one way of assessing risk in an investment project. Discounted cash flow might provide a better picture of overall returns, particularly if the investment will yield returns over a long period. But different techniques may provide different answers as to which investment projects are most appropriate.
- Another problem, explained in unit 83, is that it is difficult to predict with any certainty future revenues and costs. It can be difficult with some investment projects even to predict the initial cost of the investment. A new football stadium, for example, may be difficult to cost. Decision makers therefore have to make qualitative judgements about whether to proceed with an investment even though quantitative techniques suggest it should be profitable.

- Qualitative factors, such as the risk of a downturn in the economy or the aims of businesses, may be more important in decision making. The answers given by quantitative techniques then become just one part of the evidence used to decide whether to proceed with the investment (see unit 85).

1 Explain why a company buying a new computer would be an example of capital investment.
2 A business calculates that it will cost £100 000 to install a new computer system. Explain how this might form part of a quantitative decision.
3 What is the difference between net cash flow and cumulative cash flow?
4 Why is a cumulative cash flow of 0 important in the payback method of investment appraisal?
5 'The average rate of return on the project is 10 per cent per annum.' Explain how this might be calculated.
6 Explain why the present value of £100 available in five years' time is £62 if the discount rate is 10 per cent.
7 Explain the relationship between the initial cost of a project, the present value of its future net cash flows and its net present value.
8 What are the limitations of quantitative techniques in investment decision making?

keyterms

Average rate of return or accounting rate of return (ARR) - the total net earnings of an investment project (i.e. after its costs have been paid) divided by its initial cost and expressed as a yearly percentage.

Capital investment - expenditure on capital equipment such as machinery, vehicles and plant.

Cumulative cash flow - the running total or addition of all the net cash flows to date.

Discounted cash flow (DCF) - a stream of cash flows over a period of time which have been adjusted by a discount rate to account for the fact that cash in the future is worth less than it is today.

Discount rate - the percentage rate at which net earnings are discounted back in time to their present value; it is the equivalent of an interest rate used to calculate future returns on an investment.

Discount table - a table which shows the numbers by which net earnings must be multiplied depending upon the year in which they are earned and the discount rate.

Internal rate of return method - a method used to evaluate an investment project where the discount rate is calculated assuming net present value is zero.

Investment - any expenditure intended to raise a mix of production, sales, cash flow and profit in the future.

Investment appraisal - quantitative techniques used to evaluate investment decisions.

Net present value (NPV) - the value at a point in time of a stream of future net cash flows discounted back to the present time at a discount rate.

Net present value method or discounted cash flow method - a method of investment appraisal where the net present value (NPV) of an investment project is calculated; a positive NPV indicates that the project should be undertaken.

Payback method - a method of investment decision making where investment projects are judged by the shortness of their payback period.

Payback period - the length of time that is estimated that net earnings (or net cash flow) will cover the initial cost of an investment.

Present value - the value of future net earnings or net cash flow discounted back to the present using a discount rate.

Quantitative decision making - making decisions where decision making is based solely on numbers, exact data and mathematics.

Ladkins is a manufacturer of fireworks. It is currently replacing some of its existing equipment and investigating which one of two possible investment projects, A or B, should go ahead. Projected net cash flows for the two investment projects are shown in Table 84.10. Both investment projects foresee that the equipment will need replacing after 6 years.

The firework market has been expanding strongly over the past ten years. It used to be a highly seasonal market with most sales concentrated around November 5th, Guy Fawkes night. Today, the November period is still very important, especially since the Hindu festival of Divali occurs around that time. However, fireworks are now demanded far more frequently at other times of the year, from birthday and wedding celebrations, to corporate events and New Year. This expansion of demand is forecast to continue into the foreseeable future.

However, increasing globalisation has introduced new competition into the UK market. Chinese manufacturers are gaining some market share. Although some people have raised doubts about the safety of their products and their quality, they are sold at a substantial discount to UK made fireworks. Ladkins is becoming increasingly concerned about the effect this competition might have on future sales.

							£million
Year	0 Initial cost	1	2	3	4	5	6
Investment project A Net cash flow	3.0	1.1	1.9	0.5	0.2	0.1	0.1
Investment project B Net cash flow	2.4	0.4	0.6	1.0	1.6	1.2	0.8

Table 84.10 *Net cash flow for two investment projects, A and B*

Year	0	1	2	3	4	5	6
Rate of discount	1.00	0.87	0.76	0.66	0.57	0.50	0.43

Table 84.11 *Discount table: discount rate 15%*

1 Conduct an investment appraisal on the two investment projects. Explain which investment project should be undertaken if the decision is based solely on (a) the payback method, (b) the average rate of return method and (c) the net present value method. For the net present value method, assume that a discount rate of 15 per cent is used. Show all your workings clearly. (20 marks)

2 To what extent should Ladkins consider risk when making its investment decision? (20 marks)

85 Qualitative decision making

Hewlett Packard

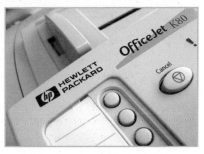

Knowledge Hewlett-Packard (HP) is a multi-billion dollar US technology company which is a market leader in printers and imaging solutions. In 2002, it launched a $2 million initiative in a range of projects in Kuppam in India.

Application The *investment*, according to HP Vice-President Maureen Conway, would have a *payback* of two years. Extra *sales* would be generated in two ways. One was *goodwill*. Positive *PR* and promotion of the *corporate image* leading indirectly to extra sales. The other was where new solutions and business model *innovation* led to *market growth* and so extra sales. On both *quantitative* and *qualitative* grounds, the investment made sense.

Analysis HP was initially motivated to become involved in Third World development projects because it would help create an image of HP as a socially responsible company. But it realised that simply giving money to development projects often led to failed development projects. Instead, it decided to enter into a partnership with the government of the state of Andrhra Pradesh to develop IT capabilities in a range of projects. By making the project semi-commercial, it would ensure the long run viability of the scheme. Local people would be buying HP equipment at commercial prices. HP would be developing and selling equipment which local people could afford to buy and operate at a profit.

Evaluation The decision by HP to invest was a shrewd one. It gained new markets, profit and good PR. There was a risk that the project would fail, but HP had the financial resources to write off the investment if it did. Ultimately, the project has led to a win-win situation. Hewlett Packard has made a profit and local people in India have benefited from access to new technology.

Adapted from the *Financial Times*, 29.9.2003 and www.ap-it.com/neelamma.html

Qualitative decision making

There are many ways in which businesses might make investment decisions. In unit 84, **quantitative** techniques were considered. Quantitative techniques take in account numbers, formulae and mathematics, using factors which are measurable to give answers to problems. However, quantitative techniques have their own problems, as explained in unit 84.

It is equally important to understand that the answers given by quantitative techniques form only one part of the investment decision making process. Qualitative factors are likely to be as important if not more important. In QUALITATIVE DECISION MAKING, businesses are making decisions which are based on criteria which may not be measurable.

There is a number of qualitative factors which can influence whether or not a business will invest.

The objectives of businesses Different businesses have different aims and objectives (see units 62 and 63). Nearly all businesses aim to make a profit, but some aim to profit maximise, whilst others might make less than maximum profit to achieve higher sales or greater market share. Some businesses put customer service above profit. Others will accept higher costs and lower profits to ensure that their production is environmentally or ethically friendly. The aims and objectives of businesses influence their investment decision making. For example, a business which puts environmental considerations high on its list of priorities might be prepared to invest in cleaner technologies even though this is not the cheapest solution. Another business which wishes to operate fair trade principles might invest more money in its supply chain than its competitors which simply buy at cheapest world prices.

Corporate image Some investment decisions are based on the image that businesses wish to project about themselves to the wider community. For example, an international oil business may build houses for local workers. This investment may make no sense from a financial viewpoint. But it may be a small price to pay for a better international image for the company as a 'caring' company. Equally, some investment projects designed to reduce pollution may be done to impress the wider community rather than for economic or regulatory reasons.

Replacement investment Many businesses tend to spend resources on investment because this is what has happened in the past. For example, a machine may come to the end of its useful life. The business may simply replace it without considering the optimum financial solution. Or a business may roll over its marketing budget from year to year without questioning its effectiveness or how it is spent.

Confidence Entrepreneurs, managers and businesses tend to have different attitudes and cultures from each other. One aspect of this is confidence or optimism. Some decision makers tend to be very cautious, seeing all the problems that might arise if things go wrong. Others are confident and optimistic. They see the future as much better and brighter than the average. This has a crucial impact on investment. The cautious, unconfident entrepreneur or manager may delay or abandon possible investment projects. In the same circumstances with the same investment projects, confident and optimistic managers will tend to go ahead and authorise the expenditure. So the deeply held attitudes of decision makers have an important influence on investment decision making.

The financial situation of a business Different businesses find themselves in different financial situations. Some businesses have borrowed heavily in the past. For companies, this could mean that their gearing ratios (see unit 79) are high. Heavily indebted businesses may find that they cannot borrow money from banks to pursue profitable investment projects. They may also choose to use spare cash flow to cut down their debts rather than spend on new investment. Different businesses will come to different decisions about whether their debt levels should stop them from committing cash to new investments.

Risk The financial position in which a business finds itself is one factor in assessing the risk of an investment project. Others include the state of the economy and the markets into which a business sells. Investment projects which have long payback periods are also riskier than ones with shorter payback periods.

Government legislation Investment may have to take place for a business to conform to government laws and regulations. So, for example, a business may have to install anti-pollution equipment to bring down its emission levels even though this investment project could make a loss for the business. Or it may have to adapt its premises to conform to various disability regulations without seeing any return on this investment.

External factors Changes in the wider economy or the market in which a business operates can influence investment. Many changes, such as the effect of a rise in interest rates on the cost of borrowing, can be quantified. But others, like the impact of an interest rate rise on consumer confidence, or the effect on sales of a new competitor entering the market, are difficult to predict. Different businesses will come to different conclusions on these based on the same change in their external environment.

Human relations Some investment may be undertaken to motivate the workforce. For example, a business may build new

premises to a much higher specification than is necessary in order to provide an excellent working environment for staff. Or a business may go beyond the minimum in terms of health and safety regulations to ensure staff feel safe. Some investment projects may be modified or even abandoned if it is felt that they would encounter trade union or staff opposition. Maintaining jobs might be important because investment which leads to redundancies can demotivate existing staff.

✓ checklist

1 Explain the difference between quantitative and qualitative investment techniques.
2 A business aims to be environmentally friendly, have a good image in the community, is confident about its future, has borrowed heavily in the past, is risk averse and currently has to trade in a recession hit economy. Explain how each of these factors might qualitatively affect its investment decision making.

"keyterms

Qualitative decision making - **making decisions where decision making is not based solely on numbers and figures.**

Mint is a large UK based oil company which has oil fields in Angola in Africa. It is currently considering whether or not to make a large £500 million investment in a new oil field off the coast of Angola. The company currently owns the drilling rights to the field and exploratory drilling has confirmed that there is a viable amount of oil to extract. At a price of $20 a barrel, the investment would yield a projected 15 per cent rate of return on capital. There is no guarantee that prices will remain above $20 a barrel but, as Figure 85.1 shows, prices in recent years have been relatively high.

Mint is under pressure from stock market investors to increase its production. Last year saw a fall in the amount of oil it produced of 5 per cent. Although the new field would not come on stream for at least three years and take a couple of years to build up to full capacity production, announcement of the investment would probably lift the share price.

Financing the new field could prove a problem. Mint is already highly geared. Shareholders would disapprove of a rights issue to cover the cost because it would dilute their holdings. On the other hand, banks might be reluctant to lend except at relatively high rates of interest.

Oil drilling in Angola is controversial. For 20 years after securing independence from Portugal in 1975, the country was engaged in a bitter civil war where some oil companies were accused of providing the cash to allow the feuding sides to continue fighting. Since the end of the war, the government has been accused of corruption and some oil companies have come under scrutiny for bribing government ministers and officials to secure drilling rights and to continue their operations. There is a risk that Mint could be exposed to negative PR if its dealings with the government were found to be illegal. Equally, it could face prosecution by UK authorities if it were found guilty of bribery. There will be a fine line between legitimate payments to Angola's government for getting permission to exploite the oil field and kickbacks to selected government officials.

Environmental groups may also object because of the danger from drilling to the local environment. Human rights groups could object too. Local people living in the area near to the oil rigs see little or nothing of the millions of pounds generated from exploitation of oil reserves. Mint could give some aid to the local area, funding the building of a few schools or perhaps a hospital. However, such initiatives in the past have had a mixed reception with aid groups saying that it is too little and local inhabitants resentful that more is not being spent.

Source: adapted from the *Financial Times*, 2.10.2003.

1 Evaluate whether, from a quantitative and a qualitative perspective, Mint should go ahead with the proposed investment in Angola. (20 marks)

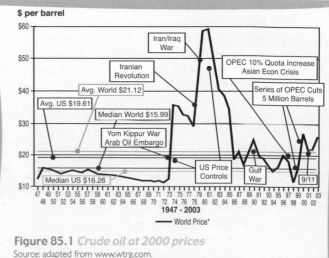

Figure 85.1 *Crude oil at 2000 prices*
Source: adapted from www.wtrg.com.

86 Communication

The meaning of communication

COMMUNICATION is the sending and receiving of **messages** between two or more individuals, groups or organisations. Messages from **senders** to **receivers** vary in their content. For example:

- they may contain **information**, such as new pay rates or new prices of products;
- they may be **instructions**, such as what work is to be carried out today or how many workers should be assigned to a particular job;
- a message could be a **question** where the sender is seeking information;
- some messages attempt to change **attitudes** and **motivation**, for example the main aim of a manager who asks employees about the health of their children might be to communicate that she cares for her staff, rather than seeking information about the health of individuals.

Internal and external communication

Communication in a business can be either internal or external.

- INTERNAL COMMUNICATION occurs when messages are passed within a business.
- EXTERNAL COMMUNICATION occurs when messages are passed from within a business to an individual or organisation outside the business like a customer or a supplier. Equally, there is external communication when an outside individual or organisation sends a message to an individual or department within the business.

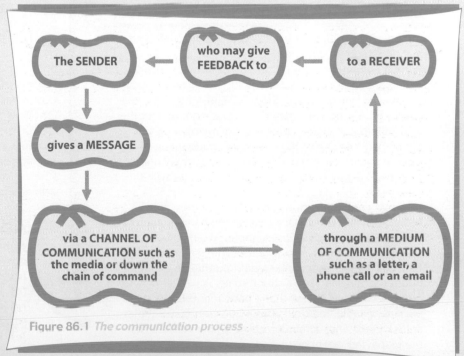

Figure 86.1 *The communication process*

The SENDER → who may give FEEDBACK to → to a RECEIVER

gives a MESSAGE

via a CHANNEL OF COMMUNICATION such as the media or down the chain of command

through a MEDIUM OF COMMUNICATION such as a letter, a phone call or an email

The communication process

Communication can be seen as a system as shown in Figure 86.1.

- **Senders** in a business can be anybody from the managing director to a shop floor worker. If the communication is external, it could be a customer, a tax official or local government officer sending a message.
- The **message** is what is communicated, such as information or a request.
- The CHANNEL OF COMMUNICATION is the route taken by the message. For example, the managing director may dictate a note to her assistant to be put up on the three notice boards in the office or the company intranet which will be read by all staff. A customer may order a bed from a sales assistant, who enters the details on a computer with the message being sent electronically to the manufacturers.
- The MEDIUM OF COMMUNICATION (or COMMUNICATION MEDIA or METHOD OF COMMUNICATION) is the method or medium used to communicate a message. This could be face-to-face communication using words, gestures and body language. It could be written communication, such as a letter, a memorandum (a 'memo'), an email, a fax, a report, a form, a noticeboard, a magazine or a newsletter. It could be oral communication, such as over the telephone, a public address system, a video conference or face-to-face communication. The medium may be paper or electronic. Messages may be transferred from one form to another for convenience. For example, a report may be sent as an attachment to an email and then printed out, to be used in a face-to-face meeting.
- The **receiver** is the person or department which listens to the message.
- FEEDBACK may be provided by the receiver. For example, a recipient may reply to an email message. A worker may acknowledge an instruction in a face-to-face conversation. However, feedback is not always given and is not always expected.

Formal and informal communication

Communication within a business can pass through both formal and informal channels.

- **Formal communication** is carried out through channels which are approved or set up by the business. For example, a manager may tell his assistant to send out a letter to a customer. A supervisor may draw up a work rota for the next month and give a copy to every member of staff concerned. Managers may meet with trade union representatives each month. A team leader may hold a progress meeting every week to discuss issues with the sales team.
- **Informal communication** is communication within a business which takes place outside of channels approved or set up by the business. For example, two members of staff may chat about their boss when playing sport after work. A manager may let slip confidential information about a future reorganisation to a subordinate. A worker may tell a customer 'off the record' that a particular product is not proving reliable. Informal communication is sometimes called 'grapevine' communication, where workers hear 'on the grapevine' about news and gossip.

Informal communication is often said to lead to **misinformation**. Stories can get distorted as they pass from one person to another. The story might not even be correct in the first place. However, formal communication may also sometimes contain information which is only partially accurate. Businesses, for example, may deny they have any plans to lay off staff and then within days announce redundancies. Customers complaining about a particular product may be told that the company has had no problems before, when in fact it may have received a large number of complaints about the product.

In practice, businesses need both formal and informal channels to function efficiently. Informal channels often supplement information coming through formal channels.

Leila likes her work routine. She gets up at 6.00 each day and is in her open plan office by 7.30. The first thing she does is make a cup of coffee and have a chat with Elle, another early bird into the office. Then she replies to any emails which came in overnight. By 8 o'clock, she is looking at her diary and reminding herself of her priorities for the day. The office is now filling up and Leila knows that for the next hour, colleagues will be dropping by her desk to say good morning, get clarification about the day's work or chat about problems. Her secretary comes in at 8.30 and she always briefs her on the day ahead. When she is not talking, she is reading briefings and memos which don't require too much concentration. 9.00 to 11.00 is Leila's time to write reports for clients based on site visits. Then it is time for a coffee and chat by the coffee machine. Often there are internal meetings in the late morning. The afternoon is typically spent on site visits to external clients. Depending on when the visit finishes, she might go home or pop back to the office to deal with emails and begin writing up the report on her visit.

I *Explain the meaning of the following using examples from the passage to illustrate your answer.*
- *(a) Internal and external communication.*
- *(b) Messages, senders, receivers and feedback.*
- *(c) Channels of communication.*
- *(d) Medium of communication.*
- *(e) Formal and informal communication.*
- *(f) Vertical and lateral communication.*

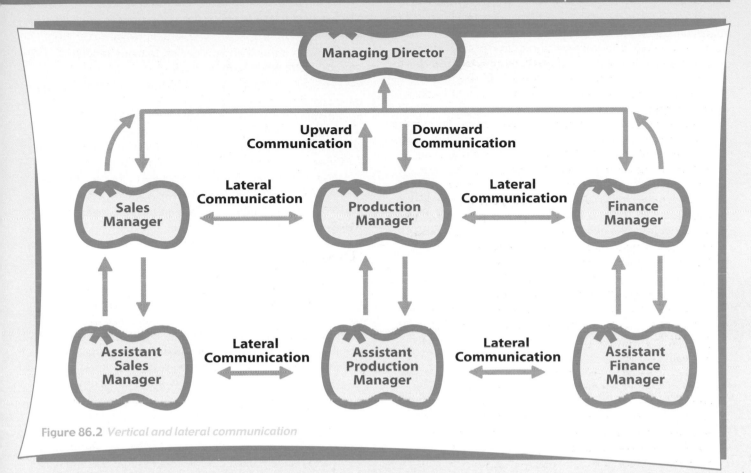

Figure 86.2 *Vertical and lateral communication*

Workers can also create communication links with other employees, which in practice function better than the official formal channels. And informal links can be an effective means of communication, particularly when staff do not want to go through formal channels for various reasons.

Vertical and lateral communication

Unit 31 explained that larger businesses tend to be organised on a **line and staff** basis. There is a **hierarchy** within the business, with a **chain of command** passing from top to bottom.

- VERTICAL COMMUNICATION occurs when there is communication up and down the hierarchy. So a manager speaking to a direct subordinate would be an example of **downward communication**. A sales assistant speaking to his departmental manager would be an example of **upward communication**.
- LATERAL COMMUNICATION occurs when there is communication between employees and departments at a similar level. So an email sent between two managers on the same grade in the finance department would be an example. So too would be a memo sent from the head of finance to the head of personnel.

Vertical and lateral communication are illustrated in Figure 86.2.

Motivation and communication

Communication is a vital factor affecting motivation (see units 34-37) and vice versa. Theories of motivation suggest different ways in which this occurs.

At Alvis Vickers, a manufacturer of armoured vehicles, Charlie Blakemore, operations director, believes that motivation is key to increasing efficiency. When the company was facing growing competition, he introduced a 'lean manufacturing programme' to counter the threat. One of the first things the business did was to install a works meeting to give workers on the shop floor a forum where they could come forward with ideas. It also made a point of implementing any good ideas very quickly so the workers could see that their ideas were valued.

Not all of the initiatives are as serious. The Bacon Sandwich Challenge involves workers getting free bacon sandwiches if they met targets. The Housekeeping Award is a scheme where the team with the best-kept area gets a bottle of wine and a trophy. Such light-hearted schemes, however, have an important place in fostering communication. As Charlie Blakemore says, 'Initiatives like the Bacon Sandwich Challenge are small things but they create awareness of the targets we are trying to achieve. Everyone takes part and has a laugh. It really does generate team spirit.'

Source: adapted from *The Sunday Times*, 16.11.2003.

1 **Explain how Alvis Vickers improved the motivation of its workforce using (a) the ideas of Elton Mayo and (b) Maslow's hierarchy of needs.**

2 **What part did improved communication play in the initiatives described in the data?**

The scientific management school Frederick Taylor's scientific management theory (see unit 34) suggests that subordinates must be given clear instructions about how best to complete tasks. It is the role of those in authority to work out what is the optimum way to complete any given task. In scientific management theory, pay is the main motivation of workers. Frederick Taylor suggested that directly linking pay to output achieved through piece rates was, in many cases, the best way to motivate workers to achieve maximum output. Although piece rates for manual workers have fallen out of fashion, bonuses, commissions and stock options for white collar workers including senior management are common in UK businesses today. Individual pay rises are also often linked to achieving targets set for a 12 month period through performance related pay (see unit 37).

Communicating the goals which workers have to achieve to gain bonuses is a vital part of the process of motivation. If workers are unclear what they have to achieve to gain high remuneration, they will become demotivated when they are judged to have failed to reach their targets. Equally, if managers have set unrealistic goals, or insist on staff working in an inefficient way, workers are likely to become demotivated.

Elton Mayo and the human relations school Elton Mayo, in his pioneering studies at the Hawthorne plant in the USA (see unit 35), showed that workers were more motivated if managers took an interest in them. Interest was expressed not just through formal channels. Communication through informal channels was also important to improve morale amongst workers.

Maslow and the hierarchy of needs Maslow (see unit 35) suggested that workers had a hierarchy of needs, from physiological needs to self-actualisation needs. Fulfilment of the higher order needs requires effective communication in the workplace. For example, workers have social needs for love and belonging. Through formal channels of communication, workers can be organised into working groups, such as cells or teams, where group members have to co-operate and communicate for the group to function effectively. Through informal channels, such as chatting over a coffee or working out at the company gym, workers can feel that they belong to a working group with shared values and shared goals. Workers also have self-esteem needs according to Maslow. So the business needs to communicate to workers that they are doing a good job. This can be done through simple verbal messages, such as just saying 'thank you', to more complex formal appraisal systems. Finally, some workers will be able to satisfy their need for self-actualisation at work. Part of fulfilling this need will be having the opportunity to communicate effectively with others.

Herzberg's two factor model In Herzberg's two factor model (see unit 35), achievement, recognition and responsibility are all motivators. A necessary part of each of these is communication. For example, a worker may get promotion, but this in itself will not be a motivator unless the worker feels that this is a recognition of achievement. That recognition comes through effective communication by the business. Equally, communication can be an important part of factors which lead to dissatisfaction. For example, good communication is vital if supervision is to be effective.

Management must communicate to their workers that their jobs are safe.

Effective communication is central to many modern innovations in working in business.

Team working When working in teams (see unit 36), workers must communicate effectively to achieve the tasks set. Failure to communicate will result in inefficiency and poor quality work. Equally, team working encourages effective communication. By working as part of a group, workers are encouraged to communicate more than if they were working in isolation. Communication then becomes motivating because team members want the group as a whole to achieve its goals.

Kaizen groups Kaizen groups (see unit 47) are teams of workers set up to consider ways of changing work practices to bring about improvements in efficiency and quality. Workers in Kaizen groups have to communicate their ideas to others. Promising ideas then need to be explored and developed. Membership of Kaizen groups is often motivating for individual workers. They feel that they are contributing something important to the group and that their skills and talents are being recognised. Communication between group members is therefore motivating both for individual workers and the group as a whole. This motivation can then spill over into the everyday activities of the workers in the group.

Single status In a single status organisation (see unit 39), every worker is offered the same conditions of work. One of the aims of creating a single status organisation is to foster effective communication between different workers at different levels and different places in the organisation. So shop floor workers should be able to communicate directly with the managing director, or a sales administrator with someone in accounts. Creating the conditions for improved communication between workers should then be motivating for staff. Instead of having a traditional 'them and us' attitude between workers at different grades or in different departments, workers should be encouraged to see every worker as one of 'us'.

keyterms

Channel of communication - **the route taken by a message.**
Communication - **the sending and receiving of messages between two or more individuals, groups or organisations.**
External communication - **when messages are passed from within a business to an individual or organisation outside the business like a customer or a supplier.**
Feedback - **a response to a message.**
Internal communication - **when messages are passed within a business.**
Lateral communication - **when there is communication between employees and departments at a similar level in the organisational hierarchy.**
Medium of communication (or communication media or method of communication) - **the method or medium used to communicate a message, such as via email, a letter, a face to face conversation or a memo.**
Vertical communication - **when there is communication up and down the hierarchy.**

checklist

1 What is meant by 'communication' in a business?
2 Distinguish between the channel of communication and the medium of communication.
3 Give one example in business of feedback in a communication (a) being given and (b) not being given.
4 Distinguish between formal and informal communication.
5 Explain how vertical and lateral communication may occur within a human relations department in a company.

6 How does effective communication motivate workers according to (a) the scientific management school; (b) Maslow's theory of a hierarchy of needs; (c) Herzberg's two factor model?
7 How might (a) working in a team and (b) single status organisations improve communication?

Northern Lights plc

Victoria Tomlinson runs Northern Lights, a Yorkshire-based public relations and research company. She has found the perfect people to do her telephone research: the mums waiting at the gates of her daughter's school. Many of these women are highly qualified. Before leaving full-time employment to look after children, several held high-powered jobs. The senior executives they interview on behalf of Northern Lights are happy to talk to them. The women do more than fill in the boxes. If the interviewing goes off on interesting tangents, they follow these up, and ask the relevant questions. The interviews over, they come back with suggestions on how the questionnaires could be improved.

JetBlue

JetBlue is a relatively young low-cost US airline. Like most airlines, it has a customer service centre where customers can ring up and book or change flights. But unlike most airlines, its customer service centre is not a physical call centre where all the operators work in one building. Instead, the 900 customer service staff work from home in Salt Lake City. The airline estimates that 70 per cent of them are stay-at-home mothers. The company provides the computer and telephone equipment they need to deal with customers. How do the staff cope during non-school hours? This is where employing mothers becomes more complicated. JetBlue employees have to be prepared to work any shift. The company does, however, encourage them to trade their hours over the company intranet. JetBlue also demands that employees ensure their workspace is quiet: no yelling or piano practice in the background. To get around the problem that working from home can be isolating, JetBlue makes sure everyone visits the office once a month.

Xansa

Xansa is a UK computer services group. Founded in 1962, the company initially specialised in computer programming done by female computer programmers working from home. Today, only 2 per cent of Xansa's 6 500 employees work from home. Valerie Huges D'Aeth, human resources director, insists that the company is still very flexible about working arrangements. However, not all jobs lend themselves to flexible working. For example, clients often insist today that computer programmers work on their premises because of security worries. Another problem is managers who do not believe people are working unless they can see them. About two-thirds of Xansa's employees came to the company through acquisitions. It sometimes takes time to persuade their managers to measure them by what they produce rather than by how much time they spend at work.

Source: adapted from the *Financial Times*, 22.9.2004.

1 Explain how the workers in the three companies described in the data communicate effectively (a) with each other and (b) with customers. (20 marks)
2 Discuss whether motivation at companies like JetBlue, Northern Lights and Xansa would be improved if workers were forced to work in an office environment rather than from home. (20 marks)

Zippo's

Knowledge Travelling circuses have a long history in the UK. Zippo's Circus is the largest of the UK's 30 travelling circuses. Each year, it replaces most of its acts to allow it to go back to the same venues with a new show.

Application Zippo's, like any *business organisation*, encounters *barriers to communication* both *internally* and *externally*.

Analysis Internally, Zippo's faces a variety of communication barriers. Almost all of the performers are hired on one yearly contracts. Most of the performers are from abroad and English is not their first language. It takes time for the performers to settle in and for them to understand the requirements of the job. Fortunately the chain of command is extremely short. Martin Burton, the circus's founder and director, is on site and deals with everything from hiring new acts to disputes about pay and dealing with the accountants. 'I'm a bit like a feudal lord', he says. 'When the staff have a problem, they come to me and justice is very swift but fair.' Externally, the major barrier to communication is with customers. The Advance Publicity Unit of the circus often has just one or two weeks to sell 13 000 seats at performances in a town on a tiny budget. The unit has to convince shopkeepers to put up their posters in exchange for free tickets, place hoardings and flyers in key locations and deal with local media. Zippo is also moving into the 21st century by using the Internet to attract customers.

Evaluation Over the past couple of years, this marketing effort has not been enough to fill all the available seats and turnover has fallen. The Internet is unlikely to become a significant way of communicating with customers. The old fashioned flyers and adverts are likely to remain key. As for internal communication, with such a transient and multinational workforce it is difficult to see how barriers to communication could be reduced. So long as the senior management team has an open door policy, problems should be capable of being resolved quickly.

Source: adapted from the *Financial Times*, 8.10.2004.

Barriers to communication for all businesses

No business communicates effectively internally or externally all the time. Messages sent might be inaccurate or poorly composed. Messages might not be sent at all. Receivers might not receive the messages or they might misunderstand them. There is a variety of causes of these barriers to communication in all businesses, however large or small.

Attitudes and perceptions Both senders and receivers can have attitudes or perceptions about each other. For example, a group of subordinates may think their boss incompetent. So when their boss passes them information, subordinates may automatically assume that it is incorrect or incomplete, even though it may this time be accurate. Or a customer may perceive a supplier to be reliable and honest. When a rumour reaches the customer that the supplier has been overcharging customers, it may refuse to accept this even though the rumour proves to be correct.

Intermediaries When there are intermediaries, messages can become distorted, as in a game of 'Chinese whispers'. The more complex the message, the more likely it is to be altered as it passes through a chain of communication. For example, the managing director of a company telling the board of directors that there 'may be redundancies in the future' could easily leak out and become, after many tellings, that there 'will be large scale redundancies now'.

Lack of common language Sometimes there is a lack of common language between sender and receiver. For example, a British speaker may have problems understanding a potential overseas customer who is talking in German and therefore get a distorted message. Or someone may use jargon in a conversation which the listener doesn't understand.

Lack of common sense of purpose When workers lack a common sense of purpose, they can often misinterpret messages. For example, an administrator in the accounts department may receive a message from the finance director that late paying invoices must be chased up more vigorously. The administrator may know that the business is experiencing cash flow problems and therefore needs to increase its inflow of cash quickly. At the same time, the marketing director is trying to expand sales to existing customers. In the event, the measures taken are too tough. Long standing large customers are threatened with being taken to court if they don't pay now, whilst other late paying customers are refused further trade credit. Although invoices are now paid more promptly, the company loses customers and the marketing director is furious. The administrator has misunderstood the message given because she failed to reconcile the goals of the marketing director with those of the finance director.

Equally, different stakeholders often have different aims and objectives which can lead to problems. For example, local residents fighting against the siting of a waste disposal factory in an area might interpret figures on pollution caused by the factory differently to the owners of the factory. The owners might argue that the figures for pollution are acceptable, whereas local residents might not.

Problems facing large businesses

Large businesses face more problems in communication than smaller businesses for a variety of reasons.

Juan Parente moved from Madrid to Leeds 10 years ago, first to work in the kitchens of a Spanish restaurant and then to open his own restaurant. A year ago, he employed Jason Belfield as an assistant chef. Initially, everything went well but, three months ago, Jason began being late for work once or twice a week. Juan took Jason aside and gave him a severe reprimand, but Jason found it difficult to understand everything Juan was saying because he spoke English with a Spanish accent and included Spanish words in sentences. As time went on, Juan became more angry with Jason's timekeeping and informed him that he may be faced with disciplinary action. Matters came to a head when Jason arrived an hour late on a day when the restaurant was fully booked for the evening and another member of the kitchen staff was off sick. For Juan, the reputation of the restaurant was at stake.

Jason began to dislike working at the restaurant. Three months ago, Jason's mother had fallen seriously ill and he had found it difficult juggling work with hospital appointments and caring for her. He had confided in Emily, another assistant chef, but she did not tell Juan about Jason's problem. The day the restaurant was fully booked Juan was incensed by Jason's lateness, but Jason could only think of his mother lying ill at home. At that moment in time, he didn't care about the restaurant and its reputation.

> 1 **Explain what barriers to communication existed between Juan and Jason.**
> 2 **Discuss how these barriers to communication could have been overcome for the benefit of both Juan and Jason.**

Communication overload In a large business, there will be a much larger amount of information available than in a small business. This information will tend to get communicated to a much larger group of employees or external contacts. The danger is that there will be communication overload. Individuals will receive so many items of communication that they will be unable to process all the information. One way of resolving this is for a business to adopt policies which restrict the flow of information on a 'need to know' basis. For example, it has become commonplace for office staff to create 'groups' on their email software. By clicking on the group symbol, a message is sent to everyone in the group. By restricting the use of email and the number of people who receive general email messages, information overload can be avoided. Another way of dealing with information overload is to make the information more accessible. For example, reports previously kept in paper form might now only be available on computer. Holding it on disk might allow the reader to find material more quickly and easily.

Many layers of hierarchy The larger the organisation, the more likely it is to have a long chain of command, with many layers in the hierarchy. This means that communication between the top and bottom of the hierarchy is likely to be difficult because messages are likely to pass through each level. At each level, the message can be distorted (the problem of 'Chinese whispers'), or simply not passed on. In large multinational companies like General Motors or McDonald's, there can therefore be a profound difference between the meaning of a message sent down the hierarchy by, say the chief executive, and the way it is received at the bottom of the hierarchy. There is also unlikely to be much feedback. When the chief executive sends a message to all employees, the workers at the bottom of the hierarchy are most unlikely to be given a chance to reply to the message.

Difficulties of communication have led some large businesses to change their organisation structure.
- Some businesses have **delayered** (see unit 31) their formal hierarchies, reducing the length of the chain of command. By cutting out layers of middle management, communication up and down the hierarchy should in theory be more effective.

- Another response has been to move away from formal hierarchies (see unit 32) to **matrix structures** where workers are organised into teams. This has the same effect as delayering a formal structure, cutting out the number of intermediaries between sender and receiver at the top and bottom of the organisation.
- A third way of dealing with problems of communication is to **decentralise** an organisation (see unit 31). Decentralisation involves pushing power to make decisions down the hierarchy. There is therefore less need for those further up the hierarchy to issue instructions and orders. By making decision making closer to those workers involved in carrying out decisions, there is less need for communication. Problems with poor communication are therefore avoided to some extent. For example, a UK engineering company may choose to set up a new subsidiary company in Spain to manufacture automotive parts. The subsidiary company is set targets by head office. How those targets are met is decided by the management of the subsidiary company. This shortens the chain of communication for many decisions and there are far fewer intermediaries when it comes to feedback.

Over-reliance on written communication In a small business, it is easy for workers to talk to each other face to face on a day to day basis. In a large company, with perhaps thousands of employees and a number of different site locations, face to face contact becomes more difficult. Hence, workers rely much more heavily on written communication, including email. Written communication, however, has its limitations. Messages can be misinterpreted because, unlike face to face communication, feedback is often slow and the signals that come from body language are missing. In large businesses, there can be an over-reliance on written communication.

Use of information and communication technology Information and communication technology (ICT) has brought about significant productivity gains for businesses. However, IT has not proved as easy to use as at first hoped. Staff need to be trained to use ICT systems. Most employees can use only a fraction of the options on ICT systems, limiting their effectiveness. Another problem is that large businesses often run several different computer software systems which may be unable to 'talk' to each other. The personnel department, for example, may not be able to access financial information because the finance department use a different software package. Information then becomes restricted rather than being open to all who might need to use it. Another problem already mentioned is information overload where ICT has given workers too much information.

Too many meetings In large businesses, there tends to be far more meetings per employee than in small businesses. Meetings are essential for effective communication. However, they can be unproductive. Some employees will be invited to a meeting although they will have little interest or understanding of the issues to be discussed. Meetings tend to go on far too long, with some employees talking too much and not concentrating on the issues in hand. Meetings may also involve unproductive travel. For example, a meeting may take place at head office of seven employees from different sites in the UK. Those involved may spend a whole day in travelling to and from a meeting which lasts perhaps only four hours. Those attending meetings will also need to be paid travel expenses, further adding to costs.

There are several possible solutions to these problems. Businesses can adopt policies which limit the number and length of meetings and the number of employees taking part. Equally, it is becoming increasingly easy to arrange telephone or video conferences to link up employees in different parts of the country or the world or simply a large site. Some businesses are able to hold meetings online through their company intranets sites or using email.

Cultural and linguistic differences The larger the business, the more likely it is that employees will come from different cultural and ethnic backgrounds. This may give rise to linguistic problems. For example, an employee in the UK may have to communicate with an employee in India about computer software. Unless both people can speak English or

Urdu there could be a barrier to communication, especially as there are technical terms involved. Even within the UK, there may be linguistic and cultural barriers to communication. Some people who move to the UK may speak little or no English, but may be employees, customers or suppliers. For example, the increasing transfers of foreign footballers to the UK may have led some football clubs to employ interpreters because some of their players or their manager speak little English. Selling to different communities, such as religious communities, may require different communication approaches to take into account specific cultural requirements.

Lord Browne is chief executive of BP oil. He recently told a UK parliamentary committee that he had instructed directors to bypass managers and talk directly to their juniors. The reason for this was that BP had issued inflated production forecasts. Three times in September and October 2002, BP had been forced to cut its production targets. The suspicion was that middle management had inflated the targets to show BP and themselves in a better light. Lord Browne told MPs that he wanted to make sure 'information is absolutely pure and not in any way distorted by trying to put things in a favourable light'. He added that by asking the middle managers to step to one side 'we went right down to the bottom of the organisation in one go'.

Lord Browne's comments point to one of the hazards facing chief executives who try to find out what is happening: that middle managers say what they think the boss wants to hear. Lord Browne clearly believes that juniors will be happier to tell him the truth. He said they would each have to sign a personal report saying what their operations were likely to achieve and would be held responsible.

Some have claimed the reasons BP got its production forecasts in a tangle was because Lord Browne had created a climate of fear that made people afraid to speak up. If so, warning junior managers they will be in trouble if they get their numbers wrong is possibly not the best way to ease their fears.

It should also be remembered that even in a flattened organisation, the distance between junior managers and the chief executive can be enormous. In a company the size of BP, the gap is very large. What is more, flattening an organisation typically widens the span of control of workers in management positions. Research conducted by Raghuram Rajan of the University of Chicago Business School and Julie Wulf of the Wharton School shows that chief executives have more managers reporting to them than ever. In a paper called *The Flattening Firm*, they state that the number of managers reporting to the chief executive grew from an average of four in 1986 to seven in 1999. This was based on a survey of 300 listed US companies.

Source: adapted from the *Financial Times* 4.12.2002.

1 **Explain why the chief executive of BP may have received inaccurate information about production forecasts.**

2 **Discuss whether delayering an organisation can reduce barriers to communication.**

checklist

1 Explain why the following might be a barrier to communication within a business:
   (a) a subordinate who does not trust the judgment of his boss;
   (b) a long chain of command;
   (c) a place of work in the UK where for half the workers English is not their first language;
   (d) management deciding that quality is the main priority in production whilst production workers are mainly motivated by their pay.

2 Explain why a large business might face more communication problems than a small business because of the following:
   (a) the amount of information available;
   (b) the length of the chain of command;
   (c) the increased percentage of written rather than oral communication;
   (d) use of ICT;
   (e) meetings;
   (f) cultural and linguistic differences.

Hovers Travel is one of the South's largest independent travel agents. Formed in 1965, it has today a sales turnover of £98 million with pre-tax profits of £1 million. It runs a chain of travel agent outlets in the South of England in towns like Bournemouth, Bath and Worthing. One quarter of its sales come from selling cruise holidays. Much of the rest is a mix of package holidays from major companies and its own package holidays.

Its main market has traditionally been older, high disposable income customers. Over the past twenty years as the population has aged, the more affluent pensioner market has become increasingly dominant in its sales and hence the very high proportion of cruise holidays sold to destinations in Europe and further afield. However, like all travel agents, the arrival of the Internet and low cost airlines has had a serious impact on turnover and profit. Five years ago, sales turnover was £110 million and pre-tax profits £7 million. The Internet has eroded sales to younger customers who have chosen to go online to book a package holiday directly or to put together their own package of flights plus hotels. Low cost airlines have encouraged customers to book directly over the Internet, eroding the market for airline ticket sales through travel agents.

Hovers Travel has been fortunate in that it has never attempted to be the lowest price agent in the market. Instead, it has concentrated on quality of service. This has been much appreciated by its most loyal customers who are prepared to pay more for a service where the needs of the customer are always put first. It has also been lucky in that its core group of customers are the least likely to own a computer and have Internet access. But over the next 20 years, this will rapidly change. The over 60s will increasingly have access to the Internet, either through their computer or through their television, and will be comfortable using it.

Within the family owned company, there are increasing divisions about how best to communicate with customers. Margaret Hovers, 68, the wife of the founder of the company, and owner of 49 per cent of the shares, is very much in charge. She believes that the downturn in sales is temporary. Her sales strategy is to open more travel agent outlets across the company and accept that some existing customers will migrate to the Internet. Richard Hovers, her son and the Sales Director, wants to compete more aggressively on the Internet. He owns 25.5 per cent of the shares. The company has had a website for the past three years which currently accounts for 5 per cent of bookings. By cutting prices, he believes the company could increase Internet sales substantially even if it means sacrificing profit margins. Jane Hovers, Margaret's daughter, owns the remaining 25.5 per cent of the shares of the company, is on the Board of Directors, but doesn't play an active role in the company. She has seen the value of the company slide as sales have fallen. She wants to sell the company as soon as possible.

The three shareholders are barely on speaking terms with each other. They communicate via memos, letters, emails and intermediaries. The Finance Director, Patrick Dagnall, a non-family employee, is the person through whom communication tends to flow. He is constantly trying to reconcile the different points of view. The problem is that a stalemate has developed where no strategic decisions are being taken or implemented. Only one Board of Directors' meeting has taken place annually in each of the past four years and only business needed to conform with the Companies Act is transacted.

The profound disagreements at the top have filtered down the hierarchy of the company. Those working in the travel agents outlets don't encourage their customers to visit the company's website. The few working on the website see themselves as the future of the company and have kept references to the physical outlets to a minimum on the website. Richard Hovers would like to see a delayering of the organisation. He believes strongly that shifting to a more web based operation would allow many middle managers to be cut, lowering costs. Margaret Hovers, on the other hand, believes that middle managers are vital to providing a high quality service. Many of the middle managers have worked for the company for at least 10 years and Margaret has got to know them well as she works at head office and travels around the outlets.

1 Evaluate how barriers to communication between Hovers Travel and its customers could be reduced and discuss whether this would benefit the company in the long term. (20 marks)

2 (a) Explain what barriers to communication exist within the company. (8 marks)

(b) Discuss whether barriers to communication would be lowered internally to the company if Margaret Hovers were to retire. (12 marks)

Germaine Ceramics

Knowledge Germaine Ceramics is a small company based in Leicester manufacturing ceramics and pottery products. There are just 35 staff with a general manager in charge. The company is owned by Liza Germaine who retired from the active running of the company two years ago.

Application There are no *trade union* members in the *company*. Pay and conditions of work are settled through *individual bargaining*. If a member of staff is away ill, it is sometimes necessary to bring in *temporary staff*. However, staff are expected to be *flexible* in their *work practices*. Some of the work of the company is *outsourced*.

Analysis The general manager, Helen Townson, has a yearly appraisal meeting with Liza Germaine where they discuss her performance and negotiate her pay and bonuses for the coming year. Helen Townson then sets pay for the rest of the staff, basing any pay increases on what the business can afford and what pay increases are being given in the local area. Work is outsourced when it would not be economic to pay a member of staff to do a particular job or when specialist expertise is needed, such as legal services. The company views its loyal workforce as a great asset. It is highly knowledgeable about the tasks that need to be done. Staff turnover is very low. There is limited flexible working but the company's operations demand that most staff turn up every day to work a 9-5 shift.

Evaluation Germaine Ceramics is lucky that it has such a dedicated and compliant workforce. It could be argued that its workers could extract higher wages from the company if they were to join a trade union and engage in collective bargaining. Equally, it could be argued that the workers are satisfied with their pay and conditions of work and have job security. There doesn't seem to be any desire on their part to become flexible workers, building up a portfolio of jobs. Like many workers in the UK, they like the security that having a permanent job brings.

Employers and employees

EMPLOYERS are businesses or other organisations such as government which hire workers to work for them. An EMPLOYEE is a worker hired to work for a business or other organisation.

Employers and employees are in a relationship together. Employers hire workers because they need their time, skills and talents to produce goods and services. Employees take on jobs for a variety of motives including pay, fringe benefits and job satisfaction. Employers and employees therefore have different needs from the relationship that exists between them. EMPLOYER-EMPLOYEE RELATIONS is the way in which employers and employees interact on key issues such as pay, conditions of work, output and productivity.

Collective bargaining

In many places of work, employees choose to join trade unions or other representative organisations, such as a professional association (see unit 89). These organisations negotiate on behalf of their members with employers. This is known as COLLECTIVE BARGAINING. It is collective because employees join together to represent themselves when dealing with their employers.

Collective bargaining can take place at many levels. In a large business or organisation, bargaining can take place:
- covering one type of worker across all places of work in the country, so, for example, the National Health Service might set the pay rates of all nurses or doctors in England and Wales;
- region by region, so London workers of a business might negotiate separately from those in Scotland;
- plant by plant, where a 'plant' is any place of work, so a factory or office in the South East might have separate pay negotiations to another factory or office in Wales owned by the same business;
- by type of worker, so office workers might negotiate a completely separate agreement to factory workers in a manufacturing company and negotiations can take place at national, regional or local level.

Collective bargaining can also take place between trade unions and a number of different businesses typically in the same industry. So, in the engineering industry there might be a minimum level of pay negotiated between the representatives of engineering employers and the trade unions of engineering workers.

Collective bargaining leads to COLLECTIVE AGREEMENTS. These are agreements signed by all parties involved in the collective bargaining on both the employers' and employees' sides. There are two types of collective agreement.

- **Substantive agreements** cover issues such as pay and conditions of work.
- **Procedural agreements** cover how bargaining should take place on issues such as pay, recruitment, dismissal, redundancy and promotion.

Collective bargaining differs from JOINT CONSULTATION. Collective bargaining is about making decisions. Joint consultation is about informing either management or workers about issues and discussing possible courses of action. In a small business, consultation is likely to be an informal chat about what is going on and how things may change in the future between the boss and individual workers. In a large business, there may be regular consultative meetings between management and workers. Under EU law, consultation must take place in certain circumstances. Under the Social Chapter of the Treaty of Maastricht, which the UK signed into law in 1998, multinational companies within the EU must have **European works councils** (see also unit 89). These must be consulted on issues such as redundancies or restructuring of work. Under the **Employment Relations Act, 1999**, businesses with union recognition must invite unions to meetings to consult on training policies.

There was a substantial shift away from collective bargaining in the 1980s and early 1990s. Partly this was due to legislation which removed power from trade unions and encouraged employers to adopt individual bargaining procedures. Partly it was caused by a major shift of employment from primary and manufacturing industry, which was heavily unionised, to private sector service industry where trade unions were poorly represented. In 1984, 71 per cent of workers were covered by collective agreements. By 1996, this was down to 36 per cent, approximately the same as in 2004.

Individual bargaining

INDIVIDUAL BARGAINING occurs when employees negotiate on their own with their employee without the support of a trade union or other association. This bargaining may cover pay, conditions of work or performance levels. Many businesses in the UK in the early twenty first century did not engage in collective bargaining with trade unions and many employees did not belong to a trade union. So individual bargaining tended to be more common than collective bargaining. This was especially true in private sector businesses since a much larger percentage of workers in the public sector belonged to trade unions than in the private sector.

Individual bargaining in practice differs widely from business to business.
- In small businesses, there is unlikely to be any formal bargaining process. In many small businesses, employees will simply accept the pay and conditions set down by the owner manager. In others, there will be informal negotiations from time to time.
- In medium to large sized businesses, there are likely to be more formal processes for bargaining. There might, for example, be annual pay reviews. There might be a clearly defined pay structure where each job is put into a particular category. Within this, however, there might be range of pay for each job. Individuals might have to negotiate to get higher in the range, or to be promoted. In many large businesses, some employees will be on performance related pay (PRP) schemes (see unit 37). With PRP, there is typically an annual review of performance where individual employees have to show that their performance during the

year justifies a particular level of pay or the award of a bonus.
- Individual one-to-one bargaining is more likely to take place the more senior or more highly paid the employee. Individual bargaining will certainly take place between the Chief Executive Officer (CEO) of a large company and the board directors responsible for pay. The workers who clean the CEO's office at the end of the day will simply be told what the rate of pay is for the job. If the cleaners don't like the pay and conditions, then their only option is to find another job.

Advantages and disadvantages of collective and individual bargaining

Collective bargaining is favoured by trade unions. They argue that it gives workers the power to gain the pay and employment rights which they deserve. Economic theory suggest that collective bargaining gives workers some monopoly power in the workplace. In many cases, this forces employers to pay higher wages and give better working conditions to employees than they would do if there were individual bargaining.

Collective bargaining can, however, have advantages for employers. The main advantage is that it can considerably reduce the cost of bargaining with employees. Instead of

According to the GMB trade union, Asda the supermarket chain has withdrawn a 10 per cent pay offer to more than 700 workers at a goods distribution centre in the north-east of England. Asda said it had put forward a package of changes to workers' terms and conditions covering areas such as overtime, holiday and premium rates, with savings being used to increase basic pay. The changes would also have seen a move away from collective bargaining to settle pay negotiations to individual bargaining. However, when balloted, the workforce had rejected the package.

Asda has two depots in Washington, Tyne and Wear, one which it has always owned and the one at the centre of the dispute, which it bought several years ago. The two depots have different terms and conditions and the dispute is understood to have arisen from efforts to put both on a similar footing.

Labour relations are a sensitive area for Asda. Its US parent, Wal-Mart, has a reputation of being staunchly anti-union. Earlier this week, Wal-Mart said it was closing a store in Canada just six months after workers there won the right to join a union.

Source: adapted from *The Guardian*, 12.2.2005.

1 **Explain what it would have meant for the workers at the Asda depot in Tyne and Wear for them to have moved from collective bargaining to individual bargaining.**
2 **What might be the advantages and disadvantages to (a) Asda and (b) the depot workers to have changed to an individual bargaining system?**

having to negotiate with workers on an individual basis, a business can negotiate a settlement for all workers which will be accepted by these workers. On the other hand, many businesses which don't have collective bargaining agreements with their workers simply impose pay settlements on them without consultation. No individual bargaining takes place and therefore there are no costs attached to individual bargaining.

Collective bargaining may encourage militancy amongst workers because as a group they feel they have more power.

Individual bargaining in theory allows an employer to pay workers exactly the amount that is needed to motivate and retain them. Wages costs are kept to a minimum whilst wages are used to maximise motivation and productivity. This might work well with high paid white collar workers where it is cost effective to negotiate a salary level each year. However, in most businesses where there is no collective bargaining, most workers tend to be put on a grade or level and paid the same as workers on the same grade. There might be bonuses linked to performance reviews. But it can be argued that these often fail to motivate workers in the way intended. Indeed, individual bargaining where different workers are paid different rates for the job can demotivate workers who are worse paid. Although their employer might argue that they don't perform as well, these workers may see the system as 'unfair'. According to Maslow's theory, this threatens both their safety needs and their esteem needs.

Flexible work practices

In the 1950s and 1960s, the UK economy was relatively stable and slow changing. Workers tended to have full time permanent jobs. However, in the 1970s and 1980s, economic conditions worsened. Primary and secondary industry (see unit 2) saw enormous change. Many businesses in these sectors became uncompetitive against foreign firms and closed. There was a rapid shift of output and employment towards the tertiary sector. There was a considerable increase in participation of women in the labour force. Part-time work became far more common.

It was against this backdrop that, in 1985, John Atkinson and the Institute of Manpower Studies put forward the concept of a **flexible firm**. This was a business which had a 'core' and a 'periphery'.

- The **core** was made up of workers who organised the essential tasks necessary for the firm's survival. They would tend to be skilled, full time workers on permanent contracts. Because of their job security, their relatively high pay and their importance to the business, they would tend to be highly motivated.
- The **periphery** was made up of a variety of workers not central to running the business. They could be employed according to how much demand there was for the firm's products. They could include temporary workers ('temps') on short term contracts and part-time workers whose hours can easily be increased or decreased. They would also include workers whose jobs had been **outsourced** (or **contracted out** see unit 43) to other businesses. This would include self-employed workers who were paid by the business for doing specific jobs. They might also include teleworkers or home workers, working from home and operating mainly via computer and email link. It is

sometimes argued that peripheral workers are motivated mainly by the pay they receive. Their loyalty to the business employing them is not as great as core workers, since they have insecure jobs and never know whether they will still be in work in 12 months' time.

The advantages and disadvantages of flexible working for businesses

There is a number of advantages of a FLEXIBLE WORKFORCE for a business.

- A flexible workforce allows a business to expand and contract quickly in response to changes in demand for its products. In contrast, a workforce made up of permanent staff is difficult to slim down quickly because of the cost and because of the time it takes to fulfil legal requirements (see unit 91). Businesses may also be reluctant to take on new permanent staff in case demand falls again and they are left with too many staff.
- Some specialist jobs need to be done but it would be wasteful to employ a permanent worker to do them. For example, most small businesses employ accountants to manage their accounts. It is far cheaper to do this than to employ an accountant within the business because the amount of work needed is relatively small.
- In some cases, temporary staff or subcontractors are cheaper to employ than permanent staff. For example, a business may not offer certain benefits to certain staff, although it must be careful not to infringe legislation (see unit 91). If the temporary staff are treated as self employed or subcontractors, the business may also be able to save on National Insurance contributions. It isn't always cheaper to employ temporary staff and in some cases it may be more expensive because temporary staff or their agencies are able to bid their pay upwards. But temporary staff can be laid off almost immediately they are not needed with little cost, which is not the case for permanent staff.
- Employers are responsible for training their permanent workers. By outsourcing work or employing temporary workers, businesses may be able to pass that cost onto subcontractors or whoever has paid for the training of a temporary worker.
- Employing workers who can job share or work flexible hours may allow a business to operate more efficiently. For example, a business may be able to employ an employee in the day and another in the evening to respond to clients' needs over a longer period. A restaurant may be able to react to increased orders by asking staff to work longer hours at certain times of the week than others.

However, using peripheral workers has its disadvantages.

- Peripheral workers may have less loyalty to the business where they work temporarily. They may be motivated mainly by financial gain.
- Some businesses have found that their outsourced work has been of poor quality, damaging their reputation with customers. The peripheral workers move on and don't have to take responsibility for the poor work. But the business may have lost customers as a result.
- Communication can be a problem. Peripheral workers are not necessarily available when the business would like to communicate with them, although IT and the mobile phone has to some extent solved this problem.

Colin Traynor, the owner and then manager of Castle Gate Hotel, decided ten years ago to slim his workforce to a minimum and buy in services wherever possible. Twenty two of his fifty permanent staff lost their jobs as work was outsourced. His hotel has a seasonal trade. In July and August, the hotel is fully booked. During the rest of the year, occupancy can fall to as low as 50 per cent despite the hotel being popular with business people and being used as a conference centre. He quickly moved to a model where he employed enough permanent staff to run the hotel at its minimum occupancy levels in the winter and then hired casual labour to cope with the rest of the year. Jobs like laundry, which used to be done in house, were sub-contracted to a local firm. Two of the workers in the accounts team lost their jobs and were re-employed by the day as and when they were needed. The marketing of the hotel was contracted out to a local business.

This year, Colin retired and management of the hotel passed to his daughter, Emma. For a long time, she had felt that the quality of service provided by the hotel to its customers was not good enough. Casual staff employed for the peak of the season often showed a lack of knowledge and a lack of commitment. Too much of her time was spent recruiting casual staff. Permanent staff were resentful of casual staff because they were always 'sorting out the mess' created by casual staff. Absenteeism amongst permanent staff was high. Emma was also unhappy with the marketing contract. It was very expensive and she questioned whether the marketing was very effective.

I Assess the possible advantages and disadvantages to Castle Gate Hotel of flexible working.

- Employing peripheral workers can be a costly process. For example, a business may put a piece of work out to tender to a subcontractor. It might get the lowest price as a result, but the efficiency gains from putting it out to tender rather than hiring core permanent staff to do the job might be more than outweighed by the costs of the tender process itself.
- Temporary staff can be excellent, well qualified and highly motivated. But equally, some temporary staff are simply workers who have found it difficult to hold down a permanent job. When employing temporary staff, there is no guarantee that they will perform their job as well as would have a permanent member of staff.
- Too many peripheral workers employed alongside core workers can cause demotivation amongst the core workers. Core workers may want to be part of a stable team to form relationships and fulfil some of their higher order needs. Constant turnover of peripheral workers may lead to core workers feeling disorientated.

The impact of flexible working on workers

There are many ways in which workers are affected by flexible work practices. Such practices can affect temporary, part time or subcontracted employees. However, they might also affect full time, permanent employees at times.

- For those on temporary contracts and the self-employed, flexible working brings greater insecurity. Temporary workers can lose their jobs at short notice. The self-employed can lose contracts or business overnight. But even workers on permanent contracts face greater uncertainty. They can find themselves being made redundant and their jobs outsourced to a contracting firm. Equally, they can find their pay fringe benefits, such as pensions, and conditions of work worsen to make them 'more competitive' against flexible workers. Insecurity makes most individuals less happy and content and is therefore generally undesirable.
- A more flexible labour force is one where workers can expect their earnings to go down as well as up. It is one where there might be periods of no income coming in to the household. It is also one where the individual worker can't expect employers to provide them with a pension. The individual worker therefore must plan to cope with this by saving more and investing in their own personal pension scheme.
- Flexible workers must be prepared to adapt and retrain to a changing job market. A self-employed photographer who finds she can't make a living out of photography may have to find another line of work to survive. Permanent workers are, to some extent, cushioned from this because their employer may pay for retraining and reassign them to other jobs within the business. A flexible market highlights the need for **lifelong learning** on behalf of workers.
- Flexible workers must be prepared to move quickly from job to job. They must also be prepared to become PORTFOLIO WORKERS. These are workers who don't have a single full time job but a mix of part time jobs. A worker might have a cleaning job in the morning and work behind a bar in the evening. Or an individual may do consultancy work for 10 days a month, and be a part time non-executive director for one company for 6 days a month and for another company for 4 days a month.

Flexible working in the UK

The UK government has increasingly encouraged the growth of flexible working in the last twenty years. Legislation has been introduced to encourage flexible work time (see unit 28), for example. However, it could be argued that it has had limited success as shown in Figures 88.1 and 88.2.

- The number of self-employed workers in 2004 was 3.6 million, almost the same as in 1990. The growth in self-employment came in the 1980s when it rose from 1.8 million in 1979 to 3.5 million in 1989.
- The number of part time employees has grown significantly, mainly due to the increased number of women in the workforce. Even so, by 2004, part time workers represented only one quarter of those economically active.
- The number of portfolio workers (workers with second jobs) has also grown. But in 2004 there were still only 1.1 million such workers, just 3 per cent of those economically active.
- The number of temporary workers has also grown, but in 2004 there were only 1.5 million such workers, just 5 per cent of those economically active.

Most workers today are still on permanent full time contracts and this is likely to remain so for the foreseeable future. Whilst some industries, such as construction, might have fairly flexible workforces, others such as manufacturing are likely to remain with more traditional work practices.

Flexible working and the Employment Act, 2002

The term 'flexible working' can be used in a different way to the one described above. In the **Employment Act**, **2002**, the government gave employees the right to request more flexible working patterns from their employer. Flexible working is then seen as ways in which the employer can give employees choices about when they work. Areas covered by flexible working then include:

- the ability of workers to choose when they start their day and when they finish;
- giving choices about which days of the week an employee works;
- options to move from full time to part time working and back again;
- maternity and paternity rights;
- opportunities to take periods of time out for an extended holiday or to look after a child;
- opportunities to job share.

The government argues that flexible working improves productivity. By giving workers greater control over their **work-life balance**, it motivates them to work harder. Labour turnover is also reduced because workers don't have to leave their jobs if their circumstances change and they have to alter their working hours. Reduced labour turnover saves the

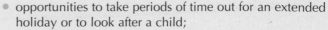

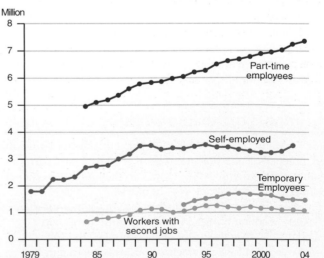

✓ *checklist*

1 Explain the difference between an employer and an employee.
2 Why can collective bargaining occur at different levels within a business?
3 Explain the difference between collective agreements and procedural agreements.
4 What is the difference between joint consultation and collective bargaining?
5 Why does individual bargaining differ from business to business?
6 What is the difference between the core and the periphery in a flexible firm?
7 What might be the advantages of outsourcing work to a business?
8 What could be the disadvantages to a business of using peripheral workers?
9 What are (a) the advantages and (b) the disadvantages to being a portfolio worker?
10 Why might small businesses suffer from flexible working rights given by the 2002 Employment Act?

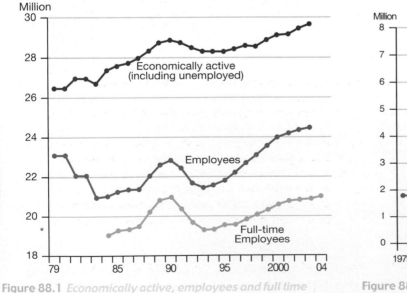

Figure 88.1 *Economically active, employees and full time employees, UK, millions*

Source: adapted from http://www.statistics.gov.uk/statbase/tsdtimezone.asp.

Figure 88.2 *Self-employed, part time employees, workers with second jobs and temporary employees, UK, millions*

Source: adapted from http://www.statistics.gov.uk/statbase/tsdtimezone.asp.

business the cost of recruiting and training new workers. It also helps retain staff who have received expensive training.

However, many smaller businesses argue that they don't have enough staff to make flexible working practical. If there are only three staff in a business, it may be impossible for one of them suddenly to start working different hours from the other staff. Equally, some aspects, such as better maternity and paternity rights, simply add to the costs of the business.

keyterms

Collective agreement - **agreements signed by all parties involved in collective bargaining on both the employers' and employees' sides.**
Collective bargaining - **when employees negotiate on behalf of many members together on issues such as pay and conditions of work with employers.**
Employees - **workers hired to work for a business or other organisation.**
Employers - **businesses or other organisations such as government or charities which hire workers to work for them.**
Employer-employee relations - **the way in which employers and employees interact on key issues such as**

pay, **conditions of work, output and productivity.**
Flexible workforce - **a workforce which can be easily adjusted in size and by skill to suit the needs of either employers or employees.**
Individual bargaining - **when an individual worker negotiates over pay and other conditions of work with his or her employer without the help of a collective group such as a trade union.**
Joint consultation - **informing management or workers about issues and discussing possible actions.**
Portfolio worker - **a worker who has a variety of part-time jobs at any one time rather than a single full time job.**

Harrington, Dutton and Partners is a firm of solicitors with a large criminal department. For some time now, it has adopted flexible work practices.

Some of the solicitors have to work night shifts and at weekends because they can be called to a police station at any time to represent a client. Some of the solicitors work part time for the firm, pursuing professional interests elsewhere, or combining work with bringing up a family. Partners own and control the practice. Their 'pay' is a share of the profits made by the partnership. About one half of the solicitors working for the firm are not partners and they receive a salary which is negotiated on a yearly basis. Solicitors wanting to become partners are expected to have worked for the firm for about ten years before being offered a partnership.

There is a core of permanent support staff, some being full time, some part time. When the firm is particularly busy, casual workers are employed and paid either by the hour

or by a fixed sum for completing a particular task. Staff turnover and absenteeism is very low. The partners put this down partly to paying competitive wages which are negotiated on an individual basis with each member of staff. They also have created a flexible working environment, with support staff being given some control over when they start and finish work during the day and, for part-time staff, which days they work.

Two of the relatively new support staff were members of T&G, the trade union, in their previous places of work. They believe that support staff could get an even better deal from their employers if they all joined the union and were able to engage in collective bargaining. Joining a trade union in a firm of solicitors is relatively rare. The partners have quietly let it be known to their support staff that they are totally opposed to the idea of a union presence in the firm. In fact, the practice might not replace permanent workers and use casual staff instead if industrial relations became difficult. For their part, the two T&G members have begun to argue that there should be less reliance on casual staff. It would be better either to take on more permanent staff to cope with sudden surges of work, or to offer existing staff overtime.

1 (a) Explain how employer-employee relations might change if support staff were to engage in collective bargaining with the partners of the firm. (8 marks)
  (b) Discuss whether the partners would be better off if there were less flexible working in the firm. (12 marks)

89 Employee participation and industrial democracy

Honda

Knowledge Honda is a Japanese car manufacturer with a factory in Swindon in the UK.

Application *Employee participation* through *teamworking* is part of the production philosophy at Honda. On the other hand, *trade unions* at Swindon have fought for an element of *industrial democracy* to be put in place. In 2001, the trade union, Amicus, achieved the right to *recognition* by Honda and with it the ability to engage in *collective bargaining*.

Analysis Honda would argue that employee participation through teamwork benefits all the stakeholders of the company. It leads to greater productivity and better quality of finished product, benefiting customers. Because customers then are more prepared to buy Honda cars, sales increase to the benefit of shareholders and workers who have more secure jobs. Employee participation is also a way to enhance the work environment for employees, with each worker gaining a 'sense of joy and pride in his or her work when he or she possesses a challenging spirit and utilises his or her own creativity and intellect to the fullest extent'. UK unions would argue that pay and conditions can be improved for workers through collective bargaining. Without some mechanism for workers to bargain collectively with management at Honda, workers could be worse off.

Evaluation The fact that trade unions have secured pay rises at Swindon in recent years which Honda has reluctantly accepted would suggest that industrial democracy benefits workers. On the other hand, Honda management is almost certainly correct to assert that employee participation is vital for the long term future of the company. Unless the energy and talents of workers are harnessed in the workplace, Honda might lose its competitive edge. In the process, workers could lose their jobs.

Adapted from *The Times*, 7.2.2003; www.amicustheunion.org and Umberto Furlan, Executive Vice President Honda, *Corporate Culture and Global Competition: The Honda Philosophy*.

The advantages and disadvantages of employee participation

EMPLOYEE PARTICIPATION occurs when employees are empowered to take part in decision making within a business. In the pre-industrial age, many workers worked for themselves in agriculture or in craft industries. They were able to set their own pace of work and determine the quantity and quality of what was produced. With the industrial revolution in the 18th and 19th centuries, the scale of business increased. Large numbers of workers might be employed in a single factory. Even so, some workers still had autonomy in how they completed their work. In coal mines, for example workers were paid on a piece rate system (see unit 37).

At the beginning of the twentieth century, Frederick W Taylor published *The Principles of Scientific Management* (see unit 34). He argued that employees could be made to work scientifically. By observing how a task could be done most efficiently, this best practice could be imposed on all workers engaged in the task. Initiative and decision making would be taken away from most workers and replaced by instructions about how the task should be performed. Taylor's work coincided with and helped develop mass production methods where workers were made to complete simple, highly specific tasks time after time. This division of labour was a key reason why the production line became a familiar sight in many factories.

However, from the 1920s, researchers such as Mayo, Maslow and Herzberg suggested that such scientific methods did not, in practice, lead to maximum efficiency. The Human Relations School (see unit 35) suggested instead that participation in decision making and taking some control of the working environment would raise the productivity of workers.

There is a number of reasons why empowering workers might raise productivity and lead to more effective decision making.

- As the Hawthorne experiments showed (see unit 35), listening to workers and paying them attention makes them feel more valued. This in turn leads to greater motivation and higher output. It can also lead to benefits such as lower absenteeism and lower turnover of staff. Empowering workers is one way in which workers can feel valued.
- Workers should be encouraged to use their skills and talents to the full. In a traditional hierarchy, subordinates receive orders whilst superiors give orders. There is little recognition that subordinates might be more skilled in certain areas than their superiors. Employee participation increases the ability of subordinates to contribute effectively to the business.
- Employee participation encourages a much greater interchange of information and ideas within a business. With more information and ideas, it is easier to make the correct decision on any issue.

Employee participation can also have its disadvantages.

- The decision making process can be slowed down. If everyone is allowed to participate, it may take several times as long to come up with a decision compared to an individual making the decision. This is particularly important at times of crisis when decisions have to be made quickly or even instantly.
- Some workers don't want to participate in decision making. They may see meetings as pointless and a waste of their time. At worst, they may use employee participation as an opportunity to disrupt the smooth workings of a business. These workers are more likely to be individuals who find it difficult to work in teams or groups.
- Some employees will pursue their own interests at the expense of the interests of the business when given the opportunity. Employee participation gives them more opportunity to do this.

- Employee participation may encourage workers to believe they have more power than they actually have. This may lead to demotivation when they feel that their advice is not being acted upon.

Methods of increasing employee participation

There is a number of ways in which a business might increase the amount of employee participation.

Teamworking Teamworking has become an increasingly fashionable method of increasing employee participation over the past 20-30 years (see unit 36 for a fuller discussion of the advantages and disadvantages of teamworking). By working together in groups, workers can contribute their ideas, skills and talents more effectively. Because workers begin to rely on others within the group, workers begin to identify with the group, increasing their motivation to ensure the success of the group.

Four different types of teams can be distinguished.

- **Advice teams** are teams set up to give advice on issues to management. An example of an advice team is a **quality circle** (see unit 47). Typically, being part of an advice team will only form part of a worker's job. In the case of quality circles, workers are expected to participate out of their formal working hours. More often than not, advice teams will be asked to give their recommendations but will not have the power to act upon them. The decision whether to implement the recommendations will lie with management. This can lead to frustration if the advice given is not acted upon. In some cases the advice team may be empowered to implement recommendations.
- **Action teams** are teams which have to perform to a very high level for some of the time. For example, an ambulance crew has to perform at peak efficiency when answering a 999 call. Other examples would include a flight crew flying an aeroplane or an orchestra giving a concert. Whilst working at their peak, workers in action teams are likely to be highly motivated, concentrating on completing the task.
- **Project teams** are teams of workers brought together to complete a specific unique task over a period of time. They are therefore temporary teams. One of the commonest types of project team is a **cross-functional team**. In these teams, workers come from different backgrounds, selected for their ability to contribute to the project to be completed. Project teams might develop a new product or redesign a work area, for example. Cross-functional teams work best when members of the group are able to relate to each other and don't see themselves as defending the interests of the department from which they have been drawn. At worst, cross-functional teams can fail because members see themselves as having to defend the importance of their department. Equally, if all the members of the team are only working part time on the team, they may all give priority to their 'proper' work within their department and neglect their work on the cross-functional team.
- **Production teams** are teams of workers responsible for day-to-day operations, for example a production cell group (see unit 36). Production teams can vary in the degree of employee participation. Individuals in teams may have little autonomy, simply completing tasks which superiors have given them. In this case the advantages of teamwork, such as increased motivation, are unlikely to occur. At the other end of the spectrum there are AUTONOMOUS WORK GROUPS (sometimes also called SELF MANAGING TEAMS). These are teams of workers who work largely without direct supervision. This means they are given a particularly high level of responsibility for the work they undertake. Because of the responsibility given to them, these teams are likely to be highly motivated and productive.

Employee shareholders Employee shareholders are workers in a business who own shares issued by the business. In the

Oxford's Cowley works faced an uncertain future in the 1990s but BMW, who now own the plant, have since invested hundreds of millions of pounds to turn it into the sole manufacturing centre for the highly successful BMW Mini.

The investment, however, has been accompanied by considerable changes in work practices designed to improve quality, harvest staff creativity and cut costs. Under the latest pay deal agreed with the unions, workers must come up with an average of three ideas to improve production and save £800 per worker to quality for a £260 annual bonus. This is in addition to meeting standard quality and productivity targets. The agreement is designed to save £3.6 million in 2003. 'It certainly focuses the employees on these targets,' says Werner Rothfuss, director of corporate communications at the plant. 'Employees can make a difference; this is to encourage their engagement.'

An example of the success of the new initiative comes from the body shop. Engineers and production line workers who work mainly on roofs for the Mini are being rewarded for coming up with the month's best money-saving idea. They realised that the number of soundproofing foam blocks could be halved without any adverse effect. The annual saving to the company will be £115 000.

Source: adapted from the *Financial Times*, 19.3.2003.

1 **Explain how BMW has increased the amount of employee participation at its Oxford Cowley plant.**
2 **To what extent do you think employee participation would have increased if a bonus had not been attached to the scheme?**

1970s and 1980s, some argued that conflict between workers and management and the 'them and us' attitude which was common in British manufacturing industry could be resolved if workers were also owners of their business. Workers would then see that going on strike, demanding high wage increases or sharply improved working conditions was against their interests as owners. The higher the cost of employing labour, the less profit the business would make. This would reduce dividends and the share price, hurting those workers who were also shareholders. A number of large companies created schemes (see unit 37) where employees could buy shares in the company for which they worked. It has been argued that too few workers took advantage of these schemes to make any significant impact on employee participation or motivation. Moreover, workers that did buy shares often bought too few for them to significantly affect business decisions.

In the 1990s, the argument and the schemes offered changed. It became fashionable to argue that **share option schemes** (see unit 37) were the way forward. These were typically only available to senior management. Senior managers were offered packages where they could buy shares at some date in the future at a very low price if they met performance targets, such as future share prices, sales or profits. For example, a chief executive might be given the right to buy 1 million shares at 200p each in three years' time. If the current share price is 220p, then the chief executive will have a significant incentive to direct the company in a way which will see its share price grow over three years. If the share price in three years' time were 300p, this is good for shareholders who have seen a 36 per cent increase in their share price. The reward to the chief executive is to be able to buy the shares in three years' time at 200p and sell them immediately for 300p, making 100p profit each on 1 million shares, i.e. a profit of £1 million.

Share option schemes are a form of payment by results. They are based on F W Taylor's view that money is the key way to motivate workers (see units 34 and 37). They have also been justified on the grounds that, when there is a vacancy, the best senior workers will not be attracted to the company if it doesn't offer generous share option schemes. However, they have been controversial in recent years. This is because schemes have benefited senior employees even when the performance of the company has been poor. Senior executives who have been sacked for poor performance have sometimes been able to exercise their share options on leaving, giving them large sums of money. It can also be argued that share option schemes are a way for senior employees to gain at the expense of other shareholders. If senior employees would have worked just as hard anyway, offering them extra in the form of share options merely reduces the amount available to shareholders.

Other methods Businesses may use a wide range of other methods to increase employee participation. These include suggestion schemes (see unit 47), company newsletters and company briefings of the workforce. Business culture (see unit 112) is also very important. Any business where workers are encouraged to question and not simply accept orders in every situation will be one where employee participation is greater. Simple things like whether workers call their superiors by their first names rather than surnames can have an impact on willingness to participate. Participation will almost certainly be greater in businesses where workers feel that their views are not just listened to but also acted upon.

Employee participation and trade unions

The trend towards employee participation in the UK in the 1980s and 1990s coincided with a reduction in the power and role of trade unions in the workplace (see unit 90). Trade unions have traditionally acted independently of management. Trade unions protect the interests of their members, not those of shareholders or other stakeholders in the business. Employee participation is about breaking down traditional barriers between workers and management. It aims to motivate workers to achieve the goals and objectives set by management. Many businesses in the 1980s and 1990s saw trade unions as an obstacle to ensuring greater employee participation. They attempted to reduce the role of trade unions in the workplace. For example, some replaced collective bargaining with individual bargaining or refused to recognise trade unions.

Changes in legislation after the year 2000 may have led to greater involvement by unions in business activity. Businesses have been increasingly willing to recognise unions. Legislation has led to unions now having representatives at employee grievance procedures, for example. Union/business partnerships have been encouraged. EU legislation has led to a greater role for employees in many business decisions. It could be argued that all these factors are likely to lead to greater employee participation in business and greater industrial democracy, as discussed in the next section.

Industrial democracy

Employee participation is a way of involving workers in the running of their business. However, the terms of the participation are often set by management. If, for example, management decides that teamworking has led to a fall in productivity and motivation of workers, then management can abolish teamworking. Equally, if the share purchase scheme no longer suits the company, then it can be wound up.

INDUSTRIAL DEMOCRACY is where workers are given the right to elect representatives who will be directly involved in the internal decision making of a business, including the highest levels of the business. It could be argued that there is a variety of ways in which might this occur.

Workers' co-operatives In a workers' co-operative, the business is owned by some or all of the employees of the business. The workers elect some of their number to the Board of the company. Important decisions are also taken at regular, often monthly, meetings of all the worker-owners. In the UK, workers' co-operatives have tended to be rare.

Worker directors Worker directors are sometimes found in the UK, but are more common in countries such as Germany. One or more directors of the company are elected from the workforce. They are on the Board of Directors to represent the interests of workers as stakeholders (see unit 56) in the company. They don't necessarily increase employee participation in practice. Sometimes the worker directors are 'captured' by the rest of the Board and act as if they were representing the interests of shareholders rather than the employees. In other situations, the rest of the Board of Directors find ways of minimising the influence of the worker directors. They might starve the worker directors of information about what is going on in the company. They might simply outvote them on any key issue where the interests of workers and shareholders don't coincide. Ordinary workers are then likely to see worker directors as of marginal importance in helping them to influence what is happening in the company.

Works councils Works councils are bodies which consist of selected managers and elected representatives of workers. The council meets to discuss issues such as conditions of work, health and safety, training, investment, redundancies and site closures. They have access to information about strategic planning, the finances of the business and company performance. Works councils have often existed in European countries such as in France and Germany. Some were set up in the UK in the 1990s. Under the EU Information and Consultation Directive, however, EUROPEAN WORKS COUNCILS (EWCs) were to be introduced into the UK from 2000. Any business with at least 1 000 employees and at least 150 employees located in two or more EU countries has to

have a European Works Council. This will therefore include UK multinationals.

Exactly what impact EWCs will have may take time to assess. In Europe, works councils have traditionally been important. This is because workers are seen as significant stakeholders alongside shareholders (see unit 62). In the UK, workers have traditionally not been seen as significant stakeholders in the business. They have certainly been seen as less important than shareholders. So it could be argued that, in the UK, European Works Councils will do little to enhance industrial democracy in business.

On the other hand, there is evidence that, where EWCs have been introduced in the UK, they provide benefits for business, such as employee motivation and the development of a positive corporate culture. Proposals for reform in future may encourage greater training and involvement for employee members. EU legislation may also continue to promote greater industrial democracy through EWCs.

Collective bargaining Workers in the past have gained rights to influence decisions through **collective bargaining** (see unit 88). Trade unions have gained **recognition** from individual employers to bargain on behalf of the workforce. Collective bargaining covers not just pay but also a wide variety of other issues including conditions of work. In the 1950s -1970s, it was widely felt that trade unions gave workers an enormous level of influence on the decisions of businesses. At their most powerful, trade unions were able to influence who was recruited for a job, who could be dismissed, how many workers were needed to do a particular task and how much time they could take to do it, as well as how much workers were paid. In many businesses, particularly small businesses, trade unions were not recognised. But throughout the non-agriculture primary sector (such as mining and oil extraction), manufacturing and public sector services, trade unions were a dominant feature in industrial relations.

In the period 1980-2000, collective bargaining became less common. The government reduced trade union powers through legislation, whilst the primary and secondary sectors shrank in size mainly due to foreign competition. The power of trade unions within collective bargaining was also reduced. Management took back control of many areas of staffing. Also individual bargaining arrangements were increasingly set in place. Approximately 35 per cent of the workforce are covered by collective bargaining agreements today.

Since 2000, it could be argued that the balance of power has begun to swing back towards trade unions. New laws have made it easier for trade unions to gain recognition from employers. However, trade unions today, for the most part, understand that the industrial climate is very different from that of the 1970s. They tend to be much more understanding that difficulties faced by employers could become difficulties faced by workers. Failure to modernise work practices, for example, could result in the closure of a business and the loss of jobs if the business is having to compete with Far Eastern producers. Trade unions would like to see increased power for themselves and their members which might involve industrial democracy. But trade unions recognise that, in most workplaces, simply maintaining collective bargaining is the most they will achieve in this area.

In October 2002, management and employee representatives at Diageo concluded an agreement which revised the workings of its European Works Council (EWC). Diageo is an alcoholic drinks manufacturer with brands such as Guinness. It has a worldwide workforce of around 25 000, with its largest operations in the UK, the USA and Ireland.

One of the new agreement's changes relates to consultation. It states that consultation - 'which must be meaningful and in good time' - is an exchange of views and establishment of dialogue. Consultation 'must provide for employee representatives' views to be heard and for management to respond to these in a timely manner'. The parties have agreed that 'for consultation to be meaningful and in good time it must occur as easily as possible and prior to a final decision being made, so that the employee representatives have the possibility of their comments being taken into account'. Furthermore, 'to ensure that consultation is meaningful ... employee representatives will be given the opportunity to propose properly formulated responses which can be taken into account by management when finalising decisions. This clear statement that consultation must occur before final decisions are taken, and that employee representatives may have a formal input into the decision-making process, should be seen in the light of a dispute in 2000, when employee representatives on the works council claimed that they had not been consulted properly about job cuts at the Guinness plant in Dundalk, Ireland.'

Source: adapted from *European Works Councils Bulletin* January/February 2003.

1 **Using Diageo as an example, explain what is meant by a European Works Council.**
2 **The passage states that there were job cuts at the Guinness plant in Dundalk in 2000. Under the 2002 agreement, how should the management have implemented the proposal to cut those jobs? In your answer explain clearly the different stages of consultation involved.**

keyterms

Autonomous work groups (or self managing teams) - **teams of workers given a particularly high level of responsibility for the work they undertake.**

Employee participation - **occurs when employees are empowered to take part in decision making within a business.**

European Works Councils - **bodies which consist of selected managers and elected representatives of workers which meet to discuss issues such as conditions of work, health and safety, training, investment, redundancies and site closures; under the EU Information and Consultation Directive, any business with at least 1 000 employees and at least 150 employees located in two or more EU countries has to have a European Works Council.**

Industrial democracy - **where workers are given the right to elect representatives who will be directly involved in the internal decision making of a business, including the highest levels of the business.**

✓checklist

1. What is the difference between employee participation and industrial democracy?
2. List the advantages to an employer of employee participation.
3. How can teamwork increase employee participation?
4. Explain the difference between an autonomous work group and a group of workers on a traditional production line where the workers have no control over how they perform tasks.
5. Why might share option schemes increase employee participation?
6. What is the difference between an ordinary company and a worker co-operative?
7. What is a worker director?
8. How might a works council create industrial democracy?
9. Explain why collective bargaining may be seen as an example of industrial democracy.

Suma is a multi-million pound company, supplying 2 500 customers across the UK and abroad. It has 100 employees and is the largest independent wholesaler in the healthfood and wholefood trade in the UK. Founded in the 1970s as a workers co-operative, it is owned by its member workers. They run the business in a democratic way.

The 'boss' of the firm is the General Meeting of members. This takes place six times a year. The General Meeting agrees strategies, business plans and major policy decisions. Any member can make proposals to the General Meeting and if passed they are mandatory on all workers. The General Meeting elects six of its number to the Management Committee which meets weekly to implement the Business Plan and other GM decisions. The Management Committee in turn appoints company officers: Personnel, Operations, Finance and Function Area coordinators.

The Management Committee monitors the implementation of the Business Plan by the Function Areas. Weekly Business Information covering finances, quality of services and labour productivity indicators are reported to the Management Committee by company officers. The Management Committee then issues Action Points when what is actually happening on the ground differs from what is laid out in the Business Plan.

Working at Suma is quite unlike other businesses. Workers must be more self-motivated and take more initiative. Suma departmental coordinators do not have an overseer role in the normal sense. Workers support each other to fulfil daily tasks and get home on time. Working as an effective member of a cooperative, not just doing the daily tasks but taking part in the management of the business, is a new skill which all new members have to learn, whether they have been shop-floor or management previously. The business can only succeed when all members share this responsibility.

All Suma workers are paid the same daily wage plus allowances and overtime or time off in lieu. It is a good wage for manual warehouse workers and the extra reflects the collective management element of the jobs. In return for the better than average wages, Suma expects much more commitment from its employees. When the need arises, when customer orders are waiting, employees are expected to work until the job is done.

Job variety is important. Drivers will drive for a maximum of three days and then work in the warehouse or office. Office people will do manual work for at least one day a week. Most members will have done a far wider range of jobs and taken on greater responsibilities within Suma than equivalent workers in other businesses. Suma encourages members to take up training and courses to bring in new skills.

Multi-skilling is the new buzzword in management theory. Suma has been doing it for 25 years. It allows the company to use labour and skills more efficiently to cope with the troughs and peaks of business. This enables Suma members to cope with high work loads. It keeps people fresher and enthusiastic for longer and it allows recuperation from stress. Many Suma members have spent 6 months throwing sacks in the warehouse after leaving a front line, super responsible position, and then re-entered the fray in a different job.

Source: adapted from About Us, Suma, www.suma.co.uk.

1 (a) Explain why 'industrial democracy' can be said to exist at Suma. (8 marks)
  (b) Discuss the possible advantages and disadvantages to Suma of industrial democracy. (12 marks)

T&G

Knowledge The Transport and General Workers' Union (T&G) is the UK's second largest trade union with over 900 000 members.

Application The T&G is a *general trade union*, representing many types of *workers* in a variety of *industries*. Like any union, it has a variety of *objectives* and *functions*. Its *organisation* is complex given that it represents so many workers. It achieves those *objectives* through gaining *recognition* and *negotiating* with individual *employers*. It also acts as a *pressure group*, campaigning on a variety of *employment issues*. Sometimes it uses the services of ACAS for *conciliation* and *arbitration*.

Analysis One of the T&G's current key objectives is to recruit more members and gain recognition from employers. Like most trade unions, it saw its membership decline in the 1980s and 1990s from a peak of 2 million in 1977 to its current membership of 0.9 million. New labour laws introduced since 1997 have made it easier for it to force anti-union employers to recognise the collective bargaining rights of the T&G. Only by gaining more members and recognition in the work place can it achieve some of its objectives, such as higher pay and greater job security for members. The T&G has also been in the forefront of campaigning on national issues, such as the minimum wage and pensions.

Evaluation The role of trade unions in a free market economy is controversial. Many businesses would argue that they push up labour costs and make them less competitive in the market place. Trade unions argue that they play a vital role in defending the interests of workers in labour markets which place individual workers in a weak and vulnerable position. There is evidence to suggest that both arguments are in part correct. Perhaps this is why the emphasis in modern industrial relations is on co-operation between employers and trade unions to achieve solutions which are mutually beneficial.

Adapted in part from www.tgwu.org.uk..

Objectives

TRADE UNIONS are organisations of workers and ex-workers which exist to promote the interests of their members. Trade unions have existed in the UK since the eighteenth century. Over time, their **objectives** or goals have remained broadly the same, although the importance of any single objective may differ from union to union. Their main objectives are to:

*   secure high wages and maximise other financial and non-financial benefits for their members;
*   prevent the loss of their members' jobs;
*   gain safe working conditions;
*   see that their members are entitled to welfare benefits if they fall ill, become unemployed or retire;
*   provide a range of other services which might increase the welfare of their members;
*   fight for causes, such as improved public services or nuclear disarmament or the election of a political party which their members support.

The functions of trade unions

Trade unions have a number of functions. These functions allow unions to achieve their objectives.

*   They negotiate with employers on behalf of their members in the workplace. This is known as **collective bargaining** (see unit 88). Negotiations include everything from pay rates to conditions of service, redundancies and health and safety.

*   They represent individual members in cases such as discrimination and dismissal. This may involve negotiating with the employer. If this fails, the union may pay to have the member represented at an **employment tribunal** (see unit 91) or a court of law.
*   Trade unions may participate in the running of a business, for example by having representatives on works councils (see unit 89 for a fuller discussion of **industrial democracy**).
*   They provide members with a range of benefits. These vary enormously from union to union, but they tend to include free legal representation and access to cheap insurance and credit cards.
*   They act as a **pressure group** (see units 56 and 106) to influence the behaviour of businesses in general, as well as to affect government and the law. Since the beginning of the twentieth century, major trade unions have sponsored Labour MPs and the trade union movement still plays an important role within the Labour Party.

The organisation of trade unions

In 2002, there were 213 trade unions in the UK. They vary enormously in size and in the way they are organised. However, they can grouped into four **types** of union.

Craft or skill unions These unions represent workers who have a particular craft or skill. For example, musicians can join the Musicians Union or journalists the National Union of Journalists. Craft unions are the oldest type of union in the UK.

Industrial unions These unions represent workers in a single industry. They don't necessarily represent all the workers in the industry, but they don't accept members from outside of that industry. Examples are the National Union of Mineworkers, the Firebrigades' Union and the National Union of Teachers.

General unions General unions represent workers from different industries and different types of workers. General unions, traditionally, recruited from unskilled workers. However, over the past twenty years there has been a trend for unions to merge to create general unions which represent both skilled and unskilled workers, and blue collar and white collar workers. An example in the UK is AMICUS, with over 1 million members made up from a variety of industries including IT, shipbuilding, energy and construction.

White-collar unions These unions represent white-collar workers. Until the 1950s and 1960s, most union members were blue-collar workers. Hence, white-collar unions were seen as a separate type of union. Today, most union members are white-collar workers. It can be argued that all white-collar unions, such as Unison or the National Union of Teachers, can be placed into one of the three types of Craft, Industrial and General Union.

The organisation of a trade union varies. However, in a typical trade union there will be both voluntary and full time trade union workers. **Shop stewards** or **trade union representatives** are ordinary workers elected within a place of work by members. This group of workers is sometimes called a **branch** of the union. The role of shop stewards is to represent workers' interests to management on issues such as pay, redundancies and working conditions. They also represent the interests of their members at local, regional or national meetings of the union. Shop stewards are typically unpaid volunteers who work for the union in their own time.

Full time officials are paid officials of the union who work full time for the union. They will be based in offices of the union. They specialise in a particular type of union work, such as recruitment, training or legal advice. The most important full time official will be the leader of the union, whose title varies from union to union, but is often called the **General Secretary** of the union. The General Secretary is elected by a postal ballot of all members.

Industrial action

Today, most conflict within the workplace is usually resolved through negotiation. However, during an INDUSTRIAL DISPUTE, both workers and management can resort to INDUSTRIAL ACTION. This is direct action aimed at putting pressure on the other side to give in to their demands. There is a variety of forms of industrial action.

- **Strikes** are when workers withdraw their labour and don't go to work. Strikes can be costly to employees because they lose pay when they are on strike. For employers, the damage is the lost output and the disruption to work. So prolonged **all-out strikes**, when all workers go out on strike for an indefinite period, are rare. Strikes tend to be **selective strikes**, where employees aim to cause maximum disruption at minimum cost to themselves. For example, there might be a **one-day strike**. In an industry like the rail industry, this can cause severe disruption. Or a particular group of key workers might be brought out on strike which brings all work to a halt. **Picketing** often takes place during a strike. Workers on strike will stand or picket outside their place of work in the hope of persuading other workers to not **cross the picket line** and therefore not to work. Equally pickets hope to discourage customers and suppliers from going into the premises to deliver supplies.

In January 2005, firefighters at Glasgow Airport went on indefinite strike and began picketing the airport. The dispute centred around plans by their employer, the British Airports Authority (BAA), to change the way in which fire safety was organised. Up to this point, the 59 firefighters at the airport were responsible both for fire safety on the runways and land of the airport, but also for the airport terminal building. To deal with the airport building, the firefighters had a fire engine crewed by four people fully equipped for firefighting and rescue duties. BAA proposed to transfer responsibility for the terminal building to Strathclyde Fire Service, the fire service provided by the local authority. Staffing levels at the terminal would be reduced to a two person fire safety team which would not be equipped with protective clothing or equipment to carry out any firefighting duties.

The Transport and General Workers' Union (T&G) said the changes would put airport staff and passengers at risk. The response times to any incident in the terminal would increase from two minutes to fourteen minutes.

BAA stated that safety would not be compromised by the changes. It suggested that the main concern of the firefighters was not safety but a loss of 'traditionally high levels' of expensive overtime that would result from the changes. It also said that the fire engine at the centre of the dispute was brought in as an extra precaution during refurbishment in the 1990s when parts of the airport were effectively a building site.

A month after the strike began, the 59 firefighters accepted a compromise solution. The new arrangements would go ahead but eight specialist officers would be recruited to improve fire safety at the terminal. The firefighters would also receive a one-off payment of £1 500 for accepting the changes.

Source: adapted from BBC News World Edition 29.1.2005 and 27.2.2005; Socialist Worker Online, 5.2.2005.

> 1 **Suggest what the Glasgow firefighters hoped to achieve by going out on strike.**
> 2 **To what extent did the firefighters achieve their possible objectives when the dispute was resolved?**

- An **overtime ban** is when workers refuse to work more than the basic working hours laid down in their contract of work. Overtime bans are particularly effective in industries where overtime is routine, or at times of the year when orders are abnormally high. For example, unions in the airline industry often choose the summer or bank holiday weekends to organise overtime bans or selective strikes in pursuit of a claim.
- A **go slow** is when workers deliberately reduce their work rate to reduce output. A **work to rule** has the same effect. Working in exact conformity to the rules and procedures laid down by employers can reduce productivity because rules and procedures may not have been updated. Both of these actions can affect the profitability of the employer. Employers too can take their own forms of industrial action.
- A **lock-out** occurs when employers don't allow their workers into work and don't pay them either. By stopping pay, employers hope to put pressure on employees to concede to employers' demands.
- Employers may threaten or actually **withdraw benefits** given to workers which are not part of their contract of employment, such as non-guaranteed overtime payments or membership of clubs.
- Rarely, an employer will make **redundant** any workers taking industrial action and employ new workers. Employees who feel that they are unfairly dismissed may take their case to an employment tribunal (see unit 91).

Conciliation and arbitration

Direct negotiations between workers and management result in a resolution of industrial issues in almost all cases. In a few cases, however, negotiations break down. Both sides refuse to move from their positions. Two ways of then resolving the dispute are CONCILIATION and ARBITRATION.

Conciliation Conciliation occurs when both sides to a dispute agree to invite an independent third party to help them resolve the conflict. The conciliator's role is not to make any judgment about who is right or wrong. The conciliator is there to find ways of getting both sides to talk to each other and explore new ways of resolving the dispute.

Arbitration With arbitration, both sides agree to the appointing of an arbitrator. The arbitrator will listen to both sides and then make a judgment about how the dispute should be resolved. In most cases, the arbitration ruling is non-binding (i.e. it is not legally binding) but it is rarely ignored. There is a strong moral pressure to accept the arbitration ruling even if it goes against you. In a few cases, both parties agree to binding arbitration where the ruling is legally binding.

Conciliation and arbitration services are offered by a number of organisations. However, in 1974, the government set up the Advisory, Conciliation and Arbitration Service (ACAS) specifically to offer such services. In addition, ACAS today offers a variety of other services.

- It gives advice to employers and employers' associations and to trade unions on a wide range of personnel issues such as the application of legislation, payment systems and contracts of employment.
- It sometimes conducts enquiries into personnel issues such as handling redundancies or the flexible use of labour. These enquiries help inform ACAS of good and bad

practice and help it to write advisory booklets on key issues.
- It issues codes of practice on industrial relations which outline good practice in this area.
- A growing workload for ACAS has been the investigation of individual cases of unfair dismissal and unfair discrimination. Today, it investigates around 100 000 such cases per year.

In January 2005, WM Morrison, the supermarket group, was pressed into rewrite a recognition agreement with the Transport & General Workers Union (T&G). The issue started in January 2004 when 87 per cent of the 1 600 T&G members working at two distribution centres at Wakefield and Northwich rejected a pay offer. Under the terms of the existing agreement, Morrisons had the right to refer any dispute to binding arbitration, where both sides were bound to accept the results of arbitration. Morrisons duly referred this dispute to arbitration. The arbiter confirmed the offer that Morrisons had originally made, much to the disappointment of the T&G.

The T&G responded by attempting to renegotiate the recognition agreement to remove the binding arbitration clause. Morrisons refused. Then the company invited other trade unions to 'bid' for T&G members. This meant asking other trade unions to enter negotiations with Morrisons with a view to changing the union to which existing T&G members belonged. Not surprisingly, the T&G were outraged by such action and in June 2004 conducted a ballot of the 1 600 members for strike action. Over 90 per cent of members supported full strike action.

With the strike ballot result in their pocket, the T&G returned to the negotiating table with Morrisons. In November 2004, the company agreed to remove the binding arbitration clause. It also offered substantial pay increases to the workers. Some drivers received as much as a 15 per cent pay increase taking their pay to £8.33 an hour.

The T&G said that it was very pleased with the outcome. It would now target the 400 non T&G workers at the two sites and hopefully persuade them to join the union. The aim was to get 100 per cent membership of the T&G in the workforce.

Source: adapted from Timesonline, 12.1.2005, *Personnel Today*, 12.1.2005, *T&G News*, January/February 2005.

1 **Suggest why binding arbitration was unpopular with T&G members at the two Morrisons distribution depots.**
2 **What might have been the advantages to Morrisons of getting another trade union to 'take over' T&G members at the two sites?**
3 **Discuss whether binding arbitration would always have acted against the interests of the union members at Morrisons.**

● It attempts to conciliate in cases before they reach a hearing at an employment tribunal. The **Employment Rights (Dispute Resolution) Act, 1998** set up an arbitration scheme for alternative dispute resolution (ADR). It aims to find solutions to disputes which do not involve court action. It has been relatively successful in this. For example, in 2003 only around 20 per cent of cases went further than this arbitration stage.

The changing face of industrial relations

Industrial relations have seen significant changes over the past 30-40 years. This has been caused by changes in the power and role of trade unions, the legislative framework for industrial relations and in perceived human resource management best practice.

Membership and union density Trade union membership has been in decline over the last 25 years, although some figures suggest there has been a slight increase in the early twenty first century. Trade unions have traditionally been strong in primary and secondary industries and public sector services. Also, membership in the past tended to be dominated by male workers. But changes in the make-up of the workforce have altered the pattern of trade union membership. There has been a significant reduction in employment in primary and secondary industries, which has contributed to a decline in overall membership of unions in the UK. Partly this has been due to growing competition from foreign companies and the trend towards globalisation. The largest growth in the workforce has come from private sector service industries where trade unions have traditionally been weak. Moreover, there has been a shift in employment between males and females. In the past there were far more male than female trade union members partly because primary and secondary industries were male dominated. Jobs created in the last twenty years have been predominantly in the service sector and have been often taken by female workers.

Trends in union membership can be seen in the changes in UNION DENSITY, the proportion of any workforce that belongs to a trade union, in the UK. The formula for calculating union density is:

$$\text{Union density} = \frac{\text{number of union members}}{\text{number of workers in the workforce}} \times 100\%$$

Figure 90.1 shows that union density in the UK fell

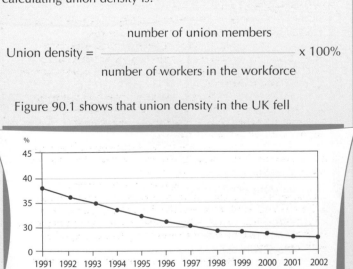

Figure 90.1 *Trade Union density, 1991–2002*
Source: adapted from Labour Force Survey.

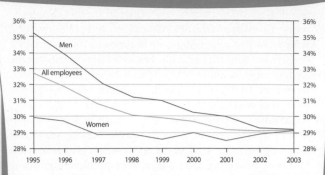

Figure 90.2 *Trade union density by gender, 1995–2003*
Source: adapted from Labour Force Survey.

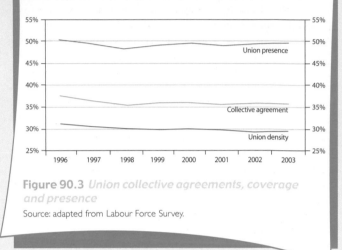

Figure 90.3 *Union collective agreements, coverage and presence*
Source: adapted from Labour Force Survey.

consistently from around 38 per cent in 1991 to over 28 per cent in 2002. This was because over that period the number of union members fell from 9.5 million to 7.7 million, whilst the number of workers in the workforce rose from around 25 million to around 27 million. In contrast, union density amongst female workers was greater in 2003 than in 1997, as shown in Figure 90.2. It has been suggested that the fall in union membership and union density have contributed to a reduction in the power of trade unions in the UK.

Legislation Another important factor in changing the power of trade unions and the nature of industrial relations has been legislative changes. In the 1980s, the Conservative government passed a number of trade union 'reform' laws which effectively curbed the power of trade unions (see unit 91). As a result, workers saw unions as less powerful and less relevant to them. Employers, on the other hand, were encouraged to refuse to **recognise** unions in their workplace (i.e. refuse to acknowledge that unions could negotiate on behalf of their members through collective bargaining). Trade unions as a result found it more difficult to recruit members and to represent them in the workplace.

However, in the late 1990s and the early twenty first century changes in legislation may have led to unions regaining some of their ability to influence business. For example, the **Employment Relations Act, 1999** allowed employees to vote for trade union recognition. Employers could be compelled to recognise unions for collective bargaining under certain conditions (see unit 91). Applications for union recognition are made to the **Central Arbitration Committee (CAC)**. This is an independent body designed to provide guidance on union recognition and make judgments about recognition if disputes occur between employees and employers. This Act led businesses to increasingly recognise unions in the early twenty first century.

Human resource management Human resource management philosophy (see units 92-94) in the last two decades has emphasised the need for individual pay bargaining and flexible workforces. Traditional union goals of nationwide pay agreements with workers getting the same rate of pay whatever their performance were seen as outdated. Moreover, the 'them and us' philosophy, associated with traditional trade unionism, was seen as contrary to a human resource management perspective, which suggested that the goals of workers should be aligned with the goals of the business (see unit 93). Existing employers were therefore encouraged by this to abandon or limit collective bargaining agreements. New businesses may have not recognised trade unions. The number of workers covered by collective bargaining agreements fell from 71 per cent to 35 per cent in the twenty years before 2002. All this meant that trade unions may have found it more difficult to recruit members in private sector industry.

The overall result is that trade unions are active and recognised in a smaller percentage of businesses than they were 30 years ago. In some businesses, workers are unrepresented and are subject to individual bargaining procedures (see unit 88). Where trade unions are recognised, there has been a significant change in industrial relations.

- Industrial action is rarer. Confrontational approaches to problems are less common. Trade unions in particular recognise that it is in their interests to reach negotiated settlements. There is a much greater realism on the part of trade unions that their actions can make businesses less competitive, putting their members' jobs at risk. Equally, more businesses have recognised that by working with rather than against trade unions, they can improve industrial relations. Trade unions can play a useful role in channelling workers' demands and in reducing the number of negotiating partners for the business. They can also exercise some discipline over their members, helping them to see what is reasonable and unreasonable.
- Some businesses have formalised their relationships with unions by signing a **partnership agreement**. Such agreements lay out medium to long term plans for industrial relations. They vary from business to business. But they typically cover pay, conditions of work, employment and training. For example, a business may agree that there will be no compulsory redundancies in return for trade unions agreeing to changes in working practices. Or a more flexible working year for workers might be agreed in the context of a three year pay deal.
- In a few high profile cases, some businesses and unions have signed a SINGLE UNION AGREEMENT. A business agrees to recognise only one trade union for collective bargaining purposes. In return, that trade union agrees to a range of conditions about how it will operate. For example, it might sign a NO STRIKE AGREEMENT where it agrees never to bring its members out on strike. Or it might agree to **flexible working practices**. Single union agreements are controversial amongst trade unions. Other trade unions will be excluded from representing workers in that business. If every business concluded single union agreements, there

would be major winners and losers amongst trade unions for members. What is more, many trade unionists see single union agreements as a 'sell out' to management. They argue that workers' interests are damaged because a union, to get a single union agreement, has to agree to unfavourable terms with the employer. In practice, single union agreements and no strike agreements have not given businesses a clear competitive advantage. For this reason, they remain the exception rather than the norm in British industry.

The number of unions Figure 90.4 shows that the number of trade unions in the UK has fallen from 446 in 1975 to 213 in

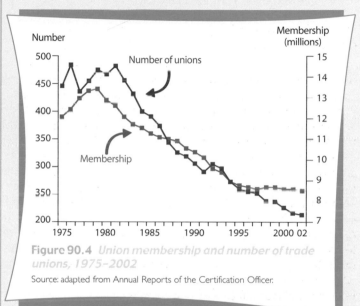

Figure 90.4 *Union membership and number of trade unions, 1975-2002*

Source: adapted from Annual Reports of the Certification Officer.

keyterms

Arbitration - **where both sides in a dispute agree to an independant party making a judgment about how a dispute should be resolved. In some cases this judgment can be legally binding.**
Conciliation - **where both sides in a dispute agree to an independant party helping to find a solution.**
Industrial action - **direct action, such as strikes or lock-outs, taken by employees or employers in the course of an industrial dispute to put pressure on the other side to agree to their demands.**
Industrial dispute - **a disagreement between employees and their employer over an issue such as pay or redundancy which has not been resolved through negotiation or other means.**
No strike agreement - **an agreement between unions and an employer that industrial disputes will not lead to any form of strike action by employees.**
Single union agreement - **an agreement between an employer and a trade union that only that trade union will be recognised for collective bargaining purposes; it effectively means that other trade unions cannot organise in that business and the business only has to negotiate with one union.**
Trade unions - **organisations of workers and ex-workers which exists to promote the interests of their members.**
Union density - **the percentage of any given workforce that belongs to a trade union.**

✓checklist

1 What might be the objectives of trade unions?
2 What are the functions of trade unions?
3 What are the different types of unions?
4 Explain the different types of industrial action that a union might take.
5 What is the difference between conciliation and arbitration?
6 Suggest why trade union power may be less today than it was thirty years ago in the UK.

2002. This has been almost entirely due to merger activity. As union membership has shrunk and total subscriptions have fallen, trade unions have found it more difficult financially to cope. By combining, they have been able to spread their overhead costs more and so survive financially. Equally, it can be argued that larger trade unions are able to give a better service to their members than very small trade unions. They are able to employ specialist staff and campaign more effectively than smaller unions. It can also be argued that very small unions do not have the industrial strength to be as effective in collective bargaining as larger unions.

Ryanair is a fast growing Irish airline company. It has based its success on offering low fares for a basic service. Costs compared to a traditional airline are low per passenger mile travelled and food, for example, is not offered for free on any flight.

The company has had a difficult relationship with trade unions. Its policy is not to recognise trade unions. Instead, it prefers to bargain with individual employees, or use the Employee Representative Committees it has established to communicate with workers. It has gained a reputation for dealing aggressively with trade unions that attempt either to gain recognition or influence the activities of the company. It has also been argued that individual employees who attempt to organise collectively are dealt with in a punitive manner.

For example, in January 2005, The Irish Airline Pilots Union (IALPA) argued successfully before the Labour Court in Ireland that Ryanair pilots should be given a copy of their Terms and Conditions of Employment. This ruling also meant that a complaint of victimisation in the workplace could be heard by an Irish Rights Commissioner. The complaints centred around training for flying new aircraft. Pilots had been informed by Ryanair that if they joined a trade union over the next 5 years they would have to commit to paying a bond of €15 000 (£10 000) for training to fly the new aircraft which is being introduced into the Ryanair fleet. If they did not undertake the training, the pilots were told they faced redundancy when the older aircraft were phased out. Others reported threats including no pay increases, no promotions, cancellation of staff travel and increased restrictions on taking holidays.

'Ryan be fair', a website critical of Ryanair employment practices, also claimed in 2004 that Ryanair was recruiting in Eastern Europe to cut wages. It said that an 'English language school' had been established in Poland where participants paid €1 900 (£1 200) for a place on a course. Some of the participants were then offered a three year employment contract with a firm called 'Crewlink', which in turn leased out the workers to Ryanair. They received two thirds of the pay of normal European Ryanair cabin crew staff.

Ryanair claims that its average wages per employee are higher than comparable unionised airlines. In September 2004, for example, it claimed that its staff earned an average of €50 582 a year, compared to the heavily unionised Scandinavian airline SAS which paid €50 425. Trade unions pointed out that Ryanair tends to contract out a number of services which use a high proportion of low paid workers compared to normal airlines. Not directly employing the same proportion of relatively lowly paid ground staff would automatically boost the average wage at Ryanair.

Ryanair also claims that its employment practices have benefited customers through lower prices. Speaking about a dispute with Siptu, an Irish trade union representing baggage handlers at Dublin Airport, Michael O'Leary, Chief Executive of Ryanair, said 'Siptu is the union that was quite happy to have £200 airfares and a monopoly (of airline flights) in and out of Ireland'. Driving down costs is central to the Ryanair strategy of competing against other low cost airlines. The 21 per cent increase in productivity achieved by staff in 2003 compared to the 3 per cent pay increase they received was one part of this relentless drive to cut costs..

Sources: adapted from www.ryan-be-fair.org, Airwise News, 6.9.2004.

1 (a) Analyse two possible objectives of trade unions dealing with Ryanair. (8 marks)
  (b) To what extent should trade unions involved with Ryanair consider the interests of passengers? (12 marks)
2 Discuss whether Ryanair's anti-union stance is beneficial to the stakeholders of the company. (20 marks)

Nationwide

Knowledge Nationwide Building Society provides a variety of financial services for customers, including banking, loans, mortgages, investments, insurance, credit cards and savings. It has a mutual status, owned by and run for the benefit of members. It is the fourth largest mortgage lender and eighth largest retail banking, saving and lending organisation by asset size and the largest building society in the world. It employs over 15 000 workers in its branches.

Application Like all businesses in the UK, Nationwide must comply with UK and EU *legislation. Individual labour law* that affects the business includes the *Equal Pay Act*, which is designed to prevent *discrimination* on grounds of gender and the *Employee Relations Act* and *Part Time Workers Directive*, designed to protect the interests of *part time* workers. Staff interests at Nationwide are represented by the Nationwide Group Staff Union. *Collective labour law* which affects the actions of the business and the *trade union* include *The Trade Union Act* and the *Trade Union Reform and Employment Rights Act*.

Analysis The Nationwide carries out regular pay reviews. It has a formalised pay structure which is designed to prevent gender bias. This helps the business to conform to equal pay and equal treatment legislation. However, a review of pay found that a 9 per cent gender pay gap existed. This was due to discretionary and ad-hoc decisions that individuals made about pay which had developed on a piecemeal basis, such as starting salaries, promotion and performance review rewards. To prevent this happening in future, the business placed controls on ad-hoc pay and trained licensed recruiters to help make more equal decisions regarding pay. In 2005 the finance industry was experiencing increased threats of industrial action. Employees at both the HSBC and Lloyds TSB were threatening to take strike action over pay. However strike action would have to be approved by a majority of employees in a secret ballot to conform with legislation in order for the strike to be legal.

Evaluation Pay reviews by Nationwide are one way in which the business can check that it is conforming to legislation. Identifying pay differentials and then taking action is likely to be an effective way of preventing pay discrimination. The business has made progress to addressing pay differentials, but accepts there is 'no quick fix'. It did accept that the equitable treatment of part timers has been more of a challenge. However, switching pay rewards to a system based on productivity rather then hours led to an increase in the number of part time applicants. This attempt to ensure equality of treatment is also likely to help contribute to a minimising of staff unrest, which may explain why, unlike other financial businesses, it was not facing threatened industrial action over pay in 2005.

Adapted from *People Management*, 10.3.2005, www.nationwide.co.uk, www.stratus.com/products/reference/nationwide.htm and www.guardian.co.uk.

Individual labour law

Employees will agree to certain conditions when they are first employed, such as the number of hours a week to be worked and how much leave they can take. Employees also have the right to be treated the same as their colleagues when applying for promotion in a business. INDIVIDUAL LABOUR LAW deals with these rights and obligations of individual employees (see unit 55). They are set out in EU and UK legislation. Employees' rights increased after the UK signed the **Social Chapter** of the EU in 1997. This meant that the UK introduced laws which reflected EU regulations. It increased the rights of workers in a number of areas, including equality of treatment and conditions of service.

Employers are obliged by law to treat employees the same in certain situations.

Equal pay The **Equal Pay Act, 1970** states that workers are entitled to the same pay and conditions as others doing broadly similar work (see unit 55). In 1983 this was amended so that workers could claim equal pay for work which made

the same demands on them. EU regulations also promote equal pay. The **Equal Pay Directive**, for example, states that men and women should receive equal pay for equal work and defines equal work as the same work or work for which equal value is attributed.

Sex discrimination The **Sex Discrimination Act, 1975** makes it unlawful to discriminate on grounds of gender or marital status, or for sexual harassment to take place. So, for example, employees cannot be refused a job simply because they are male or female. The **EU Equal Treatment Directive** also states that there should be no discrimination on grounds of gender. The **Equal Opportunities Commission** is a government body set up to work with employers to eliminate discrimination and investigate complaints by employees. Employees who feel they have been discriminated against can also take their complaint to an **employment tribunal**.

Race relations The **Race Relations Act, 1976** makes it illegal to discriminate on grounds of race, colour, nationality or ethnic origin. This was an attempt to prevent discrimination against ethnic minority groups in particular. In 2002 it was amended, particularly to take into account discrimination in bodies such as the police force and health services. It was also amended further in 2003 to include racial harassment. The **Employment Equality (Religion and Belief) Regulations, 2003** outlaw discrimination on grounds of religious beliefs. The **Commission for Racial Equality** is a non-government, publicly funded body which aims to promote fair treatment and equal opportunities regardless of race, colour nationality or ethnic origin.

Disability The **Disability Discrimination Act, 1995** makes it illegal to discriminate against a worker with a disability. Workers with disabilities cannot be treated less favourably than other workers, unless there is a justified and substantial reason. For example, refusal by a multinational to employ a disabled person because of the cost of adapting one piece of computer software is likely to be unjustified. If the costs of the adaptation involves changing all software and all hardware for the entire organisation, this may be considered justified. The **Disability Rights Commission** is an independent body set up to eliminate disability discrimination.

Older employees In the past there has been little protection for older employees, other than those set out in their contract of employment. However, EU member countries must introduce laws by 2006 to comply with the EU **Employment Framework Directive**. These regulations prevent discrimination on the basis of age unless it is justified, for example if older employees would create safety problems.

Sexual preference The EU **Employment Equality (Sexual Orientation) Regulations, 2003** outlaw discrimination and victimisation based on sexual orientation towards people of the same sex or the opposite sex.

Once employees have been appointed by a business, they are entitled to a CONTRACT OF EMPLOYMENT. The **Employment Rights Act, 1996** states that they must be given a written statement outlining the terms and conditions of their contract within two months of appointment. There is a number of laws which affect the terms and conditions of employees.

The nature and term of employment In the past there has been a tendency for the terms and conditions of part time and temporary workers to be inferior to those of full time and permanent employees. Increasingly legislation is being introduced to remove these differences. For example, the **Part Time Workers Directive, 2000** and the **Employee Relations Act, 1999** prevent part time employees from being treated less favourably than full time employees in terms of conditions such as pay, leave, holidays, redundancies and pensions. The **Employment Act, 2002** states that fixed term employees should not be treated less favourably than permanent staff.

Flexible working Increasingly businesses are making use of a flexible workforce (see unit 88). This includes employees who work from home, work from different locations, job share and work flexible hours. Some employees also taking advantage of the benefits of flexible work, such as working from home part of the week. The **Employment Act, 2002** allows employees with children to request flexibility in their terms and conditions of employment under certain circumstances. An employer can only refuse this for clear business reasons.

Minimum Wages The **Minimum Wage Act, 1998** sets national minimum wages for employees of different ages. Employers must pay at least this hourly amount to workers. For example, in 2004 the rates were set at:

- £4.25 per hour from October 2005 and £4.45 per hour from October 2006 for workers aged 18-22;
- £5.05 per hour from October 2005 and £5.35 per hour from October 2006 for workers aged 22 and over.

Hours of work The contract of employment given to an employee must state the number of hours a week or other

---

In 2005 BT was preparing to conform with the requirements of age discrimination legislation which would come into force in 2006 in the UK. It established an action team made up of human resources employees in different areas of its operating practice areas. It identified a number of possible areas of discrimination which could take place at the business if unaddressed including:

- its practice of awarding additional holidays to employees after one year's service;
- long term service awards;
- the qualifying criteria for certain roles in the business;
- its five year incremental scale for non-mangers.

Where it wanted to keep particular practices, it drew up a list of reasons why they were acceptable. Those practices it didn't think could be justified were either removed or replaced. The only real example of direct discrimination that BT found was its retirement age of 60 for employees. Previously this was used as a means of natural wastage by the business to reduce its 'headcount', although workers with essential skills and knowledge were encouraged to stay on.

The business has encouraged non-discrimination on an age basis as part of its diversity policy for many years. But it accepts that preparing for the new legislation has been 'a huge task'. The legislation unearthed a lot more issues than just age discrimination and created implications which were not initially realised.

Source: adapted from *People Management*, 21.4.2005.

(a) **Examine reasons why the current policies of the business may contravene age discrimination legislation.**

(b) **Assess why changes at the business to comply with legislation are likely to be 'a huge task'.**

time period the employee is expected to work. Legislation has been introduced to protect certain employees from working excessive hours. The **European Work Time Directive** limited the maximum amount of time employees could work to 48 hours per week. Exceptions were made, however. For example, senior executives and junior doctors were excluded.

Redundancy and dismissal Under certain circumstances, businesses may make their employees redundant (see unit 38). Employees may even chose to take voluntary redundancy. The **Employment Rights Act, 1996** gives employees who are made redundant the right to severance pay based on their length of continuous employment. A business may decide to dismiss an employee. If the employee feels that this is unfair, he or she can take a claim to an employment tribunal. The **Employment Relations Act, 1999** gives protection against unfair dismissal to employees who have been working for a business for more than one year.

Maternity and paternity leave Legislation states that parents have the right to take time off work when having children and that mothers can return to work after having children. The **Employment Act, 2002**, for example, sets out rates of pay and time for maternity leave for mothers and adoptive parents. It also states the conditions of paternity leave for working fathers.

Disciplinary and grievance procedures The nature of disciplinary procedures which businesses take against employees who have broken the terms and conditions of their contract of employment are regulated by legislation. The **Employment Rights Act, 1996** obliges employers to explain disciplinary procedures clearly and inform employees of the consequences of breaking conduct at work standards. Employees may feel that they have been unfairly treated at work and have a grievance. Businesses must set in place procedures to deal with the grievances of employees. The **Employment Act, 2002** put in place minimum standards for procedures which businesses must have.

Collective labour law

COLLECTIVE LABOUR LAW deals with legislation which affects trade union activities and industrial relations (see unit 55 and 90). Collective labour laws affect employees and businesses in a number of areas.

Industrial action Trade unions often take industrial action to further their cause in disputes with employers. This action can take a wide variety of forms, ranging from working to rule, to go slows, to official strikes. Legislation can affect the extent and form of the action taken by unions. It can also affect the extent to which unions, employees, and employers are affected by industrial action.

Legislation determines the steps which need to be taken by unions and employees when taking industrial action. For example, the **Trade Union Act, 1984** obliged unions to carry out secret ballots before they could take official action. Employees had to agree by vote before action could take place. The **Trade Unions Reform and Employment Rights Act, 1993** set up a process for postal voting in ballots on industrial action. It also forced unions to give seven days' notice to employers before industrial action could take place.

Legislation can also affect action taken by unions in the dispute. Picketing involves placing union workers outside the workplace to inform employees, employers and the public that a strike is taking place. Secondary picketing is where union members employed in a different location picket a particular office or factory. The **Employment Act, 1990** banned secondary picketing, so that only official union pickets employed at a place of work can be involved.

In certain situations unions may be held liable for the implications of their industrial action. The **Employment Act, 1982** made unions liable for actions which were not in furtherance with their dispute. In other cases union action can be restricted. The **Trade Unions Reform and Employment Rights Act, 1993** gave people deprived of goods by industrial action the right to to prevent this from happening.

Union recognition In the 1980s many employers derecognised trade unions and increasingly bargained over pay and conditions with individuals. This led to a reduction in the number of employees covered by collective bargaining agreements. In the late 1990s the UK government attempted to encourage the voluntary recognition of unions by businesses. However, the **Employment Relations Act, 1999** also set in place a legal process for trade union recognition. Employers with more than 21 workers can be compelled to recognise unions for collective bargaining automatically for a 'bargaining unit' (the workplace or group of workers the union wants to represent) where the majority of the workers are members of the union. Alternatively, union recognition may take place after a ballot where the majority of the workers and at least 40 per cent of those entitled to vote within the 'bargaining unit' want the union to act for them. Applications for union recognition are made to the **Central Arbitration Committee** (CAC).

Closed shops In the past agreements were reached between businesses and unions where a condition of employment for workers was that they must belong to a trade union. This meant that only union members would be employed. Any new employee must be a member of a union or must join one. This practice was known as a closed shop. The **Employment Act, 1990** made it unlawful to refuse to employ a non-union member, which prevented closed shops from operating.

Union membership The **Employment Relations Act, 1999** prevents dismissal for employees on the grounds of joining a trade union.

Union representatives The **Employment Act, 2002** gives trade union representatives the right to time off for training to carry out their duties.

Impact on business

Employment law can affect businesses in a variety of ways.

Business operations Legislation can influence the way in which a business carries out its human resource management. The whole process of appointing members of staff must conform with legislation. Job advertisements, selection tests, interviews and final choices of candidates must meet the requirements of equal opportunities legislation. They cannot be biased towards a particular gender or ethnic group and must not discriminate against disabled candidates, for example. The personnel department will also be responsible for ensuring that the business provides information about disciplinary and grievance procedures. Detailed knowledge and personnel management skills will be required, which could mean that the business has to train staff in personnel departments, especially when new legislation takes place. Management may also require training. And businesses may have to employ extra workers to deal with the administration and checking required for legislation.

The operation of other functional areas of the business can also be affected. Legislation which limits the number of hours worked or guaranteed leave may mean that a business requires a more flexible workforce to deal with absent staff or urgent orders. For example, if as business gets a sudden order from abroad, restrictions on the number of hours worked may mean that it cannot meet its human resource requirements from its full time staff, even with overtime. It may need to employ part time or temporary staff to meet its deadline. Organisations may also need to change. If a business employs staff who work flexibly from home, it may need to change its channels of communication (see unit 32) and make use of communication technology, such as emails and mobile phones, to ensure instructions are given and received effectively.

Negotiations between employers and employees will change as a result of legislation. Since the 1980s, the percentage of workers covered by collective bargaining agreements fell greatly. This has led the UK to be regarded as a low cost employer, which has made it attractive for the location of foreign businesses. The introduction of laws to promote union recognition may have halted this slide after the year 2000. The UK may still be regarded as having relative low wage costs compared to some its competitors, although not to others in the Far East.

The introduction of laws affecting industrial action may also have changed the nature and effects of the action on business. Today businesses are less likely to be faced by sudden unofficial strikes and may have time to put contingency plans in place before the impact of the action. On the other hand legislation in the late 1990s and the early twenty first century is likely to see unions involved in a number of business areas which involve employees, such as grievance procedures, and perhaps greater union recognition.

Costs Legislation often imposes greater costs on business. Increased costs can take a number of forms.
- Changing systems is likely to be expensive. It might involve new methods of operation, training or employing specialist workers. For example, changing a detailed company handbook to include new legislation about the rights of part time workers could be expensive for a large multinational employer of thousands of employees.
- Facilities may need to be adapted to take into account new legislation. Examples might be including different languages to take into account the needs of ethic groups if large numbers are employed or making changes to office layouts for disabled employees.
- Legislation has been introduced which can make unions responsible for their industrial action. In some cases they may be fined. Businesses may also be fined if they break individual employee legislation, such as terms in the contract of employment.
- A number of changes will directly affect the wage costs of employers. These may include giving part time and

temporary employees the same rights as full time or permanent employees or the introduction of a minimum wage.

The total costs of legislation are likely to be higher for a large company than a small business. However, the potential impact on small businesses may be greater. A small business which has sudden increased costs as a result of legislation may have working capital problems and may be forced out of business. This is why some legislation makes exceptions for firms which employ only a few workers. Some small businesses even attempt to avoid legislation because of the costs involved.

Corporate culture and motivation Legislation may lead to a change in the corporate culture of a business (see unit 64) so that employees and their contribution is taken into account to a greater extent. The introduction of European Works Councils in some businesses after the year 2000 may lead to greater involvement in decision making by employees and greater industrial democracy (see unit 89). This may also be the case if unions are recognised in business. Increased participation and industrial democracy in business is likely to motivate employees.

In October 2002, the trade union BECTU won the right to represent workers at Savoy Bingo in Cambuslang. BECTU is the independent union for those working in broadcasting, film, theatre, entertainment, leisure, interactive media and allied areas who are primarily based in the United Kingdom. A panel appointed by the Central Arbitration Committee (CAC) gave Sovereign Leisure, owners of Savoy Bingo, 30 days to agree to collective bargaining arrangements with the union.

BECTU had made a formal application in May 2002 for recognition at the company under legislation. Because BECTU had recruited more than 50% of Savoy's staff, the panel automatically awarded recognition rights without any need for a ballot of staff. Earlier attempts to win recognition through negotiations with the company had failed. The CAC award covered all grades of full time and part time staff at Savoy Bingo, except for the manager.

BECTU officials were confident that they would be able to agree a system of pay bargaining and collective negotiation by the deadline of November 1st. Sovereign was one of a number of employers to give recognition rights to BECTU as the result of CAC applications after the Employment Relations Act came into force. MTV, the music broadcaster, Meridian TV, and ITFC, the ITV teletext company, all agreed to recognise the union, in some cases before the CAC panel made a formal award.

Source: adapted from www.bectu.org.uk.

(a) **Explain why the legislation in this case is an example of collective employment law.**
(b) **Assess the importance of the factors that have affected the actions of the businesses and the union in this case.**

Image and social responsibility Legislation may affect the social responsibility and image of businesses. Businesses which follow equal opportunities policies when recruiting and offer favourable conditions of employment may be regarded as 'good' employers by potential employees. As such, they may be able to attract more able candidates.

Sales and profitability Legislation can lead to some changes in business which improve effectiveness and profitability. For example, some businesses such as B&Q have recognised that customers value the contribution of older employees. It could be argued that they have followed EMPLOYEE SEGMENTATION policies, hiring workers from a particular age group which meet the needs of its customers. Legislation to prevent age discrimination in future may encourage other businesses to take advantage of such policies. Another example is the Halifax, which recruited from the Chinese community in Manchester and found that customers for this ethnic group increased as a result.

keyterms

Collective labour law - **legislation which affects trade union activities and industrial relations.**
Contract of employment - **an agreement to employ a worker by a business which states the employee's conditions of work, such as pay, hours to be worked and holiday entitlement.**
Employee segmentation - **an employment policy where businesses hire employees who match profiles which help a business to satisfy the needs of its customers.**
Individual labour law - **legislation which deals with the rights and obligations of individual employees.**

checklist

1. What is the difference between individual labour law and collective labour law?
2. What does the following legislation make illegal?
   (i) Sex Discrimination Act.
   (ii) Race Relations Act.
   (iii) Disability Discrimination Act.
3. Explain the main features of the Minimum Wage Act.
4. State how legislation might affect:
   (i) maternity leave;
   (ii) employees with a grievance;
   (iii) employees being made redundant.
5. Explain ONE way in which the:
   (i) Trade Union Reform and Employment Rights Act;
   (ii) Trade Union Act,
   (iii) Employment Act;
   might affect union industrial action.
6. Explain briefly the steps involved in employees seeking union recognition.
7. State THREE ways in which legislation might:
   (i) change business operations;
   (ii) increase business costs.
8. Explain why employee segmentation might help a business comply with age legislation.

On 11th May 2005 the UK government suffered a blow in its campaign for flexible labour markets. MEPs voted to scrap Britain's opt-out from the maximum 48-hour working week stipulated in the EU working time directive. Unions hailed the vote as a victory in their campaign to halt a long hours culture spreading across Europe and restore the work-life balance. The UK government and business groups argued that ending the opt-out would harm UK competitiveness.

About four million British employees work more than 48 hours a week. CBI chief Sir Digby Jones said, 'The current opt-out system ... gives employees choice in the hours they work, allowing them to generate wealth for their families and companies to generate wealth for the nation. People need the opportunity to aspire and earn extra money if they want to.' TUC chief Brendan Barber, however, stated that many British businesses had not bothered to inform employees that they had the right to refuse to work more than 48 hours a week and that the decision was 'a common-sense compromise on the 48-hour working week.' The maximum working week would now be averaged over the whole year, rather than the current 17 weeks. So businesses could get workers to work long hours at certain times of the year if they let them work less at other times. The NHS was likely to be one organisation greatly affected as many staff work long hours.

'We started our clothing business five years ago. We have made great progress in that time, building up retail clients in the local area. We have recently won a regular order from a large chain. It is difficult for small businesses to break into this market. But we have a small dedicated team of staff willing to work whenever orders come in. Starting a small business takes you into another world, where you become David surrounded by an army of Goliaths, including working time directive regulations and minimum wage rules. There are around 4 million small firms in the UK, employing around 50% of the private sector workforce. Over 90% of them employ fewer than 10 people. Clearly some regulations are required, particularly to protect health and safety, but the cost and complexity of the system creates real problems for small businesses. Large employers can delegate or hire more management to cope with the additional administrative burden. Small businesses often have to divert time away from the business to cope with rules. The number of new regulations means that smaller businesses are sometimes unaware of the latest obligations with which they must comply. So time is spent trying to find out, followed by a rush to avoid penalties.'

A Guardian/ICM opinion poll in 2004 showed that people are in favour of new measures to enable more family-friendly working. The poll found that:

- 66% of people would like to see families being given a choice of deciding whether fathers or mothers should be able to take or share the six months' paid leave currently available only as maternity leave;
  - 53% wanted to see fathers given more than the current two weeks' paid maternity leave;
  - 51% wanted to see mothers given more than six months' paid maternity leave.

Legislation gives employees the right to request flexible working hours, better-paid maternity leave and two weeks' paid leave for fathers. But calls for further legislation were being made. It was suggested that a balance would need to be struck between the needs of employees and small businesses. People with young children want to spend more time with them. This could improve employee relations and motivation. Introducing flexibility does have issues for small and medium sized enterprises (SMEs), but can also help people with children who are making an economic contribution to the country.

The poll also showed the backlash against the UK's long-hours culture, particularly amongst younger workers and that people wanted a limit on the hours employees work in the UK.

Source: adapted from *The Guardian*, 17.8. 2004. 12.5.2005.

1 Examine the effects that legislation mentioned in the data may have on small businesses. (10 marks)
2 Discuss whether legislation to protect employees in small businesses should be extended. (10 marks)

Human Resource Management

INA Bearings

Knowledge INA Bearings makes high precision engine components for the automotive industry. It is part of the multinational Shaeffler group with headquarters in Germany. The business operates from a factory in Llanelli.

Application INA Bearings' *employees* had often received *task-orientated training* in the past. This is a very traditional approach to *personnel management*. After discussions with *staff* about the problems for this approach, the *business* changed its *strategy*. It wanted to operate as 'one team'. It harmonised the grades and *rewards* of *shopfloor workers*. It encouraged workers to know what the business was aiming for and become involved in discussing business strategy through a *works council*. It also developed a system of individual learning plans and training for all employees. This approach to *human resource management* recognised the contributions of employees to the business.

Analysis A number of factors contributed to the change in the human resource management approach at INA Bearings. The business had been continually losing contracts, particularly to eastern European competitors. It had been forced to cut 500 jobs and faced the possibility of losing a contract that would have used half the plant's manufacturing capacity. There was also a 'them and us' attitude between managers and employees which led to a lack of motivation and even industrial unrest, with the threat of a strike ballot. The new initiatives were designed to address these problems and improve the motivation and productivity of the business.

Evaluation Developing a shared vision for the organisation, so that everyone was working towards improving productivity, was essential if INA Bearings was to compete in the market against low cost competitors in eastern Europe and not lose further contracts. Involving staff in decision making and training them to take responsibilities were essential components of a new approach to human resource management which helped to improve the business's position. In February head office recognised the improvement by nominating the Llanelli plant to manufacture a new hi tech engine part for Jaguar.

Source: adapted from People Management, 11.11.2004.

Personnel management vs human resource management

Unit 38 explained that personnel management is the process of administering the workforce of a business. Personnel management historically arose in the first half of the twentieth century out of two distinct and separate needs.

One was the need to provide labour administration for businesses which were tending to grow larger over time. In a small business of ten workers, the owner or 'boss' might have handled the weekly payment of wages for example. The owner would almost certainly have been responsible for hiring and firing staff. But in a business of 100 or 1 000 people, it became more efficient to hire specialist staff to deal with these functions. Hence there was a growth in personnel departments in larger firms.

The second was the need to look after the welfare of staff. In the nineteenth and early twentieth centuries, there were a few pioneers such as George Cadbury, Joseph Rowntree and William Hesketh Lever who recognised that, as the owners of large and successful businesses, they had a social responsibility to care for the welfare of their workers. The First World War saw a large influx of women into the workforce and it was felt particularly important that their needs should be looked after.

As explained in Unit 38, personnel departments came to be responsible for a wide range of issues concerning staff, from administering payrolls, to selection of new staff and dismissal of existing staff, training and development and staff discipline.

However, many in personnel management felt that their function within the business organisation was considered to be of secondary importance. Personnel management was a 'client department' for the more important functions such as sales, production or finance. Very few companies had the head of personnel on the board of directors. Yet the head of sales and the head of finance might expect to sit on the board.

In the 1980s and 1990s, it was strongly argued that personnel management was just as important as the sales or production function within a business. To signify this importance, business increasingly referred to 'human resource management' (HRM). It can be argued that human resource management differs from personnel management in a number of ways.

- Human resource management sees its function as part of strategic management. Strategy is a set of plans to achieve the goals set by a business (see unit 64). HRM claims that the way human resources are managed will have a crucial impact on whether a business achieves its goals. The business must therefore plan how to use its human resources if it is to be a successful enterprise.
- Human resource management claims that human resources are as important, if not more important, than the physical or financial resources of a business. In service sector businesses in particular, the quality and effectiveness of human resources can be what gives a business its competitive edge. HRM is about ensuring that the workforce is highly committed, is of high quality and is flexible. For example, the payroll function of the personnel department is not just about organising the efficient payment of salaries to workers. It is also about motivating workers. They expect to receive an efficient and friendly service. When there are problems, such as not receiving the correct amount of overtime pay or a promised bonus, workers can become demotivated (as explained, for example, by Herzberg's two factor theory, see unit 35). The

best solution is that mistakes are not made. But if they are made, then they should be rectified quickly and efficiently and in a friendly manner. The motivation of workers can actually be increased if they see their problems being resolved quickly and fairly.

• HRM sees the management of human resources in an integrated way. So the payroll function is not just about paying workers, but is also about motivation. Recruitment is not just about getting a new worker to fill a post, it is also about identifying training needs and ensuring flexibility. Conforming with new legislation is not just about keeping to the letter of the law, it is about changing practices and policies so that the business can run efficiently and be seen to be a good employer.

Hard and soft human resource management

Human resource management today is implemented in different ways in different businesses. In some, HRM is seen as a strategic function. In others, it is seen still as very much of secondary importance to functions such as sales and finance.

John Storey (1989) in *New Perspectives on Human Resource Management* argues that there is no accepted definition of 'human resources management'. The term is used in different ways in different contexts. For example, he puts forward a distinction between 'hard' and 'soft' versions of HRM.

Hard HRM HARD HRM sees human resources in the same way that it sees physical resources such as machines, or financial resources. Hard HRM is quantitative. It is associated with **workforce planning** (see unit 38). Businesses must calculate how many workers they need and of what type.

They can then forecast how many workers they must recruit in the future from knowledge of their existing workforce and how it will change, for example, through staff turnover. Workers are then numbers to be manipulated in the production process. Their wages are costs to be minimised. Their work is output to be maximised. Training is for the benefit of the business. Workers who don't need training do not receive training because training is a cost. If it is cheaper to employ temporary workers or outsource work, then this should be the strategy pursued. Low pay, poor working conditions or work tasks which give little job satisfaction only become an issue if they affect the productivity of workers.

Hard HRM is therefore a control mechanism by management of their subordinates. Some businesses which adopt a hard HRM philosophy might superficially seem to be good employers. They might pay high wages or stress how important is the contribution of employers to the business. Working conditions might be excellent and work tasks might be designed to give high levels of job satisfaction. But all of this might be simply a structure to generate high levels of profit through maximising the output of highly efficient staff. Here, hard HRM remains a control mechanism which has been dressed up to look like 'soft' HRM.

Soft HRM SOFT HRM sees workers as stakeholders within the business. Their goals are part of the goals of the whole business. Soft HRM emphasises the importance of motivating staff and developing their skills. A work environment where staff are well paid, there is job security and high levels of job satisfaction is one where workers are likely to be highly committed. Giving staff high levels of control over their work environment will also increase job satisfaction and motivation. Soft HRM would discourage practices such as the deskilling of

Glenmorangie is best known as a producer of Scottish Whisky. In 2004 the business was sold by the Macdonald family which owned 52 per cent of shares and had been involved in the business since 1893 to LVMH (Loius Vuitton Moet Hennessy). It has just under 400 staff in three main distilleries in Tain, Elgin and the Isle of Islay, with a main site at Broxburn outside Edinburgh, where most staff are based. The change in ownership would need to be effectively handled. Communication was essential with staff.

Glenmorangie has a 'consultation and involvement' culture with staff. This involves communicating information to staff as early as possible on any changes and receiving feedback. It also includes training and development for all staff. Staff are directly involved in these training and development initiatives. The business recognises the importance of its staff as a key resource and asset of the business and values their input. The stress is very much on human resource management. But this was not always the case. Staff surveys showed that managers in the past were often too task orientated - taking a more traditional view of employees.

A survey of staff in 2001 identified a need for more people recognition at the business. Staff wanted managers to be less task centred and more people centred. This would support the culture of the business and motivate staff. The business identified its promotion strategy as perhaps leading to this problem. It often promoted people who were 'good at their job' but not necessarily good managers. The surveys helped to highlight this difficulty. Glenmorangie initiated a management development programme based on the employee feedback. Training was in the form of 'Champions' - people with a reputation in a particular area of the business. Glenmorangie argues that, without effective training, staff could not reach their true potential.

Source: adapted from *People Management*, 24.2.2005.

1 **Using Glenmorangie as an example, explain the differences between a personnel approach and a human resource management approach.**
2 **Analyse why taking a human resource management approach rather than a personnel management approach could have been more effective in the situation that Glenmorangie faced.**

Asda is one of a number of businesses that are increasingly making use of 'servant leadership'. It sees leadership as 'something you do with people, not to people'. The business argues that leadership is certainly about 'taking a lead'. But it is also about making sure you understand what makes people tick and 'how to bring them with you'.

In stores, every Asda manager is asked to know three or four things about every individual member of staff in their teams. Only then can decisions be made effectively as individuals' circumstances are taken into account. Listening is also a key factor of servant leadership. Asda has listening groups and monthly surveys which note and then react to employees' views. These try to find out the 'pulse of the workforce'.

Advertising agency St Lukes Communications also has a similar management approach. The business is not co-run, but it does argue that it takes a consultative approach. A *Sunday Times* survey found that 87 per cent of its employees felt 'cared for'. Another company which uses the idea in all but name is Happy Computers, a small business with family friendly working practices. Employees who are not happy with their manager can ask for a new one.

Is servant leadership really different from team leadership? Team leaders act as 'servants' or facilitators to teams. So is there any real difference? It is argued that under servant leadership 'its not the leader that is the servant - its the servant that is the leader'.

Source: adapted from *People Management*, 23.12.2004.

1   **Explain what type of leadership and human resource management approaches are taken by the businesses described in the article.**
2   **Examine the implications on the businesses involved.**

jobs, or the fragmentation of work tasks which demotivated workers.

Hard and soft HRM could be compared to the different approaches of the scientific management school and the human relations school of motivation (see units 34-35). Equally, hard HRM could be seen as reflecting a Theory X approach to motivation, whilst soft HRM reflects a Theory Y approach (see unit 39).

In practice, businesses tend to use both hard and soft HRM approaches. Most businesses need to make a profit to survive in the long term. Therefore they have to pay attention to the costs of the workforce and to their productivity. Equally, management in most businesses recognise that they have responsibilities to their workforce even when fulfilling these responsibilities leads to higher short term costs.

Hard and soft HRM and leadership styles

Hard and soft HRM may be linked to leadership styles (see unit 39).

Authoritarian leadership Hard HRM tends to be associated with authoritarian styles of leadership. Authoritarian leaders tend to be TASK-ORIENTATED. This means that they are focussed on completing a particular task within limits such as time and cost. They achieve this by structuring the work of their subordinates. Task-orientation can be motivating for subordinates. If a job is going well, subordinates can feel that they are part of a high achieving team. Structure and order can provide a sense of security for workers which is important in motivational needs.

Democratic leadership Soft HRM tends to be associated with democratic styles of leadership. Democratic leaders tend to be PEOPLE-ORIENTATED. They understand that there is a task to be completed. But democratic leaders are as concerned with the needs of subordinates. They listen to subordinates and take their advice. They support subordinates when problems arise with their work or outside of the workplace. By building an atmosphere of trust and respect, where subordinates are encouraged to take initiative, democratic leaders succeed in motivating workers. In all of this, effective communication (see units 86-87) is essential. A democratic leader who cannot communicate effectively is likely to fail.

Integrating plans

Human resource management stresses that the plans of the HRM department must be integrated into the strategic or corporate plan for the business. Therefore, its plans must help the business achieve its overall objectives. Its plans must also be co-ordinated with the plans of other departments such as sales and production.

For example, if the sales department plans to increase sales by 10 per cent, this is likely to have implications for both the production department and the finance department. Increased sales are likely to require increased levels of staffing. This must therefore be taken into account in the **workforce** or **human resource plan** (see unit 38). Equally, increased production may be achievable through staff training and development. A better trained workforce may be a more productive workforce. Therefore, training needs must appear in the workforce plan. The plans of the finance department also need to be taken into account. Increased sales should lead to higher revenue but increasing staff levels or increased training will also lead to higher costs. If the plans of the different departments are integrated, the finance department plan is likely to show increased profit from the higher sales. Higher profits are likely to be one of the goals of the business.

HRM and competitive advantage

Those who advocate an HRM approach argue that it can give a business a competitive advantage. P Boxall, in an article in the *Human Resource Management Journal*,1996, argues that this competitive advantage comes from two sources.

Human capital advantage HUMAN CAPITAL is the sum of all the education, training, experience and innate skills of a worker or group of workers. Just as individuals with high levels of savings will be able to earn high amounts of interest, so individuals with high levels of human capital will be able to gain high levels of earnings. Businesses offer higher earnings to workers with higher levels of human capital because such workers are more productive. The managing director of a company is paid more than a cleaner because the managing director's much higher level of human capital contributes more to the profit of the company than the cleaner.

The human capital of a worker can be increased through education and training. It can also be increased through giving a worker wider experience. Hence, workers in their 30s tend to have higher levels of human capital than workers in their early 20s starting out their career.

A business can gain a competitive advantage by building up a level of human capital within its workforce which is greater than in its rivals. Using an HRM approach, this is done through managing the HUMAN RESOURCE CYCLE.

- Workers need to be **selected** for their ability to contribute to the strategic goals of the business. Selection (see unit 40) is not just about filling vacant posts with workers. It is about questioning whether the post should exist at all, what might the post holder contribute to the business, what qualities and skills should the selectors be looking for, and if no suitable candidates present themselves, what is the most appropriate course of action at that point.
- Workers need to undergo regular **appraisal** (see unit 37). The appraisal should take place in relation to the goals of the business. The appraisal system should therefore be constructed in such a way as to ask how has the individual contributed towards achieving those goals.
- **Rewards** should be given to workers who contribute towards the business achieving its goals (see unit 93).
- Staff **development** should be linked to the needs of the business. What training and experience should an individual receive to better enable them to achieve the goals of the business? With a limited training budget, what is the optimal way to spend that budget in order to secure the firm's objectives?

The human resource cycle of selection, appraisal, rewards and development (also known as the Michigan model) affects the **performance** of employees. The better the selection, the appraisal system, the reward system and staff development,

the higher is likely to be the level of human capital in the business. This is what will then give the business its HUMAN CAPITAL ADVANTAGE.

Human process advantage The success of a football team is greater than the sum of the individual human capital of each of its players. It is about how they play as a team and not just about how they play as individual players. It is also about the network of support from everyone else at a football club. The processes of a business may be as important, if not more important, than the human capital of a business. The processes include:

- the way in which different departments within a business co-operate to achieve the goals of the business;
- the quality of the communication processes, both formal and informal (see units 85-87), which determine how knowledge, information and commands are passed through the organisation;
- the relationships between superiors and subordinates and the extent to which both superiors and subordinates are able to use their talents and skills to further the goals of the business;
- the underlying ethos of the business, and whether or not it motivates workers to achieve the goals of the business;
- the way in which a business learns over time, its **organisational learning**, to improve the way in which it conducts business, from R&D to production to marketing to HRM and finance.

HUMAN PROCESS ADVANTAGE is the competitive advantage a business gains over its rivals through the learned interaction of individual workers, which creates a business culture that is independent of any single worker.

Total competitive advantage is the sum of both human capital advantage and human process advantage. Businesses which gain a competitive advantage through human resource management policies will be more likely to survive and earn high profits than their rivals in the market. To retain that competitive advantage, human resources must be an integral part of the overall strategy of a business. This is the argument that human resource professionals use to justify why human resource management is so important to a business.

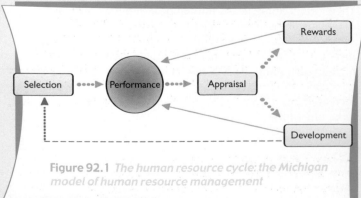

Figure 92.1 *The human resource cycle: the Michigan model of human resource management*

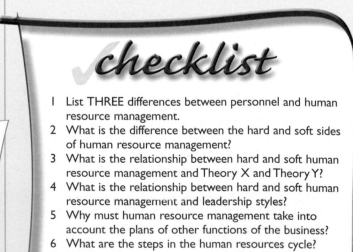

checklist

1 List THREE differences between personnel and human resource management.
2 What is the difference between the hard and soft sides of human resource management?
3 What is the relationship between hard and soft human resource management and Theory X and Theory Y?
4 What is the relationship between hard and soft human resource management and leadership styles?
5 Why must human resource management take into account the plans of other functions of the business?
6 What are the steps in the human resources cycle?
7 How can the human resources cycle affect human capital advantage?
8 Explain the difference between human capital advantage and human process advantage.

keyterms

Hard HRM – a human resource management perspective which sees human resources as no different from other resources available to the business, such as financial or physical resources. Their costs, requirements and contribution and can be quantified and businesses can manipulate these to achieve their aims and objectives.

Human capital – the sum of all the education, training, experience and innate skills of a worker or group of workers; the higher the level of human capital of workers, the higher on average will be the rewards they will be able to earn by hiring themselves out to employers.

Human capital advantage – the competitive advantage that a business gains by having a workforce with a higher level of human capital than its rivals. This advantage can be gained through the human capital cycle of selection, appraisal, rewards and development leading to improved performance of workers.

Human process advantage – the competitive advantage a business gains over its rivals through the learned interaction of individual workers which creates a business culture which is independent of any single worker.

Human resource cycle - the process through which human resources are recruited, selected, rewarded and appraised by a business.

People-orientated leadership – where a leader focuses on the needs of subordinates and gives them some autonomy to decide how best a task should be completed. People-orientated leaders tend to be democratic.

Soft HRM – a human resource management perspective which prioritises the needs and development of employees in order to motivate them and make them committed to achieving the goals of a business.

Task-orientated leadership – where a leader focuses on completing tasks rather than on the needs of the individual workers who will help complete the task. Task-orientated leaders tends to be autocratic.

Newspaper groups are not noted for their training initiatives. There is often too much pressure to meet deadlines. People issues tend to have low priority. But *Metro*, the so-called 'saviour of bored communities', is bucking the trend. Launched in 1999 it reached a 1 million circulation in September 2004. *Metro* was considered to be a classic start-up, explained Steve Auckland, its managing director. 'It was terribly autocratic and people were not the most important aspect of it all' he said. *Metro* prides itself on its different approach to readers. It give straight talking news and features that fits perfectly into a 20 minute commute to work. Now it wants to take the same approach to human resource management.

Metro's parent company is Allied Newspapers. It persuaded the company to employ a dedicated HR professional. Laura Ashworth was employed in 2003 to look after recruitment, retention and development of the paper's 180 staff. Not all people at the paper were in favour. Some wondered why there should be spending on increased skills when people were leaving to go elsewhere. After her appointment however, attrition rates of staff leaving fell from 25 per cent to 16 per cent.

Auckland argues that even although people leave, it is important to allow them to develop whilst they are at the paper. They then take the good name of the business elsewhere with them. An induction process gives employees in London a three day course and £100 to have a night out of their choice, for example. The aim is to get people to understand the audience - young ABC1 professional with high incomes - by experiencing their activities. Most newspapers work on the basis that, when you get a job with a national paper, you already have been fully trained. In contrast, *Metro* is committed to giving training to all its employees. More than 80 per cent of staff have had training now, up from 34 per cent in 2003. An internal booklet was developed showing courses that staff could take. They could pick one course relevant to their career and one to their future ambitions.

The business is now moving to the next stage. Managers are being trained in how to conduct appraisal. Members of teams also discuss how their needs can be met by courses in one to one discussions with Laura Ashworth. Commercial staff who have reached the top of their grade are also being taken into account. They can arrange special projects, such as a thank you for commercial clients who place large advertising campaigns. Projects that are successful are incorporated into the job of the person involved.

Staff surveys conducted at *Metro* in 2004 showed that 75 per cent of employees understand the goals of the business, compared to 55 per cent in 2003. 72 per cent agree that developing people is now one of the key goals of the business. For every £1 spent on training, the business calculates that there is a 1 per cent improvement in skills. Other surveys have shown that a break is occurring with the 'old school' mentality. Workers , for example, have in the past worked to the stop watch. Now they often stay later than required, just because they want to.

Source: adapted from *People Management*, 13.1.2005.

1 (a) Explain the type of approach to human resources taken by many publishing companies. (8 marks)
  (b) Identify the approach taken by *Metro* and analyse the potential benefits of this different approach. (12 marks)
2 To what extent should a new small publishing company follow the current approach of *Metro* to its human resources? (20 marks)

Volkswagon Group UK

Knowledge Volkswagen Group UK is a service business which imports and distributes cars to franchised dealers. It has 500 staff in its head office who are responsible for marketing four main brands - Volkswagen, Audi, Seat and Skoda.

Application Volkswagen Group UK has a 'total reward' *remuneration* package for its employees. This includes traditional *income* rewards, such as *salaries*, which are based on their *job description*. It is in the upper quartile of businesses when it comes to levels of *pay*. However, there is a number of other rewards, recognising the '*soft side*' of *human resources management*. These include a good *pension scheme*, exceptional *maternity benefits*, *flexible working policies*, car *leasing* at preferential rates and childcare vouchers. There is also a company performance and profit *bonus scheme*. The business even gives out ice-creams on hot days to staff.

Analysis Volkswagen Group UK changed its attitude to rewards about five years ago. It recognises that people are driven by cash rewards, but feels that these are not enough. Skills shortages in the 1990s meant that employers needed to 'maximise their attractiveness' to potential employees. The economic downturn of the early 21st century also led employers to assess the importance of non-cash benefits such as flexibility, training and career progression. Businesses came to realise that whilst some people were driven by generous fixed reward packages, others clearly were not. A further benefit is that the employer can 'brand' itself by offering cash and non-cash benefits - it can make a statement about what it is and its culture.

Evaluation As it doesn't 'make or sell anything' the business recognises that its value lies in its workforce. Its remuneration package must therefore be designed to meet the needs of its staff and motivate them. Taking a traditional approach, with strict levels of pay and little flexibility could be inappropriate for such a business or the economic and competitive situation which it faced in the early 21st century. A *Times* survey showed that 85 per cent of employees felt 'proud to work for the business' and 75 per cent felt that they could 'make a difference'. Such staff loyalty and regard is likely to be reflected in a motivated workforce, essential for a business of this nature.

Adapted from *People Management*, 29.1.2004 and www.business.timesonline.co.uk.

Traditional payment systems

In unit 37, different methods of REMUNERATION were outlined. Remuneration is the total reward given to employees for the work they do. It includes financial rewards, such as a wage or salary, as well as non-financial rewards, such as fringe benefits.

Traditionally, PAYMENT SYSTEMS were constructed around a number of factors.

- The forces of demand and supply in the labour market would set an equilibrium wage or a 'going rate' for a particular type of worker or job. If a business wanted to recruit new workers or discourage workers leaving for better paid jobs elsewhere, the job would have to be paid at a particular rate.
- There would often be a hierarchy of pay, where a superior could expect to earn more than a subordinate. The further up the hierarchy, the more a worker could be expected to be paid.
- There was an emphasis on internal equity. Different jobs would be compared with each other and a **pay differential** established. This difference in pay between different jobs would then be carried forward from year to year as average pay increased over time.
- Larger employers tended to use **pay spine** structures. This is where there would be a range of pay for a particular job, with a fixed number of points along the spine corresponding to a particular salary. A worker appointed to the job would start at some point on the pay spine. Every year they would, often automatically, move up onto the next point, thus getting a pay increase. Eventually, they would get to the top of the pay spine for that job. To earn more, they would have to seek promotion. Some employers linked movement up the pay spine to **appraisal systems** (see unit 37).
- In larger businesses, pay was administered and decided by the personnel department. Line managers in production, for example, had no control over the pay of their subordinates. This reflected a **bureaucratic** (see unit 31) approach within the business.
- Negotiations and decisions over pay were often completed through collective **bargaining** (see unit 88). Workers in the same job, but possibly of widely differing competence and performance, would all get the same rate of pay.

Human resource management and methods of remuneration

Remuneration policy is seen in a different way from a Human Resource Management (HRM) perspective. HRM is the process of administering the workforce of a business to achieve its objectives (see units 38 and 92). Remuneration policy is an important part of HRM. Effective remuneration policy, from an HRM perspective, must contribute towards achieving the goals of the business. This is done through ensuring that workers are motivated and are able to employ their skills and talents to the full. From a HRM perspective, the workforce should be highly flexible and adaptable. Team working and ongoing training are likely to be features of a business adopting a HRM approach. Payment systems which contribute towards achieving this will therefore help contribute towards achieving the goals of the business.

There is a number of key features of a payment system influenced by a HRM perspective.

Pay flexibility Instead of rigid structures, the payment system allows for considerable variation in pay for employees doing the same job. This flexibility allows managers to reward and motivate employees who are performing well. Employee goals, set through an appraisal system (see unit 37), are aligned with the goals of the business. Hence, high performing employees are helping the business to achieve its goals. Flexible pay structures include individual pay bargaining (see unit 88). Where there is collective bargaining (see unit 88), this should be done at local level, with small groups. National or even regional pay agreements should be discouraged.

Job flexibility Jobs are not rigid and do not have fixed job descriptions (see unit 40). Jobs are not boxes on a hierarchy which limit the ability of an employee to contribute to the business. Rather, jobs are flexible, allowing employees to grow into roles and to grow those roles. Their pay is then set according to the contribution they have made to the business and not according to some set amount given on a rigid pay scale. Pay systems then become people-centred rather than job-centred.

Training The development of the individual through experience and training should be linked to the payment system. It might be appropriate to link pay increases with completion of training or gaining qualifications. Part of the pay package might be an allowance for the individual worker to spend on the training which they feel is appropriate for their career needs.

Team working The reward system should encourage team working and team performance where appropriate. For example, the reward system might give bonuses to teams of workers who achieve the objectives they have been set. Or bonuses might be given to teams which have shown flexibility and the ability to adapt.

Decision making Decisions about pay and other rewards should not be decided solely by the HR (or personnel) department. Some responsibility should be devolved to line managers. They are often best placed to operate reward systems tailored to the needs of individual subordinates. For example, a worker might receive a basic pay package which was offered by the HR department when the worker was first appointed to the job. But responsibility for giving bonuses or other rewards might be passed down the line to managers. These managers would have money included in their budgets for this purpose.

Employee needs The reward given to the employee is matched to their needs. For example, many large businesses now operate flexible fringe benefit packages where an employee is given a notional amount of money and can 'buy' fringe benefits from a car, to extra holiday entitlement to private health care insurance and even simply to higher pay. By giving more control to employees of their total remuneration package, workers are able to satisfy more of their needs. This leads to increased commitment to the business and therefore higher motivation. However, the reward given to employees is not just financial. The reward system must take into account the non-financial needs and aspirations of individual employees. So some employees might be motivated by being offered extra training which will help them in their chosen career path. Others may be motivated by the ability to work very flexible hours over the year. Parents who are the main carers of their children might feel high levels of commitment to an employer who allows them to work around the needs of those children.

Recruitment and retention Payment systems should take account of recruitment and retention. In some parts of the business, it might be highly desirable for have stable teams of workers employed over time. The payment system may then give high rewards to these workers relative to the market rate. High relative rewards will discourage workers leaving to find better jobs with another employer. In other parts of the business, it might be healthy to have a regular turnover of staff to bring in new ideas and fresh enthusiasm. Paying the 'going' market rate for the job would then be an appropriate strategy.

Appraisal Many remuneration systems now incorporate appraisal (see unit 37) into the process of determining pay through performance related pay (PRP see unit 37). Appraisal is where the performance of an individual worker is reviewed against a set of criteria. Businesses use appraisal to assess the performance of an individual worker over a period of time and to feedback that assessment to the individual. Typically, goals are set for future performance and this may be linked to training needs. Assessment may also be used to discuss career development within the business. Appraisal is not always linked to pay and bonuses. However, for many workers, pay rises or bonuses are conditional upon what takes place within the appraisal process. Fundamentally, using appraisal and performance related pay is an attempt to align the goals of the individual with the goals of the business.

Hard and soft approaches to remuneration

The concepts of 'hard' and 'soft' HRM (see unit 92) can be applied to remuneration policy. Where there is a hard approach, payment methods should be linked directly to performance and the contribution of the worker to output and profit. Rewards for success should be clear and transparent to the workforce. Where there is a soft approach, payment methods should be related to the goals of workers as well as those of the business.

For example, with a hard approach to HRM, workers who were taken sick would receive exactly their entitlement under policies laid down by the business. With a soft approach, local managers would be able to 'bend the rules' where they thought this was appropriate. Equally, where a parent had to take a day off work to look after a sick child, the hard approach would be to count it as unpaid leave, or as a day's holiday entitlement. A soft approach might be either to ignore it and for colleagues to cover, or allow the worker to make up the missed hours at another time.

Where a soft approach was associated with democratic leadership, payment systems would reward those who contributed to effective decision making and were good team players. For example, bonus payments for all team members might be linked to their performance as a team. Where a hard

approach is associated with autocratic leadership, the leaders of teams alone might receive the bonuses if they motivated their team members sufficiently for the team to achieve its targets.

checklist

1 List FIVE features of a traditional payment system.
2 What is meant by flexibility in a payment system?
3 List THREE ways in which rewards can take into account employees' needs.
4 How can payments be structured to improve recruitment and retention?
5 What is the relationship between appraisal and rewards?
6 Briefly explain the relationship between:
   (i) the hard side of human resource management and remuneration;
   (ii) the soft side of human resource management and remuneration.

keyterms

Payment systems - **structures which set out how employees would be rewarded for their work.**
Remuneration - **the total reward given to employees for the work they do; it includes financial rewards such as a wage or salary, as well as non-financial rewards such as fringe benefits.**

Gerham-Nevis is a motor repair company in the North East area. It has three workshops. Each workshop employs three mechanics and two administration staff. All mechanics work a 38 hour week. At times, there is overtime work which is paid at a higher hourly rate. The two administration staff are paid at a lower rate. There is no system of progression or promotion at the business, although the manager's post at the head office in Newcastle has been filled by an experienced worker from the business each time it has become vacant. A new employee has been hired as a mechanic to take his or her place.

Last year, one of the workers at the Gateshead workshop was given a verbal warning for arriving late in the morning. He got angry and said that mechanics at other garages locally were paid more. Two weeks later, he gave in his notice saying that he had got a better paid job at a garage half a mile away. His post was vacant for three months because, despite advertising it every week in the local newspaper, the company didn't get any suitable applicants. In the end, the company had to take on a trainee. With only two qualified mechanics now at the workshop, productivity fell. Output has still not recovered as the trainee is still learning the trade.

Six months ago, management at Gerham-Nevis decided it needed to differentiate its product more. It took the strategic decision to move into the market for respraying vehicles. For example, some motorists choose to respray their car or motorcycle completely. Gerham-Nevis would also offer a service respraying individual or business vans and trucks with unique designs. Some of the mechanics, however, are opposed to the business moving into this area. They feel that they do not have the necessary skills and are concerned about the extra hours they may be forced to work. Two workers at the Newcastle workshop, in particular, have young children and have to travel to work.

One of the tasks in the office is to collate and deal with all accounts. The owners of the business would like to convert the entire system of invoicing and accounting to a computerised system using a software programme called Sage Line 50. They feel that one of the administration staff could takeover this role, although some of them are part time with young children.

1 (a) Examine the reasons why remuneration at the business may need to change. (8 marks)
   (b) Recommend and justify changes that the business could make to its remuneration. (12 marks)

EDF Associates

Knowledge

Application

EDF Associates is a manufacturer of electrical cables from a factory in Winchester. The business was founded in 1980. For many years it produced large volume orders with limited variety and was very successful.

After the year 2000 the *business* experienced a number of difficulties as a result of increased *foreign competition*. The number and size of *orders* began to fall and *labour productivity* declined. The business also calculated that over a four year period *rates of absenteeism* had risen, as had its *labour turnover*. As a result, *profits* fell and it was predicted that the business would make a *loss* in the near future.

Analysis

The business had made profits from large, uniform orders for many years. Staff were simply told what to do and got on with it without any real input to the process. But competition from abroad, a lack of both motivation and job satisfaction amongst staff, complacency of management and outdated work practices had contributed to a poor working environment and resulting rises in absences, staff leaving and falling output and profits. The business decided to introduce cell production to take into account the changing needs of the market - lower volume, higher variety orders. Five cells were set up and workers were empowered to make their own decisions. They were also allowed to operate flexibly so that orders could be met on time, yet employees could operate varied working hours if necessary. Employee productivity rose as a result and workers began to feel part of a common culture. Absenteeism rates fell from 20 per cent to 5 per cent in a short space of time. A staff survey showed that only 2 per cent of employees were considering leaving the business in the near future. Accident rates had also fallen as workers were paying more attention and could also contribute to their own health and safety practices and regulations.

Evaluation

EDF had become complacent. It had also been slow to recognise changes in the market and the effect of a stale workforce and react to these before they led to problems for the business. The change in approach to human resources and organisation of production at the business was vital if it was to avoid losses. Without these changes EDF would have made its first loss in over a quarter of a decade.

Adapted in part from www.strategosinc.com.

Measuring personnel effectiveness

Advocates of human resource management (HRM) claim that the performance of the workforce is enhanced through adopting appropriate personnel policies. In many other areas of business, such as finance or production, there is a large number of possible measures of performance, from sales revenue to profit after tax to output per day. In personnel, there are fewer key measures. Some of these only point indirectly at key variables. For example, it is not possible to measure directly:

- the motivation of a workforce;
- the ability of a workforce to accept and implement change;
- the teamworking capabilities of workers;
- the commitment of workers to the business;
- the contribution of £1 spent on personnel such as higher pay or spending on training to profit.

However, there are a few measures which can be used, including labour productivity, absenteeism rates, labour turnover, working days lost for health and safety reasons and wastage rates.

Labour productivity

In unit 34, it was explained that labour productivity is defined as output per worker. As a formula:

$$\text{Labour productivity} = \frac{\text{Total output (per period of time)}}{\text{Average number of employees (per period of time)}}$$

Labour productivity is an important measure of the efficiency of a workforce. For example, if there are two teams of workers in a factory, each with identical equipment and the same number of workers, then the team with the highest productivity could be identified as the most efficient team.

Figures for labour productivity need to be used with caution. For example, differences in labour productivity between factories or plants may be accounted for by differences in equipment used rather than the efficiency of the workforce. A plant with newer equipment is likely to have higher labour productivity than one with old equipment. Equally, productivity differs widely between processes within a business and between businesses in different industries. A highly automated section of a factory is likely to have much higher labour productivity than a labour intensive packing section in the same factory using little capital equipment. Manufacturing industry may have a higher average labour productivity than service industries simply because more capital is used per employee in manufacturing.

A business wishing to improve the labour productivity of

groups of workers can adopt a number of strategies.

- Improving the capital equipment with which they work.
- Changing the way in which workers are employed, for example, moving from an assembly line production system to a cell production system (see unit 47).
- Disappointing labour productivity may be due to a lack of training on the part of workers. Increased training may therefore raise productivity.
- Changing the reward system (see unit 93) may increase motivation and commitment and so improve productivity. There are many other ways that motivation may be increased (see unit 36). These include changing the structure of the business and devolving decision making power down the change of command.

Increasing labour productivity is generally assumed to increase the competitiveness of a business. Higher labour productivity should drive down costs, allowing a business either to lower its prices and so gain higher sales, or to keep its prices the same but increase its profit margins.

However, businesses sometimes find that they become less competitive despite increasing their labour productivity. This may occur for a number of reasons.

- Rival businesses may increase their productivity at an even faster rate.
- New rival businesses may set up which pay considerably lower wages. Many UK manufacturing businesses have become less competitive over the past 10 years due to the emergence of competition from low wage, low cost businesses in the Far East and eastern Europe.
- Other factors apart from cost may change adversely for a business. For example, a rival business may bring out a far better new product. However, productive the workforce and however low the cost, customers may prefer to buy the new product rather than a cheaper old product.

Absenteeism

Absenteeism is a problem for all businesses for a number of reasons.

- Staff who are absent often claim to be ill. The business then, in most cases, has to pay sick pay.
- If temporary staff are brought in to cover for absent staff, this leads to increased costs. Equally, costs will increase if permanent staff have to work overtime and are paid at higher rates than their basic rate of pay.
- Output may suffer if workers are expected to cover for sick colleagues or if temporary staff are not as productive as the absent workers.
- Prolonged absences can lead to major disruption if the worker is key to a particular area of work or a new project.
- If production is delayed or there are problems with quality, customers can be lost.
- Absenteeism can be demotivating to staff left to cope with the problems.
- The higher the rate of absenteeism, the more likely it is that workers will report ill. This is because a culture of absenteeism will develop where it becomes acceptable for workers to take extra days holiday by reporting in sick.

The RATE OF ABSENTEEISM or ABSENTEEISM RATE or ABSENTEE RATE can be calculated by dividing the number of staff absent by the total number of staff employed. The rate is expressed as a percentage. It can be calculated as a daily rate using the formula:

$$\frac{\text{Number of staff absent on a day}}{\text{Total number of staff employed}} \times 100\%$$

For example, if 1 000 staff are employed, and 30 are absent on a particular day, then the rate of absenteeism for that day is 3 per cent (100% x 30 ÷ 1 000). If the rate of absenteeism for a year is calculated, the total number of staff days lost through absenteeism must by divided by the number of staff days that should have been worked over the year. This is calculated using the formula:

$$\frac{\text{Total number of staff absence days over the year}}{\text{Total number of staff days that should have been worked}} \times 100\%$$

For example, assume 6 000 staff days were lost through absence. There were 500 staff, each of whom should have worked 240 days during the year. So the total number of staff days that should have been worked was 120 000 (500 x 240). The rate of absenteeism was therefore 5 per cent (100% x 6 000 ÷ 120 000).

Rates of absenteeism can be calculated for a business as a whole and compared to industry averages or national averages. They can also be compared between one part of a business and another or compared over time. Differences in rates of absenteeism occur for a number of reasons.

- Small businesses tend to have lower rates of absenteeism than larger businesses. Arguably this is because there is much more commitment and feeling of teamwork in a small business than in a large business. Workers in large businesses can feel that no one will suffer if they take a day off work and so absenteeism is acceptable.
- Health and safety is a factor. Businesses which have good health and safety procedures will tend to suffer less illness related absenteeism than those with poor procedures. Equally, some jobs are inherently more dangerous to health than others and so absenteeism is more likely.
- The nature of the tasks given to workers is another factor. Tasks which are fragmented and repetitive lead to low job satisfaction and demotivation. This encourages workers to report sick. Workers in jobs which are interesting and rewarding tend to have lower absentee rates.
- The culture of a workplace can cause absenteeism. Where workers are overworked, where there is a climate of intimidation and bullying by superiors of subordinates, and where the needs of workers are ignored, work related stress becomes much more common. Workers off through stress are a particular problem because they often take months off work at a time.
- Stress related illness is also more common where workers are oversupervised and feel that they are not trusted by their superiors to accomplish tasks.
- Workers who feel that they are grossly underpaid are more likely to take time off work. They see it as compensation for the lack of monetary reward they receive. Low pay is also a demotivator and so contributes to absenteeism.

Businesses can adopt a variety of methods to reduce absenteeism. Some assume that absenteeism is mainly caused by inappropriate or a lack of human resource management policies. Problems such as lack of commitment, low motivation, bullying, oversupervision and perceptions of low pay can be tackled through methods such as more teamwork, devolving power down the chain of command, more democratic leadership, better reward systems and policies which make bullying and harassment at work a major disciplinary offence. Health and safety issues can be addressed through the rigourous application of a well thought out health and safety policy. Adoption of lean production techniques (see units 47 and 48) are also likely to improve absenteeism rates.

The UK government in the early 2000s stressed the importance of a WORK LIFE BALANCE in dealing with a number of HR issues including absenteeism. Absenteeism can be caused by conflicts between work and family commitments, or work and leisure goals. A parent may phone in sick when in fact he or she is having to stay at home to look after his or her ill 8 year old. Or a worker may phone in sick on a Monday morning because he can't face work after a weekend's activities. The solution is for more flexible working patterns. For example, workers may be able to take a few hours off work if they work them at some other time in the week or the month. Or workers may have a number of individual days holiday a year which can be taken without giving notice. Or a worker may have the right permanently to the number of hours worked per week, changing for example from full time to 3 days a week.

On the other hand, a scientific management approach (see unit 34) would tend towards the introduction of systems of rewards and punishments. Cutting down the number of days when staff can claim sick pay is one measure. Another is for superiors to monitor closely staff who are absent. Telephoning them or even visiting them in their homes when they are off sick can be effective in deterring absenteeism. Being prepared to sack staff who abuse the system can also be an important deterrent to the rest of the workforce. Some employers offer bonuses to workers who have not had time off work due to illness. A few even offer all their staff a number of paid days off work each year which can be taken when staff don't feel like going into work or have problems with child care arrangements.

Another policy which is frequently advocated is 'back to work' interviews. Any member of staff who has been absent has to be interviewed by a superior about why they were absent. This can be seen from a human relations school perspective as supportive of the worker. Their superior cares for them enough to want to know why they were away. Equally it can be judged from a scientific management school perspective. The superior is checking up on the worker to see whether the absence was genuine.

Labour turnover

Labour or staff turnover is another measure of personnel effectiveness. **Labour turnover** is the proportion of staff leaving a business over a period of time (see unit 38). It is measured by the formula:

$$\text{Labour turnover} = \frac{\text{Number of staff leaving over a period of time}}{\text{Average number of staff in post during the period}} \times 100\%$$

For example, if 20 staff left over a year and there were on average 40 on the staff, then the staff turnover would be 50 per cent (100% x 20 ÷ 40).

As with other measures of personnel performance, labour turnover differs from department to department within a

Royal Mail's cure for Britain's £1.75bn problem of absenteeism is simple - a Ford car and holiday vouchers. Its incentive scheme has improved attendance levels by more than 10 per cent in six months, equivalent to 1 000 extra staff. It is so pleased that it is extending the scheme for 12 months. Under the initial scheme staff who worked for six months without a day off work sick were entered for a prize draw. More than half of the 170 000 employees at Royal Mail and Parcelforce Worldwide qualified. 37 won a new Ford Focus car, worth £12 000 each and 75 won the £2 000 holiday vouchers. Even the 90,000 who qualified for the draw but missed out got a £150 holiday voucher.

Royal Mail will not say how much the scheme cost, but insists it makes financial and commercial sense. 'The employees like it, as a company we like it - we have 1 000 more people every day than we would otherwise have had if nothing had changed. It benefits the customers too because good attendance goes hand in glove with good quality of service', said a Royal Mail spokesperson. Some have estimated the costs at £1.9m before allowing for any discounts.

The company denies it is putting pressure on genuinely ill workers to turn up for work. Its people and operational development director, said 'We must support and reward postmen and women. They deserve it. They do a demanding job to a high standard, day in and day out, in all weathers.'

The Communication Workers Union had a more old-fashioned explanation for the fall in absenteeism - better pay and conditions. The union's deputy general secretary said: 'Giveaways are not the reason why attendance levels have improved and they are certainly not a substitute for continuing to invest in our members' overall employment package.'

Source: adapted from *The Guardian*, 26.4.2005.

1 **Why is it important for the Royal Mail to measure absenteeism rates?**
2 **Examine the advantages and disadvantages of the scheme to reduce absenteeism at Royal Mail for (a) the business and (b) its employees.**
3 **Discuss whether the scheme is likely to be more effective than 'better pay and conditions'.**

business, from business to business within an industry and from industry to industry within an economy. Relatively high labour turnover is caused by a number of factors.

- Relatively low pay leads to higher labour turnover as workers leave to get better paid jobs.
- Relatively few training and promotion opportunities will encourage workers to leave their current jobs.
- Poor working conditions, low job satisfaction, bullying and harassment in the workplace are other factors.
- Some businesses are relatively poor at selecting and recruiting the right candidates for posts. Where workers are ill suited to their jobs, there is more chance that they will leave relatively quickly.
- In a recession, labour turnover tends to fall as the number of vacancies falls and workers become worried that if they leave their job without having got another one to go to, they will become part of the long term unemployed. In a boom, when there might be labour shortages, there are far more vacancies and so labour turnover tends to rise.

Relatively high labour turnover is usually seen as a problem for businesses for a number of reasons.

- Recruiting new staff can be costly.
- It takes time for new staff to become familiar with their roles and the way in the which business operates. High labour turnover is likely to reduce the human process advantage (see unit 94) of a business.
- Larger companies may put on induction programmes (see unit 41) which further adds to costs.
- If the post is filled internally, there may be training needs for the worker who gets the job.

However, some labour turnover is usually beneficial to a business.

- New staff can bring in fresh ideas and experience from their work with other businesses.
- Some workers may be ineffective and need to be encouraged to leave. Getting rid of ineffective staff leads to labour turnover.
- If a business is shrinking in size, reducing the size of the workforce will lead to higher labour turnover.
- Where a business pays low wages, or where conditions of work are poor, it may be more profitable to have a constant turnover of staff rather than raise wages or improve conditions of work.

Businesses can attempt to reduce their labour turnover if they see it as a problem. Higher pay and better working conditions might be one strategy. Another might be offering better internal promotion prospects to workers. Better selection procedures would be appropriate if the problem is poor recruiting. Effective procedures against bullying and harassment could help too. For senior workers, a business might offer bonuses in the future (often in the form of share option schemes, see unit 37) which can only be claimed if they are still employed by the business at the point in time.

Health and safety

The safety of the working environment can be measured in a number of different ways. For example, health and safety could be measured by the number of working days lost through accidents or injuries per thousand employees over a time period.

$$\frac{\text{Number of working days lost for health and safety reasons per time period}}{\text{Total number of workers}} \times 100\%$$

For example, if the workforce were 6 000 and there were 300 days lost through accidents or injury over a year, then the number of working days lost per thousand employees would be (6 000 ÷ 300) x 1 000, which is 20 000.

Another measure relates working days lost to the total number of working days that could have been worked over the period, expressed as a percentage.

$$\frac{\text{Number of working days lost for health and safety reasons per time period}}{\text{Total number of possible working days during the period}} \times 100\%$$

For example, if 2 000 days are lost due to health and safety reasons over a year, and the number of possible working days for the workforce over the period was 100 000, then the health and safety ratio is 2 per cent (100% x 2 000 ÷ 100 000).

A poor health and safety record may occur for a number of reasons.

- Equipment used may be dangerous. For example, it might be poorly maintained or be too old.
- The working environment itself may be dangerous. For example, unsafe levels of dangerous gases or chemicals may be found in the atmosphere in a factory building.
- There may be a lack of safety equipment. For example, workers should perhaps be wearing safety hats, but these are not provided by the employer.
- Workers may not receive sufficient health and safety training.
- The business may not enforce its own health and safety procedures. It may turn a 'blind eye' to abuses because otherwise production would be slowed down.
- Work may be contracted out to self-employed workers who prefer to disregard time-consuming health and safety procedures in order to earn more money. In the building industry, the widespread use of subcontractors is sometimes given as a reason for a poor health and safety record.

Improving a poor health and safety record may be achieved by:

- increasing expenditure on buildings and equipment to bring them up to health and safety standards;
- drawing up an appropriate set of health and safety policies and procedures;
- training all staff to ensure that they understand these policies and procedures and can carry them out;
- strictly enforcing health and safety policies, putting safety above profit and output.

Businesses which have poor health and safety records are either poorly organised and managed, or deliberately exploiting the situation to cut their costs. Lower health and safety standards is one way in which some businesses can gain a competitive advantage. One of the criticisms of **globalisation** (see unit 2) is that producers in Third World countries operate under much less stringent health and safety standards than in the UK. Hence, it could be argued that they have an 'unfair' competitive advantage.

A poor health and safety record can be a disadvantage to a business.

"key terms"

Rate of absenteeism or absenteeism rate or absentee rate - **the number of staff absent as a percentage of the total number of staff employed. It can be calculated for different periods of time, ie daily rates or annual rates.**
Work life balance - **the relationship between time spent at work and time spent away from work or the time spent at work as a proportion of total time.**

- Poor health and safety standards are likely to lead to the demotivation of staff. Their basic needs are being threatened (see unit 35).
- Such businesses are liable to have their operations closed down or be open to prosecution by health and safety inspectors. Equally, they are open to being sued by workers involved in accidents or by customers if products are put at risk. At worst, such a business could be forced to close because of this issue.
- Staff absences due to accidents may have the same costs as absences due to illness, as explained in the last section. Businesses may also be fined or sued as a result of accidents.
- A poor health and safety record could contribute towards giving a business a poor reputation with customers and so it could affect sales. In the Third World, suppliers to some Western multinationals have to conform to basic standards to win and retain orders. This is because the reputation of the multinationals in their First World markets can be at stake (see units 57 and 104).

✓ *checklist*

1 How is labour productivity calculated?
2 A component manufacturer makes 10 000 metal washers with 10 workers. After employing 5 extra workers it makes 20 000. Calculate the effect on labour productivity.
3 List FOUR ways in which a business may improve labour productivity.
4 How can a business calculate its rate of absenteeism?
5 List FIVE reasons why rates of absenteeism are different in different industries.
6 State THREE ways in which a business might reduce rates of absenteeism.
6 What is the relationship between absenteeism and a work life balance?
7 A business finds that its labour turnover falls from 20% to 15%. Should it be concerned?
8 List FOUR factors that might lead to high labour turnover.
9 State FIVE problems of high labour turnover for a business.
10 State TWO formulae that a business might use to measure its health and safety record.
11 List FIVE factors that may cause a business to have a poor health and safety record.
12 State FIVE possible problems for a business with a poor record of health and safety.

There is about a 50-1 chance that people will have an accident at work. Workplace deaths cost over £20bn a year. And yet the UK is supposed to have the best record in Europe. UK management cannot ignore long working hours and must constantly question the pressure people are under as this leads to fatigue, mistakes and accidents. Businesses face market pressures to meet deadlines, yet workplace deaths or injuries are rarely blamed on missed sales targets or late reports.

Many people do not consider an office to be a hazardous environment. They assume all workplace dangers are in a factory or on a construction site. Yet common problems include slips, trips and falls, which can lead to serious injuries. In the UK, almost a third of all accidents are in this category. A fifth of falls result in three days or more off work, adding up to 1 million days a year lost in absenteeism. The figure for the hospitality industry is four times the national average.

When carrying out safety inspections in offices, many checks must be made. Visual inspection of floors is important. Bad lighting can be a problem. Emergency lighting should be fitted where there is no natural light or where work is being carried out after dark. The strength of barriers and handrails is also important. Carpet joints at doors must be checked for loose or broken fixings. Computer cables increase tripping hazards when working and when carrying items. Modern offices have a considerable amount of electrical equipment all of which must be checked in accordance with safety legislation.

Back pain caused by manual handling is a common problem in offices. This can cost around £4bn a year. Spillages on stairs should be cleaned up as soon as possible. A hotel chain was ordered to pay out more than £20 000 following an accident in which a member of staff was scalded while carrying an unbalanced pot of coffee.

There are many ways to genuine safety culture at work. Teamwork is vital to the morale and general atmosphere. A good attitude shown to health and safety will also help. Communication is also vital. People need to be encouraged to question safety routines and procedures at work. Near misses and previous accidents should always be investigated.

Source: adapted from *The Guardian*, 15.10.2001.

1 *How might an office assess its health and safety record?*
2 *Examine the problems of offices having a poor health and safety record.*
3 *To what extent are offices likely to have a worse health and safety record than a building site?*

First there were duvet days for staff temporarily 'sick' of work - offered by companies trying to reduce absenteeism by gentle persuasion. Then there was time off for everything from a religious festival to a child's first day at school. In 2004 Tesco, opted for the stick approach instead. It cut sick pay in some of its stores and tested other schemes in an attempt to cut rates of absenteeism. Tesco spokesperson Jonathan Church said that absenteeism is a real problem. 'It impacts on our business as well as creating more work for people in the store. These trials are about encouraging people to use planned absence whenever they can. If they need to take little Johnnie to the dentist, then we will bend over backwards to make that possible.'

One scheme, introduced in two stores in the South, meant workers got no pay for the first three days off sick, but after the fourth day would get paid again with compensation for the first three days. That could encourage people to go sick for a whole week, Church admitted. 'Obviously the trial is in its early stages and these are the kinds of issues we will need to look at.' Other options are to offer staff more holiday allowance up front, but reduce it every time they take a day off sick. Tesco said there are fewer absences in stores testing the schemes. 'Our intention is not to penalise people who are genuinely ill. It is to discourage people from taking those odd days.'

Asda offers incentives to reward low absenteeism. 'There are some brilliant prizes,' said a spokesperson. 'It might be a week's extra holiday or a weekend break or vouchers. It has really helped bring absenteeism down because people think hard about whether they really need to be off.' The company already has 'carers leave' and 'first day/half day' leave for parents taking children to school.

Sick leave costs British companies around £11 billion every year through 166 million lost working days. At any one time about 6 million people are off. Stress-related absence is rising, according to the Health and Safety Executive, which estimates that 13 million days are lost a year from this problem. This has prompted organisations like The Work Foundation for businesses to look more carefully at how they treat staff and the work environment.

In 2003, seasonal workers at Asda at Christmas were entitled to benefits and job security equivalent to those enjoyed by their full-time colleagues, after the supermarket created 10 000 new permanent positions for contract workers. The new 'seasonal squad' would have the same status as permanent staff but with a contract to work an annual, rather than weekly, number of hours. They could work for as little as ten weeks of the year. The contracts would cover Christmas, Easter and the school summer holidays and cover jobs such as greeters, porters, checkout operatives and warehouse workers. 'We recognise that people are looking for flexibility across the working year, not just the working week' said Caroline Massingham, Asda retail people director. 'If you're one of the many people that want to balance long periods of leave with a fulfilling job, the options are limited'.

Asda is hoping the initiative would encourage more over 50s to join. The supermarket said that since actively recruiting older workers, it has seen absence levels drop, customer service levels rise and labour turnover fall. The flexible working package includes one week's leave for new grandparents, five days leave for IVF treatment and up to two years for a career break. Asda is hoping to make huge savings from the initiative by reducing turnover, as it has spent around £3 500 per person in recruitment costs.

Source: adapted from *The Observer*, 16.5. 2004 and *The Guardian*, 24.10.2003.

1 (a) Explain why supermarkets may want to reduce rates of absenteeism and labour turnover. (8 marks)
   (b) Examine the factors that might affect rates of absenteeism and labour turnover at supermarkets. (12 marks)
2 Evaluate the methods used by supermarkets in the article to reduce rates of absenteeism and labour turnover. (20 marks)

GSK

Knowledge GlaxoSmithKline (GSK) is one of the world's largest pharmaceutical companies with £22 billion of sales in 2003.

Application *Research and development (R&D)* is fundamental to GSK's success. Each year, *patents* on existing drugs expire and the *prices* that GSK can charge for those drugs falls as competitors bring out *generic* versions of the drug. Those drugs need to be replaced with new drugs which have *patent protection* and for which GSK can charge *premium prices*.

Analysis GSK can only survive in a fiercely competitive industry if it creates new products which have a unique selling point. The high prices it can charge for successful drugs cover the very high research and development costs for new drugs. Drugs in the pipelines are aimed almost exclusively at diseases and ailments of sufferers in the rich, developed world. For example, one possible future blockbuster drug for GSK is a treatment for furred arteries that would alleviate heart disease. Another is a cancer treatment that inhibits two 'growth factors' which tumour cells need to thrive. To go on sale, GSK has to satisfy the regulatory authorities round the world through thorough testing that its drugs are safe, and have no serious side effects. Only a few drugs make it through the research and development process.

Evaluation Developing drugs is a high risk activity. Executives at GSK know that a steady stream of new drugs and other products coming onto the market will be necessary for the success of the company. They need to place considerable management effort into R&D for the company to survive and prosper.

Adapted from *The Independent*, 3.12.2003.

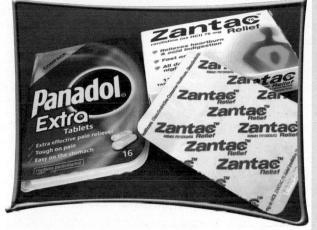

The functions of research and development

Research and development (R&D, see unit 14) is the process of scientific and technological research, and the development of that research into creating new products. Research and development has three main functions or purposes.

Creating new products Research and development can lead to the development of new products. Over the past hundred years, for example, research and development has led to the marketing of antibiotics, automatic washing machines, computers, televisions, DVDs and genetically modified foods. New products allow businesses to expand the market, creating new demands from their customers. If they are sufficiently differentiated from competing products, they will have a unique selling point (USP, see unit 10). New products are often able to command a premium price (see unit 15), allowing the developer to recoup the cost of research and development quickly and then allow it to earn high profit margins.

Improving quality Research and development can improve the quality and reliability of products. For example, in television manufacturing, R&D has helped component manufacturers reduce the number of faults in their output and extended the life of products. Improved quality can allow a business to gain a competitive advantage over their rivals. Japanese companies like Sony and Honda, for example, gained a competitive edge over rival UK companies in the 1980s and 1990s because of the greater quality of their products.

Reducing costs of production Research and development can lead to an improvement in productive efficiency (see unit 42). A business is productively efficient when it is producing at lowest cost. R&D can lead to the introduction of new production processes or the use of new materials, which in turn cause a fall in production costs.

Invention and innovation

The process of research and development can be split into two parts.

Invention INVENTION is the discovery of new processes and potential new products. Some businesses, usually large businesses, employ teams of research workers to undertake research. The future profitability of many pharmaceutical companies, for example, depends upon their ability to invent new drugs today. Electronics companies such as Lucky Gold (LG), Philips or Sony have research departments which invent new processes and products. Science is important in the invention process. As explained in unit 14, **pure scientific research** generates new ideas and theories. Very few businesses are large enough to be able to afford pure scientific research. Even fewer take the view that pure scientific research could be profitable for them and their shareholders. Pure scientific research therefore tends to be commissioned by governments, universities and charities. **Applied research** takes the results of pure scientific research and turns it into potential processes and products. However, much invention is not strictly science based. The extent to which science is used in the invention process varies from industry to industry.

Innovation Far more processes are invented than are finally used in production. Equally, far more products are invented than are finally sold to customers. INNOVATION is the process of transforming inventions into processes that are used to produce goods or products that customers will buy. Of the many drugs that are invented by pharmaceutical companies, only a few ever reach the market. With drugs, the process of innovation involves clinical trials on patients to see whether they have the effect that is intended and to see what side effects there might be. For a food manufacturing company, innovation would be producing a new recipe for, say, a frozen meal and taking that through production and marketing trials to a finished product in the freezer cabinets of a supermarket.

Product design

The process of research and development should enable researchers and designers to create marketable products. Good product design involves a number of factors.

Customer needs The product should satisfy the needs of customers. For example, if the product is a washing machine, it should wash clothes well. If it is a new medicine, it should help to cure illness without side effects.

Aesthetics A product should look good. Shape, colour and size are important. For some products, taste and smell are important aesthetically too. For example, a perfume should smell good. The bottle and packaging of the perfume then need to project and reinforce the image about the perfume.

Manufacture Some potential new products fail at the design stage because it is impossible to manufacture them commercially. For example, a chemical which can be manufactured in small quantities in a laboratory might prove impossible to manufacture in large quantities in an industrial plant. Or a new design of kitchen fan may have too many parts for it to be made reliably and cheaply in large quantities.

Quality Good design involves creating a product which meets quality standards consistently (see unit 46).

Reliability Reliability is very important for customers. When buying a television set or a new pair of shoes, customers don't want them breaking down or falling apart after being used or worn a few times. Good design should therefore build in reliability.

The environment Twenty years ago, most designers may not have considered the environmental impact of their work. Increasingly, due to pressure from governments through rules and regulations and from customers, the environment is becoming more important in the design process. For example, under EU regulations, car manufacturers will have to pay for the disposal of their cars at the end of their working life. So they are now designing cars with a view to recycling as many as possible of their parts. Newspaper and magazine companies use as much recycled paper as possible. Food manufacturers in the UK have been forced by consumer pressure to design their products without the use of genetically modified (GM) ingredients.

Michelin, the French tyre company, is the market leader of the world tyre market with a market share of 20 per cent. Founded in 1899, the company has always been an industrial innovator. This year, the company has announced a number of new inventions designed to take the company forward. One is an 'airless wheel' to weather tough road conditions in fast-growing countries such as China and India. Another is an 'active wheel' combining tyre, wheel, suspension and its own small electric motor, designed for battery or fuel-cell powered electric vehicles which, if fitted with an active wheel, would no longer need a gearbox, clutch, transmission shaft or anti-roll bar.

The commitment to innovation means that Michelin is always level with if not ahead of its rivals in bringing new products to the market. The company's culture remains firmly based on a strong belief in its technical skills. Its mission is to improve mobility of goods and people, according to Edouard Michelin, chief executive of the company and an engineer by training.

However, the company is realistic enough to realise that many of its inventions will only find a niche market, or won't become accessible to mass markets for the next 10 to 20 years. Much of its technical effort goes into making small improvements to existing products. The contribution of technology to cutting costs is also very important. Michelin has not gone down the road of closing factories in high cost European countries, particularly France, to relocate production in cheap labour countries in the Far East or Eastern Europe. Edouard Michelin says that 'in the West, our strategy is not to close plants but to pursue significant productivity improvements'.

The company's special legal structure means that it is safe from any takeover bid. This leaves it free financially to ignore demands to pursue short term profit at the expense of long term growth. Significantly, Michelin over the years has found a way of being a product led company that has secured a strong reputation for marketing products which customers want to buy. A commitment to technology and research has been key to that success.

Source: adapted from the *Financial Times*, 6.10.2004.

1 **Explain the role of invention and innovation in Michelin's success.**
2 **Discuss the advantages and disadvantages to a company like Michelin of putting resources into research and development.**

Competition Some design is meant to make a product different from those of competitors. This is to give the product a unique selling point (USP) in the market. For example, mobile phones all have different appearances and finishes. Manufacturers have different features on their products. The technology inside the machine may differ too. But some products are deliberately designed to be as similar as possible to leading products in the market. For example, in the pharmaceuticals market, once the patent on a drug expires, there is often a rush of generic products onto the market from rival companies. These are products sold often at a fraction of the price which are identical in formulation to the old patented drug. The marketing strategy is to design products which will attract customers from the best selling products on the market.

Safety Research and development should lead to the creation of products which are safe for customers to use and safe to produce. For example, there are now strict limitations on the use of asbestos in products because of safety concerns about the material.

Legislation The law often imposes limits to a designer's work. Laws about safety and the environment impact on design. Consumers are also protected by the laws such as the **Trade Descriptions Act, 1968** which makes it illegal to sell a product which does not meet the description applied to it. So glue which is designed to bond ceramics must do that job.

Profit Research and development and the design process must ultimately lead to products which are commercially viable. The supersonic passenger aeroplane Concorde, for example, was built using the best R&D. But it was ultimately a failure because it was too expensive to buy and operate. Not enough passengers were prepared to pay thousands of pounds per flight for the privilege of flying supersonically and saving a few hours on their journey times.

The product life cycle

The product life cycle (see unit 12) shows the stages through which a product passes from development, through growth and maturity to decline and withdrawal. Research and development is an inevitable feature prior to the launch of a new product. In many cases, it may be low cost and fairly quick. An independent coffee bar, for example, may introduce a new flavoured cinnamon coffee. The R&D completed may have been a few hours making coffee and adding cinnamon to get the taste right. On the other hand, a new model of car might have involved years of R&D by teams of highly skilled workers using specialist research equipment.

R&D may also be needed to create extension strategies for products. Extension strategies are strategies used to extend the life of a product and prevent falling sales. So an existing car model may get a 'face lift' every few years or a soap powder may be reformulated on a regular basis. R&D can be an important element in providing the technical knowledge to achieve a change in an existing product.

R&D expenditure for a new product will take place before any revenue has been earned on its sales. It therefore provides a negative cash flow (see unit 27) for the business. When R&D forms the basis for an extension strategy, existing cash flow generated by the product will almost certainly cover the negative cash flow generated by the R&D.

Some businesses operate in markets which demand a constant flow of new products. R&D expenditure can then be a significant part of total costs. In cash flow terms, the R&D expenditure for future products is financed by the profit made on existing mature products.

Market research

Market research may influence the direction of research and development spending. If a business is market orientated (see unit 1), the development of new products will be guided by the perceived needs of the market. Market research will be a crucial part of the process of deciding what are those needs and what products might satisfy those needs. The results of market research will drive the allocation of funds to particular R&D projects. For example, in the early days of mobile phones, there was a clear need to reduce the size of mobile handsets. So mobile phone manufacturers allocated R&D spending to achieve this.

On the other hand, a business may be product orientated (see unit 1). R&D spending is then likely to be directed towards a number of areas including:

* production processes which will reduce costs;
* products which will give a better technical performance for customers;
* processes and products which will deliver improved environmental or safety features.

Market research for a product orientated business is unlikely to have a very important influence on R&D spending. If the business is a copper mining company or a steel manufacturer, it is fairly clear what might improve sales, reduce costs and increase profit. Even for, say, pharmaceutical companies, market research is of limited value. What types of new drugs are likely to sell is already well known. What drives pharmaceutical R&D is science and the new discoveries it brings.

Patterns of R&D spending

It is often claimed that UK businesses do not spend enough on R&D. There is certain evidence which might suggest this.

* Figure 95.1 shows that of the seven largest economies in the world, the UK ranked sixth in R&D spending as a percentage of its total output measured by GDP (see unit 50). Not all R&D spending is by businesses. Charities, such as cancer research charities, higher education and government also spend on R&D. If spending by businesses alone is considered, the UK still ranks only fifth out of seven countries in Figure 95.1. The data shown in Figure 95.1 are for 2001. The rank order is little different for the previous ten years. Historically, Britain lags behind its major industrial competitors in R&D spending.
* Internationally, R&D spending is concentrated in certain product areas. Almost sixty per cent of business R&D spending worldwide is in just five industrial sectors - IT hardware, pharmaceuticals and biotechnology, electronic and electrical, software and IT services, and health. The USA dominates R&D spending in all of these apart from electronic and electrical where Japan is the number one spender. The UK comes second in only two sectors - pharmaceuticals and biotechnology, and health. Comparing the US 1000 largest companies with directly comparable 700 UK-owned companies, the UK had 50 per cent more

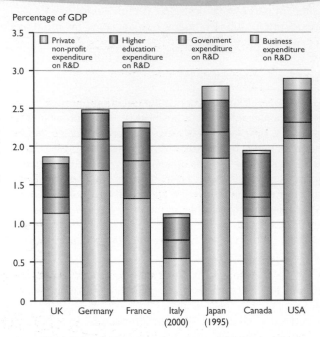

Percentage of GDP

Figure 95.1 *International comparison of R&D spending as a percentage of GDP, 2001*

Source: adapted from OECD.

relatively more important than in the UK. This encourages them to take a more long term view of investment and encourages R&D spending.
- Both short termism and the high cost of capital would tend to make UK companies more risk averse. R&D by its very nature is a risky activity. There is less incentive in the UK to undertake R&D.

The UK's failure to invest enough in R&D is likely to have damaged its economy and UK businesses in general. Spending on R&D should give businesses a competitive edge. If a British company is consistently underinvesting in R&D compared to its US, German or Japanese rivals, then over the long term it is likely to become increasingly uncompetitive. The decline in UK manufacturing compared to German manufacturing over the past 40 years, for example, could in part have been caused by a failure to invest in R&D.

For individual businesses, it is not always clear how much they should invest in R&D. As already explained, R&D expenditure varies enormously between different industries both in the UK and internationally. Table 95.1 shows that, over half of all UK R&D expenditure is concentrated in just five industries. One of them, pharmaceuticals, accounts for one quarter of all UK R&D expenditure. Not surprisingly, UK pharmaceutical companies are highly competitive internationally. But in industries such as aerospace and communication equipment, UK companies have to invest in R&D or they will be overtaken by international competitors bringing out better products. So the amount of R&D expenditure needed depends to a great extent on how much rival companies are spending.

Even then, because R&D is so risky, it is not necessarily the case that high spending will lead to success whilst low spending will lead to failure. The quality of the spending on R&D is vitally important. A culture of invention and innovation within a business might produce far more than spending large amounts on R&D projects. Also, luck plays a part in research. Some companies, despite high research spending, fail to come up with results.

companies with low R&D spending (defined as below two per cent of sales) than the US. (Statistics taken from the Department for Trade and Industry Research and Development Scoreboard 2003.)
- Anecdotal evidence suggests that major UK scientific break-throughs tend to be exploited by overseas companies. Equally, inventions may be patented by British inventors but put into commercial production by foreign companies.

Reasons for R&D spending in the UK

There is a number of reasons why UK companies may fail to invest sufficiently in R&D.
- There may be an inherited culture of lack of investment in R&D. Countries like Japan and Germany, in contrast, have had a tradition of placing importance on invention and innovation.
- The cost of financial capital to fund R&D is higher in the UK than in many other countries. This is because UK companies tend to pay out higher dividends to shareholders than, say, German, US or Japanese companies. R&D therefore has to have a higher rate of return (see unit 84) for it to be undertaken in the UK. This means that fewer R&D projects get the go ahead in the UK than in most of it's industrial competitors.
- The UK financial system encourages 'short termism'. Banks tend to lend for a few years rather than, say, 10 or 20 years, for investment projects. On UK stock markets, shareholders put pressure on companies to deliver profits now. They are less concerned about profits in five years' time because they can sell their shares if they think the company is performing poorly. In contrast, in countries such as Germany and Japan, management of companies is less worried about the views of shareholders. The interests of workers and customers are

	% of total R&D expenditure
Pharmaceuticals, medical chemicals and botanical products	25.2
Aerospace	10.3
Radio, television and communication equipment	7.3
Motor vehicles and parts	7.1
Computer and related activities	6.8
Total top five industries	56.7
Machinery and equipment	5.9
Chemicals, synthetic fibres	4.4
Research and development services	4.3
Electrical machinery and apparatus	3.5
Precision instruments	3.4
All other industries	21.8
Total all industries	100

Table 95.1 *R&D expenditure by industry as a percentage of total R&D spending, UK 2002*
Source: adapted from National Statistics, Business Enterprise Research and Development, November 2003.

Ultimately, the amount of R&D spending is constrained by the ability of the company to finance it. If a company begins to make large losses, an easy target for cost cutting is its R&D programme. R&D also has an opportunity cost. £1 spent on R&D is £1 that cannot be spent on investment in machinery, training or marketing. So the budget for R&D is always constrained.

"key terms"

Innovation - the process of transforming inventions into processes that are used to produce goods, or products that are sold to customers.
Invention - the discovery of new processes and potential new products.

✓ checklist

1 What are the functions of research and development?
2 Explain the difference between invention and innovation.
3 What factors are involved in good product design?
4 What function does R&D play in the product life cycle?
5 Explain how product orientated businesses might spend their R&D budgets differently from market orientated businesses.
6 What arguments are put forward to suggest that the UK doesn't spend enough on R&D?

A government report has found that R&D spending is boosting Britain's international competitiveness. The annual R&D Scoreboard, compiled by the Department of Trade and Industry, shows that the number of companies with sales of more than £25 million and which are spending more than 4 per cent of their turnover on research has risen from 65 in 1998 to 108 in 2004. The top five spenders are GlaxoSmithKline (£3.8bn) and AstraZeneca (£1.9bn), both pharmaceutical companies, BAE Systems (£1.1bn), the aerospace company, Unilever (£0.8bn), the food and household products company, and BT (£0.3bn), the telecommunications company.

The study shows that pharmaceuticals and biotechnology companies are the biggest spenders. The UK is catching up international competitors in IT software, a sector which up until now has been dominated by foreign, particularly US, companies. One third of the 108 UK groups defined as 'R&D intensive' are in the software business and these companies have increased their R&D spending from 4.9 per cent of sales in 1999 to 6.8 per cent in 2004. However, Britain still trails behind the USA in R&D spending.

R&D spending seems to be paying off for companies. Figure 95.2 shows that share prices for high R&D spending companies have outperformed the average in the top 100 companies in the UK.

Source: adapted from *The Times*, 25.10.2004.

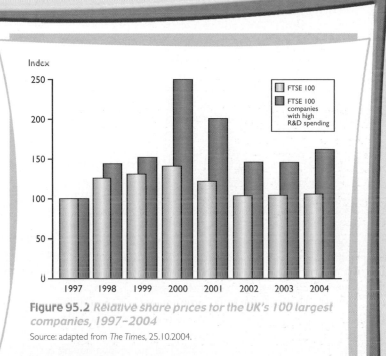

Figure 95.2 *Relative share prices for the UK's 100 largest companies, 1997–2004*

Source: adapted from *The Times*, 25.10.2004.

1 **Explain why some industries such as pharmaceuticals and software need to spend more as a proportion of sales on research and development than other industries such as hairdressing or tourism.**
2 **Discuss whether higher spending on R&D always leads to higher profits and higher share prices for a business.**

Volkswagen (VW) is counting the cost of its high spending and its faltering search for luxury. This year was supposed to a triumphal year for the company with the launch of the fifth generation of the Golf hatchback. The Golf has been VW's best selling car for many years. However, sales of the new Golf were disappointing partly due to VW's attempt to push through a price increase for the new car. It has now had to put in place a costly incentive scheme worth £823 per car in an attempt to achieve sales of 600 000 cars per year.

The projects now causing the biggest problems are part of the drive for luxury instituted by the previous chief executive of the company, Ferdinand Piëch. Today, the current chief executive Bernard Pischetsrieder, will write off €711m of investment in Britain's Bentley, the top of the range VW Phaeton and Bugatti, the sports car brand rebuilt from scratch. Part of that investment was a €186m 'glass factory' in Dresden set up to build the slow-selling Phaeton, which has its own orangery in the reception area and stores cars in a massive transparent glass tower.

However, overspending on the development of luxury cars is part of a wider problem of overspending on product development across the whole range of cars. Mr Piëch, the former chief executive, was an engineer who when he was at rival Audi developed Audi's Quattro all-wheel-drive system. Under his leadership the product development department had a mandate to produce the best car they could with little regard to cost. As a result, VW had the highest level of capital spending of any big car maker at 8.2 per cent of sales for the 2000-2003 period, according to calculations by analysts JP Morgan.

In the past, such spending made some commercial sense. VW, by developing and building a better car, has been able to charge a price premium to its competitors. Its vehicles were more reliable and move innovative than mass market rivals, justifying a 6 to 8 per cent differential in price. Marketers at VW, in order to create profits, were forced to start from the cost base and add a margin to come up with a price, rather than setting prices according to the competition and developing a vehicle that could make a profit at that level. But, as the experience of the new Golf shows, cost plus pricing can lead to disappointing sales. When the sales are too low, the price fails to cover the contribution needed per car to cover fixed costs and this leads to losses.

Mr Pischetsrieder says the strategy of luxury and technical excellence is working. He pointed out last week that car buyers interested in Golfs tend to buy the more expensive and profitable, versions. The proportion buying a Golf with more than 100 horsepower has doubled from 20 per cent to 40 per cent with the latest version of the car. But overall profit figures could suggest the contrary. Some have suggested that something has to change radically at VW if the car manufacturer is to have a successful future.

Source: adapted from the *Financial Times*, 9.3.2004.

1 (a) Explain the functions of research and development for a car manufacturer like Volkswagen.
(10 marks)

(b) Analyse why VW might be considered to have produced cars which have good product design.
(10 marks)

2 Discuss whether a car manufacturer like VW can be successful if it adopts a product orientated approach.
(20 marks)

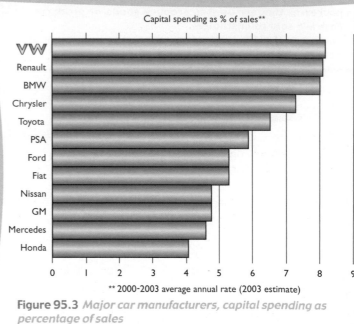

Figure 95.3 *Major car manufacturers, capital spending as percentage of sales*
Source: adapted from JP Morgan, compnay information.

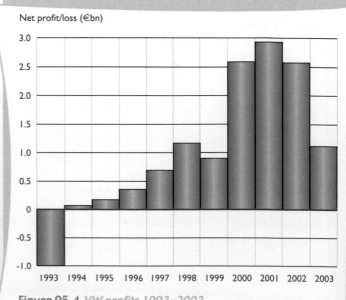

Figure 95.4 *VW profits 1993–2003*
Source: adapted from JP Morgan, company information.

96 Critical path analysis

KTL

Knowledge KLT is a UK steel manufacturer which has received a large order for steel for the construction of an exhibition hall. Much of the steel needed will be of standard sizes but some will have to be made to order.

Application Tonya Weaver has been appointed *Project Manager* by KLT for its part in the construction. She has constructed a *network* to *plan* the work using a standard piece of *network analysis* software. The software package calculates the *earliest start times* and *latest finishing times* for each activity.

Analysis Tonya has undertaken a number of similar projects in the past and has come to rely heavily on network analysis. It allows her to see quickly whether a delay in starting a particular task will have a significant impact on other activities or whether it can easily be accommodated within the production schedule. On this project, for example, a ten day delay emerged in the production of one of the special steel components due to a plant breakdown. The float, the amount of spare time within the production schedule for this activity, was 6 days. So the whole project had to be put back four days. This was acceptable given that a two week margin for completion had been built into the project at the start.

Evaluation Network analysis is a powerful tool for Tonya. However, sometimes she can become overdependent on it. Pushing numbers into a software package would seem to be the right approach in a project situation. However, sometimes Tonya needs to be a little more intuitive and look at qualitative factors in decision making. In this case, although network analysis helped Tonya complete the project on schedule, she had problems afterwards with some of the quality of the work that was done. She should have paid more attention to this at the time.

Networks

Many of the operations carried out by businesses are made up of a number of tasks. The operation is only complete when all of the tasks have taken place. For example, the tasks involved in changing a set of strings on a guitar for an instrument repairer might include:

* slacken the strings;
* remove the strings;
* clean the fretboard;
* attach new strings;
* retune the strings.

These tasks must be carried out in order for the operation to take place. Each task will take a certain amount of time. The operation is shown in Figure 96.1 on a NETWORK DIAGRAM. The operation takes 20 minutes to carry out (1 minute + 1 minute + 5 minutes + 10 minutes + 3 minutes).

Some operations are more complicated, with many tasks involved. Figure 96.2 shows a network diagram for an operation carried out by a cake manufacturer to make cakes for a wedding reception. In this operation some of the tasks can be carried out at the same time. So, for example, some of the ingredients can be prepared at the same time. Ingredient A takes 10 minutes to prepare, which is longer than any of the other ingredients. So the whole operation must take 30 minutes (5 minutes + 10 minutes + 15 minutes).

Network analysis

Businesses often have to complete large projects, which involve a series of complicated tasks or activities which must be carried out in a certain order. The use of networks helps a business to manage these projects effectively.

It is vital that a business knows the minimum length of time a project will take to complete. It is also important to know whether a delay in completing individual

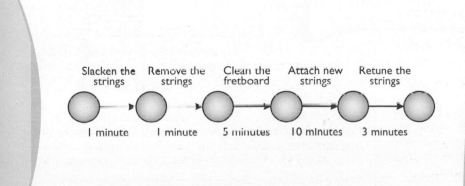

Figure 96.1 *A simple network*

Slacken the strings	Remove the strings	Clean the fretboard	Attach new strings	Retune the strings
1 minute	1 minute	5 minutes	10 minutes	3 minutes

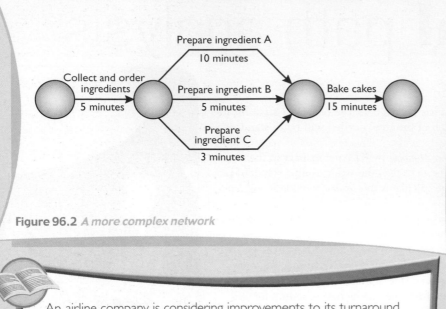

Figure 96.2 *A more complex network*

An airline company is considering improvements to its turnaround time for planes from the moment a plane arrives at the airport terminal to the time it leaves. Figure 96.3 shows a network diagram for the turnaround.

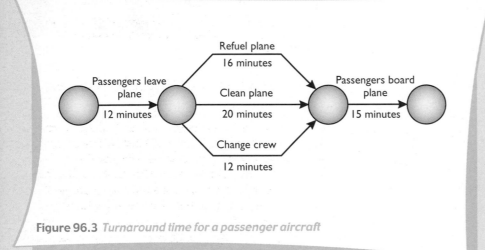

Figure 96.3 *Turnaround time for a passenger aircraft*

> **1 What is the minimum amount of time it takes for the turnaround of the aeroplane?**
> **2 If the company could cut the time it takes to clean a plane from 20 minutes to 14 minutes, would that affect the time change?**

tasks in an operation will delay the whole project or not. This is known as NETWORK ANALYSIS. It is also called CRITICAL PATH ANALYSIS as it allows a business to find the 'path' of tasks which are critical to the project and which, if delayed, will cause delays in the entire operation. In practice, businesses may use computers to manage large projects, such as the construction of a road system or hospital, or the manufacture of a large urgent overseas order for new machinery.

Before any project starts, it is important that networks are planned. This involves identifying the tasks to take place, how long each will take and the order in which they will take place. This information may be found from previous experience of projects or from research carried out by the business.

Figure 96.4 shows a network for a construction company which is renovating a cottage. There are certain features to note about the network.

- Arrows and lines show the task or activities to be carried out to complete the project. For example, Task B involves removing and replacing brickwork and flooring in the cottage.
- Some tasks can be carried out together, at the same time. For example, Tasks B and C can take place together but only after Task A has been completed.
- Arrows and lines can not cross.
- Each task takes a certain amount of time. For example, the business plans to take 4 days to complete Task B, removing and replacing the brickwork and flooring in the cottage.
- Tasks must be completed in a certain order. Certain tasks are **dependent** on others being completed. For example, Task D, fitting new windows, and Task E, rewiring, cannot begin until Task B, removing and replacing brickwork and flooring, has taken place.
- Circles on the diagram, called NODES, show the start and finish of a task or activity. For example, Task A, preparing and organising materials, starts at Node 1 and ends at Node 2.
- There is always a node at the start and end of the project.
- Nodes contain information about the timing involved in the project.

Calculating the earliest start times

The first stage in determining the critical path in the network is to calculate the earliest time at which each of the tasks or activities can start, called the EARLIEST START TIME (EST). These are shown in the top right of the nodes. Figure 96.5 shows the earliest start times for all tasks in the renovation of the cottage.

Node 1 Task A can begin immediately. So 0 is placed in the EST in Node 1.

Node 2 Task A takes 1 day to complete. Tasks B and C, which can be carried out at the same time, can only begin after Task A is completed. So they can only begin after 1 day. This is placed in the EST in Node 2.

Node 3 Task B takes 4 days to complete. Together with the 1 day to complete Task A, this means that Tasks D and E can't start until after 5 days (4 days + 1 day). This is placed in the EST in Node 3.

Node 4 Task C takes 8 days to complete. Together with the 1 day to complete Task A, this means that Task F can't start until after 9 days (8 days + 1 day). This is placed in the EST in Node 4.

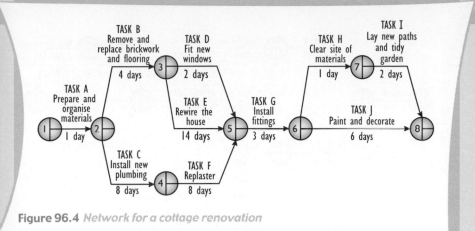

Figure 96.4 *Network for a cottage renovation*

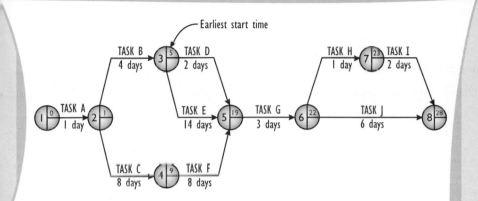

Figure 96.5 *Network showing earliest start times for a cottage renovation*

An advertising agency is working on a campaign for a large client for the launch of a new product. It has constructed a network showing the earliest start times for the different phases of the campaign.

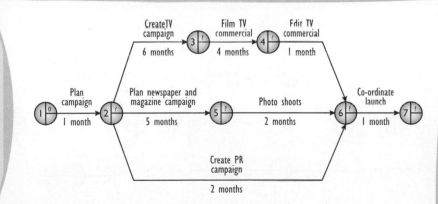

Figure 96.6 *Network for an advertising campaign*

1 **Copy out the network in Figure 96.6 and fill in the earliest start times marked by '?'.**

2 **What is the minimum amount of time the campaign will take to complete?**

3 **In the one month taken to plan the campaign at the start, the advertising agency revises its estimate of the time taken to plan the newspaper and magazine campaign to 10 months. How will this affect (a) the earliest starting times and (b) the overall time taken to complete the campaign?**

Node 5 What will be the earliest start time for Task G which begins at Node 5?

- Tasks A, B and D take 7 days to complete (1 day + 4 days + 2 days);
- Tasks A, C and F take 17 days to complete (1 day + 8 days + 8 days);
- Tasks A, B and E take 19 days to complete (1 day + 4 days + 14 days).

Task G can only begin when all preceding tasks are completed. It is dependent on earlier tasks. The longest time to complete these tasks is 19 days. So the EST in Node 5 is 19 days and Task G can't start until after 19 days. This highlights an important rule when calculating earliest start times. Always chose the **longest amount of time** when placing the ESTs in nodes.

Node 8 Another example of this can be found when calculating the final node, Node 8. Tasks up to Node 6 have taken 22 days to complete. So Tasks H and J can only begin after 22 days. The time taken to complete Task J is 6 days. This is longer than the time taken to complete Tasks H and I, which is 3 days (2 days +1 day). So the EST placed in Node 8 is 22 days + 6 days = 28 days.

As Node 8 is the final node, then 28 days is the time taken to complete the entire project.

Calculating the latest finish times

The next step involves calculating the latest times that each task can finish without causing the project to be delayed. The LATEST FINISH TIMES (LFTs) of the project to renovate a cottage are shown in Figure 96.7. They appear at the bottom right of the nodes.

Calculating the latest finish times begins at the final node, Node 8. It has already been calculated that the project will take 28 days. This is placed in the LFT of Node 8. To calculate the LFTs of earlier nodes, use the formula:

LFT at Node - time taken to complete previous task

So the LFT at Node 7, for Task H, is 28 days - 2 days = 26 days.

To calculate the LFT for Task G, to be placed in Node 6, again use the tasks which take the longest amount of time. Task J takes 6 days and Tasks H and I only 3 days (2 days + 1 day). So the LFT at Node 6 is 28 - 6 days = 22 days.

Identifying the critical path

It is now possible to calculate the CRITICAL PATH through the network. This shows the tasks which, if delayed, will lead to a delay in the project. The critical path on any network is where the earliest start times and the latest finish times in the nodes are the same. But it must also be the route through the nodes which takes the longest time.

Figure 96.8 shows the critical path and the tasks which can't be delayed if the renovation of the cottage is to be completed on time. These are tasks A, B, E, G and J. The critical path can be indicated by a broken line or crossed lines, or some other method, such as highlighting the line in colour, by pen or on computer. Other tasks in the network do not lie on the critical path.

Calculating the float

A business can use the information in the network to calculate the **float** time in the project. This is the amount of time by which a task can be delayed without causing the project to be delayed. For example, Task I takes 2 days to complete. However, as it does not lie on the critical path, it is possible that some delay can take place in this task without delaying the whole project. A delay of 1 day, for instance, would not lead to the project taking longer than 28 days.

How much delay can there be in tasks which do not lie on the critical path?

Total float The TOTAL FLOAT is the amount of time by which a task can be delayed without affecting the project. It can be calculated as:

LFT of activity - EST of activity - duration

So for Task B in Figure 96.8, for example, it would be:

5 days - 1 day - 4 days = 0 days

Activities which lie on the critical path will always have a zero total float value.

For Task C, which does not lie on the critical path, the total float is:

11 days - 1 day - 8 days = 2 days

Table 96.1 shows the total float for all tasks.

Free float The FREE FLOAT is the amount of time by which a task can be delayed without affecting the following task. It can be calculated by:

EST start of next task - EST start this task - duration

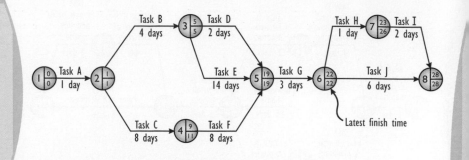

Figure 96.7 *Network showing latest finish times for a cottage renovation*

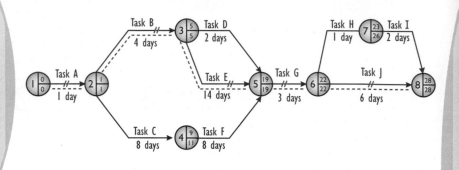

Figure 96.8 *Critical path for a cottage renovation*

Hurford's is a specialist zinc galvanising business, coating steel components with zinc to prevent them from rusting. A network for one of its processes is shown in Figure 96.9.

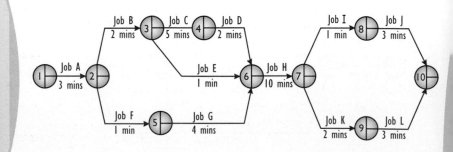

Figure 96.9 *Network for a zinc galvanising business*

1 **Copy out Figure 96.9 and fill in the latest finishing times for each job on your diagram.**
2 **Fill in the earliest starting times on the diagram.**
3 **Show the critical path on the diagram.**

| | | | | | (days) | | | |
Task/activity	LFT	EST	Duration	Total float	EST next	EST this	Duration	Free float
A	1	0	1	0	1	0	1	0
B	5	1	4	0	5	1	4	0
C	11	1	8	2	9	1	8	0
D	19	5	2	12	19	5	2	12
E	19	5	14	0	19	5	14	0
F	19	9	8	2	19	9	8	2
G	22	19	3	0	22	19	3	0
H	26	22	1	3	23	22	1	0
I	28	23	2	3	28	23	2	3
J	28	22	6	0	28	22	6	0

Table 96.1

So for Task C it would be:

$$9 - 1 - 8 = 0 \text{ days}$$

Implications for business

Critical path analysis can have a number of business implications.

Efficiency Producing a network can help a business to operate efficiently. For example, a network shows those tasks which can be carried out at the same time. This can help save manufacturing time and the use of resources. Highlighting exactly which delays are crucial to the timing of the project can help a business to meet deadlines. Inability to meet a deadline can be costly for a business. Orders may be lost if goods are not manufactured on time. In the construction industry, clients sometimes have penalty clauses on contracts. These are costs payable by a building company which does not meet its deadlines. Identifying tasks which can be delayed, without affecting the whole project, can help project management. For example, if Task A takes 3 days and Task B takes 4, then a business knows that a delay in Task A will not delay the project. However, it might be able to reduce the length of time that Task B takes to 3 days. This may reduce the length of time the entire project will take. Sometimes building firms earn bonuses for coming in 'on time' or beating deadlines.

Decision making It can influence decision making in the organisation. The use of business models such as network analysis is argued to be a more scientific and objective method of making decisions (see unit 113). It is suggested that estimating the length of time a project will take on past information and an analysis of tasks involved should lead to deadlines being met more effectively, as the implications of delays can be assessed, identified and prevented.

Time based management Some businesses operate time based management systems (see unit 48). These are techniques to minimise the length of time in business processes. Identifying tasks which have to be done in order, tasks which can be done together and tasks which may delay the whole project will all help to ensure that the least time is taken to complete an operation.

Working capital control Identifying when resources will be required in projects can help a business to manage its working capital cycle (see unit 74). Networks allow a business to identify exactly when materials and equipment will be used in a project. They can be purchased when required, rather than holding costly stocks. This is especially important if a business operates a just in time system of stock control (see unit 47). If a

business has to borrow to purchase materials then charges or interest costs may be reduced if materials are only bought when required. If delays are identified and taken into account then resources can be allocated to other operations until they are needed.

A business must not assume that simply because it produces a network its project will be completed without delay. Information used to estimate times in the network may be incorrect. For example, management might have estimated times based on past performance. But a new project may have special requirements which could take longer. Also, changes sometimes take place when projects are carried out. For example, construction companies may need contingency plans to deal with unforeseen events such as the weather (see unit 116). These would need to be taken into account when producing the network. Large projects may require detailed and extensive networks, calculated on computer.

keyterms

Earliest start time - how soon a task in a project can begin. It is influenced by the length of time taken by tasks which must be completed before it can begin.
Critical path - the tasks involved in a project which, if delayed, could delay the project.
Critical path analysis/network analysis - a method of calculating the minimum time required to complete a project, identifying delays which could be critical to its completion.
Free float - the time by which a task can be delayed without affecting the following task.
Latest finish times - the latest times that tasks in a project can finish.
Network diagram - a chart showing the order of the tasks involved in completing a project, containing information about the times taken to complete the tasks.
Nodes - positions in a network diagram which indicate the start and finish times of a task.
Total float - the time by which a task can be delayed without affecting the project.

checklist

1 Why is network analysis also known as 'critical path analysis'?
2 What is shown by a node on a network diagram?
3 Explain the difference between (a) the earliest start time and the latest finishing time; (b) the total float and the free float.
4 Why can network analysis help improve the efficiency of a business?
5 What are the implications of network analysis for working capital control?

Unett's, a Manchester building company, has won a contract to build new premises for a local drinks company. It has drawn up a network, shown in Figure 96.10, which plots the different stages of construction involved. The drinks company is anxious that the work should be completed on time because it needs the new larger premises to cope with expected increased demand for its drinks next summer. It has put into its contract with Unett's a penalty clause that states that Unett's will lose part of the contract price for every week that the work is delayed over 6 months from when work starts with the preparation of the site.

1 (a) Copy out Figure 96.10. Complete the network diagram by putting on it (i) the earliest start time and (ii) the latest finishing time for each activity. (10 marks)
  (b) Mark on the diagram the critical path. (2 marks)
  (c) Calculate the total float and the free float for (i) putting on the roof and (ii) first wall finishes. (8 marks)
2 Discuss the advantages and disadvantages to Unett's of using network analysis for this project. (20 marks)

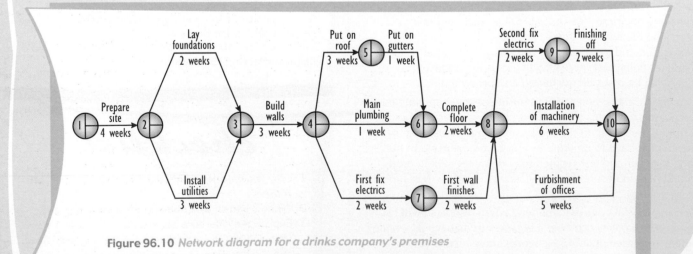

Figure 96.10 *Network diagram for a drinks company's premises*

WDS

Knowledge WDS is a firm based in Leeds which manufactures over 10 000 parts for jigs and fixtures, machines, tools and production equipment.

Application *Customers* wanting to buy parts can use an *online catalogue* to view what is available for *sale*. *Purchases* can also be made online making the service a complete *e-commerce* solution. The online catalogue offers three dimensional (3D) downloadable files. This means that a customer can incorporate the part onto its own *Computer Aided Design (CAD)* package to check that the part will fulfil the function required.

Analysis The catalogue also allows customers to order variants of parts not in the catalogue. The software allows a 'special' to be designed in as little as five minutes. Once approved, the item can go straight from a 3D model to manufacture, bringing time-to-manufacture down to a minimum. By putting its parts online with a facility to view in 3D, WDS has created a competitive advantage for itself. The service makes ordering much simpler for customers, saving time and improving accuracy.

Evaluation With no competitor offering the same service, WDS has almost certainly placed itself in a strong position within its market. As Bob Clements, the marketing director of the company which sold Solidworks the software package which has allowed the online catalogue to WDS said. 'Experience shows that the first company with a successful e-commerce solution tends to secure its position as market leader. If customers find a service useful, they become accustomed to using it and it becomes a key resource.' The service should also give WDS a key advantage in competing against lower cost Far Eastern imports. Service and speed of delivery can more than make up for any price disadvantage.

Adapted from www.ntcadcam.co.uk and www.wdsltd.co.uk.

Information technology

It is often said that 'knowledge is power'. Some argue that this is especially the case in business. Businesses which know their customers, understand their manufacturing processes, know their financial situation or understand what motivates their staff may have a **competitive advantage** (see unit 115) over their rivals.

Knowledge is held in different places within a business. Much of the key knowledge is held by individual workers. That knowledge forms a part of their individual human capital (see unit 92) and the total human capital of the business. Knowledge is held in written form, in reports, memos and accounts for example. Knowledge is also held in equipment that is bought. A machine, for example, holds the knowledge of the inventor which allows the machine to perform a particular task.

Knowledge is held in a variety of information or data in business. An increasing amount of information is held, processed and communicated through INFORMATION TECHNOLOGY (IT, sometimes also called INFORMATION AND COMMUNICATION TECHNOLOGY, ICT). Examples of IT include:

- **word processing packages** which allow information to be recorded on computer, retrieved either in paper format or electronically, and sent to another machine, for example on disk or via email;
- **databases** which allow data to be stored systematically, manipulated and then retrieved, such as a list of customer names and telephone numbers or a record of the stock held in a warehouse with arrival dates, names of suppliers and costs;
- **bar codes** which allow information about a product to be scanned and retrieved from product packaging, via product and manufacturer codes contained in the barcode;
- **spreadsheets**, used especially in finance, which allow data such as cost or revenue figures to be recorded and then manipulated and retrieved;
- **Electronic Data Interchange (EDI)**, the transfer of data between different companies using networks such as the Internet. As more companies are connected to the Internet, EDI is increasingly becoming important as an easy way for them to buy, sell, and trade information;
- the **Internet**, where information is available to everyone, often at no cost, via computer. Sometimes only selected users with a password can access information. For example, a bank may allow its customers to access their accounts and make online transactions, or a manufacturer may buy supplies over the Internet;
- business **intranets**, which operate in a similar way to the Internet, but only allow people within the organisation to access information. **Extranets** are company intranets which also allow other stakeholders such as suppliers to access information;
- **email** where messages and documents can be sent from one user to another;
- **CAM** and **CAD** programmes (see unit 58) are just two of many examples of the use of computer software systems in manufacturing. Many machines, from CNC lathes to robots, are operated by software. Increasingly, specially designed or programmed microprocessors will operate not just

production machines, but also consumer goods such as cars and washing machines. Some products, such as mobile handsets, are already totally reliant on microchips.
IT can affect every functional area of a business.

Marketing

IT can play an important role in marketing. Examples differ from industry to industry and business to business. However, they include the following.

Customer databases Businesses make use of the information in customer databases in a variety of ways. The sales representatives of a manufacturing company might phone or email every one of their customers in their database every three months to discuss possible future orders. A bank might mailshot all contacts on its database advertising its credit card services. Supermarkets, through loyalty card schemes, are able to match the names of customers with the purchases they make every time they use the loyalty card. In theory, supermarkets could target individual customers with offers based on their spending patterns. Large purchasers of wine could be invited to wine tasting evenings, for example. Customers who consistently buy special offer products could be notified of forthcoming special offers. In practice, supermarkets have found that they have too much information on customers and have been unwilling to put in the IT resources needed to analyse this data. This shows a problem with IT. In some cases, it can give far more information to a business than it can handle.

Customer databases are often used as the equivalent of a paper record which is stored on a computer. The advantage is that a number of different employees can access the record in a variety of locations. But customer databases can also be analysed. For example, customers can be ranked according to order size. Or correlations (see unit 66) can be used to see whether customers purchasing one product are likely to buy another product in the product range. Customer databases can also be used automatically to generate mailshots and for advertising email messages.

E-commerce The Internet can be a powerful marketing tool for some businesses. In a few industries, such as the tourist industry, Internet-based trading has taken a significant share of the market. From buying airline tickets to booking a hotel, companies such as easyJet or lastminute.com have made the Internet their primary marketing tool. At the other extreme, local plumbers or hairdressers may have their telephone number listed in an online telephone directory, but nothing more.

In between, there is a variety of ways in which a business can use the Internet for marketing. A business might have a website which gives details about their activities and a telephone or email address for more information. Other businesses might put up a catalogue of their products, but tell potential customers that more information such as prices or orders must be sent in writing or by telephone to the business. A few businesses offer full online ordering services, but this represents only a small part of their total sales. Supermarket

China is the fastest growing market in the world and western multinational companies want a slice of that action. One way of accessing that market is through the Internet. China already had 59 million Internet users at the end of 2002 according to analysts Morgan Stanley, making it the fourth largest Internet market in the world. To judge by the communications infrastructure being put in place, it will quickly vault to the top of the league: it already ranks first in terms of the number of mobile phone users (207m), cable TV subscribers (100m) and telephone lines (214m).

But while China is witnessing an explosion of Internet use, its adoption of e-commerce is likely to happen far more slowly. The main factors holding back growth of e-commerce are the lack of efficient systems for shipping goods and the low density of credit cards among Chinese consumers. Censorship and the general unavailability of foreign travel also limit growth. The pattern of Internet spending also may not mirror that of the western markets. For example, of China's 24 million people who pay to subscribe to their own Internet connection, as opposed to the greater number who access the Internet through colleges, work or Internet cafes, 15 million of them do so because they want to play games online. Gaming and gambling are strong interests for the Chinese, more so than in the West.

Mobile phones are also another difference. China has 3.5 times as many mobile phones as Internet users, more than double the proportion of other countries where mobile handsets are particularly popular such as Japan and Germany. In the USA, there is less than one mobile user to every one Internet user. It could be that mobile phones in China will be the main catalyst for e-commerce rather than the personal computer (PC) with Chinese customers accessing the Internet via their mobile phones rather than the PC. If so, this could influence the type of product sold over the Internet.

Age too could affect the type of goods sold. Some 70 per cent of China's Internet users are under the age of 30, compared to just 30 per cent of US Internet users. The young demographics of this Internet population will mean that they will be attracted mainly to buying products sold to young people such as fashion clothes or electronic entertainment products.

Source: adapted from the *Financial Times*, 29.11.2004.

1 Explain why 'efficient systems for shipping goods' and credit cards are essential for the growth of e-commerce.
2 In the UK, Tesco and Amazon are two of the top e-retailers by value. Which of these two companies could be most likely to sell into China today?
3 Discuss whether the Chinese are more likely to buy electronic games or foreign holidays over the Internet over the next five years.

chains in the UK like Sainsbury and Tesco are examples. Equally, a few businesses like the bookseller Amazon, have Internet only ordering systems, but e-commerce does not dominate the market and is unlikely to do so in the future.

E-commerce is unlikely totally to dominate all sales in most industries. It can, as in the airline industry, offer cost savings for businesses by cutting out expensive marketing intermediaries (see unit 19). Also, sites can be run relatively cheaply for smaller businesses, although maintaining an online site with many products, which is constantly updated, can be time consuming and will increase costs. However, some customers do not have access to the Internet, some are unwilling or unable to use sites or pay online, and some products are sold better by direct contact with customers. For example, in many industries, using the Internet to market products is not an option. The US aircraft manufacturer or the Japanese shipbuilder would be highly unlikely to sell a multi-million pound plane or ship on the Internet.

Operations management

In operations management, IT has had a powerful impact on production.

Machines and equipment Machines and equipment increasingly contain computer chips. The machines then become 'intelligent'. In some industries like finance, computerisation of processes has transformed ways of working. Labour has been eliminated in paper processing and records are stored digitally. In other industries, like car manufacturing, CNC machines and robots are now common.

Stock control Stock control is a key feature of lean production (see units 47 and 48). The use of IT can greatly help efficient stock control particularly in medium to large businesses. Stocks (often called inventory) can be recorded on a database as they are delivered. They can then be recorded as having been taken out of storage when they are used. By monitoring stock in and stock out, the level of stocks can be seen at any time. Where businesses use a just-in-time stock system, IT systems can automatically order stock to be delivered at a time when it will be needed. **Materials requirement planning** (MRP) is a computerised system which works backwards from future production schedules. Future production will determine what stock needs to be ordered and when it needs to be delivered.

Purchasing The Internet can be used for purchasing. For small businesses, ordering online can be a quick and easy way of getting supplies. Medium to large businesses can also use the Internet. One development has been the creation of web-based exchange systems and procurement sites. Examples in the construction industry include sites which auction industrial machinery and equipment online, sites which provide a marketplace for new or surplus products such as windows and doors to be sold, or sites where potential business buyers can fill out a request form detailing equipment they require, which is circulated amongst sellers.

Location IT has allowed some businesses and employees to be more footloose. For example, the move of manufacturing businesses from high wage cost developed countries like the UK or the USA to low wage cost developing countries like China or Thailand could not have happened without developments in IT. Many of the new products being manufactured are IT products themselves, such as computers or home entertainment equipment. But equally the technology to manufacture these products can be developed in countries such as the USA or Japan and then taken to low wage cost countries for use in factories. In service industries, IT has meant that some 'backroom operations' can be done anywhere in the world. For example, call centres, where customers ring up for advice or to place an order, can be located in London, Moscow, Cairo or New Delhi. The cost of routing a phone call from a customer in London to New Delhi is little more than the cost of routing it to Birmingham or Leeds.

As for workers, many 'knowledge workers' can work from home as easily as from the office. For example, operatives receiving mail order catalogue orders from customers can as easily be located at home as in a call centre. Managers can write reports at home with full access to information posted on their company computer systems. **Teleworking** has its limitations though. Many workers find it difficult to be motivated when working from home. They find there are too many distractions, from looking after children to doing the washing to looking at daytime television. Equally, most jobs require either daily face to face interaction with other workers or customers, or the use of specialist equipment which is only available in a place of work. A shop assistant or a car welder in a car assembly plant will never be able to work from home.

Finance

IT has changed the way in which financial transactions are recorded. There are still many transactions and records which use paper. But medium to large sized businesses now tend to use software packages to maintain their financial records and to generate much of the paperwork, such as invoices or receipts. There is a number of specialist accounting software

Crown Holdings is a packaging designer and manufacturer. In the mid-1990s, it realised that it needed to move from two dimensional (2D) paper drawings for its designs to three dimensional (3D) Computer Aided Design (CAD). The main limitation of the 2D approach was its lack of flexibility. Innovation Manager Chris Ramsey at Crown Holdings said: 'We wanted to be able to present some of our customers with fully rendered, curved designs. Therefore we needed a computer package that could generate curved 3D shapes, and help us to take a maximum of two or three days to draw up a design as a 'solid'. We then wanted to be able to make any further adjustments accurately and quickly in accordance with customers' instructions.'

Crown Holdings chose a CAD package called SolidWorks. Initially, it was used at its Technology Centre in Wantage, Oxfordshire. Since then other sites of the company worldwide have acquired the package.

Source: adapted from www.ntcadcam.co.uk.

1 **Explain the advantages to (a) the customers and (b) the designers of Crown Holdings of using the IT package, SolidWorks, at many of its sites across the world.**

packages available, some of which are geared towards the general business, whilst others have been specially written for certain types of business or organisation. Small businesses, too, can use cheaper accounting software packages available, although many still prefer to record everything on paper. IT packages are used for a wide variety of finance functions, such as day to day book-keeping, producing accounts, calculating cash flow and working out the wages of workers.

Financial software tends to be based on spreadsheet programs. These enable the user to add up and subtract columns or rows of figures, as well as multiply and divide figures. They can also be used instantly to calculate **financial ratios** (see units 77-81).

Software programs have the added advantage that they can help a business answer 'what if?' questions. For example, a business can prepare a **cash flow forecast** (see unit 27) and put in different scenarios about prices or sales. It can see what impact a 20 per cent fall in the average price of its products would have on cash flow. Or it could see what would happen if wages went up by 5 per cent. Large businesses may develop sophisticated computer forecasting models. These might show what would happen to sales if **macroeconomic variables** (see unit 99) such as inflation or unemployment changed, or if a competitor changed its prices. The impact on revenues and profits could then be calculated within the model.

Human Resource Management (HRM)

Personnel departments are likely to make considerable use of IT. Reports, memos, letters, application forms, employment regulations, employment history and other documents are likely to be word processed. Email is the most frequently used method of written communication today. Staff records may be kept in paper format, but increasingly they are computerised. In some industries, particularly IT, the Internet is the main medium through which jobs are advertised. Some businesses use online tests in their selection process.

It is also a vital part of KNOWLEDGE MANAGEMENT. Businesses are becoming increasingly aware that knowledge is a resource. Knowledge may be information about sales or costs. It may also be workers' knowledge. When key employees leave the organisation they often take with them intellectual property or knowledge which is a valuable asset of the business. So part of knowledge management involves ensuring that important information is retained within the business. Storing key data on processes using IT means that this information is not lost when employees leave. Another part of knowledge management is ensuring that all relevant employees have information which is essential to the performance of their tasks. For example, a multinational oil business may find that its drilling operation experiences onsite problems which it cannot solve. The solution, however, may have already been found in another part of the organisation in another country. Storing this information using IT and making it available to everyone in the business immediately might help solve the problem and ensure the efficient operation of the organisation.

Limitations of IT

IT has its limitations in business.
- IT is only a tool. If staff are not properly trained to use the IT

systems in a business, then the IT systems will underperform.
- IT can provide too much information and there can be 'information overload'. Staff must be trained to be selective about the information they use. IT systems must also be adapted to minimise information overload. One example of this is the use of emails. In many cases, they have considerably improved communication within businesses. However, often too many emails are sent to too many people. The result is that workers spend time reading emails which have no effect on their productivity or the output of the business.
- In medium to large businesses, there may be several incompatible IT systems operational at the same time. So the finance department might be using one software package whilst the production department is using another. The two systems then can't 'talk' to each other. A production budget prepared in the production department can't be read in the software package used in the finance department. This is the same problem in home entertainment where a PlayStation game can't be used on an X-box. Incompatibility severely limits the efficiency of software. There are software packages available to get around this problem, but the cost of installing and maintaining them is high.
- Some businesses have found that they have bought the wrong software systems. In extreme cases, a business might pay millions of pounds to develop a system only to find it doesn't work and it has to write off the investment. In some cases, a business may buy software which only partly does the job the business wants it to do. In other cases, IT salespeople may sell a business a system which is far too complex, and therefore expensive, when a much simpler and cheaper system would have performed just as well in practice.

keyterms

Information technology (IT) or Information and communication technology (ICT) – **the use of computers to store, handle, produce and retrieve information (information technology) whilst also allowing microchip based machines to talk to each other (communication technology).**
Knowledge management – **the collection, retention and distribution of the vital knowledge which exists in the business.**

checklist

1 Briefly explain THREE examples of IT.
2 How can a customer database be used in marketing?
3 Explain the impact that IT has had on operations management.
4 Explain the importance of spreadsheets in finance.
5 Why is IT important in knowledge management?
6 What are the limitations of IT in a business?

The NHS is currently part way through a massive £6 billion IT project, the largest in the world, due to be completed in 2010. Within this are four core projects: a universal system for electronic medical records; a hospital appointments system; a broadband infrastructure; and e-prescriptions. To build the national patient record database is forecast to cost £620 million alone, whilst the national electronic patient records system will cost £2.3 billion by 2010. The aim is for NHS professionals to be able to communicate with each other, to see a patient's records immediately online and to be able to prescribe drugs electronically. For example, a doctor treating a patient in hospital should in future be able to call up the patient's notes which have been written by his GP. Ultimately, the complete medical history of a patient from the moment of birth to the point of death will be available in one file on the NHS database.

However, there are serious doubts about the project. One is whether it will work at all. There have been several large IT projects in government which have had to be scrapped because they failed to deliver. Other IT projects have been dogged by failure to deliver on time and then the facilities promised have failed to live up to expectations. One major problem is that systems have been written by IT specialists who have consulted the end-user far too little. The result is the systems are difficult to use and fail to incorporate features which would make them more effective. In a survey completed for the television series 'File on 4' in 2004, 90 per cent of doctors questioned said either they had not been adequately consulted or that they had not been consulted

at all about the new system. Only 3 per cent of respondents thought it would deliver value for money. One doctor commented that 'It looks like it will be a step backwards several years in terms of the facilities and features that we have on current software. I am very worried about it being dangerous for patients'.

Outsiders are also worried that there will be a massive cost overrun on the project. Some commentators have put the final cost of the project at as much as £31 billion over ten years. Previous large government IT projects have seen substantial cost overruns. Concerns about cost overruns were heightened when the National Audit Office (NAO), the government watchdog responsible for checking that government spending gives value for money, announced in August 2004 that it would launch an investigation into the IT programme. A spokesperson for the NAO said that: 'The fact we are starting work does not imply any particular concern with the way the programme is going' but many suspect that it is an indication that cost overruns are likely.

Source: adapted from BBC News, http://news.bbc.co.uk, 31.8.2004, 19.10.2004.

1 Discuss the possible costs and benefits to an organisation like the NHS or to any business of implementing a complex and very costly IT project which is designed to transform the way in which it operates. (20 marks)

Minivator

Knowledge Minivator is a manufacturer of stairlifts. In 2004, it changed location by half a mile, moving into larger premises.

Application Minivator's *turnover* increased from £6 million a year in 2000 to £15 million in 2004. As a result, it was rapidly running out of room at its existing premises. *Quantitative analysis* showed that moving made financial sense for the company. *Qualitative analysis* pointed to a local move being best for the company.

Analysis Minivator made a detailed forecast of the costs and revenues associated with moving to new premises. The new premises provided almost twice as much floor space as the old premises. It also allowed for a new demonstration area with a range of fully-functional stairlifts. On the office front, it allowed the customer service, design and operational departments to come together. The higher rents would be more than covered by the increase in sales that the new premises would permit. Marketing manager Sharon Thompson said: 'We expect to double our production as a result of this move. We have also been able significantly to increase our customer service staff because of the strength of customer demand.' On the qualitative side, Barrie Payne, the managing director, said that 'The business has always been based on the Pensnett Estate but we rapidly outgrew our site at Vantage Point. Being able to relocate less than half a mile down the road and on the same estate was a huge benefit. It made the whole process far easier and our staff, many of whom are from the local area, are unaffected by the change.'

Evaluation As a medium sized company, a local move made a great deal of sense for Minivator. Moving further would probably have been highly disruptive for the company. It could have lost many key workers for little financial gain in terms of cheaper premises. It could also have lost production during the move, lowering sales and perhaps losing customers. However, moving was almost certainly the right decision given that its existing premises were too small.

Adapted from the *Express & Star*, 19.1.2004.

Making location decisions

All businesses, at some point in their life, have to make decisions about location. New businesses starting up have to decide where to locate. Existing businesses should review their location periodically to see whether relocating would bring net benefits.

Decisions about location are based on costs and benefits. Some of these costs and benefits can be **quantified** in monetary terms. However, some costs and benefits are **qualitative** rather than quantitative. They cannot be given a value in monetary terms. Any final decision about location will be based on both quantitative and qualitative factors.

A variety of business techniques can be used to help make a decision based solely on quantitative data. Two such techniques are **break-even analysis** (see unit 22) and **investment appraisal** (see unit 84). Both techniques involve identifying the costs and revenues associated with a particular project. To use break-even analysis, fixed costs need to be separated out from variable costs. For investment appraisal techniques, the timing of the costs and benefits of a project are crucial to establish an optimal solution.

Fixed costs

Fixed costs (see unit 21) are costs which do not vary with output. So fixed costs would remain the same whether production was zero or 1 million units a year. In making a location decision, two types of fixed costs can be distinguished. There are fixed costs which are incurred before any production has started and ongoing fixed costs whilst the location is in operation.

There will be a number of start up fixed costs.
- The business is likely to research a number of different possible locations. This search process is a cost.
- Most businesses locate or relocate to existing premises. These may need adapting or renovating to suit the firm's needs.
- A few business will move to purpose-built premises. Apart from the building costs, there will be architects' fees and the cost of securing planning permission. Special licences might have to be obtained if the site is to produce dangerous materials.

A decision will have to be made about whether to buy premises outright or to rent them. Cash may be paid up front if buying outright. Equally, the cash may be borrowed, with repayment spread over a period of time. If rented or leased, the rent will be a fixed cost also, spread over a period of time.

In a few cases, the business may be able to get a grant from government for setting up in an area of deprivation or high unemployment. **Regional policy** is operated both by the UK government and the European Union. Its aim is to help depressed regions by creating jobs and incomes. Grants help to reduce the fixed cost of locating.

Ongoing fixed costs vary from industry to industry. If labour is treated as a fixed cost, then wages are generally higher in the South of England than in the rest of the UK. Partly this is because unemployment tends to be lower in the South and so there is less supply of labour available to fill positions. Partly it is also because living costs, particularly house prices, are higher and so workers need higher wages to keep them from migrating to lower cost areas of the UK. This may persuade some businesses which are FOOTLOOSE and so are not fixed to any particular geographical location, to locate in cheaper labour areas outside the South of England.

Availability of labour can also lead to costs for a business. Where unemployment is low and labour is in short supply, there are likely to be shortages of different types of skilled worker. This may increase the training costs of a business because it has to train new recruits rather than expect them to have the right skills. Labour turnover may be higher because workers are able to move jobs relatively easily to more highly paid jobs. The cost of recruitment may be high and diverts scarce management time from more important issues.

Different areas of a country may have different records for absenteeism or trade union militancy. Higher absenteeism is a cost to an employer. Equally, trade union militancy is likely to push up employment costs for firms where unions are active because unions tend to push up wage costs.

Other fixed costs may relate to transport. Many businesses outsource (see unit 43) their transport and it is a variable cost. However, some businesses, particularly larger businesses, may have their own dedicated transport fleet of vehicles. Such a business located in the North of Scotland with its markets in the South of England will have higher transport costs and so higher fixed costs than a similar business located in London.

If the business is renting or leasing its premises, then the rent or lease will be a fixed cost. Again, the South of England tends to be more expensive to rent or lease property than the rest of the UK. However, there are considerable variations in rents within regions too. It is cheaper to rent commercial property in Hastings in the South of England than in Guildford for example.

Taxes can be an important fixed cost. In the UK, the local tax on businesses is Business Rates based on the value of commercial premises. When considering international location, different overall rates of tax on business varies between countries. Businesses in France and Germany, for example, pay more in tax than in the UK or the US. Different tax rates can affect location decisions.

Variable costs

For many businesses, variable costs do not alter from location to location. However, there are some manufacturing industries where variable costs are significant and these tend to be related to transport costs.

Industries which need to be near their sources of supply Some industries need to be near their sources of supply because the cost of transporting materials is so high. Traditionally, for example, iron and steel works were located in areas where iron ore and coal were mined. Coal fired electricity power stations were located next to a coal mine. In countries like China, this is still the case. In the UK, steel plants today tend to be located on the coast where coal and iron ore can be transported cheaply by ship from abroad.

Industries which need to be located near their customers In other manufacturing industries, businesses need to be located near their customers because the cost of transporting finished goods is so high. Today this is true, for example, for suppliers to

just-in-time manufacturers. In the car industry, some suppliers have chosen to locate themselves within the car assembly plant they supply to be near their customer. With just-in-time manufacturing, suppliers are committed to supplying often relatively small amounts of product on demand from the customer. The cost of transport must be kept to a minimum to make this cost effective. Note that many service businesses need to be near their customers but this is not to do with cost of supply. A supermarket or a hairdresser needs to be located in a place convenient for its customers. This might push up fixed costs in terms of premises because the hairdresser has to be on the high street rather than in an out of town industrial park. But it is unlikely to add to variable costs.

Where labour is a variable cost, such as workers paid on piece rates or solely on commissions, labour is more expensive in some locations than others. So variable costs for labour in London are more expensive than in Carlisle or Durham.

Revenues

For many businesses, location has little impact on revenues. However, in some industries, location is extremely important.

Convenience to customers Many businesses in service industries need to be near their customers. In retailing, for example, location is often crucial to success. A shop outlet on a busy high street could have much higher takings than the same shop located only a few yards away up a side street. A petrol station forecourt on a busy road, where it is easy to get in and out of the station, could have higher takings than a forecourt on a side street or one on a busy road but where there is difficult access.

Location clusters Some businesses thrive in a location because there is a cluster of similar businesses also there. Ross-on-Wye, for example, has a large number of second hand bookshops which would be unlikely to survive in other locations. Because of the cluster, customers come to the location knowing that they will have a wide choice of products to buy. In manufacturing, suppliers often locate near to their customers because local firms have an advantage in marketing. In Stoke-on-Trent, for example, there is a cluster of pottery firms and their suppliers. Harley Street for doctors and Bond Street for upmarket brands are other examples of clusters in London which raise revenues for businesses located there.

Resources, land and climate Some businesses are able to generate higher revenues because of the physical characteristics of their location. Farmers in Costa Rica can grow more bananas per hectare than a farm in Canada because of climate. Saudi Arabia has one quarter of the world's known oil reserves beneath it and so it is a major exporter of oil. Spain is a major tourist destination because of its climate and fine beaches, whereas Iceland has far fewer tourists because of its climate.

Using break-even analysis

Businesses may use break-even analysis in helping them make a decision about location. For example, a business may compare its existing site to a new proposed site. Figure 98.1 shows the break-even chart for a manufacturing company at its existing site. The break-even point is at 10 million units of output. It wants to move to larger premises because of

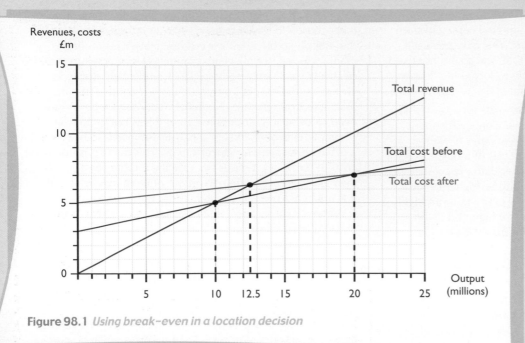

Revenues, costs
£m

Total revenue

Total cost before

Total cost after

Output
(millions)

Figure 98.1 *Using break-even in a location decision*

variable costs per unit have fallen. The break-even point at the new location would be at 12.5 million units of output. So just to break-even, the company must sell more.

However, Figure 98.1 also shows that the company will make less profit at the new site at any level of output below 20 million units of output. This is because average revenues won't change with the move but costs at any level of output below 20 million will increase. For the move to be profitable, the company must double its sales and output. This would be an unlikely scenario for most businesses. So in this case, the business is likely to reject the idea of moving to this particular new site.

increased demand for its products.

The larger site will cost more in rent and maintenance costs. The company will use the opportunity of the move to buy more machinery. This will all increase the fixed costs of the site. On the other hand, the larger site should lead to lower variable costs, for example in purchasing. The new total cost line is shown in Figure 98.1. It starts at a higher point on the vertical axis because fixed costs have increased. However, the slope of the line is less than the old total cost line because

Rollauer is a machine tool manufacturer. It is currently looking to move into larger premises because sales are expanding and its current premises are too small to accommodate expansion.

Revenue per unit sold	Variable cost per unit produced		Total fixed cost per year	
	Site A	Site B	Site A	Site B
0.5	0.3	0.4	100	60

Table 98.1 *Revenues and costs for Rollauer, £ million*

1 **Calculate the break-even point of production at site A and site B using either a break-even chart or contribution analysis.**
2 **The business is currently selling 500 units per year but is expecting within two years to have grown its sales to 700 units per year. Explain which of the two sites would be most profitable at this new level of output of 700 units per year.**
3 **If the business could raise its output to 1000 units, which site would then be the most profitable?**

Using investment appraisal

Businesses may use investment appraisal techniques (see unit 84) in deciding where to locate. Table 98.2 shows two possible sites for a business which is considering relocating its premises. It gives the initial cost of the move and then the cost savings to be made in each year compared to the existing site. The three investment appraisal methods outlined in unit 84 can be used to show which, if any, site should be chosen. It is assumed that at the end of five years, the business will be relocating again. So no cost savings will be taken into account after the end of five years.

Payback method With the payback method, the business calculates how long it will take to recoup the initial investment. In location A, the initial cost is £12 million and with annual savings (the equivalent of increased cash flows see unit 84) of £3 million, the investment will be recouped in 4 years. With location B, the initial cost is higher at £15 million, but the cost savings are £5 million per year. The result is that the investment will be recouped in 3 years. So on the payback method, location B is the preferred location.

Average rate of return (ARR) With the average annual rate of return method, the net return is divided by the initial investment and expressed as a percentage. With location A, there will be a total cost saving (i.e. increased cash flow) over 5 years of £15 million. With an initial cost of £12 million, this gives a return of £3 million (£15 million - £12 million). So the ARR is [(£3 million ÷ £15 million) ÷ 5 years] x 100 per cent, which is 4 per cent. With location B, the cost saving is £25 million over five years with an initial cost of £15 million. So the ARR is [(£10 million ÷ £25 million) ÷ 5 years] x 100 per cent, which is 8 per cent. On the average rate of return method, location B is also the preferred location.

Discounted cash flow With discounted cash flow, the value of future cash flows must be discounted back to the present. The important insight of discounted cash flow is that, just as money invested today will grow in value because of compound

	£ million	
	Location A	Location B
Initial cost	12	15
Annual cost savings/increased cash flow		
Year 1	3	5
Year 2	3	5
Year 3	3	5
Year 4	3	5
Year 5	3	5

Table 98.2 *Initial costs and cost savings of two new locations*

	Location A	Location B	Discount table	Location A	Location B
	£ millions	£ millions	15%	£ millions	£ millions
Initial cost	12	15	1.00	12.0	15.0
Annual cost savings/ increased cash flow					
Year 1	3	5	0.87	2.6	4.4
Year 2	3	5	0.76	2.3	3.8
Year 3	3	5	0.66	2.0	3.3
Year 4	3	5	0.57	1.7	2.9
Year 5	3	5	0.50	1.5	2.5
Total cost savings	15	25		10.1	16.9
Net cash flow	3	10		-1.9	1.9

Table 98.3 *Initial cost and cost savings of two new locations discounted at 15%*

interest, so the reverse is true: the value of cash available in the future is worth less today. In Table 98.3, the cost savings (or net cash flows) have been discounted back assuming a discount rate of 15 per cent. The net present value of the cost savings fall the further into the future they occur. When these are totalled up, the net present value of the cost savings at location A don't cover the initial investment needed. So moving to location A is unprofitable at this rate of discount. On the other hand, moving to location B shows a positive net cash flow. The cost savings outweigh the initial cost of the investment by £1.9 million. So this would suggest that the company should move to location B. Whatever the rate of discount used, location B would always be preferred over location A. However, if the rate of discount were much higher than 15 per cent, the discounted cash flow technique would suggest that even location B would give overall negative cash flows and therefore moving would not be profitable.

Qualitative factors

Qualitative factors are factors which cannot be measured using numbers (see unit 85). Qualitative factors are important when making location decisions partly because quantitative methods, such as investment appraisal techniques, cannot capture all the information needed to make a location decision. Qualitative factors are also important because quantitative methods can never give an accurate answer since they are based on assumptions about the future. Forecast revenues one, three or ten years from now, for example, are unlikely to match the actual revenues achieved. The further away in time the forecast, the less likely it is to be accurate. This doesn't mean to say that quantitative techniques are not important. But they must be placed alongside qualitative factors in decision making

Edney's is a manufacturer of frozen food products. It needs to move because it has outgrown its current premises. It is considering two sites, A and B. Site A has the lowest initial cost at £4.5 million but the move will cause more disruption to production initially than at Site B. In the longer term, however, the financial benefits of Site A are greater than at Site B.

The managing director has asked you to do some calculations on the two sites and make a recommendation about which site should be chosen. He has asked you to consider only any costs and cash flows over a seven year period.

	Location A	Location B	Discount table
	£millions	£millions	Rate of discount at 20%
Initial cost	4.5	6.0	1.00
Net cash flow			
Year 1	1.0	2.0	0.83
Year 2	1.5	2.5	0.69
Year 3	2.0	2.5	0.58
Year 4	2.5	2.5	0.48
Year 5	3.0	2.0	0.40
Year 6	3.0	2.0	0.33
Year 7	3.0	2.0	0.28

Table 98.4 *Initial costs and net cash flow of two sites, A and B*

1 For both sites, calculate (a) the payback time; (b) the average rate of return (ARR); (c) the net present value assuming a rate of discount of 20 per cent.
2 Explain which site you would recommend the company should choose.

and their limitations recognised.

There is a variety of qualitative factors which a business might take into consideration when making a location decision.

Laws and regulations Any location decision will have legal and regulatory aspects. In many cases, laws and regulations will determine what type of business can occupy what type of premises in what areas. Getting planning permission will be necessary if a business is building new premises. If two sites are being compared in different countries, the legal frameworks may be very different. For example, one country may have much looser regulation of pollution than another country. Health and safety regulations may differ too.

Social, environmental and ethical considerations Many businesses, particularly larger ones, may take social, environmental and ethical considerations into account. For example, a manufacturer may be reluctant to move away from a local area because it has a long history of involvement with the local area, is a major employer and moving away would severely damage the local community. Another business may decide against a particular location because the environmental impact of moving to that location would be too negative. A third business may deliberately choose a location in a high unemployment area as a positive ethical choice to create jobs. Businesses tend to make these choices for two reasons. Some businesses are set up with social, environmental and ethical goals which override the profit motive. Other businesses exploit their social, environmental and ethical decisions to promote themselves to their customers. Equally, businesses may want to avoid negative public relations (PR) which arise when they are accused of acting in an anti-social or unethical way.

Quality of life Evidence suggests that the interests of those making a location decision are very important. Small businesses, for example, tend to be located where their owner managers live. Small to medium sized businesses, when considering relocating, will typically relocate within a few miles of the present location. Owner managers don't want to move house or locality even if cheaper premises could be found just 50 miles away. Large companies will consider whether the managers who have to be sent to a location to run a plant or factory will enjoy the posting. Quality of housing, local schools and the environment are important considerations. So too are factors such as risk to employees. A multinational may choose to locate in China than, say, parts of South America or Africa for these reasons.

Political stability In the UK, political stability is taken for granted in most areas. But when large companies make decisions about where to locate around the world, political stability is a key factor. Foreign investment in certain countries may be lower than it would be if there were more political stability in these countries. At worst, political instability can lead to new governments which seize foreign owned assets or suddenly impose high taxes.

Quality of the workforce The quality of the local workforce is important. A business is unlikely to locate to a place where it is unable to recruit the right quality of local labour. China, for example, has attracted a considerable amount of inward investment because it has relatively well educated labour prepared to work for low wages. In the UK, London and the South East continue to attract new companies because, despite relatively high wages, there is a large pool of highly educated workers from which to draw.

Infrastructure Infrastructure, such as roads, railways, airports, hospitals and schools, can play an important part in location decisions. The quality of the infrastructure in a particular location will have an impact on costs and therefore will be part of any quantitative calculation. However, for a multinational company, having a local airport which takes international flights might be an important consideration. For a national company, being near the motorway network might influence a location decision. For a company located in London, which has many workers commuting in every day, nearness to a railway station or a tube station might influence a location decision.

International location

Multinational companies operate in a number of different locations across the world. International location decisions can be more complex than those made within a country.

Avoiding trade barriers Countries put up trade barriers, such as tariffs (taxes on imports) and quotas (physical limits on the quantity of a product that can be imported). They do this to protect their own national businesses from foreign competition.

One way a multinational business can get round such trade barriers is to locate within the country. For example, Japanese car producers set up car plants in both Europe and the USA in the 1980s and 1990s partly to get around trade barriers put up by EU countries and the US to keep Japanese producers of cars out of their markets.

Achieving economies of scale Multinational companies may close down plants in some countries to move production to existing plants in other countries to achieve economies of scale (see unit 42) in production. By increasing the volume of production at a particular site, economies of scale can be exploited, reducing average cost.

Cost of labour Many manufacturing multinational companies have located plants in cheap labour countries such as India or China. Cheap labour then gives them a competitive advantage. However, jobs may be retained in high labour cost countries where high quality labour is needed. Education, training and the skills of the workforce in countries like the UK are vitally important in keeping facilities such as headquarters or research in high labour cost countries.

Proximity to markets or suppliers Transport costs can be much greater over larger distances. So multinational companies may have to locate near their markets or their suppliers to remain competitive. A car component manufacturer, for example, may have to set up a factory in the Far East to be near a customer, a car manufacturer. It is not always true, though, that transport costs are significant in international location decisions. If a product is high value, transport costs may be only a small fraction of the final price charged. Equally, transport costs vary according to modes of transport. Sometimes, it can cost less to send an item thousands of miles across the globe by ship than it does to take it from the ship and transport it by lorry for the final 50 miles.

Exchange rate fluctuations Exchange rate fluctuations can be an important determinant of location decisions (see unit 52). Businesses trading internationally can experience large sudden movements in exchange rates. Sometimes these movements are beneficial to a business but sometimes they have a negative impact. For example, a UK business may import components from Germany. If the exchange rate of the pounds falls sharply against the euro, then the UK business is likely to face a larger bill for imports. One way of getting around this risk is for a company to balance its costs and revenues in a single currency through location decisions. For example, a UK company may export $20 million of goods from UK factories to customers in the USA and import €15 million of goods from a factory it owns in France to the UK. This exposes it to risks of changes in the value of the pound both against the euro and the US dollar. One way around this problem would be to close the factory in France and relocate it to the USA. Then there would be roughly equal and opposite transactions in US dollars which would considerably reduce the company's exchange rate risks.

Political stability As already mentioned above, political stability is an important qualitative factor in determining decision making. Some countries have very little inward investment by foreign companies because of chronic political instability. Equally, some countries are currently boycotted by western companies because of the nature of their political regimes. To locate in these countries, which may have a poor record on human rights, could attract consumer boycotts or shareholder disapproval.

Language barriers Language can be an important factor in location decisions. One reason why the UK is favoured as a location by US companies is because the UK and the US share a common language. Much of the foreign investment over the past ten years in China has been by companies owned by Chinese people living outside of China. Locating new facilities in China allows them the advantage of low cost labour and they share a common language.

Regional policy

Governments attempt to influence location decisions through

REGIONAL POLICY. Governments offer a range of incentives, from grants to tax breaks to subsidised land and help with the cost of training. Much of the money spent on regional policy is devoted to attracting large businesses to a particular site. Car manufacturing plants or factories making products for the computer industry are classic examples. This is because such plants create a large number of easily identifiable jobs, but also tend to create more jobs through suppliers and customers setting up locally. However, small and medium sized businesses can benefit too depending on the type of scheme in place.

Regional policy is usually aimed at bringing jobs to deprived regions. These can be measured as regions with high unemployment or where average income is well below the national average. The regions targeted can be large, such as Wales or south west England. Equally, they can be relatively small. When urban areas are targeted, regional policy is often called 'urban regeneration' because incentives are typically given to regenerate an old industrial area where many of the traditional businesses have closed down.

✓ *checklist*

1 What might be (a) the fixed costs and (b) the variable costs of a location decision?
2 How might revenues be affected by the location of a business?
3 How could break-even analysis be used to make a location decision?
4 Explain briefly the qualitative factors which a business might take into account when making a location decision.
5 What factors might a multinational company take into account when making a location decision?
6 How might regional policy affect the location decisions of firms?

keyterms

Footloose businesses - **businesses that are not tied to a particular location.**
Regional policy - **government policy aimed at attracting businesses to locate in a particular area, typically a deprived, high unemployment, low average income area.**

Pidd is a medium sized UK company which manufactures components for the aerospace industry. Approximately half its sales are to UK customers. Of the rest, three quarters are to US aerospace firms with the remaining quarter going to French and German firms. Two years ago, its turnover was £15 million but since then it has lost a number of orders because its prices were too high. This year, it expects its turnover to be down to £12 million.

John Pidd, the largest shareholder and the managing director of the company, has decided that radical measures are needed to ensure the long term survival of the business. It cannot continue manufacturing components in the UK because labour costs are simply too high. The only alternative, apart from selling the

business, is to move manufacturing abroad. After some research, John Pidd has begun to focus on two possibilities. The business could either set up a wholly owned factory in Poland or establish a partnership with a Chinese company and set up a factory in China.

The Polish alternative is attractive for a number of reasons. Polish wages are much lower than in the UK but the company should be able to recruit sufficient trained staff locally. Poland is a member of the EU and so the company would be operating within an EU framework of laws, even if Polish law can sometimes be less than business friendly. The country is not yet in the eurozone and so its currency, the zloty, fluctuates against the pound, the dollar and the euro. In the medium term, however, it is predicted that Poland will adopt the euro. The UK might join up too although there is great debate about whether this will happen. There is a possibility that the company could get an EU grant for setting up in Poland, but John Pidd would see this as a bonus and has not included it in any of the financial calculations he has made. John Pidd's mother was Polish and he speaks fluent Polish. This was the main reason why he concentrated on Poland rather than any of the other new members in Eastern Europe.

China has lower wages than Poland although there may be problems with recruiting sufficiently skilled workers. To set up in China, John Pidd has decided he must seek out a local partner. Most locations in China require that a company is at least 50 per cent owned by Chinese investors. The Chinese partner would deal with getting all the permissions needed to establish a factory and would take the lead in recruiting workers. Pidd would provide the technical expertise and the equipment. The Chinese currency, the renminbi, is at present fixed in value against the US dollar, although some expect it eventually to be revalued because of the strength of Chinese exports. John Pidd has some reservations about the safety of the investment. He has read about companies which have invested in China only to see their Chinese partner effectively seize all the assets leaving the foreign investor with nothing. He is also concerned about the political stability of the Chinese government. At some stage, there could be a transition to a more democratic government and this could be a risky change. The risk is that the change over could be used to take control of foreign assets. Transport costs will be slightly higher from China than they would be from Poland to the UK, partially offsetting the gains from lower wages. China is making rapid technological progress in the aerospace industry and forecasts predict that China will be the second largest market in the world for civil aircraft by 2020. Some of this demand is likely to be met by Chinese companies buying components from suppliers based in China.

John Pidd has made some forecasts of the costs and revenues associated with each site, along with forecast cash flows. These are shown in Tables 98.5 and 98.6.

Revenue per unit sold	Variable cost per unit produced		Total fixed cost per year	
	Poland	China	Poland	China
10	4	3	7 200	7 000

Table 98.5 *Revenues and costs for two sites in Poland and China, £000*

	Poland	China	Discount table
	£millions	£millions	Rate of discount at 10%
Initial cost	7.0	5.0	1.00
Net cash flow			
Year 1	0.5	0.5	0.91
Year 2	1.0	1.0	0.83
Year 3	1.5	1.0	0.75
Year 4	2.0	1.0	0.68
Year 5	2.0	1.2	0.62
Year 6	2.0	1.4	0.56
Year 7	2.0	1.6	0.51
Year 8	2.0	1.8	0.47
Year 9	2.0	2.0	0.42
Year 10	2.0	2.2	0.39

Table 98.6 *Initial costs and net cash flow for two new sites in Poland and China*

1 (a) Calculate the break-even level of output forecast at the site in (i) Poland and (ii) China. Show your workings carefully. (6 marks)
   (b) Calculate the payback period for the two sites. (4 marks)
   (c) Calculate the annual rate of return for the two sites. (4 marks)
   (d) Calculate the net present value of the investment in the two sites over the ten year period. (6 marks)
2 Discuss which of the two sites the company should choose. In your answer, consider both quantitative and qualitative aspects of the decision. (20 marks)

99 The macro-economic environment

Rotork

Knowledge Rotork is a UK engineering company which specialises in the manufacturer of actuations systems. These are devices that open and close valves. Its products are sold to the oil, gas, water and waste water and power generation industries around the world.

Application Rotork is a *multinational company* which has production facilities in a number of countries. Like any multinational, it is affected by *interest rates*, *exchange rates*, *inflation* and the *business cycle*.

Analysis The company is highly profitable. Part of the secret of its success is that does very little manufacturing itself. It buys in components from suppliers and then assembles them. Direct labour only accounts for around 5 per cent of costs with components making up 70 per cent. By sourcing its components competitively, often from low cost far eastern countries, it has been able to resist inflationary pressures to put up its prices. Buying components from a number of countries also means that it is able to reduce exchange rate risks. To some extent, it has been able to match foreign currency payments to suppliers with foreign currency receipts from customers. It has enjoyed considerable sales growth in recent years and was able to survive the downturns in the world economy in the early 2000s. This is because the industries to which it sells tend not to be much affected by the business cycle. Its expansion and investment programmes are not directly affected by interest rates because it has negligible borrowings and a sizeable stock of cash. It could finance any expansion or acquisition it wanted from its cash pile.

Evaluation Rotork has a reputation for being one of the best operators in the engineering sector. By concentrating on a niche market and not attempting to expand beyond its core competences, it has played to its strengths. Its results in terms of continuing sales and profits growth have been the reward for this strategy.

Adapted from the *Financial Times*, 4.6.2005; Rotork, *Annual Report and Accounts*, 2003.

Business strategy

Strategy, in a business context, is a set of plans to achieve the objectives of a business (see unit 64). The objectives of businesses (see unit 62) vary but include maximising profit or sales, maximising shareholder value, increasing market share, increasing the size of the business, benefiting customers or workers or creating wealth for the community.

Business strategies are strategies designed to give a business a competitive advantage (see unit 115). Business strategies include becoming the lowest cost producer in a market, differentiating a product or aiming a product at either a niche market or a mass market.

Business strategy will be affected by changes in the MACROECONOMIC ENVIRONMENT. This is changes in the whole of the economy. Examples of **macroeconomic variables** include interest rates, exchanges rates, inflation and unemployment; the business cycle and the labour market. These were discussed in detail in units 50 to 54. In this unit, we will consider the implications for business strategy of changes in macroeconomic variables.

Interest rates

Interest rates have a significant impact on businesses either directly through the cost of borrowing, or indirectly through their effect on spending (a thorough revision of unit 51 is advisable here).

The cost of borrowing The higher the rate of interest, the more a business is likely to pay in interest to borrow money to finance itself. For example, if interest rates rise by 1 per cent over a year, a business which has a £10 000 overdraft will have to pay £100 more a year in interest (1% x £10 000). If interest rates rise by 5 per cent, this would increase interest payments by £500.

Small changes in interest rates of up to 1 or 2 per cent are unlikely to have significant impact on costs for most businesses. Larger changes, though, can have an impact on business strategy. Significant falls in interest rates should stimulate investment by businesses. With the cost of borrowing significantly cheaper, investment projects which in the past would have been unprofitable now become profitable (see unit 84). Extra investment might make a business more competitive and allow it to expand sales or market share with the objective of increasing profit and shareholder value. Conversely, a significant rise in interest rates will increase the cost of borrowing, making investment less profitable. So a business is likely to reduce its investment.

Impact on aggregate demand Interest rates have an indirect effect on businesses through their impact on aggregate demand (i.e. total demand). Aggregate demand is partly made up of consumer spending, investment by businesses, purchases of stock by businesses and exports. A significant fall in interest rates will increase aggregate demand in the economy.

- Consumer spending rises because the cost of borrowing for consumers falls. Consumers can now afford to take on more debt to purchase consumer durables like cars or washing machines.

- Investment rises because the cost of borrowing has fallen. It also rises because businesses need to invest to cope with extra orders arising from the increase in aggregate demand.
- Businesses have to increase their purchases of stocks to cope with the increase demand.
- Export orders are likely to rise because a fall in interest rates is likely to lead to a fall in the value of the pound. This makes exports cheaper to foreigners (see unit 52).

Different businesses will react strategically in different ways to significant changes in interest rates which affect aggregate demand. In general, if interest rates fall and aggregate demand rises, this is an opportunity for a business to expand. It should increase investment and take on more workers to increase its output and sales. Conversely, a significant rise in interest rates should lead businesses to cut back their production as sales fall. Cost cutting will be vital to survival if aggregate demand falls sharply.

However, a change in interest rates leading to a change in aggregate demand affects different businesses in different ways. Businesses which rely particularly on their goods being bought on credit, such as car manufacturers, should benefit significantly if interest rates fall. So too should businesses supplying machinery and other investment goods. Construction companies building new houses and offices are likely to enjoy boom times. Businesses serving the export trade should also benefit. A significant fall in interest rates is less likely to be an opportunity for businesses which supply consumer goods not bought on credit. A manufacturer of breakfast cereals, for example, is unlikely to see much increase in sales. Neither is a hairdressing salon.

Exchange rates

The value of the pound fluctuates against other currencies on a minute by minute basis. This affects UK businesses which export and import goods and services (a thorough revision of unit 52 is advisable here). The UK's main trading partner is those countries in the European Union which form part of the eurozone and use the euro as their currency. The UK's second most important trading partner, although a long way behind the eurozone, is the USA. Changes in the value of the pound against the US dollar are important not just for the UK's trade with the USA. Some countries, like China, have unofficially fixed the value of their currency against the US dollar. So changes in the value of the pound against the dollar are important in our trade with some other countries. Equally, some world commodities, such as oil, are priced in US dollars. If their price rises, it is their dollar price that goes up. This will have more or less impact on prices in pounds depending on what is happening to the exchange rate of the pound against the dollar at the same time.

Different businesses will adopt different strategies when the value of the pound on the foreign currency markets changes.

Exporting businesses A change in the value of the pound will affect the the amount of foreign currency needed to buy £1 sterling. Exporters have two main strategies they can adopt in these circumstances. Assume there is a rise in the value of the pound.

- The UK exporter can keep its foreign currency price the same by raising its prices in pounds sterling. Because foreign customers are still paying the same price in their own currencies, they will buy the same amount as before. But the UK exporter will receive more in pounds. Its profit margins will therefore increase.
- Alternatively, the UK exporter can lower its foreign currency price by keeping its price in pounds sterling the same. This should allow it to increase sales because prices to foreign customers will have fallen. This should increase the exporter's profits because of higher sales volumes.

In practice, many UK businesses adopt a mix of these two strategies. Most don't change their prices in pounds sterling on a day to day basis as the the value of the pound fluctuates. Rather, they review prices every six to twelve months and decide on the best strategy in the light of changes in exchange rates.

A fall in the exchange rate will have the opposite effect of a rise and is likely to adversely affect UK exporting businesses. They will have to choose between lowering their UK prices and so cutting their profit margins to maintain sales volumes, or maintaining their UK prices but accepting lower sales volumes because the foreign currency prices of their products will have risen.

Businesses which buy imports Changes in the value of the pound will affect businesses which buy imported products. If the value of the pound falls, then it will take more pounds to buy the same amount of foreign currency. So the price of imports are likely to rise when the value of the pound falls. This will push up costs for businesses which buy imports. Conversely, a rise in the value of the pound will make imports cheaper. The strategic response to a fall in the value of the pound is likely to be to buy fewer imports. UK customers, for example, could switch their spending to UK suppliers. Equally, the strategic response to a rise in the value of the pound is to buy more imports.

Foreign exporting businesses have the same strategic choices as UK exporting businesses when faced with a change in the value of their currency. When the value of the pound changes, they may choose to keep their prices in pounds the same. If this happens, then UK importers will be unaffected by changes in the value of the pound.

UK businesses which compete with foreign imports Many businesses compete with foreign imports in the same market. For example, a UK components manufacturer may compete with German manufacturers. A hotel in Blackpool competes against hotels on the Costa del Sol in Spain. If the value of the pound falls, this is likely to make imports more expensive. This gives UK firms competing against imports an opportunity to gain sales and market shares against foreign imports. When the value of the pound rises, imports become cheaper on average. This will put a UK firm competing against imports at a disadvantage. It will have to decide whether to maintain its prices and possibly lose sales or whether to cut its prices and possibly see profit margins fall.

The implications for the strategy of UK businesses will vary from business to business. Some businesses are hardly affected by changes in the value of the pound. A UK hairdresser or a plumbing services business are unlikely to see any direct change in their costs or sales from a change in the value of the pound. The only significant way they would be affected is if a large change in the exchange rate were to have a major effect on inflation, unemployment or aggregate demand. However, a

Heineken drinkers in the US don't know how lucky they are. Since the dollar began to fall at the end of January 2002, it has lost about one-third of its value against the euro. But the US wholesale prices of Heineken beer, brewed in Holland and exported to the USA, have been increased just twice in that three year period, each time by an average of just 2.5 per cent. The Dutch company's annual operating profit from the USA fell over the period from an estimated €357m to €119m. Heineken has chosen to bear this pain partly because it is afraid that its US customers will migrate to a competitor beer such as Budweiser, brewed in the USA. Heineken is also aware that spirit drinks, such as whisky and vodka, have become increasingly popular in the USA in recent years with a growth in demand for cocktail drinks. Heineken could move its production to the USA but it fears that it will lose its brand image with US customers as a premium imported beer if it does so. It would also lose economies of scale in brewing at its Rotterdam brewery. Moreover, it is cheaper to ship beer from Rotterdam to California than, say, from New York to California.

However, Heineken must look enviously at some European exporters to the USA. Take for instance the luxury goods maker LVMH, which includes the Louis Vuitton brand. Yves Carcelle, president of the company's fashion and leather goods business said that it had consistently been able to raise prices in the US in response to the fall in the value of the dollar. 'We have been permanently readjusting (prices) every three to four months.' Louis Vuitton's ability to persuade its US customers to pay higher prices comes from a long term and continuing investment in its products, marketing and retail outlets in the US. Last week it opened its fifth boutique in Las Vegas, at the vast new Wynn Las Vegas casino resort

Source: adapted from the *Financial Times*, 3.5.2004.

1 **(a) Compare and (b) evaluate Heineken's strategy of dealing with a fall in the value of the dollar to that of LVMH.**

significant change in the exchange rate would have implications for the business strategy of a business which exported products, such as a car manufacturer or an engineering company, or a business which relied heavily on imports. Equally, businesses in markets where there is foreign competition will be affected by significant changes in the exchange rate.

Exporters and businesses which compete with imports, however, can reduce the impact of exchange rate fluctuations if they produce a differentiated product which has a low price elasticity of demand (see unit 17). A low price elasticity of demand means that customer demand will be relatively unchanged even if prices change. Price becomes a less important part of the marketing mix. Changes in price caused by exchange rate fluctuations therefore have relatively little

impact on quantity bought. Product differentiation is then a strategy which some businesses will be able to use to minimise the impact of exchange rate fluctuations on their profits.

Another strategy for exporters and importers is to balance their foreign exchange costs and receipts (see unit 52). For example, a company which exports $30 million worth of goods to the USA may deliberately buy $30 million worth of supplies from the USA. Any fluctuation in the value of the pound against the dollar will have no effect on the UK business because its dollar receipts will be matched by its dollar costs.

Inflation

Inflation is a general increase in prices (a thorough revision of unit 53 is advisable here). So when the government announces that the annual inflation rate last year was 2 per cent, then it means that on average prices have risen by 2 per cent. Within the average, some prices are likely to have fallen, some may have increased but by less than 2 per cent, whilst other prices will have risen by more than 2 per cent.

Inflation affects businesses in a variety of ways. For example, businesses may see rises in the prices they have to pay their suppliers. This increases their costs and could reduce their profits. Businesses may put up the price of their products to their customers. This could increase revenues. However, if competing businesses don't put up their prices, the business could become less competitive and lose sales.

In general, high inflation has mainly negative effects on businesses. Inflation rates of 1 or 2 per cent per annum are broadly neutral. Deflation (i.e. falling prices or negative inflation) can also be bad for businesses. Falling prices across the economy tends to be associated with depressions and slumps.

The main strategic responses of businesses to inflation is to push up their own prices whilst at the same time attempting to minimise the rises in their own costs.

Pushing up prices Moderate to high general inflation in an economy is likely to mean that a business is facing increases in its own costs. Suppliers will be pushing up their prices whilst workers will be demanding higher wages. Businesses can respond strategically to these cost pressures by putting up their own prices and so maintaining their profit margins. Putting up prices will be much easier if competitors are also putting up their prices. Equally, if a business is selling a popular differentiated product, this will reduce the ability of customers to buy elsewhere when prices are raised. However, there is always a danger when putting up prices that sales will fall and market share will be lost.

Reducing costs An alternative strategy to inflationary pressures is to cut costs. For example, a business may buy labour saving equipment in order to cut the cost of labour. It may seek out alternative suppliers willing to charge lower prices. It may look at all its production processes and make changes to increase efficiency in production. Cost cutting is likely to be most successful as a strategy when inflation is relatively low. When inflation is relatively high, the best a business might hope to achieve is to have lower cost inflation than its competitors.

Unemployment and the labour market

Unemployment in the UK has varied considerably over the past 40 years as Figure 54.1 shows (a thorough revision of unit 54 is advisable here). In the 1980s and early 1990s, over 3 million workers were officially unemployed. The problem was almost certainly far worse because at times of high unemployment, many workers without a job, particularly female workers, disappear from the official figures either because they are unable to claim unemployment benefits or because they stop looking for paid employment. In the early twenty first century, unemployment was relatively low.

Both high and low unemployment pose problems and provide opportunities for businesses.

Demand High unemployment is associated with weak demand in the economy. Many businesses will be struggling to maintain sales, let alone increase them. Some will experience falling sales. Luxury goods manufacturers, for example, are likely to be hit as consumers concentrate their spending on necessities. Motor car sales too are likely to be very weak. Businesses will need to respond strategically in a number of ways. Some will attempt to maintain sales by cutting prices even though this will reduce profits. Some will cut production and reduce costs. Capital investment, advertising and research and development often suffer disproportionately when unemployment rises. Businesses with strong balance sheets may attempt to trade through a period of high unemployment, accepting lower profits or even losses to take market share from businesses which are in difficulties. In contrast, low unemployment is associated with strong demand in the economy. It should be relatively easy to grow sales and earn profits in a low unemployment economy. Capital investment, advertising and research and development expenditure is often high because there are strong cash flows to support this. With high unemployment, survival becomes the strongest objective for many businesses. Low unemployment, however, does not guarantee success in the market and some businesses will still find themselves in difficulties.

Recruitment and retention At times of high unemployment, staff turnover tends to fall. Workers are more cautious about leaving because there are far fewer vacancies in the labour market. Equally, there are likely to be far more applicants for job vacancies when unemployment is high. This should allow businesses to recruit good quality workers. At times of low unemployment, staff turnover tends to rise as workers find it easier to get other jobs. Recruiting new workers becomes more difficult. However, prolonged periods of high unemployment can deskill those unemployed. This may lead to recruitment problems even when there are large numbers of workers unemployed. It leads to a mismatch in the market, with employers unable to recruit the right sort of workers whilst there are millions of workers unemployed with insufficient skills. In theory, businesses should respond by increasing their spending on training. In practice, many businesses are unwilling to train workers because they are afraid that the workers once trained will leave to get better jobs elsewhere. For this reason, governments have had to encourage training, either by offering it themselves through different training organisations, or by subsidising training offered by businesses. Another route that businesses sometimes take is to recruit from abroad. EU workers have the right to work in any EU country. So labour shortages in the UK may sometimes be resolved by recruiting workers, for example, from Eastern Europe. In the hospitality industry (e.g. hotels and restaurants) where wages tend to be low, a large proportion of workers are recruited from outside the UK.

Capital investment If unemployment is low and workers difficult to recruit, businesses may react by becoming more capital intensive in their production methods. Employing labour saving equipment may give a business a competitive edge. It may lead to lower costs and an improved quality product. High unemployment tends to discourage capital investment. Labour tends to be easy to obtain and profits are often not high enough to justify new capital spending.

Salaries for young civil engineers have risen twice as fast as inflation since 1999 owing to skill shortages. The Institute of Civil Engineers said that the wage increases were 'due to fewer graduates joining the profession after university'. Big rises in public spending in areas such as transport, health and education as well as rising infrastructure investment by water companies had increased demand for civil engineers. Students, however, were also facing competing demands for their skills from sectors such as financial services, which could offer higher salaries. Road building provided the biggest single area of work last year, accounting for 17 per cent of employment. Work on buildings accounted for another 15 per cent, while work for water companies accounted for 12 per cent.

A serious shortage of construction labourers and skilled tradespeople has encouraged growing use of immigrant labour from Portugal and eastern European countries such as Poland, Ukraine and Lithuania. The Construction Industry Training Board has estimated the industry needs 80 000 new entrants in each of the next five years to meet growth and replace those leaving.

Source: adapted from the *Financial Times*, 27.5.2005.

1 **(a) Explain why businesses have chosen to give young civil engineer graduates above average pay rises since 1999. (b) Do such high pay rises indicate that construction businesses are in trouble?**

2 **Discuss what strategies a construction business could adopt to cope with a shortfall of 'labourers and skilled tradespeople'.**

The business cycle

The business cycle (a thorough revision of unit 50 is advisable here) poses severe strategic problems for businesses. Periodic swings from booms to recessions make it difficult for businesses to plan ahead and to utilise their assets effectively over the whole cycle. In a boom, many businesses have insufficient physical assets and could sell more than they produce. In a recession, they have too many assets including too many workers. They could produce more if only demand were to pick up.

There is a variety of strategic responses to the business cycle. Some businesses expand their productive capacity to match demand in a boom. In industries such as paper manufacturing, shipping and aluminium production, there is a history of strong investment in boom periods followed by too much capacity when the economy goes back into recession. In some industries, particularly where there is little physical capital, it is easier to expand production in a boom and cut back in a recession.

Another strategic response to the business cycle is to attempt to smooth out fluctuations. In a boom, investment is not increased whilst in a recession it is not cut. In a boom, a business may cope with higher demand by taking on temporary workers or increasing overtime. In a recession, core workers are retained even if they are underutilised. This strategy works much more effectively if the business cycle only has a limited impact on the business. The greater the impact, the more a business is likely to incur unsustainable losses if it continues to spend highly through a recession. If a business is highly cyclical, such as construction or luxury goods manufacturing, failing to expand quickly in a boom can lead to a loss of profits.

In the UK, Figure 99.1 shows that there was a prolonged period of economic growth from the mid 1990s, although there was a very mild recession in 2001-2002. A smoothing out of

the business cycle like this gives businesses an ideal economic environment in which to work. Many UK businesses, particularly in manufacturing, have suffered intense competition over this period from overseas firms. But at least they haven't had to worry about unexpected falls in domestic demand.

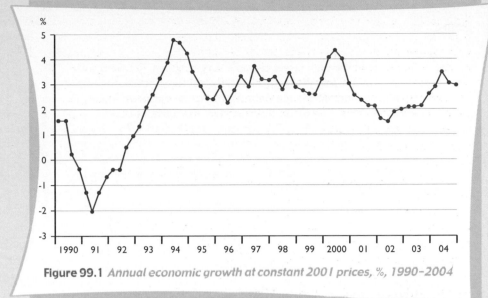

Figure 99.1 *Annual economic growth at constant 2001 prices, %, 1990-2004*

1 What is meant by a 'macroeconomic variable'?
2 Explain how a fall in interest rates can benefit a business.
3 How might a UK exporting business react to a rise in the value of the pound against other currencies?
4 What opportunities might a fall in the value of the pound give to UK businesses competing with imports?
5 How might a business react to significant levels of inflation in the economy?
6 Why might high levels of unemployment in an economy be bad for businesses?
7 What might be the disadvantages to a business of low levels of unemployment in the economy?
8 How might a business react to a downturn in the economy?

keyterms

Macroeconomic environment - **the environment of the whole economy in which a business has to operate.**

Spending in the high street remains very subdued. Retailers such as Boots, Dixons and Woolworths are feeling the pinch. 'I don't see any big macroeconomic change right now that will put more money in consumers' pockets' said Richard Baker, chief executive of Boots. 'Interest rates have gone from 3.5 per cent (in 2003) to 4.75 per cent today (in 2005). That is a 30 per cent increase in the cost of servicing debt. Electricity and fuel bills are up 15-25 per cent, so consumers just have less in their pockets than a year ago and there is nothing I am aware of that will change that.'

Boots has responded to intense competition, particularly from the ever-growing supermarket chain Tesco, by cutting its prices but this has partly contributed to an 11.4 per cent drop in profits for the year for the health and beauty retailer. Boots is now expecting between 0 and 2 per cent rise in sales in the coming year against previous predictions of 3-4 per cent.

At Woolworths, poor sales of music, books and videos has contributed to a 4.4 per cent fall in underlying sales in the first 18 weeks of the year. Nathan Cockerell, an analyst at CSFB, said there was a sense that the company was on borrowed time. 'This management hasn't really had a brainstorming session on strategy for a number of years and I think they will stay behind the curve in trading terms, with the likes of Tesco taking away their market share.'

Even Tesco is saying that it expects sales growth to be more subdued in the coming months. However, its performance shows that sales can be grown even in difficult trading conditions. In 2004, it overtook Marks & Spencer in sales of non-food items including clothing, electricals and homeware. Sales of non-food products at big grocers such as Tesco and Asda have increased by nearly 60 per cent in the past years. Its strategy has been to expand the amount of space in its supermarkets given over to non-food items. Even if sales growth per square foot of space remains subdued, expanding the floor space devoted to non-food items will produce faster growth in sales overall for the supermarket chain.

There is no solution to retailers' woes in sight. Inflation remains near the limits set by the Bank of England and it is unlikely to reduce interest rates much before the end of the year at the earliest. The eurozone remains caught in what many commentators would describe as a mild recession, unable to shift out of very low growth with average unemployment much higher than UK levels. The US economy is doing reasonably well, but many economists fear that it too could go into recession. All this means that Britain's exporters will continue to find it tough to lift their sales. The going will be even tougher if the value of pound rises against the euro and the dollar. It could be argued that the only factor preventing the British economy slipping into recession today with its consequent rise in unemployment is the strong level of government spending.

Source: adapted from the *Financial Times*, 20.5.2005, 21.5.2005, 6.6.2005 and 8.6.2005.

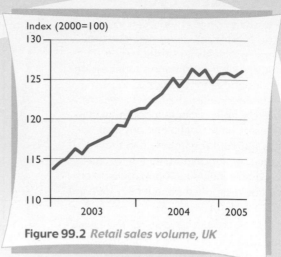

Figure 99.2 *Retail sales volume, UK*

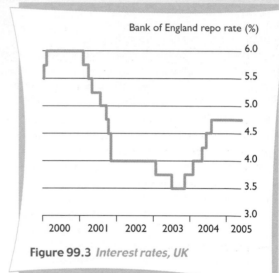

Figure 99.3 *Interest rates, UK*

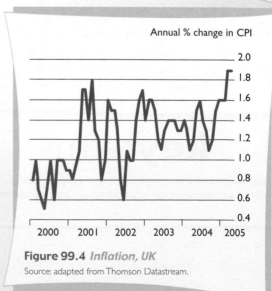

Figure 99.4 *Inflation, UK*

Source: adapted from Thomson Datastream.

1 (a) Explain how high interest rates affected UK retailers in 2004 and 2005. (8 marks)

(b) Evaluate the strategies that retailers could have adopted to combat subdued consumer spending over this period. (12 marks)

2 (a) Explain how higher exchange rates might affect UK retailers. (8 marks)

(b) Discuss whether a fall in the exchange rate would benefit both UK retailers and all other businesses in the economy. (12 marks)

Call centres

Knowledge The structure of the UK economy has been changing rapidly over the past 40 years.

Application In the 1970s, 1980s and 1990s, there was a rapid decline in *manufacturing industry* as British firms lost out to more *internationally competitive* firms, particularly in Europe and Japan. There was also a growing trend for Far Eastern countries such as Taiwan, South Korea and China to gain *international competitiveness*. Since the 1990s, some *service industries* have also been relocating internationally. One example of this is call centres. A wide variety of industries use call centres. Airlines, such as BA, use them to allow customers to book flights over the phone. Banks, such as HSBC, use them for telephone banking. Insurance companies, such as Prudential, use them to sell insurance products.

Analysis Businesses have been able to relocate their call centres because of the growing availability of cheap, educated English speaking workers in countries such as India. The cost of telecommunications has also fallen to the point where phoning, say, India, is little different to that of phoning Leeds. Staff are trained to speak with a UK English accent rather than a local, say, Indian English accent. Sometimes, staff also need be be familiarised with English customs and ways of thinking. But when you can employ graduates in India for less than the cost of unqualified staff in the UK, this is relatively simple.

Evaluation Some service industries will be difficult to export. So hairdressers and dentists are relatively safe from international competition. But other service industries will be able to take advantage of cheap labour overseas to bring down their costs and remain competitive. It can be argued that the whole British economy is under threat and that UK firms will be laying off more and more workers as they transfer jobs abroad. But history suggests that UK firms which survive will be the ones which have adapted and produce unique products which customers want to buy but are not available from other businesses. UK businesses must be encouraged constantly to seek higher value products to sell.

Adapted from *The Sunday Times*, 8.6.2003.

External influences on the business

Most businesses have to compete against other businesses. Some, however, compete on world markets. These range from relatively small businesses, which export part of their production, to large MULTINATIONAL COMPANIES, which have production facilities in more than one country.

Businesses can only survive in these markets if they are INTERNATIONALLY COMPETITIVE. Their customers must choose to buy their products rather those of rival companies. There is a number of factors which determine the extent of international competitiveness of a business.

Production

For a business to be internationally competitive in the long run, it must make sure that its production is efficient. A business will be **productively efficient** when it is producing at lowest cost (see unit 42). In markets for commodity products, such as wheat, computer assembly or call centres, price is one of the most important factors in determining sales so costs have to be kept as low as possible. How can a business improve productive efficiency?

Minimising inputs Part of productive efficiency is technical efficiency, using the least inputs to achieve a given level of output. Some of the ways of minimising inputs are to:
● ensure that employees are working to their full potential all the time. The scientific management school would encourage the use of piece rates for example (see unit 37).

Another approach might be to invest in training;
● minimising wastage of materials, for example by designing products in such a way that the least materials are used;
● using just-in-time production techniques (see unit 47) to minimise stock;
● use machinery and other equipment which will increase the productivity of workers.

Relocation or sourcing To remain internationally competitive, manufacturing businesses in rich industrialised countries have increasingly relocated production facilities in cheap labour Third World countries. Alternatively they have changed the sourcing of their supplies to Third World suppliers. China, for example, is becoming an increasingly important source of products for western markets.

Investment To remain internationally competitive, a business may have to invest in the latest equipment. This may allow it to reduce costs or produce higher quality items.

In certain cases a business may be competitive without being productively efficient.
● Not all businesses compete on price. In a niche market for example, quality or delivery times may be more important. There is less competitive pressure on businesses in niche markets to be productively efficient. However, producing at lowest cost will help maximise profit and shareholder value, which might be part of the objectives of the business.
● In markets where customers are prepared to pay higher prices, costs can be higher too, allowing products to be

produced to higher specifications.

- Ethical and marketing issues may affect production. Certain businesses have been attacked in the press and by pressure groups for using 'sweatshop' factories or child labour in the Third World to manufacture their products. The benefits of buying from cheap Third World suppliers may be outweighed if customers boycott the company in protest. In contrast, businesses such as the Co-op and The Body Shop make a point of sourcing their products from fair trade or ethical businesses around the world to appeal to customers who value this ethical stance.

Labour

Workers are important to the international competitiveness of a business. Increasingly, low skilled manufacturing jobs are being lost in rich industrialised countries to poorer Third World economies. This is because:

- there are abundant supplies of cheap labour;
- workers are prepared to work for a fraction of the wage demanded in rich industrialised countries;
- other employment costs, such as taxes on labour and fringe benefits, are often lower;
- workers are often prepared to work in conditions which would be unacceptable to European or US workers. Indeed, some Third World factories might be closed down if they had to conform to EU health and safety regulations. Not surprisingly, some multinational companies are closing

down factories in rich industrialised countries and opening up new factories in cheap labour economies. Equally, many businesses are switching their purchases of supplies from factories or premises in rich countries to those located in poor countries. The trend has mostly affected manufacturing. However, increasingly services are being affected too. For example, some UK companies are switching their call centres from the UK to Third World countries. When a UK customer rings up about their bank account or to enquire about a travel booking, the call may be answered by a worker in a call centre in India.

To remain internationally competitive, though, businesses in rich industrial countries tend to locate high value added work in their own countries. This is because the workforce is more highly skilled than in the Third World. Tasks such as research and development or complex manufacturing have tended to remain in the rich countries of the world. There are also many service jobs which have to be done locally. A computer manufacturing company might be able to assemble components in Thailand, but its UK sales force needs to be in the UK to make personal contact with customers.

With increasing globalisation, businesses have a greater choice about where to source products and locate their premises. Those which will remain internationally competitive are those which maximise the division of labour to their own advantage.

Goodyear in Wolverhampton was once a major employer in the city. In 1998, it still employed 2 200 workers and the site contained the UK national headquarters offices of the company. By 2004, only 550 workers remained and the UK national headquarters had been moved to Birmingham.

Workers at the site blame the 1998 acquisition by Goodyear of a stake in Sava Tires in Slovenia in Eastern Europe: Goodyear purchased the rest of the company in 2004. The world's biggest tyre company said at the time that the move was 'to further strengthen its position in the rapidly expanding central and eastern European market, as well as consolidating its low-cost sourcing capabilities'. Following the acquisition, Goodyear invested more than £55 million in modernisation at Sava Tires. The international company also has another three plants in Eastern Europe and the Middle East: in Debica, Poland; Izmit in Turkey; and Adapazari, also in Turkey. The four plants between them produced around 40 per cent of the 84 million tyres manufactured last year.

Workers in Eastern Europe are paid a fraction of the wages in the UK. Although wages will eventually catch up, there will be many years to come in which the wage gap will remain substantial. The security of the remaining 550 jobs at Goodyear Wolverhampton is questionable. All that is left is retread work, storage and the mixing and calendering of tyre ingredients for 'export' to other Goodyear Dunlop factories in the UK. But as the production equipment in Wolverhampton becomes due for replacement, Goodyear may decide it makes sense to set up the new lines in its Eastern European plants.

Source: adapted from the *Express & Star*, 8.4.2004.

1 **Explain why moving production from Wolverhampton to Eastern Europe might improve Goodyear's productive efficiency.**
2 **Discuss what might persuade Goodyear to retain remaining production at Wolverhampton.**

Marketing

Successful marketing is vital for businesses which aim to remain internationally competitive. International marketing is no different to other types of marketing. It centres around the '4Ps' of the marketing mix (see unit 1) - product, price, promotion and place.

Product Some multinational companies produce homogeneous goods (see unit 10). Copper, wheat, cotton and steel, whilst having many different grades and types, are the same whether they are produced in the UK, the USA or South Africa. Commodity producers can differentiate their products by entering niche markets. On the whole, however, product is not a unique selling point for such businesses.

For most businesses, their products are different from their competitors. Sony, British Aerospace, Cadbury Schweppes and Intel all attempt to differentiate their products and establish strong brands. There are two approaches to product branding in the international market place. One is to sell an identical product into all markets. For example, the Coca-Cola formulation is the same whether the product is sold in the UK or Nigeria. At the other end of the spectrum, a business may adapt its products to individual markets. McDonald's, for example, sells different menus and different products in India compared to France or the USA.

Producing one product worldwide may make sense from a technical viewpoint. A Rolls Royce aeroplane engine needs to work in exactly the same way whether it is fitted to a US aeroplane or a Saudi Arabian plane. It may also help strengthen the brand image. For Coca-Cola, a worldwide identical product enables it to market its drink as a universal drink. It also gives economies of scale (see unit 42) in areas such as product development and marketing. Choosing a strategy of selling different products into different markets is likely to increase unit costs. However, it is then possible to appeal to a wider range of customers. McDonald's, for example, has to adapt its products for local markets if only to get around religious objections to the eating of meat in various countries. But it also puts ingredients into its products in countries like India and Indonesia to cater for local tastes. Understanding local markets is likely to require market research (see units 4-8), adding to costs.

Price Producers of homogeneous goods have to accept the international market price for their output. Many businesses, however, have some market power to set their own prices. There is a variety of pricing strategies a business could adopt (see units 15 and 16).

- A business may use a competition-based strategy. It could set prices which reflect those of competitors, for example.
- A business may use the market-orientated pricing policy of price discrimination. This is where the same product would be sold at different prices in different countries or groups of countries. Audio and the visual media, books, CDs and DVDs tend to be sold at lower prices in North America compared to Europe, for example. Publishing and media companies exploit the fact that European consumers tend to be less price sensitive than North American consumers. Price discrimination allows a business to maximise its profit in the different markets into which it sells round the world.
- In some industries, cost-plus pricing is used. In defence contracts, for example, a business may win an order where the price is equal to the cost of production plus an agreed mark-up.

Promotion Promotion strategies vary from business to business. Some businesses tend to use the same promotional strategies in whichever country or region they operate. This may extend, for example, to using the same advertising slightly adapted for linguistic differences between target customers. A television commercial for a car being used across Europe would be an illustration. Or a chocolate bar may have the same name whether it is sold in the UK, the USA or Malaysia. Other businesses use different promotional strategies in different countries to reflect different cultures and different ways of doing business.

Which strategy is best depends upon a variety of factors. A business which sells only in Europe, for example, is far more likely to be successful in having one promotional approach than a business which is selling across all continents. Goods which are not culturally specific are far less likely to need targeted marketing.

Place International marketing is dependent upon 'place' in the marketing mix. If a company doesn't have a presence in Australia or China, for example, it is unlikely to sell into those countries. For some companies, like Coca-Cola, having the product available to customers where they want it and when they want it, is vital to their marketing strategies.

Different businesses will need different distribution channels for their products (see unit 19). Most businesses have their own sales teams or trade outlets in the markets into which they sell. A few use agents to seek sales opportunities.

External factors

Not all factors which determine whether a business is internationally competitive are within the control of the business. There is a number of external factors which can affect competitiveness.

Exchange rates Exchange rate movements can affect the competitiveness of individual operations in individual countries. Between 1998 and 2002, when the value of the pound was very high, some UK companies and UK based foreign firms suffered. A rise in the value of pound sterling of 20 per cent, for example, will mean that a UK-based exporter could be forced to raise its prices by up to 20 per cent in foreign currency terms (see unit 52). This would severely affect its international competitiveness.

The business cycle and economic growth When demand is growing in an economy, such as in a boom in the business cycle (see unit 50) or when there is economic growth (see unit 101), it is relatively easy for a business to expand. Often higher sales can lead to economies of scale. Lower costs can then either be used to push down prices and so increase sales further, or increase profit margins. However, if the economy suffers low or negative economic growth for a long time, like Japan in the 1990s, or there is a prolonged depression as occurred in the UK in the early 1990s, businesses are likely to experience spare capacity. This is likely to push up their average costs. In turn, this will make them less internationally competitive compared to businesses in other countries which are not experiencing these difficulties.

Taxes and government grants Governments can tax

China is attracting hundreds of foreign companies to relocate at least some of their production in its economy each year. But companies in Europe and elsewhere can compete in the Chinese market despite the 20 or 30 per cent immediate increase in costs which arise from import duties and shipping costs.

Take the example of GKN, a British vehicle parts manufacturer that is the world leader in constant-velocity joints, vital components used in steering systems, that has a plant in Shanghai in China. GKN supplies car makers such as Volkswagen, Ford and General Motors all of whom have plants in China. But GKN has problems getting top-quality supplies from local Chinese companies. It has been forced to adopt one of two policies as a result. First, it produces more components in house than it would like. Second, 30 per cent of parts bought in are imports into China, well above the company's long term target of 5 per cent.

European companies have benefited from this lack of competitiveness on the part of Chinese suppliers. For example, Precision Technologies International, a UK based company with 85 employees, sends about 40 high-tech moulds a year to GKN's China plant for use in its foundry because the automotive group has failed to find Chinese companies that can make them to a sufficiently high standard. Another example is Pioneer Weston, a British company based in Manchester. This year, it expects to ship about 35 000 small, but highly precise rubber seals to the GKN unit, each costing only about 25p. Again the problem has been poor quality from local Chinese suppliers. 'Quality control is a key part of what we do and we hope that by continuing to improve we can maintain our lead (over Chinese rivals)' explains Mark Newton, Pioneer's export manager. GKN's Shanghai unit also buys all its grease from a German-based subsidiary of the Castrol oil company, and imports special precision forged components from the Liechtenstein plant of Presta, a subsidiary of the German ThyssenKrupp industrial group.

Of course, these European suppliers to GKN could decide themselves to set up in China to service their customers in China. The problem is that the volume of potential sales into the Chinese market does not at the moment justify the investment that would be needed. European jobs may therefore be safe, at least for the moment.

Source: adapted from the *Financial Times*, 23.6.2004.

1 **Explain how companies such as Precision Technologies International remain globally competitive despite being located in the UK.**
2 **Discuss what strategies could be available to companies such as Precision Technologies International if a Chinese company were set up which could compete on quality.**

businesses in a variety of ways. Taxes on profits (corporation tax in the UK) or the employment of labour (Employers' National Insurance contributions in the UK) can have a significant impact on international competitiveness. In the 1980s and 1990s, both the UK and the Republic of Ireland pursued policies of having low taxes on businesses. This helped make factories and businesses in these countries more internationally competitive. In contrast, it is often argued that Germany has become less internationally competitive over the past 20 years because of high taxes on businesses.

Equally, sometimes governments or the EU give grants to businesses to set up factories or plants. In the UK, grants have been given to companies such as Nissan and Lucky Gold (LG) to set up factories in depressed regions of the UK. Such grants should make the difference about whether the factory will be internationally competitive or not.

Trade restrictions International competitiveness is sometimes affected by trade restrictions. For example, a US company might have to pay tariffs to sell goods manufactured in the USA to an EU customer. One way of getting around trade restrictions is to set up a production base in the country or trading bloc which is imposing the restrictions. So, major Japanese motor manufacturing companies now have car plants in the EU to get around import problems.

Education, training and wage rates The long run competitiveness of a country is crucially dependent upon the education and training of the labour force. Education and training make a workforce more productive. So the average UK worker can create more output in money terms than the average Indian or Chinese worker. However, workers in the UK are on average paid much more than the average worker in India or China. Whether a UK business can remain competitive against Indian or Chinese businesses depends therefore upon the relationship between the output and value added of workers to the wages they are paid. Over time, many jobs and businesses are being lost from rich industrialised countries like the UK to Third World countries as wages become too high in the UK and levels of education and training improve in the Third World. Textile companies in the UK, for example, have become less competitive over the past 50 years, forcing most of them to close down. There is little that an individual business can do faced with such large long term changes to remain competitive.

Strategic issues

Businesses have to decide whether competing in international markets will help them achieve their strategic objectives (see units 63 and 64). If so, they then have to decide which markets they will sell into and where they will locate their production facilities. Their decision will be partly based on costs and partly on potential sales. External constraints such as exchange rates and taxes will influence their decision making too.

Operating internationally is likely to increase the risks faced by a business in its activities. Equally, it will considerably increase marketing opportunities. For already large companies, selling globally is the only way they can expand but their domestic markets are too small. However, it opens them up to the competition of other large international companies. Strategic decision making becomes even more important at this level.

checklist

1 Name FOUR multinational companies and explain why they might be called 'multinational'.
2 Why is it important for a business which is internationally competitive to be productively efficient?
3 Why may a business be a high cost supplier and yet still be internationally competitive?
4 Why are labour costs important in international competitiveness?
5 What impact does marketing have on international competitiveness?
6 Explain how the following might affect the international competitiveness of a UK business:
   (a) a rise in the exchange rate of the pound against all other currencies;
   (b) a depression in the US economy;
   (c) a rise in taxes on profits in the UK;
   (d) a rise in UK wage rates.

"key terms"

International competitiveness - **the extent to which a business can sell products to customers in its home market or in a number of different countries.**
Multinational company - **a business which has production facilities in at least two countries, usually selling products into both domestic and export markets.**

Ten years ago, Slovakia would have been an unlikely choice for any car company. In 1998, however, a new Premier, Mikulas Dzurinda, set about reforming the economy and ensuring that it entered the European Union. His government slashed income and corporate taxes to 19 per cent, abolished taxes on dividends, liberalised labour market rules and cut social benefits to improve work incentives. The country has the lowest labour costs in central Europe and are about one sixth those in Germany and one quarter of the EU average. It also has high unemployment rates, which means that there is a large pool of labour from which to draw. The workforce, however, is relatively well educated and is comparable to other Central and Western European countries.

Slovakia has attracted $7 billion in inward investment over the past 10 years. Volkswagen already had a plant at Bratislava, whilst Peugeot chose Slovakia for a new factory in 2003. There are currently 140 automotive suppliers in Slovakia and more can be expected to set up once new car manufacturers establish plants. Slovakia is on target with current investments to have the highest per capita output of cars in the world by 2008. This is not because it is a particularly large producer but because its population, at 5.4 million, is relatively small. The automotive sector now accounts for one quarter of industrial output and 32 per cent of industrial exports.

The Slovak government is offering Hyundai an aid package worth the maximum allowed under EU rules of 15 per cent of the cost of the investment. This includes a free 250 hectare site at Zilina in the north of the country which is close to existing motor parts suppliers in Poland and the Czech Republic as well as Slovakia. Although the site is not yet connected to the motorway network, it will be by the time the site is completed. Slovakia is also offering educational facilities with English as the teaching language, a special healthcare facility, land and property tax relief and extension of public transport to the site.

In the 1990s, Poland gained the reputation of being the most forward looking of the Eastern European economies struggling to transform themselves into market economies. But by 2000 Poland seemed to have run out of steam, and red tape bogged down new investment. Problems were also caused by constantly changing tax laws and bureaucrats who issued often contradictory interpretations of tax regulations. Recently, Poland lost out when Peugeot decided to site a new plant in Slovakia whilst Toyota and Peugeot in a joint venture decided to site a car plant in the Czech Republic. To get around these problems, the prime minister, Leszek Millier, has become directly involved, guaranteeing all the provisions being negotiated with the South Korean carmaker.

Poland is offering Kobierzyce, near Wroclaw in the heavily industrialised Silesia. Although most of Poland's roads are in a poor condition, Wroclaw does have a better than average infrastructure linking it with Germany. Kobierzyce is already the site of more than 60 investment projects. It is offering a free 250 hectare plot of land, a Korean language school, as well as help with infrastructure.

Poland currently has more developed car supply industry than Slovakia, although Slovakia has a number of plant developments on stream to be completed over the next few years.

Poland is also promising to back Hyundai in the EU, contrasting its 38 million people and status as a power to be reckoned within Brussels compared to Slovakia's relatively lightweight position in the EU.

Hyundai is a fast growing South Korean company with ambitions to become the fifth largest motor manufacturing company in the world. It has spent eight years searching for a new site in Europe to expand its production. It wants to be within the European Union both to avoid trade restrictions on imports into the EU and to take advantage of lower transport costs. It has chosen to look for a site which will produce small Kia cars. Initial production is planned for up to 300 000 cars per year with a workforce of 2 800.

It has finally narrowed down its choice to two sites, one in Poland and the other in Slovakia. Both are about to become full members of the European Union.

Source: adapted from the *Financial Times*, 10.2.2004, 27.4.04; Eastern Europe, 10.12.2004, BBC News 2.03.2004.

1 Discuss which of the two sites in the data could most help make Hyundai internationally competitive. (20 marks)

UK growth

Knowledge In 2005, the UK could look back on the longest period of recorded economic growth.

Application *National income* had been rising every *quarter* since 1991. Over this period, *economic growth* or *annual growth* in *gross domestic product at constant prices* had varied from 0.26 per cent to 4.5 per cent. With low *inflation* over the period, growth in *GDP at current prices* averaged around 3 per cent more than GDP at constant prices.

Analysis Positive economic growth has benefited businesses in a variety of ways. For companies like Tesco, British Telecom and Barclays Bank, it has allowed increased sales, usually linked to increased profits. Businesses have been able to invest with some confidence that domestic markets at least are likely to grow. Stakeholders such as workers also benefit because their jobs are likely to be more secure. Economic growth can have its disadvantages. It may bring with it increased pollution and congestion. Companies which transport goods lose millions of pounds each year because their lorries are delayed in traffic jams. Industries like gas and electricity generation have higher costs because they have to limit the pollution they create.

Evaluation Economic growth is generally seen as an advantage by most businesses. The opposite, a contracting economy, is certainly harmful to most business interests. However, not all businesses benefit equally from economic growth. In recent years, for example, a booming economy has favoured mobile phone companies and computer manufacturers. On the other hand, food manufacturers have faced more difficult times because spending on food has not been rising in line with increases in income. Economic growth also doesn't guarantee success for a company in a fast growing sector of the economy. Businesses can fail whilst their competitors are recording high growth in sales.

Measurement of economic growth

Over time, economies tend to grow in size. More goods and services are produced. Economic growth (see unit 50) is defined as growth in the productive potential of the economy. This productive potential is determined by factors such as:

- the amount of **physical capital**, such as machines, factories, roads and schools;
- the amount of **human capital** (see unit 92), the education, training and experience of the population;
- the availability of natural resources, from farmland to oil reserves.

It is not possible to measure the productive potential of an economy directly. Instead, a proxy measure is used. This is the actual output of the economy, which is generally measured by gross domestic product (GDP). It is a way of putting into money terms the value of total production over a period of time.

Statisticians calculate GDP by adding together data from millions of different forms that individuals and businesses have to submit to government. These include income tax and VAT returns. The final figure is a money total, such as £105 billion. On its own, this is not a particularly useful statistic. Users typically want to compare one GDP figure with another. For example, a user might want to know by how much GDP has changed since the last period. If GDP during the last period was £100 billion, then we know that GDP has increased by £5 billion from a base of £100 billion, which is a 5 per cent increase.

Not all of this 5 per cent increase will necessarily be an increase in **physical production**. Part of it is likely to be an increase in **prices**. If the inflation rate (see unit 53) in the last period was 2 per cent, then the increase in physical output would be the other 3 per cent of the 5 per cent increase. 3 per cent is then the REAL increase in GDP. 5 per cent is the MONEY increase. Real increases are measured AT CONSTANT PRICES to show that the effect of inflation has been taken out. Money increases are measured AT CURRENT PRICES to show that measurements are being taken at whatever price level is present at the time.

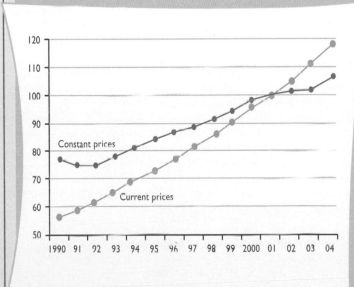

Figure 101.1 *GDP at current and constant prices, 2001=100*

	At current prices	At constant prices
1991	5.18	-1.43
1992	4.24	0.26
1993	5.05	2.23
1994	6.05	4.50
1995	5.56	2.83
1996	6.26	2.75
1997	6.01	3.38
1998	6.01	3.04
1999	5.09	2.84
2000	5.29	3.93
2001	4.60	2.25
2002	5.00	1.80
2003	5.52	2.16
2004	5.14	3.08

Table 101.1 *Economic growth: % change in GDP at current and constant prices*

Figure 101.1 shows how GDP has grown over time. GDP at current prices is much higher by the end of the period than GDP at constant prices. The price level which is being used is 2001. So the 2004 current price figure, for example, has been adjusted to take account of the inflation that has occurred over the period 2001 to 2004.

Table 101.1 shows the rate of economic growth as measured by GDP. The rate of growth of GDP at current prices is higher than that of growth at constant prices. This is because there has been inflation in each year.

Local, national and international activity

Levels of output differ from region to region and country to country. For example, the USA has the highest output in the world whatever measure is used. It has the highest GDP as a whole economy, it has the highest GDP per head of the population and it has the highest GDP at constant prices when the effects of different price levels between countries have been stripped out.

In the UK, the region with the highest output and the highest output per head of the population is the South East of England, as shown in Table 101.2. In 2003, the region with lowest output was Wales. However, if output per head is used, the lowest level of economic activity was the North East of England. Over time, economic growth rates differ between regions. Regional policy in the EU (see unit 102) and in the UK (see unit 103) attempts to raise the growth rates of poorer regions to bring their income per head nearer to the average for the EU or the UK.

Some businesses located in poorer regions may benefit because they are able to get government or EU grants for equipment or training of staff. This is a potential source of finance (see unit 25). Poorer regions also tend to have lower average wage rates. So businesses are located in these regions but sell mainly to other regions, like a manufacturing company, may gain a competitive advantage. On the other hand, levels of education and training are often lower in poor regions. So businesses located there may find it difficult to recruit the right quality staff. Service businesses located in poorer regions also tend to have to offer lower prices than average because their customers tend to have below average incomes for the country or the EU.

Globalisation (see unit 2) has allowed some former poorer countries in the world, such as South Korea, Thailand, Singapore and China to experience high levels of economic growth over the past 10 years. Other countries, such as many African countries, have actually seen a decline in their output per head. Often this has been due to a rapidly increasing population. But it may also be due to economic and political mismanagement by government. Their GDP growth has failed to keep pace with population growth, resulting in lower GDP per head over time. These trends have very important implications for both domestic businesses, exporters and multinationals, as discussed below.

	GDP £ billion	GDP per head £
United Kingdom	952	15 980
North East	32	12 736
North West	98	14 346
Yorkshire and Humberside	71	14 222
East Midlands	622	14 505
West Midlands	77	14 538
East	95	17 452
London	155	20 990
South East	149	18 411
South West	75	15 038
Wales	37	12 629
Scotland	78	15 409
Northern Ireland	22	12 971

Table 101.2 *GDP and GDP per head by region, 2003*
Source: adapted from *Economic Trends*, Office for National Statistics, February 2005.

In December 2004, a devastating tsunami, a giant wave caused by an earthquake on the sea bed in Indonesia, hit a number of coastlines bordering the Indian Ocean. Countries hard hit included Indonesia, Sri Lanka, the Maldives and Thailand. Around 220 000 people were killed and many coastal towns were destroyed.

A number of industries were affected, including fishing and agriculture. But of particular significance to some countries was the effects on the tourist industry. The World Travel and Tourism Council has estimated that the tsunami will cost the global tourism industry close to $3bn (£1.6bn) and more than than 250 000 lost jobs. Infrastructure, including hotels and roads, were destroyed. Tourists have stayed away for fear of another natural disaster or they have been diverted to other tourist destinations because resorts were too badly damaged for them to holiday there.

The effect on economic growth of these economies, however, is likely to be less than 1 per cent of GDP. The tsunami only affected some coastal regions in the countries affected. Reconstruction of infrastructure will create incomes and jobs. There was also a very large international aid response to the disaster which will have injected cash into the local economies affected.

Source: adapted from the *Financial Times*, 9.4.2004.

1 **Explain why growth in GDP will have fallen in countries affected by the tsunami.**
2 **A British couple owned a bar on the sea front in a Thai tourist resort which was completely destroyed by the tsunami and they themselves lost their lives. How might this have affected the productive potential of the Thai economy?**
3 **An international hotel group saw its hotel in the Maldives severely damaged by the tsunami. Discuss whether or not it should rebuild the hotel quickly, and what impact its decision will have on the economic growth of the local economy.**

The determinants of economic growth

Why some economies grow at a faster rate than other economies is a complex issue. There is no single factor which causes economic growth. However, economists agree that the following help to maintain or to increase the rate of growth of an economy.

Investment in physical capital Investment by businesses and by government creates the physical capital needed to increase the productive capacity of an economy. Sometimes, investment is wasted. When a business buys a new machine but it lies unused because of lack of demand, then that investment has failed to increase economic growth. However, if there is not enough investment in an economy, this can act as a constraint on growth.

Investment in education and training Workers are just as important as machines in production. In service industries in particular, output often depends on the skills of workers. It takes a long time to build up the levels of education, training and experience that is present in the rich industrialised countries of the world. It has been suggested that one of the key factors holding back economies in countries such as Pakistan, Tanzania or Peru may be insufficient investment in people.

Good governance and the institutional framework Government policies and the institutional framework of an economy are vital. For businesses to thrive, for example, laws must exist. Property rights must be enforceable. There must be institutions such as a Central Bank and a banking system which will keep prices stable and allow businesses to borrow and lend. Governments must implement sound fiscal and monetary policies (see unit 103). Taxation must not affect businesses or their customers too greatly. Government spending should be adequate in areas such as education, health care and transport. Government policies which promote long term economic growth are known as **supply side policies** (see unit 103).

Openness to international trade Many governments and businesses have believed that economic growth could be stimulated by PROTECTIONISM. This is where foreign goods are deliberately kept out through the use of measures such as TARIFFS (taxes or customs duties on imports) and QUOTAS (limits on the quantity of goods allowed to be imported into the country). The argument is that, free from foreign competition, domestic businesses could thrive. Jobs would be safeguarded, allowing more spending in the economy. New industries could grow without being driven to the wall in their early stages by strong foreign competition.

However, evidence from the past 100 years suggests that countries which open themselves to trade are likely to grow faster than those which adopt protectionist policies. Countries which have benefited from globalisation, like China, South Korea and Hong Kong, have done so by lifting trade barriers. FREE TRADE policies force domestic industries to be competitive. Only the strongest businesses survive, but they become the engines of growth for the economy.

The benefits of economic growth

Economic growth can benefit consumers and businesses.

Consumption The main benefit of economic growth to society is that is allows individuals to consume more goods and services over time. In the UK for example, current economic growth rates are allowing average incomes per person roughly to double every 25 years. Compared to 25 years ago, the average UK citizen owns far more goods, lives in better housing, takes more holidays and lives longer because of better health care.

Business opportunities Economic growth provides opportunities for businesses. In a growth environment, sales of most products increase over time. Therefore, businesses should be able to expand their own sales and earn higher profits. When GDP falls when there is a depression, as in 1990-92 in the UK, many businesses struggle just to survive. The percentage of businesses which are forced to cease trading increases. This affects all stakeholders in a business. Owners lose their capital invested in the business, workers lose their jobs, suppliers lose orders and possibly money which is owed to them and the local community in which the business operates becomes poorer.

Some businesses and industries will benefit more than others. As incomes rise, consumers spend more of the increase on some products than others. Products such as foreign holidays, education and computers have a higher income elasticity of demand (see unit 17) than products such as bread, jam and coal. Those businesses supplying products with a higher income elasticity will benefit the most from economic growth.

The costs of economic growth

Economic growth, however, also has disadvantages.

Sustainability Raw materials such as coal, oil and iron ore are used up when producing goods and services. Once used, these can never be replaced. Some argue that anywhere between 50 and 500 years time, economies will collapse because they won't have the raw materials to sustain current levels of production. Their solution is to cut back on production today, which would severely damage business interests.

Environmental problems Any production has an environmental impact (see unit 106). For example, production uses energy such as gas or electricity. Production and use of most forms of energy leads to greenhouse gas emissions which most agree is causing global warming. Governments have reacted to the environmental costs of production by introducing measures to limit production. Planning laws prevent businesses from setting up anywhere they choose. Waste disposal laws prevent businesses dumping rubbish wherever they want. EU regulations are forcing businesses to limit the amount of packaging they can use. Car manufacturers are being made responsible for the recycling of old cars. Businesses are strictly controlled in the level of emissions permitted. There are taxes on fuel and waste to discourage use. Ultimately, the costs imposed on businesses by environmental measures are passed onto customers. However, those businesses which have the highest additional costs will have to raise their prices more than businesses which are little affected. This will result in lower demand for products which have a high environmental cost. It is these businesses which will be hardest hit.

Health and lifestyle Economic growth can have other unintended negative effects. Consumers in rich countries eat more food than, say, 50 years ago. But with cars and less manual work, they take less exercise. The result is growing levels of obesity amongst both children and adults. Governments may choose in future to take measures such as raising taxes on food to discourage eating. This will harm many firms in the food industry, from food manufacturers to farmers to fast food outlets.

Quality of life Economic growth has also changed the pattern of work in society. In rich industrialised countries, the trend has been for increasing numbers of women to go from working unpaid in the home to taking on paid work in factories and offices. Whilst manual workers and junior non-manual workers have tended to see their work hours stabilised at around 35-40 hours per week, many professional white collar workers have seen their hours of work if anything increased. Stress in the workplace, arising from employers wanting to increase worker productivity, has risen. Many argue that these trends have led to a deterioration in the quality of life for individuals and families.

If the anti-growth policies of pressure groups like Greenpeace or Friends of the Earth were to be implemented, businesses in the UK would almost certainly suffer. Many would cease trading. Others would have to scale down their operations. For these reasons, pro-business pressure groups like the CBI or trade union groups like the TUC are in favour of policies which promote economic growth.

✓ checklist

1 Explain why economic growth comes about through increased availability of human and physical capital.
2 What is the difference between measuring economic growth in terms of current prices and constant prices?
3 What is the difference between the output of a region and its output per head?
4 The price of a McDonald's meal is cheaper in India than it is in the UK. Suggest why this might be the case.
5 Briefly explain what are the determinants of economic growth.
6 Why does economic growth tend to benefit businesses?
7 How can economic growth harm the interests of businesses?

Growing affluence has meant that food is now a cheap commodity available to all in the Western world. Even the poorest in society are able to afford eat quantities of food which would have been unimaginable 50 years ago. Food has also become something which consumers typically buy processed from food manufacturers. Fewer and fewer people cook from raw ingredients. Convenience food out of a packet or a tin is the growing norm. Food manufacturers, in turn, provide customers with what they most want to eat. For biological reasons, customers love high calorie, high energy food, typically with plenty of fat, sugars and salt. The result is arguably growing obesity in the affluent populations of North America and Europe.

There is a growing call for governments to step in and intervene, for example with the problem of children and advertising. In January 2001, Markos Kyprianou, EU health and consumer affairs commissioner, warned in an interview with the *Financial Times*, that urgent action was needed. He believed self-regulation in the food industry was the quickest and most effective way to tackle the problem but 'if this doesn't produce satisfactory results, we will proceed to legislation'. The European Commission can initiate legislation under rules covering the EU single market or on consumer protection grounds. It recently banned tobacco advertising under these rules.

The CIAA, the food industry's umbrella group in Europe, said it was already working with the European Commission to develop new proposals for more rigourous advertising and labelling regimes. 'There is a need for improvement, but there is no magical solution for doing this in practical terms,' it said, adding it would be pressing for self-regulation rather than legislation. The US food industry is already changing its practices in response to pressure from health campaigners. Kraft Foods said the week before the FT interview that it would stop marketing products such as the popular Orea biscuits directly to children.

Markos Kyprianou said he wanted other companies which sell products with high fat, sugar or salt content to follow suit. 'I would like to see the industry not advertising directly to children any more,' he said. He also urged food manufacturers to adopt clearer labelling 'more easily understood by a consumer who doesn't have a PhD in chemistry.' The commissioner will announce a new 'platform' in March with the food industry to agree the new self-regulatory standards, which he hoped would produce commitments by the end of 2005, or early 2006. In the UK, initiatives are being discussed to cut television advertising of junk food to children.

Source: adapted from 'EU legal threat to junk food advertising', msnbc.msn.com, 19.1.2005.

---

1 **Using the example of food, explain how economic growth might harm consumers.**
2 **Discuss whether it would be in the best interests of food manufacturers and consumers to achieve 'self-regulation rather than legislation' on advertising and food labelling.**

keyterms

Constant or real prices - prices which have been adjusted for the effects of inflation.
Current or money prices - prices which have not been adjusted for the effects of inflation.
Free trade - the import and export of goods and services with no barriers to trade such as tariffs or quotas.

Protectionism - government policies aimed at limiting the import of products into a country.
Quotas - limits on the physical quantity of products that can be imported into a country.
Tariffs - taxes, also called customs duties, on goods being imported into a country.

Tesco, the UK's largest supermarket chain, plans to open more than 40 stores in central Europe this year as it seeks growth outside its home market. Tesco, which has about 194 stores across Poland, the Czech Republic, Slovakia and Hungary, intends to increase that number to at least 234 stores.

Tesco has enjoyed enormous success in its UK market in recent years and it is continuing to take market share from other grocery retailers. Like for like sales (sales from existing stores) growth in the year to 26 February 2005 was up 9 per cent, although the company is being cautious in its prediction for 2005-2006 saying that sales growth will be only 3-4 per cent. Overall UK sales were up 11.0 per cent to £29.5bn and profits by 13.1 per cent. This included sales and profit from stores opened over the 12 month period. Non-food sales grew by 17 per cent, and within that clothing sales grew by 28 per cent. Tesco intends to continue developing its UK offering. At the moment, only 200 of its 1 900 UK stores offer clothing. It can look enviously at Asda which is now the largest clothes retailer in the UK. Tesco also has only 7 per cent of the market for all non-food items in the UK. But home entertainment sales grew by 20 per cent last year, stationery news and magazines by 26 per cent and health and beauty by 13 per cent. There is considerable room for gains in market share in all these non-food categories.

Abroad, at constant exchange rates, sales grew by 18.3 per cent in the year to 26 February 2005 and profits grew by 21.4 per cent. The strengthening of the pound meant that sales grew by 13.4 per cent and actual exchange rates and profits by 18.5 per cent. The expansion plans in Eastern Europe came against a backdrop of rising sales and profits in the region. In Hungary, Tesco is the market leader, and it plans to increase its number of stores by 16 to 85. In the Czech Republic, where profits grew by 20 per cent last year, there will be 8 new store openings this year. In Poland, floor space will be expanded by 14 per cent.

Eastern Europe states are expected to grow very strongly over the next 10-20 years as they catch up with the more mature economies of Western Europe. Countries such as Hungary, Poland and the Czech Republic which joined the EU in 2004 have the advantage that they are now within one of the world's largest trading blocs, with free access for their products to other EU countries.

Source: adapted from the *Financial Times* 12.4.2005, 13.4.2005, PricewaterhouseCoopers European Economic Outlook February 2005

1 Tesco could use the cash it is spending in Eastern Europe on expansion within the UK. Evaluate the case for and against Tesco concentrating its resources more on its core UK markets.
(20 marks)

2 Discuss the impact that the expansion of Tesco could have on the economies of Eastern Europe and its stakeholders within those countries.
(20 marks)

	2002	2003	2004 (estimate)	2005 (forecast)	2006 (forecast)
UK	1.8	2.2	3.2	2.5	2.5
Poland	1.4	3.8	5.7	4.9	4.5
Hungary	3.5	2.9	3.8	3.8	3.8
Czech Republic	1.5	3.1	3.8	3.9	4.0

Table 101.3 *Annual growth in GDP, %*

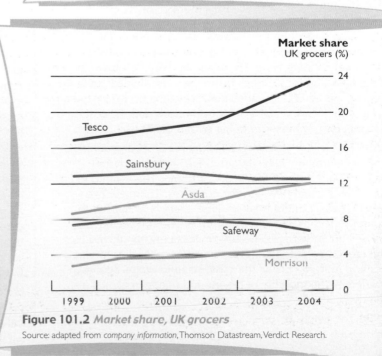

Market share
UK grocers (%)

Tesco
Sainsbury
Asda
Safeway
Morrison

1999 2000 2001 2002 2003 2004

Figure 101.2 *Market share, UK grocers*

Source: adapted from *company information*, Thomson Datastream, Verdict Research.

Vodafone

Knowledge In April 2005, Vodafone announced that it was paying $3.5bn (£1.8bn) to take control of the Romanian mobile phone group Mobifon and the Czech wireless group Oskar Mobil. These stakes were being bought from the Canadian company, TIW.

Application Vodafone is the world's largest mobile phone *company* by *revenues*. Oskar has a *market share* of the Czech mobile phone *market* of 17 per cent and is the third largest mobile phone operator in the country. Vodafone already owns 21 per cent of Mobifon and by buying the remaining 79 per cent will gain the *controlling stake* in the company. Mobifon has a market share of 48 per cent. The Czech Republic is already a member of the *European Union (EU)* and Romania is an *emerging market* which has applied to join the EU.

Analysis Vodafone is expanding its interests in two economies with high growth prospects and with a combined population of 32 million, a little over half that of the UK. Although mobile phone penetration is higher in the Czech Republic than in the UK at 105 per cent (i.e. there are 105 subscribers per 100 of the population), Oskar has been seeing sales growth of 35 per cent per annum. In Romania, mobile phone penetration is 47 per cent and Mobifon has been seeing annual sales growth of 30 per cent. In both countries, mobile phones have proved attractive because many rural homes are not connected to any land telephone line. Vodafone expects to see strong growth in revenues in the future from these companies. It will also be able to exploit purchasing, technological and marketing economies of scale, helping to reduce long run costs.

Evaluation Vodafone is already the most important world player in the mobile phone market measured by sales. These new acquisitions, although small by Vodafone's standards, will help the company maintain momentum. They fit strategically with the company's aims of increasing investment in the growth markets of Central and Eastern Europe. Both should prove to be profitable as revenues increase but average costs fall. However, there is always risk in acquisitions and there is no guarantee that Vodafone has not overpaid for these assets.

Adapted from Vodafone, Vodafone to acquire control of Mobifon in Romania and Oskar in the Czech Republic, 15 March 2005.

The history of the European Union

The UK has been a member of the EUROPEAN UNION (EU) since 1973. Around 60 per cent of UK exports and imports of goods are to and from the EU. So the EU is by far the largest trading partner for the UK.

The UK has been a reluctant partner within the EU. It refused to join when the EU was established in 1956. It has tended to resist changes which would deepen both economic and political integration. For example, the UK refused to join the Single Currency. British businesses are divided about the benefits of the EU. To understand why, it is necessary to know about the history of the EU, its institutions and the costs and benefits for businesses of being within the EU.

1956 The Treaty of Rome In 1956, six European countries, France, Germany, Italy, Belgium, the Netherlands and Luxembourg , signed the Treaty of Rome. This established a Common Market between the countries. There are two aspects to a common market. First, there is a CUSTOMS UNION. This exists when a group of countries remove all barriers to trade of goods and services between themselves but erect a common tariff (see unit 101) barrier to products coming in from outside the customs union area. Second, barriers to the mobility of labour and financial capital are removed.

1986 The Single European Act In practice, whilst barriers to trade such as tariffs and quotas had been removed between

member countries, there remained many other barriers to trade. For example, individual governments still regularly only gave contracts to domestic suppliers. Banks couldn't operate freely across the whole EU. So in 1986, member countries agreed to deepen economic links by removing these barriers to create a SINGLE EUROPEAN MARKET by December 31st 1992. This would greatly increase MARKET ACCESS for businesses in one country to another country.

1991 The Maastricht Treaty This treaty gave greater powers to the EU to create common policies in the areas of social affairs, industrial affairs, education, defence and health. For example, EU legislation states that workers should not work more than 48 hours per week. The Maastricht Treaty also set the EU the goal of creating a monetary union, abolishing individual currencies and creating one currency for the whole union.

2002 The launch of the euro On 1st January 2002, most EU countries replaced their currencies with the euro. This eliminated a major barrier to trade. The UK decided not to participate in the single currency at the time. UK companies therefore still faced exchange rate risks and the cost of exchanging pounds for euros when trading with the rest of Europe. The group of countries which have adopted the single currency is often called the EUROZONE.

Over time, the size of the European union has grown as Figure 102.1 shows. The EU started with six countries in 1956. In 1973, the UK joined along with Denmark and Eire.

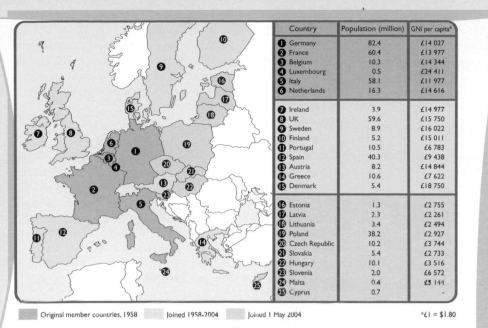

Country	Population (million)	GNI per capita*
❶ Germany	82.4	£14 027
❷ France	60.4	£13 977
❸ Belgium	10.3	£14 344
❹ Luxembourg	0.5	£24 411
❺ Italy	58.1	£11 977
❻ Netherlands	16.3	£14 616
❼ Ireland	3.9	£14 977
❽ UK	59.6	£15 750
❾ Sweden	8.9	£16 022
❿ Finland	5.2	£15 011
⓫ Portugal	10.5	£6 783
⓬ Spain	40.3	£9 438
⓭ Austria	8.2	£14 844
⓮ Greece	10.6	£7 622
⓯ Denmark	5.4	£18 750
⓰ Estonia	1.3	£2 755
⓱ Latvia	2.3	£2 261
⓲ Lithuania	3.4	£2 494
⓳ Poland	38.2	£2 927
⓴ Czech Republic	10.2	£3 744
㉑ Slovakia	5.4	£2 733
㉒ Hungary	10.1	£3 516
㉓ Slovenia	2.0	£6 572
㉔ Malta	0.4	£5 144
㉕ Cyprus	0.7	-

■ Original member countries, 1958   ■ Joined 1958-2004   ■ Joined 1 May 2004

*£1 = $1.80

Figure 102.1 *The EU, 2005*

Source: adapted from Eurostat, UNCTAD, Malta NSO.

By 2004, there were 25 countries, including several from the former Soviet bloc in Eastern Europe. The EU is now comparable in size to the United States. More countries wished to join after 2004, include Romania, Bulgaria and Turkey.

European institutions

There are four main institutions which govern the EU.

The European Commission The European Commission (EC) is located in Brussels. It is responsible for proposing policy and legislation to the European Council of Ministers. Once accepted, it is then responsible for implementing that policy and legislation. The EC is headed by the President of the European Commission who is responsible for acting in the interests of the EU. Commissioners are appointed to represent each member country.

The Council of Ministers The Council of Ministers is made up of ministers from each member country who meet on a regular basis. Twice a year, heads of government from each country also meet at the European Council. The Council of Ministers is the decision making body of the EU. It approves or rejects proposals from the European Commission about new regulations and directives.

The European Parliament The European Parliament is based in Strasbourg. Voters in EU countries elected MEPs, Members

In April 2005, a preliminary judgment from the European Court of Justice gave victory to Marks & Spencer (M&S) in a battle over taxes. M&S had wanted to offset the losses it had made in France, Germany and Belgium against profits made in the UK. This would have reduced the amount of corporation tax the company would have paid in the UK by around £30 million. The UK Inland Revenue had declared that the company could not do this. Only losses made in the UK could be offset against profits made in the UK by the company.

The preliminary ruling from the European Court of Justice agreed with M&S that the Inland Revenue's policy breached a core European treaty principle: that member states cannot hinder an EU national in one country from establishing a business in another. The preliminary ruling stated that a group relief scheme that does not allow a parent company to deduct the losses of its foreign subsidiaries under any circumstances is incompatible with European law. The ruling rejected the Inland Revenue argument that a national government cannot offer a tax advantage to a subsidiary based in a foreign country where it has no power of taxation.

However, the ruling does seem to prevent 'double dipping': where a company reclaims tax on the same losses in two countries. The ruling says that where a government allows subsidiaries of foreign companies to claim tax relief on losses made, then those tax benefits must be claimed in that country.

What made the Marks & Spencer case special was that the company pulled out of continental Europe in the early 2000s because it was making losses on these operations. So it had no prospect of future profits against which it could offset these losses in Belgium, France and Germany.

Source: adapted from the *Financial Times*, 8.4. 2005.

1 **Explain why Marks & Spencer was able to appeal against a UK tax ruling.**
2 **Both the Treaty of Rome and the Single European Act mean that 'member states cannot hinder an EU national in one country from establishing a business in another'. How could membership of the EU both (a) benefit and (b) harm the interests of a UK company like Marks & Spencer?**

of the European Parliament, to sit in the parliament. Its role is to comment on proposals put forward by the European Commission to the Council of Ministers. It does not have the power to make laws as in national parliaments. Its major power, which it has used once, is that it can dismiss the President of the European Commission and European Commissioners.

The European Court of Justice The European Court of Justice is the final court of law within the European Union. Its decisions are binding. Individual citizens and businesses can appeal to the European Court of Justice against decisions made in local or national courts. The European Court of Justice bases its decisions on EU law.

EU laws are called **directives**. In some cases, these have to be agreed by all member countries through the Council of Ministers. In other cases, they can be passed if a majority of countries agree. Directives become EU law by being made law in each individual national parliament. The European Commission then has the power to issue **regulations** based on these directives. Directives tend to be broad and general in nature. Regulations are specific and detailed.

Creating a pan-European strategy

The EU provides UK businesses with export opportunities. The low barriers to trade which exist within the EU make it easier on the whole for a UK company to export into the EU than to, say, the USA or Japan.

However, the EU is also a threat for some UK businesses. Just as the EU makes it easier for UK exports to sell into Europe, so it is easier for other EU businesses to sell into the UK. When products are traded, the EU increases the potential competition in the domestic market.

To survive in a competitive EU market, UK businesses which face increased imports or have the opportunity to increase exports must therefore develop a pan-European strategy. A strategy is a set of plans which when implemented will achieve the objectives of the business (see unit 64). Strategies should be realistic and therefore they should take account of the current trading position of the business and, its strengths and weaknesses in areas such as products, marketing and human resources. They also need to reflect the ability of the business to change. For example, plans must not be so ambitious that they cannot be financed.

Pan-European strategies can include a number of different ways of dealing with the opportunities and threats that come from larger markets and increased competition.

Operations management The production operations of a business may be affected by Britain's membership of the EU.
● The Single Market means that businesses can source supplies relatively easily across the EU. Transport costs and the need for fast deliveries may make foreign supplies uncompetitive. However, in many cases, businesses can reduce their costs by taking advantage of the large market.
● A more radical measure to reduce costs is to relocate. Some foreign companies from the USA and Japan, for example, have closed factories in the UK and relocated them in lower wage EU countries. Some UK companies have closed their factories and relocated in the EU to take advantage of transport links. This allows them to gain

economies of scale in production. Conversely, businesses in other EU countries have developed plants in the UK.
● Some businesses have to set up near to their customers. Service businesses like Tesco, the supermarket chain have established outlets in some EU countries. Equally, just-in-time delivery systems may force UK manufacturers to set up near their customers to retain orders.

Marketing A pan-European strategy will be centred around the 4Ps of the marketing mix.
● The EU gives UK businesses the opportunity to sell into a much larger market than just the UK. To take advantage of this, a business may have to increase its product range. For example, national preferences may have to be recognised. Different standards and specifications may have to be adhered to. Competition though may force a business to slim down its product range. By concentrating on fewer products, perhaps become a niche player in the market, a business can specialise and so gain a competitive advantage. Businesses also have to make strategic decisions on names and packaging. Should the same product be sold under the same brand name across the EU? Should common packaging be used whether the product is sold in the UK, Italy or Poland?
● Increased competition within the EU may force a business to lower its prices. Increased size to achieve economies of scale may be one way of achieving this. Many businesses price differentiate in different national markets. Charging different prices allows them to maximise profits. Alternatively, some businesses may charge the same prices across the EU, reducing marketing costs.
● Businesses face the same decisions about promotion. Should they have different promotional campaigns in each country or region of the EU or should they adopt a common approach across the EU? Adopting a common approach gives economies of scale in marketing. However, national markets may differ depending upon what product is being sold.
● The importance of place varies from product to product. Service industries, such as retailing or hotels, depend on location for their success. A component manufacturer, on the other hand, may find that it can be located anywhere in the EU so long as its products can be transported safely within a given time to its customers. With more and more trade occurring between EU member countries, businesses have to make sure that their logistics systems can meet the demands placed on them by customers.

Human resources Operating across the EU may have human resource implications. Whilst English is commonly understood throughout the EU, it may be easier to sell into markets outside the UK if some staff have foreign language skills. If a UK business has operations abroad, it will need to understand the labour law in each country in which it operates. Some middle and senior management workers may expect as part of their work to spend time abroad. This may benefit the business because it helps in creating a single culture within the organisation. However, human resource departments need to develop policies about how such workers are to be treated in the case of issues such as housing, salaries or company cars.

Finance Selling into foreign countries within the EU has major implications for finance departments. Will foreign customers be given trade credit and if so on what terms? How can the creditworthiness of a customer in, say, Poland or Italy be checked? Will the price of exports be quoted in euros or pounds sterling? If it is in euros, how will the business cope if the value of the euro changes significantly between the time a contract is signed or an order placed and the time the payment is received? If the business has sites abroad, profitability could be significantly affected in pounds sterling by significant movements of the exchange rate. What strategy does it have to cope with this? Does the business with sites abroad have sufficient knowledge of local accounting and tax regimes? What is the strategy for a UK multinational raising finance abroad?

The external environment The external environment may differ in the EU than in the domestic UK market. For example, interest rates may differ between the UK, the eurozone and EU countries not in the eurozone such as Denmark, Sweden and Poland. The exchange rate of the pound fluctuates against the euro. Some countries may be in a recession, whilst the UK market is in boom. Pressure groups may have different concerns from country to country. A business must therefore adopt strategies to deal with the risks and opportunities that a fast changing external environment can present.

Overall, evidence suggests that being a member of the EU favours those with two distinct strategies. Some businesses remain successful because they are small and can target niche markets. However, the opportunities offered by larger markets pushes other businesses to increase in size. By becoming larger, they can gain economies of scale and thus become more competitive. In a wide variety of industries, from steel to pharmaceuticals to chemicals and cars, the past 20 years have seen the creation of European multinationals through the takeover or merger of national companies.

A few companies have set up JOINT VENTURES. This is where a company in the UK, joins with a company in Poland, for example, to set up a jointly owned subsidiary. In this subsidiary company, the two companies work together supplying their own expertise. The UK company might want to expand in Poland and so the Polish company supplies knowledge about the country, its business environment and potential customers. The UK company might provide technology, brands or finance capabilities. The UK company may also transfer some of its production from the UK to Poland to take advantage of cheap labour, exporting the goods back into its UK markets for sale.

The Single European currency

On 1st January 2002, 12 EU countries abandoned their own currencies to launch a SINGLE EUROPEAN CURRENCY, the euro. EUROPEAN MONETARY UNION represented a further step towards creating a single market with no barriers to trade. Separate national currencies created barriers to trade for a number of reasons.

- Exports and importers had to pay commission to banks to exchange their currency for another. This increased the cost of trade between member countries, a cost which was not present with trade within one country.

- Currencies fluctuated against each other. This tends to impose risks upon either the buyer or seller in an international transaction depending on who has to buy the foreign currency. There is a variety of ways of getting

BWD Entertainment is a UK based media company. Originally a magazine company, it has diversified into radio and trade newspapers and also runs a book publishing business. In the 1990s, it acquired stakes in magazine publishing companies in Spain, the Netherlands and Italy and owns radio companies in both Germany and France.

The directors of the company have recently completed a strategic review and have decided that the new entrants to the EU in Eastern Europe should be targeted for acquisitions. Their economies are likely to grow at a faster rate than the EU average over the next 10-20 years and this should give plenty of scope for increasing sales over time.

They are particularly looking at the largest new entrant country, Poland, with a population of 38.2 million. One strategy would be to buy an established Polish magazine company and use its editorial expertise and distribution system to push a number of new magazines based on ones which have proved popular in the UK, Spain and Italy. A different strategy would be to buy a Polish magazine company which already had strong market share. By giving new finance, BWD would allow the existing Polish management greater opportunities to launch new magazines aimed at the local market. A third possible strategy would be to set up a company from scratch, recruiting editors and other workers from established Polish magazine companies, but also putting in staff from existing BWD operations in other European countries. This would probably be the highest risk strategy.

1 **Explain why there might be greater scope for marketing magazines in Poland than in, say, the UK or Italy over the next 10 years.**
2 **By considering the possible advantages and disadvantages of each of the three strategic options, discuss which is likely to be the most successful for BWD. In your answer, identify what other information would be needed to make an informed choice.**

around this problem, such as by buying foreign currency **forward**. For example, a business could enter a contract with a bank to buy euros at a fixed exchange rate for delivery in six months time. However, banks charge extra to **hedge** transactions like this. Alternatively, a large UK business could source its supplies so that supplies from the eurozone roughly equalled exports to the eurozone. This way its revenues in euros roughly match its costs in euros. But this places artificial restraints on sources of supply or export markets for a business. Ultimately, most businesses which try to minimise the risk of currency fluctuation find that there is a cost. By introducing the euro, businesses within the 12 member states found they could trade with each with no foreign currency risk, thus lowering their costs.

- Separate currencies make prices less transparent. This is particularly important for small, unsophisticated businesses. For example, a small London based business knows the monetary value of a product from a Scottish based business when it is quoted at £200 a tonne. But it doesn't necessarily know the monetary value if a Polish firm quotes a price of 1 200 zlotys a tonne. It is relatively easy to find out the exchange rate of pounds for zlotys. But for a small firm, prices in different currencies may discourage it from buying or selling because it is not immediately obvious what is the price.

Problems of the Single European Currency

Many UK businesses think that the UK should have joined the single currency in 2002 because of the benefits to trade. Some multinational businesses have threatened to reduce investment in the UK or pull out altogether and relocate within the eurozone because of the UK's failure to join.

However, other UK businesses think that the UK should remain outside the European Monetary Union for a variety of reasons.

● Joining the Single Currency means that the UK has to give up control of both monetary policy and exchange rate policy. At present, the Bank of England sets interest rates for the UK and this in turn has a significant effect on the value of the pound (see unit 103). For eurozone countries, a single interest rate is set by the European Central Bank. Both central banks have the control of inflation as their main priority when setting interest rates. But interest rates also affect demand and the business cycle in individual countries (see units 50 and 99). So the European Central Bank may set high interest rates because most of the eurozone is in boom and inflation is rising. But Spain may be in recession, with high interest rates only making matters worse. With its own currency, the UK has the power to set interest rates to match its booms and recessions. Some businesses fear that if the UK adopted the euro, its economy would suffer with inappropriate interest rates.

● Another concern is that on entry, too low a value for the euro against the old pound (or too high a value of the pound against the euro) would be set. This would lock too high a euro price for UK exports into the system, making it difficult for UK exporters to compete. Equally, existing eurozone countries would find that their prices for imports into the UK would now be low, giving them a competitive advantage against UK firms.

● Joining the single currency would make it easier for further steps to be taken towards European integration. Many UK businesses believe that the UK has a better overall business environment that countries like France or Germany. Taxes on average are lower, for example, and there is less 'red tape'. These UK businesses don't want to see more power going from the UK to the EU.

The views of British business are therefore divided between those in favour of entry and those against. It could be argued that it is unclear whether UK businesses are better off or worse off by being currently outside the euro.

Emerging markets

EMERGING MARKETS are markets in countries which have a relatively low output per capita compared to the rich industrialised nations of the world but which are relatively open to trade with markets in industrialised countries. Over the past thirty years, countries such as Hong Kong, Singapore, South Korea and Taiwan have seen very fast economic growth through trade links with rich industrialised countries. Over the past ten years, it is countries such as China, India and Thailand which have opened their markets to foreign trade. They have benefited considerably through much faster economic growth.

Emerging markets present both opportunities and threats to businesses in existing industrialised countries such as the UK.

Opportunities Emerging markets allow UK businesses to source raw materials and components more cheaply, taking advantage of cheap labour. This may mean buying goods and services from emerging markets. Or it may mean setting up offices and factories in those countries to exploit their competitive advantage directly. Reducing costs allows a UK business either to raise its profit margins, or to lower its prices and remain competitive in the market place. Another opportunity is that UK businesses can sell products into emerging markets. Typically, emerging markets sell low technology, low value added products, although this is rapidly changing over time. They buy high technology, high value added products. For example, a Chinese company may buy state of the art manufacturing machines from a UK company, or financial services from the City of London.

Threats Emerging markets pose an enormous threat to UK businesses which are in direct competition with goods and services produced in those markets. UK manufacturing has shrunk in size because production has moved overseas. Some service jobs are also being lost. For example, call centre work has been moving from the UK to India. So too has some computer programming work. Businesses which face these threats can only survive by continually moving into higher value added markets, providing goods and services which emerging markets can produce because of a lack of skilled labour or a lack of technical know-how.

1 Explain briefly the terms of (a) the Treaty of Rome; (b) the Single European Act; (c) the Maastricht Treaty.
2 Compare the roles of the European Commission, the Council of Ministers, the European Parliament and the European Court of Justice in the EU.
3 A British company manufacturing gardening equipment is coming under intense pressure from two Czech Republic companies which are taking away its export sales and taking market share away in its UK home market. Briefly outline how the UK company could respond in the areas of (a) operations management; (b) marketing; (c) human resources.
4 What might be the advantages and disadvantages to a UK company which imports components from Europe and exports finished products to Europe of Britain's failure to adopt the Single Currency?
5 What might be the opportunities and threats to a British company making components for the car industry from emerging markets?

keyterms

Customs union - a union of countries which establish free trade amongst themselves and put up a common tariff to imports from outside the union.

Emerging markets - economies which have previously had relatively low output per capita but which have markets open to trade and are now expanding, in some cases rapidly.

Eurozone - the group of countries which have adopted the Single European Currency, the euro.

European Union - a customs union whose aim is economic integration with a single market and which also has political and defence objectives.

European Monetary Union - a union of countries which have adopted a **Single European Currency**, the euro.

Joint venture - when two companies create a jointly owned subsidiary company to produce an agreed range of products.

Market access - the extent to which a business can enter a market and buy from or sell into the market.

Single European market - the market for goods and services produced within the European Union, a market which is free of trade barriers and and restrictions to trade.

Single European Currency - the euro, the common currency of the European Monetary Union.

The Japanese motor manufacturer, Nissan, has consistently said that Britain should join the euro. The company has a plant in Wearside in the North East of England which currently makes the Micra, the mid-size Almera model and the Primera. It was the first Japanese company to open a car plant in the UK in 1984, built on a greenfield site. Japanese work practices, including a single union agreement, were imported into the UK and today the plant is consistently the most productive in Europe in terms of output per worker of cars.

The problem that Nissan faces is that it imports car components from across Europe and exports finished cars back to Europe and the rest of the world. Because the UK is not in the euro, the price it has to pay for imported European components and the price it receives for finished cars exported to the eurozone is unpredictable.

Every time Nissan brings out a new model to replace one being made in Wearside, the plant has to convince headquarters that the site will be the best one for that model. Currently, the replacement for the Almera model has to be decided upon. There is no guarantee that Wearside will get the replacement. If it doesn't, thousands of the 4 500 workers employed at the site could lose their jobs. Suppliers based in the UK also stand to lose contracts if the new model goes to another EU country because they too would be outside the eurozone.

Source: adapted from *The Guardian*, 7.1.2004.

'Mr Ghosn, Nissan's President Chief Executive, has repeated warnings that its Sunderland plant could lose production of one of its most important cars if Britain remains outside the euro. Mr Ghosn made his comments during a round table meeting with journalists at the Detroit Motor Show.

A Nissan Motor Manufacturing UK (NMUK) spokesman said:

'Mr Ghosn has been very consistent in what he has been saying in response to questions about the single currency issue. The UK's exclusion from the euro adds an element of unpredictability when having to make an investment decision. Given the high cost of investment involved when introducing a new model, this lack of long term economic visibility is one of several factors that have to be taken into consideration when deciding where to site production of future models for sale in Europe. Every new model is subject to a thorough manufacturing feasibility study before any production decision is taken. If the UK is still outside the eurozone when the next decision on new model allocation has to be made, this will be one factor that will be considered as part of that study - together with logistics, production cost, manufacturing efficiency etc. On a local level, NMUK is doing what it can to offset any disadvantages caused by the UK's exclusion from the Single Currency by working to become the best it can possibly be in terms of cost, flexibility, productivity and efficiency. As with all new models, NMUK will endeavour to attract the replacement to the Almera on this basis.'

Source: adapted from *The Guardian*, 7.1.2004.

Ranking	Manufacturer	Plant	Country	Vehicles produced per worker
1	Nissan	Sunderland	UK	99
2	Renault	Valladoid	Spain	89
3	Toyota	Valenciennes	France	88
4	Ford	Saarlouis	Germany	87
5	GM	Antwerp	Belgium	83
6	Renault	Novo Mesto	Slovenia	82
7	Honda	Swindon	UK	82
8	Toyota	Burnaston	UK	81
12	Fiat	Melfi	Italy	77
15	Ford	Valencia	Spain	72
18	Fiat	Tychy	Poland	66
21	PSA	Ryton	UK	63
23	Renault	Palencia	Spain	61
28	Fiat	Cassino	Italy	53
31	Skoda	Various	Czech Republic	48
32	GM	IBC Luton	UK	47
33	PSA	Mangualde	Portugal	45
36	Renault	Bursa	Turkey	42
39	GM	Ellesmere Port	UK	41
42	Volvo	Torslanda	Sweden	36

Table 102.1 *European Automotive Productivity Index*
Source: adapted from World Markets Research Centre, *Japanese plants lead the way in WMRC European Automotive Productivity Index*, 2003102.

1 Using Nissan as an example, evaluate the case for Britain joining the euro. (20 marks)
2 'It is in Nissan's best interests to build the replacement for the Almera at its Wearside plant.' Discuss whether this ever could be the case if Britain is unlikely to join the euro in the foreseeable future. (20 marks)

skill gaps

Knowledge British industry needs skilled workers to survive and remain competitive. In a survey published for the Learning and Skills Council, 22 per cent of employers said that there were 'skills gaps' – staff who were not fully proficient to do their jobs – in their workforce. Employers also suggested that 11 per cent of all employees – 2.4 million – were 'incompetent'.

Application The UK government adopts an *interventionist approach* to education and *training*. Education is paid for as part of *public spending*. The government sees improved education and training as key to its *supply side policies*. Such policies are designed to raise the *economic growth rate* of the *economy* and to help reduce *unemployment*.

Analysis Businesses in all sectors of industry rely upon government to provide education and training for workers. Businesses themselves also have to fund specialist training. Where businesses are unable to recruit appropriately qualified staff, they either have to leave the vacancy unfilled or train a worker to fill the gap. The survey found that around one fifth of job vacancies went unfilled because an appropriately qualified person could not be found.

Evaluation Businesses would like the government to fund more education and training. On the other hand they would like to see lower taxes and less red tape affecting business. This policy a dilemma which is impossible to resolve. Inevitably there are trade offs to be made. The less interventionist the government, the more businesses are free to make their own decisions. On the other hand, a laissez faire approach could lead to underfunding of essential services and ultimately lead to business being less competitive rather than more competitive.

Intervention vs laissez faire

The role of government has changed over time. Traditionally, government had two main functions. One was to maintain armed forces in time of war. The second was to administer justice. Taxes were raised to pay for both of these. Gradually, the role of government has expanded. Today, various branches of government in the UK are responsible not just for defence and the justice system, but also for education, health care, roads, welfare benefits as well as many other areas. Government is also responsible for running the economy as a whole and for regulating many areas of economic and social activity.

There is a debate, however, about the extent to which government should interfere in the workings of the economy and society.

Laissez faire approach The LAISSEZ FAIRE approach is that government should intervene as little as possible. 100 years ago, for example, government did not feel it had any responsibility for unemployment or inflation. There was little regulation of the labour market. 'Red tape' was minimal. Those who favour a laissez faire approach argue as follows.

- Government intervention has to be paid for by taxes. The more government intervention, the higher the taxes needed, whether to pay for inspectors to monitor health and safety legislation, or doctors to provide a free health service. The money raised in taxes would be better used if it were in the hands of those being taxed, consumers, workers and businesses. High taxes also discourage investment and enterprise. Foreign companies thinking of setting up in the UK would be discouraged by a high tax regime.
- Government intervention often does more harm than good. For example, attempts to reduce inflation can lead to higher inflation or very high unemployment. Protecting workers rights by setting minimum wages can lead to firms being forced out of business because of higher wage costs and unemployment increasing. Heavy regulation discourages investment and reduces international competitiveness because it adds to the costs of running a business. Foreign businesses wanting to set up in the UK could be discouraged by a heavy regulatory framework.
- Free markets usually provide a better outcome than regulated markets or no markets at all. Everything from health care to railways and even motorways can be more efficiently provided by markets.
- Where free markets fail, it is usually better for government to persuade firms in the industry to regulate themselves, for example by adopting voluntary codes of practice (see unit 55). In advertising, the Advertising Standards Authority regulates advertising without the need for government intervention.

Intervention approach Those who argue in favour of government INTERVENTION would disagree with the laissez faire approach.

- Macroeconomic management of the economy is essential to avoid the dangers of high inflation and high unemployment. Governments have not always been successful at this but a pure laissez faire approach would result in very deep recessions and unsustainable booms (see unit 50).
- Consumers, workers and citizens demand ever more

stringent regulation from government (see unit 55). Consumers demand that they are fairly treated by businesses from which they buy goods and services. Workers want protection from employers who treat them unfairly. Citizens want the environment to be clean and healthy.

Governments can intervene in the economy in a number of ways. In this unit, macroeconomic intervention and privatisation are considered. Other types of intervention include involvement in consumer and labour markets (see units 55 and 91), environmental intervention (see unit unit 106) and competition law (see unit 55).

Red tape is a constant complaint of UK businesses, particularly if they are relatively small. Giles Henschel is the owner of Olives Et Al and has grown the business to the stage where he now employs 20 people. But having to deal with government red tape is a contrast problem for him. Administration costs, such as payroll and employment regulations, are now higher than production costs. In the case of payroll costs, for example, government red tape requires him to deduct income tax and National Insurance contributions at the appropriate rate. Payrolls are also now used to pay back student loans and give working tax credit. Some time ago, Mr Henschel decided that it was no longer worth his while to deal with this personally. So he now employs an accountant at £150 a month to deal with his payroll work.

The cost of dealing with payrolls is inverse to the size of the business. A study by the University of Bath found that while it costs some big firms just £5 a year per employee to comply with payroll rules, the cost for small firms is up to £288 per employee. John Whiting, a partner at Pricewaterhouse-Coopers commented: 'Take just one of the employer's responsibilities in this area - dealing with student loan repayments. What has this got to do with employing? Why should the employer have to grapple with such systems on behalf of the government?'

Source: adapted from *The Times*, 12.2.2004.

1 **(a) Calculate how much it is costing Olives Et Al per employee per year to administer payrolls. (b) Explain, using the example of payroll regulations, why companies such as Olives Et Al might prefer the government to adopt a more laissez faire approach.**
2 **Suggest and explain TWO arguments the government might use to justify the burdens it imposes on businesses with regard to payrolls.**

The objectives of macroeconomic policy

The government's attempt to influence the economy as a whole is known as MACROECONOMIC POLICY. In particular, government attempts to influence four key variables:
- inflation (see unit 53), to keep price increases low;

- unemployment (see unit 54) to keep the number out of work as small as possible;
- economic growth (see unit 101) to maintain a steady rise in levels of output (typically measured by GDP);
- the current account on the balance of payments to keep its balance roughly at zero over a period of time; the current account balance is calculated by taking away imports from exports.

Macroeconomic conditions change over time. However, in the early twenty first century the UK government wanted to achieve:
- low inflation of around 2.0 per cent (measured according to changes in the CPI, the Consumer Price Index);
- low unemployment of less than 1.5 million measured on the claimant count method;
- economic growth of between 2.5 and 3.0 per cent per annum;
- a current account balance of zero.

Figures 103.1 - 103.3 show how the UK economy has actually performed on these four key economic variables since 1990.

Achieving objectives

Responsibility for achieving government objectives in the UK is split between the government, in particular the Treasury department, and the Bank of England. The Bank of England is responsible for achieving low inflation through use of monetary policy (see below). The government is responsible for the other variables.

Achieving policy goals is not easy because the four variables are interlinked.
- If GDP growth is too fast, say at 4-5 per cent per annum for the UK, there is a danger that inflation will begin to rise. Too high a growth in GDP probably indicates too fast a growth in demand for goods and services (see unit 53). So demand outstrips supply, with a resulting rise in prices.
- If GDP growth is not high enough, unemployment begins to rise. This is because the productive potential of the economy is growing at between 2-3 per cent per year. More investment by businesses and a better trained workforce means that more can be produced each year. If aggregate demand (total demand in the economy, see unit 53) fails to keep up with this increase in aggregate supply, then unemployment will begin to rise.
- Too fast a growth in GDP is likely to increase imports at a faster rate than the increase in exports. When consumers and businesses have fast rising incomes, they spend part of that on imported products. Hence, economic growth which is too fast will cause a deterioration on the current account of the balance of payments. Since too fast a rise in GDP is linked to rising inflation, so rising inflation tends to be associated with a worsening current account position on the balance of payments.

Government economic policy which acts on aggregate demand can take a number of forms.
- Expansionary policy - designed to increase aggregate demand from what it would otherwise have been. This is used when economic growth is too low, unemployment is rising and inflation is subdued.
- Neutral policy - designed to keep the economy going on

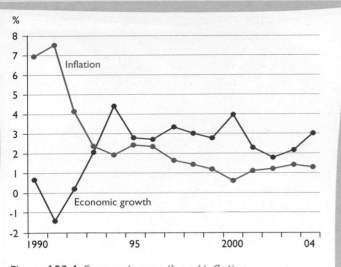

Figure 103.1 *Economic growth and inflation*

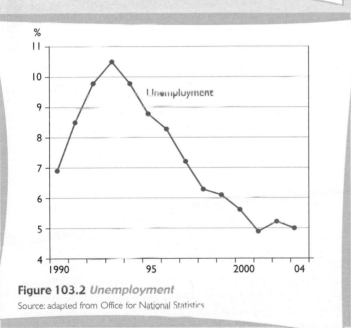

Figure 103.2 *Unemployment*
Source: adapted from Office for National Statistics

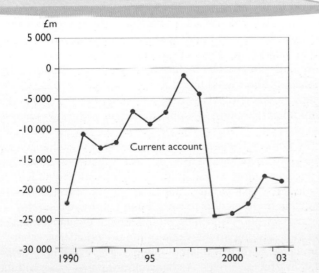

Figure 103.3 *Balance of payments on current account*
Source: adapted from Office for National Statistics.

its current course because this is achieving the objectives set by government.
● Restrictive or contractionary policy - designed to reduce aggregate demand from what it would otherwise have been. This is used to slow down the economy when GDP is growing too fast, inflation is rising or the current account on the balance of payments is in unsustainable deficit.

Fiscal policy

One way in which the government can influence aggregate demand is through fiscal policy. This is the attempt by government to influence the economy through changes in taxes, government spending and government borrowing or repayment of the national debt. If government spending is greater than government revenues, most of which are tax revenues, then there is a government BUDGET DEFICIT. If government spending is less than government revenues, then there is a BUDGET SURPLUS. When there is a budget deficit, the government has to borrow the money to finance this deficit. When there is a surplus, the government pays back some of its past borrowings. The total accumulated amount of past government borrowing is called the NATIONAL DEBT.

Expansionary fiscal policy If taxes fall or government spending rises, this is likely to make fiscal policy expansionary. Falling taxes or rising government spending will mean that government borrowing will also rise or the budget surplus will fall.
   Expansionary fiscal policy affects the economy in a number of ways.
● If government spending rises, this is a direct increase in total spending (i.e. aggregate demand) in the economy. More spending should push down unemployment and lead to a rise in GDP from what it would otherwise have been. However, it will add to inflationary pressures. It is also likely to lead to a deterioration in the current account on the balance of payments because some of the extra spending will be on imports.
● If taxes fall, this puts more money into the pockets of taxpayers. This will be some combination of consumers, savers, workers and businesses. They will spend part or all of this fall in taxes, improving the unemployment and growth situation but possibly leading to a deterioration in inflation and the current balance on the balance of payments.

Restrictive fiscal policy Restrictive fiscal policy has the opposite effect. Rising taxes or falling government spending will reduce total spending in the economy. In turn this should lead to a fall in inflation pressures and an improvement in the current account on the balance of payments, but a rise in unemployment and a fall in economic growth.
   Fiscal policy is often used to moderate the effects of the business cycle (see unit 50). When the economy is threatening to grow at too fast a rate at the top of a boom, the government can adopt restrictive fiscal policy measures. When the economy is in a recession or depression, the government can help lift the economy out of this by applying expansionary fiscal policy.

Next, the retail chain which sells clothes and household furnishings, must be hoping that the Bank of England doesn't put up interest rates this year. After several years of high sales growth, Next announced a 0.9 per cent fall in like-for-like sales in the seven weeks to March 20. The company forecast a slump in fashion sales and said that it could last 6 months.

Simon Wolfson, the chief executive, said that Next would be unwilling to fight for market share with price cuts in the coming autumn. He said that price cuts would be limited to 2-3 per cent in the autumn compared to 6-9 per cent for this spring's ranges. Clothing prices on the high street fell by 6.2 per cent on average in the year to February as competing chains forced prices down. Over the past three years, the average selling price of products at Next has fallen by up to 12 per cent while volumes increased by 73 per cent.

The Bank of England's Monetary Committee is having to grapple with whether or not inflation is rising. In April 2005, the CPI rose by 1.9 per cent, the highest rise for seven years but this is still below its target of 2 per cent. On the supply side of the economy, high oil and other commodity prices are likely to put upward pressure on inflation. On the other hand, as the figures from Next show, there are many sectors of the economy where prices are actually falling. On the demand side, the Bank of England will certainly be looking at the likely increase in consumer spending this year. If this remains subdued, there is less likelihood that interest rates rise will need to rise. Subdued consumer spending, however, is just as bad news for Next as interest rate rises.

Source: adapted from *The Times*, 24.3.2005.

1 **Why might the Bank of England have raised interest rates in 2005?**
2 **What impact might a rise in interest rates have on a company like Next?**
3 **(a) If the Bank of England were to raise interest rates, explain what would be the likely effect on the exchange rate value of the pound. (b) Explain what impact this possible change in the exchange rate could have on clothing retailers like Next.**

Monetary policy

Monetary policy is policy which uses interest rates, the supply of money, the supply of borrowed funds and the exchange rate to influence the economy. A rise or a fall in interest rates can have a number of effects.

- It was explained in unit 51 that a rise in interest rates will reduce total spending or aggregate demand in the economy. A rise in interest rates encourages people to save more and spend less. More importantly, a rise in interest rates discourages borrowing both by consumers and businesses. This results in a fall in aggregate demand, which then leads to higher unemployment and lower growth in GDP. But it has the beneficial effect of reducing inflationary pressures and improving the current account position on the balance of payments as explained earlier.
- A fall in interest rates leads to a rise in total spending or aggregate demand. This rise in aggregate demand then leads to inflationary pressures and a deterioration in the current account position on the balance of payments situation. But it has the beneficial effect of reducing unemployment and stimulating economic growth.

The Bank of England, through its Monetary Policy Committee, sets an interest rate each month. It is given a target to achieve by the government on inflation. In 2004, this was to keep inflation at less than 2 per cent per annum measured by the Consumer Price Index (CPI), a measure of inflation. When it judges that inflationary pressures are too great and inflation might exceed the 2 per cent on a long term basis, it will raise its interest rate. This then has a ripple effect on other interest rates throughout the economy. For example, banks and building societies tend to match changes in the Bank of England's interest rate with changes in their own interest rates. The higher the interest rate, the lower the demand for borrowed funds and hence the lower the money supply. Today, the only way in which the Bank of England manipulates the money supply in the UK is through interest rate policy.

The Bank of England is also responsible for exchange rate policy. By changing interest rates, it can have an impact on the exchange rate. A rise in interest rates will tend to lead to a rise in the exchange rate. This is because it becomes more attractive for foreigners to save in the UK, increasing the demand for pounds sterling on the foreign exchange markets and thus pushing up the value of the pound against other currencies. Similarly, a fall in interest rates will tend to lead to a fall in exchange rates. A change in exchange rates will then affect both exports and imports (see unit 52).

The Bank of England cannot choose both to fix the value of

the pound against other currencies and fix the value of interest rates. Either it fixes the value of the pound and is forced to raise or lower interest rates to achieve this. Or it fixes the level of interest rates it wants and allows the exchange rate to be determined by market forces. Since September 1992, when the UK left the Exchange Rate Mechanism (which existed to create the stability required before the creation of the euro), the Bank of England has chosen to fix interest rates and allow exchange rates to float freely. This is the UK's exchange rate policy today.

Supply side policies

Fiscal policy and monetary policy are used to affect aggregate demand. By adjusting its total spending, level of taxes or interest rates, the government can increase or reduce the amount of total spending in the economy. This can then have a short term impact on inflation, unemployment, GDP growth and the current account on the balance of payments.

However, a key long term aim of the government is to increase the productive capacity of the economy (see unit 101). Growth in capacity is often called the 'underlying rate of economic growth' to distinguish it from growth in GDP. Policies to increase the productive capacity of the economy are called SUPPLY SIDE POLICIES. This is to distinguish them from fiscal and monetary policies which affect aggregate demand. There are three main ways in which supply side policies can increase the productive capacity of the economy.

Increasing investment The government can use policies to promote investment by businesses. For example, it can give tax relief on money used to buy investment goods. Or it can give grants to pay for investment. It can also invest itself. Building new roads and bridges or reclaiming derelict land are examples of infrastructure spending which will benefit business.

Improving the quality of the labour force A workforce which is better educated and trained and has more experience will be more productive than one which is less well trained. So the average UK worker might be able to produce more in money terms than the average Indian or Thai worker. Through better education and promoting training, the government can therefore increase long term economic growth.

Making sure that both capital and labour are fully utilised Businesses can invest in new machines but if those machines stand idle, they won't be productive. Similarly, if workers are out of work or their skills are underutilised, then the economy will not grow as fast as it could. So a key role of government is to ensure that resources are being used productively. Policies which encourage employment, such as the New Deal or increased vocational training, help to achieve this. So do macroeconomic policies which avoid the economy from going into frequent deep slumps and booms (see unit 50). In a slump, resources are underutilised. Sound financial policies which result in low inflation will encourage investment. So too will a legal system which allows businesses to own property, sign enforceable contracts and trade goods without too much fear of crime. Countries that do not have a sound legal and financial framework often fail to grow as fast as they could as a result.

There are other examples of supply side policies used by government in an effort to increase the efficient use of resources in the economy. For example, there are regular attempts by government to simplify 'red tape', the rules and regulations ranging from tax returns to health and safety inspections to labour laws. Red tape imposes considerable costs on businesses, particularly small businesses. There are also regular changes to the amount of tax paid by businesses or workers to encourage them to work more efficiently.

Privatisation

One example of a supply side policy is privatisation. This was a policy introduced in the 1980s where state owned industries and assets were sold off to the private sector. For example the gas, electricity, coal, water, steel, post office, telecommunications, airline, airports and railway industries were all partly or fully owned by the UK government before 1980. The arguments in favour of the government owning assets and providing services are:
- by providing on a large scale, as with the National Health Service, the government can gain economies of scale and so lower costs of production to citizens;
- essential services can be provided which would otherwise not be provided in sufficient quantities by free markets;
- by eliminating the profit made by businesses, the cost to the citizen of those products would be lower.

However, there have been major criticisms of state owned industries and strong arguments in favour of privatisation.
- State owned monopolies did not have the profit or competitive incentives to reduce cost wherever possible. Hence, when industries such as gas and electricity were privatised, their new private owners stripped out huge layers of costs making them far more efficient than before. Despite now earning large profits, the new businesses were able to lower their prices to customers.
- There was no incentive for industries to innovate. Privatised industries have often introduced new services better able to cater for the needs of their customers.
- Government often starved industries of investment because it wanted to reduce its spending. The result was a lack of essential investment in industries such as water and the railways. When these industries passed into private hands, investment increased because the privatised businesses saw that they could increase their profits by investing more.
- As a one-off advantage to taxpayers, the government sold off these assets to the private sector for billions of pounds. This was used to pay off part of the government debt, reducing interest payments and allowing for lower taxes.

Some privatised industries, such as gas, electricity, water, telecommunications and the railways, were privatised in such a way that there was not always enough competition in the industry to prevent the new businesses charging high prices and exploiting customers. For this reason, the industries were given REGULATORY BODIES (see unit 55). These include OFTEL for the telecommunications industry and OFWAT for the water industry. They have the power to fix maximum prices in the industry. In the case of the telecommunications industry, OFTEL has tended to force prices down to take account of increased efficiency in providing telecommunication services. They also have the power to force existing monopoly businesses to open up individual markets to competition. For example, BT has been forced to allow competitors to provide broadband services which use BT landlines to reach customers.

The impact on businesses of fiscal, monetary and supply side policies

Different businesses are affected in different ways by government policy.

The business cycle Some industries are much less affected by the business cycle than others. For example, soap powder manufacturers see much less fluctuation in sales than car manufacturers over the business cycle. So the industries which would be most affected by restrictive monetary and fiscal policies at the top of a boom would be those which are sensitive to interest rate rises and which have higher income elasticities of demand (see unit 17). Industries benefit at the bottom of a business cycle when the government uses expansionary policies. Their sales would fall more if the government were not using policies to increase aggregate demand.

Borrowing Businesses which borrow heavily are most affected by changes in interest rates (see unit 51). They are hardest hit when the Bank of England puts up interest rates. They enjoy the most gain when interest rates fall.

Exporting Businesses which export goods or suffer competition from imports will be most affected by government policies which affect exchange rates. For example, an exporting business will suffer if a rise in interest rates leads to a rise in the value of the pound.

Taxation Tax changes hit businesses differently.
- DIRECT TAXES are taxes on incomes of individuals and businesses. For example, income tax and corporation tax are direct taxes. The Chancellor of the Exchequer might lower the corporation tax rate (the rate of tax on company profits) on the first £20 000 of profits earned. This would disproportionately benefit smaller companies. Or employers' National Insurance contributions, a tax paid by businesses on the wages they pay to their workers, might be raised. This would disproportionately affect labour intensive businesses.
- INDIRECT TAXES are taxes on spending like VAT and excise duties. A decision to raise the excise duty on tobacco hits tobacco manufacturers. A decision to impose VAT on children's clothing would hit all the businesses in the child clothing chain from retailers to manufacturers. A rise in excise duties on petrol will mainly raise costs for transport companies. Petrol garages and oil companies are unlikely to be affected much because customers will carry on buying almost the same amount as before (i.e. the demand for petrol is highly price inelastic, see unit 17).

keyterms

Budget deficit - when referring to government, a budget deficit occurs when government spending is greater than government revenues over a period of time.

Budget surplus - when referring to government, a budget surplus occurs when government spending is less than government revenues over a period of time.

Direct taxes - taxes on income and profits, such as income tax and corporation tax.

Indirect taxes - taxes on spending such as VAT and excise duties.

Interventionism - an economic philosophy which argues that government should intervene in the workings of the economy whenever the free market mechanism fails to optimise society's welfare.

Laissez faire - an economic philosophy which says that government should intervene in the workings of the economy as little as possible because free markets are the best way to maximise welfare for society.

Macroeconomic policy - the attempt of government to influence the economy as a whole.

National debt - the amount the government now owes from the accumulation of past borrowing.

Regulatory bodies - bodies set up in the UK by government which oversee the workings of certain privatised industries where competition is restricted.

Supply side policies - government policies aimed at increasing the productive capacity of the economy.

checklist

1. Briefly summarise the arguments in favour of (a) a laissez faire approach to the economy and (b) an interventionist approach.
2. What are the objectives of government macroeconomic policy?
3. Explain the four variables of unemployment, inflation, economic growth and the balance of payments.
4. Explain the differences between expansionary fiscal policy and restrictive fiscal policy.
5. What is the difference between fiscal policy and monetary policy?
6. What might be the impact of a rise in interest rates?
7. Explain briefly how supply side policies can increase economic growth.
8. What are the possible advantages and disadvantages of privatisation as a supply side policy?

Penny Streeter runs a healthcare recruitment company, Ambition 24hours. It has 200 employees, 19 branches, 13 500 professionals on its books and last year made a profit of £4.2 million on a turnover of £60 million.

Ms Streeter initially established a recruitment company for supply teachers. But then she heard that a nursing home was desperate for staff. 'It didn't take us long to realise that they were all desperate for staff, particularly at short notice. Often they needed people at 7pm to do a night shift. But by then all the other recruitment agencies had closed.' Immediately, she saw a gap in the market for round-the-clock cover and set about recruiting the healthcare staff to her books. 'Initially, it was just me and my mobile phone. But at least it was a real live person who could help, not an answer machine that said to ring back in the morning.' Word soon spread, and the company had five nursing homes on its books. Today, it has 1 600.

Ambition 24hours has branched out and offers medical and social work staff as well as nursing and other healthcare professionals to private, local authority and NHS establishments. On average, 2 000 staff on her books are working each week. The company has an open-all-hours operations centre at its headquarters in Surrey. 'There, all staff details are kept, enabling trained professionals to be dispatched to homes and hospitals across the UK, often at a moment's notice.' Customer service is an obsession for Ms Streeter. 'Let someone down in this business', she says, 'and they'll tell somebody quicker than if you do a good job.'

Last year, Ambition 24hours spent £500 000 upgrading its information systems to cope with all aspects of the work. The days of the card index are long gone.

The company has managed to grow without any bank loans. Partly this has been due to very careful control of costs. Ambition 24hours scrutinises every purchase to see if it is necessary.

Source: adapted from the *Financial Times*, 23.11.2004.

1. Discuss how the following might affect Ambition 24hours.
   (a) A fall in the growth of government spending on healthcare.
   (b) An increase in government spending on benefits to pay for nursing home fees.
   (c) The Bank of England raising its interest rate.
   (d) Increased tax relief for businesses buying computer equipment. (20 marks)
2. To what extent is Ambition 24 hours more threatened by changes in government policy than by the ups and downs of demand of the business cycle? (20 marks)

Anglo American

Knowledge Anglo American is a company with operations in dozens of countries in sectors ranging from paper and packaging to mining and forestry. Its activities have a significant impact on the local environment wherever it operates in the world.

Application To help local *managers* understand the *social* and *economic impact* of the *company's* activities, it has devised a tool called the Socio-Economic Assessment Toolbox (SEAT). Sent out to *staff* in the form of a *manual*, it has been particularly useful in helping the company to make long-term *plans* that look towards the eventual *closure* of an *operation* such as a mine. It allows managers to identify some of the *externalities* created by Anglo's operations and appreciate the full *social* cost of an activity.

Analysis Planning for closure using SEAT involves four steps: identifying the most important local issues; measuring the social and economic impact of a project; developing initiatives to address these impacts and planning for eventual closure; and reporting the result of the assessment. The idea is that once managers understand better what local communities really require they will be able to draw up initiatives to help Anglo to make up for its depletion of natural resources by, among other things, fostering free-standing local enterprises, creating jobs in the area and maximising the use of local suppliers who will live on after Anglo has pulled out. 'It's what you do to ensure that, by the end of the extraction process, you leave behind something that is more than a hole in the ground', says Edward Bickham, executive vice-president of external affairs and the person who has spearheaded much of the work on the toolbox.

Evaluation Companies are sometimes criticised for exploiting both the environment and local populations. SEAT is an indication that Anglo American is taking its social, ethical and environmental responsibilities seriously. Inevitably, there will be disagreements about the true social costs of its activities. However, without mining and forestry, modern economies could not operate. The world's prosperity is based upon activities which inevitably have some effect on the environment.

Adapted from the *Financial Times*, 29.11.2004.

Social responsibility and business ethics

Units 56 and 57 give a detailed account of social responsibility and business ethics. In unit 56, it was explained that businesses have social responsibilities. Businesses act in the interests of their owners. But social custom, the law and the market force them also to acknowledge responsibilities to their other **stakeholders**, such as their workers, their customers and suppliers and the communities in which they operate. Equally, as explained in unit 57, businesses have to act within an ethical framework. If nothing else, businesses should operate within the law.

However, there is a considerable difference between businesses in the way in which they operate in these areas. Businesses like the Co-operative Bank or The Body Shop make a point of acting in a socially responsible and ethical way. Other businesses like arms manufacturers, by the very nature of the products they make, can be accused of being socially irresponsible.

For many businesses, there is a direct trade-off between the interests of different stakeholders. The opportunity cost (see unit 21) for a business which spends £1 million a year supporting charity projects in the local area could be £1 million which is not paid in dividends to shareholders, or £1 million which is not paid to employees in higher wages. The best case scenario for a business is when acting in a socially responsible and ethical way brings benefits to all stakeholders. For example, a doughnut manufacturer may have a policy of sponsoring children's sporting activities. If sales rise as a result, the owners and employees can benefit through higher dividends and more jobs. The local community also benefits from the sponsorship of its young people. Even then, there could be disadvantages. The sponsorship may encourage customers to eat more doughnuts, which could be argued to be unhealthy. The sugar used in the product might have been produced by child labour. There will also be those who will accuse the company of sponsoring children's sporting activities as a mere PR (public relations, see unit 18) exercise.

Many businesses do not have a carefully thought out attitude to social responsibility and ethics. However, large companies are increasingly being forced by the law and by pressure groups to develop policies in these areas. For example, some companies have published social and environmental audits (see unit 56). Others have developed ethical codes of practice (see unit 57).

For some businesses, attitudes to social and ethical responsibility form part of the wider culture (see unit 64) of the business. If there is a strong culture of caring towards all the stakeholders, there is more likely to be a strong social and ethical culture. In businesses where the emphasis is mainly on financial targets, social and ethical issues may play little part in decision making.

In some companies, there could also be a clash of cultures between different layers of the organisation, or different parts of the company. Newly appointed senior executives, for example, may put social and ethical policies in place. But these may not filter down the organisation hierarchy (see unit 31). Or head office in London may follow a strong ethical stance but a subsidiary of the company in another country may conceal from head office poor work conditions and the use of labour on very low wages in its factories in order to boost profits.

Changing business culture is often difficult, whether it is aimed at increasing profitability, cutting costs or adopting more ethical codes of conduct. In an autocratic organisation,

Vodafone, the world's largest mobile phone operator, has a two-person team dedicated to developing products for people with disabilities and other under-served groups. 'These products will produce a revenue stream as soon as they are launched, albeit quite small,' according to Charlotte Grezo, Vodafone's director of corporate responsibility. 'They are designed to give a commercial return. That's the way you get a product line that is sustainable.' The team is based in the marketing department, where Vodafone's new products originate. 'This is really in the heart of the business', she says. 'Its not a CSR (Corporate Social Responsibility) bolt on.'

One product already on the market in the UK, South Africa and Ireland is a speaking phone for people with impaired sight. It can read e-mails, calendars and address book entries aloud to the user. In Germany the group is developing a handset that allows disabled or elderly people to send an alarm to a call centre if they need medical help. 'The team will also investigate ways of using mobile telephony to aid development, for example by speeding the administration of micro-finance schemes in low-income countries. These initiatives are part of Vodafone's core strategy and an important way to differentiate the company', says Ms Grezo.

Source: adapted from the *Financial Times*, 29.11.2004.

1 **Explain how Vodafone's work on products for people with disabilities and other under-served groups can help to 'differentiate the company'.**
2 **Discuss whether Vodafone should continue work on products for people with disabilities and other under-served groups if it failed to make a commercial return.**

change is only encouraged if it comes from above (see unit 39). Change may then encounter resistance as it passes down the management hierarchy. Ultimately it may be frustrated because of the unwillingness to change of those at the bottom of the hierarchy. With more democratic leadership, there will be an increased emphasis on consultation, delegation and empowerment. But this too can frustrate change. If social responsibility and ethics are not seen as high priority by all within the organisation, it becomes very difficult for a few, even if they are at the top of the hierarchy, to get their message across. Delegating responsibility and empowering workers is only successful if those workers share the same goals as the business. Getting everyone to share those goals can take a long time.

The environmental problem

Society faces major environmental challenges today.
- The world's non-renewable natural resources are being depleted at a rapid rate. Oil, coal, natural gas, iron ore and copper are just some examples. There is only a finite amount of these resources. By using up huge quantities today, society is depriving future generations of their use. Businesses, motivated by profit, play a key part of this depletion.
- Renewable resources are being squandered too. Rainforests in South America and Asia are being cut down faster than they can be grown again. Farming land in many areas of the world is being degraded to the point where some of it becomes unusable. Thousands of species of plants and animals are becoming extinct each year, resources which are important for bio-diversity. Fisheries are being fished to the point of extinction.
- Pollution of the planet by business activity continues

especially in Third World countries. Businesses are responsible for noise pollution, water pollution and air pollution on a local basis.
- Global warming, caused by excessive emissions from industrial activity of greenhouse gases, could have enormous consequences for life on this planet. Rising sea levels and shifts in temperature zones could force the relocation of large numbers of peoples and businesses at considerable cost.
- Depletion of the ozone layer, again because of industrial emissions, raises the possibility that harmful rays from the sun could increase skin cancer levels.

Business and external costs

Businesses do not always pay for the pollution they create. When this happens, the business is said to create an EXTERNAL COST or EXTERNALITY. The external cost is the difference between what the business pays, its PRIVATE COSTS, and the full cost to society of the production, the SOCIAL COSTS. External costs are therefore the difference between social and private costs.

External costs = social costs - private costs

For example, a business may recycle tyres. Its private costs include the wages of its staff, purchases of old tyres from suppliers, the transport costs of taking the tyres once recycled to customers and the energy used by the plant. However, the plant may also emit air pollution which at times can create nasty smells within a quarter of a mile radius from its plant. The people who live in that area may suffer as a result. The business is unlikely to give compensation to the local residents for this pollution. The external cost is then the value that the local inhabitants place on their loss of clean air. So the social cost is the private costs of the business plus the external cost of the air pollution.

When businesses create externalities, they are not paying the full cost to society of production. This then creates a situation of MARKET FAILURE. When markets work properly, the value that society places on a product, which is shown by the price that is paid for it, is equal to the cost to society of making the product, shown by the private costs to the business. If there are substantial externalities, the cost to society is much larger than the benefit gained by customers. The costs (the social cost) of production is much greater than the price paid by customers. This leads to overproduction of the good or service. If the price paid by the customer is low, reflecting only the private costs of production, the customer will buy more than if it is high and reflects all the costs of production, the social cost.

Pollution controls

Over the past 60 years, there has been increased pressure for government to intervene and reduce pollution levels in the UK. The government has a number of ways that it can achieve this.

Physical limits One way is for governments to pass laws and issue regulations which set limits on pollution levels or ban certain types of activity. Examples in the early twenty first century included:

- UK legislation, such as **The Environment Act, 1995**, which set up the Environment Agency which was given various functions relating to the monitoring and control of pollution, and put in place regulations regarding contaminated land, abandoned mines, national parks, air quality and waste to ensure conservation and pollution control;
- EU directives, such as Directive 2002/3/EC which became the **Air Quality Limit Values Regulations, 2003** in the UK. This set targets for levels of ozone in the air by 2010.

There are also agreements between countries to control pollution. Examples included:

- international agreements, such as the Kyoto Protocol signed in 1997 by around 180 countries, where 38 industrialised countries agreed to cut greenhouse gas emissions by 5.2 per cent from 1990 levels between 2008 and 2012;
- voluntary agreements between governments and manufacturers, such as the European, Japanese and Korean manufacturers' agreement to cut carbon dioxide emissions to 140 grams per kilometre by 2008.

Taxes Another approach is to raise the price to the customer of a product through taxation. In theory, the size of the tax per unit sold should equal the cost of the externality. This way, the customer has to pay the full social cost of the product, equal to the private cost which the business charges plus the indirect tax equal to the externality. Petrol and tobacco are two examples. The high taxes on petrol go some way to cover the environmental costs which cars and lorries impose on society. This environmental cost includes noise pollution, air pollution from emissions and the destruction of the landscape through road building. For tobacco, the high taxes help pay for the medical treatment that smokers are likely to have to receive due to smoking. It also pays for medical treatment for non-smokers who suffer illness through 'secondary smoking', breathing in fumes from smokers in a room. Taxes affect consumption. However, their impact depends upon the price elasticity of demand (see unit 17) for the product. In the cases of fuel and tobacco, both products are price inelastic, i.e. there needs to be large percentage increases in the price of the product to achieve even a relatively small fall in quantity bought. Adding a couple of pence to a litre of fuel, for example, will have almost no impact on demand.

Subsidies An alternative approach to taxation is for the government to subsidise anti-pollution policies. For example, the government could pay bus companies to buy buses which use less damaging hydrogen or natural gas powered engines. Loft insulation materials could be subsidised instead of being taxed to encourage homeowners to insulate their lofts. Grants could be given to businesses to buy more fuel efficient machinery.

Compensation In some circumstances, businesses can be sued by those affected by their pollution. For example, if houses next to a factory were destroyed in an accidental explosion at the factory, the homeowners could sue the

---

Airbus and shipping port authorities are in urgent talks with the Environment Agency in Wales this week to try to resolve a problem that could delay Europe's biggest engineering project. Airbus is the world's second largest civilian aircraft manufacturer and has a factory at Broughton in North Wales. The company employs 12 000 workers in the UK. It wants to deliver wings made for the A380 aircraft at Broughton to Toulouse in France where the aircraft are being assembled. Its chosen port is Mostyn in North Wales. However, the entrance to the port is too shallow and the Dee estuary would need to be dredged to accommodate the ships being used to transport the wings. The Environment Agency has refused to allow this dredging because it could have a serious impact on the sandbanks in the estuary which are protected habitats for birds and cockles.

Ian Gray, managing director of Airbus UK, criticised the lack of appreciation in Britain of the importance of the aerospace industry. He pointed out that in the past two years Airbus had invested £510 million in the UK with another £120 million planned for this year. Airbus UK contributes a net £1 billion in exports to the economy, which would rise to £1.5 billion as the A380 wing deliveries hit their peak.

Source: adapted from *The Times*, 17.3.2004.

---

1 **What external costs might Airbus create according to the Environment Agency?**
2 **To what extent would market failure occur if the Dee estuary were dredged?**

owners of the factory for compensation. In many cases, it is not clear who owns what is being destroyed and who is responsible. When a business emits greenhouse gases and helps raise the temperature of the earth, there is no single owner of the atmosphere being affected. Also, no single business could be said to be responsible for global warming. It is millions of businesses worldwide that collectively are responsible. But it is impossible to sue industry in general. However, there are a few examples where compensation has had some success. Asbestos manufacturers and companies which used asbestos in their products have been sued by former workers who develop asbestosis, a disease which kills. Tobacco manufacturers in the United States have also been forced to pay compensation, not to individual smokers, but to individual states which have to pick up the health bill for smoking.

Pollution permits Tradable POLLUTION PERMITS are a method of reducing pollution favoured by economists. They are issued by government or government agencies to businesses. The government decides an absolute amount of a certain type of pollution that it will allow. It then issues permits to individual businesses which total that amount. The permits will typically be allocated on the basis of levels of production. The permits give the business permission to pollute to a given level. However, the permits can be bought and sold. For example, one business might have invested heavily in anti-pollution equipment and not used up all its permit allocation. It can then sell its spare permits to another producer which might have invested very little in anti-pollution equipment. The business which has invested in anti-pollution equipment is rewarded whilst the other business is penalised. Over time, the government may issue fewer and fewer permits to reduce overall pollution levels. Businesses therefore have an incentive to buy more and more equipment which will reduce pollution.

Encouraging self regulation The government could encourage industries to produce their own targets for reductions in pollution or for recycling. Self regulation tends to be a weaker option because businesses may try to resist any measures which will make any significant impact on their costs. However, in some industries, consumer pressure can force businesses to take action. In the newspaper and magazine industry, for example, publishers have set themselves targets in terms of using recycled paper. In practice, the extra cost of them doing this is small. What is more, there are some who argue that it would be more ecologically friendly to use paper made from virgin wood pulp. This is because growing trees helps reduce the amount of CO_2 in the atmosphere which in turns reduces the global warming effect. However, self regulation can be an important marketing tool which encourages consumers to believe that they are being ecologically friendly by buying one product rather than another.

The business response to environmental issues

Environmental issues offer both threats and opportunities to businesses. Businesses which stand to gain the most from growing environmental regulation are those selling pro-environmental and anti-pollution products. These businesses range from engineering companies selling equipment

designed to reduce emissions, to service companies which advise other businesses on how they can comply with regulations, to businesses selling environmentally friendly products, such as managed wood.

Those which stand to lose the most are companies which are high polluters and who face competition from other businesses which don't face similar problems. For example, a specialist chemicals company may cease trading because there are many good substitutes to its products which have only a fraction of the environmental impact in production. Or a heavily regulated UK company may face competition from a Third World producer whose government places little restriction on its activity.

Marketing Environmental issues can be a highly effective marketing tool for some businesses. Companies such as the Co-operative Bank and The Body Shop have made a particular point of pursuing environmentally friendly policies. Many businesses on their packaging or in their advertising claim to be environmentally friendly in some way. However, some businesses have found that environmental issues pose a marketing threat. Oil companies, for example, are accused by environment pressure groups such as Greenpeace or Friends of the Earth of harming the environment. In the 1990s, when Shell planned to dispose of a disused oil platform by sinking it in the middle of the Atlantic, environmental pressure groups organised a consumer boycott of Shell petrol stations in Germany. This anti-marketing pressure was successful enough to influence the business to abandon its plans. Perrier was one of the leading brands of bottled water in Europe in the 1990s and in the UK was the top brand by sales. However, a contamination scare affected the image of the brand. Such examples show that businesses must take quick and positive action when an environmental issue suddenly arises. It also shows that some businesses have to work constantly to improve their environmental image.

Finance In some cases, responding to environmental concerns or new laws and regulations can have a positive financial impact on a business. Energy saving measures, for example, can lead to a business having lower costs than before because of previous inefficiencies. In most cases, though, taking environmental action is likely to lead to higher costs. If all businesses in the industry also face these higher costs, prices are likely to rise to reflect the higher costs. Profits would then be largely unaffected. But if higher costs fall more heavily on one business than another, then some will gain a competitive advantage and others lose it. This in turn will have different impacts on profitability. Installing expensive new equipment will also have a negative impact on cash flow. In the nuclear power industry and the car industry, businesses must also make investment decisions knowing that there will be heavy costs at the end of a product's life. In the case of the nuclear power industry, this is in terms of decommissioning plant. For motor manufacturers, they have to take back old cars for recycling. This will affect the outcomes of appraisal methods like the payback method and discounted cash flow.

Operations management Pollution controls and other environmental measures could have an impact on how a product is made. This could range from changes in the type of materials used, to production methods to storage and after sales service. For example, asbestos was widely used in industry years ago but its use today is severely restricted.

Improvements in river water quality have started to stall, leaving some of the country's most important waterways in need of more protection from pollution, the Environment Agency said yesterday. The agency said that nearly one in five rivers designated as sites of special scientific interest is failing to achieve top water quality classifications because of pollution from sewage treatment and agriculture. Water quality improved during the 1990s after a £5bn programme by water companies aimed at improving discharges to rivers by upgrading sewage treatment works and sewerage systems. But the rivers are still suffering from 'diffuse pollution' caused by phosphates and nitrates from agricultural and other sources.

Source: adapted from the *Financial Times*, 24.9.2003

1 **Discuss whether farmers should be taxed for using phosphates and nitrates as fertilisers**

Industries such as electricity generation and chemicals have had to introduce much cleaner production methods to reduce emissions. The landfill tax encourages businesses to reduce the amount of waste they produce.

Human resources Environmental concerns and policies have human resource implications. Staff will need to be recruited and trained to deal with ever increasing government regulations concerning the environment. Some businesses may choose to outsource (see unit 43) the guidance they need. Larger businesses are likely to put environmental policies in place. This could include an environmental audit (see unit 56) where key measures relating to the impact of the business on the environment are audited each year and the results are made public. Implementing policies means that staff throughout the organisation are aware of the policies and what they must do to comply with the policies. As with any policy, unless there are good procedures and training in place to ensure compliance, staff will tend to interpret the policies as they see fit. Effective communication up and down the hierarchy is therefore essential. The very small minority of businesses which make environmental concerns an important business objective can use this as a way of motivating staff. Over time, it will tend to attract employees who are interested in this aspect of business. However, a tension between meeting financial targets such as profits targets and meeting environmental targets is likely to arise. For a business to survive, it must at least break even. In this sense, financial targets tend to be more important than environmental targets. This tension between targets could demotivate staff who want to see environmental targets as the most important for the business.

Contingency planning

Contingency planning (see unit 116) is planning for what might happen in the future. In environmental terms, for example, a chemical company might plan for what would happen if there was a fire at one of its plants. Or a factory which discharges clean water into a river might plan for what would happen if there was an accidental leak and polluted water was discharged instead.

As penalties and fines become larger for environmental damage over time with new legislation, it becomes ever more important for businesses to undertake contingency planning in this area. Contingency planning is also important for marketing purposes. Food and beverage manufacturers should have contingency plans for what to do if their products are found to be contaminated for whatever reason. Experience suggests that prompt recalls, together with an openness about the source of the problem, is the response which will bring least long lasting damage to the brand.

'keyterms'

External cost or externality - the difference between the private cost to an individual or business of a product or activity and its full cost to society, its social cost. So external cost equals social cost minus private cost.

Market failure - when resources are inefficiently allocated due to imperfections in the working of the market mechanism, such as when social costs do not equal private costs.

Pollution permits - permits issued by government which allow a business or other organisation to pollute the environment to a given level over a period of time. The permits are tradable and so a low pollution business can sell its spare permits to another high pollution business.

Private cost - the cost to an individual or business of a product or activity. For business, this is likely to be roughly equivalent to the accounting cost.

Social cost - the cost to society of a product or activity. this includes the private cost born by the individual or business together with the external cost which is borne by those other than the initial producer.

✓checklist

1 To whom might a business have social responsibilities?
2 Explain the difference between a social and environmental audit and an ethical code of practice.
3 To what extent do all businesses have a strong social and ethical culture?
4 What might be the conflict between implementing ethical decisions and delegation?
5 Explain the difference between private and social costs.
6 Explain briefly how businesses might be affected by pollution controls imposed by governments.
7 How might a business respond to environmental issues from the viewpoint of (a) marketing; (b) finance; (c) operations management; (d) human resources.
8 How might contingency planning be affected by environmental issues?

Last month, the European parliament confirmed that the minimum recycling target for packaging waste would be raised from 25 to 55 per cent by 2008 to cut 'the amount of discarded packaging that pollutes the environment'. The new targets will oblige manufacturers and packaging companies to recycle materials thrown away by households.

On average, a consumer is likely to handle dozens of pieces of packaging a day, but there are questions about whether it is all necessary. Do cakes really need to be wrapped in foil? Does computer software have to be sold in a box 10 times its size? When the packaging industry set up a watchdog to examine complaints such as these in the 1990s, it judged that excessive packaging was used in about half the cases it investigated. Yet the industry denies it uses too much packaging. The increase in the number of packaged items over the past 20 years has been offset by packaging becoming lighter. As a result, it is the only element of the municipal waste stream that has not increased by weight or volume in the past 20 years.

'Packaging is not a waste problem but part of the solution', says the Industry Council for Packaging in the Environment (Incpen). 'Packaging protects at least 10 times its own weight of goods and prevents them being wasted.' It says environmental concerns about packaging distract attention from bigger issues such as climate change. Incpen cites research showing that swapping a four-wheel drive car for a more fuel-efficient family saloon would, in one year, save the same amount of energy as recycling a family's bottles for 400 years.

Friends of the Earth accepts that packaging is a small part of the overall waste stream. But focusing on packaging is 'a route into peoples' awareness' of their impact, says Clare Wilton of Friends of the Earth. Elaborate packaging might create marketing advantages but squanders resources and creates waste. Maxine Holdsworth of the National Consumer Council, says: 'If you look at the average household bin and see how much is packaging, you have to say there is further to go in minimising it'.

Environmentalists are unimpressed by current regulations that require packaging to be kept to a minimum. The rules, enforced by trading standards officers, have led to just two prosecutions since they were in force. The packaging industry accepts that the current system gives little incentive to minimise packaging. However, the new rules that require a minimum of 55 per cent of packaging to be recycled will certainly be a much greater incentive to minimise packaging.

Even so, there is a row brewing between industry and local authorities about who should pick up the bill for the recycling. Local authorities want industry to pay them a fee for picking up waste and recycling it. Local authorities argue that it costs them more to have separate collections for bottles, cans and other recyclable materials, than simply picking all the rubbish up from one bin. Reaching the 2008 targets is likely to raise local authority recycling costs from its current level of £100 million a year to £300 - £400 million a year.

On the other hand, industry says that it is already doing its bit for recycling. Alupro, the UK aluminium recycling organisation, for example, says that 'we are hopeful that we will win this battle' to have local authorities pay the cost. Richard Hands of Tetra Pak UK, the carton manufacturer, says: 'We feel we have done our bit in helping the recycling capacity to be established' referring to a newly commissioned paper mill in Fife in Scotland that can recycle 20 per cent of the UK's cartons. 'The industry cannot afford to fund collection schemes across the UK.'

Source: adapted from the *Financial Times*, 28.2.2005.

1 (a) Explain why packaging might cause externalities to arise. (10 marks)
  (b) Discuss whether it should be the responsibility of businesses making the packaging to pay for its recycling or disposal. (10 marks)
2 Discuss how a frozen food manufacturer specialising in convenience meals should react to the proposals to deal with packaging described in the passage. (20 marks)

Romania

Knowledge Romania is a country which, between 1945 and the early 1990s, was a communist state. Businesses were owned by the state. The communist government was replaced in 1989 and for the first time in over fifty years, democratic elections decided who would be in government.

Application The return of democracy co-incided with the start of a process of *privatisation*. Foreign *multinational companies* bought some of the *privatised assets*, looking to make a *profit* from this *emerging market*. One business which *invested* in Romania was the US *company* Noble Ventures. It paid $4.5 million for the Resita steel mill and promised to invest a further $85 million to upgrade the plant. According to Noble Ventures, the Romanian *government* agreed, as part of the deal, to put back payment of unpaid *tax* and utility *debts*, which would allow Resita to operate its *bank accounts* normally. But then there was a general election and the new government stopped talks about rescheduling the debts. Operating the business became almost impossible and in 2001, the government forced Resita into a *financial restructuring* which led to its *renationalisation*. In 2004, the same government cancelled all Resita's debts and resold the mill to TMK, a Russian steelmaker, for a nominal €1 (66 pence). Noble Ventures has since launched a law suit against the Romanian government, accusing it of sabotaging its *acquisition* of the steel mill and illegally renationalising it in 2001.

Analysis Noble Ventures argues that illegal practices led to its failures in Romania. Instead of the rule of law, individual politicians or government officials used their power to benefit themselves. Noble Ventures lost out in the short term, but Romania could lose out in the long term if such problems are not tackled. Foreign investors will be reluctant to invest in Romania if they think that their money is at risk. In the rest of Eastern Europe and in China, economic development has gone hand in hand with inward investment by foreign companies.

Evaluation Romania needs to abide by its own laws. It desperately needs foreign cash and foreign expertise since it is one of the poorest countries in Europe and, economically, is relatively uncompetitive. Moreover, if illegal practices take place, it will find it difficult to join the European Union, a political aim of the country. At present, foreign investors are cautious of investing in the country and that is not good news for the Romanian economy.

Adapted from the *Financial Times*, 19.4.2005.

Political change in the UK

For the past 60 years, the UK has enjoyed stable government under two major political parties, the Labour Party and the Conservative Party. Political ideology, however, has changed. This has posed both opportunities and threats for UK businesses.

Nationalisation Sixty years ago, the Labour Party began a process of nationalisation (see unit 103) which saw industries such as railways, coal, gas, electricity and health pass into public (i.e. state) ownership. In the 1980s, this process was reversed by a Conservative government. Privatisation presented opportunities for UK and foreign businesses. Some state assets were sold to existing businesses. Others were floated on the London Stock Exchange (see units 25 and 61). Subsequently, some of the companies, such as some of the water and electricity companies, have been taken over by other businesses. Privatisation has therefore allowed some businesses to enter profitable new markets which before were closed to them because of state monopolies.

Deregulation In the 1980s, policies of DEREGULATION and CONTRACTING OUT gave UK businesses further opportunities. Deregulation is the process of removing legal restrictions on certain types of economic activity. For example, before the 1980s, only what is now National Bus could provide long distance coach services. Deregulation meant that any operator could now offer this service. A number of businesses then entered the market resulting in much greater competition. Contracting out is the process of the state buying in services from private sector businesses rather than producing the services themselves. Today, for example, everything from waste collection services and hospital cleaning to prisons and cataract operations are contracted out to the private sector. This provides business opportunities for private sector businesses. For example, Rentokil provides hospital cleaning services and Group 4 provides prison services.

Fiscal policy There is a difference in ideology between the Labour Party and the Conservative Party on the issue of tax and regulation. The Conservative Party has tended to argue for lower taxes and less regulation on business than the Labour Party. Higher taxes hit businesses directly if they are taxes on profits (corporation tax) or on property (business rates). If a government raises indirect taxes like VAT, businesses will attempt to pass on the higher tax in higher prices to customers, but in some cases they will be forced to absorb part of the tax increase themselves, lowering their profits. Changes in direct taxes on workers, such as income tax, will feed through to changes in spending. Rising direct taxes could lower aggregate demand and so hit sales and profits. However, it should be remembered that political changes occur over long periods of time. The tax burden measured as a percentage of GDP has been lower since 1997 under a Labour government than it was in most years under the Conservatives between 1979 and 1997. The economy under the Labour Party since 1997 has also been far more stable than in the 1970s and 1980s. Macroeconomic stability helps businesses plan for the future with greater certainty.

There are strong differences of opinion both between

parties and within parties about whether the UK should join the euro. The arguments for and against are discussed in more detail in unit 102.

Political change outside the UK

In the developed world, in Western Europe, North America, Japan and Australia, there has been considerable stability over the past 50 years. Like the UK, there have changes in economic fashion with regard to issues such as nationalisation and privatisation, and the level of taxation and regulation of business. However, other areas of the world have seen considerable political change which have been both opened up opportunities for UK businesses but also pose considerable threats to them.

The most significant political change has occurred in Communist and former Communist countries. In China, there is still a Communist government, but since the mid-1970s, it has been gradually opening up its markets to overseas companies. It has also been steadily increasing its exports to rich industrialised nations like the UK. In Eastern Europe, Communist parties were toppled from power in the late 1980s. Their economies have since been undergoing transformation from one where private businesses were small and were discouraged, to one where private businesses are encouraged and where free markets operate in many sectors of the economy.

Business opportunities In both China and Eastern Europe, UK businesses have a number of opportunities.

- They can increase sales by exporting to these countries. Selling into Eastern Europe or China is not as easy as selling into, say, France or the USA. UK businesses have first to find businesses prepared to buy their products. They may use agents (see unit 19) in those countries to find customers for them. They could exhibit at trade exhibitions. Sales may come if the UK company establishes a joint venture (see unit 102) with an Eastern European or Chinese company.
- UK businesses could establish plants, outlets or businesses in these countries to promote sales from the UK. They could also buy up all or part of existing companies. In China, many Western companies have found it is easier to find a Chinese partner company when doing this so that the business becomes a joint venture. The Chinese partner can often unlock legal and financial difficulties which a foreign company could not do. However, some joint ventures have been failures because the foreign partner has not carried out what it promised to do.
- Establishing a business in China or Eastern Europe may also be motivated by the desire to secure a cheap manufacturing base. The UK business may have too high costs in its UK factories and plants. Moving production to Eastern Europe or China can make the UK company more competitive (see unit 100).
- A UK company may license technology to a foreign business. This will earn the UK company royalties. It has the advantage that the UK company will lose little if the foreign company fails. Sometimes it is possible to license technology to competing firms in the same country. This makes it more likely that this strategy will be successful.

Business threats However, the changed political situation in Eastern Europe and China poses threats to UK businesses.

- The UK company may invest heavily in marketing to these countries. Alternatively, it may acquire businesses and set up joint ventures. But there is no guarantee of success. The investment may be completely lost in the worst case scenario. In most cases, doing business with Eastern Europe or China is riskier than doing the same business with, say, France or the USA. Partly this is because the legal framework is not always clear and certain. A UK company, for example, may buy a piece of land but find when they have built a factory on the land that ownership is disputed. Illegal practices take place, with local officials expecting bribes. This raises ethical questions for the UK company as well as legal ones since it is illegal under UK law for businesses to offer bribes. Red tape may make it almost impossible to conduct business effectively.
- The opening up of markets in Eastern Europe and China means that many UK companies, particularly manufacturing companies, face much fiercer price competition than before. Just as the UK can sell to China, so Chinese companies can sell into the UK market. Each year, thousands of UK jobs are being 'exported' to low wage economies and UK businesses are being forced to close due to the competition. On the other hand, this is a process which has been happening for hundreds of years. To remain competitive, the UK has to produce technologically advanced goods and services which are one step ahead of foreign competition.

Although Eastern Europe and China are changing particularly rapidly, other countries and parts of the world have also experienced significant change. In the 1970s, 1980s and 1990s, the 'Tiger economies' of the Far East including South Korea, Taiwan, Singapore and Hong Kong, experienced very fast growth. Today, India is tipped to be the next China, especially if it continues to open its economy to trade and foreign investment.

keyterms

Contracting out - getting an outside supplier to provide a good or service which was previously made within the business or organisation.
Deregulation - the process of removing legal restrictions on certain types of economic activity such as providing long distance coach services.

✓*checklist*

1 Explain the difference between nationalisation and privatisation.
2 Explain the difference between deregulation and contracting out.
3 Explain the difference between fiscal policy and monetary policy.
4 Analyse two opportunities and two threats which UK businesses face from the growing economy of China.

Kinson Electricals is a small electrical contracting business with 20 employees. The company picks up around 60 per cent of its work from local authority and central government contracts. For example, the company tends to get most of the work for the schools in its area.

Dabba is a medium sized company making high precision seals for a variety of engineering industries employing 261 workers. Around 40 per cent of its work is exported to Europe and to the Far East.

ITV plc is a media company which owns all of the regional Channel 3 broadcasting licences in England and Wales. The company's main source of revenue is advertising from its main broadcast channel ITV1 (Channel 3), but it is expanding its digital offering with channels such as ITV2.

In May 2005, a general election was held in the UK. In the previous six weeks, the parties launched their manifestos and the battle lines were drawn.

Michael Howard, leader of the Conservative Party, set out to re-establish his party as the party of business yesterday with a withering attack on a bloated public sector 'where money is no object'. He promised a systematic assault on government waste and red tape. He vowed to act like 'every decent manager in every business' by scrapping 168 public bodies and cutting 235 000 civil service jobs.

'There are two Britains today,' Mr Howard told a British Chambers of Commerce conference in London. 'Private sector Britain, where people are struggling just to make ends meet. And bureaucratic Britain, where money is no object, you spend what you like and employ who you like.' Mr Howard said a Conservative government would curb the rise of public spending and reverse the spread of red tape which had damaged competitiveness. As Prime Minister, he would appoint a cabinet minister for deregulation. Each department would have a regulatory budget to cap, then cut the cost of red tape issued each year. New rules would carry sunset reviews - dates by which they would be revalidated or scrapped. Small businesses would be exempt 'wherever possible'.

Bill Midgley, president of the British Chambers of Commerce, said Mr Howard's promise not to raise business taxes in the first year of a Conservative government was welcome, 'but businesses are looking for long-term stability of the tax regime'.

Business is uncertain about how well it would be served by a Conservative government. A Mori survey for the *Financial Times* found 49 per cent of finance directors believed the Tories had the best policies for business, twice as many as backed Labour.

Source: adapted from the *Financial Times* 26.4.2005

From 63 business leaders

Sir, The general election campaign offers the business community a unique opportunity to focus on the choice that is before the electorate regarding the future strength and dynamism of the UK economy.

Since 1997, Labour has presided over a period of economic stability and growth unprecedented in modern times. We live without the spectre of inflation, unemployment levels have continued to fall, and interest rates have remained at their lowest and most stable since the 1960s.

Britain has also become a more entrepreneurial society. Labour has fostered an environment in which the starting of a business is easier, faster and cheaper than in many of our major competitors. Over 1 000 businesses a day now start up under Labour.

Economic stability and a competitive tax framework have created the environment for business investment for the long-term, raising competitiveness and creating wealth and employment across the UK. We back the Government's investment in science innovation, skills and business support, and we support the continued commitment to cut excessive regulation and in maintaining a competitive position on overall corporate taxation

The future economic success of the country does not lie in plans to cut £35bn in public spending, which would be damaging to the skill, science and business support agenda.

Business has always desired one thing above all others - a stable economic climate in which to operate. In Government, Labour has delivered such an environment. Now is not the time to put such hard won stability at risk.

Source: *Financial Times*, 25.4.2005.

The fight for the business vote is intense, but industry is sceptical about what the parties are promising to deliver. For example, Labour, Conservatives and the LibDems have promised to make large public sector savings by reducing waste and inefficiency. But industry finds it difficult to believe that such large savings are possible.

What industry would really like is a promise from all three parties that they will not raise taxes on business over the next 5 years. But none of the parties will give this pledge, partly because there is a strong likelihood that, whichever party gets into power, taxes will have to rise to pay for promised increases in public spending.

Source: adapted from the *Financial Times*, 25.4.2005.

---

1 Discuss whether or not each of the three businesses described in the data (Kinson Electricals, Dabba and ITV plc) would have benefited more from a Conservative Party victory in the 2005 general election than a Labour Party victory. (20 marks)

WAAG

Knowledge In 2003, City Hopper Airports Ltd, the owners of Halfpenny Green Airport near Wolverhampton, announced plans to transform the airfield. Currently it is used by light aircraft, typically for training or pleasure use. City Hopper Airports would like to extend the runway to allow passenger jets to land. The renamed Wolverhampton Airport would then be used by half a million passengers a year on domestic flights. An action group, Wolverhampton Airport Action Group (WAAG), was immediately set up to counter the proposals.

Application WAAG is a *pressure group*. Within days of being set up, it began *lobbying* local councils, MPs and the government to turn down the plans. One way of analysing the proposals is to consider the various interests of the *stakeholders* in the airport.

Analysis The owners of the airport are motivated by the desire to gain extra profit. If the expansion went ahead, there would be considerable local demand for domestic flights. The owners would then probably want to expand into international flights, yielding further profit. WAAG is mainly made up of local people who would suffer from the development. There would be noise pollution from the aircraft and increased congestion on local roads. Whilst new jobs would be created, benefiting the local economy and creating extra demand for houses, at least some houses would fall in value because of the pollution and congestion. Those locally outside of the area affected by pollution and congestion, which would include much of the western side of the Birmingham conurbation, would probably benefit. They would have access to an airport which was nearer than Birmingham International, Manchester or East Midlands Airport. It would be an added attraction to some businesses setting up locally. Jobs would be created both directly and indirectly in this local area. Some local councils have supported the proposals recognising the benefits that the airport would bring. Others that would be more affected by the pollution and congestion have tended to oppose the plans.

Evaluation Most of those opposing the expansion of the airport could be described as 'Nimbys' - not in my back yard. They are happy to fly away on holiday so long as the airport they use is not just down the road from them. Arguably they are failing to see the bigger picture of how the airport could benefit the local economy of the West Midlands. On the other hand, the owners of the airport are likely to be acting in their own self interest. In these situations, it could be argued that there might be some fairness if those who benefited compensated those who lost out. In practice, the economic and legal system is not that sophisticated. It is hardly any wonder, then, that those who stand to lose most have created a pressure group which to date could be argued to have been successful in preventing the plans going ahead.

Adapted from www.wolverhamptonbusinessairport.co.uk; www.waag.uk.com.

Pressure groups

Pressure groups are groups which attempt to influence the policies and actions of business, government and individuals (see unit 56). They can differ widely in their aims and objectives. They are also supported, sponsored and run by a variety of individuals and organisations.

- Many pressure groups are set up by individuals to campaign on specific issues. Most have charitable status in the UK. For example, Greenpeace and Friends of the Earth are environmental pressure groups. Amnesty International campaigns for human rights worldwide. The RSPB (Royal Society for the Protection of Birds), the RSPCA (Royal Society for the Prevention of Cruelty to Animals) and the WWF (Worldwide Fund for Nature) campaign on behalf of animal issues.
- Some pressure groups are set up by the business community to protect their interests. Local Chambers of Commerce lobby on behalf of businesses in their area to local and central government. The CBI (Confederation of British Industry) represents the interests of a wide variety of British companies. Individual industry associations, such as the National Union of Farmers or the Surface Engineering Association, lobby on behalf of firms in their industry.
- Pressure groups exist to lobby on behalf of workers. The main example is trade unions and, in the UK, the umbrella organisation for trade unions, the TUC (Trades Union Congress).

- There are also political pressure groups. Various 'think tanks', such as the Adam Smith Institute or the Institute for Public Policy Research, produce policy proposals for everything from road pricing to ways of funding health care to corporate tax policy. Political parties such as the Labour Party or the Conservative Party can be seen as pressure groups.
- Pressure groups can sometimes be short term or local groups set up to address particular issues, for example a local campaign to prevent the siting of an incinerator or a local authority waste disposal site in a rural area.

The impact of pressure groups on business

Pressure groups exist to promote their own interests. There is a variety of ways in which the activities of pressure groups can have a direct impact on businesses.

Changing the law Some pressure groups lobby local MPs and Parliament at Westminster as well as various EU bodies such as the European Commission to change the law which affects business. For example, the Consumers Association would like much tougher consumer protection laws in the UK. Ash, the anti-smoking group, lobbies the Chancellor of the Exchequer annually to raise the tax on cigarettes. The TUC would like to see legislation which gave greater powers to trade unions. Friends of the Earth has lobbied for government to ban GM crops being planted in the UK.

LOBBYING can take various forms. Pressure groups may

speak directly to ministers, and possibly even the Prime Minister, concerned with the legislation they wish to see changed. They may write to MPs setting out their case. Reports may be published which will be circulated to government ministers, opposition parties and MPs. There may be direct action in the form of marches or demonstrations, for example outside the Houses of Parliament. Pressure groups may encourage their members to write to their MPs or the government minister. Some pressure groups employ professional lobbying firms to organise the lobbying on their behalf. Pressure groups will attempt to bring the press onto their side to get as much media coverage as possible for their campaigns. Press releases, for example, will be used to inform the press of activities. Press support for a campaign can have enormous influence. At times, it can influence a government to change its mind.

Lobbying businesses directly Some pressure groups lobby businesses directly. For example, Friends of the Earth lobbies the major oil companies in the UK in an attempt to make their policies more environmentally friendly. In some cases, a pressure group may mount a campaign over a particular issue. As with attempting to change the law, lobbying can range from sending letters and information to direct action such as demonstrations outside the premises of a business. Some pressure groups attempt to influence individual businesses on a long term basis. The pressure group is then attempting to become a **stakeholder** (see unit 56) in the business. It wants to have a say in the decision making of the firm. Businesses are likely to resist any attempt by a pressure group to become a long term stakeholder. However, as some companies have found, it may be easier to form a long term relationship with pressure groups like Friends of the Earth rather than be the subject of continual negative lobbying.

Using customers to change business strategy Some pressure groups have been successful in using customers to change business strategies. Nestlé has been the focus of a consumer boycott of its products for selling powdered milk in the Third World. Shell petrol stations in Germany were boycotted by customers over Shell's decision to sink a disused oil platform in the middle of the Atlantic. Consumers have been encouraged not to purchase products made from fur through media advertisements. The response by business varies. Shell, for example, opted to dismantle the oil platform in Norway.

Changing the climate of opinion Some pressure groups have been successful at changing the climate of opinion within society. Friends of the Earth and Greenpeace, for example, have helped to create greater environmental consciousness in society. This inevitably affects businesses. Owners, management and workers will be more prepared to change their strategies and policies in line with the new opinion. Other stakeholders, such as customers and suppliers, will put pressure on businesses to change too.

How businesses can deal with pressure groups

There is a variety of ways in which businesses can react to pressure groups.

Lobbying government Just as pressure groups can lobby government for change, so too can businesses. They use the same techniques for lobbying as pressure groups, including seeing government ministers, writing to MPs, publishing reports and sometimes even organising demonstrations.

FOREST (Freedom Organisation for the Right to Enjoy Smoking Tobacco) is a pressure group dedicated to defending the interests of smokers in the UK. Founded in 1979, it exists to 'defend the interests of adults who choose to smoke; we promote freedom of choice for employers and proprietors who wish to accommodate smokers on their premises; and we speak out against those who want to discriminate against smokers or ban smoking completely; last but not least, we promote greater courtesy and tolerance between smokers and non smokers.' It does not 'deny the health risks of smoking'.

Most of its funds come from grants from tobacco companies but it also raises money from private individuals who support the group. It claims to be independent of the tobacco companies which fund its activities although their interests usually coincide.

In recent years, FOREST has campaigned on a range of issues including tobacco advertising, smoking in public places, smoking at work, tobacco taxation and the treatment of cross-Channel shoppers. FOREST spokespersons are frequently quoted in newspapers and on radio and television. Letter writing, for instance to the press and to politicians, is a major activity.

Because FOREST is a vociferous pressure group, it is regularly invited to submit its views to government bodies, such as the Department of Health, the Health and Safety Commission and the Scottish Parliament Community Care Committee.

Source: adapted from FOREST, www.forestonline.org.

1 *Suggest why tobacco companies give funds to FOREST.*
2 *FOREST has chosen to campaign on the issue of freedom to smoke. Discuss why it might have chosen to campaign on this issue.*

Establishing their own pressure groups Businesses can create their own pressure groups to counter the effects of hostile pressure groups. Chambers of Commerce and the CBI are two such examples. Even sensitive areas such as smoking might be targeted. For example, in the UK the pro-tobacco group, FOREST (Freedom Organisation for the Right to Enjoy Smoking Tobacco), attempts to defend the interests of smokers through research, campaigns, and practical advice and information.

Working with pressure groups Businesses may choose to work with pressure groups, listening to their views and allowing them to influence decision making. The most common form of this is businesses working with trade unions where trade unions become significant stakeholders in the business. This has the advantage that the pressure group is likely to moderate its demands and be more realistic in what it wants to achieve. The cost of working with the pressure group may also be lower than the cost of having to deal with the pressure group as a hostile body. The change in strategy may affect other stakeholders, such as owners, adversely. Better working conditions could be at the expense of lower profits. On the other hand, there may be a win-win situation. Better working conditions could improve motivation on the part of workers and so increase productivity and profits. Or more environmentally friendly policies might lead to customers choosing to buy from that particular business.

Resisting the demands of pressure groups In many cases, businesses will choose to resist the demands of pressure groups. This is because it would be costly to give in to their

keyterms

Lobbying - making a case for a particular course of action to those in power with the view to getting them to implement that course of action.

demands. At worst, it could mean the closure of the business. For example, Huntingdon Life Sciences is a company which conducts experiments on animals for a variety of companies including cosmetic companies. Animal rights activists have conducted a campaign to close down the company. Similarly environmental pressure groups have an ongoing campaign to close down the nuclear power industry in the UK, whilst anti-war groups would like to see the closure of most of the UK's defence businesses. In this sort of case, there is no room for compromise on the part of the business.

For most businesses, pressure groups are only likely to affect them through changes in legislation. On a day to day basis, they can therefore be ignored. However, the larger the business, the more likely that pressure groups will have a direct impact. Again, in most cases, businesses will attempt to ignore the pressure group. Polite letters thanking a pressure group for its comments and saying that they will be taken into consideration when decisions are made, are a good PR response without promising any change. Some large companies have chosen to ignore consumer boycotts rather than change their strategy.

Huntingdon Life Sciences (HLS) is a commercial animal testing laboratory in Huntingdon, near Cambridge. It is the largest commercial laboratory in the UK. It handles animal testing for both human and veterinary medical drug approval, as well as studies on agricultural chemicals, industrial chemicals and foodstuffs. It has clients worldwide, particularly in the UK, the US and Japan.

HLS has been criticised by animal rights and animal welfare supporters because they believe that there is animal abuse taking place at the laboratory. In 1999, video footage was recorded inside HLS which the company agreed showed breaches of animal protection laws. However, HLS claims that these breaches were isolated cases and the staff responsible were sacked and prosecuted. In response, animal rights activists set up a pressure group called SHAC (Stop Huntingdon Animal Cruelty). It aimed to close the HLS facility within three years. It campaigned using traditional techniques, such as picketing the laboratory, lobbying politicians and getting the media to cover its campaign sympathetically. Other action took place, although SHAC disclaimed all knowledge of these activities. They included threats made to members of Huntingdon staff and damage to cars. The managing director of the company was also attacked in his home in 2001. In 2004, the police recorded more than 100 attacks on staff at the company.

Suppliers were also targeted by SHAC for direct legal action. These ranged from suppliers of bottled gas to bankers and stockbrokers who bought and sold its shares. Some direct action included picketing and demonstrations. However, some staff at these companies also received death threats, had their cars vandalised and were intimidated. One campaign against a farm which breeds guinea pigs for use in animal experiments included the owner and family being bombarded with hate mail, telephone calls, hoax bombs and arson attacks.

The direct action against suppliers has been successful to some extent. Many suppliers targeted pulled out of their contracts with Huntingdon, although the company has managed to replace these suppliers with new ones. In the case of banking, the UK government authorised the Bank of England to run bank accounts for the company.

The UK government has provided more general support to HLS. In 2005, it tabled a new bill to make it a criminal offence to cause 'economic damage' though campaigns of intimidation. Companies which deal with the animal research industry will be protected from intimidation. Police will also be given powers to arrest anyone protesting outside the homes of scientists and to ban protesters from approaching a person's property for three months. HLS has lobbied government for stronger measures to be put in place, but accepts that the new law will help it fend off pressure from groups like SHAC.

Source: adapted from www.answers.com/topic/huntingdon-life-sciences; news.telegraph.co.uk/news/main.jhtml?xml=/news/2005/01/31/nanim31.xml.

SHAC has acquired notoriety for its aggressive campaigning techniques. Not only has it targeted Huntingdon Life Sciences (HLS), but it has deliberately chosen to campaign against all the suppliers to HLS. For example, in April 2005, it demonstrated against a number of supplier companies in Surrey and Sussex. It used its website to report the following. 'On to UPS (a parcel delivery company). We started at the top of this industrial estate today and played the beagle tap and held up the banners as we made our way to UPS, bringing out loads of workers from other firms and we made sure they knew that UPS is involved with animal killers. We handed out leaflets to the few we hadn't reached before and kept it noisy until we made our way back again ... just stopping to inform the 3 carloads of police that this is a democracy. We won't give up, UPS, so you might as well give in now.'

Source: adapted from www.shac.net.

Two key messages in SHAC's campaign are about cruelty and freedom. On their website, for example, it says that 'WE WON'T STOP until every animal trapped inside or destined to be thrown in a cage at HLS sees a better world, where they no longer have to live in fear of the next day or of human kind'. It also says that: 'Remember that we're not fighting for a petty little cause, we're not fighting for something that can be controlled by money or status. We're fighting for freedom!' Their aim is simply to close down Huntingdon Life Sciences: 'No matter how much the people who think that they can take these animals' freedom and lives away try to stop us, that won't distract us because WE WON'T STOP until Huntingdon Life Sciences is just a ... distant memory.'

Source: adapted from www.shac.net.

Animal experimentation is controversial, but many scientists argue that it is necessary for research. Huntingdon Life Sciences (HLS), for example, says that 'There are stages in any research programme when it is not enough to know how individual molecules, cells or tissues behave. The living body is much more than just a collection of these parts, and the need to understand how they interact or how they are controlled is essential. There are ethical limits to the experiments that we can perform in people, so the only alternative is to use the most suitable animal to study a particular disease or biological function.'

   HLS argues that animal research has contributed to 'an ever growing number of successes and advances in the field of human medicine. For many years, humans have benefited from the healthcare advances that animal based research has achieved.' It also argues that 'key-hole surgery, organ transplantation, skin grafting and the latest research into the prevention of genetic diseases are all benefiting from animal research.'

Source: adapted from www.shac.net;www.huntingdon.com.

1 Discuss whether the pressure group, SHAC, has adopted an effective strategy to achieve its aims. (20 marks)
2 You are the managing director of a small company. An animal research laboratory has approached you with a view to a contract to supply it with chemicals. Evaluate whether or not you should accept the contract and, if so, under what terms. (20 marks)

Barratt Developments

Knowledge Barratt Developments PLC is a UK house builder.

Application The *company* had a *turnover* of £2.5 billion in 2004 and built a total of 14 021 dwellings. Its *economic activities* had an impact both socially and environmentally. It attempted to quantify some of this impact in its *Corporate Social Responsibility Report* for the year.

Analysis The Corporate Social Responsibility Report covered three main areas. Human Resources included objectives such as 'launch Employee Handbook' and 'expand careers webpages of current websites to advertise all job roles'. The Environment included objectives such as 'minimise waste from our our business operations' and maximise the use of natural features in our developments wherever possible'. Occupational Health and Safety included objectives such as 'reduce accidents that cause injury to persons working on or visiting any of our places of work' and 'provide competent staff through a structured training programme'.

Evaluation The published Social Responsibility Report 2004 shows some of the successes and difficulties in this area. Barratt is able to point to improvements over time in some areas such as incident rates per employee of accidents reported in recent years. But this is only one of three examples in the whole report of tables or charts of statistics measuring performance. A number of other statistics are cited in the text of the report such as the percentage of timber waste recycled (100%) or the total waste recycled (76%). But there is no comparison over time or with other similar companies. Therefore, it could be agreed that it is difficult to judge from the report alone whether Barratt is an environmentally friendly company or whether it is a responsible employer. Reporting of corporate social responsibility may have some way to go before it becomes meaningful in the same way that, say, financial accounting is meaningful.

Source: adapted from Barratt Developments plc, *Annual Report and Accounts*, 2004, *Corporate Social Responsibility Report*, 2004.

Corporate social responsibility

Over the past ten years, there has been growing interest, particularly by large companies, in the issue of CORPORATE SOCIAL RESPONSIBILITY (CSR). This is the responsibility that a business has towards all stakeholders and not just to owners or shareholders. In units 56, 57 and 104, it was explained that social responsibility includes taking the considerations of workers, local communities and the environment seriously, as well acting in an ethical manner when making decisions.

Social and environmental audits

Corporate social responsibility can be shown in a wide variety of ways. Staff may be encouraged to do voluntary work, food products may be discontinued or their formulations altered to fit the latest thinking on diets, or pollution may be lowered. However, there is a trend for large companies to compile social and environmental audits (see unit 56). Auditing involves inspecting evidence against established standards. Auditors can then say that the evidence presented by the business is 'true and fair'.

In accounting, standards for accounting audits are set by accounting bodies such as the Accounting Standards Board. In contrast, social and environmental auditing is voluntary and there is no body which draws up rules about how audits should take place. At present, companies are free to choose what standards they should be measured against and who the auditors will be. Indeed, the vast majority of businesses do not undertake any social or environmental accounting.

Businesses which do compile social and environmental audits use a wide range of measures, which differs from business to business. An oil company, for example, may measure the number of oil spills for which it is responsible. This would not be appropriate for a drinks company which might use other indicators such as levels of air pollution created by its breweries and distilleries. Social and environmental audits might include some of the following.

Employment indicators How well does the business treat its staff? This might include indicators about pensions, healthcare benefits, trade union representation, training and education, number of accidents involving staff, payment of minimum wages, equal opportunities and the level of women in higher management or director positions.

Human rights indicators How well does the company perform on human rights issues? For example, does it encourage its workers to join trade unions and give those trade unions negotiating rights with the company? Does it have works councils? Does it or its suppliers use child labour? Does the company operate in, buy supplies from or sell products to countries which have poor human rights records? Does it discriminate on grounds of race, gender or age when recruiting or promoting staff?

The communities in which the business operates What impact does the business have on the life of the communities in which it operates? For example, how much does it give to charities? How much is spent on local schools, hospitals and housing?

Business integrity and ethics How ethical is the business in its activities? For example, have there been any cases of trading which breaks legislation involving the company? Did the company make political contributions and to whom? Was the company involved in cases associated with unfair competition?

Product responsibility What was the social impact of the products sold by the business? For example, were there customer health and safety issues? Was after sales service adequate? Was advertising true and fair? Did the company manage its information on customers and suppliers in such a way as to preserve their privacy?

The environment These indicators can form a separate **environmental audit**. Some businesses may only compile an environmental audit and not include any of the other social indicators described above. Indicators might include the amount of energy or other raw materials such as water or pesticides used by the business. How much waste or effluent was produced? What were levels of greenhouse gas or ozone-depleting emissions? What percentage of materials used were recycled? What was the company's impact on bio-diversity? What impact did it have on protected and sensitive areas? How many times was it fined during the period for failure to comply with environmental regulations and what was the total level of fines?

Some of these measures are **financial**, i.e. they are measured in money terms. Many, however, are **non-financial**. For this reason, it is difficult to get a quick and easy overall measure of how well a business is doing from its social and environmental audit. In contrast, with a financial audit like a set of financial accounts, it is possible, for example, to look at the profit and loss account and say that the business has performed better or worse in terms of revenues, costs and profit. The data from social audits are therefore more difficult to assess and compare from year to year than from financial accounts.

Exposing social costs or just PR?

Social and environmental auditing can be controversial. Those in favour argue that businesses should be encouraged to conduct social and environmental audits for a number of reasons.

- It helps both businesses and their stakeholders to understand the **social costs** (see unit 104) of their activities and not just the private costs shown in their financial statements.
- It is a way for management of a business to manage the business in a more socially responsible way and identify issues of **market failure** (see unit 104).
- It allows the stakeholders of a business to evaluate its success using wider criteria than simply financial measures.
- It might be used to plan more effectively for the future. For example, a business might be able to identify new markets, different sources of supply, and different production methods which might suit the needs of its stakeholders, including customers.
- It might prevent some stakeholders, such as pressure groups, from distorting facts to suit their own agendas.
Many pressure groups (see unit 106), however, argue that social and environmental auditing is inadequate. Businesses have the freedom to choose on what they report. It can also be difficult for auditors to verify the statistics produced by the company. In the case of illegal trading, for example, it is in the interests of both the employees and those they are trading

with to keep illegal deals away from the eyes of auditors. Investigative journalism also uncovers instances of issues such as use of child labour and poor working conditions in Third World factories which have not been reported in the official social audit. So social and environmental audits may be misleading.

Pressure groups would like to see tough uniform standards for social and environmental audits with which all businesses would have to comply. Then it would be possible to compare the performance of one business with another. It would also force businesses to account for externalities (see unit 106) which at present they prefer to ignore or, at worst, conceal from their stakeholders.

Current social auditing, pressure groups would argue, is little more than a PR (public relations) exercise. To make themselves look socially and environmentally aware, companies publish social and environment audits. They can use this when talking to the press, to their shareholders and to pressure groups to say that they understand the issues and are taking tough action to combat externalities.

Voluntary social auditing might also be an obstacle to the introduction by government of tougher laws and regulations on social and environmental issues. Companies could argue that their social audits show that they are responsible organisations which have the best interests of the community amongst their goals. Introducing laws and regulations would mean more red tape and higher costs to business without necessarily improving current practice. On the other hand they may be more concerned with maximising shareholder value. Social auditing is therefore an obstacle to what might really be needed - tough laws and regulations to control anti-social businesses.

keyterms

Corporate social responsibility - **the responsibility that a business has towards all stakeholders and not just to owners or shareholders.**

checklist

1 What is an audit?
2 Why are recognisable and accepted standards important in auditing?
3 What measures might be used when conducting a social and environmental audit?
4 What are the arguments (a) in favour of and (b) against conducting social and environmental audits?

British American Tobacco is one of the world's largest cigarette manufacturers. In its Social Report 2003/4 it said: 'Our vision is to achieve leadership of the global tobacco industry through strategies focussed on growth, productivity and responsibility. By growth we do not mean 'selling smoking', but growth in our share of the global market, growth in profit, and continuing growth in shareholder value. We believe that because our products pose risks to health, it is all the more important that our business is managed responsibly and we see responsibility as fundamental to building long term shareholder value. Our Business Principles are Mutual Benefit, Responsible Product Stewardship and Good Corporate Conduct. In our Social Report, we aim to demonstrate how we are working to live by them.'

Source: adapted from British American Tobacco, *Social Report*, 2003/4.

Gross turnover (including duty, excise and other taxes)	£25 622 million
Operating profit	£2 781 million
Profit after tax	£788 million
Worldwide excise and tax contribution	£14 360 million
Group environmental, health and safety expenditure	£34.8 million
Group charitable and community donations	£12.7 million
Employees (including associate companies)	86,941
Factories	87 in 66 countries

Table 107.1 *British American Tobacco: key statistics, 2003*
Source: adapted from British American Tobacco, *Social Report*, 2003/4.

Can the maker of a lethal product be socially responsible? Martin Broughton, the outgoing chairman of British American Tobacco, says of corporate social responsibility (CSR) that: 'To say it's not important for controversial industries to operate responsibility is a very strange way of looking at life. I think because the product is controversial and dangerous, it is more important that the industry is in responsible hands than what you might call a "normal" industry.'

BAT's claims of responsibility, however, face a credibility gap. A survey of MPs and non-governmental organisations has just named it the worst of Britain's top 50 companies for corporate social responsibility. 'It would seem that no matter what tobacco companies try to do on the subject of CSR, its the nature of the product that is the key issue and the two are incompatible', says BPRI, the WPP group consultancy that carried out the survey.

Source: adapted from the *Financial Times*, 28.9.2004.

	20002	2003	
	Metric tonnes	Metric tonnes	% change
Non-hazardous waste			
Sent to landfillls	50 701	41 456	-18.2
Recycled	98 909	99 630	0.7
Incinerated	1 456	1 276	-12.4
Other	4 345	759	-82.5
Total	155 411	143 121	-7.9
Hazardous waste			
Sent to approved landfills	110	117	6.4
Recycled	362	363	0.3
Incinerated	263	495	88.2
Other	176	35	-80.1
Total	911	1 010	10.9
Hazardous and non-hazardous waste, total	156 322	144 131	-7.8
Per million cigarettes equivalent produced	0.153	0.144	-5.9

Table 107.2 *Total amount of waste generated by BAT by type and destination* (Destination = method by which waste is treated, including composting, reuse, recycling, recovery, incineration or landfilling.)
Source: adapted from British American Tobacco, *Social Report*, 2003/4.

	Management trainees	Level 1 (junior management)	Level 2 (middle management)	Level 3 (senior management)	Level 4 (senior management)
Male	61%	73%	78%	87%	94%
Female	39%	27%	22%	13%	6%
Male to female ratio	1 to 1	2.7 to 1	3.6 to 1	6.7 to 1	15.7 to 1

Table 107.3 *Diversity and opportunity: composition of management (including the board of directors), male and female ratios*
Source: adapted from British American Tobacco, *Social Report*, 2003/4.

British American Tobacco (BAT) supports community and charitable projects. In its Social Report 2003/4, it said that in 2003, it had donated £12.7 million for community and charitable purposes, £2.4 million of which was in the UK. 'We believe that our companies should work with the communities where they operate to contribute to economic, social and environmental development. While we see it as the role of governments and regulatory authorities to create environments where business can thrive and can thus contribute, we believe that we can take the initiative by striving to be a good corporate citizen wherever our companies operate.'

British American Tobacco companies around the world support local community and charitable projects and initiatives. For example, in March 2004, British American Tobacco Vietnam was involved in poverty relief in Vietnam's two largest cities, Ho Chi Minh City and Hanoi. Funds were made available to families as interest free loans for one to three years. According to BAT's Social Report, 'sixty households in the Can Gio area of Ho Chi Minh City received $25 000 (£15 244) to enable them to raise shrimps and build a home-based business and the same donation was given to 83 households in the Soc Son district of Hanoi for families to build a water pump station and raise cows'.

Source: adapted from British American Tobacco, *Social Report*, 2003/4.

1 Using BAT as an example, discuss the extent to which the maker of a potentially 'controversial and dangerous' product (Box 2) can be socially responsible. (20 marks)

The Medieval Bar

Knowledge Greg Deacon has had a successful career in the brewery trade, managing pubs and then working for a national chain expanding their network of themed pubs. Two years ago, he decided to go it alone and set up his own chain of themed bars based on Medieval England. Greg Deacon was lucky in having a rich enough family to put down most of the first £½ million needed to set up the first bar in Stratford.

Application The Medieval Bar was *profitable* in its first year. Greg set about looking to expand the chain. He was faced with a number of choices. He could set up a *franchise*. Alternatively, he could try to interest a *venture capitalist* to buy into the equity of the business. A third option was to rely on *retained profit* and *borrow* the extra funds needed. He was determined to maintain a *positive cash flow* through the expansion phase. He also wanted to avoid *overtrading*.

Analysis Although franchising would have provided most of the extra finance needed for expansion, Greg didn't want to lose control of the business at this stage. So he put aside the franchise option. Introducing a venture capitalist would equally have meant losing some control of the business. He knew that the aim of the venture capitalist would be to make a profit over a 3-5 year time period and then sell out. He also knew that many entrepreneurs left their businesses at this stage unable to make the transition to being involved in a public limited company. So he decided that his preferred route would be using profit and borrowing. In its first year, the bar generated £75 000 profit. This year, he is hoping for £100 000. So he needs to borrow around £400 000 to open the second bar at a site in Birmingham which he has looked at. Despite interest charges of around £70 000 a year, he estimates that the new bar will have positive cash flow in its first year. If he negotiates medium term borrowing for the £400 000, he should also avoid any problems with overtrading.

Evaluation Greg Deacon is taking a risk in opening his second themed pub. He is probably right in avoiding franchising at this stage. He will have a much stronger proposition to make to potential franchisees when he is successfully running five pubs. As for losing control by issuing new equity to venture capitalists, he should be realistic in understanding that at some stage, if he is successful, he will sell out. As it is, most of the equity is owned by family members, not himself. Using retained profit and borrowing is probably the most risky option, but it does at least mean that control remains within the family.

Business growth

Businesses can be split into three main types. Some businesses are growing in size. Others remain the same size over a period of time. Others are declining in size. The size of a business can be measured in a number of different ways.

- By value of sales. A business might, for example, see its sales rise from £500 000 to £600 000 over a 12 month period;
- By volume of sales. A shipbuilding business might complete 10 ships this year compared to 8 ships last year;
- By number of workers. A business might have 600 workers this year compared to 550 last year;
- By the value of the business. For a public limited company, this could be measured by its stock market valuation. Alternatively, the value of capital employed on the balance sheet could be used;
- By market share. For example, a business might see its market share rise from 50 per cent to 60 per cent.

None of these is an adequate measure of business size on its own. A car manufacturer, for example, will have a much higher value of capital employed for the same level of sales as a supermarket chain because the car manufacturer is capital intensive whilst the supermarket chain is labour intensive. However, a growing business in one that is likely to have growing sales both by value and volumes, an increasing number of workers and a need to investment in new capital equipment, which could be reflected in a growing value of capital employed.

Financial capital

A growing business is likely to need more financial capital than before. It will need increased financial capital to increase its:
- working capital (see unit 28), such as stocks, debtors and cash;
- physical capital such as machinery, equipment and premises.

This financial capital can come from two sources.

Internal finance This is likely to be mainly retained profit, but could also include sales of assets, tighter credit control or reducing stock levels (see unit 24).

External finance This be achieved through a number of different sources (see units 25 and 61) including:
- borrowing money through overdrafts;
- loans and trade credit;
- hire purchase and leasing;
- gaining new equity finance, for example for a limited company through the issue of new shares;
- gaining grants, mainly from government.

Some businesses also have the option to grow through franchising their idea to other businesses or individuals. For example, McDonald's uses franchising in some countries. Typically, in return for a lump sum payment up front and a share of the revenues, a franchisee can use the business idea and brand name of the original company, the franchisor. The franchisor typically provides support in getting the franchisee started and then provides marketing support. The advantage to the franchisor is that it doesn't have to put up the financial capital to expand the business but does get a share of the revenues from the original idea.

Growth and cash flow

The higher the rate of growth of a business, the more pressure it will put on its cash flow position. Net cash flow (see units 27 and 28) is the difference between the cash flowing into a business and the cash flowing out. If a business is growing, cash flowing out of a business tends to grow at a faster rate than the cash flowing into the business. This means that over time, the net cash flow position becomes more and more unfavourable.

The reason for this deteriorating cash flow position is that a business tends to have to pay out cash to make its products in advance of when it receives cash for their sale. For example, a car battery manufacturer might see a steady rise in sales of 2 per cent a month over a year. It will initially have to buy in more materials. It doesn't have to pay for these immediately

because the supplier extends trade credit but it still has to pay within 30 days. Assuming it was using its workforce efficiently before, rising output will mean that workers will have to work longer hours. Towards the end of the period, the business will probably be hiring more workers. So there will be rising wage costs. By the end of the 12 month period, sales will be approximately a third higher than at the beginning. By this stage, the business is likely to be buying new capital equipment to cope with higher production levels.

Contrast this with its inflow of cash. Invoices for the delivery of batteries will inevitably go out weeks and possibly even months after invoices have been received for payment for materials. Workers too will probably have to be paid before the business receives the cash for the sale of the batteries they made. As for capital equipment, the business might have to outlay, say, £100 000 and only see a payback (see unit 84) on that investment in two or three years time.

To cope with this negative cash flow, growing businesses need to increase their financial capital. So a small but growing medium sized business might look to a venture capitalist (see unit 25) for an equity injection. A large plc might issue new corporate bonds (see unit 25) onto the market. A small business might arrange for its overdraft limit to be raised. A profitable business might be able to finance its growth by retaining profit (see unit 24).

Overtrading

Too many growing businesses tend to ignore the financial implications of their success. It is relatively easy for a business to slip into a position of **overtrading** (see unit 26). This occurs when a business has too little working capital (see unit 28). For example, if the the battery manufacturer were in this position, it would almost certainly delay paying invoices for as a long as possible. Other cash outlays, like paying tax to the Inland Revenue or Customs and Excise, could be delayed too. It would attempt to get its bank to increase its overdraft limit so it could borrow more money on a short term basis. It might even begin to delay payment of wages to its staff. So basic pay might be paid on time, but overtime payments would be kept back a few weeks or even months.

Overtrading in the long term is an inefficient way of running a business. Too much scarce management time will be devoted to manipulating the financial position. Long term investment will almost certainly be put off which may limit the growth of the business in the long term. Overtrading can also endanger the business. Suppliers might in the end refuse to supply because of constant late payments. The bank might decide to reduce its overdraft limit or even call in its overdraft (i.e. say that the overdraft must be repaid in full immediately). The result at best would be that the business would have to refuse some new orders, stopping growth. At worst, the business could be forced to cease trading because it did not have enough cash to carry on.

Bio-degradable packaging should be a sure-fire winner in an age when we are more than ever conscious of the environment. Toby Matthews moved into this area when he worked on an order in the early 1990s from the Glastonbury music festival. The festival wanted to reduce litter and demonstrate its green credentials. Today, his company, Potatopak, makes disposable trays for food from potato starch. It currently supplies a few small customers and supermarket group J. Sainsbury. Potentially, the global market for packaging is enormous, valued at billions of dollars. Potatopak's failure to take advantage of this reflects the financial problems that the company has faced.

One big problem is cost. Currently its trays sell for 6p-7p, or roughly twice as much as the rival standard plastic product. The conventional wisdom is that the price of bio-degradable articles will come down if made in high enough volumes. However, Terry Robins, packaging innovations manager at Sainsbury, says this theory does not necessarily hold. He says machinery to make starch-based trays is slower than the much more rapid moulding systems that turn out plastic products. 'It is not necessarily an insuperable problem', says Mr Robins, 'but it may require someone to invent a new form of machine (for making the starch-based trays at an acceptable speed)'.

Another problem is cash flow. The company last year lost £370 000 on sales of around £70 000. Potatopak is now losing about £20 000 a month. Alan Bracher, company secretary and one of the shareholders, says that 'to make the most of the potential of the company we have to find a way to make it in much higher volumes'. At present, Potatopak's moulding machines are underutilised, making just 100 000 trays a month. The large losses are due to high overheads dwarfing the small sales revenues. But the losses could be cut dramatically, says Mr Bracher, if the company could increase its production rate to perhaps 500 000 trays a month, at which point its unit prices could fall.

A third problem is long term capital. Shareholders so far have put £1.2 million into the company, with a substantial proportion of this coming from Mr Matthews and his family. But more cash is necessary to pay for the expensive moulds needed to turn out the variety of products a broader range of customers would require. Cash is also needed to undertake more technical work to improve its machines. The company has hopes of persuading a financial group to take a sizeable stake and probably to introduce new management that would release Mr Matthews for a more ambassadorial, marketing related role, with a specific job selling licensing rights to the Potatopak process to packaging companies around the world.

Source: adapted from the *Financial Times*, 20.03.2003.

1 To what extent could Potatopak's financial problems be solved if it found an equity backer ready to put an extra £1 million into the business? (20 marks)
2 Discuss whether a bank would be willing to loan Potatopak £1 million to finance its growth. (20 marks)

Natasha's Fitness Centre

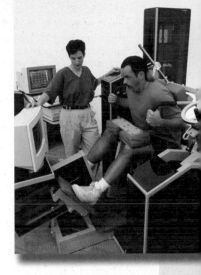

Knowledge Natasha's Fitness Centre was the inspiration of Erin Mitson. She had a background in relaxation therapy, exercise techniques and sports injuries, eventually managing a small leisure centre and then moving into a co-ordination middle management job with her employer, a large health centre in London. Four years ago, she decided to branch out on her own and opened her first centre called Natasha's Fitness Centre after her sister, a former athlete. It offered a variety of treatments, therapies and fitness regimes.

Application The *finance* for the business came from a mixture of her own savings, *borrowing* from the bank and and *equity* injection from her parents. The first centre was an enormous success and within twelve months she had opened a second. Within three years, she had a chain of five centres in the South West. However, *growth* of the *business* proved disastrous and the *company* went into *receivership*.

Analysis The problem was that Erin found it impossible to control effectively her growing chain. She appointed managers for each new centre, but they lacked the drive and energy she had with her first outlet. The managers also failed to control costs. In the centres it was easy for costs to escalate, either through increases in supplier's costs which were not monitored, ordering stock which was not used or giving expensive treatments to family or friends who were not charged. Standards of service were not as good as in the original Natasha's and some of the sites chosen for subsequent openings were not ideal.

Evaluation Scaling up a business is not easy, as Erin found out. She failed to keep control of quality and costs. In retrospect, she should have either managed her centres more closely, or spent more time finding and then training the right managers who would be able to deliver what she wanted. Alternatively, she should have found a new equity partner who would have both put new cash into the business and taken an active role in its management.

Growth of the business

Growth of a business can happen in a number of different ways. Growth can take place, for example, from a very small to a very large business, or from a small medium sized to a large medium sized business. Growth can also take place rapidly or very slowly. For example, a business which grows its sales by approximately 2.5 per cent a year will roughly double its sales over a period of 25 years. A business growing sales at 10 per cent a year will double its sales over a 7 year period.

The pace of growth and the starting point for growth will influence heavily how a business reacts to it. One aspect which needs to be addressed is that of management structure and human resources.

From single owners to a management structure

Almost all businesses start small but remain small. They may see little growth after their first couple of years and statistics show that the majority will cease to exist after five years. A very few will grow from very small to being medium sized. Even fewer will grow to become a large public limited company.

However, when there is such growth, it imposes challenges upon the original **entrepreneurs** (see unit 32). In a very small business, which could be a sole trader or a private limited company, there is usually one person who dominates the running of the business. In a partnership, there is likely to be two or more. These entrepreneurs will tend to do a number of key tasks. They will:

- set the aims and objectives;
- plan how these objectives can be achieved;
- do much of the physical work needed to execute the plan;
- monitor how well the business is doing and change strategy when the existing strategy is failing to meet objectives.

In a small business, the entrepreneur is unlikely to have a written down **strategy**. If one exists, it is likely that it was written as part of a **business plan** (see unit 62). This, almost certainly, would have been drawn up as part of the process of applying for a government grant or a loan from a bank. Even if there is a written down strategy, most entrepreneurs would see it as just a 'piece of paper', written to gain finance, but not important in the day to day running of the business. The larger the business, however, the more important it becomes to have written down strategies and procedures. Employees need to understand their role in the business and how they can help a business to achieve its objectives. As a business gets larger, it becomes ever more important to have documents such as job descriptions (see unit 40), health and safety procedures (see unit 55) or marketing budgets (see unit 69).

Equally, as the business grows, there will be a growing need to **delegate** (see unit 31) work. When the business is very small, the owner might do everything from managing the accounts, to being a salesperson to making the product. As the business grows, there will be an increasing division of labour, with specialists being employed to do these jobs (see unit 42). The original owner will have to let go of doing tasks and concentrate on managing the business. Further growth will see the need for middle managers to be employed to supervise and co-ordinate the work of small groups of specialist workers. Eventually, a growing firm will need a group of senior managers, probably organised on a **functional basis**, to run the business. Departments, such as the marketing department or the finance department, will have been created. By this time, the firm will almost certainly be a limited company. Senior managers will be sitting on the board of directors.

Risks of growth

As a business grows in size, it faces a number of risks.

Creeping inefficiency Growth can lead to a loss of control over costs. New employees might not be committed to cost minimisation. They might not work as hard as the original employees in the small business. Equipment may be more roughly treated and need replacing more often. In theory, growth should lead to lower average costs because of economies of scale. However, the benefits of economies of scale can, in some cases, be more than outweighed by the higher costs caused by increasingly inefficient production due to poor working practices.

Loss of focus and direction Some small businesses, as they grow in size, lose their focus and direction. The original entrepreneurs who made a success of the business might have moved on, selling the business to new owners who fail to understand the business. Or the original entrepreneurs might have to appoint a number of senior and middle managers to cope with the expanding workload of the business. New owners or new managers might then, for example, expand the business into markets which they don't understand. Or they might introduce new production processes which in practice lead to a loss of efficiency rather than a gain. Or they might introduce new products which fail to be attractive to customers. As a result, the business may get into financial difficulties and may even be forced to close down.

Failure to delegate A common problem in small growing businesses is the inability of the original entrepreneur to delegate. At the start, entrepreneurs may be involved in everything from production to marketing to finance and personnel. But as the business grows, they cannot continue to have a 'hands on' approach to everything. They have to delegate responsibility to existing and newly appointed staff. What all too often happens is that entrepreneurs continue to interfere in every aspect of the business. This typically undermines and demotivates staff given the responsibility for that task. The entrepreneurs themselves also don't have the time or energy to do the work in which they should be specialising.

Growth which is too fast Some businesses are in the fortunate position of growing at an exceptionally fast rate. But fast growth brings its own problems. Hiring a large number of new staff may mean that the business loses the very advantages that gave it a competitive edge in the first place. A large number of new staff starting at roughly the same time can create their own **culture** (see unit 112) which may be far less productive than the business culture of the original staff. Large numbers of new staff may need considerable resources to integrate them effectively into the business, resources which could have been used elsewhere. There is also always a risk in hiring new staff because once

in post their performance may be disappointing. If fast growth has led to a rushed job in hiring staff, there is even more risk that ineffective workers will be hired.

Financial problems Growth in sales and costs of a business can outstrip its financial resources. A common problem is that growth in the business is financed from short term sources, such as overdrafts and trade credit. However, there comes a point where there is so little working capital in the business that it prevents any further growth. The solution is to increase working capital by an injection of long term funds, such as long term loans or new equity. But it may be very difficult for the new business to find such long term finance. Often, the solution is to appoint a finance director, or to find an investor willing to inject equity capital into the business and manage the business financially.

Loss of internal control In a rapidly growing business, there is always the danger that the original founders or their new managers lose control of the business. Fast growth can mean that workers lower down the hierarchy are given large amounts of independence to make decisions simply because there are not the structures in place to ensure proper supervision and effective decision making. The business becomes effectively out of control. Those lower down the hierarchy will tend to have less understanding of the strategic direction of the business, if indeed there is a clearly articulated strategic direction from on top. They will tend to make decisions which they see as being in the best interests of the business, or will begin to make decisions which they see as being in their own best interest. Confusion, muddle and inefficiency are likely to be the result. In some cases, this will even destroy the business.

Loss of legal control Fast growing businesses often need extra finance. One way of resolving this problem is to gain new equity partners. By the far the most common solution is for an individual to take a share of the company and become part of the management team. In a few cases where the company is the right size, a venture capital company might put up new equity finance. However, the original owner might then lose legal control by owning less than 50 per cent of the shares. New shareholders coming in typically want to see a return on their investment in the medium term of, say, 3-5 years. If the company is successfully, they will often want to sell their stake to move on to investing in another small growing business. The original owner and founder often feels 'betrayed' by this behaviour and leaves the business. However, owners of small growing businesses seeking finance for expansion need to have a much more objective view of why investors would put money into the business in the first place.

✓ checklist

1. What functions might entrepreneurs perform in their own businesses?
2. Why might entrepreneurs have to delegate and set up management structures if their business grows in size?
3. Why might a business lose focus if it grows?
4. What problems might arise if a business grows too fast?
5. Why might the original owner of a business lose control of the business as it expands in size?

For Geena and Neil Gourlay, it was not difficult to spot that working parents needed nurseries. But when they did the rounds of local private nurseries for Sara, their own child, they realised there was a gap in the market for good quality nurseries. The few that they liked had a six month or more waiting list. Most of the rest which they didn't like were full and could only promise a place when another child left. A small number had vacancies, but they felt that these were not up to standard and wouldn't want Sara to go there. Staff seemed more interested in talking amongst themselves than looking after the children. There was also a heavy emphasis on paper work and filling in forms and care charts. The managers seemed to be about 21 and giving a well rehearsed pre-prepared sales talk as they showed prospective parents around.

Geena and Neil had a background in marketing. Geena left her job before the arrival of Sara when she moved with Neil to Leeds. After a year when they took turns at working from home or in part time jobs, they both decided that they wanted to work full time. But they also wanted to make sure first that Sara would not suffer.

At this point Geena and Neil saw an opportunity to set up their own nursery. As part of the research for the business plan, Geena took a part time job in two nurseries for four months and was able to see from the inside their strengths and weaknesses.

Sara's, their first nursery, was an enormous success. Great care was taken in selecting staff, finding a suitable location and equipping the premises. Within two months, it had a sizeable waiting list as parents of children at the nursery spread the word about how pleased they were. After a year, they decided to open a second nursery, also in Leeds. They had to decide whether to appoint managers for both nurseries and adopt a less hands-on approach or whether to remain day to day manages for one of the nurseries and appoint a new manager for the second. Finance was also a problem. They needed around £30 000 to establish the second nursery and give adequate working capital for the whole business. One of the mothers, Samantha Higgins, had already approached them and offered to put money into the business in return for a part share. Samantha had some accountancy qualifications and had been working as a bookkeeper for a local company, but was finding the work boring. She offered to come and work for the business, running the accounts and general administration.

Geena and Neil were worried that quality control could be lost by setting up a second nursery. They had seen what could happen in large chains of nurseries when they had done research for the business plan. They also didn't want to lose control of the business. There was a market out there for high quality nursery care and Sara's had the potential to grow much larger. Loss of control could spell disaster.

1 Discuss the problems that Geena and Neil Gourlay faced in setting up a second nursery and evaluate possible solutions to these problems. (20 marks)

Boots

Knowledge In 2003, Boots, the UK high street retailer, announced that it had signed a deal with two US groups, Target and CVS, to test Boots-branded areas in their own stores. Boots has a poor record overseas. In the mid 1970s, it bought Sephora, the French perfume and cosmetics chain, but sold up 17 years later. In the 1980s, the company opened a series of shops in Canada, but by 1988 all had been closed. In the 1990s, Boots expanded into South-East Asia, mainly Thailand and Japan. By 2001, Boots had withdrawn from Japan and in 2002, it announced that it was closing 19 outlets in Thailand and Taiwan to stem losses.

Application The US trials will *cost* less than £10 million. This compares to the £4 million loss Boots made on its *international operations* in the six months to September 2003 on *sales* of £21 million. Boots hopes that it will have the same *competitive advantage* in US markets as it enjoys in UK markets. However, its experience overseas over the past 30 years has been one of *expansion* and then *retrenchment*.

Analysis Boots faces a difficult trading environment in the UK where it faces growing competition from supermarket chains like Tesco and Asda, keen to expand in the health and beauty sectors of the market. Successful overseas growth would, to some extent, mitigate problems of loss of competitiveness in the UK market. However, it has found it difficult to translate its UK success into a formula which overseas customers find attractive. Working within other stores rather than setting up stand alone shops reduces both the risk and cost of failure.

Evaluation Given Boots' previous record internationally, it may be argued that the chances of the new US venture succeeding will be small. However, Boots needs some good news. A £10 million 'bet' on what is potentially a huge market in the USA may seem a risk worth taking to Boots. If it fails, it should reinforce the message to Boots management that the long term survival of the company is linked solely to the UK market. Management needs to address the ever growing competitive pressure with products that customers find attractive at the right price.

Source: adapted from *The Times*, 15.11.2003.

Changing legal organisation

In units 60 and 61, it was explained that there are four main types of legal organisation for businesses in the UK. These are sole proprietorships, partnerships, private limited companies and public limited companies. Each has its own particular advantages and disadvantages. However, in general, as a business grows in size, it becomes more common for it to become, first, a private limited company and then a public limited company. There is a number of reasons for this.

● The owners of sole proprietorships and many ordinary partnerships have unlimited liability (see unit 60). However, the risks of unlimited liability for the owners become too large once a certain size has been reached. By forming a limited company, the owners can keep their private assets separate from those of the business. If the business failed, they could only lose their money invested in the business and not their private assets.

● Sources of finance are limited for sole traders and partnerships (see unit 26). By becoming a private limited company or a public limited company, a growing business can issue new equity.

● Once a business has reached a certain size, there are tax advantages to the owners of being a limited company rather than an unlimited business.

● If an owner wants to sell, it is usually easier to do this is if it is a company rather than an unlimited business. Equally, it is easier for a business to find individuals wishing to buy part or all of the business if it is a limited company than if the business has unlimited liability.

Sole traders, partnerships and limited companies

Businesses do change their legal organisation as circumstances change. For example, a partnership may dissolve because one of the partners wants to retire. The remaining partners may then decide to cease working together and set up in business on their own. Very small private limited companies may become sole traders if tax rules change shifting the advantage towards being a sole trader.

Private limited companies which become public limited companies may make themselves private again at a later date. One reason is that the main shareholders (usually the original founders of the business) may see a chance to increase the long term value of their holdings in the company by buying out other shareholders when the share price is low. They then hope that the performance of the company will improve, increasing its value and therefore the price of the shares in the new private limited company.

Another reason for a shift back to a private limited company is conflict about how to run the company. Public limited companies may become 'short termist' in their day to day running of the business. This means that managers seek to achieve short term goals such as raising profits this quarter (i.e. three months) or raising the dividend this year or increasing sales over the half year. They are less concerned with the medium and long term. Indeed, their strategies to maximise short term goals may conflict with the best long term interests of the business. For example, an easy way to increase profits in the short term is to cut back on investment. But this could lead to less sales and profit in the medium term. It is often argued that shareholders in a public limited company and the financial media put pressure on the company to maximise short term profits because this can lead to a higher share price. Entrepreneurs who have floated their companies on a stock exchange can become frustrated with these pressures. They may then decide to buy back shares from other shareholders and return the company to being a private limited company.

National to international

Businesses may be able to gain a competitive advantage over their rivals as a result of growth. Larger businesses can exploit economies of scale, reducing their average costs of production, for example. But growth and large scale bring their own problems. These become particularly apparent if a business is attempting to go from operating on a national scale to operating on an international scale.

Control The larger the organisation, the more difficult it becomes for senior management to control the business. The chain of command becomes longer and it becomes more difficult to communicate up and down the hierarchy of the company. When a company goes international, problems are compounded by different business cultures between countries. US employees might interpret a message in a slightly different way to UK employees. If a UK company had a Japanese or South Korean subsidiary, there might be different perceptions of the same strategy or ways of achieving it. Different languages can sometimes be a barrier to effective communication. So too can simple things such as different time zones which can make it difficult for executives to talk over the telephone, although email has solved this problem to some extent.

Marketing A marketing formula which works well in one national market may not work in another. Many businesses which expand internationally find that best selling products in the UK fail to find a market in, say, Japan, Saudi Arabia or the USA. They may also face much fiercer competition in a new market than in the UK market. Established foreign businesses may have a very strong brand image whilst the products of the UK company may have no brand image for the foreign customer. Distribution channels ('place' in the marketing mix) may be radically different in a foreign market than in the UK. Selling to consumers in Japan, for example, is often different to selling to consumers in the UK or the USA. Pricing policies may have to be adjusted to compete abroad. A UK business used to charging premium prices in its UK market may find that the only way to compete in a foreign market is to charge a low price.

Production and human resources Establishing production facilities abroad can be difficult too. A UK company setting up abroad, for example, would have to become familiar with local work customs. It would have to understand employee legislation, as well as legislation governing issues such as health and safety. It needs to find out what laws will be strictly enforced and which may be ignored. It might have to gain planning permission to allow the setting up of a factory or obtain import licences. Issues such as quality control also need to be addressed, to ensure that goods manufactured abroad meet company standards.

Finance UK businesses establishing themselves abroad must decide how to finance this expansion. Finance could come from the UK or money could be raised abroad through foreign banks. In the medium term, much foreign investment should be financed through the retained profit of foreign operations. Some of the profit made abroad will be repatriated to the UK to pay as dividends to UK shareholders. Equally, profits made abroad could be used to help UK operations if they were making a loss or a particularly large investment had to be made.

UK businesses need to be aware that foreign operations can be a threat financially as well as an opportunity. Occasionally, foreign operations will make substantial losses which could threaten the whole business. Fraud is another problem. Sometimes fraud in a foreign operation can bring down the whole company. For example, in 1995, fraud committed by a foreign exchange dealer based in Singapore, led to the collapse of Barings Bank in the UK. For this reason, UK companies often set up foreign subsidiary companies which each have limited liability. If a subsidiary company abroad makes enormous losses, the UK company can close down the subsidiary company and not be liable for its losses.

Retrenchment

Some businesses are growing in size, but others are becoming smaller. RETRENCHMENT occurs when a business is forced to shrink. There is a number of reasons why retrenchment may take place.

Loss of control of costs Some businesses grow in size, but lose control of their costs in the process. This is one reason why diseconomies of scale occur (see unit 42). Sooner or later, the business will move into loss and be forced to take action. Such action may involve reducing the size of its operations.

Falling market demand Some businesses make products which are declining in demand. If there is a steady fall in demand, the business may be forced to cut output and reduce the size of its operation unless it can move into new markets.

Increasing market competitiveness Businesses may find that their competitive advantage is being eroded by other businesses in the market. One business may have developed a new product or a new cost saving production process which means that its sales rise at the expense of its competitors. In the UK, industries such as coal, steel and textiles have all suffered because of new low cost competition from businesses in the Third World. Similarly, some businesses in the photography market, such as Kodak, have been forced to reduce film output as a result of the impact of digital cameras.

Recession In a recession, many businesses may be forced to reduce the size of their operations as lack of demand throughout the economy leads to lower sales. A world recession may see sales falling in all the markets into which a business sells.

There is a number of different ways in which a business may carry out retrenchment depending upon the severity of the situation.

Freezing recruitment and investment A quick and easy short term measure is to reduce spending by freezing recruitment of new workers or freezing investment. This investment may be in physical equipment such as new machinery or it could be investment in marketing, such as an advertising campaign. If the freeze is maintained too long, however, it will lead to inefficiency. Key workers may leave whose work cannot be covered by other employees or an investment project may be scrapped which would have been highly profitable. The danger is that a freeze, if maintained too long, will make the business uncompetitive compared to its rivals.

Systematically making cutbacks throughout the business In the medium term, a business could carry out retrenchment throughout its business operations. It could make cuts where products or processes are either loss making or are barely profitable. In many cases, a business may be able to remove 'fat' from its operations - costs which made the business inefficient. For example, a business may delayer (see unit 31) its management structure, removing layers of management which contribute little to output. It could remove the least profitable products from its product range. It may make workers redundant that it had hoped to keep on if sales had picked up. Such cutbacks may be unpopular with workers because they fear that their jobs may go next. This could be demotivating because it threatens their basic need for security (see unit 35). A business therefore should attempt to make such cuts quickly to restore stability and minimise the impact on motivation.

Cutting factories, plants, areas or divisions Another approach is to cut out whole parts of the business. A whole factory could be closed, or just a product or geographic division of the company (see unit 32) could be shut down.

✓*checklist*

1 Why are most medium to large businesses limited companies?
2 Why might a public limited company shift back to being a private limited company?
3 What problems might a business encounter if it moves from being a national company to an international company?
4 Why might a business reduce its size?

For example, if the North American division has not made a profit in five years, it might be an immediate casualty of a policy of retrenchment. Businesses are often reluctant to close down unprofitable parts of the business when times are good because they hope that these parts are just about to turn the corner and make a profit. It also means that management doesn't have to make difficult and unpopular decisions. But in time of need, management tends to become more focused. Problem parts of the business become the first casualties of retrenchment.

In the long term, a smaller, more focused company may be more profitable than a larger, less focused company. Retrenchment can be a necessary part of long term expansion. Alternatively, continued retrenchment may be the only strategy available if a business is in a market which is in long term decline.

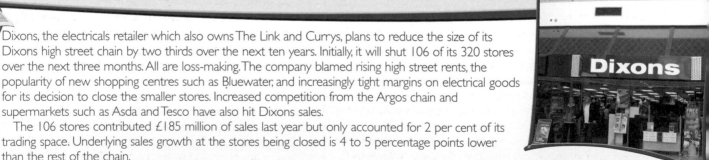

Dixons, the electricals retailer which also owns The Link and Currys, plans to reduce the size of its Dixons high street chain by two thirds over the next ten years. Initially, it will shut 106 of its 320 stores over the next three months. All are loss-making. The company blamed rising high street rents, the popularity of new shopping centres such as Bluewater, and increasingly tight margins on electrical goods for its decision to close the smaller stores. Increased competition from the Argos chain and supermarkets such as Asda and Tesco have also hit Dixons sales.

The 106 stores contributed £185 million of sales last year but only accounted for 2 per cent of its trading space. Underlying sales growth at the stores being closed is 4 to 5 percentage points lower than the rest of the chain.

Dixons plans to replace its remaining 214 high street stores that are 3 000 sq ft in size with 130 of its new larger format Dixons XL, which are 10 000 sq ft to 30 000 sq ft in size. As a result, the Dixons chain will have fewer stores, but slightly more selling space. However, management admitted Dixons was not ready to 'push the button' on a rapid expansion of the XL stores, of which there are only five at present. Just four new XL stores are planned this year. XL stores were an expensive investment at £500 000 to £1 million each, and Dixons needed to be sure that it had got the format right.

Dixons admitted that it was 'unrealistic' to expect to be able to claw back all the £185 million sales being lost by closing stores over the next three months. Most of the 1 000 staff affected by the closures will be employed elsewhere in the business. Shutting the stores will cost Dixons an estimated £48 million.

Source: adapted from *The Times*, 29.04.2004.

1 **Explain why Dixons is retrenching.**
2 **Dixons argues that the retrenchment will leave it in a stronger position in the market. To what extent to do you think this will prove to be the case?**

Anthony Preston is the founder of Pets at Home, Britain's biggest pet store chain. Expansion has come fast. Today, it has 155 stores with 1.5 million square feet of sales space, nearly 2 000 staff and 2003 sales of £219 million. Operating profits are now £14.4 million and the company is investing £55 million in opening another 200 stores over the next five years, by which time it hopes to have more than doubled its sales to £500 million a year.

Anthony Preston, an Oxford graduate in German, spent the first four years of his working life at ICFC, a venture capitalist. He then joined his family's long standing domestic hardware wholesaling business in the late 1970s. His first job was to drive around the back streets of northern mill towns looking out for new clients at a time when the number of small hardware shops was steadily declining under pressure from competition from new large DIY superstore chains like B&Q. He spotted that there were as many small pet shops as hardware shops and they were suffering less from competition. So the business added pet supplies to its traditional wholesaling distribution operation. In 1984, it bought R&B Pet Supplies, a small wholesaler with three staff and sales of around £300 000. By the end of the 1980s, the business was up to a £6 million turnover with pre-tax profits of £350 000 a year.

Anthony recognised, though, that the future was not very bright. Big supermarkets were beginning to eat into the market share of small backstreet pet shops. He sensed an opportunity to create a whole new image for pet stores by building spacious, bright and airy stores offering a much wider range of pets and products in out of town retail parks with good parking facilities. The first Pets at Home store opened in 1991 and by 1994, there were 10 stores. This had been helped by a £5 million equity injection by the venture capitalist 3i. This made Pets at Home independent of the traditional wholesaling business.

But 1995 proved a turning point. A southern company, Pet City, had raised money on the stock market to finance a plan to have 150 UK pet supermarkets by 1999. A year later, Pet City was bought for £150 million by a US company PetsMart. This US company saw itself as a 'category killer' - a large company that dominates a market category by offering a cheaper and wider range of products that puts less efficient and highly specialised shops out of business. Pet City was intended to be the launchpad for the roll-out of 300 US-style pet superstores in the UK followed by 700 on the Continent. It was to be the Toys R Us or Wal-Mart of the UK pet world market.

The new US venture proved a disaster. It made losses each quarter despite having a £120 million turnover. In 1999, the US owners pulled out, selling the chain to Pets at Home for just £30 million, a fifth of the price they had paid three years before. Pets at Home by that time had a turnover of £60 million a year and made a profit of £3.5 million. The deal more than doubled the size of Pets at Home's business and eliminated its biggest competitor. It added 1 million square feet of extra retailing space very cheaply at a time when planning constraints were limiting the supply of new retail warehouses. By 2003, the £10.2 million profit generated showed the benefits of the integration of the two businesses.

Anthony Preston said that there was 'no magic formula that we could apply to sort out the business'. It was a host of little things. Pet City's national advertising budget was scrapped, its logistics overhauled and in-store working practices changed to reduce sharply the number of times stock was handled, freeing up more staff time for customers. The product mix was skewed back towards higher margin items, such as pet accessories and toys, and Pets at Home substituted its 'soft-sell' approach for the hard-selling tactics imported from the US.

Since then, veterinary surgeries have been added to more than a third of its stores along with a growing number of grooming parlours. The new services, often provided by third parties, increase the customer flow through the stores.

Pets at Home's profit margins remain lower than its US rivals, which suggest there is still plenty of potential to squeeze more profits out of the existing group. However, it faces a great deal of competition. The supermarket chains have half the pet food market, and rivals such as Halfords and Wyevale Garden Centres are having a small impact on Pets at Home's more lucrative accessories business. There is also a chance that the two largest US competitors, PetsMart and Petco, could enter the market. PetsMart is under new management and is much further ahead than Pets at Home in developing new value-added pet services.

If Pets at Home wanted extra finance for faster expansion, it could always float itself on the stock market. Anthony Preston, however, says that 'we enjoy our independence' and says he has no plans for a float.

Source: adapted from the *Financial Times*, 8.06.2004.

1 Evaluate what were the most important factors in the successful growth of Pets at Home. (20 marks)
2 Discuss the challenges that Pets at Home might face if it decided to expand into the German market. (20 marks)

Lego

Knowledge   Lego, the toy company, launched its famous Lego bricks in 1958. Since that time, it has grown into a company which has sales worldwide and operates a number of theme parks, including the Legoland in Windsor.

Application   Lego is a *multinational company*. However, by the late 1990s, it was in financial trouble. Subject to intense *competition* from computer games, mobile phones and music players, it found its *market* amongst older children shrinking. To help turn the company around, management decided to *divest* itself of its Lego theme parks. The theme parks would be highly attractive to a *bidder* looking for an *acquisition* or *takeover* of a product with a strong *brand name*.

Analysis   Selling Legoland was just one part of Lego's strategy to put itself on a sounder financial footing. The company cut costs through cutting jobs and was considering moving some of its production to the Far East. As for the companies interested in buying Legoland, they were mainly investment companies which already owned and managed theme parks. For example, Dubai International Capital owns Alton Towers through its Tussauds company. Palamon acquired the European division of Six Flags, the world's largest regional theme park operator, in 2004. Advent International is another investment company which has shown interest in bidding for Legoland. It bought Parques Reunidos, the Spanish leisure park operator, in 2003. Buying Legoland would add to their portfolio of leisure parks, creating synergies which could cut costs or expand revenues. Ultimately, these investment companies might want to divest themselves of their leisure park divisions if the price was right.

Evaluation   Legoland is a very attractive proposition to buyers seeking a strong brand name. A buyer would probably want to cut costs and increase revenues in order to make the theme parks more profitable. A buyer might also have more cash than Lego to invest, either in existing parks or in new parks. Expanding the chain organically might lead to a higher rate of return on capital employed as economies of scale increase and the benefits of marketing are spread across a wider chain of parks.

Adapted from *The Times*, 7.04.2005 and the *Financial Times*, 30.4.2005.

Takeovers and mergers

Most businesses which grow in size do so through INTERNAL GROWTH (also called ORGANIC GROWTH). This is where sales and profits grow through means such as increased investment, new product development or better marketing. However, sometimes a business will grow in size through EXTERNAL GROWTH. This can be a TAKEOVER or ACQUISITION, where one business buys another business. Or it can be through a MERGER where two (or more) businesses join together to become one business.

Takeovers and mergers can take place in any sized business with any legal organisation. For example, a sole trader who owns two chemist shops may buy up, and therefore takeover, a third chemist shop from its owner. Two partnerships may merge to become one partnership.

However, takeovers and mergers tend to be associated more with limited companies. Usually, one company must acquire more than 50 per cent of the shares of the company which is being taken over. They buy these shares from existing shareholders. There is a variety of takeover rules for public limited companies in the UK. For example, the same offer must be made to all shareholders. The takeover company cannot offer a higher price to some shareholders and a lower price to others. The takeover company has a limited amount of time to make its offer. If, after this period, it has failed to receive offers to sell from existing shareholders, then the takeover bid lapses.

Some takeovers are **contested** or are **hostile**. This means that the board of directors of the company recommends to its shareholders that they should not accept the bid. Some takeovers, however, are **agreed takeovers**. The board of directors recommends to its shareholders that they should sell. Often a company will make a takeover offer which the board of directors rejects because the price is too low. The takeover company must then raise its bid, which the board of directors of the company being targeted may accept or reject.

In a merger, the boards of directors both agree to the merger having negotiated the terms of the merger. These terms include how may shares in the new company each existing shareholder will get. It also typically includes who will become the new chairman and chief executive of the company, and who will become its directors. Cost cutting plans may also be announced. For example, if each company has a headquarters, then it may be announced which headquarters will be closed and which will become the new headquarters.

Occasionally, a business will DEMERGE. This is when the business splits into two or more independent businesses.

Types of integration

Integration takes place when one business takes over or merges with another business. There are three main types of integration.

Horizontal integration HORIZONTAL INTEGRATION occurs when two businesses making similar products join together. One car manufacturer buying another car manufacturer would be an example of horizontal integration. So too would be a supermarket chain buying another supermarket chain, or an aerospace company buying another aerospace company.

Vertical integration VERTICAL INTEGRATION occurs when a business integrates with either a supplier (backward vertical integration) or a customer (forward vertical integration). It is vertical because the integration takes place between two businesses at different points on the chain of production for a product. For example, a car manufacturer buying a car component company would be an example of backward vertical integration. A catering company buying a chain of fast food outlets would be an example of forward vertical integration.

Conglomerate integration CONGLOMERATE INTEGRATION takes place when two businesses making unrelated products join together. For example, a cigarette manufacturer buying an insurance company would be a conglomerate take over. A steel manufacturer merging with a health care company would be a conglomerate merger.

Reasons for integration

There is a variety of reasons why a business may takeover or merge with another business. Some relate to the SYNERGIES to be gained from combining two organisations, including cutting average costs and increasing sales and profits. Others relate to the potential for asset stripping, the reduction of risk through diversification or the potential for gains by management.

Cost savings The most frequently cited reason is cost savings.

Cost savings can take place in a number of ways. The larger business may be able to cut duplicated expenditure. For example, a merged business would not need two headquarters. Marketing budgets could also be merged to produce cost savings. Further, a larger business should be able to buy in greater bulk, forcing down its suppliers prices, or borrow on better terms than a smaller business (see unit 42).

Greater control of markets A takeover or merger may allow a business to gain greater control of its markets. For example, the merger may give a business control of important brands needed to strengthen its product range. Forward vertical integration may allow a supplier to buy out an important customer and so secure orders. There is always a danger that a proposed merger or takeover may be blocked as a result of UK and EU regulation (see unit 55). In the UK mergers may be referred to the Competition Commission (CC) by the Office of Fair Trading (OFT), for example, under the **Enterprise Act, 2002**. The CC must then determine if the merger has or might result in a lessening of competition. It may then take action it feels is reasonable and practical to address any adverse effects of the merger.

Undervalued assets The management of one business may see that another business is undervalued. For example, one company may be able to buy another company for £2 million. It then sells off key assets of the company taken over for £3 million and is still left with assets it values at £1 million. In the past, some companies have specialised in this sort of asset stripping. Their main profits have come from buying other companies and selling off their most valuable assets rather than the sale of products from the existing

In April 2005, Pernod Ricard announced a £7.5bn agreement to take over Allied Domecq. Pernod Ricard is the world's third largest spirits business with brands such as Ricard, Chivas Regal, Martell and Jameson. Allied Domecq also has a number of world famous spirits brands including Malibu, Sauza tequila and Courvoisier cognac. The deal would make Pernod number two in the world spirits market behind the market leader, Diageo.

Costs are one of the main reasons for Pernod to buy Allied Domecq. Selling spirit brands across the world has high fixed distribution costs. Pushing more product through the same distribution channels will bring lower average fixed costs. There should also be gains in marketing. A single sales force offering a wider range of brands should be more effective in gaining sales.

The deal is complicated by the fact that Allied Domecq owns some brands which are in direct competition with those of Pernod. For example Allied's Courvoisier cognac competes directly with Pernod's Martell congnac. To get around the competition authorities, it will sell these brands to a conglomerate, Fortune Brands, for £2.8 billion. It is also likely to sell Allied's food interests. Allied Domecq owns the Dunkin Donuts coffee chain and the ice cream franchise Baskin Robbins. These sales will reduce the ultimate price that Pernod pays for Allied Domecq.

Finance for the £7.5bn deal is complicated. A fifth of the price will be paid by issuing new Pernod shares. Fortune Brands will contribute £2.8 billion. The rest will borrowed through the international money markets.

Source: adapted from the *Financial Times*, 6.4.2005, 21.04.2005 and 22.04.2005.

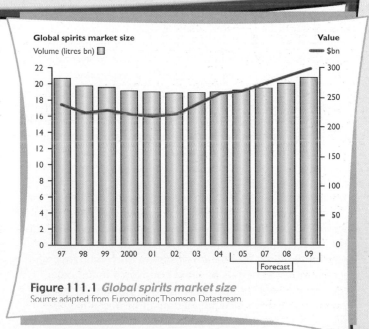

Figure 111.1 *Global spirits market size*
Source: adapted from Euromonitor, Thomson Datastream.

---

1 *Discuss whether the global spirits market is a growing market.*
2 *Evaluate the possible costs and benefits to Pernod of its takeover of Allied Domecq.*

operations. Alternatively, the company being taken over or merged may have significantly underperformed. New management may be able to reduce costs and raise sales with little extra investment. By turning round a poorly performing business, the value of the business will increase substantially.

Diversification A business may want to diversify (see unit 9). This means expanding into new product markets. Diversification can allow a business in static or declining markets to move into growth markets. Or a business may wish to reduce the risks it faces from being in a particular market. For example, a steel manufacturer which faces large swings in demand and prices according to the business cycle may want to enter a market which is less volatile. Diversification and the creation of conglomerate companies was fashionable in the past. By the 1990s, many conglomerates were breaking up. It was argued that conglomerates had no synergies between the different parts of the business. If a steel manufacturer owned an electricity generation business, there was little of benefit that the steel manufacturer would contribute to the electricity generation business and vice versa. More importantly, it was argued that senior management of a business could not be experts in running both a steel manufacturer and an electricity generation company. Parts of the business would suffer from poor management. Hence conglomerates were particularly likely to be affected by managerial diseconomies of scale (see unit 42). Less profitable or low growth parts of the business could also be starved of investment as finance was channelled into more profitable or high growth parts. If the less profitable business was an independent business, it might make higher profits because of more specialised management or more investment. Finally, many conglomerate companies had a relatively low share price. The highest growth and highest profit parts of the business were undervalued because they were lumped in with low growth, low profit businesses. It was suggested that shareholder value would increase if the conglomerate was split up into separate companies.

Rewards to management Studies of public limited company takeovers and mergers suggest that most destroy shareholder value. For example, the share price of the new company tends to perform worse, compared to the average for companies in the industry, than the share price of the two previously separate companies. Cost savings promised before the takeover or merger often fail to emerge after integration. Sales don't increase as much as was predicted or actually decline. It may prove difficult to create one corporate culture from two companies which might have had very different ways of working. Motivation of staff in one company may decline if less generous pay and conditions in the other company is imposed upon them. The computer systems of the two companies may be incompatible and it may be necessary to completely replace them at considerable cost to the new company.

So why are there so many takeovers and mergers if they clearly don't benefit shareholders? The answer may be in the divorce of ownership from control (see unit 61). In public limited companies, it is the senior management and not the owners, the shareholders, who initially suggest the takeover or merger. Senior management is likely to gain from the merger or takeover. The new senior management of the merged company is likely to be paid more than before

because senior managers are running a larger company. In the case of friendly mergers, senior personnel who lose their jobs may receive generous pensions if they are in their 50s and 60s. Or they may get a generous redundancy package which more than covers them in the time taken to get another job. The only management losers are likely to be the management team of a company taken over in a hostile bid. They may lose their jobs, with minimum compensation. So there is an incentive for senior management to look for mergers or to agree to friendly mergers.

Reasons for demergers

Sometimes businesses break themselves up into separate parts. They may sell off parts of their business to other businesses. More rarely and radically, they may split into two or more separate parts. In a public limited company, existing shareholders often end up owning shares in the two or more new companies created. Demergers occur for a number of reasons. Some have already been discussed earlier when explaining why conglomerates have fallen out of fashion.

- For public limited companies, the combined share price of the new separate companies may be above that of the old single company. Hence it increases shareholder value.
- Demergers allow management to concentrate on running a smaller, more focused business. This business may perform better than it would have done as part of the former larger business. This implies that the previous large business was suffering from diseconomies of scale.
- Parts of the business which before had been starved of investment may now see greater investment as a separate business. This should allow it to increase sales and profits.
- Demergers may take place for financial reasons. A business may have heavy debts. A simple way of reducing this debt is to sell off substantial parts of the business.

Financing a takeover or merger

In a takeover, the shareholders of the company being targeted for takeover may be offered cash for their shares. Or they may be offered shares in the company making the takeover bid. Or they may be offered a mixture of the two. For example, shareholders of the target company may be offered £1.20 plus 2 shares in the company making the offer for every 1 share they own in the target company.

In a merger, shareholders of both companies have their existing shares converted into new shares. For example, in a merger of Company A and Company B, shareholders in Company A may get 1 new share for every existing share they own, whilst shareholders in Company B may get 2 new shares for every existing share they own.

The price which is paid depends on a variety of factors.

- Physical assets will be valued. From an accounting viewpoint, these are valued on the balance sheet of a company. However, the accounting value could be different from the market value. For example, the market price of property could have risen sharply since purchase. But on the balance sheet the value of property is likely to have gone down because of depreciation. So the accounts of the business must be treated with caution when valuing assets.
- Intangibles such as brand values must be taken into

account. For a chocolate manufacturer like Nestlé, the brand value of KitKat, the best selling chocolate bar in the UK, is considerable. For a shop, there is a value in the customer loyalty that has been built up.
- Current profitability will be considered. A business making £5 million profit a year will be worth more than a business making £1 million profit a year, all other things being equal.
- A business may be prepared to pay a higher price than otherwise to prevent a rival company from buying up the target company. Equally, a business may get into a bidding war with other companies over a take over target simply to force up its price. Ideally, then, the competitor which finally buys the take over target is forced to pay too high a price and then suffers commercially as a result.

The final price paid will reflect a mix of these considerations. Ideally for the takeover company, it will pay less than the real worth for the company being taken over. It can happen, however, that companies find that they have overpaid. Assets can be overvalued. Profits can be overstated. Intangible assets may be worth far less than estimated. Paying too much for a company is one reason why takeovers can destroy shareholder value.

Management buy-outs

A MANAGEMENT BUY OUT occurs when the management of a company buys the company from its current owners. Opportunities for management to buy may arise because:
- a company has gone into receivership and the receivers are looking for someone to buy the company and continue to operate it;

- an individual or family wish to sell the business, perhaps because they want to retire;
- a large company wishes to sell off a subsidiary which is either performing poorly or which does not sell products which are part of a newly defined 'core' for the business.

Managers rarely have enough financial capital to buy the business outright. Instead, they put together a financial package which includes their own investment in the new company, loans from banks and, crucially, equity investment from a venture capitalist company (see unit 25). Venture capitalist companies specialise in buying shares in medium sized companies which they think have growth potential. Their aim is to support the company for a number of years and then float the company on a stock exchange, selling their stake in the company hopefully for a large profit. Or the company may be sold to a larger company in a takeover. In a successful management buy-out, managers who have put money into buying shares at the time of the buy-out tend to sell too at this stage. The rewards to management of a successful management buy-out are potentially very high.

Management buy-outs have tended to be successful for a number of reasons.
- Becoming the owners of the company means that managers become highly focused on making a success of the new company. Venture capitalist backers, who often have at least one seat on the board of directors, will also be very focussed on success. The main objective (see unit 63) is likely to be maximising profit to ensure short term survival.
- Management is uniquely placed to know the strengths and weaknesses of the company. Before the buy-out, they were

Littlewoods has decided to close its Index store chain. Index is a rival to Argos, using the same formula where shoppers in high street stores choose goods from a catalogue. Littlewoods has sold 33 of the Index stores to Argos as well as the brand name and associated website for £44 million. Argos said that it had 'cherry picked individual Index stores either for their size or location'. The company does not intend to use the Index brand name. By purchasing it, Argos will be able to prevent a competitor using the name to challenge its new monopoly in high street catalogue shopping.

The remaining 126 Index stores, 33 of which are stand-alone stores and 93 that trade within Littlewoods shops, will be closed with the loss of 3 200 jobs. David Simons, Littlewoods chairman, said: 'All the job losses are to be regretted. We will seek to redeploy where we can - for example with the Index concessions in Littlewoods stores, or with the jobs at the Index call centre in Sunderland - but we won't be able to offer the majority or even a significant number a new job.'

Explaining the reasons for the sale, David Simons said that 'the decision to divest the business has not been an easy one to make but it is the only solution to a difficult and unsustainable situation. Index has made a loss in nearly every year of its 20-year history, and has accumulated losses of over £100 million despite many attempts by different management teams to turn the business around.'

Source: adapted from *The Daily Telegraph*, 17.04.2005.

1 **Explain whether Argos buying Index is an example of horizontal or vertical integration.**
2 **Evaluate the synergies that Argos might gain from its takeover of Index.**
3 **What benefits might Littlewoods gain from the closure of Index?**

often unable to formulate their own strategy as to how the business should be run. Implementation of a new strategy after the buy-out often leads to the turn round of the company.

- The previous owners may have starved the company of cash. This limited the ability of management to invest, to promote products more widely and to train staff. By spending more in key areas, buy-out managers are able to raise revenues and increase profits.
- If the company had been bought from the receivers, it would almost certainly have come without very much debt. Equally, if it was bought from a larger company, the larger company might have sold it relatively debt free. Previously, payment of debt might have been a serious financial problem for the company. If it was an independent company, it would have been the ultimate reason why it might have gone into receivership. A lack of debt would give the new management a much greater chance to make a profit.
- Management buy-outs are often associated with a downsizing of the business. The buy-out will create the conditions in which the new management is faced with taking difficult decisions. If they don't make them, they face losing their investment. So, for example, the new management may make significant cuts in the workforce or close down factories. This helps reduce costs and so improve the company's profit position.
- If the buy-out company had been part of a larger company, some management time would have been spent liaising with headquarters. Decision making might have been slow because of the constant need to refer them back to headquarters to gain approval. The more centralised (see unit 31) the organisation, the more this could have been an obstacle to the success of the company. The new management will be free to make its own decisions quickly. This may help it to improve the efficiency of decision making.

Management buy-outs are sometimes criticised because investors in the new company can make millions of pounds profit in a short space of time by turning round the company and then selling it. In the process, many workers might have lost their jobs. Remaining workers may have received no financial gain from the turn round of the company, even though they worked hard to ensure its success.

Such criticisms, however, could be said to be criticisms of the capitalist market system. Investors can make large profits. Equally, they can lose their whole stake in the business in which they invest. Workers in businesses which make continued losses will lose their jobs. A management buy-out may at least save some of them. Most of the earnings of employees are not linked to the success of the business. Their earnings are likely to be more stable than the earnings of investors because profits and share prices tend to go down as well as up over a period of time.

Management buy-ins

A MANAGEMENT BUY-IN (MBI) occurs when a group of managers from outside a business buy it from its owners. In an ordinary takeover, one working business takes over another working business. The two are put together to create

one new business. With a management buy-in, typically an individual will get a small team of managers together and that team will buy a company to run it. Management buy-ins tend to be successful for the same reasons as management buy-outs. What managers buying-in may lack in terms of the knowledge of the individual business, they typically make up by in-depth knowledge of the industry. So management buy-ins are often successful.

keyterms

Conglomerate integration - when two businesses making unrelated products integrate into one business.
Demerge - when a business splits into two or more independent businesses.
External growth - when the size of a business increases through the takeover of another business or a merger with another business.
Horizontal integration - when two or more businesses making similar products integrate.
Internal growth - when the size of a business increases, for example by sales and profits growing through increased investment, new product development or better marketing.
Management buy-in - when a group of managers from outside a business buy it from its owners.
Management buy-out - when the management of a company buys it from its current owners.
Merger - when two (or more) businesses join together to become one business.
Synergy - when two or more activities or businesses, put together, create a greater outcome than the sum of the individual parts.
Takeover or acquisition - when one business buys another business.
Vertical integration - when one business integrates either with a supplier (backward vertical integration) or a customer (forward vertical integration).

checklist

1 Explain the difference between (a) internal and external growth and (b) a takeover and a merger.
2 Explain, giving examples, the difference between horizontal, vertical and conglomerate integration.
3 What synergies might be created by a merger between two companies?
4 Why might a company wish to diversify?
5 What is the possible link between mergers and the divorce of ownership from control?
6 How might a takeover be financed?
7 Explain how a price for the takeover of a company might be determined.
8 Why might managers buy their company from its owners?

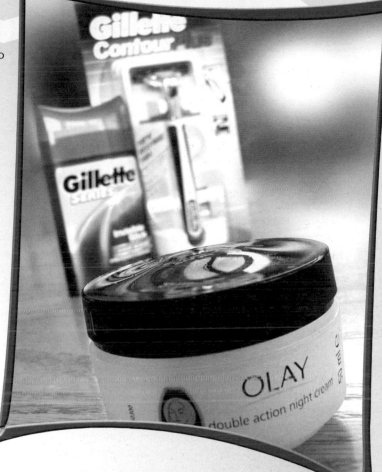

In January 2005, Procter & Gamble announced that it was to buy Gillette for $30 billion. Procter & Gamble is one of world's largest household products manufacturers. It has 16 brands with worldwide sales of more than $1 billion per year including Pampers nappies, Ariel washing powder and Pringles crisps, and total sales of around $50 billion. Gillette has a strong presence in some markets, including a 74 per cent share of the $7 billion global wet-shaving market. It has five brands with annual sales of more than $1 billion including Gillette, Duracell batteries and Oral-B.

Procter & Gamble forecast that the merger will bring about cost savings. Around 6 000 workers, or about 4 per cent of the combined workforce, will lose their jobs as functions are merged. A combined group will be able to strike even harder deals with suppliers, although the companies are already so large that purchasing economies are unlikely to be that much greater. In advertising, the new company will become an even more dominant advertiser, giving it more power over agencies and media outlets. The company will be able to use existing distribution channels for both sets of products, thus cutting costs.

The merger should increase sales from the combined group. There is very little overlap between the two company's products and so there will be little incentive to close down product lines to concentrate on better performing brands. However, the two companies use similar distribution and marketing channels. This will be particularly important in emerging markets. Procter & Gamble is particularly strong in Japan and China and will be able to leverage more Gillette products through those channels. Gillette, on the other hand, is particularly strong in Brazil and India and so the combined group should be able to increase sales of Procter & Gamble brands through these channels. In a market like the UK, the combined group will have more power with the supermarket chains to stock their products. So, for example, small domestic brands like Brylcream and King of Shaves could find themselves squeezed out as Procter & Gamble negotiate more shelf space for its products.

There was a time when manufacturing giants like Procter & Gamble could dictate terms to a fragmented retailing market. Today, household product manufacturers like Procter & Gamble are faced with a high degree of concentration in their retailing customers. One fifth of all Procter & Gamble sales worldwide are to a single retailer, Wal-Mart, which owns Asda in the UK. The British consumer now spends £1 in every £8 of all household spending at just one supermarket chain, Tesco.

The merger should help redress this imbalance in power, even if only a little. It will give Procter & Gamble a small increase in its ability to resist calls from retailers for further price cuts. It also might give greater leverage for the company to dictate shelf space and how its products are displayed in supermarkets.

The declining power of manufacturers can be seen from the increase in own brand products in supermarkets from 21.5 per cent of products in the 1980s to 38.9 per cent in 2000.

Stock markets reacted to the acquisition by sending Procter & Gamble share prices down by 2 per cent. Shares in Gillette, however, jumped 12 per cent because Procter & Gamble was offering a higher price per share than the existing stock market price. Warren Buffet, the US investment guru, whose company Berkshire Hathaway is Gillette's largest shareholder, owning 9 per cent of the shares, said that 'it's a dream deal'. He went on 'this merger is going to create the greatest consumer products company in the world'.

Stock market analysts, however, thought the deal was overpriced. They doubted whether Procter & Gamble could secure the $14-15 billion worth of cost savings it forecast and Gillette's current profits did not justify the high price being paid by Procter & Gamble.

Source: adapted from The Sunday Times, 30.1.2005.

1 Discuss whether any of Procter & Gamble's stakeholders will gain from its merger with Gillette. (20 marks)

Southwest airlines

Knowledge Southwest Airlines is a US airline company, founded in 1971.

Application Unlike many US airlines over the past ten years, Southwest Airlines is *profitable*. Arguably this can be explained by the *organisational culture* of the company. The same values exist at all levels of the *organisation*, from *surface manifestations*, to *organisational values* summarised in its *mission statement*, to *basic assumptions*.

Analysis There are many surface manifestations of this organisational culture. For example, the airline tells and retells its story of its beginnings and rapid growth as a low cost, customer friendly company to both employees and customers. It puts all its workers through some training each year where it can instil company values. It encourages workers to take responsibility and make decisions which will benefit the customer. Its flat organisational structure makes for rapid decision making and good communication. It has a policy of not laying off workers if there is a downturn in demand for flights. The organisational values of the company are expressed in its mission statement: 'The mission of Southwest Airlines is dedication to the highest quality of Customer Service delivered with a sense of warmth, friendliness, individual pride, and company spirit.' Throughout everything it says, it emphasises its commitment to providing a high quality service to the customer. The basic assumptions of the company on the whole tie in with its surface manifestations and organisational values. Partly it achieves this through recruiting workers with a sense of humour and an outgoing attitude. Also having a very stable workforce helps established workers pass on company values to new recruits.

Evaluation Southwest Airlines has been one of the few success stories of US aviation over the past forty years. Nearly all the US major airlines over that time have been through bankruptcy and destroyed shareholder value. Southwest Airlines has avoided this arguably through having a strong and distinctive organisational culture which has delivered a good service to customers.

Adapted from www.scils.rutgers.edu.

Mission statements

In unit 63, it was explained that a **mission statement** is a statement by a business of its purpose and values. It is meant both to state the aims of the business and to provide a vision for its stakeholders. Mission statements tend to be brief, ranging from a single sentence to a few sentences. Peter Drucker, the business guru, for example, has suggested that a mission statement should 'fit on a T-shirt'. But they can be longer, including more detailed statements of aims and objectives.

There is a wide variety of content that can be included in a mission statement. For example, a mission statement might:
● make reference to customers, such as 'delighting customers';
● give financial targets, such as 'maximise shareholder value' or 'achieve sustained growth in profitability';
● prioritise issues, such as 'putting the customer first';
● talk about market share, such as 'being the market leader';
● mention products, such as 'to provide transport solutions';
● comment on social issues, such as 'providing educational and youth support systems';
● comment on the competition, such as 'our approach is significantly different from other companies we have seen'.
Mission statements, to be effective, must be working documents. They must influence the everyday operations of a business. This means that employees must understand the mission statement and put it into practice. For example, if the mission statement of a business says that it 'puts customers first', then all employees must understand that customer service is top of their list of priorities. In practice, too many mission statements are written by senior personnel in a business and are then not communicated down to more junior employees. The mission statement then becomes meaningless. Ideally, the mission statement is written in a

process which involves all employees. They must 'own' the mission statement. When new staff are appointed, it then becomes vital to get them to 'own' the mission statement too. This could come about through formal training or on-the-job training (see unit 41).

Organisational culture

Mission statements should be reflected in the ORGANISATIONAL or ORGANISATION CULTURE (sometimes also called corporate culture or business culture, see unit 64) of a business. Organisational culture is the values, attitudes, beliefs, meanings and norms that are shared by people and groups within an organisation.

Edgar Schein, a US writer, suggested in *Organisational*

Figure 112.1 *Organisational culture at three levels*

Culture and Leadership (1985) that organisational culture exists at three levels within a business. These three levels are shown in Figure 112.1.

Surface manifestations These are examples of organisation culture which can easily be seen by a wide range of stakeholders. They include:

- artifacts, such as furniture, clothes or tools; wearing a uniform would be an example;
- ceremonials, such as award giving ceremonies or the singing of the company song at the start of work;
- courses, such as induction courses, or ongoing training courses for workers used to instil organisational culture;
- heroes of the business, living or dead, such as Bill Gates, Richard Branson or Walt Disney, whose way of working provides a role model within the business;
- language used in a business specific way, such as Asda referring to its workers as 'colleagues' or McDonald's calling its workers 'crew members';
- mottoes, which are short statements which never change, expressing the values of an organisation such as John Lewis's motto 'Never knowingly undersold';
- slogans, which are short statements that can change over time, such as British Airways 'the worlds favourite airline';
- stories, which tell of some important event which exemplifies the values of the business;
- myths, which are frequently told stories within a business about itself but there is not necessarily any evidence that these stories are literally true;
- norms, which are the ways in which most workers behave, such as not worrying if you turn up for work late, always being prepared to cover for workers who are off sick, or thinking it is acceptable to use the company's telephone to make personal calls;
- physical layout of premises, such as open plan offices, 'hot desking', or allocating the size of an office according to a manager's place in the hierarchy;
- rituals, which are regular events that reinforce the culture of an organisation, such as always supporting Red Nose Day (we are a caring organisation), having a weekly 'dress down day' (we are a relaxed organisation), or holding an annual Christmas party (we are a sociable organisation);
- symbols, which are signs that represent the business, such as McDonald's 'Golden Arches', or the apple logo of Apple computers.

Surface manifestations are a constant reminder to stakeholders of the culture of an organisation. They are visible and frequently used to create and reinforce that culture. However, they are not the culture itself.

Organisational values Organisational values are located below the surface manifestations of organisational culture. They are consciously thought out and expressed in words and policies. The values expressed in a mission statement would be an example. Often these are the values which have come from the top of an organisation. Perhaps they have come from

Dodgeville, Wisconsin USA, is home to the corporate headquarters of Lands' End, the mail order clothing company selling everything from shirts to swimwear. Founded in 1963, it came to the UK in the 1990s setting up in Oakham in Rutland. Just in case you were wondering about why there is an apostrophe at the end of 'Lands', when the first letterhead was produced, the printers put the apostrophe in the wrong place and the company couldn't afford to change it. The story says something about the genuineness of the company and its ability to own up to making mistakes.

Mindy Meads is president and chief executive officer. She is your typical corporate American executive, perfectly pleasant yet unable to see outside the tunnel vision of the company's culture. Asked to describe Lands' End, she replies 'If you were to sum up what Lands' End is for the apparel, it is very high quality, with the fabric we use, some of the workmanship that we put into the product.' Summing up the company ethos, she says: 'We have a very unique culture in our company; so customer driven. Everybody is working together to one goal: to get what the customer wants.'

To illustrate this, she talks about the customer, on the eve of her wedding, ringing and asking a Lands' End saleswoman to give her a 5am wake-up call. She was happy to oblige. Then there was a rogue batch of turtleneck sweaters. Lands' End voluntarily sent out 800 000 replacements to customers who had already bought the defective product. 'That was quite a bit of money', Mindy Meads conceded, insisting that the goodwill it engendered with customers made it worthwhile. She also talks about Lands' End's stain resistant trousers, perfect for coping with hazardous spills. As the brochure puts it: 'The moment a rogue splash of coffee lands, you'll be thankful for the Teflon technology that causes liquids to simply bead up and roll off.'

On the Lands' End website, you can find 'The Lands' End Principles of Doing Business'. Included in the eight principles are phrases like 'we do everything we can to make our products better', 'we price our products fairly and honestly', 'we accept any return for any reason, at any time', 'we believe that what is best for our customer is best for all of us' and 'we encourage our customers to shop for our products in whatever way they find most convenient'.

Source: adapted from *The Times*, 6.3.2004.

1 **What (a) surface manifestations and (b) organisational values are described in the passage of Lands' End's organisational culture?**
2 **If the surface manifestations and organisational values permeate the whole organisational culture, what sort of beliefs would you expect Lands' End's workers to have and how would you expect them to behave?**

the original founder of the business. Or perhaps they have come from the current senior management which has attempted to impose a culture on the business. Organisational values might reflect the actual culture of a business. But, equally, they might not. Workers at the bottom of the hierarchy might have very different values from the ones that senior management want them to possess.

Basic assumptions Basic assumptions are the organisation's culture. They represent the totality of individuals' beliefs and how they then behave. They are 'invisible' and below the surface and therefore often difficult to see, understand and change.

In practice, there may be discrepancies between the three levels. For example, a company might organise regular social events for employees (a surface manifestation). It might say in documents that it is a 'friendly and caring employer' (its organisational values). Yet, throughout the organisation there might be a culture of competitiveness which tends to make people 'look out for themselves' and makes everyone distrustful of everyone else. In this situation, the actual organisational culture is different from the surface manifestation and the organisational values. In contrast, another organisation might call its employees 'partners' (the surface manifestation). Its mission statement may say that it is committed to 'rewarding employees as well as shareholders' (its organisational values). It may then, year after year, pay employees above the average for the industry and give regular annual bonuses based upon how much profit the business has made during the year (the organisational culture). Here the underlying organisational culture fits with the stated values and the surface manifestation. There is a culture of rewarding employees because they are stakeholders.

Types of organisational culture

There are many ways of classifying organisational culture (i.e. grouping the organisational cultures of different businesses into categories and then describing the general characteristics of these cultures). One attempt to classify organisational culture was made by Charles Handy in *Understanding Organisations* (1981). He argued that there were four main types of organisational culture.

Power culture A power culture is one where there is a central source of power who is responsible for decision making. There are few rules and procedures within the business and these are overridden by the individuals who hold power when it suits them. There is a competitive atmosphere amongst employees. Amongst other things, they compete to gain power because this allows them to achieve their own objectives. This creates a political atmosphere within the business. Relatively young, small to medium sized businesses, where a single owner founded the firm and is still very much in control, could typically have power cultures.

Role culture In a role culture, decisions are made through well established rules and procedures. Power is associated with a role, such as marketing director or supervisor, rather than with individuals. In contrast to a power culture, power lies with the roles that individuals play rather than the individuals themselves. Role cultures could be described as bureaucratic (see unit 31) cultures. The Civil Service could be an example of a role culture.

Task culture In a task culture, power is given to those who

can accomplish tasks. Power therefore lies with those with expertise rather than with a particular role, as in a role culture. In a task culture, teamworking is common, with teams made up of the experts needed to get a job done. Teams are created and then dissolved as the work changes. Adaptability and dynamism is important in this culture. Examples of task culture could be businesses which operate cellular manufacturing of components (see unit 47), teamworking in the manufacturer of cars (see unit 36), scientific or medical project research operations or exploration of raw materials.

Person culture A person culture is one where there is a number of individuals in the business who have expertise but who don't necessarily work together particularly closely. The purpose of the organisation is to support those individuals. Examples of person cultures could be firms of accountants, lawyers, doctors or architects.

Changing organisational culture

Some writers, such as Tom Peters and Robert Waterman in *In Search of Excellence* (1982) have claimed that organisational culture can give a business a competitive advantage. Companies such as Microsoft, McDonald's or Virgin have been successful because they had an appropriate organisational culture for their industry. When the organisational culture is not right, then the organisation is likely to suffer from a competitive disadvantage.

For example, in the 1970s and 1980s, Japanese motor manufacturers gained a competitive advantage over the US and European rivals through the introduction of lean manufacturing techniques. Part of this was an attention to quality. Poor quality work became unacceptable within the Japanese car industry. The business used the slogan 'zero defects'. The values were expressed in the work procedures of car plants. But underlying all this was an understanding amongst workers that quality standards had to be met all the time. Quality was put above maximising output. In contrast, US and European manufacturers at the time paid lip service to quality but on the factory floor, poor quality workmanship was a daily fact of life. In the 1990s, US and European car manufacturers copied Japanese lean production techniques simply to survive. Part of that was completely changing the attitudes of workers to quality. Through training and changing the way in which employees worked, quality has improved enormously.

Changing business culture can, however, be difficult. The CULTURE GAP, the difference between the current culture and the culture that is desired by certain stakeholders such as senior management, can be very large. There is a variety of obstacles which need to be overcome if culture is to change.

Workers' and managers' views Both management and workers can be resistant to change. Many will have worked within the business for a long time. They will be used to certain ways of working. Change can threaten this. Change may also threaten their jobs or pay. One way of dealing with such problems is to work with managers and workers to change their attitudes and beliefs. Careful and sensitive implementation of change over a period of time can lead to a change in culture. For example, training can be used to explain why change is needed and how it is to be implemented. Equally, where there are performance-related pay systems, increases in pay or bonuses can be linked to changes in work methods and work attitudes. A more radical method is to make managers and workers redundant who resist change. Or they might be redeployed to jobs where they cannot influence the changes taking place. In extreme cases, businesses have been known to close a whole site and move the work elsewhere. In the UK motor industry, for example, some car plants have been told that unless they make the changes to lean production techniques, they would be closed. Sacking workers is more likely to take place where there is some urgency to change the culture. For example, if managers at a factory are told that they must raise productivity by 40 per cent over the next twelve months or risk closure, this can lead to very rapid change.

Technology and the physical environment Culture can often be maintained and promoted by the physical environment in which the business operates. An office building made up of small rooms will not promote open communication between staff. A production line where workers are stationed in isolation along the line, performing repetitive tasks, is unlikely to promote responsibility and quality assurance. Changing culture often means changing the physical environment in which workers operate. Building a new facility and hiring mostly new workers presents a real opportunity to completely change organisational culture. Few businesses, however, can do this. Instead, they have to make a large number of small changes, such buying new equipment or moving the office furniture around, to create a change in culture. The inability to make a completely new start means that changes in culture can take a long time. It also explains why some new businesses can be so successful at winning market share from older more established businesses.

The external environment Sometimes it is the external environment which is the obstacle to changing organisational culture. For example, health and safety legislation or employment law might limit the ability of businesses to encourage a new culture within the business. A lack of competition in the market might reinforce a culture of complacency and no change. There were significant changes in those industries that were privatised (see unit 55 and 103) and opened up to competition in the UK in the 1980s and 1990s. National and regional cultures can also have an important impact on organisational cultures. It can be argued that French companies have different organisational cultures to Japanese or US companies. Trying to make a business more entrepreneurial, for example, might be easier in the USA with its strong focus on individualism than in a country with a strong focus on collectivism.

Shell was once considered to have one of the best corporate cultures in the world. Yet in 2004, it became apparent that it had mislead shareholders about the size of its oil reserves and in the wake of this scandal had to reorganise itself.

In the 1970s and 1980s, Shell's reputation was very much based on its scenario planning methods. By researching factors in depth which were likely to affect the oil industry, Shell's planners would come up with a variety of scenarios about the future. It could then take account of these in making long term decisions and avoid making strategic mistakes. For example, Shell's planners foresaw the likelihood of an explosion in the price of oil in the mid-1970s and the collapse of the Soviet Union in the late 1980s.

However, by the mid-1990s some at Shell were questioning this culture. Cor Herkströter, then chairman of the committee of managing directors (CMD), had arrived at the conclusion that Shell had become too set in its ways, immobile and overstaffed. The Brent Spar crisis seemed to confirm this conclusion. The Brent Star was a disused North Sea oil platform which Shell attempted to tow out into the Atlantic and sink. Although it had researched that this was the most environmentally friendly way of disposing of the platform, environmental pressure groups such as Friends of the Earth and Greenpeace objected and forced Shell to alter its plans. In the aftermath, Mr Herkströter acknowledged that Shell had been arrogant and secretive about the issue and he set about trying to change the culture at Shell.

Out went jobs for life and in came outsourcing. The complex internal structure of the company was altered from one based on geographical divisions to one based on operating divisions. Controls were lifted to encourage managers to act more entrepreneurially rather than bureaucratically. A senior figure at the company recalled that people walked around with yellow T-shirts saying 'Grow 15 per cent a year'. In 2001, Sir Philip Watts became chairman of the CMD, the top job in Shell, but remained chairman of the executive committee of exploration and production. He was concerned that Shell was not finding enough new reserves of oil to replace oil which was being extracted from the ground. He put pressure on subordinates to find those new reserves. They in turn began increasing the volume of reserves from existing fields in a way which was not approved of by the regulatory authorities in the USA. Despite knowing that there was disquiet about this in his department, Sir Philip Watts approved the new increased figures. Subordinates were encouraged in what they were doing because employees who met the targets set were first in line for promotion.

With Sir Philip Watts gone, Shell insiders have revised their view of what makes a good corporate culture. For instance, in getting rid of staff because Shell was deemed to be 'overstaffed', today's managing chairman Jeoen van der Veer, said: 'Has excessive job movement created too many gifted amateurs in a world that needs more professionalism, commitment and discipline?' Commenting on outsourcing, another senior executive said: 'We destroyed the best skills and resource management in the world. If you remove your technical knowledge, you erase your corporate knowledge.'

Source: adapted from the *Financial Times*, 18.6.2004.

1 **What aspects of the organisational culture at Shell attracted criticism in the mid-1990s?**
2 **Discuss why the changes in organisational culture at Shell from the mid-1990s may have led to more problems than it solved.**

"**key**terms"

Culture gap - the difference between the current culture and the culture that is desired by certain stakeholders such as senior management.
Organisational or organisation or corporate or business culture - the values, attitudes, beliefs, meanings and norms that are shared by people and groups within an organisation.

✓ checklist

1 Why should mission statements be working documents?
2 Explain the difference between surface manifestations, organisational values and basic assumptions of corporate culture.
3 Explain the differences between a power culture, a role culture, a task culture and a person culture.
4 How can organisational culture give businesses a competitive advantage?
5 How can a culture gap hold back a business?

Brian Strode was appointed Chief Executive of Radigan's two years ago. Radigan's is a medium sized food manufacturing company with 750 employees. Once the company was much larger, with at its peak some 5 000 employees spread over three sites. Today, the company is based on one site reflecting the need to concentrate resources to gain competitive advantage.

When Brian Strode came into the company, he could see that it faced massive problems. Previous management had underinvested in every part of the business. Equipment was old, products were not at the cutting edge in the field and training of staff was non-existent. It was not surprising that Radigan's was struggling to maintain sales.

When talking to workers and managers about change, most seemed to think that the attitudes of other staff could not be changed. They put forward a variety of reasons why change was almost impossible. Some pointed to the main trade union representing shop floor workers as a major obstacle. They said it would resist any changes in the conditions of service of employees. Others said that staff were too set in their ways to change. They had always done the job like this and it would be impossible to get them to do it a different way. Half the workforce, including most of the managers, were over the age of 45 and there were only two employees under the age of 25. Another problem often cited was the strong division of workers into separate informal groups with distinct identities. Typically, there would be around 10-15 people in a group who took their breaks together, socialised informally together at work and formed friendship patterns outside the workplace. Each group built up a 'them and us' mentality. Each thought it was doing the hardest work in the company whilst other groups were contributing little or nothing to the organisation. Workers on the shop floor saw managers as 'pen pushers' who knew nothing about the 'real' work of the company that they were doing in making products. Managers saw shop floor workers as lazy and inflexible, always ready to find an excuse why something couldn't be done. Overall, most workers were highly cynical about the contribution that other workers made to the company. Equally, most workers and many managers had little idea of the competitive pressures that the company was now facing.

Looking through the paperwork, Brian Strode could find little that was written down that could inspire change. The company had no mission statement. There was nothing coherent about a vision for the future. Most of what was there seemed to be reacting to events rather than shaping them. He was surprised that there didn't seem to be much that even supported the very conservative nature of the company.

Looking round the site, Brian observed that everything was very boxed in. The very walls of the factory and offices seemed to emphasis the small group mentality of the workforce. Office staff, for example, were all working in small cramped offices, mostly on their own. Amongst the office staff, there were a lot of posters and stickers on walls or mugs with little work slogans like 'I'm the boss' or 'Overworked and underpaid'. By 5.30 each evening, the place was deserted. Shop floor workers, office staff and most managers worked to the clock. The minute they were due to leave, they were out like a shot.

Brian set about trying to change the culture of the business. It had to be more responsive to the needs of customers. Costs had to be reduced to maintain sales. Quality needed to be considerably improved. To achieve this, he wanted to see a more flexible and far better trained workforce, probably working in teams and whose goals were aligned to those of the company.

1 Discuss how Brian Strode could change the organisation's culture from its surface manifestations to its basic assumptions. (20 marks)

Decision making

Center Parcs

Knowledge Center Parcs is a company which runs family vacation resorts in the UK and Europe. It manages four holiday villages in the UK. It is now looking to opening a fifth site somewhere in the South of England.

Application Center Parcs is involved in a variety of *decision making* tasks. These include *routine decisions*, such as what shifts workers should do *operational decisions*, such as whether to paint a chalet, *tactical decisions*, such as whether to increase spending on advertising, and *strategic decisions* such as whether to open a new holiday village. In making strategic decisions, Center Parcs might want to consider using *scientific decision making models*, such as the *Ansoff Matrix* or the *Boston Matrix*.

Analysis Tactical decisions which Center Parcs have made include its policy of differential pricing. It charges more in season, and particularly during school holidays, than out of season and during term times. This has enabled it to maximise its revenues whilst spreading demand for its holidays over the year. In 2003, it was so successful at managing demand that its four holiday villages were 93 per cent full, which is as close to operating at full capacity as it gets in the tourist industry. Strategically, because its existing sites are full, it can only grow the business significantly by opening new sites or growing externally. Hence it is currently working on opening a new site in the South of England. It has also done 'analytical work' on three or four potential takeover targets. Champneys, the upmarket health spa, Warner Holidays and Shearings are tipped as possible candidates for an acquisition.

Evaluation Center Parcs is, operationally, a highly successful company. However, to be more successful, it needs to grow in size. Growth will introduce more risk for the business because the additional business taken on might not be successful. At this stage, increased risk is probably a small price to pay for higher sales and profits. This risk could be reduced if it used a range of scientific decision making models to help it make its choices.

Adapted from The Sunday Times, 15.8.2004, www.centerparcs.co.uk.

Types of decision

All businesses have to make decisions. The type of decision will vary, depending on its nature and the likely effect on the business.

Routine, low level decisions These have to be made on a day to day or week to week basis. Examples include which workers will work which shift or what stationery will be ordered for the next month by an office. Routine decisions will be made by all levels of workers within a business.

Operational decisions These are likely to be non-routine low level decisions. Examples include whether to call out a maintenance engineer immediately to fix a broken machine or wait until the regular weekly visit from the engineer, or whether to increase staffing on a particular production line to cope with higher than expected orders. Like routine decisions, operational decisions are likely to be made by all levels of workers within a business. However, the more hierarchical and centralised the organisation, the more likely it is that operational decisions will be made at a more senior level, and the less likely it is that workers at the bottom of the chain of command will have scope to make such decisions.

Tactical decisions These are medium term decisions made by middle or senior management. They address specific issues and problems. For example, a business may have to decide whether to produce a new colour for its range of dishwashers or whether to increase spending on promotion for its dishwasher range.

Strategic decisions These are long term decisions about the direction of the whole business. They are made by senior management and directors. For example, should the business turn away from its traditional UK suppliers to buy from cheaper suppliers in the Third World? Should the business diversify away from its current core range of products?

The higher the level of decision making, the greater the impact on the business if the wrong decision is taken. Strategic decisions are far riskier to the long term survival of the business than operational decisions. For example, Marconi's strategic decision in the 1990s to sell most of its traditional manufacturing subsidiaries and concentrate on the manufacture of IT and telecommunications equipment almost bankrupted the company when the new technology bubble burst at the end of that decade. Microsoft's strategic decision to bundle its Explorer Internet browser with its Windows operating system has helped Windows maintain a 90 per cent share of the computer operating system market and has generated large profits. Virgin has made strategic decisions to move into air and rail transport and financial markets which are unrelated to its previous operations in music and the media. This has helped the organisation to grow and help to establish a well known corporate brand.

Terry Hooton owns and runs a small engineering company employing 32 people. Over the past twelve months, he has been hard hit by a doubling in the price of steel, a crucial raw material for the company. What's more, he has often been unable to buy steel because it is in short supply. The steel crisis has been caused by a significant increase in demand for steel by Chinese industry. The steel crisis couldn't have come at a worse time for the company. Two years ago, Terry Hooton made the decision to expand capacity by moving into larger premises, taking on more workers and investing in a £90 000 welding robot. The business is now being forced to run at less than full capacity.

On a day to day basis, the steel shortage is having a considerable impact on how the business is run. Yesterday, for example, Terry Hooton had to decide which order to make up because he didn't have enough stocks of the right sort of steel for the two orders he had in hand. This meant that one customer would be receiving its order late. The weekly rostering of staff is also having to be adjusted on a day to day basis. Terry hopes to be able to get supplies of steel for the second order tomorrow. Staff will then be taken off other jobs to make the order. His workers don't like having their rosters changed at the last minute and sometimes this can cause bad feeling.

In the short term, Terry Hooton is trying to push up his prices to cover the extra cost of the steel. But he is having difficulty passing on the higher costs. Customers are threatening to take their business elsewhere and Terry knows that his competitors are sometimes winning orders because they aren't putting up their prices. These are difficult times for Terry Hooton and he expects his profits this year to fall substantially.

1 **By using examples from the passage, explain what is meant by (a) routine decisions; (b) operational decisions; (c) tactical decisions; (d) strategic decisions.**
2 **Discuss whether Terry Hooton made the right decision to expand his business two years ago.**

In contrast, an operational decision which led to too many paper clips being ordered for a company in the month of March is unlikely to have much impact on its performance in the long term.

Decision making and objectives

In many cases decisions are made quickly and informally. Workers and managers have a good understanding of what they want to achieve. They then use their knowledge and experience to make day to day decisions to achieve those objectives.

The more important and complex the decision, however, the more likely it is that they will use a formal or scientific model of decision making. One such model is shown in Figure 113.1.

Setting or identifying objectives First, decision makers have to understand what they are aiming to achieve. Objectives might already have been set, such as to purchase the best machine for less than £100 000, or to launch a new product which will gain at least 2 per cent of the market. Or decision makers might have to set their own specific objectives in the context of wider objectives. For example, a business might have an objective of increasing profit by 10 per cent per year. The manager of a particular factory within the company might then decide that the objective of the factory will be to cut its costs by 10 per cent a year.

Gathering ideas and data Decision making should be based on evidence. So decision makers need to gather ideas and data relating to the decision. This can be quite a chaotic process spread over a period of time. It will become apparent that some data is impossible to obtain. Some initial ideas might prove to be a dead end, whilst others, generated late in the whole process, might prove to be the most valuable.

Analysing ideas and data Ideas and data need to be brought together and analysed. Several possible courses of action may emerge with advantages and disadvantages for each one.

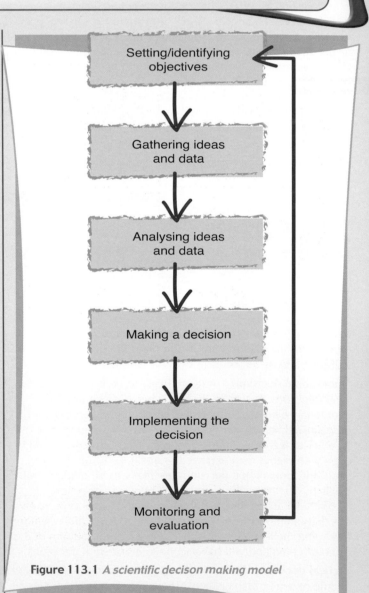

Figure 113.1 *A scientific decison making model*

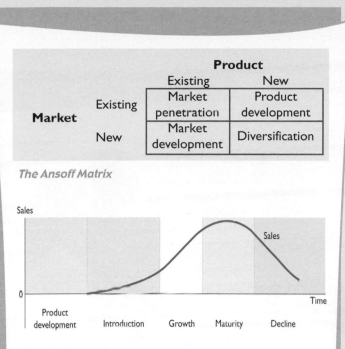

The Ansoff Matrix

The product life cycle

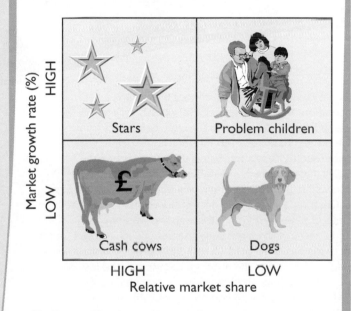

The Boston Matrix

Figure 113.2 *Examples of models used in decision making*

SWOT analysis or PEST-G analysis (see unit 64) might be used at this stage. Some outcomes may be quantifiable (i.e. measurable in numbers) in terms such as output, raw material inputs or cash. Other outcomes may prove unquantifiable, such as consumer satisfaction or staff morale.

Making a decision The culmination of thought and research will be the decision making itself. There is a variety of ways in which this can be done. It might be an individual person who makes the final decision. It could be a committee which recommends a decision to a higher committee such as the board of directors of a company. A provisional decision might be made and then that is put out to consultation before a final decision is made. A decision might be postponed if it is not vital to make the decision immediately.

Implementing the decision The decision then needs to be implemented. This can take place immediately or might be a long term decision where a course of action takes years to implement.

Monitoring and evaluation Once the decision has been made, the outcome of the decision should be monitored and evaluated. Some decisions can be reversed quickly if the outcome is unsatisfactory. For example, a shop may decide to stock a new line of frozen ready meals. If sales are not satisfactory within the first month, it can quickly and easily cease to stock the line. Other decisions are likely to be irreversible. For example, the decision to build the Channel Tunnel proved to be a commercial disaster for Eurotunnel, the company which now owns and runs it.

Scientific decision making

Figure 113.2 shows a SCIENTIFIC DECISION MAKING MODEL. It is 'scientific' because it relies upon evidence to make decisions. There are other scientific decision making models or models which can be used to help make decisions. For example, the marketing model (see unit 9) shows how a business can develop a marketing strategy, from clarifying objectives to implementing marketing plans to reviewing and evaluating outcomes.

A business may also choose to use models such as the Ansoff Matrix (see unit 9), the product life cycle model (see unit 12) or the Boston Matrix (see unit 13) shown in Figure 113.2. The advantage of using these models is that they provide a way of seeing a problem from a particular perspective. Any model is an abstraction from reality. It is never 100 per cent realistic because if it were it would be as complex to use as real life. However, models such as the Ansoff Matrix can be a powerful tool in focusing on a particular issue because they simplify issues and are easily understood.

In unit 114, another model, decision trees, is outlined which can help businesses arrive at appropriate decisions.

keyterms

Scientific decision making models - an abstraction of reality based upon empirical evidence used to make decisions.

Hunkins is a supermarket chain in the UK. It is in direction competition with the market leader, Tesco, and other chains such as Asda and J Sainsbury. Over the past ten years, it has seen steady expansion and an increase in market share, although the increased market share has come mainly from taking away sales from small independent grocers. Trading conditions over the past two years have been very difficult and whilst sales have seen some increase, profits have stagnated. The chief executive of Hunkins is looking at a variety of options to take the company forward.

One option that has been presented to him is to launch an Internet home delivery service. Tesco and Sainsbury already have well established e-commerce services although both are finding it difficult to make the services profitable. The scale of operation of Internet grocery services is very small. For example, Tesco, the largest online grocery retailing, is selling around £500 million a year through its Internet home delivery service, a drop in the ocean of the £109 billion value of the UK food retail market. If an Internet home delivery service is launched, Hunkins would have to decide whether to take the route used by Tesco and Sainsbury which is to have produce picked at local stores, or whether to have purpose built warehouses dedicated to home delivery services such as Ocado, linked to Waitrose, has done. Using existing stores would mean low start up costs but high ongoing costs because having shop assistants picking orders alongside customers is inefficient. Creating a warehouse distribution system would be high cost initially but more efficient in the long term if sufficient volumes of sales were going through the warehouse.

Another option for future strategy is to invest in price reductions. Most of the large supermarket chains in recent years have been cutting their prices in a bid to attract more customers. Asda has attempted to make low prices a unique selling point for its operations. Cutting prices is expensive in terms of lost revenues. For the strategy to succeed, the loss of revenues needs to be covered by increases in sales. The danger is that any price reductions made by Hunkins would be matched by competitors. On the other hand, Hunkins can't afford to be much out of line on prices with Asda and Tesco.

Tesco and Sainsbury have set up their own financial services operations. Up till now, Hunkins has not responded to this, but such a diversification of the product range is another possibility for investment. Tesco and Sainsbury have reduced the cost of entering financial markets by buying in the services of established banks and insurance companies. Tesco and Sainsbury market the products and put their own brand name on them, but the actual service is offered by an existing banking or insurance provider. Hunkins could do the same offering, say, credit cards, motor and household insurance or even bank accounts. The forecast profit margins on such products are low if they are competitively priced, but it might help retain customer loyalty and keep bringing customers back to the Hunkins stores.

1 (a) Use the Ansoff Matrix to analyse the three different options for growth being considered by Hunkins. (10 marks)
   (b) Explain how the decision making model shown in Figure 113.1 could be used to analyse the Internet home delivery service option. (10 marks)
2 If Hunkins only had the financial resources to develop one of the three options, discuss which of these it should undertake. (20 marks)

114 Decision trees

Beville Tools

Knowledge Beville Tools is a specialist toolmaker for the automotive industry. It is considering whether to buy an £800 000 compression moulding machine.

Application The *investment* would represent a major financial outlay for the company. As part of its *decision making process*, the *finance director* has drawn up a *decision tree* showing the *expected values* of the two alternatives, to invest or not to invest. He has estimated *probabilities* as well as factoring in the initial *cost*. The finance director has used this *quantitative model* in the context of a much wider *report* which also takes into account *qualitative* factors.

Analysis Decision tree analysis shows clearly that the investment should go ahead. The expected value of making the investment is 30 per cent higher than not making it. Qualitative factors would also point toward making the investment. To survive competition from low cost producers, Beville Tools has to retain an edge in terms of quality of product and speed of delivery. The investment will help it lower its own costs whilst improving quality and speed of production. The main argument against the investment is the strength of demand from motor manufacturers. The collapse of the car manufacturer, Rover, in April 2005 showed how fragile the market can be.

Evaluation Overall, it can be argued that the investment should go ahead. There is a risk that the motor industry could go into recession or that Beville Tools might lose a major customer. However, like much of UK manufacturing, the company will only survive competition from producers in low cost countries by investing heavily and moving upmarket in terms of either the product or the service provided. If the numbers show that the investment should be profitable, then Beville Tools has little choice but to invest if it is to ensure its long term survival.

Alternatives

In business, decision makers are constantly faced with alternatives. A personal assistant has to decide whether to make a phone call or sort out the appointments diary. A marketing manager has to decide whether to pursue a client for further orders or spend the time contacting new clients. A large business, faced with inefficiency, may have to decide whether to buy updated machinery, retrain employees, give incentives or simply accept it and carry on its operations in the same way.

The more important and complex the decision, the more likely it is that a scientific model would be used to aid the decision making. One such model is a DECISION TREE. This is a method of decision making where alternative courses of action are stated, their costs and benefits calculated and probabilities attached to outcomes so that the optimal decision can be taken.

Decision trees are **quantitative models**. This means that numerical values are given to different alternatives and the best alternative is then calculated. The numbers can be measured in money terms such as pounds or euros, or in output terms such as tonnes of production, or sales such as quantity sold.

Decision trees take their name from the diagrams used. They resemble a tree with branches, which has been put on its side.

The construction of decision trees

Decision trees are constructed in a particular way. They all have the same basic features, but some can be made more complicated if the decision requires this.

Decision points Decision points are where a decision maker has to make a decision. On a decision tree diagram, such as Figure 114.1, decision points are shown by a **square box**. Decision trees always start off on the left hand side with such a box. But with more complicated decisions, there may be decision points in the middle of the decision tree as well. In Figure 114.1, the decision is whether or not to change production output.

Alternatives Flowing out from the square decision box are various alternatives which are to be evaluated. They are shown by lines, as in Figure 114.1. In this case, three

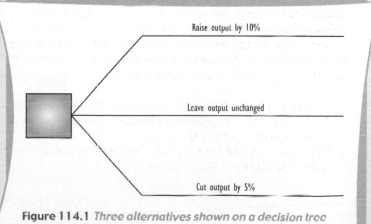

Figure 114.1 *Three alternatives shown on a decision tree*

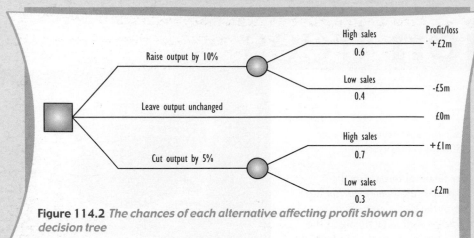

Figure 114.2 *The chances of each alternative affecting profit shown on a decision tree*

alternatives are being considered:
- to raise output by 10 per cent;
- to leave output the same;
- to cut output by 5 per cent.

Chance nodes Each alternative will have different possible outcomes. These outcomes are shown on a decision tree diagram as flowing from a circle. These circles are called chance nodes. For example, in Figure 114.2, if output were raised by 10 per cent, then it is estimated that there will be two possible outcomes. Either:
- there will be high sales raising profit by £2 million;
- there will be low sales which will result in a loss of £5 million.

Probability Managers drawing up decision trees have to show the probability or likelihood of each individual outcome occurring. The probability of any outcome occurring lies between 0 and 1. If the probability is one, then the outcome will definitely happen, i.e. there is a 100 per cent certainty of it happening. If the probability is zero, then there is no chance of that outcome occurring. Such an outcome would, in practice, not be shown on a decision tree precisely because it would not occur. If the probability is 0.5, then there is a 50-50 chance of it happening. An example of a 50-50 chance is a coin being spun and landing 'heads'. If the probability is 0.66, then in two out of three cases, this outcome will occur. For example, there is a 0.66 chance that when a six sided die is rolled, a number from one to four will appear on the top of the die. So, the higher the likelihood of an event happening, the near to one will be the value of its probability. The closer to zero the probability, the less likely it is that an event will happen.

On a decision tree, all the possible outcomes will be noted. Therefore, the sum of the probabilities of any course of action will add up to 1. The probabilities are shown below the line extending out from a chance node. For example, in Figure 114.2, managers calculate that if output were raised by 10 per cent, then there would be a 0.6 probability that this would raise profits of £2 million because of high sales. However, there is a 0.4

probability that there will be low sales. If this occurs, then profits will fall by £5 million. The 0.6 probability plus the 0.4 probability add up to 1.

Expected value The expected value of a particular course of action can be calculated. This is done by multiplying each possible outcome by its probability and adding these up for each course of action. On Figure 114.2:
- the expected value of raising output by 10 per cent is (0.6 x £2 million) + (0.4 x -£5 million). This is equal to £1.2 million -£2 million = -£0.8 million;
- the expected value if output were left unchanged is zero as there would be no effect on profit;
- the expected value of cutting output by 5 per cent is (0.7 x £1 million) + (0.3 x -£2 million). This is equal to £0.7 million - £0.6 million = +£0.1 million.

As an equation:

$$\text{Expected value} = (\text{probability}_1 \times \text{outcome}_1) + (\text{probability}_2 \times \text{outcome}_2) + ... (\text{probability}_n \times \text{outcome}_n)$$

where n is the number of possible outcomes.

The final decision Decision trees are drawn so that the expected values of different outcomes can be compared. The alternative which has the highest expected value should be chosen. In Figure 114.2, raising output by 10 per cent gives an expected value of -£0.8 million. Cutting output by 5 per cent gives an expected value of £0.1 million. Leaving output unchanged has no effect. Therefore cutting output by 5 per cent is the alternative the business is likely to choose.

Figure 114.3 shows a business which has to decide whether to invest in new machinery or make no new investment. Calculating the expected values of each alternative will help a business to choose which decision to make.

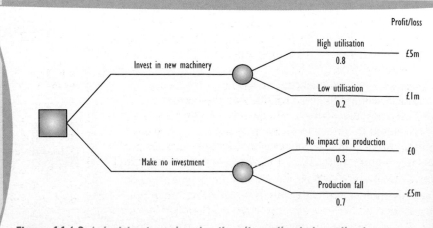

Figure 114.3 *A decision tree showing the alternative to investing in new machinery*

Lancorn Ltd imports kit models from the USA. When the models arrive they have to be assembled and painted, which can take time and is a very labour intensive process. The business has recently experienced problems with its lead times. Some deliveries have not arrived and others have been late. It has been assured that this will not continue in future, but the business must consider alternative strategies just in case. Three possible strategies are shown in Table 114.1.

> 1 Fill in the gaps in the table shown by ?.
> 2 Calculate the expected values of the three decisions.

Strategy	Effect	Probability	Profit/loss
Change supplier			
	Very effective	0.3	£4 000
	Moderately effective	0.4	£1 000
	Ineffective	?	-£3 000
Leave unchanged			
	Very effective	0.2	£2 000
	Moderately effective	?	£1 000
	Ineffective	0.2	-£1 000
Speed up production			
	Very effective	?	£4 000
	Moderately effective	0.2	-£800
	Ineffective	0.3	-£1 000

Table 114.1 *Alternative strategies when faced with delivery problems*

The expected value of investing in new machinery is:

$$0.8 \times £5m = £4m$$
$$\text{and } 0.2 \times £1m = \underline{£0.2m}$$
$$\underline{£4.2m}$$

The expected value of making no investment is:

$$0.3 \times £0 = £0m$$
$$\text{and } 0.7 \times -£5 = \underline{-£3.5m}$$
$$\underline{-£3.5m}$$

Clearly the business should invest, as the expected value is £4.2m compared to the -£3.5m as a result of making no investment.

More complex decision trees

Decision trees can be more complex than those shown in Figures 114.1-114.3. In Figure 114.4, for example, there is more than one decision point and various chance nodes on the decision tree. Greater complexity is likely to make the decision tree more realistic.

Decision points In Figure 114.4 a business is considering its marketing expenditure for the coming year. It has to make a decision and has three main alternatives:
- to allocate funding to the development of a new version of Product A, its most successful product;
- to promote another leading product, Product B;
- to promote the business as a brand in itself.

If it allocates funding to developing a new version of Product A, there is another decision to make. Does it launch the new version nationally, just in the UK market, or does it launch it internationally?

Costs There are costs involved in a particular decision. Figures 114.1-114.3 showed profit or loss figures. The costs had already been accounted for in these figures. It is also possible to show the revenues and costs of decisions on a decision tree, as in Figure 114.4. For example, the cost of promoting Product B is £6 million. The revenue from a successful promotion is £10 million, but only £3 million from an unsuccessful promotion.

Calculating expected values Working out the expected value of different outcomes is more complicated in Figure 114.4 than on a simpler decision tree. In Figure 114.4, the most complicated outcome to work out is the top one, of allocating funding to a new version of Product A. To find the expected value of this decision it is necessary to work back from right to left (known as using a **rollback technique**).

- If a new version of Product A is allocated funding and launched nationally, the expected value at the decision point of where to launch is:

(0.7 x £10 million) + (0.3 x £2 million) minus the cost of the launch, £5 million.

This equals £7 million + £0.6 million - £5 million, which is £2.6 million.

- If a new version of Product A is launched internationally, the expected value at the decision point of where to launch is:

(0.6 x £20 million) + (0.4 x £5 million) minus the cost of launch, £10 million.

This equals £12 million + £2 million - £10 million, which is £4 million.

Launching a new version of Product A internationally has a higher expected value than launching it nationally. The alternative to launch nationally is 'closed' by drawing a line across it, as indicated in Figure 114.4.

Again working from right to left, it is possible to calculate the expected value of allocating extra funding to developing a new version of Product A. This is:

(0.8 x the expected revenue from launching internationally, £4 million) plus (0.2 x the expected revenue from a failed launch, £0) minus (the cost of the extra funding, £5 million).

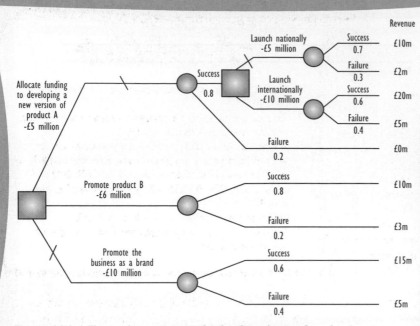

Figure 114.4 *Three alternative methods of marketing for a business*

This is greater than the loss of -£1.8 million from the development of a new version of product A. The option to develop Product A is now 'closed' as in Figure 114.4.

The expected value from promoting the business as a brand is:

0.6 x £15m =£9m

0.4 x £5m = £2m
    _____
    £11m - £10 m (costs) = £1m.

This expected value is less than the alternative to promote Product B and so the alternative to promote the business as a brand is 'closed' in Figure 114.4.

The business would make the decision to promote Product B in this decision tree.

Advantages and disadvantages of using decision trees

Using decision trees has important advantages for a business.

- Managers have to work out what alternatives they face.
- Alternatives have to be quantified both in terms of their outcomes and the probabilities that they will occur. This avoids vague and superficial thinking.
- By estimating probabilities, it is possible to expose the risks of a particular course of action. Decision tree techniques suggest that the alternative with the highest expected value should be chosen. However, the risks associated with this alternative may be judged to be too great by decision makers. An alternative with a lower expected value may be chosen because the risk associated with that alternative is much lower.

This equals £3.2 million + £0 - £5 million, which is -£1.8 million.

The final decision The decision the business chooses will be the one which yields the highest expected value. The expected value from the decision to promote Product B is:

0.8 x £10m = £8m

0.2 x £3m = £0.6m
    _____
    £8.6m - £6m (costs) = £2.6m

Commersall plc is a UK based manufacturer. It values the quality of its production methods highly and has operated lean production techniques for a number of years. Its latest ISO 9000 review suggested that some of its machinery was at the end of its useful life with no resale value and investment would be required in the near future. However, this is likely to be expensive, especially considering the size and nature of the production processes used by the business. An alternative action may be to leave these machines operating unchanged for another year, despite the possible effects on the business.

Figure 114.5 shows a decision tree with alternatives facing the business. If investment does take place then the company has the option of buying a smaller new machine or a larger second hand machine, although this is likely to be from abroad and will require shipping to the UK. Whichever it chooses, work practices may need to change and training will be required, which may affect the success of the changeover in the first year.

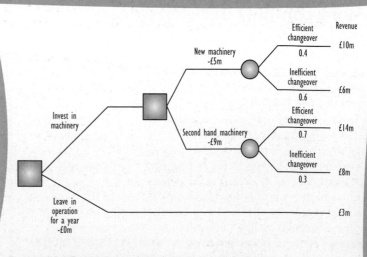

Figure 114.5 *Alternatives facing Commersall plc*

1 **Calculate the expected values of the alternatives and advise the business on the decision it should take.**
2 **How might the decision change if:**
   (a) the cost of the new machinery fell to £4m;
   (b) the revenue from an efficient changeover to new machinery rose to £11m?

keyterms

Decision tree - a method of decision making where alternative courses of action are stated, their costs and benefits calculated and probabilities attached to outcomes so that the optimal decision can be taken.

However, decision trees as a decision making technique have disadvantages too.

- Values placed on alternatives may be difficult to estimate with any accuracy. For example, the cost of an alternative may be difficult to estimate. The profit or loss associated with a particular outcome may be difficult to quantify. Probabilities attached to different alternatives may be more guesses than reliable estimates. There may be unexpected time lags in costs and benefits which make an outturn from a decision different from the prediction made for it. So decision trees, by forcing managers to put numbers onto the diagram, may give a spurious impression of accuracy to a situation.
- Decision trees need to be used alongside other decision making techniques. In particular, non-quantifiable costs

checklist

1 Why are decision trees an example of a quantitative model?
2 Explain the difference between a decision point and a chance node on a decision tree.
3 Calculate the expected value of a particular course of action if the probabilities and outcomes were: (a) 80% of £10m and 20% of £5m; (b) 60% of £100 000 and 40% of £50 000; (c) 25% of £1m and 35% of £10m and 40% of £5m.
4 What is meant by the 'rollback technique'?
5 Explain briefly the advantages and disadvantages of using decision trees.

and benefits of a particular alternative course of action must be taken into account when making a decision. Sometimes, non-quantifiable factors are more important than the profit forecast by a decision tree.

Rushton is a company which owns a number of coffee shop and fast food chains in the UK. It has built up its portfolio of brands over the past ten years partly through organic growth and partly through acquisitions. It now wants to expand internationally and is initially looking at the US market. Although fiercely competitive, the senior management at Rushton feels that the US market has more similarities to the UK market than, say, continental Europe or the Far East.

Bob Rushton, the founder of the company and its chief executive, asked Michael Yao, a senior manager, to draw up some figures for the options available. He came back with a detailed report about the US market which included the decision tree shown in Figure 114.6. The decision tree showed three options: to build up a franchise network; to build up a wholly owned network; or to buy an established US chain. The first two options would involve exporting and adapting the formula for the most successful of Rushton's chains in the UK. Franchising would be a much cheaper alternative to setting up a wholly owned chain because the franchisees would put up much of the financial capital to start their businesses. On the other hand, it would also yield less profit because the franchisees would keep much of the profit they make rather than it being passed on to Rushton. All three options assume that the chain would be made up of 100 outlets. The costs shown on the decision tree are the initial costs of each of the three options. For example, establishing a wholly owned chain would involve purchasing of leases for premises, refitting premises and providing working capital. Taking over an established chain would involve a one off payment to buy the chain. The resale value shows the estimated value of the chain at the end of five years if it were sold to another buyer assuming that any profits made in the US operation were retained within the US subsidiary. The difference between the initial cost and the estimated resale value would be the overall profit or loss which the parent company, Rushton, would make on the venture for its five year investment. She calculated that taking over an existing chain would be the most profitable option.

In his report, Michael pointed out that

many assumptions had to be made to construct the decision tree. For example, the average cost of establishing a single outlet had been estimated at £1 million based on factors such as average lease prices in the USA and fitting out costs together with apportionment of overheads. Equally, the resale value at the end of five years depended on factors such as the performance of the US economy over the period. If the USA was in a recession at the end of five years, the chain would be worth less than if the US economy were in boom.

Three months after submitting her report, an opportunity came up to buy up an existing US chain of 150 outlets almost all on the East Coast of the USA. It was owned by a large drinks company which had acquired the chain as part of another takeover. The chain had made a small loss in each of the past three years and so the asking price of £120 million was relatively cheap. Michael Yao formed part of a team which quickly put together another report about whether or not to buy the chain. As part of that report, he prepared the decision tree shown in Figure 114.7. This showed two scenarios if a decision were made to buy. One was to expand the chain to 250 outlets and the other was to keep it at its current 150 outlet size. Again the resale value showed the estimated value at the end of five years. The conclusion of the report was that Rushton should buy the company and that it was marginally more profitable to expand the chain to 250 outlets.

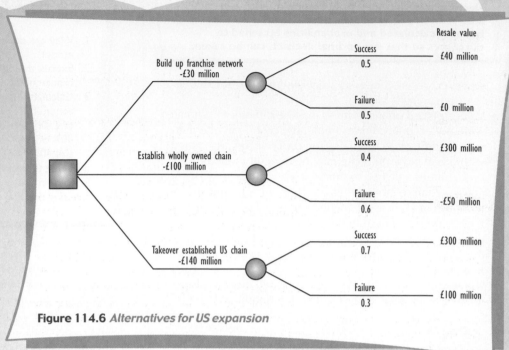

Figure 114.6 *Alternatives for US expansion*

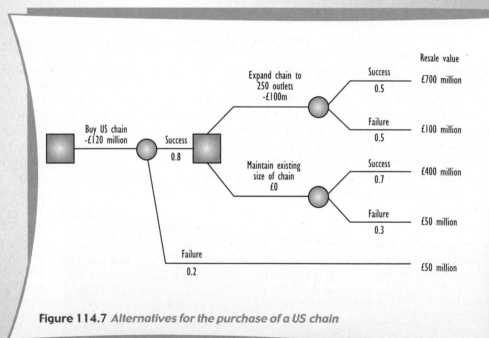

Figure 114.7 *Alternatives for the purchase of a US chain*

1 By calculating expected values, show why (a) in his initial report, Michael Yao suggested that 'taking over an existing chain would be the most profitable option' and (b) the second report concluded that 'Rushton should buy the company and that it was marginally more profitable to expand the chain to 250 outlets'. (20 marks)
2 Discuss the advantages and limitations to Rushton of using decision trees for making its decision about whether or not to expand in the USA, and if so, how to organise that expansion.

Kraft

Knowledge Kraft, the maker of Dairylea cheese and Shredded Wheat breakfast cereal, announced in 2004 that it was selling many of its famous food brands including its cereals division.

Application The US *company* had reviewed its *corporate strategy* and decided that many parts of its business were *underperforming*. Their *sales* were stagnant, or even, as with the case of the cereals *division*, were declining. *Divesting* itself of poorly performing parts of the business would give it the cash to buy higher *growth brands* from other companies or return the proceeds to *shareholders*. This called for a change in *strategic direction*.

Analysis Kraft has been hit in recent years by a number of factors. One is changes in eating habits, such as low-carbohydrate diets. This has affected, for example, sales of cereals. Another is the soaring cost of raw materials, with an extra $700 million expected this year alone from rising prices of ingredients. The company has been unable to pass on the increased cost to consumers in higher prices and so it has reduced Kraft's profitability. Its Oscar Mayer Meats division has been hit by rising competition from large slaughterhouse companies that have moved into its packaged and prepared meats market. Unable to develop effective business strategies to counter these problems, Kraft has decided to change strategic direction.

Evaluation Kraft is faced with a difficult situation. Shedding some of its more poorly performing brands is one way of giving the whole group higher sales and profits growth figures. However, the companies that buy those brands will hope to improve their performance. The question is why Kraft cannot develop the business strategies which would do the same. Shareholders should also worry about how Kraft will use the cash it raises from the sale. It could end up spending the money without raising sales or profits. Changing corporate strategy can be a high risk option. The stock market perhaps thought this as Kraft shares initially fell in price on hearing the news.

Adapted from *The Times*, 19.10.2004.

Strategies, plans and tactics

In unit 64, it was explained that a strategy is a plan to achieve given objectives. The objectives of a business might be to maximise profit, increase market share or maximise shareholder value. Plans show how a business may set about increasing market share or maximising shareholder value. For example, a business may plan to launch new products, or increase its marketing spend. Alternatively, it may plan to cut costs and prices.

It was also explained in unit 64 that a strategy is a medium to long term plan to achieve given objectives. In the short term a business may use tactics to achieve short term objectives. For example, sales may be faltering. So to boost sales, a business may launch a short term promotional campaign. A clothing retailer might find that its pre-Christmas sales in early December are disappointing. It might bring forward its January sales to mid-December to shift stock.

Strategic decisions, therefore, are often seen by businesses as choices made from alternatives which will help a business to achieve its objectives in the long term. They are often taken by senior management and have far reaching effects on the whole business. **Tactical decisions** tend to be choices made in the short or medium term with reasonably certain outcomes. They can be changed more easily in the face of changing businesses conditions. Unit 64 explains the nature of the strategic and tactical objectives of a business.

Functional level strategies

FUNCTIONAL STRATEGIES (see unit 64) are strategies to improve the effectiveness of the different functional operations within a business. It can be argued that there are four main functional operations within a business - production, marketing, human resources and finance. There are different ways of improving each of these operations.

The production function Production includes research and development (R&D) as well as production itself. A business might be able to cut costs by exploiting economies of scale (see unit 42). Improved stock control, including just-in-time production techniques, will lead to efficiency savings (see unit 45). Improved quality procedures will cut costs too as well as delivering a better product to the customer (see unit 46). Lean production techniques will cut costs by minimising the resources needed in production (see units 47-48). More focussed R&D will lead to more products getting to the launch stage for less cost (see unit 95).

The marketing function Market research can be more focussed and more cost effective (see units 4-8). Equally, too many businesses fail to conduct appropriate market research when there would be a positive rate of return on the investment. Products could be better positioned in the market. More thought could be given as to whether a product should be a mass market product or a niche product for example (see unit 11). Greater care in managing the product life cycle could increase profits. The 4Ps of marketing of promotion, production, price and place could be more effectively used (see units 14-19).

The human resource function Proponents of Human Resource Management argue that a variety of techniques from more team work, devolving power down the hierarchy and flexible pay structures can motivate staff and make them more committed (see units 92-93). Improving communication within a business can lead to greater efficiency (see units 86-87). On the other hand, the Scientific Management school would argue that greater control of workers, the division of labour and rewards strictly linked to performance will lead to greater efficiency in the work place and a workforce more focussed on achieving the goals that have been set for it (see unit 34). What is not in dispute between these different philosophies is that changing the management of workers can lead to improvements in labour productivity as well as other measures of personnel effectiveness, such as absenteeism rates and labour turnover (see unit 94).

The finance function Production, marketing and human resources must all be managed strategically, but for a business they must all lead to its financial survival. For most businesses, that means making a profit over the medium to long term. So the finance department at a strategic level must coordinate the workings of the other three functional areas to deliver that profit. Equally, the day to day workings of the finance department from sending out invoices to paying wages to keeping accounts must be conducted efficiently. Strategies must be put in place to secure the smooth flow of cash through the business. Also the finance department must comply with legal requirements such as paying taxes on time and submitting accounts to the relevant authorities.

Business strategies

BUSINESS or GENERIC STRATEGIES (sometimes also called business level strategies) are strategies which can be used by a business to give a COMPETITIVE ADVANTAGE over business rivals.

There are different ways of analysing business strategies. For example, Michael Porter, in his book *Competitive Advantage: Creating and Sustaining Superior Performance (1985)* argues that there are three ways in which a business can achieve superior performance to competitors.

Cost leadership One way is for the business to become the cost leader in the market. This means being the lowest cost producer for a given quality of product. For example, Wal-Mart in the USA and its subsidiary Asda in the UK have gained market share over time by offering lower prices to customers than competing hypermarket chains. Low cost in itself will not guarantee success. It has to be accompanied by the level of quality of product which a customer expects. So Asda in the UK may have been more successful than its rivals because it has offered a wide range of products, including well known branded products, at very low prices. Sainsbury's on the other hand may be regarded as a higher cost, higher price competitor but offering better quality products.

Differentiation A second way is for the business to differentiate its product from rivals. Differentiation is about making a product within a product range different from competitors. It is about giving a product a unique selling point (USP, see unit 10). Differentiation is in itself not sufficient to give a competitive advantage. It has to be a differentiated product which customers want to buy. So Heinz or Coca-Cola have been successful because they have products made to unique formulations which customers prefer over other formulations.

Focus A third way is for the business to focus on a particular sector of the market, i.e. to select a market **niche** (see unit 11). There are two forms of focus. **Cost focus** occurs when a business drives down its costs in the market segment to undercut the prices of competitors. **Differentiation focus** occurs when a business sells a unique and differentiated product within the market segment. In many cases, a business adopting a focus strategy will see its main competitors as larger businesses serving the much broader mass market. Because they serve the mass market, they are not always very competitive in individual niche markets. This gives businesses targeting niche markets an opportunity to become more competitive than much larger rivals. However, a focus strategy does not necessarily guarantee success. There may be other highly competitive niche businesses in that market already. Equally, a business may find it difficult either to cut costs compared to mass market businesses or to produce a differentiated product which customers value.

These strategies are summarised in Figure 115.1.

Cost leadership can be developed in the broad market. Wal-Mart has developed its cost strategy in the broad market of retailing. Differentiation too can be developed in the broad market. Coca-Cola has developed its differentiation strategy in the broad market of soft drinks. A business may also seek a competitive advantage in a narrow market. This competitive advantage can be either a cost advantage or a differentiation advantage. For example, BMW has developed a differentiated product in the narrow market for luxury cars.

There are many other ways of considering competitive advantage. Business strategies, for example, can centre around:
- product design and development (see unit 14);
- pricing (see units 15 and 16);
- promotion (see unit 18);
- place in the marketing mix (see unit 19);
- economies of scale (see unit 42);
- quality of production (see unit 46);
- delivery times including just-in-time production (see unit 47);

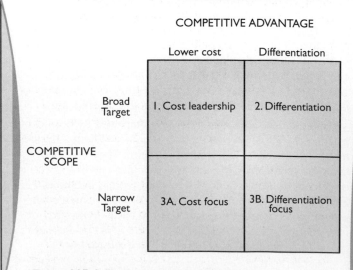

Figure 115.1 *Business or generic strategies*

In 2001, Sir Peter Davis, chief executive of Sainsbury's had told shareholders that his 'business transformation' programme would deliver a saving of £600 million every year by the end of the programme in 2004. In October 2004, a new chief executive, Justin King, said the programme had failed. He wrote off £260 million against ineffective supply chain equipment and ineffective IT systems. Worse than that, the failure had lost loyal customers and those still shopping at Sainsbury's were spending less.

At the heart of the problems were four brand new automated warehouses designed to handle all the products being delivered to the Sainsbury's chain in the UK. They should have delivered cost savings through economies of scale in distribution. Instead, they led to a breakdown in communication between the individual stores and the suppliers. IT systems should have matched what was being sold in a store with deliveries from the automated warehouses. What actually happened was that stores were failing to get deliveries on time. The result were 'stockouts': empty shelves in the stores where there should have been products for sale. If it isn't on the shelves, the customer can't buy it and so sales fall. Equally, some Sainsbury's customers got so frustrated by continual stockouts that they abandoned Sainsbury's altogether and did their regular shop at another supermarket.

But there was another problem. Stock was in the system but not in the right place. So, for example, fresh fruit and vegetables which should have been on display for sale in a supermarket was languishing in one of the warehouses undelivered. The result was a considerable increase in wastage. Instead of being bought by customers, it was being thrown away.

When Justin King took over as chief executive in 2004, he quickly appointed Lawrence Christensen, the former operations manager at Safeway, to sort out the supply chain problem. Lawrence Christensen put in place a number of solutions which haven't completely solved the problem but, where fully implemented, have resulted in a fall in stockouts of 75 per cent. He went back to Witron and Siemens, the two groups behind the equipment IT systems, to try to make improvements. He put in extra labour to manually sort products where needed. He is also implementing a 'step change' programme across all Sainsbury's stores to put clear systems in place around deliveries, stock auditing and making sure the inventory was correct.

Sainsbury's supply problems were symptomatic of much wider problems. In the 1990s, Sainsbury's lost market leadership to Tesco. Today, Tesco has nearly 30 per cent of the grocery market compared to Sainsbury's 16 per cent. Justin King has to address the fact that it isn't the cheapest supermarket at which to shop. Moreover, customers don't seem to value the differences between it and its competitors and yet it aims to be a distinctive mass market grocery retailer. Sainsbury's has been widely tipped as a takeover target for a buyer who has the skills to turn the company around.

Source: adapted from the *Financial Times*, 5.5.2005.

1 The 'business transformation' programme was a functional level strategy which went wrong. **Explain why.**
2 Explain why Sainsbury's in 2005 needed to develop a successful business strategy.

- the skill and motivation of the workforce (see units 35-37 and 41);
- a low cost labour force (see unit 100);
- the flexibility of workers (see units 36 amd 88);
- an ethical stance for the business (see unit 57).

Global strategy

A GLOBAL or INTERNATIONAL STRATEGY needs to be considered by any business which sells products to overseas customers or which is potentially large enough to move part of its production abroad. A business has four main strategic choices in its global strategy (see unit 98 for a more detailed discussion of some of these issues).

- It can export the same products or a service format that have been highly successful in its domestic market. For example, a UK chocolate manufacturer could export a new chocolate bar launched in the UK to Hungary or Thailand. A UK furniture retailer could set up identical stores in France and Germany. The advantage of this strategy is that the product or service has already proved successful in one market and the cost of introducing it into a new overseas market will be less than if the product were adapted. It allows for greater economies of scale to be achieved. Coca-Cola is an example of how successful this strategy can be. However, the main disadvantage is that what is successful in one country may be not appeal to customers in another country.

- A second strategy is to take a successful product in one market and adapt it for overseas markets. For example, McDonald's sells different food in India from France from the USA. The advantage is that there should be more chance that the product will prove attractive to local customers. The main disadvantage, apart from the risk that the product in practice doesn't appeal, is that economies of scale will be lost. Producing a number of slightly different products, each for a different market, is likely to be more costly per unit than a single mass produced product.

- A third strategy is to concentrate on minimising production costs by locating wherever in the world it is least costly to produce (see unit 98). Manufacturing industries in the industrialised countries of the world have been migrating to a small number of developing countries, including China and South Korea, over the past twenty years. They have relocated low skill jobs to countries where workers are paid a fraction of the wages paid to similar workers.

- A fourth strategy is to combine both customising products

to local markets with locating where costs are lowest. This is the most difficult strategy to implement because it requires the business to pay attention both to product and to costs.

Corporate strategy

CORPORATE STRATEGY (see unit 64) differs from business strategy. Business strategy is concerned with how a business can gain a competitive advantage in the market place. Corporate strategy is concerned with what range of activities the business needs to undertake in order to achieve its goals. It is also concerned with whether the business organisation is capable of achieving the objectives set.

For many businesses, concentrating on a single industry or market is the appropriate corporate strategy. By doing this, they can exploit their knowledge of the industry and develop their competitive strategies. A business pursuing such a strategy has to decide on its optimal size. Could it create value by growing in size or perhaps downsizing?

However, a business may be able to create value for its owners by moving into other markets. It may grow **vertically** (see unit 111), moving into markets which either its sells into or buys from. It may grow **horizontally**, expanding into its existing market. Or it may become a **conglomerate** (see unit 111), moving into unrelated markets. Equally, it may grow organically from within. It may grow by **taking over** or **merging** with other businesses. A key issue in growth is whether it will create **synergies** (see unit 111). Will the sum of the parts being greater than the individual parts working as completely separate businesses?

Equally, a large business should consider whether it can create value by divesting itself of businesses. Parts of the business may be underperforming. This may be because it is in a low profit industry. Or perhaps it is a relatively small part of the whole business and insufficient management time is being devoted to its running. Equally, since the 1990s, there has been a growing trend for businesses to **outsource** (see unit 53) functions. The argument is that a business needs to concentrate on its core competences (see unit 64). For example, a business which specialises in manufacturing canned food does not necessarily have an expertise in logistics (getting raw materials to the business and then transporting finished products to customers). It might be more cost effective to outsource logistics to a specialist logistics company.

Fifty years ago, it became fashionable for large businesses to be conglomerates (see unit 111). A conglomerate is a business which produces a range of products in widely differing markets. A steel producer which also owns a fast food chain would be an example. Today, it is more fashionable for businesses to focus on a narrow range of markets in which

Paul Burns, a 28 year-old TV producer from London, has been using Nokia mobile phones for more than 10 years. But just before Christmas he broke his Nokia allegiance and bought a snazzy new colour-screen camera phone from Sony Ericsson. 'I wanted to buy a Nokia but they didn't have a reasonable priced camera phone,' he said. 'The Sony Ericsson phones also look a lot better than the Nokia ones. Nokia just does not seem to have changed its look much over the last 10 years'.

Nokia, it seems, is facing its greatest challenge since it transformed itself from a small Finnish conglomerate to a highly-focused multinational telecommunications group in the early 1990s. It rode the mobile phone boom to become the world's biggest maker in 1998. But last month it was forced to admit that it was losing market share and seeing profits shrink. A series of factors has contributed to Nokia's problems.

First, it appears to have lost its way in an increasingly fashion-led and complex business. It has generally stuck to the tried and tested 'candy bar' format for its phones while rivals have been bringing out more innovative models. Nokia has admitted that it failed to anticipate how successful 'clamshell' mobile phones would be. It has also lacked competitive products in other segments of the market such as colour screen phones.

Second, Nokia is now subject, perhaps for the first time, to fierce competition from companies which fully understand the market. Samsung is targeting Nokia at the high end of the market, Sony Ericsson in the middle segment and Siemens at the low end.

Third, Nokia is suffering because of a desire by mobile operators to launch handsets that promote their own 'look and feel' and their own brand. Vodafone, for example, launched Vodafone Live! in 2002 and chose Sharp to produce its flagship handset. Nokia initially refused to cooperate with phone companies but it is now signalling that it is prepared to go down the co-branding route.

Source: adapted from the *Financial Times*, 16.04.2004.

1 In 2003-2004, Nokia's sales and profits failed to reach their targets. Discuss how Nokia might have been able to close the strategic gap which opened at the time.

senior management have an expertise. A water company should therefore concentrate on providing water management services. A train operator should concentrate on providing train services. A key feature of corporate strategy is deciding what part of the business should be retained and which should be sold off or closed down.

Strategic direction and strategic gaps

Corporate, business and functional strategies are plans which show how a business can achieve its objectives in the short, medium and long term. The plans may be to do what the business is currently doing, only more effectively. So the business may see itself making the same products in the same places and selling into the same markets in three to five years time. Alternatively, plans may be to move the business in a new direction. For example, a UK manufacturer may have a plan which says that the value of products sourced (i.e. made) in the UK should fall from 60 per cent to 25 per cent as production is shifted off shore to low wage economies such as eastern Europe or the Far East. Or plans may be to move into adjacent higher profit margin markets. A fixed line telephone company, for example, may plan to acquire a mobile telephone company in the medium term. The STRATEGIC DIRECTION of a business is the path which a business plans to follow to achieve its goals.

Once the strategic direction has been established, a detailed set of plans will be produced. These will enable lower and middle management to make the correct decisions to ensure the success of the plan. The period of time for which detailed plans can be made is called the PLANNING HORIZON. This might be from one to three years in a business in a stable market environment.

Sometimes, though, a STRATEGIC GAP may emerge between what a business wants to achieve and its objectives. For example, a company may have as one of its objectives

that it will achieve a 20 per cent growth in sales each year. A new strategic plan is worked out and senior managers find that, given the existing strategic direction of the company, it is most unlikely that that objective will be realised over the next 3 to 5 years. Senior management therefore either has to produce a different strategy to **close the strategic gap**, or it has to modify its objectives. A new strategy might be to expand sales overseas. It might be to enter new product markets. Or sales might be increased by spending more on R&D to develop new products in existing markets.

Porter's 5 forces analysis

A business will use many theories and pieces of information to formulate its strategy. One model it might use is Porter's 5 forces analysis. In his book, *Competitive advantage: creating and sustaining superior performance (1985)*, Michael Porter outlined five forces or factors which determine the profitability of an industry. He argues that the ultimate aim of competitive strategy is to cope with and ideally change those rules in favour of the business. Where the collective strength of those five forces is favourable, a business will be able to earn above average rates of return on capital. Where they are unfavourable, a business will be locked into low returns or wildly fluctuating returns. The five forces, shown in Figure 115.2, are as follows.

The bargaining power of suppliers Suppliers, like any business, want to maximise the profit they make from their customers. The more power a supplier has over its customers, the higher the prices it can charge and the more it can reallocate profit from the customer to itself. Limiting the power of its supplier, therefore, will improve the competitive position of a business. It has a variety of strategies it can adopt to achieve this. It can grow vertically (backward vertical integration, see unit 111), either acquiring a supplier or setting up its own business by growing organically upwards. It can seek out new suppliers to create more competition amongst suppliers. It might be able to engage in technical research to find substitutes for a particular input to broaden the supply base. It may also minimise the information provided to suppliers in order to prevent the supplier realising its power over the customer.

Bargaining power of buyers Just as suppliers want to charge maximum prices to customers, so buyers want to obtain supplies for the lowest price. If buyers or customers have considerable market power, they will be able to beat down prices offered by suppliers. For example, the major car manufacturers have succeeded in forcing down the price of components from component suppliers because of their enormous buying power and the

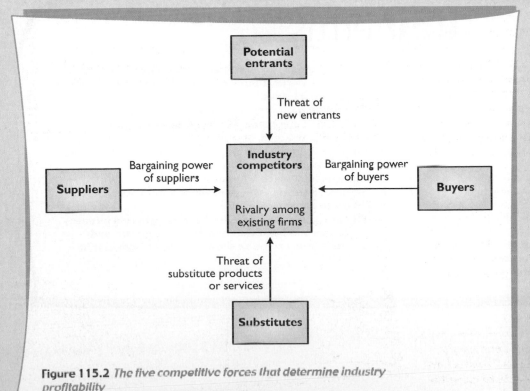

Figure 115.2 *The five competitive forces that determine industry profitability*

relatively few number of major car manufacturers in the world. One way a business can improve its competitive position viz-a-viz buyers is to extend into the buyers' market through forward vertical integration. A car manufacturer might set up its own component manufacturing division, for example. It could encourage other businesses to set up in its customers' market to reduce the power of existing customers. It could also try to make it expensive for customers to switch to another supplier. For example, one way in which games consol manufacturers keep up the price of computer games for their machines on which they receive a royalty is by making them technically incompatible with other machines.

Threat of new entrants If businesses can easily come into an industry and leave it again if profits are low, it becomes difficult for existing businesses in the industry to charge high prices and make high profits. Existing businesses are constantly under threat that if their profits rise too much, this will attract new suppliers into the market who will undercut their prices. Businesses can counter this by erecting **barriers to entry** to the industry (see unit 49). For example, a business may apply for patents and copyright to protect its intellectual property and prevent other businesses using it. It can attempt to create strong brands which will attract customer loyalty and make customers less price sensitive. Large amounts of advertising can be a deterrent because it represents a large cost to a new entrant which might have to match the spending to grow some market share. Large sunk costs, costs which have to paid at the start but are difficult to recoup if the business leaves the industry, can deter new entrants.

Substitutes The more substitutes there are for a particular product, the fiercer the competitive pressure on a business making the product. Equally, a business making a product with few or no substitutes is likely to be able to charge high prices and make high profits. A business can reduce the number of potential substitutes through research and development and then patenting the substitutes itself. Sometimes, a business will buy the patent for a new invention from a third party and do nothing with it simply to prevent the product coming to market. Businesses can also use marketing tactics to stop the spread of substitute products. A local newspaper, for example, might use predatory pricing (see unit 15) if a new competitor comes into its market to drive it out again.

Rivalry among existing firms The degree of rivalry among existing firms in an industry will also determine prices and profits for any single firm. If rivalry is fierce, businesses can reduce that rivalry by forming cartels or engaging in a broad range of restrictive practices (see unit 55). In UK and EU law, this is illegal but it is not uncommon. Businesses can also reduce competition by buying up their rivals (horizontal integration). Again, competition law may intervene to prevent this happening but most horizontal mergers are allowed to proceed. In industries where there are relatively few businesses, often businesses don't compete on price. This allows them to maintain high profitability. Instead they tend to compete by bringing out new products and through advertising, thus creating strong brands. As a result their costs are higher than they might otherwise be, but they can also charge higher prices than in a more competitive market creating high profits.

❝key terms❞

Competitive advantage - an advantage which a business has that enables it to perform better than its rivals in the market.

Business or generic strategy - strategies which can be used by a business to give a competitive advantage over business rivals, including pursuing cost leadership, product differentiation or focusing on a market segment.

Corporate strategy - is concerned with what range of activities the business needs to undertake in order to achieve its goals. It is also concerned with whether the business organisation is capable of achieving the objectives set.

Functional level strategies - strategies aimed at improving the effectiveness of the main functions with a business of production, marketing and human resources.

Global or international strategy - the range of activities across the world a business needs to undertake in order to achieve its goals.

Planning horizon - the period of time for which detailed plans have been made which will allow a business to achieve its strategic objectives. This may vary from business to business, from a few months to a few years, in part depending upon the pace of change of the markets into which a business sells.

Strategic direction - the path which a business plans to follow to achieve its goals.

Strategic gap - the difference between where a business predicts it will be in the medium to long term and where it wants to be as shown by the objectives it has set itself.

General Motors has been losing market share for the past 50 years. In 1960, one car in every two sold in the USA was a GM car. Today, that is under one quarter. Financially, the past 50 years have seen ups and downs, but yesterday, 20 April 2005, GM announced a quarterly loss of $1.1bn, the worst in more than a decade. So what has gone wrong with what was for many years the world's largest company? The key to GM's problems are its US operations.

Outside the US, its numerous subsidiaries vary in profitability. In Europe, GM has struggled for a long time with its main Opel subsidiary (badged under the Vauxhall brand in the UK) and in the quarter to April 2005, GM has written off $1.7bn on restructuring its operations and settling a dispute with Fiat over a proposed merger. But there are no structural reasons why GM should not be profitable in Europe. Equally, its operations in the rest of the world are potentially profitable.

In the US, however, GM's largest and core market, it faces a number of pressures. One comes from sales. The US market has been intensively competitive over the past 20 years with Japanese car manufacturers entering the market and gaining significant market share. They have been able to get a substantial share of the market by providing cars which have appealed to customers and been reliable. Over the past few years, GM has increased the number of new models it has offered to its US customers. The driving force behind profitable production, however, has been sales of pick-up trucks and SUVs (sports utility vehicles). In the early 2000s, GM was a market leader in this high price segment of the market. To maintain sales of the rest of its car range in a very difficult US market, GM has resorted to savage price cutting, done through offering customers zero per cent loans to buy cars. Winning the price war helped increased its market share in 2001 and 2002, the first time since 1977 that it had achieved this in two successive years. It also helped financially. GM has enormous fixed costs and pushing larger volumes of production through its factories helped maintain the contribution that each car made to overheads. But profit per vehicle in 2004 was just $125 compared to $2 000 at Toyota, the world's second largest car manufacturer.

Another problem is manufacturing costs. GM, like all car manufacturers, has transformed its production over the past ten years through use of just-in-time manufacturing techniques. The company is also beginning to exploit global economies of scale in design, purchase and production of components. Traditionally, GM has given its regions the freedom to design and engineer cars locally. Its competitors such as Toyota and Volkswagen, however, have moved to using the same production system in every factory, sharing components and models between regions, and they have centralised engineering facilities. The ultimate goal for a company like GM is to produce thousands of different models of car worldwide each focused on a particular market. All these superficially different models, though, would share the same pool of say, 10 different gear boxes, 12 braking systems, 8 chassis or 16 wheel types.

In North America, GM's production costs are still too high despite years of successful cost cutting. It has too many plants and too many workers. It is planning to close three US plants in summer 2005 whilst other plants will be subject to temporary shutdowns to reduce the number of unsold cars GM holds. But these measures are probably not tough enough. One of the main obstacles to plant closures and layoffs is the main trade union representing car workers, the United Auto Workers (UAW) union. The company is midway through a deal with the UAW signed in 2003 and which ends in 2007. For example, workers who are laid off continue to receive at least 75 per cent of their pay. This makes it very difficult to achieve cuts in costs when sales fall.

Workers and ex-workers present a more intractable problem for GM. In 1950, GM agreed to pick up some of the cost of medical insurance and pensions for its workers. By 1973, in agreements with the UAW, it was providing free private medical insurance for workers and ex-workers and their families, and had a pension scheme where workers could retire on full pensions after 30 years of service, irrespective of their age. The cost of these benefits has exploded. Health care costs have been rising in the USA at well above the rate of inflation for years. The cost of providing pensions has also risen fast as life expectancy has increased. In 2001, GM paid $3.9bn in health care costs for 1.2 million workers, ex-workers and family members. In 2005, this is forecast to increase to $5.6bn for 1.1 million members. Of the 1.1 million, no less than 0.8 million of these are retired workers and their families. As for pensions, GM is making pension contributions for existing workers. In 2003, it put an extra $18.5bn into its pension fund as a one-off payment in an attempt to make it solvent. But with falling investment returns and increased longevity, there is a fairly good chance that GM will have to make further large extra one-off payments into the fund. For every car sold, GM pays $1 800 in health care and pension contributions to its retired workers. This is an enormous 'legacy cost' which it will be difficult to negotiate away.

The chief executive officer of GM, Rick Wagoner, said in March 2005 that the company had made a lot of progress on reducing structural costs. 'What we have saved on the operating side has been filled in by higher legacy costs.... We need to be more creative and more effective in addressing legacy costs. They are kind of swamping a competitive operational performance.'

Matters would be even worse if it were not for the performance of the General Motors Acceptance Corporation (GMAC), a subsidiary of GM which provides loans to customers buying GM cars. Its profit in the first quarter of 2005 was $727 million and it paid its parent, GM, a dividend of $500 million. GM says it has no plans to sell off GMAC, but some commentators see such a sale as one answer to GM's huge problems with paying for health care and pensions in the future.

Source: adapted from the *Financial Times*, 30.9.2004, 20.4.2005, www.wsws.org, 18.3.2005.

1 To what extent could a change in strategy help General Motors resolve its difficulties? In your answer, consider functional level, business, global and corporate strategy. (20 marks)

Perrier

Knowledge Perrier is a brand of bottled water which in 1990 was owned by the French Perrier company. In February 1990, US regulators found traces of benzene, a poisonous liquid, in bottles. Perrier decided to recall around 70 million bottles in the USA and Canada and announced that it thought the contamination was probably the fault of an employee using Benzene to clean machinery at the bottling plant. However, traces of Benzene were then found in bottles sold in Holland and Denmark. Perrier recalled all its bottled worldwide. It then said that Benzene was naturally present in carbon dioxide used to make Perrier a sparkling rather than still water. Workers had failed to change the filters used to remove the Benzene at the bottling plant in France.

Application At the time, Perrier was a *market leader* in many countries around the world including the UK. In the USA, it had the highest *market share* of any imported bottled water. The contamination scare proved a *public relations* disaster for Perrier. In retrospect, it didn't seem to have any *contingency plan* for such an event. *Sales* plummeted and have never regained their 1990 level in many *markets*.

Analysis Perrier made a number of mistakes. It failed to ensure quality control at its bottling plant. Then it failed to give a correct explanation of why the failure occurred and changed its story. It was slow to recall its product. Instead of being in charge of the situation, carrying out a well rehearsed contingency plan, it seemed to be constantly reacting to events. All this meant that it lost the trust of consumers. Whilst Perrier was off the market, consumers tried out other branded bottled waters and many found that they were just as good, if not better, than Perrier. A final blow to Perrier was when the FDA (Food and Drug Administration), the US government body responsible for ensuring food standards, made Perrier drop the words 'Naturally Sparkling' from its labels. In the wake of the recall, the FDA had found that Perrier was artificially carbonating its water. There was nothing natural about the sparkle.

Evaluation Perrier paid a very heavy price for its failure to respond adequately to problems with its product. It arguably should have acted decisively, recalling all its products promptly and giving customers correct information about the cause of the problem. It could then have appeared to have been dealing openly and honestly with the problem. If it had reacted promptly, it might be argued that it could have suffered minimal damage and still be the market leading brand of bottled water.

Adapted from www.consumerbehavior.net..

Crises

Every business faces crises in its day to day operations. A CRISIS is usually an unforeseen event which threatens the business in some way. Crises in a business occur for a variety of reasons.

Production Production crises are common in business. On a day to day basis, machinery and vehicles may break down, causing production delays. Over a short period a company might receive unexpectedly large orders, causing it to run out of stock of raw materials. More rarely, a fire might destroy premises or flooding might bring work to a halt for several days. In winter, construction businesses, for example, may lose time because of abnormal weather conditions. Snow may also can prevent workers getting into work.

Finance Many businesses experience financial crises. A common financial problem is a cash flow crisis (see units 27 and 28). This is when a business does not have enough cash to pay its bills. However, some businesses face a financial crisis because of unforeseen events, such as the sudden loss of a major customer. Another problem that can arise is that a firm's bankers may suddenly decide to withdraw an overdraft facility or recall a large loan, which could force the business into receivership.

Human resources Human resource problems are as common as production and finance problems for businesses. A crisis may take place simply by a worker not turning up for work.

In a restaurant, for example, if there are just two cooks in the kitchen and one fails to turn up on a business night, the kitchen might be in crisis. Equally, a sudden walkout by staff over an industrial relations issue can cause chaos within the business. Other events which can cause problems include key workers suddenly leaving for a better job elsewhere, a flu virus sweeping through a workforce leaving many unable to come into work, or the sacking of a popular manager.

Product quality Most businesses at some time experience a problem with the product they make or with the quality of supplies coming into the business. In a bakery, a whole batch of bread might have to be thrown away because it was overcooked. In the car industry, a car model might have to be recalled because a fault is found. Production might come to a sudden stop because supplies of a key component are found to be faulty and unusable.

Public relations Some large businesses have faced public relations crises. A newspaper, for example, may run a story about how a company is sourcing materials from Third World producers which use cheap labour. A television company may broadcast a programme about poor work conditions in one of the company's factories. These stories can have an immediate effect on sales, with some customers boycotting the company.

Environmental issues Some businesses face considerable environmental challenges. Nuclear power, the chemicals industry or any form of mining may suffer crises because of

In February 1997, Aisin Seiki, a brake manufacturer in Japan making parts for Toyota, was completely destroyed by fire. The impact on Toyota was devastating. The brake manufacturer was the sole supplier of brakes to Toyota plants in Japan and Toyota used a just-in-time delivery system for the brakes. Within hours, Toyota plants were running out our brake parts and overall, 18 of Toyota's Japanese plants were shut down for almost two weeks. Estimated sales losses were 70 000 vehicles worth $325 million.

The fire didn't just affect Toyota. Hundreds of Toyota's other suppliers were forced to shut down because they could no longer supply Toyota's assembly lines whilst they were out of action.

Toyota resolved the problem in the short term by working with other brake manufacturers that usually supplied Toyota's rivals, Nissan and Honda. These brake manufacturers agreed to supply Toyota with brake parts at a competitive price. In the long term, Toyota has diversified its component purchases to ensure that no single plant can bring Toyota's production to a standstill again.

Source: adapted from www.converium.com.

1 **Explain, using the example of Toyota, why just-in-time manufacturing can lead to a crisis which shuts down a factory.**
2 **Discuss whether manufacturers should hold large stocks of components and raw materials to avoid the problem experienced by Toyota.**

environmental issues. For example, a crisis might occur because of the breakdown of safety equipment, a sudden spillage of waste into a river or a fire which releases toxic chemicals into the atmosphere.

Corporate crises Some crises threaten the business as a whole. For example, a company may suddenly face a takeover bid. Major shareholders may decide to sell their shares, threatening to destabilise the share price.

Contingency planning

Most businesses recognise that crises will arise in the future. However, it could be argued that relatively few have effective plans in place to deal with unforeseen eventualities. Those that do have plans tend to be larger businesses or well planned SMEs. Planning now, about how to do deal with a crisis in the future, is called CONTINGENCY PLANNING.

The first step in contingency planning is to identify the possible crises that could affect the business. The second step is to think about possible ways of dealing with each crisis. Then the best solution can be identified and plans drawn up showing how the business will respond. In some cases, it may be desirable to carry out practice exercises to familiarise staff with how the crisis will be dealt with. For example, a business may identify fire on the premises as a possible risk which would threaten the lives of employees. Escape routes would then be planned and employees notified of what to do in the event of a fire. There may follow regular fire practices, where staff practice evacuating the building.

Contingency planning is a cost for a business. Management time has to be spent on this activity. Most potential crises are either too trivial or too unlikely to be worth considering. So contingency planning has to be limited to:

- situations where contingency planning is required by law, such as under the Health and Safety Act (see unit 55);
- crises with a relatively high probability of occurring, such as an incident which could potentially generate negative public relations (see unit 18);
- crises with a relatively low probability of occurring, but which if they did occur would have a very high cost for the business.

For example, a particular crisis which could cost a business £5 million might have a 20 per cent probability of occurring in any 12 month period. The cost to the company if the crisis occurred over the next 12 months is mathematically £1 million (£5 million x 20 per cent). If the cost of contingency planning for the event is £5 000, then there is a clear advantage to the business of carrying out contingency planning. Equally, if a particular crisis would cost a business £100 million and there is a probability of 0.1 per cent of the event happening, then the potential cost is £100 000 (£100 million x 0.1) If the cost of carrying out contingency planning for this event is £5 000, then there is still an advantage to the business of doing this despite the low probability of the event. On the other hand, if the cost of a crisis were to be £5 million, but there is a 0.01 per cent chance of the event happening over the next 12 months, then the potential lost is only £500 (£5 million x 0.01 per cent). If the cost of formulating a contingency plan for this event is £5 000, it may not be worth carrying out.

Contingency planning and crisis management

Contingency planning and CRISIS MANAGEMENT will involve a number of different areas of the business.

Finance A crisis may have financial implications. For example, if a fire destroys a factory, output will be lost and so revenue will fall. Then there will be costs of rebuilding. The cost of replacing machinery of buildings due to fire and flooding, and the interruption to a business's activity, can be insured against. However, a loss of profit caused as a result of a downturn in the market, the failure of a product due to poor design or industrial action cannot be insured against. A business may also hold contingency funds. These are reserves of cash held back to deal with the financial implications of a crisis. Equally, a business may arrange for an overdraft or loan facility with its bankers to be drawn down in a crisis.

All these methods lead to extra costs for the business. Insurance premiums have to be paid, holding cash means that it cannot be used productively elsewhere in the business and banks charge fees for arranging overdrafts and loan facilities even if no money is borrowed.

Production Potentially, there are many different crises which involve production. A simple problem is machinery breaking down. A business may plan to transfer production to another machine, or it may have a 24 hour 365 day a year call out contract with a machine repair business. A more serious crisis would occur if a large company used just-in-time production techniques and its sole supplier of a key component suffered a fire which stopped all production. The company's contingency plan may identify an alternative source of supply. Or it may have drawn up plans with the supplier to organise a resumption of production within 48 hours by using rented equipment and new rented premises.

Human resource management If a crisis is to be successfully resolved, it must be clear who is responsible for dealing with the crisis. A contingency plan must therefore include the names of who will take charge in the crisis and what roles they will fulfil. Chains of command and channels of communication should be clearly set out. For example, a holiday company may run coach tours in Germany. There is a risk that a coach may suffer a crash, with casualties amongst the passengers. A contingency plan for such a risk may give responsibility for dealing with the problems resulting from the crash to a senior manager. Underneath the senior manager may be another manager responsible for setting up a crisis call centre where relatives can ring to get information. The plan may state that call operatives have the authority to offer relatives affected a free flight to Germany. A more senior employee may have the authority to give out immediate hardship grants of £1 000 to families affected. Meanwhile, it may be planned that a small team will fly out to Germany to deal with victims in hospitals and to deal with the dead. The team would also be responsible for looking after the relatives as they arrive in Germany. An individual may be made responsible for dealing with the press, issuing press releases and giving interviews.

Equally important in a crisis is the motivation of staff. In practice, employees tend to react positively in a crisis. If there is a fire or flood, for example, staff will typically work long hours to deal with the aftermath. However, the contingency plan should consider how employees will be rewarded for their positive response in a crisis. If a fire completely destroys a factory, and it takes three weeks to start up again in new premises, will the staff be paid for those three weeks even though they stay at home not working? Should staff be given a bonus for dealing with a crisis? If temporary staff need to be taken on to deal with a crisis, what in the contingency plan deals with possible friction between existing employees and the new staff leading to poor morale?

Marketing Marketing may pose considerable problems in a crisis. The contingency plan must deal with these marketing challenges. For example, if there is a fire which disrupts production, how will the business look after its customers? The contingency plan may say that supplies should be bought from rival producers and delivered to customers. Or customers may be contacted individually to explain the problems and given a timetable for when supplies will be resumed. Compensation may be offered to customers for the disruption caused by a temporary loss of supply. If the crisis is caused by a fault with a product, the contingency plan may state that all existing supplies will be recalled with the company paying for the recall. Compensation may be offered to customers who have already bought faulty products.

The contingency plan may outline how public relations will be handled in the event of a crisis. An individual may be nominated to deal with the press. The amount of information to be given out may be decided in advance in the contingency plan.

Jocelyn Milne is the office manager at Reid Architecture, a small business employing 100 staff with an Office in Oxford Circus, London. Chatting with staff from some of the businesses nearby, she was shocked to learn that they were working in an area that was a possible terrorist target. A few months ago, she was asked by the firm's professional-indemnity insurers what contingency plans had been put in place should disaster strike. She discovered that nothing had been organised.

As a result, Mark Taylor, a director at the company, began formulating an action plan. 'When we discussed this at board level, everyone had seen what had happened since September 11 and realised how real problems could be. But we didn't quite realise how complex it was to formulate a disaster plan.' On September 11 2001, terrorists flew two planes into the World Trade Centre into New York destroying the building. Taylor had to develop a brief that identified the company's key workers and set out what to do if staff could not get into the building, how to make sure that all important information stored on the computers was saved or retrieved, and how to maintain internal and external lines of communication. He planned for a variety of scenarios, ranging from being evacuated for a day to a week or permanently.

Source: adapted from the *Sunday Times*, 29.6.2003.

1 **Explain why Reid Architecture needed a contingency plan to deal a situation such as its location being a terrorist target.**
2 **Suggest why the measures in the contingency plan drawn up by Reid Architecture, such as making sure all computer data was retrievable, was important to an architectural practice.**

Success and failure

When faced with a serious crisis, such as the destruction of premises, a small business which does not have contingency plans may be forced to cease trading. Even large companies without plans can be forced out of business by a single catastrophe. When a foreign exchange trader working for

Barings Bank lost $1 billion, the bank was forced to put itself up for sale to survive. Lesser crises are still likely to harm a business. Fires, floods and faulty products all tend to lead to one off costs to a business which are not offset by gains elsewhere. Without contingency planning, these costs are likely to be higher than if there is planning in place.

Occasionally, however, crises can have an overall positive impact on a business. An airline, for example, which looks after its customers when it has to suspend flights may gain positive public relations. A devastating fire may be an opportunity to rebuild to allow more efficient production.

Contingency planning does not guarantee that a business will survive a crisis. For example, a business may have planned for a range of crises, except for the one that actually occurs. Or the plans may have been drawn up too long ago to reflect the current situation in which the business finds itself. The planning itself may have been faulty. When tested, solutions may prove inadequate.

Because of the changing business environment, contingency plans need to be reviewed on a regular basis. Current assumptions about potential crises must be constantly questioned and methods to deal with them constantly updated.

keyterms

Contingency planning - the creation of plans of how particular crises which might affect a business will be dealt with should they arise.
Crisis - usually an unforeseen event which threatens the business in some way, such as a sudden drop in sales, a fire which destroys premises or the discovery of a fault in a product.
Crisis management - dealing effectively with an unforeseen or unplanned event.

checklist

1 What type of crises might a small engineering company face?
2 Explain how a contingency plan might be drawn up.
3 Should every contingency be considered by a business in contingency planning?
4 How might a business react to a crisis in (a) finance; (b) production; (c) human resources; (d) marketing?
5 Why do contingency plans need to be reviewed regularly?

Maya Lim found her life turned upside down when a leak, followed by an explosion, effectively destroyed her premises which were part of a shopping centre. Maya was ill prepared for such a disaster. She, along with all the other people in the shopping centre at the time, were safely evacuated so at least there was no loss of life and few injuries. However, her business was one of a number of firms that never recovered.

Part of the problem was that her business had not been doing particularly well financially. Table 116.1 shows the profit and loss account for her last year of full trading. She had an agreed overdraft limit of £8 000 with her bank and on the day of the explosion, she was overdrawn on her bank account by £7 854. She had also £10 450 of outstanding trade credit, much of it already overdue to her suppliers from the run up to the previous Christmas which had seen very disappointing sales.

In the aftermath of the explosion, Maya, along with other retailers in the centre were unable to visit the premises for a number of days. She didn't know what she was going to find, but it was worse than she imagined. Her entire stock was so damaged that none of it was saleable and fixtures and fittings were not worth salvaging. The small office at the back of the outlet where she kept most of her business records was particularly badly affected. Some of the records were completely destroyed, whilst others were only useable with difficulty.

Maya spent days worrying about what she would find. Seeing the premises in such a condition worried her considerably. She knew she had to decide what to do about her business, but she found she couldn't face up to the difficult decisions that lay ahead. The management of the shopping centre let her know that it would have to be completely rebuilt and so premises would not be available certainly in the short term and possibly for more than a year.

Profit and loss account for year ended 31.5.2005

	£
Turnover	83,890
Cost of sales	41,498
Gross profit	42,392
Expenses	37,720
Net profit	4,672

Figure 116.1 *Profit and loss account of Maya Lim*

So she would have to look for new premises. Then she would have to buy in new stock. But she had no cash. The insurance payout for the damage would take months to come. It would only cover the cost of the stock and fixtures and fittings anyway. She had no insurance for loss of earnings whilst she couldn't trade. She couldn't see how her bank would increase her overdraft limit. Nor could she see any supplier giving her more trade credit given her existing debts.

By the time her unit in the centre had been repaired, Maya had got a management job paying £30 000 a year and she was no longer interested in taking back the premises.

1 Explain the nature of the crisis that faced Maya Lim from the perspective of finance, marketing, production and human resources. (20 marks)
2 Discuss whether any amount of contingency planning would have saved Maya's business in the aftermath of the crisis. (20 marks)

Index